The First
One Hundred
Years of
Christianity

The First One Hundred Years of Christianity

AN INTRODUCTION
TO ITS HISTORY, LITERATURE, AND DEVELOPMENT

UDO SCHNELLE

TRANSLATED BY JAMES W. THOMPSON

B
Baker Academic
a division of Baker Publishing Group
Grand Rapids, Michigan

Originally published as Udo Schnelle, *Die ersten 100 Jahre des Christentums*, 3. veränderte Auflage © 2019 by Vandenhoeck & Ruprecht GmbH & Co. KG, Göttingen. All rights reserved.

English translation © 2020 by Baker Publishing Group
Published by Baker Academic
a division of Baker Publishing Group
PO Box 6287, Grand Rapids, MI 49516-6287
www.bakeracademic.com

Printed in the United States of America

Library of Congress Cataloging-in-Publication Data
Names: Schnelle, Udo, 1952– author. | Thompson, James W., translator.
Title: The first one hundred years of Christianity : an introduction to its history, literature, and development / Udo Schnelle ; translated by James W. Thompson.
Other titles: Ersten 100 Jahre des Christentums. English
Description: Grand Rapids : Baker Academic, a division of Baker Publishing Group, 2020. | Includes bibliographical references and index. | Summary: "This major work by a senior international scholar traces the historical, cultural, and theological influences and developments of the early years of the Christian movement"—Provided by publisher.
Identifiers: LCCN 2019031832 | ISBN 9781540960153 (cloth)
Subjects: LCSH: Church history—Primitive and early church, ca. 30–600.
Classification: LCC BR165 .S36513 2020 | DDC 270.1—dc23
LC record available at https://lccn.loc.gov/2019031832

20 21 22 23 24 25 26   7 6 5 4 3 2 1

Contents

Illustrations

Tables

Translator's Preface

In the last generation, the works of Udo Schnelle have had a major impact on English-speaking scholars and students, who have benefited from his encyclopedic knowledge and depth of insight about a wide range of topics related to the New Testament. Translations of *Antidocetic Christology in the Gospel of John*; *The Human Condition: Anthropology in the Teachings of Jesus, Paul, and John*; *History and Theology of the New Testament Writings*; *Theology of the New Testament*; *Apostle Paul: His Life and Theology*, and numerous articles that have appeared in English have been valuable resources for scholars who do not have access to his original publications. These works in English translation, however, represent only a small part of the scholarly productivity that has been available for decades to German readers.

The First Hundred Years of Christianity builds on the results of the previous works and advances beyond the traditional questions of New Testament introduction and theology by offering a coherent vision of the historical development of the Christian movement from roughly 30 CE to about 130 CE. Beginning with the Greco-Roman and Jewish context, Schnelle demonstrates the variety of streams within the Jesus movement of the first generation and the historical forces that led to the spread of Christianity during this period.

This book reflects an extraordinary knowledge of both primary and secondary sources. As one of the editors of the *Neuer Wettstein* (cited here as NW), a collection of texts from the Hellenistic world, Schnelle has a rare mastery of primary sources, which he demonstrates throughout the book. Using more than 1,700 secondary sources representing current scholarship, Schnelle engages the most recent scholarship on the environment of early Christianity.

The First Hundred Years of Christianity has a unique place in current New Testament scholarship. In moving beyond the traditional questions that occupy scholars, the book is unparalleled in current literature. Thus it will be a valuable reference work for scholars and graduate students. I have learned much about early Christianity from the book, and I am pleased to participate in making it available to English readers.

At the request of the author and publisher, I have supplied the English titles and appropriate page numbers for all references where an English translation exists. I have also added works written in English to the secondary sources. Translations of classical sources are from the Loeb Classical Library.

This translation was read by the author and by the editors at Baker Academic, all of whom made valuable suggestions. Professor Schnelle has been a gracious conversation partner, offering clarification for the translation, and the Baker editors' attention to clarity and accuracy has been helpful in the process of preparing the book for publication.

James W. Thompson
October 27, 2019

Author's Preface
to the American Edition

This book is an introduction to the complex history, literature, and theology of early Christianity. One major question is the focus of this study: How did the insignificant Jesus movement in Galilee and Jerusalem become a powerful religious community and spread in a brief period throughout the Roman Empire? Three factors played a crucial role:

1. Early Christianity was a diverse movement. This diversity ensured its survival, for the demise of one stream (e.g., the early church) did not result in the end of the entire movement.
2. The history of events and ideas formed a unity at the beginning of Christianity; events gave rise to theological interpretation, and ideas made history.
3. An astonishing factor is the high literary production of the new movement and the related intellectual and cultural achievements. Early Christians created and were surrounded by literature, and therefore early Christianity must be regarded as an educational phenomenon.

Thus very early an independent identity emerged, and the developing Christianity possessed a charismatic, social, and intellectual power of attraction.

Udo Schnelle
Halle, December 2019

Abbreviations

General and Bibliographic

//	parallel to
§(§)	section(s)
BCE	before the Common Era
ca.	*circa*, about
CE	Common Era
cent.	century
chap(s).	chapter(s)
Diels-Kranz	reference system for works of pre-Socratic philosophers
diss.	dissertation
ed(s).	edition, editor(s)
e.g.	*exempli gratia*, for example
Eng.	versification of English Bible versions
enl.	enlarged
esp.	especially
et al.	*et alii*, and others
frag(s).	fragment(s)
FS	Festschrift
Gk.	Greek language
Hb.	Hebrew language
i.e.	*id est*, that is
LCL	Loeb Classical Library
LXX	Septuagint, Greek Old Testament
MT	Masoretic Text
NT	New Testament
orig.	original
OT	Old Testament
par.	parallel(s)
p(p).	page(s)
$\mathfrak{P}^{52}$	a second-century papyrus of parts of John
$\mathfrak{P}^{66}$	a papyrus of parts of John, dated around 200 CE
$\mathfrak{P}^{75}$	a papyrus of parts of Luke and John, dated around 200 CE
Ps.	Pseudo
pub.	publication
Q	Quelle, dominical sayings source; e.g., Luke 10:7Q
repr.	reprint
rev.	revised
S. or St.	Saint
Sup.	Supplement
theol.	theological
trans.	translated by, translation, translator(s)
v(v).	verse(s)
vol(s).	volume(s)

Old Testament

Gen.	Genesis
Exod.	Exodus
Lev.	Leviticus
Num.	Numbers
Deut.	Deuteronomy
Josh.	Joshua
Judg.	Judges
Ruth	Ruth
1 Sam.	1 Samuel

2 Sam.	2 Samuel		1 Tim.	1 Timothy
1 Kings	1 Kings		2 Tim.	2 Timothy
2 Kings	2 Kings		Titus	Titus
1 Chron.	1 Chronicles		Philem.	Philemon
2 Chron.	2 Chronicles		Heb.	Hebrews
Ezra	Ezra		James	James
Neh.	Nehemiah		1 Pet.	1 Peter
Esther	Esther		2 Pet.	2 Peter
Job	Job		1 John	1 John
Ps(s).	Psalm(s)		2 John	2 John
Prov.	Proverbs		3 John	3 John
Eccles.	Ecclesiastes		Jude	Jude
Song	Song of Songs		Rev.	Revelation
Isa.	Isaiah			
Jer.	Jeremiah			
Lam.	Lamentations			
Ezek.	Ezekiel			
Dan.	Daniel			
Hosea	Hosea			
Joel	Joel			
Amos	Amos			
Obad.	Obadiah			
Jon.	Jonah			
Mic.	Micah			
Nah.	Nahum			
Hab.	Habakkuk			
Zeph.	Zephaniah			
Hag.	Haggai			
Zech.	Zechariah			
Mal.	Malachi			

Old Testament Apocrypha / Deuterocanonical Books

Bar.	Baruch
1–4 Macc.	1–4 Maccabees
Sir. (Ecclus.)	Sirach (Ecclesiasticus)
Tob.	Tobit
Wis.	Wisdom (of Solomon)

New Testament

Matt.	Matthew
Mark	Mark
Luke	Luke
John	John
Acts	Acts
Rom.	Romans
1 Cor.	1 Corinthians
2 Cor.	2 Corinthians
Gal.	Galatians
Eph.	Ephesians
Phil.	Philippians
Col.	Colossians
1 Thess.	1 Thessalonians
2 Thess.	2 Thessalonians

Old Testament Pseudepigrapha

2 Bar.	2 Baruch (Syriac Apocalypse)
1 En.	1 Enoch
Jos. Asen.	Joseph and Aseneth
Jub.	Jubilees
LAB	Liber antiquitatum biblicarum (Pseudo-Philo)
Let. Aris.	Letter of Aristeas
Pss. Sol.	Psalms of Solomon
Sib. Or.	Sibylline Oracles
T. Ash.	Testament of Asher
T. Ben.	Testament of Benjamin
T. Iss.	Testament of Issachar
T. Jos.	Testament of Joseph
T. Jud.	Testament of Judah
T. Levi	Testament of Levi
T. Mos.	Testament of Moses
T. Naph.	Testament of Naphtali
T. Zeb.	Testament of Zebulun

Qumran / Dead Sea Scrolls

CD	Cairo Geniza copy of Damascus Document

1QH	Hodayot/Thanksgiving Hymns
1QM	Milḥamah/War Scroll
1QpHab	Pesher Habakkuk
1QS	Serek Hayaḥad/Rule of the Community
1QSa	Rule of the Congregation (appendix a to 1QS)
1QSb	Rule of the Blessings (appendix b to 1QS)
4QFlor	Florilegium, also Midrash on Eschatology[a]
4Q246	Apocryphon of Daniel
4Q394	4QHalakhic Letter[a]
4Q521	Messianic Apocalypse
11QT[a]	Temple Scroll[a]

Rabbinic Writings

b.	Babylonian Talmud
Ker.	tractate Kerithot
m.	Mishnah

Apostolic Fathers

1–2 Clem.	1–2 Clement
Did.	Didache
Herm. Sim.	Shepherd of Hermas, Similitudes
Herm. Vis.	Shepherd of Hermas, Visions
Ign. *Eph.*	Ignatius, *To the Ephesians*
Ign. *Magn.*	Ignatius, *To the Magnesians*
Ign. *Phld.*	Ignatius, *To the Philadelphians*
Ign. *Pol.*	Ignatius, *To Polycarp*
Ign. *Rom.*	Ignatius, *To the Romans*
Ign. *Smyrn.*	Ignatius, *To the Smyrnaeans*
Ign. *Trall.*	Ignatius, *To the Trallians*
Pol. *Phil.*	Polycarp, *To the Philadelphians*

Patristic Writings

1 Apol.	Justin, *First Apology*
Dial.	Justin, *Dialogue with Trypho*
Haer.	Irenaeus, *Adversus haereses* (*Against Heresies*)

Hist. eccl.	Eusebius, *Historia ecclesiastica* (*Ecclesiastical History*)
Pan.	Epiphanius, *Panarion* (*Refutation of All Heresies*)
Pol. *Phil.*	Polycarp, *To the Philippians*
Ref.	Hippolytus, *Refutatio omnium haeresium* (*Refutation of All Heresies*)

Classical and Hellenistic Writings

Ag. Ap.	Josephus, *Against Apion*
Ann.	Tacitus, *Annales* (*Annals*)
Ant.	Josephus, *Jewish Antiquities*
Apol.	Plato, *Apologia* (*Apology of Socrates*)
Aug.	Suetonius, *Divus Augustus*
Ben.	Seneca, *De beneficiis*
Cal.	Suetonius, *Gaius Caligula*
Claud.	Suetonius, *Divus Claudius*
Creation	Philo, *On the Creation of the World*
Diatr.	Epictetus, *Diatribai* (*Dissertationes*)
Diss.	Musonius, *Dissertationes*
Dom.	Suetonius, *Domitianus*
Ench.	Epictetus, *Enchiridion* (*Handbook*)
Ep.	Pliny the Younger, *Epistulae* (*Epistles*)
Ep.	Seneca, *Epistulae morales* (*Moral Epistles*)
Eth. Nic.	Aristotle, *Ethica nicomachea* (*Nicomachean Ethics*)
Flacc.	Philo, *In Flaccum* (*Against Flaccus*)
Good Person	Philo, *That Every Good Person Is Free*
Hist.	Herodotus, *Historiae* (*Histories*)
Hist.	Tacitus, *Historiae* (*Histories*)
Is. Os.	Plutarch, *De Iside et Osiride*
Jul.	Suetonius, *Divus Julius*
J.W.	Josephus, *Jewish War*

Leg.	Cicero, *De legibus*	AJEC	Ancient Judaism and Early Christianity
Leg.	Philo, *Legum allegoriae* (*Allegorical Interpretation*)	AKG	Antike Kultur und Geschichte
		ALGHJ	Arbeiten zur Literatur und Geschichte des hellenistischen Judentums
Legat.	Philo, *Legatio ad Gaium*		
Life	Josephus, *The Life*	AMMTC	Ancient Mediterranean and Medieval Texts and Contexts
Mem.	Xenophon, *Memorabilia*		
Mor.	Plutarch, *Moralia*	ANF	*The Ante-Nicene Fathers: Translations of the Writings of the Fathers down to A.D. 325.* Edited by Alexander Roberts and James Donaldson. Revised by A. Cleveland Coxe. 10 vols. New York: Christian Literature, 1885–87. Reprint, Peabody, MA: Hendrickson, 1994
Nat. d.	Cicero, *De natura deorum*		
Or.	Dio Chrysostom, *Orationes* (*Orations*)		
Peregr.	Lucian of Samosata, *The Passing of Peregrinus*		
Phaed.	Plato, *Phaedo*		
Phaedr.	Plato, *Phaedrus*		
Pol.	Plato, *Politicus* (*Statesman*)		
Prelim. Studies	Philo, *On the Preliminary Studies*	ANRW	*Aufstieg und Niedergang der römischen Welt: Geschichte und Kultur Roms im Spiegel der neueren Forschung.* Edited by H. Temporini and W. Haase. Berlin: de Gruyter, 1972–98
Res gestae	Augustus, Res gestae divi Augusti (Record of Deeds of Divine Augustus)		
Resp.	Plato, *Respublica* (*Republic*)		
		ANTC	Abingdon New Testament Commentaries
Sat.	Juvenal, *Satires*		
Spec. Laws	Philo, *Special Laws*	ANTZ	Arbeiten zur neutestamentlichen Theologie und Zeitgeschichte
Tib.	Suetonius, *Tiberius*		
Tim.	Plato, *Timaeus*		
Tusc.	Cicero, *Tusculanae disputationes*	ARGU	Arbeiten zur Religion und Geschichte des Urchristentums
Vesp.	Suetonius, *Vespasianus*	ARW	*Archiv für Religionswissenschaft*

Modern Secondary Sources

AASF	Annales Academiae Scientiarum Fennicae	ATANT	Abhandlungen zur Theologie des Alten und Neuen Testaments
AB	Anchor Bible		
ABD	*The Anchor Bible Dictionary.* Edited by D. N. Freedman et al. 6 vols. New York: Doubleday, 1992	ATDan	Acta theologica danica
		BAFCS	The Book of Acts in Its First Century Setting
ABG	Arbeiten zur Bibel und ihrer Geschichte	BAK	Beiträge zur Altertumskunde
		BAL	Blackwell Ancient Lives
ABRL	Anchor Bible Reference Library	BAW	Bibliothek der Alten Welt
AcBib	Academia Biblica	BBB	Bonner biblische Beiträge
ACW	Ancient Christian Writers	BBET	Beiträge zur biblischen Exegese und Theologie
AGJU	Arbeiten zur Geschichte des antiken Judentums und des Urchristentums		
		BBJ	Beihefte der Bonner Jahrbücher

BDAG	W. Bauer, F. W. Danker, W. F. Arndt, and F. W. Gingrich. *A Greek-English Lexicon of New Testament and Other Early Christian Literature*. 3rd ed. Chicago: University of Chicago Press, 2000		CP	Clavis pansophiae
			CPJ	*Corpus Papyrorum Judaicarum*. Edited by Victor A. Tcherikover. 3 vols. Cambridge, MA: Harvard University Press, 1957–64
BEATAJ	Beiträge zur Erforschung des Alten Testaments und des antiken Judentum		CRINT	Compendia rerum iudaicarum ad Novum Testamentum
BETL	Bibliotheca ephemeridum theologicarum lovaniensium		CTM	Calwer theologische Monographien
BEvT	Beiträge zur evangelischen Theologie		DK	Dialog der Kirchen
			DNP	*Der neue Pauly: Enzyklopädie der Antike*. Edited by Hubert Cancik and Helmuth Schneider. Stuttgart: Metzler, 1996–
BFCT	Beiträge zur Förderung christlicher Theologie			
BG	Biblische Gestalten		*DPL*	*Dictionary of Paul and His Letters*. Edited by Gerald F. Hawthorne and Ralph P. Martin. Downers Grove, IL: InterVarsity, 1993
BGK	Beiträge zur Geschichtskultur			
BH	Beiträge zur Historik			
BHT	Beiträge zur historischen Theologie			
Bib	*Biblica*		Dtv	Deutsch Taschenbuch-Verlag
BKP	Beiträge zur klassischen Philologie		*EC*	*Early Christianity*
			ECCA	Early Christianity in the Context of Antiquity
BN	*Biblischen Notizen*		EdA	Erbe der Alten
BTS	Biblisch-theologische Studien		EdF	Erträge der Forschung
BTZ	*Berliner Theologische Zeitschrift*		*EDNT*	*Exegetical Dictionary of the New Testament*. Edited by Horst Balz and Gerhard Schneider. Translated by James W. Thompson and John W. Medendorp. 3 vols. Grand Rapids: Eerdmans, 1990–93
BU	Biblische Untersuchungen			
BVB	Beiträge zum Verstehen der Bibel			
BWANT	Beiträge zur Wissenschaft vom Alten und Neuen Testament			
BZ	*Biblische Zeitschrift*		EKKNT	Evangelisch-katholischer Kommentar zum Neuen Testament
BZAW	Beihefte zur Zeitschrift für die alttestamentliche Wissenschaft		ETS	Erfurter theologische Studien
BZNW	Beihefte zur Zeitschrift für die neutestamentliche Wissenschaft		EURHS	Europäische Hochschulschriften
			EvT	*Evangelische Theologie*
CBNT	Coniectanea biblica: New Testament		FAT	Forschungen zum Alten Testament
CBQ	*Catholic Biblical Quarterly*		FB	Forschung zur Bibel
CC	Continental Commentaries		FMS	Foundations of Modern Sociology
CHANE	Culture and History of the Ancient Near East		FRLANT	Forschungen zur Religion und Literatur des Alten und Neuen Testaments
COQG	Christian Origins and the Question of God			

FzB	Forschung zur Bibel
GFAW	Göttinger Forum für Altertumswissenschaft
GFC	Geschichte des frühen Christentums
GGP	Grundriss zur Geschichte der Philosophie
GK	Geschichte kompakt
GNT	Grundrisse zum Neuen Testament
GTA	Göttinger theologischer Arbeiten
GTF	Greifswalder theologische Forschungen
GuL	Glaube und Lernen
HABES	Heidelberger Althistorische Beiträge und Epigraphische Studien
HAW	Handbuch der Altertumswissenschaft
HBS	Herders biblische Studien
Here.	Hereditas: Studien zur alten Kirchengeschichte
Herm.	Hermeneia: A Critical and Historical Commentary on the Bible
HNT	Handbuch zum Neuen Testament
HThSt	Hamburger theologische Studien
HTKNT	Herders theologischer Kommentar zum Neuen Testament
HTKSup	Herders theologischer Kommentar Supplement Volume
HTS	Harvard Theological Studies
HTS	Hervormde Teologiese Studies
HUT	Hermeneutische Untersuchungen zur Theologie
ICC	International Critical Commentary
JAC	Jahrbuch für Antike und Christentum
JAJSup	Journal of Ancient Judaism Supplement
JBTh	Jahrbuch für biblische Theologie
JSJ	Journal for the Study of Judaism in the Persian, Hellenistic, and Roman Periods
JSNT	Journal for the Study of the New Testament
JSNTSup	Journal for the Study of the New Testament Supplement Series
JThF	Jerusalemer Theologisches Forum
JTS	Journal of Theological Studies
Jud	Judaica
KE	Kirchengeschichte in Einzeldarstellungen
KEK	Kritisch-exegetischer Kommentar über das Neue Testament (Meyers Kommentar)
KG	Kunst und Gesellschaft
KGAW	Kulturgeschichte der antiken Welt
KP-II	Kleiner Pauly II
K-ST	Kohlhammer-Studienbücher Theologie
KTA	Kröners Taschenausgabe
KuD	Kirche und Dogma
KuI	Kirche und Israel
LBS	Linguistic Biblical Studies
LEC	Library of Early Christianity
LNTS	Library of New Testament Studies
LTT	Library of Theological Translations
MBAH	Marburger Beiträge zur antiken Handels-, Sozial- und Wirtschaftsgeschichte
MBPF	Münchener Beiträge zur Papyrusforschung und antiken Rechtsgeschichte
MJS	Münsteraner Judaistischen Studien
MSH	Making Sense of History
MTA	Münsteraner theologische Abhandlungen
MTS	Marburger theologische Studien
MTZ	Münchener theologische Zeitschrift

NBL	*Neues Bibel-Lexikon.* Edited by Manfred Görg and Bernard Lang. Zurich: Benziger, 1988–2001
NEB.AT	Neue Echter Bibel: Ergänzungsband zum Alten Testament
NET	Neutestamentliche Entwürfe zur Theologie
NHC	Nag Hammadi Codices
NovT	*Novum Testamentum*
NovTSup	Supplements to Novum Testamentum
NTA	Neutestamentliche Abhandlungen
NTAK	Neues Testament und Antike Kultur
NTD	Das Neue Testament Deutsch
NTL	New Testament Library
NTOA	Novum Testamentum et orbis antiquus
NTS	New Testament Series
NTS	*New Testament Studies*
NTSI	New Testament and the Scriptures of Israel
NTTS	New Testament Tools and Studies
NW	Georg Strecker, Udo Schnelle, et al., eds. *Neuer Wettstein: Texte zum Neuen Testament aus Griechentum und Hellenismus.* Berlin: de Gruyter, 1996–.
ÖBS	Österreichische biblische Studien
OGIS	*Orientis Graeci Inscriptiones Selectae.* Edited by Wilhelm Dittenberger. 2 vols. Leipzig: Hirzel, 1903–5
ÖTK	Ökumenischer Taschenbuch-Kommentar
PaSt	Pauline Studies
PaThSt	Paderborner theologische Studien
PhAnt	Philosophia antiqua
PKNT	Papyrologische Kommentare zum Neuen Testament

PW	A. F. Pauly. *Paulys Realencyclopädie der classischen Altertumswissenschaft.* Edited by G. Wissowa. 49 vols. in 58. New ed. Munich: Druckenmüller, 1894–1980
QD	Quaestiones disputatae
RAC	*Reallexikon für Antike und Christentum: Sachwörterbuch zur Auseinandersetzung des Christentums mit der antiken Welt.* Edited by T. Klauser et al. Stuttgart: Hiersemann, 1950–.
RGG	*Religion in Geschichte und Gegenwart Handwörterbuch für Theologie und Religionswissenschaft.* Edited by Hans Dieter Benz et al. 4th ed. Tübingen: Mohr Siebeck, 1998–2007
RGRW	Religions in the Graeco-Roman World
RM	Religionen der Menschheit
RNT	Regensburger Neues Testament
RVV	Religionsgeschichtliche Versuche und Vorarbeiten
SAC	Studies in Antiquity and Christianity
SAG	Studien zur Alten Geschichte
SANT	Studien zum Alten und Neuen Testaments
SBB	Stuttgarter biblische Beiträge
SBibSt	Sources for Biblical Study
SBIR	Studies of the Bible and Its Reception
SBLDS	Society of Biblical Literature Dissertation Series
SBS	Stuttgarter Bibelstudien
SBT	Studies in Biblical Theology
SdU	Schriften des Urchristentums
SESJ	Suomen Eksegeettisen Seuran julkaisuja
SFEG	Schriften der Finnischen exegetischen Gesellschaft
SGKA	Studien zur Geschichte und Kultur des Altertums
SHAW	Sitzungen der heidelberger Akademie der Wissenschaften

SHR	Studies in the History of Religions (supplements to *Numen*)
SIG	*Sylloge Inscriptionum Graecarum*. Edited by Wilhelm Dittenberger. 4 vols. 3rd ed. Leipzig: Hirzel, 1915–24
SIJD	Schriften des Institutum judaicum delitzschianum
SJ	Studia Judaica
SNT	Studien zum Neuen Testament
SNTSMS	Society for New Testament Studies Monograph Series
SNTW	Studies of the New Testament and Its World
SPB	Studia Post-Biblica
SPK	Schriften zur politischen Kommunikation
SQAW	Schriften und Quellen der Alten Welt
SRLT	Schriftenreihe des Rheinischen Landesmuseums Trier
StA	Studienhefte zur Altertumswissenschaft
STAC	Studien und Texte zu Antike und Christentum
StAns	Studia Anselmiana
Str-B	H. L. Strack and P. Billerbeck. *Kommentar zum Neuen Testament aus Talmud und Midrasch*. 6 vols. Munich: Beck, 1922–61
SUNT	Studien zur Umwelt des Neuen Testaments
SVF	*Stoicorum Veterum Fragmenta*. Edited by H. F. A. von Arnim. 4 vols. Leipzig: Teubner, 1903–24. Repr., Stuttgart: Teubner, 1964
TANZ	Texte und Arbeiten zum neutestamentlichen Zeitalter
TB	Theologische Bücherei: Neudrucke und Berichte aus dem 20. Jahrhundert
TBei	*Theologische Beiträge*
TBLNT	*Theologisches Begriffslexikon zum Neuen Testament*. Edited by L. Coenen and K. Haacker. Rev. ed. Wuppertal: Brockhaus, 1997–2000
TDNT	*Theological Dictionary of the New Testament*. Edited by G. Kittel and G. Friedrich. Translated by G. W. Bromiley. 10 vols. Grand Rapids: Eerdmans, 1964–76
TdT	Themen der Theologie
TheolViat	*Theologia Viatorum*
THK	Theologischer Handkommentar zum Neuen Testament
TI	Theologie interdisziplinär
TKNT	Theologischer Kommentar zum Neuen Testament
TLZ	*Theologische Literaturzeitung*
TPQ	*Theologisch-praktische Quartalschrift*
TRE	*Theologische Realenzyklopädie*. Edited by G. Krause and G. Müller. Berlin: de Gruyter, 1977–2007
TSAJ	Texte und Studien zum antiken Judentum
TTZ	*Trierer theologische Zeitschrift*
TUGAL	Texte und Untersuchungen zur Geschichte der altchristlichen Literatur
TynBul	*Tyndale Bulletin*
TZ	*Theologische Zeitschrift*
TzF	Texte zur Forschung
TzNT	Texte zum Neuen Testament
UaLG	Untersuchungen zur antiken Literatur und Geschichte
UNT	Untersuchungen zum Neuen Testament
USU	Das Urchristentum in seiner Umwelt
UTB	Uni-Taschenbücher
VCSup	Supplements to Vigiliae Christianae
VuF	*Verkündigung und Forschung*
WBC	Word Biblical Commentary
WdF	Weg der Forschung

WKGLS	Wissenschaftliche Kommentare zu Griechischen und Lateinischen Schriftstellern	ZDPV	*Zeitschrift des deutschen Palästina-Vereins*
WMANT	Wissenschaftliche Monographien zum Alten und Neuen Testament	Zet	Zetemata
		ZGKJ	*Aschkenas: Zeitschrift für Geschichte und Kultur der Juden*
WS	*Wissenschaftliche Studien*	ZKG	*Zeitschrift für Kirchengeschichte*
WuD	*Wort und Dienst*	ZNT	*Zeitschrift für Neues Testament*
WUNT	Wissenschaftliche Untersuchungen zum Neuen Testament	ZNW	*Zeitschrift für die neutestamentliche Wissenschaft und die Kunde der älteren Kirche*
ZAC	*Zeitschrift für Antikes Christentum / Journal of Ancient Christianity*	ZPE	*Zeitschrift für Papyrologie und Epigraphik*
		ZTK	*Zeitschrift für Theologie und Kirche*
ZBK.NT	Zürcher Bibelkommentare: Novem Testamentum	ZWT	*Zeitschrift für wissenschaftliche Theologie*

1

On Writing a History of Origins

Jesus of Nazareth is a figure of history, and the Christian movement is a witness to the impact of this person. One who writes a history of early Christianity from a distance of two thousand years inevitably confronts the basic problem of historical research and knowledge. How does history take place? What happens when a document of the past is interpreted in the present with a claim on the future? How do historical reports and their arrangement relate to the contemporary framework of the historian/exegete's understanding?

1.1. History as Interpretation of the Present and the Past

Interests and the Acquisition of Knowledge

The classical ideal of historicism, to "demonstrate what happened,"[1] turns out to be an ideological postulate in a variety of ways. With its transition into the past, the present irrevocably loses its character as reality. Thus it is not possible to make the past to be present in unbroken form. The temporal interval means a distance in every respect. It denies historical knowledge in the sense of a comprehensive recovery of what happened. Rather, one can only make known one's own interpretation in the present of what happened in the past. The past meets us exclusively in the mode of the present, in an

---

1. Ranke, "Geschichten der romanischen und germanischen Völker," in Ranke's *Sämtliche Werke: Zweite Gesamtausgabe* 33/34:vii, "People have conferred on history the responsibility of restoring the past, to make it useful for the instruction of years to come. The present work does not accept such a high office; it only wants to set forth what actually happened."

interpreted and selective form. What is relevant from the past is only that which is no longer past but rather influences the contemporary world formation and world interpretation.[2] The historians' social settings, including their geographical location and political and religious value systems, necessarily shapes what they say in the present about the past.[3] The writing of history is never a pure image of events because it has a history of its own, the history of the writer. The subject does not stand over history but is entirely entangled in it. Therefore, "objectivity" is not appropriate as the opposite of "subjectivity" in describing historical understanding.[4] Rather, one should speak of "reasonableness" or "plausibility" of historical arguments.[5] The actual event is not accessible to us, but rather only the various interpretations from the standpoint of the interpreter. Only through our attribution of meaning do things become what they are for us. History is not reconstructed, but rather it is unavoidably and necessarily constructed. That is, "it becomes history, but it is not history."[6] The writing of history involves much more than a mere relationship to the past. It is a way of establishing and shaping meaning, without which individual and collective life would not be possible.

Facts and Fiction

History turns out to be always a selective system, with which interpreters arrange and interpret not only the past but also their own world.[7] The linguistic construction of history that takes place, therefore, is always a process that bestows meaning on both the past and the present. Historical interpretation involves creating a coherent framework of meaning. With the production of a historical narrative, the facts become what they are for us. Thus historical reports must be made accessible to the present and articulated so that in the presentation or narration of historical events, "facts" and "fiction,"[8] data and

2. Cf. Droysen, *Outline of the Principles of History*, 11. "The data for historical investigation are not past things, for these have disappeared, but things that are still present here and now, whether recollections of what was done, or remnants of things that have existed and of events that have occurred." Cf. Schnelle, *Theology of the New Testament*, 28.

3. Cf. Straub, "Über das Bilden von Vergangenheit."

4. Cf. Goertz, *Umgang mit Geschichte*.

5. Cf. Kocka, "Angemessenheitskriterien historischer Argumente."

6. Droysen, *Historik*, 69. Concerning the historical subject matter, Droysen correctly observes: "They are only historical because we grasp them historically, not objectively in and of themselves, but in our own perspective and through them. We must, so to speak, transpose them."

7. Cf. Cassirer, *Versuch über den Menschen*, 291: "Historical study is not the knowledge of outward facts or events; it is a form of self-knowledge."

8. "Fiction" designates not simply the popular sense of "unreal" or "untrue" but is intended in a functional and communicative sense and approximates the original meaning of "fictio": construction, formation. Cf. Iser, *Act of Reading*, 53–54.

the creative work of an author, are combined with each other. As historical reports are combined, empty historical places must be filled in, and reports out of the past and their interpretation in the present come together as something new.[9] Through the interpretation, the event takes on a new structure that it never had before. Facts must be given a significance; the structure of this process of interpretation constitutes the understanding of the facts. The fictional element opens an access to the past and makes possible the essential rewriting of the presumed events.

Reality as Given

At the same time, statements are always interwoven with the conceptions of existing reality and time, without which construction and communication are not possible. There undoubtedly exists a reality, which is before, alongside, and after, but above all independent of our perception and description. Every person is genetically preconstructed and is constantly being coconstructed by sociocultural dynamics. Reflection and construction are always later actions that refer to something that is already given. Thus self-consciousness is never based on itself but necessarily requires reference to something beyond itself that grounds it and makes it possible. The fact that the question about meaning is even possible, and that meaning can be attained, points to an "unimaginable reality,"[10] which precedes all existence and gives it the status of reality. A basic principle thus emerges: History comes into being first, after the underlying event takes place, and becomes elevated into the status of the past that is relevant to the present. Thus history does not have the same claim to reality as the underlying events. It is not our world and life that is a construction, but rather our perspective about it. For us, the two cannot be kept apart.

1.2 History and Method

The indispensable fictional or creative element of any writing of history requires a comprehensive inclusion of all relevant sources, a consideration of the central cultural presuppositions and contexts, and a combination of various

---

9. Cicero, *Orator* 2.54 (the historian Antipater is singled out with praise: "the others do not embellish the story, but are only chroniclers"); Luke 1:1–4; Plutarch, *Alexander* 1.1 (οὔτε γὰρ ἱστορίας γράφομεν ἀλλὰ βίους, "For I do not write history, but instead I draw life portraits") indicates that ancient authors had a clear consciousness of these relationships. Cf. also Thucydides, *Historiae* 1.22.1; Lucian, *Historia* 51; Quintilian, *Institutio Oratoria* 8.3.70.

10. Cf. Rüsen, "Faktizität und Fiktionalität der Geschichte," 31.

questions in order to guard the natural subjective element from subjectivistic reductionism.[11]

Sources

The main sources are naturally all writings of the NT, especially the letters of Paul, Acts, and the Gospels. In addition one must also consider the Greek OT (Septuagint) and the entire Jewish literature from about 200 BCE to 100 CE insofar as they are relevant to early Christianity (see 3.3.1). In addition there are the writings of Flavius Josephus (ca. 37/38 CE–100 CE), whose main works, *Bellum Iudaicum* (*Jewish War*, written around 78/79 CE) and *Antiquitates Iudaicae* (*Antiquities of the Jews*, 94 CE) are of greatest significance for the understanding of ancient Judaism. From the Greco-Roman world the major sources are Tacitus (ca. 60–120 CE; major works *Historiae* [*Histories*], ca. 105 CE; *Annales* [*Annals*], ca. 115 CE), Suetonius (ca. 70–140/150 CE; major work *De vita Caesarum* [*Life of the Caesars*], 120 CE), and Dio Cassius (ca. 160–235 CE; major work, Ῥωμαϊκὴ ἱστορία [*Historia romana*, *Roman History*], ca. 230 CE).[12] They had access to numerous (no longer extant) sources and transmitted valuable information about the relationship of the Roman state to Judaism and to emerging early Christianity. Also noteworthy are individual noncanonical witnesses to Jesus and to early Christianity that indicate how this person/movement was perceived. A distinctive source for the perception of Christians by the Romans appears in the exchange of letters between the governor Pliny and the caesar Trajan (ca. 110 CE), which offers an insight into the thinking of the imperial leadership over legal questions (see 12.4 below). The great philosophical movements in the first century are also significant: in contrast to today, philosophical-religious thinking influenced a large segment of the population. Finally, the inscriptions, coins, and architectonic witnesses (e.g., the Titus Arch in Rome) are to be considered, especially when they are significant for early Christianity.

Chronological Basis

In any historical depiction, a chronological framework is a starting point. The direct and indirect presuppositions must be expressed, including the central lines of development and the major events. The places of the events and the influential persons must be connected to the chronology. Geographic/

---

11. On the world of the historical disciplines, cf. Jordan, *Theorien und Methoden*; on methods, approaches, and problems, cf. Maurer, *Aufriss der Historischen Wissenschaften*, vols. 1–6.
12. Cf. Flach, *Römische Geschichtsschreibung*.

local history and cultural-religious aspects complement each other, for, as a rule, it is no coincidence that relevant developments occur only or primarily in specific places.

Cultural Contexts and Personae

Early Christianity can neither be viewed in isolation nor explained in a monocausal way. Rather, the starting point for depicting it is its embeddedness in the multifaceted world of Hellenism. Judaism, indeed, as the first reference point of early Christianity, is a part of Hellenism. Hence an intentional further methodical horizon must be chosen, with which the religio-history and societal history, including the world of politics, economics, and culture, are included (see chap. 3 below). Likewise, individual and collective actors are not mutually exclusive in historical developments. Thus Paul is undoubtedly the most influential individual within early Christianity, but at the same time the individual unknown communities and nameless missionaries in the beginning period are of great significance for the development of the empire-wide movement of the "Christians" (cf. Acts 11:26). Likewise, a plausible, logical intentionality may be inherent in historical processes yet also may cause or support accidental developments.

The interaction of individual actors and comprehensive developments must thus be complemented by an understanding of those who thought otherwise ("opponents") in specific communities in specific places. They played a significant, but not always comprehensible, role in the history of early Christianity, for they are known only indirectly from the perspective of later literature that has been preserved (see 11.3). They are nevertheless indispensable for the understanding of the total development of early Christianity. Theologically revealing and historically necessary controversies are intelligible only when the positions of respective dissenters are included in the depiction.[13]

History of Ideas and Social Conditions

A purely materialistic basis of history, according to which the genetic configuration and social reality alone determine the thought and action of humanity, is reductionistic, as is the idealistic concept of the historical personality or powerful idea/ideology that determines the course of history. The world of

---

13. Discourse analysis is helpful for the understanding of these positions. It is a method/ formulation of a question intended to understand and demonstrate the formation and establishment of discourses in history and the associated linguistic expressions/views/arguments/ intentions/interests/claims to power. Cf. Keller, *Diskursforschung*; Landwehr, *Historische Diskursanalyse*.

ideas is a formative element of history, as are the actual relationships. Thus
the history of ideas and social history should not be considered antithetical;
rather, ideas and theological concepts in their concrete social and literary
manifestations as a rule merge into one another in a positive development.
With the early Christians this connection is immense, for faith in Jesus Christ
was experienced in a new social form, the Christian house church, in which
fundamental distinctions of the ancient world were abolished (cf. Gal. 3:26–
28). Furthermore, early Christianity was, at the level of the history of ideas,
a highly creative phenomenon (see chap. 13), for it developed forward-looking
interpretations of God and the world, a distinctive language of faith, its own
forms of literature, and new forms of living, which were obviously perceived
as attractive, made history, established the success of the new movement, and
thus belong in the depiction of this history.

Microhistory

The history of early Christianity is a form of microhistory, which is reflected
almost exclusively in its own literature. It was a movement that had only small
groups of followers (house churches with ca. 30–40 people) at the beginning
and was only slowly recognized by outsiders. Thus from the earliest time only
those witnesses exist that were recognized as relevant at a later time in the
process of the formation of the canon. Furthermore, literature from the beginning period simply became lost, including, according to 1 Cor. 5:9, a letter of
Paul and, according to Luke 1:1–4, early (pre-)forms of the gospel literature.
At the same time, one must affirm that the number and the quality of the witnesses that have been preserved are distinctive in the history of religions: (1) In
comparison with the original phase of other world religions (e.g., Judaism
and Islam), the number, the age, and the various authors of the writings from
the beginning era are remarkable. After an initial phase of oral tradition and
the earliest written activity (see 6.7), the first independent witness of the new
movement was 1 Thessalonians, written around 50 CE, about twenty years
after the death of Jesus. With the logia source (Q) came the first account of
the life and proclamation of Jesus Christ around 50–60 CE.[14] (2) With more
than 5,000 manuscripts of the NT,[15] the production of texts and traditions in
antiquity is unique to early Christianity and a reliable foundation for historical
questions. (3) Inasmuch as texts come from every important stream of early
Christianity, one cannot speak of the history written by the victors.

14. For the basis of this dating, cf. Schnelle, *History and Theology*, 44–45.
15. Cf. K. Aland and B. Aland, *Der Text des Neuen Testaments*; Parker, *New Testament
Manuscripts*.

Macrohistory

Finally, the history of early Christianity clearly demonstrates that each element of microhistory is part of a macrohistory in many respects:

1. In its emerging phase the movement of Christ-believers was a part of Jewish history (see chap. 5).
2. This brought them into the tense relationship between the Jews and the Romans in a parallel history.
3. With the successful Pauline mission in Asia Minor and Greece, the emerging Christianity was part of the Jewish (diaspora) history and was perceived in this way by the Romans (Edict of Claudius; Paul before Gallio). At the same time the new movement developed its own dynamic in actual Roman history (the fire of Rome under Nero).
4. The destruction of Jerusalem in 70 CE had great significance for early Christianity (see chap. 9) but affected it less than it affected Judaism.
5. The larger early Christianity became, the more it participated in Roman history and was at the same time destined for a long-lasting confrontation with the Romans. The special arrangement by which Judaism was tolerated as a religion did not apply to the Christians. The imperial cult made conflict with Christians inevitable (see chap. 12).[16]

What is generally true applies to the writing of history: To be human is to interpret; that is, to be able to understand oneself and others, one relies on an interpretation of the self and the world. This interpretative process must be consciously shaped and reflected upon. One considers the historical sources as well as the history of interpretation and the conditions of the contemporary construction of history. Multiple perspectives as well as one's own standpoint are not mutually exclusive but complement each other. Both the origin and basis of a historical phenomenon must be distinguished but can never be separated.

16. The frequently used concept of "religio licita" for Judaism is misleading because it was never officially recognized from the Roman side; cf. D.-A. Koch, *Geschichte des Urchristentums*, 548–50. As a rule, the Romans accepted "ancient" cults and religions and provided Judaism special rights only from time to time and from caesar to caesar.

2

Definition and Demarcation of the Epoch

2.1 Primitive Christianity or Early Christianity?

Since the end of the eighteenth century the term *Urchristentum* has prevailed as a *terminus technicus* in German scholarship for the earliest historical epoch of the origin of Christianity. Within itself it includes multiple meanings that are different categories and must be analyzed separately. In a temporal-descriptive sense it refers to the moment of beginning, and primitive Christianity means the original Christianity. With the term *primitive* (German: with the prefix *ur*), a value judgment is commonly made that equates the beginning of Christianity with its essence. Primitive Christianity then means the original Christianity, the original condition. By this understanding "primitive Christianity" and "the primitive church" presuppose the concept of a pure, unadulterated origin in contrast to the later development of a history of decline.[1] The beginning of Christianity is equated with its essence, and in most cases unity is regarded as the characteristic of the beginning, and opposition/conflict is characterized as a sign of the later decline. However, this usage involves value judgments, that is, views of history that cannot be verified in the texts.

Thus neutral terms have been suggested in order to characterize the beginning stage of Christianity. Terms such as "apostolic/postapostolic era" or "primitive Christianity" have not been widely accepted because they include many value judgments. On the other hand, in German and in English-language

1. Cf. Alkier, *Urchristentum*, 261ff.

8

scholarship, the term "early Christianity" (*Frühchristentum*) is used[2] because it most clearly makes possible a purely phenomenological understanding and neutral designation; it concerns the beginning era of a movement that has existed for 2,000 years. A normative element still resonates since a special meaning for all time is attributed to the beginning. This term does not prejudice how one describes the beginning—whether as unified movement or as a multistructured or even divided entity. Thus "early Christianity" is used in this book as the most neutral *terminus technicus*.

2.2 The Chronological Framework

From what point can one speak of early Christianity? First of all, the term "early Christianity" is an interpretative category that emerges from the impact of the movement but was not used by its members. Acts 11:26 ("the disciples were called Christians first at Antioch") and the letters of Paul indicate that, between 50 and 60 CE, the new movement developed a consciousness of its distinctiveness and separate identity (see 8.7). At this point we may speak of the beginnings of the movement of Christ-believers (see chap. 4): people who believed in Jesus as the Messiah were followers of Christ. First the Pauline mission creates the presuppositions and the consciousness of an independent entity (see 8.7), which then creates in the Gospels the basic narrative (9.4). From this point in time the designation "early Christianity" is a historical category. The term is not used for the time before that, except in popular discourse.

How does one structure the epoch of the origin of early Christianity? First of all, it is evident that the new movement of Christ-believers begins where the earthly life of Jesus of Nazareth ended (in the year 30 CE).[3] Two reasons support this conclusion: (1) Jesus of Nazareth proclaimed the coming of the kingdom of God[4] and did not understand himself as founder of a new and lasting movement; (2) the appearances of the Resurrected One (see chap. 4)

---

2. Alkier, *Urchristentum*, 265, offers a variant: "I propose to replace the term 'primitive Christianity' (*Urchristentum*) by the term 'early Christianity' [*Frühchristentum*], which is already in common use." Lüdemann, *Primitive Christianity*, prefers to keep the term "primitive Christianity" (*Urchristentum*), but without the idealizing connotation; similarly D.-A. Koch, *Geschichte des Urchristentums*, 24, gives a chronological indefiniteness to the term "early Christianity."

3. Jesus of Nazareth was crucified probably on Friday, the 14th of Nisan (= April 7) of the year 30 in Jerusalem as a rebel against the Romans. Cf. A. Strobel, "Der Termin des Todes Jesu"; Riesner, *Paul's Early Period*, 52–63. Skeptical about this dating is Bond, "Dating the Death of Jesus," who favors a period between 29 and 34 CE.

4. On the proclamation of Jesus, cf. Schnelle, *Theology of the New Testament*, 61–155.

introduced something new, for now Jesus Christ was worshiped as a divine being and as the founder of a new (inner Jewish) discourse.[5]

The next turning point that can be established is around 50 CE.[6] The apostolic council in 48 CE (see chap. 7) and the associated second (48–51/52 CE) and third missionary journeys (52–55 CE) with the crossing into Europe mark a new theological and geographic orientation within the emerging early Christianity. The independent circumcision-free Pauline mission turned programmatically to people from the Greco-Roman culture, universalized the movement, and transferred its primary location to Asia Minor and Greece.

The third decisive turning point was undoubtedly the year 70 CE (see chap. 9). Between 60 and 70, the epoch of the founders ended with the deaths of Peter, Paul, and James (see 9.1). With the destruction of the temple and of the Jerusalem church, early Christianity lost its previous center and had to establish itself elsewhere. The origin of new literature emerged out of this radically changed situation. The new literary form, *gospel*, and the pseudepigraphical apostolic letters (deutero-Pauline, letters under the name of Peter, James, and Jude) indicate the consciousness of a new epoch. The Jesus traditions had to be secured, and the personal ministry of the apostles at the beginning had come to an end. These were challenges to be overcome in a new literature. The year 70 introduces the last epoch of early Christianity, but the end is difficult to determine. To be sure, in the period around 130 CE a clear shift occurs at several levels.

    a. *New issues.* The early apologists defend themselves to the outside world against persecution and slander of Christians, first with apologetic,[7] directing their defense to the Roman caesar. Around 125/126 CE, Quadratus wrote to caesar Hadrian[8] to protest against the unproven accusations against Christians. Around 127 CE the Athenian philosopher Aristides likewise turned to Hadrian, explaining the teaching of the

5. Similarly, Conzelmann, *History of Primitive Christianity*, 7: "Jesus' life and teaching are the *presupposition* of church history." Totally different is the view of Hengel and Schwemer, *Jesus und das Judentum*, 3–20, who begin their history of early Christianity with the appearance of John the Baptist and the ministry of Jesus. The second epoch is the period from 30–72 CE; the third epoch encompasses the time from 70–138 CE (the death of Hadrian).

6. Cf. also Schramm, *Fünf Wegscheiden*, 151.

7. Apologetic is present also in the NT, especially in Acts. Both the leaders of the Jews and the people persecute Jesus and ultimately the Christians (Mark 15:16–20, omitted in Luke; cf. also Acts 13:50; 17:5–7, 13; 21:17ff.); at the attack of the Jews, the Roman authorities intervened and protected them.

8. See the dating and texts (particularly Eusebius, *Historia ecclesiastica*), in Fiedrowicz, *Christen und Heiden*, 24–25.

Christians and appealing for understanding.[9] A common feature of the
early apologies is a new perspective and a new self-understanding: The
Christians see themselves as a significant group within the society, placed
permanently into history, and as loyal citizens of the Roman Empire
who demand their natural rights of protection.[10] Thus, as believers in
God, they distinguish themselves from Jews and Greeks, as attested in
the Kerygma Petrou (ca. 125 CE): "For what has reference to the Greeks
and Jews is old; but we are Christians, who as a third race worship him
in a new way."[11]

b. *New literary forms.* A new literary form came into being that had not
existed before: the apologies. These were works of exhortation and
especially of argumentation, which were intended for the caesar and/
or the senate and similar to the literary form of a petition. It is striking
that the authors of the early apologies appeared as philosophers in order
to gain the attention of the caesar.

c. *New mass movements.* Gnosticism developed around the end of the first
century CE (see under 14.2), and then from the first third of the second
century it grew into an independent mass movement within Christianity.
Around 180 CE it had spread and gained so much power that Irenaeus
saw the church as endangered and published his foundational work,
Adversus haereses (Against Heresies).

d. *The Bar Kokhba Rebellion (132–34 CE).* This event marks a turning
point. As a result of it, the national status of Judaism, which had already been severely constrained, came to an end (see under 3.3). This
strong and sustained weakening of Judaism led to a strengthening of
the independence and self-assurance of emerging Christianity, which is
evident in the "dialogue" between Justin and the Jewish philosopher
Trypho (*Dialogue with Trypho*, ca. 155 CE).

> As a rule, historical processes in antiquity cannot be established to a specific year.
> Rather, the developments occur as the old still dominates while the new emerges.

9. Cf. Fiedrowicz, *Christen und Heiden*, 25–28.

10. Other early apologists: Justin (around 155 CE); Athenagoras (around 177 CE); on the
history of apologetic, cf. Conzelmann, *Gentiles, Jews, Christians*, 275–342.

11. Kerygma Petrou (Preaching of Peter) 2d, trans. Schneemelcher.

Thus the structuring, the demarcation, and the dates merely indicate the basic
movements in early Christianity.[12]

12. While in almost all outlines the year 30 CE is given as the beginning of primitive/early
Christianity, the transition to the ancient church is established in various ways. Paulsen (*Zur
Wissenschaft vom Urchristentum*, 210) proposes 150–180 CE. Lüdemann, *Heretics*, 15, suggests the end of the second century; J. Becker, *Das Urchristentum als gegliederte Epoch*, 12,
assumes 120/130 CE; D.-A. Koch, *Geschichte des Urchristentums*, 153–56, argues for 150 CE,
because only now are the new developments set in motion by apologetic and gnosis. Justin in
particular speaks against such a late dating of gnosis. He probably made a comprehensive attack on Gnostic systems in his (now lost) *Syntagma*, written around 145 CE. Thus one must
assume an origin and spread of gnosis and thus its origin must be earlier, e.g., in the first third
of the second century.

3

Presuppositions and Contexts

E arly Christianity is bound up equally with the history of Judaism and the Greco-Roman world. It came into being as a movement within Judaism and developed into a new, Greek-speaking, universal religion in the Roman Empire. The precondition for this development was Hellenism, which created a new world culture from the fourth century BCE. The NT also came into existence in this setting.

3.1 Hellenism as a World Culture

The term *Hellenism* as a designation of a historical epoch was first coined by the historian Johann Gustav Droysen (1808–84).[1] Hellenism (Ἑλληνισμός = Greek language and customs) designates the spread of Greek language, customs, administrative structures, art, architecture, literature, philosophy, and religion in the Near and Middle East that occurred with the rise of Alexander the Great (356–323 BCE). This movement encompassed the region from Macedonia to the edge of India, from the north coast of the Black Sea and the shores of the Danube to Nubia in the Sahara. The cultural expansion of Hellenism was founded especially on the Greek cities, which were perceived as attractive.[2] With the founding of new cities, with their imposing architecture,

1. On the political, economic, and societal aspects of Hellenism that are not treated here, see Gehrke, *Geschichte des Hellenismus*, 165ff.; Meissner, *Hellenismus*, 97ff.
2. Cf. Metzler and Kolb, *Die Stadt im Altertum*, 121–40.

3.1. The military campaigns of Alexander the Great

CELTS

THRACE
Pella
Illion (ancient Troy)
Granicus
Gordium
PHRYGIA
CAPPADOCIA
Pergamum
Ephesus
Miletus
Halicarnassus
Delphi
Athens
Sparta
CRETE
CYPRUS
Issus
SYRIA
Damascus
Tyre
Gaza
Alexandria (Iskenderun)
Cilician Gates
Alexandria
Memphis
EGYPT
Alexandria
Siwa Oasis
Cyrene
LIBYA

Black Sea
Mediterranean Sea
Red Sea
Nile

Danube R.

ARABIA

Euphrates R.
Tigris R.
Babylon
Opis
Susa
Gaugamela
Echatana
MEDIAN EMPIRE
Caspian Gates
Caspian Sea
Aral Sea

Ispahan
Persian Gates
Persepolis
PERSIA
PARTHIA
Zadrakarta

Persian Gulf
Harmozia
Journey of Nearchus (325 BCE)
GEDROSIA
Pura
Alexandria (Bela)
Pattala
Indian Ocean

Alexandria (Farah)
Alexandria (Herat)
Alexandropolis
Alexandria (Mary)
Oxus R.
Jaxartes R.
Marakanda
SOGDIANA
Balkh
BACTRIA
Alexandria (Charikar)
Kabura
ARIA
Alexandria (Ghazi)
Alexandria (Kandahar)
Path of (the Macedonian general) Craterus

Taxila
Alexandria (Chudshand)
Bukaphata
Nikaia
Altars of Alexander
INDIA
Indus R.
Hydaspes R.
Hyphasis R.

Macedonia before Philip II
Conquered by Philip II
States subject to Alexander

Cities besieged by Alexander
Cities founded by Alexander
Important battles

Border of Alexander's kingdom
Military campaigns of Alexander
Further military campaigns

(Mary) Modern place names
Desert and plain areas
Pass

0   100   200 mi
0 100 200 km

military and economic potential, and open forms of life, Alexander's brief military success had a long, enduring effect.

Hellenism did not come to an end with the rise of the Roman Empire:[3] it gained influence in the entire Roman world. It was significant for the course of history; both Byzantium and the renaissance of the Middle Ages are unimaginable without Hellenism. The primary marker of Hellenism is the increased blending and saturation of various cultures in which national cultures were transformed by Greek life and thought. At the same time, however, Greek and later Roman culture became open to oriental influences.[4] The new global culture did not remove the existing national or regional cultures: it transformed them at the same time. Thus a relatively unified cultural area emerged that allowed cultural peculiarities and differences without coming apart.

Greek as a World Language

The spread of the Greek language must be regarded as an excellent example of this process. In the NT era, the Greek language was the world language. Inscriptional discoveries indicate especially that in Palestine of the first century CE, two linguae francae overlapped.[5] Greek was spoken along with Aramaic, even in the simplest levels of society.[6] A comparable linguistic situation existed in Syria, where Aramaic and Greek dominated.[7] After Alexander's conquest, Asia Minor came under Greek influence, so that Greek defined the linguistic face of Asia Minor in the first century CE.[8] Alongside Greek, the local dialects continued to be spoken (e.g., Acts 2:5–11; 14:11). The linguistic situation in Greece was clear, in contrast to Italy and Rome, where the linguistic situation is difficult to ascertain.

Educated Romans had a good knowledge of Greek; so also did many of the slaves who had been brought to Rome from the East. Thus in a limited sense

---

3. The temporal delimitation of "Hellenism" is determined in a variety of ways. While a relative consensus exists that with Alexander's conquest a new epoch began (year of death is usually given as 323 BCE and the beginning of Hellenism), the end of the period is judged in various ways: with the incorporation of Egypt into the Roman Empire (30 BCE) or with the end of the Roman Empire, that is, with the end of antiquity. Cf. Timpe, "Hellenismus."

4. Interaction between Greece and the Orient naturally already existed; cf. Dihle and Feldmeier, *Hellas und der Orient*.

5. Cf. Rosén, "Die Sprachsituation im Römischen Palästina"; Millard, *Pergament und Papyrus*, 81–114.

6. Cf. Rosén, "Die Sprachsituation im Römischen Palästina," 236–37.

7. Cf. R. Schmitt, "Die Ostgrenze von Armenien über Mesopotamien, Syrien bis Arabien," in *Die Sprachen im Römischen Reich der Kaiserzeit*, 195–205.

8. Cf. G. Neumann, "Kleinasien."

one can say that Rome was bilingual.[9] All authors of the NT write in Greek. For example, Paul conducts his mission with one language and communicates with all levels of society. The language of the diaspora Jews was also Greek. Besides the Septuagint and the other numerous writers of Hellenistic Judaism, Philo and Josephus are especially important. Philo of Alexandria called Greek "our language,"[10] and Josephus writes his history of the Jewish War around 78/79 CE in Greek for a predominantly Roman audience.[11]

Judaism and Hellenism

From the time of the *diadochoi* (from ca. 300 BCE), ancient Judaism (see under 3.3) was politically and culturally a part of Hellenism. The Hellenistic influence was stronger in the diaspora than in Palestine. This fact is especially evident in the development of Hellenistic-Jewish literature.[12] The most significant literary production was the Greek translation of the OT, the Septuagint (LXX).[13] Because increasingly fewer Jews in the diaspora understood Hebrew, there was a great need to translate the Scriptures into Greek, the language of the worship service. The Septuagint is especially significant in the history of culture: with it, the greatest work of translation in antiquity, the Semitic and Greek language cultures meet in the third century BCE (probably from 250 BCE in Alexandria) and form a distinctive literary tradition. Beyond the Hebrew tradition, besides the additions and revisions of the Hebrew Bible, the Septuagint includes nine other books: Wisdom of Solomon, Jesus Sirach, Psalms of Solomon, Judith, Tobit, and 1–4 Maccabees. While in the Septuagint, Greek cultural influence is disputed, it is obvious among other authors: Aristobulus (beginning of the 2nd cent. BCE), the Greek Jesus Sirach (132–117 BCE), Joseph and Aseneth (2nd cent. BCE), 4 Maccabees (1st or 2nd cent. CE) and, of course, Philo of Alexandria (see below, 3.2.1), who interpreted the Jewish religion with the help of allegorical interpretation and

9. Cf. Kajanto, "Minderheiten und ihre Sprachen in Rom," 84ff. On the significance of Greek as an international language in the Roman Empire, cf. Zgusta, "Die Rolle des Griechischen im römischen Kaiserreich." Cicero offers an instructive example, in *Pro Archia* 23: "For if anyone thinks that one gains a smaller gain of glory from Greek verses than from Latin ones, he is greatly mistaken, because Greek poetry is read among all nations, Latin is confined to its own linguistic area, which is rather small."

10. Cf. Philo, *Prelim. Studies* 44.

11. Cf. Josephus, *J.W.* 1.3.

12. Nickelsburg gives an overview in *Jewish Literature*, 191–221. See also Gruen, *Heritage and Hellenism.*

13. It received this name because, according to the tradition of the Letter of Aristeas, this work was produced by seventy-two scribes in seventy-two days; on the Septuagint, cf. Tilly, *Einführung in die Septuaginta.*

thus employed a Platonic hermeneutic, portraying it as the old and, at the same time, supreme philosophy.

The influence of Hellenism was by no means limited to the diaspora but rather was also present in Palestine. Beginning in the third century BCE, increasingly more Jews adopted the Greek way of life, which was contained by the Maccabean Revolt (see under 3.3) but not defeated. Evidence of the influence of Hellenism may be seen not only in the Greek inscriptions and sarcophagi but also in the numerous theaters, amphitheaters, and hippodromes.[14] As an expression of the Hellenistic way of life, the culture of public baths was integrated into Judaism, and regional rulers such as Herod the Great (40–4 BCE) and his sons conducted themselves like Hellenistic princes. The architectural program of renovating the Jerusalem temple under Herod also exhibited Greek influence: splendid architecture with giant columned halls and Corinthian and Ionic capitals. In Galilee, Sepphoris and the new capital Tiberias (beginning in 19 CE, named for the caesar Tiberius) showed a Hellenistic stamp. Herod Antipas (4 BCE–39 CE) was, like his father Herod the Great, a Hellenistic ruler with a Roman orientation who nevertheless emphasized his Jewish identity. The marriage of Herod Antipas to Herodias, who previously was married to his half-brother, was denounced by John the Baptist (cf. Luke 3:19–20; Mark 6:14–29). This political-cultural (anti-Hellenistic?) critique resulted in the execution of the Baptist (see under 3.3). Herod Antipas evidently feared the Baptist as he also feared Jesus (cf. Luke 13:31–32) as leaders of messianic movements.

> Hellenism did not abolish the identity of Judaism, but changed it as it learned to understand itself as a part of global culture, from which no one could withdraw.

The NT is also a part and expression of Hellenism, for Hellenism undoubtedly benefited the emergence of new religious movements and the associated process of the blending of cultures. All writings of the NT exist in the Greek language. No single writing was produced in Palestine; instead, they were produced primarily in Asia Minor, Greece, and Rome. Very early the area of activity of the new movement took place outside Palestine and with the Pauline mission moved especially into genuine Greek territory. Paul was a diaspora Jew from the Hellenistic metropolis of Tarsus. He had been educated as a Pharisee in Jerusalem (cf. Acts 22:3) but had a Greek education.[15] In the

---

14. Cf. Kasher, *Jews and Hellenistic Cities in Eretz Israel*.

15. Cf. Vegge, *Paulus und das antike Schulwesen*, 423: "The creation of a text completed with an appropriate disposition and style requires a basic education in grammar and rhetoric."

Pauline churches, the majority lived in the Greco-Roman tradition. They did not then come into contact with Hellenism but rather came originally from Hellenism. The literary genres of the NT, including the letters of Paul, the Gospels, and Acts, have their closest parallels in Hellenistic literature. Early Christianity did not develop out of Judaism into Hellenism but was a part of Hellenism from the beginning. The question of the influence of Hellenism cannot be reduced to the thesis that all of Hellenism in early Christianity was mediated through Hellenistic Judaism.[16] Thus it is evident not only in Paul that the early Christians participated in debates that were current in both Judaism and the Greco-Roman environment.

One cannot deny that the anchor of early Christianity was (primarily Hellenistic) Judaism. The early Christians lived with the understanding of their basic continuity with the history of God with Israel. They lived with the Septuagint, and here the believers found anticipations of God's act in Jesus Christ and formed their religious life in the living encounter with Scripture (e.g., the Psalms). Thus one should not create false alternatives, for the early Christians operated in an expansive cultural region, to which, of course, the Greco-Roman culture belonged. A combined heritage in Judaism and Hellenism was one of the decisive presuppositions for the successful reception of the new faith in mixed communities and thus was characteristic of early Christianity.

3.2 Greco-Roman Culture

Greek Religion

Greek religion is very complex and diverse. Geographically it encompasses not only Greece itself but from the eighth century BCE also extended to southern Italy and the Black Sea coast. From the time of Alexander the Great it extended to Asia Minor, Syria, Egypt, Iraq, and Iran. Local and informal

---

Thus the quality of Pauline texts attests the solid general literary education, a familiarity with the form and content of rhetorical and philosophical discourse of their authors." Cf. also T. Bauer, *Paulus und die kaiserzeitliche Epistolographie*, 404–18, who assumes a higher schooling and rhetorical education of Paul. Arzt-Grabner, *Gott als verlässlicher Käufer*, 412, concludes from the frequent use of commercial terminology in Paul's letters: "As a trained handworker, who presumably had a leading function in shops for handworkers, Paul was familiar with sales and work contracts."

16. Contra Hengel, "Das früheste Christentum," 198: "Whatever pagan influences in early Christianity were assumed can be traced fully to Jewish mediation. One can nowhere demonstrate a direct, continuing influence by pagan cults or non-Jewish thought. What one calls 'Hellenistic' in the New Testament originates as a rule out of Jewish sources, which neither could or wanted to withdraw from the 'religious koine' of the Hellenistic period."

customs form the foundation of this religion, which has these characteristics: (1) a mythologically oriented polytheism, (2) a highly developed art, with images and temples, and (3) a public cult praxis concentrated on animal sacrifice at festivals determined by the local calendar. In Greek religion there is no (1) revelatory writing,[17] (2) religious founder, or (3) organized priesthood extending throughout the land.

Within Greek religion, Homer (8th cent. BCE) and Hesiod (ca. 740–670 BCE) handed down the genealogy of the gods, preserved their epithets, and established their area of responsibility.[18] For our epoch, the Homeric gods, considered to be a great family living on Mount Olympus, are especially crucial. All of the powers that determine life and make it intelligible are visible in the Olympic gods. In most cases twelve gods are attributed to Mount Olympus, although the number varies.[19]

1. In the first place stands Zeus (Ζεύς, genitive Διός, Roman Jupiter), for the Greeks in particular, the weather god who throws lightning bolts and is the mightiest of all gods. Hesiod relates the myth of how Zeus overthrew the old gods, including Kronos and the Titans, and chained them in the underworld. Zeus represents victorious order to which all must submit and which provides the benefits that the sons of Zeus share. Zeus stands over all beings and has no one over him. He is also the only god who could be elevated to be the supreme god: the god of earth, heaven, and the universe.

2. Hera (Ἥρα, Roman Juno) is the jealous and quarreling spouse of Zeus. In the cult she was revered as the great maternal goddess who was enthroned over the festivals.

3. Poseidon (Ποσειδῶν, Roman Neptune) is the brother of Zeus, the lord of the sea, and patron of fishermen and horsemen.

4. Athena (Ἀθηνᾶ, Ἀθήνη, Roman Minerva), the goddess of the citadel of Athens, originated from the head of Zeus; she is the armed protector of her city.

17. Cf. Baumgarten, *Heiliges Wort und Heilige Schrift*, 223: "There is no evidence of an effort by the Greeks to put old religious traditions in writing in a systematic way."

18. Herodotus (ca. 484–425 BCE) handed down the legend of the founding of Greek religion: "Hesiod and Homer flourished not more than four hundred years earlier than I; and these are the ones who taught the Greeks the descent of the gods, and gave the gods their names, and determined their spheres and functions, and described their outward forms" (*Hist.* 22.53.2). In the critique of anthropomorphism of the Homeric gods, one also finds very early the idea that there can only be one god among the gods; cf. Xenophanes (ca. 570–475 BCE) frag. B23 (Mansfeld 1.224): "A single god is the greatest among the gods and humans" (εἷς θεὸς ἔν τε θεοῖσι καὶ ἀνθρώποισι μέγιστος).

19. Cf. Otto, *The Homeric Gods*; on the distinction between Greek and Roman polytheism, cf. Ebner, *Die Stadt als Lebensraum*, 120–22.

5. Apollo (Ἀπόλλων) is the radiant son of Zeus. He embodies the flower of youth. Placed on the famous sanctuaries of Delos and Delphi, he is the most widely venerated god of the Greeks.

6. Artemis (Ἄρτεμις, Roman Diana) is the twin sister of Apollo, the goddess of animals and virgin huntress. She assists women in childbirth.

7. Aphrodite (Ἀφροδίτη, Roman Venus) is the goddess of spiritual and physical love; Eros is her son.

8. Hermes (Ἑρμῆς, Roman Mercury) is the messenger of the gods, who invents sacrifice and music and brings culture to humankind.

9. Hephaestus (Ἥφαιστος, Roman Vulcan) is the god of fire and of the forge and the patron of the crafts.

10. Ares (Ἄρης, Roman Mars) is the violent god of war.

11. Demeter (Δημήτηρ, Roman Ceres) is the mother of the earth and of grain.

12. Dionysus (Διόνυσος, Roman Bacchus) is the the god of wine.

The distinguishing feature of the Olympian family of gods is an anthropomorphic polytheism[20] (cf. Euripides, *Alcestis* 1159: "The divine knows many forms [πολλαὶ μορφαὶ τῶν δαιμονίων]"). At the center of classical Greek thinking is the divine nature in human form. Homer reports, "The gods take on many forms as they wander through the cities in the guise of strangers from a distant place."[21] The gods are a category of their own, distinct from humans yet nevertheless concerned about humans. The origin of culture was traced back to the intervention of the gods. Thus Zeus sends Hermes to teach humanity justice and reverence.[22] Hermes, Heracles, and Apollo take on human form as messengers of the gods; that is, they work as gods among humankind. Gods in human form can have an eternal as well as an earthly origin. Among the heroes (demigods),[23] Heracles (Roman Hercules) ranks first; he was venerated continuously from Homeric times until the imperial

20. Cf. Burkert, *Greek Religion*, 182–215.

21. Homer, *Odyssey* 17.485–86; also Homer, *Iliad* 2.167–72; 5.121–32; 15.236–38; Homer, *Odyssey* 7.199–210; Euripides, *Bacchae* lines 1–4 and 43–54; Plato, *Sophista* 216a–b; Diodorus Siculus 1.12.9–10; Dio Chrysostom, *Or.* 20.27, "As long as life was newly established, the gods visited us in person and sent from their midst leaders, a type of governors, who looked after us; for example, Heracles, Dionysus, Perseus, and all of the others who, we are told, stayed with us as sons or descendants of the gods."

22. Cf. Plato, *Protagoras* 322c–d.

23. Cf. Plato, *Cratylus* 398c–d, where Socrates says, "Do you not know that the heroes are demigods [οὐκ οἶσθα ὅτι ἡμίθεοι οἱ ἥρωες]? . . . All of them sprang either when Eros provided a god to a mortal or a goddess to a mortal." On this topic, see Burkert, *Greek Religion*, 203–11.

3.2. Greek temple in Paestum, south of Naples (fifth cent. BCE)

period. Heracles destroyed injustice and lawlessness on the earth, and Zeus conferred immortality upon him because of his virtue (ἀρετή).[24]

Greek religion is shaped by ritual practices, the actions determined by the custom of the ancestors or the city. The central concern (also among the Romans) was purification. "Our ancestors believed that every sin and every cause of ill could be wiped out by rites or purgation. Greece set the example: she deems that the guilty can rid themselves of their crimes by being purified."[25] By the ritually proper execution of the sacrifice dedicated to the gods,[26] through ceremonial slaughter and eating, through ceremonial purification rituals, the disturbances in the relationship between the gods and humankind and of humans with each other were taken away.[27] The basis of this practice was the generally valid religious conception, the principle: *do ut des* (I give so that you might give). By means of the sacrifice by the people, the gods preserve the order and stability of public and private life. The gods are the guarantors of life, and those who neglect them or turn away

24. Cf. Isocrates, *Orationes* 1.50; Epictetus, *Diatr.* 2.16.44; *Ench.* 15 (Diogenes and Heracles are, because of their exemplary character, coregents of the gods, "and thus they are deservedly called divine").

25. Ovid, *Fasti* 2.35–37.

26. Cf. Plato, *Leges* 4.716d: "To engage in sacrifice and communion with the gods continually, by prayers and offerings and devotions of every kind, is a thing most noble and good and helpful towards the happy life, and superlatively fitting also, for the good man."

27. Cf. Burkert, *Greek Religion*, 75–84.

3.3. The sanctuary of Delphi

from them endanger the cosmic order. The usual animal sacrificed was the
sheep, but they also sacrificed goats and pigs. The highest sacrifice was the
bull. Sacrifices were understood as festive performances of the communion
between humankind and the gods. Alongside the animal sacrifice, the gift offering was also significant, especially in the sanctuary the gift of the first of
the harvest from the field or the fruits from the orchard. Similarly basic was
the drink offering (libation) and the prayers that accompanied it.[28] Sanctuaries
were pervasive in Greece, normally encircled and marked by stones or trees,
and most often connected with a spring.[29] The altars on which the sacrifices
were offered consisted normally of simple rectangular stones. As a rule, the
sacrificial festivals were held at the temple by local functionaries rather than
a select group with a special training and consecration. They were not representatives of a distinct "theology" or "religion" but rather practitioners
for the cult at a particular place. Numerous social functions were associated
with the cult, for the community defined itself through participation in it.
The family defined itself by the hearth. Groups of families came together for

28. Burkert, *Greek Religion,* 70–73.
29. On the architectonic program, cf. Gruben, Irmer, and Hirmer, *Griechische Tempel und
Heiligtümer*; on the theological dimensions, cf. Burkert, *Greek Religion,* 84–92.

festivals, and city associations had their own sanctuary. Within the city this was documented with a festal calendar, which defined the specific festivals and the related cultic activities.[30] In Greco-Roman antiquity, religion was a public and therefore a political matter.

Because no revelatory literature existed, the observation of signs as messages of the gods played a major role. The flight of birds and the entrails of chickens were interpreted by seers. Besides the seers, the oracles at sanctuaries took on great significance, especially the sanctuary of Apollo at Delphi.[31] The oracles primarily gave options for actions to politicians and the military concerning war and the founding of colonies, and also advice for daily problems.[32]

Roman Religion

According to common understanding, Roman religion is the official religion of the city of Rome, and thus the religion of the entire Roman Empire. Little is known about the Roman religion in the early period. It probably originated in the eighth century BCE as various tribes between the Alban Hills and the Tiber came together and began the original settlement.[33] At the beginning period the dominant influence was that of the Etruscans, whose traditions are reflected in both temples and images of the gods. Under the influence of the Etruscans, from the fifth century BCE the Roman religion came under the influence of Greek mythology. Consequently, an increased overlapping and blending of Roman and Greek deities took place. Roman religion also was defined by multiple deities, each of which was responsible for a particular area of life. The three chief Roman gods and the highest gods of the state were Jupiter, Juno, and Minerva. Jupiter, like Zeus, reigned over all as the highest gods of heaven. Juno stood at the side of Jupiter like her model Hera. Minerva probably became the protector of artists and handworkers in accordance with the analogy of Athena. As the god of war, Mars had a great significance; every five years a great sacrificial festival was celebrated at his altar on the field of Mars. Other significant deities include Janus, the god of doors, entrances, and beginnings; and Vesta, the goddess of the hearth. A distinct feature of Roman religion was the veneration of household gods,

---

30. On the basic function of public religious festivals and processions, cf. Burkert, *Greek Religion*, 99–109; André, *Griechische Feste, Römische Spiele*.

31. Plutarch, *Mor.* 116c–d organizes his philosophy around two central inscriptions at Delphi: "'Know yourself' and 'Avoid extremes,' for in these principles is self-knowledge."

32. Cf. here Ebner, *Die Stadt als Lebensraum*, 306–28.

33. Cf. Kolb, *Röm*, 27–114; see under 3.4.1.

whose altars stood in the home: the Lares and the Penates.[34] The spirits of the deceased members of the family, good spirits that continued to live and protect the family, the Romans called Lares. The Penates were the gods of the cupboard, who ensured that all went well with the family and that they always had enough to eat. As with the Greeks, the religion of the Romans was primarily defined by the cult, which established and ensured the communication with the gods. A religious act was regarded as a necessary obligation that was to be fulfilled conscientiously. Cicero derived the concept of *religio* etymologically from *relegere* (reread, retrace).[35] Religion is constituted thus through praxis, the exercise and practice of customs that have a ritual character, and through the observing of regulations. The definitive role of cults and rites in Roman religion can be explained from the conviction that only by holding on to what has been passed down is there the guarantee of a happy life for the individual and for the state as well. Rituals served to determine the will of the gods and to ensure their favor. The tradition, more precisely, what has been passed down from the ancients (*mos maiorum* = customs of the ancestors), formed the second basic pillar of Roman religion. According to Cicero, "one may not introduce anything new that is not in accordance with the exemplary precepts of the ancestors."[36] Fides (trust, faith, loyalty, commitment) was not only venerated as a goddess but was also considered the highest virtue in all areas of life. The encounter with the gods occurred in the cult; thus great significance was attributed to the images of the gods in the temple. The offering of sacrifices to a specific deity served as an additional central element of Roman religion in order to reinforce its effective power. Products of nature, such as fruit, wine, milk, and honey, were given as sacrifices without bloodshed; cattle, sheep, and bulls were also sacrificed. Thus the proper performance of the cultic activity was essential in order to protect the state through the appeasement of the gods. In the private realm, a wide variety of expiatory acts were used for purification in order to restore the earlier innocence and thus to avoid the wrath of the gods, again under the principle of *do et des*. Magical practices also took on meaning; thus the Romans adopted from the Etruscans the technique of interpreting omens

34. Cf. Cicero, *Leg.* 2.27: "Furthermore, the holy custom of the family and the ancestors should be maintained."

35. Cf. Cicero, *Nat. d.* 2.72: "Those, on the other hand, who carefully reviewed and, so to speak, retraced all the lore of ritual were called 'religious,' from *relegere* (to retrace or reread)." He also speaks of the "religious norms and precepts" and of religious rituals, customs, and ceremonies (*Nat. d.* 2.8; 3.5: sacrifices, augury, and prophetic warnings as the foundation of Roman religion).

36. Cicero, *Pro Lege manilia* (*De Imperio Cn. Pompeii*) 60; cf. Cicero, *Leg.* 2.25–26.

(portents, such as the flight of birds or the appearance of lightning).[37] The Romans understood themselves as a religious people. Religion was a social reality of the greatest importance for the stability of society; for prosperity and success were considered by the Romans as a sign of the continuing favor of the gods.

Mystery Religions

In the Hellenistic Age the classical Greek and Roman religion experienced a period of increased, reciprocal saturation and fertilization. Greek deities— such as Zeus, Apollo, Artemis, Dionysus, Heracles, or Hermes—were revered in the entire East and entered (primarily with Roman names) into the Roman pantheon. Greek and Roman religion shared a common basic perspective. One is religious who honors the gods, the ancestors, and the parents in the maintenance of tradition. At the same time, Greek and Roman religion influenced the cults of the East. Alongside the Homeric gods of heaven and the official or public national, state, and house gods, the ancient world knows a further form of religiosity, the so-called mystery cults (μυστήριον = mystery).[38] They are distinguished from the official cults by their secret knowledge and hidden rites, into which one was initiated after a time of testing. Because participants had to be silent, the secrecy (Latin *arcanus* = secret) is one of the main reasons that little is known about these cults.[39] The basic distinguishing marks of the mystery cults were (1) secret discipline, (2) rites of initiation, (3) common meals, (4) identification with the fate of a deity, and (5) hope for the afterlife/conceptions of rebirth.[40]

The mystery cults were primarily a matter of personal option within the polytheistic system of antiquity. The initiates received a new status

37. Cf. Valerius Maximus, *Facta et dicta memorabilia* 1.1, where the characteristic features of Roman religion are enumerated: "Likewise, according to an old custom people employed the following forms: prayer, . . . vows, . . . thanksgiving, . . . the plea for favorable omens, . . . sacrifice."

38. Introductions and surveys are found in Cumont, *Oriental Religions in Roman Paganism*; Burkert, *Ancient Mystery Cults*; D. Zeller, "Mysterien/Mysterienreligionen," *TRE* 23; Klauck, *Religious Context of Early Christianity*, 81–148; Kloft, *Mysterienkulte der Antike*; Giebel, *Das Geheimnis der Mysterien*; Ebner, *Die Stadt als Lebensraum*, 236–73. Images of the sanctuaries of the mystery cults and their rites are found in D.-A. Koch, *Bilder aus der Welt des Urchristentums*, 224–49.

39. An exception is the novella *Metamorphosis* by Apuleius (composed around the end of the second century CE, with older materials included), in which an Isis initiation in Corinth is described. The bad reputation of the mystery cults is documented by Philo (as in *Spec. Laws* 1.319–20), who associates them with darkness and forbids the Jews to be initiated into these rites, for "both the teaching and the learning of the mysteries is no small sin."

40. I am dependent largely on Colpe, "Mithra-Verehrung, Mithras-Cult."

when they participated not only in the festivals and rites of the cult but
also in the fate or the benefits of the deity. In this way the mystery cults
had similarities with early Christianity, for in contrast to most local Greek
cults, the mystery religions combined an expectation of a favorable afterlife
with their rites.

The mysteries of Eleusis (ca. 8th cent. BCE) were probably the oldest of the
Greek mystery cults. They were conducted near Athens, where a sanctuary of
Demeter stood.[41] As the goddess of grain and fertility, Demeter symbolized
the eternal cycle of rebirth and dying, which gave the initiate the hope for a
better life after death. The cult reached its greatest period of activity in the
Roman period, and thus Cicero and Roman caesars such as Augustus and
Hadrian were initiated there.

The cult of Dionysus belongs to the most significant and yet puzzling
phenomena in ancient religiosity.[42] Dionysus (son of Zeus and the princess
Semele), also called Βάκχος (Latin Bacchus), is a polymorphic and multilayered deity. He stood for unrestrained nature, metamorphosis, and ecstasy,
often associated with indulgence in wine, with music, dancing, and to some
extent, debaucherous sexuality. In the retinue of Dionysus belonged libidi-
nal mixed beings such as the satyr, the shepherd god Pan, and the Maenads,
the ecstatic followers of the god. In addition, Dionysus (that is, his masks)
played an important role in theatrical and cultic performances. Originally,
Dionysus was probably a god of vegetation who was venerated on islands
(Crete) toward the end of the second millennium BCE and in time took on
influences from Thrace and Asia Minor and then migrated into the central
area of Greece. Thus from the sixth century BCE the cult was in evidence. In
the cities numerous Dionysus festivals and sanctuaries and theaters and processions dedicated to him attest to his great popularity.[43] In the year 185 BCE
the secret cult of the Bacchanalia was temporarily forbidden by the Roman
senate because the nocturnal meetings with orgiastic elements were regarded
as a conspiracy that threatened public order (Livy 39.8–18). Afterward the
Dionysius cult established itself also in Italy, as numerous archaeological, ar-
tistic (e.g., in Pompeii), and literary witnesses attest. Rules from the Dionysus
associations indicate that the ecstatic elements remained an essential element
of the myth but were no longer practiced. Dionysus was especially regarded
as the guarantor of a good afterlife, which, according to ancient conceptions,

41. Cf. here Giebel, *Das Geheimnis der Mysterien*, 17–53.
42. Cf. Burkert, *Greek Religion*, 161–66.
43. Cf. Merkelbach, *Die Hirten des Dionysos*, which depicts the pervasive Dionysus festivals and mysteries of the imperial period. Texts on Dionysus and his cult are provided in *NW*
I/2:112–18.

involved drunken orgies. "Passports of the dead"[44] secured the passage of the initiate into the afterlife, where the festival of the mystery would be continued and the initiate would lead a good or better life. Dionysus became more and more a redeemer who did not just make it easy to forget earthly cares; rather, the elements of his myth were interpreted symbolically and allegorically by many as saving events.

Evidence indicates that the cult of Isis existed at the end of the third millennium BCE in Egypt. In the Hellenistic Age it took on strong Greek elements and spread to almost every province in the Roman Empire.[45] Isis mysteries are attested, for example, in Alexandria, Corinth, Thessalonica, Puteoli, Pompeii,[46] and Rome. According to the basic myth,[47] Osiris, the brother and consort of Isis, was drowned in the Nile and dismembered by his evil brother, Seth, who then scattered the body parts all over the land. Isis finds her husband and conceives from him the son Horus in order to mourn and bury Osiris along with her sister Nephthys. Osiris came to power in the land of the dead, while Horus grew up and then, with the help of Isis, defeated Seth. Finally, Horus became the true ruler of the world. While Horus rules the earth, Osirus and Isis rule in the underworld. In the course of the Hellenization of the cult, Isis is in part identified with Serapis and increasingly takes on features of the all-powerful Zeus. The myth of the killing of Osiris and his revitalization by Isis symbolizes not only the eternal cycle of decay and renewal; it also opens numerous connecting points. In the initiation into the Isis cult, the initiates experience the journey to the boundary of death; they experience a "voluntary death" that prepares them for the future, as reported by an initiate in Apuleius who describes the central event of an Isis initiation: "I came to the boundary of death and entered the threshold of Proserpina. I have traveled through all elements and then returned. In the middle of the night I saw the sun in dazzling bright light. I came face to face with the gods above and below and paid reverence to them in the closest proximity."[48] Isis, the "queen of heaven,"[49] promises to

44. Cf. two Thessalian gold tablets on Rom. 6:3 in *NW* II/1:122–23; also Fritz Graf and Johnston, *Ritual Texts for the Afterlife*. Plutarch reports in *Mor.* 611d–f about hopes for the afterlife in the cult of Dionysus, into which he was initiated.

45. Cf. Merkelbach, *Isis regina—Zeus Sarapis*.

46. The significance of Isis in the public life of Pompeii is indicated by the fact that, after the earthquake in 62 CE, the Isis temple was rebuilt before the other temples.

47. The most important text is Plutarch, *Isis and Osiris*, which is available in Görgemanns, *Drei religionsphilosophische Schriften*, 132–35.

48. Apuleius, *Metamorphoses* 11.23.8. In Firmicus Maternus, *Die errore profanorum religionum* 22, an Isis priest says, "Be of good courage, initiates, since your god is redeemed. For salvation from suffering will be yours" (θαρρεῖτε μύσται τοῦ θεοῦ σεσωσμένου· ἔσται γὰρ ὑμῖν ἐκ πόνων σωτηρία).

49. Cf. the prayer in Apuleius, *Metamorphoses* 2.1.

Following Hadrian, CC BY-SA 2.0 / Wikimedia Commons

3.4. The temple of Isis in Pompeii

the initiate not only a happy life but also an escort into the world below.[50] As co-ruler of the world below, mistress, and mother, Isis guides the initiates in the path through the dangerous realm of the dead and grants salvation. The Isis mystery is distinguished by a comprehensive cultic-ritual system of levels through which the initiate must pass in order to attain the full protection of the goddess. These levels include holy meals[51] as well as numerous festivals and processions. In Italy especially, Isis became the goddess of women, a miracle worker and all-powerful and omnipresent goddess.[52] Plutarch demonstrates how intellectuals around 100 CE could understand these remarkable stories from Egypt about hostilities within families of the gods, the animal deities, holy numbers, and rites. "One does not worship them, but through them one worships the divine, insofar as they, by their nature, are mirrors of the divine."[53] The symbolic interpretation enabled them to apply the entire myth, with all of its specific features, to the divine logos and open it to reason.

50. Cf. Apuleius, *Metamorphoses* 11.6.6: "A life full of happiness and glory awaits you under my guardianship. And once the span of your life has been completed and you have gone to the world below, there also, even in the hemisphere under the earth, I will illuminate the darkness of hell and command the palace of the dead."
    51. Apuleius, *Metamorphoses* 11.24.
    52. On these roles, see, e.g., the Isis-aretalogy from Kyme [in Asia Minor] 1–65, which originated in the first or second century CE (NW I/2:370–71).
    53. Plutarch, *Isis and Osiris*, in Görgemanns, *Drei religionsphilosophische Schriften*, 76.

The cult of Cybele (= the Great Mother) came from Asia Minor, originating in Phrygia around 1000 BCE.[54] The region between Phrygia and Galatia
soon developed into the center of the cult. Here a great priesthood called
Galloi came into existence. At the top stood the high priest, who bore the
name of Attis. The priests emasculated themselves in honor of the deity
and celebrated—similar to Dionysus—an ecstatic cult with musical processions, warriors, and wild animals. Cybele combined several motifs; she was
the goddess of the mountains and the earth, of nature, and of animals. As
ruler of nature, she became associated, in many characteristics of the myth,
with the becoming and passing away of vegetation. In association with that,
the mother goddess Cybele had a beautiful young lover, usually called Attis.
When he became unfaithful, she punished him with madness. As a result, he
emasculated himself and died. Cybele was remorseful, and she asked Zeus
to restore her beloved to life, but this did not happen. From the sixth century
BCE, Cybele is attested in Athens, and from the second century BCE in Rome.
In many public festivals madness, castration, death, and partial reanimation
were associated with the cult of Cybele. As a result, it is not surprising that
the cult—despite its spread and its acceptance in the Roman pantheon—was
always regarded with suspicion. At the same time, the Great Mother cult
blossomed at the beginning of the imperial period.

The cult of Mithras can be traced back to the Iranian deity Mithras, who
was originally the god of the oath.[55] The cult spread beyond Asia Minor to
Rome and the western provinces, going through such a major process of
transformation that one may consider it a new beginning.[56] The Roman cult
of Mithras may have originated in the last third of the first century and then
spread into the entire empire in the second century CE. Besides Rome/Ostia,
its center was particularly in military installations along the Limes (frontier:
Britain, Germany) and in the provinces of the Danube.

The cult of Mithras was reserved for men only, knew no feminine deities, and found a great following among soldiers but also among slaves and
freedmen who worked in the administration in the border provinces (e.g., as
tax officials). The cult was also passed on within families, from grandfather
to father to son. The particular virtues associated with the followers of the
cult were bravery, honesty, justice, and piety. A second distinctive feature of
the cult was that it was the only exclusively private mystery cult, whereas

54. Cf. Vermaseren, *Cybele and Attis.*
55. On the history and the changes in the Mithras cult, cf. Merkelbach, *Mithras*; Clauss,
Roman Cult of Mithras; H. Betz, "Mithras Liturgy."
56. Cf. Clauss, *Roman Cult of Mithras*, 7–10, who disputes a direct continuity between the
Iranian and the Roman Mithras cults.

Dionysus, Isis, and Cybele were worshiped with numerous festivals in the cities. The basic myth tells how Mithras killed a bull, the epitome of vitality, in a cave. The cave probably symbolizes the cosmos, which now benefits from the life power of the bull, embodied by the participants in the cultic meal. Thus the mysteries of Mithras were celebrated in cavernous spaces. The cosmic dimension of the cult is indicated by the association of Mithras with the unconquerable sun god, Sol Invictus, who repeatedly went up and down. On cult images Mithras is accompanied by the sun god;[57] he is regarded as invincible, and his birthday on December 25 coincided with that of the sun god. In the fourth century CE, this date became the birthday of Jesus Christ, who embodied the true sun.

> On two points Greek and Roman religions as well as the mystery religions are different from early Christianity: (1) they produced no primary revelatory writings, and (2) they had no comprehensive, intentional solicitation of members.

3.2.1 Major Philosophical Movements

Because in antiquity an ethical life was synonymous with philosophy, and philosophy teaches behavior,[58] it can be compared to the proclamation and the ethical instructions of early Christianity. In antiquity philosophy and theology belonged together as concrete ways of life. Philosophical, religious, and moral themes are intertwined and were not considered separate areas of knowledge or of life.[59] Every philosophy had a religious potential, and every religion had philosophical potential,[60] particularly since the philosopher is the one "who, with his understanding [λόγῳ], most truly and perfectly explains and proclaims the nature of the divine."[61] God and the successful life are the central themes of ancient philosophy and theology. Almost all members of Pauline churches in cities such as Ephesus, Corinth, Philippi, and Athens would have

57. Cf. Clauss, *Roman Cult of Mithras*, 146–54.
58. Cf. Seneca, *Ep.* 20.2: "Philosophy teaches us to act, not to speak"; also Musonius, *Diss.* 3, according to whom people seek to know "how to live an ethical life, which is synonymous with philosophy."
59. Cf. Hadot, *Philosophie als Lebensform*, 142–219.
60. All great thinkers in the NT world were theologians (e.g., Cicero, Philo, Seneca, Epictetus, Plutarch, Dio Chrysostom). This fact is not surprising, for every significant system of Greco-Roman philosophy culminated in a theology; cf. Jaeger, *Theology of the Early Greek Philosophers*; Weischedel, *Wesen, Aufstieg und Verfall*; Verweyen, *Philosophie und Theologie*, 39–127.
61. Dio Chrysostom, *Or.* 12.47.

been acquainted with major philosophical movements of their time, at least in rudimentary form (cf. Acts 17:18).

The creative development of philosophy in Hellenism was of major significance for intellectual life in the Roman Empire. On the one hand, it drew on the philosophical schools of Plato and Aristotle, while on the other hand new influential schools emerged, including the Cynic, Stoic, and Epicurean philosophies. Undoubtedly, the most influential figure for all of Hellenistic philosophy was Socrates (ca. 470–399 BCE),[62] who was considered the prototype of the wise man who followed his convictions and was truly free.[63] The influence of Socrates followed in a variety of ways:[64] While the Cynics and Stoics oriented themselves to the "wild" ethical Socrates, Platonism and the Academy placed at the center the questioning, discovering Socrates, who sought knowledge.

CYNICS

The Cynics traced their origins to Antisthenes (ca. 445–365 BCE), the student of Socrates.[65] Their name (κυνικός, Cynic; derived from κύων, dog) is probably based on the lifestyle of Diogenes Sinope (ca. 400–325 BCE), their chief protagonist, who, in part, behaved and dwelled like a dog. The chief representatives of the earlier epoch of Cynicism were Crates (ca. 365–285 BCE), his brother-in-law Metrocles, Menippus (ca. 350–270 BCE), Bion (ca. 335–245 BCE), and Teles (mid-third cent. BCE).[66]

The Cynics had the radical understanding of philosophy as ethics. Antisthenes formulated their foundational insight: "Virtue [ἀρετή] is sufficient [αὐτάρκης] to ensure happiness [εὐδαιμονία] and requires in addition only the strength of a Socrates. Virtue is a matter of deeds, and requires neither words nor learning" (Diogenes Laertius 6.111). Consequently, the result was the relativizing of traditional cultural values, including the rebellion against wealth and possessions,[67] contempt for luxury and acquisitiveness and greed,[68]

---

62. Cf. Döring, *Exemplum Socratis*.

63. Cf., e.g., Xenophon, *Apologia* 16, where Socrates asks, "Who among humankind is as free as I, for I take no money or payment from anyone?"

64. On Socrates, cf. Döring, "Sokrates."

65. On Cynicism, see Dudley, *History of Cynicism*; Branham and Goulet-Cazé, *Cynics*; Döring, "Antisthenes, Diogenes und die Kyniker vor Christi Geburt"; Luck, *Die Weisheit der Hunde*; Goulet-Cazé, "Kynismus."

66. Noteworthy is the fact that famed Cynics came from Gadara in the land east of the Jordan and south of the Sea of Gennesaret (cf. Mark 5:1–20; Matt. 8:28–34); cf. Menippus (ca. 350–270 BCE), Meleager (most productive ca. 100 BCE), Oenomaus of Gadara (second cent. CE).

67. Cf. the example in Diogenes Laertius 6.87–88, in which Crates sells his possessions and gives the money away.

68. Diogenes Laertius 6.50, "Greed is the homeland of all evils."

distancing from marriage and family,[69] the insignificance of background (as a free Greek man),[70] the rejection of traditional power politics (e.g., war), and skepticism about the traditional state, cultural, and religious rituals. The Cynics did not engage in the elaborate explanatory claims of the great theories (e.g., Plato) but placed the personal example, the praxis of the successful existence, in the foreground, appealing especially to Socrates as an example. In positive terms, they commended and practiced a lifestyle oriented to nature and to reason, which eradicates false passions from the soul (lust, craving, anger) and leads to a simple life without needs. Thus the Cynic is truly free and independent; he represents free, unadorned speech and does not allow anything or anyone to instrumentalize him. No fate breaks him; as a wise man he is sufficient and thus like the gods. The development of an understanding of individual freedom belongs to the crowning cultural achievements of Hellenism,[71] especially of the Cynic-Stoic philosophy. It is the mark of the philosopher to live in freedom (Epictetus, *Diatr.* 2.1.23). According to Diogenes Laertius, "To pursue the same way of life as Heracles, who preferred freedom to everything" (Diogenes Laertius 6.71). The Cynics demonstrated restraint concerning theories of the afterlife. According to Diogenes Laertius, "The dying Diogenes commanded that he be thrown out unburied as prey for wild animals or thrown into a ditch with dust sprinkled over him" (6.79; cf. 6.52; Lucian, *Demonax* 35.66).

The Cynics understood themselves as cosmopolitans. Diogenes answered the question of where he came from: "I am a citizen of the world" (Diogenes Laertius 6.63, κοσμοπολίτης),[72] and Plutarch praised Zeno explicitly for his universal concept, which Alexander the Great was the first to implement. "That we not live separated in separate cities and villages . . . but consider all people to be fellow countrymen and fellow citizens, and that we should have a common life and order" (*Mor.* 329a–b).[73] Because most people have false conceptions of a life that is in accordance with nature, the Cynics come to them as messengers and offer insights in the form of anecdotes, aphorisms, and maxims (*chreiai*, χρεῖαι) that can be useful for all the vicissitudes of life. One's actions must always be oriented to the circumstances, for suffering originates from a false view of things. "Thus one must not attempt to change

69. Marriage and family hinder the Cynic from his essential task of being a scout and herald of the deity among humankind (Epictetus, *Diatr.* 3.67–82).

70. Cf. Diogenes Laertius 6.1.4. Numerous Cynics were slaves (e.g., Epictetus) and did not come from the great cultural centers (e.g., Menippus of Gadara in the land east of the Jordan).

71. Cf. the claim in Nestle, *Die Griechen*; Nestle, "Freiheit"; Pohlenz, *Griechische Freiheit*, 104–13.

72. Epictetus, *Diatr.* 1.9.1, attributes this saying to Socrates.

73. Cf. also Diogenes Laertius 6.38, 72, 98.

the relationships, but to adapt to the situation, just as seamen do. They do not attempt to change the wind and the sea, but they prepare themselves. . . . So you must conduct yourself in relation to your circumstances. You have become old; leave the play of youth. You are weak; take the hands from your work that demands strength" (Teles, frag. 2).

In the first and second centuries CE, Cynicism had a second flourishing, so one can scarcely distinguish between Cynics and Stoics. Famous Cynics or propagandists of Cynic thought of this time were Demetrius (lived under Nero and Vespasian), Dio Chrysostom (ca. 40–120 CE), Epictetus (ca. 55–135 CE), Favorinus (ca. 80/90–150 CE), and Demonax (born 80/90 CE). The polemics of Dio Chrysostom, Epictetus, or Lucian of Samosata (ca. 120–180 CE) against a false understanding of Cynicism indicate clearly that Cynicism was an empire-wide phenomenon. The Cynic traveling philosophers did not form an elite school, but they traversed the Roman-Hellenistic world and gained a hearing for their message of ethical renewal in the streets and plazas, in front of theaters and temples.[74] In order to be a messenger of the gods, the Cynic must "stand entirely in the service of the deity, free to go about among men, not tied down by domestic duties, not bound by personal relationships" (Epictetus, *Diatr.* 3.22.69).[75] Because of their unconventional appearance (cloak, satchel, walking stick, and long, unkempt hair) and especially because of their taking up of current themes and problems from daily life, they frequently caused a stir and provoked the hostility of rulers.[76] Many wandering philosophers had no fixed residence; they went about with bare feet, begged, and slept on the floor of public buildings. A center of the newly revived Cynic movement in the first century CE was Corinth. Diogenes stayed here happily, and the famous Demetrius also lived and taught in this city.[77]

74. Cf. Dio Chrysostom, *Or.* 32.9: "And as for the Cynics, as they are called, it is true that the city contains no small number of that sect, and that, like any other thing, this too has had its crop—persons whose tenets, to be sure, comprise practically nothing spurious or ignoble, yet who must make a living—still these Cynics, posting themselves at street-corners, in alleyways, and at temple-gates, pass round the hat and play upon the credulity of lads and sailors and crowds of that sort, stringing together rough jokes and much tittle-tattle and that low badinage that smacks of the market-place."

75. Epictetus, *Diatr.* 3.22, gives a programmatic description of the true Cynic (cf. M. Billerbeck, *Epiktet*); cf. also Epictetus, *Diatr.* 4.8.30–31: "For such a man is the true Cynic, whom Zeus has deemed worthy of the scepter and diadem; who may say: So that you may see yourselves, O men, that you do not seek happiness and tranquility where it is, but where it is not, See, that I have been sent to you by God as an example. I have neither house nor property, neither wife nor children, not even a bed or shirt or my own plate, and yet observe how healthy I am."

76. Cf. Liefeld, "Wandering Preacher as a Social Figure."

77. Cf. M. Billerbeck, *Der Kyniker Demetrius.*

STOA

Cynicism and the Stoa are connected with each other in many ways through both their origins and their intellectual profile. The founder of the school was Zeno (ca. 334–262 BCE) from Citium on Cyprus, the student of Crates. Around 300 BCE he founded a philosophical school, which took its name from the place of instruction, a painted portico at the agora in Athens (στοὰ ποικίλη, colorful hall). The movement then acquired the name οἱ στωϊκοί (the Stoics, or ἡ στοά, the Stoa).[78]

The most significant difference between Cynicism and the Stoa was that Cynicism dealt exclusively with ethics (cf. Diogenes Laertius 6.103). In contrast, the Stoa developed, in addition to ethics, a complex scientific system that included logic, linguistic philosophy, the theory of knowledge, and especially physics. The history of the Stoa can be divided into three phases. The "old" Stoa spanned the period from 300 to 150 BCE. Here Cleanthes (ca. 300–230 BCE), the head of the school after Zeno, and Chrysippus (ca. 282–209 BCE) were active. The most significant representatives of the "middle" Stoa in the period from 150 to the end of the millennium were Panaetius of Rhodes (ca. 180–100 BCE) and Posidonius (ca. 135–50 BCE). The Stoicism of the imperial period was characterized not as much by theoretical investigation as by a focus on the ethical-political arena (in connection with elements of Cynicism). The chief representatives of Stoicism in this period[79] were Seneca (ca. 4 BCE−65 CE), Musonius Rufus (ca. 25–85 CE), Epictetus (ca. 55–135 CE), and Marcus Aurelius (121–180 CE).

Stoicism assumes a divine structure of reality.[80] It represents a monistic pantheism in which the deity is active in all forms of existence. The deity is immanent in the world and omnipresent, but at the same time intangible. Chrysippus teaches, "The divine power lies in the reason and soul and spirit and all of nature, and explains further that the world itself and the world soul that permeates it is God."[81] Nothing exists above the substance of all

78. On the Stoa, cf. Rist, *Stoics*; Colish, *Stoic Tradition from Antiquity*, vol. 1; Pohlenz, *Die Stoa*, vols. 1–2; Steinmetz, "Die Stoa"; Hossenfelder, *Stoa, Epikureismus und Skepsis*, 44–99. Anthologies: Hossenfelder, *Antike Glückslehren*, 63–162; Long and Sedley, *Hellenistic Philosophers*, 1:158–487; Weinkauf, *Die Philosophie der Stoa*; Nickel, *Stoa und Stoiker*, vols. 1–2; Thorsteinsson, *Roman Christianity and Roman Stoicism*; Dienstbeck, *Die Theologie der Stoa*.

79. Cicero (106–43 BCE) belonged to no philosophical school, but he was a Skeptical sympathizer and important transmitter of Stoic thought.

80. Cf. Forschner, *Die Philosophie der Stoa*, 10: "In recent scholarship on the Stoa, broad agreement has emerged that the intellectual center of the philosophy of the Stoa is in (pantheistic) theology."

81. Cicero, *Nat. d.* 1.39. According to Diogenes Laertius 7.135–36, Chrysippus says, "God is one and reason and fate and Zeus; he has many other names [ἕν τ᾽ εἶναι θεὸν καὶ νοῦν καὶ

that exists; there is neither a transcendent creator God nor a metaphysical beginning of the world. The deity dwells as a developing power, as πνεῦμα (spirit, breath) or λόγος σπερματικός (fructifying logos) within things that it created. The logos is the finest material and penetrates the entire cosmos as a guiding and shaping power. Nothing in the cosmos happens without the assistance/influence of the logos, which can also be called "divine." According to the Stoa, the destiny of the human is embedded in the concept of a divine, purposefully arranged nature, which humankind should follow. When one lives in agreement with nature (= ὁμολογουμένως τῇ φύσει ζῆν) and oneself, the authentic self-understanding of the one who lives according to reason takes place. One who is oriented toward the life in accordance with nature[82] chooses what is beneficial for one's natural inclinations (doctrine of *oikeiosis*, οἰκείωσις, beneficial for self-preservation). One seeks to reach the goal of life by living in accordance with nature.

In order to realize this, one must make good judgments and then act. False judgments result from the passions,[83] which are based on false conceptions.[84] It is the task of reason, and thus of philosophy, through reason not to let the passions arise. It is only in a struggle with oneself and, should the occasion arise, against oneself that one can find the good. "An overpowering impulse that is not under control of the choices made by reason" or an (unreasonable) movement of the soul against nature is what the Stoics call passion.[85] The passions include desire, fear, grief, lust, displeasure, anger, strong love, and hate.[86] Thus the goal of the Stoic is freedom from the passions, meaning

εἱμαρμένην καὶ Δία πολλὰς τ' ἑτέρας ὀνομασίας προσονομάζεσθαι]. At the beginning he was by himself; he transformed the whole of substance through the air into water. And just as the germ is contained in the seed, so he remains as the productive power of reason [σπερματικὸν λόγον] of the cosmos in moisture and by himself enables nature in its continual creation."

Aëtius says about God, "He is a stream of breath that flows through the whole world and, depending on the substance through which he comes, takes on a variety of names" (*SVF* 2:1027).

82. Cf. Cicero, *De finibus* 3.31: "The highest good consists of a life that applied the knowledge of the nature of things, deciding on what is according to nature and rejecting what is against nature. That means to live in harmony and agreement with nature." Seneca, *De vita beata* 3: "I follow the guidance of Nature—a doctrine upon which all Stoics are agreed. Not to stray from Nature and to mold ourselves according to her law and pattern—this is true wisdom. The happy life, therefore, is a life that is in harmony with its own nature, and it can be attained in only one way."

83. On the complex Stoic doctrine of the passions, cf. Forschner, *Die stoische Ethik*, 114–41.

84. "The things themselves do not disturb people, but rather their opinions and judgments about things. For example, death is not a thing to be feared; otherwise it would have appeared so to Socrates. Rather, the opinion that it is fearful is what is to be feared" (Epictetus, *Ench.* 5).

85. *SVF* 3:378 (cited in Hossenfelder, *Antike Glückslehren*, 81; see 80–96 for further examples).

86. Cf. Diogenes Laertius 7.113: "Desire or craving is irrational appetency, and under it are ranged the following states: want, hatred, contentiousness, anger, love, wrath, resentment."

apathy (ἀπάθεια), which is the attribute only of the wise man.[87] For the one who lives by reason, virtue (ἀρετή) is the only good, and only in it does one find happiness. The chief virtues are φρόνησις (practical wisdom), σωφροσύνη (moderation), ἐγκράτεια (self-control), δικαιοσύνη (justice). In order to avoid the passions and to attain virtue, and thus to reach αὐτάρκεια (self-sufficiency, independence), according to Epictetus,[88] it is necessary to distinguish between that which one does not have at one's disposal and that over which one has control. This involves the distinction between what is external and what is one's own. This is accomplished by προαίρεσις (free self-determination/free will). It involves the basic and essential characteristic that enables humans to act ethically. *Proairesis* includes the use of the elements of reason, has a proximity to the freedom of the will, and is never merely theoretical but is related to concrete ethical activity. Our self-determination is free and cannot be interfered with by anyone, not even by God,[89] for it constitutes the essential nature of the human. A self-realization by the individual is required and active with the use of reason, which is the true nature of the human. One's task is to prove oneself καλὸς καὶ ἀγαθός (noble and good) in every place and every situation. For the Stoic (as well as for the Cynic), individuals carry the true quality of life in their inner being and do not need to fear any other fate when they use these internal powers correctly in every situation. Thus Epictetus describes the famous saying of Socrates as a memory aid: "Anytus and Meletus can kill me, but they cannot hurt me."[90] When self-determination/reason recognizes that the outer things are indifferent and that value comes only to the one who has the appropriate conception of things, then no passions emerge and one arrives at happiness. The essence of the individual is the inner being of the person who stands in full sufficiency. The goal of ethics is to recognize the nature of the good that is available to us, to realize it, and thus to be truly free. For Epictetus, freedom is identical to inner independence. "You should give up everything, your body and possession, good reputation and your books, association, office and your private life. For wherever your inclinations draw you, you have become a slave, a subordinate, firmly shackled, oppressed; in short, you are entirely dependent" (*Diatr.* 4.4.33; cf. *Ench.* 11). Just as no one can actually give to the Stoic, so

87. Cf. Zeno in Diogenes Laertius 7.125: τῶν σοφῶν δὲ πάντα εἶναι, "Everything belongs to the wise man"; also Cicero, *Paradoxa Stoicorum* 33 ("Only the wise man is free, and every fool is a slave"); Epictetus, *Diatr.* 3.22, 49, 63, 95; Seneca, *Ben.* 7.2.5.

88. On Epictetus, cf. Long, *Epictetus*; Schnelle, "Paulus und Epiktet"; Vollenweider et al., *Epiktet: Was ist wahre Freiheit?*

89. "You may put my legs in fetters, but not even Zeus can take away my free will/free self-determination [τὴν προαίρεσιν]" (Epictetus, *Diatr.* 1.1.24).

90. Epictetus, *Ench.* 53.4 (according to Plato, *Apology* 30c–d).

nothing can be taken away from him.[91] His goal is to live in agreement with himself and thus to integrate himself into the harmony of the cosmos. The renunciation of anything and thus the inner independence from it is to be considered greater than the possession of it.[92] Epictetus (*Ench.* 11): "Do not say of any matter: 'I lost it'; rather, 'I returned it.' Your child died? The child was given back. Your wife died? She was returned. 'Someone stole my land.' Even it was returned." Philosophy imparts all of these insights; and it offers true life to one who follows it: "calmness, fearlessness, freedom" (ἀταραξία, ἀφοβία, ἐλευθερία).[93]

EPICURUS

Epicurus (341–270 BCE), who came from Samos and founded his school in Athens shortly before 300 BCE, created a distinctive and influential form of ancient philosophy.[94] He represents a therapeutic thought that aimed to take from humankind the fear of the gods, fear of death, and their ignorance of the nature of desire and displeasure in order to lead people to rest for the soul (ἀταραξία) and well-being (εὐδαιμονία). "Hollow is the speech of the philosopher from whom no passion of humankind is healed."[95] The basis of Epicurean thought is the insight that knowledge can be attained only from the experience of the senses. As long as the senses remain purely receptive and reason remains within its possibilities, no error can take place. This is the case with cosmology, which aims at explaining natural occurrences in and of themselves. Neither earthquake nor heavenly appearances come from God and must not therefore be explained as punishment of fate or the gods.[96] Thus Epicurus rejects the common opinion that the gods rule the world and that they intervene in the course of time to reward or punish. There is neither divine foreknowledge (πρόνοια) nor a determined fate (εἱμαρμένη), but rather everything comes into existence of itself. According to Epicurus, the gods live a blissful, timeless life without bothering with humankind. "For a god

91. When the Stoic Stilpon was asked about what still remained after the loss of his wife and children: "Everything that is mine is with me: justice, virtue, wisdom, and even this: Not to regard anything of value that can be taken away from me" (Seneca, *Ep.* 9.19).

92. Cf. Epictetus, *Diatr.* 4.9.1–3.

93. Epictetus, *Diatr.* 2.1, 21.

94. On Epicurus, cf. Rist, *Epicurus*; H. Jones, *Epicurean Tradition*; Hossenfelder, *Epikur*; Erler, "Epikur." Text editions: Krautz, *Epikur*; Long, *Hellenistic Philosophy*; Nickel, *Epikur*; Rapp, *Epikur*.

95. Porphyry, *Ad Marcellam* 31 (cited in Nickel, *Epikur*, 69).

96. Cf. Diogenes Laertius, *Herodotus* 76 LCL: "Nay more: we are bound to believe that in the sky revolutions, solstices, eclipses, risings and settings, and the like, take place without the ministration or command, either now or in the future, of any being who at the same time enjoys perfect bliss along with immortality."

does nothing, is entangled in no affairs, is not concerned about any work, but rather enjoys himself in his wisdom and virtue and trusts that he will always live in the highest and, especially, in eternal delight."[97] As immortals, the gods can neither suffer nor turn to the world in love.[98] They are removed from the sorrows of life and have nothing in common with humankind.[99] Thus Epicurus rejects the common Hellenistic-Greek conception of the deity, but he definitely does not represent an atheistic point of view: he attempts to preserve a concept of the deity in all of its purity and unfalsifiability. If the Stoics were pantheists, the Epicureans were deists.

The fear of the gods, whose punishing deeds were spuriously seen in the heavens, was connected to the fear of death. Epicurus represents a unique and still fascinating theory of death as timelessness. "Death has no meaning for us, for whatever is dissolved is without feeling, and that which has no feeling has no meaning for us" (Diogenes Laertius 10.139 = Epicurus, *Sententiae* 2). With death the soul also dies, a belief that Epicurus attempted to prove in his teaching on nature. Death appears to humankind as so horrible because it causes pain. The myths tell of the horrors after death and thus cause already in the present debilitating fear and a loss of possible happiness. In contrast, the conduct of the wise person is characterized by tranquility about death. He does not spurn life, "nor does he fear the absence of life, for neither is life for him disagreeable, nor does he assume that the absence of life is an evil . . . because the practice of a perfect life and of a perfect dying is the same" (Epicurus, *Letter to Menoeceus* 126).

The ethic of Epicurus was also based on a theory of knowledge determined by sense perception. The point of departure is the simple observation that people are drawn to feelings of pleasure, while they avoid feelings of pain. "For we need pleasure, therefore, when we feel pain because we have the absence of pleasure. When we are no longer in pain, we do not need pleasure. For this reason, as we say, pleasure is the origin and goal of the happy life" (Epicurus, *Letter to Menoeceus* 128). Pleasure (ἡδονή), according to Epicurus, means not the maximization of pleasant yet fleeting feelings or situations[100] but a natural orientation in life, which can be described as the freedom from unease caused by fear, desire, and pain, which is *eudaimonia*

97. Cicero, *Nat. d.* 1.51.
98. Cf. Cicero, *Nat. d.* 1.95.121; Diogenes Laertius 10.76–77.
99. Cf. also Diogenes Laertius 10.123, where Epicurus challenges his pupils to have a correct concept of God. "First, consider god an immortal and blissful being, corresponding to the commonly held concept of god, and ascribe to him nothing that is not consistent with his immortality or is in conflict with his blissfulness."
100. Cf. Epicurus, *Letter to Menoeceus* 131–32: "When we say that pleasure is the goal, we do not mean pleasures of the profligate and those that consist in indulgence, . . . but rather a

(good fortune, joy, confidence). The striving for happiness corresponds to human nature. Thus the goal of the individual must be to lead a life withdrawn from the alternation between pleasure and displeasure. The insight is thus of special importance that having no needs makes life more carefree and independent than a life with abundance. The sayings (κύριαι δόξαι) of Epicurus, which are to be understood as practical instructions for a life of happiness, serve the implementation of this individual and nonpolitical ethic.[101] Epicurus established a school, and the transmission of his sayings ensured the influence of his school for centuries.

Skepticism

Among the most influential philosophical movements in antiquity is that of the Skeptics.[102] Its founder was Pyrrho of Elis (ca. 365–275 BCE), from whom no written work has been preserved. Skepticism stands in the tradition of the academy and, in the course of its history, borrowed from the Stoics and Epicureans. At the same time, it was distinguished by an unmistakable profile, for the foundation of Pyrrhonic thought is the insolubility of the problem of knowledge, the unknowability of things, and the resulting suspension of judgment. "He denied that anything was honourable or dishonourable, just or unjust. And so, universally, he held that there is nothing really existent, but custom and convention govern human action" (Diogenes Laertius 9.61 LCL). After Pyrrho, Skepticism underwent a decline and did not gain significance until the first and second centuries CE. Sextus Empiricus, who was considered as its most significant representative, lived in the second half of the second century CE.

Because for every argument an equal contrary argument can be made, things are not really distinguishable, and there is no distinction in value between them (adiaphora = ἀδιάφορα). For the Skeptic cannot really seek happiness because one does not know what it is or where to find it. Nevertheless, the Skeptic himself must live and act. "We adhere to the appearances and live undogmatically according to the daily experience of life, for we cannot be totally inactive."[103] Happiness does not come from the conscious search for

---

sober understanding that examines the bases for every choice and avoidance and drives out the assumptions from which the most common turmoils overcome the soul."

101. Texts in Krautz, *Epikur*, 66–79.

102. On Skepticism, cf. Hossenfelder, *Stoa, Epikureismus und Skepsis*, 147–82; Görler, "Älterer Pyrrhonismus." Texts in Hossenfelder, *Antike Glückslehren*, 287–369; Long, *Hellenistic Philosophy*, 3–27, 559–82.

103. Sextus Empiricus, *Pyrrhoneae Hypotyposes* 23 (cited from Hossenfelder, *Antike Glückslehren*, 307–8).

truth, for the questions that cannot be definitely answered set humankind in constant distress. The Skeptic, however, pauses: "Skepticism is the art of setting in opposition all possible appearances and judgments to each other; from this standpoint we attain restraint and quietude."[104]

One can explain and practice certain customs and types of behavior, but the question of right and wrong cannot be solved. Thus from the equivalence of things there emerges a reservation in judgment. A perfect *ataraxia* (ἀταραξία = calm) is thus not possible, but rather the attainable happiness under the circumstances that have been given. The Skeptic thus leads a life in "quotation marks."[105] He did not seek it, and he did not assent to it, but rather he is subjected to it. This is a situation that, because of inadequate knowledge, he can neither undo nor change. Indeed, the doubt about the possibility of assured knowledge is not certain. "We do not know anything; we do not yet even know that we do not know."[106] At the same time, this insight protected against constant restlessness. Thus Skepticism is a form of therapeutic philosophy.

Middle Platonism

In the history of philosophy[107] of the first century CE to the second and third centuries CE, Middle Platonism was a rather marginal phenomenon,[108] but it is of great significance for the study of the intellectual climate and educational ideal of the NT era as well as the examination of the crosscurrents of intellectual traditions. Two basic conceptions shape Middle Platonism: the existence of a transcendent God and the immortality of the soul. Numerous other Platonic concepts were combined with that, while also Middle Platonists such as Philo of Alexandria (ca. 20 BCE–45 CE), Plutarch (ca. 45–120 CE), Apuleius (ca. 125–75 CE), and Maximus of Tyre (ca. 125–85 CE) incorporated Stoic, Epicurean, and Neopythagorean traditions, combining them with their own basic assumptions.

According to Plato, true being is intelligible being (οὐσία ὄντως ὄν, ὃ ἔστιν ὄν), the world of ideas. As essential reality, it underlies all perceptions, while the world of perception is subject to change, illusion, decay, and appearance

---

104. Sextus Empiricus, *Pyrrhoneae Hypotyposes* 4 (cited from Hossenfelder, *Antike Glückslehren*, 303).

105. Cf. Hossenfelder, *Antike Glückslehren*, 292.

106. Sextus Empiricus, *Adversus Mathematicos* 7.87–88 (cited from Long and Sedley, *Hellenistic Philosophers*, 1:14).

107. Plato (ca. 427–347 BCE) founded the Old Academy around 385 BCE, which existed until around 268 BCE. Middle Platonism covered the years from about 80 BCE to 220 CE. Neoplatonism was dominant in the period from 240 to 550 CE.

108. Cf. Dillon, *Middle Platonists*; Krämer, *Platonismus und hellenistische Philosophie*; Zintzen, *Der Mittelplatonismus*.

(δοκεῖν, δόκησις). Thus God (or the gods) belongs to the ideal, intelligible, transcendent, incorporeal world, the only real level: the world of ideas. The highest deity is identical with the highest idea: the good ("That is, the divine is the beautiful, the wise, the good, and whatever is similar"; *Phaedr.* 246d) [109] Because God in every respect is perfect (*Resp.* 381b), he cannot change or come near to humankind,[110] but must abide in himself (*Resp.* 381c). "Thus it is impossible for the gods to change" (*Resp.* 381c). In contrast to the immutable gods, the world and heaven were "created, for it is visible and tangible and in possession of a body" (*Tim.* 28b). The Platonic body-soul emerges from the principle that ascribes a higher status to the transcendent world. Socrates defines death as the separation of the soul from the body, a process that already begins in life, "the separation of the soul as far as possible away from the body and its getting used to being gathered and assembled by itself, withdrawn from all parts of the body and living as far as possible both in the present circumstances and in the future alone by itself, released, as it were, from the chains of the body" (Plato, *Phaed.* 67c). The soul resembles the divine, but the body is like the mortal (Plato, *Phaed.* 80a).[111] After death, and thus after the dissolution of the body, the soul goes to a glorious place willed by God. This occurs because the soul "is pure when it separates off and drags nothing of the body with it since it has not willingly had any association with it in life, but has avoided it and drawn itself together into itself, since this has always been its habit—that is nothing other than practicing philosophy correctly" (*Phaedo* 80e). Plato gathered and systematized the Greek concepts of the afterlife and gave them the form that was dominant from the fourth century BCE on.[112]

A significant representative of Middle Platonism was Philo of Alexandria. He descended from a rich family in Alexandria, and he attempted, more thoroughly than his predecessors (e.g., Demetrius, Aristobulus), to combine Jewish tradition and Greek philosophy. He applied the allegorical method of interpretation to the Jewish Bible, particularly to overcome the offensive

109. On the Platonic understanding of the gods, cf. Erler, *Platon*, 464–73.

110. Cf. Erler, *Platon*, 472: "An essential characteristic of Platonic theology is the rejection of proximity to humankind. God is unapproachable and beyond human knowledge."

111. On the Platonic doctrine of the soul, cf. Erler, *Platon*, 375–90.

112. For example, cf. Plato, *Phaed.* 113d–14c, where Socrates and his conversation partner recall the old myths about the events after death. After the separation of body and soul, the deceased go into Hades, where they, in accordance with their deeds, await their fate. For example, "Those who have been purified through a love of wisdom will live forever entirely without bodies and come into still more beautiful dwellings than these, which are neither easy to describe nor is there the time to do so." For an overview of particular conceptions, see Burkert, *Greek Religion*, 277, 293–95.

anthropomorphisms. He made the appeal to worship the one and true God and to strive for a life in piety and virtue. The Torah appears as the true way to virtue and bliss, and Moses as the greater philosopher and teacher[113] of a life that is pleasing to God. God's works can be recognized in creation and in the order of the cosmos, but God himself is understood to be a purely spiritual being. Philo commented on the prohibition of making gods out of silver or gold: "Whoever believes that God has a quality, or whoever denies or disputes that God is one, or that he is uncreated, eternal and unchangeable commits injustice against himself, not against God, as it is said, 'do not make for yourselves.' For one must believe that he belongs to no type, that God is one, eternal, and unchangeable. One who does not believe this fills his soul with a false and ungodly opinion" (*Leg.* 1.51). In his appropriation (especially) of the Stoa and of the "sacred Plato,"[114] Philo understands himself as a legitimate interpreter of the Jewish tradition for his time.

The most significant Middle Platonist was undoubtedly Plutarch of Chaeronea,[115] who combined in his person all of the major intellectual traditions of his time. He ran a philosophical school in his hometown, had contact with major philosophers of his time, undertook journeys (e.g., to Rome and Egypt), and was one of the two main priests at Delphi for about twenty years. He attempted to rejuvenate the Greek religion, had wide interests in the history of cultures, and produced a synthesis of Greek spirit and Roman power. The strong emphasis on the absolute transcendence and otherness of God, his categorical separation from everything human, and his unapproachable distance are characteristic of the negative theology of Middle Platonism, especially its view of God,[116] which was formulated by Plutarch: "What is true being? The eternal, without beginning and end, to which no length of time brings change" (*Delphi* 19). For Plutarch, god/the gods are the only reality removed from time and becoming. They stand beyond movement, of becoming and passing away. For Plutarch, the transcendence of the deity is clearly connected with the tendency toward monotheism.[117] Just as the sun and the moon and the heavens and the earth and the sea are common to all but are called by different names by different peoples, "so for that one rationality

---

113. Cf. Philo, *De opificio mundi* 8–9: "Moses . . . had been taught the summit of philosophy and by divine revelation had been instructed about the greatest and most essential things of nature."

114. Philo, *Good Person* 13; cf. also Philo, *De aeternitate mundi* 52: "the great Plato" (ὁ μέγας Πλάτων).

115. For an introduction to the life and work of Plutarch, see Klauck, *Plutarch.*

116. On the conceptions of God in Plutarch, cf. Hirsch-Luipold, *Gott und die Götter bei Plutarch*; Lanzillotta, *Plutarch.*

117. On pagan monotheism, see below, 13.2.

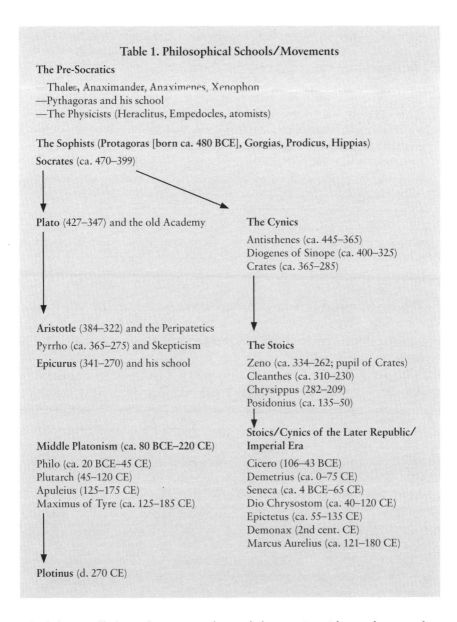

Table 1. Philosophical Schools/Movements

The Pre-Socratics

Thales, Anaximander, Anaximenes, Xenophon
—Pythagoras and his school
—The Physicists (Heraclitus, Empedocles, atomists)

The Sophists (Protagoras [born ca. 480 BCE], Gorgias, Prodicus, Hippias)

Socrates (ca. 470–399)

Plato (427–347) and the old Academy	**The Cynics**
	Antisthenes (ca. 445–365)
	Diogenes of Sinope (ca. 400–325)
	Crates (ca. 365–285)
Aristotle (384–322) and the Peripatetics	**The Stoics**
Pyrrho (ca. 365–275) and Skepticism	
Epicurus (341–270) and his school	Zeno (ca. 334–262; pupil of Crates)
	Cleanthes (ca. 310–230)
	Chrysippus (282–209)
	Posidonius (ca. 135–50)
	Stoics/Cynics of the Later Republic/
Middle Platonism (ca. 80 BCE–220 CE)	**Imperial Era**
Philo (ca. 20 BCE–45 CE)	Cicero (106–43 BCE)
Plutarch (45–120 CE)	Demetrius (ca. 0–75 CE)
Apuleius (125–175 CE)	Seneca (ca. 4 BCE–65 CE)
Maximus of Tyre (ca. 125–185 CE)	Dio Chrysostom (ca. 40–120 CE)
	Epictetus (ca. 55–135 CE)
	Demonax (2nd cent. CE)
	Marcus Aurelius (ca. 121–180 CE)
Plotinus (d. 270 CE)	

which keeps all these things in order and the one Providence that watches over them and the ancillary powers that are set over all."[118]

The concept of an absolute, transcendent deity inevitably raised the question of how communication between god and humankind was possible.

118. Plutarch, *Is. Os.* 67.

Plutarch maintains the existence of intermediary beings that maintain contact with the true deity and maintain an indispensable function for humankind. He illustrates with the myth of Isis and Osiris:

> Better, therefore, is the judgement of those who hold that the stories about Typhon, Osiris, and Isis are records of experiences of neither gods nor men, but of demigods, whom Plato and Pythagoras and Xenocrates and Chrysippus, following the lead of early writers on sacred subjects, allege to have been stronger than men and, in their might, greatly surpassing our nature, yet not possessing the divine quality unmixed and uncontaminated, but with a share also in the nature of the soul and in the perceptive faculties of the body, and with a susceptibility to pleasure and pain. . . .
>
> . . . Plato calls this class of beings an interpretative and ministering class, midway between gods and men, in that they convey thither the prayers and petitions of men, and thence they bring hither the oracles and the gifts of good things. (*Is. Os.* 360–61)

The concept of divine intermediary beings and the tendency toward monotheism in Plutarch indicate how it was possible for people from a genuine Greco-Roman cultural sphere to find access to the new religion of the Christians.

In his ethics, Plutarch expresses himself as a philosopher dedicated to human improvement; he wants to lead humankind to the overcoming of the passions and to the active exercise of the virtues in order to liberate them from all false conceptions. Thus he gives advice on almost all areas of ethics, from political advice to the training of children. According to Plutarch, true friends of God are the people whose "refined and chastened mind recognizes God as the ultimate source of all good, the father of all beauty, the one who can neither do evil nor tolerate it. He is good and knows nothing of malevolence, fear, wrath, or hate."[119] With reason/the logos, God gives a share in his justice, truth, and mercy and enables humankind to turn to the good.

Ancient philosophy was always a form of pagan theology. The gods were considered the guarantors and companions of human existence. At the beginning of the new millennium a therapeutic philosophy dominated that was intended to make individuals the masters of their fate. As a way of life and technique of well-being, as a science of living,[120] its task was to awaken the virtues that are present—that is, to challenge the insight of humankind to orient their lives to these virtues.

119. Plutarch, *Mor.* 1102.
120. *Cicero, De finibus 3.4*, "Philosophy is the science of living."

Thus the soul is led back to itself as it rejects strange demands and false wishes. In order to be happy, rich, and free, the wise person is content with virtue. Thus philosophy is a salutary means for living well and dying well. Here it becomes clear: The followers of Jesus of Nazareth practiced a comparable lifestyle, treated comparable subjects, and produced comparable literature.

3.3. Judaism

The Term "Judaism"

As a generic term "Judaism"[121] (in ideal terms, "Israel") designates the history of Judea beginning with the conquest of Babylon by the Persians (539 BCE) and the Jewish diaspora under the military-cultural foreign occupation by the Persians, Greeks, and Romans.[122] Under Darius I new administrative and economic forms were created around 520 BCE in the Persian province of Yehud. Under this condition, a return of exiles followed in several stages. The temple was rebuilt (ca. 520–515 BCE), and social and cultic reforms took place under Ezra (458 BCE?) and Nehemiah (445–433 BCE). In this period the standard form of Judaism came into existence. At the center of the activities was the high evaluation and implementation of the law of Moses (cf. Ezra 7 with Neh. 8 and 10),[123] by which the introduction of the festivals (Passover, Ezra 6:19–22; Festival of Booths, Neh. 8:13–18; Sabbath, Neh. 13:15–22) and the prohibition of mixed marriage took on a special significance (cf. Ezra 9–10; Neh. 13:1–3, 23–31). Deuteronomy transmitted the program that stood in the background and reflected this process as it took place. The rebuilding of Jerusalem is interpreted as the story of divine guidance and covenant. Yahweh returns to his people their old/new identity. Yahweh-monotheism, election,

121. The word Ἰουδαϊσμός (Judaism) appears in 2 Macc. 2:21; 8:1; 14:38; 4 Macc. 4:26 and designates "the way of life according to the law" (also used by Paul in this way in Gal. 1:13–14). Probably it involves a Jewish self-designation that originated in the second century BCE, formed in analogy to the Greek Κυνισμός = "the Cynic way of life" (Diogenes Laertius 6.2, 104; cf. Στοϊκός = "Stoic way of life," as in Diogenes Laertius 4.67; 6.104). On the thesis of Mason, "Das antike Judentum," that Ἰουδαϊσμός is exclusively ethnic (in the sense of "Judean"), cf. the convincing critique by Sänger, "Ἰουδαϊσμός." Cf. Amir, Studien zum antiken Judentum, 101–13.

122. It is significant that the concept "Israel" designates the preexilic, older form of the people, while "Judaism" designates the postexilic, later form. In the last thirty years the designation "early Judaism" is used for the postexilic epoch in place of the negative connotation of "late Judaism." Cf. B. Lang, "Judentum (Frühjudentum)," NBL 2:404–9.

123. Cf. K. Schmid, Literaturgeschichte des Alten Testaments, 174: "The formation of the Torah, thus the limitation and literary determination of Genesis–Deuteronomy as a single entity, is one of the most important literary-historical acts of the Persian period."

the Torah of Moses, the temple, the Sabbath, the covenant, and the land of "Israel" stood, from this point onward, at the center of religious thinking and formed the religion of Judaism (see under 3.3.1).

In connection with the conquests of Alexander the Great in the Near and Middle East (between 336 and 323 BCE), Judea remained a largely autonomous province that was led by high priests according to the instructions of the Torah. Under the Ptolemies (ca. 301–200 BCE) and the Seleucids (ca. 200–63 BCE), Judea experienced an identity crisis because of the massive pressure for Hellenization (see under 3.3.1). These events led to the beginning of movements (apocalyptic, wisdom) and to the formation of those groups (Pharisees, Essenes, Zealots), which are of great significance for the NT. Also, after the conquest of Palestine by the Romans (Pompey in 63 BCE), Judea was not under direct Roman rule. Vassal kings (especially Herod the Great, 37–4 BCE) ruled the land with the recognition of its traditional religious-political structures.

The Diaspora

The origin of the Jewish diaspora (διασπορά, dispersion) is associated with the Babylonian exile and deportations in the sixth century BCE.[124] In the fifth century, not only did a flourishing Jewish culture exist in Babylon, but also a diaspora community is attested on the Egyptian Nile island Elephantine. In Asia Minor the Jewish diaspora expanded especially under the Seleucids (from 200 BCE). In Egypt, Alexandria became the most significant cultural center of diaspora Judaism. Other centers of the diaspora were Syria (Antioch, Damascus), Cyprus, Greece with Crete, Rome, and Cyrenaica.[125] Overall, more Jews lived in the diaspora by far than in Palestine; in the first century CE they numbered five to six million people.[126] Most Jews outside Palestine lived in Egypt, whose number Philo gives as around one million.[127] The Jewish diaspora communities had an extensive internal self-administration. Nevertheless, their well-being always depended on the goodwill of the ruler and the particular non-Jewish population. The basic goal for the diaspora community was to live according to the "laws of the fathers" and the Jewish customs, that is, particularly to follow the marriage and food laws as well as to keep the Sabbath. Although the pilgrimages to Jerusalem were an important bond between Palestine and the diaspora, the distance from the Jerusalem temple

---

124. For a thorough portrayal, cf. Barclay, *Jews in the Mediterranean Diaspora*.

125. Cf. Barclay, "Die Diaspora in der Kyrenaika."

126. On the numbers, cf. Kasher, "Diaspora"; Conzelmann, *Heiden—Juden—Christen*, 18; Ben-David, *Talmudische Ökonomie*, 41–57; Stemberger, *Juden und Christen*, 172–73.

127. Cf. Philo, *Flaccus* 43; on the distribution, cf. Stemberger, *Juden und Christen*, 162–65.

required the emergence of the synagogue (συναγωγή, assembly) as a new cultural and religious center for Jewish communities. The first evidence of the synagogue is found from the third century BCE in Egypt. From the first century BCE the synagogue slowly prevailed in Palestine.[128] The dominance of the Greek language and the cultural influence of Hellenism did not just require a translation of the OT into Greek (Septuagint), but its own branch of literature also emerged with the Jewish-Hellenistic writings of the diaspora, which partially opened them to Greek thought.

The Political Situation of Judaism in the First Century

The history of Judaism in the first century BCE and the first century CE can be understood only in the context of the conflicts involving Hellenization in the second century BCE. The Seleucid Antiochus IV Epiphanes (reigned 175–164 BCE) conducted an aggressive political program of Hellenization. In 169 BCE he plundered the temple and entered the most holy place (cf. 1 Macc. 1:21–23; 2 Macc. 5:15–16, 21); in 168 BCE he issued a religious edict, which was basically a prohibition of the exercise of the Jewish religion (cf. 1 Macc. 1:44–50). In addition, in 167 BCE he introduced the cult of the god Zeus Olympus in the Jerusalem temple (cf. Dan. 9:27; 11:31, "abomination of desolation") and had altars set up everywhere at which everyone could sacrifice to the foreign religion. The goal of the Seleucids was a complete Hellenization, and thus an integration, of Judea into the Seleucid world empire.

The Maccabean Revolt and the Formation of Groups

An opposition movement formed within Judaism to combat this violent effort at assimilation. The advocates of forced Hellenization within Judaism were probably a minority that lived primarily in Jerusalem and profited personally from this development.[129] However, most Jews—especially those in the countryside—responded to these efforts at Hellenization either with skepticism or rejection. The beginning of the open resistance against Antiochus is recorded in 1 Macc. 2:15–28. A Jewish priest named Mattathias, out of zeal for the law, struck dead another Jew who was about to offer a sacrifice at a pagan altar. Along with him, he also struck the royal official who wanted to

128. Cf. Stemberger, *Juden und Christen*, 169–70, 182–83, 194–95, 211–13; Claussen, *Versammlung, Gemeinde, Synagoge*, 83–112; Olsson and Zetterholm, *Ancient Synagogue*.
129. Cf. Dan. 11:39, which describes Antiochus: "Those who acknowledge him, he will make more wealthy. He makes them rulers over many and distributes to them land and reward."

force them to offer a sacrifice, and he tore down the altar. Then he fled into the mountains with his sons and organized the resistance.

Soon after the beginning of the uprising in the year 167 BCE, Mattathias died, and his son Judas came to be the head of the movement. He is mentioned in 2 Macc. 5:27 alone as the military leader and was called "the Maccabee" (ὁ Μακκαβαῖος),[130] from whom the whole movement received its name. Soon the "pious" (Gk. Ἀσιδαῖοι, Hb. חֲסִידִים), who were true to the law, united with the Maccabean movement, as 1 Macc. 2:42 reports: "Then the community of the Hasideans, brave men from Israel, who were true to the law, united with them" (cf. 1 Macc. 7:13; 2 Macc. 14:6). The phrase συναγωγὴ Ἀσιδαίων ("community of the Hasideans") indicates that this group had already existed for a long time and was formed before the Maccabees. Priests and significant scribes (γραμματεῖς, Hb. סֹפְרִים) probably belonged to this group (cf. 1 Macc. 7:12–13). Beginning with the Persian period, they were the bearers of the tradition defining Jewish identity and wrote apocalyptic literature, in which is evident political and theological protest against the pressure for assimilation from the great powers (see under 3.3.1).

One may assume the common origin of the Pharisees and Essenes in the environment of this movement,[131] for the Hasideans, like the Pharisees and the Essenes, distinguished themselves publicly by a strict obedience to the Torah and a determined rejection of the appearance of foreign influence on the Jewish faith.[132] Josephus appears to confirm this interpretation, for he mentions the existence of three Jewish schools—the Pharisees, Sadducees, and the Essenes (cf. Josephus, Ant. 13.171–73)—among the circles of those who were true to the Torah in the time of the disputed non-Zadokite priest Jonathan (152–43 BCE).

The Pharisees[133] take on a recognized identity during the period of John Hyrcanus (135/134–104 BCE), when they appear as an established group with a great reputation (cf. Josephus, Ant. 13.288–92) and oppose the king. The Pharisees demanded from Hyrcanus the abdication of the office of high priest, possibly because his mother had earlier been a prisoner of war. This concern indicates

130. Schürer, History of the Jewish People, 1:158. In 1 Macc. 3:4 Judas is described: "He was like a lion in his deeds, like a lion's cub that roars for prey."

131. Cf. the argument in Hengel, Judaism and Hellenism, 1:175–247.

132. On the critical discussion of the problem, cf. Stemberger, Pharisäer, 91–98, who comes to this conclusion: "A precise history of the origins of the three religious schools cannot be reconstructed any more than one can trace its direct origin from the Hasidean movement" (98).

133. On the Pharisees, cf. Meyer and H.-F. Weiss, Φαρισαῖος; Neusner, Das pharisäische und talmudische Judentum; Stemberger, Pharisaer, Sadduzaer, Essener, passim; Schäfter, "Der vorrabbinische Pharisaismus," in Hengel and Heckel, Paulus und das antike Judentum, 125–72; Deines, "Pharisaer"; Meier, Companions and Competitors, 289–388.

agreements with the original ideals of the Maccabean movement, which was interested primarily in a legitimate temple cult and the correct observance of the Torah. The Pharisees took a dominant role at the time of Salome Alexandra (76–67 BCE). Josephus emphasizes their continually growing influence on the queen (cf. *J.W.* 1.110–12). Under Herod the Great (40–4 BCE) the influence of the Pharisees was probably diminished.[134] Josephus gives their number during this period as six thousand (*Ant.* 17.42).[135] They were an influential minority of the Jewish population. Around the end of Herod's time, the Pharisees turned from being a political group to being a movement of piety.[136]

A significant event was the separation of a radical group among the Pharisees, the Zealots (Ζηλωταί), who associated their ideal with Phinehas (Num. 25) and Elijah (1 Kings 19:9–10). This group emerged in 6 CE under the leadership of the Galilean Judas of Gamala and the Pharisee Zadduk (cf. also Acts 5:37).[137] The Zealots were distinguished by their intensification of the first command of the Decalogue, strict Sabbath observance, and a rigorous keeping of the commands for purity. They strove for a radical theocracy and rejected Roman rule over the Jewish people on religious grounds.[138]

The Sadducees (see under 5.4), who descended primarily from the aristocratic families of Jerusalem and sought to maintain their dominant position in the political and religious system of Judaism (especially in the Sanhedrin through their cooperation with the respective major powers), took a rather opposite political stance.

As at the beginning period of the Pharisees, the legitimacy of the high priestly office and the purity of the temple cult played a decisive role among the Essenes. The accession of the high priestly office by the non-Zadokite Jonathan in the year 152 BCE probably led to the entrance of the Teacher of Righteousness (as former high priest) into the movement of the "new covenant" (cf. CD 1.5–11), which had already existed for twenty years.[139] This

134. Cf. Stemberger, *Pharisäer*, 107–10.

135. On the numbers of Pharisees, cf. Schaller, "4000 Essener—6000 Pharisäer," 172–82 (round numbers as a widespread means of historical fiction).

136. Cf. Stemberger, *Pharisäer, Sadduzäer, Essener*, 110.

137. Cf. Hengel, *Zealots*, 337–43.

138. Cf. Josephus, *J.W.* 2.117–18: "The territory of Archelaus was now reduced to a province, and Coponius, a Roman from the Roman equestrian order, was sent out as procurator, entrusted by Augustus with full powers, including infliction of capital punishment. Under his administration, a Galilaean, named Judas, incited his countrymen to revolt, upbraiding them as cowards for consenting to pay tribute to the Romans and tolerating mortal masters, after having God for their Lord. This man was, however, a Sophist who founded his own sect, having nothing to do with other Jews."

139. Cf. H. Stegemann, *Die Essener, Qumran*, 205ff.; the Teacher of Righteousness probably died around 110 BCE.

Hasidic group, together with the Teacher of Righteousness and his priestly followers, comprised the Essenes (Ἐσσηνοί = the pious). The history of their origin explains the constantly strong polemic against the actual temple cult in Jerusalem that was characteristic of the Essenes. According to Philo there were four thousand Essenes[140] who lived in villages and avoided the cities. However, Josephus mentions an Essene gate in Jerusalem (*J.W.* 5.145) that apparently refers to a part of the city inhabited by Essenes.[141] He also indicates that the Essenes differed among themselves with respect to marriage: one section permitted marriage, while another rejected it (cf. *J.W.* 2.160). Finally, the written discoveries at Qumran indicate that here, in direct proximity to the Dead Sea around 100 BCE–68 CE, a spiritual center of the Essenes existed.[142] The Essenes were probably not a uniform movement; it is noteworthy that they are not mentioned in the NT. According to the Qumran texts, the Essenes represented a radical obedience to the Torah (cf. CD 20.19–21), which involved a deep understanding of sin (cf. 1QH 4.30; 1QS 11.9–10) and an elite concept of election.[143] They regarded themselves as the opposition to the (cultically desecrated) Jerusalem temple, where the "wicked priest" ruled (cf. 1QpHab 8.8–13 and passim). As the alternative, the Qumran Essenes practiced the ideal cult and, as "sons of light," resisted eschatological temptations that had come over Israel. Its perfect orientation to the Torah and its penitence for ritual and ethical offenses correspond to the gracious work of God in the end time through the revelation of God's will by the Qumran community of the pious. Nevertheless, the pious need the mercy of God. The righteousness of God is God's fidelity to the covenant and the community, from which the righteousness of humankind grows (cf. 1QH 12.35–37).

From the Maccabean Revolt to the Jewish War, the office of high priest was the central point of dispute between the Jews and the occupying powers, but also within Judaism. The high priest was the head of the Jerusalem priesthood (cf. 1 Kings 4:2). He anointed the king (cf. 2 Kings 11:12) and bore the responsibility for the temple cult. After the exile he took an

---

140. Philo, *Good Person* 75.

141. Cf. Riesner, *Essener und Urgemeinde*, 14–30.

142. In the ongoing Qumran debate, I follow the basic thesis of Hartmut Stegemann, according to which Qumran is to be understood as an Essene settlement (so also Pliny the Elder, *Natural History* 5.17.4), and the texts found in the caves have something to do with the settlement. Hirschfeld (*Qumran—die ganze Wahrheit*) documents the new, disputed development: the texts and the settlement stand in a causal relationship; additionally, there is a new evaluation of the archaeological discoveries. For current scholarship on the topic, see Xeravits and Porzig, *Einführung in die Qumranliteratur*, and Stökl Ben Ezra, *Qumran*. Both works argue for a connection between the place and the writings. See also Flusser, *Judaism of the Second Temple Period*, 1:25–31.

143. Cf. O. Betz, "Rechtfertigung in Qumran."

increasingly political role as the primary leader of the Sanhedrin. The high priest made sacrifices for sins on the Day of Atonement (Lev. 16). He wore a special robe (Exod. 28:1–39) and offered the sacrifice on the altar of incense (Exod. 30:7, 10). The holiness of the office of high priest required specific rules of conduct (Lev. 21:10–15). The office was hereditary (Lev. 6:14; Num. 20:26ff.), and the one who held the office had to be a Zadokite (cf. 1 Chron. 5:27–41 LXX = 6:1–15 Eng.). With Menelaus (cf. 2 Macc. 4:23–29; Josephus, *Ant.* 12.237–41) and Alcimus (2 Macc. 14:3–14; Josephus, *Ant.* 12.382–88), two non-Zadokites took over the high-priestly office as the office of high priest was now purchased. Under the Hasmoneans, the office of high priest remained exclusively in the hand of the ruler and was, from the perspective of the pious, illegitimate. In the Assumption of Moses (6.1) the writer speaks of this period: "Then kings will rise as rulers over them, and they will become high priests. Yet they will commit ungodliness in the most holy place." Under the Romans the principle of heredity and the holding of the office for life was finally abandoned, and the high priest was appointed according to the will of the ruler alone (often for a very brief period).[144] The discrepancy between the ideal institution of the high-priestly office (cf. Sir. 50) and the reality could not have been greater. The highest office in Judaism became increasingly the plaything for political and financial interests. From the view of the Jews who were true to Torah, this situation was a continuing harsh provocation, for with illegitimate priests the Jerusalem cult was also illegitimate, and atonement for the people became impossible.

Messianic Figures and Movements

The fracturing of Judaism into both theologically and politically different movements that began with the Maccabean Revolt shaped the history of the first century CE and is of great significance for the history of early Christianity. After the success of the Maccabean period and the relative independence under the rule of the Hasmoneans (ca. 142–63 BCE), the Jewish state fell under the Roman demand for tribute beginning in 63 BCE. While especially the rule of Herod the Great (40–4 BCE) gave Israel relative independence once more, the division of the kingdom under Herod's sons in 4 BCE led to a development that, not coincidentally, led to the First Jewish War. In the context of the horrors of the rule of Archelaus (4 BCE–6 CE) and the associated transformation of Judea into a (significant) division within

---

144. A list of the high priests that can be reconstructed is given by Zwickel, "Hohepriester."

the Roman province of Syria,[145] the result was not only the formation of the Zealot movement but also revolts in many places that were brutally suppressed by the commander Varus (cf. Josephus, *J.W.* 2.55–79).[146] Messianic prophets such as Simon Athronges and Judas the son of Hezekiah appeared;[147] other local leaders, reformers, and insurrectionists also protested against Roman power for political, social, and theological reasons and aspired to rule.[148] Josephus characterizes the tense situation in summary: "Thus Judea was full of brigandage. Anyone might make himself king as the head of a band of rebels whom he fell in with, and then would press on to the destruction of the community" (*Ant.* 17.285). Behind the groups that Josephus called "robber bands" stood messianic and social hopes that strove for a liberation from Roman rule and for a just order. According to Pss. Sol. 17.21ff., the king and Anointed One sent by God would not only drive out the gentiles but would also rule over his people in righteousness. Judea and Galilee remained territories with unrest in which revolts constantly occurred. Thus Josephus[149] reported about a Samaritan prophet (around 36 CE) and mentioned Theudas (around 45 CE), who is also mentioned in Acts 5:36.

The appearance of John the Baptist and Jesus of Nazareth must also be seen in this context.[150] Their renewal movements were evidently perceived to be politically dangerous. The preaching of repentance by the Baptist (Mark 1:2–8; Matt. 3:7–12 par.) induced his sovereign Herod Antipas (4 BCE–39 CE) in 28 CE to get him out of the way.[151] Herod also followed Jesus of Nazareth with suspicion (cf. Luke 9:7–9; 13:31–33) but could not arrest him. The events in Jerusalem in the year 30 indicate clearly that Jesus's public

---

145. Until 66 CE the province of Syria was ruled by an imperial legate of senatorial rank; the prefect/procurator in Judea was subordinate to him and responsible for public order in Judea; cf. Eck, "Die römischen Repräsentanten in Judäa."

146. Ca. 6–4 BCE, Legate in Syria; 7–9 CE, in Germania.

147. Cf. Josephus, *Ant.* 17.273–74: Simon, the slave (after 4 BCE); *Ant.* 17.278–80: the shepherd Athronges (after 4 BCE); Josephus, *J.W.* 2.55–56: Judas the son of Hezekiah (after 4 BCE).

148. Cf. Meyer, *Der Prophet aus Galiläa*; Hanson and Oakman, *Palestine in the Time of Jesus*, 80–89; Riedo-Emmenegger, *Prophetisch-messianische Provokateure*, 245–75.

149. Cf. Josephus, *Ant.* 18.85–86; 20.97–98; also *Ant.* 20.102: death of the sons of Judas (between 46 and 48 CE); *Ant.* 20.167–68; *J.W.* 2.258–59: anonymous prophets (52–60 CE).

150. Cf. Riedo-Emmenegger, *Prophetisch-messianische Provokateure*, 276–309.

151. Cf. Josephus, *Ant.* 18.116–19: "When others too joined the crowds about him, because they were aroused to the highest degree by his sermons, Herod became alarmed. Eloquence that had so great an effect on mankind might lead to some form of sedition, for it looked as if they would be guided by John in everything they did. Herod decided therefore that it would be much better to strike first and be rid of him before his work led to an uprising than to wait for an upheaval, get involved in a difficult situation, and see his mistake. Because of these suspicions, Herod had John brought in chains to Machaerus, the stronghold previously mentioned, and there put to death."

appearance was considered politically dangerous for both the Jewish authorities and the Romans. The messianic ovation at Jesus's entry into Jerusalem (cf. Mark 11:8–10), the purification of the temple, and especially the inscription on the cross indicate that Jesus elicited messianic expectations and aroused unrest. The inscription on the cross—ὁ βασιλεὺς τῶν Ἰουδαίων, The king of the Jews—was probably derived not from the Jews or Christians but from the Romans and attests that they executed Jesus of Nazareth as a (political) messianic pretender.[152]

A severe crisis in the relationship between Rome and Jerusalem occurred at the end of the time of Caligula's rule (39/40 CE). Caligula intensified the ruler cult and was obviously not prepared to accept the special place of the Jews in relationship to the cult of Caesar.[153] In Alexandria anti-Jewish pogroms occurred in 38/39 CE because the Jews refused to participate in the cult of Caesar. As a result, Caligula commanded Petronius, the governor of Syria, to erect a golden statue of Caesar as "Zeus Epiphanes Neos Gaius" in the temple in Jerusalem (cf. Josephus, *J.W.* 2.184–203; *Ant.* 18.261–88; Philo, *Legat.* 200–207). Philo interpreted this action as an intentional war against Judaism and leaves no doubt: "But what Gaius altered was no small matter, but rather the greatest atrocity, the attempt namely to transform the created mortal nature of a man into the uncreated, immortality of God according to his own preference" (*Legat.* 118). This action of Caligula aroused the bitter resistance of the Jews, who successfully requested that he delay the execution of this command (cf. Philo, *Legat.* 222–53). The murder of Caligula finally resulted in his statue not being erected, thus hindering an open war (for the time being) between Jews and Romans.

The brief rule of Agrippa I (41–44 CE), the friend of Claudius, over almost the entire territory of his grandfather Herod the Great was only a brief interlude, for after his sudden death the greatest part of Palestine came again under direct Roman administration. The provocations of the Jews by Roman soldiers and procurators continued, and the anti-Roman mood grew as a prelude to the Jewish War.[154] The political-religious concept of the holiness and purity of Israel was not, in the long run, consistent with an occupying power that raised political-religious claims in the form and the presence of

152. Cf. Hengel, "Jesus der Messias Israels," 50. This view is supported by the fact that, according to Matt. 27:38, 44 and John 18:38b–40, Barabbas, the one set free in Jesus's place, is called a "brigand" (λῃστής), i.e., insurrectionist, Zealot.

153. Cf. Philo, *Legat.* 115–18; on the specific course of events, cf. Bernett, *Der Kaiserkult in Judäa*, 264–87.

154. On the detailed history of the events, cf. Bernett, *Der Kaiserkult in Judäa*, 328–51; she describes especially the accumulation of the violations of the Torah under Roman rule after the death of Agrippa I (44 CE).

the cult of Caesar.[155] Under the procurator Tiberius Alexander (46–48 CE),[156] there was a great famine that was catastrophic for the impoverished population in the countryside. A bloody conflict that took place in Jerusalem during the period of the procurator Ventidus Cumanus (48–52 CE) was set off by an incident during the Passover festival. Josephus attributed the incident to the Zealots: "Many of them, however, emboldened by impunity, had recourse to robbery, and raids and insurrections, fostered by the more reckless, broke out all over the country" (*J.W.* 2.238–39). Under the procurator Felix (52–60 CE), the situation became worse: Roman rule disintegrated, and at the same time the Zealot movement grew in influence. Uprisings occurred, as Acts 21:38 reports, when Paul was asked: "Are you not the Egyptian who recently stirred up a revolt and led four thousand rebels into the wilderness?" Josephus also reports about the Egyptian with his large number of followers.[157] Felix quelled this revolt with powerful weapons. The Jerusalem church was also affected by the anti-Roman sentiment within Judaism. The execution of James the brother of Jesus around 62 CE (see below, 9.1) by conservative Sadducean circles probably caused the Jerusalem church, with its connection with Christians from the Greco-Roman tradition, no longer to be regarded as a part of Judaism. Directly before the outbreak of the war, prophets appeared who sang a lament over Jerusalem; thus Jesus ben Ananias (62–64 CE) announced the fall of the city.[158]

The Jewish War

The direct trigger for the Jewish War was the conduct of the last Roman procurator, Gessius Florus (64–66 CE),[159] who interfered with the temple treasure,[160] provoking an open uprising by the people in April/May 66 CE in Jerusalem and other Jewish territories. In Jerusalem the daily sacrifice for the caesar ceased, causing an open break with Rome. At the same time, bitter conflicts within Judaism occurred. The high priest, the Pharisees, and the Herodians wanted to avoid a larger conflict with the Romans, while the Zealots

---

155. Cf. Bernett, *Der Kaiserkult in Judäa*, 310–27.

156. Because of the usage of Josephus, the designation for the office (procurator or praefectus) is not entirely clear in every case; cf. Eck, *Rom und Judaea*, 1–51. Prefects from the equestrian order ruled Judea 6–41 CE (documented by the Pilate inscription from Caesarea Maritima); procurators ruled 44–66 CE.

157. Cf. Josephus, *Ant.* 20.169ff.; *J.W.* 2.261ff.

158. Cf. Josephus, *J.W.* 6.300–309; cf. also the prophecies for the year 66 CE mentioned in *J.W.* 6.312–15.

159. See Mason, *History of the Jewish War*.

160. Cf. Josephus, *J.W.* 2.293.

especially favored the conflict with Rome, which they followed through with brutal violence. They represented a radicalized political theology that saw the fulfillment of the will of God in the enforcement of the cultic "purity" of the temple and of all Israel.[161] Therefore the "impure," most of all the Romans, had to be driven from the land. The Zealots were under the leadership of Menahem, a son of the Zealot founder Judas of Galilee, who had himself honored in Jerusalem as king and probably made messianic claims.[162] The war party under the leadership of the Zealots torched the palace of the high priest and burned the city archive. Josephus gives the reason: "They next carried their combustibles to the public archives, eager to destroy the creditors' contracts and to prevent the recovery of debts, in order to win over a host of grateful debtors and to cause a rising of the poor against the rich, sure of impunity" (*J.W.* 2.427). Thus it is evident that a motive for the uprising was the social and economic injustice in Judea. Evidently some of the Zealots wanted a new distribution of the land, which was primarily in the hands of the upper class. Added to this were the conflicts based on ethnicity, for in many regions of Palestine, conflicts arose between Jewish and Greek parts of the population in something like a civil war, as some favored and others rejected the struggle against Rome. There was also a conflict between city and countryside that was less obvious, for while the majority in cities influenced by Greek culture, such as Sepphoris and Tiberias, were against the war, most of the poor people in the countryside supported it. Further aspects of the war were multilayered.[163] After the initial success of the resistance, Caesar Nero commissioned his general Vespasian with the task of putting down the rebellion in Judea. He began his campaign in the early part of 67 with his son Titus. They had about sixty thousand well-trained men at their disposal. Vespasian continued to come closer to Jerusalem but had to suspend the operation because of the death of Caesar Nero (68 CE) and the related uncertain situation in Rome. On July 1, 69, Vespasian was proclaimed emperor by the Egyptian legions, and within a brief period he was recognized as caesar in the entire eastern portion of the empire. Vespasian now concentrated on the events in Rome and commissioned his son Titus to continue. In early 70 CE the siege of Jerusalem began.

161. The demand for "holiness" was represented in numerous Jewish texts; cf. Pss. Sol. 17.22 ("to purify Jerusalem from the gentile peoples"); 17.28 ("and no stranger and foreigner will live anymore among them"); 4Q394 frag. 8 col. 4 line 9 ("Jerusalem is the camp of holiness").
162. Cf. Josephus, *J.W.* 2.433: "At this period a certain Menahem . . . took his intimate friends off with him to Masada, where he broke into King Herod's armory and provided arms both for his fellow-townsmen and for other brigands; then, with these men for his bodyguard, he returned like a veritable king to Jerusalem, became the leader of the revolution, and directed the siege of the palace."
163. On the details, cf. Schwier, *Tempel und Tempelzerstörung*, 4–54.

Finally, in August of that year, the temple was conquered and burned down, and the whole city was almost totally destroyed. The outcome of the war was thus decided, although the Zealots maintained their resistance at the fortress Masada. Josephus primarily blames the appearance of the prophets for the resistance of the Jews in Jerusalem, for they had proclaimed the coming of a messianic savior and thus goaded the people onward (*J.W.* 6.285, 311–12).

The consequence of the defeat was disastrous for the Jews. It changed their political status, for Judea became an independent Roman province, for which the Syrian legate was no longer responsible. A standing legion was now stationed there. Whole settlements were destroyed and depopulated. Many people died in battle or as a result of the battles, while others were sold into slavery. A total of about a third of the population died. Property went to the caesar; it is unclear whether this involved all property or the so-called crown properties. The people of the countryside, already at a strong disadvantage, were impoverished even more. Almost all Jewish farmers became tenant farmers, who worked the land as renters.

The former religious life, which was oriented for centuries toward the Jerusalem temple cult, could no longer be continued. The Jews had to live not only without a state but also without the temple. This also resulted in the end of the high-priestly office. Of the religious parties that existed before 70 CE, the Zealots, Sadducees, and Essenes disappeared. Only the more moderate Pharisees/scribes remained, who then entered into Jewish history as the rabbis. Early Christianity was strongly affected by the events of the year 70, for the Jerusalem church perished in the wreckage of the war (see under 9.2). Thus the movement lost its point of origin and abiding point of orientation. However, at the same time the missionary activities of Paul in Asia Minor, Greece, and Rome preserved Christianity from disappearing.

For the Romans, the victory over the Jews was not counted only as one among many. Titus returned to Rome and, with his father, Vespasian, celebrated a triumphal march in the year 71.[164] This event was unusual, for normally such a triumphal march was held only with the conquest of a new province. Here it celebrated merely the pacification of a part of an existing province of Syria.[165] Moreover, in the entire empire coins were minted with the inscription *Judaea capta* (Judea conquered). The victory of Jupiter over Yahweh is documented also in the introduction of the *fiscus Judaicus*, a tax (see under 9.2) that was levied on every Jew (also in the diaspora) and that,

---

164. Weikert, *Von Jerusalem zu Aelia Capitolina*, 63–73, who demonstrates how powerfully the victory over the Jews served to legitimize the rule of the Flavian family.

165. Cf. Schwier, *Tempel und Tempelzerstörung*, 317–30.

A. Hunter Wright, CC BY-SA 3.0 / Wikimedia Commons

3.5. Arch of Titus in Rome (today Forum Romanum). After the victory, the spoils of war from the temple were transported to Rome, among them the table of showbread, the seven-armed menorah, and two silver trumpets.

in reality, took the place of the temple tax.[166] The Titus arch, erected in Rome after the death of Titus (81 CE), indicates how strongly the Flavians used the victory over the Jews for propaganda purposes.

Judaism survived after 70 in Palestine under harsh conditions. Of the Jewish groups the only ones who survived were the Pharisees and the scribes, who led the effort for the transformation of rabbinic Judaism oriented totally in the Torah (see below, 11.5). The diaspora remained a center of Judaism but was affected by the outcome of the war. Especially in Syria, Egypt, and Cyrenaica, hatred against the Jews erupted into open hostility, which increased because of the flight of radical Zealots to these places. In Cyrene, Jonathan the Weaver staged a messianic revolt around 73/74 CE that resulted in a bloody defeat by the Romans.[167] Between 115 and 117 CE, there were revolts on Cyprus and in Egypt and Cyrenaica, which all came to a bloody end.[168] The Bar Kokhba Revolt (132–35 CE) marked the ultimate end of any Jewish state.[169]

166. Cf. Josephus, *J.W.* 7.218; Dio Cassius 65.7.2.
167. Cf. Josephus, *J.W.* 7.437–42.
168. Cf. Dio Cassius 68.32; *Historia Augusta, Vita Hadrian* 14.2.
169. On the history of the events, cf. P. Schäfer, *Geschichte der Juden in der Antike*, 159–75; Eck, "Der Kochba-Aufstand der Jahre 132–136."

The caesar Hadrian probably commanded the transformation of Jerusalem into a Hellenistic city with the name Aelia Capitolina around 130 CE;[170] he intensified the prohibition of circumcision and in Jerusalem erected a sanctuary of Jupiter on the ruins of the old temple. After that, a revolt broke out under the leadership of Simon bar Kokhba, whom Rabbi Akiba called "Son of the Star" (Bar Kokhba),[171] using the messianic predicate from Num. 24:17. In a guerilla war (e.g., with surprise attacks from subterranean cave complexes), primarily in the southern part of Judea, the insurrectionists had great success, but they were ultimately annihilated. Then the caesar issued an edict that no Jew was permitted to enter Jerusalem and the neighboring territories. The name of the province was changed to Syria Palestine so that there was no longer a land of the Jews.

3.3.1 The Jewish Religion

The theological thought of Judaism is characterized by a profound transformation as a result of the Babylonian exile (598/587–537 BCE), for the collapse of the preexilic order had to be theologically overcome. In the center of the religion was exclusive monotheism, knowledge of election, the Torah, and the land as the gifts of God along with the temple as the place of God's presence. Despite the afflictions of the present, Israel hoped for God's unfailing fidelity and attempted to define itself anew through ritual separation from the other peoples.[172]

The oneness and uniqueness of God is the basis of Jewish faith;[173] there is only one God, besides whom there is no other God (Deut. 6:4b, "Hear, O Israel, the LORD our God is one!"; cf. Isa. 44:6; Jer. 10:10; 2 Kings 5:15; 19:19; and passim). In the Letter of Aristeas (132) an instruction about the nature of God begins with the affirmation that "there is only one God, and his power is evident through all things, for everywhere is full of his power." In sharp contrast to ancient polytheism, Philo emphasizes: "We want to affirm the first and holiest commandment among us; to acknowledge and honor the highest

170. Cf. Dio Cassius 69.12.
171. An indirect reference to the messianic claims of Bar Kokhba appears in Justin, *1 Apol.* 32.13: "A star shall rise out of Jacob, and a flower shall spring from the root of Jesse—this is the Christ." The antichristian attitude of Bar Kokhba is noteworthy. According to Justin (*1 Apol.* 31.6), Bar Kokhba had Jewish Christians executed when they did not deny Jesus Christ.
172. On this historical process, cf. Maier, *Zwischen den Testamenten*, 191–247; on the fundamental theological assumptions, cf. Nissen, *Gott und der Nächste*, 99–329.
173. On the development of monotheism within the history of Israelite religion, cf. Albani, *Der eine Gott und die himmlischen Heerscharen*; cf. also Schrage, *Unterwegs zur Einheit und Einzigkeit Gottes*, 1–35 (primary texts for the OT and Jewish monotheism), 35–43 (important texts of pagan monotheism).

God; the doctrine of polytheism must not ever touch the ear of the one who seeks the truth in purity and without falsehood."[174] Monotheism was the basis for the uniqueness but also the fascination with Judaism in antiquity.[175]

The concept of election was closely related to belief in the true God. Thus Deut. 7:6–8 ("The LORD has chosen you out of all the people of the world to be his people") and Deut. 14:2 ("You are the people who are consecrated to the LORD, your God, and the LORD has chosen you from all of the people of the earth to be his own people") give the classic formulation of the basic idea of election: God chose Israel from all the peoples and established Israel's special place as a free decision and because of affection and not any other reason. Thus the exodus from Egypt was regarded as the permanent commitment and as the fundamental model of the saving act of God (cf. Deut. 7:8, "Because the LORD loves you and keeps his oath that he swore to your fathers. Thus he led you out with a strong hand and liberated you from the house of slavery, out of the house of Pharaoh, the king of Egypt"). This preexilic concept of election in the Deuteronomic-Deuteronomistic theology was combined with the concept of the covenant (cf. Exod. 19:4–8) and defined the thought of all of Judaism. In Qumran especially, the concept of election is dominant, as, for example, the Rule of the Community (1QS) indicates, describing the "Sons of Light." God elected them to "an eternal covenant." Jewish apocalyptic is also shaped by the consciousness of election (cf. 4 Ezra 5.27: "You have chosen one people out of many peoples, and to this people whom you have loved, you have given the law, which is recognized by all").

The gift of the Torah is the expression of God's binding himself to his people.[176] The Torah is primarily a gift for life and order (cf. Deut. 30:15–16: "See I have set before you today life. . . . I command you this day, to love the LORD, your God, and to follow in his ways, and to keep his commandments and decrees").[177] The Torah is understood as a gift of grace and a testimony of his covenant (cf., e.g., Sir. 24; Jub. 1.16–18). To keep it means to enter into God's rule, to recognize it, and to follow it. As observance and respect for God's will, fidelity to the Torah is thus the answer expected of Israel to election

---

174. Philo, *On the Decalogue* 51 and 65; *Creation* 171; *Spec. Laws* 1.30; cf. also Josephus, *Ant.* 3.91; Josephus, *Ag. Ap.* 2.167.251ff. The ancient polytheism with its numerous images of the deity was also a topic of ridicule among pagan philosophers; cf. Cicero, *Nat. d.* 1.81–84.

175. Cf. Tacitus, *Hist.* 5.5.4: "The Jews have purely mental conceptions of deity, as one in essence."

176. On the theology and social history of the Torah, cf. Crüsemann, *Die Tora*; Nissen, *Gott und der Nächste*, 330ff.; Weber, *Das Gesetz im hellenistischen Judentum*; Weber, *Das "Gesetz" bei Philon von Alexandrien und Flavius Josephus.*

177. On the power of Torah to give salvation and life, cf., e.g., Sir. 17:11; 45:5; Bar. 3:9; 4:1; Pss. Sol. 14.2; 4 Ezra 7.21ff.; 9.7ff.; 14.22, 30; 2 Bar. 38.2; 85.3ff.

by God. The Torah does not mediate the relationship to God, but is rather the guide to the order of creation given by God. Within this whole concept, righteousness is not the result of human achievement, but rather God's promise to humankind (cf. Jub. 22.15: "May he renew his covenant with you, that you might be a people for him, his inheritance forever. And he will be God in truth and righteousness for you and for your seed in all of the days on the earth"). The measure of the righteousness of God and of the righteousness of humankind is the law. Moses gave the law "for the sake of righteousness and for pious observance and for the formation of character" (Let. Aris. 144). "Everything regulated in the law is for the purpose of righteousness" (Let. Aris. 168; cf. 147). Fidelity to the Torah maintains righteousness and life. However, over a long period the Torah is no verbatim fixed document, but rather what the Torah is in each case is differently unfolded through individual writings (e.g., the pre-Qumran Temple Scroll, the book of Jubilees, Philo).

The gift of the land is connected to election, as in Deut. 7:1: "When the LORD your God brings you into the land, into which you go, in order to take it as a possession . . ." The promise of the land and the occupation of the land are the central features of the acts of God in history (cf. Deut. 11:29; 15:4; 18:9; 26:1; 30:5; Josh. 21:43; Ps. 25:13; and passim). The land of Israel is Yahweh's possession (cf. Lev. 25), in which the Torah has unlimited authority and in which no idolatry is permitted. Thus the keeping of the Torah is connected with continuation in the land (cf. Deut. 4:1, 26). Inseparable from the land are Jerusalem as the holy city and the temple as the dwelling place of God. The temple in Jerusalem is the throne of God, where God is king (cf. Isa. 8:18; 1 Kings 8:12ff.; Pss. 9:12; 74:2; 76:3; 132:13). Here is the place where God appears and meets the people (cf. Exod. 29:43–45). Similarly, the temple mountain is the "holy mountain" (cf. Pss. 2:6; 48:3) and Jerusalem is the "city of God" (cf. Pss. 46:5; 48:2, 9; 87:3). From the Persian period onward, the Sabbath becomes increasingly the central sign of Jewish identity.[178] The relatively brief passages of Exod. 23:10; 34:18–23; 35:1–3 (cf. also Exod. 16:23–30; Lev. 25:1–7) were constantly expanded in the framework of a rigorist priestly interpretation, as indicated by the comparison with Jub. 50, the Damascus Document (CD) 10.14–11.18, and the Mishnah tractate Shabbat. The obligation for rest on the seventh day commanded by God increasingly develops into a comprehensive system of rules; for example, Shabbat 7.2 lists "forty less one" forbidden kinds of work.

Two other influential streams of thought were also connected with the basic construction of Judaism based on monotheism, election, and the Torah:

---

178. Cf. Doering, *Schabbat*; Grund, *Die Entstehung des Sabbats*.

apocalyptic and wisdom. Both of these streams were major influences on early Christianity.

Apocalyptic

Apocalyptic is both a way of thinking and a literary phenomonen that strongly shaped both Jewish and early Christian thought, especially between 200 BCE and 100 CE.[179] Apocalyptic (ἀποκάλυψις, revelation/unveiling) is a specific manner of interpreting history with the help of otherworldly knowledge that is written down in apocalypses as a literary form.[180] The basic assumption is the concept that ideal figures of Jewish history had an extraordinary insight/illumination/revelation that unveiled God's plan for the future and was recorded for the orientation of later generations. One considers oneself to be at the end and hopes for God's imminent intervention in order to turn things fundamentally to the good. Those phenomena that form the matrix of apocalyptic thought include (1) pseudepigraphy as the appropriation of a legendary figure of the past (e.g., Enoch, Baruch, Moses, Ezra) in order to legitimate new knowledge; (2) visions with revelations about the history (primarily of the Jewish people); (3) journeys in heaven with descriptions of the heavenly world that have been communicated to the apocalyptist; (4) historical summaries that are frequently based on a concept of wisdom and history divided into periods, according to which the sufferings of the present will be replaced by the joys of the future; (5) the hope for a turn in history as it moves toward a final situation that corresponds to the original situation; (6) a lively and colorful imagery that is partially encrypted and intelligible only to the group; (7) paraenesis and *paraclesis* (encouragement), which are intended to resist the temptations of the present; (8) prayers for help and salvation from the present situation, which is understood as the end time; (9) claims of one's own election and the rejection of others that are often expressed with deterministic and dualistic statements; and (10) the expectation of a saving figure in the future who, in many instances, engages in a final battle against evil powers/eschatological opponents and is appointed by God to a position as ruler (e.g., Son of Man, Messiah). Apocalyptic is at the same time a literary and theological phenomenon that interprets history

---

179. The concept of "apocalyptic" is an artificial and technical academic word that was coined at the beginning of the nineteenth century; on the history of research, cf. J. Schmidt, *Die jüdische Apokalyptik*; Zager, *Begriff und Wertung der Apokalyptik*; Förg, *Die Ursprünge der alttestamentlichen Apokalyptik*, 16–38. A very restrictive definition of the term *apocalyptic* is found in Wolter, "Apokalyptik als Redeform im Neuen Testament," 171–91.

180. Apocalyptic/apocalypses are not uniquely Jewish phenomena; they can be found also in Iran and Greece; cf. the contributions of Hellholm, *Apocalypticism in the Mediterranean World*.

by interpreting the coming history and the present situation reciprocally. This results in a comprehensive, partially encrypted image of the history of the world and of the end of the world in the form of a catastrophe that is under God's control. The main texts of Jewish apocalyptic are Ethiopic Enoch (1 Enoch: extensive collection of Enoch literature, of which the oldest parts come from the pre-Maccabean period), Daniel, the Isaiah apocalypse (Isa. 24–27), the book of Jubilees, Ascension of Moses, Sibylline Oracles, 4 Ezra, Slavonic Enoch (2 Enoch), 2 Baruch, Apocalypse of Abraham, parts of the Qumran scrolls, and 3 Baruch.[181]

The book of Joel, which originated in either the fourth or third century BCE, can be read as a prime example of Jewish apocalyptic. It develops in an exemplary way the entire apocalyptic scenario:

a general distress precedes the day of the Lord (1:2–20);

a general destruction follows (2:1–11);

God initiates a new era for those in Israel who are willing to repent (2:12–27);

the outpouring of the Spirit and the salvation of Israel is promised (2:28–32);

there is destruction of the gentiles (3:1–16);

the destruction of the gentiles and the salvation of Israel comes in the end (3:17–21);

and a holy war of Yahweh against the gentiles follows at the end of time (3:9).

Numerous texts of apocalyptic were, in the course of their transmission, copied and revised.[182] In Jewish apocalyptic several motifs flow together from tradition history: those connected with the figure of Enoch, the theme of the heavenly journey and mediation of revelation influenced by Ezekiel, and especially Sinai traditions connected to Moses.

Relevant bearers of Jewish apocalyptic were probably the scribes, those who were knowledgeable of the Torah, whose task was the interpretation of

---

181. Förg, *Die Ursprünge der alttestamentlichen Apokalyptik*, 47ff., sees also in Daniel the apocalyptic book in the full sense but asks at the same time about the older apocalyptic texts (royal Yahweh Psalms: 47; 93; 96–99; Zech. 1–6; Haggai; Ezekiel). His conclusion: "The thesis that Old Testament apocalyptic begins with Daniel is improbable when one considers the present investigation. Haggai and Zechariah are to be regarded as representatives of earlier apocalyptic. With the classification of Ezekiel already as early apocalyptic literature, apocalyptic may be regarded as preexilic."

182. On specific instances, cf. Nickelsburg, *Jewish Literature*; Lichtenberger and Oegema, *Jüdische Schriften*.

the Torah, the education of pupils in the Torah, and adjudication of legal matters according to the Torah. From the fourth century BCE, the position of the "scribes" emerged from the priesthood. They saw in Ezra the original ideal type (Ezra 7:6, 11, with Ezra as scribe and priest). Jesus Sirach described an ideal image of the wise scribe around 180 BCE (Sir. 38:24–39:11), whose wisdom and insight are praised before God and the world and who concentrates himself totally on the Torah. The majority of scribes in the early period belonged to the lower priesthood, serving the temple aristocracy (cf. Sir. 39:4), and were at the same time bearers of Jewish tradition and preservers of Jewish identity. While the temple aristocracy—especially the high priest and the circles of the higher priesthood who stood around him—were open to Hellenistic assimilation or even supported it, the majority distanced themselves from it.[183]

Scribes formulated their protest against Hellenistic assimilation in apocalypses. Thus 1 Enoch ("Enoch the scribe") says that behind the extensive Enoch literature that developed over centuries stood the circle of scribes (cf. also Jub. 4.16, 17). Daniel 1:4; 11:33; and 12:3, 10 refer to scribes as a circle of those who are schooled in every topic. From the time of the Maccabean Revolt, they probably fell into a far-reaching conflict, for the distinctiveness and the purity of the elect people of God stood in jeopardy and had to be protected. More and more scribes separated themselves from the temple and thus introduced the opening for nonpriests. Apocalyptic was thus in many instances an expression and means of political agitation, particularly against the Seleucids and later against the Romans (cf., e.g., Pss. Sol. 2; 17; T. Mos. 7; 10.7–10).

Apocalyptic is a challenging phenomenon. It is rooted in prophetic (announcement and unveiling of future events) as well as wisdom (pseudonymity, observation of nature, interpretation of dreams, reports on heavenly journeys, an overview of the periods of history) and priestly tradition (preservation of the heritage of the fathers, high value of the Torah, ideal temple, cultic purity, questions of the calendar).[184]

WISDOM

Jewish wisdom literature[185] belongs within the larger realm of ancient oriental wisdom literature, which was especially prominent in Egypt and

---

183. Cf. Hengel, *Judaism and Hellenism*, 1:304–14; Horsley, *Revolt of the Scribes*, 31–32.

184. Apropos Förg, *Die Ursprünge der alttestamentlichen Apokalyptik*, 496: "Apocalyptic is the result of the flowing together of prophecy and wisdom."

185. Cf. the classic description in von Rad, *Wisdom in Israel*. See also J. Collins, *Jewish Wisdom*.

Mesopotamia. Wisdom was a phenomenon of education that conveyed insight into all the essential areas of experience and thus had the purpose of ordering itself positively in the principles of individual and social life. The clever conduct of life is a gift of God (Sir. 1:1–10) and at the same time a human capacity that is open to everyone (Sir. 51:21–24). The basic themes of wisdom are the knowledge of God as the guarantor and the founder of world order, the relationship of the wise man and the fool, the righteous man and the sinner in their deeds and actions, poverty and wealth, and the right time for a happy life. The beginning of wisdom is, according to Prov. 9:10, "the fear of the LORD." The source of wisdom is primarily the Torah, which in Sir. 24:23 and Bar. 3:9–4:4 is identified with wisdom (cf. Pss. 19:8; 119:98). As a literary form, wisdom literature consists primarily of wisdom sayings and the collection that emerges from it. These were cultivated in schools for scribes, that is, handed on and directed in the didactic forms of admonition and instruction on the complete realm of knowledge, education, and status and conduct of life. Like apocalyptic, wisdom cannot be cleanly separated from other areas; instead, the concept of wisdom is preserved in almost all traditional forms in Jewish thought.

A crisis of wisdom thought is documented in the outer frame (chaps. 1–2; 42:7–14) of the book of Job (fifth to fourth cent. BCE), where the pious man sees himself unexpectedly, through no fault of his own and without understanding, abandoned to the enmity of God and no longer understands the logic of the connection between deed and blessing.[186] The credibility of God and the order established by God is on the line: Why is the sinner happy, and why does the righteous one suffer although he has done nothing wrong? While in Job, trust in God's power and sovereignty are restored (cf. Job 38:1–42:6), another position is argued in Ecclesiastes (Qohelet) around 200 BCE.[187] Here also the connection of deed and blessing is recognized (cf. Eccles. 7:15–16; 8:12–14), but the conclusion is different from that of Job. God is unpredictable; his just order is not ascertainable, and thus "everything is nothing/absurd" (cf. Eccles. 1:2; 8:14; 12:8). A religious-philosophical pessimism dominates, which shows a proximity to Greek Skepticism, and also to Epicurus. What matters is to seize the few moments of joy in life and of happiness (cf. Eccles. 5:17–19; 9:7–10; 11:9) that happen to be granted. This carpe diem no longer trusts in the unshakable order of God but knows itself placed in a world determined by nothingness.

186. Cf. Oorschot, *Gott als Grenze*.
187. Cf. Kaiser, "Die Botschaft des Buches Kohelet."

Judaism in both centuries at the turn of the millennium was characterized by an inner differentiation and pluralizing that is most evident in the division into groups. A massive power conflict is associated with this process. Individual groups struggled for the high ground of interpreting Jewish existence. This struggle was intensified by the Roman presence in Palestine. The appearance of John the Baptist and of Jesus of Nazareth must be understood as an aspect of this development.

Table 2. Chronology of Jewish Literature

400–300 BCE	formation of the Hebrew canon, with major sections closed
3rd cent. BCE	Ethiopic Enoch (1 Enoch: The Book of the Watchers)
3rd cent. BCE	Ethiopic Enoch (1 Enoch: The Astronomical Book)
3rd cent. BCE	Temple Scroll (11QT)
ca. 250 BCE	beginning of the translation of the Septuagint
ca. 200 BCE	Ecclesiastes/Qohelet
200–150 BCE	Book of Jubilees
ca. 190 BCE	Testament of the Twelve Patriarchs
ca. 180 BCE	Sirach/Ecclesiasticus
ca. 170 BCE	War Scroll (1QM); Proverbs
165/164 BCE	final redaction of the book of Daniel
ca. 100 BCE	Rule of the Community (1QS); Cairo Genizah copy of the Damascus Document (CD); 1 Maccabees
ca. 50 BCE	Psalms of Solomon
ca. 0–30 CE	Assumption of Moses
ca. 15–45 CE	writings of Philo
ca. 50–70 CE	2 Enoch (Slavonic Apocalypse)
ca. 100 CE	4 Ezra
ca. 120 CE	2 Baruch (Syriac Apocalypse)

3.4 The Political and Economic Situation in the Roman Empire in the First and Second Centuries CE

A decisive presupposition for the origin of early Christianity is the reality of the Roman Empire as a global political, economic, and cultural matrix. In this relatively unified realm, early Christianity found the best conditions for its expansion, with the politically and economically stable environment in the first and second centuries CE.

3.6. The Roman Empire in New Testament times

Imperial border at the death of Augustus (14 CE)

Provincial borders

Senatorial provinces

Emperial provinces and areas under procurators

Vassal states

Acquisitions until the death of Trajan (117 CE)

The Roman Republic,[188] beginning with the end of the second century BCE, entered into a lengthy crisis that escalated in 52 BCE. The civil war resulted in the emergence of Julius Gaius Caesar as victor in 49 BCE, and in 48 BCE his stubborn rival Pompey died. In the moment when Caesar extended his hand to be the sole ruler, he was murdered (March 15, 44 BCE).[189] However, the murderers of Caesar could last only a brief period. Then Octavian and Antony, who had been allies in the fight against the murderers of Caesar, disbanded their rule (42 BCE). The victors divided the empire: Antony took over the rule in the East, lived in Alexandria, and determined from there the fate of Syria and Palestine. Octavian ruled in Rome over Italy and the west of the empire. However, this arrangement could not last long: a disagreement soon occurred between the two rulers. After the victory in the sea battle at Actium (31 BCE), Octavian became the sole ruler over the Roman Empire.

The position of Octavian was secured[190] when his adoptive father Caesar was elevated among the gods on the decision of the senate. Octavian then called himself son of the divine Caesar. Although the ancient Roman constitution was again in force, the actual ruling power was Octavian's alone. When he laid down his special authority and returned it to the senate in an official public event in 27 CE so that the old order would be restored, the senate requested that he keep this position so he could maintain the peace and also care for the welfare of the state. Then Octavian took the full authority from the senate that he had just given up. Thus a new form of government emerged. The senate remained the highest authority, but Octavian, who guided its destiny as princeps, was the first citizen of the state. At the same time the name "Augustus" (exalted one) was conferred, giving his rule a sacral aura. However, he was wary of breaking with Roman tradition, which clearly distinguished between gods and humankind, while he nevertheless allowed himself to be called August, unmistakably bringing incomparable majesty to his power. At the same time, Augustus succeeded in having his power regarded as a steadfast service to Rome. He introduced a comprehensive program of sacralizing that was evident in the buildings (in Rome and all over the empire), on coins, and finally, in literary works (Ovid, Vergil, Horace).[191] With Augustus, a new literary activity and visualization began that had not been known before. After the highest priestly office of the pontifex maximus was conferred on Augustus,[192]

188. Cf. Bleicken, *Geschichte der romischen Republik*.
189. On Caesar, cf. Will, *Caesar*.
190. On Augustus, cf. also Kienast, *Augustus*; Bringmann, *Augustus*.
191. This process is described by Hoff, Stroh, and M. Zimmermann, *Divus Augustus*, 129ff.
192. Cf. Plutarch, *Numa* 9.4: "The chief of the Pontifices, the Pontifex Maximus, had the duty of expounding and interpreting the divine will, or rather of directing sacred rites, not only

the list of honorific names again increased, as the senate conferred the title *pater patriae* (father of the fatherland) in 2 CE. The clever and restrained policy with which Augustus ruled the empire had almost total support.[193] After the long-lasting horrors of war, peace was finally present, and Augustus was celebrated throughout the empire as the ruler of peace.[194] Everywhere in the empire, new cities were founded; temples, theaters, aqueducts, and other public facilities were built; and roads were laid out. Economic activity and trade blossomed and expanded over the entire empire all the way to the Atlantic, the Baltic Sea, and Africa. Roman citizenship was extended beyond Italy to worthy inhabitants in the provinces. Every citizen of the empire could travel around freely; only at the provincial borders was a small tax levied. The population of the entire empire experienced a feeling of security that it had not known before, for they were finally free from the threat to body and life. The new order of the empire that was attained during the long peaceful time of the rule of Augustus was so secured that it extended beyond his death.

When Augustus died in 14 CE at the age of seventy-six, his adoptive son, Tiberius (14–37 CE), took over the government. He was an experienced commander and skillful politician when he assumed the rule at the age of fifty-five.[195] The institution of the principate was so established that he could enter his rule without controversy. Indeed, Augustus did not regard him as his successor, but after other possibilities faltered, he finally agreed. Tiberius executed his duties conscientiously; as a clever administrator of the legacy that was left to him, he continued the politics of his predecessor zealously and according to plan. Gaius Caligula (37–41 CE) took over the reign when he was only twenty-four years old. In contrast to his predecessor, he conducted himself as a Hellenistic ruler and surrounded himself with a circle of young Hellenistic princes, among whom was Herod Agrippa, who gained influence and the rule in Palestine. He was the first caesar to have himself worshiped as a god by the Roman aristocracy (Suetonius, *Cal.* 22.3).[196] He openly humiliated the

---

being in charge of public ceremonies, but also watching over private sacrifices and preventing any departure from established custom, as well as teaching whatever was requisite for the worship or propitiation of the gods" (LCL).

193. Cf. the Res gestae (= record of deeds) of Augustus (as the greatest known inscription in antiquity, a classic example of ancient self-presentation). On the development of Octavian Augustus, cf. Clauss, *Kaiser und Gott*, 54–75; Christ, *Geschichte der römischen Kaiserzeit*, 158–68.

194. Cf. the inscription from Priene from the year 9 CE (NW II/1:7–9); Seutonius, *Augustus* 22.

195. On Tiberius, cf. Yavetz, *Tiberius*.

196. It is disputed whether the divine honor demanded by Caligula arose from a greater conviction about himself (cf. Philo, *Legat.* 162: "But Gaius built himself up, for he said not only that he believed that he was god") or was only engaged in conscious political calculation. Winterling, *Caligula*, argues for the latter.

senatorial class of leaders and carried through his absolutist tendencies. His dissolute life and excessive striving for divine-like transcendence of his ruling position hindered Caligula from fulfilling the tasks of his office. He also did not stop short of demanding that the Jews place his image in the temple in Jerusalem (see above, 3.3). In the few years of his rule, he made so many enemies that a palace revolt defeated his government (41 CE).

The praetorian guard called Claudius to be the new caesar (41–54 CE). In contrast to Caligula, he was modest with respect to divine reverence for his person (cf. Suetonius, *Claud.* 12). He wanted to revive the Roman religion anew and was an admirer of Greece.[197] His position regarding Judaism appeared to have fluctuated. On the one hand, he protected the rights of the Jews in Alexandria at the beginning of his reign;[198] on the other hand, he expelled the Jews from Rome in 49 CE (cf. Acts 18:2). The Edict of Claudius (see below, 6.5) was of great significance for early Christianity, for the expulsion of Jewish Christians from Rome (primarily to Asia Minor) that accompanied it changed the composition of the Roman church and had an influence on the Pauline mission. Claudius was poisoned by his wife in 54 CE, preparing the way for Nero (54–63 CE), her son from her first marriage, to take the throne.[199] The new ruler was only seventeen years old, and thus the business of the office was led by prefects of the praetorium and the philosopher Seneca, one of the most prosperous and influential men in Rome.[200] The years of their regency were fortunate. As Nero himself took over the government, he developed into a capricious despot and self-promoter. He loved to appear as an artist, conducting himself as a friend and promoter of Greek culture[201] and seeking to adorn his ruling position with divine glory. Thus he transgressed the recognized moral and political boundaries and had men put out of the way who could be an obstacle to him. In 68 CE, when there was a conspiracy against him, he took his life. Nero was significant for early Christianity because of the fire of Rome (64 CE) and the resulting first great persecution of Christians (see below, 12.2). Nero's sudden end was celebrated by many people; others, however, were bewildered and assumed that he had not died and that he lived still in a hidden place. Consequently, the expectation arose that he would return from the East as the head of the Parthian army. Conceptions of a "Nero redivivus" (cf. Sib.

---

197. On a comprehensive study, cf. Cineira, *Die Religionspolitik des Kaisers Claudius.*
198. Cf. Josephus, *Ant.* 19.280–85.
199. On Nero, cf. Malitz, *Nero*; Waldherr, *Nero*; Merten, *Nero.*
200. Cf. Fuhrmann, *Seneca und Kaiser Nero.*
201. As an actual classical witness, cf. the declaration of freedom to the Greeks in 67 CE; *SIG* 3:814 = NW I/2:249–50.

Or. 4–5; Tacitus, *Hist.* 2.8–9) spread. The description in Rev. 13:1–18 and 17:11–17 of the beast from the abyss may be an allusion to the terrifying caesar of the last days.

With the death of Nero, the ruling power of the Julian-Claudian house came to an end, and the period of the Flavians (see below, 9.3) began. In 69 CE Vespasian succeeded in bringing the ruling power to himself and, supported by his army, in creating peace and order. Vespasian continued the renewal of the principate created by Augustus and secured the succession of his sons. When he died in 79 CE, his son Titus, who had conquered Jerusalem, became caesar. In 81 CE Titus's brother, Domitian (81–96 CE), followed him. He appears to have become increasingly tyrannical during the course of his rule (see below, 12.3), demonstrating publicly the power and sacredness of his person. With Nerva (96–98 CE) the series of caesars began who considered themselves obligated to the teachings of the philosophers and attempted to make them a reality for the well-being of the community. The Stoic ideal of the ruler prevailed, according to which the best ruler should rule and conduct his office as servant of the people. Nerva adopted the general Trajan, who took over the rule as successor in 98 CE and remained in that position until 117 CE.[202] Through the process of adoption, it was assured that, out of the circle of candidates under consideration, the most capable one could be chosen and declared the ruler. Hadrian (117–38 CE), who understood himself as a cosmopolitan ruler, followed Trajan.[203] He traveled throughout the empire, gladly spent time in Greece, had splendid buildings erected, and was committed to the welfare of the provinces. The Bar Kokhba Rebellion (132–35 CE), which resulted in the final downfall of Judaism (see above, 3.3), occurred during the period of his rule.

3.4.1 Basic Features of the Social and Economic History of the Early Imperial Era

It is only possible in a limited way to ascertain precisely (in the modern sense) the social and economic structure of the early imperial period because of the enormous size of the Roman Empire, the scanty available sources, and the very different relationships in the city and country as well as between the individual provinces. Nevertheless, one can recognize basic structures.[204]

202. On Trajan, cf. K. Strobel, *Kaiser Traian.*
203. Cf. Opper, *Hadrian.*
204. Cf. the methodological considerations in Drexhage, Konen, and Ruffing, *Die Wirtschaft des Römischen Reiches*, 19–21.

THE STRUCTURE OF SOCIETY

The society of the Roman Empire was distinguished by a relatively rigid vertical structure.[205] At the top stood the imperial ruling class, whose leadership function encompassed the entire empire. All of the crucial responsibilities in political leadership in war, administration, and law lay in their hands; only rarely did they involve themselves in the realm of the economy. The ruling class included not only the caesar and his family but also those senators who had served in the consulate at least once. Leading military people, administrative officers, jurists, and friends who belonged to the aristocracy and regularly advised the caesar are also to be considered in the ruling class. Under individual rulers (e.g., Claudius, Nero, Domitian), slaves or freedmen who had gained the special trust of the caesar had central administrative offices.[206]

In contrast to the imperial ruling class, the imperial upper class did not have active leadership functions over the whole empire. They were privileged by origin, property, and wealth.[207] This class included vassal kings/princes, especially members of the senatorial equestrian order.[208] Beginning with Augustus, members of the senate had to be from old families (of Rome) and possess considerable wealth.[209] After the senators (*ordo senatorius*), equestrians (*ordo equester*) formed the second level; it involved—sponsored by the caesar—wealthy and successful people from all the provinces, especially those who played a leading role in the provincial administration of the empire, the judiciary, and the military. The leading priestly families of Rome also belonged to the imperial upper class. The regional and local upper class (*ordo decurionum*), as a third level, exercised local leadership functions, for example, in the city councils or in the assemblies of the individual provinces.[210] This class was privileged primarily by local anchoring, property, and wealth. Among them were the leading administrative officials of large and moderately large cities. Military people, rich citizens, large landowners,

---

205. Cf. Christ, *Geschichte der römischen Kaiserzeit*, 350–433; E. Stegemann and W. Stegemann, *Urchristliche Sozialgeschichte*, 58–94.

206. According to Alföldy, *Römische Sozialgeschichte*, 198, ca. 160 persons belonged to the imperial ruling class.

207. On wealth and its display, cf. Weeber, *Luxus im alten Rom*.

208. Cf. Alföldy, *Römische Sozialgeschichte*, 138ff., who equates the political elite with the socioeconomic elite in essential matters during the imperial period (cf. the graphic on p. 196); he counts ca. 300,000 men in the empire-wide upper class (p. 198).

209. On the wealth of the senators and equestrians, cf. Drexhage, Konen, and Ruffing, *Die Wirtschaft des Römischen Reiches*, 163–70; the richest man in the empire at the time of Nero was the philosopher Seneca.

210. On the concept of *ordo*, cf. A. Weiss, *Soziale Elite und Christentum*, 23–28.

and merchants, as well as individual scientists and intellectuals, were numbered among them.[211]

As a relevant criterion for membership in the middle level of the empire,[212] one must feed himself and his family through independent work and thereby at the same time obtain some surplus. Diligence, success, wealth, and influence rather than background qualified one for the middle class. The greatest part of free citizens of Rome, as long as they were not impoverished, belonged to it along with independent free citizens of the cities of the empire who had at their disposal some wealth. Thus successful landowners, merchants, and bankers as well as independent qualified handworkers and service providers also belonged to it. This also included officials in the middle-sized and larger cities of the empire. Members of the military, such as centurions and lower officers, may also be considered a part of the middle class. It likewise included members of special formations and privileged veterans. Finally, those freedmen who stood in the service of the caesar and had great influence and earned a certain wealth belonged to it. Even individual slaves of the family of the caesar belonged to the middle class. As a whole this class was not homogeneous, but at the same time it offered many people in the upwardly mobile economy of the first and second centuries CE the opportunity to climb within the society. It was possible, therefore, to leap over the limitations of one's background through (newly acquired) wealth and to gain influence and societal prestige.[213]

Like the middle class, the broad lower class was also heterogenous. As a deciding criterion for membership in the lower class, the various kinds of dependence must be considered that prevented them from independently earning a living.[214] Also to be considered are the grave differences between

211. E. Stegemann and W. Stegemann, *Urchristliche Sozialgeschichte*, 78, reckons that between 1 and 5 percent of the total population belonged to the upper class.

212. It is disputed whether in Roman society there was a middle class at all in the modern sense; negative conclusions are given by, e.g., Alföldy, *Römische Sozialgeschichte*, 138–217 (he speaks in the plural of upper and lower classes); E. Stegemann and W. Stegemann, *Urchristliche Sozialgeschichte*, 70ff. (they distinguish between "elite" [the upper-class groups] and "non-elite" [lower classes]). The distribution of the entire Roman society into merely two strata (lower and upper classes) is criticized as heuristically unproductive and with a historically leveling result; cf. Christ, "Grundfragen der römischen Sozialstruktur"; Vittinghoff, "Gesellschaft."

213. Instances of this were parodied, especially in the satires; cf. Juvenal, *Sat.* 1.23ff. ("in his youth he was still a barber, but today he holds wealth with all the aristocrats"); Petronius, *Satyr* 76–77 (the career of the former slave and newly rich Trimalchio). The satirists are (despite their exaggerations) an important source of the reality of the life of the people; cf. especially Horace, ca. 65–8 BCE; Petronius, ca. 25–66 CE; Martial, ca. 40–102 CE; Juvenal, ca. 55–130 CE.

214. E. Stegemann and W. Stegemann, *Urchristliche Sozialgeschichte*, 85, want to distinguish between various (urban and rural) groups of the underclass, in which the "supposed" minimum existence is considered a criterion.

urban and rural as well as between individual regions of the giant empire that led to a flight from the countryside[215] and thus to a creeping impoverishment of the cities.[216]

In the cities[217] dependent workers and those involved in service especially were included, for example, small handworkers such as shoemakers, potters, smiths, textile workers, harbor workers, bakers, masons, metal workers, and carriage makers. In addition, small merchants, teachers, musicians, hairdressers, sailors, recipients of state benefits, those who were dependent on the gifts of their patrons, the aged, widows as well as day laborers, beggars, and the chronically ill must be counted among the lower class. Great numbers of the population of Rome were dependent on the public distribution of grain.[218] Likewise, in addition to the *plebs urbana* there was also the *plebs rustica*. In the rural areas the small farmers (free or dependent), the tenant farmers, and especially the day laborers were dominant. In the cities there were small handworkers, service providers, shepherds, beggars, and the sick.

The most predominant group in the lower class were the slaves, who constituted an essential component of all ancient societies and economic forms.[219] Ancient slavery was a very complex phenomenon that was never questioned in theory or in practice.[220] From the second century BCE, the number of slaves greatly increased. Around the end of the first century BCE, slaves made up about 15–20 percent of the total population of the Roman Empire (ca. 50 million),[221] in absolute numbers, about ten million people.[222] Causes of slavery were primarily imprisonment from war, birth in slavery, kidnapping, human trafficking, children being abandoned, and being sold because of indebtedness.

215. On this influx (especially out of the Greek-speaking East to Rome), cf. Kolb, *Rom*, 457–63. Juvenal, *Sat.* 3.57–125, begins his mean-spirited parody of the situation in Rome with the comment "Roman citizens, I cannot bear a Rome overcome by Greeks."

216. Dio Chrysostom, *Or.* 7.105–6, says about the poor: "For the poor of this type suitable work may perhaps be hard to find in the cities, and will need to be supplemented by outside resources when they have to pay house-rent and buy everything they get, not merely clothes, household belongings, and food, but even the wood to supply the daily need for fire, and even any odd sticks, leaves, or other most trifling thing they need."

217. On city life, cf. Weeber, *Alltag im Alten Rom*.

218. Cf. Kolb, *Rom*, 514–39. For Augustus, Res gestae (5.15.18) speaks repeatedly of the matter that he donated to the Romans grain and money valued at 250,000 and 100,000 denarii, respectively.

219. On the history of slavery in Greece and Rome, cf. Herrmann-Otto, *Sklaverei und Freilassung*, 51–110, 111–202.

220. On the ancient discussion of the theory, cf. Herrmann-Otto, *Sklaverei und Freilassung*, 16–34.

221. Cf. Drexhage, Konen, and Ruffing, *Die Wirtschaft des Römischen Reiches*, 24.

222. So L. Schumacher, *Sklaverei in der Antike*, 42; other numbers in Herrmann-Otto, *Sklaverei und Freilassung*, 124.

Slaves were engaged primarily in farming; hard physical labor with the military and in mills, baths, and mines also had to be done by slaves.[223] However, slaves could, depending on their capability and the needs of their masters, be engaged as teachers, cooks, wet-nurses, midwives, physicians, writers, and administrators, or for normal service in the household. Finally, slaves were active in all areas of handwork and trade.[224]

Masters possessed unlimited power over their slaves, who had neither property nor the right to marry. They stood at the disposal of their owner, either for personal use or to be made available for a business partner. They could be bequeathed, pledged, or given away. On the other hand, they had to be fed and given a place to live, even when there was no need for their work.

There were also privileged slaves, especially the slaves of the upper classes in the big cities, who had good living conditions. If they belonged to caesar's household (*familia caesaris*), that is, to caesar's administration, they could even be influential and prosperous.[225] Frequently slaves did not remain in bondage for a lifetime, especially in the exalted Roman households but also when they had labored as handworkers or service providers. Inasmuch as the emancipation of slaves was legally regulated, the freedmen belonged to Roman society almost without limitations.[226]

THE ANCIENT ECONOMY

The basis of the ancient economy was agriculture. Other central areas included handwork, trade, and various services.

As in all preindustrial societies, the Roman Empire was an agrarian society.[227] Approximately 90 percent of the population lived in the country.[228] Primarily grain was cultivated, which had a key role in providing the basic food supply for the population, especially the centers for urban and military consumption. North Africa in particular (with Egypt as the center) was the granary for the empire. Bad harvest and problems of transport affected the urban population especially and led frequently to empire-wide famine.[229] When there was a

---

223. Cf. the comprehensive analysis of L. Schumacher, *Sklaverei*, 91–238.
224. A list of slave occupations is given in Herrmann-Otto, *Sklaverei und Freilassung*, 78f.; cf. also the inscriptions and text collections in Eck and Heinrichs, *Sklaven und Freigelassene*.
225. Cf. Herrmann-Otto, *Sklaverei und Freilassung*, 177–90.
226. Cf. here Herrmann-Otto, *Sklaverei und Freilassung*, 190–202.
227. Cf. Drexhage, Konen, and Ruffing, *Die Wirtschaft des Römischen Reiches*, 59–100.
228. On life in the country, cf. Weeber, *Alltag im Alten Rom*.
229. Tacitus, *Ann.* 12.43, reports about the time of Claudius (51 CE) that only a fifteen-day food supply was available in Rome: "We work the land in Africa and Egypt, and Rome depends on the changing fortunes of sea travel." According to Suetonius, *Dom.* 7, Domitian prohibited the planting of new vineyards so that the production of grain could be improved.

surplus in the harvest of grain, it was gathered into barns (cf. Luke 12:16–21), but in many instances the concern was bare survival. Bakeries ground the grain and delivered baked bread to the Roman cities. The cultivation of wine and olives was a second focus of agriculture. Other points of emphasis were the breeding of animals, pasture farming, cultivation of fruit, and fishing. Bees produced honey; birds furnished meat and eggs; sheep, goats, and cattle provided milk, wool, meat, and hide. The farmers themselves usually brought the surplus products of small farms to the market. A few of them may have possessed donkeys, mules, and carts. At the markets, which were held in the city squares or outside the city gates, grain, fruit, wine, oil, meat, and wool were for sale.

The distribution of land ownership was varied; a major part of the land was owned by the Roman elite, inherited or acquired from insolvent neighbors or as spoils of war. Evidently large-scale landholding of more than one thousand hectares expanded in the first century CE at the expense of the free small farmers.[230] Large estates were, as a rule, run by managers and worked by slaves. Large areas could be divided into small portions and assigned to tenants (cf. Matt. 21:33–42). When interest was high and bad harvests occurred, these tenants quickly fell into great dependence on their masters (to the point of slavery). The free middle and small farmers—with few hectares of land guaranteed and with field crops, animal breeding, and vegetable gardens—formed the self-sufficiency of larger parts of the rural area and with their surplus contributed also to the supply of the smaller cities. From the second century BCE onward, the severity of life in the country and the constant danger of social and legal downfall through famine and debt led to a continuing flight from the land.[231]

Handwork, trade, and service occupations were booming in the early imperial period.[232] Small businesses dominated in this economic sector. These were conducted by free citizens, freedmen, and even slaves in the service of their masters. In cities, the businesses were most often integrated in rental houses; in the large cities there were entire sections named for particular trades. In the businesses, potters produced bowls and vases for daily use; fullers and weavers produced clothing; leather workers sewed shoes and tarpaulins; smiths made

230. Pliny the Elder, *Natural History* 18.35, complained about the landed estates in Italy and commented that six men owned half of Africa before Nero killed them; cf. also Seneca, *Ep.* 89.20, who castigated the greed of Roman landowners.

231. Sallust, *Catalina* 37.7, gives an interpretation of this phenomenon: "Besides this, the young men who had maintained a wretched existence by manual labor in the country, tempted by private and public doles, had come to prefer idleness in the city to their disagreeable toil."

232. On handwork, cf. Drexhage, Konen, and Ruffing, *Die Wirtschaft des Römischen Reiches*, 101–17.

agricultural instruments and tools for handworkers; carpenters made furniture and carriages; and sculptors made statues and decorative reliefs. Other craftsmen included basketmakers, cobblers, bakers, roofers, builders, metal workers, and copper- and goldsmiths. Normally they used raw material that could be found nearby and sold their finished products in their own stores or in the markets. Along with the small businesses, there was also mass production, especially of bricks, terra cotta lamps, dishes, and glassware. These products were frequently sold regionally or even internationally.

Intensive trade dominated in and between all regions of the Roman Empire.[233] Local trade in the nearby areas and those farther away between villages and cities involved primarily agricultural and craft products (grain, oil, meat, livestock, items for daily use), which were offered in the market. In trade between regions—between big cities and the particular provinces—food (olive oil, wine, fish sauce) and craft products (ceramic oil lamps, building materials, textiles) were transported in amphorae. On land, the transport could be by people as porters, by donkeys, mules, and camels, or by carriages led by draft animals. River and sea transport had great significance for trade with distant places. Rivers such as the Nile, the Rhine, and the Danube were important. Also important was sea travel in the Mediterranean and nearby areas (e.g., the Black Sea). In commerce with distant places (e.g., India, China, Arabia), oil and wine were sent in amphorae; valuable clothing, metals, weapons, and luxury items were sold. The Romans especially desired amber from Germany. Of course, sea trade brought with it many dangers, including shipwrecks and piracy, but people with the means to invest and sufficient daring could acquire great wealth.[234]

Along with agriculture as the primary area and handwork as the secondary area of economic activity, service occupations were the tertiary area. Here occupations involving banking and gold had a significant place. Along with it came the changing of money, testing of coins, and involvement in credit. Banking activities were often a part of societal relationships. Within the higher class one borrowed money from friends when there was a need or loaned to friends when they were in need. Members of the higher classes were often asked for loans from their subordinates and clients as a constituent part of the continuing fidelity to them. The educational sector belonged to the most important service activity, inasmuch as it was not provided primarily by the state. Teachers, child-care workers, wet-nurses, and scribes worked in this

233. On trade and service providers, cf. Drexhage, Konen, and Ruffing, *Die Wirtschaft des Römischen Reiches*, 119–47, 149–60.
234. Cf. Trimalchio in Petronius, *Satyricon* 76; James 4:13.

capacity. Further service providers were physicians and jurists. Among the greater areas of service were also those of food service and entertainment, including prostitution.

> In the Roman Empire of the first century CE, the distinction between ruler and ruled was fundamental. However, this principle was mitigated by the economic and cultural dynamic that enabled members of all classes to expand their worlds.

EARLY CHRISTIANITY IN ITS CONTEXTS

The overview of history, philosophy, religion/theology, and economics of the Hellenistic age is fundamental for the following portrayal of the history of early Christianity in a threefold way.

1. Early Christianity participated totally in the social reality of the Roman Empire of the first and second centuries CE and was embedded in a very complex and attractive religious-philosophical environment. Religious conceptions and activities determined all areas of life for ancient people. Thus early Christianity developed in a multireligious society and in no way entered into an areligious realm. As a result, the nonreligious society that is suggested by the Jew/Christian/pagan distinction never existed. To the contrary, no society was as religious as that of Hellenism, including also the Roman Empire in the first century CE. Thus it is inappropriate to speak of the non-Jew and non-Christian as a pagan.[235] Rather, such people were involved in Greco-Roman religiosity and, upon becoming Christians, affiliated with the early congregations.[236]

2. An additional matter follows from the first: The early communities with their members from a variety of cultural contexts (Palestinian, Hellenistic Judaism, Greco-Roman religiosity, local cults, and societies) were from the beginning enmeshed, both through their members and through the actual environment, in the political and cultural-religious debates of the time. The success of the early Christian mission can be explained only with the assumption that a strong capacity existed for incorporating the Jewish and Greco-Roman

235. The German word *Heide* is probably derived from the Gothic word *hethnos*; that is, "those belonging to a foreign group": cf. Colpe, "Das deutsche Wort 'Judenchristen,'" 40f. Translator's note: The English word *heathen* probably has the same roots.

236. On the question of whether and how extensive terms such as "Jew," "Judean," "Jewish," and "Christian" can be assumed or meaningfully used for the first century CE, cf. Holmberg, "Understanding the First Hundred Years." I assume that the linguistic textual evidence and the traditions of academic nomenclature may be and must be used (see below, 8.7; 10.5; 13.1).

streams of tradition.[237] This capacity for incorporating took place, not from repudiation, but through a conscious participation in the debates, which took place in the world of the churches. Anyone who wants to understand the history of early Christianity must identify these communication fields; one must also determine which answers to these questions were given and why the answers in theory and practice were apparently considered plausible by many people. A new cultural system such as early Christianity could come into existence only because it was capable of networking with existing cultural streams and creating new organizations, conceptions, and traditions and could adopt the prior understandings of the respective cultures. Intentional communication and desired conviction are present at the beginning!

3. Finally, early Christianity not only had its own history but was also enmeshed in the history of others. As a movement within Judaism, the Christ-believers (especially in Jerusalem) fell increasingly into conflict with the other Jewish groups, especially with the Sadducees but also with the Pharisees. As a movement coming out of Judaism, the Christians participated in the stressful history of Jews in the Roman Empire (see below, 6.5, the Edict of Claudius). At the same time they were also drawn into a massive conflict with the Roman government, especially where the caesar cult was involved. Thus the history of early Christianity always has a religious-political dimension.

237. Cf. Schnelle, "Historische Anschlussfähigkeit."

Table 3. Chronology of World History and Palestine

356–323 BCE Alexander the Great

World History	Palestine
ca. 301–200 Ptolemaic power (reign/ dominion)	ca. 301–200 Ptolemaic power (reign/ dominion)
ca. 200–63 Seleucid power (reign/dominion)	ca. 200–63 Seleucid power (reign/dominion)
197 Roman victory over Philip V of Macedonia	
175–164 Antiochus IV Epiphanes	ca. 175–172 Jason
	ca. 172–163 Menelaus
	167 beginning of the rise of the Maccabees
	166–161 Judas Maccabeus
	161–142 Jonathan
	ca. 150 Teacher of Righteousness
	142–135/134 Simon
	100 BCE–68 CE Qumran community
	The Hasmoneans
	135/134–104 John Hyrcanus I
	104–103 Aristobulus I
	103–76 Alexander Jannaeus
	76–67 Salome Alexandra
64 Pompey conquers the Seleucids	67–63 Aristobulus II
	63 conquest of Jerusalem by the Romans
	63–40 Hyrcanus II
40 Parthian invasion	40–4 Herod the Great
31 BCE—14 CE Augustus	ca. 4 BCE birth of Jesus
	4 BCE—33/34 CE Philip Tetrarch
	4 BCE—39 CE Herod Antipas
	4 BCE—6 CE Herod Archelaus
	6–41 Judea under Roman administration
	6/7 census
14–37 Tiberius	26–36 Pontius Pilate
	27/28 appearance of John the Baptist and Jesus of Nazareth
	30 death of Jesus
37–41 Caligula	
41–54 Claudius	41–44 Agrippa I
54–68 Nero	50–92/93 Agrippa II
69–79 Vespasian	66–73 (74) Jewish War
	70 fall of Jerusalem
	73/74 fall of Masada
	74–132 period of Jamnia
79–81 Titus	
81–96 Domitian	
98–117 Trajan	
117–138 Hadrian	132–135 Bar Kokhba Rebellion

4

The New Movement of Christ-Believers

Jesus of Nazareth was probably crucified as an insurrectionist on Friday, the fourteenth of Nisan (April 7) of the year 30 in Jerusalem by the Romans (see above, 2.2). What developed later into Christianity as an independent religion began as an inner-Jewish renewal movement. The disciples of the Jewish healer and preacher Jesus of Nazareth were not, like the followers of other messianic prophets after the crucifixion of their revolutionary leader, persecuted or killed. After a brief phase of scattering and disorientation, they formed—primarily in Jerusalem—the community of the Christ-believers, that is, those who believed in Jesus of Nazareth as the Messiah of Israel. Thus they were primarily one small and largely invisible group among others. They stood on the foundation of Jewish belief but developed at the same time—like other Jewish groups—their own world of narrative, signs, and rituals, and were relatively soon drawn into conflict with the dominant Jewish groups.

Four different sources give direct or indirect information about the Easter events and the resulting formation of the first church in Jerusalem: the Synoptic Gospels (Mark, Matthew, Luke), the Acts of the Apostles, the authentic Pauline letters (1 Thessalonians, 1 and 2 Corinthians, Galatians, Romans, Philippians, Philemon), and the Gospel of John.

4.1 The Easter Events

The events immediately after the crucifixion and death of Jesus lie in obscurity. Probably after the arrest of Jesus, many followers of Jesus took flight in order to avoid possible arrest by the Romans (cf. Mark 14:50, "And they left him and all fled"; cf. also Mark 14:27–28). They left Jerusalem and, after Jesus's crucifixion at the latest, returned to Galilee, as the stories in Mark 14:28 and 16:7 of the appearance of Jesus assume.[1]

The Burial of Jesus

Both the Synoptic Gospels (cf. Mark 15:42–47; Matt. 27:57–61; Luke 23:50–56) and the Gospel of John (cf. John 19:38–42) agree that Joseph of Arimathea requested the body of Jesus from Pilate and buried him.[2] The tradition according to which Joseph of Arimathea laid Jesus in an empty stone grave (cf. Mark 15:46) could derive from a later interpretation, for in that case Jesus, who had died as a criminal, received an honorable burial. Moreover, how did Joseph of Arimathea so quickly have at his disposal a grave that was laboriously hewn out of the rock?[3] This could be an ancient Jerusalem local tradition, which told of a prosperous sympathizer of Jesus who made his own burial place available for the burial of Jesus. Was Jesus buried in a private grave or in an anonymous mass grave? Victims of crucifixion were either not buried at all,[4] placed in an anonymous mass grave, or buried by relatives.[5] Through the discovery of a tomb in northeast Jerusalem, the burial of a crucified man in a private tomb is attested.[6] Probably the approaching Sabbath caused Pilate to release the body for burial in order not to provoke more unrest. The secret sympathizer Joseph of Arimathea took the body of Jesus and buried it. The fact that Joseph of Arimathea would hardly have asked for the body of Jesus in order to put him in a public mass grave—which the Romans would have done—suggests that Jesus had a private burial. Probably he placed Jesus in an individual tomb, about which no one can say with certainty. The place of the tomb was probably known to the Jerusalem church, for Mark 15:47 emphasizes that the women who followed Jesus observed the burial ("But

1. The Lukan portrayal, according to which the disciples hid in a house in Jerusalem because of their fear of the Jews (cf. Luke 24:36–49), is probably secondary; cf. L. Schenke, *Die Urgemeinde*, 13–14.

2. Contra Lüdemann, *Resurrection of Jesus*, 40–41, who sees the tradition of Joseph of Arimathea in Mark as already a Christian legend and regards John 19:31–37 as historical (the Jews ask for the body of Jesus). According to John 19:31, the Jews indeed ask that the bones of Jesus be broken and that he be taken down from the cross, but the removal action, according to John 19:38, was carried out by Joseph of Arimathea.

3. The early tradition was concerned with this question. Matthew 27:60 gives an answer: Joseph of Arimathea buried Jesus in his own tomb.

4. Cf. Tacitus, *Ann.* 6.29.

5. Cf. Philo, *Flaccus* 83.

6. Cf. H.-W. Kuhn, "Der Gekreuzigte von Givcat hat-Mivtar."

Mary Magdalene and Mary, the mother of Joses, saw where he was laid").[7] Moreover, the inhabitants of Jerusalem knew about the usual burial places. Because Jesus's appearance, his trial, and crucifixion had drawn much attention in Jerusalem, the burial would scarcely have been fully anonymous.

Experiences of the Resurrected One

The experiences of the men and women disciples—that the crucified Jesus of Nazareth did not remain in death but rather was raised from the dead by God—determined the next events. The central theological insight stated: Jesus of Nazareth has given his life "for us" in order to receive it anew from God. In the perspective of the resurrection, a new meaning was given to the cross, which was no longer the place of separation from God (Deut. 21:22–23) but a place of the love of God. As the oldest core of the resurrection message,[8] statements such as Rom. 10:9 must be considered: "God has raised Jesus from the dead" (cf. 1 Cor. 15:15; 2 Cor. 4:14; Gal. 1:1; Rom. 4:24; 8:11a). Characteristic is the strongly theological structure: God is the one who acts, and Jesus is the object. In numerous twofold and larger formulas, the resurrection/ raising of Jesus is mentioned, according to which Jesus, meaning Christ, is the respective subject: "Jesus died and arose" (1 Thess. 4:14; cf. 2 Cor. 5:15; Rom. 4:25). The resurrection is the basis for an epithet for God: The God of the resurrection is the one who "gives life to the dead and calls into existence the things that do not exist" (Rom. 4:17b NRSV; cf. 8:11). God identifies himself so much with the crucified Jesus of Nazareth that his power as revealed in the resurrection is still at work. "For this reason has Christ died and returned to life so that he may become Lord over the dead and the living" (Rom. 14:9).

Paul leaves no doubt about the significance of the resurrection as the foundation of the new faith. "If Christ has not been raised, then our proclamation is vain, and your faith is also vain" (1 Cor. 15:14); and also "If Christ has not been raised, so is your faith void, and you are still in your sins, . . . and we are the most miserable of all people" (1 Cor. 15:17, 19b).

The reality of the resurrection for the Christ-believers was based on the appearances of the Crucified One as the Resurrected One. This event was apparently the initial force that ignited the basic knowledge of the first Christ-believers. The Jesus who died shamefully on the cross is not a criminal, but

7. Contra Lüdemann, *Resurrection of Jesus*, 44, who maintains that the earliest church did not know where Jesus was buried. He argues that no tradition of the burial of Jesus would have developed.

8. On the subject of the resurrection, cf. Viering, *Die Bedeutung der Auferstehungsbotschaft*; Marxsen, *Resurrection of Jesus*; Wilckens, *Auferstehung*; Hoffmann, "Die historisch-kritische Osterdiskussion," 15–67; Schnelle, *Apostle Paul*, 410–29.

rather he has been raised from the dead and belongs eternally on the side of God. From the extraordinary quality of Jesus before Easter emerged the unsurpassing quality of Jesus after Easter. The point of departure for the traditions of the appearance[9] is the proto-epiphany of Jesus to Peter (cf. 1 Cor. 15:5a NRSV, "and that he appeared to Cephas"; Luke 24:34, "The Lord is truly risen and has appeared to Simon")[10] since it is the basis for the elevated place of Peter in early Christianity.[11] The Gospel of John begins with an initial appearance to Mary Magdalene (John 20:11–18); only then did Jesus appear to the disciples.

Both Luke 24:34 and John 20:11–18 point to Jerusalem as the place of the appearances (John 21:1–14, however, takes place in Galilee). In Mark, the appearances of Jesus are proclaimed in Galilee (Mark 14:28; 16:7: "Go forth and say to his disciples and Peter that he goes before you to Galilee, and there you will see him, just as he told you"), without narrating the event. In Matthew, the announcements of the appearances in Galilee are adopted (Matt. 26:32; 28:7); then Jesus appears first to Mary Magdalene and to the other Mary in Jerusalem (cf. Matt. 28:9–10), then to the disciples in Galilee (Matt. 28:16–20). Luke concentrates the appearances exclusively around Jerusalem, first to the Emmaus disciples (Luke 24:13–35), then to all the disciples (Luke 24:36–49). The reports suggest that Jesus probably appeared first to Peter and Mary Magdalene[12] or several women. The reports of the appearances obviously pursue no apologetic interest,[13] for although women under Jewish law were not qualified as witnesses, they played an important role in almost all of the reports of the appearances. First Corinthians 15:3–8 reports about numerous individual and group appearances. Along with Peter (v. 5a), the Resurrected One appeared to the Twelve (v. 5b), to more than five hundred brothers (v. 6), to James (v. 7a), to all the apostles (v. 7b), and finally to Paul (v. 8). The appearance to Paul happened near Damascus; nothing is said about the places of the other appearances. It is conceivable that those to the "Twelve" and the "five hundred brothers" happened in Galilee; for the other appearances to James and "to all the brothers," Jerusalem is a possibility. First Corinthians 15:3–5 is the oldest literary tradition that includes all the elements of the Easter faith: Jesus's death, his burial, his resurrection, and his appearance as the Resurrected One ("that Christ died for our sins in accordance with

9. For the analysis of the texts, cf. Wilckens, *Auferstehung*, 15–61.
10. Mark 16:7 indicates the differentiation between Peter and "the disciples," indicating that Jesus first appeared to Peter.
11. Cf. Campenhausen, *Der Ablauf der Osterereignisse*, 15.
12. Cf. Petersen, *Maria aus Magdala*.
13. Cf. Campenhausen, *Der Ablauf der Osterereignisse*, 41.

the scriptures, and that he was buried, and that he was raised on the third day in accordance with the scriptures, and that he appeared to Cephas, then to the twelve" [NRSV]). The apostle Paul was called about 32 or 33 CE. He received instruction in the Christian faith in Antioch, and thus the tradition cited by him certainly originated before 40 CE. Along with the individuals and groups, further appearances probably took place that are only indirectly recorded. Romans 16:7 is possible: "Greet Andronicus and Junia, my relatives and fellow prisoners, who are famous among the apostles and were in Christ before I was." The prominent place of this married couple could be based on appearances to them.[14] In any case, it is evident that with Paul, around 32/33 CE, the special epoch of appearances of the Crucified and Resurrected One came to an end. If one dates the crucifixion in the year 30 CE, then the appearances lasted about two to three years.

The Empty Tomb

Reports about the empty tomb are inseparable from the reports about the appearances of the resurrected Christ. The women disciples of Jesus go to the tomb in the early morning on the first day of the week and find the stone rolled away and the tomb empty (cf. Mark 16:1–5; John 20:1, 11–13; Matt. 28:1–6; Luke 24:1–6). The women report this event immediately to the disciples (cf. Mark 16:7; John 20:18; Matt. 28:8; Luke 24:9). Like the evangelists, Paul presupposes the empty tomb.[15] He does not mention it explicitly, but the logic of the burial and resurrection of Jesus in 1 Cor. 15:4 (and also the concept of being buried with Christ in Rom. 6:4) presupposes an empty tomb, for the Jewish anthropology assumes a bodily resurrection.[16] In addition, a fundamental argument must be considered: The message of the resurrection could not have been proclaimed so successfully if the body of Jesus had remained in a mass grave or in an unopened private tomb.[17] It would have escaped neither the notice of Jesus's enemies nor his followers where he had been buried.[18] Jesus's crucifixion had created a stir, and when, a short

14. On Andronicus and Junia, see below, 5.2 under "Other Concepts of Apostleship."

15. Contra Bultmann, *Theology*, 1:48: "Accounts of the empty tomb, of which Paul still knows nothing, are legend."

16. See the argument of Martin Hengel in his work "Das Begräbnis Jesu bei Paulus."

17. Cf. Althaus, *Die Wahrheit des christlichen Osterglaubens*, 25: "In Jerusalem, at the place of the execution and of the tomb of Jesus, it was proclaimed not long after his death that he was raised. This fact indicates the existence in the circles of the first church in Jerusalem of reliable witnesses that the tomb was discovered empty."

18. Contra Lüdemann, *Resurrection of Jesus*, 44, who argues without a basis: "Because neither the disciples nor closest family members concerned themselves with the body, it is

time after the event, the disciples came preaching that he was raised from the dead, then the question of the tomb must have had a central significance from the beginning (cf. Matt. 27:62–66). The success of the Easter proclamation in Jerusalem would have been inconceivable without an empty tomb. The discovery of the crucified person in the northeastern part of present-day Jerusalem from the time of Jesus indicates that the body of one who had been executed was turned over to relatives or friends and buried by them. Nevertheless, the empty tomb alone remains ambiguous; it is a conclusion drawn only from the appearances of the Resurrected One. One cannot prove the appearances and the resurrection as a historical fact, but neither can one exclude the possibility. In historical terms, one can only say that followers of Jesus—the itinerant Jewish preacher, Jesus of Nazareth—affirmed that, after his death, he appeared to them alive.

Evaluations of the historical reality of the resurrection event for both those who support it and those who deny it move at the level of the statements involving the theory of knowledge, experiences in life history, and historical consideration. The truth content of the event cannot be historically demonstrated, but also it cannot be negated! It is certain, however, that the Easter events set off a creative interpretative process. In light of the Easter event, it must be determined anew who Jesus of Nazareth was and is as the Resurrected One. The interweaving of new experiences with new categories of interpretation led to the formation of a new knowledge of Christology.

4.2. The Origin of Christology

Because of the cross, resurrection, and appearances, Jesus gained a new significance, which led to the formation of a complex Christology. With it the earliest communities could already build on the pre-Easter claim of Jesus.[19]

Jesus's Pre-Easter Claim

Jesus of Nazareth did not intend to establish a church, but (like John the Baptist) he gathered a circle of disciples around him (Mark 1:16–20; Luke 8:1–3), called a circle of twelve (Mark 3:14; 6:7; 14:10; 1 Cor. 15:5),

---

hardly conceivable that they could be informed about the remains of the body in order to bury the bones later."

19. Cf. Konradt, "Stellt der Vollmachtsanspruch des historischen Jesus?"

and appeared with the claim of gathering the eschatological Israel (cf. Luke 22:28–30). He bound the establishment of the kingdom of God exclusively to his person so that his activity appeared as the coming of the kingdom of God (cf. Luke 11:20). When he made his person the criterion of the final eschatological judgment (cf. Luke 12:8–9 par.), he appeared as a miracle worker (Mark 1:40–45; 7:31–37), forgave sins as God does (cf. Mark 2:1–12), and placed himself above Moses (cf. Matt. 5:21–48); then he had necessarily to be drawn close to God and be considered alongside God. The singular quality of the pre-Easter Jesus[20] is an essential reason an explicit Christology emerged after Easter. Already the pre-Easter Jesus made a distinctive claim that was changed and strengthened by the resurrection and post-Easter appearances. Because of the cross and resurrection, the transformation of meaning was inevitable, for such an event as the resurrection of Jesus of Nazareth from the dead required an interpretation and new conclusions. The first Christ-believers in Jerusalem stood before the task, like all later early Christian authors, of creating theological meaning in narrative form concerning a once-for-all event and the extraordinary nature of the cross and resurrection. Christology is the means by which the nature and meaning of Jesus of Nazareth as Messiah of Israel and of the peoples is conceptually shaped and transformed. Within this process, Easter took on the status of the founding story of the new movement.[21]

The origin of early Christology, however, is based not only in the personal claim of Jesus and the Easter event but also in the content of Jesus's teaching: (1) Jesus did not connect the will of God to ritual acts but instead emphasized the ethic of love for God and neighbor. On this basis an ethic of love could be developed in early Christianity that was not directly connected with the Torah. Jesus's ministry was, as a whole, perceived and interpreted as a saving reversal of the distorted relationship of humankind to God and of humans to each other. (2) God's unlimited love opens perspectives that transcend the election of Israel. Although Jesus understood himself to have been sent only to Israel, the signs signifying a turning to gentiles enabled the early Christians to take their message beyond Israel. (3) Jesus apparently attributed little significance to the temple; thus, for the early Christians, the worship of God in a single place played no particular role. Jesus interpreted the basic pillars of the Judaism of his time obviously in a way that was open for a transformation to universalism.

20. For a summary of the ministry and teaching of Jesus, see Schnelle, *Theology of the New Testament*, 61–162.
21. Cf. Bendemann, "Die Auferstehung von den Toten."

The Work of the Spirit

Along with the appearances of the Resurrected One, the work of the Spirit was the second dimension of the experience that effected the formation of early Christology. While the appearances were limited, the work of the Spirit was subject to no limitation. In terms of the history of religion, God and the Spirit always belong together. In the Greco-Roman cultural sphere, the work of the deity takes place, according to the teaching of the Stoics, in the sphere of the spirit.[22] In ancient Judaism the concept is of great significance. In the end time the Spirit of God is poured out (cf. Ezek. 36:25–29; Isa. 32:15–18; Joel 3:1–5 LXX [2:28–32 Eng.]; 1QS 4.18–23 and passim). The Messiah is conceived as a figure endowed with the Spirit, and the temple/dwelling metaphor is connected with the Spirit.[23] In the legendary ornamentation that at its core is historically reliable, Acts describes the activity of the Spirit in the earliest churches. The Holy Spirit appears as the "power from on high" (Luke 24:49 NRSV; Acts 1:5, 8) promised by Jesus that was given to the disciples at Pentecost (Acts 2:4). The Spirit falls on all who accept the preaching of the apostles and are baptized (cf. Acts 2:38). The reception of the Spirit is also recognizable as outward phenomena (cf. Gal. 3:2; Acts 8:18), especially in miraculous healings (1 Cor. 12:9, 28, 30), ecstatic glossolalia (Acts 2:4, 11; 4:31 and passim), and prophetic speech (cf. 1 Cor. 12; 14; Acts 10; 19). According to earliest tradition, the ministry of Jesus was already shaped by the Holy Spirit (cf. Mark 1:9–11; Acts 10:37). It was the Spirit of God that was at work in the resurrection of Jesus (Rom. 1:3b–4a; 6:4; 8:11; 1 Pet. 3:18; 1 Tim. 3:16) and determined the new manner of existence and activity of the Resurrected One (2 Cor. 3:17: "But the Lord is the Spirit"; cf. 1 Cor. 15:45). The oldest Christian statements about the work of the Spirit of God declare that the Jewish hope for the *Pneuma* that inspires and gives life for the end time has now reached its fulfillment. In the work of the Spirit, the Christ-believers recognized the reality of the resurrection of Jesus Christ from the dead.

The Interpretation of Scripture

Christology finds its language especially from Israel's Scripture, as 1 Cor. 15:3–5 indicates: "in accordance with the Scriptures." The Christ-believers lived in and out of the Scripture of Israel. This reading occurred, of course, under changed conditions for understanding, for the Jewish Christians read (most notably in the Septuagint) in a new way from the perspective of the

22. Cf. the texts in NW I/2:226–34.
23. Cf. specific evidence in Horn, *Das Angeld des Geistes*, 61ff.

Christ event. The reading of Scripture took place in a twofold movement. The Scriptures were read within the framework of Christology, and Christology gave the Scripture a new meaning.[24] The christological reading of Scripture in early Christianity leads to various models for demonstrating the continuity of God's promises in history. Through God's saving activity in the cross and resurrection of Jesus of Nazareth, it was evident to the first Christians that a connection existed between this event and the saving activity of God with Israel. Within the framework of typology (prefiguring, cf. 1 Cor. 10:1–6), promise and fulfillment (cf. Matt. 2:17–18 and passim), the exegetical methods of allegory (cf. Gal. 4:21–31) and of midrash (cf. Acts 7; 2 Cor. 3)—and in combinations of citations (cf. Rom. 9:25–29), adaptations of citations (cf. Rom. 11:3), and allusions—one may see models for expressing this fundamental conclusion. A few individual texts have a special place in the early Christian reception of the OT. Paul, with his interpretation of Gen. 15:6 and Hab. 2:4b, actually takes away the force of all other passages in the OT. With the interpretation of Hab. 2:4b LXX in Gal. 3:11 and Rom. 1:17, the apostle binds the faithfulness of God to faith in Jesus Christ as the event of justification rather than righteousness from the Torah. The chronological distance between Gen. 15:6 and Gen. 17 is theologically significant for Paul. While in Jewish tradition circumcision was a full proof of Abraham's fidelity to the commandments of God, Paul separates circumcision from the righteousness by faith, which preceded circumcision. Thus circumcision can be understood as merely a later recognition and confirmation of the new status of believers.

A key passage in the development of early Christology is Ps. 110:1 LXX: "The Lord said to my Lord: Sit at my right hand, until I make your enemies a footstool."[25] Here the early Christians found the relevant text for Jesus's heavenly dignity and function: He was exalted to the right hand of God, participates in the power and glory of God, and exercises his rule from there (cf. 1 Cor. 15:24; Rom. 8:34; Mark 12:36; 14:62; Matt. 22:44; 26:64; Luke 20:42; 22:69; Acts 2:34; Col. 3:1; Eph. 1:20; Heb. 1:3, 13; 8:1; 10:12). In this context the first Christians very early transferred the common address "Lord" to Jesus (cf. the reception of Joel 3:5 LXX in Rom. 10:12–13; also 1 Cor. 1:31; 2:16; 10:26; 2 Cor. 10:17), expressing a singular authority to distinguish it from other claims.[26] In the development of the christological title Son (cf. 1 Thess. 1:9–10; Rom. 1:3b–4a; Mark 1:11; 9:7), Ps. 2:7 ("I will tell of the decree of the

24. For an overview, see Moyise, *Old Testament in the New*.
25. Cf. Hengel, "Psalm 110 und die Erhöhung." On the reception of the Psalms as a whole, cf. Moyise and Menken, *Psalms in the New Testament*.
26. Cf. Jonge, *Christologie im Kontext*, 177–78.

Lord. He said to me, 'You are my son; today I have begotten you'" [NRSV]; cf. 2 Sam. 7:11–14) had a major significance.

As an intertextual phenomenon, the christological reading of the Scripture had a twofold result. It placed the OT passage in a new horizon of meaning and also legitimated the theological position of the NT authors. Thus God's eschatological saving action in Jesus Christ, rather than the weight of the Scripture itself, shaped their central thinking. The central contents of Jewish theology (Torah, election) were reconceived, and the scriptural passage underwent a productive intertextual interpretative process.

4.3 The Founder of a New Discourse and New Thinking

Beginning with the proclamation and ministry of Jesus[27] and newly inspired by the Easter event, the early Christians from the beginning reflected on the lasting significance of the Christ event in various ways. They had to determine the status of Jesus Christ in a new way, especially in his relationship to God. Thus they made use of categories from the Jewish and Hellenistic tradition, made extensive attributions, and introduced Jesus Christ as the founder of a new discourse, from which they conceived of a new religious world.

Jewish Foundations

The foundation of this new world came from basic Jewish claims, which offered important categories for understanding: God is one; he is the creator, the Lord and preserver of the world; he elected Israel from the peoples; he gave Israel the land and the Torah and chose the temple in Jerusalem as his dwelling place (see the first subheading under 3.3; see 5.3 below). Traditions of ancient Judaism[28] enabled Israel to maintain monotheism yet at the same time to designate Jesus of Nazareth as Χριστός (Messiah), κύριος (Lord), and υἱὸς τοῦ θεοῦ (Son of God). According to Jewish thought, there is only one God, but he is not alone. Many heavenly intermediaries such as Wisdom (cf. Prov. 2:1–6; 8:22–31; Wis. 6:12–11:1), the Logos, or the Name of God have their home in heaven in proximity to God.[29] Biblical patriarchs such as Enoch

---

27. Luz, "Das 'Auseinandergehen der Wege,'" 62–64, correctly emphasizes that the earthly Jesus can be seen as the starting point for the separation of Judaism and Christianity, for he had expressed an open understanding of Israel and taught and practiced radical love and had relativized the temple. Thus, taken as a whole, Jesus was "a unique Jew" (63).

28. Cf. Hurtado, *One God, One Lord*, 17–92.

29. For example, cf. Wis. 9:9–11; Philo, *Confusion* 146–47.

(cf. Gen. 5:18–24)[30] or Moses and the archangel Michael[31] surround God and act on his behalf. As participants in the heavenly world, they are subordinate to God, and in no way do they endanger the belief in the one God. As created and subordinate powers, they do not compete with God. The language of human hierarchy is used to describe the activities of God for the world and in the world.

Judaism, with its hope for the resurrection of the dead, provided the framework and conceptual background within apocalyptic thought in the third to second century BCE.[32] The only unambiguous resurrection text in the OT is Dan. 12:2–3: "Of those who sleep in the ground, many will arise to eternal life, the others to the shame of eternal contempt. Those who are wise will shine like stars in the heavens, and those who lead many to righteousness will shine like the stars eternally." Isaiah 26:19 is a second central text in a redactional addition from the Hellenistic Age: "Your dead will live, the bodies will stand again; those who lie in the earth will arise and rejoice, for the dew that you send is a dew of light; the earth gives back the dead" (cf. Isa. 25:6–8). The hope for the resurrection expressed in both texts has a prehistory in the OT. One may note Hosea 6:1–3 and Ezek. 37:1–14. In the second and first centuries BCE, numerous texts attest the hope for the resurrection: Wis. 3:1–8; 1 En. 16.6; 48.9–10; 51.1; 91.10; 93.3–4; 104.2; Pss. Sol. 3.11–12; LAB 19.12–13; 2 Macc. 7:9; T. Ben. 10.6–10. Of special significance is the fact that among the Qumran Essenes there was faith in a resurrection of the dead. In 4Q521 2.ii.12 God is praised with the words "Then he will heal the wounded, and revive the dead and bring good news to the poor."[33] In addition, there are the experiences of the Spirit already mentioned and the reading of Scripture (see above, 4.2), which, along with other motifs, especially from Jewish apocalyptic (judgment, expectation of the end, appearances of the Messiah, salvation of the faithful), also illustrate the Jewish background of numerous christological perspectives of the early period.

Greek Concepts

From the beginning, a genuine Greek-Hellenistic conception stood at the center of the faith of the new movement: God has become human in Jesus of Nazareth. The incarnation of gods or godlike beings (and the divinization of a man) is a genuine Greek idea (see above, 3.1; 3.2, first subheading)

---

30. Cf., e.g., 1 En. 61.
31. Cf., e.g., Dan. 10:13–21; 1 En. 20.5; 71.3; 90.21.
32. Cf. Schwankl, *Die Sadduzäerfrage*, 173–274.
33. Translation by Vermès, *Complete Dead Sea Scrolls*, 413.

and reflects a motif from Hellenistic culture that played an important role in the formation and reception of the earliest Christology.[34] The concept of a being that was both divine and human, such as Jesus Christ, was acceptable for Greeks and Romans on the basis of their own cultural background. The pagan narratives about gods in human form, about heroes such as Heracles or others, were significant for the socialization of many gentile Christians, especially in the cities of Asia Minor and Greece. On the other hand, for Jews the thought was unacceptable that men such as the Roman caesar Caligula claimed to be divine and demanded to be worshiped (cf. Philo, *Legat.* 118).

New Thinking

Along with the permanent anchor of the Christ-believers in the Jewish tradition and the acceptance of Greek concepts, a new way of thinking also determined the earliest theology, which was not actually compatible with Jewish and Greek views. The affirmation that a crucified man was the messiah was perceived as blasphemy within the context of Deut. 21:22–23 ("for whoever hangs on a tree is cursed by God"), according to the Jewish perspective (cf. Gal. 3:13). With the Greeks it was judged as "sheer nonsense" (1 Cor. 1:23: "But we preach Christ crucified, for Jews an offense, for gentiles foolishness"). To worship a crucified man as God's son appeared to the Jews as a theological offense[35] and to the Greco-Roman world as lunacy.[36] With the central place given to a crucified man among early Christians, any idea of cultural plausibility was turned on its head, for now the cross appeared as the central characteristic of divine wisdom.

Additional major differences are also present.[37] First, the personified divine attributes in Jewish tradition mentioned above were not equal to the deity or godlike persons with their own areas of action and cultic worship. From the beginning, Jesus was elevated to a unique proximity to God. The name of God was given to him (Phil. 2:9–10). He is like God, as the image of God (Phil. 2:6; 2 Cor. 4:4), and bearer of the glory of God (2 Cor. 4:6; Phil. 3:21).

34. Cf. D. Zeller, "New Testament Christology." On the history-of-religions background of the concept of incarnation and its early Christian manifestation, cf. Schnelle, *Das Evangelium nach Johannes*, 65–71.

35. Cf. H.-W. Kuhn, "Jesus als Gekreuzigter," 36 37.

36. Cicero describes the horror that the thought of crucifixion evoked: Cicero, *Pro Rabirio postumo* 5.16: "Even if we are threatened with death, we may die free men. But the executioner, the veiling of the head, and the very word 'cross' should be far removed not only from the body and life of Roman citizens, but also from their thoughts, eyes, and ears. For all of these things are unworthy of a Roman citizen and a free man"; Pliny the Younger, *Ep.* 10.96.8, "confusing, wasted superstition."

37. Cf. Hurtado, *One God, One Lord*, 93–124.

In Rom. 9:5, the former Pharisee Paul equates the Χριστὸς κατὰ σάρκα who descends from Israel with God: "From the fathers, from whom is the Christ according to the flesh, who is God over all; may he be praised forever."[38]

As a preexistent being, he participated in the divine act of creation (Phil. 2:6; 1 Cor. 8:6); phrases originally referring to God are now applied to him (cf. 1 Cor. 1:31; 2:16; Rom. 10:13). His place is in heaven (1 Thess. 1:10; 4:16; Phil. 3:20) at the right hand of God (Rom. 8:34); from there he rules over all things (1 Cor. 15:27; Phil. 3:21) and over the heavenly powers (Phil. 2:10). As one sent by God, he is at work presently in the church (Gal. 4:4–5; Rom. 8:3). He is the divine agent who initiates the eschatological judgment at his parousia (1 Thess. 1:10; 1 Cor. 16:22; 2 Cor. 5:10). In the worship service he was addressed as God (cf. 1 Cor. 12:3; 16:22, *Maranatha*, our Lord come).[39] He made possible the new access to God, which is known in the prayer Ἀββα (*Abba*, Father; Gal. 4:6; Rom. 8:15; Mark 14:36) in the worship service. In liturgical practice it was expressed as "Praise the God and Father of our Lord Jesus Christ" (Rom. 15:6). Baptism, the Lord's Supper, and acclamations are exclusively in the name of Jesus. Alongside the theological reflections came liturgical invocation and ritual adoration of Jesus as a further starting point for the formation, development, and spread of early christological conceptions.

At the beginning of the new movement stood a thoroughly creative process: With Jesus Christ the Christ-believers introduced nothing less than the founder of a new discourse into the existing religious world and ascribed to him an unlimited soteriological power. Attributes were ascribed to him that in Jewish thought belonged exclusively to God. Thus Moses was not only relativized as the founder of a discourse, but because Jesus Christ was given divine worship, the Christ-believers transcended the limits of Jewish thought and established a new world of discourse in teaching and cult.[40] A second aspect followed the first. The incarnation of God and a human's becoming God is a Greek idea, which in its alien character and offensiveness cannot be relativized for Jewish ears. However, over against Greco-Roman thought, the earliest Christology

38. This involves the interpretation that is grammatically most obvious with content that is the most difficult interpretation; cf. Kammler, "Die Prädikation Jesu Christi als 'Gott' und die paulinische Christologie"; for positive and negative arguments, cf. Wilckens, *Der Brief an die Römer*, 2:189.

39. On the significance of the worship service for the formation of early Christology, see Schrage, *Unterwegs zur Einheit und Einzigkeit Gottes*, 158–67; Hengel, "Abba, Maranatha, Hosanna," 154: "Already in the Aramaic-speaking early church, the acclamations *abba* and *maranatha* express elementary certainties."

40. Cf. Luz, "Das 'Auseinandergehen der Wege,'" 64: "Soon after the death of Jesus, the ways began to separate." See also Dunn, *Parting of the Ways*.

had its own accent, for the idea of a crucified man becoming Son of God remained an alien and offensive thought (cf. 1 Cor. 1:23). Similarly, Jesus's exclusive soteriological position conflicted with Greco-Roman tradition, in which deities were responsible for specific areas.

With Jesus as the founder of a new discourse and the new forms of knowledge of Christology, the foundation was already established to see early Christianity as an independent movement. There was no possibility of integrating the crucified Son of God easily into an existing religious world. This could take place in neither the Jewish nor the Greco-Roman tradition of thought. The witness of Christ was not accepted as a possible form of pluralizing of the OT. This was indicated already shortly after Easter in Jerusalem. Although the Christ-believers understood themselves as a legitimate part of Israel, from the beginning they were not accepted as such. Thus it is not surprising that the Jerusalem church fell into conflict with official Judaism from the beginning.

5

The Jerusalem Church

The Jerusalem church is designated usually as the "primitive church" in order to express its special significance for the history of early Christianity. There are four primary reasons for the special place of the Jerusalem church: (1) Jerusalem was the religious center of Judaism, and also from it came the first Christ-believers; (2) Jerusalem was the place of the crucifixion and resurrection of Christ; (3) Jerusalem was where the appearances of the Resurrected One were first experienced (cf. Luke 24:34; John 20:11–18); and (4) Jerusalem, with its religious traditions that had been handed on, was the place where the first Christ-believers awaited the parousia of the Messiah Jesus of Nazareth (see below, 5.1). The special place of the church is indicated in the (delayed) visit of Paul (cf. Gal. 1:18), as the place of the apostolic council (Gal. 2:1; Acts 15:4) as well as its significance in the Pauline rationale for the collection: It is a ministry for the "saints" in Jerusalem (2 Cor. 8:4–5; 9:1, 12; Rom. 15:25–27), who received a material reciprocation for their spiritual gifts.[1]

Even if Jerusalem was the center of the post-Easter movement of Christ-believers, it was not the only place and especially not *the* place for the origin of Christianity as an independent movement.[2] Presumably also in Galilee there were communities of Christ-believers from the beginning (see below,

---

1. This information disputes the claim of Smith, "What Do We Really Know about the Jerusalem Church?," 243, "that the Jerusalem 'church' as a power broker in Christian origins was a mythological construct from the outset. . . . The actual *ekklēsia* in Jerusalem, such as it was, most likely played a minor role in Christian origins."

2. Contra Dunn, *Beginning from Jerusalem*, 2:133–37; and D.-A. Koch, *Geschichte des Ur-christentums*, 164–68: both concentrate exclusively on Jerusalem and do not consider Galilee.

6.3; 6.4). With the spread of the new movement and especially of its thought, Damascus and primarily Antioch played a more important role than Jerusalem (see below, 6.4). The evidence suggests that in Jerusalem the mission to the uncircumcised (primarily by Paul) had much opposition, leading to the attempts to hinder it and subsequently to correct it (see below, 7.6; 8.5). Moreover, a significant church such as Rome was founded, independent of Jerusalem; one may assume that the same situation was the case in Damascus, Antioch, and Alexandria. Thus it is more appropriate to speak of the Jerusalem church and not of the "early church" as the mother of all things, whereby the special place of Jerusalem is in no way diminished.

5.1 The Beginnings

One can trace the basic information about the origin of the Jerusalem church.[3] The turmoil surrounding the appearance, the trial, and the crucifixion of the Galilean healer and preacher, Jesus of Nazareth, appears to have taken place in a brief period of time. Probably the Romans and Jews returned rather quickly to the order of the day, thinking that the matter of Jesus and his message had come to an end with the death of Jesus. Because the disciples of Jesus had fled (see above, 4.1), the entire movement appeared to have dissolved, so the authorities saw no occasion to pursue the disciples of Jesus. With the execution of John the Baptist and the crucifixion of Jesus, two messianic-prophetic figures and movements appeared to have been defeated, both of which had power, not in weapons, but in their subversive religious and ethical message. As a whole, the time shortly after 30 was relatively peaceful. Major events were reported neither for the Roman Empire nor the Jews. The leading Jewish groups, the Pharisees and Sadducees, probably saw the brief appearance of the Galilean preacher Jesus of Nazareth and his Galilean followers as a failure and at an end.

The First Events

Then began a multilevel movement. (1) The Galilean disciples of Jesus who had fled from Jerusalem (cf. some women: Mark 15:47; 16:1) probably remained for a while in Galilee. Then the pre-Easter impulse of Jesus, in connection with the appearances (Mark 16:7; 1 Cor. 15:5, Cephas and the Twelve; 15:6: "five hundred brothers"), and the commissioning by the Exalted One

---

3. Cf. Colpe, *Die erste urchristliche Generation*, 62; contra Lüdemann, *Die ersten drei Jahre Christentum*, 11: "The history of the earliest church remains almost unknown."

(Peter, Matt. 16:16–18), and new experiences of the Spirit (Acts 1:11; 2:7) led to the pre-Easter circle of disciples who had remained in Galilee or returned from Jerusalem. (2) At the same time sympathizers of Jesus remained in Jerusalem, including Joseph of Arimathea (and Joseph Barsabbas, Matthew?),[4] without engaging in any known activities. There were also appearances (Luke 24:34; John 20:11–18) and experiences of the Spirit (cf. Acts 1:16; 2:1–36; 4:31). (3) Parts of the Galilean Christ-believers gradually returned—without being noticed by Jews and Romans—to Jerusalem under the leadership of Peter (cf. Acts 1:12, 13a), and there, along with others who revered Jesus, came something totally new: the first church of Christ-believers. Then other members of the inner-Jewish movement joined: from Galilee especially parts of the family of Jesus (Mary, James; cf. Acts 1:14b), but also unknown people who had been impressed by the ministry of Jesus and acted as sympathizers. Jerusalem is the holy city (Isa. 48:2; 52:1), the dwelling of the Most High (Ps. 46:4), where God will establish his kingdom (cf. Isa. 33:20–22; 54:10–14; 60:1ff.). In Jewish eschatology, Jerusalem was traditionally the place of the coming, that is, the return of the Messiah, so it was apparent that the disciples should await the arrival of the Messiah Jesus of Nazareth in Jerusalem.[5] In Pss. Sol. 17.21–22, 26, written around 50 CE, we read, "Behold, Lord, and raise up their king, the son of David, to rule over your servant Israel, and undergird him with strength to destroy unrighteous rulers in the time known to you, to purify Jerusalem from the gentiles. . . . And he will gather a holy people, that he will lead in righteousness" (cf. also 2 Bar. 40.1; 1 En. 90; Sib. Or. 5.414ff.). There where Jesus was crucified, died, arose, and appeared, his followers hoped for his return.

With these events, a key position was probably occupied by Peter (see below, 5.2). As the first one called and the first witness of the Resurrected One, despite his failure in the passion, he had a special authority. He apparently led the community that was being formed. Peter is named first in the list of disciples (Acts 1:13); he determines the action (cf. Acts 1:15ff.), makes the programmatic speech (cf. Acts 2:14–36), and performs the first miracles (cf. Acts 3). Peter is the one who summarizes the first proclamation, according to Acts 2:38: "Repent and be baptized, everyone of you in the name of Jesus Christ for the forgiveness of your sins, and you will receive the gift of the Holy Spirit."

---

4. The report in Acts 1:23 ("they proposed two, Joseph, named Barsabbas who was also known as Justus, and Matthew") probably refers to two actual members of the Jerusalem church (noteworthy is especially the first, with the threefold name!), even if the election is indebted to Lukan ecclesiology; cf. Roloff, *Die Apostelgeschichte*, 34–36.

5. Cf. L. Schenke, *Die Urgemeinde*, 22.

First Structures

We know little about the original organizational forms and structures of leadership in the Jerusalem church. In the earliest post-Easter group, questions of organization and leadership probably played only a small role. The sociological conditions of the city of Jerusalem probably had an impact on the first church in Jerusalem. According to Acts 1:13, the church met in Jerusalem first in an upper room of a house. Along with the apostles and Galilean disciples of Jesus (cf. Acts 1:11, 13; 2:7) were also women (Mark 15:40, 47; 16:1: Mary Magdalene; Mary, the mother of Joses; Mary, the mother of James; Salome) as well as Mary, the mother of Jesus, and his brothers. There were also sympathizers such as Joseph of Arimathea (Mark 15:43), Matthias (Acts 1:23, 26), and Joseph Barsabbas, named Justus (Acts 1:23); Mary, the mother of John Mark, with her servant Rhoda (Acts 12:12–15); Alexander and Rufus, the sons of Simon of Cyrene (Mark 15:21); the Emmaus disciples (Luke 24:18: Cleopas and the unknown disciple), Barnabas (Acts 4:36–37), Mnason from Cyprus (Acts 21:16), perhaps also Silvanus/Silas (1 Thess. 1:1; Acts 15:22, 27), and Judas Barsabbas (Acts 15:22, 27). Andronicus and Junia (see below, 5.2), who came to faith prior to Paul (Rom. 16:7), probably also belonged to the early church. Perhaps they were numbered among those who immigrated to Rome, having come into the church after the experience of the Spirit described in Acts (cf. Acts 2:10).[6] In a somewhat later phase of the development of the community, Ananias and Sapphira (Acts 5:1–11), Hellenistic Jews from the diaspora (cf. the widows among the Hellenists in Acts 6:1), the prophet Agabus (Acts 11:28; 21:10), and Jewish priests (Acts 6:7) could have come into the church.[7]

Acts 2:46 reports that the church came together daily for the breaking of bread. As customary, these communal meals comprised more people than belonged to the respective house communities. Corresponding to the size of the houses in Jerusalem, about twenty to thirty people participated in the fellowship meals. Houses in and around Jerusalem are presupposed in Mark 14:3 (Simon of Bethany); Luke 24:13, 29 (the Emmaus disciples), Acts 1:13 (an upper room); 12:12–13 (Mary, the mother of John Mark); 21:16 (Mnason from Cyprus); and Gal. 1:18 (Peter can accommodate Paul for two weeks). Very soon there must have been smaller groups, house churches, within the entire church in Jerusalem. This is indicated by the linguistic distinction between

6. Cf. Robert Jewett, *Romans*, 964. A list of possible members of the Jerusalem church may be found in Bauckham, "Jesus and the Jerusalem Community"; Dunn, *Beginning from Jerusalem*, 178–80.

7. Riesner, "Zwischen Tempel und Obergemach," 78f., includes among the additional ones (cf. Acts 2:41, 47) also Essenes, who joined from the nearby Essene quarter.

the Greek-speaking Hellenistic Jews and the Aramaic-speaking Palestinian Jews (see below, 5.5). Such meetings naturally required a certain organization and leaders. These could have been selected leaders or the respective heads of the households.

One can only estimate the size of the church; the information about the numbers in Acts 1:15 (120 brothers) and Acts 2:41 (3,000 people became members of the community in one day) is probably the ideal concept of the beginning. One can, however, assume that the church grew quickly and that a large number of men and women became members (Acts 5:14). If one assumes many house churches in Jerusalem, then one could speak of about one hundred and more church members. After they reached a certain size, the place of assembly for the church, the temple area with its courtyards and halls, becomes a possibility. In general, the development occurred quickly and with turbulence.

Religious Experiences

What is certain for the Pauline communities (cf. only 1 Thess. 5:19; 1 Cor. 12) was probably also the case for the Jerusalem church; intensive experiences of the Spirit shaped the religious world of the first Christ-believers. In its present form the Pentecost story in Acts 2:1–36 derives from Luke and is integrated fully into the Lukan theology. According to Acts 1:6–8, the gift of the Holy Spirit is the decisive instrument for the witnesses of Christ in the time of the absence of the Lord. Acts 2:33 describes the activities of the Spirit, describing Jesus as the one who is exalted into heaven: "After he had been exalted to the right hand of God and received from the Father the promised Holy Spirit, he poured out what you see and hear." The gift of the Resurrected and Exalted One is thus the foundation for the worldwide mission and the gathering of the holy community.[8] For Luke, Pentecost is the fulfillment of the baptism of the Spirit announced by John the Baptist (cf. Luke 3:16; Acts 1:5; 2:4). The disciples and all of the hearers in Jerusalem were empowered by the Spirit for proclamation (Acts 2:1–13). Thus Pentecost is an anticipation of what happens later: the proclamation of the resurrected Jesus Christ, under the power of the Spirit, is understood and accepted by people from entirely different cultures. Despite its integration into Lukan theology, behind the Pentecost event is a historical core:[9] new and intensive experiences of the Spirit by Christ-believers in Jerusalem.[10] Both in the OT (cf. Ezek. 36; Joel 3)

8. Cf. Kremer, "Weltweites Zeugnis für Christus."
9. Cf. Roloff, *Die Apostelgeschichte*, 38.
10. Cf. Colpe, *Die erste urchristliche Generation*, 59: "Undoubtedly, Jewish Christianity begins with pneumatic experiences after the death of Jesus."

and in ancient Judaism (cf. 1 En. 61; Jub. 1.20ff.; 1QS 4.18–23; 1QH 7.6–7; 16.11–12; 17.26), the gift of the Spirit was considered a sign of the coming of the end time.[11] The gift of the Spirit on the Messiah (Isa. 11:2; 28:6; 42:1; 61:1; 1 En. 49.3; 62.2; Pss. Sol. 17.37; 18.7) and the gift of the Spirit on the entire people (cf. Ezek. 36:26–27; 37:5, 14; 39:29; Isa. 32:15; 44:3; Zech. 12:10; Hag. 2:5; Joel 2:28–31; 1 En. 1.23) witness similarly to the presence of God and his initiating of the end-time act of bringing salvation. Even if the experience of the Spirit among the first Christ-believers in Jerusalem was not as spectacular and extensive as the Pentecost narrative portrays it, they were able to come to a similar conviction, for example, as among the Christians in Corinth: God and the Resurrected One are present in the Spirit. The appearances of the Resurrected One and the work of the Spirit made the church certain that God had acted through Jesus Christ and will act in the future. Miraculous deeds probably accompanied the work of the Spirit. Indeed, the miracle stories in Acts 3:1–9 and the associated events (cf. Acts 4:7, where the chief priests ask Peter and John: "By what power or in whose name have you done this?"), which are shaped by Luke, probably reflect a historical core. In 2 Cor. 11–12, in a conflict with the strict Jewish Christian "super-apostles" (2 Cor. 12:11), Paul emphasizes to the Corinthians that "the signs of an apostle" (2 Cor. 12:12, σημεῖα τοῦ ἀποστόλου) had occurred among them. It was the nature of the apostolic office to perform miracles. In this way an apostle identified himself and others recognized him (see below, 5.2). This pneumatic understanding of the apostolic office could scarcely have developed outside Jerusalem or independent of Jerusalem. Rather, it reflects the initial events in Jerusalem, where the apostles performed miracles under the power of the Spirit.

5.2 Groups and Persons

The first phase within the Jerusalem church was a kind of eschatological gathering; closely connected was a phase of the first institutionalization: groups and persons appear in the foreground and firm structures emerge.[12] According to Luke's depiction, two groups play a significant role at the beginning of the Jerusalem church, for the Exalted One appeared to the apostles (cf. Acts 1:2), who, according to Luke's portrayal, are identical with the Twelve (cf. Acts 1:15–26).

11. Cf. H. Kuhn, *Enderwartung und gegenwärtiges Heil*, 117–20; Horn, *Das Angeld des Geistes*, 26–60.

12. Cf. Dunn, *Beginning from Jerusalem*, 206–12.

The Twelve

The circle of the Twelve[13] had probably already been initiated by Jesus of Nazareth.[14] Four arguments support its historicity: (1) The post-Easter church would scarcely have come to the statement that Judas, as a member of the closest circle of disciples, betrayed Jesus (cf. Mark 14:10, 43 par.) if this were not a historical fact.[15] (2) The Twelve are named in the pre-Pauline tradition of 1 Cor. 15:5, according to which Christ "appeared to Cephas, then to the Twelve." "The Twelve" are here an established institution, although Judas no longer belonged among them and Peter is mentioned separately. (3) In 1 Cor. 15:5, 7 Paul distinguishes between "the Twelve" and the apostles; he knows about its early origin and its special function. (4) The Twelve play no historical role after Easter. Those who were called to be an apostle by an appearance of the Resurrected One are more important. Only at a later time, in Mark, Matthew, Luke, and the Revelation of John (Rev. 21:14), are the Twelve identified with the apostles. The group of twelve probably extends back to the pre-Easter time; its significance can be seen primarily in Luke 22:28, 30Q: "You, who have followed me, will sit on thrones and judge the twelve tribes of Israel." The Twelve evidently had the function of representing the twelve tribes of Israel as an anticipation of the eschatological totality of Israel, analogous to the kingdom of God, which had already begun in secret. The Twelve thus correspond to the present aspect of the kingdom of God, for they signal the beginning of the totality of Israel created by God.

A (limited) post-Easter significance of the Twelve is indicated in the reports of the appearances. According to 1 Cor. 15:5, "then he appeared to Cephas, then to the Twelve." The place of the event is uncertain. Inasmuch as the appearances to Cephas and to the Twelve belong closely together and Cephas receives his appearance in Galilee (cf. Mark 16:7), the appearance to the Twelve was probably in Galilee.[16] After the appearances to him, Peter then probably reconstituted the group of twelve, which had also been granted an appearance, in Galilee. Then the traces of the circle of twelve disappear, for it is doubtful that the entire group returned to Jerusalem. That the Twelve did

---

13. Those who belonged to the group of twelve were the brothers Peter (Mark 1:16; 3:16; Acts 1:13) and Andrew (Mark 1:16; 3:18; Acts 1:13); James (Mark 1:19; 3:17; Acts 1:13) and John (Mark 1:19; 3:17; Acts 1:13), the sons of Zebedee; Philip, Bartholomew, Matthew, Thomas (twin), James the son of Alphaeus, Simon the Canaanean/Zealot, and Judas Iscariot (Mark 3:18; Acts 1:13, 16). Other figures are Thaddeus (Mark 3:18) and Judas, the son of James (Acts 1:13) or brother of James (Luke 6:16).

14. On the argument, cf. D.-A. Koch, *Geschichte des Urchristentums*, 149–51.

15. Cf. Rigaux, "Die 'Zwölf' in Geschichte und Kerygma."

16. Lüdemann, *Die ersten drei Jahre Christentum*, 112.

not have a leading role in the Jerusalem church is indicated by the fact that it is mentioned only twice: (1) in the list in Acts 1:13 and the selection of Matthias (Acts 1:15–26); and (2) in the establishment of the group of seven (Acts 6:2–7). Both texts reflect the basic thought of Lukan ecclesiology, according to which the Twelve apostles are the connecting link between the time of Jesus and the time of the church. Thus the Twelve "must" be complete, and only the "Twelve" could legitimate a new group (see below, 5.5). First Corinthians 15:5, 7 indicates clearly, on the other hand, that the Twelve, contrary to Luke's portrayal, are not identical with the apostles, for here he distinguishes between the "Twelve" and the apostles. In fact, only specific people from the Twelve (especially Peter and the sons of Zebedee) play a role in the Jerusalem church. This fact is confirmed by Paul, who in his first visit to Jerusalem circa 35 CE, according to Gal. 1:18–19, had extensive contact only with Cephas. "I did not see the other apostles, except for James the brother of the Lord." After Easter, the Twelve were significant only for a brief period. Peter gathered the group in Galilee; then the traces disappear. A few members remained in Galilee, while others went to Jerusalem. The book of Acts gives indirect confirmation, for only individuals hold leadership roles in the Jerusalem church. It is not the Twelve, but the apostles, who have a major significance.

The Apostles

In nonbiblical Greek, the noun ἀπόστολος is used primarily in the sense of "sending out" in the context of military activities.[17] Neither is it the designation of an office nor does it appear as a fixed term in religious contexts. When it is used of persons, then it, like the passive participle of ἀποστέλλειν (send) and πέμπειν (send), means "to be sent from someone to someone" and has no established meaning.[18] The spectrum extends from "authorized agent/leading negotiator" to "messenger/mediator." In the Septuagint the call and sending of prophets are connected with ἀποστέλλειν (cf. Isa. 6:8 and passim). Moreover, according to Isa. 61:1–2 the prophet who is sent to the poor proclaims the good news (εὐαγγελίσασθαι). However, Epictetus also uses the verb ἀποστέλλειν in a philosophical-religious context: The Cynic has been sent by Zeus as messenger of the good and the true.[19] Early Christianity took the concept of ἀπόστολος

17. Cf. M. Lohmeyer, *Der Apostelbegriff*, 133–41; cf. 18–122, on the history of scholarship (there is also critique of a derivation from the Jewish messenger).

18. On the analysis of the verbs, cf. M. Lohmeyer, *Der Apostelbegriff*, 141–54.

19. Cf. Epictetus, *Diatr.* 1.24.6: Diogenes was sent out as a scout (κατάσκοπος ἀποστολεὶς Διογένης); 3.22.46: Epictetus answered the question of how anyone without house, homeland, or slaves could lead a happy life. "See, God has sent you a man who can show you that it is

and shaped it (probably from the verb ἀποστέλλειν) with a new content.[20] The concept of one "sent" referred exclusively to persons, which developed into various conceptions,[21] of which two may be distinguished: one transmitted by Luke, and the other represented above all by Paul.

The Lukan Concept

Luke connects "the Twelve" exclusively with "the apostles." For him the twelve apostles are the archetype of the church, for they are witnesses of the earthly Jesus (Luke 6:13: "And when it was day, he called his disciples and selected twelve of them, whom he named apostles"); they are the representatives of Israel (Luke 22:30), whom Jesus commissions and sends out (Luke 24:47). They become eyewitnesses of the ascension and exaltation (Luke 24:48; Acts 1:21–22), and the Spirit is sent to them (Luke 24:49; Acts 1:8).[22] The twelve apostles are thus the primary witnesses of the Christ event and the essential bearers of tradition. To some extent they represent for Luke the completed Israel, for they portray the continuity between the time of Jesus and the church that is being formed. In this function, they can have no successors because they are historically and theologically the once-for-all guarantors of the Jesus tradition and prototype of the ecclesiastical officeholder. Thus, according to Acts 1:21–22, only those in this circle would be accepted: "one of the men who was together with us for the entire time that the Lord went in and out among us, beginning from the baptism of John until the day that he was taken away from us." Matthias filled both criteria of being a continuous pre- and post-Easter eyewitness and is thus qualified (by the Spirit) for this office. Evidently the Lukan conception of the twelve apostles served to ensure the portrayal of the certainty of the instruction in the Jesus tradition mentioned in Luke 1:1–4. In order to do this, Luke equates the pre-Easter circle of disciples with the "Twelve" and identifies the "Twelve" with the post-Easter

possible" (ἰδοὺ ἀπέστακλεν ὑμῖν ὁ θεὸς τὸν δείξοντα ἔργῳ ὅτι ἐνδέχεται), "See, I have been sent by god as an example" (ἰδοὺ ἐγὼ ὑμῖν παράδειγμα ὑπὸ τοῦ θεοῦ ἀπέσταλμαι); cf. also 22.23.56, 69.

20. On the basis of this conclusion, see M. Lohmeyer, *Der Apostelbegriff*, 121ff. (for both the external and the NT realm, it can be shown that the verb and noun were closely connected).

21. The range of meaning extends from a possible sending of disciples by the earthly Jesus (Luke 10:1, 3, 16Q; Mark 6:7, 20) to the interpretations of Jesus as the one sent at the end time (Luke 13:34Q), one sent by Wisdom (Luke 11:49–50Q), the Baptist as one sent by God (Luke 7:27Q; John 1:6), the self-understanding of the Q missionaries as "sent" (Luke 10:1, 3, 16Q), in a neutral sense for those sent out by the church (Acts 14:4, 14; John 13:16). On the analysis of all relevant texts, conceptions, and models, cf. M. Lohmeyer, *Der Apostelbegriff*, 160–343.

22. On the Lukan concept of apostle, cf. G. Klein, *Die zwölf Apostel*; Roloff, *Apostolat, Verkündigung, Kirche*, 169–235. Mark 6:30 could have been a source for Luke, for there "the apostles" are identified with the Twelve (cf. Mark 6:7–13).

circle of apostles. After Easter the twelve apostles bring the Jesus tradition into the missionary proclamation (Acts 2:22–23; 4:10ff.; 6:4) and make it the foundation of the Jerusalem church, as Acts 2:42 indicates: "They continued in the teaching of the apostles." Within this framework, for Luke, Paul cannot be an apostle because he, as one called after Easter (Acts 9:1–19), is not a bearer of the original Jesus tradition.[23] Paul is himself subordinated to the apostles in the history of salvation, but he is a witness of the Christ event (cf. Acts 20:24; 22:15; 23:11; 26:16; 28:23) and surpasses them by far in his work, as the second part of Acts demonstrates.

The Pauline Concept

While Luke associates the concept of apostle with both the ministry of the earthly Jesus and the resurrected Christ, in the Pauline letters another conception is present.[24] Here an appearance of the Resurrected One and the call/mission is the decisive, if not the only, legitimation for the apostolic office. This interpretation is suggested in particular in 1 Cor. 9:1; 15:8–11; Gal. 1:16, in which "last of all" in 1 Cor. 15:8 indicates that Paul understood himself to be the last legitimate apostle. Especially in the churches in which his apostolic office was disputed (Corinth, Galatia), Paul refers to his authority as an apostle called by God, that is, Christ.[25] In Gal. 1:15–16 and Rom. 1:1, the Pauline apostolate takes on an incomparable dimension in salvation history: Paul speaks of his (pretemporal) election by God for the service to the gospel (cf. also Rom. 11:13, "I am the apostle to the nations"). The Pauline apostolate has divine authority and can thus claim this authority from the churches (cf. 1 Thess. 2:7), even if Paul does not use it. It is not only the call and sending that in Paul legitimate the permanent apostolic office but also the capacity of the apostle to establish the church and to represent the gospel convincingly as the norm of grace in the churches (cf. 2 Cor. 1:13–18). The apostle himself becomes the norm (cf. 1 Thess. 1:6; 1 Cor. 4:16; 11:1; Phil.

23. The exceptions in Acts 14:4 and 14 are to be attributed to pre-Lukan tradition. Cf. Roloff, *Die Apostelgeschichte*, 211. Luke allowed—consciously?—the tensions with his original conception to remain. More convincing is the assumption that Luke understands Barnabas and Paul simply as men sent out by the church.

24. On the Pauline understanding of apostleship, cf. Frey, "Apostelbegriff," 126–33; see also Rengstorf, "ἀπόστολος," *TDNT* 1:407–47.

25. Undoubtedly, in the conflicts in Corinth and Galatia, Paul indicates his understanding as an apostle; cf. Frey, "Apostelbegriff," 132–33. In 1 Thessalonians, Paul's earliest letter, the ἀπόστολος concept does not appear in the prescript; similarly, it does not appear in Philippians or Philemon. In all three cases the relationship to the church was not in question. In addition, 1 Thess. 2:7 indicates that, from the beginning, Paul knew and used the wider understanding of an apostle as an emissary sent by a church.

3:17). In his public activity and his work, he embodies the servant character of the gospel (cf. 2 Cor. 4:7–18); he demonstrates the freedom of the apostle (1 Cor. 9:19), for the refusal of the financial support to which he was entitled (1 Cor. 9:14) alone serves the unhindered spread of the gospel. However, Paul indicates explicitly that the apostle has a right of support by the churches, and he supports this conclusion with a word of the Lord (cf. 1 Cor. 9:14 with Luke 10:7Q).[26] His refusal of material support from the Corinthians (cf. 1 Cor. 9:12, 15, 18) secures his own theological independence (cf. 1 Cor. 9:19–23) and demonstrates his theological principle: God's strength is powerful in weakness (cf. 2 Cor. 13:3–4). Paul maintains that powerful deeds also belong to the apostolate; in Corinth, "signs and wonders" occurred (2 Cor. 12:12: σημεῖα καὶ τέρατα)[27] "primarily in healings of the sick, along with conversions accompanied by special circumstances, impressive public appearance in relation to unbelievers, glossolalia, and other pneumatic activities, including miraculous punishments within and outside the church."[28]

For Paul, the call and mission belong exclusively to the Easter event, and thus the characteristics of the apostolate are the capability of establishing, leading, and guiding the church. The special capacity of Paul was that, after the initial preaching and time spent with the church, he remained present with them through coworkers and letters.[29] Paul recognizes the right for financial support and the legitimation through miracles as signs of the apostles but exercises this right only rarely. For him the existence of his churches is the primary seal of his apostleship and his boast at the judgment (cf. 1 Thess. 2:19–20; 1 Cor. 9:2; 2 Cor. 3:2).

Other Concepts of Apostleship

Neither the Lukan nor the Pauline concept of apostleship were completely maintained,[30] for before, beside, and beyond these conceptions, there were independent and/or rival models. In the earliest period of the new movement, the concept of apostleship was concentrated in Jerusalem (cf. 1 Cor. 15:7; Gal. 1:17, 19) but was in no way limited there. On numerous occasions Paul himself indicates that there were before and besides him—other than

---

26. Paul probably knew the traditions of Jesus's missionary discourse in Luke 10Q; 1 Cor. 4:11–13 points to the reference to the word of the Lord in 1 Cor. 9:14 and the metaphor in 1 Cor. 9:10–11; for the analysis, cf. M. Lohmeyer, *Der Apostelbegriff*, 409–35.

27. Cf. Kollmann, "Paulus als Wundertäter."

28. Windisch, *Der zweite Korintherbrief*, 397.

29. In 2 Cor. 8:23 and Phil. 2:25, ἀπόστολος designates a function of someone sent by the church.

30. Cf. M. Lohmeyer, *Der Apostelbegriff*, 120–21.

Peter, "the Twelve," those to whom Jesus appeared (cf. 1 Cor. 15:7; also Gal. 1:19), and James, who was legitimated by being a member of the family of Jesus—other apostles (cf. 1 Cor. 9:5, "as the other apostles"; 1 Cor. 12:28, "for God has established first apostles"; 1 Cor. 15:7, "then Christ appeared to all of the apostles"; Gal. 1:17, "those who were apostles before me"; 1:19, "by the other apostles").

Noteworthy is the couple Andronicus and Junia mentioned in Rom. 16:7:[31] "Greet Andronicus and Junia, my relatives who were with me in prison, who are famous among the apostles and were in Christ before me." Junia, a woman, was probably a liberated slave; likewise, Andronicus may have been a freedman.[32] Inasmuch as they were apostles before Paul, they must have entered the movement of Christ-believers around 31–32 CE. Jerusalem is the likely place; that is, they were, as Jews by birth, members of the Jerusalem church. They could have emigrated from Rome (cf. Acts 2:10) and belonged to the Hellenist group and worked with Paul for a time before returning to Rome. In 2 Cor. 11:23 Paul speaks of many imprisonments so that the place of imprisonment cannot be determined. Similarly, one cannot answer the question of the means by which they became apostles. They could have been witnesses of an Easter appearance (cf. 1 Cor. 15:6–7) or have simply worked as emissaries of a church (cf. ἀπόστολος in 2 Cor. 8:23; Phil. 2:25; Acts 14:4, 14). Certainly the early period of their apostolate suggests an appearance of the Resurrected One. The fact remains that, already before Paul, a woman was an apostle, a historical fact that indicates the noteworthy place of women at the beginning phase of Christianity in general and in the Pauline mission in particular (see below, 8.3). In the logia source (Luke 10:2–16Q)[33] and in 2 Corinthians one cannot find an apostolic concept that can be integrated with the concepts in Luke and Paul. The concept of the one sent in the logia source and the "super-apostles" (cf. 2 Cor. 11:5; 12:11) against whom Paul battled indicates a number of striking agreements: (1) They are (Palestinian) Jews by birth and give value to their origin. Those sent in the Q tradition raise the claim of proclaiming salvation and judgment to their Jewish countrymen (cf. Luke 10:5–12Q). Paul says about his opponents in 2 Cor. 11:22, "Are they Hebrews? So am I! Are they Israelites? So am I! Are they descendants of Abraham? So am I!" (2) They are traveling missionaries who move from church to church (cf. Luke 10:5–8Q; cf. 2 Cor. 11:4: "If someone comes

---

31. Cf. Jewett, *Romans*, 961–64. He convincingly demonstrates that the phrase ἐπίσημοι ἐν τοῖς ἀποστόλοις does not mean "by the apostles," but rather "among the apostles" because the adjective ἐπίσημος always expresses a comparison at the same level.

32. On the questions involving the text and social history, cf. the detailed study by Epp, *Junia*.

33. See Q's reconstruction in Hoffmann and C. Heil, *Die Spruchquelle Q*, 52–57.

to you and . . ."). (3) They apparently understand themselves as "workers" (ἐργάτης) and thus take over an honorific title for early Christian missionaries (cf. Luke 10:2, 7Q; 2 Cor. 11;13; cf. Phil. 3:2). (4) They make a claim for material support from the churches in which they work; they have an apostolic right (cf. Luke 10:4, 7–8Q; 1 Cor. 9:4, 14; 2 Cor. 11:7–9, 20–21; 12:13, 16–18). (5) They perform signs and wonders (cf. Luke 10:9aQ; 2 Cor. 12:12). (6) They proclaim Jesus as eschatological Son of Man and judge (cf. Luke 10:9b, 11, 12, 13–15Q; 2 Cor. 11:4: "If anyone comes and preaches another Jesus than what we proclaimed"), and the opponents in 2 Corinthians apparently do not preach the crucified Jesus but orient themselves primarily to the earthly Jesus, which Paul strongly rejects (cf. 2 Cor. 5:16).

Despite these common features, the most striking difference is that the Q missionaries probably did not claim the title of apostle.[34] Nevertheless, their self-understanding as "sent people" was no less a claim than the title of apostle. The Q missionaries and the opponents of Paul in 2 Corinthians (and Philippians) apparently represented—with differences—an independent concept of apostleship that goes back to the early time of the mission. They oriented themselves primarily to the earthly Jesus whom they identified with the eschatological one to come, and understood themselves as "workers" in the eschatological judgment. They understood themselves to be in possession of the Spirit (cf. Luke 12:10Q; 2 Cor. 11:4) and claimed the right for support. This concept of apostleship is still present at the beginning of the second century CE, for in Did. 11.3–6 strict rules are laid down for traveling apostles and prophets (see below, 10.5.2).

Four basic common features can be observed within the various concepts of the apostle/sent one, in which apostolic function, apostolic authority, and apostolic rights form a unity: The apostle is someone (1) called by God and (2) sent by the earthly Jesus and/or by the Crucified and Resurrected One. (3) The apostles demonstrated their apostleship through signs and wonders and (4) had a right for support from the churches

Peter

Peter is the one from the beginning to whom the Pauline and Lukan concept of apostleship applies in a preeminent way: (a) He is the first disciple to be called (cf. Mark 1:16–17) and leads the circle of disciples of Jesus of Nazareth

34. For additional differences, see M. Lohmeyer, *Der Apostelbegriff*, 428–29.

(cf. Mark 8:29; 9:2). (b) The first appearance of the resurrected Christ that was given to him legitimates him after Easter as the first disciple, as apostle, and as the first leader of the Jerusalem church (cf. Acts 1:13). Five traditions that are independent of each other demonstrate his special place.

1. In 1 Cor. 15:5, Peter becomes the first witness (cf. Luke 24:34) explicitly distinguished from "the Twelve" and listed before them.

2. In Luke 22:31–32, Peter's elevated role at the beginning of the Jerusalem church is indicated by the ancient word, "Simon, Simon, behold, Satan has asked for you in order that he might sift you as one sifts wheat. But I have prayed for you so that your faith does not fail. But you, when you have repented, strengthen your brothers." This passage is a retrospective of the situation of the disciples before the passion of Jesus and ascribes to Peter a special place before and after Easter.

3. Mark 16:7 assumes a first appearance to Peter in Galilee ("Go forth and say to his disciples and to Peter that he will go before you to Galilee; there you will see him, as he had said to you"). In his person Peter combines the two concepts of apostleship mentioned above, composing the ideal: he was an extraordinary companion of the earthly Jesus and at the same time the first witness of the resurrection.

4. Galatians 1:18 indicates the leading role of Peter in Jerusalem. In Paul's first visit to Jerusalem after his call as missionary to the nations, he visits only Cephas for two weeks in order to become acquainted with him; besides that, "he saw only James the brother of the Lord" (Gal. 1:19).

5. In Matt. 16:17–19, Jesus's word to Peter also indicates the position of Peter.[35] The word has a complex structure: (a) The macarism in verse 17 ("Blessed are you, Simon Barjona, for flesh and blood have not revealed [this] to you, but rather my Father in heaven") refers directly to the preceding confession. (b) To the introductory formula in verse 18a, three similarly constructed sayings are appended, which concern the building of the church (v. 18b: "You are Peter, and on this rock I will build my church, and the gates of Hades will not prevail against it"), the conferring of the keys to the kingdom (v. 19a: "I will give to you the keys of the kingdom"), and the giving of authority to bind and loose (v. 19b: "And whatever you bind on earth, will be bound in heaven, and whatever you loose on earth will be loosed in heaven"). A very old tradition may be preserved in verse 18b, for a wordplay with

---

35. In addition to the commentaries, cf. also the analysis by F. Hahn, "Die Petrusverheißung Mt 16,18f."; Hoffmann, "Der Petrus-Primat im Matthäusevangelium."

Πέτρος (Peter) and πέτρα (rock) is present here.[36] The conferring of a name and the meaning of the name are connected, indicating that the name is also associated with the function. The saying may go back to a very early period, but not to Jesus himself, for the phrase μου τὴν ἐκκλησίαν (my congregation/church) presupposes a post-Easter situation. Nevertheless, the text points to Peter as the guarantor of the tradition and prototype of the disciple who confesses Christ and of the Christian teacher.

The book of Acts also depicts the leading place of Peter at the beginning phase of the Jerusalem church. In Acts 1–5, Peter dominates at all levels.[37] (a) Peter calls for the selection of the "twelfth" apostle (Acts 1:15–26) and formulates the criteria for the selection (Acts 1:21–22). (b) Peter initiates the proclamation at the beginning of the Jerusalem church (cf. Acts 2:14–36, Pentecost; 3:12–26, temple sermon; 4:8–12, before the Jewish rulers). (c) Peter formulates the decisive theological insights of the beginning period (cf. Acts 2:38; 4:12; 5:29). (d) Peter demonstrates the power of the Resurrected One through miracles (cf. Acts 3:1–11; 5:9–10). He is, along with Paul, the miracle worker of Acts. (e) Peter's special status is indicated in the phrase "Peter and the apostles" (Acts 2:37; 5:29). Even when the texts in Acts 1–5 are thoroughly shaped by Luke, a historical core of the portrayal undoubtedly exists: Peter, from about 31 to 43 CE, was the first leader of the Jerusalem church and the preeminent figure of the beginning period.

James

Along with Peter in the initial period of the Jerusalem church, James the brother of Jesus emerges (cf. Mark 6:3 par; 1 Cor. 15:7; Gal. 1:19; 2:9, 12; Acts 12:17; 15:13; 21:18; Jude 1).[38] He was not a companion of his brother (cf. Mark 3:21, 31; John 7:3ff.) but rather became a part of the church shortly after the death and resurrection of Jesus Christ. His authority rested on three pillars: (1) James the brother of the Lord was—along with Peter, Mary Magdalene, and Paul—one of the people about whom an acknowledged special revelation of the Resurrected One is reported (cf. 1 Cor. 15:7, "he appeared to James, then to all of the apostles"). In addition to Gal. 1:19 ("I did not see other apostles, except for James, the brother of the Lord"), 1 Cor. 15:7 indicates

---

36. Cf. Lampe, "Das Spiel mit dem Petrusnamen"; Hengel, *Der unterschätzte Petrus*, 21–44.
37. Cf. Böttrich, *Petrus*, 143–57.
38. On the analysis of the texts, cf. Pratscher, *Der Herrenbruder Jakobus*, 13–102.

that James was considered an apostle.[39] (2) James was a physical brother of the Lord, and the blood relationship apparently played an increasing role in his position. (3) James was considered as faithful to the law, that is, he represented a strong Jewish Christian standpoint. This was indicated in the Antioch conflict (see below, 7.6) and the tradition about his death in Josephus (see below, 9.1). All three factors may have contributed to James's emergence as the leading figure of the Jerusalem church. In Paul's first visit to Jerusalem (after his baptism) in the year 35 CE, Peter is apparently the leader of the church. Paul says explicitly in Gal. 1:18 that he went to Jerusalem to meet Cephas and then in verse 19 adds that he saw no other apostles except James. The apostolic council in the year 48 CE indicates a changed situation. Now James, Cephas, and John, according to Gal. 2:9, are the pillars in Jerusalem. The sequence is noteworthy, for now James is listed first. If Cephas was the authority until Paul's first visit to Jerusalem, James the brother of the Lord appears to have become the dominant personality before the apostolic council.[40] This major change was occasioned by the departure of Peter from Jerusalem. According to Acts 12:17–18, Peter fled from Jerusalem circa 43/44 CE because of the persecution by Herod Agrippa (see below, 6.5) and, not coincidentally, he had James informed about it first (Acts 12:17c: "tell James and the brothers"). Moreover, James and Peter probably represented differing theological positions. While Peter was increasingly open to the mission to the gentiles (cf. Acts 10; Gal. 2:12; 1 Cor. 9:5), it was apparently the goal of James to anchor the movement of Christ-believers within Judaism.

The Family of Jesus

Not only James but also other members of the family of Jesus joined the movement of Christ-believers after Easter.[41] The only record of the family of Jesus appears in Mark 6:3: "Is that not the carpenter, the son of Mary and the brother of James, Joses, Judas, and Simon? And do not his sisters live among us?" During the lifetime of Jesus, his relationship with his family was apparently very uneasy, for after his first public activity, according to Mark 3:21, "as his family heard it, they went out to restrain him, for they believed that he was out of his mind!" The reserved relationship to his family is reflected in Mark 3:31–35, where he answers the report that his mother

39. Pratscher, *Der Herrenbruder Jakobus*, 35–46, sees in 1 Cor. 15:7 an old rivalry and a legitimating formula that is intended to legitimate James in relation to Peter and the other apostles. The family relationship to Jesus was not sufficient to justify the special place of James.

40. Cf. Lüdemann, *Paulus, der Heidenapostel*, 67–84; Lüdemann, *Opposition to Paul*, 40–63.

41. On the family of Jesus, cf. Reiprich, *Das Mariageheimnis*, 119–49.

and brothers have come: "Everyone who does the will of God is my brother
and sister and mother." Finally, according to John 7:5, "His brothers did not
believe in him." After Easter, the situation appears to have changed. James
was not the only post-Easter follower of his brother, for Paul speaks in 1 Cor.
9:5 of "the brothers of the Lord," who take their wives along on missionary
journeys. While Joseph disappears into obscurity, Mary, the mother of Jesus,
appears in the story of Jesus, according to Luke 1–2, Matt. 2, and John 2:4;
19:25; according to Acts 1:14, Mary and the brothers of Jesus belong to the
Jerusalem church from the beginning. James in particular, and perhaps also
Mary,[42] presumably connected their family relation to claims of leadership
within the first church.

The Sons of Zebedee

Along with Peter and Andrew, the sons of Zebedee, the second pair of
brothers, followed Jesus from the beginning (cf. Mark 1:19; 3:17; Luke 5:10)
and belonged to the inner circle of disciples (cf. Mark 1:29; 9:2; 13:3; 14:33).
Like Simon, they were fishermen (cf. Luke 5:9–11) and later played a special
role in the Jerusalem church. According to Mark 3:17, they bore the nickname "Boanerges" (Βοανηργές), that is, "Sons of Thunder." Inasmuch as
thunder is a feature of epiphanies in the OT, this designation suggests that
God reveals himself in the activities of the two brothers.[43] Mark 10:35–41
presupposes the simultaneous martyrdom of the two sons of Zebedee, but
it may be a *vaticinium ex eventu*: according to Acts 12:2, James the son of
Zebedee was executed under Agrippa I around 42/43 CE (see below, 6.5);
according to Gal. 2:9 his brother John is one of the three pillars of the Jerusalem church in the year 48 CE. Thus he could not have died together
with his brother James. Within the Jerusalem church the significance of
John appears to have been greater, for James is not mentioned anywhere
but in the list of disciples in Acts 1:13 and the reference to his death in
12:2. In contrast to James, John the son of Zebedee appears in Acts 3:1,
3, 4, 11; 4:13, 19 as a leading figure of the earliest period. He is, like Peter,
a proclaimer and stands with him before the high council. In addition,
Acts 8:14 and especially Gal. 2:9 attest to the influence of John the son of
Zebedee in the early history of Christianity. John is counted, along with
Peter and James, as the three "pillars" of the Jerusalem church. The word
στῦλος (pillar) appears also in 1 Tim. 3:15; Rev. 3:12; 10:1, where it refers
to the pillars of the Jerusalem temple. This could also have an overtone for

42. J. Becker, *Maria: Mutter Jesu.*
43. Cf. A. Collins, *Mark*, 220.

the background of the metaphor in Gal. 2:9. A broader understanding is present in 1 Clem. 5.2, where Peter and Paul are called "the greatest and most righteous pillars."[44] In any case, it is an honorific title that emphasizes the significance of a person or group of persons who are foundational. John the son of Zebedee was such a foundational person, even if we know nothing about his theology.

Barnabas

Another preeminent personality of the Jerusalem church was Barnabas (see below, 6.2), who, according to Acts 4:36, was a Levite from Cyprus and a Greek-speaking Jew; he probably stood close to the circle of Hellenists. It is reported of him that he sold a field in Jerusalem and placed the money at the disposal of the church (Acts 4:36–37). The reserve with which this story is told suggests its historical reliability, especially since it stands in tension with the general community of goods mentioned in Acts 2:45; in Acts 4:37 Barnabas's action is specifically emphasized. The special significance of Barnabas, however, lies elsewhere. He was apparently the contact person between two of the most important churches in the earliest period: Jerusalem and Antioch. According to Acts 11:22ff., Barnabas was the representative of the Jerusalem church in his visit to the church in Antioch, which had been established by the Hellenists. He brought Paul to Antioch (Acts 11:25–26) and introduced him to the church. As a leading personality (cf. Acts 13:1), from Antioch he undertook the first missionary journey with Paul and represented the Antiochian church at the apostolic council in Jerusalem in the year 48 CE. Inasmuch as he participated crucially in the resolution of difficult fundamental questions, such as the mission to the gentiles apart from circumcision, one may assume that he was highly regarded in Jerusalem and later in Antioch as a significant missionary and theologian (and apostle?).

One cannot yet speak of a structure of offices in the early Jerusalem church, although there were influential individuals (especially Peter, James the brother of the Lord) and groups (especially the "Twelve," the apostles, the family of Jesus). Personal position with respect to the earthly Jesus finally prevailed, resulting in an increasing role for Peter and John the son of Zebedee, and then finally for James the brother of the Lord.

---

44. Cf. Euripides, *Iphigenia Taurica* 57, where the sons appear as "στῦλοι of the house."

5.3 Places: The Temple

The Jerusalem temple, first built presumably under Solomon (ca. 965–926/25 BCE), was destroyed by the Babylonians in 587/86 BCE (cf. 2 Kings 25:9).[45] After the exile the temple was rebuilt (ca. 520–515 BCE); from the fourth century BCE, it increasingly became the center of religious, cultural, and economic life in Judea. Under Herod the temple was modified and enlarged into a magnificent building in 20/19 BCE, the area of land extending to almost 1,550,000 square feet (144,000 m²).

Several theological concepts were associated with the temple cult, especially the idea of the throne of God or of his name in the most holy place (cf. 1 Kings 8:12ff.); God appears in the temple (cf. Lev. 16:2) and may be met there (cf. Exod. 29:43–45). The temple is the place of the ark of the covenant (cf. 2 Sam. 6; 1 Kings 8:1–6) and of the kingship of God (cf. Pss. 24; 68). In the postexilic period, the motif of holiness takes on increased meaning. Only the high priest was permitted to enter on the Day of Atonement (cf. Lev. 16). Because of the holiness of the temple, non-Jews were forbidden to enter the actual temple area (cf. Philo, *Legat.* 212; Acts 21:27–29; Josephus, *J.W.* 6.126).

Because there was no free flow of capital or banking system in antiquity, the temple always served as an economic and administrative center and, as a rule, had a temple treasury. This treasury in Jerusalem consisted of vessels for the temple cult and materials for sacrifice (cf. 1 Chron. 26:20; 28:12) as well as spoils of war and gifts to the Jerusalem kings (cf. 2 Sam. 8:11; 1 Kings 7:51). Regular receipts included the temple tax and the tithe collection. The temple tax had to be paid by every male Israelite beginning in the twentieth year of life. Included also was the tax from the diaspora[46] of one-third or one-half shekel (cf. Exod. 30:11–16; Neh. 10:33–34; 2 Chron. 24:9). The tithe in Jerusalem served especially for the care (cf. Neh. 10:38) of the priests, Levites, gatekeepers, singers, and temple servants who were on official duty at and in the temple.[47] In addition, private and state funds were stored in the temple. There were also further revenues, for example, from landed estates (e.g., Philo, *Spec. Laws* 1.76). As a cultic center, the temple was the destination of numerous pilgrims who came to the major festivals, for every Jew was obligated to come to Jerusalem at Passover, the Festival of Weeks, and the Feast of Tabernacles, to offer

45. Cf. Zwickel, "Tempel."
46. Cf. Philo, *Spec. Laws* 1.76–78.
47. According to Jeremias, *Jerusalem in the Time of Jesus*, 203–6, in the time of Jesus there were in Israel ca. 7,200 priests and ca. 9,600 Levites. They served at the temple every twenty-four weeks, and at the three great festivals about 300 priests and Levites served. Inasmuch as their cultic activities were limited to two weeks and the three great festivals, they otherwise performed their tasks in their home area and engaged in their occupation (primarily handwork).

a sacrifice there (cf. Deut. 16:1–17). At the festivals the number of inhabitants of Jerusalem grew considerably.[48] Consequently, the necessary infrastructure for accommodating and supplying the people as well as providing the great number of sacrificial animals had a great economic impact on Jerusalem.[49]

Against this background, one can understand why the cleansing of the temple by Jesus (Mark 11:15–18 par.)[50] was understood, especially by the Sadducees but also by the Romans, as an act against the cultic, political, and economic order. The extent of the cleansing of the temple cannot be precisely reconstructed, but Jesus appears to have acted with force against (some) animal sellers and money changers. Closely associated with the temple cleansing was the threatening word against the temple, the core of which is shaped by Mark: "Here no stone will be left on another that will not be torn down."[51] The temple cleansing and the word about the temple do not aim at the restoration of a new temple cult that is pleasing to God, like the one that was expected in the history of Judaism.[52] Rather, Jesus expected that with the present and approaching kingdom of God, the temple had lost its function as the place for the sacrifice for sins. Because the rule of evil is coming to an end, there is no longer a need for sacrifice. Thus when members of the Jerusalem church assembled in and around the temple, as Acts reports (cf. Acts 2:46, "and they were daily of one accord together in the temple"), and taught in the temple (cf. Acts 5:20–21), one is not surprised that the Sadducees also proceeded against the followers of Jesus.

5.4 Conflicts

The violent death of Jesus did not signify the end of his message or his movement. To the contrary, very early and openly Jesus of Nazareth, the Crucified

48. Cf. Jeremias, *Jerusalem in the Time of Jesus*, 83–84; he argues that the population of Jerusalem (ca. 25,000–30,000) multiplied during the festivals in Jerusalem. In recent research, the population is estimated to be considerably higher (cf. Riesner, *Zwischen Tempel und Obergemach*, 69–70), probably as many as 60,000, to which were added tens of thousands during the festivals. Söllner, "Jerusalem," 155.

49. Cf. Philo, *Spec. Laws* 1.69: "Thousands and thousands stream from thousands of cities, some over the sea, and others over land, from East and West, from North and South, to every festival to the sanctuary."

50. Cf. Söding, "Die Tempelaktion Jesu"; Paesler, *Das Tempelwort Jesu*, 233–49; Ådna, *Jesu Stellung zum Tempel*, 300–333.

51. Cf. the argument of Paesler, *Das Tempelwort Jesu*, 76–92 (Mark 14:58 is a post-Easter variant of the original statement in Mark 13:2).

52. Cf. Paesler, *Das Tempelwort Jesu*, 244: "a visual demonstration of the nullification and revocation of the Jerusalem cult."

One, was proclaimed as the Messiah of Israel and the Son of God. This called for action from old and new opponents. Twice it is reported that apostles had to appear before the Sanhedrin (Acts 4:1–22; 5:17–42). They were beaten and forbidden to speak anymore in the name of Jesus (Acts 5:40). From the beginning the Christ-believers in Jerusalem were regarded as a religiously illegitimate and politically destabilizing movement.

The Sadducees as Opponents of the New Movement

The passion narrative indicates clearly that the Sadducees were the most tenacious opponents of Jesus. In the reports about the decision to put Jesus to death, the Sadduceean ἀρχιερεῖς (chief priests, high priest) took the lead (cf. Mark 11:18, 27; 14:1; 15:31; Matt. 26:3; Luke 22:2). A secondary role is placed by the scribes (cf. Mark 11:18; 14:1; 15:31; Matt. 21:15; Luke 22:2) and/ or the elders (Matt. 26:3 and passim; Acts 4:23; 23:14; 25:15). This hostility continued, for according to Acts 4:1, the Sadducees joined the priests and the captain of the temple guard,[53] who proceeded against the Christ-believers. According to Acts 5:17, the opponents are the high priest "and all who were with him, that is, the party of the Sadducees."

The origins of the Sadducees (Σαδδουκαῖοι) lie in obscurity. According to textual witnesses, the Sadducees may be traced back to Zadok, a leading priest at the time of David who is mentioned in 2 Sam. 15:24, 27, 29, 35; 17:15; 19:11. In the conflict over the successor to David, the priest Zadok stood on the side of Solomon and anointed him to be king (1 Kings. 1:32ff.) and became high priest in Jerusalem (1 Kings. 2:35). After the Babylonian exile, a Zadokite priest took over the office of high priest that was being reconstituted (cf. Hag. 1:1 with 1 Chron. 5:40, where Joshua ben Jehozadak is identified as a Zadokite; cf. also Ezek. 40:46). The Zadokites presumably held the office of high priest until the conflicts under Antiochus IV. With the usurpation of the office of high priest by the Maccabees, a twofold development occurred. On one hand, the Zadokites fled from Jerusalem and joined the opposition to the Jerusalem temple; thus, among others, the Teacher of Righteousness was probably a former high priest and thus a follower of Zadok.[54] Important Zadokite traditions are present in the Qumran literature (cf. CD 4.2–4, "The priests are the converts of Israel, who departed from the land of Judah, and the Levites are those who joined them. The sons of Zadok are the elect of Israel, the men called by name, and will stand at the end of days"; cf. also

53. On the Sadducees, cf. Schürer, *History of the Jewish People*, 2:404–14; Meyer, "Σαδδου-καῖος," *TDNT* 7:35–54.
54. Cf. H. Stegemann, *Die Essener, Qumran*, 205–6.

1QS 5.2.2; 1QSa 1.2, 24; 2.3). On the other side stood the great majority of
the Zadokite families who remained in Jerusalem. They were the religious,
economic, and political leading priestly aristocratic families, the influential
religious party of the Sadducees, who had great power at their disposal in
the Sanhedrin. Josephus confirms this when he says of the Sadducees, "They
win over only the wealthy for themselves; they do not have the people on their
side."[55] "This teaching reached but few, but these are men with the highest
standing."[56]

The hostility of the Sadducees against the Christ-believers may be accurately described in Acts 4:2: "They proclaimed in Jesus the resurrection
from the dead." This was a provocation for the Sadducees in two ways: (1) In
contrast to the Pharisees, the Sadducees rejected the doctrine of the resurrection of the dead (cf. Josephus, *J.W.* 2.164, "They reject the continuance of
the soul and the punishment and reward in Hades"; cf. Mark 12:18–27).[57] It
is no coincidence that the appearance of the Sadducees in Acts (cf. Acts 4:1–
22; 5:17–42; 23:6–9) is always connected to the question of the resurrection.
(2) When the Christ-believers proclaimed the resurrection of one crucified
by the Romans, they also endangered the relationship between the Jews and
the Romans. As a leading political group, it was incumbent on the Sadducees
to get along with the occupying Roman power (cf. Acts 5:28). In the year 62
CE the stoning of the conservative James the brother of the Lord, which was
initiated by a Sadducean high priest (see below, 9.1), further confirms the
enduring hostility of the Sadducees to the new movement.

Paul as Persecutor

The Pharisees were also hostile to the Christ-believers. Once more one
finds continuity with the ministry of Jesus, for alongside positive encounters
between Jesus and the Pharisees, there are many texts reporting conflicts

---

55. Josephus, *Ant.* 13.298.

56. Josephus, *Ant.* 18.17, trans. Schürer, *History of the Jewish People*, 2:404.

57. In addition, there are two other important differences from the teaching of the Pharisees reported by Josephus. (1) In the traditional understanding, "I want to make clear that the
Pharisees had passed down to the people certain regulations handed down by former generations and not recorded in the Laws of Moses, and thus they [these regulations] are rejected
by the Sadducean group, who hold that only those regulations should be considered valid
which were written down in the law of Moses, and that those written by the traditions of the
fathers need not be observed" (*Ant.* 13.297.2 LCL). (2) On the question of the freedom of the
will, "the Sadducees, the second of the orders, do away with Fate altogether, and move God
beyond, not only the commission, but the very sight of evil. They affirm rather that man has a
free choice of good and evil, and that it rests with each man's will whether he follows the one
or the other" (*J.W.* 2.164 LCL).

between Jesus and the Pharisees (cf. Mark 2:13–17, 23–28; 3:1–6). Thus it is not surprising that after Easter radical Pharisees, especially Paul, proceeded in their opposition to the new movement of Christ-believers.

The reports about his activities as a persecutor belong to the oldest traditions about Paul. Very early, the churches in Judea heard from another church: "The one who once persecuted us . . . proclaims the faith that he once tried to destroy" (Gal. 1:23). Similarly stereotypical is the report of the apostle in 1 Cor. 15:9; Gal. 1:13, and Phil. 3:6 that he had persecuted the church, that is, the church of God. Paul apparently recalls his activity as a persecutor in instances where his apostolate is disputed. In the conflict with the opponents, Paul says of his activity as a persecutor that only God could bring about the change from a merciless persecutor of Christians to the worldwide proclaimer of the gospel.[58] While Paul offers no specific information about the place and manner of his activity as a persecutor, Acts graphically describes the action of Paul against the Jerusalem church. Paul went from house to house in the Jerusalem church and had men and women thrown into prison (Acts 8:3); he gave the sentence of death against Christians (cf. Acts 22:4; 26:10) and forced them to recant their faith (cf. Acts 26:11). He arranged the beating of Christians (Acts 22:19) and legitimated the persecution of Christians in Damascus (Acts 9:2). The dark portrayal of the merciless persecutor Paul certainly goes back to Luke so that he can let the deeds of the apostle to the gentiles shine brightly.[59]

Where did Paul persecute the first churches of Christ-believers? Both Luke and his traditions (cf. Acts 8:3; 9:1c–2; 22:19) presuppose Jerusalem as the place of the persecution. Galatians 1:22, however, explicitly says, "I was unknown by sight to the churches in Judea." It was only from the other churches that the Christ-believers heard that the former persecutor now preached the faith (Gal. 1:23). Paul always includes Judea with Jerusalem (cf. 2 Cor. 1:16; Rom. 15:31), and thus the Jewish metropolis may be excluded as the place of Paul's persecution.[60] Otherwise one must explain how the unrelenting persecutor remained unknown to the first churches! This problem cannot be resolved through the assumption that Paul persecuted only the "Hellenists"

58. Cf. Dietzfelbinger, *Die Berufung des Paulus*, 6.

59. On the analysis of the texts, cf. Löning, *Die Saulustradition in der Apostelgeschichte*, 12–25, 93–95; Burchard, *Der dreizehnte Zeuge*, 40–51, cf. 50f.: "The persecution taken over and accomplished by Paul against all Christians in Jerusalem and presumably leading to execution or recantation is essentially a Lucan construction."

60. Contra Hengel and Schwemer, *Paul between Damascus and Antioch*, 37–39, who maintain Jerusalem as the place of persecution and the persecuted "Hellenists" as the origin of the tradition in Gal. 1:23.

in Jerusalem but not the Aramaic-speaking members of the church.[61] Indeed, there was a relatively independent church of Christ-believing diaspora Jews in Jerusalem, whose leaders are mentioned in Acts 6:5, and which developed an independent mission after the death of Stephen (cf. Acts 8:4ff.; 11:19ff.). If the persecution by Paul had been a purely internal matter of the Greek-speaking synagogue in Jerusalem, it would still not explain why the Aramaic-speaking Christ-believing Jews had not learned anything about it. Against this view, one must consider the modest number of Christ-believers in Jerusalem and the close contact between both sides.[62] Moreover, the theological profiles of both groups were not so different that only one would face systematic persecutions while the other remained fully unaffected! Galatians 1:17 offers a suggestion about the place of persecution. Here the apostle mentions that, after his call, he did not go directly to Jerusalem but instead went into Arabia and then again to Damascus. He was thus in Damascus before or at his conversion, where he probably acted against the local Christ-believing community and attempted to carry out punishments in the synagogue.[63] "There where he acts against the message of Jesus, he is won over to it."[64]

Paul justifies his activity as persecutor in Gal. 1:13–14 and Phil. 3:5–6 by recalling his former life in Judaism and his zeal for the traditions of the fathers.[65] Thus Paul stands in the tradition of the Jewish zeal for the Torah, which defended the Torah as the all-encompassing norm of Jewish life, following the example of Elijah (cf. 1 Kings. 18:40; 19:10, 14) and Phinehas (cf. Num. 25:7–11; cf. Sir. 48:2; 1 Macc. 2:54, 58). The zeal for the Torah as the preeminent characteristic of the Jewish way of life was not unique

61. Contra Hengel, *Pre-Christian Paul*, 68–71; Niebuhr, *Heidenapostel aus Israel*, 58–59; Kraus, *Zwischen Jerusalem und Antiochia*, 40.

62. Cf. Dietzfelbinger, *Die Berufung des Paulus*, 21–22. Those who argue against a Pauline persecuting activity in Jerusalem include, among others, Conzelmann, *Geschichte des Urchristentums*, 65; Schneemelcher, *Das Urchristentum*, 107; L. Schenke, *Die Urgemeinde*, 186; J. Becker, *Paul*, 60–61.

63. The depiction in Acts 9:1–2, according to which Paul was commissioned by the high priest in Jerusalem to arrest the followers of the new movement and bring them back to Jerusalem, is historically improbable because no legal foundation existed for him to carry out this activity over several governmental regions; cf. Hengel and Schwemer, *Paul between Damascus and Antioch*, 80–81. Since the church in Damascus understood itself within the local group of synagogues there around 32/33, it is plausible that Paul attempted to carry out synagogue punishments (admonishment, imposition of a ban, beating, exclusion) there.

64. Dietzfelbinger, *Die Berufung des Paulus*, 22. For Damascus as the place of the persecution, see also Haenchen, *Acts*, 320–21; Suhl, *Paulus und seine Briefe*, 26–27, 30; Schneemelcher, *Das Urchristentum*, 136; G. Strecker, "Der vorchristliche Paulus," 730; J. Becker, *Paul*, 60–62; H. Betz, "Paul," *ABD* 5:187; Lüdemann, *Die ersten drei Jahre Christentum*, 11–12; D.-A. Koch, *Geschichte des Urchristentums*, 207–10.

65. Cf. Schröder, *Die "väterlichen Gesetze."*

to the militant Zealots but also defined the Essenes (cf. 1QS 4.5–6, 17–18) and radical Pharisees such as Paul. The manner of Paul's actions against the Christ-believers is indicated with the verb πορθεῖν (destroy; Gal. 1:13, 23; Acts 9:21), which apparently involves violent activities (cf. Josephus, J.W. 4.405).[66]

What led to Paul's activity as a persecutor? Probably the proclamation of the Christ-believers that a crucified man was the Messiah of Israel appeared to the Pharisee who was zealous for the law as a *skandalon*.[67] The significance of the cross of Jesus Christ for Pauline theology (cf., e.g., 1 Cor. 1:17–18, 23; 2:2, 8; Gal. 3:1; 5:11, 14; 6:14; Rom. 6:6; Phil. 2:8; 3:18) indicates that what Paul once considered an offense became the center of his proclamation. According to Deut. 21:23, the one who "has been hanged on a tree" is under the curse of God. In 11QT^a 64.15–20, this curse is transferred to the one who is executed on a cross.[68] The proclamation by the Christ-believers of Jesus of Nazareth as Messiah, the one who died as a blasphemer, was unbearable for Paul, for it called into question the foundation of his faith. Galatians 3:13 confirms this interpretation, for here Paul the Christian reinterpreted Deut. 21:23 LXX and arrived at the insight: Christ took the curse of the law upon himself and thus redeemed us from the curse. God did not put Christ under the curse, for Jesus, the innocent one, took the curse of the law/the Torah upon himself for our sake.[69] The concept of a crucified Messiah must have been for Paul not only absurd but also a blasphemy against the holiness of God and thus a conflict with Jewish faith. Therefore, he especially denied the right of existence of the followers of Jesus Christ within the group of synagogues. Thus what followed was probably an organizational dynamic among synagogues; that is, the Christ-believers were increasingly an identifiable group, which through its own rituals (baptism, Lord's Supper) and continuing popularity transcended the boundaries of Judaism as they were understood in the synagogue.[70]

---

66. On the manner of forced measures and punishment in the synagogue, see Str-B 4.1:292ff.

67. Undoubtedly, from the Jewish perspective, not all crucified people were cursed by God (correctly argues G. Friedrich, *Die Verkündigung des Todes Jesu*, 122–30), for Jewish martyrs had also been crucified (cf., e.g., Philo, *Flaccus* 27, 83–85). Of course, the concept of a crucified Messiah stands outside the Jewish perspective, as Justin's *Dialogue with Trypho* indicates (cf. *Dial.* 90.1, where Trypho says, "You must prove to us whether he had to be crucified and die such a shameful and dishonorable death, cursed in the law, for such a claim we would never consider").

68. Cf. 11QT^a 64.7–8, 12–13: "When a man . . . curses his people, the Israelites should hang him upon the tree so that he dies, . . . cursed by God, and the man is the one who hangs on a tree, and you should not desecrate the land that I give you as an inheritance."

69. Paul cites Deut. 21:23 LXX with two significant changes; he leaves out ὑπὸ θεοῦ and changes the perfective passive κεκατηραμένος into the passive ἐπικατάρατος (cf. Deut. 27:26 LXX).

70. According to D.-A. Koch, *Geschichte des Urchristentums*, 211, the movement beyond the boundaries of Judaism was already taking place in Damascus, for "through the baptism

The early hostility of the Sadducees and the persecution by Paul indicate that this alternative version of Judaism practiced by the Jerusalem church was regarded critically and was fought against. The later departure of Christ-believers/Christians from Judaism was in no way a one-sided process; rather it was also driven from the Jewish side!

5.5 Theological Institutions and Discourse

Baptism and the Lord's Supper belonged among the first basic aspects of the institutionalization of the Christ-believers in Jerusalem (and Galilee). Because rituals are concentrations of religious worldviews,[71] baptism and the Lord's Supper became the catalysts of a new identity. The ritual expresses the theological and social construction of the new man "in Christ."[72]

Baptism

The baptism of Jesus in the Jordan by John the Baptist (cf. Mark 1:9–11 par.) may explain why from the beginning the early churches practiced baptism as the normative rite of initiation. The ritual washings at Qumran (cf. 1QS 2.25–3.12; 1QS 6.16–17; 5.13), proselyte baptism (cf. Sifre, Bamidbar 108; b. Ker. 9a), and the washings in some mystery cults (cf. Apuleius, *Metamorphoses* 11.33) indicate a few analogies, but these cannot be considered as a historical presupposition and source for early Christian baptism.

After Easter the opinion apparently prevailed that the announcements of the Baptist were unexpectedly fulfilled with the event around Jesus of Nazareth. In this continuity of the eschatological new reality, one finds the deepest reason for the adoption of the practice of baptism that originated with John the Baptist. The continuity of the baptism of John is indicated in the characteristic features of early Christian baptismal practice: (1) The early Christian baptism is not a self-baptism but rather was carried out by a baptizer (cf. 1 Cor. 1:14, 16; Acts 8:38; 10:48). (2) Like the baptism practiced by John the Baptist, the baptism among Christians was a once-for-all act and is thus distinguished from the ritual washings in ancient Judaism and Hellenism.

---

of individual sympathizers to Judaism, the boundary of the people of God was taken away, an arbitrary act that no traditions of the fathers permitted, but rather was contrary to all fundamental Pharisaic convictions (as well as others)."

71. On ritual theory, cf. Turner, *Ritual Process*.

72. Cf. Theissen, "Die urchristliche Taufe," 107ff.

(3) Early Christian baptism was probably practiced in running water (cf. Acts 8:38; Did. 7.1ff.). (4) As with John's baptism, Christian baptism was for the forgiveness of sins (cf. 1 Cor. 6:11; Acts 2:38) and thus had an eschatological and a soteriological dimension.

At the same time the baptism of the Christ-believers differed from John's baptism in a threefold way: (a) It understands the Christ event as the eschatological saving moment that is present in the baptism "in the name of the Lord Jesus"/"in the name of Jesus Christ." Several old formulaic expressions give evidence of a baptismal practice that attaches a central meaning to the "name of Jesus": εἰς τὸ ὄνομα τοῦ κυρίου (in the name of the Lord Jesus, Acts 8:16; 19:5; cf. 1 Cor. 1:13, 15; Gal. 3:27; Rom. 6:3; Matt. 28:19); ἐν τῷ ὀνόματι Ἰησοῦ Χριστοῦ (in the name of Jesus Christ, Acts 10:48; cf. 1 Cor. 6:11); ἐπὶ τῷ ὀνόματι Ἰησοῦ Χριστοῦ (in the name of Jesus Christ, Acts 2:38). A precise linguistic derivation of these formulaic phrases can be found neither in pagan Hellenism nor in the LXX.[73] Rather, its variability and breadth of content suggest that it is to be considered a specific early Christian formation that was founded on the resurrection of Jesus Christ from the dead and finds its meaning in the respective literary contexts. As a supporting thought, behind all of the phrases was a fundamental experience. Through the baptism in the name of Jesus, the one who was baptized was conveyed to Jesus Christ, brought into the messianic community of salvation, and sacramentally sealed in anticipation of the coming world judgment. In the saying of the name of κύριος Ἰησοῦς Χριστός, God's saving work is present in baptism and from this point onward defines the life of the one who is baptized. (b) Early Christian baptism is connected to the gift of the Spirit. The experience of the presence of the Spirit in the event of baptism not only marks the difference from the baptism of John but also distinguishes the center of Christian baptismal theology (cf. Mark 1:8; Acts 1:5; 8:14–25; 9:17–18; 11:16; 1 Cor. 6:11; 12:13; 2 Cor. 1:21–22; Gal. 5:24–25; Rom. 5:5; John 3:5). The Spirit separates the person from the power of sin, confers righteousness (cf. 1 Cor. 1:30; 6:11; Rom. 3:25), and determines the new life as the effective power of God (cf. Rom. 8:1–11). (c) In baptism the believer is incorporated into the eschatological community of salvation. Those who are baptized now live in the unity of the body of Christ (1 Cor. 12:13) and already participate in the power of the coming world (cf. 2 Cor. 1:22; 5:5; Rom. 8:23).

73. Cf. the variety of positions, as in Heitmüller, *"Im Namen Jesu"*; Delling, *Die Zueignung des Heils in der Taufe*. On the recent discussion, cf. Schnelle, *Gerechtigkeit und Christusgegenwart*, 37–46, 178–83; Hartmann, *Auf den Namen des Herrn Jesus*, 39–52.

The distinction between (John's) baptism with water and the baptism of the Spirit (cf. Acts 1:5; 11:16; 18:25; 19:3–6) in Acts serves as the demonstration of the superiority of Christian baptism in salvation history. With this distinction, Luke can depict the connection between baptism "in the name of Jesus," reception of the Spirit, forgiveness of sins (Acts 2:38; 22:16), and the unity of the apostolic church. It is now self-evident that those who come to faith are immediately baptized (cf. Acts 2:41; 8:12–13, 26–40; 9:18; 10:47–48; 16:33; 18:8; 22:16). Very early within the baptismal celebration, evidently, the reception of the Spirit was coordinated with the laying on of hands. This offered Luke the possibility of connecting the preceding baptism with the laying on of hands by an apostle and demonstrating the continuing connection with the Jerusalem church. For Luke, the laying on of hands, the conveying of the Spirit, and baptism belong closely together, even if the laying on of hands can precede baptism (Acts 9:17–19; 10:44–48) or follow it (Acts 8:4–25; 19:1–7).[74]

Early Christian baptism was both historically (onetime immersion in running water) and theologically (forgiveness of sins, participation in the saving event) a new ritual. It could take place either before or during the normal worship service. Undoubtedly, baptism took a central place in forming the identity of the new movement; now besides circumcision, baptism was another initiatory rite in which also women (and children?)[75] participated and in which fundamental theological reflection was connected. As a ritual that transformed status, baptism not only effected a new perception of reality, but the baptized person and reality itself also changed.[76]

The Lord's Supper

As with the case of baptism, with the Lord's Supper also an impulse from the life of Jesus was of decisive meaning for the development of the

74. On the statements connected to baptism, cf. Avemarie, *Die Tauferzählungen der Apostelgeschichte.*

75. At the time of the New Testament, the baptism of adults was practiced; children in antiquity were legally and religiously not of age. For a different view, see Lindemann, commenting on ἐκτρέφετε αὐτὰ ἐν παιδείᾳ καὶ νουθεσίᾳ κυρίου (Eph. 6.4): "Kinder in der Welt des frühen Christentums." On the basis of Mark 10:13–16; 1 Cor. 1:16 ("house of Stephanus"), and Eph. 6:4, he maintains that the baptism of children (not babies) is historically possible.

76. On the perspective of cultural anthropology, cf. Geertz, "Thick Description," 122: "Having ritually 'leapt' . . . into the framework of meaning which religious conceptions define, and the ritual ended, returned again to the common-sense world, a man is—unless, as sometimes happens, the experience fails to register—changed. And as he is changed, so also is the common-sense world, for it is now seen as but the partial form of a wider reality which corrects and completes it."

sacrament.[77] Jesus's last meal with his disciples in Jerusalem directly before his arrest (cf. 1 Cor. 11:23c) is probably historical. This meal took on a special character because of Jesus's consciousness that he would die. Jesus associated his impending death apparently with the expectation that the kingdom of God would fully come (Mark 14:25: "Truly, I say to you, I will certainly not drink of this fruit of the vine until that day when I drink it anew in the kingdom of God").[78] The reference to the dying of Jesus could not be considered detached from this unique relation to God and his developed knowledge of God, which was demonstrated especially in his proclamation of the kingdom of God and his miracles. Jesus's consciousness of his exalted role required an interpretation of the impending event! This interpretation could not stand in simple continuity with the meals of the earthly Jesus, for the impending death raised the larger question about the meaning of his mission. A central significance was attached to his person, for already the presence of the kingdom of God and the miracles depended on it (cf. Luke 11:20). Correspondingly, the imminent event required an interpretation in view of the person of Jesus, which only he himself could give.[79] Jesus probably understood his death as a sacrifice for the "many" (cf. Mark 10:45b), based on Isaiah 53.[80] The death thus stood in continuity with the life of the earthly Jesus, who came and lived "for others." Jesus verbalized this sacrifice in the course of the last meal metaphorically in the words of institution: τοῦτο ἐστιν τὸ σῶμά μου (this is my body) and τοῦτο ἐστιν τὸ αἷμα . . . ὑπὲρ πολλῶν (this is my blood . . . for many).

These words of interpretation are not oriented to what is essential in the foreground of the Passover meal but take on another dimension: The common participation in drinking from the cup could indicate that Jesus, before his death, wanted the fellowship that he had established to continue beyond his death. Jesus thus celebrated the last meal in the consciousness that the kingdom of God would come and with it the judgment. He gives his life in order that "the many" will receive salvation at the end. Jesus's expectation of the coming of the ultimate revelation of the kingdom of God with his death was not fulfilled (cf. Mark 15:34). With the resurrection from the dead, God acted on him in an unexpected way, but also in continuity: Jesus's death is and remains the saving act of God for "the many."

77. On the concept in 1 Cor. 11:20, Paul calls the celebration of the meal a κυριακὸν δεῖπνον (Lord's Supper); Luke repeatedly speaks of the breaking of bread (cf. Acts 2:42, 46; 20:7–12).

78. The pre-Easter origin of Mark 14:25 is indicated by the fact that Jesus's fate does not stand in the midpoint, but rather the kingdom of God is the focus. Cf. Merklein, "Erwägungen zur Überlieferungsgeschichte," 170–74. He correctly maintains that Mark 14:25 is the hermeneutical key to the question of the Last Supper.

79. Cf. Schürmann, "Jesu Tod im Licht seines Basileia-Verständnisses."

80. On Mark 10:45b, cf. Roloff, "Anfänge der soteriologischen Deutung," 129–41.

From the perspective after Easter, the Last Supper became an occasion for thanksgiving and praise (cf. 1 Cor. 11:17–24; Mark 14:22, 23) as well as a sign of fulfillment and remembrance (1 Cor. 11:24–25; Luke 22:19, "in memory of me") of the one who suffered for others (Mark 14:24, "poured out for the many"; Luke 22:20, "poured out for you"). In the power of the Holy Spirit, the Resurrected One in the present is himself the living and powerful subject of his memory; he is the founder of a new covenant (1 Cor. 11:25; Luke 22:20), whose saving work ("my body"/"my blood") can receive the believing community. The κύριος Ἰησοῦς (Jesus the Lord, 1 Cor. 11:23) is known as the coming Lord of humanity and of the world (1 Cor. 11:26: "you proclaim the death of the Lord until he comes"; cf. Mark 14:25). Despite the various formulations of this basic idea, all traditions of the Lord's Supper are shaped by this basic concept. The reference to the "breaking of bread" in Acts 2:42, 46 gives no direct information about the basic form of the Lord's Supper in the Jerusalem church. However, Luke indicates what he presupposes for Jerusalem: community worship in house churches with liturgical elements such as "breaking of bread" and prayer (cf. 2:42, 46) connected with a common meal (cf. v. 46b) and an eschatological perspective (v. 46b, "with rejoicing").

The pre-Pauline tradition preserves a more precise view into the early Christian practice of the Lord's Supper in 1 Cor. 11:23–36: "I received from the Lord what I delivered to you: In the night in which he was betrayed, the Lord Jesus took bread, blessed it, broke it and said, 'This is my body, which (was given) for you. Do this in my memory!' In the same way, after supper, he took the cup and said: 'This cup is the new covenant in my blood; do this, as often as you drink it, in my memory.' For as often as you eat this bread and drink this cup, you proclaim the death of the Lord until he comes." In Corinth the sacramental action was connected with a common meal, and originally the action with the bread and cup provided the frame for the meal (μετὰ τὸ δειπνῆσαι, after supper, in 1 Cor. 11:25; cf. also Acts 22:20). The gesture and the word over the bread initiated the common meal; the gesture and word over the cup concluded it; between the two acts, a full meal took place. This initial practice gave way to meals before the sacramental activity. Consequently, the distinctions between poor and rich members of the congregation emerged, and one group feasted while the other group hungered (cf. 1 Cor. 11:21–22, 33–34). As in pagan sacrificial meals, table fellowship occurred among the wealthy, while the poor were excluded. This development is sharply criticized by Paul (1 Cor. 11:17–22); he argues for a separation of the meals from the celebration of the Lord's Supper (1 Cor. 11:22: "Do you not have houses to eat and drink in?"). The realism of the Pauline understanding of the sacrament and the thought of the purity of the church are noteworthy, as 1 Cor. 11:30 indicates: Because some participate in the Lord's Supper in an unworthy manner, many in the church are weak and sick, and some have died. Here Paul makes a direct connection between the participation in the sacrament and the fate of the people. Undoubtedly, the basis of this statement is the concept that unworthy participation in the sacrament itself has deadly consequences.[81] As with vicarious baptism in 1 Cor. 15:29, a power is present in the Lord's Supper that is at work independently of individuals, either for the good or the bad.

The significance of baptism and the Lord's Supper for the movement of Christ-believers at the levels of theology, institutionalization, and the theory of identity formation can hardly be overestimated. In theological terms, both sacraments attest the breaking in of the end time; the exalted Christ is considered to be present in them, and the sacraments point to the anticipation of the future. In institutional terms, baptism and the Lord's Supper contribute decisively to the formation of the community's identity. Indeed, the Jerusalem church may have understood their practice of baptism and the Lord's Supper within the context of Judaism. At the same time, they distinguished baptism and the Lord's Supper sharply from Jewish practices of purification and meals by the centrality of Christ and the soteriological claims. Moreover, baptism and the Lord's Supper were soon detached from the Jewish context outside Palestine in the churches of Syria, Asia Minor, and Greece; that is, from the perspective of identity formation, they were the catalysts for a transethnic consciousness and contributed significantly to the process of becoming an independent movement of Christ-believers.

New Social Forms?

Luke describes the initial period of the Jerusalem church as an epoch of unity: unity in prayer and teaching (cf. Acts 2:42), in the Eucharist, and in conduct. The portrayal of the social and economic relationships within the church stands under the motif of unity, which is emphasized in the summaries in Acts 2:42–46; 4:32–35. The Christ-believers were a voluntary

---

81. Peter Lampe takes a different view. Cf. Lampe, "Das korinthische Herrenmahl," 211n79: "ὑπὸ κυρίου excludes a magical automatism in the elements; the elements do not have the effect of a poison that makes people sick when they participate in an unworthy manner. Instead, the kyrios lets them become sick." This view cannot be an alternative, as the direct connection between participation in the elements and the judgment in 1 Cor. 11:29 indicates: "For all who eat and drink . . . eat and drink judgment on themselves."

loving community: they renounced property for the sake of those who were in need (Acts 2:45; 4:34) and placed private property at the disposal of the community (Acts 4:32, "The multitude of believers were of one heart and one soul, and no one called anything that he possessed his own, but rather they had all things in common"). Acts 2:45 reports about the role of the apostles in the selling and sharing of goods: "They sold their goods and possessions and shared everything, as anyone had a need." Further differentiation is indicated in the second summary, which, like Acts 2:44, takes up the ancient motif of friendship in the phrase ἅπαντα κοινά (all things in common; cf. Acts 4:34). It is first mentioned here that members of the Jerusalem church possessed lands and houses (cf. Acts 4:34). The proceeds of the goods that were sold were laid at the feet of the apostles, who had the authority of distributing them; they then distributed to anyone in need. Acts 4:36–37 mentions the sale of land by Barnabas, who also gave the proceeds to the apostles.

The missing dimensions of this form—summaries based on the ancient ideal of friendship—are obvious.[82]

1. The conduct of the Jerusalem church is economically irrational, for through the sale of their property, they lose their economic and social basis for existence.

2. When Luke emphasizes that the church met daily in houses for the breaking of bread (Acts 2:46), this claim presupposes that Christ-believers still owned houses. They placed their houses at the disposal of the church for common use (cf. Acts 12:12–13).

3. If the prosperous members of the church sell their property and lay the proceeds at the apostles' feet, one could expect that all members of the church would be cared for out of this fund. We hear, however, that the money was divided according to need (cf. Acts 2:45; 4:35). After the selling and distribution of property, there were still some who were in need, but others apparently did not depend on support. Furthermore, the conflict over the care of the widows (Acts 6:1) and the collection for "the poor among the saints" (Rom. 15:26) confirms that social and economic problems continued in the church.

82. Otherwise Theissen, "Urchristlicher Liebeskommunismus," 707, who assumes a historical core to the story: "The early Christian 'love communism' could have been an idea of reform within the Jerusalem church. The idea in this case would not have followed the reality that remained behind (the usual view); rather, it could have preceded it." For critique, cf. Horn, "Die Gütergemeinschaft," 378ff.

4. According to Acts 4:32, there continued to be property owners in the church who made their property available to all. They did not hold to their property but placed it at the disposal of others without selling it, allowing others to share in it.

5. The image of the Jerusalem church described by Luke is also contradictory. The story of Ananias and Sapphira in Acts 5:1–11 presupposes that not all "had all things in common" and that it was not expected.

6. In the Pauline churches, private property is assumed; if the community of goods in Jerusalem had taken place in the way it is described, it would have had no successors.

Based on these observations, one may conclude that Luke generalized particular cases of the selling of property for the sake of the church. This fact is suggested by the mention of Barnabas in Acts 4:36–37, for it would not have been reasonable if Barnabas had only done what everyone else had done anyway. Probably the proceeds from the sale of a few houses or lands were distributed in the church, each in response to a specific need.

With the community of goods, Luke takes up a central topos of ancient concepts of state and societal utopia.[83] He could have gone back to Pythagoras, of whom Iamblichus, *De Vita Pythagorica* (167–68) records, "The origin of justice is community, equal rights and a solidarity in which all consider themselves entirely as one single body and one single soul, and 'mine' and 'yours' designate the same thing. . . . Together everything belongs to everyone without distinction, and no one possesses anything. If one enjoyed community, then he used the common goods in the most just way; otherwise, he took his own goods and even more than he had contributed to the common possessions and went from there" (cf. also Diogenes Laertius 8.23, "To deem nothing their own"). Plato described the ideal state in which "friends have all things in common" (*Pol.* 424A, 449C) and private property is to be avoided (*Pol.* 416D; 464D; 543B). Aristotle (*Eth. Nic.* 8.11 [1159b]) says about friendship: "And the extent of their association is the extent of their friendship, as it is with the extent of justice. And the saying 'What friends have is common property' is correct. For friendship depends on community." Cicero also (*De officiis* 1.51) sees in the common use of possessions a characteristic of the ideal state: "This, then, is the most comprehensive bond that unites together men as men and all to all;

83. For ancient parallels, cf. also Diogenes Laertius 6.72 (the Cynic Diogenes); Philo, *Good Person* 75–91; Josephus, *J.W.* 2.119–61; see the detailed collection of texts in Wacht, "Gütergemeinschaft," *RAC* 13:1–59.

and under it the common right to all things that Nature has produced for the common use of man is to be maintained, . . . in the light indicated by the Greek proverb: 'Amongst friends all things in common'" (LCL). An impressive parallel to the community life of the Jerusalem church described by Luke is found among the Essenes.[84] The married members of the Essene settlements that were scattered all over Israel had at their disposal private property and private assets (CD 9.14ff., 22). They possessed houses (CD 11.7–11) and land and employed slaves and day laborers (CD 11.12; 12.10). Anyone who was accepted into the community had to provide information about his financial relationships, and false statements were punished (CD 14.20–21). The members made monthly contributions into the community treasury, which was administered by an overseer (CD 14.12–16). From this community treasury the needy were supported. "From it one should give to the orphans, and from it one should support those in distress and the poor; and also for the aged who lay dying, and for the man who is homeless and for anyone taken into prison, and for the virgin who has no redeemer" (CD 14.14ff.). As the center of the Essene movement, Qumran had more radical rules. Anyone who entered this community had to contribute his property and his funds into the possession of the community (1QS 6.19–20). The control of the property lay with the priests: "Only the sons of Aaron control legal rulings and property, and every rule for the men of the community shall be determined according to their word. As for the property of the men of holiness who walk in perfection, it shall not be merged with the property of the men of injustice who have not purified their life and separated themselves from a life of iniquity and walking in the way of perfection" (1QS 9.7–9).

Luke took individual cases of voluntary renunciation of possessions or of shared usage within the Jerusalem church as a starting point for his narrative and connected it with the common ideal of ἅπαντα κοινά. He created the original scenes and gave to the events a paradigmatic aura. The radical lifestyle of the earthly Jesus and his disciples as well as that of Paul and his coworkers may have also inspired this portrayal. Moreover, he sees in the church the realization of the social utopia of the ideal community that was frequently mentioned in ancient philosophy. This portrayal of the church indicates that, with the new community of Christ-believers, a new culture of sharing came into existence, which actually occurred in some cases. With this description of social utopia, Luke also created an impulse that has lasted through the ages,

---

84. Riesner, *Essener und Urgemeinde in Jerusalem*, 100–104, sees connections between the Essenes and the Christ-believers in Jerusalem.

which demands that communities, like the Jerusalem church, give, share and have all things in common.[85]

Hebrews and Hellenists

The narrative perspective of Acts changes in chapter 6; the portrayal of a harmonious life in the Jerusalem church that is depicted in Acts 1–5 is disrupted. Until now, the church grew in an extraordinary way (Acts 2:41; 4:4; 5:14). It is held in high regard by the people (Acts 5:13b), and all are of "one heart and one soul" (Acts 2:44; 4:32) and have all things in common (Acts 2:44ff.; 4:32) so that no one has to suffer from need (Acts 4:34). Now another reality dominates; the high regard of the people toward the church has given way to severe quarrels and persecutions, which culminate with the martyrdom of Stephen (cf. Acts 6:11–14; 7:57–58). Outcries against the new movement occur, causing many to flee from Jerusalem (Acts 8:1), and even among Christ-believers there emerges a dispute between the groups of "Hellenists" and "Hebrews." In chapter 6 no further mention is made of the community of goods in Acts 2:44–47 and 4:32–37. Even if the narrative depiction belongs to Luke, behind Acts 6:1–8:3 one may recognize historical conflicts within the Jerusalem church and between parts of the church and the Judaism of Jerusalem.[86]

In Acts 6:1–7, Luke describes two groups of leaders: the Twelve and the Seven. "The Twelve" appears only in Acts 6:2 (cf. Luke 6:13; 9:1; 18:31; 22:3, 30); in Acts 6:6 Luke speaks of "the apostles." The Twelve is probably a group appointed by Jesus, who symbolically represented the totality of the twelve tribes of Israel and were significant for only a brief period after Easter (see above, 5.2). The Seven was a fixed concept in early Christianity, for in Acts 21:8, Philip is called "one of the Seven." The origin of the number seven could be derived from the interpretation of Deut. 16:18, for Josephus mentions that in every Jewish city seven men should rule.[87] Luke connects the formation of the Seven with a conflict within the Jerusalem church: "In those days, as the number of the disciples grew rapidly, there was a murmuring of the Hellenists against the Hebrews; their widows were being overlooked in the daily distribution of alms" (Acts 6:1). The widows of the Hellenists felt overlooked

---

85. Noteworthy is that the Hellenistic satirist and philosopher Lucian of Samosata (ca. 120–80 CE) reports about the Christians of his time: "They despise all worldly things in the same way and keep everything as a common possession and accept such without proof of trustworthiness" (*Peregr.* 13).

86. Cf. Zugmann, *"Hellenisten" in der Apostelgeschichte*, 300–309.

87. Cf. Josephus, *Ant.* 4.214, 287.

or neglected in the fair distribution within the church, leading to a conflict between Hellenists and Hebrews. As an explanation Luke indicates that the "Twelve" were overburdened with the double task of *diakonia* and proclamation. This situation led to the first expansion of the organization of the church, as seven men were selected to care for the poor, having been appointed by the apostles. Luke's portrayal in Acts 6:1–7 contains several inconsistencies. (1) It remains unclear whether the widows of the Hellenists—because of the growth of the church—were not considered in the newly established system from the beginning or were neglected at a certain point within an existing system. (2) Why were the Hellenist widows overlooked? Did they live separately in their own church? (3) All seven "deacons" bore Hellenistic names;[88] one is even a proselyte from Antioch. (4) Why did they select only Hellenists and not a mixed group for caring for the poor? (5) Particularly striking is the fact that, later in Acts, Stephen and Philip appear in no way as servants of the poor. Rather, they are spirit-filled missionaries. (6) Similarly, "the Twelve" do not continue with the task that is declared (Acts 6:4: "But we want to remain in prayer and the service of the word") within the narrative; instead, they disappear and are replaced by the apostles (cf. Acts 6:6).[89] (7) A connection with the previously mentioned community of goods (Acts 4:32–37) is not made by Luke, although it was evident. If the purpose of the program was to determine that "no one among them was in need" (cf. Acts 4:34), the dispute over the care for the widows indicates that it did not function in reality (or was entirely fiction).

As a historical fact, one can ascertain from the Lukan depiction that in the Jerusalem church there were very early two groups: The "Hellenists" and the "Hebrews." The concept of Ἑλληνισταί and Ἑβραῖοι suggests that the conflict had, to a considerable extent, roots in the two languages. The Ἑβραῖοι are Aramaic-speaking Jewish followers of Jesus, while the Ἑλληνισταί are Greek-speaking Jews from the diaspora who have returned to Jerusalem and become followers of Jesus (cf. Acts 2:5).[90] Thus they did not speak Aramaic or were limited in the language. On the other hand, there were among the "Hebrews" certainly a few who spoke Greek as a foreign language, but most of the time they spoke exclusively Aramaic. Because language is a primary mark of identity,

88. Acts 6:5: "Thus they selected Stephen, a man full of faith and the Holy Spirit, Philip, Prochorus, Nicanor, Timon, Parmenas, and Nicolaus, a proselyte from Antioch."

89. Neither the "Seven" nor the "Twelve" engage in the tasks indicated in the narrative and actually disappear as a group after they are mentioned; that observation speaks against the thesis of Theissen, "Hellenisten und Hebräer," 328, according to which the "Seven" are local authorities in Jerusalem, while the "Twelve" on the other hand are transregional authorities.

90. On the evidence, cf. Hengel, *Between Jesus and Paul*, 8–9; Zugmann, *"Hellenisten" in der Apostelgeschichte*, 11–88.

it is not surprising that it here led to conflicts. Social distinctions probably also existed, for the majority of Hellenistic Jews from the diaspora were financially prosperous,[91] while at least the Galilean followers of Jesus in Jerusalem relied on support. Furthermore, the Jews who had returned from the diaspora had a certain linguistic-cultural identity that was maintained by synagogues of their countrymen in Jerusalem, which is indicated both in Acts 6:9 ("synagogue of the freedmen and of the Cyrenaeans and of the Alexandrians") and especially by the so-called Theodotus inscription.[92] The language differences, the variety of places of origin, the social distinctions, and a certain respective independence within the Judaism of Jerusalem before the beginning of the new movement of Christ-believers led to the development of two separate groups relatively early.[93] A consequence of the language differences was the development of respective independent worship services. According to Acts 2:46, the believers gathered for daily worship services "in the houses," a suggestion that the Jerusalem church was divided into house churches for practical reasons. The "Hellenists" probably organized assemblies in houses from the beginning, in which worship services were held in the Greek language. The liturgical-cultic separation brought with it also a separation in service, which is described in Acts 6:1–7. This setting explains the difficulties in caring for the poor. Apparently, the care for the poor was originally organized by the Hebrews, who then from a certain point in time ceased to care for the Hellenistic widows because they were no longer regarded as members of their own community.[94]

Theological differences apparently were connected with the neglect of the widows of the Hellenists. The Seven did not carry out the social tasks given to them, and Stephen, as an outstanding figure of this group, was something other than an organizer of care for the widows.

Stephen and the Ensuing Events

Stephen appears suddenly in Acts 6:8–15 and is apparently something like a leading theological spokesman within the Hellenistic part of the Jerusalem

---

91. Those who came from the diaspora to Jerusalem wanted to live according to the Torah and to die in Jerusalem, the place of the end-time gathering of Israel, the appearance of the Messiah, and the resurrection. Cf. Zugmann, *"Hellenisten" in der Apostelgeschichte*, 271–94.

92. Text and interpretation in Zugmann, *"Hellenisten" in der Apostelgeschichte*, 278–82: one named Theodotos, who returned from the diaspora, built a synagogue and a lodging for pilgrims in Jerusalem.

93. Contra Theissen, "Hellenisten und Hebräer," 340, who does not speak of a "division."

94. Another possibility for explanation: The Hellenistic widows were at the beginning not participants in this system because they were considered prosperous. At a certain point in time they demanded to be cared for. This could be connected to the fact that increasingly more widows without relatives in Jerusalem were in need. Cf., e.g., Roloff, *Die Apostelgeschichte*, 109.

church. His theological profile may be stated briefly. He is charismatic, performs miracles, and acts as a teacher of wisdom and a pneumatic (v. 8, "full of grace and power, he performed signs and great wonders among the people"; v. 10, "they were not able to withstand the wisdom and the Spirit with which he spoke"). Then Hellenistic Jews rose up and were not able to withstand him (vv. 9–10). Consequently, a prejudicial polemic takes place (v. 11, "We have heard him say blasphemous words against Moses and God"), and in a formal accusation, they charged him with being critical of the temple and the law, a charge that was brought forth by false witnesses (v. 13, "This man never stops speaking against this holy place and the law"). Only with difficulty can one say the extent to which this theological position represents the historical Stephen (and the Hellenists) because Acts 6:8–15 is infused strongly with a Lukan redaction.

First, the intended parallel between Stephen and Paul (cf. Acts 6:13 with 21:28)[95] suggests that the motif of criticism of the law is to be regarded as a Lukan contribution, which presupposes a knowledge of Paul's circumcision-free mission.[96] In the initial period of the Jerusalem church, a position critical of the Torah could scarcely have developed that would have transcended what was possible in Judaism at the turn of the millennium and would have justified a persecution.[97] Rather, one may assume that the successful proclamation of the crucified Jesus of Nazareth as Messiah in connection with a critical attitude toward the temple[98] and the developing organizational independence and missionary activity led to the persecution. Two arguments support this view: (1) Stephen and the other Hellenistic Jewish Christians saw in the cross and resurrection of Jesus Christ the breaking in of the universal eschatological saving act of God, with the result that the temple was relativized as the place of God's atoning action (cf. Rom. 3:25).[99] The Hellenistic Jews who loved

95. Weiser, *Die Apostelgeschichte*, 1:173: "According to Luke, Stephen already represented the basic position that Paul later took (cf. 6:13–14 and 7:48 with 21:21, 28; 7:58 with 9:29)"; cf. Löning, "Der Stephanuskreis," 86; Zugmann, *"Hellenisten" in der Apostelgeschichte*, 325–33; Hill, *Hellenists and Hebrews*, 41–100.
96. Cf. Zugmann, *"Hellenisten" in der Apostelgeschichte*, 331.
97. Of course, a charge of blasphemy against Moses would have evoked aggression; on the contemporary rigor with respect to the Torah, cf. Josephus, *J.W.* 2.145 (among the Essenes, everyone who blasphemes Moses the lawgiver is punished with death); *J.W.* 2.228–31 (a Roman soldier tore a Torah scroll and was immediately executed by the procurator Cumanus in order to pacify the Jewish plaintiffs).
98. Emphasized by Rau, *Von Jesus zu Paulus*, 15–77; cf. also Haacker, *Stephanus*, 31–40.
99. Cf. Löning, *Der Stephanuskreis*, 86–87, who considers neither Acts 6:8–15 nor the speech of Stephen that follows critical of the law and assumes: "The pre-Lucan core of the accusation against Stephen is the dispute about the temple as the place of the presence of God and eschatological atonement" (Löning, *Der Stephanuskreis*, 86); similarly Kraus, *Zwischen Jerusalem*

the temple would have considered this a provocation that justified the charge of blasphemy by Hellenistic Jews (Acts 6:11)[100] and the lynch-mob justice that followed (death penalty by stoning, according to Lev. 24:10–16; Num. 15:30–31). Along with this, the same charge was made against the followers of Jesus, which also played a significant role with Jesus himself. This is indicated in the rudimentary transference of the temple logion (cf. Mark 14:58b–c) to Stephen in Acts 6:14b ("This Jesus of Nazareth will destroy this place"). Possibly the Hellenists classified the existing temple as "made with hands" and thus as temporary in order to contrast the one "not made with hands" as the abiding place of the presence of God (cf. Acts 7:48–50).[101] (2) The criticism of the temple by the Hellenists could (perhaps) explain the remarkable comment in Acts 8:1, according to which, with the persecution that began with the stoning of Stephen, only the Hellenistic Jewish followers of Christ, and not the apostles, were persecuted. While the Aramaic-speaking members of the Jerusalem church in Acts 1–5 are portrayed as especially related to the temple, Stephen and his group apparently represented a critical stance so that only they, not the other Christ-believers, were driven out. Thus a changed situation from that in Acts 1–5 is to be assumed.[102] The locale of the conflicts was in the synagogues of the Hellenistic Jews; that is, new people appear in new places. While the Galilean Christ-believers who came predominantly from Galilee remained in the area of the temple, Stephen and his associates operated in the Hellenistic synagogues with intellectual brilliance. More than any other Christ-believers, the group around Steven could be noticed. It recruited aggressively and successfully for the Messiah Jesus Christ among the Hellenistic Jews in Jerusalem and was thus identifiable. The appearance of the Hellenists probably led the Pharisees to give up their previous cautious position (cf. Acts 5:34–39). Consequently, like the Sadducees, they became opponents of the new movement (especially in the person of Paul).

---

und Antiochia, 55: "In view of the issue discussed here about the persecution of the 'Hellenists,' the thesis that the critique of temple and cult played a decisive role in their expulsion from Jerusalem has the greatest plausibility." Also Zugmann, *"Hellenisten" in der Apostelgeschichte,* 333, emphasizes that "with Stephen and the Jewish Christian Hellenists in Jerusalem, the criticism of the temple had both factual and temporal priority."

100. On the charge of blasphemy, cf. Haacker, "Die Stellung des Stephanus," 1522, who indicates that βλασφημεῖν in many Jewish texts signals the separation from the religious community.

101. Zugmann, *"Hellenisten" in der Apostelgeschichte,* 333–57, assumes that Jesus's statement about the temple was already rendered into Greek and propagated; then in Acts 6:14 Luke replaces "the second positive part of the saying that Jesus speaks about building another temple 'not made with hands,' with the saying about the change of the customs of Moses" (355). Zugmann also considers Stephen's speech as tendentious evidence for the criticism of the temple by the Hellenists (cf. 357–71).

102. Cf. Haacker, "Die Stellung des Stephanus," 1519–21.

The successful missionary activity of the group around Stephen within the Hellenistic synagogues of Jerusalem, their proclamation of a crucified one as the Messiah of Israel, and especially their relativizing of the temple cult by affirming that Jesus is God's eschatological place of atonement—these were all perceived as a provocation, which ended with mob justice in the stoning of Stephen (cf. Acts 7:54–60). The precise temporal sequence of this event is difficult to establish. The question involves the year 33 or 36 CE. After the departure of Pilate and the appointment of Marcellus by the Syrian legate Vitellius,[103] a power vacuum emerged, which the new high priest Jonathan exploited in order to proceed against the Jewish Christian Hellenists.[104]

Against this assumption, one may note that the connection between the martyrdom of Stephen and Paul requires an earlier calculation, for Paul was called to be apostle to the nations at the latest in 33 CE.[105] Thus the activity of the Hellenists and the death of Stephen must be dated in the year 32/33 CE.

The significance of the Hellenists for the further development of early Christianity cannot be overestimated. Already their return from the diaspora to Jerusalem indicates that the Hellenists were very religious people who accepted faith in Christ and took it beyond Jerusalem (into the diaspora). Although the Hellenists may not be regarded as a closed group,[106] already in Jerusalem and later in Damascus (cf. Acts 9:2) and in Antioch (cf. Acts 11:19) they developed their own theological perspective and christological conceptions with a universalistic tendency, which opened the movement of Christ-believers to a mission beyond the boundaries of Palestine (see below, 6.2). They were probably the first to give theological consideration to the spontaneous gifts of the Holy Spirit to non-Jews (cf. Acts 2:9–11; 8:17–39). Paul's entire missionary work is inconceivable apart from the work of this group. The Hellenists were probably the ones who very early transmitted the Jesus tradition into Greek and thus opened the message of Jesus to the Greek world.

5.6 Texts: The Passion Narrative

The successful proclamation of the Jerusalem church is only conceivable where convincing content of the proclamation existed. Here first of all one must consider the oral preaching, which in a special way would have had the

103. Cf. Josephus, *Ant.* 18.90–95.
104. Löning, "Der Stephanuskreis," 89, argues for 36 CE.
105. Cf. Schnelle, *History and Theology of the New Testament*, 17–27.
106. According to Acts 11:20, "a few of them" went to Antioch in order to preach the gospel also to the Greeks.

focus on the fate of Jesus in light of the OT promises. An exclusively orally delivered tradition that was passed on is conceivable only for a short period of time, but already one or two years later the worship services in the house churches as well as the baptismal and Lord's Supper celebrations required a certain stabilization of the tradition and thus a process of committing it to writing. For the Jerusalem church, what probably stood in the foreground was the event that also happened in Jerusalem: the passion.

From the beginning, the foundational narrative of the new movement of Christ-believers in Jerusalem was certainly the passion narrative. Paul confirms this indirectly when he introduces the Lord's Supper tradition with the comment "I received from the Lord what I also handed on to you, 'The Lord Jesus, in the night when he was betrayed . . .'" (1 Cor. 11:23). The report transmitted by Mark depicts not only the literary, but also the earliest, version in the history of the tradition. It existed already long before the Gospel of Mark, as the differing chronologies between the pre-Markan tradition (Jesus dies on the day of preparation of Passover) and the Gospel of Mark indicate (Jesus dies on Passover).[107]

All four Gospels agree that Jesus was crucified on a Friday (Mark 15:42; Matt. 27:62; Luke 23:54; John 19:14, 31, 42). According to the Synoptic Gospels, this Friday falls on the first day of the Passover festival, Nisan 15 (cf. Mark 14:12 par.). In John Jesus dies on the Day of Preparation, Nisan 14 at noon (cf. John 18:29; 19:14, 31),[108] exactly at the time that the Passover lambs were slaughtered at the temple.[109] The Markan tradition supports the Johannine tradition, for, according to Mark 14:1, Jesus should be arrested before the festival (v. 2, "not during the festival"), and Judas should hand him over "at an opportune time" (εὐκαίρως); that is, the arrest of Jesus followed in the night from Nisan 13 to 14.[110] All textual signals, which emphasize the speed of the event (Mark 14:30, "today, in this night"; 15:1, "and immediately, in the morning"; 15:34, for a crucified one, Jesus died very quickly, already in the "ninth hour," that is, after six hours; 15:44, Pilate is astonished that Jesus has already died), point likewise to the Day of Preparation. The note in Mark 15:20–21 also suggests this dating; Simon of Cyrene has come from the field and was forced to carry the cross. On Passover all work ceased so that also here one must consider the Day of Preparation for Passover as the time, a fact that is presupposed

---

107. Cf. Theissen, *Gospels in Context*, 166–69.

108. The convincing argument of P. Billerbeck (Str-B 2:812–53) remains basic for all of the problems.

109. Cf. Josephus, *Ant.* 17.213; *J.W.* 6.423.

110. Cf. A. Strobel, "Der Termin des Todes Jesu," 73.

in the additional phrase ὅ ἐστιν προσάββατον ("this is before the Sabbath") in Mark 15:42. The trials before the Sanhedrin and Pilate are also not conceivable on a Sabbath.

The following passages probably belong to the oldest passion tradition: Mark 14:1–2 (decision about the death); 14:10–11 (Judas); 14:22–25 (Last Supper); 14:43–46 (arrest); 14:53–65 (trial before the chief priests and elders); 14:66–72 (denial by Peter); 15:1–5 (Jesus before Pilate); 15:16–20a (mocking); 15:20b–27 (crucifixion); 15:42–47 (burial). The following passages may be regarded as later additions: Mark 14:3–9 (anointing in Bethany); 14:12–17 (preparation for the meal); 14:18–21 (the traitor); 14:26–31 (announcement of the denial by Peter); 14:32–42 (Gethsemane); 14:47–52 (events at the arrest); 15:6–15 (Jesus again before Pilate); 15:29–41 (events at the crucifixion). Presumably the oldest individual traditions originated relatively early, and the somewhat later traditions were brought together into a pre-Markan passion narrative and then reworked by Mark and integrated into his Gospel. The oldest collection of the passion narrative originated at the place of the event, in Jerusalem, and was put into writing between 35 and 40 CE, then translated into Greek.[111] This took place first because of the needs in the Jerusalem church, for with the passage of time, the traditions had to be secured and established and made accessible to both primary languages, Aramaic and Greek. Furthermore, around 40 CE other large churches (Damascus, Antioch) and other new ones were being established (Rome), in which the fate of Jesus was being told; that is, they were dependent on a written (Greek) form of the passion narrative. One may assume that in the worship service, particularly at the Lord's Supper, the passion narrative or parts of it were read. With the passion narrative, the Jerusalem church provided a cult etiology, that is, a narrative basis for the existence of this cultic practice.

5.7 The Theological Development of the Early Jerusalem Church

Within the Jerusalem church, texts in the Jesus tradition other than the passion narrative were established, orally or in writing, even if one cannot trace the process. However, one can determine which theological foundational perspectives originated in the Jerusalem church that had greater meaning for its later development.

---

111. Theissen, *Gospels in Context*, 198–99, also reckons with a process of putting into writing from 40 CE; Pesch, *Das Markusevangelium*, 21, dates the pre-Markan passion narrative in the year 37 CE at the latest "in the Aramaic-speaking earliest church in Jerusalem."

The Titles of Christ

The worship of Jesus alongside God was shaped by the overwhelming religious experiences of the Christ-believers in Jerusalem, including especially the appearances of the Resurrected One, the present work of the Spirit, and the intensive experiences in the service of worship (see above, 4.1–2). Along with the invocation and ritual worship of Jesus came the christological titles, which were the first elements of theological reflection. They are the abbreviations of the entire saving event; they express who and what Jesus of Nazareth is for the believing community.[112]

The central title Χριστός or Ἰησοῦς Χριστός goes back to the oldest pre-Pauline confessional tradition (cf. 1 Cor. 15:3b–5; 2 Cor. 5:14–15) and summarizes the entire saving event.[113] In Paul (and probably before him) sayings about the crucifixion (1 Cor. 1:23; 2:2; Gal. 3:1, 13), the death (Rom. 5:6, 8; 14:15; 15:3; 1 Cor. 8:11; Gal. 2:19, 21), the resurrection (Rom. 6:9; 8:11; 10:7; 1 Cor. 15:12–17, 20, 23), the preexistence (1 Cor. 10:4; 11:3a–b), and the earthly existence of Jesus (Rom. 9:5; 2 Cor. 5:16) are combined with Χριστός. From the basic creedal statement summarizing the entire salvation event, the Χριστός sayings become associated with a variety of themes. In the Gospels also the title name Ἰησοῦς Χριστός takes a central place, as, for example, Mark 1:1; 8:29; 14:61; Matt. 16:16 clearly demonstrate. The self-evident use of Χριστός in churches that are shaped in the Greco-Roman environment is no coincidence, for the addressees could interpret Χριστός on the basis of the anointing rites of their own cultural-historical background. The anointing rites that are widespread in the entire Mediterranean world attest the common terminology, according to which "who/whatever is anointed, is holy, near to God, devoted to God."[114] Both Jewish Christians and Christians from the Greco-Roman tradition could understand Χριστός as a predicate for the unique proximity to God and the holiness of Jesus so that Χριστός (or Ἰησοῦς Χριστός) became a title for an ideal concept of mission.

A changed situation occurs with κύριος as a title (cf. Ps. 110:1 LXX);[115] it already had a central significance in the Jerusalem church, as 1 Cor. 16:22 indicates (*maranatha*/μαράνα θά, our Lord come). When believers call Jesus

112. Comprehensive description in Hurtado, *Lord Jesus Christ*, 98–118.
113. Cf. F. Hahn, *Titles of Jesus in Christology*, 175–239, 347–51; Vermès, *Jesus the Jew*, 129–59; F. Hahn, "Χριστός," *EDNT* 3:477–86; Karrer, *Der Gesalbte*; D. Zeller, "Messias/Christus"; Hengel, "Jesus der Messias Israels"; Frey, "Der historische Jesus und der Christus der Evangelien," in Schröter and Brucker, ed., *Der historische Jesus*, 273–336.
114. Karrer, *Der Gesalbte*, 211.
115. Cf. Kramer, *Christos Kyrios Gottessohn*, 61–103, 149–81; F. Hahn, *Titles of Jesus in Christology*, 68–135; Fitzmyer, "κύριος"; Vermès, *Jesus the Jew*, 103–28.

"Lord," they indicate the authority of the exalted κύριος who is present in the community. Κύριος expresses the unique and exalted dignity: he was exalted to the right hand of God and participates in the power and glory of God and from there exercises his rule. The aspect of the presence of the Exalted One that is associated with the title κύριος demonstrates in the acclamation and the Lord's Supper tradition that it is the focal point of the tradition. In the church's acclamation that Jesus is Lord, it confesses itself to him (cf. 1 Cor. 12:3; Phil. 2:6–11). The God of the Christians is at work through his Spirit so that the Spirit cries out in the worship service (1 Cor. 12:3): κύριος Ἰησοῦς (the Lord is Jesus) and not ἀνάθεμα Ἰησοῦς (cursed be Jesus). Κύριος frequently appears in the Lord's Supper tradition (cf. 1 Cor. 11:20–23, 26ff., 32; 16:22). The church assembles in the powerful presence of the Exalted One, whose saving, but also punishing, powers (cf. 1 Cor. 11:30) are at work in the celebration of the Lord's Supper. Along with the liturgical dimension of the *Kyrios* [Lord] title, in Paul ethical components are also present. The Kyrios is the decisive reality who determines all realms of daily life (Rom. 14:8, "If we live, we live to the Lord; if we die, so we die to the Lord. Whether we live or die, we are of the Lord").

The title υἱὸς (τοῦ) θεοῦ stands particularly in continuity with the tradition history of Ps. 2:7 (cf. also 2 Sam. 7:11–14) and is connected with various christological conceptions.[116] Paul took the title from the tradition (cf. 1 Thess. 1:9–10; Rom. 1:3b–4a) in which the particular position of υἱός indicates that he ascribed a great theological significance to this title. The title of Son expresses both the close relationship of Jesus Christ to the Father and his function as the mediator of salvation between God and humankind (cf. 2 Cor. 1:19; Gal. 1:16; 4:4, 6; Rom. 8:3). In Mark υἱὸς (τοῦ) θεοῦ becomes a central theological title that equally encompasses Jesus's heavenly and earthly dignity (cf. Mark 1:1, 9–11; 9:2–8; 12:6; 14:61; 15:39). Matthew also develops an established Son of God Christology (cf. Matt. 1:22–23, 25; 3:17; 4:5–7), while in Luke the title does not have a central place.

In the Jerusalem church, the title "Son of David" (υἱὸς Δαυίδ) probably played a significant role, for the Messiah was considered a descendent of David (cf. Pss. Sol. 17.21). A central text is the old tradition in Rom. 1:3b–4a, according to which the earthly Jesus was the son of David. God, in his power as creator, appoints him Son of God as a result of the resurrection and makes

116. The relevant material is discussed in Hengel, *Son of God*, 22, 44–64; A. Collins and J. Collins, *King and Messiah as Son of God*; cf. also Hurtado, "Son of God"; A. Labahn and M. Labahn, "Jesus als Sohn Gottes bei Paulus." On Qumran (besides 4QFlor 1.11–13; 1QSa 2.11; esp. 4Q 246), cf. Fitzmyer, "'Son of God' Document from Qumran"; J. Zimmermann, *Messianische Texte aus Qumran*, 128–70.

him the decisive figure of the end time (cf. 2 Tim. 2:8). In the tradition of
the Gospels, the title dominates particularly in the healing of the blind (cf.
Mark 10:46–52; Matt. 9:27; 12:23). Matthew gives the title a special shape.
By divine intervention, Jesus is conceived as the legitimate descendant of the
Davidic dynasty and thus the Messiah, in accordance with Jewish tradition
(Matt. 1:1–17). Then he is at work as the son of David in his healings (cf.
Matt. 9:27; 12:23; 21:14–16).

A central role in the Christology of the Jerusalem church is played by the
concept of the Son of Man.[117] The basic Jewish texts are Dan. 7:9–14 and
1 En. 46.1–48.7. According to this tradition, the Son of Man is described as a
preexistent (1 En. 48.6) heavenly being "whose face was like that of a human
being" (1 En. 46.1). He is the bearer of righteousness and God's chosen (1 En.
46.3); the wisdom of God rests on him, and he appears as the eschatological
judge (1 En. 48.7; cf. 47.1–3). According to 1 En. 48.4ff., the Son of Man is a
"support and a staff for the righteous, a light to the nations, and the hope of
those who are in grief." His heavenly majesty is indicated in that all people
who dwell on earth will fall down and worship him" (1 En. 48.5). Probably
Jesus referred to himself as Son of Man,[118] so that it is not surprising when
the Jerusalem church employed this title in order to designate the special
significance of Jesus. It probably handed down the logion about the Son of
Man (cf. Luke 7:31–34; 9:58; 12:8–9, 40; 17:24, 26, 30; Mark 2:10, 28) and,
in addition, developed the original form about the suffering Son of Man that
stands behind Mark 8:31.[119]

Wisdom and Preexistence

Wisdom and speculation about preexistence also became significant in the
Jerusalem church. In the concept of the Son of Man, the ideas of both preexistence and wisdom were connected. Stephen and the Hellenists in particular
apparently shaped the thought of wisdom (cf. Acts 6:3, 10). Along with the
Logos, Wisdom belongs among the heavenly mediating figures (cf. Prov. 2:1–6;
8:22–31; Wis. 6:12–11:1), whose home is especially near to God.[120] Wisdom is
preexistent, the mediator in creation, and sent by God; the pious pray that God

117. Cf. Tödt, *Der Menschensohn in der synoptischen Überlieferung*; F. Hahn, *Titles of Jesus in Christology*, 13–53; Colpe, "υἱὸς τοῦ ἀνθρώπου"; M. Müller, *Der Ausdruck Menschensohn in den Evangelien*; Hampel, *Menschensohn und historischer Jesus*; J. Collins, "The Son of Man in First-Century Judaism"; Vögtle, *Die "Gretchenfrage" des Menschensohnproblems*; Kreplin, *Das Selbstverständnis Jesu*, 88–133.
118. Cf. Schnelle, *Theology of the New Testament*, 148–53.
119. Cf. Hoffmann, "Markus 8,31."
120. On the analysis of early wisdom traditions, cf. Lips, *Weisheitliche Traditionen*, 267–80.

will send Wisdom to them (cf. Wis. 9:9–11). In 1 En. 42.1–2 the old conception is depicted, according to which Wisdom found no place on the earth to dwell and thus returned to heaven. This motif of the rejected Wisdom was very early applied to Jesus. Wisdom attests that the Son of Man came and found no home among humankind (cf. Luke 7:34–35). Thus for this generation only judgment remains. The children of Wisdom, however, who respond to the call of the Baptist and the Son of Man, are spared from judgment.

If one looks at the full scope of the first years of the Jerusalem church, surprising variety and creativity become apparent. The composition of the church is very heterogeneous; along with the immediate disciples of Jesus and the larger circle of disciples (with many women) from Galilee, the family of Jesus, especially his mother and his brother James are also present. There are also the sympathizers in Jerusalem who advocate for Jesus at the time of the crucifixion and burial. Finally, Jews from Jerusalem and all of Palestine join, and besides them Jews from the Hellenistic diaspora come in considerable numbers. This diversity was the basis for a new culture of sharing and a dynamic theological development. This development was manifested in worship services filled with the Spirit, in which prayer and acclamation stood at the middle point; in the establishment of baptism and the Lord's Supper as new rituals shaping identity; in the creation of the first textual documents; and in the transference of numerous titles for deity to Jesus, who was not rejected by God but was exalted and now holds the office of Anointed One, Lord, Son of God, and Son of Man and will appear again at the parousia.

6

Early Churches and Early Mission outside Jerusalem

The spread of Christ-believers occurred in several stages. Both the events in Jerusalem and the existence of a church in Damascus already in 32/33 CE indicate that the new movement expanded from the beginning. The activities of the churches in Antioch and the related planned activity of Paul and his coworkers were of decisive meaning for a new missionary religion. Both outward conditions and inner factors were favorable for the expansion.

6.1 Contexts: Mobility and Religious-Philosophical Variety in the Roman Empire

External Factors

The period circa 30–130 CE was an epoch of (relatively) outward and inner peace and of economic growth within the Roman Empire. An essential external factor for the success of the early mission was the existence of a well-developed infrastructure for communication in the Roman Empire of the first century CE, which was determined by the dominance of the Greek language (see above, 3.1). In addition, excellent possibilities for travel existed in the Roman Empire of the first century CE.[1] The network of roads comprised 300,000 kilometers (186,411 miles), of which about 80,000 kilometers

1. Riesner, *Paul's Early Period*, gives a good overview, 307–17.

(49,710 miles) were well-built roads.[2] The quality of this network of roads is indicated by the fact that it remained intact in the High Middle Ages and is even partially intact for walking today. Thus Paul and his coworkers were either on the way by foot or they used a ship, for the NT never mentions Paul traveling in carriages. On the road a traveler on normal terrain could cover a distance of thirty kilometers (18.6 miles) per day.[3] In travel by ship with a favorable wind, an average speed of about 4.5–6 knots could be reached so that one could travel, for example, from Corinth to Roman Puteoli in four to five days. In the first century CE, a bustling traveling activity dominated. Merchants as well as those making educational journeys were on the road; travelers moved from city to city, and pilgrimages enjoyed much popularity, not just among diaspora Jews.[4]

A decisive factor for the expansion of the new movement of Christ-believers was the existence of Jewish diaspora communities (see above, 3.3), whose center in the first century CE was the synagogue. In the big cities they were present in the Jewish section of town or at least on Jewish streets. According to the description of Acts, Paul first made contact in the synagogue when he arrived in a new city and recorded the first missionary successes (cf. Acts 9:20; 13:5, 14–43; 14:1–2; 16:13–14; 17:1–3; 18:4; 19:8). This was a natural procedure, for Paul was a diaspora Jew with knowledge of the structures of communication in the synagogue, and the emerging Christianity began first to detach itself from Judaism. The synagogue was the center of all activities within the Jewish community. Here they assembled for a worship service with prayer,[5] the reading of Scripture, instruction, and blessing. Community meetings and other events also took place. The significance of the synagogue as a cultural and communication center was enhanced by libraries, schools, hostels, and homes for the aged. Pilgrimages from the diaspora to Jerusalem not only required a connection with the temple and the holy city but also provided a brisk exchange of news between Palestine and the various centers of the diaspora. Thus the already-existing system of communication between diaspora communities offered the early missionaries (especially Paul and his coworkers) the first opportunity for proclaiming the new message.

The addressees of this proclamation included, along with those who were Jews by birth, especially proselytes and Godfearers. "Proselytes" (προσήλυτοι,

---

2. Cf. Höcker, "Straßen- und Brückenbau," 1032; Reck, *Kommunikation und Gemeindeaufbau*, 82.

3. Cf. Reck, *Kommunikation und Gemeindeaufbau*, 86; Riesner, *Paul's Early Period*, 10–11, calculates 20 to 30 km; Weeber, "Reisen," even calculates 37.5 km.

4. Cf. Friedländer, *Sittengeschichte Roms*, 1:389–488; Giebel, *Reisen in der Antike*, 131–214.

5. Cf. P. Schäfer, "Der synagogale Gottesdienst."

those who have come in) are former non-Jews who converted fully to Judaism by the offering of a sacrifice, immersion in water, and in particular through circumcision.[6] Those called "Godfearers" (σεβόμενοι or φοβούμενοι τὸν θεόν)[7] were people from among the gentiles who adopted monotheism and the basic ethical standards of Judaism, attended the worship service, were instructed in the Torah, and held to important parts of the Sabbath and food laws without being circumcised. This group was naturally larger than the Pharisees; however, it remains doubtful whether they were regarded as members of the synagogue by the Jewish side.[8] The early Christian mission probably had its greatest success among the "Godfearers" (cf. Acts 10:2; 13:16, 26; 16:14; 17:4, 17; 18:7, 13),[9] for Christianity offered them—as Judaism also did—a monotheistic teaching and an attractive ethic without refusing them a full-fledged status within the fellowship.

The religious variety and openness in the Roman Empire also provided a favorable climate for the expansion of Christianity. The existence of strange gods as a rule was not doubted among Romans and Greeks, resulting in a coexistence and merging of religions. Greco-Roman religion (see above, 3.2) was traditionally inclined not toward conflict but toward integration. It was not familiar with any mission and had no obligation to convert other people to another religion. It expanded by diffusion and was able, at least partially, to integrate other cults. The Romans exercised tolerance in questions of religion under the basic principle that the disregard for the gods was their own concern (cf. Tacitus, *Ann.* 1.73.4). This principle is evident especially in the great expansion of Greek and oriental mystery cults (see above, 3.2), which could not be overlooked in Rome.[10] While the numerous cults from the east of the Roman Empire were disputed in the republican period, in the imperial period they could again be freely practiced and found acceptance in public calendars of festivals. Those who were responsible for this expansion to Rome included especially slaves, tradesmen, travelers, and soldiers from the eastern provinces. In the first century CE, however, people from every cult in the population

---

6. Cf. K. Kuhn and H. Stegemann, "Proselyten." A significant example is the conversion of the royal house of Adiabene to Judaism; cf. Josephus, *Ant.* 20.34–48; cf. also Matt. 23:15.

7. For proximity to Judaism, the term Ἰουδαΐζειν was also used; cf. Plutarch, *Cicero* 7.6.

8. D.-A. Koch, "The God-Fearers between Facts and Fiction," refers to (later) inscriptions clearly indicating that Godfearers were not regarded as members of the elect people of God from the Jewish perspective.

9. Cf. Siegert, "Gottesfürchtige und Sympathisanten"; Wander, *Gottesfürchtige und Sympathisanten*. On sympathizers toward the Jewish religion from the Roman perspective, cf. Juvenal, *Sat.* 14.96–106.

10. Cf. Kolb, *Rom*, 607–20. The great expansion of oriental cults is indicated in that in Rome about forty sanctuaries of these cults can be identified; frescos, inscriptions, and literature attest to the wide expansion of these religions.

joined. Rome developed into a center of all the popular cults of the empire. The common polytheism and the loyalty to the caesar required the acceptance of such cults. The classic Roman and Greek deities were partially identified with these new gods, and others, including the healing god Asclepius, gained great significance.[11] This religious variety was in no way limited to a special class; rather, throughout the population a certain openness to new cults was present, which had a positive effect for the emerging Christianity.

The recruitment by the early Christian missionaries was probably familiar to their contemporaries to a certain extent, for Paul and the other early Christian missionaries were not the only ones who appeared with religious-ethical claims in the cities of Greece and Asia Minor, and in Rome. A thoroughly comparable established and highly influential group in the Roman imperial period were the philosophers/rhetoricians/sophists in the various schools (especially the Stoics, Cynics, Platonists, and Epicureans). They were not only active in the realm of private or public education but also appeared with a public claim that encompassed every area of life, including politics.[12] Luke knew this and, not coincidentally, depicted Paul at the center of the metropolis of philosophy in a dispute with them (cf. Acts 17:16–34). The philosophical symbolism was present everywhere in cities such as Corinth, Ephesus, Rome, and Athens:[13] (1) The true philosopher does not decide himself to enter this profession, but rather he is called by the deity.[14] This experience of conversion is made publicly and attests the credibility of the philosopher.[15] (2) The philosopher had long hair and a chin beard, wore a simple garment, carried a stick and a satchel, and worked especially to recruit women.[16] The appearance was not only an external matter in the present sense but also signaled membership in a school, competence, and was thus considered a matter of substance.[17] (3) The philosopher did not flatter and deceive but instead spoke the truth and rebuked others.[18] He spoke the unvarnished truth with boldness (παρρησία) and without fear. Thus he made use of all forms of rhetoric and

11. On Asclepius, cf. D.-A. Koch, *Bilder aus der Welt des Urchristentums*, 213–20.

12. Cf. J. Hahn, *Der Philosoph und die Gesellschaft*, 55: "The philosopher—whether he is called and understood to be a teacher [διδάσκαλος], everyone's educator [κοινὸς παιδευτής], pedagogue [παιδωγογός], guide [καθηγητής], everyone's leader [ἡγεμών] or helmsman [κυβερνήτης]— should give answers to the needs of his environment for self-understanding and orientation, for larger aims and making sense."

13. Caricatured in Lucian's work *Philosophies for Sale* (*Vitarum auctio*).

14. Cf. Dio Chrysostom, *Or.* 13.1–11; Epictetus, *Diatr.* 3.22.2.

15. Cf. J. Hahn, *Der Philosoph und die Gesellschaft*, 58–60.

16. Dio Chrysostom, *Or.* 72.1–3; Artimidor, *Traumbuch* 1.18.30.

17. Cf. J. Hahn, *Der Philosoph und die Gesellschaft*, 33–45; Malherbe, *Paul and the Popular Philosophers*, 103–4.

18. Cf. Dio Chrysostom, *Or.* 33.10.13.

did not shy away from addressing the public. (4) The true philosopher was not quarrelsome and greedy.[19] (5) Because the philosopher is considered an example and teacher of the *ars vitae*, the ethos (ἔθος) and conduct of life (βίος) agree. (6) It is characteristic of the true philosopher that he is the teacher and educator of all; he appeals to the broad public, participates in social life, and also looks after hearers/students personally.[20] (7) The philosopher does not shy away from associating with, or giving a critique of, the Roman leadership elite, including the caesar. Not coincidentally, this conduct repeatedly resulted in persecution or expulsion of (Stoic) philosophers by the Roman caesar (especially under Nero, Vespasian, and Domitian).[21]

Few actors fit the ideal program of philosophical existence,[22] and the critique of the great divide between claim and reality is varied.[23] Nevertheless, the philosophers/rhetoricians/sophists and the expectations connected to them are important, especially for understanding the Pauline letters. All essential elements that characterize the philosopher apply to the early Christian preachers/missionaries. First Thessalonians 2:1–12 indicates that Paul knew and used the topic of the true philosopher.[24] Second Corinthians 10–13 also indicates that he was measured by this standard, and numerous conflicts (especially in Corinth) may be understood against this background.[25]

19. Cf. Xenophon, *Apologia* 16, where Socrates asks, "Who among humankind is as free as I, for I take neither gold nor payment?" According to Diogenes Laertius 7.188, Chrysippus wrote an entire book about this question; cf. J. Hahn, *Der Philosoph und die Gesellschaft*, 81–85.

20. Cf. Seneca, *Ep.* 108.3.

21. For the year 71 CE, cf., e.g., Dio Cassius 65.12.2: "And thus Vespasian drove the philosophers out of Rome, except for Musonius"; on the subject, cf. Malitz, "Philosophie und Politik im frühen Prinzipat."

22. Ideal philosophers were, among others, Demetrius (the teacher of Seneca), Euphrates (cf. Pliny the Younger, *Ep.* 1.10.2), and Demonax (cf. Lucian, *Demonax*). The quintessential philosopher was naturally Socrates; cf. the encomium to Socrates in Plutarch, *Mor.* 11.581c: "Rather, the decisions of Socrates in everything apparently possessed a high degree of power and firmness, as they were drawn from a straight and strong judgment and foundation. That he voluntarily remained in poverty his entire life, although he could have been prosperous if he had taken from those who offered help with desire and joy; that he did not forsake philosophy despite so many obstacles; and that he at the end, when his friends had made every effort to rescue him and to enable him to flee, neither yielded to their entreaties nor recoiled from death, but in the most extreme danger remained unbending by his decision—that is not the act of a man who changes his mind in response to voices or sneezes, but a man who is guided to the good by a higher authority and a deeper foundation."

23. Cf. Dio Chrysostom, *Or.* 32.9; 71 (about the "true" philosopher); Epictetus, *Diatr.* 3.22 (the "true" Cynic); Lucian, *Icaromenippus* 5.

24. With regard to the conversion experience, self-presentation, ethical instructions, and the response to the adversities of life (catalog of sufferings), one may observe the agreements between Paul and ancient philosophers; cf. Divjanović, *Paulus als Philosoph.*

25. Cf. B. Winter, *After Paul Left Corinth.*

Internal Factors

Alongside the external factors, internal factors were also favorable for the expansion of early Christianity. The first factor is the different understanding of mission. Religious propaganda was everywhere in the Roman Empire, from local cults to the cult of the emperor; as with Judaism, the numerous cults had no purposeful program of mission. If one understands by mission an activity of intentional recruitment and action based on a global, established eschatological (i.e., with the end of the world in view) claim to exclusive truth in order to win others to a clearly definable group,[26] then early Christianity brought a new dimension into the history of ancient religions. The aim of the early Christian mission was not to offer people an additional religion; rather, it combined with the exclusive claim a requirement for the abandonment of all previous religious commitments. The goal of early Christian preaching was not the adhesion to another religion but the conversion to the one true God (cf. 1 Thess. 1:10). It required a conscious decision with a high level of commitment! Although Judaism and emerging Christianity represented respective exclusive claims, the concepts of mission were different. Of course, in Judaism in the first century, there was, to a considerable extent, a concept of the eschatological turning of the nations to Yahweh (cf., e.g., T. Levi 18.9; T. Jud. 24.5–6; 25.3–5; T. Ben. 9.2; 10.6–11; T. Ash. 7.2–3; T. Naph. 8.3–4; 1 En. 90.33–38; Sir. 44:19–23; Pss. Sol. 17.31; 2 Bar. 68.1–8; 70.7–8; 4 Ezra 13.33–50; Jub. 22.20–22).[27] However, Judaism conducted an intentional mission within a limited framework,[28] trusting especially in its power of attraction to outsiders. In contrast, the emerging Christianity did not remain isolated but saw very early the whole world as its forum.

Where are the origins of this new concept?[29] Three major reasons account for it. (1) One may observe traditions such as Matt. 8:5–13 (centurion from Capernaum) and Mark 7:24–30 (Syrophoenician woman) as well as Jesus's openness to non-Jews compared to the discriminatory practice of the Torah. This openness is apparent in the parable of the banquet (Luke 14:16–24) and in the prophetic threat in Q at Luke 13:29, 28, in which the priority of Israel is brought into question and the nations appear as possible guests. (2) This pre-Easter impulse is strengthened by the appearances of the Resurrected

---

26. Cf. Zangenberg, "Mission in der Antike und im antiken Christentum," 12–13; cf. also Schnabel, *Early Christian Mission*, 4; Schmeller, "Mission im Urchristentum."

27. Cf. the analyses in Kraus, *Das Volk Gottes*, 12–110.

28. Diaspora Jews may have also been involved in mission, as suggested by Matt. 23:15 and Horace, *Sermones* 1.4.142–43. However, one cannot speak of a general concept of mission. For an analysis, see Riesner, "Pre-Christian Jewish Mission?"

29. Cf. Hengel, "Origins of the Christian Mission."

One, and especially the experience of the Spirit, which made those who were Jewish by birth as well as those from among the nations equal. These are experiences that Luke compressed into the story of Pentecost or the narrative of the centurion Cornelius (cf. Acts 2:1–13; 10:44; also 11:21), giving the insight to Peter, a Jew by birth: "In truth I understand that God is not a respecter of persons, but among all people one is welcome who fears him and does righteousness" (Acts 10:34–35). (3) An additional important factor was undoubtedly the cultural mobility of the Hellenists, who shaped the expansion of the new movement in its earliest stages. They were theologically interested; in the diaspora they had become acquainted with the culture of the other peoples, and they were in a position to overcome geographical and cultural boundaries.

The weakness of the old traditions also called for the success of the new.[30] Plutarch and Pliny lament the decline of the temple culture and of the oracle.[31] The official cults could no longer sufficiently satisfy the needs of the people, as the success of the Greek-oriental cults indicates (see above, 3.2). Thus the "mystery" cults frequently offered answers in the form of myths to the existential questions of the people, such as "Where do I come from, where am I going, how do I protect myself from a dangerous world?" In particular, the ceremonial and religiously laden initiation into the cult gave the initiates the feeling of participating in a higher reality that transcended their lives. This receptivity to cults "from the East" benefited the emerging Christianity.

An additional reason for the success of the new movement is monotheism, which already created a fascination with Judaism in antiquity. The large number of gods and depictions of the gods in the Greco-Roman world obviously led to a loss of plausibility. Because of the philosophical critique of polytheism,[32] pagan monotheism already took on significance,[33] preparing the way for Christian monotheism. While polytheism did not make a personal relationship with God possible, the God proclaimed by the early Christians had in himself two attractive basic principles: He is both lord of history and also lord of one's personal life. This God is one, but not alone; he has a name, a history, and a face: Jesus Christ. This formed a binitarian monotheism, for

---

30. For the cultural and historical conditions of the early Christian mission, see Speyer, "Hellenistisch-römische Voraussetzungen der Verbreitung des Christentums": decline of the classical Greek and Roman culture, development of monotheism, the concept of the divine origin of a particular man, significance of the ethic.

31. Cf. Plutarch, "Über die eingegangenen Orakel"; Pliny the Younger, *Ep.* 10.96.9–10.

32. Cf. above, 3.3 under "Messianic Figures and Movements" and 13.5.2 under "The Synoptic Gospels."

33. Cf., e.g., Cicero, *Nat. d.* 3.47; Plutarch, *Is. Os.* 67.68; Dio Chrysostom, *Or.* 12; on the subject, cf. S. Mitchell and Nuffelen, *One God: Pagan Monotheism.*

Jesus Christ was taken up into the power and realm of activity of the one God. Christians lived in the consciousness of belonging to the group of people whom God had chosen for the sake of the salvation of the world but also to reveal his judgments. They were convinced that God through Jesus Christ had also given meaning and purpose to history and to every individual life. This meaning included both daily life and the hope for life beyond this one. Early Christian proclamation addressed equally the everyday life of the believers as well as the basic questions of life, as, for example, death. Here the difference between the emerging Christianity and its milieu was considerable. The God of the Christians was a God of life who demanded a relationship but also allowed freedom, was accessible already in the present but also guaranteed the future for the believers. It was not the capricious fate,[34] which played a central role in the thought of the Greeks, but rather the God who revealed himself in Jesus Christ is the one who determines the present and future life. Early Christianity offered a comprehensive and consistent concept that took up the afterlife hopes of antiquity and also gave to the individual a convincing perspective on life.

In addition, the hope for a complete participation in the divine socio-structural elements also made the emerging Christianity attractive. In addition to a novel teaching, Christianity provided an ambitious love ethic and new social forms. A key to the success of Christian churches was the openness for people of all kinds, all ages, all occupations. This openness was the greatest difference between Christianity and the pagan associations. The conversion of "entire houses" (cf. 1 Cor. 1:16; Acts 16:14–15; 18:8) indicates that members of all levels of society could belong to this new community (cf. Gal. 3:26–28). There was no barrier of rank, position, family origin, or gender. Because of the community's rejection of formal conditions for admission, many women and members of the lower levels of society (especially slaves) became members of the new churches in great numbers.[35]

The early Christian missionaries moved within a political, economic, and linguistic realm that, despite its regional characteristics, was perceived to be a unified world. These favorable external conditions were combined with a novel, expansive

---

34. Cf., e.g., the statement of Cleanthes recorded in Epictetus, *Ench.* 53, "O Zeus, and you almighty fate, lead me on to the goal assigned to me long ago. I will follow without faltering. If my will is weak and craven, still I will follow you!" The significance of the belief in fate can be seen explicitly in the tomb inscriptions; cf. Peres, *Griechische Grabinschriften*, 34–41; on the theory and practice of the Greco-Roman belief in fate, cf. Cicero's *De fato* and *De divinatione*.

35. Cf. Ebel, *Die Attraktivität früher christlicher Gemeinden*, 214–21.

concept of mission expansion as well as attractive teachings and ways of living. The combination of these factors considerably fostered the expansion of the new movement of Christians.

6.2 Persons

Which persons conducted the earliest missionary activity outside Jerusalem? The information is sparse, but in the earliest period three names come to the foreground: Philip, Peter, and Barnabas.

Philip

Acts 8:4 reports that the scattered Hellenists proclaimed the saving message outside Jerusalem; however, it identifies only Philip. After Stephen, Philip was apparently the most prominent member of the Hellenists; in the enumeration of the "Seven" in Acts 6:5, he stands in the second position. As "Philip the evangelist" (Acts 21:8), he is probably not to be identified with the apostle Philip (cf. Acts 1:13). By around 33 CE, missionary activity outside Jerusalem had probably begun. Its mission fields were Samaria (Acts 8:5ff.) and the Hellenistic cities of the coastal region; it occurred between Ashdod and Gaza (Acts 8:26, 40) as well as in Caesarea on the coast, the residence of the Roman procurator (Acts 8:40). A mission among those who worshiped God[36] in Samaria suggests itself on historical and geographic grounds, especially since Samaria already played a prominent role in the Jesus tradition (see below, 6.4). According to Acts 8:5–25, Philip appeared as a charismatic miracle worker in Samaria (cf. vv. 7–8) and became a competitor of the local sorcerer Simon, who may have regarded himself as the incarnation of "the great power of God" (Acts 8:10).[37] Behind the legendary ornamentation of the narrative, a conflict is visible that runs through the entire early history of missions: the conflict of early Christianity with local cults, sorcerers, and magical practices (cf. Acts 13:4–12; 14:8–20; 16:16–24; 19:11–20).[38] Magic—in the sense of influencing the gods, powers, and fate by extraordinary powers and/or ritual action—belonged to the assumed worldview of antiquity.[39] Interaction between microcosm (the world of humans) and macrocosm (universe/the

36. Cf. Acts 8:5, which speaks only of the proclamation of Christ; i.e., the worship of the one true God is presupposed.
37. On Simon, cf. Theissen, "Simon Magus"; Zangenberg, *Dynamis tou theou.*
38. Cf. Klauck, *Magie und Heidentum in der Apostelgeschichte des Lukas.*
39. Cf. the collection of sources in Luck, *Magie und andere Geheimlehren;* also Ebner, *Die Stadt als Lebensraum,* 347–57.

world of the gods) had to be activated by definite rules and practices, which could be exercised only by specific people or in special places. The appearance of Spirit-endowed Christian missionaries was apparently perceived by local sorcerers and cults as a danger to their own influences and thus evoked defensive reactions (cf. Acts 13:8–12). According to Acts 8:26–40, Philip appears as the first missionary to the gentiles, for he converts the finance minister of the queen of Ethiopia. He may have conducted himself among the Ethiopians as a "Godfearer," but as a eunuch he was definitely not a proselyte (cf. Acts 8:27). Acts 21:8–9 reports about a missionary endeavor established by Philip: "On the next day we went further and came to Caesarea, where we stayed with Philip the evangelist, one of the Seven. He had four unmarried daughters who possessed the gift of prophecy." The "four daughters" may have been prophetically endowed schoolgirls;[40] that is, Philip was the leader of a charismatic-pneumatically oriented mission center, as suggested by the fact that he provided lodging for Paul and his companions. Ancient church tradition placed Philip finally in Hierapolis in Asia Minor.[41] Philip was apparently a very active and successful pneumatic charismatic (cf. Acts 8:6–7, 29, 39) who worked in Samaria and the Hellenistic cities of the coastal plain (Gaza, Ashdod, Caesarea) and established churches there very early.

Peter

According to the portrayal in Acts, Peter was not only the first leader of the Jerusalem church (see above, 5.2) but soon worked outside Jerusalem also (Acts 9:32: "And so Peter went here and there among the saints living in Lydda"). Peter performed miracles in Lydda and Joppa (Acts 9:32–35, 36–43) and then in Caesarea by the sea in order to baptize the centurion Cornelius (Acts 10:1–48). Cornelius is portrayed as a God-fearing sympathizer toward Judaism (cf. Acts 10:2, 22, 35) who sought out contact with Peter (cf. Acts 10:7–8). The length and the place of the narrative within Acts demonstrate clearly the intention of Luke to attribute the programmatic transition of the mission to the nations as well as its theological basis (Acts 11:1–18) to an extraordinary figure at the beginning. As in Acts 8:14–17, the activity of the Spirit is connected to the authority of those who were apostles with gifts from the first hour. Only then could unknown Hellenistic missionaries appear in Antioch who historically probably established the programmatic mission beyond Judaism (cf. Acts 11:19–30). Even if Peter cannot be considered the

40. For the evidence, cf. Dobbeler, *Der Evangelist Philippus*, 217–48.
41. Eusebius, *Hist. eccl.* 3.31.3; 5.24.2; on the analysis of the texts, cf. Dobbeler, *Der Evangelist Philippus*, 230–33.

initiator of the universal mission, he would have been engaged in missionary activity in Lydda, Joppa, and Caesarea.[42] This view is supported by the course of his life, which brought him beyond Jerusalem to Antioch, Corinth, and Rome (see below, 9.1).

Barnabas

A leading figure in the history of the early Christian mission from Jerusalem to Antioch was Barnabas. According to Acts 4:36–37, "But Joseph, whom the apostles called Barnabas—translated 'Son of exhortation'—a Levite from Cyprus, possessed a plot of land, which he sold and then brought the money and laid it at the feet of the apostles." The names "Joseph" and "Barnabas" can be explained from the custom in which a second name was added to a common first name ("Joseph"). To the Jewish name Joseph an additional Jewish epithet "Barnabas" was added, which means either "Son from Nob/Naba" or "Son of Prophecy."[43] He himself or his family originally came from Cyprus. As a Levite (cf. Ezek. 44:9–14), he stood firmly in the Jewish tradition and had a basic knowledge of theological and cultic matters. The origin from Cyprus indicates furthermore a Hellenistic background, that is, knowledge of the Greek language and the cultural breadth of diaspora Judaism. Whether Barnabas came from Cyprus to Jerusalem as a pilgrim, immigrated, or was a descendant of a Jewish family from Cyprus cannot be determined. Inasmuch as he had at his disposal a plot of land in Jerusalem or nearby, he probably had lived there for a long period of time and attained some wealth. With the sale of the land, Barnabas appears to be a benefactor of the Jerusalem church; his extraordinary deed remained in the memory of the emerging Christianity. First Corinthians 9:5–6 throws further light on Barnabas when Paul defends his apostolate and the resulting rights: "Do we not have the right to have a sister as a wife like the other apostles and the brothers of the Lord and Cephas? Or are we alone, Barnabas and I, not permitted to refrain from working for a living?" Paul counts not only himself but also Barnabas among the group of apostles; that is, Barnabas was a witness of an appearance of the Resurrected One and thus a legitimized proclaimer of

42. Whether he established churches there remains an open question. For Acts 9:32, 36 (Tabitha) and 9:43 (Simon the tanner) presuppose at least individual Christians in that place. On Peter as missionary, cf. also Böttrich, *Petrus*, 161–82; Hengel, *Saint Peter*, 79–99; other views are in Reinbold, *Propaganda und Mission*, 43–79, who strongly minimizes the activities of Peter and attributes to him only the role of a type of supervisor. "The journeys of the apostle Simon Peter apparently served, as a rule, as visits to already existing churches not founded by him" (79).

43. For the discussion, cf. Öhler, *Barnabas*, 21–28, who comes to no definite solution. If it means "son from Nob/Naba," then the place of origin was intended (cf. Nob in 1 Sam. 21–22); if it means "son of prophecy," the reference was to *nabi* (prophet).

Jesus Christ. Furthermore, the text indicates that Barnabas—like Paul—had an occupation that he could practice. Barnabus was, as apostle and benefactor, a recognized member of the earliest Jerusalem church, and he combined Jewish and Hellenistic culture in his manner of life. Thus it is not coincidental that he became a key person in the gentile mission that had begun.

According to Acts 9:27, Barnabas met with Paul for the first time shortly after Paul's call; this report is rather historically improbable, for Paul explicitly emphasizes in Gal. 1:16–17 that only after three years past the Damascus event did he come to Jerusalem (35 CE).[44] More probable is a different sequence. According to Acts 11:20, unknown missionaries from Cyprus and Cyrene founded the church in Antioch and went on a systematic activity of preaching the gospel "also to the Greeks." Then Barnabas is sent from the Jerusalem church to Antioch in order to examine and endorse the new development. However, it is noteworthy that he does not return to Jerusalem; this suggests that the "sending construction" corresponds to the Lukan schema of apostolic legitimation of every step of the salvation history. One may assume rather that, after the death of Stephen—there is no record of a persecution of Barnabas—he went to Antioch around the year 35 in order to join the church there or, along with others, to establish churches. In any case, Barnabas belonged among the most prominent members of the Antioch church from the beginning. He introduced Paul to the church (cf. Acts 11:25); and it was not Paul, but Barnabas, who led the first missionary journey (Acts 13:1–3).

The theological profile of Barnabas cannot be precisely determined, but two aspects may be noted: (1) In the early period of the new movement, Barnabas was one of the most important representatives of the proclamation of the message of Christ beyond Jerusalem and Israel. Even before Paul, he initiated a systematic mission to the gentiles. (2) At the same time, the events of the incident in Antioch indicate (see below, 7.6) that he had not fully detached himself from the strict Jewish Christian position of the Jerusalem church (Gal. 2:13, "even Barnabas was carried away into hypocrisy"). Acts 11:24 may reflect his position most clearly: "He was an admirable man, filled with the Holy Spirit"; that is, he was considered by everyone to be an upright and reliable apostle and missionary.

Paul

At the beginning, Paul was in no way the preeminent figure in the history of the early Christian mission, as he is portrayed in Acts and the letters. After

---

44. Cf. Öhler, *Barnabas*, 54–55.

his call (32/33 CE, according to Paul's own statement), he neither consulted with others nor went to Jerusalem to those who were apostles before him, "but instead I made my way to Arabia and returned again to Damascus" (Gal. 1:17b).[45] Arabia probably stands for the rocky desert area southeast of Damascus, which formed the northern part of the Nabatean kingdom. Damascus also belonged to the economic realm of influence of the Nabatean kingdom (2 Cor. 11:32), to which Paul returned and worked for the first time for an extended period. According to Acts 23:12, Paul was introduced into the church at Damascus by Ananias, who was highly regarded as a God-fearing man by the Jews. Thus one may conclude that Christianity first spread to Damascus. According to 2 Cor. 11:32, "The ethnarch of King Aretas guarded the city in order to take me prisoner, but I was let down in a basket through the wall and escaped his hands" (cf. Acts 9:23–25). This ethnarch was presumably the overseer of the Nabatean trade colony and represented the interests of the Nabatean state.[46] Such an intervention of the ethnarch was probably caused by the missionary activity of Paul in Damascus, which caused unrest among the Jewish population as well as among the Nabateans. The relationship between Nabateans and Jews was tense during that period because continuing disputes over boundaries, bellicose arguments, and the conduct of Rome damaged the relationships (cf. Josephus, *Ant.* 18.109ff.).

Not until the third year after his call to be an apostle (35 CE) did Paul visit the Jerusalem church (Gal. 1:18–20).[47] He remained there only fifteen days in order to get acquainted with Cephas. Of the other apostles, he saw only James the brother of the Lord. Nothing is known about the content of the conversation between Peter and Paul.[48] The self-understanding of the apostles is reflected in the manner of the portrayal of this visit. Because the Resurrected One himself called him, Paul needed no legitimation by the Jerusalem authorities. He sought the contact with Jerusalem, but at the same time avoided any appearance of dependence and subordination.

45. Why did Paul go into Arabia? A possible answer appears in Hengel, "Attitude of Paul to the Law," 37: "The Arabians as descendants of Ishmael were genealogically and geographically the closest relatives of the Israelites among the 'pagans.' For they were also the descendants of Abraham." Here Hengel defines Arabia in the following way: "With Arabia, the apostle probably meant the Nabatean kingdom bordering on the south and east of Eretz Israel, including a few cities of the Decapolis beyond the Jordan."
46. Cf. Knauf, "Zum Ethnarchen des Aretas."
47. According to Acts 9:26–30, Paul returned immediately to Jerusalem after his flight from Damascus, and there he spoke to the apostles; a harmonization with Paul's own statements is not possible. Hengel and Schwemer, *Paul between Damascus and Antioch*, 137–39, acknowledges the contradiction.
48. Contra Hengel and Schwemer, *Paul between Damascus and Antioch*, 144–50.

The revelation of Christ granted to him has the same quality as the appearances of the Resurrected One to Peter and the other apostles, even if Paul is the least among the apostles because of his activity as a persecutor (cf. 1 Cor. 15:3b–8). Following the brief stay in Jerusalem, Paul went into the regions of Syria and Cilicia (Gal. 1:21). By Syria the reference could be the region around Antioch on the Orontes, and with Cilicia he probably meant Tarsus.[49] Paul was probably active first in Tarsus in the area of Cilicia, but the character of this mission can be determined neither from the Pauline letters nor from Acts. Was Paul alone? How long did the stay in Cilicia last? When did he make the transition to Antioch? Was his mission in Cilicia successful? Or did he continue his missionary activity in Antioch after a few years because of the failure? Convincing answers to these questions do not exist; one can only make assumptions. Tarsus, the hometown of Paul and the metropolis of Cilicia, possessed a large Jewish community; thus it ideally offered itself as an area for missions. The reference to Christian churches in Cilicia in Acts 15:23, 41 could be a reflection of the Pauline missionary activity in and around Tarsus. This six-year activity[50] could not have been particularly successful, for Paul joined the Antiochian mission around 42 CE as the "junior partner" of Barnabas.

Apollos

Acts 18:24 says of Apollos: "Now a Jew named Apollos, who came from Alexandria, an eloquent/learned man [ἀνὴρ λόγιος] who was extraordinarily versed in the Scriptures, came to Ephesus." Apollos, apparently a diaspora Jew, was already educated in the Scriptures of the OT in Alexandria and found there (or later in Asia Minor/Greece) a new movement of Christ-believers.

---

49. Cf. Gal. 1:21 with Acts 9:30f., according to which Paul was sent to Tarsus in order to bring him into safety from the Jews in Jerusalem. Galatians 1:23 indicates further that Paul did not view Judea as a part of Syria and that he did not understand Syria to be the Roman province. Cf. H. Betz, *Galatians*, 79–80. On this section of the Pauline mission, cf. also Riesner, *Paul's Early Period*, 235–43.

50. The duration of time of this mission is difficult to determine. One may note the arguments for the period of time that is in question: (1) In Acts 12:1a, Luke explains "at that time" as the period when Barnabas and Paul were beginning their activity in Antioch; he puts this in a temporal relationship to the persecution of the Jerusalem church by Agrippa I (cf. Acts 12:1b–17). This persecution probably took place in the year 42 CE (cf. Riesner, *Paul's Early Period*, 105–10). (2) The famine mentioned in Acts 11:28 and the support of the Antiochian church for Jerusalem (Acts 11:29) occurred in the period between 42 and 44 CE (cf. Riesner, *Paul's Early Period*, 108–21). Somewhat different is the view of Hengel and Schwemer, *Paul between Damascus and Antioch*, 151–60, who calculate a stay of three to four years in Cilicia (between 36/37 and 39/40 CE) before Paul joined the missionary activity of the Antiochian mission after that independent and successful missionary activity.

Alexandria (founded in 331 BCE) was, along with Rome, the cultural-scientific metropolis of the empire and a center of diaspora Judaism.[51] Here the Septuagint and the Jewish wisdom literature were produced. How strong was the influence of Greek thought on Alexandrian Judaism is evident especially in the writings of Philo, in which the attempt was made to express Jewish thought with the help of contemporary Greek categories. The numerous connections between Jerusalem and Alexandria and the large number of Jews in Alexandria (at the turn of the millennium certainly more than five figures) makes it appear possible that there (as in Rome) followers of the movement of Jesus Christ were at work very early.[52] Of course, in this period there is only the reference to Apollos in Acts 18:24–25, where it remains open in which place his "instruction in the way of the Lord" took place.[53] Apollos was active at the beginning of the 50s in Ephesus (Acts 18:24) before Paul and in Corinth (Acts 18:27; 19:1; 1 Cor. 3:4ff.) both after and alongside Paul. It is noteworthy that Paul accepted the (not unproblematic) ministry of Apollos in "his" churches (cf. the parties in 1 Cor. 1:10–17); that is, Apollos was apparently a known missionary who probably worked in other areas before Ephesus and Corinth and whose theological orientation Paul recognized.[54] Presumably he was also the founder of the church in Ephesus, as the textual sequence in Acts 18:24–28 and 19:1ff. presupposes. Consequently, this explains why Paul accepted him or had to accept him.[55] Apollos had great missionary success in Corinth (cf. Acts 18:27–28), which evidently was because of his Alexandrian origin and education.

Apollos was a gifted exegete, rhetor, pneumatic, and debater (cf. Acts 18:24–25, 28), whose theological orientation was associated with the concept of wisdom. This orientation is suggested by the existence of an "Apollos party" in 1 Cor. 1:12 and the apparently related argument of Paul against those who equate divine and human wisdom in 1 Cor. 1:18–4:21.[56] The fol-

51. Cf. Schimanowski, *Juden und Nichtjuden in Alexandrien.*

52. See the critique of this view in D.-A. Koch, *Geschichte des Urchristentums*, 434–35, who mentions the strong anti-Jewish attitude in Alexandria after 38 CE and the tight organization of Judaism there. Thus he doubts an (early) origin of a Christian community. Against his view, one may object that, despite the differences also in Rome, Jews as well as the early Christians were subject to continuing repression and persecution, which did not prevent the formation of a Christian community and perhaps was actually useful to them.

53. However, Codex D (05) in Acts 18:25 renders "who was instructed in the word in his home city."

54. The comment in Acts 18:25d–26 that Apollos knew only the baptism of John and had to be instructed theologically by Aquila and Prisca goes back to Luke, who consciously minimized the significance of Apollos. Cf. Wolter, "Apollos und die ephesinischen Johannesjünger."

55. Cf. Witetschek, *Ephesische Enthüllungen*, 1:350–58.

56. Cf. Merklein, *Der erste Brief an die Korinther*, 134–45.

lowers of Apollos represented a Hellenistic wisdom theology (see below, 8.5) and considered themselves superior to others in the church. The act of baptism for them was probably an incorporation into a pneumatic wisdom, which was mediated essentially by the one who baptized (Apollos).

From their superimposing of wisdom on the message of Christ followed a comprehensive "now already" view of salvation, which the twofold ἤδη in 1 Cor. 4:8 indicates. They understood the gift of the Spirit primarily as the overcoming of the limitations of the previous creaturely existence and as the increase of vitality and expectations for life. With their focus on the present and the individualistic approach, they had a negative view of suffering and minimized hamartiology (personal sin). The central focus was the maximizing of life's possibilities through the deity, whose destiny was to overcome the boundary of death and guarantee the total presence of life beyond in the present time. Paul argues against this overemphasis on the present and the attempt to play him and Apollos off against each other (cf. 1 Cor. 4:6). However, he does not argue against Apollos. Paul, Apollos, and Peter are merely coworkers of God, but not the master builders of the truth (cf. 1 Cor. 3:6–10. "No other foundation can one lay than the one that has been laid, Jesus Christ" (1 Cor. 3:11). Although Paul depicts himself unambiguously as the founder and father of the Corinthian church (1 Cor. 3:8, 10; 4:14–16), he accepts Apollos as an independent and equal missionary/apostle and encourages him, according to 1 Cor. 16:12, numerous times to travel again to Corinth. If one compares this approach with Paul's generally aggressive reaction to other missionaries who wanted to set foot in his churches (cf. 2 Cor. 10–13; Gal. 1:6–10; Phil. 3:2–11), then one may draw the conclusion: Apollos was an independent and highly regarded missionary (apostle?)[57] of the early period, a successful founder of churches (Ephesus), with whom a particular theological program was associated (wisdom theology); for a time he worked with Paul and then went his own way.

Prisca and Aquila

Like Apollos, Prisca (Priscilla) and Aquila were independent missionaries who worked for a period of time with Paul but also were active alongside and after him. The Jewish Christian missionary couple Prisca and Aquila came to Corinth around the year 50 from Rome and met Paul there.[58] According

57. Whether Apollos was called, or claimed the title of, apostle cannot be definitely determined. The enumeration of Paul, Apollos, Cephas in 1 Cor. 1:12; 3:22; and 4:6 suggests that Apollos is included as an apostle. On the other hand, Paul calls him "brother" in 1 Cor. 16:12 (in 1 Cor. 3:9 Paul and Apollos are "coworkers").

58. On Prisca and Aquila, cf. Lampe, *Die stadtrömischen Christen*, 156–64.

to Acts 18:2–3, "There he met a Jew named Aquila, who came originally from Pontus and had recently come from Rome with his wife, Prisca, because Claudius had expelled all Jews out of Rome. Paul went to see them; because he had the same trade as handworkers, he lived with them and worked with them; for they were tentmakers." Aquila came originally from the Roman province of Pontus on the Black Sea. As a Jew by birth, he practiced his profession as handworker in Rome. In the first century CE, this was no exception, for numerous merchants and tradesmen as well as freed slaves streamed into the capital of the empire.[59] This married couple is counted among the first Christians in Rome, possibly among the founders of one of the Roman house churches. After the expulsion from Rome in 49 CE, the couple went first to Corinth, where they engaged in missionary activity and worked (cf. Acts 18:18). Like Paul himself,[60] the two, as independent tent-makers (σκηνοποιοί), belonged to the middle class. They primarily provided tents to private customers,[61] possibly also to the military. Linen tents or linen tent covers were widespread for private use in the Mediterranean world in order to protect from the heat of the sun.[62] Of course, 2 Cor. 11:9 indicates that the financial success of Aquila and Paul in Corinth could not have been very great, for brothers in the faith from Macedonia helped Paul in his time of pressing need.[63] Prisca and Aquila were certainly involved in missionary activity in their workplace-shop; conceivably as many as twenty believers could assemble in a house church.[64] From Corinth the couple moved to Ephesus, where they and Paul worked together and founded a house church (cf. 1 Cor. 16:19). After the relaxation of the Edict of Claudius, Prisca and Aquila returned to Rome around 55/56 CE, where they again led a house church (cf. Rom. 16:3–5). Paul's exuberant expression of thanks in Rom. 16:4 suggests that Prisca and Aquila not only supported Paul in his missionary activity and established a basis for work and living but also intervened for him in dangerous (political?) situations: "Greet Prisca and Aquila, my coworkers in Christ Jesus, who risked their head for my life, to whom not only I, but also all of the churches among the gentiles are indebted." In many instances Prisca (contrary to the usual convention) is named before Aquila (cf. Acts 18:18, 26; Rom. 16:3, but not in 1 Cor. 16:19), a fact suggesting that she participated in

59. Cf. Juvenal, *Sat*. 3.61ff.
60. On Paul as a member of the middle class, cf. A. Weiss, "Das Kapital des Paulus."
61. Lampe, "Paulus—Zeltmacher," 256–61; Hock, *Social Context of Paul's Ministry*, 33–34, who maintains, in contrast to Lampe, that Aquila and Paul made leather tents.
62. Cf. Lampe, "Paulus—Zeltmacher," 258–59.
63. Cf. Lampe, *Die stadtrömischen Christen*, 160.
64. Cf. Lampe, *Die stadtrömischen Christen*, 161.

the churches in a stronger way than her husband. It would be completely false to reduce the activities of Prisca and Aquila to mere assistants of Paul. They were a very mobile couple who worked fully independently, sometimes with Paul. They established many house churches and cared for communication among the churches of Asia Minor, Greece, and Rome. Their significance is indicated by the fact that their names are connected to three large churches (Rome, Corinth, Ephesus) and are mentioned in three early Christian traditions (Paul, Acts, and 2 Tim. 4:19).

6.3 Groups: The Jesus Movement

Along with Jerusalem (see above, chap. 5) and later Antioch, there was a third significant line from the very beginning within emerging Christianity: the Jesus movement in and around Galilee (see below, 6.4). This includes especially the proclaimers and tradents of the Jesus tradition who primarily were responsible for the logia source[65] (Q) and the Gospel of Mark. Because these texts always say something about the self-understanding of their bearers, only limited conclusions about the conceptual world and social milieu of the Jesus movement are possible. While Jerusalem was strongly oriented to the passion and resurrection of Jesus, was centered in the temple, and was structured in a static/hierarchical manner and the Hellenists/Antioch/Paul oriented themselves universally to the exalted Kyrios (Lord) Jesus, the Jesus movement understood itself primarily as a radical inner-Jewish renewal movement in direct continuity with Jesus of Nazareth.

The Jesus movement came into existence presumably in northern Palestine (especially Galilee, later also the surrounding areas including the southern part of Syria),[66] for it is theologically oriented toward Israel. The preaching of judgment at the beginning and end of the logia source (cf. Luke 3:7–9Q; Luke 22:28–30Q) is addressed to Israel,[67] and numerous logia have references to the place and living conditions in Galilee and the surrounding areas (cf. Luke 7:1Q; 10:13–15Q). The beginnings of the Jesus movement could be

---

65. On the origin and redactional theories of the logia source, cf. Schnelle, *History and Theology of the New Testament*, 179–97. As a primary document of the Jesus movement, the logia source was produced before the destruction of the temple; the statement against Jerusalem and the temple in Luke 13:34Q does not presuppose any events connected to the war. A more precise determination of the time of its composition must remain hypothetical. However, a few indicators suggest a period between 40 and 50 CE.

66. Freyne, *Jesus-Movement and Its Expansion*, 257–58, argues for "upper Galilee/southern Syria."

67. The logia source is cited according to the presumably Lukan sequence as a reconstruction of the text: Hoffmann and C. Heil, eds., *Die Spruchquelle Q*.

extended back to the pre-Easter period,[68] but only after Easter did the formation of the tradition and the shaping of the traveling mission and of the church structures begin.

Structures

Supporters of the Jesus movement included groups of men (cf. Luke 10:1) and women (cf. Mark 15:40–41; Luke 8:1–3), most of whom followed Jesus already before Easter. Also included were individual men and women disciples of Jesus such as the ones healed by Jesus (cf. Luke 8:1–3; Mark 5:25–34; 10:46–52; 14:3–9). After Easter other people joined, presumably primarily from Galilee. From the textual world, one can envision day laborers (cf. Luke 15:11–32; Matt. 20:1–16), slaves (Luke 12:35–48Q), women at the margins of society (cf. Luke 7:36–38), people who lived a minimal existence (cf. Luke 14:22–24; 16:19–31; Matt. 22:9f.), but also farmers (cf. Matt. 13:44), a merchant (cf. Matt. 13:45f.), or a fisherman (cf. Matt. 13:47–52; Mark 6:45–56). Individual tax collectors (cf. Luke 18:9–14; 10:1–9) could likewise have joined the movement as people of means (cf. Mark 10:17–27).

The Jesus movement was probably not very large (Luke 10:2Q, "The harvest is great, but the laborers are few"). The organization was probably structured in a twofold way; besides traveling missionaries (cf. Luke 9:57–62; 10:1–12, 16; 12:22–31, 33–34Q) there was a considerable number of followers who remained at home (cf. Luke 13:18–21; 16:18Q; 12:39f.Q).[69] Such a manner of life was no real exception within the history of early Christianity, for already Paul and his closest coworkers practiced a comparable radical life and mission style (cf. 1 Cor. 9:5, 14–15), and the Didache attributes this phenomenon also to the Syro-Palestinian area at the beginning of the second century (cf. Did. 11.13). The sympathizers who remained at home in the local churches offered the traveling missionaries material support, providing lodging (Luke 9:58Q) and upkeep (Luke 10:5–7Q). Many logia assume followers who remain at home,[70] as in the parables of the mustard seed and the leaven (Luke 13:18–21Q; Mark 4:30–32), the prohibition of divorce (Luke 16:18Q; Mark 10:1–12), or the word about the householder and the thief (Luke 12:39–40Q).[71] In the local churches the logia were collected,[72] and here was probably the first redactional activity

68. Cf. the sketch in Sato, *Q und Prophetie*, 375–79.

69. Cf. Sato, *Q und Prophetie*, 375ff.

70. On the traveling charismatics and the sedentary disciples, cf. Theissen, *Die Jesusbewegung*, 55–90.

71. Cf. also Q in Luke 6:43, 47–49; 7:32; 11:11–13; 14:42–46; 12:58; 13:25.

72. In the first century CE, ca. 200,000 inhabitants lived in Galilee. Cf. Ben-David, *Talmudische Ökonomie*, 48; the majority of the people lived in villages and small towns with 100–2,000

of the material. One may assume two social strata within the Jesus movement. Numerous logia reflect material poverty (Luke 6:20–21; 7:22; 11:3Q), but at the same time the demand for a decision between God and mammon (Luke 16.13Q) or between heavenly and earthly treasures (Luke 12:33–34Q) and the readiness for unlimited giving in Luke 6:30Q have a material basis in reality (cf. also the parable of the great banquet in Luke 14:15–24Q). The relationship between traveling preachers and sedentary followers must not be regarded as a static condition; certainly there was interaction, and the two groups reciprocally recruited each other.[73] One must consider the existence of a thick network between city and countryside and between various social and ethnic strata.[74] Both the traveling missionaries and the sedentary scribes collected and transmitted words of the historical Jesus (cf., e.g., Luke 6:20–21Q; 10:4–6Q; 11:20Q; 17:26–27, 30Q). They appeared piecemeal in the name of Jesus and repeated or actualized his message. In addition, spirit-endowed prophets created new Jesus traditions, for in their self-understanding the Exalted One spoke through them (cf., e.g., Luke 6:22–23Q; 10:21–22Q; Matt. 12:31Q; Matt. 19:28Q).[75] Overall, the words of Jesus and narratives about Jesus served the purposes of catechesis and mission.

> The Jesus movement practiced the message of Jesus; they took the words of Jesus seriously at the existential level; they implemented and lived by the words; their entire form of life was proclamation and mission.

Life and Ethic

The model text for such a conduct of life and mission is Jesus's speech commissioning the disciples (Luke 10:2–12Q).[76] Despite the greatest external

---

inhabitants. The population of Capernaum was about 1,000–1,500; Sepphoris and Tiberias, as major cities, each had ca. 8,000–12,000 inhabitants. Cf. Crossan and Reed, *Jesus ausgraben*.

73. Contra Schmeller, *Brechungen*, 93–98, who regards the traveling missionaries of the Q community as sent out. He formulates the result of his analysis in the following way: "(1) Q is a document of a community. (2) The Q community sent out missionaries who lived as traveling charismatics. (3) Which (or whether specific) Q sayings were transmitted exclusively by such traveling charismatics cannot be reconstructed. (4) The commissioning speech as a community tradition comes near to a constructive witness evaluating the lifestyle of the traveling missionaries" (96).

74. Cf. Dulling, "Die Jesusbewegung und die Netzwerkanalyse."

75. Cf. the thorough study by Boring, *The Continuing Voice of Jesus*, 15–234; also F. Hahn and H. Klein, *Die frühchristliche Prophetie*.

76. A sketch of the traveling radicalism of the Q community is given by Tiwald, "Der Wanderradikalismus als Brücke zum historischen Jesus."

danger (Luke 10:3Q, "Go! Behold, I send you as sheep among wolves"), the missionaries should deny themselves not only money but also any amenities (necessary for existence) during their travels (Luke 10:4Q). The ethic is especially a way of life in the logia source, which springs from the consciousness of announcing the kingdom of God as authorized disciples of the Son of Man of Israel who has come and will come as salvation and judgment. The ethical radicalism indicates that the disciples of Jesus in the logia source understand themselves to be in direct continuity with the life and the power of his words (cf. Luke 6:20–49Q).[77] The promise of the kingdom of God in the Beatitudes (Luke 6:20–23Q) determines the foundation, the command of love for enemies (Luke 6:27Q), the fundamental norm of the ethic. The absolute command of love for enemies is expanded and made more precise in Luke 6:28Q around the prayer for persecutors and in the two double logia in Luke 6:29–30Q. They define the relationship between law and justice in a new way, for here a renunciation of resistance and vengeance as well as the unlimited readiness to give is demanded. Thus the logia source extends even Jesus's conception, for the commandment of the love of enemies extends beyond the personal opponent to every group that takes a hostile position toward their own community.

Despite danger and hostility, the societal situation should be positively changed through the power of love that overcomes boundaries. The creator God is the model, and the promise of becoming "sons of God" functions as a motivation (Luke 6:34c–d, 35–36Q). The basic issue is to rely on the principle of reciprocity (Luke 6:32aQ: "When you love only those who love you, what reward do you have?") and to do what is extraordinary: not to judge and first to pay attention to one's own blindness or limitation (Luke 6:37–39, 41Q). The golden rule is presented in its positive form and extended to all people by the expansion of the addressees into a universal dimension in the programmatic speech: "As you wish that others do to you, so do to them" (Luke 6:31Q).[78]

In the logia source a radical ethos of existence without home and possessions is combined with the renunciation of violence and retaliation. The homelessness of the Son of Man (Luke 9:58Q) becomes a model for the disciple, for whom the hatred of father and mother is the presupposition for the participation in the *familia Dei* (Luke 14:26Q).[79] The bonds to the family that were fundamental to ancient life and thought lose their significance (Luke 12:51, 53Q): "Do you think that I came to bring peace

77. On the analysis, cf. Fleddermann, *Q: Reconstruction and Commentary*, 266–335.

78. On the traditional background in the history of religions, cf. Dihle, *Die goldene Regel*; all relevant texts appear in *NW* I/1.2 (1):699–713.

79. Cf. Kristen, *Familie, Kreuz und Leben*, 55–155.

on the earth? I did not come to bring peace, but a sword. . . . I came to divide the son against his father and daughter against her mother and the daughter-in-law against her mother-in-law." Social conventions such as the burial of parents (Luke 9:59–60Q) or the greeting (Luke 10:4dQ) are nullified. Finally, wealth is subjected to a fundamental critique (cf. Mark 18:25: "It is easier for a camel to go through the eye of the needle than for a rich man to enter into the kingdom of God"); according to Luke 16:13, no servant can serve two masters, "for either he will hate the one and love the other or be devoted to one and despise the other. You cannot serve God and mammon." In a society shaped by hate and violence, the followers of Jesus proclaimed the message with credibility because they practiced nonviolence and the abandonment of possessions and cared for nothing other than the kingdom of God.

In the Conflicts of the Time

The Jesus movement proclaimed its radical message in an atmosphere that was politically and religiously volatile.[80] Like the movement of John the Baptist (see below, 6.5), it was a part of a diverse Judaism (see above, 3.3) that increasingly drifted apart between 30 CE and the outbreak of the Jewish War in 66 CE and finally was destroyed. The followers of the Baptist and Jesus were considered charismatic spiritual renewal movements,[81] which stood opposite to the rather conservative Sadducees; the Pharisees, who concentrated on exercising religious authority; and the Essenes, who rejected the actual temple cult in Jerusalem. There were also the radical theocratically oriented Zealots,[82] who were ready for violence; and the Sicarii, who, like the messianic prophets, advocated the overthrow of political relationships that would be brought about by God. Inasmuch as the Baptist and Jesus were threatened by their ruler Herod Antipas (cf. Luke 3:19–20; Mark 6:14–20; Luke 13:31–32) and finally executed by Herod Antipas (or the Romans), it is not surprising that the followers were subject to repression. The logia source presupposes persecutions for the young churches by Jews in Palestine (cf. Luke 6:23; 11:49–51; 12:4f.; 12:11Q), to which they responded with a demonstrated trust in God, fearless confession (Luke 12:8f.Q), and the loyalty of a true servant (Luke 12:42–46Q). It is significant that 1 Thess. 2:14–16, written around 50

---

80. A summary is given by Theissen, *Die Jesusbewegung*, 131–241.

81. On the possible sociological characterizations of the Jesus movement, see Theissen, *Die Jesusbewegung*, 99–129.

82. Noteworthy is Josephus, *Ant.* 20.102, according to which, between 45 and 48 CE, Simon and James—the sons of the Zealot founder, Judas the Galilean—were crucified under the procurator Tiberius Alexander as rebels.

CE, mentions persecutions of Christ-believers that have already occurred, which could have affected the Jesus movement.

In addition, numerous social and political tensions existed in Galilee, which largely came to a violent end in the Jewish War, but certainly existed previously.[83] Conflicts existed between Jews and gentiles; in Tiberias, those of the gentile minority were murdered at the beginning of the war,[84] while on the other hand in neighboring cities the Jewish minorities were killed.[85] Thus there were tensions between the (relatively Jewish-permeated) land and the (relatively gentile-permeated) cities,[86] which are visible in the synoptic tradition. It is scarcely conceivable that Jesus and the Jesus movement did not know and did not work in the Hellenistically shaped cities of Sepphoris and Tiberias (only John 6:23); indeed, a city environment is presupposed in Luke 12:58f.Q (cf. also Matt. 6:2, 5, 16; Luke 13; 15; 19:11ff.). However, the two most important cities of Galilee are not mentioned in the NT because both Jesus and the Jesus movement that followed—as people from the countryside—worked there unsuccessfully. There were also conflicts between rich and poor, especially between the large landowners and the small tenants (cf. Mark 12:1–12; Matt. 20:1–16). Finally, Galilee cannot be called un-Jewish; it had its own cultural and religious profile. Encounters and intermingling with non-Jews in Galilee were an everyday experience; and in contrast to Jerusalem, the problems of ritual purity would have been handled with more latitude. Moreover, with the limited presence of the Pharisees, the motivating control mechanisms were not in place. This fact is reflected in a few texts in the Gospel of John, where Galilee is regarded as religiously inferior (cf. John 1:45–46; 7:49; 7:52).

The Jesus movement entered into the context of these ethnic, social, and cultural tensions[87] with a message that was both surprising and provocative. The confession of Jesus of Nazareth as the coming and returning Son of Man determined salvation or condemnation (Luke 12:8–9Q): "To everyone who confesses me before men, the Son of man will confess before the angels. But whoever

83. Introductions and surveys on Galilee may be found in Bösen, *Galiläa als Lebensraum und Wirkungsfeld Jesu*; Meyers, "Jesus und seine galiläische Lebenswelt"; Reed, *Archaeology and the Galilean Jesus*; Freyne, *Jesus: A Jewish Galilean*; Voigt, *Die Jesusbewegung*, 34–77.

84. Cf. Josephus, *Life* 67: "The people of Jeschu immediately killed all non-Jews of the area as well as those who were their enemies before the war."

85. Cf. Josephus, *J.W.* 2.457–58, 466ff., 477–78, 559ff.

86. Cf. Josephus, *Life* 375, 384 (the Galilean rural population hates the inhabitants of Sepphoris and Tiberias).

87. Ostmeyer, "Armenhaus und Räuberhöhle?," is critical of this characterization of Galilee as a place of unrest. He emphasizes accurately: "Jesus' message and the movement that he initiated are not primarily to be explained as the consequence of the pressure of social or political relationships." At the same time, both the synoptic tradition and Josephus indicate that in Galilee numerous tensions existed within which Jesus and later the Jesus movement operated.

denies me before men, will be denied before the angels."[88] The logia source is especially filled with the call to decision (cf. Luke 11:23, 33Q); the acceptance or rejection of the message of Jesus determines salvation or condemnation (Luke 14:16–23Q). Because the confession of the coming Son of Man determines one's place in the judgment, the people are called to watchfulness: "Be ready, for the Son of Man comes at an hour in which you do not expect it" (Luke 12:40Q; cf. Luke 17:24, 26, 30Q). The woes against the Galilean cities (Luke 10:13–15Q), the words of judgment on "this generation" (Luke 11:31–32, 49–51Q), the woes against the Pharisees (Luke 11:42–44Q) and against the teachers of the law (Luke 11:46b–48Q), and the saying about the judgment of Israel in Luke 13:24–35Q indicate that Jesus appears as eschatological judge and thus forcefully legitimates the claim of Son of Man for himself and his disciples. With this message an extraordinary ethical concept comes together that aims toward the rejection of violence, mitigation of judgment, and an egalitarianism of love. The exercise of power is deliberately avoided, and serving is praised as the ideal (cf. Mark 9:35–41; 10:35–45; Luke 14:11Q). In a society stamped by violence at several levels, both would have been perceived as attractive, impractical, or even provocative. The radical and undivided action that is demanded is oriented toward the words and life of the Son of Man, Jesus of Nazareth, who declared the unlimited love of God and promised his disciples God's care in his kingdom. The missionaries of the Jesus movement regarded themselves as living in a shared destiny with their Lord. They lived and acted as he did and awaited the eschatological rule with him and from him (cf. Luke 22:28, 30Q; in addition, the promises in Mark 10:29–30; 14:25; Luke 7:28; 13:28–29Q; Matt. 5:19). It remains noteworthy that within this concept the death of Jesus is assumed (cf. Luke 14:27Q) but not theologically interpreted (see below, 6.7).

Jesus as Miracle Worker

In parts of the Jesus movement, Jesus was worshiped and proclaimed not only as a narrator of parables and a wise interpreter of the Torah, but especially as a healer/miracle worker. In the logia source this aspect does not stand in the center of the tradition (however, cf. Luke 7:1–10, 22f.; 10:9, 13–15; 11:20Q).[89] In the special material in Matthew and Luke, miracle stories appear only rarely; thus Mark and his tradition are the essential bearers of the miracle traditions in the NT.[90] The extent of the narrative form is con-

---

88. Cf. M. Labahn, *Der Gekommene als Wiederkommender*, 271–92.
89. Cf. Hüneburg, *Jesus als Wundertäter in der Logienquelle*.
90. Cf. Kertelge, *Die Wunder im Markusevangelium*; L. Schenke, *Die Wundererzählungen des Markusevangeliums*; Theissen, *The Miracle Stories of the Early Christian Tradition*; D.-A. Koch, *Die Bedeutung der Wundererzählungen*.

siderable: (a) exorcisms: Mark 1:21–28; 5:1–20; 9:14–27; (b) healings/thera-
pies: Mark 1:29–31, 40–45; 5:21–43; 7:31–37; 8:22–26; 10:46–52; (c) rescue
miracles: Mark 4:35–41; (d) epiphany narratives: Mark 6:45–52; (e) gift
miracles: Mark 6:30–44; 8:1–9; (f) mixed forms: Mark 2:1–12; 3:1–6; 7:24–
30; (g) summaries of miraculous activity of Jesus: Mark 1:32–34; 3:7–12;
6:53–56. In the center of the pre-Markan miracle stories stands the miracle
worker himself so that these narratives can be regarded as miracle stories that
unfold a Christology of healing and were probably transmitted in Galilee.
In the history of the tradition, they echo the Elijah tradition (cf. Mark 5:7
with 1 Kings. 17–18) and the Moses tradition (cf. Mark 6:32ff.). There are
also motifs that are parallel to the Hellenistic tradition of the "divine man"
(θεῖος ἀνήρ). These include miraculous knowledge/foreknowledge: Mark 2:8;
3:3; 4:39–40; 5:30; 6:37; 8:4–5; fear and trembling: Mark 4:41; 5:15, 17, 33,
42; 6:49–50; trust as the recognition of the miracle worker: Mark 4:40; 5:34,
36; *proskynēse* (bowed down): Mark 5:6; divine power becoming visible:
Mark 5:20; power over nature: Mark 4:41; 6:48–50; a desire not to be in
the public eye: Mark 5:40; wonder-working words/acts: Mark 7:33–34. As
in the Hellenistic miracle stories, the pre-Markan miracle tradition has its
focus on the capability of the miracle worker, who demonstrates his special
qualification by his deed. The miracles of Jesus are the central content of the
preaching in the pre-Markan community (as with Mark himself). In many
acclamations one can hear the reaction of the listeners to the missionary
preaching (cf. Mark 2:12; 4:41; 5:20; 7:37; 10:52). Because Jesus empowered
the disciples to perform miracles (cf. Mark 3:15; 6:7, 13; 9:28, 38ff.; Luke
10:9Q), and through them the early Christians also, the empowered acts of
Jesus continue in the church; as a result, it called forth a continually renewed
faith. Thus the church regards its own reality as based on the miracles of the
earthly Jesus and continually tells the stories about him. The pre-Markan
miracle tradition indicates especially how strongly Jesus was worshiped and
preached as a healer/miracle worker.[91]

The Variety of the Jesus Movement

The Jesus movement was not a monolithic unity but instead included
various streams. Undoubtedly the bearers of the logia tradition stood in
the center, with their provocative Son-of-Man theology and their radical
ethos. In addition, there was the pre-Markan miracle tradition and also the

---

91. On Jesus of Nazareth as a healer and miracle worker, cf. Theissen and Merz, *Historical Jesus*, 256–83; Kollmann, *Jesus und die Christen als Wundertäter*; L. Schenke, "Jesus als
Wundertäter."

collections of conflict stories in Mark 2:1–3:6, of parables in Mark 4:1–34, and of traditional catechesis in Mark 10, where the evangelist has redacted traditions about marriage (10:1–12), possessions (10:17–31), and striving for rank (10:35–45). The "Synoptic apocalypse" may be regarded as a tradition independent of the Jesus movement (Mark 13 par.). It was probably written in Judea, for in Mark 13:14 the readers are challenged to flee to the mountains of Judea at the approach of the eschatological affliction.[92] Numerous narrative traditions of the Lukan (e.g., Luke 10:29–37, 38–42; 12:13–21; 13:10–17; 14:1–6; 15:8–10, 11–32; 16:1–13, 19–31; 18:1–8, 9–14; 19:2–10) and Matthean special material (e.g., Matt. 13:47–50; 18:23–35; 20:1–16) are to be attributed to the Jesus movement. Despite numerous differences, they share a biographical and theological interest in the life of Jesus, to which they (unlike James the brother of the Lord or Paul) give fundamental significance.

The appearance of the missionaries of the Jesus movement and their extraordinary claim apparently found only a limited acceptance in Palestine. The argument with "this generation" in Luke 7:31; 11:29, 30, 31, 32, 50–51Q and the emphasis on the judgment of Israel in response to the appearance of Jesus and the work of his disciples (cf. Luke 13:24–27, 28–29, 30, 34; 14:16–18, 21–22; 22:28, 30Q) indicate that the majority of Israel refused the message of the Jesus movement. The largely failed mission to Israel and the activity of missionaries in the cities of Phoenicia (Luke 10:13f.Q) and in the north (Mark 8:27, Caesarea Philippi) indicate that the Jesus movement sought to win others to their message outside the Jewish heartland. In the south of Syria, the reception of the logia source may have been adopted by Matthew (cf. Matt. 4:24). Finally, the positive reference to gentiles (cf. Luke 10:13–15; 11:29–31Q; Matt. 8:5–13; 5:47; 22:1–10Q) suggests an opening toward a mission to the nations,[93] which is conceivable in the period between 40 and 60 CE. In this period, numerous Jesus traditions could have found their way into the churches of Mark, Matthew, and Luke and then been transformed into the gospel literary genre.[94] The Jesus movement probably disappeared at the latest during the initial havoc of the Jewish War in Galilee (66/67 CE).

92. Theissen, *The Gospels in Context*, 140–65, connects Mark 13 with the Caligula crisis (39/40 CE).

93. Cf. Schmeller, *Brechungen*, 97; Horn, "Christentum und Judentum in der Logienquelle," 363. According to Luke 10:7–8Q, the food laws no longer apply to the missionaries.

94. Theissen offers a sketch in *New Testament: A Literary History*, 19–58: the tradition's beginnings derive from Jesus himself; next it follows the Jesus movement after Easter as bearers of individual traditions; then it follows the logia source as the first and the Gospel of Mark as the second written records, by which a public claim was connected with the gospel genre.

In an agonistic society imbued with the contrast between ruler and ruled, the Jesus movement lived a fully new religious and societal model: love instead of hate, renunciation of violence instead of suppression, shared participation in the gifts of the Creator. The transition to the synoptic tradition secured for the Jesus movement its lasting influence in early Christianity.

6.4 Lands and Places

The book of Acts awakens the impression that there was at first only a church in Jerusalem (cf. Acts 1–6), from which the other churches then developed so that Christianity came into existence.[95] This image is probably not accurate, for several observations suggest the probability that the new movement of Christ-believers existed in Jerusalem and Galilee from the beginning.

Galilee

Three observations suggest that Christ-believers were present in Galilee immediately after Easter.

1. Mark 14:28 and 16:7 assume appearances in Galilee. In Mark 16:7, the angel says to the terrified women: "Go and say to his disciples and Peter that he goes before you to Galilee; there he will see you, as he told you." For Mark, the oldest Gospel, only Galilee is the place where Jesus will appear. Matthew follows Mark in principle, for he adopts Mark 14:28 (= Matt. 26:32) and 16:7 (= Matt. 28:7), inserts a brief appearance in Jerusalem in Matt. 28:9–10, and then finally has Jesus appear to his disciples in Galilee (Matt. 28:16–20). In addition, the appearance of the Resurrected One to more than five hundred brothers, as reported by Paul (see above, 4.1), would most likely have happened under the open sky in Galilee and not in the narrow alleys of the big city Jerusalem. This view is supported by the previous reference to Peter and the Twelve (1 Cor. 15:5), to whom Jesus appeared in Galilee as well. By contrast, Luke, who omits Mark 14:28 and Mark 16:7, radically alters the interpretation: "He is not here, but he has been raised! Remember how he told you when he was still in Galilee" (Luke 24:6). According to Luke, Jesus appears to his disciples alone in Jerusalem (cf. the Emmaus disciples in Luke 24:13–35 and then all the disciples in Luke 24:36–49), which coheres unambiguously with the Lukan concept of the unified origin of Christianity beginning in Jerusalem. John

---

95. This image of Acts appears fully in Dunn, *Beginning from Jerusalem* (note the title of the book), 27, 135f., who does not actually treat Galilee as a place of Christian churches.

records three appearances in Jerusalem (John 20:11–18, Mary Magdalene; 20:19–23, the disciples without Thomas; 20:24–29, the disciples and Thomas). The post-Johannine tradition in John 21:1–14 adds another appearance in Galilee. The result is clear:[96] The oldest traditions (Mark 16:7; 1 Cor. 15:6) assume appearances in Galilee. Mark presupposes only Galilee. Matthew also knows about appearances in Jerusalem; thus into the course of events, he inserts the narrative in 28:9–10 that in the tradition-history is connected with John 20:14–18 (Mary Magdalene). Luke omits Galilee, consistent with his theology, while in John the appearance traditions in Jerusalem are dominant. This evidence supports the assumption that there were appearances in both Jerusalem and Galilee.[97] Less convincing, therefore, is the assumption that the appearances of the Resurrected One in Jerusalem led to the founding of the church there but not in Galilee.[98] Indeed, Peter and a core of the group of disciples probably moved to Jerusalem soon after the appearances in Galilee, but not all followers of Jesus from Galilee disappeared.[99] Instead, the majority of the followers of Jesus in Galilee probably remained in Galilee, where they had family, work, and a living environment.

2. The logia source and the Gospel of Mark, as the oldest discernible written witnesses, presuppose that both Jesus and the movement that followed him appeared in Galilee.[100] Why should the development not continue, especially in the place where Jesus and the Jesus movement were active?[101] Local tradi-

96. D.-A. Koch, *Geschichte des Urchristentums*, 185f., wants to minimize the weight of the appearances in Galilee and speaks of indirect "conclusions and presumptions" (186). However, he also offers an assumption: "The oldest reference to the appearances in Galilee, Mk 14:28; 16:7 is an expression of the theology of Mark" (186).

97. This thesis was firmly established by E. Lohmeyer, *Galiläa und Jerusalem*, 52, who even suggested that, with Luke, "Galilee and Jerusalem were both the home of the early Christian gospel."

98. This is the view of Dunn, *Beginning from Jerusalem*, 135–36: the primary argument, along with the skepticism about the existence of Q, is the silence of the sources about a Galilean Christianity. Similarly with reference to the silence of the early sources, see Zangenberg, "From the Galilean Jesus to the Galilean Silence," where on p. 108 he concludes: "Galilean Christianity seems more an offshoot from Jerusalem than a product of continuation of Jesus' Galilean ministry"; D.-A. Koch, *Geschichte des Urchristentums*, 166: "A parallel Jewish Christianity in Galilee is not yet apparent; with the relocation of James (and his brothers), it is not to be expected."

99. See D.-A. Koch, *Geschichte des Urchristentums*, 187–88: "The logia source indicates an actual interest in the Jesus tradition and presupposes tradents who had access to the pre-Easter proclamation of Jesus and knew his manner of existence as a traveling prophet. Such a personal continuity with the pre-Easter activity of Jesus is attested only for Jerusalem and indeed within the circle of the traveling followers who came with Jesus from Galilee to Jerusalem with the Twelve as a core."

100. The logia source could scarcely have originated in Jerusalem, as is assumed by Frenschkowski, "Galiläa oder Jerusalem?"; cf. the opposing view in M. Labahn, *Der Gekommene als Wiederkommender*, 94–98.

101. On the early churches in Galilee, cf. L. Schenke, *Die Urgemeinde*, 198–216; Schnabel, *Early Christian Mission*, 747–59; on the group that stands behind the logia source, cf. Reed, *Archaeology and the Galilean Jesus*, 170–96, on "The Sayings Source Q in Galilee."

tions from Capernaum (cf. Mark 1:29–31; Luke 7:1–10Q), Bethsaida (cf. Mark 8:22–26), Caesarea Philippi (cf. Mark 8:27–29), or Cana (cf. John 2:1–11; 4:46; 21:2) especially were passed on from churches in the places where the events took place. This is also the case for numerous other words or narratives that take place around the Sea of Gennesaret (cf., e.g., Mark 1:16–20; 2:1–12, 13, 17; 4:35–41; Luke 5:1–11).

3. A fundamental consideration must be added: The transmission of the oral traditions from Jesus and about Jesus up until the first written records is not conceivable without the post-Easter churches in Galilee![102] Where should this crucial process in the history of early Christianity have taken place, if not particularly in Galilee?[103] Of course, Galilean traditions were also transmitted in Jerusalem, but that fact in no way leads to the conclusion that, because of Jerusalem, Galilee—the place of the historical activity of Jesus, the place of residence for numerous followers of Jesus (cf. the missionary discourse in Luke 20:1–16 par.), and the locale of many texts—is not to be considered as the place where traditions were being formed.[104]

The book of Acts does not report a mission in Galilee. However, in Acts 9:31, Luke indicates that, at the time of the call of Paul around 32/33 CE, there were various churches in Galilee: "Thus the churches in all Judea, Galilee, and Samaria had peace and were built up; walking in the fear of the Lord, it grew through the comfort of the Holy Spirit." For two reasons, the near silence of Acts is not surprising: (a) Luke is interested in an organized expansion directed from Jerusalem. An independent movement in Galilee alongside Jerusalem does not fit the image, nor does a division in the Jerusalem church (cf. Acts 6:1–7) or the transition to a mission to the gentiles without the legitimation by the apostles (cf. Acts 10); (b) Luke could have omitted Galilee in Acts deliberately because churches already there were simply assumed in the Lukan Gospel.

Churches also existed in bordering regions such as the Decapolis,[105] as the tradition that is critical of the Romans suggests (Mark 5:1–20). The demons that were driven out by Jesus bore the name Legion, which is not coincidental (v. 9); they went into the pigs, which were unclean animals for Jews (and strict Jewish Christians). Mark 5:20 explicitly reports the reaction to this event in establishing a community, saying about the one who was healed: "And he went

---

102. Literacy is to be assumed not only in Jerusalem but also in Galilee; M. Labahn, *Der Gekommene als Wiederkommender*, 83–88.

103. Even Epictetus knew the Christians as "Galileans"; cf. *Diatr.* 4.7.6: "Therefore, . . . madness can produce this attitude of mind toward the things that have just been mentioned (that is, fearlessness before tyrants), and also habit, as with the Galileans."

104. Cf. C. Heil, "Die Q-Gruppe in Galiläa und Syrien." He maintains that a network of Q groups existed in Galilee; the final redaction of Q then follows in southern Syria.

105. Cf. Wenning, "Dekapolis."

away and began to proclaim in the Decapolis what a great thing Jesus had done for him, and all were astonished." The resurrection of the boy in Nain (Luke 7:11–16) and the narrative of the Syrophoenician woman in Mark 7:24–30 suggest that churches existed in the bordering areas surrounding Galilee.

Judea

Other communities of Christ-believers probably existed very early in Judea besides the one in Jerusalem. Other local traditions suggest that these communities existed in places such as Jericho (cf. Mark 10:46–52, the blind man in Jericho), Emmaus (cf. Luke 24:13–35, the Emmaus disciples), or Bethany (cf. Mark 11:1, 11–12 par.; Mark 14:3–9, anointing in Bethany; Luke 24:50, place of the ascension; John 11:1, 18; 12:1; Luke 10:38–42, Lazarus, Mary, and Martha). In addition, the early mission of Philip (already mentioned, see above, 6.2) in the Hellenistic cities of the coastal plain (Gaza, Ashdod, Caesarea, cf. Acts 8:26, 40) and of Peter outside Jerusalem in Lydda/Joppa (cf. Acts 9:32–35, 36–43) and Caesarea on the seacoast (cf. Acts 10:1–48) suggest that beyond Jerusalem further churches existed in Judea and the bordering regions.

> Galilee and Judea were probably connected to each other in a network of places and settlements in which Christ-believers lived. They formed small house and local churches and understood themselves as a movement within Judaism, who believed in Jesus of Nazareth as the resurrected Messiah and the Son of Man. Beginning with the proclamation and activity of Jesus and newly inspired by the Easter events, these communities developed a comprehensive, predominantly oral textual preservation of the tradition and meaning in order to preserve the records in their permanent condition and also through interpretative activity to mediate its meaning in the past into the present.

Samaria

In addition to Judea and Galilee, Samaria was the third center of Christ-believers in Palestine. The origin of the Samaritans is disputed.[106] Previous scholarship connected them with the syncretistic worshipers of Yahweh who, according to 2 Kings 17:29, lived in Samaria in the eighth to seventh centuries

---

106. On the Samaritans, cf. Kippenberg, *Garizim und Synagoge*; Coggins, *Samaritans and Jews*; Lowy, *Principles of Samaritan Bible Exegesis*; Dexinger and Pummer, *Die Samaritaner*; Egger, *Josephus Flavius und die Samaritaner*; Schur, *History of the Samaritans*; Zangenberg, *ΣΑΜΑΡΕΙΑ*; cf. also Lindemann, "Samaria und Samaritaner im Neuen Testament"; Zangenberg, *Frühes Christentum in Samaria*.

BCE. They are to be distinguished from the adherents of a cult on Mount Gerizim who appeared in the fourth century BCE as a new religious community in competition with Jerusalem. According to Josephus (*Ant.* 11.306–12), the occasion for this Samaritan schism was a dispute within the Jerusalem priesthood over mixed marriage. One influential group among the priests regarded the marriages of priests with non-Israelite women as a danger to Jewish identity. In the ensuing conflict, a group of priests left Jerusalem and settled in the Samaritan region. From this time, Zadokite priests carried out their duties not only in Jerusalem but also on Gerizim, a mountain lying southwest of Shechem.

In recent scholarship, a very different model of the origin of the Samaritans has been proposed: "In conclusion, all the evidence shows that the Samaritans are not a sect that broke off from Judaism but rather a branch of Yahwistic Israel in the same sense as the Jews."[107] This view can be supported especially by archaeological and textual-historical evidence. The claim that a sanctuary to Yahweh was not erected on Mount Gerizim until around 330 BCE, as Josephus suggests, is incorrect. Instead, it is certain that a sanctuary to Yahweh (ca. 98m × 98m) existed in the Persian period around the middle of the fifth century BCE. Indeed, it far surpassed the Jerusalem temple of that period.[108] Like the Sadducees, the Samaritans accepted only the Pentateuch (in their own recension) as revelation.[109] It was on this foundation that they developed an eschatology according to which Moses is the only prophet and Gerizim stands in the middle as the only legitimate place for the cult.[110] Around 180 BCE the sanctuary on Gerizim was considerably expanded, but it was later destroyed in 128 BCE by John Hyrcanus. However, the place continued to retain a cultic meaning. In Israel there were probably two competing Yahweh sanctuaries for a long time (from the eighth/seventh century BCE?): the one on Gerizim and the one in Jerusalem. Jerusalem gradually gained the upper hand, and its point of view not only won militarily but also in the textual tradition.[111] A prominent example is Deut. 27:4b–6, where in the Masoretic tradition Moses commands that a Yahweh altar be erected on the cursed Mount Ebal, but a Qumran fragment has "Gerizim" (cf. Deut 11:29; Josh. 8:33–34) and not "Ebal" as the original reading.[112] Here the Jerusalem circles disqualify (around 150 BCE) Mount Gerizim as a place for the cult. In any case, it is evident that, after a lengthy political and religious history of hostility, a final

107. Pummer, *Samaritans*, 25.
108. Pummer, *Samaritans*, 80–81.
109. Cf. Schorch, "Der Pentateuch der Samaritaner."
110. Cf. Kippenberg and Wewers, "Texte aus der samaritanischen Tradition," 97ff.
111. Pummer, *Samaritans*, 195ff.
112. Cf. Kreuzer, *Geschichte, Sprache und Text*, 144–55; Pummer, *Samaritans*, 204–5 (here additional examples).

break came between Jews and Samaritans in the Hasmonean period when the temple on Gerizim was conquered and destroyed.[113] From the end of the second century BCE, tensions (even hostility) existed between Samaritans and Jews, about which the Bible and Josephus report.[114]

In the NT the conduct of Jesus toward Samaritans is described in predominantly positive ways (negatively in Luke 9:51–56; Matt. 10:5f.); especially in the story of the good Samaritan (Luke 10:25–37), they are equated with the Jews (cf. also Luke 17:11–19). According to rabbinic tradition, contact with Samaritans causes impurity, as in a statement attributed to Rabbi Eliezer (around 90 CE): "Anyone who eats the bread of a Samaritan is like one who eats meat from a pig."[115] The early Christian missionaries did not recognize these barriers; Samaria is mentioned programmatically in Acts 1:8 as a mission field, and in Acts 8:4–25 Philip implemented this mission. Jesus appears programmatically as a missionary in John 4:5–42.[116] As Jesus recognizes the identity of the Samaritan woman and discloses her past, she recognizes the messianic significance of the person of Jesus. She led the Samaritans to Jesus (4:27–30), and through Jesus's words she came to crucial knowledge: "This is truly the Savior of the world" (4:42). The harvest metaphor in John 4:48 reflects the post-Easter missionary activity of the disciples, which stands in continuity with the ministry of Jesus. The woman from Samaria who had come to faith becomes a missionary, for she proclaims Jesus to the people of her country (4:29) and bears witness to him (4:39).

Damascus

In the first century CE, Damascus was a Hellenistic commercial metropolis with about 45,000 inhabitants.[117] Around 30 CE, the city stood under Nabatean influence (cf. 2 Cor. 11:32); it had numerous synagogues (cf. Acts 9:2, 20) and a significant Jewish population.[118] The beginning of the church of Christ-believers

---

113. Cf. Pummer, *Samaritans*, 89: "It was not the erection of the temple that caused the division between Judeans and Samaritans, but most likely its destruction by a Judean ruler." The report of Josephus (*Ant.* 12.257–64) and 2 Macc. 6:1–3 is probably tendentious, according to which influential circles of the Samaritans supported the Hellenizing politics of Antiochus IV and contributed to the break.

114. Cf. Josephus, *J.W.* 2.232–46; 3.307–15; *Ant.* 12.257; 13.254–56; 18.29–30, 85–89; 20.118–36; also Sir. 50:26.

115. See m. Shevi'it 8.10.

116. Cf. Okure, *Johannine Approach to Mission.*

117. Cf. Stark, *Rise of Christianity*, 131–42.

118. The information given by Josephus is exaggerated. Josephus, *J.W.* 2.561; 7.368; according to Josephus, 10,000 to 18,000 Jews fell victim in Damascus to a bloodbath.

in Damascus lies in obscurity.[119] The new movement could have made its way on the trade route,[120] or the church could have been formed by the wave of Hellenists fleeing from Jerusalem. It would have understood itself to be a part of the Jewish synagogue community. The report of the call of Paul in Acts 9:1–24 is the only witness that gives a limited view into the early period of the church there. The resurrected Jesus Christ appeared to Paul circa 32/33 CE near Damascus[121] and brought about a life turning point. The fact that Paul earlier had proceeded against Damascus is evidence of its significance and also of its reputation! Paul acted as a militant Pharisee (cf. Gal. 1:13–14; Phil. 3:6), probably on his own, against the new group, in which he saw a danger to Jewish identity. The task commissioned by the high priest mentioned in Acts 9:1 is not legally permissible because the Jerusalem high priest had no authority in Damascus.[122] According to Acts 9:2, Paul wanted to take the followers of the (new) "way" (cf. Acts 19:23; 24:14, 22) prisoner. Perhaps this designation of Christ-believers employed by Luke had its origin in Damascus. Both the place name "Straight Street" (Acts 9:11) and the names "Ananias" and "House of Judas" (Acts 9:10–12) suggest house churches in the center of the city. There Spirit-filled worship services took place, as the calling out of "the name of the Lord" (Acts 9:14) and the baptism of Paul (Acts 9:18) indicate. Damascus was undoubtedly a key church at the beginning. However, all traces of it are soon lost.[123]

Antioch

The Syrian city Antioch on the Orontes was the third largest city in the Roman Empire;[124] at the end of the first century CE, it had a population of

119. On the city of Damascus, cf. Bietenhard, "Die Dekapolis von Pompejus bis Trajan"; Freyberger, "Damaskus"; on the history of the Christian church there, cf. Hengel and Schwemer, *Paul between Damascus and Antioch*, 24–60, 127–32.

120. Intense commercial activity between Jerusalem and Antioch (distance ca. 130 miles) had existed for a long time.

121. Cf. Schnelle, *Apostle Paul*, 87–102.

122. Cf. D.-A. Koch, *Geschichte des Urchristentums*, 203–4.

123. Contra Lüdemann, *Die ersten drei Jahre Christentum*, 156–59, who connects the church in Damascus with texts such as Gal. 3:26–28 and maintains that it is the predecessor of the Antiochian church. According to Lüdemann (159–63), the two crucial churches at the beginning were Jerusalem and Damascus, not Jerusalem and Antioch. Three arguments may be offered against this construction: (1) The limited temporal distance to the original events; (2) no text of the NT attests a significant development for Damascus; and (3) according to Acts 11:19–30, Antioch was the place where the new movement programmatically crossed the boundaries of Judaism.

124. Cf. Josephus, *J.W.* 3.29: Because of its size and general prosperity, Antioch was incontrovertibly the third greatest city ruled by Rome, after Rome and Alexandria. On Antioch, cf. also Kolb, "Antiochia in der frühen Kaiserzeit."

about 300,000.[125] Josephus assumes the existence of a large Jewish community in Antioch (cf. *J.W.* 7.43–45), which probably had about 20,000 to 30,000 people. For the early Christian mission, Antioch offered the best possibilities, for here numerous Greeks sympathized with the Jewish religion.[126] From Antioch came the proselyte Nicolaus (Acts 6:5), who belonged to the group around Stephen; according to Acts 11:19, the Antioch church was founded by Christians who, as a result of the persecution of Stephen, had to leave Jerusalem. The founding probably followed in 34/35 CE.[127] Hellenistic Jewish Christians from Cyprus and Cyrene then went to Antioch to preach the gospel with success among the Greek population (cf. Acts 11:20: "and they preached the Lord Jesus also to the Greeks").[128] Antioch is thus the place where the crucial epoch of early Christianity was introduced: the programmatic proclamation of the gospel to the gentiles without circumcision. The renunciation of circumcision probably resulted from the missionary work itself, for circumcision had previously naturally been a major hurdle (for men). In the ancient world, circumcision had a negative reputation and was considered barbarian.[129] In addition, a model already existed with the Godfearers (see above, 6.1), to which the early churches could orient themselves: participation in monotheism, the ethic, and the promises of Judaism without circumcision. Finally, one could become a full member of the elected community through baptism and the gift of the Spirit, a status that was probably not granted to the Godfearers in the synagogue. In any case, the treatment of circumcision as adiaphora (cf. 1 Cor. 7:19, "Neither circumcision nor uncircumcision matters, but the keeping of the commandments") signified

---

125. Norris, "Antiochien I," maintains for "greater Antioch" at the end of the first century CE a total population of about 300,000 to 600,000.

126. Cf. Josephus, *J.W.* 7.45. The Jews "induced a large number of Greeks to come to their services and, to a certain extent, made them a part of them." On Antioch, cf. also Hengel and Schwemer, *Paul between Damascus and Antioch*, 178–204; Haensch and Zangenberg, "Antiochia."

127. D.-A. Koch, *Geschichte des Urchristentums*, 195, argues for 32/33 CE; Hengel and Schwemer, *Paul between Damascus and Antioch*, 178–79, however, date it around 36 CE.

128. The historicity of these reports is supported by the fact that they do not cohere with Luke's own view, according to which the missionary activity in Cyprus was first conducted by Paul and Barnabas (cf. Acts 13:4; 15:39). It was not Peter but rather unknown Christian missionaries who first initiated the crucial epoch in the history of early Christianity; for the analysis of Acts 11:19–30, see Weiser, *Die Apostelgeschichte*, 1:273–80. Of course, this fact does not mean that before Antioch there was no preaching to Greek-speaking non-Jews! The mission in Samaria, Damascus, Arabia, and Cilicia certainly included these groups; cf. Hengel and Schwemer, *Paul between Damascus and Antioch*, 260–67.

129. Cf. Juvenal, *Sat.* 14.98; Petronius, *Satyricon* 68.8; Josephus, *Ag. Ap.* 2.13; cf. also 1 Macc. 1:15, which reports about hellenized Jews in Jerusalem around 175 BCE: "They removed the marks of circumcision and abandoned the holy covenant" (cf. Josephus, *Ant.* 12.241). It appears that there was a small movement within Hellenistic Judaism that regarded the renunciation of circumcision as a position within Judaism; cf. Philo, *Migration* 89–93. Cf. Blaschke, *Beschneidung*.

the rejection of the validity of the Torah, which was summarized in the love command.[130]

According to the portrayal in Acts, Barnabas and Paul did not belong to the Antiochian church at its beginning; rather, they began their work only after the start of the mission to the gentiles (cf. Acts 11:22, 25). Apparently, Paul first came into contact with the Hellenists from Jerusalem in Antioch.[131] The mission of the Antiochian church among Jews and especially among gentiles must have been successful, for according to Acts 11:26 ("in Antioch the disciples were first called Christians"), in Antioch the term *Christianoi* was a designation by outsiders for the predominantly gentile Christian followers of the new teaching. The origin of this designation from Antioch was confirmed by Ignatius, who uses it in his letters as a normal term for Christians.[132] Thus at the beginning of the 40s, the Christians were perceived as their own group along with Jews and gentiles. From the pagan perspective, they were considered a non-Jewish movement and must have taken on a recognizable theological profile and their own organizational structure.[133] The term *Christianoi* is a Grecized Latinism,[134] a fact indicating that the Roman provincial administration already had an interest in the new movement.[135] In addition, the formation of the word indicates that the title Χριστός had already become a proper name among outsiders.

Why was the Christian proclamation so successful in Antioch in particular? In the first place, the gospel was comprehensively preached in a large city where numerous sympathizers toward the Jewish faith lived, and the ties to the synagogue were probably not as close as in Palestine. This led to the formation of house churches, in which the orientation was to the new rather than to the old. The previous religious, social, and national distinctions now lost meaning, and a pneumatically defined community emerged (cf. Gal. 3:26–28) that was perceived by outsiders as a new religion. With the separation from the synagogue, the portion and influence of Christians from the gentiles increased.[136] Consequently, the later disputes over the function of the Torah for uncircumcised Christians became unavoidable.

---

130. Cf. Horn, "Der Verzicht auf die Beschneidung," 496, who comments correctly of "a changed emphasis within the Torah."

131. Cf. Wellhausen, *Kritische Analyse der Apostelgeschichte*, 21.

132. Cf. Ign. *Eph.* 11.2; *Magn.* 4; *Rom.* 3.2; *Pol.* 7.3.

133. Cf. Harnack, *Mission and Expansion of Christianity*, 399–418.

134. Cf. Blass, Debrunner, and Rehkopf, *Grammatik* §5.

135. Cf. Mehl, "Sprachen im Kontakt," 198, who sees in the creation of the word an action by the authorities, primarily for use among government authorities. Cf. also D.-A. Koch, *Geschichte des Urchristentums*, 199, who suggests "that the designation is derived from Roman provincial authorities." Hengel and Schwemer, *Paul between Damascus and Antioch*, 350–51, see analogies to the Piso Inscription, where followers of the ruler Piso are called "Pisoniani."

136. Cf. Hengel and Schwemer, *Paul between Damascus and Antioch*, 173–83.

Rome

In the first century CE, Rome was undoubtedly the world capital, with around one million inhabitants.[137] The origin of Christianity in Rome cannot be understood apart from the Jewish community there, which is mentioned for the first time in 139 BCE.[138] The Jews in Rome lived through a history full of changes. The community grew very quickly. Josephus (*Ant.* 17.300) mentioned that eight thousand Roman Jews accompanied the arriving delegation after the death of Herod. Augustus was favorable toward the Jews; he respected their customs and sanctioned the status of their communities as an "ancient religion."[139] It is reported about Claudius that in 41 CE, because of the great number of the Jews, he did not drive them out of Rome but forbade them from assembling (Dio Cassius 60.6.6). The Jews organized themselves in individual communities with their own assemblies and their own administration.[140] Approximately 30,000 to 40,000 Jews lived in Rome at the turn of the millennium.[141] Although there were continuing conflicts between the authorities and the Jews, this religion was tolerated and accepted as an ancient religion. The expulsion under Tiberius in 19 CE and under Claudius in 49 CE was a harsh blow for the Jewish community. The Edict of Claudius presupposes conflicts between Jews and Christians over "Chrestus" and is evidence of the success of the Christian mission in the synagogues. Like Judaism before it, Christianity made its way to Rome by the trade routes, probably at the beginning of the 40s CE. It is not coincidental that there were pre-Pauline churches in Puteoli (Acts 28:12) and Rome (Rom. 1:7; Acts 28:14). Here existed not only two large Jewish communities, but also the primary trade route connecting the eastern part of the empire with Rome ran through Puteoli. Probably unknown early Christian missionaries brought the gospel to Rome, entering the capital of the empire as slaves, freedmen, tradesmen, and

---

137. Cf. Kolb, *Rom*, 457.

138. On Judaism in Rome, cf. Wiefel, "Jewish Community in Ancient Rome"; Lichtenberger, "Josephus und Paulus in Rom"; Rutgers, *The Jews in Late Ancient Rome*; Noethlichs, *Das Judentum und der römische Staat*; Claussen, *Versammlung, Gemeinde, Synagoge*, 103–11; Margaret Williams, "Jewish Community in Rome in Antiquity."

139. Cf. Philo, *Legat.* 156–57: "Thus it was known to Augustus that they possessed synagogues and gathered especially on the holy Sabbath, where they were publicly instructed in the philosophy of their fathers. . . . Nevertheless, he did not drive them from Rome and did not take away from them their rights as Roman citizens because they held their Jewish nationality in high esteem. He introduced no changes against the synagogues; he did not hinder them from assembling to interpret their laws, and he placed no obstacle to the offering of their sacrifices."

140. Cf. Wiefel, "The Jewish Community in Ancient Rome," 86–92; Lampe, *Die stadtrömischen Christen*, 367ff.; Lichtenberger, "Josephus und Paulus in Rom," 247–48.

141. Cf. Noethlichs, *Das Judentum und der römische Staat*, 10; Kolb, *Rom*, 621.

businesspeople.[142] Initially Jewish Christians were the majority in the church. This situation changed with their expulsion that was dictated by the Edict of Claudius (see below, 6.5). When the Letter to the Romans was written in 56 CE, the gentile Christians were already in the majority (cf. Rom. 1:5, 13–15; 10:1–3; 11:13, 17–32; 15:15–16, 18).

One may draw conclusions cautiously about the social stratification within the Roman church, based on Rom. 16:3–16, in which twenty-eight individuals are listed (twenty-six by name). Thus Prisca and Aquila (Rom. 16:3–4) were independent free traders who possibly employed dependent employees or slaves.[143] Romans 16:10–11b mentions as fellow Christians the members of the households of Aristobulus and Narcissus, who were slaves or freedmen working in the house of their master. The analysis of names from Rom. 16:3–16 found in inscriptions indicates that, of thirteen comparable names, four indicate a person who was free and nine indicate that the one bearing the name was of slave origin.[144] Many tasks in the church were performed by women, for it is said only of them that they "labor" (κοπιάω in Rom. 16:6, 12; cf. also v. 13b). Of the twenty-six who are named in Rom. 16:3–16, twelve came from the East to Rome and are personally known by Paul, an indication that a great flood of Christians came from the eastern part of the empire into the Roman church. One may assume similar relationships for the beginning, however in smaller numbers and primarily under Jewish Christian control; mostly slaves, freedmen, and women probably would have been brought to the Christianity that existed in Rome.

Romans 16:3–16 also provides information about the organizational forms of the Roman Christians. Paul mentions not only the house church of Prisca and Aquila (Rom. 16:5), but at least Rom. 16:14 and 16:15 offer evidence for the existence of several independent house churches in Rome.[145] From the beginning in Rome there was probably no established Christian church with a large room for assembling. Rather, as time went by, several house churches developed. In any case, Christianity in Rome grew, primarily very quickly through the flow from

142. On the conditions for the origin of the Roman church, cf. Lampe, "Urchristliche Missionswege nach Rom," who assumes that Jewish freedmen and slaves of pagan masters in Rome served as bridgeheads "by whom the Jewish Christians in the 40s CE traveled from the Syro-Palestine East into the world capital Rome" (127).

143. Cf. Lampe, *Die stadtrömischen Christen*, 156–64.

144. Cf. Lampe, *Die stadtrömischen Christen*, 141–53.

145. Cf. Lampe, *Die stadtrömischen Christen*, 301ff. The separation into house churches was of great significance, according to Lampe, "Urchristliche Missionswege nach Rom," 126. In the 50s CE at least seven separate Christian islands existed in the world capital. Evidence of a space that would be a center for the various scattered groups existed neither in this period nor later in the first two centuries. Every group probably celebrated its own worship service in a dwelling, so one may speak of them as house churches.

the eastern part of the empire. Paul expected material and personal support in 56 CE for his mission to Spain. The persecution of Christians under Nero in 64 CE presupposes the expansion of Christianity as well as a recognition of Christians.

Alexandria

At the beginning of the 50s, the Alexandrian missionary Apollos (see above, 6.2) appeared in Corinth (cf. 1 Cor. 1:12; 3:4ff.; 16:12). According to Acts 18:24–28, he worked earlier as a founder of the church in Ephesus. Inasmuch as Paul valued and accepted his work in Corinth, Apollos had probably already been a Christian for some time. Whether he became a Christian in Alexandria or later in Jerusalem (cf. Acts 2:10; 6:9), Asia Minor, or Greece is an open question. However, it remains possible that the missionary activity of the Hellenists reached Alexandria and that there Apollos became acquainted with the teaching of the new religion. Relationships between Alexandria and Jerusalem had existed for centuries, for the largest Jewish diaspora community lived in Alexandria.[146] The city was one of the centers of Jewish wisdom literature; thus it is not surprising that Apollos in Acts 18:25 is portrayed as the representative of a wisdom Christology. No evidence exists for an early church in Alexandria, but the possibility cannot be ruled out. Indeed, Alexandria/Egypt at the end of the first and beginning of the second century became a center of Christian theology, as especially the NT papyri and the appearance of Gnostic teachers indicate.[147]

6.5 Competitors and Conflicts

In the period between about 30 and 50, numerous disputes occurred in the earliest churches, which in those churches led to the development of their own identity and at the same time called for separation from the Jewish mother religion.

The Baptist Movement

John the Baptist[148] was a Jewish prophet of repentance, about whose history one can speak with great certainty:[149] (1) According to Luke 3:1, his activity

---

146. Cf. Schimanowski, "Alexandria."

147. $\mathfrak{P}^{52}$ (John 18:31–33, 37–38) was written around 125 CE. The Gnostics appeared under Hadrian (117–138) in Alexandria; see below, 14.2 under "The Beginnings of Gnosticism."

148. On John the Baptist and his movement, cf. Böcher, "Johannes der Täufer"; Ernst, "Johannes der Täufer"; Backhaus, Die "Jüngerkreise" des Täufers Johannes; H. Stegemann, Die Essener, Qumran, 292–313; Meier, Mentor, Message and Miracles, 19–233; U. Müller, Johannes der Täufer.

149. Three independent sources provide information about John the Baptist: (1) Mark (cf. Mark 1:2–8 par.; 6:17–29 par.), (2) the logia source (Luke 3:7–9, 16–17Q; Luke 7:18–19, 22–23, 24–28, 33–34; 16:16Q), and (3) Josephus, Ant.18.116–19.

began in the time of Tiberius, that is, in the year 28 or 29 CE. The duration of
his activity is unknown; it did not last long, for when Jesus was thought to be
John redivivus (cf. Mark 6:14–15; 8:28), this presupposes that Jesus appeared
after the demise of John the Baptist. (2) The place of his activity is, according
to Mark 1:4–5, "in the wilderness" (cf. Matt. 11:7), and he baptized in the
Jordan. (3) The preaching of John was entirely determined by the eschatological imminent expectation (cf. Matt. 3:7–12 par.). His preaching is focused on
judgment and repentance; he appeals to the entire people, including the pious,
and calls them to a radical repentance. John's baptism of repentance is to be
considered an original creation of the Baptist. He lived in the consciousness
that the eschatological forgiveness of sins that only God can give already takes
place sacramentally in his work. The judge of the world himself will ratify
in fire what John's baptism already determines. (4) John was executed at the
command of Herod Antipas (cf. Mark 6:17–29; Josephus, *Ant.* 18.118–19).
While the anecdote in Mark 6 gives as the reason for the execution the familial
relationship of the Herodians, Josephus (more probable historically) gives
political reasons: John was so successful that all of the people ran to him,
and so Herod Antipas had this successful competitor put out of the way.

Whether John the Baptist gathered a circle of disciples around himself
during his lifetime must remain an open question.[150] Among those who were
baptized by John, Jesus was certainly included (cf. Mark 1:9–11 par.); he probably belonged among the disciples of John for a certain period.[151] After the
death of the Baptist, a Baptist movement developed, which apparently saw in
John the messiah of Israel (cf. John 1:20). A characteristic of this group was
regular fasting (cf. Mark 2:18 par., "And the disciples of John and the disciples
of the Pharisees fasted") and their own prayer (Luke 5:33; 11:1). The disciples
of John and the developing Christian communities resembled each other and
were compared to each other by their contemporaries (cf. Luke 7:33–34). Thus
it is not surprising that a competition on several levels developed after Easter.
The first level of conflict between the two movements involved a personal
exchange, especially of the disciples of John who changed to the (more successful) Jesus movement (cf. John 1:35–51; 3:22–23; 4:1). The second conflict
involved the question of the priority in salvation history. The Baptist, who
made an extraordinary eschatological claim, becomes in the gospel tradition
the "forerunner" and the one who prepares the way for Jesus (cf. Mark 1:2
par.). The Gospel of John finally nullifies the independence of the Baptist and
makes of him a mere witness for Jesus as Son of God (John 1:23, 27–34, 36;

150. E.g., Ernst, *Johannes der Täufer*, 349–52, argues in favor of this view.
151. Cf. Schnelle, *Theology of the New Testament*, 78–80.

3:27–30). The miracles of Jesus were apparently another point of conflict; from the Christian viewpoint they were the indicators of the superiority of Jesus (cf. Mark 6:14 par.; Luke 7:18–23Q; John 10:40–42). Finally, ascetic tendencies existed within the Baptist movement that were not shared by the Jesus movement (cf. Mark 2:18 par.; Luke 7:33–34Q). In Jesus of Nazareth the Christ-believers recognized the Messiah promised by John the Baptist and adopted from him the practice of baptism. However, they distinguished their baptism from that of John through the experience of the Spirit; while John baptized only with water, they baptized with water and the Spirit (cf. Mark 1:8 par.; Acts 18:25; 19:1–7). Nevertheless, the Baptist movement existed over a lengthy period and was active beyond the Palestinian-Syrian region in Asia Minor, as Acts 18:24–19:7 indicates.[152]

The Persecution under Agrippa I

When Claudius became emperor after the death of Caligula (January 24, 41 CE), he made the effort, in contrast to his predecessor, to preserve the status quo with respect to the Jews. In the year 39/40 CE, Caligula had provoked a grave conflict with Judaism (see above, 3.3), for after the destruction of a newly erected altar to Caesar in Jamnia by the Jews, he commanded that an image of the caesar be placed in the Jerusalem temple with the force of arms (cf. Philo, *Legat.* 200–207).[153] The intervention of Agrippa I in Rome and the clever involvement of Petronius as commander of the Syrian army resulted in a delay in placing the statue in the temple until the conflict could be resolved with the murder of Caligula. After this event, Claudius set out to stabilize the relationship with the Jews. He confirmed the special rights that Augustus had granted to the Jews,[154] but at the same time he made it clear that no further unrest by the Jews would be accepted. An Edict of Claudius, which he issued in the first year of his rule (41 CE), illustrates his concern for the avoidance of unrest. "The number of Jews has become so great that it has become difficult to ban them from Rome without an uproar. Thus Claudius declined expelling them, but commanded them to remain in their way of life and not

---

152. On the further historical impact of the Baptist and his disciples, cf. Ernst, *Johannes der Täufer*, 363–83.

153. On the Caligula crisis, cf. Philo, *Legat.* 197–337; Josephus, *J.W.* 2.184–203; *Ant.* 18.256–309; on the analysis of the texts in the Caligula crisis as a whole, cf. Theissen, *The Gospels in Context*, 142–44.

154. Cf. Josephus, *Ant.* 19.280–91, 299–311; 20.10–14. The special rights granted to the Jews included the right of assembly, the temple tax, internal administration of justice, Sabbath rest, the keeping of food laws, and no sacrifice to pagan gods; cf. Cineira, *Die Religionspolitik des Kaisers Claudius*, 165–70.

to assemble" (Dio Cassius 60.6.6). The text assumes the existence of unrest among the Jews that arose in their assemblies. Noteworthy is the command of the caesar to maintain the traditional manner of life, which made conflicts on this point inevitable. Those who caused these conflicts may have included those who believed in Jesus of Nazareth as Messiah.[155]

Agrippa I (ca. 7 BCE–44 CE) was in Rome at the time of the change of emperors from Caligula to Claudius in the year 41 and probably knew the basic elements of the policy toward religion of his friend, the new caesar.[156] In 41 CE, Claudius made him the king over the entire kingdom of his grand-father Herod the Great. Agrippa knew about the endangered situation of Jews throughout the Roman Empire in other conflicts; according to his view, it was logical to proceed against the new group of Christ-believers, which could cause conflicts. According to Acts 12:1–4, "About this time, Herod laid his hand on some in the church in order to mistreat them. But he killed James the brother of John by the sword. And as he saw that it pleased the Jews, he continued and imprisoned Peter also. But these were the days of unleavened bread. After he had seized him, he put him in prison and handed him over to four squads of four soldiers each in order to watch him. For he intended to place him before the people after the festival." Although the charges against James the son of Zebedee and the other Christ-believers certainly could be made only on religious grounds, James was killed by the sword, an indication of political motives. Evidently this procedure against the Christ-believers was popular, for Peter also was taken prisoner in order to be taken later before the people. He was able to flee from Jerusalem and avoid the fate of the son of Zebedee. Although according to the witness of Acts only James was killed, Mark 10:35–40 appears to presuppose the martyrdom of both sons of Zebedee. However, the reference to John the son of Zebedee in Gal. 2:9 along with James the brother of the Lord and Cephas confirms the report of Acts. Prob-ably the son of Zebedee was able, like Peter, to escape the persecutions.[157] The repression probably had various grounds: (1) In the Caligula crisis, Agrippa had forcefully involved himself in support of the cultic purity of the temple; hence the Christians' distancing themselves from the temple could have justi-fied his actions (cf. Mark 14:56–58; Acts 6:13–14).[158] (2) As a motivation for his persecution, Acts 13:3 states that he wanted to be beloved by the Jews.

---

155. Cf. Botermann, "Das Judenedikt des Kaisers Claudius," 103–40.
156. On Agrippa I, cf. especially Schwartz, *Agrippa I*.
157. Cf. also Theissen, "Die Verfolgung unter Agrippa dem I." He interprets the metaphor of the cup as a reference to a violent death while, on the other hand, the metaphor of baptism is understood as rescue from danger. Cf. also Schwemer, "Verfolger und Verfolgte bei Paulus."
158. Cf. Theissen, *Die Jesusbewegung*, 290–93.

The newly strengthened Sadducees rejected every form of hope for the resurrection so that they must be regarded as opponents of the Christ-believers. This action would accommodate them. (3) The success of the early Christian mission placed in question the status quo in relation to the Romans, which had been reached only with much effort. It undermined the differentiation between non-Jews and Jews, which was equally important for Romans and Jews. Consequently, Agrippa I proceeded against the new movement because, from his political and religious perspective, they were primarily a cause of unrest. Inasmuch as Acts 12:18–25 regards the sudden death of Agrippa as the consequence of his activity against the Christ-believers, the events probably took place in 43/44 CE. Paul may have referred to the persecution under Agrippa in about 50 CE in 1 Thess. 2:14–15: "For you have become imitators, brothers, of the churches of God in Judea, as you suffered the same persecutions from your countrymen as they suffered from the Jews, who killed the Lord Jesus and the prophets and persecuted us." A great persecution of the churches in Judea by the Jews is assumed, about which the Thessalonians were informed.

The persecution under Agrippa I had severe consequences for the Jerusalem church and the history of early Christianity. Peter, the leader of the church, had to leave Jerusalem (Acts 12:17). As a result, James the brother of the Lord took over the leadership of the church around 43/44. Both Acts 12:17 (Peter says: "Tell James and the brothers") and a comparison of Gal. 1:18–19 and 2:9 point to this change in leadership. When Cephas was the leader of the Jerusalem church during Paul's first visit to the city in 35 CE and Paul interacted almost exclusively with him, Peter stands in the list of the "pillars" after James the brother of the Lord. At the apostolic council, James the brother of the Lord led the debate as a member of the Jerusalem church, and he claimed authority over Peter at the conflict in Antioch (cf. Gal. 2:11–12).

> With James the brother of the Lord, the political direction of the Jerusalem church changed. As a consequence of the conflict under Agrippa I, James steered a new politics of rapprochement toward official Judaism and a distancing from Paul's mission to the gentiles apart from the requirement of circumcision.

The Edict of Claudius

Wide-ranging consequences for relationships among Christianity and Judaism, the Roman church, and the early Christian history of missions grew out of the Edict of Claudius.[159] Suetonius (*Claud.* 25.4) reports about Claudius, "Iudaeos impulsore Chresto assidue tumultuantis Roma expulit" (He drove the Jews out of Rome because they, incited by Chrestus, continually caused unrest).[160] This event is dated in the ninth year of the rule of Claudius (49 CE) by the later Christian historian Orosius (fifth cent.).[161] The chronologically oldest reference to the Edict of Claudius appears in Acts 18:2, where it is reported that Aquila and Prisca had recently come to Corinth "because Claudius had mandated that all Jews must leave Rome." The occasion for the edict was the success of the Christian mission among the synagogues in Rome (and other regions of the empire), which had resulted in strong defensive reaction within Judaism. They were so intense that the caesar considered it necessary to intervene in order to prevent greater unrest. The Edict of Claudius scarcely led to the expulsion of all the approximately 30,000 to 40,000 Jews from Rome. However, numerous leading personalities of both groups had to leave the world capital.[162] Consequently, a dangerous situation emerged for the Jews. If in the heart of the Roman Empire a notorious instigator of unrest attracts attention, then that could mean for the Romans that it would be only one more small step to take further harsher measures against Judaism, for example, to drive all Jews from Rome and to declare Judaism a religion that was no longer tolerated. Indeed, Claudius had confirmed the special rights of the Jews conferred by Augustus, but further unrest could lead to a loss of the privileged status.[163] In addition, the action of the caesar was quickly known in the provinces so that it no longer involved a local conflict. That was sufficient reason for the Jews to clarify the relationship to the new group, in order not to provoke more dangerous conflicts. The Jews, from their perspective, had to regard Christianity as a destabilizing factor. It won over its members from the synagogue to a considerable extent and, as a supposed part of Judaism, endangered the peaceful relationship to the Roman state.

159. Cf. Cineira, *Die Religionspolitik des Kaisers Claudius*, 187–216.

160. For the evidence that "impulsore Chresto" is not the name of an unknown Jewish insurrectionist or messianic pretender with the common slave name "Chrestos," cf. Botermann, *Das Judenedikt des Claudius*, 57–71; Cineira, *Die Religionspolitik des Kaisers Claudius*, 201–10; Cook, *Roman Attitudes toward the Christians*, 15–22.

161. Cf. Orosius, *Historia adversum paganos* 7.6.15.

162. Cf. Riesner, *Paul's Early Period*, 157–80 (he calculates a considerable number of expelled Jews or Jewish Christians). Acts 18:2 indicates, in any case, that it was not only a symbolic act.

163. In the years 47–49 CE, Claudius intensified his efforts to revive the Roman religion; in 49 the expansion of the pomerium falls, i.e., the realm in which the Roman gods were to be worshiped; cf. Riesner, *Paul's Early Period*, 93–95; Cineira, *Die Religionspolitik des Kaisers Claudius*, 39–54.

The Edict of Claudius is connected to the expulsion of Jews from Rome, who always stood in the context of missionary-syncretistic activities.[164] The expulsions mentioned by Valerius Maximus[165] in 139 BCE were the result of the propagation of a Jewish-Asia Minor mixed cult by syncretistic Jews in Rome.[166] As a result of aggressive proselytizing,[167] in 19 CE, in an action against oriental cults,[168] Tiberius expelled the Jews and followers of the Isis cult from Rome.[169] From the Roman perspective, the Edict of Claudius cohered with these decisions; in addition, Claudius also forbade the exercise of the Druid religion.[170] Barbarian cults could be as little tolerated as aggressive missionary developments. In the year 41 two events happened that belong to the prehistory of the Edict of Claudius. In the first place, Dio Cassius (60.6.6) reports in an enumeration of the measures of the new caesar: "The Jews had increased so much in numbers that, because of their numbers, it had become difficult to expel them from the city without causing unrest. Thus Claudius refrained from expelling them, but commanded that they maintain their customary manner of life, and that they not organize assemblies." In Alexandria a massive anti-Jewish riot occurred in 41 BCE in a dispute over tax increases, to which Claudius reacted with a letter to the Alexandrians. On the one hand, Claudius confirmed the privileges of the Jews; but on the other hand, he made unmistakably clear that the Jews should restrain themselves and especially

164. The Baccanalian trial recorded by Livy 39.8–18 in 186 BCE indicates clearly that the religious tolerance of the Romans ended where they feared a destabilization of public order by cultic activities (secret worship assemblies, orgies, danger of conspiracies). On the relationship of Roman religions to other religions, cf. Berner, "Religio und Superstitio."

165. Valerius Maximus, *Facta et dicta memorabilia* 1.3.3: The same praetor (Cornelius Hispalos) forced the Jews who had sought to infect the Roman rites with the cult of Jupiter Sabazius to return to their houses; texts and commentaries in Stern, *Greek and Latin Authors on Jews and Judaism*, 1:358–60; Conzelmann, *Gentiles, Jews, Christians*, 110.

166. Cf. Hengel, *Judaism and Hellenism*, 1:263.

167. Cf. Suetonius, *Tib.* 36: "He forbade the introduction of strange religious customs, particularly the Egyptian and Judean, who had confessed to such superstitions, and he forced those who had confessed to such a superstition to burn the clothes and other items associated with the cultic activities. . . . He expelled those people who belonged to the cult and all of those who held to similar beliefs." Cf. Josephus, *Ant.* 18.81–83, who reports that a Jewish teacher of the law in Rome was able to win prominent women to Judaism. The result was that Tiberius expelled all Jews out of the capital city.

168. Cf. Seneca, *Ep.* 108.22: "The days of my youth coincided with the early part of the reign of Tiberius Caesar. Some foreign rites were at that time being inaugurated, and abstinence from certain kinds of animal food was set down as a proof of interest in the strange cult."

169. Tacitus, *Ann.* 2.85.5 (4,000 followers of Egyptian and Jewish cults were deported to Sardinia in order to battle against piracy); Suetonius, *Tib.* 36.1–2; Josephus, *Ant.* 18.65–83.

170. Cf. Suetonius, *Claud.* 25.5: "He prohibited the religious customs of the Druids from Gaul with their gruesome, barbaric character. At the time of Augustus participation in it was prohibited only for Roman citizens."

"that they should not invite or bring in other Jews, who travel from Syria or Egypt. In that case I will be forced to create the strongest suspicion. If you do not, I will proceed against those in every way who incite trouble in the entire world."[171] When political freedom was endangered by the unimpeded migration of Jews into the large cities or by the conflicts caused by the Jews, the caesar saw himself forced to energetic action.

In addition, critical statements by Cicero[172] and Seneca indicate that the Roman leadership class had nothing to do with the Jews. Statements of Seneca, a witness of the period, are informative, as recorded in Augustine; even then the Christians were the hated enemies of the Jews. Seneca says of the Jews: "However the manner of life of this shameful people has gained such influence that they have found an entry. The defeated have given laws to the victors."[173] The dangerous political and cultural total constellation of factors must have led the Jews to the insight that they should distance themselves from the Christian movement because of the latter's offensive missionary-oriented and syncretistic character.

The Edict of Claudius not only affected the Jews in Rome; it was also significant for the Christian movement in several respects. (1) It hastened the separation of Judaism from emerging Christianity. (2) The expulsion of Jews and Jewish Christians crucially changed the composition of the Roman church. Whereas the Jewish Christians constituted the majority until the Edict of Claudius, they were in the minority after the relaxation of the edict (after the death of Claudius in 54 CE). In the persecution of Christians under Nero in 64 CE, the authorities distinguished between Jews and Christians.[174] (3) The edict probably hindered Paul from coming to Rome earlier (cf. Rom. 1:13; 15:22). (4) The Edict of Claudius made clear to the young Christian church that it must find its way in the tense atmosphere between the synagogue and the Roman authorities.

Local Conflicts

In some passages in the letters of Paul and Acts, it becomes evident that Jews took actions against the early Christians after the Edict of Claudius. Acts 17:1–9 reports about the Pauline mission in Thessalonica and the conflict that

171. CPJ 153 (text in Leipoldt and Grundmann, Umwelt, 2:250–53); somewhat different is the report of Josephus, Ant. 19.279–85.
172. Cf. Cicero, Pro L. Valerio Flacco 66, where Cicero comments about a Jewish group in the trial against Flaccus: "You know how strong it is, how it holds together, and what roles it plays in assemblies."
173. Augustine, De civitate dei 6.11; cf. Seneca, Ep. 95.47; 108.2.
174. Cf. Tacitus, Ann. 15.44.

arose. Paul was present in Thessalonica in 49 and the beginning of 50 CE;[175] he had great success in the environment of the synagogue (Acts 17:4). This success resulted in a tumult incited by the Jews. Christians were dragged before the city officials as two political charges were made against them: (1) The Christians incited uproar throughout the world (Acts 17:6), and (2) they violated the decrees (δόγματα) of the caesar. The plural δόγματα probably refers to the Edict of Claudius,[176] and the charge of causing uproar throughout the world is to be understood in this context. When the early Christians proclaimed that, in view of the imminent parousia of Christ, *Roma aeterna* is temporary and God had appointed the crucified Jesus of Nazareth as king, this was a provocation to the Roman authorities. First Thessalonians 2:14–16 confirms that actions during this period against Paul and his coworkers were taken, in which the Jews also participated,[177] for only in this context is the sharp anti-Jewish polemic in 1 Thess. 2:14–16 to be explained. Apparently, the Jews accused the apostle before the Roman authorities, claiming that he disturbed the peace and violated Claudius's political policy toward religions. The Pauline mission to the gentiles was not only viewed critically by the Jerusalem church but was also fought against by Jews in Asia Minor and Greece. Their intent was probably to portray the new movement as no longer a part of Judaism with its special rights but rather as a *collegium illicitum*.

6.6 The Development of the Community's Own Cult Praxis and Theology: The First Forms of Institutionalization

About 40–50 CE not only did the transition to a mission to the gentiles without circumcision take place, but also the final development of the movement's own cultic practice and of a new theological world occurred. Thus the transfer of norms, the variation of norms, and the development of new norms played a decisive role. This process occurred especially on three levels: (1) Within Judaism, the Christ-believers increasingly distanced themselves from the previous rites, developed new norms, and established their own new identity. (2) In churches outside Palestine also, in a predominantly Hellenistic environment, the formation of the community's own tradition and the new praxis associated with it began. (3) With the first missionary journey, a successful expansion of the new movement took place, for a programmatic mission to the gentiles

---

175. Cf. Riesner, *Paul's Early Period*, 323.
176. Cf. Cineira, *Die Religionspolitik des Kaisers Claudius*, 268.
177. Cf. Riesner, *Paul's Early Period*, 312; Cineira, *Die Religionspolitik des Kaisers Claudius*, 280–86.

apart from circumcision had not existed before. Churches were formed in the originally Greco-Roman cultural sphere, which must have had an impact on churches within the Jewish environment and on the self-understanding of the movement of Christ-believers.

New Norms in the Jewish Context

A differentiation and distancing of the Christ-believers from the Judaism shaped by Pharisaism were inevitable. The Pharisees, with their "oral Torah," had created a rule-and-power system[178] that cast a comprehensive net over the people and identified it with God's will. The early (oral) synoptic tradition indicates especially how new traditions were created and legitimated with Jesus's words.[179] The discourse about the original will of God encompassed especially the following themes.

1. *Sabbath*. Here the expansion of a religious world is especially evident. The central disputed question was Who is lord over the Sabbath? Especially the pre-Markan tradition gives a clear answer: "Thus the Son of Man is Lord also over the Sabbath" (Mark 2:28).[180] While the Damascus Document (CD 1.16–17) specifies that no one who has fallen into a water hole on the Sabbath "may be rescued with a ladder or a rope or any other object," in Mark 3:4 Jesus defends the healing of the man with the withered hand on the Sabbath with the subversive question, "Is it allowed to do good or evil, to heal or to kill, on the Sabbath?" Luke 13:14–16 also emphasizes the legitimacy of healing the sick on the Sabbath. In the Pauline churches, the Sabbath played no role at all;[181] in the synoptic tradition one may observe the tendency to become emancipated from the dominant Pharisaic interpretation and to develop the community's own Sabbath praxis.

2. *Forgiveness*. Directly related to the Sabbath question was the question of the forgiveness of sins (on the Sabbath). The early churches probably created

178. Josephus reports on the Pharisees' particular understanding of tradition: "The Pharisees have given to the people regulations from the successors of the fathers, which are not written down in the laws of Moses" (*Ant.* 13.297). The Pharisaic understanding was taken up in m. Avot 1.1, "Make a fence around the Torah."

179. For this process, see Dibelius, *From Tradition to Gospel*; Bultmann, *History of the Synoptic Tradition*.

180. In Mark 2:23–28 the problem of work in the field is addressed directly; the larger Sabbath issue is addressed indirectly; cf. CD 10.20–21: "One may not go out into the field to do business on the Sabbath. He shall not walk more than ten thousand cubits from his town." Concerning whether an animal can be rescued from a ditch on the Sabbath, see Matt. 12:11; Luke 14:1–5; cf. CD 9.13–14. An extreme form of the priestly Sabbath rigorism is found in Num. 15:32–36, where a man gathers sticks on the Sabbath and is then stoned.

181. In 1 Cor. 16:2 "on the first Sabbath" means the first day of the new week, the Sunday of the resurrection.

their own practice of the forgiveness of sins in the context of baptism and the Lord's Supper (cf. Mark 1:4; 14:22–24; 1 Cor. 6:11), in which they called on the Jesus tradition (according to Mark 2:5, Jesus says to the lame man, "My son, your sins are forgiven"). The objection of the scribes (Mark 2:7, "He blasphemes God! Who can forgive sins except God alone?") can be derived from texts such as Ps. 130:4, "For forgiveness is with you."[182] The explosive nature of the theme is obvious, for in this case the temple lost its meaning as the place of atonement, and Jesus Christ as the Son of God took its place.

3. *Pure/impure.* An additional focus was the departure from the fundamental religious distinction between "pure" and "impure," which is stated in a programmatic way already in Mark 7:15: "Nothing that comes in from outside the person into him can make him impure, but rather what comes out of the man, which makes the person unclean."[183] From the beginning of creation, the fundamental distinction of "pure" and "impure" did not exist; rather, not until Gen. 7:2 does the separation of clean and unclean animals appear. The purity laws and especially the food laws[184] lost their meaning as the legitimizing boundary markers for Jesus and the early churches because, for Jesus, uncleanness comes from another source. The variants of Mark 7:15 in Mark 7:18b, 20 and the acceptance of Mark 7:15 in Rom. 14:14 as words of the Lord attest to an actual relativizing of the purity and food laws of Lev. 11–17. Jesus's interactions with the cultically impure (Mark 1:40–45 par.; Luke 7:1–10Q; Luke 7:36–50; 17:11–19; 18:9–14; 19:1–10) and the critique by the Pharisees (cf. Luke 11:39–42; Matt. 23:25) are evidence of this change. Finally, Luke 10:7Q is further evidence, where Jesus says to his disciples in his commissioning speech: "Eat and drink whatever they give you." The churches thus place themselves in opposition to the Pharisees, Sadducees, and Qumran Essenes, for whom the cultic ritual norms maintain their essential significance, despite some differences in praxis. These functioned not only as distinguishing signs to the gentiles and to the religiously indifferent of their own people; they were also an expression of obedience to the Torah and the continuing validity of the word of God delivered by Moses.[185]

4. *Fasting.* Just as the cultic boundary and the food laws lost their significance for the relationship between humankind and God and between humans

---

182. According to Str-B 1:495–96, this was the principle of the entire rabbinic tradition.

183. Kümmel offers a convincing, exemplary analysis in "Äußere und innere Reinheit."

184. The food laws (cf., e.g., Deut. 14:3–21) during this period comprised the central content of the Jewish understanding of the law. Cf. C. Heil, *Die Ablehnung der Speisegebote.*

185. On the Pharisees, cf. Neusner, "Die pharisäischen rechtlichen Überlieferungen"; Neusner and Chilton, *In Quest of the Historical Pharisees*; on the position of the Sadducees, cf. Schürer, *History of the Jewish People*, 2:404–14; on Qumran, cf. H.-W. Kuhn, "Jesus vor dem Hintergrund der Qumrangemeinde."

themselves, with the impending coming of the kingdom of God, the present is not a time for fasting (cf. Mark 2:18b–19a; Matt. 11:18–19//Luke 7:33–34). What was true for the Pharisees and the disciples of the Baptist was no longer the case for the early churches.

5. *Hand washing.* The churches also took a new position concerning ritual hand washing (cf. Mark 7:1–6) and vows (cf. Mark 7:7–13).

6. *Divorce.* The issuance of a certificate of divorce in conformity with the Torah (cf. Deut. 24:1)[186] was rejected, and new regulations were developed for separations in Paul (cf. 1 Cor. 7:10–12), in the pre-Markan tradition (cf. Mark 10:1–12), in the logia source (cf. Luke 16:18Q), and in Matthew (cf. Matt. 5:32, "with the exception of sexual immorality"). In 1 Cor. 6:1–11 and Matt. 18:15–18[187] one finds documentation of the development of the Christian's own law and disciplinary institution, which is the alternative to the worldly courts and the disciplinary measures of the synagogue.[188]

7. *Exorcism.* Of great significance was the controversy over the exorcism of demons by Jesus, as the double tradition in Mark 3:22–30 and the logia source (Matt. 12:22–37Q) indicate. The dispute involved the evaluation of Jesus's activity as an exorcist. Did the exorcisms indicate divine authority or (as in the Jewish accusation) an alliance with the devil? The demand for a sign in Luke 11:16, 29–35Q belongs within the sphere of the conflict between the early churches and Judaism over the legitimacy of Jesus.

8. *Love commandment.* A significant new theological dimension associated with Jesus of Nazareth[189] was the determination of the double commandment of love as the "greatest command" in Mark 12:28–34.[190] When the scribe asks, "What is the first of all commands?" Jesus answers: "The first is, 'Hear, O Israel, the Lord, our God is the one God, and you shall love the Lord your God with all your heart and all your soul and your whole mind and with all your power.' The second is this: 'You shall love your neighbor as yourself.' No other commandment is greater than this" (vv. 30–31). The combination of Deut. 6:5 and Lev. 19:18 is indeed already prepared in Judaism,[191] but they are not

---

186. Cf. m. Gittin 9.10: "The School of Shammai says, One may divorce his wife only if he has found something shameful in her, for it is said, 'Because he has found something shameful in her' (Deut. 24:1). But the School of Hillel says, Even when she has burned the food, for it is written, 'Because he has found something shameful.' And Rabbi Akiba says, Even when he has found one prettier, for it is written, 'When she finds no favor in his eyes.'"

187. On the interpretation, cf. Goldhahn-Müller, *Die Grenze der Gemeinde*, 164–95; S. Koch, *Rechtliche Regelung von Konflikten*, 66–83.

188. On punishment in the synagogue, cf. Str-B 4.1:292ff.

189. Cf. Theissen, "Das Doppelgebot der Liebe," 57–72.

190. Cf. Burchard, "Das doppelte Liebesgebot"; Ebersohn, *Das Nächstenliebegebot*.

191. Cf. only the Let. Aris. 131; Philo, *Spec. Laws* 2.63, 95; 4.147; T. Iss. 5.2; 7.6; T. Zeb. 5.3; T. Jos. 11.1. Numerous other texts are given in Berger, *Die Gesetzesauslegung Jesu*, 99–136;

ranked in the Torah.[192] The extended spread of the double commandment in three strands of the tradition (cf. Mark 12:28–34 par.; Gal. 5:14/Rom. 13:8–10; John 13:34–35) indicates that the essential element of successful proclamation by the early churches was found in the abandonment of religious and ethnic boundaries for the obligation of love.

New Norms within the Hellenistic Context

Along with the early synoptic tradition, the pre-Pauline traditions[193] especially offer an insight into topics and the store of knowledge in the earliest theological and social development in churches shaped in the Hellenistic context. These traditions have fixed formulaic texts, which came into existence before the Pauline production of letters, primarily between 40 and 50 CE in the churches of Syria (e.g., Antioch) and of southeast Asia Minor. They provide an insight into the life and thought of churches outside Palestine, which were open very early to the universalistic direction within the new movement. The early Pauline letters (1 Thessalonians, 1 Corinthians) indicate which problems shaped the first churches in the Hellenistic environment. Most pre-Pauline texts probably had their *Sitz im Leben* (life setting) in the praxis of communal worship,[194] so that they reflected the independent religious praxis of the early churches. In order to introduce detachment from the previous religious world, the early Christians had to institutionalize their own norms. Thus especially baptism, the Lord's Supper, and the worship services together were ritual places in which the new religious experiences were practiced and solidified (see above, 5.5).

The development of a new self-understanding and ritual forms in a predominantly Hellenistic context involved the following areas:

1. The turn toward a true God involved the turning away from polytheism. According to the pre-Pauline kerygmatic mission, 1 Thess. 1:9–10 says, "How you turned to God from idols in order to serve the true God and to wait for his Son from heaven, Jesus, whom he raised from the dead, and who saves us from the coming wrath."[195]

Nissen, *Gott und der Nächste*, 224–46, 389–416; Str-B 1:357–59; 3:306; Wischmeyer, "Das Gebot der Nächstenliebe," 162ff.

192. Cf. Hengel, "Jesus und die Tora," 170.

193. Criteria for the determination of such texts are (1) citation formulae (1 Cor. 11:23a; 15:3a), (2) participial phrases (Rom. 1:3a–4b; 3:24), (3) relative clauses (Rom. 3:25; 4:25), (4) *parallelismus membrorum* (Rom. 1:3b–4a), (5) rare or singular vocabulary (Rom. 3:25; 4:25), (6) strophic arrangement (Phil. 2:6–11), (7) unusual theological conceptions (Rom. 1:3b–4a); cf. Schnelle, *Einführung in die neutestamentliche Exegese*, 134–36.

194. On the early Christian worship service, cf. F. Hahn, "Gottesdienst III: Neues Testament."

195. Cf. the analysis by Bussmann, *Themen der paulinischen Missionspredigt*, 38–56.

2. Monotheism was connected to the concept of a salvation, a central motif of ancient philosophy and religion. In the Greco-Roman area, this especially involves salvation from the inexorable rule of fortune. As Seneca complains, "We have come into the realm of fortune, and harsh and invincible is her power; things deserved and undeserved must we suffer just as she wills."[196] The early churches proclaim a dependable and predictable God, who declares his will in Jesus Christ and from whose wrath people are saved through faith and baptism (cf. Rom. 1:16).

3. The pre-Pauline baptismal traditions in 1 Cor. 1:30; 6:11; 12:13; 2 Cor. 1:21–22; Gal. 3:26–28; Rom. 3:25; 4:25; 6:3 indicate the significance of rites and the association of conceptions of transfer for the formation of the church's own identity and at the same time indicate the departure from previous value systems. (a) The overcoming of sin occurs in baptism "in the name of Jesus" (cf. 1 Cor. 6:11; Rom. 6:3–4). Purity before God can be attained neither through repeated cultic washings nor through the temple cult or animal sacrifices; instead, the believers are "washed and sanctified" (1 Cor. 6:11), "anointed and sealed" (2 Cor. 1:21–22). (b) Righteousness cannot be attained by correct ritual acts but is the result of divine activity (cf. 1 Cor. 6:11; Rom. 3:25; 4:25; 6:3–4). (c) The Spirit is granted in baptism as the power and presence of God in baptism (cf. 1 Cor. 6:11; 12:13; 2 Cor. 1:21–22) and is at work powerfully in the worship service (cf. 1 Thess. 5:19; 1 Cor. 12:14).

4. The interpretation of the cross as a once-for-all and ultimate sacrifice must be understood as a fundamental break with both Judaism and Greco-Roman concepts (Rom. 3:25), which makes all other sacrifices superfluous.

5. The baptismal tradition unfurls a revolutionary and at the same time utopian concept in Gal. 3:26–28:[197] "For you are all (through faith) sons of God in Christ Jesus. As many as have been baptized into Christ have put on Christ. There is no longer Jew or Greek, nor slave or free, male and female, for you are all one in Christ Jesus." The change of status effected by baptism includes a transformation of the actual social relationships! The opposite "neither Jew nor Greek" is directed both against the Jewish antithesis "Jew-Gentile" and the Greek distinction "Greek-Barbarian."[198] The OT legislation on slaves can be called relatively humane,[199] but slavery was considered self-evident. This was also the case for the Greek tradition of the distinction between δοῦλος

196. Seneca, *Ad Marciam de consolatione* 10.
197. On the analysis of the text, cf. Schnelle, *Gerechtigkeit und Christusgegenwart*, 57–62; C. Strecker, *Die liminale Theologie des Paulus*, 351–59; Hansen, *"All of You Are One,"* 67–106.
198. Cf. the texts in NW II/1:3–6.
199. Cf. only Exod. 21:2–6, 26–27; Deut. 15:12–18; 23:16–17; Lev. 25:8ff., 39–40; Job 31:13, 15; cf. Gülzow, *Christentum und Sklaverei*, 9–21.

(slave) and ἐλεύθερος (free); indeed, according to the Sophists it derives from human establishment rather than from a natural distinction,[200] but both Plato and Aristotle considered slavery essential.[201] Thus the antithesis "slave-free" was a reality that was assumed by both the Jews and the Greeks and was the economic and ideological basis for the ancient world. The third pair of opposites, "man and woman" (ἄρσεν καὶ θῆλυ, Gen. 1:27 LXX), also had a fundamental significance for Jews and Greeks, for according to the Jewish view the woman was not and is not fully able to participate in the cult, and among the Greeks the view was pervasive that the man is superior to the woman.[202] These new perspectives probably originated in those Hellenistic cities that were the missionary region of Antioch and Paul and in which the abolition of old traditions was conceivable. One text illustrates the religious, political, and social power of these concepts, for it reflects the values of antiquity: "Hermippus ascribes to Thales what others ascribe to Socrates: namely, that he was thankful to fortune for three things: that he was born [1] as a man and not an animal, [2] as a man and not a woman, and [3] as a Greek and not as a barbarian."[203] The early Christians met this static social situation with a movement of change. Thus they bear a resemblance to the Cynics,[204] who regarded themselves as comopolitans (Diogenes is asked: "Where do you come from? . . . His answer: "I am a citizen of the world").[205] They defined slavery and freedom in a new way[206] and accepted the equal place of women.[207]

6. In the Lord's Supper also a new identity was being formed that was especially in sharp contrast to the one associated with Hellenistic practices. Indeed, the misconduct at the Lord's Supper criticized by Paul[208] in 1 Cor. 11:17–34 refers to events at the beginning of the 50s, but Paul cites a very old tradition in 1 Cor. 11:23b–25, which explains the early forms of the praxis of the Lord's Supper.[209] Originally the action over the bread and cup provided the frame around a common meal (cf. μετὰ τὸ δειπνῆσαι, "after the meal," in 1 Cor. 11:25). This praxis changed, and a meal before the essential

200. Cf. Aristotle, *Politics* 1253b.20–23; on the Greek or Hellenistic understanding of slavery, see above, 3.4.1; also the texts in NW II/1:1065–72.
201. Cf. Plato, *Laws* 7.806d–e; Aristotle, *Politics* 1253b.
202. On the place of the woman in antiquity, cf. E. Stegemann and W. Stegemann, *Urchristliche Sozialgeschichte*, 311–46.
203. Diogenes Laertius 1.33.
204. Cf. Downing, "A Cynic Preparation for Paul's Gospel."
205. Diogenes Laertius 6.63.
206. Cf. Epictetus, *Diatr.* 3.22.45–49.
207. In the Cynic Epistles, cf. Crates 28: "The women are not by nature less than the men." See also Musonius, *Diss.* 3; Diogenes Laertius 6.12.
208. Cf. Klauck, *Herrenmahl und hellenistischer Kult*, 287–97.
209. See above, 5.5 under "The Lord's Supper."

sacramental action became the rule. As with pagan sacrificial meals, it became table fellowship among the wealthy so that the poor were pushed to the margins as outsiders (cf. vv. 21–22, 33–34). Moreover, not a few members of the community participated in both the Lord's Supper celebration and in the meals in pagan temples. Paul declares to them, "You cannot drink the cup of the Lord and the cup of demons. You cannot participate at the table of the Lord and participate in the table of the demons" (1 Cor. 10:21). The situation of the church in Corinth demonstrates what was also the case for other churches in a predominantly Hellenistic environment. The new cultic praxis became the occasion for withdrawal from the previous environment. The formation of new identities, the abandonment of the old, and the remaining in the familiar are not to be regarded strictly as opposites but rather as a fluid process. Of special significance for the formation of identity was the frequency of the communal meals, which probably took place in Corinth at least weekly (cf. 1 Cor. 16:2). In the churches more communal meals were held than in pagan associations. There is no parallel in pagan associations for the frequency of the meetings and "the weekly rhythm of the gathering of Christians."[210]

7. In the early celebrations of the Lord's Supper, eschatology stood theologically at the center. The memory of the death of Jesus as the source of salvation (cf. 1 Cor. 11:24–25, "Do this in my memory") has the coming of Christ firmly in view: "As often as you eat this bread and drink this cup, you proclaim the Lord's death until he comes" (1 Cor. 11:26). This eschatological perspective is the emotional and conceptual source of power for the early churches and at the same time marks the crucial difference from the pagan cults. The church gathers in the powerful presence of the Exalted One, whose saving but also punishing powers (cf. 1 Cor. 11:30) are active in the celebration of the Lord's Supper.

8. Thus in the worship services a new lordship is proclaimed that features a high degree of affectivity and goes beyond the purely spiritual. The saving faith is publicly confessed: "For if you confess with your mouth that Jesus is Lord and believe in your heart that God raised him from the dead, you will be saved. With the heart one believes toward righteousness, but with the mouth one confesses for salvation" (Rom. 10:9–10).[211] The believers understand themselves as "called to be saints" (cf. 1 Cor. 1:2; 2 Cor. 1:1) who, through their turning to the one true God, are spared from the coming judgment (1 Thess. 1:9–10) and participate in the eschatological salvation (1 Thess. 5:10).

---

210. Ebel, *Die Attraktivität früher christlicher Gemeinden*, 217.
211. Cf. Conzelmann, "Was glaubte die frühe Christenheit?"

9. In addition, the new determination of the "holy day," Sunday, occurs.[212] The oldest literary reference is found in 1 Cor. 16:2, where Paul says, in connection with the collection: "On the first day of the week [κατὰ μίαν σαββάτου] everyone should lay something aside." The first day of the Jewish week after the Sabbath is, according to Mark 16:2, the day of the resurrection, in which the worship services were celebrated (cf. Acts 20:7) and considered the "Lord's Day" (cf. Rev. 1:10).

Generalization of Values

The new message and the new norms indicate that those who joined the new movement of Christ-believers as Jews by birth or Greeks/Romans by birth inevitably restructured their worlds. This took place not as an absolute break with the past but rather, as a rule, as a process of connecting, of demarcation, of reinterpretation, of discarding, of redefinition, in which all of these concepts did not depict opposites, but over a period of time ran their course either one after the other or alongside each other. Thus one may observe a basic movement: In early Christianity a generalization of values took place as a cultural synthesis, in which various value systems were brought together to a higher level.[213] Believers from both the Jewish and the Greco-Roman world could discover areas in common with their own religious roots in the traditions of values in the new early Christian world in which they were at least partially connected. With the generalization of values, there was the regulation and the balancing of cultural traditions that, as a rule, are the result of communication, integration, and new definition. Examples: In the whole ancient world the temple is the place of the presence of God and communication with the deity. The early Christians adopted this and defined the church as the temple of God (1 Cor. 3:16–17) or the body of believers as the temple of the Holy Spirit (cf. 1 Cor. 6:19–20). They maintained the idea of cultic purity but associated it with the once-for-all act of baptism and thus restructured it in content and ritual. In addition, the concept of sacrifice is maintained, but it is personalized (Jesus Christ) and separated from every human activity (cf. Rom. 3:25).

Nevertheless, boundaries from the previous religious and cultural life were inevitable. For those who were Jews by birth among early church members,

---

212. On the development of Sunday, cf. Rordorf, *Sunday*. Alikin, *Earliest History of the Christian Gathering*.

213. Cf. Parsons, *System of Modern Societies*, 27, according to which societal processes of change "must be complemented by *value generalization* if the various units in the society are to gain appropriate legitimation and modes of orientation for their new patterns of action."

there could no longer be a permanent separation of "pure-impure," no ritual
and legal behavior oriented to the Torah, and no sacrifice at the Jerusalem
temple. Likewise, the new Christian rituals took the place of the Jewish festal
calendar. Greeks and Romans could no longer participate in the pagan cultic
meals (cf. 1 Cor. 10:21), the worship of the household gods or local deities,
or cultic processions or sacrifices to pagan gods (including the caesar). For
both groups this change meant not only the abandonment of previous bonds
but also the departure from customary social and family relationships. They
either did not participate at all or only in a reduced way in the numerous
religiously structured festivals of their families and environment and thus
withdrew from the recognition of this way of life. This process probably did
not take place abruptly but was rather fluid. This fact is evident especially in
the incidents in Corinth, where one observes how church members seek to find
their way in matters between the old and new norms, including questions of
sexuality (1 Cor. 6:12–21), law (6:1–11), marriage/singleness (7:1–16, 25–40),
status in society (slavery, widows, 7:17–24, 39–40), and participation/invita-
tion to pagan meals (chaps. 8 and 10). The incident at Antioch, the continuing conflict between the strong and weak in Corinth and Rome (cf. 1 Cor. 8;
Rom. 14:1–15:13), and the conflict over circumcision in Galatia and Philippi
indicate that the questions about the theological and ritual orientation of the
new movement were disputed for a long time.

6.7 Texts

An additional crucial factor within the formation of early Christian identity
was the astonishingly large production of texts and literature of the new
movement, as is indicated in a variety of ways in the letters of Paul and the
early synoptic tradition. They offer an insight into the new formation of
identity and are at the same time its historically effective result. In addition,
they represent the store and system of knowledge that creates identity.

Early Traditions

From 40 CE at the latest, one must consider the growth of the synoptic
tradition. The oral tradition of the words/narratives from Jesus Christ and
about Jesus Christ were probably established from this period;[214] that is, traditions were collected, established in writing, and transmitted in larger blocks.

214. On the state of scholarship regarding the higher estimation of the oral traditions, cf.
most recently Riesner, "Die Rückkehr der Augenzeugen"; Baum, *Der mündliche Faktor und
seine Bedeutung*; Dunn, *Oral Gospel Tradition*.

In the period 35–40 CE the passion narrative came into existence (see above, 5.6); between 40 CE and 50 CE, numerous other texts followed, as the references to traditions in the Pauline letters (cf. 1 Cor. 11:23; 15:1–3a; Rom. 6:3–4) especially indicate.

In the texts the Christians' new understanding of God, the world, and the self is articulated. The expression of this is found primarily in the form of myth (ὁ μῦθος, speech/narrative about God or the gods), for the history had to be opened for something that can no longer be depicted in purely historical terms: God became man in Jesus of Nazareth. This nexus of the divine world with human history could be formulated and received only in the form of myth. Myth is a cultural interpretative system that offers the meaning of the existence of history and human life, leads to identity formation, and has an impact on actions.[215] In the center of the mythical speech in the NT is the divinization of Jesus of Nazareth, which began in all areas of emerging Christianity. This mythicizing did not result from the adoption of preexisting concepts; instead, on the basis of Jewish (monotheism) and Greco-Roman conceptions (a god becoming a man/divinization of a man), Jesus's pre-Easter claim and the Easter event were taken up, resulting in a new myth. Thus the history is not abandoned through myth but integrated into a new overall reality. Probably the oldest mythical narrative and a central witness of early Christology is the pre-Pauline hymn in Phil. 2:6–11,[216] where Paul says about Jesus Christ, "who, although he was in the form of God, counted it not as robbery to be equal to God, but emptied himself and took on the form of a servant; he became in the likeness of a man. He humbled himself and became obedient to death (death on a cross.) Therefore, God has highly exalted him and given him a name above all names so that in the name of Jesus every knee in heaven and on earth and under the earth will bow so that every tongue will confess that Jesus Christ is Lord, to the glory of the Father." Already before Paul the christological reflection extended the change of status from the postexistence to the preexistence. The basis of this process lies in the thought that determines the Christology of numerous Scriptures in the NT. One can become only what one has always been. In the hymn the transformation of status is emphatically emphasized by the contrast between the μορφὴ θεοῦ (v. 6, form of God) and μορφὴ δούλου (v. 7, form of a servant). Jesus Christ leaves his Godlike position (without losing it!) and takes on the most degrading conceivable opposite. The basic event is described and reflected upon as a series of stages in the hymn. This leads to the unlimited

---

215. On the concept of myth, cf. Barthes, *Mythen des Alltags*; Kolakowski, *Die Gegenwärtigkeit des Mythos*; K. Hübner, *Die Wahrheit des Mythos*; Sellin, "Mythos."

216. On Phil. 2:6–11, cf. E. Lohmeyer, *Kyrios Jesus*; Hofius, *Der Christushymnus Philipper 2,6–11*; Vollenweider, "Der 'Raub' der Gottgleichheit."

praise as ruler that places Jesus Christ as the unlimited lord of the whole world and (consciously or unconsciously) over the Roman caesar.[217]

An additional central text of early Christology is the pre-Pauline tradition in 1 Cor. 15:3b–5, in which the basic structure of integration and interpretation is characteristic:[218] "That Christ died for our sins according to the Scriptures and that he was buried, and that he was raised on the third day according to the Scriptures and appeared first to Cephas, then to the Twelve." Linguistically, the subject of the sentence is Χριστός, and the topic is the destiny of the decisive figure of humanity, who unites individual and universal history in himself. This is possible because God is to be considered the consistent actual subject of the event. The series—died, buried, raised, appeared—describes the events in their chronological sequence. Christ has been raised from the dead, and the resurrection of the Crucified One has a lasting effect. The passive ὤφθη in verse 5 emphasizes in connection to OT theophanies that the appearances of the Resurrected One correspond to the will of God.

Fixed formulations about the death and resurrection of Jesus (confessional statements) appear also in 1 Thess. 4:14 ("for if we believe that Jesus died and arose" [ὅτι Ἰησοῦς ἀπέθανεν καὶ ἀνέστη]); 1 Cor. 15:12, 15; 2 Cor. 4:14; Gal. 1:1; Rom. 4:24; 8:34; 10:9 ("and if you believe that God raised him from the dead" [ὁ θεὸς αὐτὸν ἤγειρεν ἐκ νεκρῶν]); 14:9; Col. 2:12; 1 Pet. 1:21; Acts 3:15; 4:10. The "dying formula," "died for us"—which appears in 1 Thess. 5:9–10; 1 Cor. 1:13; 8:11; 2 Cor. 5:14; Rom. 5:6, 8; 14:15; 1 Pet. 2:21; 3:18; 1 John 3:16[219]—emphasizes the soteriological dimension of the Christ. The "giving formula" emphasizes the act of God in the Son as an event "for us" (Gal. 1:4; 2:20; Rom. 4:25; 8:32; 1 Tim. 2:5f.; Titus 2:14).[220] Noteworthy is the pre-Pauline tradition in Rom. 1:3b–4a, which may be called the "Son formula."[221] Here Christ is regarded in his fleshly existence as the son of

217. The appearance of the Armenian king Tiridates before Nero in 66 CE illustrates this (Dio Cassius 63). He had to bow down to Nero and say, among other things, "And I have come to you, my God, to worship as Mithras. I will become what you wish; you are my fortune and my fate." Nero responded to him in the following way: "You have done well to come here personally so that you can experience my grace face to face" (63.2–3).

218. On the interpretation of this text, cf. Conzelmann, "Zur Analyse der Bekenntnisformel 1 Kor 15,3–5"; Wolff, *Der erste Brief des Paulus an die Korinther*, 354–70; Schrage, *Der erste Brief an die Korinther*, 4:31–53; Merklein, *Der erste Brief an die Korinther*, 247–83.

219. Cf. Wengst, *Christologische Formeln*, 78–86.

220. Cf. Eschner, *Gestorben und hingegeben*, 1:511, on Pauline usage: "Following an analysis and investigation, one may conclude that Paul formulated the Pauline 'dying and giving formulas' in unmistakable echo of the concept, widely attested in the literature of Hellenism and the imperial period, of the death that averts calamity."

221. Besides the commentaries, cf. the analysis in Schweizer, "Röm 1,3–4f. und der Gegensatz von Fleisch und Geist."

David but in his pneumatic existence as Son of God. He is the Son of God as a result of the resurrection, which the πνεῦμα ἁγιωσύνης (Spirit of holiness), the Spirit of God, effects, according to Rom. 1:4. Only by the resurrection is Jesus enthroned as Son of God; the preexistence and the sonship of the earthly one is not presupposed. The sending of the Son is also described in fixed formulations in Gal. 4:4 and Rom. 8:3, which presuppose the concept of preexistence, as in Gal. 4:4, "But when the fullness of time had come, God sent his son, born of woman, born under the law."

In the realm of early Christian liturgy are acclamations with which the lordship of Jesus Christ is confessed (cf. 1 Cor. 12:3; 16:22). Of preeminent significance is the Pauline εἷς tradition in 1 Cor. 8:6,[222] in which the narrative of the one God is connected with Jesus Christ in a bold way: "Thus there is for us [only] one God, the Father, from whom everything is and we are unto him, and one Lord Jesus Christ, through whom everything is and we through him." The text reflects the relationship of *the*ology and *Christ*ology within the horizon of monotheism; the εἷς formula describes God as well as Jesus Christ. Thus one cannot divide the one God into two gods; rather, the one Kyrios is incorporated into the realm of the one God. In relation to his origin and nature, Christ belongs fully on the side of God. At the same time the one Kyrios remains subordinate not only in the textual sequence, for the creator God is father of the Kyrios Jesus Christ.[223] The traditions transmitted by Paul include, besides the baptismal and Lord's Supper tradition already mentioned (see above, 6.6), also words of the Lord.[224] He cites them in 1 Thess. 4:15ff.; 1 Cor. 7:10–11; 9:14; and 11:23ff., without in any case mentioning the words known from the synoptic tradition. Traditional topoi of paraenesis are present in 1 Cor. 5:10–11; 6:9–10; 2 Cor. 12:20–21; Gal. 5:19–23; Rom. 1:29–31; 13:13.[225]

The early traditions are artful linguistic creations and witnesses of the early theological reflection and, at the same time, the source of knowledge for the emerging Christianity. They succinctly summarize the heart of the new message; they are brief and striking but at the same time rich in content and

222. On the evidence of the pre-Pauline character and classification of numerous references in the history of religions, cf. Schrage, *Der erste Brief an die Korinther*, 216–25; also D. Zeller, "Der eine Gott und der eine Herr."

223. The uniqueness formula (of God) probably originated independently in the seventh/sixth century BCE both in Judaism (Deut. 6:4) and in early Greek philosophy (Xenophanes, frag. 23). In the first century CE the formula apparently underwent a renaissance from which early Christianity profited; cf. the comprehensive study of Staudt, *Der eine und einzige Gott*.

224. Neirynck (*Evangelica*, 2:511–68) offers a critical survey of the literature in "Paul and the Sayings of Jesus."

225. Cf. W. Popkes, *Paränese und Neues Testament*.

with aesthetic appeal. Traditions are thus formative elements in the cultural maintenance of a group/author and are of crucial significance because they are points of orientation amid unavoidable changing times.[226]

Early Forms of the Gospels

Luke 1:1 confirms that there were earlier forms of the Gospels ("Inasmuch as many have undertaken to draw an orderly account about the events that have been fulfilled among us"). Besides the passion narrative (see above, 5.6), the early forms included a pre-Mark collection in Mark 2:1–3:6 (conflict stories), Mark 4:1–34 (parables), and Mark 10, where the evangelist provides an edited version of a catechetical collection on the themes of marriage (10:1–12), possessions (10:17–31), and striving for honor (10:35–45).[227] An additional focus of the early traditions was the miracle stories, which are pervasive in the pre-Markan tradition (cf. Mark 1:21–28, 29–31, 40–45; 4:35–41; 5:1–20, 21–43; 6:30–44, 45–52; 7:24–30, 31–37; 8:1–9, 22–26; 9:14–27; 10:46–52). Both oral and written traditions were integrated into the Markan apocalypse (Mark 13).[228] When one adds the parable tradition (besides Mark 4//Matt. 13 especially, cf. Matt. 18:23–35; 20:1–15; 22:1–14; Luke 10:25–37; 15:11–32), the types of texts/textual units mentioned above form the basis of the new genre, gospel.

The Logia Source

The logia source can be understood as a protogospel (see above, 6.3),[229] for it is the first (comprehensible) outline of the story of the life and proclamation of Jesus of Nazareth. The logia source (Q) went through a process of formation that occurred primarily in the period between 40 and 50 CE and ended around 60 CE. In the present form the logia source is a carefully created composition.[230] In the section giving the introduction and subject,

---

226. The present boom in narrative and synchrony should not block our view that a genuine understanding of the essence of texts is possible only when one observes their development; cf. Gadamer, *Truth and Method*, 303: "The task of historical understanding also involves acquiring an appropriate historical horizon so that what we are trying to understand can be seen in its true dimensions."

227. Cf. H.-W. Kuhn, *Ältere Sammlungen im Markusevangelium*; Kiilunen, *Die Vollmacht im Widerstreit*; W. Weiss, *Eine neue Lehre in Vollmacht*.

228. On the analysis, cf. Theissen, *Gospels in Context*, 133–76.

229. Text reconstruction in Hoffmann and C. Heil, *Die Spruchquelle Q*; Robinson, Hoffmann, and Kloppenborg, eds., *Critical Edition of Q*; Fleddermann, *Q: Reconstruction and Commentary*. Additional basic literature: Kloppenborg, *Formation of Q*; Sato, *Q und Prophetie*; Hoffmann, *Tradition und Situation*; Schröter, *Erinnerung an Jesu Worte*; Kloppenborg, *Excavating Q*; Lindemann, *Sayings Source Q*; M. Labahn, *Der Gekommene als Wiederkommender*.

230. Evidence in M. Labahn, *Der Gekommene als Wiederkommender*, 169–90.

Luke 3:1–7:35Q functions as the introduction of the Baptist; the temptation narrative in Luke 4:1–13Q functions as the narratival and christological pivot of the logia source, for the testing of Jesus is here demonstrated as the presupposition for the complete orientation to the words of the earthly Jesus. The foundational speech of Jesus (Luke 6:20–49Q) follows the beginning of the story of Jesus. The centurion from Capernaum (Luke 7:1–10Q) obviously signals the inclusion of gentiles in the eschatological act of God that is directed first to Israel. This section also includes the saying of the Baptist and the instruction on discipleship (Luke 7:18–35Q). The very positive statement about the Baptist points to the competing Baptist movement, which is now taught by its master about his own honor and the significance of Jesus. In the middle section, Luke 9:57–11:51Q, the sending of the disciples (Luke 10:2–16) marks the beginning point for the conflict between the preachers of the coming Son of Man (Luke 9:57–60; 10:21–11:13Q) and the opposition to this message (Luke 11:14–52Q). In the key section, Luke 12:2–22:20Q, the return of the Son of Man is powerfully proclaimed (Luke 12:2–13:21Q) and the crisis of Israel on hearing the message of the Q missionaries is emphasized (Luke 13:24–14:23Q). At the end of the logia source stands the subject of discipleship amid hardship (Luke 14:26–17:21Q); the sudden coming of the Son of Man and the ultimate rule of the disciples over Israel is in the center (Luke 17:23–22:30Q).

The logia source is the first (reconstructable) document that conceives the life and work of Jesus in a narratival biographical way and develops a theological reflection. It is significant for the history of Christianity in a threefold way: (1) With it Jesus of Nazareth makes an appearance as a formative phenomenon of memory. In contrast to Paul, the central point is not just the total significance of the work of Jesus Christ. (2) The theology of the logia source is rooted in the basic conviction that relevance to salvation is attributed to the place of Jesus and his message. The basic movement of the life of Jesus and the basic data of his preaching are characterized by the tension between the Son of Man who has come and is coming. (3) The logia source develops this concept without an explicit passion kerygma. The death of Jesus and his resurrection are presupposed (cf. Luke 11:49–51; 13:34–35, 14:2/Q) but not christologically interpreted. The reception by Matthew and Luke alters this plan, but at the same time the logia source, with its radical image of Jesus, continued to define the thought of Christianity in the tradition of the major Gospels.

6.8 The First Missionary Journey and the Mission to the Gentiles without the Requirement of Circumcision

The early mission outside Jerusalem, the first missionary journey (ca. 45–47 CE),[231] reached a high point with which other important turning points and future conflicts were in turn connected. The universal perspective of the church at Antioch (see above, 6.4) introduced a development that was irreversible. Of course, the portrayal in Acts 13:1–14:28 poses numerous problems. While Paul in Gal. 1:21 speaks of missionary activity in the territory of Syria and Cilicia before the apostolic council, Luke further reports of missionary activity on Cyprus and in the area of Pamphylia, Pisidia, and Lycaonia.

In Acts 13:1 Barnabas and Paul appear in a traditional list of names of the Antiochian church: "In Antioch there were in the church prophets and teachers: Barnabas, Simeon called Niger, Lucius of Cyrene, Manaen, a member of the court of Herod the Tetrarch, and Saul." The position of Barnabas at the head and of Paul (Saul) at the end of the list probably goes back to Luke, who thus highlights the main actors of the following event.[232] The church in Antioch apparently knew no fixed leadership offices. Former traveling missionaries now were active in this place, who nevertheless were ready at any time to resume their travels (cf. Acts 13:2–3), in which the functions of prophet and teacher were exercised by the same persons.

The description of the Cyprus mission in Acts 13:4–12 corresponds to the interests of the Lukan portrayal.[233] Luke shapes individual traditions into a dramatic event that finds its goal in the conversion of the proconsul Sergius Paulus.[234] After the centurion Cornelius in Acts 10, now even a Roman proconsul converts to the Christian faith. It is probably no coincidence that Sergius Paulus, the first convert of the apostle Paul, bears that name by which Paul himself is known in the early history of missions.[235] Here Luke introduces the Roman name of the apostle because the universal mission of Paul has begun. Cyprus is traditionally connected with the name of Barnabas, who came from there (cf. Acts 4:36); according to Acts 15:39, Barnabas, together with John Mark, sets out for Cyprus. The present literary form of Acts 13:4–12 clearly goes back to Luke, as is suggested, not least, by the Lukan narrative

---

231. Basis: The death of Agrippa I in 44 CE (cf. Acts 12:18–23) and the apostolic council in the spring of 48 CE, according to the Lukan portrayal, bracket the time during which the first missionary journey took place.

232. Cf. Lüdemann, *Das frühe Christentum*, 153.

233. On the analysis, cf. Lüdemann, *Das frühe Christentum*, 154–58.

234. On the historical location of Sergius Paulus, see below, 10.6, and further literature there.

235. Cf. the introduction of the name of Peter in Luke 6:14; noteworthy is also the parallel in the change of names of Barjesus-Elymas (Acts 13:6, 8).

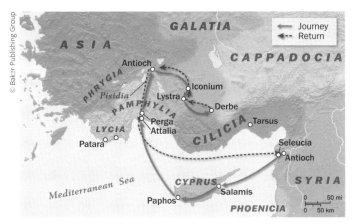

6.1. The first missionary journey

interests depicted and the inconsistency in the content of the present text.[236] Nevertheless, the mission to Cyprus by Barnabas and Paul must be considered historical in its main features, for it is obvious that Barnabas, because of his previous contact with his home area, chose it as the goal of the first mission work. Moreover, in Acts 13:4–12 Luke shapes numerous local and personal traditions, whose historicity can scarcely be disputed.[237] This view is suggested by the longer route, for on the one hand, a trip by Barnabas and Paul to Perga, Antioch of Pisidia, and Iconium is not directly confirmed by the letters of Paul; on the other hand, the connections of Sergius Paulus with Antioch of Pisidia strengthen the assumption that Barnabas and Paul were active in southern Asia Minor after the stay in Cyprus (cf. also 2 Tim. 3:11).[238] They would have determined the direction for the larger mission from their

236. The essential points are described by Lüdemann, *Das frühe Christentum*, 155–56: The conflict between Paul and the sorcerer Barjesus that is anticipated in Acts 13:6 does not take place. Instead, a new person is introduced with Sergius Paulus. In v. 8 the sorcerer is suddenly called Elymas without his explicitly being identified with Barjesus. The miracle of punishment effected the faith of the proconsul; as in Acts 8, Luke's concern is the differentiation and superiority of Christianity over competing religious groups.

237. For the support of the historical credibility of the basic features of Acts 13:4–12, see Riesner, *Paul's Early Period*, 242–43; Breytenbach, *Paulus und Barnabas*, 76–93; Dunn, *Beginning from Jerusalem*, 419–27; D.-A. Koch, *Geschichte des Urchristentums*, 221–22. For an alternative view, see Lüdemann, *Frühe Christentum*, 157: "The Cyprus mission can have no basis in the tradition."

238. See the evidence in S. Mitchell, *Anatolia*, 2:6–8, that Lucius Sergius Paulus came from Antioch of Pisidia; the family of Sergius Paulus is attested in inscriptions in Rome and Asia Minor; A. Weiss, *Soziale Elite und Christentum*, 73: "The connections sketched above between Sergius Paulus, Antioch of Pisidia, and the lands of the family in the Anatolian hinterland are thus significant for the question of the historical value of Acts because they give a plausible explanation of the course of the narrative in Acts 13:13–14 and the path taken by Paul and Barnabas from Cyprus."

contact with Sergius Paulus. The fact that Paul appears here as an apostle of
the church in Antioch subordinate to Barnabas (cf. Acts 14:12) also suggests
the historicity of such a mission (cf. Acts 14:4, 14). The programmatic speech
of Paul in Antioch of Pisidia, on the other hand, arises from Lukan redaction.
Within the structure of Luke-Acts, it corresponds to the inaugural sermon of
Jesus in Nazareth (Luke 4:16–30).[239] In its present form the description of the
missionary activity of Barnabas and Paul in Iconium (Acts 14:1–7) and Lystra
(Acts 14:8–20) derives essentially from Luke but at the same time includes
old traditions.[240] Whereas the previous sermon was intended for Jews and
Godfearers (cf. Acts 13:43, 50; 14:1), Barnabas and Paul turn for the first time
to the pagan population in Lystra (cf. Acts 14:11–13).[241] As a reaction to the
preaching of the apostle (14:14–18), Acts 14:19–20 reports in summary form
about the stoning of Paul, in which verses 19–20a may derive from an old
Pauline tradition.[242]Apart from the action described in this verse, Paul himself
mentions a stoning in 2 Cor. 11:25 (cf. also 2 Tim. 3:11). Probably he suffered
a life-threatening punishment in Lystra. It is no longer a question of whether
Jews or the local people were responsible for the stoning. It probably involved
an act of spontaneous lynch-mob justice in which the victim was pursued for
a time and collapsed lifelessly from the throwing of stones.

The frequently discussed alternative "history or story" does not apply to
Acts 13:1–14:28. In this section Luke shapes numerous older traditions but
at the same time combines a theological concept with the first journey of the
apostle Paul.[243] The phrase τὸ ἔργον (the work/the task) frames the report (Acts
13:2; 14:26) and signals the theological significance of the event. Sent out by
the Holy Spirit, Barnabas and Paul perform the task that is given, empowered
by God to open the door of faith to the nations. Thus the clarification of the
apostolic council is prepared, which then follows in Acts 15:1–35. While the
gentile mission has been miraculously accepted (cf. 10:1–11:18), according
to the Lukan portrayal, an official unification between the Jerusalem church
and Paul now follows. As a result, from Acts 15:36 the focus of the reader
rests only on the essential hero of Acts: Paul.

239. Cf. Radl, *Paulus und Jesus im Lukanischen Doppelwerk*, 82–100.
240. Cf. Breytenbach, *Paulus und Barnabas*, 29ff.; Dunn, *Beginning from Jerusalem*, 427–38.
241. Contra Reiser, "Hat Paulus Heiden bekehrt?," who maintains that Paul did not convert
pagans in the classical sense but converted exclusively Godfearers. Against this view, one may
observe unambiguous texts such as 1 Thess. 1:9–10; 2:16; 1 Cor. 12:2, 13; Gal. 2:3; 3:26–28; 4:8–9;
5:2–3; 6:12; Rom. 1:13–15, 18ff.; 10:1–3; 11:13, 17–18, 24, 28, 30–31; 15:15–16, 18. However,
Reinbold, *Propaganda und Mission im ältesten Christentum*, 164–82, indicates, appropriately,
that the pagans were the goal of Paul's missionary activity.
242. For the basis of this claim, cf. Lüdemann, *Das frühe Christentum*, 170–71.
243. Cf. Burfeind, "Paulus *muß* nach Rom," 78.

Three highly significant developments accompany the first missionary journey. (1) The mission loses the coincidental character that it had at the beginning. It does not depend any longer on individual journey routes, life stories, or places. Rather, it is now planned and places the focus on islands such as Cyprus and entire areas of land. (2) Along with this comes a new self-understanding. The early Christians regard themselves not as one among many religious movements, but instead make an exclusive claim and demand a conscious rejection of the deities and a turning to the one true God (cf. 1 Thess. 1:9–10). Geographical and cultural barriers do not stop the early Antiochian mission; such obstacles are consciously overcome because the saving gospel of Jesus Christ must be preached to the whole world. (3) The crucial presupposition for this expansive conduct was the programmatic rejection of circumcision for non-Jews (see above, 6.4), which took place first in Antioch. In terms of missionary strategy, it was clear to both the Antiochian church and Paul that large-scale universal preaching to the nations was not possible with the demand for circumcision. Consequently, the theological insight emerged that God would integrate the nations into the elect people in a new way, that is, through baptism and the giving of the Holy Spirit. Through baptism, the alternative circumcision-uncircumcision has been "overcome" (cf. Gal. 5:6, "In Christ it is neither circumcision nor uncircumcision, but faith working through love that matters"; cf. 1 Cor. 7:19; Gal. 6:15). The events that follow (apostolic council, incident at Antioch, conflict in Galatia) indicate, of course, that the question of circumcision remained a highly disputed subject. This is not surprising, for the character of the new movement had yet to be finally determined. Was it to be a variant of Judaism? Or did a new independent and universal religion emerge out of Judaism?

> The first missionary journey marks a crucial turning point in the history of emerging Christianity. With a planned mission, an exclusive claim, and the renunciation of circumcision, the previous geographic and theological boundaries are transcended and a universal perspective is now opened.

6.9 The Three Great Currents at the Beginning

The analysis given above has indicated that in the period of about 35–50 CE fundamental decisions and turning points take place for the new movement of Christ-believers/Christians. For the initial period after the crucifixion of Jesus (April 7, 30) and the appearances of the Resurrected One (ca. 32/33 CE), one may assume that a first period of consolidation of the movement took place after the initial confusion. Paul's visit to Jerusalem in the year 35 CE already signals a changed situation; one may observe both structural and preaching activities of the Jerusalem church (see above, chaps. 4 and 5). Then a natural process of geographical, sociological, theological, and literary differentiation takes place, resulting in three different directions within early Christianity,[244] which were determinative for the entire development in the first century CE.

The Jerusalem Church

The Jerusalem church always understood itself as the starting point and center of the new movement. In the first two decades of its existence, it went through a turbulent history and was initially not a monolithic unity. As the first leader of the church, Peter was, like the Hellenists, open to an expansion of the movement. Another group was present, however, that was represented by the family of Jesus, with James as the head; it stood for the principle of stability. For the local stability Jerusalem stands as the place of suffering and of the crucifixion of Jesus; moreover, it was the place of the appearances of Jesus. Similarly, all central theological hopes of Judaism and of the new movement were connected with Jerusalem, especially the expectation of the coming of the Messiah in glory. Thus one can speak of the stability of the traditions, which is accompanied by theological stability. It is understood as a structural type of a diverse Judaism of the first century CE that carries out partial differentiation, limits its missionary activities to the Jews, and makes circumcision the unquestioned sine qua non for the acceptance of non-Jewish members. Finally, in view of James (and Mary), one can speak of a biological stability.

The Jesus Movement

The Galilean Jesus movement is the second crucial impulse at the beginning. While the Jerusalem church, corresponding to its own history, concentrated on the end of the ministry of Jesus (passion and exaltation), at the center of the Jesus movement was the authoritative appearance and ministry of the pre-Easter Jesus of Nazareth in Galilee. For them, the death of Jesus and his saving significance was not ignored, but it was not actually a major theme. In direct continuity with Jesus, the Jesus movement connected salvation and judgment to its radical message and did not avoid conflict with Israel. The disciples of Jesus saw themselves in a direct community of destiny with

---

244. Cf. Parsons, *Societies*, 22–25, 33, 43, who maintains that differentiation is the presupposition for every higher level of development.

Jesus, lived and acted as he did, and awaited from him and with him the eschatological rule (cf. Luke 22:28–30Q). The special significance of the Jesus movement consisted in the fact that it created the presuppositions for the new literary genre, gospel. Without their collection and transmitting of the words of Jesus and words about Jesus, the knowledge about Jesus of Nazareth would have been considerably less and more limited.

Antioch and Paul

Both the Jerusalem church and the Jesus movement limited themselves in their preaching activities and theological content in principle to the land of Israel and Judaism. This geographical and theological limitation was overcome by the Hellenists, who were driven out of Jerusalem, and by the many unknown diaspora Jews (e.g., from Cyprus) beginning circa 40 CE. Especially in Antioch a new subgroup of the movement came into existence that soon became publicly recognized (cf. Acts 11:26, "Christians") and then developed its own theological and geographical program. Theologically, the universal saving significance of the death and resurrection of Jesus stood in the center and was expressed in succinct formulae. Geographically and theologically, this wing of the new movement moved beyond the borders of Israel and the boundaries of Judaism inasmuch as it conceived of the Christ event as salvation for all people.

Plurality from the Beginning

From the beginning, the new movement of Christ-believers/early Christianity was divided into two groups, and after about 40 CE there were three subgroups. They were united in the saving significance of the death and resurrection of Jesus Christ from the dead, but at the same time they developed diverse images of Jesus and the theological concepts that resulted: First was the rather static conception of the Jerusalem church; then the very dynamic but also restricted Jesus movement; finally came the universal variation in Antioch. Two aspects are connected with this development: (1) The much-discussed relationship of Jesus to Paul must be treated in a larger context. Paul has often been made the second founder and thus the essential creator of Christianity and placed in opposition to Jesus.[245] It is said of Paul: "Everything, on the other hand, is said when we say that he made Christianity the

---

245. An influential study was that of Wrede, *Paul*, 179: "It follows then conclusively from all of this that Paul is to be considered the second founder of Christianity." See also 163, "Jesus knows nothing of what for Paul is one and everything." On the recent debate, cf. Dunn, *Beginning from Jerusalem*, 519, on Paul, "the second founder of Christianity."

religion of redemption."[246] At the beginning is a twofold gospel: here Jesus's message of joy for the poor and meek, while there is the Pauline message that the Son of God who came down from heaven and "brought salvation from sin, death and the devil to believers through his death and resurrection, making the eternal plan of God a reality."[247] This view misjudges the fact that, from the very beginning, various models of the interpretation of Jesus existed and that the Antiochian-Pauline movement was merely one of several. (2) Along with them was the Jerusalem church and the Galilean Jesus movement, which made the family relationship, the life and ministry of Jesus of Nazareth in its biographical aspects, the central content of their self-understanding. It is not true that at the beginning the "pure" gospel of Jesus existed, which then was falsified by Paul into a Hellenistic cult deity. There was never the "pure" Jesus; instead, from the beginning there were only various interpretations and receptions of his activity and significance. In this respect it is misleading to place Paul in the foreground and to ignore the significance of the two other subgroups. Paul undoubtedly developed an impressive historical impact, but the Jesus movement, with the logia source and the Synoptic Gospels, shaped the image of Jesus and the history of early Christianity. Finally, the Jerusalem church left behind an abiding theological concept that continued especially in the Gospel of Matthew and the Letter of James.

A complete unity of Christ-believers/Christians never existed. Rather, the plurality is the characteristic also of the beginning. Subsystems differentiating themselves from one another explain the successful history of the mission of the new movement, for only it made possible the adaptation to the variety of the requirements of their own mission fields.

Excursus: Did an Early Fourth Line of Development Exist?

Since the 1960s, especially in the US, alternative models have developed for the interpretation of Jesus and the earliest history of Christianity. Despite considerable variation, a basic idea is dominant: The boundaries between canonical and noncanonical, heresy and orthodoxy, lose their significance; and in particular, esoteric and Gnostic-wisdom thinking stands not at the end but rather at the beginning of early Christianity. In order to support this view, the argument until today is based primarily on two claims: (1) Actual or

246. Wrede, *Paul*, 177.
247. Harnack, "Das doppelte Evangelium im Neuen Testament," 2:215.

postulated noncanonical traditions are raised to the level of the pre- or present forms of the Synoptic and Johannine Jesus tradition.[248] The purpose of such a construction is undoubtedly the attempt to undermine the interpretative power of the canonical Gospels and to establish an alternative view of Jesus and an alternative history of early Christianity. (2) In order to gain media attention, some postulate theories of falsification, suppression, or conspiracies in the early church. Added to this is the desire for the sensational (Jesus and the women, same-sex love) and mere presumption as a method.[249] These theories are advanced in particular by alleged or actual new "gospel discoveries" that supposedly document the "hidden" initial history of Christianity.[250]

The methodological basis for these theories is, for the most part, a new classification of the earliest gospel tradition in which neither Mark nor another Synoptic Gospel is the earliest, but the logia source and, in analogy to it, the Gospel of Thomas and a pre-Johannine signs source[251] are declared to be the oldest witnesses of the tradition. This claim is made, first of all, on the basis of form-critical arguments. J. M. Robinson understands the logia source and the Gospel of Thomas equally as collections of wisdom sayings,[252] and an ancient collection of miracle stories of a "divine man" (aretalogy) lies behind the "signs source" and an ancient pre-Markan collection of miracles. J. D. Crossan considers the Gospel of Thomas to be the oldest source for the life of Jesus,"[253] whom he calls a peasant Jewish Cynic, a type of a healing teacher of wisdom.[254] The starting point for the rise of Christianity was not the bodily resurrection of Jesus, but a kind of general resurrection. All disciples share in the memory of Jesus when they orient themselves to him as the incarnation of

248. The actual development is laid out by Schröter, "Jesus im frühen Christentum."

249. Cf. Heiligenthal, *Der verfälschte Jesus*; Frenschkowski, *Mysterien des Urchristentums*.

250. Included among these are especially (1) the so-called Secret Gospel of Mark (an alleged letter from Clement of Alexandria with two citations from an unknown "Gospel of Mark"), which was found in 1958 by the historian of religion Morton Smith. Only photographs of the discovery exist, which have no convincing evidential value. Falsification of the document is claimed by Carlson, *Gospel Hoax*. On the authenticity with contemporaneous dependence on the Synoptic Gospels and a dating in the second century CE, see recently Klauck, *Apokryphe Evangelien*, 48–52; Rau, *Das geheime Markusevangelium*. (2) The Gospel of Judas is a writing produced circa 160 CE, which gives a new and positive evaluation of the person of Judas; cf. P. Nagel, "Das Evangelium des Judas."

251. Cf. Fortna, *Gospel of Signs*.

252. Cf. Robinson, "ΛΟΓΟΙ ΣΟΦΩΝ: On the Gattung of Q."

253. Cf. Crossan, *Historical Jesus*, 427–28 (to the oldest stratum of the tradition, according to Crossan, belong also the Gospel of the Hebrews, the logia source, and a pre-Markan or pre-Johannine collection of miracles. The "cross gospel" is added at another place, which Crossan considers to be a source of the Gospel of Peter and which contains an alternative passion narrative. Cf. Crossan, *Birth of Christianity*, 120, 503–4).

254. From the German-speaking world, cf. B. Lang, *Jesus der Hund*.

divine righteousness and remain in his spirit, that is, practice righteousness.[255] This intra-Jewish and fully individualistic movement was then totally altered by Paul, who introduced a flesh-spirit dualism and devalued the this-worldly in favor of the otherworldly.[256] Another example: E. Pagels understands the Gospel of John as a polemical reaction to the content of the Gospel of Thomas. She invokes in particular the narrative figure of "doubting Thomas" (cf. John 20:24–29), who supposedly represents the group that stands behind the Gospel of Thomas. John, with his consistent reference to Jesus Christ as the Son of God, argues against "what the Gospel of Thomas teaches, that is, that God's light shines not only in Jesus, but rather—at least potentially—in everyone. The Gospel of Thomas encourages the hearers not so much 'to believe in Jesus,' as John demands, but instead encourages them, because all people are created in the image of God, 'to strive toward knowledge of God' with their God-given potential."[257] John appears, therefore, as a representative of the victorious Christians who suppressed the alternative images of Jesus. At the beginning was not the faith in the Crucified and Resurrected One but a new consciousness of one's own inner power. This construction functions—along with numerous specific problems—only if the Gospel of Thomas originated in the first century before the Gospel of John.

In principle, it is thoroughly possible to give new dates to writings or to assume that late writings have preserved early tradition. With the Gospel of Thomas, one faces two models for dating: that it was produced either in the middle of the first century[258] or in the middle of the second century.[259] Serious objections can be made against the early dating: (1) External evidence supports a date not in the first century but rather in the second century: Hippolytus (*Ref.* 5.7.20) assumes that the Gospel of Thomas comes from the beginning of the third century; Papyrus Oxyrhynchus 1.643, 655[260] indicates

255. Cf.. Crossan, *Birth of Christianity*, xxi: "The birth of Christianity is the interaction between the historical Jesus and his first companions and the continuation of that relationship despite his execution."

256. Cf. Crossan, *Birth of Christianity*, xxv, a statement about Paul: "He takes that first distinction of Jew and Gentile out of the soul and puts it onto the body, out of spirit and onto the flesh."

257. Pagels, *Beyond Belief*, 40.

258. A representative of this line of argument is Köster, *Ancient Christian Gospels*, 75–128.

259. Cf. Schröter and Bethge, "Das Evangelium nach Thomas" (not before the 2nd cent.); B. Blatz, "Das koptische Thomasevangelium"; Fieger, *Das Thomasevangelium*, 7 (middle of the 2nd cent.); Klauck, *Apokryphe Evangelien*, 162 (early 2nd cent.); E. Popkes, *Das Menschenbild des Thomasevangeliums*, 161 (2nd half of the 2nd cent.); Plisch, *Das Thomas-Evangelium*, 16–18 (after 135 CE); Gathercole, *Composition of the Gospel of Thomas* (2nd cent. CE); Goodacre, *Thomas and the Gospels* (middle of the 2nd cent.); P. Nagel, *Codex apocryphus gnosticus Novi Testamenti*, 102 (last decade of the 2nd cent.).

260. Texts in Lührmann, *Fragmente apokryph gewordener Evangelien*, 106–31.

the end of the second century. Logion 68 of the Gospel of Thomas ("Jesus says: Blessed are you when they hate you and persecute you. But they themselves will find no place where they have persecuted you") probably refers to the transformation of Jerusalem into a Roman city after the Bar Kokhba Rebellion in 135 CE.[261] Together these three indications of the time period argue for a dating of the Gospel of Thomas around 150 CE. (2) The central structural analogy to the logia source likewise is refuted by the fact that, unlike the Gospel of Thomas, the logia source indicates a conscious literary form with a narrative frame and is more than a "collection of sayings" (see above, 6.7). (3) The Gospel of Thomas may have taken up old traditions in individual logia (cf. logion 98), but as a whole it presupposes an acquaintance with the Synoptic Gospels. This acquaintance is indicated both by the reception of redactional passages in the Synoptics[262] and the editorial work on specific passages.[263] (4) The consistent decontextualizing of the words of Jesus, the secondary stylizing of traditional forms, and the total detachment from the history of Israel especially suggest the later dating of the Gospel of Thomas. (5) Anti-Jewish elements—as in logia 14, 39, 53, 85, 102, and 104—are scarcely conceivable for the earliest tradition. They are instead an indication of a process of emancipation and estrangement. (6) In addition, the dominant orientation of the content of the Gospel of Thomas in Christology (deliberate omission of almost all christological titles: "Christ" does not appear), soteriology, and anthropology,[264] as well as the actual absence of a theology (God appears only in logion 30), clearly points to the second century. In particular, the absence of a passion narrative and appearance stories probably reflects the author's own perspective, for salvation is not associated with the cross but is instead present in Jesus's words. All of these factors point to a second-century place for the Gospel of Thomas in the history of theology. The other postulated early "sources" for an alternative history of early Christianity likewise cannot withstand the scrutiny of historical-critical analysis: In the recent investigation of John, the existence of a pre-Johannine

261. Cf. Plisch, *Das Thomas-Evangelium*, 177.

262. Cf. Tuckett, "Thomas and the Synoptics."

263. Evidence for this view is given convincingly by Fieger, *Das Thomasevangelium*, 26, and passim; an alternative view is given by Plisch, *Das Thomas-Evangelium*, 17–18, who avoids commenting on the whole document and always treats only individual sayings.

264. Cf. E. Popkes, *Das Menschenbild des Thomasevangeliums*, 356–57: "Regarding the image of humankind in the Gospel of Thomas, it is evident that this work is not derived from a tradition that is independent of the Synoptic, Johannine, or Pauline traditions," i.e., a "fourth line of development of early Christian theology, which was inspired by Jewish-wisdom concepts. . . . The Gospel of Thomas rather assumes a continuing progressive intra-Christian process of identity formation."

"signs source" is overwhelmingly rejected,[265] and the genre of "aretalogy" is not attested in ancient literature.[266]

> These are unconvincing attempts to find the cofounders of early Christianity in the later literature of outsiders. The wish is obviously the father/mother of the idea. Thus what remains are the three great streams [the Synoptic Gospels] at the beginning of early Christianity, to which the Johannine was added in the last third of the first century, before a new and idiosyncratic interpretation of the Christian faith appeared at the beginning of the second century CE with the rise of Gnosis.

265. Cf. Schnelle, *Antidocetic Christology*, 150–63; Belle, *Signs Source.*
266. Cf. Du Toit, *Theios Anthropos.*

7

The Apostolic Conference

The apostolic conference in the spring of 48 CE was the most significant historical event in the history of early Christianity.[1] The differing theological conceptions of the three subtypes of early Christianity and the continuing success of the mission from Antioch among the nations/non-Jews made a clarification of an unavoidable problem necessary. Must believers from the gentiles be circumcised in order to belong to the elect people of God? Or, in other words, must a pagan first become a Jew in order to be a Christian? Thus the issue involved the questions of membership, boundaries, identity, and the capacity of the new movement to remain connected to Judaism. One possibility was to remain within the previous Jewish identity, to expand it, and to concentrate the relationship only on the capacity to remain in Judaism. A second possibility was to create an alternative: to form a totally new identity transcending Judaism and intentionally to establish a new capacity for connection with the surrounding culture.

1. Concerning the terminology: The predominant name in scholarship, "apostolic council," suggests a conference of all relevant persons and movements as well as a resolution with binding provisions according to the model of medieval councils; this terminology does not apply to this meeting. In fact, it involves a meeting of the Jerusalem and Antiochian churches (absent are the Jesus movement, Damascus, and Rome), and binding resolutions of all movements/parties to the conflict were not given. H. Betz, *Galatians*, 81, speaks of the "conference at Jerusalem." Reinbold, *Propaganda und Mission*, 62 and passim, calls this a "Jerusalem Conference"; Wolter, *Paul*, 38, an "apostolic conference."

7.1 The Initial Conflict

At the conclusion of the first missionary journey, Barnabas and Paul return to Antioch. Here, according to Acts 15:1, "certain individuals" come from Judea, teaching the brothers in Antioch, "Unless you become circumcised according to the custom of Moses, then you cannot be saved" (Acts 15:1b). As a result, a vehement dispute arose between these strict Jewish Christians from Judea on one side and Barnabas and Paul on the other. The Antiochian church decided to send Barnabas and Paul and other coworkers to Jerusalem in order to discuss the matter with Jerusalem leaders and to resolve the problem (cf. Acts 15:2; Gal. 2:1). Paul gives a somewhat different portrayal of the concrete occasion for the trip to Jerusalem in Gal. 2:2a: "I went up because of a revelation."[2] He thus does not place his presence at the apostolic conference within the framework of the missionary activity in Antioch. One can assume that the linkage of Barnabas and Paul at the beginning of the apostolic conference is indebted to Lukan historical perspective. On the other hand, however, Paul's description is also tendentious, for he emphasizes his independence from Jerusalem and other churches. Moreover, he indicates the concrete occasion for his participation in the apostolic conference: "so that I was not running in vain or had run in vain" (Gal. 2:2c). Torah-observant Jewish Christians had intruded into the house churches of the apostle, where they observed the freedom (from the Torah) that was practiced, and now they are present at the apostolic conference in order to demand the circumcision of Christians among the gentiles (Gal. 2:4–5).[3] Paul obviously feared that his previous gentile mission without the requirement of circumcision (thus from the Jewish and strict Jewish Christian view without the Torah)[4] could be brought to nothing by the agitation of these opponents and a decision in Jerusalem influenced by them. Then his apostolic commission to establish churches (cf. 1 Thess. 2:19; 1 Cor. 9:15–18, 23; 2 Cor. 1:14) would not be fulfilled. Besides, he offers another reason: The apostle saw his boast on the day of Christ and thus his eschatological salvation in danger, for he would fail in his own primary task (cf. Phil. 2:16).[5]

---

2. Paul follows ancient argumentation; cf. Xenophon, *Anabasis* 3.1.5–7; Philo, *Moses* 1.268.

3. With Wehnert, *Die Reinheit*, 115–16, I understand Gal. 2:4–5 as a reference to both the events in the Pauline/Antiochian church and the context of the conversation in Jerusalem.

4. Paul was never engaged in a mission to the gentiles that was, in principle, "law free," for the central content of the Torah (e.g., the Decalogue) applied also to gentile converts. The renunciation of circumcision for non-Jews, along with the concurrent affirmation of their membership in the elect people of God, was certainly tantamount to a mission apart from the law, for the contents of Pauline ethics could be received and integrated without problems from the cultural background of the gentile Christians.

5. Cf. T. Holtz, "Die Bedeutung des Apostelkonzils für Paulus," 149–50.

7.2 The Essential Problem

The basic problem that was discussed at the apostolic conference is obvious: What criteria must be satisfied in order to belong to the elect church of God and at the same time preserve continuity with the people of God of the first covenant? Should circumcision, as a sign of the covenant (cf. Gen. 17:11), thus of the membership in the elect people of God, be obligatory for Christians from the nations?[6] From the Jewish perspective, if one became a proselyte by means of circumcision and a ritual washing and thus a member of the elect people of God, then for Jewish Christians it follows that only baptism in the name of Jesus Christ *and* circumcision mediate the new status in salvation.[7]

The problems debated at the apostolic conference (and in the Antiochian conflict) occurred in a time in which the definition of what, at the ritual and social level, constitutes Christianity had not yet been concluded and was not yet defined. Neither the Christian identity markers nor the resulting pattern of life were yet clarified. Could gentile Christian churches be recognized in the same way as Jewish Christian churches, which, to a considerable extent, continued to live within the association of synagogues? Must the unity of an ethnic and religious community that had been constitutive for Jewish self-understanding be abandoned? What brings about holiness and purity? By what means do those who believe in Jesus participate in the people of God? How do they become bearers of the promises of the covenant of God with Israel? To what extent should Jewish identity markers such as circumcision, table fellowship among only the people of Israel, and Sabbath apply to the gentile Christian churches that are being formed? Does the change of status that has taken place also include other status changes? In the same way, can one find regulations for believers from Judaism and the gentiles, or must they take differing paths? Are baptism and circumcision binding initiation rites for all Christ-believers, or does baptism alone allow full acceptance into the people of God?

The resolution of these problems is made more difficult by the fact that no clear statements can be found in the Torah regarding the life together of Jews and non-Jews outside Israel. The young churches composed of Jewish and gentile Christians were a sui generis reality,[8] for the Torah did not anticipate such a situation. The Torah was instruction for Israel, and it did not apply to non-Jews

6. Cf. O. Betz, "Beschneidung II."

7. There had probably never been a fully valid conversion to Judaism without circumcision; cf. the analysis of texts in Kraus, *Das Volk Gottes*, 96–107.

8. In the OT and in ancient Jewish literature, the idea merely appears that also "the gentiles" will glorify and worship Yahweh (cf. Isa. 19:16–25; Mal. 1:11; Zeph. 2:11; 3:9–10; LAB 1.1.1–2; Sib. Or. 3.716–20; Tob. 14:6–7).

(cf. Exod. 34:10–17; Lev. 20:2–7). Nowhere does it require circumcision or the keeping of the Sabbath for non-Jews. Indeed, the gods of the other peoples are accepted as allotted by Yahweh (cf. Deut. 4:19). Also the attempted solution in the apostolic decrees (see below, 7.3) to regulate the relationship of Jewish and gentile Christians in a way analogous to the relationship of the people of Israel to the "strangers" in the land could not be a lasting solution, for this model is determined not by equality in living together but by the idea of subordination.

7.3 The Process

The process of the apostolic conference in its main features can be discerned from Acts 15:1–34 and Gal. 2:1–10, even if both reports deviate from one another in specific details. (1) Paul and Barnabas appear in Jerusalem as leading representatives of the Antiochian church (Acts 15:2, 4; Gal. 2:1, 9).[9] (2) The topic of the conference is the fundamental justification and practical execution of the mission to the gentiles without requiring circumcision (Acts 15:12; Gal. 2:2, 9). (3) At the conference one group demands the circumcision of the gentile Christians (Gal. 2:4–5, "the false brothers"; Acts 15:5, "sect of the Pharisees"). (4) The conference takes place at two levels: at the level of the church (Acts 15:12; Gal. 2:2a) and in a smaller group (Acts 15:6: the apostles and the elders came together; Gal. 2:9: Paul speaks with the "pillars"). This distinction determines the Pauline portrayal of the apostolic conference, for Gal. 2:3–5 reports of the events of the full gathering, and Gal. 2:6–10 reports the agreements with the leadership of the church. (5) After both reports, the mission to the gentiles without the requirement of circumcision is recognized (Acts 15:10–12, 19; Gal. 2:9). Here the Lukan report deviates sharply from Paul's own account. According to Luke, the people in Jerusalem combine their agreement with the condition that the non-Jews keep a minimum of the ritual requirements (Acts 15:19–21, 28–29; 21:25: abstention from idolatry, food offered to idols, sexual immorality, things strangled, and blood).[10] The four prohibitions are oriented to the regulations for Jews and foreigners in Lev. 17–18 and were understood as a model for the interaction of Jewish and gentile Christians.[11] The apostolic decree is limited to specific territories (Acts

9. D.-A. Koch, *Geschichte des Urchristentums*, 229–30, assumes that the Antiochian delegation was led by Barnabas.

10. The three traditions vary slightly: "They should abstain from the pollutions of idols, sexual immorality, things strangled, and blood" (Acts 15:20); that you abstain (keep yourselves free) "from food offered to idols, blood, things strangled, and sexual immorality" (Acts 15:29; 21:25).

11. On the cultic minimal demands of the Holiness Code (Lev. 17–26) for the strangers in the land, cf. Lev. 17:10–14; 18:6–18, 26; cf. also Exod. 12:43–49; 20:10; 23:12; Lev. 16:29; 20:2;

Table 4. Sequence of the Jerusalem Conference according to Paul and Luke

Galatians 2:1–10	Acts 15
date (2:1)	—
Paul and Barnabas travel to Jerusalem (2:1)	Paul and Barnabas travel to Jerusalem (15:2)
Titus (2:1)	—
Jerusalem trip due to a disclosure (2:2)	Paul and Barnabas as emissaries of Antioch (15:2)
Paul presents "his" gospel (2:2)	—
no circumcision of Titus (2:3)	—
the "false brothers" (2:4)	believing Pharisees (15:5; cf. 15:1, 24)
Paul resists the false brothers (2:5)	dispute of Paul and Barnabas with Judaizers in Antioch and Jerusalem (cf. 15:2, 7)
no requirement for the gentile believers by the members of repute in the Jerusalem church (2:6)	"apostolic decree" (15:19–20) as a decision of James: "to abstain from uncleanliness from idols, from unchastity, from things strangled and from blood" (cf. 15:28–29; 21:25)
"gospel of circumcision" by Peter; "gospel of uncircumcision" by Paul (2:7–8)	—
recognition of the apostleship of Paul (2:9a)	recognition of the apostleship of Paul (cf. 15:12)
the pillars: James, Peter, John (2:9b)	Peter, James (cf. 15:7, 13)
handshake of the "pillars" with Paul and Barnabas (2:9c)	handshake of the "pillars" with Paul and Barnabas (15:25)
collection for the "poor" in Jerusalem (2:10)	collection for the "poor" in Jerusalem (but cf. 11:29–30; 12:25; 24:17)

15:23, Antioch, Syria, Cilicia) and can be partially compared to the regulations for pagan associations, where disputes can be mediated by internal rules of conduct.[12] It undoubtedly has an integrative function, but it remains enclosed in ethnic thinking and thus cannot be regarded as an actual solution to the problem. Luke also does not mention the disputes about the gentile Christian Titus (Gal. 2:3), and he does not connect the agreement about the

---

22:18–20; 24:10–22; Num. 9:14; 15:30; 19:1–11. For the apostolic decree's comprehensive background in tradition history, cf. Wehnert, *Die Reinheit*, 213–38; cf. also Avemarie, "Die jüdischen Wurzeln des Aposteldekrets," 5–32; Pratscher, "Der Beitrag des Herrenbruders Jakobus" 33–48 (with a review of recent research).

12. Cf. Ebel, "Regeln von der Gemeinschaft?," who on p. 337 points out agreements (internal rules for conduct in the form of prohibition) but also differences (no conditions for admission are formulated; consequences for violation remain unclear). Her conclusion: "When compared to the regulations for ancient associations, the apostolic decree turns out to be a deficient and confusing document that raises more questions than it answers."

collection with the conference (Gal. 2:10; cf., however, Acts 11:29–30; 12:25; 24:17). Moreover, in the Lukan portrayal, only a minor role is attributed to Paul, for the real decisions were made by Peter (Acts 15:7–11) and James (Acts 15:13–21).

Galatians 2:1–10 depicts the event differently. Here the essential decision is made in a conversation between Paul, on the one hand, and James, Peter, and John on the other hand. While in Acts 15:5ff. a discursive clarification of the problem is described, Paul does not place the content of his gospel up for debate (cf. Gal. 1:7, 12) since it was received by revelation. He instead emphasizes that the Jerusalem authorities recognize the revelatory theological quality of his gospel (cf. Gal. 2:9, "As they knew the grace given to me"),[13] so that the foundation of the intended unity was laid. According to Paul, this unity included a distribution of the world mission along ethnographic lines: "We to the gentiles, but they to the circumcision" (Gal. 2:9c). Thus the apostle confirms his right for the mission to the gentiles, but at the same time Paul recognizes the right of a Christian mission that considers faith in Jesus Christ and the keeping of the regulations of the Torah as compatible.

7.4 The Result

What was the result of the apostolic conference? Were there many results? According to the Pauline portrayal, the unity at the apostolic conference consisted of three points: (1) The agreement for the collection (Gal. 2:10),[14] (2) freedom from circumcision for gentile Christians, connected with (3) a division of the areas of responsibility: Barnabas and Paul to the gentiles, Jerusalem disciples to the circumcision (Gal. 2:9c). Is this division really a solution? It is unclear, first, whether the decision is conceived in ethnic or geographic terms. If it is understood in ethnic terms, two authorities would be responsible, and the formation of two separate churches in each place would have been inevitable. No evidence exists for this arrangement, not even in Antioch. Furthermore, the Jerusalem church would have been totally overburdened if it had to bear the strategic mission responsibility for the entire Jewish diaspora. However, a geographic understanding does not actually solve the problem. Jerusalem would have been responsible for Palestine, and Antioch for the rest of the world, including the Jewish diaspora. Would the Jerusalem church have been ready to give up the diaspora, which was inseparable from the holy city? The

13. Cf. Jürgens, *Zweierlei Anfang*, 214–15.
14. In addition to the theological-symbolic meaning of the unity of the church, the collection "for the poor" also had a material dimension; according to Josephus, *Ant.* 20.101, a great famine prevailed in Palestine at the time of the procurator Tiberius Alexander (46–48 CE).

second major problem arises: Are the Pauline "gospel of the uncircumcised" and the Petrine "gospel of the circumcised" in Gal. 2:7 congruent in content? In content, one can observe in these formulations major agreements: Both sides understand the core of the gospel in such a way as it is transmitted, for example, in 1 Cor. 15:3. Furthermore, typical Jewish identity markers were undisputed, such as monotheism and numerous ethical precepts. Finally, everyone proceeded from the conviction that salvation could be attained for those who believe in Jesus only in continuity with Israel.

Yet the differences between the two formulations should not be prematurely overplayed, for Paul normally speaks of the "gospel of Christ" or "gospel of God" (εὐαγγέλιον θεοῦ).[15] With these two phrases Paul probably renders the formula that the two negotiating partners were united on.[16] The crucial difference certainly lay in the significance of circumcision in salvation history and the extent of Torah observance. Circumcision was by no means an adiaphoron, for it was the precondition and the entry gate to the law (cf. Philo, *Spec. Laws* 1.1ff.). It documented Israel's special place among the people, secured its identity (cf. Jub. 15.25–34),[17] and separated it from all of the peoples (cf. Josephus, *Ant.* 1.192; Tacitus, *Hist.* 5.5.2). For the strict Jewish Christians, a natural connection existed between faith in Jesus of Nazareth the Messiah, circumcision as a sign of election, and observance of the Torah. Baptism did not take the place of circumcision, for salvation could not be attained beyond the law. Paul, however, can point to the evident activity of God among the peoples, for God elects without respect of persons (cf. Gal. 2:6).[18] By baptism and the reception of the Spirit, the gentile Christians are already complete and equal members of the people of God (cf. Gal. 3:1–5; 3:26–28; Acts 10:44–48); any further sign of legitimation would place God's previous saving action on the gentiles in question. Thus James, Cephas, and John recognize the grace given to Paul (Gal. 2:9a), and he in turn accepts both the collection for Jerusalem (Gal. 2:10) and the "gospel of the

15. On εὐαγγέλιον Χριστοῦ, cf. 1 Thess. 3:2; 1 Cor. 4:15; 9:12; 2 Cor.2:12; 4:4; 9:13; 10:14; Gal. 1:16–17, 11–12; Rom. 1:9; Phil. 1:27; on εὐαγγέλιον τοῦ θεοῦ, cf. 1 Thess. 2:2, 8–9; 2 Cor. 11:7; Rom. 1:1, 15–16, 19.

16. On the other hand, many exegetes correctly see the core part in Gal. 2:7–8 as a pre-Pauline tradition; cf., e.g., Dinkler, "Der Brief an die Galater"; G. Klein, "Galater 2,6–9 und die Geschichte der Jerusalemer Urgemeinde," 110–11; Cullmann, "Πέτρος," 100n16; H. Betz, *Galatians*, 97.

17. Jubilees 15.25–26: "And this command [for circumcision] is for all the eternal generations. . . . And anyone who is born and whose flesh is not circumcised on the eighth day is not from the sons of the covenant, which the Lord made with Abraham."

18. One may not overlook that the vague formulations in Gal. 2:6 ("What they actually were makes no difference to me") depicts a distancing from the Jerusalem "pillars"; cf. Jürgens, *Zweierlei Anfang*, 215–16.

circumcision." It is clear, however, that "the gospel of the uncircumcision" and the "gospel of the circumcision" are not totally identical. The concern with this singular contrast is not on the "one" Pauline gospel, a fact that is indicated not least by the phrase φοβούμενος τοὺς ἐκ περιτομῆς (fear of those from the circumcision) in Gal. 2:12. The people from James demand the keeping of the "gospel of the circumcision," whose "identity markers" Peter had transcended.

According to the Lukan portrayal, the result consisted of two points: (1) believers from the nations are not required to be circumcised (cf. Acts 15:7–11, 19, 28), but (2) the minimal ritual requirements of the apostolic decree (Acts 15:20, 29; 21:25) must be observed. Acts 15:1–35 does not speak of a collective agreement or of a division of the entire mission into ethnographic areas. How does one explain this different portrayal of the results of the apostolic conference? It is noteworthy that, with the apostolic decrees, the basic topic of the Antioch incident, which is not mentioned in Acts, is alluded to: What rules must Christians observe in order to attain the status of purity that is demanded by God and have fellowship with Jewish Christians? It is thus conceivable that Luke has woven together two problems that were originally separate:[19] (1) the ruling of the apostolic conference, according to which gentile Christians are not required to be circumcised; (2) the ruling in the apostolic decree, as formulated in the context of the Antioch incident, that should apply in the interaction of Jews and gentile Christians in the region of the Antiochian/Pauline mission (cf. Acts 15:23).

Traces of this process of fusing may be observed in Acts 15:1–29. It corresponds to Lukan redaction in keeping with the earlier narrative of Acts 10:1–11:15, in which Peter first speaks, and then James presents the solution and Paul is actually silent.[20] Peter's speech again fundamentally and without reservation legitimates the right of the gentile mission unconditionally (cf. Acts 15:10). The speech reaches its climax in the Pauline-sounding statement in Acts 15:11: "On the contrary, we believe that we will be saved through the grace of the Lord Jesus, just as they [the gentile Christians] will." Through the mouth of Peter, the Pauline position legitimates the gentile Christians' freedom from circumcision without further conditions and thus stands in tension with the apostolic decree that follows. The argument of James in Acts 15:19, 28 indicates that he agreed with the unlimited freedom from circumcision for the gentiles at the apostolic conference ("Therefore I consider it right not to lay a burden on the gentiles who turn to God, but . . ."; cf. v. 28: "For the Holy

19. For example, see the argument in Weiser, *Die Apostelgeschichte*, 2:375–77.
20. Only in Acts 15:12 do Barnabas and Paul report (note the sequence!) a summary of their missionary success.

Spirit and we have determined not to lay a burden on you, except . . ."). Thus
the restricting connection with the apostolic decree is derived from Luke.

The traditional content of the Lukan version of the apostolic conference
confirms the substance of the Pauline portrayal. The negotiating partners were
Paul and Barnabas on the one side and James and Peter on the other side. The
crucial result of the conversation was that Christians from among the nations
were not required to be circumcised in order to become full members of the
people of God (Gal. 2:9). In addition, the mission was probably established
along ethnographic lines (Gal. 2:9). This resolution leaves unclear how and
especially whether they had united.[21] In addition, there was the agreement
about the collection (Gal. 2:10).[22]

7.5 Interpretations of the Outcome

At the apostolic conference both sides thus recognized that the one God calls
humankind (with or without circumcision) by the gospel in various ways and
that the believers serve the will of God in different ways.[23] Besides, different
concepts of mission led to the apostolic conference, which did not actually
unite but were instead recognized as legitimate expressions of the Christian
faith. The equal status but not the identity of the two gospels (of the circumcision, of the uncircumcision) was affirmed at the apostolic conference![24] For
Paul this was already obvious because he was the new one; for circumcision,
observance of the Torah, and faith in Messiah Jesus of Nazareth were before
Paul and during his mission self-evident signs of membership in the people

21. Probably Luke knew about the discussions (and failures) and placed a later, restricted
ethnographic agreement (see below, 7.6) as the solution reached already at the apostolic
conference.

22. Acts 24:17 indicates that Luke knows about the collection. Whether he refers to the agreement about the collection in Acts 11:29–30; 12:25 remains uncertain. Probably Luke incorporates
the agreement about the collection into the apostolic conference because the collection was
not accepted by the Jerusalem church (see below, 8.5), thus contradicting the Lukan concept
of the unity of the church.

23. This was recognized already by Baur, *Paul*, 130–31, "The κοινωνία was always a division; it could be brought into agreement only by one party going εἰς τὰ ἔθνη, the other going
εἰς τὴν περιτομήν; i.e., the Jewish apostles could allege nothing against the principles on which
Paul founded his evangelistic labors; they were obliged to recognize them in a certain manner,
but this recognition was a merely outward one; they left it to him to work on these principles
still further in the cause of the gospel among the gentiles; but for themselves they did not want
to know anything more about them. The distinct apostolic regions are thus strictly separated;
there is a εὐαγγέλιον τῆς περιτομῆς and a εὐαγγέλιον τῆς ἀκροβυστίας (Gal. 2:7), an ἀποστολὴ εἰς
τὴν περιτομήν (Gal. 2:8) and an ἀποστολὴ εἰς τὰ ἔθνη, in which the Mosaic law applied to one
and not to the other, but both stand parallel to each other."

24. Wehnert, *Die Reinheit*, 120, even speaks of a "resolution for separation."

of God. From the Pauline view the apostolic conference sanctions not only the mission to the gentiles without circumcision and without restrictions; according to his perspective, it confirms the special place of the apostle to the gentiles as an equal partner alongside the Jerusalem "pillars."

This interpretation of the apostolic conference was by no means undisputed, as the Antioch incident, the later agitation by Judaizers in the Pauline churches, and especially the Lukan tradition of the apostolic decree demonstrate.[25] While, according to his version, Paul regarded the agreement at the conference as a binding obligation, other streams within early Christianity understood it as a onetime concession or interpreted it in a different way. The juxtaposition of theological concepts of identity that were ultimately irreconcilable was only codified but not overcome. After the apostolic conference there were at least three different positions on the crucial question of the validity of the Torah for gentile Christians: (1) freedom from circumcision and thus actual freedom from the Torah with the exception of the core elements from the Decalogue (Paul, parts of the Antiochian church?, Apollos?); (2) limited Torah observance without circumcision (apostolic decree); (3) total validity of the Torah, including the requirement of circumcision for gentile believers (Jewish Christian missionary opponents in Galatia and Philippi, parts of the Jerusalem church).

7.6 The Incident at Antioch

The incident at Antioch occurred in both topical (and temporal)[26] proximity to the apostolic conference (summer/fall 48 CE). At the apostolic conference the mission concept of the Jerusalem church and the basic freedom from circumcision for gentile Christians were recognized, and a division of missionary responsibility was intended. The problems of churches with a mixture of Jewish and gentile Christians was not on the agenda, or it was ignored or at least not resolved. The problems erupted in Antioch, where table fellowship

25. The Pauline letters betray no knowledge of the apostolic decree; it is disputed whether it was known to Paul (those who argue against a knowledge include, among others, Roloff, *Die Apostelgeschichte*, 227; for another view, cf., e.g., Lüdemann, *Paul: Apostle to the Gentiles* 1:71–75).

26. In Gal. 2:11 the linguistic signal ὅτε indicates that Paul depicts the events in chronological order; for evidence, see Wechsler, *Geschichtsbild und Apostelstreit*, 297–305; Wehnert, *Die Reinheit*, 120–23. Konradt ("Zur Datierung des sogenannten antiochenischen Zwischenfalls") dates the incident at Antioch to 52 CE and connects it with Acts 18:22; against this view in particular is the fact that Paul follows a temporally structured sequence in Gal. 1:10–2:14, which does not allow for a four-year distance from the apostolic conference (cf. the critique in Schnelle, *History and Theology of the New Testament*, 20–21).

was a common practice between Jewish Christians and the uncircumcised who, according to Jewish law, were unclean gentile Christians. According to Gal. 2:11, Peter participated in the mixed meals in Antioch. He thus verifies that the Jewish regulations for food and purity do not apply to Christians from the nations, that Jewish Christians cannot place gentile Christians on the same level with unbelievers. This liberal position changed abruptly with the arrival of τινες ἀπὸ Ἰακώβου (some people from James).[27] Peter withdrew himself and abandoned the table fellowship. He separated himself, as is recommended in Jub. 22.16: "And you, my son Jacob, remember my words and keep the commandments of Abraham your father! Separate yourself from the nations and do not eat with them, and do not perform deeds like theirs and do not be their associates! For their work is impure and all their ways are defiled and despicable" (cf. also Dan. 1:8ff.; Tob. 1:10–12; Jos. Asen. 8; Let. Aris. 139–42; 182–83; 4 Macc. 1:33–35; Tacitus, *Hist.* 5.5.5. On the Torah's requirement of separation, cf. 4 Ezra 10).[28] At this time the food laws (cf., e.g., Deut. 14:3–21) were the central content of the Jewish (and thus the Jewish Christian) understanding of the law;[29] its existence led the people from James to the rejection of common meals.[30] The application of the demand for cultic separation from the impure to the relationship between gentile and Jewish Christians would not only have assigned a lower status to gentile Christians but particularly would have made table fellowship at the Lord's Supper between both groups impossible. Paul identifies a motivation for this momentous conduct of Peter in Gal. 2:12: "Because he feared the people of the circumcision."[31] Apparently the consistent Jewish Christian point of view under the leadership of James in the Jerusalem church induced Peter to change his conduct. The attempt to remain as Christians within Judaism was, for James and his followers, certainly possible only with consistent obedience to the Torah. Although Peter had already abandoned this standpoint through his previous practice in Antioch (cf. also Acts 11:3), he now adopted it again.

27. The "people from James" are not identical to the "false brothers" in Gal. 2:4, for the people from James accept the agreement of the apostolic conference; cf. H. Betz, *Galatians*, 203–4, who correctly places James in the background.

28. Cf. also Str-B 4.1:374–78.

29. Cf. the comprehensive evidence in C. Heil, *Die Ablehnung der Speisegebote*, 23–123, cf. 299: "According to the widespread early Jewish view, God had revealed the food laws, and any non-observance meant ipso facto a rejection of God."

30. The assumption of Dunn ("Incident at Antioch," 15–16) that insufficient tithing of the food motivated the people from James to interfere is inadequate.

31. The phrase οἱ τῆς περιτομῆς does not designate an additional group but signifies the "people from James." Peter's fear can be explained only with the appearance of an influential authority, even an emissary of James; cf. G. Klein, "Die Verleugnung des Petrus," 83n205. The οἱ λοιποὶ Ἰουδαῖοι in Gal. 2:13 are Jewish Christians from Antioch.

Therefore Paul reproaches him: he condemns himself by his conduct (Gal. 2:11b). This inconsistency of Peter then led the other Jewish Christians, even Barnabas, into hypocrisy and to abandon the table fellowship that Peter had previously practiced with the gentile Christians (Gal. 2:13). Paul regarded this conduct as theological inconsistency because it involved the abandonment of fellowship between gentile and Jewish Christians. Thus Peter, Barnabas, and the other Jewish Christians are not conducting themselves according to the truth of the gospel (Gal. 2:14), just as previously at the apostolic conference false brothers had done when they wanted to demand circumcision for gentile Christians (cf. Gal. 2:4f.). The verb ὀρθοποδέω (walk in the right way) and the phrase ἀλήθεια τοῦ εὐαγγελίου (truth of gospel) indicate precisely that for both Paul and his opponents practical and theological issues were permanently intertwined. The truth of the gospel did not require the obligation of gentile Christians to keep the ritual demands of the Jewish law (cf. Gal. 2:5, 14). Consequently, Paul speaks to Peter's face: "If you, though a Jew, live in a gentile and not a Jewish way, how can you compel the gentiles to live according to Jewish customs?" It is not necessary for Jews to give up, but at the same time non-Jews do not have to Ἰουδαΐζειν (live in a Jewish manner). The requirement that gentile Christians live in a Jewish manner, as the context indicates (v. 12, συνήσθιεν, he ate together), refers primarily to the keeping of Jewish food laws.

A consequence of the Antiochian conflict was probably the apostolic decree (see above, 7.3), which was secondarily inserted into the decision of the apostolic conference. Theologically, James the brother of the Lord, who is presupposed in Acts 15:20, 29; 21:25 as speaker or author, probably stood behind the apostolic decree. At the apostolic conference James had agreed to the freedom from circumcision for gentile Christians only with reservations. He held firmly to this position; but after the incident at Antioch, he took a more specific and restrictive position as he formulated halakic demands: Table fellowship between Jewish and gentile Christians can occur only when minimal standards of ethical-ritual regulations apply to the gentile Christians,[32] that is, the abstention from the polluting contacts with the gods, from things strangled and blood, and from sexual immorality. James evidently counted Antioch, Syria, and Cilicia (cf. Acts 15:23) as the area of responsibility for the Jerusalem church and from that made the claim to issue such a decree. In fact, he intervened in a limited way into the rights of gentile Christians.

---

32. An alternative between "ritual" and "ethical" is inappropriate for the apostolic decree because "sexual immorality" is interwoven with both.

The apostolic conference did not resolve the basic problem of early Christianity: What conditions must be fulfilled in order to become completely a member of the new movement? Does Christianity remain an open, liberal variation of Judaism, or does it become its own independent universal movement? If an agreement was reached in the spring of 48 CE, both sides probably interpreted it in their own way. In particular, the strict Jewish Christian orientation around James the brother of the Lord could not be satisfactory for a long period, for among them the central question of purity was not actually resolved. It wanted the new movement to remain permanently within Judaism and thus, in view of the surrounding Jewish context, had to insist on a minimal level of cultic purity. A solution would have been the model behind the Antiochian conflict, but it would have made, for example, table fellowship of the Christ-believers from Judaism with the gentiles impossible at the Lord's Supper and was vehemently rejected by Paul. Thus the conflict remained under the surface until it exploded in the Galatian crisis (see below, 8.5).

Table 5. Chronology of Early Christianity to 50 CE

30	death of Jesus
ca. 30–32	establishment of the Jerusalem church/first conflicts
from 30	activities of the Jesus movement in Galilee, at first oral transmission of the Jesus traditions
31–43	Peter leads the Jerusalem church
31/32	formation of a church in Damascus
ca. 32	Hebrews and Hellenists in Jerusalem
32/33	Stephen
32/33	calling of Paul
from 33	mission of Philip
ca. 33–34	Paul in Arabia
ca. 34	founding of the church in Antioch
35	first visit of Paul to Jerusalem
ca. 35	Barnabas works in Antioch
ca. 35–40	oral/written establishment of the passion narrative, first targeted collections of Jesus traditions
ca. 36–42	Paul in Syria and Cilicia (Tarsus)
ca. 40	founding of the church in Rome, "Christians" as their own group in Antioch
ca. 40–50	origin of pre-Pauline traditions
ca. 42	Paul unites with the church at Antioch
43/44	persecution under Agrippa I, Peter leaves Jerusalem, and James takes over the leadership of the church
ca. 45–47	first missionary trip
48	apostolic council (spring), incident at Antioch (summer/fall)
49	edict of Claudius

8

The Independent Mission of Paul

The events surrounding the apostolic conference and the Antiochian conflict led to a separation between Paul and Barnabas and to the ultimate separation of the apostle from the Antiochian mission. The portrayal in Acts must be considered without historical basis for two reasons: (1) The apparent conflict over John Mark on a personal level (cf. Acts 15:36–39) was scarcely the actual occasion for the separation of Paul and Barnabas. More probable is the assumption that the incident at Antioch was the precipitating factor, for Paul and Barnabas evidently represented different concepts of purity. (2) Paul's appearance in Acts 16:4 as the leading protagonist of the apostolic decree does not correspond to the historical truth. One cannot say with certainty whether Paul knew the apostolic decree; his conduct in the Antiochian conflict (Gal. 2) suggests that he totally rejected the concept of purity that stands behind the apostolic decree. Paul probably separated himself from Barnabas and Antioch because he, in contrast to Barnabas, did not accept the apostolic decree that applied to the area of the Antiochian mission (cf. Acts 15:23).[1] With the course of events, Paul traveled further west. Strengthened by the decision of the apostolic conference and now homeless because of the application of the apostolic decree in his previous area of work, Paul at the end of 48 CE began to conduct an independent mission.

1. Contra, e.g., Öhler, *Barnabas*, 124–25, who accepts the authenticity of the Lukan version.

8.1 Perspective, Process, and Conflicts

Paul breaks through the previous restriction of the Antiochian mission to the regions of Palestine, Syria, and southeast Asia Minor and turns toward western Asia Minor and Greece with the proclamation of the Christian message. Finally, he includes Rome and Spain in his plans (cf. Rom. 15:22–33). He takes the gospel into the cultural and political centers of the ancient world. With this movement he clearly changes the perspective of his activity. Apparently he had first been engaged in missions without much success in the Syrian desert areas (cf. Gal. 1:17) and his Cilician homeland (cf. Gal. 1:21); then he joined the Antiochian opening to the gentiles (cf. Acts 11:25f.); now after an evaluation of the success of the first missionary journey, he takes on a universal perspective. He shares the view of a victorious general (2 Cor. 2:14–15) and thinks in geographic and religious-political categories of the entire Roman Empire (cf. Rom. 15:19–20, "from Jerusalem to Illyricum";[2] 15:26, "Macedonia and Achaia").[3] He had the task of extending the "obedience of faith" (Rom. 1:5) worldwide. Paul understands himself to be called by God (cf. Gal. 1:15–16; Rom. 1:1–2), an apostle/sent one (Rom. 1:1), and a *presbeutēs*/ambassador (2 Cor. 5:20) of the true/only Kyrios, Jesus Christ. He proclaims to the whole world (Rom. 1:14, "I am a debtor to the Greeks and the barbarians, the wise and the foolish") the only gospel: "Be reconciled to God" (2 Cor. 5:20). Thus Luke's description of the events indicates the extent to which the success of Paul led him increasingly into conflict with Judaism, the Jerusalem church, local cults, and the Roman authorities.

The Second Missionary Journey

According to the Lukan portrayal, the second missionary journey included the events in Acts 15:36–18:22[4] and took place from the end of 48 to spring 52 CE. Luke traces the specific locales of this missionary expansion and presents the image of a tirelessly active missionary. The path leads Paul with

---

2. Whether he thinks of Isa. 66:19 here (so Riesner, *Paul's Early Period*, 245–53) or of the table of nations in Gen. 10 (so Scott, *Paul and the Nations*, 135–49) must remain an open question. Paul does not cite Isa. 66:19 directly, and he evidently thinks in Roman territorial categories (Macedonia and Achaia in 1 Thess. 1:7–8; province of Asia in 1 Cor. 16:19; 2 Cor. 1:8; and Rom. 16:5; Illyricum, founded as a Roman province in 9 BCE, in Rom. 15:19). For a critique of these theses, cf. Peerbolte, *Paul the Missionary*, 248–52. As before, the assumption of Käsemann, *Romans*, 395, is still correct: Jerusalem and Illyricum designate the "boundaries of Paul's missionary activity."

3. Cf. Wischmeyer, *Die paulinische Mission*, 105.

4. On the Lukan schematization of the Pauline missionary journeys, see D.-A. Koch, *Geschichte des Urchristentums*, 562–69.

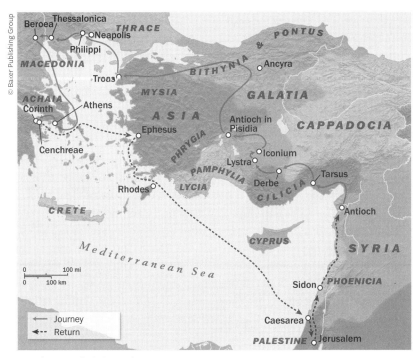

8.1. The second missionary journey

companions Silas and Timothy[5] from Syria through Cilicia and Phrygia to Galatia, thence to Troas, and from there they proceeded to Macedonia in order to set foot on European soil for the first time. While Luke ascribes the transfer of the gospel to Europe directly to a revelation (Acts 16:9–10), he underlines the significance of the Pauline decision for salvation history.

At the beginning of 49 CE, Paul begins his missionary activity in Philippi.[6] The city of Philippi was established circa 356 BCE by Philip II of Macedonia. In 42 BCE an intensive colonizing program began, which intensified in 31 BCE (the victory of Octavian over Antony). Philippi developed as colonia Julia Augusta Philippensis (from 27 BCE) into a Roman military colony, in which veterans especially were settled. The Romans were the most influential

5. Timothy came from Lystra in southern Asia Minor and, according to Acts 16:3, was circumcised there by Paul. This tradition is scarcely reliable, for it stands in sharp contradiction to the position of Paul at the apostolic council, where the Greek Titus was not required to be circumcised (cf. Gal. 2:3). The tradition of Acts 16:4, according to which Paul and his companions propagated the apostolic decree, is also not reliable. For a thorough examination, cf. Lips, *Timotheus und Titus*, 123–27.

6. On Philippi, cf. Elliger, *Paulus in Griechenland*, 23–77; Pilhofer, *Philippi*, vol. 1; Bormann, *Philippi*; Verhoef, *Philippi*.

population group. However, Greeks and Thracians also shaped the linguistic, cultural, and religious life of the city.[7] The economic significance of the city (agriculture, crafts, commerce) was the result of the city's position on the Via Egnatia, part of the primary connection between the eastern and western parts of the Roman Empire. Philippi is an example of the religious syncretism of the first century CE (cf. Acts 16:16–22), for along with the cult of the caesar as well as Greek, Roman, and Egyptian deities, the cults of the indigenous Thracian population enjoyed great popularity, in which above all the gods of the land and of fertility were worshiped. The mission in Philippi was very successful. In the environment of the synagogue, Paul converted Lydia, the seller of purple, a God-fearing woman.[8] The radiating power of the Jewish faith had led many people to turn from the worship of pagan gods and toward monotheism without formally converting to Judaism through circumcision (see above, 6.1). From within this group and especially in Asia Minor, Paul was able to win over many to the new faith. Noteworthy is also the fact that Lydia, a prosperous woman, turned to Christianity along with her family (Acts 16:15: "When she was baptized with her house"). Consequently, a conflict was preprogrammed: The Godfearers probably belonged predominantly to the middle and higher social levels; they were an important link to the Greek and Roman populations, and they frequently supported the synagogue communities as patrons. The Pauline mission achieved great success especially with these people and drew important sympathizers away from each local Jewish community. In addition, two further conflicts arose: the virulent conflict with pagan magic, which Paul had already faced (cf. Acts 13:6–12) on the first missionary journey (cf. Acts 16:16–19, the slave girl with the spirit of divination), and the resulting charge of violating local laws (Acts 16:20–22, "These men are disturbing our city. They are Jews and they proclaim customs, which we as Romans neither accept nor observe"). Probably Paul was primarily perceived by the Roman population as a Jewish missionary and confronted by anti-Jewish prejudices. The apostle and his coworkers were led before the Roman magistrates in the city, beaten, and thrown into prison. While the narrative in Acts 16:16–40 has legendary embellishment, its historical core is confirmed by 1 Thess. 2:2 ("although we suffered before in Philippi and were mistreated"; cf. Phil. 1:30: "You suffer the same struggle that you have seen in me").

---

7. The Roman element is strongly emphasized by Bormann, *Philippi*, 11–84; Pilhofer, *Philippi*, 1:85–92, also emphasizes the Roman character of Philippi but in addition points to the not-insignificant influence of Greeks and Thracians. Judaism evidently played no role. There was probably no synagogue in Philippi, but only a Jewish place of prayer (cf. προσευχή in Acts 16:13, 16); cf. Pilhofer, *Philippi*, 1:165–274.

8. Cf. Pilhofer, *Philippi*, 1:234–40; Ebel, *Lydia und Berenike*, 21–76.

From Philippi, Paul traveled on the Via Egnatia in the westward direction toward Thessalonica. The city of Thessalonica was founded around 315 BCE. In every period, its favorable location at the innermost corner of the Thermaic Gulf and on the Via Egnatia established the constant significance of Thessalonica as a harbor city, a trading venue, and commercial hub.[9] As a cultural and religious center, Thessalonica had great appeal; excavations and literary witnesses attest to the worship of cult deities such as Serapis, Isis, Dionysus, or the Cabiri.[10] The description in Acts and the information from 1 Thessalonians agree on two basic points: (1) Paul had great missionary success (cf. 1 Thess. 1:6–10; Acts 17:4), and (2) the Jews reacted with persecutions that, according to Acts 17:5ff., were directed at Paul and his coworkers. According to 1 Thess. 2:14–16, the church in Thessalonica was persecuted especially by its own countrymen (v. 14); the sharp polemic against Jews in verses 15–16 also indicates participation by the Jews. Paul probably began his mission within the area of the synagogue and was successful among some Jews, many Godfearers, and (prosperous) women (cf. Acts 17:4). The leadership of the Jewish community could apparently bring the city authorities to proceed against Paul. Once more, the agitation against Paul involved a political charge: "They turn the entire world in an uproar. . . . And they also violate the laws of Caesar when they affirm that there is only one king, named Jesus" (Acts 17:6–7). Acts 17:2 reports that Paul stayed a brief month in Thessalonica. A somewhat different picture comes from Phil. 4:15–16, according to which the church in Philippi supported Paul twice while he was in Thessalonica. In Thessalonica, Paul and his coworkers labored for their livelihood in order not to be a burden to the church (1 Thess. 2:9). Both facts suggest a somewhat longer stay, perhaps about three months[11] in the middle of 49 CE. After his departure Paul sought to visit the young church again but was not able to do so (cf. 1 Thess. 2:17–18).

In Berea also, Paul worked successfully; one of the companions on the journey with the collection for Jerusalem came from this church (Acts 20:4, Sopater; cf. Rom. 16:21). From Berea, Paul and his companions traveled to Athens (cf. 1 Thess. 3:1–2). There Paul stayed for a longer time at the end of 49 CE, and from here he sent Timothy to Thessalonica. Except for the fact of his stay, Paul says nothing about his effectiveness in Athens. The preaching to Jews and Greeks in Athens, the encounter with Greek philosophers, and the impression made by the many statues and pagan altars in the city as described by Luke are never mentioned by Paul. The Areopagus speech (Acts

9. On the history of the city, cf. Elliger, *Paulus in Griechenland*, 78–116; Riesner, *Paul's Early Period*, 337–41; Brocke, *Thessaloniki*, 12–101.

10. Cf. Donfried, "Cults of Thessalonica"; Brocke, *Thessaloniki*, 115–38.

11. Cf. Riesner, *Paul's Early Period*, 364.

8.2. The Stoa of Athens

17:22–31) was probably not made in this form.[12] In particular, the concept of a natural kinship of humankind to God in Acts 17:28–29 is inconceivable for Paul inasmuch as he assumes an alienation of humankind from God caused by sin. Apparently the apostle had only limited missionary success in Athens. Acts 17:32–34 confirms this assumption, for only Damaris and Dionysius the Areopagite were mentioned by name as Christians.[13]

Paul entered Athens as one of many traveling preachers, and he apparently did not leave a lasting impression. Whether his visit resulted in the establishment of a church in Athens is not reported. Athens played no role among the Pauline churches in Greece and in the larger history of early Christianity. Reports of a Christian church in Athens do not appear until 170 CE (Eusebius, *Hist. eccl.* 4.23.2).

12. The basic analysis still holds: Dibelius, "Paul on the Areopagus," correctly calls this section the "high point of the book" (26). For the analysis, cf. also Lüdemann, *Das frühe Christentum*, 196–202; Manfred Lang, *Die Kunst des christlichen Lebens*, 251–314.

13. That Dionysius was a member of the Areopagus and thus a member of the city elite is to be doubted; cf. D.-A. Koch, *Geschichte des Urchristentums*, 256. A. Weiss, *Soziale Elite und Christentum*, 100–101, argues for his elite status: "The objections that have been raised against the possible conversion of Dionysius in the sense of a conversion to Christianity have turned out to be not cogent, so his conversion may also be considered historically plausible. The Areopagus probably functioned from the time of Sulla's reorganization, with certainty in the middle of the first century CE, as the equivalent of an *ordo decurionum*, and thus one is probably justified in regarding Dionysius the Areopagite as a Christian member of the *ordo*."

At the beginning of 50 CE, Paul entered Corinth, where he met the married couple Prisca and Aquila, who had been expelled from Rome (cf. Acts 18:2); then Timothy and Silas/Silvanus soon followed (Acts 18:5). Caesar established the city (which had been destroyed in 146 BCE but was by no means uninhabited in the meantime) as a Roman colony for veterans in 44 BCE.[14] In 27 BCE Corinth became the capital of the senatorial province of Achaia. Besides the strong Roman element, the Greek and eastern population must have been large. Philo mentions a noteworthy Jewish colony in Rome (*Legatio ad Gaium* 281); Acts reports the existence of a synagogue (Acts 18:4).[15] The strategic location of the city with the two harbors, Cenchreae and Lechaum, explains the significance of Corinth as an economic center between Asia and Rome/Greece. Corinth was considered a rich city, in which trade, financial activities, and the production of crafts blossomed.[16] In Corinth there was a variety of Hellenistic cults. Pausanius reports on altars and temples of Poseidon, Artemis of Ephesus, and Dionysus as well as a temple of Asclepius and sanctuaries of Isis and Serapis in Corinth in the second century CE.[17] An Isis initiation described by Apuleius took place in Corinth (cf. *Metamorphoses* 11.22.7ff.), and it was a center of the newly revived Cynic movement in the first century CE. Diogenes gladly stayed here,[18] and the famous Cynic Demetrius lived and taught also in Corinth. Moreover, the Isthmian Games took place there (cf. 1 Cor. 9:24–27); after the Olympian games they were the most important athletic championship in antiquity. Finally, in the northern part of the city, an Asclepius temple was excavated. With its three dining rooms it illustrates the problem that stands behind 1 Cor. 8–10.[19]

Paul remained in the city about one and one-half years (cf. Acts 18:11); along with Ephesus, Corinth developed into a center of missionary activity. In Corinth, Paul worked successfully among the Godfearers (cf. Acts 18:7, Titius Justus) and Jews so that even Crispus, the head of the synagogue, and his house were converted (cf. Acts 18:8). The Corinthian church was relatively large, and above all the life of the worship services was vibrant (cf. 1 Cor. 11–14).[20]

14. On Corinth, cf. especially Wiseman, "Corinth and Rome I"; Elliger, *Paulus in Griechenland*, 200–251; Murphy-O'Connor, *St. Paul's Corinth*; B. Winter, *After Paul Left Corinth*, 7–25; Schowalter and Friesen, *Urban Religion in Roman Corinth*; Elliger, "Korinth"; Belezos, *Saint Paul and Corinth*, vols. 1–2.

15. In inscriptions only a synagogue from the second or third century CE is attested. Cf. Klauck, *Herrenmahl und hellenistischer Kult*, 234n3.

16. Cf. Strabo, *Geography* 8.6.20–21, 23 (NW II/1:235–36).

17. Cf. Pausanias, *Description of Greece* 2.1.7–5.5.

18. Cf. Dio Chrysostom, *Or.* 6.3.

19. Cf. Murphy-O'Connor, *St. Paul's Corinth*, 186–91.

20. Cf. Balode, *Gottesdienst in Korinth*.

8.3. The sanctuary of Apollo in Corinth

House churches in the homes of Gaius (cf. 1 Cor. 1:14; Rom. 16:23), Stephanas (cf. 1 Cor. 16:15), Titius Justus (Acts 18:7), Crispus (Acts 18:8), and Erastus (Rom. 16:23) may be assumed. In Corinth, as in Philippi previously, the Jews similarly attempted to criminalize Paul before the Roman authorities, but the effort failed before the Roman proconsul Gallio (cf. Acts 18:12–16). The apostle wrote at least three letters to the church at Corinth (1 and 2 Corinthians and a lost prior letter mentioned in 1 Cor. 5:9) and undertook numerous attempts through visits or emissaries (2 Cor. 1:12–2:11; 8:6ff.) to maintain contact with the church. Both 1 and 2 Corinthians give a unique insight into the very intensive and contentious relationship between the apostle and this church.

The summary travel report in Acts 18:18–22:23 raises major problems: Paul spends a few more days in Corinth in order to go to Syria, leaving behind the married couple Prisca/Priscilla and Aquila in Ephesus. He had a discussion with the Jews in the synagogue but declined the resulting mission possibilities there in order to leave Ephesus. Although Acts 18:18 mentions Syria as the essential destination of Paul, in Acts 18:22 he lands in Caesarea, goes up (ἀναβάς) to Jerusalem, and then travels further from Jerusalem to Antioch.[21]

21. On the analysis of Acts 18:18–23, cf. esp. Weiser, *Die Apostelgeschichte* 2:496ff. A distinction between redaction and tradition gives the following result: traditional elements are probably contained in vv. 18a–c, 19a, 21b–23; on the other hand, vv. 18d, 19b–21a correspond to the Lukan portrayal of Paul.

These stations on the journey prior to the resettlement of Prisca and Aquila from Corinth to Ephesus cannot be confirmed in the Pauline letters. Moreover, the course and the motivation for the trip cannot be satisfactorily explained. What did Paul want to accomplish in Antioch in the middle of his successful missionary activity in Macedonia and Asia Minor? Also inexplicable are the reports of the landing in Caesarea and the visit to Jerusalem, for according to Acts 18:18 Syria is the destination, and according to Acts 18:22 Antioch is the actual destination. Furthermore, the fourth visit to Jerusalem cannot be historical, according to the Lukan reckoning,[22] for it stands in conflict with the statements of the early Pauline letters. What justifies striking off Jerusalem and Caesarea and regarding Antioch as original? On the other hand, the pre-Lukan tradition spoke of a trip of the apostle to Antioch, the place from which he visited the Galatian and Phrygian regions on the way to Ephesus. After all attempts fail to coordinate the redacted traditions of another Jerusalem visit in Acts 18:22–23,[23] we must be content with the insight that, according to the traditions available to Luke, after Paul's stay in Corinth, he returned to Antioch by way of Ephesus in order to return to Ephesus. If the historicity of these details is considered, a visit to Jerusalem on this trip must be ruled out.

The Third Missionary Journey

The journey described in Acts 18:18–22 depicts a period from summer 51 to spring 52, after which Paul stayed about two to two and three-fourths years in Ephesus (cf. Acts 19:8, 10; 20:31), from the summer of 52 to the spring of 55.[24] At all times Ephesus belonged among the most important cities of Asia Minor.[25] In the first century CE, as the capital of Asia Minor, it numbered about one hundred thousand inhabitants. The great theater alone could seat twenty-five thousand people. Ephesus had grand boulevards, large libraries, and numerous imposing religious structures. Local and oriental cults, mystery religions, the imperial cult, and the predominant cult of Artemis, with

22. Cf. Weiser, *Die Apostelgeschichte*, 2:502; Roloff, *Die Apostelgeschichte*, 277.

23. Cf. Weiser, *Die Apostelgeschichte*, 2:495–502.

24. The section Acts 18:23 21:14 is traditionally designated as the third missionary journey, which takes place in 52–55/56 CE. Luke apparently intends such an arrangement into periods with the return of Paul to Antioch in Acts 18:22. However, the problems mentioned in connection with Acts 18:18–23 indicate how difficult such a demarcation is. While the first missionary journey (Acts 13:1–14:28) and the beginning of the second missionary journey (Acts 15:36) are clearly definable, the transition from the second to the third missionary journey is not clearly marked.

25. On Ephesus, cf. Elliger, *Ephesos*; Karwiese, *Groß ist die Artemis von Ephesos*; Murphy-O'Connor, *St. Paul's Ephesus*.

Austrian Archaeological Institute, CC BY-SA 3.0 / Wikimedia Commons

8.4. The theater in Ephesus

its variety of (including magical) practices, determined the religious-cultural situation in Ephesus.[26]

It was not Paul but rather Apollos who evidently founded the church in Ephesus (see above, 6.2), for according to Acts 18:24–28, he was active there before the beginning of Paul's activity (cf. Acts 19:1). Paul was supported primarily by Prisca and Aquila, whose house church (cf. 1 Cor. 16:19) formed the core of Ephesian Christianity. Next to Corinth, Ephesus became the second center of the Pauline mission and remained as a central place for the history of Christianity, as the Johannine literature and the letters of Ignatius indicate (see below, 14.1).[27] In Ephesus, Paul, like a traveling philosopher, rented the lecture hall of the rhetor Tyrannus (Acts 19:9) for two years and proclaimed the gospel to Jews and Greeks. In Ephesus, miracles took place (cf. Acts 19:11–12), leading to conflicts with Jewish sorcerers (cf. Acts 19:13–16), reaching their high point in the public burning of valuable magical books (cf. Acts 19:19). Thus Luke illustrates an

26. On the religious infrastructure of Ephesus, cf. Friesen, *Twice Neokoros*; Köster, *Ephesos*; Witetschek, *Ephesische Enthüllungen*, 1:66–139.

27. On the history of Ephesian Christianity, cf. Thiessen, *Christen in Ephesus*; Günther, *Die Frühgeschichte des Christentums in Ephesus*; Trebilco, *Early Christians in Ephesus*; Tellbe, *Christ-Believers in Ephesus*; Witetschek, *Ephesische Enthüllungen* 1.141ff. Pichler and Rajič, *Ephesus als Ort frühchristlichen Lebens*.

Carole Raddato, CC BY-SA 2.0 / Wikimedia Commons

Daniel Villafruela, CC BY-SA 3.0 / Wikimedia Commons

8.5. Two portrayals of Artemis of Ephesus

important consequence of the early Christian mission: the distancing from the pervasive magic. The Christian mission resulted not only in religious and political conflict but also in economic confrontation. The Artemis temple in Ephesus, which was considered one of the seven wonders of the world, was also the most significant bank. Many craftsmen, particularly dealers in devotional items, earned their livelihood from the temple. In Acts 19:23–40, Luke with dramatic words describes the uprising of the silversmiths under the leadership of Demetrius.[28] Once more, the political and the religious are connected, for the early Christian polemic against the pagan cults (cf. v. 26) was considered a disturbance and a destabilizing element in the province of Asia (cf. v. 27). In Ephesus this was a dangerous accusation, for it was a center of the imperial cult, and here the provincial assembly of Asia met under the Roman proconsul. Only the prudent intervention of the town clerk finally calmed the situation (cf. vv. 31, 35–40) so that Paul could leave the city. The Pauline letters also indicate that the mission in Ephesus was

28. Cf. Oster, "The Ephesian Artemis as an Opponent"; Lampe, "*Acta* 19 im Spiegel der ephesischen Inschriften"; A. Weiss, "Der Aufruhr der Silberschmiede (Apg 19,23–40)."

8.6. The Celsus library, built around 120 CE

full of conflict. Thus Paul speaks in 1 Cor. 15:32 metaphorically of a battle with "wild beasts," that is, adversaries; the apostle also mentions "many adversaries" in Ephesus in 1 Cor. 16:9 (cf. also 1 Cor. 4:9). Whether the danger of death in 2 Cor. 1:8–10 refers to events in Ephesus is uncertain; one can assume that Paul here speaks either of extreme resistance against him and his coworkers or of a severe illness (cf. 2 Cor. 12:7).

The journey through Macedonia and Achaia with the collection is connected with Paul's stay in Ephesus. According to Acts 19:21 and 1 Cor. 16:5, Paul wanted to travel through Macedonia to Corinth. Acts 20:1–3 also indicates that the destination for the journey was Corinth, where Paul probably arrived at the beginning of 56 CE and remained for three months. Originally, Paul intended to travel directly from Corinth to Syria by ship. Jews prevented him, however, so that he had to return by way of Macedonia. These statements in Acts 20:3 stand in tension with Rom. 15:25, where Paul announces his return to Jerusalem in order to deliver the collection. Romans 15:25 does not speak of a direct trip from Corinth to Jerusalem, so no contradiction exists between the information of Acts and the witness of Paul that has to be constructed. According to Acts 20:6, Paul traveled from Corinth to Philippi, then to Troas, in order to go to Miletus by way of Assos. The apostle set out by ship for his trip to Caesarea in order to reach Jerusalem by Pentecost of 56 (cf. Acts 20:16).

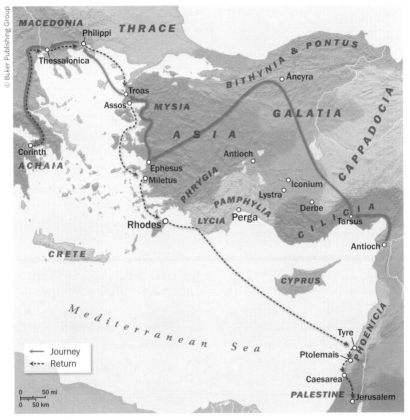

8.7. The third missionary journey

Mission Strategies

The letters of Paul and Acts indicate in a few passages how the mission took place in specific situations.[29] Paul proclaimed the gospel not only in the local synagogues but also in private houses (cf. Acts 18:7–8; 20:7–11; 28:30–31; also Rom. 16:23),[30] in public places (cf. Acts 17:16–34),[31] and in prison (cf.

---

29. On the modalities of the Pauline mission, cf. Reinbold, *Propaganda und Mission*, 182–225. Reinbold strongly emphasizes the function of personal contacts of the apostle. "They were the small units and structures in which he began: chance acquaintances, relatives, families, colleagues, small interest groups, and similar connections" (195).

30. Cf. the detailed study in Gehring, *House Church and Mission*, 119–29.

31. Cf. Brocke, *Thessaloniki*, 151n37, who maintains, on the basis of Thessalonica, what was probably the case for other cities: "It is scarcely conceivable that Paul did not make use of the large auditorium of the agora with its many shops and public establishments. Besides the harbor, there was scarcely any other place in the city where public and commercial life was more strongly vibrant than here."

Acts 28:30–31; Phil. 1:12ff.; Philemon). He rented public halls (cf. Acts 19:9f.)[32] and also used his craftwork in order to be active as a missionary (cf. 1 Thess. 2:9).[33] The contact with businesspeople, customers, colleagues, coworkers, and slaves offered Paul numerous possibilities for conversation and preaching.[34] As among Cynic preachers,[35] Paul's work secured for him financial independence (cf. 1 Cor. 9:18) and spiritual freedom. The first preaching preceded the origin of the church [in an area]. According to Rom. 15:20, Paul saw as his specific task "to proclaim the gospel where Christ has not yet been named so that I not build on another man's foundation."

The methods of preaching corresponded to the content of the gospel. The advancement and the zeal for the gospel (cf. 2 Cor. 11:2; Gal. 4:18) must agree with the preaching of the crucified Christ (cf. 1 Cor. 1:17; 2 Cor. 13:4). Neither secrecy, cunning, nor desire for gain characterize the conduct of the apostle (cf. 2 Cor. 4:1–2; 7:2; 11:7–11). Rather, he provides for his churches like a mother with her children (1 Thess. 2:1–12; 1 Cor. 4:14–16; 2 Cor. 12:14; Gal. 4:19). The care for "all of the churches" (2 Cor. 11:28) characterizes the tireless life of the apostle. He is a pastor to his churches and the individual members (cf. 1 Thess. 2:11). From the beginning, words of encouragement and the corresponding conduct of the apostle belong to the basic practice of his missionary activity.[36] He meets with his churches with openness and love; he battles for them when they appear to be abandoning the truth of the gospel (2 Cor. 11:4, 29; Gal. 3:1–5). Although Paul is driven by the concern that he might have worked in vain for his churches (cf. 1 Thess. 3:5; Gal. 2:2; 4:11; Phil. 2:16), his mission is not oriented only toward success. He is independent of the recognition of others and obligated only to his call as apostle to the nations (cf. 1 Thess. 2:4, 6; 1 Cor. 9:16; Gal. 1:10). Paul trusts in the convincing power of the truth; thus he works tirelessly for the truth (cf. 1 Cor. 3:10–11). He takes upon himself the effort and the dangers of the preaching activity (beatings in 1 Cor. 4:11; 2 Cor. 6:5; and 11:23–24; imprisonments in 2 Cor. 6:5; 11:23; and Phil. 1:7, 13f., 16; stoning in 2 Cor. 11:25; danger of death in 1 Cor. 15:32; 2 Cor. 4:11; 11:23;

32. Cf. Epictetus, *Diatr.* 3.23, 30.

33. Cf. Hock, *Social Context of Paul's Ministry*, 37–42.

34. Cf. Arzt-Grabner, *Gott als verlässlicher Käufer*, 412: "An essential part of the Pauline mission probably took place in craft shops and in contact with businesspeople. The use of the concept of ἀρραβῶν [pledge] by Paul is thus more intelligible against this background."

35. Texts in Ebner, *Leidenslisten und Apostelbrief*, 70–71. Especially instructive is Musonius, *Diss.* 11: "It is clear that it is to be expected of free men rather to work for life's necessities, than to take from others. It is more honorable to use no other person for the basic needs than to rely on him."

36. Cf. Gebauer, *Paulus als Seelsorger*.

Phil. 1:20–23) because he knows that God himself acts on others through the activity of preaching (1 Thess. 2:13). The lasting significance of the initial proclamation is documented in 1 Thess. 1:6–10; 2:1; 4:2ff.; 1 Cor. 3:6, 10–11; 4:15; Gal. 4:13; 5:21; Phil. 1:5; 4:15. Paul reminds the churches of this foundational event and derives his authority from it. As ambassador of the gospel (cf. 2 Cor. 5:19–21; Rom. 10:14–17), he finds an entrance into the hearts of people because the gospel itself has convinced the people about Jesus Christ (cf. 1 Cor. 15:11). The Spirit is at work through the preaching of the gospel by the apostle (cf. 1 Thess. 1:5; 1 Cor. 2:4–5; 4:19–20; Gal. 3:5). The preaching of the word and the demonstration of power were a self-evident unity for Paul (cf. 1 Thess. 1; 1 Cor. 2:4–5; 4:19–20; 2 Cor. 6:7; 12:12; Gal. 3:5; Rom. 15:18–19).

> The geographic sequence of the Pauline mission, locality, and methods; its public claim; and the information in the letters (cf. 1 Thess. 1:9–10; 1 Cor. 12:2; 4:8) indicate that the greatest number of the members of the churches came from the Greek and Roman worlds.[37] In addition many Godfearers and Jews by birth came into the community.

8.2 Persons

The image of Paul as a solitary thinker and missionary is false. Instead, Paul was integrated his entire life in networks, from which he profited, but which he especially inspired and led.

Paul and His Coworkers

To a considerable extent, coworkers carried out and shaped the Pauline mission, without whom the success of his undertaking would be inconceivable.[38] The proto-Pauline letters mention approximately forty persons who may be considered coworkers of the apostle. Those who belonged to the closest circle of Paul's coworkers included first Barnabas; with the beginning of the independent mission were Silvanus and Timothy, and later Titus. Silvanus (1 Thess. 1:1) and Timothy (1 Thess. 1:1; 2 Cor. 1:1; Phil.

---

37. Löhr, "Speisefrage und Tora im Judentum," indicates that, already in Paul, the issue of food (cf. 1 Cor. 8–10; Gal. 2:11–21; Rom. 14–15) was not treated any more on the basis of Jewish food halakah, a clear indication of the pagan context of the discourse.

38. A detailed list and discussion in Ollrog, *Paulus und seine Mitarbeiter*, 162.

1:1; Philem. 1) functioned as cosenders of Paul's letters (cf. also Sosthenes in 1 Cor. 1:1), thus documenting their shared responsibility for the work in various Pauline churches. In particular, Timothy and Titus appear as independent missionaries who were commissioned by Paul to resolve problems in the mission churches (cf. 1 Cor. 4:17; 2 Cor. 8). The majority of the coworkers mentioned in the Pauline letters were sent from the churches. They came from the churches established by Paul and participated in the mission work as delegates of these churches (e.g., Erastus, Gaius, Aristarchus, Sosipater, Jason, Epaphras, and Epaphroditus). They maintained contact with their home churches, supported Paul in various ways, and served as missionaries independently in the surrounding area of the churches founded by Paul. Paul himself, with his widening mission work, could maintain contact with the churches only occasionally. His letters indicate how dissatisfied the churches were with care that was perceived as limited and how difficult it was for Paul to dampen this discontent with plausible explanations (cf. 1 Thess. 2:17–20; 1 Cor. 4:18). Within the large circle of coworkers, Paul's labor was scarcely limited to purely organizational questions. The συνεργοί (coworkers) were not commissioned by Paul but rather taken into service by God (cf. 1 Cor. 3:9). Like Paul, they were engaged in the same "work" of proclaiming the gospel among the nations (cf. 1 Thess. 3:2; 1 Cor. 3:5–9; 16:10, 15–18; 2 Cor. 8:16–23; Phil. 2:22). One can assume an intensive theological work, particularly in the closely connected group of coworkers.

The Pauline School

This work did not take place by chance but took place within structures: the school of Paul.[39] The evidence for a Pauline school includes the following: (1) Luke already uses the concept αἵρεσις in the sense of "direction, party, school" for Paul.[40] In Acts 24:5 (Paul before Felix), Paul is called a "ringleader of the movement/school of the Nazarenes" (πρωτοστάτην τε τῆς τῶν Ναζωραίων αἱρέσεως). The Nazarene is the school founder, and his successor is Paul. Luke designates the movement of Christians as the "new way" (Acts

39. Cf. Conzelmann, "Paulus und die Weisheit"; Ludwig, "Der Verfasser des Kolosserbriefes," 201–29; Conzelmann, "Die Schule des Paulus"; Standhartinger, *Entstehungsgeschichte und Intention des Kolosserbriefes*, 1–10, 277–89; Alexander, "Paul and the Hellenistic Schools"; Witetschek, *Ephesische Enthüllungen*, 1:402–10; Schnelle, "Denkender Glaube." Schmeller, *Schulen im Neuen Testament?*, 182, is critical of the idea of a Pauline school: "One must speak with great reservations about a Pauline school during Paul's lifetime."

40. Diogenes Laertius discusses the question at the beginning of his works, which can be considered as a philosophical movement/school, and says, "We designate as a school [αἵρεσις] a philosophical orientation that in its appearance follows or seems to follow a basic principle [λόγος]" (1.20).

19:23) and makes Paul its leader, who appears programmatically as teacher.[41]
(2) In Paul himself there are clear suggestions of the formation of a school,
for he himself went through a school tradition that shaped him for his whole
life, that is, as a Pharisee. According to his own statements, he exceeded his
peers in the knowledge and application of the traditions of the fathers (cf.
Gal. 1:13–14). Furthermore, after his conversion Paul was introduced to the
foundations of the Christian faith, labored as a coworker in the church at
Antioch, and thus learned a second school tradition. (3) The letters of Paul
demonstrate that in no way did Paul belong to the social and educational lower
class, but he definitely had a higher education (see above, 3.1). (4) Paul was
not only well acquainted with Jewish religion and culture, but as a diaspora
Jew he was also able to receive a genuine Hellenistic education at a high level.
He was apparently familiar with ancient philosophical schools, for Tarsus
was considered a center of Hellenistic philosophy.[42] (5) In the proto-Pauline
letters coauthors always appear with the exception of Romans (1 Thess. 1:1;
1 Cor. 1:1; 2 Cor. 1:1; Gal. 1:2; Phil. 1:1; Philem. 1), and the letters were written
down by secretaries (Rom. 16:22) or scribes (Rom. 16:22; Philem. 19). Thus
although Paul is the primary author, the letters have the character of collab-
orative works.[43] The coworkers/pupils of Paul probably worked together on
the content of the letters in the context of a Pauline school. (6) The deutero-
Pauline letters (Colossians, Ephesians, 2 Thessalonians, Pastorals)[44] attest
that, at least after the death of Paul, a Pauline school existed that attempted
to maintain the Pauline legacy under changed conditions. But are the deutero-
Pauline letters also an indication of the existence of a Pauline school during
the lifetime of the apostle? The coauthorship by pupils already mentioned
above is, in my opinion, a clear indication that, for example, Timothy did
not become theologically active only after the death of the apostle. Because

41. Cf. Heininger, "Einmal Tarsus und zurück."
42. On Tarsus, cf. H. Böhlig, *Die Geisteskultur von Tarsos*.
43. All of Paul's letters were probably written over a period of several days or a longer period.
This is suggested by the careful arrangement (the entire texts of the letters could not simply
have been "in Paul's head"), the length (only Philemon corresponds to a "normal" letter), and
the conditions for the writing of the letters (writing materials and scribes had to be available
always). This fact is evident in Romans (cf. Rom. 16:22: Tertius, the writer of the letter; cf. also
Gal. 6:11); it is probable for the Corinthian letters (sixteen and thirteen chapters respectively).
High-ranking persons in Roman life, such as Pliny the Younger, were served naturally by a
secretary and outlined their works/letters similarly over a longer period: "I reconsider what
work I have, reconsider it, as if I write it down word for word and correct, some less, some
more, afterward. How easy or difficult it is to plan or to leave it. Then I call my secretary, let
the daylight in, and dictate to him what I have outlined. He leaves, is called again, and again
sent away" (*Ep.* 9.36.2).
44. P. Müller, *Anfänge der Paulusschule*, 270–320; Frenschkowski, "Pseudepigraphie und
Paulusschule," limits the phenomenon of the Pauline school to the deutero-Pauline letters.

the proto-Pauline letters originated with the collaboration of coworkers, the pupils could justifiably claim the authority also after his death inasmuch as they took his thoughts, developed them further, integrated them into oral Pauline traditions in the letters, and introduced them into the letters in their own arguments, corresponding to the situation of the church.

The existence of a school during Paul's lifetime is an essential presupposition for the reception of the deutero-Pauline letters. For early Christian churches it would have been thoroughly plausible that Paul wrote letters to his closest coworkers, Timothy (cf. 1 Thess. 3:2; Rom. 16:21; Phil. 2:19–23) and Titus (cf. 2 Cor. 8:16). One would expect letters to the most significant churches in Ephesus (cf. 1 Cor. 15:32; 16:8; Acts 18:19, 21, 24; 19:1, 17, 26; 20:16–17) and Colossae and a second letter to a church founded by Paul (2 Thessalonians). These letters could have been "found" in churches and/or issued with the authentic letters as a collection. Indeed, the deutero-Pauline letters differ in essential points from the genuine Pauline theology; nevertheless, they show evidence of a familiarity with the thought of the apostle. The author of Colossians is especially shaped to a great extent by the Pauline tradition, especially Romans. He acquired his knowledge of basic Pauline theology in the Pauline school in order to develop it further in accordance with the requirements of his time. Acts must also be read as a witness to the Pauline school tradition, for it is actually the first biography of Paul.[45]

The work within the Pauline school probably took place in the following areas: (a) study of Scripture (especially LXX citations); (b) maintenance and transmission of early Christian traditions; (c) discussion and solving of numerous problems in the context of the formation of a new identity (e.g., death/eternal life, place of the Torah, relation to the pagan environment and to the Roman state, sexual ethics, questions about slavery, relation to cults, rich-poor [relations], organization of the churches); (d) development of their own theological language (e.g., "in Christ," emphasis on faith and sin as a destructive power), and thus the development of their own theological conceptual worlds, for example, the doctrine of justification in Galatians and Romans, which had not only a theological but also a religio-philosophical potential. Ephesus presents itself as a setting for the Pauline school.[46] This city, shaped by the variety of cultural currents, was the center of the early Christian mission. Paul remained in Ephesus longer than in any other city. Here he gathered a large group of coworkers and, according to Acts 19:9, preached for two years in the lecture hall of the rhetor Tyrannus. Not only

---

45. Cf. Alexander, "Acts and Ancient Intellectual Biography," 34, who regards Acts as "not just a biography of Paul, but it contains a Pauline biography."

46. Cf. Conzelmann, "Paulus und die Weisheit," 179.

was 1 Corinthians written in Ephesus, but some of the deutero-Pauline letters (Colossians, Ephesians [?], Pastorals) probably also originated there.

Finally, the similarities between ancient philosophical schools and the Pauline school are unmistakable:[47] (a) founding personality (Paul), (b) founding by a group of sympathizers (coworkers), (c) discussion and interpretation of writings (e.g., Septuagint), (d) common meals and the ideal of friendship, (e) development of an identity in adaptation and demarcation in relation to the external world, (f) teaching activity in various locations, (g) journeys accompanied by the pupils, and (h) successors (Timothy, Titus, deutero-Paulines).

8.3 Structures

The large number of coworkers/emissaries from the churches is originally linked to the new missionary methods of Paul. He did not pursue the traveling mission as it had been practiced but developed an independent mission center. Whereas other missionaries or early Christian prophets traveled from place to place, Paul attempted to establish a church, that is, more concretely, one or several house churches. He remained until the house church had built its own leadership structures and his presence was no longer necessary. From the Pauline mission center other independent churches grew, which in turn formed the basis for the wider Pauline mission and took over their own responsibility for missionary work (1 Thess. 1:6–8).

House Churches

Within this concept the house/apartment[48] as the center of religious life formed the natural link, particularly because the early Christian churches did not have public buildings at their disposal. As the center of religious life, the house had a long tradition in a twofold way: (1) In both the Greco-Roman and Jewish tradition, it was a place of worship, the place of the religious life of a family on a daily basis (*religio domestica*).[49] Particularly, the pagan house cult shaped the religious practice of Greeks and Romans (worship of the house deities, house altars, food and drink offerings, prayers, images, statues, little rooms for worship) in which the head of the house/family (paterfamilias) also

---

47. Cf. the survey by Schmeller, *Schulen im Neuen Testament?*, 46–92.

48. Both central lexemes οἶκος and οἰκία can (each according to context) mean both "house/one's own house" as well as apartment (cf. BDAG 695, 698). In this framework I assume that no further difference exists; i.e., whether the reference is to "house" or to "apartment" depends on the context.

49. See above 3.2; cf. Öhler, "Das ganze Haus"; Ebner, *Die Stadt als Lebensraum*, 166–77.

led the religious ceremonies.[50] This is presupposed in 1 Cor. 1:16 ("But I did, however, baptize also the house of Stephanus"); 1 Cor. 1:11; Acts 16:13–15; 16:25–34; 18:8. What is assumed: Along with the head of the household, the dependents and (often) the house slaves converted to the new cult. The Christian faith was now the cult of the house; that is, concretely, the worship of the previous gods was abandoned, altars were removed, magic books were burned (cf. Acts 19:19), and they no longer bought statues of the gods (cf. Acts 19:26f.). (2) The house was also a natural place for the assembly, and that included more than the family. It was the place for the gathering of private cultic associations, mystery adherents, and philosophical schools.[51] The Jewish communities also organized themselves in house synagogues,[52] and the Christian mission began first in the environment of the synagogue.

It is thus not surprising that Christian house churches are assumed as self-evident in the letters of the apostle Paul.[53] One must distinguish here between

1. house churches, which (at first or permanently) represent the whole church at a location—Philippi (Lydia, Acts 16:14–15), Thessalonica (Jason, Acts 17:6–7), Cenchreae (Phoebe, Rom. 16:1–2), and Colossae (Philemon, Philem. 1–2)—and

2. larger churches that consist of several house churches—Corinth (Prisca and Aquila, Acts 18:2–3; Titius Justus, Acts 18:7; Crispus, Acts 18:8; Stephanus, 1 Cor. 1:16; 16:15;[54] Gaius and Erastus, Rom. 16:23), Ephesus (Prisca and Aquila, 1 Cor. 16:19; "all of the brothers greet you," 1 Cor. 16:20), and Rome (Prisca and Aquila "and the church in their house," Rom. 16:5a; Epaenetus, Rom. 16:5b; dependents of two house churches, Rom. 16:14, 15; cf. also "those from the house of Aristobulus," Rom. 16:10b; and "those from the house of Narcissus," where the reference is probably to Christian house fellowships in non-Christian houses, Rom. 16:11).[55]

50. Cf. the inscription of a house cult from Philadelphia (Asia Minor) from the first century BCE, in which regulations are given for the behavior of each status (men, women, free, slaves). Texts in Berger and Colpe, *Religionsgeschichtliches Textbuch*, 274–75.

51. Cf. Klauck, *Hausgemeinde und Hauskirche*, 83–97.

52. Cf. Claussen, *Versammlung, Gemeinde, Synagoge*, 160–64.

53. House churches are demonstrable in Thessalonica, Philippi, Corinth, Cenchreae, Ephesus, and Rome. In the Pauline and post-Pauline period, they are also evident in Colossae and Laodicea; on the analysis, cf. Gehring, *House Church and Mission*, 130–55.

54. First Corinthians 16:15–16 indicates that specific house churches could take a leading role in the entire church, for in v. 16 the Corinthians are encouraged, "Submit yourselves under them"; cf. Horn, "Stephanus und sein Haus."

55. The phrase ἡ κατ᾽ οἶκον ἐκκλησία (the church constituted in the house) is found in 1 Cor. 16:19; Rom. 16:5; Philem. 2; also cf. Rom. 16:23; Acts 12:12; 18:7; Col. 4:15.

This categorization is suggested by the phrase ἡ ἐκκλησία ὅλη (the whole church) in 1 Cor. 14:23; Rom. 16:23,[56] for it presupposes a juxtaposition of both forms of community. However, this categorization is only a picture of a particular moment, for in the dynamic early history the number and structures of the house churches probably changed continually. The married couple Prisca and Aquila themselves worked in Corinth, Ephesus, and Rome!

The house/apartment church was a special place to practice the Christian life in an environment that was at least partially hostile. Here the community prayed (cf. Acts 12:12), preached the word (cf. Acts 16:32; 20:20), participated in baptisms and the Lord's Supper, and hosted missionaries (cf. Acts 16:15). Church assemblies in a house are attested in 1 Cor. 14:23, and Paul's letters were read publicly in house churches (cf. 1 Thess. 5:27; also Col. 4:16). As a center of early Christian missions, the house church thus facilitated a relatively undisturbed practice of religious life and enabled an efficient competition with the synagogue communities and ancient cultic associations. Finally, the house church offered the place where ancient regulations and concepts of value could be violated and believers could maintain the new identity in Christ (cf. Gal. 3:26–28), for in the Greco-Roman society people lived between the poles of polis (city) and family, in which both areas were structured in a strictly hierarchical way. At the top stood the male citizens; women, people without the right of citizenship, children, and slaves could participate in the life of the society in only limited ways. In the Christian house churches, these distinctions between people lost their meaning. All had been torn out of the old life and placed into a new reality, which Paul describes as life in Christ. With their eschatological orientation, the self-designation ἐκκλησία, the absence of a structure of offices, and the diverse membership, the young churches broke through ancient norms (along with men with Roman citizenship, there were foreign men without citizenship, women, and slaves).[57]

In the perception of outsiders, the Christian churches appeared to be associations like the Hellenistic Jewish synagogues.[58] Thus just as social life in Roman-Hellenistic antiquity took place in associations[59] and reached its high

---

56. Cf. Gehring, *House Church and Mission*, 139–42. According to Lampe, "Urchristliche Missionswege nach Rom," 126, "At least seven separate Christian islands [population clusters] existed in the capital of the world in the 50s CE."

57. Cf. E. Stegemann and W. Stegemann, *Urchristliche Sozialgeschichte*, 243–44.

58. Cf. the basic study by Heinrici, "Die Christengemeinden Korinths"; also Hans-Josef Klauck, *Religious Context of Early Christianity*, 42–54; Schmeller, *Hierarchie und Egalität*; E. Stegemann and W. Stegemann, *Urchristliche Sozialgeschichte*, 237–48; Ascough, *What Are They Saying?* (comprehensive history of research); Kloppenborg and Ascough, *Greco-Roman Associations*.

59. The legal situation of associations is summarized by Öhler, "Römisches Vereinsrecht und christliche Gemeinden," 61: "Not later than Augustus there was a precise regulation regarding

point and central focus in communal meals,[60] communal life among Christians was structured around the communal meal. In the communal meal, one thought of the founder, who had "given" more than a great sum of money: his life. Thus the Christians in their self-understanding were much more than an association: they understood themselves not as a community for the regulation of social or cultural interest but rather as the beginning of a new humanity (cf. 2 Cor. 5:17). The establishment of a new group could take place, however, only in the framework of regular assemblies and communal meals in houses. A striking fact in relation to the pagan associations and for the feeling of community in the churches is the frequency of the times for the meal, which at least in Corinth (cf. 1 Cor. 16:2) probably took place weekly. The Christian churches surpassed all others in the frequency of the common meals: "Among the communities competing for members in the first and second century CE, the Christian churches occupied the leading position on this point; no one met more frequently for a meal."[61] How did one become a member of an early Christian church? First of all, through baptism. Furthermore, it is possible—in analogy to ancient associations—that there was a list of members.[62] However, no evidence exists for this in Paul; the first significant reference appears in 1 Tim. 5:9 ("should be enrolled as widows"). In addition to the fundamentally different orientation, three major differences existed between pagan associations and early Christian churches:[63] (1) the churches had no articles of

---

the approval of associations. A collegium could apply to the senate for approval, which it received when there were no activities that endangered the state and a public usefulness was present. Specific ancient associations such as the Jewish synagogues were always licensed on the basis of their tradition. In addition, there was a host of associations that had not been approved, which were tolerated until they committed crimes or other offenses." The early Christians could present themselves first as an inner-Jewish movement and thus as a tolerated collegium. From the middle of the 50s CE, this probably became no longer possible, as the persecution under Nero indicates. There was the possibility to exist like the pagan collegia as long as the political peace lasted. Thus they were not legally recognized because they in no way met the legal requirements (e.g., "public benefit"). Furthermore, the Romans were always suspicious of cult associations (cf. Eckhardt and Leonhard, *Juden, Christen und Vereine im römischen Reich*). On the structure of ancient associations and the parallels with the early churches, cf. also Ebner, *Die Stadt als Lebensraum*, 190–235, esp. 228: "Both in their social forms and structures as well as their self-stylization, the early Christian churches resemble ancient associations in an extraordinary way—and want to do otherwise. The greatest similarity to the ancient associations was the communal meal in remembrance of the founder."

60. Cf. Klinghardt, *Gemeinschaftsmahl und Mahlgemeinschaft*; Ebel, *Die Attraktivität früher christlicher Gemeinden*, 151–80, presents in detail the similarities and differences between the fellowship meals of the early Christians and private or communal meals of associations in the environment.

61. Ebel, *Die Attraktivität früher christlicher Gemeinden*, 163.

62. Cf. Kloppenborg, "Membership Practices," 206–10.

63. Cf. also Judge, "Kultgemeinde (Kultverein)," 420, who mentions, besides the entirely different "purpose for existence," the absence of formal networking of associations and the

association; (2) onetime or continuing financial obligations as a condition of membership did not exist among the Christians; and (3) as a member of a Christian church in Ephesus, one would be welcomed as an equal member in a Christian church in Corinth. The transregional dimension of membership did not exist in the pagan association; that is, whoever belonged to a Dionysus association in Athens had to join the local association in Corinth again.

One can only conjecture about the size of the first churches. One can conclude from 1 Cor. 11:20; 14:23 ("when the whole church comes together in the same place") that the entire Corinthian church assembled in one place, that is, in a large private house. The atrium of a dwelling could accommodate thirty to a maximum of fifty persons, so thirty to forty persons could be assumed to be the approximate beginning size of a church.[64] If several house churches existed in a larger city (e.g., in Rome), then the membership in the church was correspondingly larger. The whole church probably met in worship services and assemblies at the same place; certainly meetings took place in much smaller apartments. As meeting places, besides houses and apartments/rental apartments (cf. Acts 20:8–9), the other possible meeting places were public places, shops, taverns, and gardens.[65] In large churches such as Rome, Ephesus, and Corinth/Cenchreae (with the surrounding area), surely the number of church members soon increased after a period of time to over one hundred.[66]

Ekklēsia

Paul selects a political concept in order to designate the nature and local assemblies of the new community: ἐκκλησία (assembly).[67] In the Greek-Hellenistic usage, ἐκκλησία does not mean a constant group, but the actual

---

networking of the churches among each other as a major difference from contemporary associations.

64. Cf. Murphy-O'Connor, *St. Paul's Corinth*, 178–91, calculating 30 to 40 persons on the basis of floor plans of Roman houses. Gehring, *House Church and Mission*, 313–20, assumes 40–50 persons for a house church. Horrell, "Domestic Space and Christian Meetings at Corinth," 349–69, considers it probable that church assemblies in Corinth took place in shops and rented houses, where around 50 persons could meet.

65. Cf. Balch and Weissenrieder, *Contested Spaces*.

66. The size of pagan associations probably ranged mostly between 20 and 100 members; cf. the lists in Kloppenborg, "Membership Practices," 211–15.

67. On specific theories of derivation of the term, cf. Roloff, "ἐκκλησία"; Kraus, *Das Volk Gottes*, 124–26; D.-A. Koch, *Geschichte des Urchristentums*, 272–74 (justifiably critical of Jürgen Roloff). In a debate early in the twenty-first century, Trebilco, *Self-Designations and Group Identity*, 164–207, again argues for a Septuagint background of ἐκκλησία; Kooten, "ἐκκλησία τοῦ θεοῦ," emphasizes the influence of the political significance of the concept, "which the early Christians adopted, varied, and surpassed" (cf. Acts 19:32, 39–40 with Acts 20:28).

8.8. The *ekklēsiasterion* in Paestum (fifth cent. BCE)

assembly of free men who had the right to vote,[68] a usage that is present also in Acts 19:32, 39. The building where the Greek assembly of the people met was called the *ekklēsiastērion* (τὸ ἐκκλησιαστήριον); a member/speaker in the assembly is an *ekklēsiastēs* (ὁ ἐκκλησιαστής). First Thessalonians 2:14 ("You, brothers, became the imitators of the churches of God in Judea"); 1 Cor. 15:9; Gal. 1:13; and Phil. 3:6 ("I persecuted the church [of God]") indicate the possibility that already in Jerusalem the designation ἐκκλησία τοῦ θεοῦ (assembly, church of God) had emerged for the new movement. Thus one connected it on the one hand with the rendering of קהל as ἐκκλησία in the Septuagint,[69] associating the Christian community with the people of God in Israel; on the other hand, the avoidance of συναγωγή (synagogue) expresses the self-understanding of the earliest churches in demarcation from Judaism. With Paul as the essential carrier of this semantic new usage,[70] it is apparent that,

68. Cf. an inscription from the first century CE, where, in the context of a tribute to the Corinthian woman Junia Theodora, an assembly of citizens in Patara in Asia Minor is called an ἐκκλησία ("wherefore most of our citizens have given a witness for her when they appeared before the assembly"); translation [into German] and interpretation of the text in Klauck, "Junia Theodora und die Gemeinde in Korinth."

69. Cf. Deut. 23:2–4; Mic. 2:5; 1 Chron. 28:8; קהל can also be rendered with συναγωγή (cf. Num. 16:3; 20:4; Isa. 56:8; Jer. 38:4; Ezek. 37:10).

70. The Greek syntagma ἐκκλησία τοῦ θεοῦ is attested only by Paul (1 Thess. 2:14; 1 Cor. 1:2; 10:32; 11:16, 22; 15:9; 2 Cor. 1:1; Gal. 1:13) and in the literature influenced by him (Acts 20:28;

with the phrase "church(es) of God," he expresses the new self-understanding of Christians as a separate group in relation to Jews and Greeks. *Ekklēsia* can designate both the local church (1 Thess. 1:1; 1 Cor. 1:2) and the whole church (1 Thess. 2:14; 1 Cor. 10:32; Phil. 3:6). The whole church is present in the local congregation, and the local congregation is a part of the whole church. Thus as the association of Christians in a particular place, *ekklēsia* should be translated as the "congregation," while the universal totality of all Christians should be translated as "church."[71]

Paul describes the nature and form of the *ekklēsia* with three basic metaphors: "in Christ," "body of Christ," and "people of God."[72] With "in Christ," Paul designates the close and salutary community of every individual Christian and of all together with Jesus Christ (1 Cor. 1:30; Gal. 3:26–28). In baptism the believers are incorporated into the sphere of Christ and are a new creation (2 Cor. 5:17). Closely related is the concept of the church as the "body of Christ." Here Paul's concern is primarily the unity of the church and the equality of the gifts of the Spirit. Thus as the body is one and yet has members, so there is in the church a variety of callings and gifts, but only one church (1 Cor. 1:10–17; 12:12–27; Rom. 12:5). The individual members of the body are not all the same but are dependent on each other; thus they are of the same mind with love as the highest gift (1 Cor. 13).[73] The activity of the Spirit and the *charismata* as gifts of the Spirit work together for the building up of the church (cf. 1 Cor. 14:12).[74] The metaphor of the "people of God" is connected with the problem of continuity and discontinuity of the church with Israel (1 Cor. 10:7; Rom. 9:25–26; 10:21; 11:1–2; 15:10). It involves the unity of God's activity and thus the continuity of the people of God in salvation history.

Gifts, Functions, and Offices

How are charisma and office related in Paul?[75] They are not alternatives because structure, order, and consistency are natural elements of the free work

---

2 Thess. 1:4; 1 Tim. 3:5, 15). Comparable phrases are found only in the LXX (Judg. 20:1; Neh. 13:1; 1 Chron. 13:4; 28:8; Mic. 2:5; Deut. 23:1–2; cf. also Philo, *Leg.* 3.8.5).

71. Translator's note: In English, translations of *ekklēsia* can be used for both the local and universal church. "Church" and "congregation" can be used interchangeably as renderings of *ekklēsia*.

72. On the ecclesiological concept of Paul, cf. Roloff, *Die Kirche*, 86–143; Schnelle, *Apostle Paul*, 560–69.

73. On the concept of love in Paul, cf. Wischmeyer, *Der höchste Weg*; Wischmeyer, "Das Gebot der Nächstenliebe"; Söding, *Das Liebesgebot bei Paulus*; J. Thompson, *Moral Formation according to Paul*, 157–80.

74. On the metaphor οἰκοδομή (building), cf. Vielhauer, "Oikodome," 11–68.

75. On the history of research and exegetical discussion, see Brockhaus, *Charisma und Amt*; Kertelge, *Das kirchliche Amt*; Tiwald, "Entwicklungslinien kirchlichen Amtes," 101–28.

of the Spirit.[76] This fact is clearly indicated in 1 Cor. 12:28, where Paul names
the tasks of apostles, prophets, teachers, and the gifts of miracle working,
healing, giving aid, leading/steering, and speaking in tongues in one breath:
"And God has appointed in the church first apostles, second prophets, third
teachers; then [those who possess] the gift of healing, who [perform] works
of assistance, [exercise] leadership, who [have] various types of tongues." The
emphasis on the divine appointment, the enumeration, the personal designation; the parallels in Acts 13:1; and the sequencing of the following charisms
with ἔπειτα (then) emphasize the first three functions clearly: For a fixed
duration a fixed circle of persons exercises a concrete function on behalf of
the church. In this sense, with Paul one can speak of offices. The office of
apostle emphasizes in a special way the calling, the basic responsibility, and
the leadership function of early Christian missionaries (see above, 5.2). This
office is centered in Jerusalem in the early period (1 Cor. 15:3–11; Gal. 1:17,
19) but in no way can be limited to the Twelve, the Jerusalem church, or men
(1 Cor. 15:7; Rom. 16:7). Early Christian prophets appear as an independent
group in a variety of NT groups:

Acts 13:1; 15:32; 20:23; 21:4, 10 presuppose early Christian prophets in
  Syria, Greece, and Asia Minor.
Ephesians 3:5; 4:11; and 1 Tim. 1:18; 4:14 look back to the church at the
  beginning, in which prophets were self-evidently at work.
Revelation 1:1, 18; 16:6; 18:24; 22:9 see in the prophets the central indepen-
  dent group in the universal church.[77]

The prophets were a part of a process of traditioning and interpretation, for
they transmitted the words of the historical Jesus and also shaped new Jesus
traditions in the consciousness of the presence of the Spirit and interpreted
the current situation of the church in the authority of the Spirit. In this sense
they already play a central role in the Pauline churches (cf. 1 Thess. 5:20, "Do
not despise prophetic speech!"; also 1 Cor. 12:10; 14:1, 6, 22). The functions of
early Christian teachers are concentrated on the interpretation of the (oral or
written) kerygma as well as the interpretation of the written text. The functions
of early Christian teachers presuppose a timely, accurate, local, and thus also
personal presence and continuity; thus we can speak here also of an office.[78]

76. Cf. Roloff, *Die Kirche*, 139: "The Spirit itself establishes the practice, for it emphasizes
certain functions as binding."
77. Cf. the comprehensive study by Boring, *The Continuing Voice of Jesus*, 59–85; also
Dautzenberg, *Urchristliche Prophetie*; Aune, *Prophecy in Early Christianity*.
78. Cf. A. Zimmermann, *Die urchristlichen Lehrer*.

The list of charisms in Rom. 12:6–8 confirms the close coordination of functions, offices, and areas of responsibility in the churches. Indeed, Paul does not mention personal functions as in 1 Cor. 12:28a, but the functions of prophecy, service, teaching, and pastoral care are clearly connected with each other by εἴτε (whether [not translated in NRSV]); the connection of prophecy and teaching is parallel to 1 Cor. 12:28a). In addition, Rom. 12:8b includes giving, leadership (cf. 1 Thess. 5:12), and energetic mercy. Here prophecy, service (at the table), teaching, and encouragement belong in the realm of the worship service, while the giving, the leadership, and the care for the sick concern the organization of the church.

In Phil. 1:1 ἐπίσκοποι (overseer, administrator) and διάκονοι (helper, servant)[79] appear. The bishops are probably the leaders of house churches (cf. 1 Cor. 1:14; 16:15, 19; Rom. 16:5, 23; Acts 18:8), who make their houses available for the gathering of the Christians and support the respective churches in various ways. Deacons/servants function as helpers of the bishops and were probably responsible especially for the preparation of the Lord's Supper. They were also responsible for the collection and administration of gifts.[80] Finally, 1 Cor. 5:4 ("when you come together in the name of our Lord") refers to an assembly in which it remains unclear whether it involves spontaneous or regular gatherings.

> In the Pauline churches one finds a parallel existence and an interaction of continuing offices related to persons (apostles, prophets, teachers, church overseers) and functions that were recognized by various church members based on their respective charisms. Probably the relationships between them were fluid, varying from church to church.

Social Stratification

To a great extent the social stratification of the Pauline house churches was certainly a reflection of the society of the period (see above, 3.4.1).[81] Members

---

79. The plural indicates that here the "bishop" of the Pastoral Epistles is not yet the meaning intended (see below, 11.4).

80. The use of both terms is probably to be explained as pertinent to the specific situation in Philippi; cf. Pilhofer, *Philippi*, 1:144–46.

81. Cf. Judge, *Social Pattern of Christian Goups*, 60: "Far from being a socially depressed group, then, if the Corinthians are at all typical, the Christians were dominated by a socially pretentious section of the population of the big cities." Cf. the view of Theissen, "Social Stratification in the Corinthian Community," 69: "The majority of the members, who come from

8.9. The Erastus inscription reads as follows: Erastus pro aedilit[at]e s[ua] p[ecunia] stravit (Erastus, in return for his aedileship, laid [the pavement] at his own expense).

of the empire-wide ruling class (the caesar, the caesar's family, senators, highest military officers) or the provincial upper class (senators, proconsuls, members of the imperial family, military) probably did not belong to the early churches (possible exception: Acts 13:7, Sergius Paulus).[82] Local members of the upper class, however, probably belonged in the Pauline churches from the beginning.[83] In Rom. 16:23 Erastus is called οἰκονόμος τῆς πόλεως (economist/financial administrator of the city). As a member of the *ordo decurionum* (city council), he held a high office. It remains disputed, however, how precisely one can define this office.[84] It must have been significant, for it is the only time

the lower classes, stand in contrast to a few influential members who come from the upper classes." An alternative view is that of, e.g., Justin J. Meggitt, *Paul, Poverty and Survival*, 99: "The Pauline Christians en masse shared fully the bleak material existence, which was the lot of more than 99% of the inhabitants of the Empire, and also, as we have just seen, of Paul himself." Friesen, "Poverty in Pauline Studies," discusses the methodological problems of a social-historical classification of ancient society as a whole and of the Christian churches in particular (he also emphasizes the lower-class character of the early Christians); a critical history of research appears in A. Weiss, *Soziale Elite und Christentum*, 5–22 (he demonstrates the problems involved in the thesis of Christians as the lower class [held by Adolf Deissmann] and assumes that in the early churches there were individual members of the *ordo*). An overview of the current discussion is given in Still and Horrell, *After the First Urban Christians*.

82. See below, 10.6.

83. Contra D.-A. Koch, *Geschichte des Urchristentums*, 268, who rules this out.

84. In scholarship three serious possibilities are discussed: (1) Erastus was quaestor (administrator), i.e., a high city administrative official (in a senatorian career path); so Theissen, "Social Stratification in the Corinthian Community," 80–83; Jewett, *Romans*, 981–82; Goodrich, "Erastus, Quaestor of Corinth"; according to A. Weiss, "Keine Quästoren in Korinth," there were no quaestors in Corinth. (2) οἰκονόμος τῆς πόλεως (Rom. 16:23) is to be understood as the aedile office; so Clarke, "Another Corinthian Erastus Inscription," 151; A. Weiss, *Soziale Elite und Christentum*, 139: "As aedile Erastus held the office as member of the Corinthian *ordo decurionum*." (3) While the first two theories for the most part identify the Erastus of Rom. 16:23 as the Erastus of the inscription, Friesen, "The Wrong Erastus," dates the inscription to the second century CE and regards οἰκονόμος τῆς πόλεως as merely a general designation that could refer to a variety of possible functions in the city financial administration.

that Paul explicitly emphasizes the professional/societal position of a church member. Had Erastus been only one of innumerable (lower) employees in the city of Corinth, Paul would scarcely have emphasized him in the Letter to the Romans! If the Erastus inscription near the great theater at Corinth refers to the Erastus of Rom. 16:23, it would be further evidence for his prominent position in the city.

In addition, the household of Caesar mentioned in Phil. 4:22 could have belonged to the local upper class;[85] and Dionysius the Areopagite as well (cf. Acts 17:34). Members of the city's upper class are greeted in Rom. 16:10–11. Those who belonged to the prosperous group of the city included Gaius (1 Cor. 1:14; Rom. 16:23), Phoebe (Rom. 16:1–2), Stephanus (1 Cor. 1:16; 16:15, 17), Jason (Acts 17:5, 7), and Philemon (1–2). They owned houses and some owned slaves, but especially they supported the church as patrons.[86] The collection for Jerusalem that was organized by Paul is not conceivable apart from the existence of patrons in the congregation. The deposit that Jason provided for Paul and his coworkers (Acts 17:9), the legal disputes in Corinth before pagan judges (cf. 1 Cor. 6:1–11), and the grievances at the Lord's Supper (1 Cor. 11:22, "Do you not have houses to eat and drink in?)[87] indicate a level of prosperity. In 1 Cor. 1:26, when Paul emphasizes that there were not many wise, not many influential people, and not many of noble birth, he assumes the existence of a few rich and prominent people in the church.

Those who belonged to the middle class were probably, like Paul himself,[88] primarily artisans and tradespeople (cf. Prisca and Aquila, Rom. 16:3; Acts 18:2; 18:26; Lydia, the seller of purple, Acts 16:14–15; also the congregational leaders mentioned in 1 Thess. 4:11–12), for they could generate their own livelihood. In addition, prominent coworkers such as Timothy and Titus also belonged to the middle class. The predominant number of the members of the church must be regarded as belonging to the lower class (cf. 1 Cor. 1:26–28, "not many wise according to the flesh, not many powerful, not many of noble birth, . . . for God has chosen the ignoble of the world and those who are despised"), among them numerous women and slaves (cf. 1 Cor. 7:21–24; Gal. 3:28; Onesimus, and the female and male slave names in Rom. 16:8–9, 22). They were in numerous dependent relationships and were not capable of

---

85. Cf. Oakes, *Philippians*, 66: "Those of Caesar's household" (Phil. 4:22) are slaves or *liberti*, "employed by the Emperor in a wide range of roles, particularly administrative ones."

86. On Roman patronage, cf. Garnsey and Saller, "Patronal Power Relations."

87. Here Paul addresses the owners of houses in Corinth specifically; cf. D. Zeller, *Der erste Brief an die Korinther*, 368.

88. For the evidence, see Schnelle, *Apostle Paul*, 62–63.

generating their own livelihood. In Corinth, problems emerged at the Lord's Supper because those "who have nothing" were shamed (1 Cor. 11:22). In the collection, the Macedonians gave "out of their deep poverty" (2 Cor. 8:2). As a whole, major parts of the Pauline churches lived at the level of minimal existence or below.

Slaves and Masters

Belonging predominantly to the lower class were the slaves, who were an essential element of all ancient societies and economic forms (see above, 3.4.1). In the early churches, the slaves probably formed an important and large group.[89] Regarding the names in Rom. 16:3–16, of the thirteen comparable names, four are of those who are free and nine are of an origin that is not free.[90] In 1 Cor. 7:21–22 Paul explicitly addresses slaves and advises them, in view of the world that is passing away (1 Cor. 7:29–31), to remain in their status.[91] The interpretation of this unclear passage (v. 21, "Were you a slave when called? Do not let it bother you. But if you can become free, use it all the more") is determined by the context in 1 Cor. 7:17–24, where the emphasis of the paraenesis is on one's "remaining" (μένειν in 1 Cor. 7:20, 24, also 7:8, 11, 40) in one's respective calling. The clarifying verse 22 also points in this direction: "For the slave who has been called is free in the Lord; likewise, whoever was a free person when called is a slave of Christ." Paul defines freedom here as inner freedom, which is made possible and has its goal in Jesus Christ alone. With this concept of freedom, social structures are insignificant, for they can neither grant freedom nor annul it. Paul stands in clear proximity to Cynic-Stoic thought. Thus Seneca can say about slaves: "'He is a slave.' His soul, however, may be that of a freeman. 'He is a slave.' But shall that stand in his way? Show me a man who is not a slave; one is a slave to lust, another to greed, another to ambition, and all men are slaves to fear. I will name you an ex-consul who is slave to an old hag, a millionaire who is slave to a serving-maid; I will show you youths of the noblest birth in serfdom to pantomime players! No servitude is more disgraceful than that which is self-imposed" (Ep. 47 LCL). For Epictetus, freedom is identical to inner independence: "You ought to give up everything, your body, your property, your reputation, your books, society, office, and private life. For wherever your inclination draws you, there you have become a slave, a

---

89. On the total evidence, cf. Harrill, *Slaves in the New Testament*; on Paul, cf. P. Müller, *Der Brief an Philemon*, 54–67.

90. Cf. Lampe, *Die stadtrömischen Christen*, 141–53.

91. Detailed exegesis is given by Vollenweider, *Freiheit als neue Schöpfung*, 233–46; Schrage, *Der erste Brief an die Korinther*, 2:138–44.

subject, shackled, under compulsion; in summary, you are totally dependent on others" (*Diatr.* 4.4.33; cf. *Ench.* 11).[92] In the cosmos that is passing away (cf. 1 Cor. 7:29–31), Paul advises inner freedom in relation to the things of the world and to remain in one's own calling.

With the exception of the Letter to Philemon, we learn nothing about the (Christian) masters of the slaves in Paul's time. Philemon was a Christian (Philem. 5, 7), and is addressed as an ἀδελφός (brother) and συνεργός (fellow worker, Philem. 1) He was probably converted by Paul (v. 19b), collaborated actively in the church, and possessed at least one slave; his house served as the meeting place for the church. Thus he belonged to the local upper class (or artisan/tradesman middle class). The central theological theme of the letter appears in verse 11: the conversion of Onesimus has consequences not only for Onesimus but also for the relationship of the slave Onesimus to his master Philemon. Philemon should recognize and accept the new status of the slave Onesimus as beloved brother: "both in the flesh and in the Lord" (Philem. 16, καὶ ἐν σαρκὶ καὶ ἐν κυρίῳ) Thus Paul expects Philemon to break through the ancient social fabric of the house and recognize Onesimus in a new social status as beloved while the legal status remains the same.[93] By identifying himself emphatically with Onesimus (Philem. 12, 16–20), Paul clarifies the situation to Philemon. Because of his relationship to Paul, he should shape the new relationship to Onesimus. Christian slaveholders are now required to define not only their own status but also the new relationship to their Christian slaves as brothers and sisters.

It remains unclear whether Paul supported manumission in individual instances, for he argues (intentionally?) in 1 Cor. 7:17–24 (cf. 1 Cor. 7:2, "make use even more," i.e., of what, freedom or slavery?) and in the Letter to Philemon (cf. v. 21, "However, I know that you will do more than I say") overtly or indirectly with many indications. The exhortations in 1 Tim. 6:1–2 suggest that, at the latest, conflicts in the post-Pauline churches between believing slaves and believing masters arose, in which slaves possibly understood Paul's statements in the sense of manumission (1 Tim. 6:2, "But those who have believing masters should not regard them with disrespect because they are brothers, but should serve them more zealously because they are believers and beloved").

---

92. The two speeches about freedom and bondage/slavery in Dio Chrysostom (*Or.* 14 and 15) indicate how strongly this theme defined the philosophical-religious self-understanding of humankind.

93. Cf. Wolter, *Der Brief an Philemon*, 233–34: "Philemon should now see his slave as a brother (15–16), that is, without lessening the radicality of this extraordinary demand through a formal judicial lifting of Onesimus's legal status by manumission."

Men and Women

The entire ancient society[94] is shaped by the concept of the superiority of the man over the woman[95] and the related distribution of functions: The man is responsible for the "outside world," that is, for the securing of the livelihood and politics. The woman, on the other hand, concentrates on activity within the "house," that is, food, household management, and the raising of children.[96] Of course, there were exceptions[97] in all periods, but ideas claiming the equality of women developed only in the Cynic tradition (cf. Crates, *De cynicorum epistulis* 28: "The women are by nature not less than the men"). According to Musonius, the "seed of virtue" (σπέρμα ἀρετῆς) is implanted in every person, and thus the women also have a share in virtue and can study philosophy (*Diss.* 3). Daughters and sons should be educated in the same way, for both sexes must be just in life (*Diss.* 4). All vices are present among men and women so that both are capable of overcoming them.

From the beginning in the Pauline churches, a model of joint participation and responsibility between men and women was practiced in a way that, by ancient standards, was open.[98] According to Acts 17:4, 12 women from the local upper class in the city of Thessalonica joined the church. Phoebe probably belonged to the local upper class of Cenchreae, for she supported Paul and others as patroness (cf. Rom. 16:1–2). Lydia belongs to the middle class in Philippi (Acts 16:14). The social status of Damaris in Athens is unknown (Acts 17:34). Women obviously led house churches or were in the leadership team[99] (Acts 16:14, Lydia in Philippi; Rom. 16:1–2, Phoebe as "overseer/leader" [προστάτις] in Cenchreae; 1 Cor. 16:19 and Rom. 16:4–5, Prisca in Ephesus and Rome; 1 Cor. 1:11, Chloe in Corinth; Philem. 2, Apphia in Colossae); Junia (Rom. 16:7) belonged as a woman to the group of the earliest apostles. Many leadership tasks in the church were administered by women. Paul uses the verb κοπιάω (work)[100] for the activities of Mary (Rom. 16:6),

94. On the status of women in antiquity, cf. Mayer, *Die jüdische Frau*; Späth and Wagner-Hasel, *Frauenwelten in der Antike*; E. Stegemann and W. Stegemann, *Urchristliche Sozialgeschichte*, 311–46.

95. Cf. only Plato, *Resp.* 5.451–57, in which a pseudepigraphical letter of the Pythagorean Melissa says to Cleareta: "For the wishes of the man should be unwritten law for the woman, law by which she must live" (Pythagorean Epistles 3.2); Josephus, *Ag. Ap.* 2.24, declares in brief that "the woman is inferior to the man in every respect."

96. Cf. Homer, *Iliad* 6.486–92; Plutarch, *Mor.* 142c–d; Philo, *Spec. Laws* 3.169–71.

97. Prosperous women in particular could escape the conventions and lead a self-determining life; in the middle and lower classes, women also took financial and social responsibility. Cf. Rottloff, *Lebensbilder römischer Frauen*.

98. For a comprehensive analysis of the texts, cf. Payne, *Man and Woman*.

99. Cf. here Gielen, "Die Wahrnehmung gemeindlicher Leitungsfunktionen."

100. Cf. Schreiber, "Arbeit mit der Gemeinde."

Tryphena, Tryphosa, and Persis (Rom. 16:12); this is the term that he uses for his own work/preaching of the gospel in 1 Cor. 15:10; Gal. 4:11; Phil. 2:16. Concerning the disputing Euodia and Syntyche, Paul says in Phil. 4:2–3, "They contended with me for the gospel." Both married (1 Cor. 7:2–5) and divorced women (1 Cor. 7:10–12) belonged to the churches. Single women and widows (1 Cor. 7:8, 39) as well as women whose husbands were not members (1 Cor. 7:13, 15–16) belonged to the churches. Paul regards marriage as a reciprocal partnership with mutual obligations (cf. 1 Cor. 7:3–4, "The man should fulfill his conjugal obligation to his wife, and likewise the wife should fulfill her obligation to her husband. For the wife does not have authority over her husband, but the husband does; likewise, the man does not have the right over his body, but the wife does"); this is a virtually revolutionary perspective for antiquity! Women appear as patronesses of churches (Lydia in Philippi, Phoebe in Cenchreae) or individuals (Rom. 16:13, the mother of Rufus supported Paul). The proportion of women in the churches is difficult to determine; if one takes as a starting point the names that are mentioned, it may have been about 20 percent.[101] On the other hand, the Pauline letters, especially 1 Corinthians, Rom. 16, and Philippians (of the five known names, three are women), suggest that the proportion must have been greater in some churches. Particularly in Corinth, there were apparently emancipatory efforts led by women involving the role of women in the worship service (1 Cor. 11:1–16). Women appear in the worship service praying and prophesying with uncovered hair (cf. 1 Cor. 11:5, "But every woman who prays or prophesies with an uncovered head, disgraces her head, for it is the same as if she were shorn").[102] Paul, however, argues with a creation theology when he explicitly refers to Gen. 1:26–27 in 1 Cor. 11:7: "For the man must not cover his head because he is the image and reflection of God; but the woman is the reflection of man. For the man was not made from the woman, but the woman from the man." The participation of women without a head covering at the worship service was apparently a new practice, unknown in the other churches but a sharply disputed issue (cf. 1 Cor. 11:16, "If anyone wishes to be contentious"). The Pauline argumentation indicates that the apostle does not move away from the common ancient view of the superiority of the man over the

---

101. So E. Stegemann and W. Stegemann, *Urchristliche Sozialgeschichte*, 332, in connection with the thorough analysis of the stratification of Pauline churches by Meeks, *First Urban Christians*, 51–73.

102. The saying "The women should be silent in the churches" (1 Cor. 14:33b–36) is a gloss, as judged by three reasons: (1) the silence demanded of women in the worship service contradicts 1 Cor. 11:5; (2) the gloss clearly interrupts the discussion of prophecy; and (3) the insertion reflects the thought world of 1 Tim. 2:11–15; cf. the argument in Roloff, *Der erste Brief an Timotheus*, 128ff.; Payne, *Man and Woman*, 217–67.

woman.[103] However, he permits common participation in his churches as long as the boundaries are not crossed. An essential dimension for this development was the equal admission to the sacraments. In particular, baptism as an initiation ritual was totally independent of gender, and the associated gift of the Spirit probably advanced the emancipatory developments, as Gal. 3:26–28 and 1 Cor. 12:13 (Col. 3:11) indicate. All receive the same baptism and the one Spirit, which makes them sisters and brothers in Christ. The full participation in the rituals and cultic practices resulted in the abandonment of fundamental differences in status, even between man and woman (Gal. 3:28, "Here is neither man nor woman"). The pneumatic equivalence through baptism and the associated charismatic variety (cf. 1 Cor. 12:12–31; 14:31–32) obviously raised the position of the women in the church, for they were the bearers of numerous charisms.

Greeks and Jews

Since Homer, the Greeks were defined by their cultural superiority in contrast to the "barbarian" (ὁ βάρβαρος, one who is not Greek),[104] particularly as a result of the Persian War. This term referred to one who did not speak perfect Greek;[105] it also referred to all areas of culture, technology, and leadership in war.[106] The barbarians were considered cruel, licentious, and without culture, while the Hellenes were considered brave, civilized, and noble. This view is evident in both poetry and systematic philosophy:[107] The Hellenes are born to rule, while the barbarians are born to slavery. In the ranking of cultures, the Greeks naturally placed themselves first.[108] The Romans understood themselves as successors of the Hellenes and took over this view. Nevertheless, in antiquity national consciousness of the smaller nations was of great significance. Neither the Hellenization after the conquests of Alexander nor Roman rule led to a unified culture; instead, under and alongside the dominant Greco-Roman culture, numerous ethnicities existed: for example, Judaism continued to exist as one of the linguistic and cultural entities. The Jews divided the world into two groups: Jews and non-Jews. In the face of

---

103. Cf. also Plutarch, *Mor.* 142E: "As long as the wives are subject to their husbands, they deserve praise."

104. Cf. Homer, *Iliad* 2.867.

105. Cf. Zeno, according to Diogenes Laertius 7.59: "By good Greek is meant language that is faultless in point of grammar and free from careless vulgarity" (LCL).

106. Cf. the thorough study by Jüthner, *Hellenen und Barbaren.*

107. Cf. Euripides, *Iphigenia at Aulis* 1400–1401; Aristotle, *Pol.* 1252b: "It is right that the Greeks rule the barbarians."

108. In Rom. 1:14, Paul employs the common duality "Greeks and barbarians" in naming all humanity as the target audience of his preaching.

this constellation, assessments and discrimination were the order of the day.[109] Here the early Christians stood before a double problem: (1) Many members were Godfearers or Jews by birth and thus followers or members of a people that regarded itself as chosen and from which the new movement came. Yet in the view of the Greeks and Romans, the Jews were "barbarians" because of their separation and practice of circumcision.[110] (2) The Greeks and Romans in the church gave up their privileged heritage and joined an obscure movement from the eastern part of the empire.

The related problems were overcome in the Antiochian-Pauline mission by a transethnic concept. The one Spirit of the one God was poured out over many people and nations and no longer allowed ethnic boundaries (cf. 1 Cor. 12:12–13). All have drunk of the one Spirit and have received the one baptism so that "here there is neither Jew nor Greek" (Gal. 3:28). They regarded themselves as a "third race" in relation to Jews and Greeks (cf. 1 Cor. 1:22–23); consequently, according to Paul, "You are one in Christ Jesus" (Gal. 3:28).[111] For the many members of the Pauline churches in Asia Minor and Greece, it was naturally clear that their new faith was neither a variant of Judaism nor an additional form of pagan religiosity. Indeed, the consciousness of the new was a decisive factor in the growth of the churches! Membership in the elected people was defined no longer by national or family heritage but rather through the "new birth" or "rebirth" in baptism. The theological construction of a new identity and its social realization in Paul's churches in Asia Minor and Greece formed the basis for the origin of a new religion, yet one with an attractive content! Again, this relativizing way of thinking has a parallel among Cynics, who understood themselves as cosmopolitans[112] and did not follow the alternative: Greeks and barbarians.[113] Epictetus develops a universal model based on the relationship of all humankind in reason. Socrates is neither a citizen of Athens nor of Corinth, but a "citizen of the world." "Why should not such a person be called a 'citizen of the universe'

109. Cf. Epictetus, *Diatr.* 2.9.19: "Why do you act the part of a Jew, when you are a Greek? Do you not see in which sense men are severally called Jew, Syrian, or Egyptian?" (LCL).

110. As an example, cf. the section about the Jews in Tacitus, *Hist.* 5.3–5: "Everything there is unholy that we consider holy; on the other hand, everything is permitted for them that we consider shameful" (5.4.1).

111. Cf. the excellent study by Harnack, *Mission and Expansion of Christianity*, 267–78, who sees the origin of the concept of Christians as a "new people" or "third race" already in Paul.

112. Diogenes of Sinope, according to Diogenes Laertius 6.63, "I am a citizen of the world"; 6.72, "The only true commonwealth is as wide as the universe"; also Epictetus, *Diatr.* 3.22.47, "I am without a home, without a city" (LCL); Ps.-Anacharsis 5, "My camp is the entire earth."

113. Plutarch, *Mor.* 329c–d; Dio Chrysostom, *Or.* 4.4–6: Alexander the Great is praised because he did not follow the advice of his teacher Aristotle and did not treat the barbarians as slaves.

(κόσμιος)? Why not 'son of God'? . . . He is really free and must fear no one, for he is related to God alone, his creator, father, and protector."[114] In Paul, people become "sons of God" through faith and baptism, while in Epictetus they are because of their relationship with God. The crucial result in both cases is a relativizing/abandonment of membership based on natural descent. Of course, there is a crucial difference. For Epictetus, the philosopher alone who has such insights is able to realize this goal.[115] For Paul this elite barrier does not exist.

> Within the ancient world, the Pauline churches represented something new: Without preconditions (such as origin, gender, property, status, education), they were open for the people of all levels without regard for gender and occupation. This lived reality of faith had the power to attract peopie from a variety of ethnic groups, cultures, social levels, and environments. In a society shaped by Greco-Roman ethnocentrism, the Christians practiced a model of openness and equality among brothers and sisters that contained utopian elements, left behind the values of antiquity, and created a new kind of community.

8.4 External Discourse

Paul proclaimed a public message with a universal claim. Consequently, during his entire life he was involved in a variety of discourses and conflicts that he partially set in motion or unleashed and aggressively led, but also was drawn into at times. External conflicts, including direct and indirect dialogue with Judaism and Roman authority, define his way as missionary.

The Discourse with the Jews

According to the narrative of Acts, Paul regularly began his activities in a new city in the respective synagogues (cf. Acts 9:20; 13:15, 14–43; 14:1–2; 16:13–14; 17:1–3; 18:4; 19:8). This depiction is probably Lukan;[116] however, one may assume that for strategic missionary reasons, Paul turned first to the local synagogue and its sympathizers. Here he proclaimed the crucified Jesus of Nazareth as the Messiah of Israel and of the entire world. Thus he engaged directly in the interpretation of the eschatological traditions

114. Epictetus, *Diatr.* 1.9.1, 6–7.
115. Cf. Epictetus, *Diatr.* 1.9.9.
116. Cf. Pervo, *Acts*, 323: "The Lucan principle of 'Jews first.'"

of Israel and interpreted them in new ways that were perceived by many Jews as a provocation. Paul himself notes this response in 1 Cor. 1:23: "But we preach Christ as the crucified one, to the Jews a scandal, to the nations foolishness." What caused him at first to persecute the Christ-believers (see above, 5.4) has become the content of his preaching. If, according to Deut. 21:23, a crucified person can only be under a curse from God (cf. Gal. 3:13), then as the Resurrected One, according to Paul, he is the Anointed One, Christ, Lord, Kyrios, and Son of God. Thus the claim to be the true "Israel of God" (Gal. 6:16;[117] Rom. 9:6ff.) is connected with the fulfillment of the traditions of Israel. As a Jew by birth, during his entire life Paul hoped that his entire people would be converted. However, statements on this topic are varied; on the one hand, there are critical texts such as 1 Thess. 2:14–16; 2 Cor. 3; and especially Gal. 4:21–31;[118] on the other hand, in Rom. 9–11 Paul struggles with the conduct of God toward the elect people Israel and the validity of his promises.[119] According to Rom. 11:25–27, he expects an act of God at the end, with the appearance of the parousia of Christ, that leads to a conversion and thus to the salvation of Israel. Paul concludes, "All Israel will be saved" (Rom. 11:26a).

Paul connected his appeal to the Jewish concept of salvation with the postulate of its being fulfilled or surpassed and having gained success, especially among the Godfearers. This led to the conflicts in Philippi, Thessalonica, and Corinth described above (see 8.1), which are indirectly confirmed in the Pauline letters. "From the Jews I received the forty lashes less one; . . . once I was stoned"; stoning was the death penalty for blasphemy (Lev. 24:16), idolatry (20:2), or violation of the Sabbath (Num. 15:35). For Paul, one may assume the accusation of blasphemy; he was perceived by the Jews as apostate; his message was received as a provocation and by no means a legitimate variant of Judaism. This perception is confirmed by his foreboding in Rom. 15:31 and, of course, by the arrest in Jerusalem, which was explicitly connected with the charge of apostasy (Acts 21:21: "They have reported about you that you teach all Jews who live among the gentiles to forsake Moses, and that you tell them that they do not need to circumcise their children or observe the customs"). The arrest of Paul in Acts 21:27–30 was concretely set in motion when he is reported to have taken a gentile Christian from Ephesus named Trophimus

117. H. Betz, *Galatians*, 323, is apposite: "Taken as it stands, the expression 'Israel of God' is redundant: it makes no sense to speak of an Israel that is not "of God." Yet such an expression does make sense as a critical distinction between a 'true' and a 'false' Israel."

118. Cf. here the critical analysis of Sellin, "Hagar und Sara," 137: "Beyond the fleshly descent there is one that is 'spiritual,' which basically proceeds outside genealogy."

119. On the interpretation of Rom. 9–11, cf. Schnelle, *Apostle Paul*, 342–52.

into the temple. With this action the temple law was violated, according to which no non-Jew was permitted to enter the sanctuary.[120] Luke explicitly describes this charge as false (Acts 21:29); Paul, like Stephen before him, was arrested on the basis of false eyewitnesses. The exact circumstances for the arrest of Paul and his transfer to the Romans can no longer be illuminated.[121] The following report about the trial of Paul also includes numerous historical inconsistencies.[122] It is nevertheless clear that, for the Jews (and rigorous Jewish Christians), Paul was no longer considered a part of Judaism; he was regarded as belonging to another movement, against which one must battle. That a connection existed between Jews and strict Jewish Christians is indicated in Gal. 6:12: "Those who want to make a good show in the flesh compel you to be circumcised so that they will not be persecuted because of [the preaching of] the cross."

This verse contains two valuable historical facts: (1) In order to avoid the persecution threatened by the Jews, the strict Jewish Christian opponents of Paul in Galatia required the practice of circumcision (cf. Gal. 5:3; 6:12, 13; also 2:2; 6:15) and the observance of cultic times for gentile Christians (cf. Gal. 4:3, 9, 10). The essential occasion for the Judaizers in Galatia is thus the pressure of Judaism on the Jewish Christians, probably in Jerusalem especially (see below, 8.5). The Judaizers apparently believed that they could avoid assimilation of the gentile Christians into the wider realm of Judaism only through this pressure. (2) With μόνον (Gal. 6:12) Paul marks the crucial distinction between himself and his Jewish Christian opponents. They distort the gospel only in order not to be persecuted; that is, Paul also was persecuted by the Jews without betraying the truth of the gospel. A reflection of these actions is present also in Gal. 4:21–31, where Paul alludes to the present relationship between Jews and Christians, particularly in verse 29: "Just as at that time the one who was born according to the flesh persecuted the one born according to the Spirit, so it is now also." With the phrase οὕτως καὶ νῦν (so also now), Paul alludes to the present persecutions by Jews and Jewish Christians. Galatians 5:11 must be understood within this context: "But I, brothers and sisters, if I still preach circumcision, why am I still persecuted? In that case the offense of the cross has been removed."

---

120. Cf. Philo, *Legat.* 212 ("a merciless death penalty is laid down for non-Jews who cross the boundary of the innermost area of the temple"); Josephus, *J.W.* 5.192–94; cf. also the temple inscription found in 1871 (text in Barrett and Thornton, *New Testament Background*, 53).

121. On the possible legal background, cf. Rapske, *Book of Acts and Paul*, 135–49 (events in Jerusalem); Omerzu, *Der Prozess des Paulus*, 309–84.

122. On the events in Caesarea, cf. Rapske, *Book of Acts and Paul*, 151–72; Omerzu, *Der Prozess des Paulus*, 396–501.

The fact of the persecution alone attests the truth of the Pauline preaching of the cross. In contrast to his opponents, Paul does not falsify the gospel under the threat of persecution.

The Pauline mission to the nations, which did not require circumcision—and thus did not require observance of Torah (but did include acceptance of the basic ethical requirements of the Torah)—was embattled from two directions that were, for their part, involved in a major conflict.[123] The Jews exercised pressure not only on Paul but also on his Jewish Christian opponents. Their purpose was certainly not to allow the new movement to be regarded as a part of Judaism, with its established privileges, but as a questionable political-religious group. The events of the burning of Rome in 64 CE indicate that this goal was attained. The Christians were regarded as an independent movement that one could make responsible for evil apparently without a reason and without opposition.

> Probably the success of the Pauline mission in diaspora Judaism and in Palestine, with the increasing nationalism in anticipation of the Jewish War, led to pressure not only on Paul but also on the strict Jewish Christians, who understood themselves as still a part of Judaism and thus attacked Paul themselves.

The Discourse with the Imperium Romanum

According to Acts 16:37–38; 22:25; 23:27, Paul was a Roman citizen,[124] probably a descendant of a Jewish slave who had been freed (cf. Acts 22:28).[125] As a Roman citizen, Paul took a Roman name,[126] and in his missionary planning he thought in the geographic categories of the Imperium Romanum (see above, 8.1). He is oriented to the provincial capital cities and expands

123. Cf. Wander, *Trennungsprozesse*, 244–62.

124. The historicity of this claim is disputed by, among others, W. Stegemann, "War der Apostel Paulus ein römischer Bürger?"; Wengst, *Pax Romana*, 94–95; Cineira, *Die Religionspolitik des Kaisers Claudius*, 348–70; D.-A. Koch, *Geschichte des Urchristentums*, 336–40; on the current discussion, cf. Schnelle, *Apostle Paul*, 60–61; A. Weiss, "Paulus und die *coloniae*," who points out that, in Roman colonies such as Philippi, the great majority of the population had Roman citizenship. Thus "in all probability, a considerable number in my opinion, even the overwhelming majority—of the Christians in Philippi were Roman citizens" (352).

125. Cf. Omerzu, *Der Prozess des Paulus*, 28–39. Philo, *Legat*. 155, reports that the majority of Jews living in Rome were freedmen and Roman citizens.

126. The apostle did not only take on the name Παῦλος in order to facilitate social context within the sphere of his missionary activity (cf. Acts 13:7–12); rather, Παῦλος is the Roman name that Σαῦλος (cf. Acts 7:58; 8:1, 3; 9:1, 8, 22, 24, and passim) as a Roman citizen took from the beginning; cf. Hengel, *Pre-Christian Paul*, 6–7; Omerzu, *Der Prozess des Paulus*, 39–42.

his missionary activity constantly toward the west. Luke describes the conduct of the Roman authorities toward Paul almost totally in positive terms. Only in Acts 16:16–22 are accusations raised against Paul and Silas by the Roman authorities because they introduce new (Jewish) customs. Otherwise the theme is that it is the Jews (cf. Acts 13:50; 17:5–7, 13, 21, 27ff.), not the Roman authorities, who persecute Paul. They proceed with illegal measures against Paul (cf. Acts 23:12–15; 25:3), or they turn to the state authorities (cf. Acts 18:12ff.; 24:1ff.; 25:5) but are regularly rejected by them. According to the Lukan view, the state must act against iniquity and crime, but it does not have the task of intervening in religious disputes (cf. Acts 18:12–17). Thus for both Gallio (Acts 18:15) and Festus (Acts 25:18, 25) there is no basis for bringing charges against Paul. According to Roman law, Paul was innocent and should be set free (cf. Acts 25:25; 26:31–32), and only corruption and failure by the Roman authorities (cf. Acts 24:26–27; 25:9) forced Paul to appeal to Caesar.

The Pauline letters offer a different portrayal: Paul was in prison many times; according to 2 Cor. 11:25, he received the Roman punishment of beating with rods (cf. also 2 Cor. 6:5; 12:10). Both the "battle with wild beasts" in Ephesus (1 Cor. 15:32) and the danger of death in the province of Asia (2 Cor. 1:8–9) indicate life-threatening conflicts (cf. also Rom. 16:4). He was accused before the Roman prefect Felix of causing riots (Acts 24:5: "riots among all the Jews in the world"). Paul wrote the letters to the Philippians and Philemon from Roman prisons (cf. Phil. 1:13; Philem. 1). Thus it is not surprising when, particularly in Philippians, allusions to the imperial Roman world appear. The Philippians receive their citizenship not from Roman authorities but from heaven (Phil. 3:20, "Our citizenship is in heaven; from there we await the Kyrios Jesus Christ as Savior").[127] The concept πολίτευμα (citizenship) designates the legal status of a citizen. Thus just as the Roman citizens of Philippi were registered in the list of the citizens of *tribus* Voltinia, the Christians of Philippi are registered in a heavenly list of citizens.[128] Consequently, only in Phil. 1:27 does Paul describe the conduct of believers with the verb πολιτεύεσθαι (conduct yourselves as citizens). Against the background of a church shaped in a colonial Roman environment, the hymn in Phil. 2:6–11 takes on a political dimension. A man crucified by the Romans receives the highest status through the direct intervention of God, and worship (*proskynēsis*) and confession (*exhomologēsis*) are due to him alone. While kings and rulers gain their power through violence and predatory actions, Jesus Christ humbles himself and becomes the true ruler. He embodies the

127. Epictetus has a comparable saying in *Diatr.* 3.22.47, claiming explicitly that the true Cynic is ἄπολις (without a home city) and thus is truly free.
128. Cf. Schinkel, *Die himmlische Bürgerschaft*, 100–122.

antithesis of the ruler who exalts himself.[129] The *Kyrios* title in Phil. 2:11 and the title of Savior in Phil. 3:20 also contain anti-imperial connotations. A Greek inscription from the time of Nero contains the formulation: "Nero the kyrios of the whole world,"[130] and the Roman caesars allowed themselves to be praised as savior, especially in the eastern part of the empire.[131] Over against this political-religious claim, the hymn declares a new reality that surpasses any earthly power. Paul, who is probably a prisoner in Rome, offers his new countermodel. Powerlessness and domination are in truth distributed differently than it at first appears.

Thus Paul finds himself in a dialogue with the Pax Romana. The Romans sought to restrict and channel the numerous religious and cultural movements within the empire through a common bond: the Pax Romana.[132] At the center of this concept since Augustus[133] stood the person of the caesar, who, as pontifex maximus, guaranteed the continued existence and cohesion of the Roman Empire with respect to sacral-legal matters, held together the commonwealth, and secured peace and prosperity through clever politics.[134] With its military power, the Pax Romana maintained the political unity of the empire, the basis for economic growth and legal stability. The external peace made possible an intact infrastructure and a booming commerce between the east and the west of the empire, creating the conditions for the spread of the gospel by tradesmen, travelers, and slaves. The economic boom was connected

129. Cf. Vollenweider, "Der 'Raub' der Gottgleichheit," 431. In this context, Plutarch, *Mor.* 330d, is frequently cited, where Plutarch defends Alexander the Great as the exemplary world ruler: "For Alexander did not overrun Asia like a robber, nor did he have the intention to treat it as if it were booty and plunder to tear and to rend, bestowed as unexpected fortune."

130. Cf. *NW* I/2:249.

131. Cf. texts in *NW* I/2:239–56.

132. Cf. Wengst, *Pax Romana*, 19–71.

133. For example, cf. the Res gestae of Augustus; for the religious development of Octavian/Augustus, cf. Clauss, *Kaiser und Gott*, 54–75; Christ, *Geschichte der römischen Kaiserzeit*, 158–68.

134. As an example, cf. in Freis, *Historische Inschriften zur römischen Kaiserzeit*, 17, the inscription from Halicarnassus (2nd cent. BCE): "Since the eternal and immortal nature of the All grants the greatest good to humankind out of overflowing friendship, bringing forth Caesar Augustus, the [line 5] father for a happy life among us and father of his native goddess Roma, the native Zeus and savior of the human race, whose wishes in all providence are not only fulfilled, but also surpassed, for land and sea live in peace; cities shine in legal order [line 10], harmony, and abundance; it is an encouraging high point for every good, for good hopes for the future, for good courage for the presence of humankind, who fulfill . . . with festivals, statues, sacrifices and songs." Cf. Seneca, *De clementia* 2.1, from a later time, where he says about Nero: "That kindness of your heart will be recounted, will be diffused little by little throughout the whole body of the empire, and all things will be moulded into your likeness. It is from the head that comes the health of the body; it is through it that all the parts are lively and alert or languid and drooping according as their animating spirit has life or withers. There will be citizens, there will be allies worthy of this goodness, and uprightness will return to the whole world; your hands will everywhere be spared" (LCL).

with social mobility. The boundaries between classes were more permeable, giving the possibility for social mobility among the lower classes.[135]

The discourse with the Pax Romana is evident in other passages in the Pauline letters. In 1 Thess. 5:3, the apostle signals in the introductory phrase εἰρήνη καὶ ἀσφάλεια (peace and security) that he is taking up a slogan of the Pax Romana: "When they say 'peace and security,' then suddenly destruction comes over them like birth pangs, and they will not escape."[136] The apostle places the Roman ideology[137] of peace, security, and prosperity in opposition to his view of the imminent end: Perfection is not achieved in this world by the Roman Empire, but rather God's intervention as judge is the goal of history. In 2 Cor. 2:14 Paul takes up the metaphor of the imperial victory processional; he is a participant in a universal triumphal processional, and he takes the perspective of a general: "Thanks be to God, who leads us always in a triumphal procession in Jesus Christ and reveals the fragrance of the knowledge of him in every place." God has achieved the victory in Jesus Christ and commissions Paul to appear as his herald and bearer of the incense burner (cf. v. 15, "we are the aroma of Christ"). Paul employs secular terms such as εὐαγγέλιον (good news, e.g., of the elevation of the caesar), ἐκκλησία (the assembly of free men with voting rights), κύριος (Lord, Caesar, God), ἀπόστολος (messenger) or πρεσβεύειν (official representative), which he uses with a transcendent dimension. Thus, on the one hand, he creates the connection with the vocabulary of Rome, but at the same time makes it clear that his message surpasses the realities of the Roman Empire by far.

In the discourse of the Neronian period, Paul addresses the issue explicitly in Rom. 13:1–7.[138] This passage is filled with secular terms and concepts. The Roman church is encouraged to submit to the structures of the world in accordance with the creation. The general exhortation for obedience in verse 6 becomes concretized in a striking example: The Romans pay taxes and thus recognize the powers ordained by God. In their collection of taxes and

---

135. Cf. Gülzow, "Pontifikalreligion und Gesellschaft."

136. Cf. Wengst, *Pax Romana*, 97–99; Brocke, *Thessaloniki*, 167–85; Malherbe, *The Letters to the Thessalonians*, 303–5; Riedo-Emmenegger, *Prophetisch-messianische Provokateure*, 165–68.

137. Cf., e.g., Seneca, *De clementia* 1.2: "All those many thousands of swords which my peace restrains will be drawn at my nod"; *De clementia* 1.5: "This pronouncement, Caesar, you may boldly make, that whatever has passed into your trust and guardianship is still kept safe" (LCL); Epictetus, *Diatr.* 2.13, concerning the peace that is maintained through philosophy: "If one has this freedom, it is not the same as the one that the Caesar has called forth." Aelius Aristides, *Roman Oration* 104: "Now a general security recognized by all has been given to the earth and its inhabitants."

138. Cf. the thorough analysis of A. Strobel, "Zum Verständnis von Röm 13"; Krauter, *Studien zu Röm 13,1–7*.

customs, the imperial officers are nothing less than λειτουροὶ θεοῦ (servants of God). In verse 7 Paul concludes his exhortation with the general statement, "Pay to all what you owe—taxes to whom taxes are due, revenue to whom revenue is due, respect to whom respect is due, honor to whom honor is due." Romans 13:1–7 reflects a twofold political dimension: (1) Paul's demand for the recognition of governmental authorities may be understood against the background of the increasing tension between the Christian church as it is developing as an independent movement and the Roman authorities. They now perceive the Christians as a group that worships as God an executed criminal and proclaims an imminent end of the world. (2) The striking emphasis on the payment of taxes could have a background in the current situation, for protests in Rome against the increasing pressure of taxes under Nero had erupted, and Paul could have been trying to urge the Roman Christians not to participate in the protests and not to have an attitude of protest.[139]

All of these connections, echoes, and aspects, however, are by no means identical with a comprehensive and intentional "anti-imperial" theology of Paul.[140] First of all, one may not attribute to Paul a modern concept of politics in order to make of him a critic of the empire. Paul directed a theological revolution that affirmed a change already taking place that is more fundamental than any political revolution was capable of achieving.[141] Furthermore, Paul moved (1) with his mission, not in "the" Imperium Romanum but rather in subcultures (Judaism, Hellenistic cities, provinces, countryside).[142] (2) His churches form alternative ways of life, but they were by no means a world in opposition (cf. 1 Cor. 10:32, "Give no offense"). It is scarcely coincidental that (3) there are no direct (!) statements that are anti-Roman or critical of Rome in Paul. Rather, (4) Rom. 13:1–7, as the only statement of Paul about the Imperium Romanum, demands (despite all undertones and secondary tones) this recognition. Furthermore, (5) the imminent return of the exalted Christ already places earthly matters in a provisional light (1 Cor. 7:29–31).

---

139. According to Tacitus, *Ann.* 13.50–51, in 58 CE continued protests against the oppressive taxation occurred, which probably had a longer prior history, however; cf. J. Friedrich, Stuhlmacher, and Pöhlmann, "Zur historischen Situation und Intention von Röm 13,1–7."

140. Cf. especially the collection of essays in Horsley, *Paul and Empire*; Horsley, *Paul and Politics*. The current discussion is reported with a critique by Harrill, "Paul and Empire."

141. Cf. Wright, *Paul and the Faithfulness of God*, 1306–7: "Paul did not, however, advocate the normal sort of revolution. . . . A different kind of revolution. A different kind of 'subversion'—and Paul would have said, a more powerful and effective one."

142. One may also ask to what extent, at the time of Paul, the imperial cult was practiced in the cities visited by him. For a rather negative answer for 30–60 CE, see Miller, "The Imperial Cult in the Pauline Cities," 316: "The archaeological evidence reveals that, in the cities Paul visited, in Paul's time, the emperor cult was marginal."

8.5 Internal Discourse

While the external discourse and conflicts can, for the most part, be examined only indirectly, the internal discourse essentially shapes the argumentation in the Pauline letters. They offer insights into the problems of the early churches and indicate how Paul worked through social, cultural, ethical, and ethnic conflicts theologically.

Pneumatic Enthusiasm

In the Corinthian church especially, an enthusiastic, Spirit-filled Christianity developed that regarded itself as already united in the Spirit with Christ and carried away from earthly limitations. The Corinthians' consciousness of superiority and perfection (cf. 1 Cor. 4:8, "Already you are filled; already you are rich; without us you now rule";[143] 1 Cor. 6:12; 10:23; also 1 Cor. 2:6; 4:10, 18, 20; 5:2; 10:1ff.; 15:12) is derived from its high evaluation of the gift of the Spirit in baptism (cf. 1 Cor. 6:11; 12:13; also 1:10–17; 10:1–4; 15:29). Because, according to ancient thought, God is Spirit/Reason (πνεῦμα/νοῦς) or works in and through the Spirit,[144] the Corinthians believed that they were already participating in the full salvation. They regarded this extraordinary activity of the Spirit in the worship service (1 Cor. 11; 14) and in the charismatic gifts (cf. 1 Cor. 12–14) as confirmation of their new status. Paul attempts to clarify to the church that was striving for perfection in the present that this wisdom is revealed where humankind sees foolishness (1 Cor. 1:18ff.). At the cross one can see the action of God, who elects the lowly and the despised (1 Cor. 1:26–29) and leads the apostle to an existence and manner of thinking determined by the Lord (1 Cor. 2:2). The Corinthians confuse worldly wisdom, that is, their own wisdom, with the wisdom of God. There is no wisdom and glory other than that of the Crucified One (1 Cor. 2:6ff.), and one can speak of the resurrection only of the Crucified One. Thus Paul says, "For the word of the cross is foolishness to those who are lost, but to us, who are being saved, it is the power of God" (1 Cor. 1:18).[145]

They believed that they could do without a future bodily resurrection because they imagined that they were already raised (cf. 1 Cor. 15:12–19).

143. On the analysis of the Corinthian position and the comments by Paul, cf., besides the commentaries, Wilckens, *Weisheit und Torheit*; Horn, *Das Angeld des Geistes*, 157–301; B. Winter, *After Paul Left Corinth*, 31ff.; Schnelle, *Apostle Paul*, 192–234.

144. Cf., e.g., Stobaeus 1.34.26–35.2 about the Stoa: "Posidonius defines God as gifted with spirit and reason [πνεῦμα νοερόν] and a fiery life form, which has no form, but takes on every random form and can adapt to everything"; cf. also texts in *NW* I/2:226–34.

145. On the Pauline theology of the cross, cf. Weder, *Das Kreuz Jesu bei Paulus*; Söding, *Das Wort vom Kreuz*; Voss, *Das Wort vom Kreuz und die menschliche Vernunft*.

They probably thought in terms of a dichotomy; that is, they distinguish between the invisible "I soul" and the visible body.[146] In contrast to the later Gnostic point of view, the Corinthians did not hold to a negative view of the body; instead, they believed that it, as an earthly temporary reality, was excluded from the eschatological redemption. An expectation for the afterlife was limited to the higher part of humankind, the Spirit-endowed "I soul." As an earthly dwelling not relevant to salvation, the body, according to the Corinthians, was of secondary importance; thus both sexual promiscuity and asceticism were expressions of this way of thinking (cf. 1 Cor. 6:12–20; 7:1–9, 25–28). The apostle shared the reality of such an understanding of the Spirit; for him also, "The Lord is the Spirit" (2 Cor. 3:17), and the Spirit has a supernatural quality (cf. 1 Cor. 3:15–16; 5:5). In contrast to the Corinthians' theology, however, for Paul the human as an "I" cannot be separated from the body. Corporeality constitutes being human; it is not excluded from present (1 Cor. 6:17, "Whoever is united with the Lord is one Spirit with him") and future salvation (cf. 1 Cor. 15:44, "It is sown a natural body; it is raised a spiritual body"). Thus Paul inverts the Corinthian sequence: "But it is not the spiritual that comes first, but instead the physical, and then the spiritual" (1 Cor. 15:46).

The Corinthians wanted to escape their creaturely limitations. It was not lowliness but rather power and rule that appeared to them as an appropriate presentation of the salvation that is attained. In contrast to them, the apostles are "fools for Christ's sake" (1 Cor. 4:10). They offer another exemplum, for they constantly live in weakness, danger, and poverty for the sake of the church (cf. 1 Cor. 4:11ff.). Thus they represent the example of the truly wise person, for they live independently of all external matters in their calling and their message. Correspondingly, the form of apostolic existence is shaped by the Crucified One (cf. the catalogs of suffering in 1 Cor. 4:11–13; 2 Cor. 4:7–12; 6:4–10; 11:23–29).[147]

In 2 Corinthians Paul takes this argumentation further into a different context.[148] At the center is the theme of the paradox of lowliness: "For we preach not ourselves, but Jesus Christ as Lord, but we are your servants for Christ's sake" (2 Cor. 4:5). The lowliness of Christ creates an obligation for both the apostle (2 Cor. 10:1; 11:23, 30) and the church (2 Cor. 8; 9). The

---

146. Cf. Sellin, *Der Streit um die Auferstehung der Toten*, 30: "The Corinthians totally rejected the resurrection of the dead because they could not accept the related idea of the corporeality of eternal salvation."

147. On the analysis, cf. Ebner, *Leidenslisten und Apostelbrief*, 196ff.; Schiefer-Ferrari, *Die Sprache des Leids*, 201ff.; Hotze, *Paradoxien bei Paulus*, 252–87.

148. Cf. the introduction in Schnelle, *Apostle Paul*, 228–55; Fitzgerald, *Cracks in an Earthen Vessel*.

Crucified and Resurrected One shapes the paradoxical form of apostolic existence in weakness and power. Paul employs this argument against early Christian traveling preachers of Hellenistic-Jewish background, who place value on their own origin (cf. 2 Cor. 11:22) and pneumatic capabilities (cf. 2 Cor. 12:12). They work with letters of recommendation (cf. 2 Cor. 3:1b) and commend themselves (cf. 2 Cor. 10:18). Paul speaks ironically, calling them "super-apostles" (cf. 2 Cor. 11:5; 12:11). The Corinthians themselves were fascinated with preachers who were able to excite their listeners by their personality. Rhetorical education, the claim of special knowledge, and impressive external appearance characterized the traveling missionaries (cf. 2 Cor. 10:5). In addition, they boasted of special gifts; they could demonstrate ecstatic visions as well as signs and wonders (cf. 2 Cor. 11:6; 12:1, 12). Thus, from the perspective of the Corinthians, the opponents belonged to the large group of traveling preachers who shaped the religious and intellectual climate in the cities during that time. They attempted to impress the people by an unconventional appearance, a self-sufficient lifestyle, and rhetorical pathos (see above, 6.1). Paul, however, could boast of his accomplishments only as a fool (cf. 2 Cor. 11:21b–12:10;[149] his weak outward appearance and lack of the gift of speech (cf. 2 Cor. 10:10) led many Corinthians to disregard the quality of his message also. The strength of the gospel that was desired did not cohere with the weakness of the apostle. Paul, however, declared clearly that God's glory is revealed paradoxically in the weakness of suffering and death. Just as the life-giving power of God is present in the cross, God's power is at work in the apostle's weakness.

"Strong" and "Weak"

A second intrachurch discourse is connected with Corinth and Rome, which indicates the concrete difficulties involved in the life together of Christians from various ethnic, social, and cultural backgrounds (cf. 1 Cor. 8:1–13; 10:14–33). Practical questions of church life are the point of departure: Are Christians permitted to buy meat (dedicated to the gods) at the market (1 Cor. 10:25)? Are they allowed to accept invitations from pagan fellow citizens (1 Cor. 10:27–28)? Is it compatible with the new faith to participate in meals (1 Cor. 8:10) or cultic celebrations (1 Cor. 10:14–22) in temples?[150] Both gentile Christians and liberal Jewish Christians belonged to the group of the "strong"; they certainly belonged to the upper social class, for whom it was possible

---

149. Cf. U. Heckel, *Kraft in Schwachheit*.

150. On the determination of the historical situation that is assumed, cf. Gäckle, *Die Starken und Schwachen*, 183–218.

to resolve traditional religious viewpoints through their religious knowledge (cf. 1 Cor. 8:1, 4; 10:23).[151] Nevertheless, the "strong" are not to be equated simply with the social upper class in the community, for a monotheism that was known to both Jewish and gentile Christians (cf. 1 Thess. 1:9–10) is expressed in knowing the existence of one God and the nonexistence of idols and demons. They ate food offered to idols without reservation (1 Cor. 8:9; 10:25–30), were also invited by Greeks/Romans (1 Cor. 10:27), and even participated in pagan cultic celebrations (1 Cor. 14:20–21). Indeed, their place in society made it impossible for them to forgo the consumption of food offered to idols. As a justification for this practice, the "strong" appealed to their "knowledge" (cf. γνῶσις in 1 Cor. 8:1–2, 4). They understood the gospel and its message of freedom apparently as primarily individual independence, as emancipation from traditional religious and moral concepts.[152] Presumably the "weak" in the Corinthian church were primarily a gentile Christian minority (cf. 1 Cor. 8:7).[153] Some of this group probably abstained from the consumption of food offered to idols out of fear of the gods in general. Others were forced, because of physical necessity, to participate in public religious celebrations, where they ate meat within a cultic context and thus burdened their consciences.[154] Others were led away by the conduct of the "strong" to eat food offered to idols against their conscience, while the "strong" participated without reservation when they were not in need.

Although Paul basically agrees with the position of the "strong" (cf. 1 Cor. 8:4–6), he draws two boundary markers: (1) the participation of Christians in pagan sacrificial and cult meals is prohibited (cf. 1 Cor. 10:21); and (2) when sacrificial meat is specifically identified at a private invitation, the Christians should not eat it (cf. 1 Cor. 10:28). In both instances the honor of the one true God is damaged (cf. 1 Cor. 10:31).[155] Beneath these clear boundaries, no other inquiry is necessary; one can buy at the marketplace and accept

---

151. Theissen emphasizes this aspect in "The Strong and the Weak in Corinth," 130–36. For a different view, cf. Gäckle, *Die Starken und Schwachen*, 197, who observes: "There is much to suggest that the conflict between the strong and the weak was not primarily a social issue; rather, it was a cognitive and ethical problem." He regards the "strong" as representatives of an elite intellectualism shaped by Stoicism, which was related in content to the Apollos group (1 Cor. 1:12); cf. Gäckle, *Die Starken und Schwachen*, 203–4.

152. Cf. Söding, "Starke und Schwache," 70–75.

153. Cf., e.g., Söding, "Starke und Schwache," 75–77. Gäckle, *Die Starken und Schwachen*, 205–15, understands the "weak" as no particular defined group, but rather individuals, primarily gentiles. They had become "accustomed" to the eating of meat offered to idols in their earlier pre-Christian life and now stood in danger of "falling away" again.

154. Cf. Theissen, "Strong and the Weak in Corinth," 127–28.

155. D.-A. Koch, "Seid unanstößig für Juden und für Griechen," 155–56, correctly emphasizes that Paul arrives at the interpretation in this specific situation.

private invitations (cf. 1 Cor. 10:25, 27). Paul insists that the conduct of both groups be appropriate to a proper understanding of the gospel, in which the love command is the standard. Agape "builds up," because it bears the weaknesses of the other: "Everything is permitted, but not everything serves the good. Everything is permitted, but not everything builds up" (1 Cor. 10:23). The Corinthians are guided to an intentional action that must balance anew between the current situation, the conscience of the brother, and their own knowledge. Paul formulates his agreement with the position of the strong without disregarding the respect for the weak so that the two groups can have a conversation on an equal footing. Moreover, the Pauline solution secures the place of the church between Jews and Greeks (cf. 1 Cor. 10:32). With respect to the Jews, the offense of participation in the idolatrous cultic activity is avoided; with respect to Greeks, no one is required to separate, and invitations from nonbelievers can be accepted.[156]

The conflict in Rome (cf. Rom. 14:1–15:13)[157] has a different setting from the one in Corinth. The majority of the "weak" were Jewish Christians, who probably abstained from eating the meat out of fear that the meat was not correctly slaughtered. In addition, they also abstained from wine and kept special days (cf. Rom. 14:2, 5, 21). The "strong" were predominantly gentiles who had no problem of adapting to the Roman-Hellenistic environment. Paul shares the position of the "strong" (Rom. 14:14, 20; 15:1: "We, the strong") yet encourages them for the sake of love to show consideration toward the "weak." Everyone had the right to remain in his own lifestyle (cf. Rom. 14:12), because the brother who thinks and acts in a different way has been accepted by God. Thus Paul says, "Accept one another as Christ has accepted you, to the glory of God" (Rom. 15:7). When love takes shape in the acceptance of the one who has different opinions, reciprocal judging is forbidden (cf. Rom. 14:4, 10, 13). God alone has the privilege of judging (Rom. 14:10–11). Thus every individual will give an account to God (cf. Rom. 14:12). The unity of the church composed of Jews and gentiles must not be obscured or put at risk by minor problems, for then the church maintains its power of attracting the outside world (cf. Rom. 15:8ff.).

The Office of Apostle

The third major discourse is also present in the Corinthian correspondence: the dispute over Paul's apostleship. This issue involves the formal and

---

156. D.-A. Koch, "Seid unanstößig für Juden und für Griechen," 158ff.

157. On the interpretation, cf. Reichert, *Der Römerbrief als Gratwanderung*, 271–311; Gäckle, *Die Starken und die Schwachen*, 292–449.

content-related definition of the apostolic office (see above, 5.2). The legitimation of the Pauline apostolate was formally a topic for discussion: May Paul
call himself a legitimate apostle at all? From diverse motives, this question was
apparently disputed, especially in Corinth and Galatia. The prescripts of the
letters already signal the significance of the topic, for they establish the basis
for the communication: "Paul, called to be an apostle of Christ Jesus through
the will of God" (1 Cor. 1:1) and "Paul, apostle of Jesus Christ through the
will of God" (2 Cor. 1:1). The manner in which Paul discusses the apostolate
in 1 Cor. 9:1 ("Am I not an apostle? Have I not seen Jesus, our Lord?") and
1 Cor. 15:8–11 indicates clearly that his apostleship was in dispute. Two objections could have been brought against Paul: (1) unlike Peter, the Twelve, and
James (cf. 1 Cor. 15:5, 7), he did not know the earthly Jesus and was—like
James—not one of his disciples; and (2) he had persecuted the earliest church
(cf. 1 Cor. 15:9). Paul refuted the first objection by claiming that Jesus Christ
appeared to him (1 Cor. 9:1; 15:8); he refuted the second objection by referring
to his missionary activity (1 Cor. 15:10: "I worked more than all of them").
The existence of churches also attests the legitimacy of his apostleship (cf.
1 Cor. 9:2b: "You are the seal of my apostleship in the Lord"). In 2 Corinthians a third charge was made against him: Paul is outwardly weak (2 Cor.
10:10–11), does not describe his achievements (cf. 2 Cor. 11:22–23), and is not
able to perform the "signs of an apostle" (cf. 2 Cor. 12:12f.), that is, the spectacular self-commendations and wonders. Paul says of the Corinthians, "You
demand proof that Christ speaks through me" (2 Cor. 13:3). Paul, however,
tells the church that his opponents are false apostles (cf. 2 Cor. 11:12) and
that he also has the expected achievements (cf. 2 Cor. 11:16ff.) but does not
use them, for God's power is demonstrated in weakness (cf. 2 Cor. 12:1–10;
v. 9: "My grace is sufficient for you, for strength is powerful in weakness").

In Galatians, Paul highlights his position in the first verse; his apostolate
is "not from men nor through men, but through Jesus Christ and God the
Father" (Gal. 1:1). Apparently, the opponents in Galatia dispute Paul's claim
of direct revelation of God in the Pauline gospel, probably regarding his
preaching as personal opinion, to which they contrasted the practice of the
Jerusalem church. Against this view, Paul depicts a reality that connects him
directly with the heavenly level and legitimates him from there.[158] The Pauline apostolate and his gospel are derived from heavenly revelation so that
even angels would be subject to an ἀνάθεμα (curse) if they preached another
gospel (cf. Gal. 1:8–9). In contrast to the argument to the Corinthians, Paul
introduces a new argument that he also uses in Romans. God himself called

---

158. On the analysis, cf. Alkier, *Wunder und Wirklichkeit*, 125–31.

him even before his birth to be an apostle to the nations (Gal. 1:15–16; cf. Rom. 1:1–2). Both his apostolate and his gospel are directly from God. What made him an apostle was not only the appearance of Christ near Damascus, for God's will from the beginning legitimated Paul's apostleship.

Paul defines the content of his apostleship in a fourfold way. (1) The Pauline mission is universal; Paul understands himself as "apostle to the nations" (Rom. 11:13; cf. Gal. 1:16, "among the nations"). This is his distinctive calling, to which he knew that he was obligated from the time of the apostolic conference (cf. Gal. 2:7). (2) In 2 Corinthians Paul characterizes himself and his apostleship with the phrase "minister of the new covenant" (cf. 2 Cor. 3:6).[159] Here, with the dichotomies of γράμμα-πνεῦμα (letter-Spirit) and "stone tablets"—"tablets on the hearts of flesh" (cf. 2 Cor. 3:3)—he emphasizes the superiority of the new relationship with God to the old relationship. The hearts of the Corinthians became temples of the living God through the reception of the Holy Spirit. The time of stone tablets is past; God does not write with letters, but in the hearts of people through the Holy Spirit in the Christ event: "For the letter kills, but the Spirit gives life" (2 Cor. 3:6b). The antithesis "old covenant–new covenant" (cf. 2 Cor. 3:6a) for Paul corresponds finally to the antithesis Moses-Christ. For Paul, Moses is the personification of the letter that kills as a way of salvation, while Christ is the personification of the new covenant in the power of the Spirit (cf. 2 Cor. 3:7–15). The new aspect of the second covenant is indicated in the liberating presence of the Spirit, through which the Resurrected One is at work: "But the Lord is the Spirit" (ὁ κύριος τὸ πνεῦμά ἐστιν, 2 Cor. 3:17a). The second covenant for Paul is actually a new and not a renewed covenant, for it is based on the power and presence of the Spirit. (3) An additional fundamental metaphor for the description of the nature and task of the Pauline apostolate is the concept of reconciliation (cf. 2 Cor. 5:14–21; Rom. 5:1–10).[160] For Paul, reconciliation is exclusively an event that proceeds from God, for at the cross God's act of reconciliation became a reality for humankind in Jesus Christ: "All of this comes from God, who reconciled us to himself through Christ and gave us the ministry of reconciliation" (2 Cor. 5:18; cf. Rom. 5:10). The reconciling deed at the cross made possible the proclamation of the message of reconciliation; at the same time the reconciliation with God occurred in this proclamation. The ministry of reconciliation takes place in the preaching of the message of reconciliation (2 Cor. 5:20c: "We appeal for Christ: be reconciled to God"),

---

159. On 2 Cor. 3, cf. Grässer, "Der Alte Bund im Neuen"; Hofius, "Gesetz und Evangelium"; Hafemann, *Paul, Moses, and the History of Israel*; Vogel, *Das Heil des Bundes*; Hulmi, *Paulus und Mose*; Schmeller, *Der zweite Brief an die Korinther*, 168–232.

160. On the Pauline concept of reconciliation, cf. Breytenbach, *Versöhnung*.

for the saving event is present in the word.[161] Paul sees his apostolic existence as anchored in the saving event itself, for the apostle's ministry of reconciliation results from the reconciling act of God. (4) The Pauline apostolate is independent and obligated to his mission. Thus Paul denies himself the essential right to receive support from the churches (cf. 1 Cor. 9:14–15) and accepts no money from them (cf. 1 Cor. 9:18; 2 Cor. 12:13). Paul takes up topoi from the Socratic tradition:[162] Like the true philosopher who accepts no payment for his instruction and appears thus truly independent and convincing, Paul waives his right for financial support by the church in order to preach the gospel freely in accordance with his apostolate.

The Mission against Paul and the Crisis in Galatia

A crucial event in the history of the Pauline mission and of early Christianity as a whole was the mission against Paul. The conflicts in 2 Corinthians and Galatians, as well as those in Romans and Philippians, indicate that, at the latest with 2 Corinthians, in progress was a countermovement, a mission against Paul.[163] It is a consequence of the apostolic conference and the associated developments. Already the variety of reports about the apostolic conference (see above, 7.1–5) and the conflict at Antioch (see above, 7.6), with the appearance of the "people from James," indicate that the question of the validity of the Mosaic law for gentile Christians was not really resolved. In addition, a contrary development took place: on the one hand was the success of the continuously expanding Pauline mission to the west; on the other hand was a mission from Jerusalem by that church, which regarded itself as a part of Judaism but increasingly under pressure from Jewish nationalists. Thus the crucial theological-political question about the character of the new movement became increasingly urgent. Should they remain as a liberal variation within Judaism or a new and independent religion associated with Judaism but without the practice of circumcision? The appropriate powers

161. Cf. Bultmann, *Theology*, 1:305–6.

162. Cf. Xenophon, *Mem.* 1.2.5–7, where it is said of Socrates: "Nor, again, did he encourage love of money in his associates. For while he checked their other desires, he would not make money himself out of their desire for his companionship. He held that this self-denying ordinance insured his independence" (LCL). Cf. also Seneca, *Ep.* 108.36. "No one has treated mankind worse than he who has studied philosophy like a remarkable trade, who lives in a different way than he advises" (LCL).

163. Cf. the detailed study by Schnelle, "Der 2. Korintherbrief und die Mission gegen Paulus." The thesis of a Judaizing mission against Paul is naturally not new; W. Wrede argued earlier: "Jewish Christianity organized in Paul's own churches a formal countermission. There are traces of it indicating that the movement was not limited to Galatia and Corinth" (cf. Wrede, *Paul*, 71–72); for recent studies, cf. e.g., Theissen, "Die Gegenmission zu Paulus."

in the Jerusalem church decided for the first option and supported (or tolerated) the attempt to integrate the Pauline churches in a type of successor countermission within Judaism.

Traces of such a countermission are present already in 2 Corinthians. The "super-apostles" (cf. 2 Cor. 11:5; 12:11) mentioned above not only invoked their rhetorical and ecstatic capabilities and their special qualification as apostles;[164] they also appealed especially to Moses and Abraham. They invoked the exclusive covenant of God with Moses (cf. Exod. 34), which Paul claims is surpassed by the "new covenant" in the power of the Spirit. They also emphasized their Jewish origin and identity (cf. 2 Cor. 11:22: "Are they Hebrews? I am also! Are they Israelites? So am I! Descendants of Abraham? I am also!") and understood themselves as the only legitimate heirs of the promises to Abraham. Finally, they emphasized Christ "according to the flesh" (2 Cor. 5:16b), that is, that they had known the earthly Jesus, while Paul did not know the Christ "according to the flesh" (2 Cor. 5:16a–c), but desires to know only the exalted Christ who is at work in the Spirit (cf. 2 Cor. 3:17). However, despite the Jewish character of the competing apostles in 2 Corinthians, there is no indication of the demand for circumcision.[165] This situation changed fundamentally with the crisis in Galatia. The (at least partially) successful attempt of strict Jewish Christian visiting missionaries to circumcise the gentile Christians in Galatia (cf. Gal. 4:8–10) after their conversion (cf. Gal. 4:21; 5:3; 6:12–13) and to observe the Jewish calendar (cf. Gal. 4:3, 9–10) led to a far-reaching conflict. This conflict altered not only the theology of Paul[166] but also the history of early Christianity. The Galatians were receptive to the arguments of the opponents, four of which are clear: (1) They appealed to Abraham[167] and persuaded with the reference to Gen. 17:7, 13, where circumcision is the sign of the eternal covenant both with Abraham and with

---

164. Cf. above, 5.2 under "Other Concepts of Apostleship" and 8.5 under "Pneumatic Enthusiasm."

165. The movement against Paul was certainly not a unified opposition; instead, from elsewhere and in specific churches the opponents or missionaries of varying positions appeared. For an overview, cf. Sumney, *Identifying Paul's Opponents*; Porter, *Paul and His Opponents*. They probably all disputed the legitimacy of Paul's apostleship and attempted to integrate the Pauline churches into a strict Jewish Christianity or reintegrate them into Judaism.

166. Cf. the basic argument in Wrede, *Paul*, 128–37, who maintains that the Galatian crisis was the starting point for the doctrine of justification. This view is supported also by G. Strecker, *Theologie des Neuen Testaments*, 149; Wilckens, *Theologie des Neuen Testaments*, 3:136ff.; Esler, *Galatians*, 153–59; Schnelle, *Apostle Paul*, 271–76; and Wolter, *Paul*, 334–48, who nevertheless distinguishes between a "context of discovery" and a "context of justification" that can evidently be placed before the Galatian controversy (Wolter, *Paul*, 392–93).

167. Of nineteen Pauline references to Abraham, eighteen are coincidentally found in Galatians and Romans (nine references each), elsewhere only in 2 Cor. 11:22.

all Israel. Anyone who is not circumcised breaks the covenant and must be excluded (Gen. 17:14). (2) The faith in the God of Israel includes membership in the currently existing people of Israel. (3) Both Jesus and Paul submitted to circumcision. (4) Membership in Jewish Christianity assures the circumcised one of social identity and stability, needed because the first emerging churches were subject to great social and political pressure from many sides.[168]

Thus Paul was faced with a totally new situation. The agreements at the apostolic conference appeared no longer to apply for the strict Jewish Christian opponents; also, the gentile Christians should totally submit themselves to the requirements of the Torah (and the claim to leadership by Jerusalem). Thus the Jewish Christians challenged the legitimacy of the entire previous Pauline mission work. The worldwide mission inaugurated by the apostle would be impossible under the mark of circumcision of gentile Christians. Paul did not conduct the mission without the requirement of circumcision primarily on the basis of missionary strategy but as an expression of a fundamental theological position. God saves the gentiles also through faith in Jesus Christ. Finally, in the conflict between Paul and his Jewish Christian opponents, the issue was the meaning of the saving deed in Jesus Christ. Does it really apply to all people without conditions, or is it determined by specific preconditions? In addition, through the opponents' demand for circumcision, the Torah moved from the periphery to the center in the churches of Asia Minor and Greece. Thus Paul saw himself compelled to revoke the concept of different paths in the question of the law/Torah that had been agreed upon at the apostolic conference (cf. Gal. 2:7; see above, 7.4) and to clarify fundamentally the significance of the Torah for Christians from Judaism and from the gentiles.[169] The question of attainment of life was naturally and irrefutably

168. Barclay, *Obeying the Truth*, 58, emphasizes that the uncertain social situation was probably an essential reason why gentile Christians accepted circumcision.

169. The weight of terms in Galatians and Romans demonstrates the importance of this topic.

	NT	Paul	1 Thess.	1 Cor.	2 Cor.	Gal.	Rom.	Phil.	Philem.
δικαιοσύνη	91	49	–	1	6	4	34	4	–
(δικαιοσύνη θεοῦ)	7	7	–	–	1	–	5	1	–
δικαιόω	39	25	–	2	–	8	15	-	–
δικαίωμα	10	5	–	–	–	–	5	-	–
δικαίωσις	2	2	–	–	–	–	2	-	–
δίκαιος	79	10	–	–	–	1	7	2	–
δικαίως	5	2	1	1	–	–	–	–	–
νόμος	195	118	–	9	–	32	74	3	–

(*continued*)

connected with circumcision,[170] that is, whether the soteriological quality of the Christ event would be undermined. Paul maintained the weakness of the Torah, for he classified it as secondary in both its point in time (Gal. 3:17) and its content (Gal. 3:19–20). Within history, its task was merely to supervise (cf. Gal. 3:24). The believers from both Judaism and the Greco-Roman world are the legitimate heirs of the promises to Abraham (cf. Gal. 3:29) apart from circumcision and the law. In Galatians, Paul annuls the hamartiological special place of Jews and Jewish Christians (Gal. 2:16) and classifies them in human history as defined by sin (cf. Gal. 3:22). Circumcision and the Torah do not belong to the soteriological self-definition of Christianity because God revealed himself directly in Jesus Christ, and those who believe and are baptized participate in the saving event in the gift of the Spirit (Gal. 3:26–28). Thus Paul also cancels the agreement of the apostolic conference, for the Petrine "gospel of the circumcision" (Gal. 2:7) confirms the special place of those who are Jews by birth and those who become circumcised after them in the new movement. Now the principle applies: "for no flesh will be justified by works of the law" (Gal. 2:16e). Thus Galatians becomes a document of a breach that can never be put back together although Paul undertakes precisely this attempt in Romans with the delivery of the collection.

Paul's Letter to the Romans is the attempt to counteract the solidifying separation between the Jerusalem church around James and his own churches in Asia Minor and Greece.[171] Paul knew that the predominantly negative statements in Galatians about the law and Israel would find only limited agreement and was no real positive solution to the problems. Consequently, in Romans he makes substantial alterations at several levels.[172] In Rom. 2:1–3:20 he disputes a special

	NT	Paul	1 Thess.	1 Cor.	2 Cor.	Gal.	Rom.	Phil.	Philem.
ἔργον	169	39	2	8	3	8	15	3	–
ἔργα νόμου	9	9	–	–	–	6	2	1	–
ἁμαρτία	173	59	1	4	3	3	48	–	–
χάρις	156	65	2	10	18	7	24	3	1
Ἀβραάμ	73	19	–	–	1	9	9	–	–

170. Gathercole, *Where Is Boasting?*, demonstrates that in numerous Jewish texts (e.g., Sir. 51:30; Bar. 4:1; 2 Macc. 7:35–38; Jub. 30.17–23; Pss. Sol. 14.2–3; Ps.-Philo 64.7; T. Zeb. 10.2–3) the observance of the Torah and acquisition of life are inseparably connected.

171. Cf. Schnelle, "Der Römerbrief und die Aporien."

172. By no means is the concern about the "deepening," as J. Becker, *Paul*, 386, suggests. Some object that the limited temporal distance between Galatians and Romans would speak against alterations (so Dunn, *Theology of Paul the Apostle*, 131). That objection is not convincing, for both the textual evidence in both letters and the changed historical situation of the apostle indicate that Paul has developed his position further. For a detailed argument, cf. Schnelle, "Gibt es eine Entwicklung in der Rechtfertigungslehre?"

place for Israel through the giving of the Torah. Because there is a common law (κοινὸς νόμος) that is given to all humankind as a reasonable measure of the just and the unjust, making possible life in the community of the polis or the state overall,[173] people from among the nations in this basic realm have no disadvantages in relation to the Jews (Rom. 2:14f.). Paul connects this negative equivalence with the introduction of the δικαιοσύνη θεοῦ (righteousness of God) as the primary concept (previously only in 2 Cor. 5:21; cf. also Rom. 1:17; 3:5, 22; 10:3; Phil. 3:9), which is then defined as the δικαιοσύνη θεοῦ χωρὶς νόμου (Rom. 3:21, "righteousness of God apart from law"; cf. also Rom. 6:14b; 10:1–4). Finally, the concept of sin moves to the center in Romans (ἁμαρτία, 48 times in Romans; in Galatians only in 1:4; 2:17; 3:22), in which sin now becomes the essential power of evil and antagonist of the Torah (Rom. 7:7ff.), a thought that is only suggested in Gal. 3:22. Thus it is now possible for Paul to evaluate the law in a much more positive light than in Galatians. He speaks of the "law of faith" (Rom. 3:27), and he once again raises up the Torah (Rom. 3:31), and above all that "the law is holy and the commandment is holy and just and good" (Rom. 7:12). In the question of Israel also, Paul offers a new accent, as he for the first time treats this topic in real detail and offers a surprising perspective: At the event of the parousia of Christ, "all Israel will be saved" (Rom. 11:26).[174] In Romans also, however, there are evident traces of ongoing agitation by the Jewish Christian opponents both in Rome and Jerusalem. In Rome his opponents are active (Rom. 16:17–20: "I encourage you, brothers, to keep an eye on those who cause divisions and offenses"),[175] attacking his theology and taking it ad absurdum (cf. Rom. 3:1–8; 6:1–2; 7:7; 9:1). In the first place, however, as the "apostle to the gentiles" (Rom. 11:13), Paul regards his position in the East as severely weakened (Rom. 15:23a: "But now I have no more place in these regions"), and with the planned mission to Spain he makes the attempt to shift the focus of the emerging Christian movement increasingly to the West (cf. Rom. 15:24). He fears particularly that the Jerusalem church will not accept the collection and that strict Jewish opponents will bring him into danger (cf. Rom. 15:31: "So that I will be saved from the disobedient in Judea and my ministry to Jerusalem will be accepted by

---

173. Cf. Chrysippus, according to Diogenes Laertius 7.87–88: "This is why the end may be defined as life in accordance with nature or, in other words, in accordance with our own nature as well as that of the universe, a life in which we refrain from every action forbidden by the law common [ὁ νόμος ὁ κοινός] to all things, that is the right reason [ὀρθὸς λόγος] that pervades all things, and is identical to Zeus, lord and ruler of all that is" (LCL). Cf. also Seneca, *Ep.* 124.14; Dio Chrysostom, *Or.* 80.5.

174. Cf. Merklein, "Der Theologe als Prophet."

175. Some regard Rom. 16:17–20 as a secondary interpolation (so, e.g., Jewett, *Romans*, 986–88); Haacker, *Der Brief des Paulus an die Römer*, 382–88, correctly argues for the originality of the passage.

the saints"). Finally, the Letter to the Philippians, presumably written in Rome, indicates that the mission against Paul continued after his imprisonment: "Beware the dogs, beware the evil workers, beware the mutilation! For we are the circumcision, who serve in the Spirit of God and boast in Christ Jesus and have no confidence in the flesh" (Phil. 3:2–3). Major parts of the Pauline letters and theology are thematically determined by the mission against Paul.

The mission against Paul was probably not a monolithic bloc but was united in the effort to integrate the predominantly gentile Christian Pauline churches again into Judaism. While the Pauline churches were on the way to becoming an independent movement in a predominantly pagan environment,[176] the opposing mission campaigned and pressed for a primarily Jewish identity that could have definitely liberal features (apostolic decrees) but consistently maintained the requirement of circumcision. This movement probably lost its power in the fall of the Jerusalem church in 70 CE. With the Galatian crisis, the unresolved and suppressed problems erupted with full severity. Paul recognized that he must resolve the problem of the law comprehensively under a changed situation. Thus a clarification was unavoidable: Until the Galatian crisis, Paul had accepted a differing view of the Torah among the Jerusalem church (and its sympathizers), on the one hand, and the young mission churches that did not practice circumcision, on the other hand (Gal. 2:7). With the Galatian crisis, the situation changed abruptly; for now the problem of the Torah confronted the Pauline churches from the outside with the demand for circumcision. Paul responded with the doctrine of justification in Galatians and Romans.

The Collection and the Jerusalem Church

The collection must be regarded in its late phase within the framework of the opposing mission. Originally it was probably merely material support by the Greek churches "for the poor among the saints in Jerusalem" (Rom. 15:26). As a consequence of the Galatian crisis, the delivery of the collection took on urgency for Paul, who now connected it with the great theological subject of the unity of the one church of God composed of Jewish and gentile Christians.[177] According to 1 Cor. 16:3, the collection is to be delivered by a delegation (v. 3, without Paul; v. 4, possibly with Paul). According to

176. Cf. Theissen, *Kirche oder Sekte?*, 90–91.
177. On the collection, cf. Georgi, *Remembering the Poor*; Beckheuer, *Paulus und Jerusalem*; Kim, *Die paulinische Kollekte*; Horn, "Die Kollektenthematik"; Downs, *Offering of the Gentiles*; D.-A. Koch, *Geschichte des Urchristentums*, 323–34.

2 Cor. 8:16–20, Paul wanted them to deliver it together with Titus. Now the apostle sees himself compelled to accept a circuitous route by Jerusalem in order to continue his mission in the West. In Rom. 15:30–31 Paul explicitly indicates the tense situation; he fears violent actions from the Jews in Judea, whose hostility against the apostle also influences the conduct of the Jerusalem church. The tensions obviously escalated in Jerusalem,[178] and Paul undertakes the last and possibly even desperate attempt with his journey to rebut the charges against him in order to bring the agitation of his Jewish Christian and Jewish opponents (in Jerusalem, Galatia, Corinth [2 Corinthians], Rome, Philippi) to a halt, to place his relations with the church in Jerusalem on a new basis through the delivery of the collection, and finally to secure his continuance in Judaism through a demonstration of his fidelity to Jewish tradition.[179]

For Paul, but particularly for the churches that participated in the collection in Asia Minor and Greece, the collection must be understood within the context of ancient patronage and the system of reciprocal benefactions.[180] "Not to return gratitude for benefits is a disgrace, and the whole world counts it as such" (Seneca, *Ben.* 3.1.1 LCL). Seneca compares the system of reciprocal benefits with the dance of the Graces in a circle with hands interlocked. "For the reason that a benefit passing in its course from hand to hand returns nevertheless to the giver, the beauty of the whole is destroyed if the course is anywhere broken" (*Ben.* 1.3.3). The gods also are involved in this circle; people should respond to their benefits especially with a noble attitude.[181] For Paul, the collection creates a just balance between Jerusalem and the primarily Greek churches (cf. 2 Cor. 8:13–14): "For if the gentiles have come to share in the spiritual blessings, then they ought to be of service to them in material blessings" (Rom. 15:27). Here material gifts and immaterial gifts come together with a spiritual dimension. Gifts and gifts in return are united in the common participation in the great blessing of the one God, the Christ event. It is noteworthy that Acts is silent as to whether the collection was accepted by the Jerusalem church. Although, according to Acts 24:17 ("After many years I came to bring alms for my people and to offer a sacrifice"), the purpose of Paul's final trip to Jerusalem is known to Luke, he does not mention the

---

178. Cf. H. Betz, *2 Corinthians 8 and 9*, 142.
179. Cf. Horn, "Die letzte Jerusalemreise des Paulus," 34.
180. Wolter, *Paul*, 41–43, emphasizes this aspect of the ethos of ancient friendship.
181. Cf. Seneca, *Ben.* 1.6.3; however, Seneca naturally knows that humankind cannot provide corresponding benefits. "God bestows upon us very many and very great benefits, with no thought of any return, since he has no need of having anything bestowed, nor are we capable of bestowing anything on him; consequently, a benefit is something that is desirable in itself" (*Ben.* 4.9.1 LCL).

collection, although the delivery of it could have been easily placed between Acts 21:19 and 21:20. This remarkable fact has been explained in three alternative ways: (1) The collection was delivered but only (unofficially) under great difficulties.[182] (2) It was within the context of the Nazarite vow (cf. Acts 21:23–24, 26)[183] that the collection was used or delivered partially or in stages.[184] (3) Luke does not report the collection because the Jerusalem church refused it.[185] In fact, there is much to commend the view that the Jerusalem church rejected the collection and that Luke is silent because the rejection did not correspond to his ecclesiology of the one church composed of Jews and gentiles. There are several other reasons for the rejection in the situation of the Jerusalem church at the time: (1) The understanding of the law in Galatians and Romans was out of the question for strict Jewish Christians, amounting to a termination of the fellowship of the churches because now the Torah had at best only a secondary function for Jewish Christians (cf., e.g., Gal. 6:15; Rom. 6:14). (2) Furthermore, the Jewish Christians who had been rejected in Galatia probably added strong support to the Jerusalem position because the rejection of the collection was an additional victory over the Pauline concept of a church of Jesus Christ composed of Jewish and gentile Christians (cf. Gal. 3:26–28). (3) For strict Jewish Christians (and Jews), Paul was nothing other than an apostate who had essentially betrayed the home of Jews and Jewish Christians, the synagogue. (4) From the Jewish perspective, a new movement caused great mistrust, creating competition in the diaspora synagogues, taking away increasingly more of the uncircumcised, and nevertheless claiming to be the "true" Israel (cf. Gal. 6:16). (5) The concern for the synagogue was probably the reason that the Jerusalem church accepted no "impure" money.[186] (6) The negative attitude and the intentional distance from Paul by the Jerusalem church indicate finally that nothing is reported of attempts by the Jerusalem church to liberate Paul from prison or to stand by him at the trial.

The separation between Paul and the Jerusalem church is no coincidence but rather the logical development that began at the apostolic conference at

182. Thus, e.g., Haenchen, *Acts*, 612–14; Georgi, *Remembering the Poor*, 125–26: "Thus the collection was . . . apparently delivered, so to speak, only in a back room and accepted only with whispers."

183. On the Nazarite vow to God, cf. the basic texts in Judg. 13; Num. 6.

184. Cf. Horn, "Paulus, das Nasiräat und die Nasiräer"; D.-A. Koch, *Geschichte des Urchristentums*, 333–34, who nevertheless grants that the collection actually failed.

185. Cf. Lüdemann, *Das frühe Christentum*, 245; J. Gnilka, "Die Kollekte der paulinischen Gemeinden"; Jervell, *Die Apostelgeschichte*, 529–30; Roloff, *Die Apostelgeschichte*, 313.

186. Cf. Josephus, *J.W.* 2.408–9, where the call for the temple priests not to accept money or sacrifices from non-Jews is called the trigger for the outbreak of the war; Haacker, *Der Brief des Paulus an die Römer*, 370–72, considers this partial aspect as the essential starting point for the rejection.

the latest. Also logical and ultimately unavoidable was the conflict with the Jerusalem church and separation from it, which proceeded not primarily from Paul but from Jerusalem. Evidently James made a claim to authority that went beyond Jerusalem and included Antioch (cf. Gal. 2:12) as well as the churches founded by Paul. The relationship between Paul and the Jerusalem church, which was never free from tension (cf. Gal. 1:18–19; 2:6), developed into open opposition at the end of the successful Pauline mission to the gentiles. The theological differences were too great and the characters were too different. Paul did not want the separation from Israel (and the Jerusalem church; cf. Rom. 9:1–3),[187] but he did not prevent it because doing so would have made him unfaithful to his basic convictions. Nevertheless, the church in Jerusalem became increasingly under both theological and political pressure because of Paul. They had to give theological reasons how the Christ-believers on one side should be considered a part of Judaism, while on the other side an expanding wing of the new movement rejected the circumcision of gentile Christians and applied the idea of the true people of God exclusively to them.

> The rejection of the collection demonstrates that, at the end of the founding epoch of early Christianity, it was not unity that existed but rather division. Neither Paul nor the Jerusalem church wanted this outcome, but both accepted it, for neither side was prepared to change its position.

8.6 Theology in Letter Form: The Pauline Letters

The letters of Paul have essentially shaped the history of early Christianity and are thus a part of it. Besides his time with the churches and the visits of his coworkers, Paul especially employed the letters as a means of communication with his churches.[188] The theological and social identity of new churches was not yet established; in particular, the conditions for membership and the ethical norms had to be defined. Many aspects were fluid and needed clarification.

187. Cf. Theissen, "Röm 9–11."

188. On ancient and Pauline letters, cf. Deissmann, *Light from the Ancient East*, 116–213; Roller, *Das Formular der paulinischen Briefe*; Koskenniemi, *Studien zur Idee und Phraseologie*; Doty, *Letters in Primitive Christianity*; Stowers, *Letter Writing in Greco-Roman Antiquity*; Schnider and Stenger, *Studien zum neutestamentlichen Briefformular*; Malherbe, *Ancient Epistolary Theorists*; Klauck, *Ancient Letters and the New Testament*; Porter, *Paul and the Ancient Letter Form*; T. Bauer, *Paulus und die kaiserzeitliche Epistolographie*, passim; Doering, *Ancient Jewish Letters*; Hoegen-Rohls, *Zwischen Augenblickskorrespondenz und Ewigkeitstexten*.

In antiquity the letter served as a substitute for a conversation (cf. Cicero, *Philippica* in M. Antonium 2.7; Seneca, *Ep.* 40.1, "I never receive a letter from you without our being immediately together"; *Ep.* 75.1–8). From the time of Epicurus,[189] the form of the letter had a firm place in philosophical-theological instruction that was intended to provide knowledge, self-knowledge, and change of behavior. The Pauline letters also aim for knowledge and impact; through coordinated and intertwining argumentation, the forms of understanding were meant to be developed, and behavioral norms to be practiced. As the initiator or a part of a communication, the Pauline letter offers the recipient a meaning that aims at the realization of the communication through the manner of its presentation. A special task was given to all of the parts of the letter within this process. The prescript opens the letter as a full text; the situation behind the communication is established, and at the same time the purpose is defined. In the body of the letter, Paul develops various strategies of action and introduces ideas and roles in order to work through a problem that was under debate. The ending of the letter had a twofold function: it summarized the main topics of the letter and at the same time discussed the future of the relationship between the writer and the recipients.

Of the many possible genres of ancient letters,[190] for the Pauline letters the letter of friendship and the philosophical letter are significant. The letter of friendship serves for the maintenance of personal contact between friends. Indeed, the letter is only an imperfect substitute for the spatial separation between writer and recipient; however, the author is present, so to speak. The letter is a reminder of the basis of the friendship, and through it the relationship is renewed and the prospect of a reunion in the near future eases the pain of separation. Paul also repeatedly reminds the churches of the basis of their common relationship (1 Cor. 15:1; Gal. 3:1); he longs for his churches (1 Thess. 2:17; Gal. 4:20) and hopes to come to them soon (1 Thess. 2:18; Rom. 1:11; 15:32; Phil. 2:24). As a substitute for his presence, he sends messengers or letters (1 Thess. 3:1–2; 1 Cor. 5:3–4). He is concerned to justify his conduct and to clear away hindrances that still stand in the way of his coming in the near future (2 Cor. 1:15–22). In the philosophical letters (e.g., Cynic letters, letters of Epicurus, Seneca, *Epistulae morales*) one frequently finds, as in Paul, a combination of didactic and ethical sections. Philosophical reflection is combined

189. Cf. here particularly the *Letter to Menoecus*, by Epicurus, as a parallel in substance; on the significant parallels between Epicurus and Paul, cf. P. Eckstein, *Gemeinde, Brief und Heilsbotschaft*.

190. Stowers, *Letter Writing in Greco-Roman Antiquity*, 49ff., proposes six types of letters: (1) letters of friendship, (2) family letters, (3) letters of praise or blame, (4) admonitory letters, (5) letters of recommendation, (6) apologetic letters.

with questions of a practical way of life. The self-portrayal and the personal witness of the author occupy a major part of the communication. Seneca repeatedly presents Socrates as a model and becomes himself an exemplum.[191] Paul also offers himself to his churches as an example (1 Thess. 1:6; 1 Cor. 11:1; 4.16–17; Gal. 4:12; Phil. 3:17; 4:9), and distinct autobiographical portions are means of his argumentation (Gal. 1:13ff.; Phil. 1:12–26; 3:4ff.). Other elements that are present in the topics in Greco-Roman letters are also in the letters of Paul: praise, blame, admonition, comfort, accusation, and defense. Paul takes on no specific genre of the ancient letter, but he employs conventions of the ancient letter and at the same time employs them for his own purpose.

This fact is evident especially in the opening and closing parts of the letter, where Paul makes characteristic expansions that go beyond ancient conventions as he establishes a three-dimensional communication: Besides the apostle as the sender and the church as the recipient, God or Christ appears as the essential subject of the event (cf. 1 Cor. 1:1–2: "Paul, called to be an apostle of Christ Jesus through the will of God, . . . to the church of God in Corinth"). The heaping up of christological titles is especially striking in the prescripts (in 1 Cor. 1:1–9 alone there are fifteen christological titles).[192] As the focus of fundamental theological perspectives, they formulate and actualize the new reality in which the apostle and the church live. In place of the wish for health and well-being, Paul has a greeting or blessing that is highly theological. With the exception of 1 Thessalonians, the salutation regularly has the words "Grace to you and peace from God our Father and the Lord Jesus Christ" (for the letter closing, cf., e.g., 1 Cor. 16:23: "The grace of the Lord Jesus be with you"). Thus the religious dimension is appealed to in each letter already in the prescript and then confirmed in the postscript; it takes place within the framework of the reality determined by God and Jesus Christ. The communication is expanded: besides the conversation between the apostle and the church that is shaped by the situation and the form of the letter, there is the appearance of God himself, the one who provides salvation and blessing in Jesus Christ and is the essential subject of the new reality and a new communication. The Pauline letters effect a realization of God or Jesus Christ,[193] who are both the subject and object of the saving message. Consequently, they proceed beyond the claim and the conventions of ancient letters, for they actively postulate the presence of God or Christ in the present (epistolary) proclamation of the gospel; the Pauline letters are "kerygmatic epistles";[194] thus

---

191. Cf. Seneca, *Ep.* 20.34–35 and passim.

192. Cf. Schnelle, "Heilsgegenwart."

193. Cf. Hoegen-Rohls, *Zwischen Augenblickskorrespondenz und Ewigkeitstexten*, 90.

194. So correctly Hoegen-Rohls, *Zwischen Augenblickskorrespondenz und Ewigkeitstexten*, 92–117 (the Pauline letters as "kerygmatic letters"). However, this definition is based on content

they are—in continuity with ancient epistolary conventions—an independent new subgenre that one can describe as an "apostolic letter."[195] This designation suggests not that the letter is necessarily written by an apostle but that the authentic Pauline letters formulate, postulate, and define the binding apostolic faith, the (only) valid form of the gospel. Significant and striking features in these letters are the thematic variety, the predominantly argumentative style, and especially their length. While Philemon corresponds largely to the scope of an ancient letter, all other Pauline letters are much longer. Thus the longest previously known private letter from the Greco-Roman period corresponds to the length of Galatians;[196] that is, the two Corinthian letters and Romans are unique in the ancient context.

The few statements about the handling of the Pauline letters attest the high value that was already attributed to them. The Pauline letters were read to the churches from the beginning (cf. 1 Thess. 5:27; Rom. 16:16), and the recipients received the original communication directly in person (cf. Gal. 6:11). The apostle himself anticipates the circulation of his letters, as the plural "the churches in Galatia" in Gal. 1:2 and the prescript in 2 Cor. 1:1b ("Corinth and all the saints in Achaia") indicate. The Pauline letters were written in response to an actual occasion; nevertheless, they were far more than occasional writings. In the time of Paul's absence, they became the substitute for the apostle and contained the Pauline gospel and the necessary ethical instructions for living in the community. In the churches they in no way disappeared into the cabinets, for with the exception of Ephesus, Paul stayed in each community for a comparatively brief period. Consequently, his letters gained great significance even during his lifetime. The convincing power of the Pauline letters is even praised by the opponents in 2 Cor. 10:10–11 ("for, as some say, his letters are weighty and strong"). This is no coincidence, for a writing such as Romans—with its sweeping argumentation, artful disposition, wealth of topics, high proportion of fully new thoughts, and lasting impact—can be included alongside every letter of Seneca or every oration of a Dio of Prusa.

First Thessalonians was written circa 50 CE in Corinth and is the oldest writing in the NT.[197] The apostle Paul enters into actual questions of the church in this advisory letter. An inquiry about the fate of Christians who have

---

and is not a convincing form-critical classification that does justice to the particularities of the Pauline letters.

195. Cf. Boring, *I and II Thessalonians*, 37: "1 Thessalonians Is a New Generic Departure, the Apostolic Letter."

196. Cf. Arzt-Grabner, *2. Korinther*, 56–57.

197. On the historical situations and theological intentions of the Pauline letters as a whole, cf. Schnelle, *Apostle Paul*, 171–358.

died before the return of Jesus has special significance (cf. 1 Thess. 4:13–18). Are they excluded from the coming reunion with the Lord? Paul answers with the indication that both Christians who have died and those who are alive will in the same way be reunited when Christ returns. First Corinthians originated in 54 CE in Ephesus and has both an advisory and instructional function. In Corinth rival groups had formed (1 Cor. 1:10–4:21). There were various opinions over questions of sexual ethics (cf. 1 Cor. 5–7), disputes about the eating of food offered to idols (1 Cor. 8–10), about conduct in the worship service (1 Cor. 11), the significance of the gifts of the Spirit (1 Cor. 12–14), and the understanding of the resurrection from the dead (1 Cor. 15). Apparently, some in the Corinthian church were followers of an enthusiastic Christianity that emphasized the Spirit, and such members regarded themselves as already united with Christ (cf. 1 Cor. 4:8; 6:12a). Paul responds to the striving for spiritual gifts and the speculative wisdom with the theology of the cross. According to the will of God, the foolishness of the preaching of the cross alone, not human wisdom (1 Cor. 1:18ff.), saves. The cross nullifies all human boasting and striving, for it powerfully expresses the paradox of the Christian faith: It was not in the height of human wisdom and knowledge, but in the depth of suffering and death that the Father of Jesus Christ demonstrated his care for humankind. Second Corinthians was written from Macedonia in circa 55 CE, not long after the writing of the first letter to Corinth. In the church at Corinth, active now were other Christian preachers who boasted of special revelations, ecstatic experiences, and a brilliant self-portrayal and interpretation of the Scripture (2 Cor. 10–13). They charged Paul, on the other hand, with a weak appearance and claimed that he did not have the qualifications of an apostle. Paul now attempts to clarify to the church that following the Crucified One also means suffering and that people should place their trust not in their own power but in God alone. Second Corinthians is, to some extent, a witness for Paul's theology of the cross as it was personally applied and lived.

Galatians is a polemical work written in the middle of battle that is probably addressed to the churches in the land of Galatia, which lies in the region of present-day Ankara. Shortly after Paul had founded these churches, he received the report of the successful appearance of the strict Jewish Christian opposing missionaries. They maintained that it was necessary, in order to complete one's faith, to keep the law of Moses and to submit to circumcision as a sign of the covenant of God with his people. Paul thus regarded his mission among the gentiles apart from circumcision as threatened and wrote (in the late fall of 55 CE in Macedonia) an intense letter, in which urgent warning, theological argumentation, and tender appeals are impressively

combined. The special situation in Galatia became for Paul the occasion to
develop his doctrine of justification clearly for the first time and to emphasize
its fundamental significance.

Romans gives precise information about the time and occasion when it was
written (Rom. 15:22–29). After the delivery of the collection for the church in
Jerusalem, Paul wants to come to Rome in order to begin his missionary work
in Spain from there. The announcement of this visit is the external occasion
of the letter, which was written in Corinth in the spring of 56 CE. Romans
is characterized by its extraordinary length (cf. Rom. 16:22) and a carefully
designed structure; thus it can be described as a discourse in letter form.[198] Because of the financial support that Paul needs, he describes in detail the basic
content of his preaching. The major theme of the letter is the righteousness
of God, that is, God's faithfulness and care, which is revealed in the gospel of
Jesus Christ (1:16–17). The conviction "that one is justified by faith without
the works of the law" (Rom. 3:28) opens for Paul the possibility of taking the
gospel to the end of the earth. The law remains for him the word and will of
God, but not the basis of salvation or a condition for salvation. The topic
of the righteousness of God through faith in Jesus also opens the possibility
of a new perspective for Israel (Rom. 9–11). Paul is thus convinced that, at
the return of Jesus Christ, Israel will be converted. Philippians is written to
a church with which Paul has been deeply connected since its founding. The
apostle writes this letter of friendship from prison in Rome, probably in 60
CE. The occasion for the letter is the gratitude for the material support of
the church, which an emissary of the church with the name of Epaphroditus
has delivered. The apostle has become old and desires to die and be with
Christ (Phil. 1:20–21). Nevertheless, he finds the strength to place before a
church shaped by conflict once more the model of the story of Jesus Christ
(Phil. 2:6–11). The Letter to Philemon was also written in Rome around 61
CE. With this letter Paul makes an intercession for a runaway slave named
Onesimus to his master, Philemon. Evidently Onesimus had caused damages
in the house of Philemon and found Paul in order to ask for mediation in
the conflict. As a result of the conflict, Onesimus became a Christian. Paul
requests that Philemon accept his slave as a brother in Christ and then place
him at Paul's disposal as a helper for his missionary work.

The letters of Paul made history. They were not only an effective means for guiding
the church and establishing its identity but also the cornerstone of the abiding

198. Cf. Keck, *Romans*, 20–25.

influence of Paul in the history of early Christianity. They formed the theoretical foundation for setting the basic course of the world mission without circumcision and the presupposition for the deutero-Pauline letters (see below, 10.3.2). In addition, either directly or indirectly they influenced almost all of the writings of the NT (see below, 13.5.2). Above all, the Pauline letters also created a theological cosmos that has been, as an abiding emotional and intellectual challenge, a source of fascination throughout the ages.

8.7 Paul and the Development of Early Christianity as an Independent Movement

From what point can one speak of early Christianity as an independent movement or even speak of it as a new religion? In order to answer this disputed question,[199] one must make methodological observations. What happens when, out of two ancient cultures, each with its own fixed religious system, something new comes into existence that has not existed before? How is one to interpret the event when more happens than merely the assimilation of Jews by birth to the Hellenistic environment or when Greeks/Romans by birth convert to the Jewish religion?

Conditions for the Development of a New Movement

If a new movement wants to establish its own identity and remain permanently, at least ten conditions must be met: (1) The new group must define its boundaries; that is, it is necessary to designate the differences and agreements between it and the world around it. (2) Inherent in this process is especially the introduction of a new founder of the discourse (see above, 4.3) or new authorities who either remove or at least surpass what existed previously.

---

199. The positions on this question are varied and almost always affected by ideological evaluations and with social-psychological theories. See the history of research in Wander, *Trennungsprozesse*, 8–39. In current scholarship two alternative concepts have been proposed. On the one hand is the view of a "parting of the ways" (cf. Dunn, *Parting of the Ways*), according to which a gradual separation of Judaism and Christianity occurred, with the actual date variously determined (the time of Paul, around 70 CE, or around 135 CE). The alternative view is that Christianity and Judaism did not finally separate until the third or even the beginning of the fourth century CE as Christianity became the religion of the empire. Just as there was a variety of churches/confessions in Christianity ("Christianities"), a variety of directions also existed in Judaism ("Judaisms"), which were sometimes in conflict with one another but nevertheless belonged to a complex unity. They stood not in opposition to each other as two distinct religions but as groups who practiced various forms of Jewish and/or Christian faith (cf. Schnelle, *Die getrennten Wege*, 2–10).

(3) With these authorities the introduction of rituals and norms is established that are central to the formation of the identity of the new movement. (4) The new movement must be able to designate its place in history, that is, its prehistory, its present, and its future. (5) Every new movement must appear with a certain public claim that makes it intelligible and familiar. (6) When a new movement develops its own language, this is a clear indication of the conscious formation of identity. (7) All of this succeeds only when a comprehensive ethical and ideological worldview and set of values is established that can be understood within the surrounding societal and cultural systems.[200] Only where a cultural-political connectivity exists can a movement last permanently.[201] (8) This worldview and value system must include signals of both differentiation and integration and distinguish itself by a normative coherence; that is, opposing values are regarded in a first step as subordinated in order then to be transferred into a higher coherent value system. Thus the claim of validity must be formulated and integration strategies developed in order to integrate competing perspectives into a higher value system. (9) This step takes place as a value generalization; central perspectives of the respective traditions are presented at such a higher level that specific currents then recognize the new norms. (10) A movement must differentiate itself permanently if it is to survive. The—intended or unintended—formation of new structural types increases the possibilities to test various strategies and to increase the capability for adaptation and survival.[202]

The System-Quality of Pauline Theology

The subsystem of early Christianity shaped by Paul especially meets these criteria.[203]

1. He intentionally and programmatically transcends ethnic, cultural, and religious boundaries and propagates a universal concept of messianic redemption that incorporates all peoples. It was not demarcation but acculturation

---

200. Cf. Parsons, *System of Modern Societies*, 7–9.

201. Cf. Parsons, *System of Modern Societies*, 8, 7–9.

Cf. Parsons, *System of Modern Societies*, 8: "Any society depends for its continuation as a system on the inputs it receives through interchanges with its environing systems. Self-sufficiency in relation to environments, then, means stability of interchange relationships and capacity to control interchanges in the interest of societal functioning."

202. Cf. Parsons, *Societies*, 22–25.

203. Cf. Theissen, "Judentum und Christentum bei Paulus," 354: "Paul is a crucial figure in the separation of the ways between Christians and Jews." Luz, "Das 'Auseinandergehen der Wege,'" 65ff.; L. Johnson, *Among the Gentiles*, 130ff. Molthagen, "Die ersten Konflikte der Christen in der griechisch-römischen Welt," describes these processes from the view of the ancient historian.

(cf. 1 Cor. 9:20–22) as well as trans-ethnic conceptions (cf. Gal. 3:26–28) that significantly defined the early Christian mission. This universalizing is the crucial precondition for the establishment of a new value system. In terms of the sociology of religion, every religion is defined by particularistic and universalistic elements/tendencies insofar as it must secure its own identity through demarcation and yet by—gradual and varied—opening for new members it guarantees its survival into the future.[204] In ancient Judaism, universalistic tendencies are present,[205] but as a whole the tendency is oriented toward election, Torah, temple, and land: the particularistic elements are predominant. The Jewish concept is primarily characterized by the view that the nations will come and participate in the unique election of Israel;[206] Israel understands itself as the "light to the nations" (cf. 1QSb 4.25–28) and expects the messiah of Israel to subjugate the nations or place them under his rule at the end of the ages (cf. Pss. 2:8f.; 72:8ff.; 110:1; Pss. Sol. 17.30). Paul is undoubtedly influenced by the universalistic elements of the OT/ancient Judaism (especially Isaiah).[207] However, from his basic understanding emerges a totally different relationship of the particularistic and universalistic elements from that in ancient Judaism: While in ancient Judaism a comprehensive active mission is not verifiable,[208] Paul actively transcends the existing boundaries through a universally oriented public mission. He not only postulates a universalism but also actively puts it into practice; thus Judaism and emerging Christianity are shaped by fully different internal and external movements. To be sure, Israel maintains its special eschatological role as the elect people of God within the Pauline concept, but in the Pauline mission it becomes actually and massively relativized. A

204. On the concept of universalism, cf. Figl, Rüterswörden, and Wander, "Universalismus/ Partikularismus," 778. The definition by Leeuw, "Universalismus und Partikularismus I," is still useful; universalism means the denial of the limitation of religious goods to a specific group: "The universalistic tendency is directed to an increasingly wider circle until it finally places humanity as such in direct relation to God."

205. The problem is discussed in all of its complexity, employing all relevant texts, in Kraus, *Das Volk Gottes*, 16–110; cf. also the analyses of Philonic and Qumran texts by G. Holtz, *Damit Gott sei alles in allem*, 87–167, 309–504.

206. Cf., e.g., Philo, *Moses* 2.44: "Each nation would abandon its peculiar ways, and, throwing overboard their ancestral customs, turn to honouring our laws alone. For, when the brightness of their shining is accompanied by national prosperity, it will darken the light of the others as the risen sun darkens the stars" (LCL). Also 1QH 6.12: "And all nations will recognize your faithfulness and all nations your glory."

207. Cf. Wilk, *Die Bedeutung des Jesajabuches für Paulus*.

208. Cf. Hengel and Schwemer, *Paul between Damascus and Antioch*, 75–90 (not "mission" but "power of attraction"); appropriate is the comment by G. Holtz, *Damit Gott sei alles in allem*, 559: "It is clear in any case that mission in ancient Judaism, as it is always in individual cases, has no comparable value as it does in Paul."

considerable distinction exists between a (partially) postulated universalism and a universalism that is (actually) realized or put into practice!

2. A new theological and sociological entity is formed in the Pauline churches: the unrestricted fellowship of Christians from the Jewish and Greco-Roman tradition on the singular basis of faith and baptism. Paul developed and practiced a new concept of identity beyond traditional religious privileges with the concept of "being in Christ." This transnational and transcultural concept mediated by baptism[209] was not really compatible with Jewish and Greco-Roman concepts of identity, which were primarily based on demarcation and the postulate of their respective superiority. The new group had to first orient itself into the social world of its environment, as the conflicts described in 1 Cor. 8–10 attest. Private invitations, buying in the marketplace, and the participation or nonparticipation in pagan cults/cultic meals confronted Christians increasingly with difficult decisions that with certainty were observed and judged by the respective social surroundings. The conflicts with the synagogue communities (cf., e.g., Acts 17:1–9, 10–15; 18:1–17) could not remain unnoticed;[210] that is, here the public activities and the public claim of the new movement could not be overlooked.

3. With his theological concept, Paul understands the movement as a third entity beyond that of Judaism and the gentiles and establishes both boundaries and points of contact. His self-understanding is evident in 1 Cor. 1:22–23; 9:20–23; 10:32; Gal. 3:26–28; 5:6.[211] If Paul, according to 1 Cor. 9:2–21, can become a Jew to the Jews and a gentile to the gentiles, then he is neither Jew nor gentile in the full sense, but the representative of a new movement and religion. The consciousness of the early Christians as a third group of people alongside Jews and Greeks is a crucial factor within the value generalization and is expressed in 1 Cor. 1:22–23 and 10:32. In 1 Cor. 1:22 Paul describes the

209. Theissen, "Die urchristliche Taufe," 90ff., correctly emphasizes that the differentiation of early Christianity from Judaism was connected with a new understanding of baptism that developed in the context of the gentile mission and was fully shaped by Paul: "The origin of baptism is closely connected with the origin of a new religion that was independent of an origin, oriented toward reconciliation, and formed a subculture, which brought together people from many nations in small communities. In the place of a relationship by birth came a relationship by rebirth. The physical birth was replaced by the construction of a new birth mediated in a ritual. The social construction of the new person is thus not an arbitrary marginal appearance of this new religion, but is its constitutive presupposition" (93–94).

210. Cf. D.-A. Koch, "Die Christen als neue Randgruppe," 366: "The developing Christianity was noticed relatively early at both the individual and the institutional level."

211. In 1 Thess. 2:14–15 (around 50 CE), Paul distinguishes between the Christian churches in Judea and "the Jews"; i.e., already here is a clear consciousness of the separate identity of the new movement: "For you have become imitators, brothers and sisters, of the churches of God in Judea, for you have suffered from your own people just as they suffered from the Jews, who killed the Lord Jesus and the prophets and persecuted us."

theology of the cross as the decisive difference from the symbolic world of Jews and Greeks. Because the word of the cross is not compatible with this worldview, it must be an offense to the Jews and foolishness to the Greeks. In 1 Cor. 10:32 Paul challenges the Corinthian church to cause no offense to the Jews, the Greeks, and the "church of God." The programmatic statement in Gal. 3:28 ("Here there is neither Jew nor Greek") also indicates the intentional relativizing and transcending of traditional cultural definitions. Paul positions the entire church as an independent entry in relation to Jews and Greek. Therefore, Paul and the early churches do not select as the self-designation συναγωγή, but the political concept ἐκκλησία.[212] They do not become a new subgroup within the synagogue, but organize themselves from the beginning as a new independent movement alongside and in competition with the synagogue.[213] Paul reclaims the concept of freedom exclusively for the new movement (cf. Gal. 4:31; 5:1). The "new covenant" is not the improved edition of the old but rather a qualitatively new event, characterized by the Spirit and surpassing glory (cf. 2 Cor. 3:6, 10). Finally, according to 2 Cor. 5:17, the baptized and Spirit-endowed believers have the status of being a "new creation," which means that the church is considerably more than a sociological entity! Paul asks the Corinthians, "Do you not know that the saints will judge the world [κόσμος]? . . . Do you not know that we will judge angels?" (1 Cor. 6:2a, 3a). If the church will judge even the world and the angels, who are heavenly beings, and the whole creation awaits the revealing of the sons of God at the end of time (Rom. 8:19–21), then the church is a cosmic entity.[214] There can scarcely be a greater autonomy and self-consciousness than that!

4. With this consciousness came the development of a new language as the direct expression of the formation of the identity (see below, 13.1). This process began prior to Paul and accelerates with him. It is evident both in the semantic reshaping of concepts and in the new accentuations or new formations. Semantic reshaping is present, for example, in εὐαγγέλιον (gospel) and ἐκκλησία (congregation/church). A new accent or expansion is evident in the concept of faith; the use and the content of πίστις or πιστεύειν go far beyond the common usage in the pagan environment. A significant new stamp is given, for example, to the phrase ἐν Χριστῷ (in Christ).[215] The external

212. Cf. Theissen, "Kirche oder Sekte?," 87–88.
213. Cf. D.-A. Koch, "Die Christen als neue Randgruppe," 361. Texts such as Acts 16:11–39; 17:1–9, 10–14; 18:1–17; 19:6–20 leave no doubt (even with Luke's schematization) that the respective local synagogues vehemently rejected the Christians and did not accept them.
214. Schnelle, "Ethik und Kosmologie bei Paulus."
215. On ἐν Χριστῷ, cf. Deissmann, *Die neutestamentliche Formel "in Christo Jesu"*; Neugebauer, *In Christus*; Schnelle, *Gerechtigkeit und Christusgegenwart*, 106–23, 225–35; Seifrid, "'In Christ'"; Roloff, *Die Kirche*, 86–99; C. Strecker, *Die liminale Theologie des Paulus*, 189–211.

evidence is significant: In all the Pauline letters, ἐν Χριστῷ Ἰησοῦ with variant forms appears sixty-four times, and the derived phrase ἐν κυρίῳ appears thirty-seven times. Paul is not the creator of the phrase ἐν Χριστῷ, as the pre-Pauline baptismal traditions (1 Cor. 1:30; 2 Cor. 5:17; Gal. 3:26–28) indicate. However, he can be considered as the essential proponent of this concept, which for him becomes a brief definition of being a Christian:[216] ἐν Χριστῷ in 1 Thess. 2:14; 4:16; 1 Cor. 1:2; 3:1; 2 Cor. 5:17; Gal. 1:22; 3:26, 28; Rom. 6:11; Phil. 1:1; or ἐν κυρίῳ in Rom. 16:1, 11, 13 means nothing other than "Christian" and is thus also an identifying and demarcating self-designation! In addition, such phrases as "called to belong in Jesus Christ" (Rom. 1:6), "baptized into Christ" (Gal. 3:27; Rom. 6:3); "joint heirs of Christ" (Rom. 8:17), "body of Christ" or "one body in Christ" (1 Cor. 12:27; Rom. 12:5), "sanctified in Christ Jesus" or "saints in Christ Jesus" (1 Cor. 1:2; Phil. 1:1); "put on Christ" (Gal. 3:27), "belonged to Christ" (2 Cor. 10:7; Gal. 3:29); "dead in Christ" (1 Thess. 4:16) document the consciousness of the identity of Paul and his churches as Christians.

5. The God of the Christians belonged—in contrast to Jewish belief—to no particular people, and—in contrast to Greek gods—he did not intervene for a particular people. This fundamental universal theological conception is not compatible with a Jewish identity oriented toward election, Torah, temple, and land.[217] The Greek and Roman world of the gods is also distinguished fundamentally from this concept. This consciousness is determined not by historical factors, ritual correctness, and trust in the powers of the tradition and of ethical virtue but by faith in Jesus Christ as the only saving authority and by belonging to the Christian faith and its worship and participating in God's eschatological salvation in the present.

6. New constructions of meaning such as early Christianity could only come into existence when they had the historical capacity to connect.[218] Inasmuch as every linguistic element includes and conveys elements of a specific

216. For the complete breadth of the concept of ἐν Χριστῷ, cf. Schnelle, *Gerechtigkeit und Christusgegenwart*, 117–22.

217. In terms of the sociology of religion, early Christianity developed very quickly from a subcultural ethnic religion (as an orientation within ancient Judaism) to a subcultural universal religion with the character of a religion of redemption and reconciliation; for a typology, cf. Mensching, *Soziologie der Religion*, 24ff. Newer models (Christianity as parallel to Judaism, Christianity as limitation of Judaism, or Christianity as transformation of Judaism) are described by Theissen, "Judentum und Christentum bei Paulus," 332ff.

218. Cf. Rüsen, "Was heißt: Sinn der Geschichte?," 38: "Historical meaning must meet the condition of genetic capacity to incorporate and combine disparate elements in which subjective constructions proceed from objective data in interpretative interaction with the human past and that develop both in relation to the given data and at the same time in relation to the needs of the subjects defined by them."

worldview, the so-called topical horizon comes into play.[219] Every linguistic expression refers beyond the concrete situation toward a summary horizon of all competing worldviews of a society. A statement is plausible and has persuasive power for the addressees when it takes up the prior knowledge specific to a culture and connects with it through variation or an alternative new interpretation. Pauline Christianity demonstrated this capacity for connection in a special way, for it integrated and transformed, so to speak, Jewish, Hellenistic-Jewish, and Greco-Roman conceptions. These value generalizations occurred especially in the following areas: (a) Paul accepted Jewish monotheism as well as the monotheistic streams in Greco-Roman thought and connected them with the exemplary story of Jesus Christ. (b) For ancient people, the spirit (πνεῦμα, νοῦς) was the natural connection to the deity.[220] Early Christianity and particularly Paul took over the linkage between the divine and the human with their language of the Holy Spirit. (c) The concept of love as the fulfillment of the whole law (cf. Rom. 13:8–10) enabled both Jews and Greeks/Romans to bring their legal traditions and basic ethical convictions into the new movement.

7. Paul especially had a new authority to become the founder of a new discourse with respect to Judaism and the Greco-Roman world: Jesus Christ (see above, 4.3). Because of Jesus Christ, he evaluated his own past in Judaism (and thus Judaism itself) in extremely negative terms. After he lists his advantages as a Pharisaic Jew in Phil. 3:4b–6, he emphasizes in Phil. 3:8: "Truly, I count all things as loss because of the surpassing knowledge of Christ Jesus my Lord. For his sake I count all things loss and consider it filth [σκύβαλα] so that I may gain Christ." Thus Paul engages in a new evaluation of the previous system of knowledge in Judaism; the term σκύβαλα is fecal terminology (poop) and designates what has been "finished," what one has left behind.[221] Paul in no way changed from one form of Judaism to another; rather, he became a part of a new movement from Judaism for the sake of the

219. The "topical horizon" is derived from basic rhetorical theory. It attempts to grasp all elements that lead to generally recognized convictions; cf. Kaiser and Oesterreich, *Die Rede von Gott und der Welt*.

220. Two examples: The rhetor Isocrates (436–338 BCE) praises the logos: "And if there is need to speak in brief summary of this power, we shall find that none of the things which are done with intelligence [φρονίμως] occur without logos [ἀλόγως], but that logos is our guide [ἡγεμών] in all of our actions as well as our thoughts, and is most employed by those who have the most wisdom [νοῦς]" (*Nicocles* 7–9 LCL). Cicero, *Academica priori* 1.29, speaks of the power that holds the world together: "And this force they say is the soul of the world, and the all-pervading reason is also perfect intelligence and wisdom, which they entitle God, and is a sort of 'providence' knowing the things that fall within its province, governing especially the heavenly bodies, and then those things on earth that concern mankind" (LCL).

221. Cf. Passow, *Handwörterbuch der Griechischen Sprache* 2/2:1468.

nations. In addition to Phil. 3:8, the following factors indicate that what Paul experienced was a conversion. (a) Paul now belonged to the movement that he once wanted to "destroy" (Gal. 1:13, πορθεῖν). (b) Within the Jewish thought world, a crucified man as messiah was unimaginable, for he was considered as cursed by God (cf. use of Deut. 21:23 in Gal. 3:13). This fundamental contradiction was known not only to Paul the former Pharisee but also to his opponents. (c) In the eyes of the Jews, Paul was considered a renegade, an apostate who, according to OT tradition, was worthy of death (cf. Acts 21:21, 27–31).[222] In conversions, external perception is always clearer than self-perception! (d) Paul could not evade the fact that his westward-oriented mission separated him increasingly from Jerusalem and from Judaism.

8. Pauline theology represents the first relatively closed early Christian system of knowledge. Every worldview, political program, philosophy, and of course, every religion generates knowledge.[223] Knowledge is socially communicated meaning that is recognized by individuals, then groups, and finally by the society. This process of recognition can take a considerable amount of time. It is formed first through discourse and then through conflict, which at the end leads to either a voluntary or a forced acceptance. Thus, as a rule, groups prevail in their conceptions of reality when they gain influence through argumentative discourse and/or by force. Pauline theology is a new system of knowledge that distinguishes itself in relation to Judaism and Hellenism not only with totally new content, but especially with fundamentally altered conditions of relevance and allocation.[224] It provides new knowledge about God and God's saving work in Jesus Christ "for us," about the place of humankind in the world between good and evil, about election as victory over capricious fate, about life after biological death, and about true ethical activity in love.

Of course, new systems are based partially on the old, but crucial is the degree of agreements and deviations between the old and the new stock of knowledge. In Paul the agreements with Judaism consist primarily of knowledge of the tradition. He deviates sharply, however, in the interpretation of this knowledge of the tradition to the point of irreconcilable conflicts. To a lesser extent the same is true for his relationship to Hellenism. Here also there are, besides the sharp contrasts (e.g., polytheism), especially in the area of ethics, common areas that can be integrated into a new foundational system.

---

222. Cf., e.g., Lev. 24:16: "Anyone who blasphemes the name of Yahweh must be put to death; the whole community should stone him"; also Num. 15:30.

223. Cf. Knoblauch, *Wissenssoziologie*, 353.

224. It involves a new structural foundation and conceptual framework; thus it is inappropriate to speak of different "identity markers" (so Tiwald, *Das Frühjudentum und die Anfänge des Christentums*, 49).

Added to this are fully new traditions that cannot be integrated seamlessly or even in any other way into the old system of knowledge. Consequently, there are necessary processes of adoption and rejection, partial acceptance, new interpretation of specific items, and/or a combination of old and new knowledge. They naturally occur again in various ways, depending on the standpoint of the participant. Thus, with great deviations, inevitably conflicts and possibly a separation take place because the common basis of knowledge no longer suffices and the new elements are evaluated in fully different ways. Moreover, knowledge systems are always associated with the changes in the times, and new challenges, questions, and problems seek new answers that cannot be given by the previous fund of knowledge. As one who knows both the Jewish and Hellenistic knowledge systems, Paul knew about the asymmetric structure of his proclamation, and the explosive force of the new message was clear from the beginning: "But we preach Christ crucified, an offense to the Jews and foolishness to the nations" (1 Cor. 1:23).[225]

The partial and continuing adoption of concepts of identity shared in Judaism by early Christian authors in the first century (e.g., Matthew, James) and the continuing conflicts (see below, 11.5) among Jews, Christians, and Romans do not undermine the thesis of an early beginning of the formation of Christianity as an independent movement.[226] Paul could unite something in his person that could not remain a unity in historical and institutional perspective. The developments took place in different places and at different times, but the Christianity shaped by Paul and the Judaism that was demarcated from it took up irreversible positions in a period of painful separation. The dichotomy "Jewish Christian" was not taken up by every author or every movement, and it was not clear in every time and place in the same way what was considered "Christian." Boundaries could be drawn in various ways. Moreover, the question remains whether polemics in texts are to be understood as a dispute or as a fracture. Finally, one can object that categories such as "Jewish" and "Christian" are a schematizing and oversimplification in reference to the diversity of

225. This concept was unacceptable to the Jews on the basis of Deut. 21:23, and for the Greeks and Romans it was highly offensive, as Cicero, *Leg.* 2.28, declares: "One may indeed deify the virtues, but not the vices."

226. A fully different view is that of Daniel Boyarin, who vehemently rejects the model of a "parting of the ways" and instead argues that the relationship of Judaism-Christianity be "understood as a circulation system in which discursive elements move from non-Christian Jews and then again return and could develop through the system as it passes through" (Boyarin, "Als Christen noch Juden waren," 120). Thus he concludes that even in the second century CE "no one can say precisely where one stops and the other begins" (121). Similarly, Frankemölle, *Frühjudentum und Urchristentum*, 437; Tiwald, *Das Frühjudentum und die Anfänge des Christentums*, 48, who understands early Christianity primarily as a reformed Judaism and places the final separation in the third or fourth century CE.

ancient Judaism and the continuing process of forming an identity. However, categories are unavoidable for one who wants to make historical process intelligible. The theories of an abiding variety, of fluid transitions, of the pluralizing of "Christianities" until the second and third centuries CE do not keep one from terminological and historical lack of clarity and must be verified in the texts. Pauline Christianity introduced two points of differentiation that (earlier or later, open or haltingly) made a separation from Judaism unavoidable: (a) the abandonment of circumcision and the food laws; (b) faith in the crucified Messiah as a decisive mark of identity. Both points were taken over by the four Gospels (see below, 13.5) and defined the further historical development. Undoubtedly, later authors established their theological worlds on this basis in various ways and in more or less proximity to Judaism, but the basic foundation given by Paul remained. Those who have their own place of assembly, new name, new rituals and rules, communal meals, new holy day with its own worship services, and their own exclusive self-understanding do not belong to any other group and are not recognized as such. Moreover, at no time was any form of the emerging Christianity recognized from an orientation within Judaism as a legitimate variant expression of Jewish existence, for then Judaism—in addition to basic theological differences—risked its religious-legal special place within the Roman Empire (see below, 12.2). Thus, for religio-political reasons, it was necessary for Judaism to keep its distance from emerging Christianity in order not to lose its privileges.[227]

Early Christianity developed as an independent movement primarily in its Pauline form. While it abandoned circumcision and food laws as the central marks of Jewish identity and placed before the Jews (and Greeks/Romans) the fully unacceptable faith in a crucified Messiah at the center of its knowledge system, it positioned itself intentionally as the third entity in the ancient world. Anyone who was "in Christ" was thus a Christian. Like the segmentation of early Christianity into three subsystems (see above, 6.9), this formed the presupposition for its survival. Drastic historical developments or catastrophes such as the fall of the Jerusalem church in 70 could be overcome because the Antiochian-Pauline subsystem had already created a fully independent missionary region, and the Galilean-Syrian subsystem was able to transmit the Jesus tradition independent of the Jerusalem church.

---

227. Cf. Stemberger, "Die Juden im Römischen Reich," 6: "In historical terms, the privileged stand at the beginning. They enable the incorporation of Jews into the Roman Empire." Cf. Schnelle, *Die getrennten Wege von Römern, Juden und Christen*, 45–70.

9

The Crisis of Early Christianity
around 70 CE

B etween 60 and 70 CE a critical culmination occurred within the history of
the theology of the early church. Problems of both the internal logic of
faith and the external influences resulted in the necessity of making a literary
and theological new orientation. Three of the most important figures of early
Christianity died as martyrs almost contemporaneously shortly before the
Jewish War. James the brother of the Lord died in 62 CE in Jerusalem; Paul
and Peter probably died in 64 CE in Rome. Their deaths constituted a clear
turning point for the self-understanding of Christianity, also precipitating a
new literature. In place of the eyewitnesses and appearances and the personal
activity of the apostles for the expansion of Christianity, the written record
now takes the form of the new literary genre of the gospel and of the pseudepigraphic letters (Deutero-Paulines and apostolic letters under the names of
Peter, James, and Jude).

9.1 The Deaths of Peter, Paul, and James and the First Persecutions

Simon (Peter), with his brother Andrew, belonged to the first group of disciples
(cf. Mark 1:16–20; John 1:41–42) and was a recognized leading personality
both within the group of disciples and in the early Jerusalem church (see
above, 5.2). The confession of the Messiah (Mark 8:27–30), the symbolic name
"Peter" ("noble rock"; cf. Mark 3:13–16), and the eschatological promise in
Matt. 16:18 clearly indicate his special place, which was not annulled by his

failure at the passion of Jesus (cf. Mark 14:54, 66–72). Peter is listed among
the purported witnesses to the resurrection (cf. 1 Cor. 15:5; Mark 16:7; Luke
24:34) and was the first leader of the Jerusalem church (cf. Gal. 1:18; Acts
1:15; 2:14ff., 38ff.; 3:1ff. and passim). He left Jerusalem in the course of the
persecution under Herod Agrippa I (cf. Acts 12:17) and gradually became an
advocate of the mission without the requirement of circumcision (cf. Gal.
2:11–12; Acts 10:1–11:18). Finally, he engaged in missions among the circle
of Pauline churches (cf. 1 Cor. 1:12; 9:5),[1] and it is totally plausible that he,
in this westward-oriented context, came to Rome, where he probably died in
the course of the Neronian persecution.[2] This fate is indicated especially in
1 Clem. 5.2–4[3] and Ign. *Rom.* 4.1–3[4] as well as 1 Pet. 5:13[5] and John 21:18–19.[6]
A tradition of Peter's martyrdom associated with Rome existed around 100 CE
at the latest. The veneration of Peter's grave in Rome began by the middle of
the second century CE.[7] Thus at the beginning, no apologetic or ideological

1. Cf. Karrer, "Petrus im paulinischen Gemeindekreis."
2. Cf. the carefully considered study (on Peter and Paul) in D.-A. Koch, *Geschichte des Urchristentums*, 415–27.
3. First Clement 5.2–4 reports: "Because of jealousy and envy the greatest and most righteous pillars were persecuted and fought to the death. Let us set before our eyes the good apostles. There was Peter, who because of unrighteous jealousy endured not one or two but many trials, and thus having given his testimony, went to his appointed place of glory" (trans. Holmes). The reference to the martyrdom of Peter and Paul is highly disputed because always the charge is made that a secondary construction stands here because in the background is the attempt to secure power interests. Compare the view in Zwierlein, *Petrus in Rom.* He assigns a late date to 1 Clement (around 125 CE), claiming that it is fully derived from Acts, the Pastoral Epistles, and 1 Peter; he maintains: "The author of '1 Clement' knows 'nothing' of the stay of Peter in Rome, of a persecution of Peter and Paul, and of the martyrdom of the two apostles" (30). For a justified critique of Zwierlein, see Lona, "'Petrus in Rome' und der erste Clemensbrief"; Riesner, "Apostelgeschichte, Pastoralbriefe"; cf. also C. Gnilka, Heid, and Riesner, *Blutzeuge*.
4. Zwierlein, *Petrus in Rom*, 31, sweeps this passage aside with the general indication of the difficulty of dating the letters of Ignatius. However, he must concede: "One may assume in this passage a stay in Rome by both apostles" (32).
5. According to Zwierlein, *Petrus in Rom*, 7–12, "Babylon" is not a reference to Rome but is to be understood as a general religious metaphor for the exile of Christians; cf. the opposing view in Baum, "'Babylon' als Ortsnamenmetapher in 1 Petr 5,13," who argues convincingly for Rome.
6. On the interpretation, cf. Schnelle, *Das Evangelium nach Johannes*, 343–44; Zwierlein, "Kritisches zur Römischen Petrustradition," 95–97, gives the date as "perhaps around 160" without any actual reason (97).
7. Literary evidence comes from the letter of Dionysius of Corinth to the Roman church, written around 170 CE. See Eusebius, *Hist. eccl.* 2.25.8, which says of Peter and Paul, "and together also [they] taught in Italy in the same place and were martyred at the same time" (LCL). Around 200 CE the Roman presbyter Gaius wrote (Eusebius, *Hist. eccl.* 2.25.7 LCL): "But I can point out the trophies of the Apostles, for if you will go to the Vatican or to the Ostian Way you will find the trophies of those who founded this church." On the disputed archaeological sites, cf. Thümmel, *Die Memorien für Petrus und Paulus*: since around 160–165 CE there is a memorial to Peter and Paul, but the previous 100 years are not available to the historian; Brandenburg, "Die

reasons played a role; rather, in the Roman culture a central significance was always given to the commemoration of the dead, which required an (actual or claimed) knowledge of the tombs of Peter and Paul.

According to Rom. 15:22–33, Paul wanted to deliver the collection from Corinth to Jerusalem in order to travel to Rome, where he hoped to receive support for his mission to Spain from the church there.[8] Luke gives a detailed report about Paul's stay in Jerusalem, his imprisonment, and the resulting trip to Rome (cf. Acts 21:15–28, 31). However, many events in this period of time lie in darkness. Theologically and historically significant is the open end of Acts. Although Paul is the obscure and—from chapter 15 onward—the clear hero of the entire work, his end remains unknown. Luke knows about the essential purpose of the last trip to Jerusalem (cf. Acts 24:17) and, in Acts 20:24–25, anticipates Paul's death without however mentioning either explicitly. Historically, one may conclude from Rom. 16 that Paul knew many members of the Roman church. Nevertheless, no actual meeting between Paul and the Roman church ever took place (cf. Acts 28:16). Instead, as was always the case in Acts, Paul made first contact with the local synagogues (Acts 28:17ff.). Only after the rejection of Paul's message did he turn to the gentiles in Rome. Thus the impression emerges that Paul established the church in Rome although in Acts 28:15 the non-Pauline origin of the Roman church is presupposed. What brought Luke to this portrayal? One may assume that, for this part of Paul's activity, he had at his disposal only a few reliable traditions.[9] Added to this is the tendency that has been observed throughout Luke-Acts to exonerate the Romans from any complicity in the death of Jesus or in the hindering of the mission. As a consequence, Luke probably was silent on the condemnation of Paul in Rome although he knew about the death of Paul (cf. Acts 19:21; 20:23–25; 21:11). As to historical information, one can say only that Paul arrived in Rome with his prisoner transport, where he, despite his incarceration, conducted missionary activity. Paul appears as a lonely man who was in no way supported by the Roman church, conducting missionary

---

Aussagen der Schriftquellen," is rather confident: "The tombs of the apostles at the Vatican and on the Ostian Way, identified since the middle of the second century by a mark, . . . impressively attest the Roman tradition, which may be traced to the turn of the second century, of the stay, teaching, and martyrdom of Peter and Paul in Rome" (380); Zangenberg, "Gebeine des Apostelfürsten?," is rather critical. As a whole, one could say that the new excavations in the Vatican and in the Basilica San Paola *fuori le mure* (outside the walls) indicate that in the middle of the second century there was a marking and veneration of the martyr tombs of Peter and Paul.

8. On the end of Paul, cf. Horn, *Das Ende des Paulus*; Omerzu, *Der Prozess des Paulus*; Schnelle, *Apostle Paul*, 381–86, 411–16; Tàrrech, Barclay, and Frey, *Last Years of Paul*.

9. Cf. Omerzu, "Das Schweigen des Lukas," who regards Acts 28:16, 23, 30–31 as the core of the tradition.

© Baker Publishing Group

9.1. The possible place of Paul's tomb is the Basilica San Paolo fuori le mura in Rome.

activity among the Jews with limited success. This situation corresponds to the personal tradition given in 2 Tim. 4:10–16, which corresponds in a decisive way to Acts 28:16–31: Paul has been abandoned by his coworkers, and only Luke is with him! Even if the strands of tradition in Acts and 2 Timothy argue in different ways in their specifics, they agree that Paul received no support from his coworkers and probably none from the Roman church. The emphasis on jealousy and conflict in 1 Clem. 5.4–5 confirms this view.[10] The conflict between Christians of Jewish origin and those from a Greco-Roman

10. Cf. 1 Clem. 5.5–7, "Because of jealousy and strife [διὰ ζῆλον καὶ ἔριν] Paul showed the way to the prize for patient endurance. After he had been seven times in chains, had been driven into exile, had been stoned, and had preached in the East and the West, he won the genuine glory for his faith, having taught righteousness to the whole world and having reached the farthest limits of the West. Finally, when he had given his testimony before the rulers, he thus departed from the world and went to the holy place, having become an outstanding example of patient endurance" (trans. Holmes).

background over the person of Paul as well as between Christians and Jews continued in Rome. Paul, like Peter, probably died alone in the course of the Neronian persecution (see below, 12.2). Such a martyrdom may lie in the background of Col. 1:24: "I rejoice in my suffering for you and fill up what is lacking in the afflictions of Christ in my flesh for the sake of his body, the church." The "completion" of the suffering of Christ can refer only to the martyrdom of the apostle, particularly since the pseudepigraphic Letter to the Colossians was probably written in Rome.[11] Clearly, Ignatius of Antioch assumes Paul's martyrdom in Rome (cf. Ign. *Eph.* 12.2; *Rom.* 4.1–3).

> The deaths of Peter and Paul as martyrs in Rome in 64 CE cannot, of course, be "proved." Nevertheless, both the life stories of the two protagonists and numerous sources point in this direction. Moreover, no alternative traditions developed in early Christianity, a fact that supports the Roman tradition. Through their life's work and the end of their lives, Peter and Paul were the significant bearers and guarantors of the tradition.

Besides Peter, Mary Magdalene, and Paul, James the brother of the Lord was one of the people of whom a recognized special revelation of the Resurrected One is reported (cf. 1 Cor. 15:7, "He appeared to James, then to all of the Twelve"). In the initial period of the Jerusalem church, he did not yet appear in the foreground (see above, 5.2). Only after the expulsion of the Hellenists from Jerusalem (cf. Acts 8:1ff.) does James, as the physical brother of the Lord and representative of a perspective that was faithful to the Torah, become a dominant figure in early Christianity. After Peter had fled from Jerusalem around 43/44 CE and before the problems caused by Herod Antipas (see above, 6.5), James assumed the leadership of the Jerusalem church. Moreover, James and Peter apparently represented different theological positions. Peter opened himself very early to the gentile mission while James apparently represented a strict Jewish Christian position that, after the apostolic conference, also turned against the Pauline mission that did not require circumcision.[12] James's faithfulness to the law is emphasized not only in post-NT Christian literature[13] but also in the report of Josephus

11. Cf. Schnelle, *History and Theology of the New Testament*, 286–87.

12. Deines, *Jakobus*, 166–76, describes James as a church leader between two fronts: "on the one side the nationalistic Judaism that regarded the conservative Jewish Christian leaders as an enemy/traitor of the Jewish people, on the other side the continually expanding gentile Christianity."

13. In the Gospel of Thomas 12 he appears as "James the Just" (cf. also Eusebius, *Hist. eccl.* 2.1.3 and passim).

about the martyrdom of James (*Ant.* 20.197–303). Josephus hands down the tradition that during the power vacuum between the death of Festus and the assumption of office of his successor, the Sadducean high priest Ananus, son of Annas of the Synoptic Gospels, acted against James and other members of the Jerusalem church. Ananus, presumably in 62 CE, called the Sanhedrin into session, and James and other Jewish Christians were condemned to death by stoning because of their breach of the Torah.[14] This judgment made by the Sadducean majority called forth crucial objection by the Pharisees, who finally intervened successfully with the Roman governor, Albinus. Although James the brother of the Lord separated from the mission concept of Paul, he was no longer able to save the Jerusalem church in a phase of increasing nationalism within a broad spectrum of Judaism.

9.2 The Destruction of the Temple, the Fall of the Jerusalem Church, and the *Fiscus Judaicus*

The loss of a central temple as a place of religious and political identity in antiquity was always a drastic event.[15] The almost total destruction of the temple by the Romans in 70 CE led ancient Judaism into a profound crisis and was also of great significance for early Christianity. Not only the Jerusalem church but also the entire new movement lost a central link to its earliest history. Jesus of Nazareth had objected to the commercialization of the temple cult (cf. Mark 11:15–19), but he did not question the legitimacy of the temple. For the Jerusalem church the temple was self-evidently the place of its relation to Judaism and center of its spiritual life and preaching (cf. Acts 2:46; 3:1, 8; 5:20, 25; 21:26 and passim). This loss was handled in two ways. (1) The integration of the destruction of the temple into an apocalyptic scenario (cf. Mark 13:2ff.) connected the event equally with the will of God and their own expectations for the end time. (2) Jesus Christ is himself understood as the temple, which would be rebuilt in three days (cf. Mark 14:58; John 2:19–21). Thus early Christianity linked itself to a broad stream within Hellenism that detached the true worship of God/the gods from religious centers.[16]

14. Cf. Josephus, *Ant.* 20.200: "And so he convened the judges of the Sanhedrin and brought before them a man named James, the brother of Jesus who is called Christ [τὸν ἀδελφὸν Ἰησοῦ τοῦ λεγομένου Χριστοῦ], and a few others. He accused them of having transgressed the law and delivered them up to be stoned."

15. For the Greek world, cf. Teichmann, *Der Mensch und sein Tempel.* For the Jewish temple theology with its concept of holiness and purity, cf. Schwier, *Tempel und Tempelzerstörung,* 55ff.; cf. also Ego, A. Lange, and Pilhofer, *Gemeinde ohne Tempel.*

16. Texts in *NW* I/2:226–34.

In the turmoil of the Jewish War and the capture of Jerusalem, the Jerusalem church also fell concurrently with the temple. No direct witnesses exist; only Eusebius, *Hist. eccl.* 3.5.3, reports about the fate of the Jerusalem church.[17] "The people of the church in Jerusalem were commanded by an oracle given by revelation before the war to those in the city who were worthy of it to depart and dwell in one of the cities of Perea, which they called Pella." In that case, the church would have survived the fall of Jerusalem in relative security. However, significant reasons call the historicity of this Pella tradition into question:[18] (1) It is a late report and is found in only one tradition. The fate of the Jerusalem church was of general interest in early Christianity. If they had possessed information about it, it would have been handed on earlier by more authors. (2) Pella was a gentile city that, according to Josephus,[19] was destroyed at the beginning of the Jewish War. (3) The actual disappearance of the Jerusalem church (not of Jewish Christianity!) after 70 CE speaks against the assumption that it survived the destruction of Jerusalem. (4) The Pella tradition can be explained as a local tradition of a Jewish Christian church that—probably in the second century CE—can be traced to the Jerusalem church. In addition, the death of James the brother of the Lord indicates that the Jerusalem church fell into the crosshairs of nationalistic circles already before the beginning of the war. If one assumes the radical action of this circle at the beginning of the war against possible or actual Jewish dissenters,[20] the conclusion is unavoidable: The Jerusalem church was destroyed in the turmoil of the war and never again had any influence on the history of early Christianity. To be sure, Jewish Christian groups existed further (see below, 10.5), but they lost their natural point of reference with the people of Jerusalem. As a result, the urban churches of Asia Minor, Greece, and Italy gained increasingly more significance.

A further event came with the end of the Jewish War that had great influence on the history of early Christianity, and especially with the separation between Jews and Jewish Christians: the *fiscus Judaicus*. Josephus writes

17. The threat in Matt. 23:37–39//Luke 13:34–35 that is frequently connected with Pella cannot be historically verified. On the relationship of comparable reports and traditions competing with that of Eusebius among other church fathers, cf. Lüdemann, *Opposition to Paul*, 203–10, 307–15.

18. Cf. the detailed study by Lüdemann, *Opposition to Paul*, 203–10. On the other hand, Wehnert, "Die Auswanderung der Jerusalemer Christen nach Pella," argues for the (generally speaking) historicity of the Pella tradition. D.-A. Koch, *Geschichte des Urchristentums*, 380–88, treats the emigration of the Jerusalem Christians before the beginning of the Jewish War; after the war the Jewish Christians returned and selected Symeon, a cousin of Jesus, to be the new leader of the church (so Eusebius, *Hist. eccl.* 3.10.11).

19. Josephus, *J.W.* 2.458.

20. Cf., e.g., Josephus, *J.W.* 2.562.

about Vespasian: "Moreover, he laid on the Jews a head tax, wherever they
lived. Every year they had to pay two drachmas to the capital corresponding to
the tax that they had previously given to the temple."[21] The question of who
was a Jew did not depend any longer on religious practice or self-identification
but became a question of administration and legal practice. A special collection authority decided about the tax obligation so that men, women, and
children had to demonstrate that they were Jews in a testing procedure.[22] The
intensification of the practice of collecting taxes under Domitian (see below,
12.3) indicates the pressure that was exercised on the Jews, for even a ninety-
year-old man had to be examined to determine if he had been circumcised
(Seutonius, *Dom.* 12.2).[23] The consequences for this development are evident:
A decision over membership or nonmembership in Judaism was inevitable,
especially for those who previously had defined themselves loosely in relation
to the synagogue.[24] Both strict Jewish Christians and Romans/Greeks who
were favorable to Judaism (Godfearers) faced the decision of defining their
legal relation to Judaism. Suetonius again attests that they stood in the focus
of the Roman authorities: "Besides other taxes, that on the Jews was levied
with the utmost rigour, and those were prosecuted who without publicly ac-
knowledging that faith yet lived as Jews, as well as those who concealed their
origin and did not pay the tribute levied upon their people" (*Dom.* 12.2 LCL).
Suspicions and denunciations increased in which the strict Jewish Christians
who were associated with the synagogue fell into a difficult situation, for a
decision was forced upon them. If they decided for the synagogue, then they
were probably forced into a break in their relationships with Christians. If
they decided to belong to a Christian church, then they lost their previous
legal status as a recognized religion and took on the insecure legal status of
the gentile Christians. Consequently, conflicts between Jewish and Christian
churches were unavoidable, as for example, the book of Revelation indicates
(cf. Rev. 3:9).[25]

21. Josephus, *J.W.* 7.218; according to Dio Cassius 65.7.2, "Thus Jerusalem was destroyed
on the day of Saturn, the place that the Jews highly venerate until this day. From that time on
it was determined that the Jews, as long as they held further to their old traditional customs,
would have to pay each year two denarii to Jupiter Capitolinus as taxes."

22. Cf. the comprehensive study in Heemstra, *The* Fiscus Judaicus *and the Parting of the
Ways*, 24–66.

23. Cf. also Martial, *Epigramme* 7.82, who reports about a Jew who attempted to conceal
his circumcision.

24. Heemstra, *The* Fiscus Judaicus *and the Parting of the Ways*, 64, enumerates seven groups
that were affected: (1) Godfearers, (2) Gentile Christians as a distinct class of sympathizers with
Judaism, (3) Jewish tax evaders, (4) proselytes, (5) apostate Jews, (6) circumcised non-Jews,
(7) Jewish Christians; the Samaritans are an eighth group.

25. Cf. Hirschberg, *Das eschatologische Israel*, 59ff.

Caesar Nerva (96–98 CE) appeared as a reformer and corrected the politics of Domitian at many points.[26] He carried out a reform of the *fiscus Judaicus*, which is primarily attested in a coin inscription from the spring of 97 CE: "fisci Iudaici calumnia sublata [false accusations with respect to the tax on Jews are annulled]."[27] Probably excesses and arbitrary acts from the time of Domitian were corrected, especially the frequent obvious practice of false accusations that someone was an adherent of Judaism. Pagan sympathizers of Judaism, Christians, and Jewish Christians were naturally affected. The *fiscus* was further lifted: it was required only for those who practiced a recognizable Jewish way of life. In each case the *fiscus Judaicus* accelerated the separation between Jews and Christians, for one could not be permanently both at the same time.[28]

9.3 The Rise of the Flavians

The period of the Flavians encompassed the rule of the caesars Vespasian, Titus, and Domitian; the term "Flavian" is derived from the family name of Vespasian: Flavius.[29] In 68 CE Nero committed suicide, and with him the last male member of the Julian-Claudian family died, who had descended directly from Caesar. Galba became caesar first, but he was already very old and had no successor from his own family. At the beginning of 69 CE, the first revolt erupted among the legions in Germania, who called Vitellius to be caesar. Galba's former follower Otho rose up against him, and Galba died in this coup. Otho lost the following crucial battle and then took his life, leaving Vitellius as the sole ruler. Continuing unrest in individual armies and Vitellius's unconvincing stature as a ruler led to the call of Vespasian in the East to be caesar in June 69. He was supported especially by the Egyptian prefect Julius Alexander and the Syrian governor Mucianus. After a series of skirmishes and battles, the troops of Vespasian finally succeeded in taking over power also in Rome, in the course of which Vitellius died. Vespasian did not descend from an old established family and had to legitimate his claim to power.[30] Thus he gave a religious dimension to his rule and presented himself

26. Cf. Dio Cassius 68.1–2.

27. Images of the coins are in Heemstra, *The* Fiscus Judaicus *and the Parting of the Ways*, 69.

28. Cf. also Frey, "Von Paulus zu Johannes," 268–75, who correctly regards the *fiscus Judaicus* as a major accelerating factor in the process of separation between Jews and Christians.

29. On the Flavians, cf. Bellen, *Grundzüge der römischen Geschichte*, 2:81–115; S. Pfeiffer, *Die Zeit der Flavier*.

30. Cf. Suetonius, *Vesp.* 1: "The empire, which had long been unsettled and, as it were, drifting, through the usurpation and violent death of three emperors, was at last taken in hand

as the long-awaited ruler from the East. Both Tacitus[31] and Suetonius[32] report this tradition, according to which Vespasian and Titus, who were victorious in Judea, were the incarnation of that prophecy, which the Jews applied to themselves. A special role in this context was played by Flavius Josephus, who became propagandist of the providential role of Vespasian. As a prisoner, he affirmed for Vespasian the world domination that had been prophesied (cf. *J.W.* 3.399–408; 4.622–29; Suetonius, *Vesp.* 5.6; Dio Cassius 65.1.4), and he placed Vespasian's inauguration to power within a religious context, connecting it with the concept of εὐαγγέλια (message of victory).[33] The portrayal of Vespasian as the one who brings peace to the world (cf. Tacitus, *Hist.* 4.3) and the Arch of Titus in Rome indicate that the Flavians consciously staged their victory over the Jews in their self-presentation.[34] Finally, the miracles ascribed to Vespasian may be regarded as political-religious propaganda.[35] Shortly after his ascent to power, he is reported to have healed a blind man, that is, both a blind man and a man with a withered hand (cf. Mark 3:1–6; 8:22–26; 10:46–52). He presented himself as a living Serapis and was venerated as the son of Ammon, the Egyptian Zeus.[36] In addition, Vespasian's

and given stability by the Flavian family. This house was, it is true, obscure and without family portraits, yet it was one of which our country had no reason whatever to be ashamed, even though it is the general opinion that the penalty which Domitian paid for his avarice and cruelty was fully merited" (LCL).

31. Tacitus, *Hist.* 5.13.1–2, in the context of the capture of the Jerusalem temple: "Prodigies had indeed occurred, but to avert them either by victims or by vows is held unlawful by a people which, though prone to superstition, is opposed to all propitiatory rites. Contending hosts were seen meeting in the skies, arms flashed, and suddenly the temple was illumined with fire from the clouds. Of a sudden the doors of the shrine opened and a superhuman voice cried: 'The gods are departing': at the same moment the mighty stir of their going was heard. Few interpreted these omens as fearful; the majority firmly believed that their ancient priestly writings contained the prophecy that this was the very time when the East should grow strong and that men starting from Judea should possess the world. This mysterious prophecy had in reality pointed to Vespasian and Titus, but the common people, as is the way of human ambition, interpreted these great destinies in their own favour, and could not be turned to the truth even by adversity."

32. Suetonius, *Vesp.* 4.5: "There had spread over all the Orient an old and established belief, that it was fated at that time for men coming from Judaea to rule the world. This prediction, referring to the emperor of Rome, as afterwards appeared from the event, the people of Judaea took to themselves [and] accordingly revolted" (LCL). Cf. the comments of Dio Cassius 64.9 about Vespasian: "Portents and dreams were given to him, which had announced his rule a long time in the past."

33. Cf. Josephus, *J.W.* 4.618, 656 (NW II/1:9–10). Noteworthy is the connection between εὐαγγέλια, the elevation of Vespasian as caesar, and the offering of sacrifices.

34. Cf. Panzram, "Der Jerusalemer Tempel."

35. Cf. Tacitus, *Hist.* 4.81.1–3; Suetonius, *Vesp.* 7.2–3; Dio Cassius 66.8.1(NW I/2:480–81); cf. also Josephus, *Ant.* 8.46–48. On the caesar as healer and miracle worker, cf. Clauss, *Kaiser und Gott*, 346–52; Leppin, "Imperial Miracles and Elitist Discourses."

36. Cf. Papyrus Fouad 8 (NW I/1.1:744); also Clauss, *Kaiser und Gott*, 113–17; H. Blatz, *Die Semantic der Macht*, 175–212.

relationship to philosophers, which ranged from disassociation to rejection,[37] indicates that he intentionally introduced the imperial cult (see below, 12.1) to secure his claims.

The Gospel of Mark, and with it the new literary genre of gospel, came into existence during a time when other forms of "good news" were being proclaimed. Caesar appeared as miracle worker and was propagated as the savior figure from the East. In the context of these claims, Mark narrates (as did the other Gospels) another story of salvation in which the one who was crucified by the Romans appears as the Son of God, miracle worker, and Messiah from the East. The propaganda of the Flavians was certainly not the factor that caused the creation of the gospel genre,[38] but it was a stimulating feature to which Mark repeatedly alludes in his narrative (cf. Mark 1:1, 11; 9:7; 10:42–45; 15:39).[39]

9.4 The Writing of the Gospels and Pseudepigraphy as Innovative Responses to Crises

A definite historical consciousness of crisis was associated with the literary form of the gospel and the production of theological writings under the pseudonymous authority of the apostles. The time of the eyewitnesses and witnesses of the appearance of Jesus was over so that the story of Jesus had to be recorded in a permanent form.

The Writing of the Gospels

It is probably no coincidence that the new gospel genre (see below, 10.1; 13.1) originated around 70 CE. First, the writing of the Gospels is the result of the natural processes within definite historical conditions.[40] The pre-Markan collections (Mark 2:1–3:6; chaps. 4; 10; 13) and the passion narrative are evidence of the tendency for smaller units to be formed into larger text complexes, and the logia source as well as Luke 1:1 explicitly confirms the preliminary stages in the writing of the Gospels. As creator of the gospel genre, Mark stands in a process that already began before him. Moreover,

37. Cf. Suetonius, *Vesp.* 13.15; Tacitus, *Hist.* 4.5.12.
38. Cf. Bellen, *Grundzüge der römischen Geschichte*, 95: "Christianity appeared in the period of the Flavians for the first time with its own genre: the gospels."
39. Cf. the thorough study by E.-M. Becker, "Der jüdisch-römische Krieg."
40. This insight is found already in early form-critical study; cf. Dibelius, *From Tradition to Gospel*; Bultmann, *History of the Synoptic Tradition*; Karl L. Schmidt, "Die Stellung der Evangelien."

the declining expectation of an imminent parousia, the multiple movements of the first century, and the concrete problems of Christian ethics required a new orientation in time and history. With the extension of time, this natural and unavoidable development was strengthened by the death of the founding leaders, the persecution of Christians in Rome, the loss of the temple and Jerusalem church, and the religious-political propaganda of the Flavians. Early Christianity stood before the task of equally preserving the continuity with the beginnings and addressing the current problems. The Gospels handled this problem particularly by the reception of salvation-historical traditions, the development of practical ethical norms, and the introduction of organized instructional authority in the churches. The trend toward historicizing, ethicizing, and institutionalizing of the traditional material becomes open and perceptible in Matthew and Luke but is also clearly recognizable in Mark.[41] Thus the literary character of the Gospels corresponds to their function in intrachurch usage as the foundation for preaching, worship, catechesis, and the management of inner church processes.[42]

In addition, an integrative and innovative function accompanies the Gospels from a pragmatic perspective. The evangelists wrote as members of a group and had to present an image of Jesus with the church traditions that were available that corresponded to the convictions of the church.[43] Thus their special integrative achievement consists of their fusion of traditions about Jesus that were either contradictory or in tension (e.g., a theology of glory and theology of the cross, particularism and universalism). An essential function of the writing of the Gospels consists of the formation of consensus, which was a presupposition for survival in a situation in crisis. The innovative potential of the Gospels is evident especially at the level of interpretation and action, which had to be developed for the external and internal perspective. The Gospels present an image of the surrounding environment and of their

41. These insights of classical redaction criticism are concentrated in G. Strecker, "Redaktionsgeschichte als Aufgabe der Synoptikerexegese."

42. The pragmatic aspects of the writing of the Gospels are emphasized by Theissen, *Gospels in Context*, 235–89.

43. A totally different view is that of Bauckham, "For Whom Were Gospels Written?" In contrast to classical redaction criticism, Bauckham regards the evangelists not as representatives of their church/churches but instead claims, "The evangelists, I have argued, did not write for specific churches they knew or knew about, not even for a large number of such churches. Rather, drawing on their experience and knowledge of several or many specific churches, they wrote *for any and every church* to which their Gospels might circulate" (46). Against this view is the following: (1) the unique narrative and theological profile of each evangelist, which is clearly evident, indicates that (2) each evangelist had at his disposal his own language, visual world, theological concept, and strategies for addressing problems, which did not give an answer to all questions and also were not intended to be used to remove whatever one desired.

own position in it, which led to a self-definition and offered an orientation. Consequently, the demarcation from the religion of their origin was of fundamental significance. Because early Christianity originated as an inner-Jewish renewal movement, it was necessary to portray the reasons for the separation plausibly. With the writing of the Gospels, the new movement gives its own basic narrative and separates itself finally from the common narrative of Judaism. From the internal perspective, models for the life together and the common maintenance of the various streams had to be developed. The relation between Christians from Jewish and from Greco-Roman traditions likewise had to be regulated, just as also there was the need for norms of the relationship of poor and rich, man and woman, Spirit-filled and "normal" Christians. All of the Gospels give an impulse in the form of narratives to enable the life together of various groups within the church. It is noteworthy that all of the Gospels presuppose the outcome of the Pauline missions. Christians from the nations do not have to be circumcised. Furthermore, norms for new authority structures and leadership offices had to be established, for with the gospel genre, the wandering charismatics, with their strong oral tradition, lost their influence. With the Gospels, the local churches became the bearers of the Jesus tradition.

Two factors favored the origin and spread of the Gospels: (1) The early Christians were predominantly a bilingual movement so that the Gospels could be received in practically the entire Roman Empire and by people of various educational levels.[44] (2) In the first century CE, the codex (stapled or folded pages) became significant,[45] for in contrast to the scroll, it had practical advantages, especially with long texts.[46] Rome appears to have been a center of this development;[47] one can assume that the Christians used this practical procedure from the beginning with their new literary genre.

Pseudepigraphy

Besides the Gospels, after around 70 CE the pseudepigraphic letters appear, in which the first witnesses are still claimed as identification and mediating figures in the time of crisis.[48] New Testament pseudepigraphy (Gk.

44. On the pagan literature, see Fantham, *Literarisches Leben im antiken Rom.*
45. Cf. U. Schmid, "Die Buchwerdung des Neuen Testaments."
46. Cf. Birt, *Das antike Buchwesen*; Trobisch, *Die Endredaktion des Neuen Testaments*, 106–24.
47. Cf. Martial, *Epigramme* 1.2, "Buy these; that parchment compresses in small pages"; 14.192, "This mass that has been built up for you with many a leaf contains the fifteen lays of Naso."
48. Speyer, *Die literarische Fälschung*; Baum, *Pseudepigraphie und literarische Fälschung*; R. Zimmermann, "Unecht—und doch wahr?"; Frey, Herzer, Janssen, and Rothschild, *Pseudepigraphie und Verfasserfiktion.*

ψευδεπίγραφος, written falsely, false writing), that is, the publication of writings with claims to authorship that are not historically true, is not unique, for both in Greco-Roman[49] as also in Jewish literature[50] there are numerous pseudepigraphical works. The NT pseudepigraphy can clearly be placed in a limited time frame; most pseudepigraphical writings originated between 60/70 and 100 CE, in which respective boundaries are the proto-Pauline letters and 1 Clement (ca. 96 CE), and the letters of Ignatius (ca. 110 CE). This period in the history of early Christianity was an epoch of upheaval and new orientation. The generation of the first witnesses had died, an organization of the whole church did not yet exist, at this time church offices for the local church began to take shape, the problem of the delay of the parousia was a concern, and the first comprehensive persecutions took place. Finally, the period was marked by both the painful separation from Judaism and the intense conflict with false teachers in their own ranks. Moreover, one can assume from 2 Thess. 2:2 that opponents of Paul made use of Paul's authority through pseudepigraphy. Within this situation, the question of offices took on a special meaning. The development of generally recognized church offices occurred in the period between 70 and 100 CE; that is, the lack of an authoritative office was an essential reason why the authority of the first witnesses was claimed through pseudepigraphy. Clement of Rome and Ignatius of Antioch, on the other hand, were supra-regionally recognized officeholders, and they wrote letters again under their own names. The office thus gave them the necessary authority that had not existed previously.

In sociohistorical terms the communal missions practice of Paul and the existence of a Pauline school (see above, 8.2) are of great significance for the origin of epistolary pseudepigraphy. In the proto-Pauline letters, with the exception of Romans, coauthors appear along with Paul (1 Thess. 1:1; 1 Cor. 1:1; 2 Cor. 1:1; Gal. 1:2; Phil. 1:1; Philem. 1); letters were written down by secretaries (Rom. 16:22) or scribes (1 Cor. 16:21; Gal. 6:11; Philem. 19); that is, the letters, following the model of Paul, have the character of cooperative works. Thus the pupils could justifiably claim the authority of Paul insofar as they could take his thoughts, develop them further, integrate oral Pauline traditions into the letters,[51] and introduce their own line of argument correspondingly into the current situation in the church. Finally, the letters from such significant personalities as Peter or James were probably not perceived as unusual. Both had an eventful history that could be claimed.

49. On pseudepigraphy among the Greeks and Romans, cf. especially Speyer, *Die literarische Fälschung*, 111–49.

50. Cf. Meade, *Pseudonymity and Canon*, 17–85.

51. Cf. Standhartinger, *Studien zur Entstehungsgeschichte*, 91–152.

A theological judgment should not be made on the basis of (contemporary) moral categories of falsification or deceit,[52] for the NT pseudepigraphy fits into its own contemporary environment as a common phenomenon, and deception is not its goal. The Cynic letters may be regarded as a parallel phenomenon to the epistolary pseudepigraphy of the NT. Around 45 Cicero cites (*Tusc.* 5.90) in a fully unbiased way a (reputed) letter of the Scythian Anacharsis (6th cent. BCE), who was considered the progenitor of the Cynics.[53] From the first century CE to the second century CE, individual letters of Pythagoras, that is, by the Pythagoreans,[54] the letters of Socrates,[55] and the Cynic letters[56] were produced. The respective "heroes" had been dead for centuries; nevertheless, their alleged letters were received. Here a "school of pseudepigraphy" was probably present: one actualized the basic philosophical teachings of a movement in the form of a letter under the name of a famous figure from the beginning, and the pseudepigraphical character of the letter was generally accepted. What mattered was the content, which, as a rule, was appropriate for the alleged authors. Whether, therefore, one may speak of an accepted "school of pseudepigraphy" with regard to the deutero-Pauline letters (as with the Cynic letters) must remain an open question. On the one hand, the appeal to Paul and the actualization of his teaching in a school context is evident; on the other hand, the temporal distance (from the death of Paul) in comparison with the Cynic letters is small. Consequently, the churches could have understood at least a few of the deutero-Pauline letters as authentic. In any case, the literary form of pseudepigraphy in the last third of the first Christian century was an effective means to resolve the new problems from the perspective of the author of the pseudepigraphic work by claiming the past authority; that is, a definite intent for reception was in the foreground. The moral category of falsification is thus unsuitable for understanding the purposes of pseudepigraphy,[57] for the truth of what was written did not depend on applicable or inapplicable information about the author, which could not be completely explained anyway. It is more appropriate to speak of "borrowed authorial information," by which the apostolic authority appears as guarantor of the validity of what is written.[58] New Testament pseudepigraphy must be regarded as the theologically legitimate and

---

52. Cf. Brox, *Falsche Verfasserangaben*, 81ff.

53. Cf. Reuters, *Die Briefe des Anacharsis* (on dating the letters to the 3rd cent. BCE).

54. Cf. Städele, *Die Briefe des Pythagoras.*

55. Cf. Borkowski, *Socratis quae feruntur Epistolae*, 16.

56. Cf. Malherbe, *Cynic Epistles*; Müseler, *Die Kynikerbriefe*, 2 vols.

57. Cf. R. Zimmermann, "Unecht—und doch wahr?," 34–35.

58. Cf. Brox, *Falsche Verfasserangaben*, 105, who emphasizes "the motif of participation in the superior past."

ecclesiologically necessary attempt to consider and preserve apostolic traditions in a process of interpretative anamnesis within changed situations. At
the same time it provided necessary answers to new situations and questions.

Table 6. Chronology of Early Christianity to 70 CE

48 (late summer) –51/52	second missionary trip
50/51	Paul in Corinth
51/52	Gallio in Corinth
51/52	Paul's trip to Antioch
52–55/56	third missionary trip
52–54/55	Paul in Ephesus
55	Paul's trip to Macedonia
55	Galatian crisis
56 (beginning of the year)	Paul's last stay in Corinth
56 (early summer)	Paul's arrival in Jerusalem
56–58	Paul's arrest in Cesarea
58	change of office: Felix to Festus
59	Paul's arrival in Rome
62	death of James
64	death of Peter and Paul
66	beginning of the Jewish War
66	flight of the Jerusalem church to Pella (?)
70	fall of Jerusalem; destruction of the temple
ca. 70	Gospel of Mark; first pseudepigraphic writings

10

The Establishment of Early Christianity

The history of early Christianity was not determined only by persons, historical events, or political developments, but primarily through experiences, ideas, utopian dreams, convictions, and expectations that were disseminated primarily in conversations and speeches so that they could find reception in texts. Texts develop an effect, have a history, and are thus a constituent part of history. This fact is evident with the Pauline letters (see above, 8.6) as well as the Gospels, with which the history of early Christianity entered a new phase. Literature is always a product of history yet is primarily itself history-making as it transports concepts, makes interpretations possible, and forms identity. Thus the astonishing production of literature of early Christianity is an aspect and driving force of its history and must naturally enter into the portrayal of this history. The innovative potential of the new movement is indicated especially in the fact that the new religious knowledge is presented in new literary genres.

10.1 A New Genre for a New Era: The Gospels

The new literary genre, gospel, presents for the first time a biographically oriented narrative of Jesus Christ and thus preserves the Jesus traditions as a memory of the program of early Christianity, keeping it from disappearing into obscurity (see above, 9.4). Among the comparable textual types, the

Hellenistic biographies come the closest.[1] The combination of historiographical and biographical sayings that dominates the Hellenistic writing of vitae is also present in the gospel form. Characteristic of the gospel form is the juxtaposition of narrative text and kerygmatic address, a narrative basic structure[2] combined with biographical, historiographical, and dramatic, kerygmatic elements. Nevertheless, the content of the Gospels is distinctive in ancient literature. Only they claim that, in a concrete and singular event of the past, history took a turn and that both the present and the future are defined by this event. Thus the narration in the Gospels is always simultaneously a re-presentation. The concern is not only memory, but also always kerygmatic re-presentation. In this sense, the gospel genre is sui generis and cannot be classified with any overarching genre. With the gospel, to a certain extent the new content created its own new literary form! The primary purpose of all of the Gospels is the clarification of the identity of Jesus of Nazareth as Christ, which then was intended to shape the identity of the church. All of the narrative and theological strategies of the evangelists serve this task.

The distinctive feature of the new gospel genre consists of the placing of divine and human reality in relation to each other. From the "beginning" (cf. Gen. 1:1; Mark 1:1; John 1:1), only the mythical could be narrated; especially the christological titles bring to expression that the Jesus who acts in history belongs to the heavenly world. The Gospels thus become the basic books of a new religion, in which its center is the Christ myth: the narrative of the Son of God, Jesus of Nazareth, who entered the world for humankind and died "for our sins" so that we could live (cf. 2 Cor. 8:9). Through the presentation of the events/characters, the geographical/chronological framework, and the course of events, the Gospels present the narratival perspectives and their theological principles, their image of Jesus Christ, and thus they define essentially their own understanding of Jesus for early Christianity. They also have an apologetic function, inasmuch as both Jews and Romans considered Jesus, as a crucified one, a rejected man. The Gospels counter this view with the demonstration that the Christians are the successors of a teacher and healer who was unjustly condemned. The Gospels agree in the basic facts in

---

1. Cf., e.g., Berger, *Formgeschichte des Neuen Testaments*, 367–71; Aune, *New Testament in Its Literary Environment*, 64 (Gospel as subgenre of ancient biography); Burridge, *What Are the Gospels?*, 212: "The Synoptic Gospels belong within the overall genre of *bioi*"; Frickenschmidt, *Evangelium als Biographie*, 508 (the four Gospels are ancient "biographies of Jesus" in the full sense of the word"); Dormeyer, *Das Neue Testament*, 199–228, on the Gospels as "kerygmatic ideal biographies."

2. Breytenbach, "Das Markusevangelium als episodische Erzählung," describes the Gospel of Mark as "episodic" narrative in which the global themes consistently appear within individual pericopes.

their portrayal of the story of Jesus Christ, yet they structure the material in various ways and emphasize in each case those aspects that were important for the formation of the identity of their own communities. Thus they acquire from Paul a fundamental decision: the mission to the gentiles without cir cumcision. In no Gospel does the key noun "circumcision" appear, although the Gospels define their relation to the Torah in thoroughly different ways.

In terms of literary history, the Gospels are by no means without literary merit [*Kleinliteratur*],[3] but instead they have at their command a high literary quality. This is evident in a highly complex literary and theological comprehensive plan; a deliberate structure; a textual sequence that shows the evidence of careful consideration within the section; the numerous linguistic and content-related linkages within the entire work; the treatment of theological, ethical, and anthropological themes; and finally in the creation and formation of a new literary genre, gospel, itself. It is a highly creative act within the history of ancient literature. The Gospels should be classified as elevated narrative literature, in which religious, philosophical, ethical, and cultural themes are treated (cf. especially Plutarch). The Gospels have the quality of a foundational narrative, a large or master narrative,[4] that is inscribed into the culture of humanity and continues to reach and move people today. The special quality of such a foundational narrative consists in the fact that "they themselves have to produce the conditions of their own narrative," for "they pass through something like a time warp that excludes them from the external conditions of their origination."[5] They create within the narrative various levels of time and reality that increase their plausibility and do not depend on external interpretative power. "The narrative gains here, in its entire inconsistency, a transcendental quality."[6]

10.2 The Synoptic Gospels and Acts as Master Narratives

"Master narratives" are texts that mediate to people "a conception of their belonging, their collective identity: stories of the founding of a nation and

---

3. The nonliterary quality of the Gospels is argued by Dibelius, *From Tradition to Gospel*, 1: "Primitive Christian literature passed through all of the stages between private notes and the borders of literature proper. Only two or three of its documents approximate the literary standards of Philo and Josephus. All the rest are either nonliterary or of minor literary significance." Bultmann takes this view and attributes no literary genre to the Gospels: "Mark is not sufficiently master of his material to be able to venture on a systematic construction himself" (*History of the Synoptic Tradition*, 350), and none of the evangelists have the educated compositional technique to produce high-quality literature (397).

4. Cf. Rüsen, "Kann gestern besser werden?"

5. Koschorke, *Wahrheit und Erfindung*, 396.

6. Koschorke, *Wahrheit und Erfindung*, 397.

its successes, religious stories of salvation."[7] They convey knowledge and establish identities and have at their command the quality that leads to their being read more and more by people. The Synoptic Gospels and Acts are such master narratives.

10.2.1 Mark: The Son of God for All

Mark wrote his Gospel probably in Rome around 70 CE for a predominantly gentile church.[8] He composed the first detailed narrative of Jesus Christ and essentially shaped the image of Jesus Christ in early Christianity through his narrative presentation and his theological insights. The new literary genre, gospel, prevailed, not least because of the complete reception of the Gospel of Mark by Matthew and Luke (and partly by John). By combining historiographical and biographical narrative texts and kerygmatic address with Jesus's path to the cross as a dramatic event, Mark preserves the historical and theological identity of the Christian faith. The logia source and Luke 1:1 suggest the existence of earlier forms of these Gospels and probably lost gospels. Thus Mark accomplishes a crucial achievement: He prevents various Jesus traditions from being forgotten, combines them in narrative form, and presents Jesus of Nazareth as both proclaimer and proclaimed. Mark is the first person in early Christianity who places the historical dimension of the appearance of Jesus comprehensively at the center; thus he prevents a dehistoricizing of the story of Jesus Christ, as will be done later, for example, in the Gospel of John. With his Gospel, Mark created a central building block for the cultural memory of early Christianity.

Mark assumes faith in Jesus as Messiah (Mark 1:1), develops this confession through his narrative arrangement, and in his Gospel portrays in what sense Jesus Christ is the Son of God all along and yet becomes the Son of God in the narrative. Thus two lines of knowledge and understanding become dominant: the revelation of the Son and the theory of secrecy.

1. For Mark, the earthly way of Jesus is at the same time the way of the Son of God. Jesus Christ stands equally in association with heaven and earth; thus his narrative is both heavenly and earthly. This fundamental connection is signified fundamentally by the narrative of the baptism of Jesus (Mark 1:9–11), the story of the transfiguration (Mark 9:2–9), and the confession

---

7. Rüsen, *Kann gestern besser werden?*, 29–30.

8. Cf. Schnelle, *History and Theology of the New Testament*, 202. I support a time of writing shortly after 70 because the contrast at the level of the narrative between the still-existing temple and the temple that is completely destroyed in the future in Mark 13:2 presupposes that the actual destruction has become a reality. A conquest of Jerusalem and of the temple by the Romans was foreseeable, but not the complete destruction of the temple.

of the centurion at the cross (Mark 15:39).[9] These three texts form the basic structure of Mark's composition insofar as here the heavenly and earthly worlds come together in a similar way and the close relationship of Jesus to God is expressed in the title "Son."[10] Baptism, transfiguration, and confession under the cross are the three basic pillars around which Mark groups his traditions in the form of a life of Jesus. The title "Son" thus marks the central content, for it is able to encompass Jesus's divine nature and his suffering and death at the same time. Jesus's existence and nature stand firmly from the beginning; he is the Son of God, and he does not change his nature. For humankind, however, he first becomes the Son of God, for people need a process of gaining knowledge,[11] which Mark effects with his vita of Jesus in the new literary genre, gospel. He first reaches the goal of this process of knowledge at the end of the Gospel at the cross; it is here that a man, not God, recognizes Jesus as "Son of God" (Mark 15:39). Previously, those who know this are only God (Mark 1:11; 9:7), the demons (Mark 3:11; 5:7), and the Son himself (Mark 12:6; 13:32). One must first stride through the entire path of Jesus from the baptism to the cross in order to come to an understanding of Jesus as the Son of God. Thus the central question of Markan Christology is answered: "Who is this?" (cf. Mark 1:27; 4:41; 6:2–3, 14–16; 8:27ff.; 9:7; 10:47–48; 14:61–62; 15:39).

With the title of Son, an enigmatic and subversive political message is combined: It is not the Roman caesar who is the Son of God, but rather the suffering, crucified, and resurrected Jesus of Nazareth. The Gospel of Mark is full of allusions and polemics against the Flavians (especially Vespasian).[12] Besides the concept of *euangelion* (good news), one may name especially the apotheosis of a Crucified One in Mark 15:39 (also 10:42–44; 16:1–8) and the healing of blind men in Mark 8:22–26 and 10:46–52, which could compete with the healings reported of Vespasian.[13] Serving enacted as a basic principle of Christian existence (cf. Mark 9:33–37; 10:35–45) is profiled over against the reality of imperial Rome: "You know that among the gentiles those whom they regard as their rulers lord it over them, and their great ones are tyrants

9. See Vielhauer, "Erwägungen zur Christologie des Markusevangeliums."

10. Cf. Weber, "Christologie und 'Messiasgeheimnis.'"

11. Cf. Weber, "Christologie und 'Messiasgeheimnis,'" 115–16.

12. Cf. Ebner, "Evangelium contra Evangelium."

13. Cf. Winn, *Purpose of Mark's Gospel*: "In conclusion, the primary purpose of Mark's gospel is to respond to Flavian propaganda that has created a crisis within the church in Rome. This response is polemical, pitting Jesus's impressive résumé against that of the current Roman emperor Vespasian. Mark's Gospel offers overwhelming evidence to its audience of Jesus's superiority to Vespasian and confirms for its audience Jesus's identity as God's Messiah and the true world ruler."

over them. But it is not so among you" (Mark 10:42–43). A relativizing of the claim of the power of the state lies also in Mark 12:13–17, for Jesus's answer (Mark 12:17, "Give to Caesar what is Caesar's, and to God what is God's") rejects the political-religious claim of the caesar and ascribes to him a functional significance that lies beneath any religious veneration. The persecutions presupposed in Mark 13:9–13 indicate that Mark wants to motivate his community to courageous confession in a hostile environment.

2. Mark's messianic secret also serves the knowledge of Jesus Christ as Son of God. The hiddenness of Jesus as a saving figure is present in Mark in various forms, each of which needs to be understood within the framework of an overarching christological theory of the messianic secret. (a) The demons' knowledge of the Messiah and Jesus's command for their silence: In Mark 1:25; 1:34; 3:12 Jesus commands the silence of the demons, who previously have made an accurate statement about the person of Jesus. Mark wants to signify with this that the knowledge of Jesus on the basis of miraculous acts is not sufficient to have a full understanding of his sonship. The miracles do not yet make Jesus the Son of God. (b) The hidden performance of the miracles of Jesus: the prohibition of spreading the story and the disobedience of this command. In Mark 5:43a and 7:36a, Jesus forbids the public reporting of the healing event to those present and to the healed man himself within the framework of a miraculous deed. This instruction is disobeyed in Mark 7:36b as well as in Mark 1:45. The command not to tell anyone should again prevent them from defining and usurping Jesus on the basis of the miracles. In the miracles the secret of Jesus is not yet totally unveiled, yet the violation of this command indicates that Jesus's epiphany as miracle worker cannot be stopped (cf. also Mark 7:24!).[14] (c) The understanding of the disciples: Until 8:27 the disciples' lack understanding of the teaching (Mark 4:13; 7:18) and person of Jesus (Mark 4:40f.; 6:52). Both the secret instruction to the disciples and the disciples' misunderstanding occur frequently. Whereas the disciples in Mark 8:17, 21 are portrayed as stubborn and hard-hearted, with Peter's confession in Mark 8:29, a break occurs. A change in the level of the disciples' knowledge has taken place, for now the disciples have a consciousness of the messianic identity of Jesus. The command to silence in Mark 8:30 and the reaction of Peter to the first passion prediction indicate, however, that the disciples in Mark 8:27–33 understand the secret of the suffering of Jesus's person as little as they do in Mark 9:5–6; 9:30–32; 10:32–34. With the incomprehension of the disciples, Mark demonstrates from the negative side, to a

---

14. Cf. Frenschkowski, *Offenbarung und Epiphanie*, 211: "The numen reveals itself; its true nature constantly glimmers through the hiddenness."

certain extent, how the person of Jesus may not be understood. A complete understanding of the person of Jesus cannot be limited to his high status and glory and at the same time ignore the suffering. Rather, both belong to a full knowledge of Jesus. (d) The command for the disciples' silence: Both commands to the disciples to be silent in Mark 8:30 and 9:9 are of great significance for the theory of the secret. With the command to silence in 8:30, Mark indicates that in Peter's confession alone there is still not a complete and definitive knowledge of the person of Jesus. This fact is indicated in the first passion prediction that follows and the reaction of Peter. Years ago W. Wrede articulated the basic theory of messianic secrecy for interpreting Mark 9:9, "As they were coming down from the mountain, he commanded them to tell no one what they had seen until the Son of Man had risen from the dead."[15] Mark then ends the command to silence until the resurrection of Jesus and from that point onward annuls the secret about the person of Jesus.[16] Furthermore, from the narrative logic of Mark 9:2–8, one can explain neither the subject of resurrection nor a termination of the command to silence. Finally, the Markan theme of the incomprehension of the disciples in verse 10 and the terminated command to silence in verse 9 are very closely related to each other. Both indicate that not until the cross and resurrection is an unlimited knowledge of Jesus Christ possible.

The theory of secrecy is the narratival and theological central feature of the discourse of Mark's Gospel, with which all other aspects are connected in various ways and in various concentrations. The individual elements of the Markan theory of secrecy do not originate from historical interest; instead, each feature aims at the reader in order to lead to a complete knowledge of Jesus Christ. At the same time, the theory of secrecy enables the evangelist Mark to combine the pre-Markan miracle stories and the passion tradition within the framework of the new literary genre, gospel, and to merge the two into a unity.[17] Here is a great achievement of integration. Mark is the essential bearer of the NT miracle tradition,[18] for he succeeded in harmonizing two

15. Cf. Wrede, *The Messianic Secret*, 69–70.

16. Räisänen, *Das "Messiasgeheimnis,"* 109–17, 161; Pesch, *Das Markusevangelium*, 39, 77, considering Mark 9:9 traditional. Against this view one may observe the substantive and formal agreements with the clearly redactional command to silence in Mark 5:43; 7:36.

17. A pragmatic function of the motif of secrecy is given by Gerd Theissen: From the parallel between the world of the text of the Gospel and the real world of the reader/hearer, one may conclude that the successive unveiling of the secret and the growing danger for Jesus correspond to the social world of the Markan community; cf. Theissen, "Evangelienschreibung und Gemeindeleitung," 405.

18. Miracle stories are almost totally absent from the logia source and appear in the special material of Matthew and Luke only occasionally. Consequently, Mark and his tradition

competing interpretations of Jesus (Jesus as miracle worker and Jesus as the suffering one). Jesus the Son of God remains the same in his suffering and in his authoritative deeds. Thus Mark preserves the fundamental unity of exalted status and lowliness in the person of Jesus Christ. He demonstrates how Jesus will gather his people in the sign of the kingdom of God through his authoritative word, his healing activity in the miracles, and his readiness to give his life for others. With the theology of the cross, Mark takes up the theological inheritance of Paul and decisively expands it with his narrative presentation of the story of Jesus Christ (see below, 13.5). The crucial insight that the crucified Jesus of Nazareth is the Son of God not only concentrates on a singular event, as Paul does, but is presented in the clarity and intelligibility of a dramatic narrative.

10.2.2. Matthew: The Salvation of Israel for All People

The Gospel of Matthew was written in Syria around 90 CE (cf. Mark 4:24) and is the witness of a painful process of identity formation, which took place both in continuity and discontinuity with Judaism. Matthew is a representative of a Hellenistic Judaism/Jewish Christianity that was familiar with the Septuagint and that knew itself to be obligated to both particularistic and universalistic aspects. The evangelist considered himself permanently bound to Israel, but at the same time he worked through the separation of the majority of Israel and the new orientation to the gentiles. He was probably himself a teacher of his community (cf. Matt. 13:52) and presents Jesus especially as the teacher of the community and of the gentiles. Not coincidentally, Matthew became the main Gospel in church history,[19] for his portrayal of Jesus as authoritative teacher and world ruler as well as the whole catechetical shape of the Gospel emphatically and for all time shaped the image that humankind has about Jesus Christ.

The Gospel of Matthew is conceived as a book (Matt. 1:1) intended for public reading in the worship service. The first citation from Scripture in Matt. 1:23 ("Behold, the virgin will conceive and bear a son, and he will be called Emmanuel"), with its Matthean interpretation ("that is interpreted, 'God with us'") and the eschatological promise in Matt. 28:20 ("And behold, I am with you always until the end of the ages") forms an inclusio that is crucial

---

are the primary bearers of the New Testament miracle tradition. Miracle stories appear in several forms in Mark: (1) exorcisms: 1:21–28; 5:1–20; 9:14–27; (2) healings: 1:29–31; 1:40–45; 5:21–43; 7:31–37; 8:22–26; 10:46–52; (3) rescue miracles: 4:35–41; (4) epiphany stories: 6:45–52; (5) miracles of giving: 6:30–44; 8:1–9; (6) mixed forms: 2:1–12; 3:1–6; 7:24–30; (7) summary statements about the miraculous activity of Jesus: 1:32–34; 3:7–12; 6:53–56.

19. Cf. Köhler, *Rezeption des Matthäusevangeliums*.

for the total understanding of the Gospel.[20] With μεθ' ἡμῶν (with us, Matt. 1:23) or μεθ' ὑμῶν (with you, Matt. 28:20), Matthew signals the basic theme of his work: God's presence and faithfulness to his people in Jesus Christ.

The five great speeches in particular demonstrate the didactic competence of the evangelist. As the first and most extensive speech, the Sermon on the Mount in Matt. 5–7 has a key place,[21] particularly as in Matt. 28:20 (again on the mountain) it is referred to explicitly. The Sermon on the Mount is the core of what the disciples should teach to all nations. Matthew combines central aspects of his Christology with its composition: The frame in Matt. 5:1–2 and 7:28–29 designates both the disciples and the people as addressees; that is, the Sermon on the Mount is not a special instruction for a few but is intended for all believers. The Beatitudes (5:3–12) are not only a rhetorically impressive introduction but also give a signal as to the content: At the beginning stands Jesus's promise of salvation so that in Matthew also the commendation is the basis for the demand. The double metaphor of salt and light (5:13–16) strengthens the commendation (5:13a, "You are the salt of the earth"; 5:14a, "You are the light of the world"). However, in 5:13b, 14b–16, the demand comes into the foreground, and then in 5:17–20 it becomes programmatically formulated. The central focus is the better, that is, greater righteousness, of which the content is heard in the antitheses (5:20–48). The theme of righteousness is developed in a threefold way, as righteousness with respect to God (6:1–18), as righteousness for the kingdom of heaven (6:19–34), and with love as the foundation of the greater righteousness (7:1–12). In the final part (7:13–27) the criterion of righteousness is emphasized as doing, and it is connected with clear warnings that neither hearing nor confession alone ensures entrance into the kingdom of heaven, but only the *doing* of God's will.

Like the Sermon on the Mount, the other speeches do not accelerate the event, but rather the hearers/readers pause in order to experience basic instructions from the mouth of Jesus.[22] The outward pause corresponds to an inner progress. With the address to the disciples (Matt. 9:36–11:1), the disciples are incorporated into the commission to proclaim (cf. Matt. 4:19; 10:7). The sending of the disciples to Israel corresponds to the ministry of Jesus to Israel. The speech that records parables (Matt. 13:1–53) comments on the situation of the church by telling the story of Jesus. Paraenetic and salvation-historical

20. Cf. Frankemölle, *Jahwebund und Kirche Christi*, 7–83.
21. On the Sermon on the Mount, cf., in addition to the commentaries, especially G. Strecker, *Die Bergpredigt*; Weder, *Die "Rede der Reden"*; H. Betz, *Sermon on the Mount*; Feldmeier, "Verpflichtende Gnade."
22. Luz, *Matthew*, 1:12, formulates the matter in this context: "The five major discourses are spoken, as it were, 'beyond the window' of the Matthean story of Jesus."

elements emerge (especially in the metaphors of sowing and harvest), both of which take on their severity against the background of judgment (Matt. 13:40–43). Ecclesiological themes are dominant in the speech about church matters (Matt. 18:1–35): the humility of the disciples and the search for the little ones and those who have gone astray are treated as well as the brotherly encouragement in prayer, the expulsion from the community, and the unlimited forgiveness. At the center of the speech stands a christological promise: "For where two or three gather in my name, I am with them" (Matt. 18:20). The position of the eschatological speech (Matt. 24:3–25:46) is anticipated in Mark 13. For Matthew, the concern is not with eschatological speculation but with the practice of faithfulness, for the argumentation moves toward paraenesis in Matt. 24:32–25:30.

The five speeches, like the work as a whole, communicate the impression and the claim that the teaching of Jesus should be understood as the binding interpretation of the will of God. As the Resurrected One proclaims the binding nature of the words of the earthly Jesus (Matt. 28:20a), these words have full authority.

The appearance of the Resurrected One, his enthronement to become world ruler, and the missionary command in Matt. 28:16–20 form not only the narrative conclusion of Matthew's Gospel but are rather the culmination toward which the entire Gospel moves and from which it should be read.[23] Matthew 28:16–20 is thus the theological and hermeneutical key to an appropriate understanding of the entire work.[24] In the center of Matt. 28:16–20 stands the concept of the universal rule of Jesus Christ. Jesus appears as the only and true teacher, whose commands are binding for both the disciples and the entire world. The authority of the Resurrected One now empowers the disciples and also the contemporary Matthean church to take the mission of Jesus to the nations, to follow the obligation to spread the teaching of Jesus, and thus to be the church of Jesus Christ. The perspective of 28:16–20 not only portrays the final chord of the work but is also present from the beginning: The way of Jesus in the Gospel appears as the way of God to the nations. The signals of this perspective in Matt. 1–2 were already portrayed; further observations may be added: after the preaching of judgment over Israel (Matt. 3:1–12) by the Baptist with the new constitution of the people

23. Appropriately, O. Michel, "Der Abschluß des Matthäusevangeliums," 21: "Only under the theological presupposition of Matt. 28:18–20 was the entire gospel written (cf. Matt. 28:19 with 10:5ff.; 15:24; Matt. 28:20 with 1:23; return to the baptism, Matt. 3:1). Indeed, to some extent, the end returns to the beginning and teaches the gospel, the story of Jesus, 'from the back.' Matthew 28:18–20 is the key to understanding the entire book."

24. For a basic analysis, cf. Bornkamm, "Der Auferstandene und der Irdische."

of Abraham in Matt. 3:9 and the reference to Galilee of the gentiles (Matt. 4:12, 15), Jesus, at the conclusion of the Sermon on the Mount, programmatically performs healings on outsiders of the society (Matt. 8:1–4, a leper; 8:5–13, a gentile; 8:14–15, a woman). Matthew 8–9, as the founding legend of the Matthean community, signals the position of the evangelist. He lives in a church composed of Jewish and gentile Christians, for whom a Roman is the first example of faith (cf. Matt. 8:10). In the narrative of the centurion of Capernaum, the Matthean church recognizes its own history. The centurion accepts the primacy of Israel in salvation history (Matt. 8:8) and at the same time becomes the first among the gentile Christians, while Israel falls under judgment (Matt. 8:11–12).[25] Matthew 10:17–18 presupposes that the disciples proclaim the gospel equally among Jews and gentiles. Matthew 12:21 and 13:38a point to the universal mission to the nations; in Matt. 12:18–21, the unrestricted mission is supported with the lengthy reflective citation (Isa. 42:1–4).[26] If the gospel is preached among the nations (cf. also Matt. 24:14; 26:13), it is only consistent if, at the final judgment, all nations stand before the throne of the Son of Man (cf. Matt. 25:31–46).

The significance of the Gospel of Matthew in the history of early Christianity consists primarily in the fact that it, like no other Gospel, defines its standpoint in continuity with Israel, preserves Jewish Christian traditions, and combines it with the opening to the universal mission to the nations. Like Paul, Matthew legitimates the mission to the nations without minimizing the significance of the Torah. The claim of the whole Torah is maintained in Matthew; however, it takes place within a new framework of interpretation. "The Torah is not an independent reality alongside Jesus. Instead Jesus was the only teacher even in reference to the law and was the key to its understanding."[27] The Matthean church grew out of Judaism and is permanently connected to it, but it does not belong to the synagogue any longer. It has its own narrative of its foundation, its own offices, and its own theological profile. Alongside the universal perspective directed to the nations, the intentional omission of the problem of circumcision indicates that Matthew cannot be explained exclusively within a continuing intra-Jewish standpoint.[28] The absence of the

25. Luz, *Matthew*, 2:12, minimizes the significance of this text when he says that the centurion from Capernaum is for Matthew "a marginal figure with a future perspective."

26. Cf. Walker, *Die Heilsgeschichte im ersten Evangelium*, 78–79.

27. Luz, *Matthew*, 1:51; cf. Deines, *Die Gerechtigkeit der Tora*, 256, who argues about the significance of the Torah in Matthew: "As an independent entity, as a means of righteousness, it has lost its function, because it is fulfilled."

28. The answers to these questions are not convincing. On the contrary, the evidence in the Gospel is clear. It is not circumcision but baptism and mission and instruction (cf. Matt. 28:16–20) that are the rites of initiation/the major principles of the Matthean community.

noun περιτομή (circumcision)[29] in the logia sources and in all three Synoptics is scarcely a coincidence, and the Jewish Christian Matthew cannot have been unaware that without circumcision[30] there is no Judaism and also no serious inner-Jewish dialogue.[31] Matthew takes away the boundary and embeds the Torah on a higher level in a new frame of reference: love in the form of love for God, self, the neighbor, and the enemy as the center of the universal will of God that is proclaimed about Jesus Christ as the Son of God. With this intriguing result, the assumption is most likely correct that the evangelist Matthew is a representative of liberal Hellenistic diaspora Jewish Christianity.[32] Baptism is now the entry into the church of God (Matt. 28:19) for all believers for all time. Rigorous historical classifications such as "Jewish Christianity" or "gentile Christianity" probably no longer correspond to the reality of the Matthean church and the self-understanding of the evangelist.[33] Matthew does not think only in terms of particular Jewish or gentile Christianity; he thinks in universal terms! Thus he could maintain the Jewish heritage and the claim associated with it in the church that was being formed. The Gospel of Matthew has an inclusive basic structure, uniting in itself disparate streams that become something new through the dominant place of Christology.[34]

10.2.3 Luke: God's Faithfulness in History

Luke introduces something new into early Christianity: he writes a two-volume history of the origin of Christianity. In the process he explicitly

29. The verb περιτέμνειν (circumcise) appears only in Luke 1:59; 2:21 (the circumcision of the infant Jesus).

30. Cf. only Gen. 17:7, 13, where circumcision is both the sign of the eternal covenant with Abraham and with all Israel. Anyone who refrains from circumcision breaks the covenant and must be cut off from the people (Gen. 17:14).

31. In contemporary German scholarship, Matthias Konradt and Wolfgang Kraus in particular represent the thesis that Matthew stands within an inner Jewish discourse and that the universalism of the missionary command is not conditioned by the failure of the mission to Israel "but rather in the acceptance and performance of the theme of descent from Abraham and the promise to Abraham for the blessing to all nations." Kraus, "Zur Ekklesiologie des Matthäusevangeliums," 212. Matthias Konradt emphasizes: "In 28:19 the emphasis is on the fact that the disciples are no longer sent to Israel alone, but to all nations. The much-debated question of whether Israel is still included is definitely not a matter for debate for Matthew; his concern is the opposite: that now all (other) people are included." Konradt, *Israel, Kirche und die Völker*, 339.

32. Cf. in this sense, e.g., H. Stegemann, "Die des Uria," 271, who maintains "that the Judaistic components of Matthean theology were Hellenistic-Jewish from the outset."

33. Cf. Wong, *Interkulturelle Theologie und multikulturelle Gemeinde*, 125–54, who wants to explain the "gentile and Jewish Christian texts" from the parallel existence and interconnected relationship of gentile and Jewish Christians in the Matthean church.

34. Cf. Backhaus, "Entgrenzte Himmelsherrschaft," 75–103.

reflects and justifies his approach (Luke 1:1–4); Luke looks back to an un-paralleled beginning (Luke 1:5–2:52) and writes a continuation with the book of Acts. This expansion of the narrative framework corresponds to a changed perspective and a new consciousness. The changed perspective: the theme of this two-volume work is the spread of the gospel into the world within its religious, economic, and political framework. For the evangelist, the existence of numerous churches in the eastern Mediterranean, extending to Rome, forms the historical framework for the composition of his two works between 90 and 100 CE. In a new consciousness, Luke not only considers himself and his churches a part of this world but also appeals to a propertied, educated, and religio-philosophically interested urban audience (cf., e.g., Luke 1:1–4; Acts 17:22–31; 19:23–40; 25:13–26:32) whom he wishes to convince of the trustworthiness of the Christian teaching. He thus understands the Gospel of Luke and Acts as a unified work for narrating, reading, and understanding.[35] Especially in the prologue in Luke 1:1–4, he demonstrates his literary ambitions as an author and his theological intentions.[36] His work is the expression of a changed historical consciousness and understanding of history! As a historian and theologian, Luke is interested in the beginnings and the continuity that develops from it. He is concerned for completeness, accuracy, and reliability through which he evidently links himself to the traditions of ancient historiography, as the synchronizing and dating in Luke 1:5; 2:1, 2; 3:1, 2; Acts 11:28, and Acts 18:12 demonstrate. Moreover, there is the distinctively Lukan characteristic in which he arranges salvation history into epochs that are woven together yet at the same time are clearly distinguishable; this is not without contemporary parallels, for in particular the historical monographs of Sallust indicate a comparable structure.[37] Thus the two books of Luke could be described as historical monographs in which the character of the Lukan portrayal of the life of Jesus remains unaffected as a Gospel.[38] However, Luke gives his own stamp to this genre, for the "reliability" (ἀσφάλεια in Luke 1:4) of the account rests not on the events themselves, but in God as the Lord of history. In literary terms, with his historical work Luke creates a document of world literature! Even as a historian he desires to be also a narrator who makes a claim on the emotions of his hearers/readers and reports on a new "way of salvation" (Acts 16:17) in faith and discipleship in Jesus Christ.

35. See the basic evidence in Tannehill, *Narrative Unity of Luke-Acts*, 2 vols.

36. On the theological program, see the argument of G. Klein, "Lukas 1,1–4 als theologisches Programm"; cf. also Alexander, *Preface to Luke's Gospel*.

37. Cf. Plümacher, "Neues Testament und hellenistische Form."

38. Cf. Plümacher, "Neues Testament und hellenistische Form," 116–17.

A guiding principle runs through Luke's twofold work. God's promises have been fulfilled, for in Jesus's story and the story of the expansion of the gospel from Jerusalem to Rome, God is active as the Lord of history. The idea of fulfillment in the form of a periodization in salvation history determines the theological plot both in the macro- and microstructure of Luke-Acts. In the macrostructure a correspondence is evident between Luke 1:1 ("about the events that have been fulfilled among us"), Luke 24:44–47 (the Resurrected One says, "These are my words, which I have said to you as I was with you. Everything must be fulfilled, that was written about me in the law of Moses and in the Psalms; . . . in my name repentance for the forgiveness of sins will be preached to all nations"), and Acts 28:28 (the last words of Paul: "Then you should now know: the salvation of God has been sent to the gentiles. They will listen!"). In the course of the Gospel narrative from Israel to the gentiles, God's original and final will is being fulfilled. God's act in history is thus an event aimed toward the goal that is carried along by God's saving will in every era.[39] The divine δεῖ determines the course of history: Jesus "must" be in the temple (Luke 2:49); he "must" proclaim (Luke 4:43), and he "must" go to Jerusalem to the passion (Luke 9:31; 13:22; 24:26, 44). Similarly, the systematic expansion of the gospel into the world stands under the divine plan. According to the first words of Peter, "the word of the Scripture must be fulfilled" (Acts 1:16). Despite all of the opposition, it is true that one must obey God rather than men (Acts 5:29); against his own will, Peter must understand that the gospel is destined for the nations (Acts 10:14–16) and that God is no respecter of persons (Acts 10:34). Finally, Luke emphasizes three times that Paul "must" go to Rome (Acts 19:21; 23:11; 27:24), and an angel says to Paul, "Fear not, Paul! You must appear before Caesar").[40] Caesar also serves the will of God, for it is by his decree that Mary and Joseph go to Bethlehem (Luke 2:1–21), and the appeal to Caesar takes Paul to Rome (Acts 25:11).

Luke thinks in terms of distinct periods, but each does not begin afresh without presuppositions. What has preceded always continues to be present and is developed further. He makes a structure in which the time of Jesus and the time of the church form the clear center. Luke characterizes the time of Jesus as a time free from Satan, and thus it is the middle of time.[41] At the end of the temptation story, Satan goes away (Luke 4:13, "He left him until a more convenient time") in order to enter into Judas in Luke 22:3 and to become active again. The vision in Luke 10:18 ("I saw Satan fall like lightning from heaven") emphasizes the special quality of the appearance of Jesus. Through

---

39. Cf. Schulz, "Gottes Vorsehung bei Lukas."
40. Cf. Burfeind, "Paulus *muß* nach Rom."
41. Cf. Conzelmann, *Theology of St. Luke*, 170–206.

this perspective, Luke emphasizes the ministry of Jesus to Israel as a time of salvation in a special way, yet without separating it from the other epochs. John the Baptist, beyond the parallel in the birth story, remains present in the world narrated in Luke-Acts (Luke 7:18–35; 16:16; Acts 1:22; 10:37; 11:16; 13:24f.; 18:24–19:7), and the time of Jesus is permanently connected with the time of the church by thoughts of fulfillment, ascension (cf. Luke 24:50–53; Acts 1:1–11), the work of the Spirit, and the proclamation of the kingdom of God.[42] The immediate time of Jesus is distinguished in content by the concentration of his ministry to Israel. With it a programmatic significance belongs to the inaugural speech of Jesus in Nazareth (Luke 4:16–30). With his teaching and miracles, Jesus carries out his attention to the poor, the sinners, and the outsiders of society (cf. Luke 6:17–49, Sermon on the Plain; 5:27–32, the tax collector Levi; 7:36–50, the sinful woman; 8:1–3, the women who accompanied Jesus). With the story of the transfiguration (Luke 9:28–36) and the two passion predictions that provide the frame for it (Luke 9:18–22, 43–45), the perspective changes, for Jerusalem, the suffering of Jesus, and his resurrection now come into view. In the travel narrative (Luke 9:51–19:27) Luke strengthens this focus, as he adds to the third (Markan) passion prediction (cf. 18:31–34) three additional references to the passion (Luke 12:49–50; 13:31–33; 17:25). The path of Jesus that begins in 9:51 is the way to suffering and glory to which, according to Luke 22:42, he must go! The reference to the ascension in Luke 9:51 ("when he would be taken up [into heaven]") also emphasizes the characteristic interlocking for Luke of suffering and glory. The travel narrative has a paraenetic orientation: in addition to the connections with the theology of the passion, Luke teaches that the path of Jesus is to be understood as a continuing care for the lost (Luke 15), the poor (Luke 16:19–31), and the Samaritans (Luke 10:25–37) and as an offer of the kingdom of God to Israel. The destination of the Lukan portrayal of the life of Jesus is Jerusalem (within the travel narrative, cf. esp. Luke 13:22; 17:11), where he works as a teacher, especially in the temple (Luke 19:29–21:38). Passion and Easter for Luke form an inseparable unity. The Easter events happen in one day and find their climax and their end (Luke 24:1–53) in the ascension.

Whereas the activity of Jesus in Jerusalem, his death on the cross, and the resurrection form the conclusion to the time of Jesus, the Emmaus story and the ascension mark the transition and at the same time the connection to the time of the church,[43] for the end of the Gospel is the stage for the beginning

42. Cf. G. Schneider, *Das Evangelium nach Lukas*, 98; contra Conzelmann, *Theology of St. Luke*, 16, who alone sees the time of Jesus as bounded by Luke 4:13 and 22:3 and as the time of salvation.

43. Contra Conzelmann, *Theology of St. Luke*, 207–15 and passim, who regards the Pentecost event as the beginning of the church.

of Acts. Allegiance to the Resurrected One comes into view with the Emmaus disciples and becomes the primary theme of Acts. Furthermore, Luke illustrates with the trusted Greco-Roman literary form of the apotheosis: God's faithfulness to his promise from the birth to the ascension continues in the universal preaching of the gospel and ends with the parousia, for the one who has gone into heaven will also return! Inasmuch as the ascension takes place before the eyes of the apostles (Luke 24:51; Acts 1:9–11), they are legitimated as eyewitnesses (cf. Luke 1:1–4). This event is crucial for the depiction of the activity of the apostles. Moreover, the "forty days" (Acts 1:3) of instruction of the apostles by the Exalted One signal that, with the ascension as the conclusion of the Easter event, a crucial transition has taken place. The ascension thus marks the continuity between the time of Jesus and the time of the church in which the apostles have a crucial role. For Luke, the time of Jesus is the central period of salvation, from which the church originates and to which it must always be drawn.[44]

Programmatically, the apostles are commissioned to give testimony "in Jerusalem, in all Judea and Samaria, and to the end of the earth" (Acts 1:8b). In the course of the narrative, this program is purposefully implemented. After the successful preaching in Jerusalem in Acts 1–5[45] and the crisis over Stephen (Acts 6:8–7:60), the preaching around Israel took place (Acts 8), reaching the climax in the story of Cornelius in Acts 10:1–11:18, which marked an additional crucial transition: God himself turns to the gentile world. Peter's experience of gradually learning the will of God illustrates the far-reaching implications of the event, which cannot be reversed by later opposing forces (cf. Acts 15:1ff.) but leads to table fellowship of Christ-believers from Jewish and gentile backgrounds (cf. Acts 15:22–29). Within this event the person of Paul takes on a crucial significance, for the portrayal of Paul is the essential center of Acts (see below, 10.3.1). For Luke, Paul the converted Jew is the chief witness for the continuity of Israel within salvation history in the transition of the history of the early Christian mission from Jews to the nations. Luke's concern is particularly the demonstration that the transition of salvation from the Jews to the nations as recipients of the promises to Israel corresponds to the initial will of God. Luke treats the increasing distance between Christianity and Judaism because it threatens to call into question the continuity of the

44. Cf. Roloff, *Die Kirche*, 191: "The church, as it has developed through the witness of the messengers of Jesus, stands in definite continuity determined by the acts of God with the story of Jesus."

45. Lohfink, *Die Sammlung Israels*, formulates the program in Acts 1–5: "In the period of the first apostolic preaching, the true Israel was gathered out of the Jewish people! The Israel that persisted in rejecting Jesus lost its right to be the true people of God—and it became Judaism."

church with Israel in salvation history and the validity of the promises. The church should understand how the divine σωτηρία (salvation; cf. Luke 1:69, 71, 77; 19:9; Acts 4:12; 7:25; 13:26, 47; 16:17; 27:34) came to the gentiles, thus finally to the (Christian) readers, and became a reality in a "church" composed of Jewish and gentile Christians. This is the background for the emphatic advocacy for the legitimacy of the mission apart from circumcision, as the second part of Acts especially demonstrates. With this perspective, Luke wants to communicate certainty, strengthen identity, and advocate Christianity![46]

The time of Jesus and the time of the church are bound together primarily by the work of the Spirit. As the Spirit of God, the Spirit is the essential subject of the story of Jesus Christ (cf. Luke 1–2) and of the history of the universal mission to the nations. The Spirit is granted to the apostles after Easter by the Resurrected and Exalted One (cf. Acts 1:6–8); the Spirit continues the work of Jesus in the church (cf. Acts 2:1–13) and thus ensures the continuity of God's saving activity in history. The Spirit not only repeatedly intervenes in the course of salvation history but is also active in the founding of historical decisions, setting the course of events (cf. Acts 10:45; 15:28; 16:6f.). Finally, at the end of this two-volume work, Luke interprets the saying about the hardening of Israel (Isa. 6:9–10 in Acts 28:25–27) as a word of the Holy Spirit. The fact that the majority of his people are closed to the gospel and do not repent corresponds to the will of God.

With the expansion of the historical-theological perspective by this two-volume work, Luke sees an opening to areas that had previously been reached in limited ways at best: (1) the evangelist has the educated people in view (Luke 1:1–4; Acts 25:13–26:32), (2) he places the urban culture in his narrative world (Acts 19:23–40), and (3) he portrays the Christian teaching within the context of and in conflict with contemporary magic/sorcery (Acts 8:4–25; 13:8–12; 16:16–22) and philosophy (Acts 17:16–34). Thus "the [new] way" (cf. Acts 19:23)[47] appeared not only as cultured but also as its own new religious culture with Jewish roots in the Roman world. Luke clearly documents the growing self-confidence of the Christians; with his two-volume work he engages in the ancient practice of writing history, gives a literary form to a new perception of his own history, and announces a claim to significance in world history.

---

46. Cf. Backhaus, "Lukas der Maler," 31: Luke "anchors the relational memory in the 'objective' depth of a first epoch in order to make visible the ancient biblical origin to his community in a vigorous forum of competing religious self-definitions, to bring to mind the memory of the founding, to place the abiding attractiveness before the eyes, and thus to give to their present existence a binding identity."

47. On this self-designation derived from Isa. 40:3 LXX, cf. Trebilco, *Self-Designations and Group Identity*, 247–71.

The Synoptic Gospels are highly significant for the history of early Christianity in many respects: (1) By granting theological importance to the life of Jesus as Christ, Son of God, and Lord, they first make possible a comprehensive reception of the figure of Jesus and thus form a crucial presupposition for a successful identity formation and mission. In the Gospels, memory, narrative, and identity form a new reciprocal unity, for narrative that is remembered aims for the formation of Christian identity. (2) If previously only single aspects of the life/preaching of Jesus stood in the foreground (passion narrative: the suffering Jesus; miracle tradition: the authoritative Jesus; logia source: the Jesus who returns), the Synoptic Gospels develop a comprehensive portrayal of the ministry and teaching of Jesus from their own perspective. (3) Thus they take very different theological-political positions. While Mark never mentions the word νόμος (law), Matthew positions himself in conscious continuity with Judaism (cf. Matt. 5:17–20), while Luke takes a somewhat mediating position. (4) However, all three Gospels assume the decision of the apostolic conference and consistently omit the problem of circumcision. (5) The Gospels and Acts formulate the new self-confidence and the new perspective of Christians in the world. In contrast to Paul's view, the imminent end no longer stands in the foreground, but the continuance of life in the world. (6) Acts especially demonstrates: Whoever writes his own history is convinced he is writing real history.

10.3 The Continuing Legacy of Paul

Of the twenty-seven writings of the NT, half are connected with the name of Paul: seven proto-Pauline and six deutero-Pauline, and Acts from chapter 15 to the end reports primarily on Paul only. This fact is no coincidence; instead, it reflects the significance of the apostle for the formation of the emerging Christianity and the shape of the Christianity that was being consolidated. The story of Paul did not end with his death; it continued in an intensive movement of reception. In this reception there was a reflection of how one regarded Paul "after Paul" and what solutions to problems were connected with his person.

10.3.1 Acts as the First Biography of Paul

Acts is not a biography of Paul, but it includes one![48] It communicates biographical information that, in part, is found neither in the proto-Pauline nor in the deutero-Pauline letters and is basic for every image of Paul.

48. Cf. Alexander, "Acts and Ancient Intellectual Biography," 34, according to whom Acts is "not just a biography of Paul, but it contains a Pauline biography."

1. *Origin.* Three times Acts mentions that Paul comes from the Cilician city of Tarsus (Acts 9:11; 21:39; 22:3; cf. 11:25).

2. *Legal status.* According to Acts 16:37–38; 22:25, 28; 23:27, Paul possessed Roman citizenship; furthermore, Acts 21:39 assumes the citizenship in his home city Tarsus.

3. *Vocation and social status.* Acts 18:3 hands on the plausible tradition that Paul and Aquila were tentmakers.

4. *Religious education.* Paul received his education from the most famous teacher of the law of his time, Gamaliel (Acts 22:3; cf. 5:34).

5. *Earliest theological orientation.* Paul was active as a Pharisee (Acts 22:3; 23:6, "son of Pharisees"). The striking emphasis on the theological category of "zeal"[49] (cf. Gal. 1:14; Phil. 3:6; Acts 22:3–4) indicates that Paul leaned toward the radical wing of Pharisaism.[50]

6. *Persecutor of the first Christ-believers.* Paul's activity as a persecutor is recorded in the oldest descriptions of him (cf. Acts 8:3; 9:2; 22:4, 19; 26:10–11; also 1 Cor. 15:9; Gal. 1:13, 23; Phil. 3:6).

7. *New direction in his life and teaching.* Luke reports the call and commissioning of Paul three times (Acts 9:3–19a; 22:6–16; 26:12–18; cf. 1 Cor. 9:1; 15:8; 2 Cor. 4:6; Gal. 1:12–16; Phil. 3:4b–11).

8. *School membership.* Paul appears first as a persecutor (Acts 9:2) of "the [new] way" (Acts 19:23), a wing of the movement that did not insist on circumcision (Acts 15:1–5), and then belonged to it and preached its message (Acts 19:9–10).

9. *The work of his life.* The three missionary journeys in particular (Acts 13:1–14:28; 15:36–18:22; 18:23–21:14) document the impressive life-achievement of the apostle.

10. *Fate.* Acts describes the destiny of its hero obliquely, from the events in Jerusalem (Acts 21:15–23:22) and Caesarea (Acts 23:23–26:32), then through the adventurous journey by ship (Acts 27:1–28:13) to his ministry in Rome (Acts 28:14–31).

Luke skillfully introduces Paul (Saul) in narrative form en passant, first as a spectator but then as an actor (cf. Acts 7:58; 8:3). Stephen as the first martyr of Christianity and Paul as the greatest martyr of Christianity stand in relationship to each other. Within the narrative, Paul increasingly enters the picture. The first close-up shot is the report about the call near Damascus (Acts

49. On the category of "zeal" in ancient Judaism, cf. Hengel, *Zealots*, 149–200.
50. Cf. Haacker, "Die Berufung des Verfolgers."

9:1–19a, 19b–31). Then Paul temporarily returns to the background so that the role of Peter (from the Lukan view) can reach its goal (Acts 10:1–11:18). A few smaller notes on Paul appear (cf. Acts 11:25, 30; 12:25) until he dominates the events from Acts 13 onward. The portrayal of Paul is the narrative and theological center of Acts,[51] in which seven motifs stand in the foreground.

1. *The one who fights against God.* First, Paul appears as a relentless fighter against God.[52] His activity as a persecutor belongs to the oldest traditions about Paul (cf. Gal. 1:23; also 1 Cor. 15:9; Gal. 1:13; Phil. 3:6). Acts vividly and dramatically describes Paul's action against the Jerusalem church. In Jerusalem, Paul goes from house to house and has men and women thrown into prison (Acts 8:3). He aims for the death penalty against Christians (cf. Acts 22:4; 26:10) and forces them to renounce their faith (cf. Acts 26:11). He causes the beating of Christians (Acts 22:19) and has himself authorized for persecutions in Damascus (cf. Acts 9:2). The especially dark foil of the merciless persecutor Paul certainly originates with Luke, who can then let the great deeds of Paul the apostle shine brightly.[53]

2. *The one who fights for God.* From being a fighter against God, Paul becomes, through God's grace, God's fighter. Three times Luke describes the turn in the life of Paul from persecutor to proclaimer of the gospel (cf. Acts 9:3–19a; 22:6–16; 26:12–18),[54] suggesting the epochal significance of this event. In Acts 9:3–19a, an old legend about Paul in the church at Damascus may be the basis for the story of Paul the persecutor of Christians, who was led to a new knowledge of Jesus Christ by the shining of a heavenly light, and his companions brought him to Damascus (cf. Acts 9:10f.).[55]

3. *The witness.* A central element of the report of Paul's call is the motif of witness. In Acts 9:15–16 Jesus says to Ananias about Paul: "For he is my chosen instrument to bring my name before the eyes of the gentiles and the kings and the Israelites. I will show him how much he must suffer for the

---

51. Cf. Lampe and Luz, "Nachpaulinisches Christentum," 186, according to whom "Acts is to be read as the story of Paul with a detailed introduction." Cf. Manfred Lang, *Die Kunst des christlichen Lebens*, 201–50.

52. Cf. Manfred Lang, *Die Kunst des christlichen Lebens*, 201–50.

53. On the analysis of the texts, cf. Löning, *Die Saulustradition in der Apostelgeschichte*, 12–25, 93–95; Burchard, *Der dreizehnte Zeuge*, 40–51, esp. 50–51: "The persecution taken on and carried out by Paul, which was aimed against all Christians in Jerusalem and was meant to lead to execution or renunciation, is thus essentially a purely Lucan construction."

54. On the analysis of the texts, cf. Burchard, *Der dreizehnte Zeuge*, 51–136; Dietzfelbinger, *Die Berufung des Paulus*, 75–82; Heininger, *Paulus als Visionär*, 211–34; different accents are given in Haacker, "Zum Werdegang des Paulus," 900–909; Hengel and Schwemer, *Paulus zwischen Damaskus und Antiochien*, 63–80.

55. On the analysis, cf. Lüdemann, *Das frühe Christentum*, 111–21; Heininger, *Paulus als Visionär*, 221–22 (reconstruction of the possibly oldest tradition).

sake of my name" (cf. Acts 22:15, "You will be a witness for him"; 26:16, "to appoint you to be my servant and witness"). This testimony takes place within the narrative at several levels; among the places where Paul gives his testimony are Philippi (Acts 16:23–40), Corinth (Acts 18:12–16), and Ephesus (Acts 19:23–40). Jerusalem becomes the central place of witnessing in Acts. Thus just as the apostles and the Jerusalem church are subject to continuing persecutions (cf. Acts 4:1–22; 6:8–15; 7:54–60; 8:1), Paul also becomes a suffering witness (cf. Acts 21:27–22:21; 23:1–11, 12–22). Finally, Acts ends with the witness of Paul to the Jews and gentiles in Rome.

4. *The teacher*. From the beginning Luke already presents the chosen Paul as a teacher.[56] He had hardly been brought from Tarsus to Antioch by Barnabas when,[57] according to Acts 11:26, "They stayed an entire year with the church and taught many. In Antioch the disciples were first called Christians." Thus Luke portrays the Christians (cf. Acts 11:26; 26:28, χριστιανοί) as a school and Paul (and Barnabas) as founders and teachers of the school. The additional stages of Paul the teacher are impressive; in Acts 13:1 (διδάσκαλοι) he begins as a junior partner of Barnabas, and Sergius Paulus believes in the "new way" (cf. Acts 13:10; 19:23), "astonished about the teaching of the Lord" (Acts 13:12). In Acts 15:35 Paul's name appears before that of Barnabas ("they teach and preach the word of the Lord with many others"). In Acts 17:16–34 Paul appears as a learned man who is familiar with philosophical traditions but knows how to formulate fully new ideas (resurrection of the dead). In Corinth, Paul "taught" for a year and a half (Acts 18:11), and in Ephesus he rented the teaching hall of Tyrannus, where he "spoke" for two years (Acts 19:9–10). With this note, Luke depicts Paul as a traveling Hellenistic teacher for whom it was typical "to wander around and to establish successful schools."[58] Finally, in Troas, Paul extended his "lesson" until midnight and, as a result, Eutychus fell asleep and fell from the third floor. In the final address at Miletus, Paul speaks of teaching both in public and in homes (Acts 20:20). In Acts 21:21, 28 he is confronted with the accusation that he "taught" against the law and against the Jews. Finally, Acts ends with Paul the teacher who, like a true philosopher, speaks "with boldness" (παρρησία) and unhindered about Jesus Christ (28:31).

5. *The miracle worker*. In Acts, the two main protagonists, Peter (Acts 3:1–10; 5:12–16; 9:32–43) and Paul (Acts 13:4–12; 14:8–14; 16:16–18; 19:11f., 13–16; 20:7–12; 28:1–10), function in a prominent way also as miracle workers

---

56. Cf. Heininger, "Einmal Tarsus und zurück."

57. Heininger, "Einmal Tarsus und zurück," 128–33, describes the stay in Tarsus between Acts 9:30 and 11:25–26 as a time for study in Tarsus.

58. So Strabo, *Geography* 675, about the philosophers Plutiades and Diogenes from Tarsus.

(cf. also the summaries in Acts 2:43; 4:30, 33; 5:12; 14:3).[59] In the miracles the Crucified and Resurrected One proves to be the one who is alive; the essential subject of the miracle is Jesus (cf. Acts 4:10). Luke takes up a frequently underestimated part of the Pauline ministry, inasmuch as miracles were nothing unusual for Paul the pneumatic (cf. 1 Thess. 1:5; 1 Cor. 2:4–5; 4:19–20; 2 Cor. 6:7; 12:12; Gal. 3:5; Rom. 15:18–19). Acts, however, goes beyond this fact. Here Paul battles with magicians for the faith of the proconsul Sergius Paulus (Acts 13:4–12), heals a lame man (Acts 14:8–14), carries out exorcisms (Acts 16:16–18; 19:13–16), awakens the young Eutychus from the dead (Acts 20:7–12), and survives a deadly snakebite (Acts 28:1–10). Even the handkerchiefs that he touches have a healing function (Acts 19:12). Like Empedocles or Pythagoras, Paul appeared as a miracle worker authorized and empowered by God, whom some even considered a god (cf. Acts 14:11–13). What is assumed on this topic in the Pauline letters, Luke describes in powerful and somewhat dramatic episodes, which reflect the image of Paul that circulated in the churches. Paul engages in conflict with magic, which was widespread in antiquity, and becomes himself a Christian magician.[60]

6. *The philosopher.* Of special significance for the Lukan understanding of Paul is the Areopagus speech in Acts 17:16–34,[61] which portrays Paul as a philosopher. The echoes of Socrates are intentional, for Socrates's mimesis was widespread in the imperial period. Luke obviously attempts to present the Christian message among the educated people of his time, for he intentionally enriches the Areopagus speech with the cultural heritage of antiquity. Paul is parallel to Socrates, who was also accused of introducing "strange *daimons*/gods" (cf. Acts 17:18 with Xenophon, *Mem.* 1.1; Plato, *Apol.* 29d). In Acts 17:28 ("'For in him we live and move and have our being,' as some of your poets have said; 'For we are his offspring'") the Lukan Paul speaks in positive terms about the basic ideas of Greek theology and philosophy.[62] A new cultural horizon is opened with the speech of Paul in Athens. In the center of ancient intellectual history, the Lukan Paul does not simply reject Greco-Roman polytheism—he argues against it (Acts 17:22–23).[63] The identification of the "unknown god" with the one true God is an explicit attempt at accommodation that aims for an integration of Greco-Roman concepts of

59. On the miracles in Acts, cf. Neirynck, "Miracle Stories"; Schreiber, *Paulus als Wundertäter*, 13–158; Kollmann, "Paulus als Wundertäter."
60. Cf. Heininger, "Im Dunstkreis der Magie."
61. Still foundational is the work of Dibelius, "Paul on the Areopagus," who is absolutely correct in describing this section as "a climax of the book" (26).
62. Cf. only Xenophon, *Mem.* 1.4.18; 4.3, 14; Plato, *Leges* 10.899d; Aratus, *Phaenomena* 1–5.
63. A different view is that of Jervell, *Die Apostelgeschichte*, 443, about the Lukan Paul: "What he finds here is thus the pure paganism. That is what Athens means for him."

God. The omnipresence of the divine is established explicitly (vv. 27–28), but his representation in objects is rejected. The crucial intellectual argument that stands in the background is that a god in the plural is no god. People who share Greco-Roman religiosity can turn to the one God without throwing their own cultural concepts entirely overboard. However, Luke marks precisely the point where theology and philosophy separate: the resurrection of the dead (v. 32).

7. *The model martyr.* A certain proximity to the Socratic tradition for ancient readers and hearers is evident in the description of the trial, for both heroes are accused of offenses against religion (Xenophon, *Mem.* 1.1.1; Diogenes Laertius 2.40; Acts 21:28; 23:29). Socrates and Paul say nothing but the truth (Plato, *Apol.* 22a; Acts 25:11), and God is their witness (Plato, *Apol.* 22e; Acts 26:19–21); they justify their actions with God (Plato, *Apol.* 22a; Acts 22:14; 23:1) and attribute their action to a revelation from God (Plato, *Apol.* 33c; Acts 26:15); both stand firmly and do not avoid their fate through flight or bribery (Plato, *Crito* 44b–46a; Xenophon, *Mem.* 4.4.4; Acts 24:26). Among the various dangers (cf. Acts 22:22–30; 23:12–22; 25:3) and interrogations, Paul masterfully resists all attacks and accusations in order that finally, at the end, he is able to confront King Agrippa II on the same level (Acts 25:23–26:32).[64] In contrast to his opponents, in an exemplary way Paul represents the virtues of justice, courage, and steadfastness. These motifs also define the subsequent narrative of the transfer to Rome.[65] Thus it is evident to the reader that neither the trial nor the imprisonment describe a loss of honor for Paul and the churches.

Acts presents the "popular" Paul, as he was probably revered in the churches and became a major historical figure: the fighter, the conqueror of supernatural powers, the authoritative missionary, the teacher and miracle worker, and finally the exemplary witness of faith to the point of death. All of these aspects have a connection in the authentic Pauline letters and complete the image of Paul.

10.3.2 The Deutero-Paulines and the Collection of Paul's Letters

The greatest group of pseudepigraphic writings is the deutero-Pauline letters. This is no coincidence, for Paul became a central role model in early Christianity because of his intellectual achievement, his impressive lifework, and finally his martyrdom. Furthermore, Pauline theology was never a fixed,

64. Cf. Manfred Lang, *Die Kunst des christlichen Lebens*, 373–85.
65. Cf. here M. Labahn, "Paulus, ein homo honestus et iustus."

closed system, but a structure of thought based on fundamental convictions that were open to historical changes and theological challenges. Students of the apostle took up this tendency and published letters under the name of Paul that reflected on Pauline theology for a different era and wanted to gain a further hearing for it. The deutero-Pauline letters took the basic concerns of the apostle and developed them further for their specific historical and theological situation. Thus they are very different from each other: While Colossians and Ephesians, in the conflict with false teaching, further develop and adapt Pauline thought cosmologically, the Pastoral Epistles concentrate on the question of church office and particular aspects of the way of life, and 2 Thessalonians treats the question of the parousia almost exclusively.

The Deutero-Pauline Letters

The Letter to the Colossians is the first letter that was written after the death of the apostle in the name of Paul (and of Timothy). Written around 70 CE by a coworker and student of the apostle, Colossians stands in historical theological continuity with Paul like no other post-Pauline letter.[66] Paul always attributed to his person and his message a prominent significance in the process of the preaching of the gospel and the development of the church (cf. only 2 Cor. 3 and 5).[67] The Letter to the Colossians goes a step further, for it places the founding of the church and the person of the apostle in direct connection.[68] It now belongs in the Pauline gospel that is preached; the apostle is, as a messenger of the gospel, part of the all-embracing pretemporal plan of God, the church, "whose minister I have become in accordance with the divine office given to me for you to complete the word of God, the mystery that was hidden for aeons and for generations, but has now been revealed to the saints" (Col. 1:25–26). If Paul preached the gospel of Jesus Christ, the μυστήριον θεοῦ/Χριστοῦ (mystery of God/Christ) appears as the central message of Colossians (cf. 1:26–27; 2:2; 4:3).[69] Behind this mystery that was hidden for ages and now revealed (beyond Israel) stands the church that is being formed, which owes its existence to the preaching of the apostle. Thus the person and the suffering of the apostle are the content of the mystery (cf. Col. 1:24–29). As a servant of the body of Christ, Paul reveals to the church the mystery of the divine will; his person is inseparable from the content of

66. On the introductory issues, cf. Schnelle, *History and Theology of the New Testament*, 281–99.
67. Cf. Schröter, *Der versöhnte Versöhner*, 74–127, 250–91.
68. On the reception of Paul in Colossians, cf. especially Merklein, "Paulinische Theologie in der Rezeption."
69. Cf. Merklein, "Paulinische Theologie in der Rezeption," 412ff.

the gospel. His suffering (as apostle and martyr) even completes the tribulation of Jesus Christ for his church (Col. 1:24). Although Paul is not present in the body, he is still present in the spirit to the church (Col. 2:5), which should now proclaim Christ, just as the apostle proclaimed him (Col. 2:6). Every other teaching is regarded as the doctrine of men (Col. 2:8), but not as apostolic tradition. The gospel is defined no longer by the content in Jesus Christ but essentially by the proclamation of the apostle. Paul is not only the apostle to the gentiles (Col. 1:27) but also the apostle to the universal church (Col. 1:23b), who preaches the gospel to all people (Col. 1:28). Thus the letter raises the challenge of being oriented to the person, theology, and significance of the martyr-apostle. A significant feature for the structuring of the growing house churches is the household code, attested for the first time in Col. 3:18–4:1[70] (cf. Eph. 5:22–6:9; 1 Pet. 2:18–3:7). Within the context of ancient concern for order, the household code, as a Christian text, formulates the respective duties of wife and husband, children and parents/fathers, slaves and masters. The household codes are a type of handbook for life in the house churches; they define the status of individual groups and determine how to avoid internal conflicts. It is remarkable that in Col. 3:20–21 (cf. Eph. 6:1–4) the children are addressed as autonomous persons who were probably also present in the church assemblies.[71]

In Ephesians also, written between 80 and 90 CE in Asia Minor,[72] Paul is the apostle of the church. In Ephesians 3:1–13 he appears as the crucial messenger of revelation for the church (cf. Col. 1:24–29), for he reveals the previously hidden mystery of the granting of salvation to the gentiles (Eph. 3:6, 8), to all humankind, and to the powers (Eph. 3:10). In the memory of his person/his work, the Pauline apostle to the nations appears after his death (Eph. 3:1; 4:1) in a dimension that is significant for salvation history. Paul is the decisive recipient of the revelation of God, which leads to the universal church composed of Jews and people from the nations. The grace given to Paul tears down the wall between the two human groups (cf. Eph. 3:3, 6) and establishes a universal church, the topic that is carefully developed in Ephesians. Christ is the cornerstone of the church, which was built on the foundation of the apostles and prophets (Eph. 2:20). The apostleship guaranteed through Paul appears as the norm for the relationship to Christ. There is no trace of the conflict over the Pauline apostolate (cf. 1 Cor. 9:1ff.) or the conflicts between Jewish and gentile

---

70. On the form criticism and interpretation, cf. Gielen, *Tradition und Theologie*; Woyke, *Die neutestamentlichen Haustafeln*.

71. Cf. Dettinger, *Neues Leben in der alten Welt*.

72. On the introductory issues, cf. Schnelle, *History and Theology of the New Testament*, 299–314.

Christians. Paul does not win his position, for it is already commended in its historical dimension for the church.[73] This role is connected to the normative function of Paul for the understanding of tradition in the letter. The apostles and prophets (and thus especially Paul) are the foundation and the norm of what is Christian, which is no longer dependent on the deceptive games of men (Eph. 4:14). Because the apostle is a messenger of the mystery of the gospel (Eph. 6:20), this mystery can be appropriately preached only by him. The recourse to Paul and the associated pseudepigraphic character of Ephesians thus results necessarily from the image of Paul communicated in the letter.[74]

Second Thessalonians goes in a completely different direction. It was a pseudepigraphic hortatory and teaching document that was written around the end of the first century from Macedonia or Asia Minor,[75] intended to serve as an instruction manual for 1 Thessalonians. The authority claimed for Paul serves to defend against a false interpretation of the eschatological statements in 1 Thess. 4:13–18; 5:1–11. The apostle himself would not have shared the eschatological slogan of the opponents (2 Thess. 2:2c: ὡς ὅτι ἐνέστηκεν ἡ ἡμέρα τοῦ κυρίου, to the effect that the day of the Lord is already here); thus 2 Thessalonians claims the authority of Paul under its own conditions without, however, communicating genuine Pauline eschatology. The entire argument of 2 Thessalonians is based on the person of Paul. The call of the church is inseparably connected with the Pauline gospel (2 Thess. 2:14). The church resists the false teachers as it holds firmly to the teaching of the apostle (2 Thess. 2:5–6; cf. 1:10b) and, as he himself does, keeps away from evil people (cf. 2 Thess. 3:6). Along with the authoritative word, the apostle's way of life (cf. 2 Thess. 3:8) should help the church orient itself in the tumult of the present and hold firmly to the apostolic proclamation. The paraenesis in 2 Thessalonians is also shaped by the reference to the apostle Paul. The instruction communicated by the apostle serves as the ethical norm (cf. 2 Thess. 2:15; 3:6, 14). Furthermore, Paul appears as an example, whom the church should imitate (2 Thess. 3:7–9). He admonishes the church (2 Thess. 3:4, 6, 10, 12) to live in accordance with God's election (2 Thess. 2:13). The orientation toward Paul, however, cannot obscure the fact that 2 Thessalonians, in contrast to Colossians and Ephesians, does not develop Pauline theology in a productive way in a changed situation.[76]

73. Cf. Merklein, "Paulinische Theologie in der Rezeption," 416–19.

74. Gese, *Das Vermächtnis des Paulus*, 275, emphasizes: "Among the post-Pauline letters, Ephesians alone offers a comprehensive and condensed presentation of Pauline theology, for which the claim of timeless validity and authority is raised. This fact justifies regarding Ephesians as the theological legacy of Paul."

75. On the introductory issues, cf. Schnelle, *History and Theology of the New Testament*, 315–25.

76. Cf. Lindemann, *Paulus im ältesten Christentum*, 132–33.

The form of the Pastoral Epistles indicates their changed perspective in comparison with the proto-Paulines (and also Colossians, Ephesians, and 2 Thessalonians). They are not letters to churches, but they are addressed to personal coworkers of Paul in their responsibility for the whole church. In form and content, they are to be understood as a complement to the letters that have been published under the name of Paul. They were probably written around 100 CE in Ephesus[77] and issued within the framework of an edition of the Pauline corpus.[78] Fundamental to the Pastoral Epistles is a reference to Paul the apostle and teacher. He is the apostle commissioned by Jesus Christ by the will of God, the servant of the gospel, whose apostolate is a constituent part of the divine order of salvation (cf. 1 Tim. 1:1; 2:7; Titus 1:1; 2 Tim. 1:1, 11). The Pauline apostolate is intended for all nations (cf. 1 Tim. 2:7; 2 Tim. 4:17), to whom Paul preaches the gospel that has been entrusted to him (1 Tim. 1:11; 2:6–7; 2 Tim. 1:10–12; Titus 1:3). This gospel is the most precious treasure of the church (cf. 1 Tim. 6:19–20; 2 Tim. 1:12, 14), to be guarded as παραθήκη (the property that has been entrusted). As the only legitimate proclaimer, Paul himself becomes the content of the preaching so that a soteriological dimension is attributed to his work.[79] The fate of the apostles becomes the message; God's saving will is fulfilled with him and in him in an exemplary way (cf. only 1 Tim. 1:16, "For that reason I received mercy so that in me, as the foremost, Jesus Christ might demonstrate the utmost patience, making me an example for those who come to faith in him for eternal life"). Paul embodies the saving message so that one can speak of a "kerygmatizing" (cf. 2 Tim. 4:17) of his person in the Pastoral Epistles.[80]

As authorized proclaimer and content of the gospel, Paul in the Pastoral Epistles becomes the guarantor of the tradition and the legitimate teacher. He instructs the churches in "sound teaching"; διδασκαλία and παραθήκη designate the totality of what is presented in the Pastorals as preaching and ethical instruction.[81] While the false teachers split the churches with their false teaching, Timothy and Titus, along with the churches that are addressed, should hold firmly to the original teaching and to the Scripture (cf. 1 Tim. 1:3–7; 6:3–5; 2 Tim. 3:10–12, 15–16; Titus 1:10–2:15). As the

77. On the introductory issues, cf. Schnelle, *History and Theology of the New Testament*, 326–48.
78. Cf. Trummer, "Corpus Paulinum—Corpus Pastorale." The corpus thesis is disputed by Herzer, "Juden—Christen—Gnostiker."
79. Cf. Wolter, *Die Pastoralbriefe als Paulustradition*, 82; Läger, *Die Christologie der Pastoralbriefe*, 128.
80. Cf. Wolter, *Die Pastoralbriefe als Paulustradition*, 52.
81. Cf. Lohfink, "Paulinische Theologie in den Pastoralbriefen," 99.

archetype of faith, Paul is at the same time also the model and example for the churches (cf. 1 Tim. 1:15–16). The churches should follow the apostle in the teaching, in the conduct of life, in faith, and in suffering (cf. 2 Tim. 3:10–11; 1:13). Just as Paul is the model for Timothy at the internal level of the text, Timothy becomes the model for the churches (cf. 1 Tim. 4:12; 2 Tim. 3:10–11; cf. also Titus 2:7). Timothy and Titus are children of the apostle in faith (cf. 1 Tim. 1:2, 18; 2 Tim. 1:2; 2:1; Titus 1:4) and represent the ideal type of the postapostolic officeholder. As a whole, the Pastoral Epistles present an exceedingly vigorous image of Paul who stands up for and battles for his churches as preacher, teacher, pastor, and church organizer. Paul is equally an apostle, church authority, supporter of a collective identity, and the ideal/model of a Christian. His dominant place in the churches does not have to be established by the author of the Pastorals, for he writes in a living Pauline tradition.

The deutero-Pauline letters offer a multilayered image. What is striking, above all, is that the doctrine of justification that is prominent in Galatians and Romans recedes into the background in all of these letters.[82] In Colossians and Ephesians, the apocalyptic motifs in the Christology lose their significance, and now a present eschatology and a static cosmology are predominant. In contrast, 2 Thessalonians makes an attempt to reactivate apocalyptic thought. The central issues involve problems of church order and ethics that emerged in the changed situation within church history (appearance of false teachers, overcoming of declining expectation of the parousia). In this situation, the suffering Paul (Colossians, Ephesians, and 2 Timothy present themselves as Prison Epistles) becomes the authority of the beginning period. Appeal is made to Paul with the attempt to perpetuate his theology under changed conditions. While the deutero-Pauline letters deviate from genuine Pauline theology at significant points, they nevertheless demonstrate a familiarity with the thought of the apostle. In particular, the author of Colossians is shaped to a great degree by the Pauline school tradition, especially Romans. He probably acquired his knowledge of the basic themes of Pauline theology in the Pauline school in order to develop them further in accordance with the requirements of his own time.

THE COLLECTION OF THE PAULINE LETTERS AND THE BEGINNINGS OF THE CHRISTIAN CULTURAL TRADITION

The Pauline school (see above, 8.2) and the deutero-Pauline letters presuppose a lasting significance in the person of Paul and his letters (see above, 8.6)

82. Cf. Luz, "Rechtfertigung bei den Paulusschülern."

so that a key function belongs to the collection of the Pauline letters.[83] Colossians already confirms this fact, for it is familiar with the Corinthian letters, Philemon, Romans, Galatians, and Philippians.[84] Ephesians, a revision and expansion of Colossians, appears to refer to 1 Corinthians, Romans, and Galatians. Second Thessalonians is oriented completely to one authentic Pauline letter, 1 Thessalonians. Of special significance are the Pastoral Epistles, whose author probably made use of 1 and 2 Corinthians, Romans, Philippians, Colossians, and probably also Philemon. While Ephesians and 2 Thessalonians are obviously oriented to individual writings, the Pastoral Epistles already presuppose a collection of Pauline letters. If the Pastoral Epistles are designated as inspired writings in 2 Tim. 3:16, this would suggest that a process of collection and demarcation has already taken place in early Christian literature.[85] The corpus Paulinum was obviously supplemented by the Pastoral Letters. Thus the author of the Pastorals could employ a living oral Pauline tradition along with the authentic Pauline letters.

One can make only hypothetical statements about the extent of the first small collection. However, 1 and 2 Corinthians, Romans, Galatians, Philippians, and Philemon probably belonged to the collection from the beginning. Paul's former area of mission work in Asia Minor certainly played a crucial role in the collection of the Pauline letters. Therefore, it is widely assumed that the first collection of Paul's letters was in Ephesus.[86] The assumption is supported by several indications: (1) The church at Ephesus, as the location of the Pauline school, assuredly had many letters of Paul at its disposal. (2) The attribution of Ephesians, which was originally without a name for the addressees, confirms the great significance of this center of early Christian mission and theology. (3) Colossians and the Pastorals were probably written in Ephesus, a fact that underlines the significance of the church for the deutero-Pauline tradition. Finally, in this multicultural city, collections of letters of famous ancient authors were known,[87] and Acts 19:19 attests to the existence of book production in Ephesus. However, in other churches

---

83. On the collection of the Pauline letters, cf. Harnack, *Die Briefsammlung des Apostels Paulus*; Mitton, *Formation of the Pauline Corpus*; K. Aland, "Die Entstehung des Corpus Paulinum"; Trobisch, *Paul's Letter Collection*; Pervo, *Making of Paul*, 25–61.

84. Cf. Lohse, *Colossians and Philemon*, 180–82.

85. Cf. Trummer, "Corpus Paulinum—Corpus Pastorale," 133: "The Pastorals could have been written and disseminated only in the course of a new edition of the previous corpus. Another origin would have had to encounter a very sensitive critique and resistance amid the credulity and the somewhat uncritical conduct of early Christian circles."

86. Cf. Goodspeed, *Formation of the New Testament*, 28; Mitton, *Formation of the Pauline Corpus*, 44–49, 75–76; Trobisch, *Paul's Letter Collection*, 94–96.

87. On ancient collections of letters, cf. Trobisch, *Paul's Letter Collection*, 48–54.

collections of Pauline letters were made, for example, in Rome, where, besides Romans, 1 and 2 Corinthians were known; and possibly also the Letter to the Hebrews was first included in a Pauline collection.[88] The smaller collections of Pauline letters that existed from the beginning probably overlapped and merged successively into "smaller corpora" and larger corpora. This merging into larger collections began around the turn of the first century.[89]

The collection of the proto-Pauline and deutero-Pauline letters indicates that Paul stood at the beginning of the Christian culture of tradition. Already during the apostle's lifetime, his letters were gathered in the Pauline school, and the deutero-Paulines in part (Pastoral Epistles) originated in the course of the publication of a collection of Pauline letters and, as a whole, indicate the enduring effect of the apostle as a "book."[90] One may also add Paul's own statements and the associated claims about himself, for Paul himself laid the foundation for his successful reception! He understood himself according to the example of the OT prophets (cf. Gal. 1:15–16; Rom. 1:1–2) as one chosen by God and seized by the πνεῦμα (cf. Isa. 42:1 LXX), one who possessed the Spirit and lived and acted according to the Spirit (cf., e.g., 1 Cor. 2:10ff.; 14:1, 18, 37ff.; Gal. 6:1; Phil. 3:15). He is the man with pneumatic power who in both the past and the present surpasses all in power, perseverance, and success. No one can surpass him, neither the "pillars of the Jerusalem church" (cf. Gal. 2:6, "what they were is of no consequence to me") nor any opponent of his gospel.[91]

Paul was undoubtedly the preeminent figure of early Christianity and made history in a threefold way: (1) He was the crucial representative of the mission to the gentiles without the requirement of circumcision. With his mission oriented to the west, he not only opened new fields for activity, but he also created the presupposition for the survival of the new movement after the fall of Jerusalem. (2) Pauline theology provided the theoretical foundation for this expansion and turned out to be extraordinarily adaptable and powerful; adaptable with respect to Jewish and Greco-Roman culture and powerful within early Christianity. (3) The impact is in no way limited to the deutero-Pauline letters, but extends both to

88. This is indicated by 1 Clement, which was written in Rome; cf. Lindemann, *Paulus im ältesten Christentum*, 177–99.

89. The earliest collection probably originated between 80 and 90 CE; cf. Aland, *Corpus Paulinum*, 336.

90. Cf. Pervo, *Making of Paul*, 61: "Yet from the early second century onward, Paul was encountered as a book from which individual letters might be cited, but with awareness of, and often in the context of, the collection."

91. See 11.3 below, under "Orthodoxy and Heresy."

Acts and to the Gospels (see below, 13.5.2). Whether in a positive or negative way, almost every NT writing is influenced by Paul.

10.4 Johannine Christianity as the Fourth Great Stream

With the Johannine literature a new, fourth great belief system and school of thought enters into the history of early Christianity.[92] The three letters of John and especially the Gospel of John[93] are characterized by a distinctive view of the Christ event, which is indicated in their own world of language, thought, and imagery, especially in a christological concentration. This is particularly evident in the Gospel of John, which opens Christianity, with its conceptual view of the world (e.g., λόγος, reason; ἀλήθεια, truth), to the Greek conceptual world and makes the new faith attractive to the upper classes. The multiple agreements in the theological outlook of the three Johannine Letters and the Gospel of John indicate the existence of a Johannine school,[94] that is, a spiritual-theological community of Christians that took shape around the end of the first century in a group of churches in and around Ephesus.[95]

With the question of the sequence of the Johannine writings, two models have been discussed. While the classic model (Gospel → 1 John → 2 John → 3 John) is shaped by an ecclesiastical understanding, the second model is dominated by the alternative (2 John → 3 John → 1 John → Gospel) concept of a continuing development and unfolding of Johannine theology. Two arguments can be made for the sequence of the second model 2 John → 3 John → 1 John → Gospel:[96] (1) The linguistic and theological independence of 2 and 3 John, which indicates particularly that the central concepts of the Gospel and of 1 John do not appear: πιστεύειν, believe; πνεῦμα, Spirit; ἁμαρτία, sin; ζωή, life; φῶς, light; σκοτία, darkness; θέλημα, will (of God). (2) One who

92. On the three other movements (Jerusalem church, Galilean Jesus movement, Antioch and Paul), see above, 6.9.

93. The Revelation of John, because of its own linguistic features and thought world, is not to be considered as part of the Johannine school; on the argument, cf. U. Müller, *Die Offenbarung des Johannes*, 46–52; on the Jewish Christian orientation of the Revelation of John; cf. chap. 11 below, under "Synoptic Gospels."

94. On the Johannine school, cf. Cullmann, *Der johanneische Kreis*; Culpepper, *Johannine School*, 261–90; G. Strecker, "Die Anfänge der johanneischen Schule"; Schnelle, "Die johanneische Schule."

95. This is indicated by ancient church tradition (cf. Irenaeus, *Haer.* 3.1.1; the impact of Johannine theology, involving Alogoi, Montanists, Acts of John, and its reception by Gnostics) and the agreements between Pauline and Johannine theology; cf. Schnelle, *History and Theology of the New Testament*, 434–35; Hengel, *Johannine Question*, 30–31, 123–29, and passim.

96. On the detailed argument, cf. Schnelle, "Die Reihenfolge der johanneischen Schriften."

reads the Johannine Letters after the Gospel and places 2 and 3 John at the end of the Johannine tradition must explain the comprehensive reduction of Christology in the two smaller letters as well as the disappearance of central theological themes of the Gospel: the relationship of Father-Son, soteriology, eschatology, pneumatology, anthropology, the concept of faith, the sacraments, and dualism. Finally, if the Johannine Letters are dated after the Gospel, the Johannine community would have become speechless and would not have used the theological argumentation model of the Gospel as it fell into the deepest crisis! If, however, one considers that the Johannine Letters originated before the Gospel and that 2 and 3 John were the beginning of the Johannine tradition, a plausible linguistic and theological explanation is possible. The two letters from the presbyter then reflect the beginnings of the Johannine school shaped by Jewish Christian thought, the conflicts between individual church leaders, and the appearance of docetic Christology.

10.4.1 The Conflicts of the Beginning Period

The first Johannine churches organized themselves as local house churches and stood at the beginning under the leadership of their founder, the presbyter John. As the one who maintained the tradition and as the teacher, he was the leader of the local community/house church as well as the leading personality/leader of a supraregional association of churches. The conflict over acceptance of traveling missionaries indicates that the authority of the presbyter was increasingly called into question. In addition, this conflict is evidence of the existence of a number of Johannine churches that were separated from each other by a considerable distance. A house church could at the same time represent the entire local church. It is also conceivable that a number of house churches formed the substructure of a local church (e.g., in Ephesus). First John suggests the existence of a number of house/local churches, for it, unlike 2 and 3 John, is not addressed to a single local church (2 John) or an individual person (3 John) but is addressed to the entire association of churches.

At least three communities/house churches are assumed in 2 and 3 John. (1) the one of the presbyter, (2) the ἐκλεκτὴ κυρία (elect lady) of 2 John 1, and (3) the church of Gaius, who is neither a member of the church of the presbyter nor of the church of Diotrephes. Diotrephes probably belonged to the church addressed in 2 John. The communication occurred (a) through official letters from church to church (2 John) or from a church to individual members/leaders of other churches (3 John); (b) through traveling missionaries, who were normally welcomed (2 John 10; 3 John 5–8), listened to, and equipped for further mission work (2 John 10; 3 John 5–8); (c) by special individuals (Demetrius as the letter carrier); or (d) by visits of presbyters, who were leaders of the association of churches (cf. 2 John 12; 3 John 10). As a whole this documents the high social and informal networking among the churches, which is comparable to the networking among Pauline churches.

At the center of 2 and 3 John stands the conflict between the presbyter John and Diotrephes (cf. 3 John), which evidently took place at several levels. Who was the presbyter? Around 130 CE Papias of Hierapolis mentions a presbyter John in clear distinction from John the son of Zebedee, whom he describes as one of the guarantors of the tradition.[97] Both the presbyter of the Johannine Letters and the presbyter John of Papias passed on the traditions; there is no serious reason not to regard the two as the same person. The presbyter was probably the founder of the Johannine school and, as such, a prominent bearer of the Johannine tradition, with a wide-ranging influence. He was held in high regard, as the preservation and inclusion of 2 and 3 John in the canon suggest.[98] During his lifetime, however, his authority was not undisputed, as the conflict over the welcoming/not welcoming of traveling missionaries indicates (cf. 2 John 10; 3 John 9–10).

Diotrephes did not welcome the brother of the presbyter and even expelled from the church those who wished to do so. He had apparently taken over the leadership of the church addressed in 2 John. He did not recognize the claim of the presbyter and in his church exercised a type of discipline by force. The presbyter now motivates his follower Gaius in 3 John to continue to welcome the missionaries of the presbyter and sends him a particularly trustworthy coworker in Demetrius. Doctrinal disputes continue, for although no christological controversy is explicitly mentioned in 3 John, one may assume that one exists. The evidence for this in both letters is the variety of ways in which connection exists between the rejection of traveling missionaries, the concept of truth (cf. 2 John 4; 3 John 3, 11–12), and doctrinal disputes. The obstinate reaction of Diotrephes cannot be reduced to a personal matter, for also 1 John and the Gospel of John presuppose a christological controversy over the correct understanding of the humanity of Jesus Christ (see below, 10.4.2). The name Diotrephes ("nurtured by Zeus") indicates clearly a Christian from a Greco-Roman tradition, who probably represented a docetic Christology on the basis of his cultural-historical background (cf. 2 John 7a, "For many deceivers have gone into the world, who do not confess that Jesus came in

---

97. Eusebius, *Hist. eccl.* 3.39.4: "If ever anyone came who had followed the presbyters, I inquired into the words of the presbyters, what Andrew or Peter or Philip or Thomas or James or John or Matthew, or any other of the Lord's disciples, had said, and what Aristion and the presbyter John, the Lord's disciples, were saying" (LCL).

98. Cf. Schnelle, *Die Johannesbriefe*, 5–6.

the flesh") and strictly rejected a limitation of the mission to Jews (cf. 3 John 7b). Diotrephes is characterized by a caustic, ironic undertone: "who wants to be the first" (φιλοπρωτεύειν). The verb appears only in 3 John 9 and the literature referring to it; it clearly expresses Diotrephes's competing claim to leadership. However, the presbyter does not argue with him in theological terms but only mentions the point of differences and directs countermeasures at the level of conduct. Since the traveling missionaries who are equipped by Gaius should accept nothing from the gentiles (3 John 7b), a practice that is explicitly commended by the presbyter (3 John 2–6), one may assume an intentional Jewish Christian position for the presbyter. This would explain why he places so much value on defending that Jesus came in the flesh, for it includes the historical Jesus of Nazareth.

Two explanatory models for the background and nature of the conflict between the presbyter and Diotrephes are significant to the present time. (1) The explanatory model in terms of ecclesiastical law was developed fundamentally by A. von Harnack. According to this view the presbyter is the leader of a comprehensive missions organization in the province of Asia; he sent out missionaries and was the head over the churches. The church of Diotrephes rebelled against this form of organization and the presbyter's claim to authority. "It is the battle of the old patriarchal and provincial missionary organization against the individual church as it was in the process of consolidating, which emphasized the monarchical bishop for the purpose of its consolidation and strict closure to the outside world."[99] Diotrephes is thus the first monarchical bishop. (2) Walter Bauer represents the dogmatic explanatory model. Here the dispute between the presbyter and Diotrephes reflects the conflict between heresy and orthodoxy. Bauer sees the presbyter as the representative of orthodoxy, who was placed on the defensive by the influence of the chief heretic Diotrephes. In his church Diotrephes was successful in driving back the influence of the presbyter, who with the writing of 3 John shows that he understood the attempt to regain terrain that had been lost to him.[100] In a reversal of the thesis of W. Bauer, E. Käsemann sees in Diotrephes a monarchical bishop, but he understands the author of 2 and 3 John to be a presbyter excommunicated on the basis of his Gnostic heresy. "It was not as the head of a sect, but rather as a monarchical bishop confronting and acting against a false teacher that Diotrephes exercised forceful church discipline on the presbyter and his followers in their own church."[101]

---

99. Harnack, *Über den 3. Johannesbrief*, 21.
100. Cf. W. Bauer, *Orthodoxy and Heresy*, 93–94.
101. Käsemann, *Ketzer und Zeuge*, 173–74.

As a whole, the presbyter probably stood on the side of the (later victorious) orthodoxy and Diotrephes on the side of the (later so-called) heresy. However, these value-laden terms of later church history are not sufficient to make an accurate judgment about the historical situation, for 2 and 3 John are witnesses to a conflict over the correct understanding of Christ in a time when general, binding dogmatic decisions had not yet been established. Furthermore, structures of ecclesiastical law cannot yet be recognized behind the letters, for neither letter speaks of an excommunication of the presbyter by Diotrephes or of a monarchical bishop. Along with the doctrinal dimension of the conflict (cf. 2 John 7–10), there is very early a conflict over leadership and a conflict over the direction of the church, that is, a conflict over power.[102] Diotrephes not only openly rejected the presbyter's claim to leadership but also had the power to enforce his position in the church. In addition, differing ecclesiological conceptions probably contributed to the conflicts. The presbyter not only made a claim for supraregional authority with respect to other Johannine churches, but he also attempted to enforce it through his emissaries/traveling missionaries/followers, thus pursuing an expansive agenda. Diotrephes apparently represented a particular concept of church concentrated in the single house/local church. Finally, the issue was a personal conflict; the presbyter and Diotrephes exhibit a comparable personality type: both make personal claims and always want to be preeminent. Such personal conflicts/rivalries were not rare in early Christianity.[103] The friendship of two former partners and traveling companions likely turned into hostility.[104]

10.4.2 1 John and Docetism

The two letters from the presbyter reflect the Jewish Christian stamp on the beginnings of the Johannine school, the conflict between individual church leaders, and the rise of a docetic Christology (2 John 7). The letters from the presbyter introduce only the beginning stage of a recognizable theological discourse; instead, they persist in personal claims to power and symbolic actions; they remain rudimentary in their theological argumentation and do not actually develop the initial christological issue. In contrast, 1 John is a

---

102. Ebel ("Ein Verein von Christusverehrern?") indicates that the reciprocal sanctions between the presbyter and Diotrephes (excommunication or breaking off all relationship also among members) go far beyond what was customary in ancient associations (warnings or fines for failing to make financial contributions and/or improper conduct in assemblies).

103. Already in Paul one must assume such personality conflicts (cf. Gal. 2:1–10, 11, 15); from a later period, cf. James 2:1–4; Herm. Vis. 3.1.8 (presbyters demand places of honor); Herm. Sim. 8.7.4.6 (dispute over the first places in the church).

104. Cf. Leutzsch, *Die Bewährung der Wahrheit*, 114–15.

witness to a new stage of Johannine theological formation. Johannine thought takes on a quality of a system and enters into a comprehensive theological discourse. Sociologically, in contrast to the letters from the presbyter, behind 1 John stands a growing association of churches,[105] in which a majority of the teachers are included in the "we" in 1 John 1:1–4 and remain viable after the division (cf. 1 John 2:19). First John attests a lively life of worship in the church that is indicated by the significance of prayer (cf. 1 John 3:22; 5:14–16) and the anointing of the Spirt (cf. 1 John 2:20, 27) as well as the dispute over the right understanding of the sacraments (cf. 1 John 5:6–8). While only a few statements offer information about the social level of the church, two points are relatively clear: (1) There were social conflicts between the rich and poor members of the church. The rich boasted about their property (cf. 1 John 2:16–17) and refused to offer concrete, active love for the brothers and sisters (cf. 1 John 3:17–18). (2) The intrachurch controversies over the understanding of sin (see below, 11.3) indicate a lively theological interest and suggest a certain level of education. (3) At least the false teachers who formerly belonged to the church (cf. 1 John 2:19) probably had an elitist self-understanding: their docetism reflecting the worldview of Platonism suggests a circle of educated people who potentially considered themselves superior to the rest of the church. Within this complex constellation, the author (authors)[106] establishes a thorough theological-political standpoint.

The starting point is a division within the church (1 John 2:19, "They went out from us, but they did not belong to us. For if they had first belonged to us, they would have remained with us. But by going out they made it plain that none of them belongs to us") connected apparently with continuing conflicts at various levels. First John seeks to restore the unity of the church by placing the major thought in the foreground: the visibility of faith in Jesus Christ as the Son of God. The concern in 1 John is the ethical form, the ethical character of Christianity! In it the knowledge of God and the knowledge of Christ are inseparable from the knowledge of love—the nature of God and the nature of true life (cf. only 1 John 2:3–6; 2:9, 10; 3:14; 4:8, 16, 21). The conflict over docetic false teachers, which had already become apparent in 2 John 7, is connected to this primary theme. Because the love command and faith in Jesus Christ belong inseparably together, one who does not believe does not love; one who does not love does not know the Son of God, Jesus Christ. Already at the beginning of the letter in 1 John 1:1–4, the emphasis on a theological eyewitness has the false teaching in

---

105. Cf. Rusam, *Die Gemeinschaft der Kinder Gottes*, 214–18.
106. Cf. the "we" in 1 John 1:1–4.

view,[107] for the Johannine language of epiphany and revelation and the touching/seeing of the Logos in verse 1 indicate that the concern in 1 John is the reality of the saving event. In the context of the division of the church in 1 John 2:19, the false teachers are reproached in 1 John 2:22–23: "Who is the liar, but the one who does not confess that Jesus is the Christ? This one is the antichrist, the one who denies the Father and the Son. Everyone who denies the Son also does not have the Father; whoever confesses the Son, however, also has the father."

The phrase "Jesus is not the Christ" (Ἰησοῦς οὐκ ἔστιν ὁ Χριστός) may be interpreted in three possible ways.[108] (1) It could refer to a Jewish denial of the messiahship of Jesus.[109] This view is untenable for two reasons. (a) The parallel between Χριστός and υἱός at the end of verses 22a and 22b makes a one-sided concentration on the problem of messiahship improbable. (b) According to 1 John 2:19 the false teachers belonged to the Johannine church and thus did not come from outside. (2) This problem would be nonexistent if the issue concerned Jewish Christians who questioned the messiahship of Jesus. Would they have rejected the Johannine Christology as a violation of Jewish monotheism?[110] Why would they have done this? They have probably entered the Johannine community because they have regarded the Jewish hope for the messiah as fulfilled in Jesus of Nazareth, seeing in him the Messiah and Son of God (cf. Ps. 2:7; 110:1). Furthermore, in the Johannine school there was probably never anything other than the "high" Christology that is present in the letters and the Gospel (with the unity of Father and Son), as is indicated, not least, by 1 John 2:22d–23! The assumption that this Jewish Christian group has returned to the synagogue[111] and caused conflict from there is not convincing, for clearly the issue is an ongoing conflict *within* the Johannine school. (3) The false teachers represented a docetic Christology;[112]

107. On the interpretation, cf. Schnelle, *Die Johannesbriefe*, 59–69.

108. A review of research is provided by Klauck, *Die Johannesbriefe*, 127–51.

109. So Wurm, *Die Irrlehrer*, 24–25 and passim; Thyen, "Johannesbriefe," 194. He designates (following A. Wurm) the opponents as "orthodox Jews" who dispute the necessity of a heavenly revealer for a knowledge of God.

110. See especially Wilckens, "Die Gegner im 1. und 2. Johannesbrief," 90: "These opponents are Christians from the Johannine church [1 John 2:19] who have emphatically rejected the confession of Jesus as Son of God as it was stated in the Gospel of John (cf. 10:30!) as a violation of the basic Jewish monotheism in the sense of Deut. 6:4 and Exod. 20:2ff. and have accordingly claimed to be Christians who are 'orthodox Jews.'"

111. See Rusam, *Die Gemeinschaft der Kinder Gottes*, 192–93; cf. also Griffith, *Keep Yourselves from Idols*, 175: "I wish to argue that [1 John] 2:19 describes a situation where ethnic Jews who had become Christians were returning to the synagogue and thereby denying their formerly held belief that the Messiah was Jesus."

112. Those who argue for an antidocetic interpretation of 1 John 2:22 include, among others, Schnelle, *Antidoketische Christologie*, 74–75; G. Strecker, *Die Johannesbriefe*, 137–38;

that is, in the view of the author, they denied the soteriological identity between the earthly Jesus and the heavenly Christ (Ἰησοῦς οὐκ ἔστιν ὁ Χριστός; cf. also the statements about identity in 1 John 4:15; 5:1, 5).

The opponents evidently represented a docetic Christology; for them only the Father and the heavenly Christ were relevant to salvation, but not the life and death of the historical Jesus of Nazareth, whom they relegated to being merely an insignificant apparent reality. This interpretation is based on the distinction in 2:22 between Ἰησοῦς and Χριστός, and especially between the synonyms Christ and Son of God. Like verse 23, this indicates that the messiahship of Jesus was not—in isolation—a matter of debate. Instead, the issue was the understanding of the Son in his relation to the Father. Thus the Χριστός title is to be associated with the title υἱός.[113] The false teachers claimed God for themselves, just as 1 John did. For 1 John, however, anyone who does not have the Father teaches the work of the Son falsely. Father and Son, Son and Father—they belong inseparably together in 1 John. He regards the earthly and heavenly existence of the Son with a clear antidocetic accent as a unity and understands the Father on the basis of the Son.

An antidocetic interpretation is also suggested in 1 John 4:2–3 and 5:6. First John 4:2–3 gives the criteria for the correct knowledge of Christ: "By this you know the Spirit of God: Every spirit that confesses that Jesus Christ has come in the flesh is from God, and every spirit that does not confess Jesus is not from God. And this is the antichrist, of whom you have heard that he is coming and now he is already in the world." Here the issue is not about an identity (as always to be defined) between Ἰησοῦς and Χριστός, but about a real incarnation of Jesus Christ. This is indicated especially by the added ἐν σαρκί, which provides emphasis in both content and rhetoric.[114] The strong emphasis on the incarnation indicates that the false teachers dispute the relevance of the incarnation of the preexistent Christ for salvation. They distinguish strictly between the saving relevance of the heavenly Christ and the earthly Jesus, although for 1 John the two form a unity. How did the false teachers conceive of the relationship between the earthly Jesus, whose real existence they, as Christians, could not deny, and the heavenly Christ? Here 1 John is silent, but the assumption remains valid that the opponents regarded

---

Hengel, *Johannine Question*, 62–70; Frey, *Die johanneische Eschatologie*, 3:72; Uebele, "*Viele Verführer*," 133–36; Schnelle, *Die Johannesbriefe*, 107–9.

113. Cf. Schnackenburg, *Die Johannesbriefe*, 157.

114. Cf. Klauck, *Der erste Johannesbrief*, 233; Uebele, "*Viele Verführer*," 120. The significance of *en sarki* is minimized by all interpreters, who prefer a Jewish background alone (so Wilckens, "Die Gegner im 1. und 2. Johannesbrief," 106), "according to whom the opponents dispute that Jesus is the Son of God in the sense of the unity of Christ with God, but not the incarnation of the heavenly nature of Christ in the man Jesus."

Jesus Christ as intrinsically and exclusively God, who could have had the appearance of a body that was not relevant for salvation. They would have thus represented a docetic Christology. The negative part of the confession in verse 3 confirms this interpretation: "Every spirit that does not confess Jesus is not from God" (καὶ πᾶν πνεῦμα ὃ μὴ ὁμολογεῖ ᾽Ιησοῦν ἐκ τοῦ θεοῦ οὐκ ἔστιν). The opponents "eliminated" Jesus from their teaching and denied the human side of the redeemer.[115] This orientation is indicated in 1 John 5:6: "This is the one who came by water and blood: Jesus Christ; not in water alone, but in water and in blood. And the Spirit is the one who testifies, for the Spirit is truth." Here 1 John proceeds beyond defining the christological relationship and places before the readers the ritual reality of the church: baptism, giving of the Spirit/anointing, and Eucharist are not only the foci of fundamental theological relationships but also emotional and social places of an abiding character. Because the incarnate, crucified, and resurrected Jesus Christ is present in baptism and the Eucharist, the false teachers, with their one-sided orientation on the divinity of the Son, minimize the saving reality and miss out on it at the same time. In both baptism and the Eucharist, the Crucified and Resurrected One is present for the believers as the embodiment of life and grants to them participation in his own fullness of life.

The cultural and historical starting points and background of docetism[116] are basic assumptions of Platonic thought that were influential in the Middle Platonism of the first century BCE to the second and third centuries CE (Philo of Alexandria, Plutarch, Apuleius, Maximus of Tyre).[117] Because becoming must be explained from being, the Platonic understanding of reality is shaped by the dichotomy εἶναι-δοκεῖν (cf. Plato, *Resp.* 2.361b–62a and passim). The essential being is the intelligible ideal being (οὐσία, ὄντως ὄν, ὁ ἔστιν ὄν), the world of ideas. As basic reality, it precedes all natural perceptions, while the world of perceptions (from the view of the docetists the bodily being of Jesus) is subject to change, to illusion, to disappearing, to appearance (δοκεῖν, δόκησις). According to Plato, "As being is to becoming, so is the truth to faith" (*Tim.* 29c). Consequently, God/the gods alone belong to the ideal, intelligible, transcendent, incorporeal, and only true level of reality: the world of ideas. Because God is in every manner perfect (*Pol.* 381b), he cannot change and

---

115. Weigandt, "Der Doketismus im Urchristentum," 105.

116. Literature on docetism: Weigandt, "Der Doketismus im Urchristentum"; Wengst, *Häresie und Orthodoxie im Spiegel*, 15–61; Brox, "'Doketismus'—eine Problemanzeige," 301–14; Kinlaw, *Christ Is Jesus*, 69–108; U. Müller, *Die Menschwerdung des Gottessohnes*, 102–22; G. Strecker, *Die Johannesbriefe*, 131–39; Uebele, *"Viele Verführer,"* 44–57; Schnelle, *Die Johannesbriefe*, 138–46; Bauspiess, "'Doketismus' als theologisches Problem"; Wahlde, *Gnosticism, Docetism, and the Judaisms*; Verheyden et al., *Docetism in the Early Church*.

117. Cf. Maas, *Die Unveränderlichkeit Gottes*, 34–118.

come near to humankind, but must remain in himself. "Thus it is impossible for God to change" (*Pol.* 381c). In contrast to the unchangeable gods is the world and the heavens: "It has come into being, for it is visible and tangible and in possession of a body" (*Tim.* 28b). From this basic idea that the transcendent world has a higher status of reality than the world of appearances emerges the Platonic body-soul dualism. Socrates defines death explicitly as a separation of the soul from the body, a process that begins already in life: "the separation of the soul as far as possible away from the body and its getting used to being gathered and assembled by itself, withdrawn from all parts of the body and living as far as possible both in the present circumstances and in the future alone by itself, released, as it were, from the chains of the body" (Plato, *Phaed.* 67c LCL). The soul is like the divine, but the body is like the mortal. After death and the disintegration of the body, the soul moves and "makes its way to another place of that kind, noble, pure and invisible: Hades in the true sense, to be with the good and wise god where, if the god wills it, my soul too must go directly" (*Phaed.* 80d LCL).

In all philosophical-theological systems, God is understood as the essential being, the good, the Logos, the Spirit, and categorically separated from the earthly world, from change, from coming into being and passing away, and thus also from corporeality. For church members educated in Platonic thought, the obvious choice was a monophysite Christology, in which the redeemer is exclusively of a divine nature; thus it was not he but rather his δόκησις (appearance) that appeared on earth.[118] Many church members probably made rational arguments (from the ancient worldview). As the polemic of 1 John demonstrates, they were successful in the Johannine churches. A docetic false teaching that resulted in a full abandonment of the earthly Jesus is found in the letters of Ignatius (see below, 14.1). An initial correspondence[119] to the Johannine Letters exists at the sociological level, for the false teachers whom Ignatius struggled against were traveling missionaries (cf. Ign. *Eph.* 7.1; 9.1; Ign. *Smyrn.* 4.1; 6.2) who upset house churches, and so Ignatius says that they corrupt households (Ign. *Eph.* 16.1). The second correspondence exists at the theological level, inasmuch as Ignatius also battles a docetic Christology. He accuses his opponents of disputing the bodily nature of Jesus Christ. They do not confess that the Lord came in the flesh (cf., e.g., Ign. *Smyrn.* 5.2, μὴ ὁμολογῶν αὐτὸν σαρκοφόρον). Finally, docetic views appear in later Gnostic systems (see below, chap. 14), suggesting the reason for the success of this form of Christology.

---

118. Cf. Weigandt, "Der Doketismus im Urchristentum," 16, 18.

119. For a thorough analysis of the texts, in addition to the commentaries, see Uebele, *"Viele Verführer,"* 38–92.

10.4.3 The Gospel of John as the First Introduction to Christianity

The Gospel of John is the climax and conclusion of Johannine theology. John stands at a turning point. He sees clearly that his era can remain faithful to Jesus Christ and to the origin of Christianity only if it takes the risk of a linguistic and intellectual new formulation of the Christ event. John carries out this new development as a productive and continuing appropriation of the revelation of Jesus with the writing of his Gospel under the guidance of the Paraclete (cf. John 14:26). John was very well aware of the basic questions of the representation of the past through the writing of history. He redacted them and transformed them literarily and theologically in his story of Jesus Christ. John takes up the issue of the perspectivity of historical knowledge, and he knows about the inseparable relationship of events and their appropriation (by the Paraclete) in and through narrative. He expands the linguistic and theological presentation of the Christ event in order to stabilize the endangered identity of his church through the new insight that has been made possible. It was clear to him that events of the past can attain the status of history only when they are appropriated through a process of historical formation of meaning. The result of such a process of appropriation is the Fourth Gospel. Three discourses/conflicts shape the Gospel of John: (1) with the world, (2) with the Jews, and (3) with the docetists. In all three cases the issue is the opposing judgments on the nature of Christ: For the world and for the Jews, he is only a man (John 10:33); for the docetists he is only God.

On conflict 1: A qualifying leading concept of the Fourth Gospel is ὁ κόσμος (the world), which is not used consistently in a negative way.[120] The world of God and the world of humankind originally belong together. Already in the creation the primordial good is present; it is a work of the Logos that exists with God at the beginning. God sent his Son into the world because of his love (John 3:16; cf. 10:36; 1 John 4:9–10, 14); Jesus Christ is the prophet, that is, Son who has come into the world (John 6:14; 11:27). As the bread that has come down from heaven, he gives life to the cosmos (John 6:33; cf. 6:51). He is the light of the world (John 9:5). Jesus came to save the cosmos (cf. John 3:17; 12:47), and he is the σωτὴρ τοῦ κόσμου (John 4:42, Savior of the world; cf. 1 John 2:2). Jesus sends his disciples into the world (John 17:18), and the capacity of knowing and believing in the sending of Jesus is given to the world (cf. John 17:21, 23). The church lives in the cosmos, but it is not ἐκ τοῦ κόσμου (cf. John 15:19; 17:14). It is not the cosmos itself that is judged in negative terms; rather, disbelief makes the cosmos a godless world (cf. John 16:9; 1:10; 7:7; 8:23; 9:39; 14:17). The cosmos is described in negative terms

---

120. Cf. Kierspel, *Jews and the World*, 155–213.

because it does not accept Jesus (John 1:10; cf. 17:25); it hates him and the disciples (cf. John 7:7; 15:18, 19; 17:14). It appears as the realm of the godless (cf. John 8:23; 12:25; 14:17, 22, 27, 30; 15:19; 16:8, 20, 33; 17:6, 11, 13f., 16; 18:36); consequently, it is subject to the judgment (John 9:39; 12:31; 16:11).

On conflict 2. As with the concept of the cosmos, a differentiated use of "the Jews" (οἱ Ἰουδαῖοι) is evident.[121] The Jews are not at all simply *the* only representatives of the unbelieving cosmos.[122] Instead, they are one (and not the only!) embodiment of the cosmos, that follows/emerges within the narrative structure of a Gospel out of the concrete historical situation of the work of Jesus and additionally in John out of the beginning of his church and the dramatic structure of his Gospel. As Jesus's enemies and representatives of disbelief, they appear primarily in John 5:10, 15–16, 18; 6:41; 7:1, 13; 8:44, 48, 52, 57; 9:18, 22; 10:31, 33; 11:8, 54; 18:36; 19:7, 12, 38b; 20:19. The negative portrayal reaches its climactic moment in John 8:44: "You are from your father, the devil, and you choose to perform your father's desires." However, the Ἰουδαῖοι are not from themselves the originators of evil, for their disbelief originates from a superhuman power of evil, the devil. Besides a somewhat neutral use of the term,[123] there are numerous positive references to the Jews. Some are Jewish sympathizers of Jesus (John 3:1; 8:30, 31; 11:45; 12:11; 19:38a, 39); Jesus is the king of the Jews (18:33, 39; 19:3, 21) and, above all, John 4:22b: "Salvation comes from the Jews" (ἡ σωτηρία ἐκ τῶν Ἰουδαίων). This fundamental and unrestricted positive affirmation indicates clearly, with respect to the Jews, that faith or disbelief determines the positive or negative perspective.[124]

On conflict 3. The continuing christological debates in the Johannine school (see above, 10.4.2) required their own Gospel.[125] How the divinity and humanity of Jesus are to be understood, how the two are related, and

---

121. Cf. Grässer, "Die antijüdische Polemik," 135–53; Schnelle, "Die Juden im Johannesevangelium"; Bieringer, Pollefeyt, and Vandecasteele-Vanneuville, *Anti-Judaism and the Fourth Gospel*; Diefenbach, *Der Konflikt Jesu mit den "Juden"*; Kierspel, *Jews and the World*, 13–110.

122. Contra Bultmann, *Theology*, 2:27–30.

123. Cf. the list in Schnelle, *Das Evangelium nach Johannes*, 214–15.

124. On the conflict with Judaism in the Gospel of John, see also below, 11.5.

125. Four (partially overlapping) answers are discussed in scholarship: (1) The supplemental hypothesis, according to which the Gospel of John is to be read as a supplement to the Synoptics (Clement of Alexandria, according to Eusebius, *Hist. eccl.* 6.14.7: "Finally John, knowing that the human nature [τὰ σωματικά] is treated in the Gospels, at the instigation of his pupils and inspired by the Spirit, wrote a spiritual gospel [πνευματικὸν ποιῆσαι εὐαγγέλιον]"); an influential variant of this thesis is given by Windisch, *Johannes und die Synoptiker*, who understands John as the absolute Gospel that supersedes the Synoptics. (2) The Gospel of John as a *missions document* for Israel (Bornhäuser, *Das Johannesevangelium*, 138, 158–67). (3) The Gospel of John as a *completed* gospel (so, e.g., Barrett, *St. John*, 121–24). (4) The Gospel of John as a "*strategy of faith*" that seeks to overcome the disbelief of the world (in the recent discussion thus Zumstein, "Das Johannesevangelium").

how they appear are not sufficiently answered by Mark or Luke.[126] The Fourth Gospel attempts this in a new way as it reflects the post-Easter perspective of faith and decisively places it in the foreground without neglecting the bond with the earthly Jesus. The evangelist John thus undertakes the attempt in his Gospel to define the nature of the Son of God, Jesus Christ, in his exalted nature and his lowliness in a comprehensive way through the narration. Thus in comparison with the Synoptics, with the portrayal of a very strong emphasis on the exalted nature and deity of Jesus, John endeavors to take up the basic concern of the docetic teachers that is shared by both the members of his church and himself, but to limit it and make it more precise in a theology of the incarnation and the cross. The exalted status/deity of Jesus is indicated in the primordial being with God and the mediation in creation by the Logos (John 1:1–5), the continuing *doxa* even after the incarnation (cf. John 1:14b; 2:11; 11:4, 40), his sovereignty over the elements and over life and death in his phenomenal and verifiable miracles leading up to and including the raising of Lazarus (cf. John 2:1–11; 4:46–54; 5:1–9; 6:1–21; 9:1–41; 11:1–44), his marvelous foreknowledge (cf. John 1:42, 48f.; 4:29; 5:5f.; 6:6; 11:11; 18:4; etc.), the "I am" sayings (John 6:35a; 8:12; 10:7, 11; 11:25; 14:6; 15:1), and his sovereign demeanor in suffering (cf. John 18:1–11, 33–38; 19:5, 25–27, 28–30). Finally, the confession of Thomas to the Resurrected One is at the same time the confession of the church: "My Lord and my God" (John 20:28).

At the same time, the incarnational focus of Johannine theology (John 1:14a)[127] and the numerous indications of a theology of the cross prevent a one-sided and deficient interpretation of the person of Christ.[128] From the beginning, the ministry of Jesus in the world stands under the perspective of the cross (cf. John 1:29, 36). The cleansing of the temple at the beginning of the public ministry of Jesus (John 2:14–22) underlines the compositional intent of John in pointing to the saving significance of the cross and resurrection.[129] Allusions to the passion are pervasive in the entire Gospel (cf. John 2:14c; 10:11, 15, 17; 11:13; 12:16, 32f.; 13:1–3, 7, 37; 15:13; 17:19; 18:32), indicating clearly that the Incarnate One is none other than the Crucified One. Incarnation and cross are equally movements of love from below, like the foot washing (John 13:1–20), in which Jesus introduces those near him into the new existence of brotherly love as he himself lives and makes it possible

126. John may have known both Mark and Luke; cf. Schnelle, "Johannes und die Synoptiker."

127. Cf. Weder, "Die Menschwerdung Gottes"; M. Thompson, *Humanity of Jesus in the Fourth Gospel.*

128. On the Johannine theology of the cross, cf. Kohler, *Kreuz und Menschwerdung*; Knöppler, *Die theologia crucis*; Frey, "Die 'theologia crucifixi'"; Schnelle, *Theology of the New Testament*, 760–61.

129. Cf. Schnelle, "Die Tempelreinigung und die Christologie."

through the death on the cross. In the Gospel of John also the revelation at the cross reaches its goal; here the Son fulfills the will of the Father (cf. John 13:1, 32; 14:31; 17:5; 19:11a and passim) and fulfills the Scripture (19:28), and the incarnate Christ says, "It is finished" (19:30). John focuses entirely on the identity of the Preexistent and Incarnate One with the Crucified and Exalted One, as the Thomas pericope in John 20:24–29 documents directly with the grasp of the hands. The one who died shamefully on the cross was exalted by God and is the Living Word of God. The exaltation of the Son coincides with the cross (cf. John 12:27–33). And the cross is the abiding place of salvation.

Besides the theological orientation of the Fourth Gospel in the incarnation and cross, the striking emphasis on the humanity of Jesus in the Gospel of John has an antidocetic orientation. Jesus celebrates at a wedding (2:1–11), he loves his friend Lazarus (11:3), he is disturbed by the mourning of the crowd (11:33–34), and he weeps over Lazarus (11:35). Jesus comes from Nazareth in Galilee (1:45–46; 4:44; 7:41, 52), not from Bethlehem (cf. 7:42!). His parents are well known (1:45; 2:1, 3, 12; 6:42; 19:26), and his brothers are also (2:12; 7:1–10). He possesses a mortal body (2:21) of flesh (6:51) and blood (19:34). He cleanses the temple because of intense passion (2:14–22); he is exhausted and thirsty from traveling (4:6–7). Prior to his imminent fate (12:27; cf. 13:21), Jesus is "troubled," that is, "moved" (ταράσσω) and asks for a drink on the cross (19:28). Pilate has him tortured by the soldiers with scourging and thorns (19:1–2) in order to affirm in a somewhat official manner: "Behold the man!" (19:5, ἰδοὺ ὁ ἄνθρωπος). A member of the execution squad clearly declares that Jesus is indeed dead (19:33); finally, the body of Jesus is officially released (19:38). With his burial, the expected smell of the corpse is averted by the fragrances that were brought (19:39f.). The disciples and finally Thomas may become eyewitnesses and be convinced that the body of the Resurrected One is identical to that of the earthly and crucified Jesus (20:20, 27). The theological culmination is evident: God commits himself in his saving care for the world entirely in this man Jesus of Nazareth and his ministry. God himself speaks and acts in Jesus, and indeed in an exclusive and unmistakable way. His word can be heard nowhere else (5:39–40); nowhere else can one experience his works (3:35; 5:20–22) than in the man Jesus.

The continuing emphasis on the incarnation, the humanity/corporeality of Jesus, and the cross as the place of salvation emerges, in the first place, from the theological and fundamental foundation and the logic of Johannine thought but is at the same time also the narrative-theological answer to the christological controversies in the Johannine school. Within the course of the narrative of the Gospel, the eucharistic section, with its emphasis on the inseparable unity of the humanity and deity of the person of Jesus Christ, causes a schism among the disciples (John 6:60–71). This schism is a reflection of the division within the Johannine school, which was ignited over the soteriological significance of the earthly existence of Jesus in reference to 1 John 2:19.

In addition to defining the relationship between the deity and humanity of Jesus Christ, the Fourth Gospel is very innovative in a second point. It is the first introduction to Christianity and the first dogmatics in early Christianity (cf. John 20:30–31). This fact is apparent in its redacting and response to all of the central questions of the new formation of meaning. The prologue already combines time and eternity with the Logos and defines the unique relationship between God and the Logos Jesus Christ, who is, as the Creator, the source of all life. God's truth and glory are visible in him alone. From the mouth of Jesus, the believers learn what birth and new birth are (John 3), who truly quenches life's thirst and gives eternal life (John 4; 6), and who already in the present is lord over life and death (John 5:11). The path of the man born blind (John 9) serves as an orientation for the distressed church, like the good shepherd speech (John 10) and Jesus's farewell speech (John 13:31–16:33), which formulate the consequence of the departure of Jesus and, like the high-priestly prayer (John 17), place the theological consequence of the passion of Jesus in a new perspective. Jesus intentionally and confidently goes the way of the cross, for he knows its significance and lets the disciples participate in the reality of his death and life (John 20:24–29). Because the coming of the Paraclete is connected to the departure of Jesus, an understanding of Easter and the event preceding Easter can occur only after Easter (cf. John 20:29b: "Blessed are those who do not see and yet believe"). Only from this perspective is the past event intelligible and accessible in its significance. The presupposition for this argumentation is the determination of the relationship of Father, Son, and Spirit, which John, as the first theologian in early Christianity, thoroughly develops. As a whole, John demonstrates that he is the master of interpretative integration: he brings together various streams of tradition under the umbrella of the love of God toward humankind in Jesus Christ in his Gospel. The numerous interconnections/emphases in the Gospel are integral parts/variations of a fundamental theological design: the revelation of the love of God in Jesus Christ as the love of God for the world and for believers, for whom abiding in God and Jesus takes place as abiding in love.

The Gospel of John is not only the conclusion and climax of Johannine theology. As a "master narrative" it also unites two major lines of the formation of early Christian theology.[130] While Paul presents a kerygmatically oriented

---

130. Cf. Theissen, *Die Religion der ersten Christen*, 255: "It forms a synthesis from two developments that run toward each other. On the one side, we find in Paul the faith in the

story of Jesus Christ, Mark unfolds a narratival story of Jesus Christ.[131] John combines both tendencies, shaping the memories of the earthly Jesus consistently from the perspective of the Exalted One. He takes over the gospel genre, expands it in continuity with Paul around the theme of a preexistence Christology, and intensifies (differently from Matthew and Luke) the orientation toward the theology of the cross that is predominant in Paul. More strongly than in Mark, the grandeur of the Exalted One is pervasive in the image of the earthly Jesus. In contrast to Paul, John does not remain principally with a structured high Christology but translates it into a dramatic narrative.

As a whole, the Gospel of John takes a key position within early Christianity in a twofold way. It not only completes the theological formation of the NT at the highest level but especially opens the way to Greco-Roman intellectual history through the concepts of the logos, truth, and freedom and thus at the same time prepares the transition to the ancient church.[132] When Jesus Christ is identified in the prologue with the guiding concept of Greco-Roman culture and history of education, a distinctive claim is suggested: In the Logos, Jesus Christ culminates the ancient history of religion and the intellectual quest; he is the origin and the goal of all being. This claim was taken up by the apologists and developed further until it flowed finally into the christological debates of the third and fourth centuries.

> Johannine theology opens early Christianity not merely to a new educated level; rather, it is an entirely new perspective on the Christ event: The nature of the Son of God Jesus Christ and the possibility of continuing participation in the divine gift of life are expressed in memorable concepts, symbols, and images.

10.5 Jewish Christianity as an Enduring Power

The separation of Christianity from Judaism during its formational stage was introduced with Paul; with the fall of the Jerusalem church around 70 CE, it became irreversible (see above, 8.7). However, this involved a long and continuing process that continued dynamically in the second and third

---

Pre-existent and Exalted One who has a status that is godlike. . . . On the other side, the tradition of the Earthly One in the Synoptic tradition is shaped and in the First Gospel increasingly permeated with the majesty of the Exalted One; yet the Synoptic Gospels lack the claim of faith in the preexistence of Jesus. In John the two strands of development are blended together."

131. Cf. Schnelle, "Theologie als kreative Sinnbildung."

132. Cf. Nagel, *Die Rezeption des Johannesevangeliums.*

centuries and finally ended in the early Middle Ages. Within this process, a crucial significance belonged to Jewish Christianity, for it formed a natural bridge to ethnic and theological Judaism. The term "Jewish Christianity" is an artificial concept of scholarly nomenclature in the English and German Enlightenment and is not attested in sources.[133] In numerous instances there are, however, circumlocutions for the churches: Gal. 2:12, "those from the circumcision"; Gal. 2:14, "to live by Jewish customs" ('Ιουδαΐζειν); Acts 9:2; 19:9, 23; 22:4; 24:14, 22: "the [new] way";[134] Acts 15:5, "Pharisees, who have become believers"; Acts 24:5, "groups/direction of the Nazarenes"; John 8:31, "Jews who believe in Jesus." Inasmuch as the concept is essential in scholarly literature, it must be defined. However, an exact definition of the subject is not possible, for a multilayered Judaism is associated here with, in turn, a new, developing, multilayered movement: Christianity. Combinations such as "Christian Judaism" or "Jewish Christianity" give emphases, but no real clarity. Thus only indicators can be given that can be regarded as characteristic for Jewish Christian self-understanding.[135] When one observes the earliest ancient terms, then, three aspects are in the foreground. (1) *Origin*. Jewish Christians are Jews by birth who joined with the new direction of Christ-believers/Christians ("those of the circumcision," Gal. 2:12; Acts 10:45; 11:2).[136] This ethnic-genetic definition is not sufficient, however, because then Jews by birth such as Paul, Peter, and James would be placed together as Jewish Christians without distinction, without a consideration of their differences.[137] (2) *Way of life*. Therefore, the Jewish way of life must be considered as a second aspect ('Ιουδαΐζειν, Gal. 2:14; Ign. *Magn.* 8.1; 9.1; 10.3). This could include circumcision, Sabbath observance, purity and food regulations, participation in the Jewish worship services and festivals.[138] (3) *Theology*. A theology is also necessarily connected with the praxis of a Jewish way of life. Inasmuch as early

133. On the history of research, cf. Lemke, *Judenchristentum*; Paget, "Jewish Christian and Jewish Christianity"; F. Jones, *Rediscovery of Jewish Christianity*.

134. Trebilco, *Self-Designations and Group Identity*, 270, considers ἡ ὁδός a Jewish Christian self-designation based on Isa. 40:3.

135. Garleff, *Urchristliche Identität in Matthäusevangelium*, 26–47, selects the concept of identity (as social, personal, and collective identity) as the starting point and attempts to communicate "story, ethos, ritus" as means of identity construction for the respective Jewish Christian concepts of Matthew, the Didache, and the Letter of James.

136. G. Strecker, *Das Judenchristentum*, 310–11, speaks of a "genetic definition"; Colpe, "Das deutsche Wort 'Judenchristen,'" 39, speaks of a "case composition" in the sense of a partitive genitive: "Christians from among the Jews."

137. Cf. G. Strecker, *Das Judenchristentum*, 311; Frey, "Die Fragmente judenchristlicher Evangelien," 567.

138. Cf. Paget, "Jewish Christian and Jewish Christianity," 49n119: "A Jewish Christian is a Jewish believer in Jesus who maintains a Jewish lifestyle."

Christianity develops its theology totally from the OT, specific conceptions must be present that are not represented by the great majority of Christians. Here, first of all, circumcision may be mentioned as a valid sign of election and identity. In addition, the distinction between "clean" and "unclean" and the related food regulations prevent table fellowship with gentile Christians. Sabbath observance and a theological reverence for the Jerusalem temple and the land of Israel as the place of election can be further signs of identity, as well as an exclusive appeal to Abraham. A preference for Matthew's Gospel and a hidden or open opposition to Paul may be observed among most Jewish Christians.

A definition of an "intentional," "strict" Jewish Christianity in this sense must always have these three points in view. The starting point is, besides the confession of Christ, the origin in Judaism, which is connected with a self-understanding consisting of full observance of the Torah and maintains the priority over gentile Christians. Diverse elements can be added to this basic position: the continuing practice of circumcision, differing approaches to food regulations, minimal ritual regulations, special forms of baptism and Eucharist, participation in synagogue worship, special understanding of Christology, rejection of the virgin birth, Jesus as "merely" a man. Such a cumulative conceptual description is necessarily not precise but is appropriate to the topic. Because Jewish Christianity appealed to two authorities (Moses and Jesus Christ) at the same time, it had to be inevitably a religious form of compromise in the positive sense, in which the boundaries in the individual churches were drawn in different ways. The apostolic decrees, for example, signify this compromise (Acts 15:20, 29; 21:25; Rev. 2:24), as does Did. 6.1–3:

> See that no one leads you astray from this way of the teaching, for such a person teaches you without regard for God. For if you are able to bear the whole yoke of the Lord, you will be perfect. But if you are not able, then do what you can. Now concerning food, bear what you are able, but in any case, keep strictly away from meat sacrificed to idols, for it involves the worship of dead gods. (trans. Holmes)

The church of the Didache holds to a maximal demand but does not make it a sine qua non. However, it draws a boundary with food offered to idols, which must not be crossed. If such a flexibility is missing and circumcision is not only continued within Jewish/Jewish Christian families but also belongs to the irrevocable ideological foundation and is demanded of gentile Christians, then one can speak of a radical Jewish Christianity or of Judaizers. For them the complete integration of the new movement of Christ-believers into Judaism and not a measured combination of the old and new (cf. Matt. 13:52) stands in the foreground.

In general, strict Jewish Christianity has a special structure of authority inasmuch as normative elements of Judaism in a variety of forms and concentrations are regarded as obligatory along with a confession of Christ.

10.5.1 Jewish Christianity before 70 CE

Emerging Christianity was exclusively Jewish Christian at the beginning, both in Jerusalem (see above, chap. 5) and in the churches in Galilee. More precisely expressed: It was first a defined, liberal form of Judaism. Circumcision was probably a self-evident practice that was connected with baptism; similarly, the Jewish Christians participated in the temple or synagogue worship services (cf. Acts 3:1 and passim). The Jewish food and ritual regulations were probably still observed. The conflict with Stephen (see above, 5.5) indicates, however, that theological controversies occurred very early (ca. 32/33 CE) both among the Jewish Christ-believers and between the new movement and the established groups. The position regarding the temple and the law played a crucial role. Presumably, the Hellenists relativized the soteriological significance of the temple and the law in light of the Christ event and evoked a negative reaction from both conservative Jewish Christians and militant Jews. The further development indicates that early Jewish Christianity was diverse and absolutely not a unified entity.[139] The mission of the Hellenists and especially the founding of the church at Antioch (see above, 6.4) are evidence of a liberal Jewish Christianity that made the transition to the gentile mission, overcame the boundaries between Judaism and the gentiles, and to a certain extent, dispersed into the emerging Christianity. In a variety of ways, Barnabas, Peter, and Paul (see above, 5.2) belonged to this orientation. The Antioch incident in Gal. 2:11–15 (see above, 7.6) indicates that Peter and Barnabas were influenced by the strict Jewish Christianity of James, while Paul rejected the significance of the food laws for the interaction of Jewish Christians and gentiles. At least one may assume that Peter's missionary path to the West (Corinth, Rome) was also a theological decision away from Jerusalem and a stance for an open Jewish Christianity.

A totally different position is taken by James the brother of the Lord (see above, 5.2), who led the Jerusalem church after 43/44 CE and must be considered a representative of the strict Judaism that remained faithful to the Torah. Even here, however, differentiations are necessary. While at the apostolic conference an influential group (cf. Gal. 2:3f., "false brothers"; Acts 15:5,

139. An overview is given by G. Strecker, *Das Judenchristentum*, 313–18.

believing Pharisees) demanded circumcision from gentile Christians, James (probably with reservations) takes a position against the strict ones; according to Paul, James does this without additional conditions; but according to Luke, James lays down conditions (cf. Acts 15:19–20, 28–29). The apostolic conference demonstrates the diversity of early Jewish Christianity (see above, chap. 7), for at least three positions may be distinguished: (1) radical Jewish Christians who demanded circumcision for gentile Christians; (2) Paul, who battled them vehemently; and (3) those who did not demand circumcision but desired minimal ritual conditions (James). The development that follows indicates that James increasingly pursued a radical Jewish Christian course. If at the apostolic conference James agreed to freedom from circumcision for gentiles without concrete conditions and with reservations, his emissaries (Gal. 2:12) at the Antioch incident demanded minimal ritual standards for table fellowship of Jews with gentile Christians. If those who demanded circumcision in Galatia (cf. Gal. 5:2, "If you let yourselves be circumcised, Christ will be of no benefit to you" [NRSV]) and the opponents in Philippi (cf. Phil. 3:2, "Watch out for the mutilators") correctly appealed to the Jerusalem church, then James would ultimately have changed to the side of the radical Jewish Christians. This possibility is completely conceivable because, in anticipation of the Jewish War, the pressure on the Jerusalem church from official Judaism became increasingly greater. The Jerusalem church stood under suspicion, in their view, of cooperating with the hated gentiles. The members of the Jerusalem church had to counter this view by demanding the circumcision of gentile Christians in order to demonstrate their abiding membership in Judaism.

The logia source is evidence of an independent type of early Jewish Christianity (see above, 6.3; 6.7). Its supporters understood themselves as an inner-Jewish renewal movement that preached the (second) coming of the Son of Man in judgment, Jesus Christ.[140] The conflict with Israel and the rejection by a major part of Israel is determinative, as indicated by the words about "this generation" (Luke 7:31; 11:29, 30–32, 50–51Q). It rejected the preaching of the Q missionaries (Luke 7:31Q); it is "evil" (Luke 11:29Q), and the Son of Man will be a sign of the judgment for them (Luke 11:30–32, 50–51Q). The crisis of Israel is evident especially in the forfeiture of its primacy in salvation history (Luke 13:24–27, 28, 29, 30; 14:16–18:21–22Q), and the consequence is the judgment (Luke 13:34–35Q). In the center of the eschatology of the logia source is the concept of the imminent judgment that stands directly before the people (Luke 3:7–9, 16b–17; 10:12–15; 17:23–37Q). Jesus's message

---

140. Arnal, "Q Document," 150, speaks of "Jewish Jesus people."

of judgment is taken up by Q and strengthened by the composition of the words about the Son of Man, for at the end of Q the Son of Man appears increasingly as judge (Luke 12:40; 17:24, 26, 30Q). The criterion for the judgment is unambiguously the acceptance or rejection of Jesus's message of the kingdom of God. Anyone who now rejects this message will not only be subject to the judgment (Luke 10:13–15; 11:31–32Q), but according to Luke 12:10 (Q), the rejection is even unforgivable. Finally, the announcement of judgment for Israel in Luke 22:28, 30 (Q) marks the end of the logia source and also the end point of Israel. Whether Israel is finally rejected according to Q, one cannot say with certainty, for the intensity of the conflict can indicate continuing proximity or increasing alienation and ultimate separation.[141] It is noteworthy that the concept of νόμος (law) appears only twice in the logia source (Luke 16:16–17 [Q]: "The law and the prophets were until John. . . . It is easier for heaven and earth to pass away, than for an iota or a stroke of a letter in the law to be dropped"). While the Baptist represents the end of the law (v. 16), in verse 17 its commandments are still valid. However, the fact stands that neither individual Mosaic laws nor Moses himself appears in Q.[142] Single texts such as Luke 9:59–60 and 14:26 (Q) call the Torah commands into question, and the woes against the Pharisees (Luke 11:42, 39b, 41, 43Q) and scribes (Luke 11:46b, 52, 47–48Q) clearly demonstrate a critique of Jewish groups that want to expand the influence of the Torah on daily life. Thus the Torah is not rejected, but the ritual regulations are relativized in comparison with the ethical sayings (cf. Luke 11:42Q). In any case, it is clear that within the logia source, it is not the Torah, but "the message and figure of Jesus, the Son of Man-Kyrios,"[143] that is the central orienting fact and soteriological principle. In addition, neither the commands for circumcision nor for purity play a role (Luke 10:7 [Q], "Eat what is set before you"); and the nations come into view, at least to some extent (cf. Luke 7:9; 13:28–29Q). All of these observations (polemic against Israel/separation from Israel, absence of the significance of Torah, circumcision as well as the nullification of the distinction "clean-unclean") justify ascribing to the logia source its own identity, with

141. Both are basically possible; hence the opinions vary correspondingly. Those who support continuing proximity are, e.g., Sevenich-Bax, *Israels Konfrontation mit den letzten Boten*, 186–90; Karrer, "Christliche Gemeinde und Israel"; Arnal, "Q Document," 150–53, sees the logia source exclusively within the possibilities of Jewish (and non–Jewish Christian) identity formation and self-description. Horn, "Christentum und Judentum in der Logienquelle," however, emphasizes within the redactions of Q an increasing distance from Israel. D. Zeller, "Jesus, Q und die Zukunft Israels," emphasizes the continuing intensity of the word of judgment over Israel that is not to be minimized.

142. Cf. C. Heil, *Lukas und Q*, 318–20.

143. Kosch, *Die eschatologische Tora des Menschensohnes*, 450.

which Judaism is no longer really compatible. One can best describe the logia source as a prophetic-eschatological Jewish Christian document, one that is fully shaped by the expectation of the future. In the time span between the coming of Jesus and his second coming as Son of Man, the church sees itself involved in great challenges for the maintenance of their faith.

An additional type of early Jewish Christianity is represented by the opponents of Paul in 2 Corinthians. They proclaim "another Jesus" and "another gospel" (2 Cor. 11:4), and Paul attacks them sharply in 2 Cor. 11:13: "For such boasters are false apostles, malicious workers, disguising apostles of Christ." Their Jewish origin is documented in 2 Cor. 11:22: "Are they Hebrews? I am also! Are they Israelites? I am also! Are they descendants of Abraham? I am also!" Since Paul ironically calls them "super-apostles" in 2 Cor. 11:5, they probably emphasized their Judaism with an appeal especially to Abraham. At the same time, they identified their credentials through impressive appearance, skillful rhetoric (cf. 2 Cor. 10:10), and "signs of an apostle" (2 Cor. 12:12), that is, miracles. In contrast to Galatians, no mention is made of circumcision. Thus they are not designated as Judaizers in the same way as in Galatia and Philippi. The opponents in 2 Corinthians were early Christian traveling missionaries of Jewish-Hellenistic origin who charged that Paul in particular lacked the Spirit; they identified themselves as true apostles by miracles, speech, and an exclusive reference to Abraham and claim to be people of the Spirit. One cannot determine to what extent they were associated with Jerusalem.

An additional variant of strict early Jewish Christianity is to be seen in the Judaizers in Galatia (and Philippi)[144] who, at least in Galatia, appealed to Abraham (cf. Gal. 3:6ff.) and demanded the subsequent circumcision of gentile Christians (cf. Gal. 5:2; Phil. 3:2–3). They advocated a reintegration of the new movement into Judaism and were thus supported by the Jerusalem church.

10.5.2 Jewish Christianity after 70

Jewish Christianity after 70 CE was no more united than before 70. The fall of Jerusalem (see above, 3.3.) was a radical turning point. The temple and the Jerusalem church were now no longer a reference point for Jewish Christianity (see above, 9.2), and the place of Judaism in the Roman Empire was weakened. Furthermore, the mission to the gentiles without requiring circumcision accelerated considerably after 70 and altered the weight of early

---

144. A survey of the history of research on the question of opponents in 2 Corinthians is provided by Sumney, *Identifying Paul's Opponents*, 13–73; Bieringer, "Die Gegner des Paulus."

Christianity to the disadvantage of Jewish Christianity. Finally, the *fiscus Judaicus* especially placed the Jewish Christians under pressure,[145] for now they were forced to choose between Judaism and Christianity. Nevertheless, the Jewish Christianity remained a weighty voice in multiple forms in the expanding Christianity.

The Gospel of Matthew

Undoubtedly the Gospel of Matthew was the most significant Jewish Christian writing after 70 (see above, 10.2.2). The following indicators suggest the Jewish Christian place of Matthew:

a. There is a fundamental "yes" to the law (cf. Matt. 5:17–20; 23:3a, 23b).[146]

b. The permanent appeal to the OT and the emphasis on the idea of fulfillment (cf. Matt. 1:22–23; 2:5–6, 15, 17–18; 3:3; 4:14–16; 8:17 and passim) are evident.

c. The mission of Jesus is basically limited to Israel (cf. Matt. 10:5–6; 15:24).

d. The Matthean community continues to keep the Sabbath (cf. Matt. 24:20).

e. The Matthean community continues to live within the association of Judaism (cf. Matt. 17:24–27; 23:1–3).

f. The Moses typology in Matt. 2:13ff.; 4:1–2; 5:1; and the five major speeches in the Gospel (Matt. 5–7; 10; 13; 18; 23–25) suggest an affinity between Jesus and Moses.

g. The language, structure, reception of the Scripture, argumentation, and impact of the Gospel of Matthew point to a Jewish Christian as author.

Of fundamental significance is the affirmation of the Matthean Jesus of the law, which is programmatically formulated in Matt. 5:17–20: "Do not think that I have come to destroy the law or the prophets. I have not come to destroy but to fulfill. For truly I say to you: Until heaven and earth pass away, neither an iota nor a stroke of a letter will pass away until all things are accomplished." This conceivable ideal regarding observance and fulfillment of the law is supported by a warning: "Whoever relaxes one of the least of the commandments and teaches others to do so will be called least in the kingdom of heaven. But whoever does it and teaches it will be called great in the

---

145. See above, 9.2.
146. Cf. above, 10.2.2.

kingdom of heaven." Here discussions within the church about the extent of fulfillment of the law are evident. These are decided as the unlimited validity of the Torah. A polemical topos about what is greatest is finally evident in verse 20: "But I tell you, if your righteousness does not exceed that of the scribes and Pharisees, you will not enter the kingdom of heaven." As always, redaction and tradition can be distinguished in Matt. 5:17–20;[147] Matthew took over the entire text; thus it is binding for him without limitations. The Torah is affected, even in the smallest letter, for Jesus has come to fulfill it. Only with this affirmation does the interpretative achievement begin, which Matthew accomplishes with his textual sequence and demands of his interpreters. The foundational presupposition for understanding is also here the preceding mercy of God in the Beatitudes and the conditional trust in the generosity of God (cf. Matt. 5:45; 6:25–34; 7:7–11). However, a tension exists between the thesis statement in Matt. 5:17–20 and the antitheses in Matt. 5:21–48, which cannot be explained away with hermeneutical artistry, for the intensification in the antitheses can be explained sufficiently neither with the citation of OT texts nor with its history of interpretation.

Therefore, one must ask: In what sense does Jesus fulfill the law according to Matthew? It is certainly not only as a mere repetition of the will of God as it is formulated in the OT, but rather it is as an authoritative interpretation. The correspondence between Matt. 5:20 and 5:48 indicates that the antitheses are the concretizing of the better righteousness demanded by the evangelist, which formulates the "better" of this righteousness. Therefore, the law remains a constituent part of the righteousness, while at the same time the authority of the speaker defines its content.[148] In the first antithesis Jesus radicalizes the Torah prohibition of killing. The second antithesis, concerning adultery (Matt. 5:27–30), is also a radicalizing of the Torah within the possibilities of contemporary interpretation. In contrast, the third antithesis, concerning divorce (Matt. 5:31–32), depicts an annulment of the Torah command (cf. Deut. 24:1, 3). The absolute prohibition of oaths in Matt. 5:33–37, which bursts OT-Jewish thought, is based on the authority and majesty of Jesus. Matthew makes this commandment feasible for his church, as he had previously done with the prohibition of divorce, without nullifying the original intention of the

147. For the analysis, cf. G. Strecker, *Die Bergpredigt*, 55–64; Luz, *Matthew*, 1:213–25; Deines, *Die Gerechtigkeit der Tora*, 257–428. In any case, it is clear that Matt. 5:17 is predominantly redactional and v. 20 is entirely redactional; v. 18 is an inextricable ball of threads; v. 19c–d may go back to Matthew.

148. Cf. Deines, *Die Gerechtigkeit der Tora*, 649: "In its previous function, the Torah can contribute nothing to this eschatological righteousness, but it remains an expression of the will of God that is present in that which leads to the ἐντολαί of Jesus. In Matthew, only Jesus makes possible the path into the universal kingdom."

proclamation of Jesus. With the rejection of the OT principle of retaliation in Matt. 5:38–42 and the absolute command for love of enemies, the preacher of the sermon leaves behind Jewish thought[149] and emphasizes that the true will of God lies in unlimited and perfect love and righteousness. The antitheses demonstrate how Matthew understands the fulfillment of the law by Jesus: the validity and the binding nature lie not in the text of the OT tradition but exclusively in the authority of Jesus. The ἐξουσία of Jesus enables one to override a valid command, at the same time bringing the true will of God into reality. Thus for Matthew the intensification of Torah and the nullification of the Torah do not stand in opposition to each other because both are based on and held together by the authority of Jesus alone. For the Matthean community, it is not the OT law as such that is binding but the authoritative interpretation of the OT by Jesus.[150] Therefore, the authority of Jesus does not simply nullify a mistaken interpretation of the Torah; rather, Jesus claims, sometimes against the actual wording of the Torah, to unveil again its original intention.

The Jewish Christianity of Matthew is necessarily a new interpretation of Judaism from the perspective of the Christ event and portrays a new form of a universalistic Jewish Christianity by its opening to the nations (Matt. 28:16–20).[151] It demonstrates the character of a compromise, which is particularly evident in two points: (1) The golden rule as the goal of the Sermon on the Mount (Matt. 7:12) is not only a universal ethical axiom[152] but also reflects a fully different logic from the programmatic word in Matt. 5:17–20, which is oriented to single commands. It is based on the principle of reciprocity and one's own assessment and now makes practicable, above all, the rigorous ethical demands of the Torah and of the teacher Jesus Christ. The Golden Rule, like the command for love of neighbor (Matt. 5:21–26), the command for love of enemy (Matt. 5:44), and the twofold command for love of neighbor and love of God in Matt. 22:34–40, likewise indicates that, for Matthew, obedience to the law consists not in the observation of many single regulations, commands, and rules, but in the act of love and righteousness. Thus one may speak of a "transformation of the Torah by the gospel."[153] (2) The intentional

---

149. On the parallels in the history of religion, cf. NW I/1.2:484–522.

150. Deines, *Die Gerechtigkeit der Tora*, 648: "The Torah no longer has its own function besides the command of Jesus, not even for Jewish Christians. Rather, the disciples (and their successors in the churches) are instructed to pass on the commandments of the 'one teacher' (S. Byrskog). On the other hand, the Torah nowhere appears as an obligatory norm independent of the teaching and interpretation of Jesus; i.e., the διδάσκειν of the Christian teacher is determined exclusively in christological perspective in reference to righteousness."

151. Cf. Garleff, *Urchristliche Identität im Matthäusevangelium*, 203.

152. Cf. the texts in NW I/1.2:699–712.

153. So Deines, *Gerechtigkeit der Tora*, 645.

omission of the noun περιτομή indicates clearly[154] that Matthew also assumes the historic legacy of Paul's mission to the gentiles. It was obviously apparent to the Jewish Christian Matthew that, without circumcision, neither Judaism nor inner-Jewish dialogue could exist for an extended period! The intentional omission of the problem of circumcision within an exclusively inner-Jewish standpoint of Matthew can scarcely be explained.[155] Rather, in this Gospel it is not circumcision but baptism as well as mission and teaching (cf. Matt. 28:16–20) that are the rites of initiation/the guiding principles of Matthean Christianity. Matthew comes from Judaism and considers himself permanently bound to it. However, he considers himself a strict Jewish Christian within a new coordination system and opens himself and his church, after the failure of the mission to Israel, to the universal mission to the nations. "Matthew's gospel is an answer to the 'no' of the great majority of Israel to Jesus. It is the attempt to come to terms with this by defining the community's position and to contribute to forming and preserving its identity in a situation of crisis and transition."[156]

THE LETTER OF JAMES

In the Letter of James another indicator of strict Jewish Christianity is emphasized in addition to the emphasis on Torah: anti-Paulinism. The Letter of James is an early Christian pseudepigraphic wisdom document that makes the claim to be written by James the brother of the Lord.[157] This attribution is no coincidence, for James the brother of the Lord, as leader of the Jerusalem church, was probably considered the primary opponent of Paul and, with his loyalty to the Torah, was a symbolic figure in strict Jewish Christianity.[158] The Letter of James is intended, in the post-Pauline period between 80 and 100 CE, to define endangered Jewish Christian identity. Soteriology, anthropology, and ethics are closely interwoven in James. The soteriological basic concept is shaped not by christological but rather by theocentric wisdom: the "wisdom [of God]" given "from above" (James 3:15, 17) enables the believer to follow

154. Cf. above, the sidebar under 10.2.3.
155. The very striking fact that the evangelist omits circumcision as the entry gate into the Torah cannot alleviate the assumption "that he himself and the Jewish believers in his group practiced circumcision" (so Davies and Allison, *Matthew*, 3:703). If Matthew does not have "his teacher" Jesus of Nazareth teach circumcision, how can one argue that he nevertheless practiced it?
156. Luz, *Matthew*, 1:55.
157. On the introductory issues, cf. Schnelle, *History and Theology of the New Testament*, 383–98; a survey of research is provided by Konradt, "Theologie in der 'strohernen Epistel'"; Niebuhr, "'New Perspective on James'?"
158. In the Gospel of the Hebrews, frag. 5, he is called "James the Just."

the "perfect law of liberty" (James 1:25; 2:12) as a unity of faith and works/deeds. For James, the law in the full sense is a gift of God. However, it is not the law that saves,[159] but instead it is the activity of God (cf. James 1:17–18). This "word of truth" is identical with the "law of liberty" (James 1.25),[160] which is consistently connected with doing or not doing (James 2:8–12; 4:11–12).[161] The act of God is understood by James as an obligating event that demands a total response from the people in his community. Thus James ascribes to the work/the deed (ἔργον in James 1:4, 25) or the works/deeds (ἔργα in James 2:14, 17–18, 20–21, 24–26; 3:13) in the soteriological event a crucial and lasting significance in a positive sense in a way that is different from Paul (cf. Rom. 3:21). The double minded (δίψυχος in James 1:8; 4:8), the doubters (James 1:6, 8), the wavering (James 4:8), the proud (James 2:1ff.; 4:6), those driven by desires (James 1:14), and the rich (James 1:11; 5:1–6) are challenged and motivated to restore the unity of their Christian existence. Their own deeds bring the people into judgment so that they must always be conscious of their consequences. As James 2:8–13 says explicitly, the judgment takes place according to the criterion of observance of the law (James 2:12–13: "So speak and act as those who will be judged by the perfect law of liberty. For judgment without mercy comes to those who do not exercise mercy. Mercy triumphs over the judgment"). By the "law of liberty," James means primarily the "royal law," namely the command for the love of neighbor (Lev. 19:18 in James 2:8),[162] which unmistakably obligates the believer to keep "the whole law" (ὅλον τὸν νόμον): "For whoever keeps the whole law but fails in one point is guilty of all" (James 2:10). This soteriological concept is an expression of a conscious Jewish Christian identity, which directly links together the mercy of God and the mercy of humankind toward the neighbor and judges according to the criterion of deeds according to the law.

The differences between James and Paul are apparent: While for Paul sin is a supraindividual power that serves the law and deceives the person (cf. Rom. 7:7ff.), with James sin is overcome by the keeping of the whole law (James 2:9; 4:7; 5:15b, 16, 20); that is, sin in James is a concept of a deed and act against God's law.[163] Consequently, for him there is no opposition between faith and works/deeds, contrary to the view of his conversation partner. Is the conversation partner Paul? Inasmuch as the opposition between πίστις-ἔργα (νόμου) is

159. Cf. Burchard, *Der Jakobusbrief*, 90.

160. Cf. Burchard, *Der Jakobusbrief*, 88.

161. Appropriately, according to Konradt, "'Geboren durch das Wort der Wahrheit,'" 12: "Faith without works, however, is soteriologically ineffective."

162. Cf. W. Popkes, *Der Brief des Jakobus*, 180–81.

163. Cf. Burchard, *Der Jakobusbrief*, 74.

nowhere attested before Paul,[164] a reference to Paul in James is likely.[165] Moreover, James 2:10 appears to refer to Gal. 5:3 (ὅλον τὸν νόμον in the accusative only here; elsewhere, Matt. 22:40), and the allusion to Rom. 3:28 in James 2:24 is evident, as is indicated in the linguistic/subject agreements and the polemical-rhetorical μόνον.[166] Finally, contacts with the theme of Abraham are present (cf. Rom. 4:2; James 2:21), and the citation from Gen. 15:6 in Rom. 4:3 and James 2:23 agrees in deviating from the LXX text at two points: Ἀβραάμ instead of Ἀβράμ, and the addition of δέ after ἐπίστευσεν.[167] These contacts indicate that James is to be read as a document of anti-Paulinism. But is the letter at the same time a document against Paul?[168] Paul is not the target in James 2:14–26: indeed, for Paul there is no faith apart from works (cf. only Rom. 1:5; 13:8–10; Gal. 5:6). James could have alluded to or misunderstood the Pauline position. Perhaps he did not know Galatians or Romans but knew only unknown oral and/or literary intermediary stages. Possibly he argues against Christians who practiced faith without works and in so doing appealed to Paul.[169] Second Thessalonians 2:2 and 2 Tim. 2:18 give evidence of an eschatological enthusiasm in the post-Pauline missionary churches of Asia Minor and Greece, which possibly led to a neglect of works/deeds, a position that is opposed by James. In any case, in James there is a combination of the high view of the law and a sharp critique of the theological position attributed to Paul.

The Epistle to the Hebrews

Whether Hebrews exhibits an intentional Jewish Christian profile is disputed. In support of its Jewish Christian nature, one could observe the title "To the

164. Cf. Hengel, "Der Jakobusbrief als antipaulinische Polemik," 526; Avemarie, "Die Werke des Gesetzes," 291.

165. Cf. W. Popkes, "Traditionen und Traditionsbrüche," 161: "A decisive fact in favor of the assumption that James takes up traditions derived from Paul (but not necessarily genuinely Pauline) is, in my opinion, that James reacts negatively to positions that are attested in this form only in Paul."

166. Cf. Hengel, "Der Jakobusbrief als antipaulinische Polemik," 527: "It cannot be disputed that James 2:24 argues against a Pauline polemical statement such as Rom. 3:28."

167. Cf. Lindemann, *Paulus im ältesten Christentum*, 244–51; Lüdemann, *Opposition to Paul*, 143–49.

168. This view is affirmed by M. Mitchell ("James as a Document of Paulinism?"), according to whom James is intentionally directed against Galatians and Romans in the context of post-Pauline Christianity and at the same time recalls 1 Corinthians.

169. Wischmeyer, "Polemik im Jakobusbrief," 375, does not regard James as anti-Pauline: "The theme of James as a teaching document is ethics, which concentrates on two classical areas, the ethic of the word or the ethic of speech and about the ethic of deed or works. . . . The polemic of the letter, which to some extent is very intense, is intended correspondingly to the correct modeling of ethics, not the theological dispute with an opposing front. Opponents are present, but the opponent is evil or Satan, not Paul."

Hebrews" (attested from ca. 200 CE onward) as well as the total embeddedness of the author and his church in the language and thought world of the OT and early Judaism. A theology of the word is pervasive from the prologue throughout the entire document.[170] In addition to the overture, this is evident especially in Hebrews 1:5, 13; 2:1–4; 4:2, 12; 5:12; 11:3; 12:25; 13:7. The speaking of God as the basic dimension of God's acts is emphasized literarily by numerous LXX citations in which God speaks (ca. 22 times),[171] an abundance and density that is unique in the NT. Besides the approximately thirty-five literal text citations, there are approximately eighty allusions to OT texts. Hebrews cites exclusively from the LXX; any deviations can be explained by the assumption that other LXX codices were available to the author or that he cited from memory.[172]

The conception of cult theology is also developed from the theme of the theology of the word in Hebrews. The opening, which is concentrated on the speaking of God, leads to and culminates in the central thesis of the atoning high priest in Heb. 2:17–18: "Therefore he had to be like his brothers in every respect so that he might be a merciful and faithful high priest for the service to God, to make atonement for the sins of the people. For because he has suffered when he was tempted, he is able to help those who are tempted." From Heb. 5:1 onward, the theology of the high priest dominates the entire argument.[173] The dominant motif of the surpassing greatness of the event in the history of revelation, announced already in Heb. 1:1–2, remains definitive. Jesus the high priest does not serve in an earthly temple but instead is active in the heavenly sanctuary and is thus superior to all other cultic activities. As the frame for the major section of Hebrews, 4:14–16 and 10:19–23 present the basic thesis of the high-priestly theology. The sinless suffering Jesus, as Son of God, is installed as high priest; he goes through the heavens and enables the believing church to have free access to God. Historically, the destruction of the temple in Jerusalem is a presupposition, for with it the OT-Jewish cult has come to its earthly end. In terms of the history of religions, the sayings about the high priest in Philo of Alexandria offer the material for a completely transcending and universalizing of the high priest.[174]

---

170. Cf. here Grässer, "Das Wort als Heil"; Hegermann, "Das Wort Gottes als aufdeckende Macht"; Wider, *Theozentrik und Bekenntnis.*

171. Cf. Theobald, "Vom Text zum 'lebendigen Wort.'"

172. For an analysis, cf. Schröger, *Der Verfasser des Hebräerbriefes,* 35–197, 247–56. Parallels to the interpretative methods in ancient Judaism are evident in Hebrews; cf. the detailed list, 256–99.

173. Cf., besides the commentaries, especially H. Zimmermann, *Die Hohepriester-Christologie des Hebräerbriefes;* Loader, *Sohn und Hoherpriester.*

174. Numerous parallels between Hebrews and Philo exist besides the high-priestly speculation; besides the commentaries, cf. Hegermann, *Der Brief an die Hebräer;* and H.-F. Weiss,

The covenant theology adopts OT–early Jewish linguistic conventions (cf. the reception of Jer. 31:31–34 and Exod. 24:8 in Heb. 8:8–12; 9:20; 10:16) but transforms their central focus and shapes them in a new way. The variety of OT covenant traditions is not within the focus of Hebrews; instead, he concentrates on the motif of the breach of the covenant and the blinding of the people of the old covenant. The central connection between the covenant and the law is not addressed.[175] The essential connection between the OT concept of covenant and the covenant theology in Hebrews lies in its theocentric nature: God is the origin, middle, and goal of the covenant.[176] However, this theocentric aspect is christologically filled, taking on a new profile, for the Christ confession is the center of the covenant concept in Hebrews. A further central metaphor of ecclesiology is the concept of the wandering people of God (cf. esp. Heb. 3:7–4:11).[177] While the entry into the promised place of rest remains closed to the pilgrim people of God because of their disobedience, the task for the present is to draw the consequences and hear the voice of God "today" and not to close the heart (Heb. 3:7–8). Those who belong to the people of God are at the same time former Jews and gentiles, who hear the same message that the wilderness generation heard (Heb. 4:2). Hebrews does not contain reflections about the relationship of the church and Israel in salvation history; instead, the concept of one people of God combines with the word-of-God theology, for the speaking of God in the word has constituted the people of God in all times.

First conclusion. The entire argument, the metaphors, and the images are developed by Hebrews from the intertextual link with the Scriptures of Israel, and the author indicates a consciousness of an election theology, describing the readers as "seed of Abraham" (Heb. 2:16). All of this could suggest an intentional Jewish Christian position of Hebrews in the environment of the synagogue.[178]

Other observations conflict with this view.[179] (1) First Clement (see below, 14.1), written in Rome and contemporaneous with Hebrews, indicates that an

---

Der Brief an die Hebräer; esp. Williamson, *Philo and the Epistle to the Hebrews*, who explores all relevant parallels.

175. Cf. Backhaus, *Der neue Bund*, 333.

176. Cf. Backhaus, *Der neue Bund*, 350.

177. Cf. Grässer, "Das wandernde Gottesvolk," 231–50; Roloff, *Die Kirche*, 282–87.

178. The Jewish Christian setting for Hebrews is supported by Gelardini, "*Verhärtet eure Herzen nicht*"; Vogel, "Der Hebräerbrief als ständiger Gast"; R. Hays ("'New Covenantalism'") sees in Hebrews a document of a group that self-evidently regards itself within Judaism. "The Epistle to the Hebrews nowhere allows the conclusion that the new covenant is meant for anyone other than 'the house of Israel and . . . the house of Judah' (Heb. 8:8). A gentile church is nowhere in sight. . . . The thought of the new covenant does not aim toward rejection [of Israel], but for the restoration of Israel."

179. Cf. esp. Backhaus, *Der Hebräerbrief*, 24–25.

intensive study of the Scripture was made and detailed citations were made in predominantly gentile Christian churches. Themes from the OT or ancient Judaism are not a certain indicator of a specific Jewish Christian standpoint. (2) Central Jewish and Jewish Christian identity markers such as circumcision or Sabbath are never mentioned in Hebrews. (3) The Levitical high priesthood and the law do not have the power to lead humankind to its goal: to arrive at participation in the holiness and nature of God and receive free access to God (cf. Heb. 2:17; 7:15–19; 9:11–12). The law is definitely removed, for the power of sin that separates from salvation cannot be removed by the law. The law belongs to the outward realm and does not give life (Heb. 7:16); it is not capable of leading to perfection (Heb. 7:18, 19a) because it is weak and unable to take away sin (Heb. 10:1–2, 11). (4) The Sinai covenant is not a part of the community's original history (cf. Heb. 12:18–24). (5) The warnings against apostasy from "the living God" (Heb. 3:12) and the repentance from "dead works" (Heb. 6:1; 9:14; 12:22) suggest terminology used in the mission to the gentiles. (6) Hebrews is primarily, however, the main document of a theological comparative in the NT. It depicts the superiority of the new way of salvation in antithetical terms, in which the history of revelation is described as the superiority of Jesus's status in the history of revelation, even over the angels and the earthly priests (cf. only Heb. 1). The dualistic reading of the OT under the influence of Jewish-Hellenistic and Middle Platonist traditions[180] is an expression of a comprehensive process of reevaluation that is shaped by the idea of qualitative superiority.

Second conclusion. The question of whether Hebrews is to be regarded as a document of a conscious Jewish Christian position can scarcely be answered, depending ultimately on the theological-political standpoint of the interpreter. Probably Hebrews pictures its own world beyond our conventions of interpretation.

Like Hebrews, the Letter of Jude is also interwoven into a very complex OT-Jewish tradition.[181] The OT is employed in numerous references and allusions.[182] What is striking is the reference to traditions from ancient Judaism that are unique in the NT for their density. The series of examples in Jude 5–7 develops the connection between a misspent life and divine judgment; there are parallels in Sir. 16:6–15; CD 2.17–3.12; 3 Macc. 2:4–7; T. Naph. 3.4–5. Jude 6 stands in a long line of Jewish interpretations of Gen. 6:1–4; comparable

---

180. On the influence of Middle Platonism, cf. Eisele, *Ein unerschütterliches Reich*; Backhaus, *Der Hebräerbrief*, 24–25; J. Thompson, *Beginnings of Christian Philosophy.*

181. Cf. Heiligenthal, *Zwischen Henoch und Paulus.*

182. On the language of Jude (14 hapax legomena) and its use of the OT (primarily MT, but with knowledge of the LXX), cf. Bauckham, *Jude, 2 Peter*, 6–8.

texts appear in 1 En. 10.4–6, 11–13; 12.14–13.1. The destruction of Sodom and Gomorrah, invoked in Jude 7, is considered in numerous Jewish and Christian texts (cf. 3 Macc. 2:5; Jub. 16.6; 20.5; 22.22; T. Ash. 7.1; Josephus, *J.W.* 5.566; Matt. 10:15; 11:24; Luke 10:12; 17:29). Apocryphal Moses traditions are taken up in Jude 9, 11;[183] the reference to Cain, Balaam, and Korah gains its impact only against the background of its reception history in Judaism.[184] In Jude 14b–15, the author cites 1 En. 1.9[185] in order to emphasize the ungodliness of the opponents and the necessity of the impending judgment over them. The citations, the allusion, and the technique of scriptural argument in the Letter of Jude indicate how strongly the author thought and lived within the traditions of ancient Judaism.

THE REVELATION OF JOHN

Like Hebrews and Jude, the Revelation of John is totally embedded in the Jewish tradition, but at the same time it is disputed, as with Hebrews and Jude, whether Revelation represents a known Jewish Christian standpoint. The seer John (cf. Rev. 1:3; 10:11; 19:10; 22:7, 9–10, 18–19) treats traditional material in a variety of ways. Numerous cultic and Scripture references are evident, which indicate that he is a scribal prophet.[186] However, numerous motifs and borrowings from the Greco-Roman world are present,[187] which document his cultural-historical breadth. A Jewish Christian position becomes especially visible in the conflicts with opposing streams within the churches (see below, 11.3). In Pergamum, church members follow the teaching of Balaam, which John designates as the eating of food offered to idols and sexual immorality (cf. Rev. 2:14). In addition, there is the teaching of the Nicolaitans (Rev. 2:6), and in Thyatira a prophetess (Jezebel) appears,[188] who also entices church members to eat food offered to idols and to engage in sexual immorality (Rev. 2:20). John sharply attacks the opposing streams and explains that the consumption of food offered to idols is a central point of dispute. Only those who refrain from earthly sacral meals can eat "the hidden manna" (Rev. 2:17). The crucial difference between the seer and his opponents is evident especially in Rev. 2:24–25. Similar to the apostolic decree (Acts 15:28–29), a

183. On possible sources, cf. Paulsen, *Der zweite Petrusbrief*, 66–67.

184. Cf. Heiligenthal, *Zwischen Henoch und Paulus*, 42–61.

185. On the specific instances, cf. Paulsen, *Der zweite Petrusbrief*, 74ff.

186. Cf. the thorough study by Tóth, *Der himmlische Kult*; for Rev. 12 the following is exemplary evidence: Dochhorn, *Schriftgelehrte Prophetie*, 393: "Rev. 12 has been interpreted as a product of scribal prophecy."

187. Cf. Böcher, "Hellenistisches in der Apokalypse"; Karrer, "Apoll und die apokalyptischen Reiter."

188. Cf. 1 Kings 16:29–33; 18:19; 19:2.

kind of compromise formula is communicated to the church in Thyatira: "I do not lay any other burden on you; only hold fast, until I come." Thus βάρος in Rev. 2:24, as also in Acts 15:28, designates the minimal legal requirements that apply to gentile Christians.[189] The entire Jewish law is not the point of dispute, for the issue is the keeping of minimal ritual standards. They were not observed by the opponents, who claimed for themselves special insight (cf. the "deep things of Satan" in Rev. 2:24 with 1 Cor. 2:10). As with the strong in Corinth, the knowledge enabled them to have an understanding of the true God (cf. 1 Cor. 8:4, 6) that allowed a relatively unrestricted contact with pagan society. In contrast, John the seer rejected this form of accommodation and strictly rejected the eating of food offered to idols and any form of sexual immorality. Although Jewish themes such as the Sabbath or the law do not appear in Revelation (νόμος and σάββατον are missing), and the gentile mission is assumed (cf. Rev. 7:9), John's scribal ability, his roots in the Jewish world of thought and imagery, and the demand for minimal ritual standards demonstrate the seer's conscious Jewish Christian standpoint.

Didache

The Didache gives insight into the life of a Jewish Christian group of communities shaped in an agrarian environment (cf. Did. 11.6; 13.3) and standing in the tradition of the Gospel of Matthew[190] in Syria at the beginning of the second century.[191] The setting is the instruction of people who are asking for baptism and want to join the new movement of Christians (cf. Did. 7.1).[192] The two-ways teaching in the introductory section in Did. 1–6[193] clearly indicates the crucial situation that stands before the one to be baptized. They must choose between life and death (Did. 1.1). The didachist describes the "way of life" (Did. 1.1–4, 14) and the "way of death" (Did. 5.1–2) with the norms of traditional Jewish ethics; one should stay far away from every kind

---

189. For the analysis, cf. U. Müller, *Die Offenbarung des Johannes*, 97, 120.

190. Evidence for this is especially Did. 15.3, which refers to Matt. 18:15: "Correct one another, not in anger, but in peace, as you have it in the gospel."

191. Cf. Wengst, *Didache*, 62–63; Niederwimmer, *Die Didache*, 79 (110 or 120 CE). Draper, "Die Didache," 20–21, supports a date at the end of the first century. Antioch of Syria is often assumed to be the place of origin; cf. Zetterholm, "Didache, Matthew, James—and Paul." However, there is no compelling evidence for this view; one cannot go beyond the general information "Syria."

192. The Didache is not a "church order" (as argued by Schöllgen, "Die Didache als Kirchenordnung"), but belongs to the genre of "teachings/instructions"; cf. the detailed study of Pardee, *Genre and Development of the Didache*. Garleff (*Urchristliche Identität im Matthäusevangelium*, 206) understands it as an "actualizing amendment" to Matthew's Gospel. D.-A. Koch, *Geschichte des Urchristentums*, 390, calls the Didache a "church order."

193. Probably based on a Jewish source; cf. Niederwimmer, *Die Didache*, 83–88.

of evil, especially from pagan gentile practices (augury, astrology, magic practices). In Did. 3.8–10 and 4.1–9, a distinct piety of poverty, which formulates the ideal group, is evident. They are the poor and the oppressed who hope for the Lord in humility and await the promise of the land from him. The repeated challenge to give alms (cf. Did. 2.6; 4.5–8; 5.2) and the paraenesis to slave owners (Did. 4.10–11: masters and slaves in the household belong to the same new religion) presuppose the presence of rich members of the church and indirectly give evidence of a powerful social system. The teachers enjoy high regard within the church (Did. 4.1, "You should honor him as the Lord"); they, along with the prophets, form the teaching and charismatic position of the church. The conclusion of the two-ways teaching in 6.2–3 clearly indicates the Jewish Christian standpoint of the Didache.[194] The church members should keep the food laws as much as possible: "Keep strictly away from meat sacrificed to idols, for it involves the worship of dead gods" (6.3). In Did. 3.4 and 5.1, idolatry appears as the ultimate sin. The strong Jewish or Jewish Christian influence is in the source employed by the didachist (Did. 1.1–6, 9–10), as evident in the designation "holy vine of David" in 9.2 and the practice of giving the firstfruits in 13.3. The agenda-driven section in Did. 7.1–10.7 offers a singular insight into early Christianity, where baptism (7.1–4), fasting and prayer (8.1–3), and the Eucharist (9.1–5; 10.1–7) are discussed. Didache 10.1 ("After you have had enough, give thanks as follows") suggests that the preceding meal is a full dinner, but it nevertheless remains unclear whether it was actually part of the Eucharist. The reversed sequence cup-bread (9.2–3) suggests otherwise, and especially the absence of the words of institution. On the other hand, the entire sequence of the formula (after baptism the details about the Eucharist are to be expected)[195] suggests the relationship of the meal to the Eucharist. The *terminus technicus* εὐχαριστία (Eucharist, 9.1),[196] the exclusion formula in 9.5, the conditions for admission as well as the eschatological outlook in 10.6 (μαράνα θά, Our Lord, come!; cf. 1 Cor. 11:26; 16:22) make sense only if it involves the eucharistic celebration. It probably involves a eucharistic celebration on Sunday (cf. Did. 14.1), in which a full meal and the elements of the Eucharist are connected, referring to one another and understood as a unity (cf. 1 Cor. 11:23–26).[197] In Did.

194. Cf. Draper, "Holy Vine of David," 280: "The Didache provides evidence for the life and thought of an early Christian Jewish community and its interpretation and practice of Torah in Christian halakah, which has been preserved in its present form by accident."

195. Cf. Lietzmann, *Mass and Lord's Supper*, 189.

196. At the beginning of the second century, Ignatius (*Eph.* 13.1; *Phld.* 4; *Smyrn.* 8.1) attests εὐχαριστία as a *terminus technicus* (technical term) for the Eucharist.

197. Contra Lietzmann, *Mass and Lord's Supper*, 211–12, it does not involve two types of meals: "We have before us an agape, which was introduced by the eucharistic celebration."

11–15 a comprehensive church order is presented that regulates the conduct of the churches in relation to various groups. At the beginning, there are rules for traveling charismatics (apostles and prophets) who, as a rule, should be welcomed for only a day. If they remain three days or demand money, they demonstrate that they are false prophets (Did. 11.3–6). Apparently, apostles[198] and a considerable number of prophets traveled from church to church and created significant problems for accommodating them. What is presupposed is a larger association of churches, in which the churches were not separated by great distance (one- to two-days' walk). As with the prophets (Did. 11.7–12), individual traveling brothers (Did. 12.1–5) should be welcomed and their truthfulness examined. Anyone who settled among them, worked, and did not seek benefits was welcome. As a fourth group besides the apostles, prophets, and individual brothers, the teachers appear in Did. 13.2. When they settle among them, the same rule applies to them as for the prophets who live and minister in that location. They receive material support in the form of the gift of the firstfruits (Did. 13.3–7). The Didache attests, like no other writing, the significance of hospitality for the followers of the new faith and demonstrates the material capacity of the churches in the problem of abuse of the hospitality. In Did. 15.1 the churches are instructed to select bishops and deacons; that is, besides the traveling prophets and teachers there were local officeholders. The instruction not to despise them (15.2) indicates that there must have been conflict particularly between the representatives of the local churches and the traveling prophets who were not bound to a location. An eschatological outlook forms the conclusion of the Didache (16.1–8). The *theology* of the Didache is concentrated on the almighty God, while only little is said of the *Christology*, inasmuch as "Christ" does not appear. The weight undoubtedly lies in the ecclesiology, with the elevated position of the prophets, and on eschatology, which determines the conclusion of the document.

The churches of the Didache found themselves evidently in a transition process at multiple levels. (1) The separation from Judaism is complete, and the community now seeks its own moderate Jewish Christian standpoint (cf. Did. 6.3). (2) The introductory two-way teaching is evidence that the ethical orientation of the church still needed a foundation. (3) The ritual world of the church had to be more precisely adjusted, as the instructions on baptism,

---

Niederwimmer, *Die Didache*, 201, assumes that a celebration similar to the agape then became the sacramental communion. Against the thesis of two different meals or types of celebrations, one may observe that the term εὐχαριστία appears only at the beginning in 9.1, 5 and that the entire event is described as a Eucharist.

198. Here another concept of "apostle" is apparently present in the sense of "one who is sent," a term that stands in the tradition of Jesus's commissioning speech (Matt. 10; Luke 10).

prayer, fasting, and Eucharist indicate. (4) The relationship of the offices to each other, particularly between the prophets who went from church to church and the local officeholders, demanded a more precise definition and demarcation in order to prevent or correct developments in the wrong direction. The Didache not only pursues the goal of accompanying and promoting this process but also of directing it and implementing its concepts or regulations in order to strengthen collective identity.[199]

JEWISH CHRISTIANITY AS REFLECTED IN THE POLEMIC AGAINST OPPONENTS

The existence of Jewish Christian groups/churches or practices can be inferred indirectly in a few polemical passages against opponents. The demands of the opponents within the church of Colossae probably included the circumcision of gentile Christians (cf. Col. 2:11, "In him you were circumcised with a circumcision not with the hands, in the putting off of the flesh, in the circumcision of Christ"). The singular comparison between baptism and circumcision makes sense only if both were required and practiced.[200] The ascetic food regulations and festivals (cf. Col. 2:16–17, 21–22, 23b), the observation of the elements (cf. Col. 2:8, 15, 20),[201] the worship of angels (cf. Col. 2:18), and the imposition of regulations point to a known Jewish Christianity[202] that was, however, part of a syncretistic teaching, which is called a "philosophy" in Col. 2:8. The false teachers who are opposed in the Pastoral Epistles also clearly have strong Jewish Christian features. They claim to be "teachers of the law" (1 Tim. 1:7, νομοδιδάσκαλοι; cf. Titus 3:9) and dispute over endless genealogies (1 Tim. 1:4). According to Titus 1:10 the deceivers come "from the circumcision" (οἱ ἐκ τῆς περιτομῆς), and in Titus 1:14 the mythological speculations are called "Jewish myths" (cf. 1 Tim. 4:7; 2 Tim. 4:4). These Jewish Christian elements are a part of a comprehensive syncretistic teaching,

199. Cf. Garleff, *Urchristliche Identität im Matthäusevangelium*, 199.

200. Cf. Lindemann, *Der Kolosserbrief*, 41.

201. The Qumran texts especially attest to the great significance given to issues of the calendar in ancient Judaism as well as the firm connection between the Torah and the ordering of time (cf., e.g., 1QS 1.13–15; 9.26–10.8; 1QM 2.4; 10.15; CD 3.12–16; 16.2–4; 1QH 1.24; 12.4–9, also Jub. 6.32, 36, 37; 1 En. 72.1; 75.3f.; 79.2; 82.4, 7–10); cf. the comprehensive evidence in Lührmann, "Tage, Monate, Jahreszeiten, Jahre."

202. Häfner, *Die Pastoralbriefe*, 463–65, assumes a single opposition group in whose teaching Jewish Christian and Gnostic elements merge. A contrasting view is that of Herzer ("Juden—Christen—Gnostiker"), who argues against the existence of a single opposing front. Instead, Jewish influences are present in a Cretan context (Titus 1:12); those opponents in 2 Timothy must be read within the context of the correct understanding of Pauline eschatology (2 Tim. 2:17–18); finally, the opponents of 1 Timothy exhibit Gnostic influences (1 Tim. 6:20).

which contains both ascetic elements (cf. 1 Tim. 4:3: prohibition of marriage) and elements of over-realized eschatology (cf. 2 Tim. 2:18) and is described as "falsely called knowledge" (see below, 14.2).

OTHER WITNESSES

Valuable information about the continuing presence of strict Jewish Christian positions in Asia Minor at the beginning of the second century CE appears in a very polemical context in the work of Ignatius of Antioch (see below, 14.1).[203] He warns about "strange doctrines" (ἑτεροδοξίαις) in the churches (Ign. *Magn.* 8–11), that is, "old myths that are worthless," and then warns, "If we continue to live in accordance with Judaism [κατὰ Ἰουδαϊσμὸν ζῶμεν], we admit that we have not received grace" (trans. Holmes). Both the first-person plural and the time specification "until now" (μέχρι νῦν) indicate that the warning concerns a contemporary strict Jewish Christian element within individual (Christian, not Jewish!) communities in Asia Minor.[204] Its actual profile is difficult to determine, for in some passages docetic and Jewish motifs are combined (cf. Ign. *Magn.* 9.1; 11; *Phld.* 4). The agreements in the "old myths" with 1 Tim. 1:4; Titus 1:14; 3:9, and the reference to the Sabbath (*Magn.* 9.1, "no longer keeping the Sabbath, but living in accordance with the Lord's day") indicate clearly that conflicts arose over the significance of Jewish genealogies and Sabbath observance. Ignatius speaks further of the replacement of Judaism by Christianity (Ign. *Magn.* 9) and combines this view with the charge now "to live in accordance with Christianity" (10.1, κατὰ Χριστιανισμὸν ζῆν). Here the concept "Christianity" appears for the first time in literature, obviously shaped as a contrast to the concept of Judaism. "It is utterly absurd to profess Jesus Christ and to practice Judaism, for Christianity did not believe in Judaism [ὁ γὰρ Χριστιανισμὸς οὐκ εἰς Ἰουδαϊσμὸν ἐπίστευσεν], rather Judaism in Christianity, in which every tongue believed and was brought together to God" (Ign. *Magn.* 10.3). In addition, when Ignatius (*Magn.* 11.1) emphasizes that there is no Judaizing Christianity in the Magnesian church, he nevertheless appears to be aware of such people. Also, in *Phld.* 6–9 he alludes to a Judaizing Christianity.[205] He warns the church: "But if anyone expounds Judaism to you, do not listen to him. For it is better to hear about Christianity from a man who is circumcised than about Judaism from one who is not. But if either of them fails to speak about Jesus Christ,

---

203. Cf. Barrett, "Jews and Judaizers."
204. Schoedel, *Ignatius of Antioch*, 124–25, correctly argues that a separate Jewish Christian element and not a docetic-Jewish Christian one is intended.
205. Cf. Schoedel, *Ignatius of Antioch*, 204–11.

I look on them as tombstones and graves of the dead" (*Phld.* 6.1). Evidently among both uncircumcised and circumcised church members, there was an interest in following the Jewish law; they oriented themselves to what they found "in the archives" (Ign. *Phld.* 8.2), that is, the OT. Ignatius interpreted this as a lessening of faith in Christ, whose cross, death, and resurrection are the true "archives."

The polemical reports from the church fathers and the fragments of Jewish Christian gospels[206] also give limited information about the life and teachings of the later Jewish Christian groups, for their time period and content are difficult to classify. Somewhat comprehensible are the Ebionites,[207] whom Irenaeus classifies in the context of Cerinthus, Cerdo, and Marcion at the beginning of the second century CE. Whether Irenaeus had primary knowledge of the Ebionites is doubtful; nevertheless, he transmitted somewhat useful reports: "The so-called Ebionites agree [with us] that the world was made by the true God, but regarding the kyrios they speak as Cerinthus and Carpocrates do. They use only the Gospel of Matthew, and they reject the apostle Paul because they regard him as an apostate from the law. They endeavor overzealously to interpret the prophetic writings. They practice circumcision and keep the customs that are demanded in the law as well as the Jewish way of life, and thus they revere Jerusalem as the dwelling place of God."[208] The name Ἐβιωναῖοι (Latin Ebionaei or Ebionitae) is derived from אֶבְיוֹנִים (poor), probably a self-designation in the tradition of the Jewish pious (the poor, the elect before God).[209] A connection to the "poor" in the Jerusalem church (Gal. 2:10; Rom. 15:26) mentioned by Paul is conceivable, although Paul means with it only an economically disadvantaged small group (Rom. 15:26, "for the poor among the saints in Jerusalem"). The Gospel of Matthew used by the Ebionites cannot be identical with the canonical Matthew, for they rejected the virgin birth[210] and represented a natural Christology, as men-

206. The Jewish Christian Gospels (Gospels of the Hebrews, Nazarenes, Ebionites) probably originated after the Bar Kokhba Rebellion in the middle of the second century and are not treated more here. They exist only in the fragments transmitted by the church fathers and raise numerous historical and theological questions; cf. Klauck, *Apokryphe Evangelien*, 53–76; Markschies and Schröter, *Antike christliche Apokryphen*, 593–654 (text and commentary).

207. Still basic is G. Strecker, "Ebioniten"; cf. Markschies and Schröter, *Antike christliche Apokryphen*, 607–10.

208. Irenaeus, *Haer.* 1.26.2; the second important report is found in Epiphanius, *Pan.* 30.

209. Cf. Ps. 86:1; Pss. Sol. 10.6; 1QpHab 12.3 and passim.

210. Cf. Irenaeus, *Haer.* 3.21.1, according to which Jewish proselytes rejected the virgin birth. "The Ebionites, following these, assert that he was the child of Joseph"; cf. also Irenaeus, *Haer.* 5.1.3.

tioned in Justin, *Dial.* 48.4: "There are, my friends, I said, among your people those who acknowledge that Jesus is the Christ, but claim that he was a man of purely human origin." Circumcision and practice of the law, the rejection of Paul, the significance of Jerusalem, and a peculiar interpretation of the prophets and eucharistic practice[211] could be considered further characteristics of this group, which probably was primarily spread east of the Jordan.[212] One can say nothing certain about the wider history of the Ebionites.[213] Justin, in his *Dialogue with Trypho* (ca. 155 CE), alludes repeatedly to churches that had a strict Jewish Christian orientation. Trypho asks him (*Dial.* 46.1) "But is salvation possible when someone at the present time still wants to observe the regulations of Moses in his life, although he believes in the crucified Jesus and recognizes that he is the Christ of God, that the judgment over all has been given to him, and that the eternal kingdom belongs to him?" According to Justin (*Dial.* 46.2), the regulations of Moses include observance of the Sabbath, circumcision, the observance of months, and the washing, if anyone has touched what Moses has forbidden, after sexual intercourse. According to Justin (*Dial.* 47.2), these strict Jewish Christians appear to have avoided all contact with gentile Christians ("There are some who would not ever join with such in conversation or in meals"). Justin replied to this among other things, "O Trypho, when, on the other hand, I continue, your people who affirm that they believe in our Christ, compel the gentile Christians in every manner to live according to the Mosaic law, or refuse to associate with them, in this case, in turn, I do not recognize them" (*Dial.* 47.3). This probably involved contemporary disputes from the middle of the second century CE, but this strict Jewish position was probably older. These churches consisted of a majority of ethnic Jews who maintained their full Jewish identity while believing in Jesus Christ and maintained separation from uncircumcised gentile Christians. But gentiles also found the way into such communities, were circumcised, and then, in some instances, fell from the Christian faith and went into Judaism (cf. *Dial.* 47.4).

211. Cf. Irenaeus, *Haer.* 5.1.3: "They reject the mixing of water and heavenly wine and want nothing other than to be the water of the world."

212. Cf. Eusebius, *Hist. eccl.* 1.7.14.

213. Similarly vague are the reports about the appearance of the Jewish Christian syncretistic teacher and prophet Elchasai ("hidden power"), who appeared in the borderland of Syria-Parthia between 115 and 117 CE. He received a fragmentary revelatory book, according to Hippolytus and Epiphanius, from which a second repentance-baptism bath was derived. In addition, the Elchasites were characterized by circumcision, observance of the Sabbath, prayer facing Jerusalem, and anti-Paulinism. All essential texts are analyzed by G. Strecker, "Elkesai"; Lüdemann, *Opposition to Paul*, 129–39, 279–85.

Both the NT and the church fathers attest the existence of a diverse strict Jewish Christianity before and after 70 CE. This fact is not surprising, for the original form of emerging Christianity was a Jewish Christianity oriented to the Torah. Already from the middle of the first century, the Jewish Christians were exposed to a double dissonance. They were put under pressure from both the gentile church and official Judaism, and sometimes they were fought against. From the beginning Jewish Christianity was no uniform phenomenon. In particular, the level of Torah orientation and the determination of the relationships to both Judaism and the gentiles were determined in different ways. There were groups that asked, from a primarily Jewish standpoint, how much Christianity they wanted to have, and others who asked, how much Judaism was necessary for them as Christians. For the second and third century, especially, Jewish Christianity was in general a complex phenomenon that took on syncretistic elements and was historically elusive.

10.6 Perceptions by Outsiders

When were the Christians noticed as an independent new movement by the surrounding world? Luke depicts a local tradition for the beginning of the 40s from Antioch (see above, 6.4), according to which, for the first time, the outsiders used the designation "Christians" for the new group (cf. Acts 11:26). While it is here only a limited perception, a greater significance possibly belongs to another tradition. In Acts 13:6–12, Luke reports about the first missionary success on Cyprus (see above, 6.8), where the proconsul Sergius Paulus became a believer (Acts 13:12).[214] The present form and position of the text indicate that Luke is presenting a model story.[215] The first convert on the first missionary journey is a proconsul and thus a member of the Roman upper class who bore the name from which Saul (according to Luke) also received his Roman name (Acts 13:9,[216] "But Saul, who was also called Paul"). Thus the beginning and end of the ministry of Paul correspond, for Paul then appears to the governors Felix and Festus and appeals to the caesar (cf. Acts 24–26). For the Roman readers of Acts, from the very beginning, the acceptance and the extraordinary place of the new movement are not in doubt. Thus the question is not yet answered whether Luke is here transmitting an old and historically reliable local tradition, according to which the proconsul of

214. On Sergius Paulus, cf. also above, 6.8.
215. Cf. Haenchen, *Acts*, 394–404.
216. It is very probable that Saul took the Roman name Paul from the beginning; cf. Hengel, *Pre-Christian Paul*, 9.

Cyprus converted to the new faith. It is thoroughly probable that the Sergius Paulus of Acts is identical with a Lucius Sergius Paulus[217] who is mentioned in an inscription in Rome,[218] whose senatorial family, the Sergii Paulli, came from Pisidian Antioch. He was probably proconsul of Cyprus in the period between about 45 and 48 CE.[219] In southern Galatia and Cyprus, such an event would have brought attention to the new movement of Christians.

The Christians drew local attention to themselves relatively early (beginning/middle of the 50s) in important cities such as Corinth, Athens, and Ephesus. In Corinth, the finance official Erastus (cf. Rom. 16:23), a leading council member (*ordo decurionum*), belonged to the new movement.[220] Likewise, Dionysius the Areopagite in Athens (cf. Acts 17:34) was a member of the council in Athens.[221] When members of the city elite joined this strange group, then the interest of the entire state was probably awakened. In Ephesus the riot of the silversmiths and the associated religious and economic conflicts (cf. Acts 19:23–40) led to a considerable stir in the city and possibly in all of Asia Minor.[222] Then again the Christians drew attention from the populace as the cause of conflict.

217. Roman spelling: Sergius Paullus; in the NT: Sergius Paulus.

218. Text of the inscription in Breytenbach, *Paulus und Barnabas*, 180; A. Weiss, *Soziale Elite und Christentum*, 62–66 (text and interpretation). Breytenbach, *Paulus und Barnabas*, 38–45, offers a critical analysis of all possibilities and is inclined toward an identification with the Sergius Paulus of Acts; cf. in this sense also Riesner, *Paul's Early Period*, 137–38; Schnabel, *Early Christian Mission*, 1085–88; A. Weiss, "Sergius Paullus," argues explicitly for an identification with Lucius Sergius Paullus and rejects a reference to Quintus Sergius Paullus, whose time in office on Cyprus was not under Claudius but under Caligula between 37 and 41 CE; A. Weiss, *Soziale Elite und Christentum*, 78–79: "The narrative in Acts 13:4–12 of the conversion of Sergius Paullus, the proconsul of Cyprus, to Christianity is historically plausible. The proconsul is most likely to be identified with the Tiber curator L. Sergius Paullus. On the social background of Sergius Paullus, despite many uncertainties, one can say with certainty that the Sergii Paulli belonged to the most highly regarded and well-known families in Antioch and enjoyed a high name recognition. . . . If, however, Luke reports an actual event with the conversion of Sergius Paulus, and this appears to be the case, then we do not see here a person who suffered from little social recognition, but someone who came from an important local family and who was successful in rising politically into the narrow circle of senators, and thus to the pinnacle of society." After a comprehensive discussion, S. Mitchell, *Anatolia* (2:7), concludes, "The proconsul of Cyprus at the time of St. Paul's visit should be identified with the curator of the banks of the Tiber under Claudius, L. Sergius Paullus, the only senator attested from the generation of the family." See also Heil and Wachtel, *Prosopographia Imperii Romani*, VII/2, 213.

219. Cf. A. Weiss, *Soziale Elite und Christentum*, 65: "If the dating of the Tiber curator L. Sergius Paullus in the year 41/42 as concluded above is correct, according to the conventions of a senatorial career, he probably assumed the proconsulship over the praetorian province of Cyprus sometime between the years 45 and 48."

220. See under 8.3 above, "Social Stratification."

221. See above, under 8.1.

222. Cf. here A. Weiss, "Der Aufruhr der Silberschmiede (Apg 19,23–40)."

Undoubtedly, the first instance was the persecution of Christians in Rome under Nero in the year 64 (see below, 12.2). The Edict of Claudius indicates[223] that the Roman authorities in 49 CE were not yet able to distinguish between Jews and Christians. On the other hand, in 64 CE the Christians appear already as a group to be punished, although Tacitus (around 116/117 CE) affirmed their innocence. They must have been known in Rome even in the house of Caesar[224] and, because of their worship of one who was crucified, considered an obscure and hidden criminal movement from the East. In any case, the Christians were known and recognized for the first time in the center of the Roman Empire.

Probably the oldest pagan witness to Jesus and the Christians comes from the Syrian Stoic Mara bar Serapion, who came from Samosata and in 73 CE wrote a letter to his son from a Roman prison.[225] Here, besides numerous admonitions and the recommendation to seek wisdom alone, is the following section:

> What advantage did the Athenians gain from putting Socrates to death? Famine and plague came upon them as a judgment for their crime. What advantage did the men of Samos gain from burning Pythagoras? In a moment, their land was covered with sand. What advantage did the Jews gain from executing their wise king? It was just after that that their kingdom was abolished. God justly avenged these three wise men: the Athenians died of hunger; the Samians were overwhelmed by the sea; the Jews, ruined and driven from their land, live in complete dispersion. But Socrates did not die for good; he lived on in the teaching of Plato. Pythagoras did not die for good; he lived on in the statue of Hera. Nor did the wise king die for good; he lived on in the teaching which he had given.[226]

What is noteworthy is the positive perception and depiction of Jesus as a philosopher in an illustrious group with Socrates and Pythagoras. Relatively early there was apparently a tradition in which Jesus was considered a teacher of wisdom. In terms of content, Jesus appears as king of the Jews, which could be a reference to the inscription on the cross (cf. Mark 15:26) or royal traditions in the NT (Matt. 2:1–12; John 18:33–40). In addition, the punishment of the Jews as a consequence of their conduct toward Jesus is derived from NT traditions (cf. 1 Thess. 2:15; Acts 4:10). In particular, Jesus is perceived to be a new

223. Suetonius, *Claud.* 25.4: "Since the Jews, who were stirred up by Chrestus, constantly caused unrest, he drove them out of Rome."
224. An indirect witness could be the Letter to the Philippians, written in Rome ca. 61 CE, where in 1:13 a praetorium is mentioned, and in 4:22 the family of Caesar is mentioned; cf. Schnelle, *History and Theology of the New Testament*, 129–43.
225. The text is in a manuscript from the seventh century; on the various aspects of the text, cf. the comprehensive study by Merz and Tielemann, *Letter of Mara bar Sarapion in Context*.
226. Translation Bruce, *Jesus and Christian Origins*, 31.

lawgiver, according to whose laws the Christians live and in which Jesus himself lives on. This probably refers to the ethical commands of Jesus and the praxis in the Christian churches that are oriented toward them (rejection of differences in status, love of enemies, nonviolence, sanctity of marriage, relationships as brothers and sisters, social care for each other). Mara bar Sarapion probably acquired his knowledge about Jesus and the Christians in the Syrian region. As a Stoic, he obviously had a positive view of the ethical orientation of the new movement.

As a Pharisee already in Jerusalem or Galilee, Flavius Josephus may have heard of Jesus. In the *Jewish Antiquities* (around 94 CE), he mentions Jesus twice. In an indirect reference (*Ant.* 20.200), Josephus reports the killing of James the brother of Jesus: "He gathered the high council before the court and placed before it the brother of Jesus, who is called Christ [τὸν ἀδελφὸν Ἰησοῦ τοῦ λεγομένου Χριστοῦ], with the name of James and a few others, whom he accused of transgression of the law and allowed them to be stoned." In the context of the description of the cruel deeds of Pilate, Josephus speaks of Jesus (*Ant.* 18.63–64). This so-called Testimonium Flavianum has certainly been given a Christian redaction in the course of its transmission,[227] but in its original form it may nevertheless be traced back to Josephus. The original source could have read as follows:

> [63]About this time Jesus lived, a wise man [Ἰησοῦς σοφὸς ἀνήρ]. He performed extraordinary deeds and was the teacher of people who accepted the truth gladly. He won over many Jews and Greeks. [64]When Pilate, upon hearing him accused by the men of the highest standing among us, had condemned him to be crucified, his first followers were not unfaithful. And until this day the tribe of Christians who are named for him still exists.

Like John the Baptist (*Ant.* 18.116–19), Jesus is, according to Josephus, an ethical teacher and miracle worker who attracted great crowds. His violent death, brought about by the Jewish leaders, did not result in the end of his movement; that is, Josephus assumes a certain knowledge of this group by his readers.

The relatively neutral to positive portrayals by Mara bar Serapion and Josephus indicate that Jesus and the Christians were positively regarded by educated non-Romans in the eastern part of the empire.[228] This view changes among the Roman elite around the turn of the century (see below, 12.4).

227. Cf. Meier, *Roots of the Problem and the Person*, 56–69; Theissen and Merz, *Der historische Jesus*, 74–82 (both argue for an original edition that can be reconstructed).
228. Nevertheless, around the end of the first century CE, Epictetus from Hierapolis in Phrygia calls the Christians "Galileans" (cf. Epictetus, *Diatr.* 4.7.6): "if madness can produce this attitude of mind toward the things which have just been mentioned (namely, fearlessness before tyrants), and also habit, as with the Galileans" (LCL).

11

Dangers and Threats

E very new movement in history must preserve itself. This fact applies not only to outward threats but especially to dangers from within.[1] The latter is the greater danger, for outward pressure as a rule strengthens the feeling of solidarity, while a wavering of inner certainty can introduce an inevitable process of decline. Early Christianity also saw itself subjected to massive inner dangers to its identity that it had to overcome. The delay of the return of Jesus Christ was undoubtedly the greatest problem.

11.1 The Delay of the Parousia

Within early Christianity a basic unified perspective quickly developed: the resurrection of Jesus Christ from the dead and the experience of the Spirit made the believers confident that Christ would come quickly (μαράνα θά, 1 Cor. 16:22) as "Son" (cf. 1 Thess. 1:9–10), "Lord" (cf. Phil. 4:5; Rev. 22:20), or "Son of Man" (cf. Mark 8:38; 13:24–27; 14:62; Matt. 10:23; Luke 18:8; etc.) to execute judgment. His revelation is imminent (cf. 1 Thess. 5:23; 1 Cor. 1:7; 15:23) and determines the thinking and conduct of the Christians. At the same time, the lapse of time placed the early Christians before a considerable task of thought and interpretation, for the certainty and the delay of the imminent coming of the Lord still had to be explained and believed. Thus it is

---

1. An excellent survey is given by Lampe and Luz, "Nachpaulinisches Christentum." See also C. Hays, *When the Son of Man Didn't Come.*

not surprising that Paul already had to incorporate the delay of the parousia into his thought.

Paul

The first existing statement on the subject was forced upon Paul by the unexpected deaths in Thessalonica before the parousia (arrival/appearance)[2] of the Lord (1 Thess. 4:13–18). Paul answers (1 Thess. 4:13–18), for the first time connecting the concept of the parousia of the Lord with the resurrection of Christians who had died. It is clear in 1 Thessalonians that the death of Christians before the parousia is still the exception. Paul assumes that he himself and the church will be alive at the return of the Lord (vv. 15, 17), in the conviction that the return of the Lord was imminent. The question of how the resurrection of the deceased members of the church would take place as well as the place of all believers in the heavenly world has not been discussed.[3] The passage of time, the situation of the Corinthian church with its own theological formation, and Paul's own reflection on the Corinthian church cause the subject to appear in a different light in the two Corinthian letters. Paul continues to affirm an acute imminent expectation (1 Cor. 7:29; 10:11; 16:22), and instances of death in Corinth before the parousia are no longer unusual (cf. 1 Cor. 7:39; 11:30; 15:6, 18, 29, 51). In 1 Cor. 15:50–54 Paul introduces a new category with the metaphor of a bodily transformation in contrast to 1 Thess. 4:13–18 and the preceding argument in 1 Cor. 15.[4] A new incorruptible existence is granted to those who are already deceased and to those who are alive at the parousia. Whereas Paul in 1 Thess. 4:13–18 and 1 Cor. 15:51–52 had indicated his place at the end time as one who was still living, using the personal pronoun ἡμεῖς ("we," 1 Thess. 4:17; 1 Cor. 15:52), in 2 Cor. 5:1–10 he for the first time reckons with his own death before the parousia (vv. 1, 9).[5] This radical change of Paul's situation is reflected in the reduction of apocalyptic elements in the description of the end-time events and the associated acceptance of Hellenistic concepts and the tendency toward

---

2. The word παρουσία is not a *terminus technicus* of pre-Christian Jewish apocalyptic; cf. Radl, "παρουσία"; Köster, "Imperial Ideology and Paul's Eschatology." In Hellenism it designates, among other things, the visit of a ruler to a place, for which the people must prepare. The early Christians may have taken this concept over from this context. "Christ is awaited as savior and Lord. If, however, the caesar can be greeted not only as ruler but also as savior, then such an official concept of the parousia with its sacral elements suggested itself for Christian usage" (Radl, "παρουσία").

3. Cf. Walter, "Leibliche Auferstehung?," 110–11.

4. Cf. Walter, "Leibliche Auferstehung?," 114–15.

5. On the analysis, cf. Vogel, *Commentatio mortis*.

dualism and individualization. In Romans also, death before the parousia is
no longer the exception but is now the rule (cf. Rom. 14:8b: "Whether we live
or die, we belong to the Lord"). The parousia of the Lord is still considered
to be an event that stands directly before them (cf. Rom. 13:11–12; 16:20),
but the comparative in the phrase "now salvation is nearer than when we first
believed" (Rom. 13:11c) suggests a consciousness of a delay. As the eschatological object of hope, the phrase "eternal life" (ζωὴ αἰώνιος) is significant in
Romans, where four of the five Pauline references to the topic are found (cf.
Gal. 6:8; Rom. 2:7; 5:21; 6:22, 23). It designates the future mode of existence
of the saved, for whom there is no end of time. Paul does not elaborate further
on the course of the events of the end and on the how of the new existence
in a programmatic way in Romans, but Rom. 8:11 and 8:23 indicate that now
the concept of the transformation of the body stands in the foreground.[6]

In Philippians two tendencies that were previously noticeable are compressed: Paul reckons openly with his death before the parousia and concentrates his eschatological conceptions on the fate of the individual.[7] In Phil. 1:20
the apostle speaks of his earthly body in which Christ is glorified "whether
through life or through death." In Phil. 1:21–24 Paul wavers between the expectation of living longer and death in the near future, which is connected with
the confidence that he will immediately "be with Christ" (v. 23, σὺν Χριστῷ
εἶναι) after his death. Philippians 1:23 points to immediately being with Christ
after death without mentioning the parousia and the resurrection of the dead.
The singular formulation "whether I attain to the resurrection of the dead"
(εἰς τὴν ἐξανάστασιν τὴν ἐκ νεκρῶν) in Phil. 3:11, with the double ἐκ (counting
the prefix), also suggests an early resurrection immediately after death.[8] Indeed
here, as in all of the Pauline letters, the parousia is the focus of the sayings of
the apostle (cf. Phil. 4:5b, "the Lord is near"; 1:6, 10; 2:16; 3:20b), but at the
end of his life Paul defines his destiny in a new way. Because he anticipates that
he will die before the parousia, the parousia and the subsequent resurrection
of the dead can no longer be his exclusive point of orientation. Because of
the delay of the parousia, in the central area of Pauline eschatology, one can
speak of changes, that is, of a progression of Paul's thought corresponding
to the changing situation.[9] However, the imminent expectation of the field
of vision and both the present and future Christ event remain the foundation
of Pauline eschatology, but the place of the individual and the course of the

6. Correctly observed by Walter, "Leibliche Auferstehung?," 120: "thus not the redemption
'from the body' or 'out of the body,' but the salutary transformation of the bodies."
7. Cf. Wiefel, "Die Hauptrichtung des Wandels," 79–81.
8. Cf. Hunzinger, "Die Hoffnung angesichts des Todes," 87.
9. Cf. Schnelle, *Wandlungen im paulinischen Denken*, 37–48.

end-time event change with the passing of the extended time. Paul obviously holds to a belief in the imminent coming of the Lord, but at the same time he makes appropriate changes in his statements about the end that became necessary with the lapse of time.

Synoptic Gospels

At the center of the eschatology of the logia source (as an earlier form of the Gospels) stands the concept of the imminent, immediate coming of the Son of Man and the judgment that is associated with it (Luke 3:7–9, 16b–17; 10:12–15; 12:40; 17:23–37Q).[10] Despite or even because of the delayed imminent expectation, the topic of the delay of the parousia becomes a common theme. Thus Luke 12:39–40Q emphasizes the unpredictability and suddenness of the coming of the Son of Man, and the parable of the faithful and unfaithful servants (Luke 12:42–46Q) affirms: "But when that slave says in his heart, 'My master delays' [χρονίζει] and begins to beat his fellow slaves." The theme of the indefiniteness of the time also dominates in the parable of the money that has been entrusted: "A man who wanted to go on a journey called ten of his slaves. . . . [After a long time] the master comes to those slaves and demands an accounting from them" (Luke 19:12–13, 15Q). Luke 17:23Q warns of false prophecies about the coming of the Son of Man and challenges the believers, "Do not follow him!" Thus come the themes of the indefiniteness of the time and of vigilance: "For just as lightning comes from the East and illuminates the West, so will it be on the day of the Son of Man" (Luke 17:24Q). In Luke 19:12–13, 15–24Q a consciousness of a delay is evident and is forced back by a massive threat of judgment.

Mark integrates the expectation of the parousia into an eschatological itinerary in order to affirm equally the certainty and the temporal indefiniteness of the imminent coming of the Son of Man (cf. Mark 13:24–27). Through the destruction of the temple, he connects the expectation of the end time with an event within history (cf. Mark 13:2–3) but severs it from a historical event because only God knows the time of his coming (cf. Mark 13:27). It is evident in Mark that the delay of the parousia must not mean a de-eschatologizing, for he connects it with an intensification of the expectation (cf. Mark 13:14, 17, 18, 30: "This generation will not pass away until all these things take place"), with a clear consciousness of the delay (cf. Mark 13:10, "And before that the gospel must first be preached to all nations"; 13:1, 33–36). The intensification of the imminent expectation opened the possibility to work through the lapse

---

10. A survey is given by D. Zeller, "Eschatologie in der Logienquelle," esp. 75. See also Johnson-Debaufre, *Q, Eschatology, and the Construction of Christian Origins.*

of time and to strengthen the church's consciousness of its election (cf. Mark 13:20); that is, the imminent *expectation and the consciousness of a delay do not stand in opposition to each other around 70 CE.*

Matthew and his community lived in imminent expectation, as, for example, his appropriation of Mark 13:28–32 in Matt. 24:32–36 indicates (cf. also Matt. 3:2; 4:17; 10:7, 23; 16:28; 24:22). This is suggested by the singular formulation of the "kingdom of the Son of Man" (Matt. 13:41; 16:28) or the "kingdom of Jesus" (Matt. 20:21), for it indicates that Matthew distinguishes between the "kingdom of heaven" and the "kingdom of the Son of Man" that breaks in with the resurrection and extends to the parousia.[11] At the same time a consciousness of the delay is obvious: in the parable of the faithful and evil servants (Matt. 24:45–51), the evil servant says, "My master delays his coming" (24:48); he mistreats his fellow servant and is then punished by the master, who comes when he is not expected. The parable of the ten virgins (Matt. 25:1–13), which is about watchfulness, comments explicitly: "Then the bridegroom was delayed; they all became tired and went to sleep" (Matt. 25:5). It ends with a warning: "Therefore, watch, for you know neither the day nor the hour" (25:13). The imminent expectation of the parousia of the first and second early Christian generations could not simply remain unchanged and repeated because the lapse of time made it no longer a plausible future (see above, 10.2.3).[12] Thus the third evangelist made an adjustment in the eschatology in which the ascension has a fundamental significance in the structure. With the theme of the ascension, Luke took over the Greco-Roman tradition of apotheosis (divinization), which played a central role in the imperial cult.[13] The ascension signifies three fundamental aspects of the abiding presence and future of Jesus Christ to the church and thus leads to a slowing down of the end-time events: (1) The Crucified and Resurrected One instructed the apostles for forty days as the Exalted One and instructed the church about

11. Cf. Roloff, "Das Reich des Menschensohnes"; Sim, *Apocalyptic Eschatology.*

12. On Lukan eschatology, cf. Zmijewski, *Die Eschatologiereden des Lukasevangeliums*; G. Schneider, *Parusiegleichnisse im Lukas-Evangelium*; Merk, "Das Reich Gottes"; Ernst, *Herr der Geschichte*; G. Schneider, "Anbruch des Heils und Hoffnung"; Wolter, "Israels Zukunft" (cf. also the literature under 10.2.3).

13. The reception of a Roman caesar into heaven after his death, guaranteed by witnesses, led to a final divinization; noteworthy in this context is Seneca's essay, *Apocolocyntosis (divi) Claudi*, which makes fun of this ritual. On apotheosis, cf. Pilhofer, "Livius, Lukas und Lukian"; relevant material from the history of religions appears in Bickermann, "Die römische Kaiserapotheose." Plutarch transmits the basic model in *Romulus* (27.3) about the legendary founder of the city, who, according to reports, suddenly disappeared in the midst of an unusual storm in the presence of the senators. The nobles of the city did not permit the people to inquire about his disappearance, but exhorted them all to honor and revere Romulus since he had been caught up into heaven and was to be a benevolent god for them instead of a good king.

the kingdom of God (Acts 1:3) so that it was well equipped for the present and the immediate future. (2) The Exalted One sends the Holy Spirt as the power of God, which remains with the church (Acts 1:8). (3) The one who was received in heaven will also return. Upon this foundation it was possible for Luke to determine the signs, the time, and the nature of the parousia without eliminating it. The ascension changes the architecture of the end-time events, for suddenly with the catastrophic events the expectation of the parousia stands in continuity with the ascension in a limited way. Rather, the ascension suggests the continuity of the saving activity of God that is aimed toward a goal, which Luke describes in his twofold work.

The end time has by no means become irrelevant for Luke. However, eschatology is no longer the pervasive and defining power of his theology. This fact is evident also in the rejection of speculation about the time of the parousia. Luke 17:20–21 has a foundational character: "When he was asked by the Pharisees when the kingdom of God would come, he responded to them: 'The kingdom of God does not come in such a way that one can calculate it. One cannot say, "See here! Or There!" For behold, the kingdom of God is among you.'" This statement about certainty, indefiniteness, and present time corresponds to Acts 1:6–7: "'Lord, will you at this time restore the kingdom to Israel?' He answered them: 'It is not for you to know the times and the hour which the father has determined in his power.'" Acts 3:21 provides a similar perspective ("whom heaven must receive until the time of the restoration of all things, which God has promised through the mouth of his holy prophets from the beginning"), for on the one hand a termination is established until the Exalted One appears again, while on the other hand the course of this event remains open. The placement of Luke 19:11 before the parable of the entrusted pounds and the expansion of Mark 13:6 in Luke 21:8 ("He said, 'See that you not be led into error! For many will come in my name and say, "I am the one!" and "The time has come!" Do not follow them!'") also served as a correction to an expectation of the end that can be calculated with a fixed time (Luke 19:11, "But as they heard this, he continued and told them a parable because he was near Jerusalem and they thought that the kingdom of God would come immediately"). Luke replaces the summary of the preaching of Jesus in Mark 1:15 with the inaugural sermon of Jesus in Nazareth (cf. esp. Luke 4:21) and corrects the logion about the imminent expectation in Mark 9:1 in Luke 9:27 (omitting "when it comes with power"). Thus Luke does not give up on the expectation of the parousia[14] but combines the uncertain

---

14. Contra Haenchen, *Acts*, 96: "The Third Evangelist also denied the imminent expectation"; cf. the alternative view of G. Schneider, *Die Apostelgeschichte*, 1:142: "He holds on energetically to the parousia, but disputes that one can determine the date."

time of the coming of the Lord (cf. Luke 12:40, "Be ready, for the Son of Man comes at an hour when you do not expect it"; Luke 17:24, 26–30; Acts 1:7) with the call for patience (cf. Luke 8:15: "That which falls on the good ground are those who have heard the word with right and good hearts, keep it, and bring fruit in patience") and watchfulness (cf. Luke 12:35ff.; 21:34, 36). The words about the imminence of the rule of God (cf. Luke 10:9, 11) indicate that the evangelist does not fundamentally abandon the imminent expectation but sees a behavior in responsible readiness corresponding to the nature of the parousia. It is not the expectation of the parousia as such but the calculation of the time of the parousia that Luke rejects! According to Acts 1:6–8, the end time will not begin until the missionaries have reached the end of the earth. One cannot determine chronologically when this event will take place or when the parousia begins. What this means in positive terms is that God creates a period of time in which the preaching of the gospel can proceed and the nations can become participants in "salvation for Israel" (Luke 2:30; Acts 28:28).[15] Thus the lapse of time has an eminently positive function; it first establishes the presuppositions for the accomplishment of the universal saving acts of God in history. The readers of Luke-Acts recognize the significance of this period that has been planned by God and may now, as a result of the ascension of Jesus, hope calmly and confidently for his return. The existence of the church for Luke is thus neither directly nor indirectly a replacement for the expectation of the parousia.[16]

Realized Eschatology

An independent and new solution to the problem of the delay of the parousia is realized eschatology, which intentionally places the (complete) presence of salvation in the middle point and thus minimizes the future events, makes them superfluous, or entirely excludes them. The basis of the realized eschatology in Colossians is a cosmic Christology, which is characterized by thoughts about spheres and spaces of divine rule. Christ rules over all things (cf. Col. 1:15–20); thus "Christ is all in all" (Col. 3:11d). In the foreground stands the static place of the present rule of Jesus Christ, while a dynamic eschatology that focuses on a comprehensive end-time event is pushed to the background. In baptism the believers have died with Christ and been

---

15. Appropriately stated by Wolter, *Israels Zukunft*, 423: "The delay of the parousia is not a part of the problem; rather, it belongs to the solution."

16. However, one may observe the influential thesis of Conzelmann, *Theology of St. Luke*, 127: "If Luke has definitely abandoned belief in the early expectation, what does he have to offer on the positive side as an adequate solution of the problem? An outline of the successive stages of the redemptive history according to God's plan."

raised with him so that other powers may not rule over them (Col. 2:12, "You were buried with him in baptism, in which you were also raised with him through faith in the power of God, who raised him from the dead"; Col. 3:1, "You have been raised with Christ").[17] As in Rom. 6:3–5, one may observe a comprehensive understanding of total participation in the destiny of the Lord, with one basic difference: While Paul never speaks of a resurrection of believers that has already taken place and clearly avoids this idea in the logic of the pre-Pauline tradition in Rom. 6:3b–4, Colossians transfers the time of the past event to the resurrection of the believer. However, the author thus does not represent an unreflected-on concept of realized eschatology, for he makes the determination "through faith" (Col. 2:12) more precise and limits the resurrection event to the insight of faith.

In Ephesians (as in Colossians) the tense of the past event is not only consistently transferred to the eschaton, but in addition to that there is the idea of being placed in heaven. Thus as Christ has already achieved the victory (cf. Eph. 1:20–23), the elect community (cf. Eph. 1:5, 9, 11, 19; 2:10; 3:11) is already in a present place of salvation: the church as the body of Christ. Believers are now saved by grace in baptism (Eph. 2:5–6, 8); with Christ (cf. 1:20) they have been "made alive," "raised," and "exalted" in heaven (2:5–6). As fellow citizens of the saints and members of the household of God (Eph. 2:19), they have full participation in the redemption through the blood of Christ (cf. Eph. 1:7). The clear shift in comparison to the eschatology of Paul occurs through the receding of the category of time and the emergence of spatial categories; the tension between the present and future loses its meaning. The strong emphasis on the presence of salvation in Ephesians leads to a theology in which it is not the future that determines the present, but the present determines the future. In particular, the head-body metaphor, with its spatial dimension, and the related theology of unity demand a strong emphasis on the present, or it involves the current overcoming of the divisions and (in the face of the ruling Roman caesar) the demonstration of the comprehensive present rule of Jesus Christ. With this concept, the problem of the delay of the parousia no longer exists.

The Epistle to the Hebrews also deals with the problem of the delay of the parousia. The author holds firmly to an expectation for the near future (cf. Heb. 10:25 NRSV, "and all the more as you see the day approaching"; 10:37, "For in yet a little while the Coming One will come and not delay") but gives precedence to spatial sayings in order to emphasize strongly (under the influence of Middle Platonism) the ontological status of existence that transcends

17. A penetrating analysis of Col. 3:1–4 is given by Grässer, "Kolosser 3,1–4."

time.[18] Jesus has gone into heaven "to appear before the face of God" (Heb. 9:24b). The cosmology of Hebrews is essentially shaped by a dualistic view of the world, according to which the visible/changeable passes away while the invisible/unchangeable is the abiding and true reality. Behind the visible world stands the invisible heavenly world as a pattern of the visible world. Faith knows "that the aeons were made by the word of God so that the visible came into existence from what is not perceptible" (Heb. 11:3). God created both worlds, but only the heavenly world is permanent. The unshakeable world of heaven into which Christ entered at the exaltation, which is subjected to him and in which the believer participates, is for Hebrews the central eschatological reality (Heb. 8:1, "We have such a high priest who has been seated at the right hand of the throne of the majesty in heaven"). While the earthly cult in Jerusalem is a "copy" and "shadow" of the heavenly (Heb. 8:5), the promise of the new covenant consists of the fact that the believers have access to God in the most holy place in heaven through Jesus, the great high priest: "Therefore, let us who receive an unshakeable kingdom be thankful" (Heb. 12:28a).

The present eschatology of the Gospel of John has a system quality.[19] This concept results from the Christology of the Fourth Evangelist, which presents Jesus as the one who brings time to completion: He is preexistent (cf. John 1:1–5), incarnate without the surrender of his divinity (cf. John 1:14), exalted to the Father (cf. John 3:14f.), and glorified (cf. John 17:1–5) in order to be present in his church in the Paraclete after the exaltation (cf. John 14:16, 26; 15:26; 16:7). Thus not only the fundamental distinction between heaven and earth is taken away, but Jesus Christ is the Lord over time; he breaks through the times and in him the future becomes present. Thus the decision about life and death takes place in the present encounter with Jesus Christ as faith or unbelief. In faith the reality of eternal life is present; as a consequence, the step from life to death takes place not in the future but lies already in the past for the believer (John 5:24: "Amen, amen, I say to you: Whoever hears my word and believes in the one who sent me has eternal life and does not come into judgment, but has been rescued from death into life"). Thus "whoever believes in the Son has eternal life, but whoever does not obey the Son will

---

18. Cf. Eisele, *Ein unerschütterliches Reich*, 132: "The author of Hebrews indicates no interest in a detailed description of the events to come. With him, the traditional temporal schema of apocalyptic recedes into the background. In the place of the tension between the already and the not yet, the author has the dichotomy between the shakeable and unshakeable world, both of which exist alongside each other now." Backhaus, *Der Hebräerbrief*, 340, in reference to the eschatology of Hebrews, speaks of the model of a "Christian interim period."

19. Cf. Schnelle, *Neutestamentliche Anthropologie*, 154–58; Frey, *Die johanneische Eschatologie*; Kammler, *Christologie und Eschatologie*; H.-J. Eckstein, "Die Gegenwart im Licht der erinnerten Zukunft."

not see life, but rather the wrath of God rests on him" (John 3:36; cf. also 6:47; 8:51; 11:25–26). Because the decision about the future has taken place in the present, believers have already gone through the judgment (John 3:18; 12:48). Faith guarantees full participation in life. Believers thus know that they have passed from the realm of death, for their existence as a new creation from water and the Spirit is "from God" and is no longer imprisoned in the cosmos (John 3:3, 5, 7). In the Eucharist, the Johannine community receives the bread of life that has come down from heaven (John 6:51a–b: "I am the living bread that has come down from heaven. Whoever eats this bread will live in eternity"; cf. John 6:33, 50, 58). But whoever does not obey the Son and persists in unbelief will not see life; rather, the wrath of God remains over him (cf. John 5:14, 22). Despite this unambiguous dominance of the present in Johannine eschatology, present and future are not opposites; rather, they complement each other: That which was determined in the present will continue in the future (cf. John 5:25, 28–29; 6:39–40, 44, 54; 14:2–3; 16:20–22). Because Christology is interrelated with eschatology (cf. John 5:19–30), the present eschatological and future eschatological sayings are not in contradiction, for Jesus Christ is the true giver of life in the present and the future. At the same time, it is true that the dominant focus in John is not on the returning Christ but on the certainty of the present salvation.

Second Thessalonians argues firmly against a present eschatology. It affirms that the eschatological parousia-Kyrios will be revealed with the angels: "When he comes to be glorified with his saints and to be marveled at on that day among all who have believed" (2 Thess. 1:10). But when is "that day"? Second Thessalonians indicates that a bitter dispute existed over this question in the church. One group represented the view that "the day of the Lord has already come" (2 Thess. 2:2c). The representatives of this present eschatology appealed to insights that came from the Spirit to a word of the apostle and an (allegedly or actual) Pauline letter (cf. 2 Thess. 2:2, 15). Against this view, 2 Thessalonians presents an eschatological timetable that indicates all of the things that will still happen before the parousia. Before the parousia of Christ the "man of lawlessness" (2 Thess. 2:3) must appear, who establishes himself in opposition to God in God's place. The complete epiphany of this opponent is yet to come (2 Thess. 2:6–7). Nevertheless, he is already at work in the present and deceives the unbelievers. Still the adversary of God is being restrained, but at the parousia Christ destroys him, and the judgment comes over those who persist in unbelief.

The Letter of James remains in somewhat conventional course, which calls for patience and confidence before the (postulated) imminent parousia of the Lord (James 5:8). The church should not be impatient, for as the farmer waits patiently for the fruit to ripen, the church may now be certain of the coming of the Lord.

How acute the problem of the delay of the parousia was at the end of the NT age is indicated in 2 Peter (written around 110 CE). The author opposes false teachers, who reject the essential elements of traditional eschatological teaching (angels, parousia, final judgment, destruction of the world) and only ridicule these beliefs (cf. 2 Pet. 3:4: "They say, 'Where is the promise of his coming?' For ever since our ancestors died, all things remain as they were from the beginning of creation"; also 1:16; 3:3, 5, 9). The opponents "deny" the Lord (2 Pet. 2:1); they "malign" and "despise" the truth and the heavenly powers (2 Pet. 2:2, 10); they are proud and arrogant, and they proclaim a false doctrine of freedom (2 Pet. 2:18a, 19). Apparently, the foundation for a skepticism that spread at the beginning of the second century is the dying of the ancestors and the delay of the parousia (cf. 1 Clem. 23.3–4; 2 Clem. 11.2–4),[20] which regarded as μῦθος (myth) Jewish and Jewish Christian concepts of the end time (cf. 2 Pet. 2:1: Christology of the atoning death; 2 Pet. 1:16: the conceptions of the parousia that had been passed on) and thus considered them as no longer valid. Thus they appealed to the letters of Paul (cf. 2 Pet. 3:15–16). The massive objections are answered in 2 Peter in a twofold way: (1) He introduces a new way of reckoning time, as he, on the one hand, affirms the unpredictability of the time and the suddenness of the coming of the Lord (2 Pet. 3:10), while on the other hand he affirms: "This should not remain unknown to you, that one day with the Lord is as a thousand years, and a thousand years as one day" (2 Pet. 3:8). (2) He indicates the true reason for the delay of the parousia: "The Lord is not slow in keeping his promise, as some think of slowness, but is patient with you, not wanting any to perish, but all to come to repentance" (2 Pet. 3:9). As Lord of creation and of history, God does not just have a different perspective on time; rather, it is actually his goodness that is being ridiculed by the opponents!

In view of the eschatological conceptions of other religions and cults, the delay of the parousia presented a challenge not only to other religions and cults but also to the imperial eschatology. The rule of Augustus was already interpreted by himself as the fulfillment of the wishes of the Roman people: "Of their own free will all Italy has sworn loyalty to me and called for me to be the leader in war, in which I was the victor at Actium. The provinces of Gaul and Spain, Africa, Sicily, and Sardinia have sworn the same oath."[21] His contemporary and biographer, Nicholas of Damascus,

20. For the pagan evidence (esp. Plutarch, *On the Delays of the Divine Vengeance*), see Berger, "Streit um Gottes Vorsehung," 124–25.
21. Augustus, Res gestae 25.

says about Augustus: "The people have named him this as a recognition of his reputation and worship him in temples and with sacrifices. . . . For after this man had reached the pinnacle of power and of wisdom, he ruled over more people than anyone in human memory."[22] Vergil identified the birth of the child with which the golden age would arise with Augustus:[23] "Do not prevent this young prince from coming to the aid of this broken age."[24] Horace praises Augustus as a peacemaker and a "man of integrity";[25] "in this sense, Pollux and the restless Hercules won the fiery heights, in the center of which Augustus will one day drink nectar with rosy lips."[26] Vergil's Aeneas, in which the hero of the new national epic appears as the embodiment of Roman piety and courage, is applied to Augustus. In a way that is previously unknown, Augustus is presented as peacemaker and as champion of the empire, of tradition, and of prosperity: as the embodiment of Roman virtues and guarantor of a golden future.[27] A new way of reckoning time,[28] the name of a new month,[29] and numerous impressive buildings attest the greatness of the caesar, to whom unlimited divine adoration was given.[30] With Augustus, a development began in the context of an ancient adoration of the ruler oriented toward Alexander the Great, which ascribed an immanent saving function to the caesar and required and promoted a cult of his person and position (see below, 12.1). A politically shaped present eschatology emerged that stylized the caesar as guarantor of peace and prosperity as the central saving figure. After Augustus, the emperors Nero,[31] Domitian (see below, 12.3), and Hadrian demanded the ruler cult and regarded Rome not only as a political power giving order to the world but also ascribed to it a larger eschatological role for the world (*Roma aeterna*).[32] This form of realized

22. Nicholas of Damascus, *Life of Caesar Augustus* 1.1; cited from Malitz, *Nikolaos von Damaskus*, 27.
23. Cf. Hoff, Stroh, and M. Zimmermann, *Divus Augustus*, 113–14.
24. Vergil, *Georgica* 1.500–501.
25. Cf. also Suetonius, *Aug.* 22: he has "made peace on land and on sea."
26. Horace, *Odes* 3.9–12.
27. Cf. Hoff, Stroh, and M. Zimmermann, *Divus Augustus*, 143–203.
28. On the *saeculum Augustum*, cf. Suetonius, *Aug.* 100.3.
29. In the year 8 BCE, the month of Sextilis was renamed Augustus.
30. Cf. below, 12.1.
31. Cf. especially *Eclogue* (1.33–99) of Calpurnius Siculus, Paul's contemporary, about Nero: "A golden era with peace without danger is reborn" (43); "All wars are cast then into the dungeon of Tartartus" (53); "The goddess of peace shines" (55); "the reign of Numa" (65); "All people should rejoice who live below in the south and as well as those who live above in the north, who extend to the east and the west, or those who burn with heat under the middle of heaven."
32. Cf. Kytzler, *Roma aeterna*. The Roman speech of Aelius Aristides (around 155 CE) is undoubtedly a high point of this genre (Rome is the peacemaker and common capital of the world; there is no other way of life than the Roman; the divine caesar is the guarantor of this order).

eschatology existed everywhere in the cities where Christians were present (in various texts and buildings) and exercised a great attractive power, especially at the end of the first century and beginning of the second century CE. The early Christian eschatology was not directly influenced by it but was indirectly influenced by it. Both the emphasis on the cosmological place of Christ and the present eschatology as a whole ascribed to Jesus Christ, the crucified Son of God, a unique dignity and power that the Roman caesar himself never attained.

> The delay of the parousia was undoubtedly the greatest theological problem and challenge of early Christianity. It is thus astonishing that the various strategies for resolving the problem were apparently convincing, although they were no real solution to the problem. The more Christ was considered the perpetual ruler of the world in heaven with a position above Caesar's, the less the solution to this question pressed upon them. Eternity also included the future so that the chronological dynamic of the beginning receded into the background, being replaced by a hierarchical state of eternity.

11.2 Poor and Rich

The Pauline mission churches were not a sociologically homogeneous group; instead, the members came from all social levels, and there were already conflicts very early between rich and poor members of the church (cf. 1 Cor. 11:17–22). In the post-Pauline period, the conflicts apparently intensified because rich people increasingly came into the Christian communities,[33] and the gaps between the specific social groups grew. Theological models had to be developed in order to preserve the unity of the churches and to enable the interaction of various groups.

Luke

Luke attempts in a special way to address this problem. At the close of the first century, respected and prosperous people belonged to the Christian churches (cf. Acts 17:4; 18:8). The proper use of money and property

---

33. Critique of wealth is also a central theme of Cynicism and the Stoa in the early imperial period; cf. only the Cynic Demetrius (first century CE), who is presented by Seneca as a shining example; cf. Seneca, *Ben.* 7.8.2–12.1 (NW I/1.2:192–95); also Seneca, *Ep.* 62.3: "The shortest way to wealth is the contempt of wealth." Cf. N. Neumann, *Armut und Reichtum.*

developed into a central problem of the Lukan ethic (cf. Luke 3:11; Acts 2:45; 4:34–37). The rich in the community are self-righteous and avaricious (cf. Luke 12:13–15; 16:14–15), they despise the poor (cf. Luke 18:9), and they stand in danger of falling away from faith because of their striving for wealth (cf. Luke 8:14; 9:25). Luke confronts these negative features within his church with a multilayered argument. John the Baptist already stands in the service of an ethical conception, as his preaching in Luke 3:10–14 indicates.[34] The adoption of the baptism of repentance is realized in a new way of life that proceeds from the question, "What shall we do?" (Luke 3:10, 12, 14; cf. 10:5; 16:3; 18:18; Acts 2:37; 16:30) and suggests a generous giving, while in verses 12–14 the illegal collecting by the tax collectors and extortion by the soldiers are forbidden. In the Sermon on the Plain (Luke 6:20–49), Luke interprets the command for the love of neighbor and love of the enemy with an ethic of generosity. He rejects behavior built on reciprocity (Luke 6:32–34) and offers a different model: "Rather, love your enemies and do good to them, and lend when you hope for nothing in return. Then your reward will be great, and you will be sons of the Most High, for he is good to the unthankful and the evil" (Luke 6:35). In the thematic blocks in 12:13–34; 16:1–31 the evangelist comprehensively demonstrates the problem of wealth, for life does not consist in the abundance of possessions (cf. Luke 12:15); the desire for gain and greed do not correspond to the will of God (cf. Luke 12:15; 16:14). In the dispute of the disciples about greatness (Luke 9:46–48; 22:24–27) and the banquet (Luke 14:7–24), Jesus criticizes the conduct of the rich. The call to discipleship and the renunciation of possessions mutually depend on each other (cf. Luke 5:11, 28; 8:3; 9:3; 10:4; 18:28); thereby Luke 14:33 is programmatically formulated: "Thus no one of you who does not give up all of his possessions can be my disciple." The requirement not to love possessions is associated with the readiness to give alms (cf. Luke 11:41; 12:21, 33–34; 16:9, 27–31). The programmatic demand in Luke 12:33a goes back to the evangelist: "Sell your possessions and give alms!" Thus the call to discipleship given to the rich ruler (Luke 18:18–23) is connected with the requirement to sell "everything" (πάντα only in the Lukan parallel, 18:22!) and to give to the poor. "For it is easier for a camel to go through the eye of a needle than for a rich person to enter into the kingdom of God" (Luke 18:25). Thus Luke holds firmly to the voluntary nature of the gifts (Acts 5:4) according to the capabilities of the individuals (cf. Acts 11:29).

How are the care for and the critique of the rich (Luke 1:53; 6:24–25; 8:14; 12:13–21; 14:15–24; 16:14–15, 19–31), the promises to the poor (Luke

---

34. For the analysis, cf. Horn, *Glaube und Handeln*, 91–97.

1:53; 4:18–19; 6:20–21; 7:22), and the call for the renunciation of possessions
(Luke 5:11, 28; 12:33; 14:33; 18:18–30) and for charity (Luke 3:10–11; 6:33–38;
8:1–3; 16:9; 19:1–10; 21:1–4) connected in Luke? Luke focuses primarily on
the rich in his church and calls on them not to pursue wealth because of the
danger of falling away from faith. His purpose is not the absolute critique
of the rich but the realization of a community of love between rich and poor
members of the church that requires the readiness of the rich to give alms.[35]
Thus the renunciation of possessions by the disciples of Jesus as well as the
Jerusalem church itself (see above, 5.5) serve Luke as models, just as the
Roman sympathizer does. His "prayers and alms before God" are explicitly
mentioned twice (Acts 10:4, 31). The unconditional nature of discipleship
and the community of love that was practiced should become a reality in the
Lukan community. As the evangelist portrays the church as a community of
love, he takes up the claim of Jesus as the legacy of the church, which Paul
summarizes in the farewell address to the church in Miletus in Acts 20:35: "It
is more blessed to give than to receive."

Pastoral Epistles

The Pastoral Epistles reflect the reality of multiple social classes in post-
Pauline Christianity. Christian homeowners are mentioned several times (cf.
1 Tim. 3:4–5, 12; 5:4, 8; 2 Tim. 1:16; 4:19; cf. also 1 Tim. 5:13; 2 Tim. 3:6;
Titus 1:11); large houses with valuable furnishings were apparently not unusual (cf. 2 Tim. 2:20). The Christian house serves as the primary model for
the self-understanding of the church. The ecclesiology of the Pastoral Epistles
is oriented to the metaphor of the house (cf. 1 Tim. 3:4, 15). Women's jew-
elry (1 Tim. 2:9), the slaves of Christian masters (cf. 1 Tim. 6:2), the warning

35. Horn, *Glaube und Handeln*, 231 and passim, regards the paraenesis about alms given by
the rich as the social-ethical conception of Luke; against this view is Schottroff and W. Stegemann, *Jesus and the Hope of the Poor*, 150, who speak of an equality of possessions within the
community. Mineshige, *Besitzverzicht und Almosen bei Lukas*, 263–64, categorizes the subject
within the Lukan view of history: "Luke thinks of three different eras: the time of Jesus, the
initial period of the church, and his own time. The renunciation of possessions applies to the
time of Jesus. The first disciples have left their entire property to follow Jesus. However, such
renunciation is no longer required in the time of the church. What is required for the initial
period of the church is the community of goods. . . . In contrast to the earlier periods, neither the
renunciation of goods nor the community of goods is required in the time of Luke. Christians
of his time, i.e., his readers, are instead called upon to support the poor church members with
voluntary donations." Petracca, *Gott oder das Geld*, 354, considers the central theme of Luke
the saving of the lost at two levels, which are made concrete in the topic of possessions: "The
seeking of the lost leads to the salvation of the poor and the outsiders. It also makes possible
the salvation of the rich and the respectable as they, as an expression of undivided devotion
to God, care for the poor and the outsider rather than strive for property and social prestige."

against the desire for gain and greed (cf. 1 Tim. 6:6–10; 2 Tim. 3:2; Titus 1:7), and the separate instruction to the rich in 1 Tim. 6:17–20 indicate that members of the upper class belonged to the churches.[36] The churches had at their disposal considerable financial means, for the elders were paid (as certainly the bishop, who held the highest office). Furthermore, a church treasury existed for the care of the widows (cf. 1 Tim. 5:16). The misuse of this institution (cf. 1 Tim. 5:4–15) is indirect evidence of the financial capability of this system of welfare. Besides the rich, who apparently dominated congregational life, the Pastoral Epistles mention slaves (cf. 1 Tim. 6:1; Titus 2:9f.), widows (cf. 1 Tim. 5:3ff.), artisans (cf. 2 Tim. 4:14), and lawyers (cf. Titus 3:13) and call for the care of the poor (cf. 1 Tim. 5:10). As a whole, the warning about the dangers of wealth and greed (cf. 1 Tim. 6:10: "For the love of money is the root of all evil; for some have longed for it, have wandered away and pierced themselves with much pain") dominates the instructions. Scarcely coincidentally, 1 Timothy ends with a general admonition to the rich (1 Tim. 6:17–19). The contrast is a life of good works, readiness to share and help, and self-sufficiency (cf. 1 Tim. 6:6–8, 18), the positive model of the Pastoral Epistles.

The Letter of James

The situation of the churches addressed in the Letter of James is marked by social tensions.[37] The provision for the needy is not succeeding (James 1:27; 2:15–16); rich and poor are treated unequally (James 2:1ff.), and envy, quarreling, and fighting (James 3:13–14; 4:11–12; 5:9) are dominant. In the worship service the rich are given preferential treatment (James 2:1ff.), and the poor are dismissed with religious clichés. The rich trust in themselves and not in God (James 4:13–17). Landowners also exploit their workers (James 5:1–6). Finally, the churches are subject to local legal discrimination (cf. James 2:6). The numerous sayings about poor and rich in James in no way originate from a spiritualized piety of poverty,[38] but this topic must have a background in the experience of the churches that are addressed; it aims at a change in the conduct of the Christians.[39] The advocacy for the poor (James 1:27) and criticism of the rich (James 2:1–13; 4:13–5:6) correspond to the will of God,

36. Cf. Dschulnigg, "Warnung vor Reichtum."

37. On the ethic of James, cf. Tsuji, *Glaube zwischen Vollkommenheit und Verweltlichung*; Konradt, *Christliche Existenz nach dem Jakobusbrief*; Gemünden, Konradt, and Theissen, *Der Jakobusbrief*; Garleff, *Urchristliche Identität im Matthäusevangelium*, 222–321; Hoppe, "Arm und Reich im Jakobusbrief."

38. Contra Dibelius, *James*, 135–37.

39. Cf. Schnider, *Der Jakobusbrief*, 57–58; Frankemölle, *Der Brief des Jakobus*, 57–62, 251–59.

for "has not God selected the poor in the world as rich in faith and heirs of his kingdom that he promised to those who love him?" (James 2:5).

James does not (like Luke) aim at an inner-church balance between poor and rich, but he represents an inner-church solidarity (James 2:14–16) and supports the equality of the church members (James 2:1–7).[40] James opposes the claim of the rich to a special position and treatment by indicating that God has elected the poor (James 2:5) and thus determines a new definition of status between rich and poor: because the rich person as well as his wealth will pass away, he should boast in his lowliness alone (before God), and on the other hand the lowly should boast of his high position (cf. James 1:9–11). It is not the usual social status that matters; rather, the conduct according to the measure of the love command (as the guiding principle of the law) is the visible expression of the unity of Christian existence and of the church. Thus hearing (James 1:19) stands at the beginning, which is perfected in the unity of speaking and conduct and continues into the judgment (James 2:12: "So speak and act as those who will be judged by the law of liberty"). Good words or thoughts are not sufficient; instead, concrete conduct oriented to the law is required. From here the Letter of James develops—alongside a few other NT writings—the foundations for a social and economic ethic because the demand of the love command is unlimited for all areas of life. James sharply criticizes an autonomy oriented to the world, which is evident especially in the self-serving plans of the merchants (James 4:13–17) and the antisocial conduct of the landowners (James 5:1–16). Instead of the false self-security that ignores God's sovereign rule, they should say, "If the Lord wills, we will live and do this or that" (James 4:15 NRSV). Christians cannot at the same time orient themselves to God and the world; egoism and love of the world stand in opposition to the will of God. Thus at the end of the letter, the warning about the judgment on the rich is not coincidental: "Come now, you rich, wail and mourn about the misery that is about to come over you. Your riches have decayed" (James 5:1–2). James advocates an ethical perfection in humility and lowliness, which (essentially) excludes a division in the church into rich and poor members.

The Revelation of John

A critique of the rich shaped by Jewish Christianity appears in the book of Revelation. It involves a reversal of the relationships established by God; thus

---

40. Cf. Garleff, *Urchristliche Identität im Matthäusevangelium*, 269; Theissen, "Nächstenliebe und Egalität," who emphasizes about James: "No New Testament author has so clearly understood the love command as obligation to equal treatment as James; at the same time he relatively openly formulates it for outsiders" (120–21).

the seer can say to the economically poor and oppressed church of Smyrna: "I know your affliction and poverty, but you are rich" (Rev. 2:9). This is to be contrasted to the church in the commercial city of Laodicea, which is considered rich, but in truth it is not: "For you say, 'I am rich and have property, and I lack nothing!' Thus you do not know that you are needy, miserable, poor, blind, and naked" (Rev. 3:17–18). The church gains true riches only when it purchases "white robes" in order to be seen, that is, when it stays away from material wealth and the pagan cults. The general increase in prices of the basic foods such as wheat and barley is evidence not only of an increasing division of the society into the hungering, the poor, and the rich (cf. Rev. 6:5f.) but is also a sign of the approach of the end time. Christians may have been among those merchants who are attacked in Rev. 18:11ff. They engaged in trade with the whore Babylon and became rich. However, they had to wear the mark of the beast in order to be able to buy and sell; that is, they subjected themselves to the totalitarian religious-political claim of the state in order to avoid any economic disadvantages (cf. Rev. 13:16–17).[41]

11.3 Controversies, False Teachers, and Opponents

Early Christianity was a movement in dispute from the beginning. In terms of the history of religion, this was no exception, for conflicts and division as a rule accompany new, emerging religions/philosophies/political systems. The correct path must first be found, and opinions about where this path lies and where it should lead frequently go in different directions at the initial phase of movements. The concept of "one heart and soul" in Luke (cf. Acts 4:32) was probably already not the case in the Jerusalem church (see above, chap. 5). The determining and naming of the conflicts that are identified, suggested, or assumed in the NT present a methodological and conceptual problem: (1) Methodologically, one must consider how to determine the content of a position that is either fought against or rejected. Thus one must consider the dangers of "mirror reading,"[42] for we know the position of the opponents as a rule only partially from polemical statements, the "reflections" of the NT authors, which include conscious distortions, polemical exaggerations, and frequently stereotypical accusations. In order to avoid a circular conclusion, it is appropriate to ask precisely which statements come into question for the historical standpoint of the position that is criticized and where a NT author takes up a common polemic against opponents (e.g.,

41. Cf. Klauck, *Das Sendschreiben nach Pergamon*, 178–79.
42. Cf. Barclay, "Mirror-Reading a Polemical Letter."

the appearance of opponents as a sign of the beginning of the end time, the accusation of sexual immorality).[43] One may not exclude the possibility of a purely constructed opposing front with which a NT author hopes to make his argument. (2) Conceptually, what should we call the deviating groups or opinions? As a rule, only the designations of others and not self-descriptions/ designations can be found. This begins already with Paul who, for example, calls the outside missionaries "evil workers" in 2 Cor. 11:13 or "dogs, evil workers, and the mutilation" (Phil. 3:2); in each case these are polemical and insulting expressions. They do correspond to ancient conventions, for we find ourselves in a contentious society, and it was commonplace to engage in polemic in a rhetorically effective way.[44] Nevertheless, these descriptions from others should not simply be taken over; instead, neutral expressions should be found without, of course, concealing the objective bases for the conflict: dissenters, foreign missionaries, antagonists, divergent concepts, false teachers. Where, to be sure, from the texts an objectively based opposition can be derived, one should speak further of opponents.

Conflicts in the Post-Pauline Churches

Massive conflicts already accompanied the Pauline mission, in which the pneumatic enthusiasm in Corinth and the demand of circumcision for gentile Christians in Galatia stood at the center (see above, 7 and 8.6). In the deutero-Pauline writings after 70 CE, one can observe, besides the conflicts about the time of the parousia (see above, 11.1: 2 Thessalonians), further conflicts within the church: the relationship of rich and poor (see above, 11.2: Pastoral Epistles) and early Gnostic streams (see below, 14.2: 1 Timothy).

Colossians confronts a "philosophy" (φιλοσοφία) in which the teaching can be determined (cf. Col. 2:8):[45] (a) They required circumcision for gentile Christians (cf. Col. 2:11). (b) Ascetic food regulations and observance of special days were among the characteristic features of the "philosophy" (cf. Col. 2:16, 21, 23b). Sexual abstinence may have been required (Col. 2:21a). (c) A central component of the teaching was the observation of the elements and powers (cf. Col. 2:8, 15, 20). (d) The worship of angels was also practiced (cf.

43. Cf. Berger, "Die impliziten Gegner."
44. Cf. Wischmeyer and Scornaienchi, *Polemik in der frühchristlichen Literatur.*
45. A survey of research and interpretations is given in Bornkamm, "Die Häresie des Kolosserbriefes" (earlier discussion); Wolter, *Der Brief an die Kolosser*, 155–63; Maisch, *Der Brief an die Gemeinde in Kolossä*, 30–40; P. Müller, "Gegner im Kolosserbrief." On the key term τὰ στοιχεῖα τοῦ κόσμου, cf. Delling, "στοιχεῖον"; Lohse, *Colossians and Philemon*, 127–31; Schweizer, "Altes und Neues zu den 'Elementen der Welt'"; Rusam, "Neue Belege zu den στοιχεῖα τοῦ κόσμου"; Wolter, *Der Brief an die Kolosser*, 122–24.

Col. 2:18). One may conclude additional elements of this teaching from the polemic of the writer. He opposes regulations that are required by the opponents (Col. 2:20) and describes the teaching of the opponents as so-called wisdom (cf. Col. 2:23) and being puffed up in the flesh (cf. Col. 2:18, 23). Evidently the rhetorically trained opponents (Col. 2:4) established norms, and by keeping them the Christians in Colossae were supposed to become liberated from the power of the elements (cf. Col. 2:14).[46] In the Colossian "philosophy," elements flow in from Hellenistic Judaism and contemporary Stoic, Neopythagorean, and Middle Platonist philosophy as well as from the mystery cults so that a monocausal derivation from a single source in the religious environment appears impossible. The opponents in Colossians evidently practiced their teaching and their cult within the church. They did not understand themselves as heretics but rather saw in their philosophy a legitimate form of expressing the Christian faith. The sharp contrast between the *stoicheia* (powers) of the world and Christ in Col. 2:8 indicates that in the "philosophy" the *stoicheia* were conceived as personal powers. They appear as forces that want to exercise their authority over humankind (cf. Col. 2:10, 15). In any case the tendency is clear: to display the obligatory worship to the powers and elements alongside Christ in the cosmic order.

Colossians answers this totally plausible challenge with the basic assumptions of that era, making cosmology the foundation and center of Christology. Christ is the firstborn of all creation; in him the All was created; it has continued existence through him and for him (cf. Col. 1:15–17). As Lord of creation, he rules over every created thing, both invisible and visible. Christ is the head over all powers (Col. 2:10) and triumphant over the cosmic forces (Col. 2:15). The cosmos endures in him, and he assigns to all their significance. In the present, the church already participates in the sovereign rule of Christ. Through his death he reconciles the believers with God (Col. 1:22) and blots out the accusing record of indebtedness (Col. 2:14). Now Christ can be proclaimed to the gentiles as Lord of the cosmos (Col. 1:27). Colossians 3:11d expresses the Christology of the letter succinctly: "Christ is all in all" (τὰ πάντα καὶ ἐν πᾶσιν Χριστός).[47]

Apparently there was in the post-Pauline era a conflict, with an appeal to Paul over the legitimacy of angel worship. Thus Col. 2:18–19 and the

46. P. Müller, "Gegner im Kolosserbrief," 369–74, discusses in detail the danger of "mirror reading" and indicates that at least "partial aspects of the opponents' views" (388) can be ascertained: philosophy and wisdom, appeal to traditions, elements of the world, worship of angels, precise "investigation, humility toward transcendent beings, keeping of special days, and the tabu with regard to food and special days."

47. In 1 Cor. 15:28, *God* is "all in all" (ὁ θεὸς τὰ πάντα ἐν πᾶσιν)!

Letter of Jude (cf. Jude 6, 9) refer to a connection between "regulations of the law and service to angels" on the one hand, and "antinomianism and despising of angels on the other hand."[48] The connecting line to the Pauline/ deutero-Pauline tradition suggests that the opponents of Jude represented an enthusiastic teaching (and practice). They despised the angelic powers, saw themselves as pneumatics, and believed that they had risen above traditional limitations. One may not exclude the possibility of a purely constructed opposition front against which a NT author hoped to establish his argument.

The Letter to the Ephesians takes up Colossians and extends its cosmological perspective, but at the same time it carries on another discussion within the church. Ephesians outlines the concept of a church composed of Jewish Christians and Christians from the Greco-Roman tradition who form the body of Christ. Thus the author reacts to a contrary development in the churches of Asia Minor. Jewish Christians are already a minority, and the gentile Christians regard them no longer as equal partners.[49] The unity of the church is thus the exemplum envisaged for the cosmic peace established by Christ. Therefore, the election of Israel (in contrast to Colossians) is emphatically emphasized: "That you at that time were without Christ, excluded from the citizenship of Israel, and strangers to the covenant of the promise, without hope and without God in the cosmos" (Eph. 2:12), at a distance but now "brought near" (Eph. 2:13). Here the dominant focus is not the thought of incorporation into the elect people but rather reconciliation as the overcoming of hostility (Eph. 2:14–18).[50] And now the new situation: "You are no longer strangers and aliens, but fellow citizens [συμπολῖται] of the saints and members of the household [οἰκεῖοι] of God" (Eph. 2:19).[51] The overcoming of the existing tensions between Jews and Greeks/Romans in the society is to a certain extent affirmed with these political concepts. Against the background of an increasing anti-Judaism in the church (and in the whole society), Ephesians advocates the equal inheritance of Jewish Christians in the body of Christ. Thus the letter stands in opposition to the tendencies that were taking place in the church of Asia Minor. Of course, the subject of Israel was perceived as an issue within the church and no longer (as with Paul) a universal problem in salvation history.

48. Sellin, "Die Häretiker des Judasbriefes," 222.

49. Cf. K. Fischer, *Tendenz und Absicht*, 79.

50. Cf. Roloff, *Die Kirche*, 241–42.

51. Cf. K. Fischer, *Tendenz und Absicht*, 80: "The thesis of Ephesians is clear and unambiguous: Israel is the people of God and has the covenantal promises; the gentiles have nothing. That is the starting point. Then, however, the incomprehensible miracle occurred in which Christ tore down the wall with its commandments separating gentiles and Jews, and thus he opened up the access of gentiles to God in one church (2:11ff.)."

Colossians and Ephesians (along with the Gospel of John) depict a new independent form of early Christian thought. The dominant thought of creation, rule, and space marks a Christian position in the continuing ancient religious philosophy of rule and nature. The observation of, the accommodation to, and the subjection under the powers that determine destiny were natural components of ancient thought. It was self-evident and appropriate to pay tribute to the powers of fate.[52] Furthermore, it was considered a mark of effective philosophical discourse to explain the cosmos and its phenomena and to derive from it the meaning of human existence. The Letter to the Colossians contrasts the reality of the Christ event to the natural and at the same time highly attractive message of the opponents' teaching; the Christ event stands above the cosmos and makes superfluous any other attempt to gain the certainty of salvation. The new identity cannot be intensified and given certainty by additional ancient practices; instead, it rests exclusively in God's saving act that brings peace and reconciliation in Jesus Christ. Consequently, a countermodel is outlined for the competing doctrine, which permits the reception of this form of Christian thinking in the Greco-Roman environment through the dimension of sovereignty and space.

Second Repentance and Forgiveness of Sins

In many cases affiliation in the early churches did not involve an exclusive and lasting membership. Instead, one could, in the tradition of Greco-Roman practice, belong to various religious groups and alternate in participating in the cults. Paul already confronts this practice in Corinth (1 Cor. 10:21: "You cannot participate at the same time in the cup of the Lord and the cup of demons"), and the variety of temples and sanctuaries in ancient Pompeii illustrates impressively the wide diversity in the religious infrastructure in the Roman Empire. Apparently numerous people either concurrently participated in Christian and pagan cultic activities or temporarily joined the Christian communities, left them, and then returned to Christianity. Thus the theological problem emerged, whether the sin of falling away can be forgiven or which sins could be forgiven or not forgiven.

The question of forgiveness/nonforgiveness of sins and the related question of exclusion is already presupposed in 1 Cor. 5:1–13, for Paul demands that the church definitively separate from a church member in a charismatic-pneumatic act. This issue becomes a topic in the Gospel of Matthew and in

---

52. Cf. Seneca, *Ep.* 107.11: "Lead me, O Master of the lofty heavens, My Father, wherever you wish. And I shall not falter, but obey with speed. . . . Aye, the willing soul Fate leads, but the unwilling drags along."

Hebrews.[53] Like the wilderness generation, the church in the Letter to the Hebrews stands in danger of disparaging God's grace (cf. Heb. 3:7–4:13; 12:15). Thus the apostasy from faith and the related problem of second repentance is a current topic in the church (cf. Heb. 6:4–6; 10:26–29; 12:16–17; also 3:12; 12:25). Here the argument of Hebrews becomes compressed: Anyone who denies the faith tramples the Son of God under the feet and profanes "the blood of the covenant" (Heb. 10:29). As the consequence of the once-for-all nature and enormity of the sacrifice of Jesus Christ, the author gives the warning not to despise the saving work of Jesus by apostasy. Those who fall away cannot return, for then Jesus's death on the cross would be emptied of its meaning (cf. Heb. 6:4–6; 10:26–29; 12:16–17). The one baptism corresponds to the once-for-all nature of the sacrifice of Christ, but a second repentance does not. The ἐφάπαξ that is fundamental for the Christology and soteriology of the saving event does not permit a repetition of the μετάνοια.

The question of the forgiveness of sins has a central place in the Gospel of Matthew,[54] for Jesus is the one who redeems his people from their sins (Matt. 1:21), and the authority to forgive sins has been given to the church (Matt. 9:8; 26:28). This authority is reflected in the rule for discipline in Matt. 18:15–17, which is to be understood as an institutionalized measure for discipline by the church. A three-stage process is established in accordance with OT traditions: (1) A private conversation with the church member (v. 15); (2) a further conversation in the presence of one or two witnesses if this conversation does not have the proper result (v. 16); and finally (3) the treatment of this case before the full assembly. When the admonition before this group does not end in an appropriate resolution, excommunication is the result (v. 17b: "he may be like the gentiles and the tax collectors"). The goal of this process is the regaining of every church member who threatens to fall away from discipleship. A discussion over forgivable and unforgivable sins is assumed in the puzzling logion in Mark 3:28–29 and Luke 12:10Q: "Everyone who speaks a word against the Son of Man will be forgiven, but anyone who speaks against the Holy Spirit will not be forgiven." This word may belong to the conflicts of Q missionaries with their opponents and have a pre- and post-Easter perspective.[55] The pre-Easter rejection of the Son of Man can be forgiven, but not the post-Easter rejection of the Q missionaries, for it is the

53. For an analysis of the text, cf. Goldhahn-Müller, *Die Grenze der Gemeinde*, 75–114, who discusses the problem of exclusion from/return to the community at the turn of the century and in 1 Tim. 1:20; 5:19–20; Titus 3:10–11; James 5:14–16, 19–20.

54. On the interpretation, cf. Goldhahn-Müller, *Die Grenze der Gemeinde*, 164–95; S. Koch, *Rechtliche Regelung von Konflikten*, 66–83.

55. Cf. Wiefel, *Das Evangelium nach Matthäus*, 238.

equivalent of rejecting Jesus as the Son of God as well as the blasphemy of the Spirit of God.

Besides the conflict with a docetic Christology (see above, 10.4.2), 1 John indicates that a conflict occurred in the Johannine churches over the forgivable and unforgivable sins.[56] While in 1 John 1:8–10 it is explicitly said that any Christian's claim to be without sin is against the truth, 1 John 3:9 emphasizes: "Those who have been born of God do not sin because God's seed abides in them; they cannot sin because they have been born of God." To be born of God and to be bound to Christ excludes sin. A clear separation exists between the children of God and the children of the devil (1 John 3:10). Another direction is indicated in 1 John 5:16–17: "If anyone sees his brother committing a sin that is not mortal, he should ask, and God will give him life, to those who do not commit a mortal sin. There is a sin that is mortal; I do not say that one should pray about that. All wrongdoing is sin, but there are sins that are not mortal." Those who sin are not within the realm of the Spirit and life, but belong in the realm of death. On the other hand, the author of 1 John takes into account the reality within the church when he speaks of sins that do not lead to death. The brother within the church may ask God for forgiveness of this person. It is scarcely coincidental that both in 1 John and in the Gospel of John there is no definition of the two types of sins. The church members thus maintain the freedom to decide themselves in each case which sin is forgivable and where a sin is mortal. With this concept the essential contrast between sins and being a Christian is fundamentally maintained, and at the same time the imperative intensifies: There are sins that destroy the relationship with God so that also one who has been baptized can fall from the realm of life in God.[57]

In the early church a variety of positions on the question of a second repentance are present.[58] A rigorist position in the line of tradition in Hebrews is represented by the earliest Montanists (last third of the second century), the Montanist Tertullian (around 203 CE), Acts of John 107 (end of the second century), Acts of Thomas 34 (around 230 CE), and the Roman presbyter Novatian, who died around 258 CE (cf. Eusebius, *Hist. eccl.* 6.43.1–2). A somewhat more moderate position is represented by the Jewish Christian Elkesai (around 110 CE in Syria), who proclaimed a onetime repentance for mortal sins (cf. Hippolytus, *Ref.* 9.15.1–2, 3). The Shepherd of Hermas (Rome, around 130 CE) also allows a second repentance "because of human

---

56. On the analysis of the texts, cf. Goldhahn-Müller, *Die Grenze der Gemeinde*, 27–72.

57. On the agreements and differences in the concept of sin between the Gospel of John and 1 John, cf. Metzner, *Das Verständnis der Sünde*, 325–27.

58. On the interpretation, cf. Goldhahn-Müller, *Die Grenze der Gemeinde*, 225–351.

weaknesses" (cf. Herm. 5.2.5). The development of the institution of penance that gives authority to the clergy to forgive any kind of sin at any time can be observed in Ign. *Phld.* 8.1; 2 Clem. 8.3; Dionysius of Corinth (around 170 CE; cf. Eusebius, *Hist. eccl.* 4.23.6), Irenaeus, *Haer.* 1.6.3; 13.5, 7, and in the Catholic Tertullian (before 203 CE).

Opponents in the Revelation of John

The conflicts in the churches of Revelation are especially sharp. In the letters to the churches, the seer engages intensively in a conflict with the internal situation of the churches and attacks opposing streams.[59] The use of διδαχή (teaching, Rev. 2:14, 15, 24) and διδάσκειν (teach, Rev. 2:14, 20) indicates that disputes over teaching form the background of the controversies. In the church at Pergamum are Christians who hold to the teaching of Balaam; the seer calls this the eating of food offered to idols and participation in sexual immorality (Rev. 2:14). Balaam appears also in Jude 11 and 2 Pet. 2:15–16 as a prototype of the greedy false teacher. In both places the seer follows Jewish tradition.[60] The teaching of the Nicolaitans (cf. Rev. 2:6) is described in parallel terms in Rev. 2:15 with the views of those who have already been attacked. In Thyatira, Jezebel appears as a prophetess[61] who has induced numerous church members to eat food offered to idols and to engage in sexual immorality (Rev. 2:20). John probably confronts relatively similar opposing fronts.[62] Led by prophets and prophetesses, they gained influence in the churches of Ephesus, Pergamum, and Thyatira[63] in varying ways. John discredits the other teaching, using assumed names from the OT, and raises the question of the consumption of food offered to idols to a central point of conflict. The "hidden manna" will be given to those who distance themselves from the earthly sacral meals (cf. Rev. 2:17). The eating of food offered to idols was scarcely to be avoided in the normal contacts with the pagan environment and was the source of conflict in Paul's churches (cf. 1 Cor. 8–10). The decisive difference between the seer and his opponents may be evident in Rev. 2:24–25, where, in a striking similarity to the apostolic decree (Acts 15:28–29),[64]

---

59. The opponents in Smyrna and Philadelphia do not belong in this group, for among them the tension between the Christian and Jewish communities is the dominant issue (cf. Rev. 2:9f.; 3:9).

60. The positive image in Num. 22–24 changes already in Num. 31:16; cf. also Philo, *Moses* 1.296–99; Josephus, *Ant.* 4.129–30.

61. Cf. 1 Kings 16:29–33; 18:19; 19:2.

62. Cf. U. Müller, *Die Offenbarung des Johannes*, 112, 118; Klauck, "Das Sendschreiben nach Pergamon," 166.

63. The influence of the false teachers in Sardis also must be considered (cf. Rev. 3:4).

64. Cf. U. Müller, *Zur frühchristlichen Theologiegeschichte*, 17–21.

the church at Thyatira is told: "I do not lay on you any other burden; only what you have, hold fast until I come." As in Acts 15:28, βάρος (burden, in Rev. 2:24) refers to minimal legal requirements that apply also to gentile Christians. Probably in their teaching, the opponents required the minimal legal requirements and claimed for themselves special insights (cf. the "deep things of Satan" in Rev. 2:24 with 1 Cor. 2:10). The knowledge of the true God (cf. 1 Cor. 8:4, 6) enabled them to have unlimited contact with pagan society. They were, in the eyes of the seer, ready for false compromise and a dangerous strategy of accommodation. For John, the ultimate sin was assimilation to the gentile-Roman world and the related distancing from the Jewish tradition. Over against this assimilation, he requires a minimum of distance from the pagan state and its various forms of religious exercises in order to flee from food offered to idols.[65]

How may one classify the opposing groups in the history of early Christianity? The names given to the opponents may suggest the answer. The proselyte Nicolaus (Acts 6:5) fits well into the gallery of forebears of a radicalized post-Pauline Christianity that invoked the position of the beginnings of Christianity in the Jerusalem church. The Nicolaitans denied any binding by OT laws and based this view on their special knowledge. They appeared as traveling apostles or prophets (cf. Rev. 2:2, 20)[66] and successfully advocated interaction with the gentile environment, its institutions, and its meaningless rituals.

Orthodoxy and Heresy

Was a specific claim to truth the basis of conflicts in early Christianity from the beginning, resulting in a defense against falsifications of the "pure, true" teaching? Later church historians, such as Irenaeus of Lyon (around 180 CE), attempt to give this impression, introducing the concepts of apostolic succession[67] and the rule of faith,[68] granting the primacy of the Roman church,[69] and depicting the canon that was being formed as a determining factor in salvation

65. Cf. also S. Schreiber, "Häresie im Kanon?," who maintains that two opposing streams existed in Asia Minor, represented by the Pastoral Epistles and Revelation: "In stream 1 the opening to Roman culture was present, along with assimilation and the reduction of the distance 'to the integration of the societal order.' . . . In stream 2 the demarcation from Roman culture, the resistance to the tendencies to assimilation in prophetic radicality; the latter view appealed for support to the Jewish Christian tradition" (206).

66. Cf. U. Müller, Die Offenbarung des Johannes, 101.

67. Cf. Irenaeus, Haer. 3.3.1: "And we can enumerate the bishops who were installed in individual churches by the apostles as well as their successors until our time."

68. Cf. Irenaeus, Haer. 1.10.1–2: The church "has received from the apostles and their pupils the faith in one God . . . and in one Christ Jesus, the Son of God, who came in the flesh . . . and in the Holy Spirit. This message, which it has received, and this faith that, as reported, preserves the church, although it has spread throughout the world, so carefully as if it lives in one house."

69. Cf. Irenaeus, Haer. 3.3.2–3.

history.[70] This depiction was fundamentally challenged by Walter Bauer, for whom the later classifications of "orthodoxy" and "heresy" can be used in only a limited way or not at all for the understanding of the historical course and theological concepts of the initial period of Christianity. One cannot exclude the possibility that positions later branded as "heretical" at the time of their origin were not perceived as such and were represented in many Christian churches.[71] This perspective developed to become common knowledge among exegetes of NT and patristic exegesis,[72] who undoubtedly correctly observe that from the beginning there were competing concepts in early Christianity (Jerusalem church, Paul), and for the most part we do not know which groups were in the majority. In addition, it was not yet decided which interpretation of the Christ event would prevail. However, was early Christianity a kind of laboratory[73] in which one experimented and still had no fully developed consciousness of truth?

As the oldest literary documents, the letters of Paul already speak another language.[74] Paul not only challenges his churches repeatedly to imitate him (cf. 1 Thess. 1:6; 1 Cor. 4:16; 11:1; Phil. 3:17) but also defines his interpretation of the Christ event in Gal. 1:6–9 as the only possible form of the gospel: "But if we or an angel from heaven preach to you a gospel other than what we preached to you, let him be accursed. As we said previously, so I say to you now: If anyone preaches to you a gospel other than what you have received, let him be accursed." Paul here makes his gospel the norm and permits no other interpretation. In addition, he berates those who think otherwise as "false apostles," "evil workers" (2 Cor. 11:13), "dogs," or "mutilators" (Phil. 3:2–3). One can scarcely conceive of a greater claim, a more sharply laden critique, and a more pronounced consciousness of truth! Paul indicates that, from the

70. Cf. Irenaeus, *Haer.* 4.9.1.

71. Cf. W. Bauer, *Orthodoxy and Heresy*, xxii, "Perhaps—I repeat, *perhaps*—certain manifestations of Christian life that the authors of the church renounce as 'heresies' originally had not been such at all, but, at least here and there, were the only form of the new religion—that is, for those regions they were simply 'Christianity.' The possibility also exists that their adherents constituted the majority, and that they looked down with hatred and scorn on the orthodox, who for them were false believers."

72. For the scholarly discussion after Walter Bauer, cf. Markschies, *Kaiserzeitliche christliche Theologie und ihre Institutionen*, 337–83 (main topic: Can one speak at all of orthodoxy and heresy before Nicaea?).

73. So Markschies, *Kaiserzeitliche christliche Theologie*, 380–81, for the second and third centuries.

74. Cf. Horn, "Wollte Paulus 'kanonisch' wirken?"; E.-M. Becker, "Form und Gattung," 144: "Thus, as a historical letter writer, Paul presents himself finally in his letters as a literary person in whom the dimensions of biographical, letter writing, and theological argumentation of an author come together—an authorial concept that the pseudepigraphical Pauline letters and the pseudepigraphic Petrine letters adopt (in contrast to James)."

beginning, there was a consciousness of truth and falsehood, appropriate and inappropriate, with respect to the Christ event. In the first place it involved three areas of concern: (1) How is the relationship of the new movement of Christians to Judaism to be determined? Does the universal event of the cross and resurrection require a universal perspective or merely a new orientation within Judaism? (2) How is one to understand and define the humanity and divinity of Jesus Christ? What significance is given to the shameful death of Jesus on the cross? (3) How does one deal with the delay of the parousia? Paul provides the standard for all three questions. (1) No NT document requires the circumcision of non-Jews as a condition for acceptance into the eschatological community; that is, the Pauline position (see above, 7.4) has prevailed on this issue, although the Gospel of Matthew and the Letter of James (theoretically) maintain a complete keeping of the Torah. (2) The Pauline theology of the cross was accepted with varying intensity (positively in Mark and John). The core idea, however, is foundational in all NT writings. A soteriological significance is given to the death of Jesus and thus also to his earthly existence. (3) Despite the obvious delay, Paul held firmly to a belief in the imminent parousia (cf. Phil. 4:5: "The Lord is near"). No NT writing has abandoned the expectation of the parousia, but the late writings especially have undertaken independent solutions.

Apparently, a foundation was laid with the Pauline gospel, which (primarily), in connection and (in part) in contradiction, served as a criterion for the further development. Paul functioned "canonically" in three ways. (1) By his tireless engagement for the gospel and by his version of the gospel (cf. Gal. 1:6–9), he wanted to be canonical in the sense of a "norm of the gospel." (2) Paul acted "canonically" with regard to the formation of the canon. A collection of the Pauline letters formed the nucleus of the canon.

As a "book," Paul exercised a lasting effect (see above, 10.3.2). (3) It is no coincidence that all of the writings accepted in the canon have in some way something to do with Paul (see below, 13.5.2). This fact is apparent in the proto- and deutero-Pauline literature as well as in Luke (Paul in Acts) and the Letter to the Hebrews (cf. Heb. 13:22–25). As with the deutero-Pauline literature, Jude and 2 Peter can be understood within the framework of conflict over the Pauline legacy. The Markan and Johannine theology have been influenced by Paul (Jesus Christ as Son of God, theology of the cross); likewise, 1 Peter ("in Christ") is influenced by him. In the Revelation of John, the letters to the churches (Rev. 2:1–3:22) also address issues in the Pauline or post-Pauline churches. Finally, both the Letter of James and the Gospel of Matthew can be understood as writings against Paul or Pauline pupils. The conflicts over the correct understanding of the Christ event were naturally not ended with Paul but lasted into the NT and post-NT time. In the initial period also, it was in no way determined which position the majority held and who would prevail. At the same time, however, no one could ignore the Pauline legacy. In this sense the Pauline claim of truth exercised a great influence, and Paul actually founded that form of Christianity (see above, 8.7) that was later understood as ὀρθός, that is, as "going straight" and "true." At the beginning neither heresy nor orthodoxy stood, but rather at the beginning stood Paul!

11.4 Structures and Offices

After the death of the founding figures, the fall of the Jerusalem church, increasing social problems, conflicts over doctrine, and the further delay of the parousia, it is only natural and necessary when the early Christian churches after 70 CE had to reorient themselves at various levels. A natural level was the question of the organization and leadership of the churches. New leadership structures emerged into the foreground, especially the offices of presbyters and bishops.

Paul and Luke

In the authentic Pauline letters, presbyters do not appear, and they are to be assumed neither in the Pauline churches nor (in the early period) in Jerusalem.[75] This is evident in Paul's writings, for presbyters are not mentioned by him, and he has a different concept of the structure of the church. With the model of presbyter, the matters that make the elders effective in a church are the wisdom and experience of the "older" men. They were probably "elder" in a twofold sense, as they already belonged to the church for a sufficient period of time, possessed a good reputation, and at the same time in most cases they were older in years. With Paul, on the other hand, there was a charismatic concept of the church that is not oriented toward age or gender (see above, 8.3). Instead, what mattered was the call by the Holy Spirit and

---

75. The office of presbyter is of Jewish origin; cf. Campbell, *Elders*, 1–67; Karrer, "Das urchristliche Ältestenamt." It is, of course, disputed when one can assume an office of the ruling elder in the diaspora (of Asia Minor) in the synagogue communities. The office of presbyter probably did not have the prominent position within the Jewish synagogue communities that is often assumed; cf. Ameling, "Die jüdischen Gemeinden." Claussen, *Versammlung, Gemeinde, Synagoge*, 264–73, emphasizes the variety of concepts of presbyter in the Jewish tradition and designates it as "an umbrella concept for all types of leadership positions" (273). D.-A. Koch, *Die Entwicklung der Ämter*, 196, emphasizes: "At any rate there is no evidence in Asia Minor for a collective leadership council."

the capability of being coworkers with their own gifts for the building up of the church (cf. 1 Cor. 12).

Luke depicts another image of the development: In Acts 11:30, Barnabas and Saul are sent to the elders, who are unexpectedly assumed to be in the Jerusalem church. According to Acts 14:23, Barnabas and Paul install elders in the church on the first missionary journey: "They prayed and fasted and entrusted them to the Lord, in whom they had come to believe." In Acts 15:2, 4, 6, and 22, the "apostles and elders" are the ones who negotiate with the Antiochian delegation and determine the essential resolution. Two reasons indicate why a Lukan construction is present here, which does not correspond to historical reality: (1) According to Gal. 2:1–10 the three pillars—James, Peter, and John—determine the destiny of the Jerusalem church and not the "apostles and presbyters/elders." (2) Luke evidently has the task of providing a solid historical and theological foundation for the office of presbyter that exists in his own time. For him the Twelve merge into the group of apostles so that the pre- and post-Easter periods flow together continuously. The presbyters in turn follow the apostles, with whom they already at the apostolic conference establish the most important direction for the history of early Christianity. The Lukan view of continuity anchors the presbyters already in the time of Paul and the Jerusalem church.[76] Thus Luke receives a continuous line of tradition that proceeds from Jesus to the Twelve and the apostles until the presbyters of his own time. The speech at Miletus in Acts 20:17–38 confirms this conception; here the Lukan Paul establishes the elders as representatives of all of the elders in Asia Minor as bishops/overseers (Gk. ἐπίσκοποι) of the church, who have the task by the will of the Holy Spirit to protect the church of God when faced with inner and outer dangers (Acts 20:28–30).[77]

The term ἐπίσκοπος has a Greek origin and designates an official or overseer of an association or a political community.[78] In Paul, only in the late Letter to the Philippians are the ἐπίσκοποι (overseers, administrators) and διάκονοι (helpers, servants) mentioned as offices (Phil. 1:1), yet without more precise explanation. It presumably involves multiple persons who take on generally recognized tasks and whose special position is underlined by being mentioned in the prescript. The linguistic usage suggests that the ἐπίσκοποι occupied a position of leadership within the Philippian church. The term probably refers to leaders of house churches (cf. 1 Cor. 1:14; 16:15–16, 19; Rom. 16:5, 23; Acts

---

76. Cf. D.-A. Koch, *Die Entwicklung der Ämter*, 168ff.

77. For an analysis, cf. H.-J. Michel, *Die Abschiedsrede des Paulus*; Prast, *Presbyter und Evangelium*; Ballhorn, "Die Miletrede—ein Literaturbericht"; Manfred Lang, *Die Kunst des christlichen Lebens*, 316–37; Lindemann, "Paulus und die Rede in Milet."

78. For the semantic analysis, cf. Beyer, "ἐπίσκοπος."

18:8), who placed their houses at the disposal of the church for the meetings and supported the respective churches as a patron in various ways. Their natural authority qualified them for this office as the church in Philippi grew and divided into multiple house churches.[79] Servants (διάκονοι) functioned as helpers of the overseers and were probably responsible for the preparation of the Lord's Supper; furthermore, they were appointed for the collection and administration of the gifts.[80]

On the other hand, especially in the Miletus speech, the Lukan Paul represents an already advanced understanding of the office, for it documents the transition from the presbyter organization to the position of the overseer (ἐπίσκοπος). By the work of the Spirit, "Paul" is a model for the elders in Ephesus (Acts 20:17), who have the instruction "to feed the church of God" (as a shepherd leads the sheep to pasture; cf. Acts 20:28). A responsibility for the entire church is thus given to the overseers. The Miletus speech clearly indicates that Luke implicitly transfers to Paul those functions that previously belonged to the apostles: Paul becomes the determining witness of the tradition and continuity in the church, and he is the one who fulfills the commission by the Exalted One from Acts 1:8 and becomes the essential hero of Luke-Acts.

Conclusion. The office of presbyter cannot be assumed for the Pauline churches, and its existence is unlikely in the Jerusalem church in the early period (at least until the apostolic council), for the model of the three "pillars" is oriented to the familial relationships and the place within the group of disciples. The office of presbyter evidently originated in the second and third generation, as is confirmed in 1 Pet. 5:1–4; James 5:14; Heb. 11:2; 2 and 3 John; and the Revelation of John. Around 80–90 CE, Luke is a representative of this development; for him the office of presbyter is already widespread and progresses toward the office of *episkopos* (overseer), which, in contrast to Phil. 1:1, now has a special, exalted meaning. The merging of the offices of elder and of overseers/*diakonoi* is attested for the end of the first century also in 1 Pet. 5:1–5; 1 Clem. 40–44, especially around 100 CE in the Pastoral Epistles.

The Pastoral Epistles

It was no longer the individual house churches but the local community divided into separate houses modeled after the ancient household that formed the organizational structure commended by the Pastoral Epistles.[81] With a new structure of offices, the isolated churches, threatened by false teaching,

---

79. Cf. Gehring, *House Church and Mission*, 130–96.
80. Cf. Roloff, *Die Kirche*, 143.
81. Cf. Roloff, *Die Kirche*, 255; Campbell, *Elders*, 176–204.

should be brought together as those who belong to one house of God, over which an ἐπίσκοπος (*episkopos*, overseer/bishop) presides.[82] This concept is connected with the basic reference to Paul, as 1 Tim. 3:15 indicates as an example: "but if I am delayed in coming, so that you know how to behave in the house of God, which is the church of the living God, the pillar and ground of the truth . . ." (cf. 2 Tim. 2:20–21; Titus 1:7). The connection with Paul gives the office of leadership in the church its authority.[83] The service in the gospel entrusted by God (cf. 1 Tim. 1:12) is now taken up by Timothy and Titus, who are prototypes of the church leaders. Since Paul was entrusted with the truth of the gospel, the task is given to the church leader to preserve the tradition legitimated by the Pauline proclamation (cf. 1 Tim. 6:20; 2 Tim. 1:14). The author of the Pastoral Epistles stood before the task of merging and giving a new interpretation to two (probably already existing in the churches)[84] forms of church governance. In the Pastoral Epistles one finds statements about both a governance by elders (1 Tim. 5:17–18, 19; Titus 1:5–6) and qualifications and duties for bishops and deacons (1 Tim. 3:2–13; Titus 1:7–9).

The author's goal was not the blending of two structures of governance, for only in Titus 1:5–9 do both offices stand alongside each other without being connected. Instead, the author of the Pastorals favors an episcopal organization, connected with the office of deacon.[85] According to 1 Tim. 3:1 the office of bishop is a good thing, toward which one should strive. The *episkopos* (bishop) has not only authority over the house church but also responsibility for the leadership of a local church, surrounded by deacons as well as elders who carry out their responsibilities. The deacons were clearly subordinate to the bishops; nevertheless, the qualifications are similar (cf. 1 Tim. 3:8–13); the deacons should, according to 1 Tim. 3:9, "hold the mystery of the faith with a pure conscience." The "good conscience" in the Pastoral Epistles is

82. Cf. Dassmann, "Hausgemeinde und Bischofsamt."

83. Cf. Roloff, *Der erste Brief an Timotheus*, 169–89.

84. According to Roloff, *Der erste Brief an Timotheus*, 170, the author does not introduce any new office, but his task is "to integrate the existing offices and ministries as much as possible into an overall view and to transform them with a deeper new interpretation that could correspond to the challenges and demands of his ecclesiastical situation." On the other hand, Merkel, *Die Pastoralbriefe*, 13, explains the tensions between the sayings about church office in the Pastoral Epistles: "The simplest explanation is the assumption that in the churches the office of presbyter was known, while the author wants to introduce the *episkopos/diakonos* (overseer, deacon)." A critical view of these models is given by D.-A. Koch, "Die Einmaligkeit des Anfangs," 209–10, who rejects the idea of a "fusion": "Neither was there a Pauline *episkopos* form of church governance, nor is the office of presbyter characteristic for the Jewish synagogue communities of the first and second centuries CE. The organization and structure of offices in the Pastoral Epistles is thus a new development of the third generation."

85. Cf. Roloff, *Der erste Brief an Timotheus*, 175; Oberlinner, *Titusbrief*, 91.

not, as in Paul, a neutral authority judging the person, but the consciousness of standing in agreement with correct teaching and expected conduct. The deacons should especially "serve well" (1 Tim. 3:13), including functions in the worship service and social tasks in the churches.

The restructuring of the office of *episkopos* that was aimed toward the gradual overcoming of the governance by presbyters is evident in the ordination of Timothy in 1 Tim. 4:14. Indeed, the presbyters lay hands on Timothy (according to 2 Tim. 1:6, Timothy was ordained by Paul); he is ordained to be ἐπίσκοπος of the entire community. Ordination as a spiritual and legitimating institutional act is intended to confer authority on the officeholder for the purpose of preserving the tradition.[86] It was the appearance of the false teachers and their success in the house churches that accelerated the establishment of a functioning leadership office, for the ἐπίσκοπος must be responsible for the entire church (cf. 1 Tim. 5:1–21). As a holy building founded on God, in which the truth that appears in Jesus Christ the only Savior is present (cf. 1 Tim. 3:15–16; 2 Tim. 2:20–21), the church must separate itself from false teaching. Nevertheless, legal categories do not grasp the essence of the office of *episkopos*, which is primarily a spiritual office, for the ability to teach qualifies the church leader (1 Tim. 3:2; Titus 1:9). The bishop is addressed as a householder of God (Titus 1:7–9), who holds on to correct teaching and resists the opponents. The bishop does not rule, but he is the personal guarantor of the unity of the church!

The development of the office of presbyter and *episkopos* continued in the second and third generation and is to be understood as the reaction to new challenges. The collective leadership associated with the office of presbyter of the churches became necessary, as the tasks became increasingly more comprehensive and varied, especially with numerous cells and house churches in one place. Moreover, the various ethnic, social, and theological currents in the church could be better represented by the presbyters.[87] The office of bishop presented a further step within the development, for it responded to an increasing plurality of issues of doctrine and way of life that were perceived as a danger for the unity of the church. Already in Paul the teachers were among the basic offices (1 Cor. 12:28), and for the post-Pauline time Eph. 4:11 attests their continuing importance ("And he himself appointed apostles, prophets, evangelists, shepherds, and teachers"). In the growing diverse churches around

---

86. Cf. Lips, *Glaube, Gemeinde, Amt*, 279: "The significance of ordination as authorization and qualification for the officeholder aims at its official function and authority in the church on the one hand and for the preservation of the tradition by maintaining official continuity on the other hand."

87. Cf. D.-A. Koch, *Die Entwicklung der Ämter*, 198.

the end of the first century, there were increasingly more disputes over doctrine (especially in the churches of the Pastoral Epistles), which led to the concentration on the office of *episkopos*. A clear ethical and theological set of requirements was connected with this office (cf. 1 Tim. 3:1–7); it was concentrated on one person; it contained institutional features (metaphor of the house); and as the superior office, it took on not only a regulative but also an added constitutive significance. The task of the *episkopos* was to ensure the unity of the church by teaching the truth that had been handed on and by demonstrating an exemplary way of life. Ignatius of Antioch can be regarded as a first terminus of this development, for the office of *episkopos*/bishop takes on a major significance (see below, 14.1). The office of deacon, attested already in Paul (Rom. 16:1; Phil. 1:1), is finally coordinated with and subordinated to the office of the *episkopos*. It responds to the increasing social tasks within the church, in which the strict requirements placed on the officeholders (cf. 1 Tim. 3:8–13) witness to the growing significance of this ministry.

11.5. Conflicts with Judaism after 70 CE

After the destruction of the temple, Judaism took on a new form. Of the Jewish groups, only the moderate Pharisees and scribes survived the catastrophe of 70 CE. Together with the surviving priests, not coincidentally, they became the nucleus of the slowly emerging rabbinic Judaism (from rabbi/*rabbouni*, my teacher/my master), for because of the elimination of the temple as the cultic center, the Torah became the absolute center, and the synagogue became the central place of the Jewish religion.[88] The Pharisaically minded rabbis especially played a crucial role in the interpretation of the Torah. In retrospect, this development connected the rabbinic tradition with the coastal town of Jabneh, which became a spiritual center of Judaism under the leadership of Johanan ben Zakkai.[89] A comprehensive legitimation in the form of a succession is given in the tractate Pirqe Avot (Sayings of the Fathers): "Moses received the Torah from Sinai and delivered it to Joshua, Joshua to the elders, and the elders to the prophets. And the prophets handed it to the men of the great synagogue. They said three words: Be deliberate in judgment; raise up many disciples; and make a fence around the Torah. Simon the Just belonged to the remainder of the great synagogue. He said. 'The world rests on three things: on the Torah, on worship, and on the works of mercy.' . . . Hillel and

88. On rabbinic Judaism, cf. Stemberger, *Das klassische Judentum*.
89. Whether this occurred with the consent of the Romans is disputed; on the discussion, cf. P. Schäfer, *Geschichte der Juden in der Antike*, 166–70.

Shammai received the Torah from them.[90] Rabbi Johanan ben Zakkai received the Torah from Hillel and Shammai" (m. Avot 1.1, 11; 2.8). Holiness is no longer bound to the temple and mediated by the cult, but by the Torah as applied by the rabbis, who could trace themselves back to Moses. This practice of the Torah, based on the Pharisaic sanctification of every day, placed regulations relating to purity and food as well as legal issues in the foreground and, not coincidentally, fell into conflict with an (originally) other variant of Judaism, which (predominantly) had become its own movement: Christianity.

In the period after 70 CE, the Gospels (see above, 10.2) are the primary sources reflecting this conflict. Here three different levels are interwoven with each other, which cannot always be disentangled: the level of the conflicts of the historical Jesus with the Pharisees, the level of the church before the writing of the Gospels, and the level of the evangelists themselves. In the final text of a Gospel, they form a unity and document for the time of the evangelist the past and present story of conflict with Judaism. In the Gospel of Mark, written outside Palestine and Syria, no current conflicts with Judaism are evident. Instead, it clearly reflects a distance in relation to Jewish religious practice; individual commands of the Torah and the Sabbath are subordinated to human need (cf. Mark 2:1–3:6), and a clear ethicizing of the tradition is evident (cf. Mark 7:1–23; 12:28–34). The Gospel of Luke and the book of Acts are intensively reflective on the relationship and continuing connection between Christians and Judaism (cf. Luke 1:69, 71, 77; 19:9; Acts 4:23; 7:25; 13:26, 47; 16:17; 27:34–35). At the same time there is also here an ethicizing of the tradition in the interpretation of the law (cf. Luke 10:25–28; 18:18–27; 19:1–10; Acts 10:28; 11:9; 15:10–11) and in the critique of the hypocrisy of the Pharisees (cf. Luke 11:37–54; 18:9–14). Here is a clear distance from Judaism as a religion that is practiced.[91] Current conflicts with forms of Pharisaic-rabbinic Judaism are not evident in Luke.

The situation is totally different in the Jewish Christian Gospel of Matthew (see above, 10.2.2/10.5.2), which was written in Syria (cf. Matt. 4:24). The evangelist Matthew was probably a Jewish scribe (Matt. 13:52: "Therefore every scribe who is trained for the kingdom of heaven is like the master of a household, who takes out of his treasure what is new and what is old"),[92]

90. That is, from the rabbis already named.

91. On the subject of Israel and the law in Luke, cf. the various positions in Klinghardt, *Gesetz und Volk Gottes*; Wolter, "'Reich Gottes' bei Lukas"; Korn, *Die Geschichte Jesu in veränderter Zeit*; Pokorný, *Theologie der Lukanischen Schriften* (cf. also the literature under 10.2.3).

92. Cf. Konradt, *Israel, Kirche und die Völker*, 375: "One may almost say that Matthew has become like a scribe who has become a disciple of the kingdom of heaven, taking out of his treasure something new and something old (Matt. 13:52) and connecting it to a complex theological concept."

who understood himself along with his church as part of Judaism. But the church opened itself to the gentile mission (cf. Matt. 28:16–20) and in a painful process increasingly distanced itself from Judaism.[93] This separation met massive resistance from the Jewish side, as the repression and persecutions against the Matthean Christians indicate (cf. Matt. 10:17–18; 23:34). Distance and conflict with Israel are evident also in the level of language, for example, in the stereotypical speech of "their/your synagogues" (cf. Matt. 4:23; 9:35; 10:17; 12:9; 13:54; 23:34; also 6:2, 5; 23:6) and references to the "scribes and Pharisees" (cf. Matt. 5:20; 12:38; 15:1; 23:2, 13, 15, 23, 25, 27, 29). Matthew unmasks and surpasses the "hypocritical" conduct of the Pharisees and scribes (cf., e.g., Matt. 6:1–18; 23:1–36) with a "better righteousness" (Matt. 5:20) and the complete fulfillment of the original will of God (cf., e.g., Matt. 5:21–48; 6:10b; 12:50; 15:4; 18:14; 19:3–9; 21:31), which appear as the basis for the entry into the kingdom of heaven (cf. Matt. 23:13). The sharp polemic against the scribes and Pharisees is concentrated in the charge that they make false priorities and thus they bar people from entering the kingdom of God.

The Gospel of John also (see above, 10.4.3) contains a reflection of an intensive conflict with Judaism and the related process of separation. At the core of the theological controversy is the charge of ditheism: "Thus the Jews wanted even more to kill him because he not only broke the Sabbath, but also called God his father and made himself equal to God" (John 5:18; cf. 10:33, "It is not because of a good work that we want to stone you, but because of blasphemy, because you have made yourself God, although you are only a man" (cf. also John 10:36; 19:7).[94] The charge of ditheism hit the Johannine community at its core. The evangelist expresses the counterargument: the claim is the sonship of the Son, not a usurpation of godlike dignity or an abandonment of monotheism, but rather it is a precise definition of the

93. On this position and the current scholarly discussion, cf. Schnelle, *History and Theology of the New Testament*, 217–37. The textual evidence is and remains contradictory: On the one side, the fundamental "yes" to the law (cf. Matt. 5:17–20; 23:3a, 23); the limitation of the mission of Jesus to Israel (cf. Matt. 10:5f.; 15:24); the Matthean community may have kept the Sabbath (cf. Matt. 24:20) and oriented itself further to Jewish authorities (cf. Matt. 17:24–27; 23:1–3). On the other hand, consider the universalism of salvation in the Gospel (cf. Matt. 28:18–20; 8:11–12; 10:18; 12:18, 21; 13:38a; 21:43–45; 22:1–14; 24:14; 25:32; 26:13), the abandonment of ritual regulations (cf. Matt. 15:11, 20b; 23:25f.), the ignoring of circumcision, the Matthean critique of the law in the antitheses (Matt. 5:21–48), and the polemic against the Pharisaic casuistry (cf. Matt. 5:20; 6:1ff.; 9:9ff.; 12:1ff., 9ff.; 15:1ff.; 19:1ff.; 23:1ff.). Thus the rejection of Israel has long been a reality for the Matthean church (cf. Matt. 8:11–12; 21:43; 22:9), and the gentile mission is an established practice.

94. Cf. also Mark 14:61–64 par. According to Lev. 24:15–16, the punishment for blasphemy is death by stoning. According to Deut. 21:22–23, the body is to be hanged on a tree; cf. details in Bock, *Blasphemy and Exaltation*.

will of the Father (cf. John 5:19–27 etc.). A further area of conflict was the descent from Abraham (John 8:37–47). Jesus explicitly recognizes the appeal of the Jews (who believe in him) to be Abraham's children (John 8:37);[95] at the same time he says, "If God were your father, you would love me. For I have come from God and now I am here. For I did not come on my own, but that one has sent me" (John 8:42). To be a child of God and Abraham is determined by faith or unbelief in God's Son. The source of unbelief is not in the Jews themselves; instead, unbelief originates in the superhuman power of evil, the devil. "You are from your father, the devil, and you choose to do your father's desires" (John 8:44a). John describes the history of the separation from Judaism likewise in a dramatic way. While in John 1–4 the Jews are depicted positively (cf. John 4:22b: "Salvation comes from the Jews") or neutrally, chapter 5 introduces the increasing conflict of Jesus with hostile Jews, which finds its climax in the sentence of death in John 11:47–53. Both threads are taken up in the passion narrative. Here the Jews appear again as opponents of Jesus (cf. John 18:36; 19:7, 12, 38b), but at the same time, for John, Jesus is "king of the Jews" in a deep and absolute sense (cf. John 19:3, 14, 19, 21–22). Individuals such as Nicodemus (cf. John 3:1–12; 7:50; 19:39), the man born blind (John 9:1–41), or Lazarus (John 11:1–45) also illustrate the division within Judaism. Nicodemus becomes, in contrast to the other leaders of Israel, a follower of Jesus; the healing of the man born blind resulted in either faith or unbelief from the Jews (cf. John 9:16). The resurrection of Lazarus leads many Jews to faith (John 11:45); at the same time the greatest miracle of Jesus becomes the occasion for one to betray Jesus (John 11:46).

Apparently these conflicts led to the expulsion from the synagogue of individual members of the Johannine churches. The term ἀποσυνάγωγος (expel from the synagogue) in John 9:22; 12:42; 16:2 presents the formation of a new term, which appears only in John. Often this process is connected with the insertion of the so-called benediction on heretics (בִּרְכַּת הַמִּינִים) in the Eighteen Benedictions arranged by Shmuel the Small, who is supposed to have completed them under Gamaliel II at the so-called Synod of Jabneh between 85 and 90 CE:[96] "May there be no hope for the apostates, and may the kingdom of the arrogant be quickly uprooted in our days, and may the Nazarenes

---

95. According to the present sequence of the text, Jesus responds to Jews who believe in him (cf. John 8:30–31), so that the sharp critique of Jesus also reflects a conflict with strict Jewish Christians and indicates that John is scarcely to be designated as a Jewish Christian Gospel.

96. For the basis of this argument, cf. Teppler, *Jews and Christians*; for critique, cf. Stemberger, "Birkat ha-minim and the Separation"; Frey, "Von Paulus zu Johannes," 269–71. A direct connection between Jabneh and the Gospel of John is maintained by Martyn, *History and Theology*, 37ff.; Wengst, *Bedrängte Gemeinde*, 48–61.

and the Minim instantly perish, and may they be blotted from the book of
the living and not be written with the righteous. Blessed are you, O Lord,
who humbles the arrogant."[97] The following important reasons indicate the
implausibility of such a direct connection:[98] (1) The events at Jabneh can be
neither historically illuminated nor dated.[99] Jabneh is actually a symbolic place
of the Jewish tradition. (2) The original text of the *birkat-ha-minim* cannot be
precisely reconstructed from later rabbinic tradition. (3) The מִינִים (heretics)
are not primarily Jewish Christians but currents within Judaism that deviated
from the rabbinic course. The insertion of נוֹצְרִים (Jewish Christians) did not
occur until a later period.[100] Very probably the addition of the *birkat-ha-minim*
into the Eighteen Benedictions was aimed at all groups who, from the rabbinic perspective, endangered Jewish unity; it must be considered primarily
an inner-Jewish statement.[101] The text of the Gospel of John is not simply
a reflection of historical events but also a subtle interpretation of the story
of Jesus Christ and the Johannine community aimed at identity formation.[102]
Undoubtedly there were in the history of the Johannine community massive
conflicts with Judaism and probably also separations by both sides, which,
of course, belonged to the past by the writing of the Gospel of John around
100 CE.[103] Three major reasons may be considered: (a) The Johannine Letters
as writings addressed to the contemporary situation of the church nowhere
mention the Jews or Judaism; one finds no OT citations! (b) In the "farewell
address" in the Gospel of John (John 13:31–16:33), which also refers to the
situation of the church, the Jews do not appear. The Fourth Gospel already
looks back to the separation from Judaism.[104] (c) In the theological world of
the Gospel of John, the Jewish religion—in a positive sense as it was lived—
plays no role; rather, John develops its own universal language of images and

97. Cited according to Barrett and Thornton, *New Testament Background*, 211.

98. For further details, cf. Schnelle, *Antidocetic Christology*, 25–30.

99. Cf. Maier, *Zwischen den Testamenten*, 288: "The frequently mentioned 'synod of Jabneh,' conceived according to the model of Christian councils, never took place."

100. For the argument against the originality of נוֹצְרִים, e.g., Johann Maier, *Jüdische Auseinandersetzung*, 137ff.; P. Schäfer, "Die sogenannte Synode von Jabne," 60; P. Schäfer, *Geschichte
der Juden in der Antike*, 168–69.

101. Cf. P. Schäfer, "Die sogenannte Synode von Jabne," 60; Günter Stemberger, "Die sogenannte 'Synode von Jabne,'" 18; Maier, *Jüdische Auseinandersetzung*, 140. The practice of a
curse on Christians is not attested until Justin, *Dial.* 16.4; 47.5, in the middle of the second
century in the synagogue.

102. Cf. Zumstein, "Ausgrenzung aus dem Judentum."

103. Hengel, *Johannine Question*, 298, correctly emphasizes that the Johannine school had
long been separated from the synagogue: "The 'expulsion' lies quite far in the past, and it took
place presumably in various ways."

104. Cf. also Hengel, *Johannine Question*, 121: "The immediate controversy with the Jews
has long ceased to be the main theme of the school." Frey, *Die johanneische Eschatologie*, 2:295.

theology (Logos, truth, grace, life, faith, etc.).[105] The Gospels of Matthew and John primarily indicate that there was a painful history of separation and continuing rivalry between Judaism (after 70) and Christianity. It was even intensified by the *fiscus Judaicus* (cf. above, 9.2), for this compulsory tax necessitated that not only proselytes and Godfearers but also Jews drawn to Christianity, Jewish Christians, Christian Samaritans, and gentile Christians sympathetic to Judaism examine and define (negatively) their relationship to Judaism.

---

105. Hakola ("Johannine Community as Jewish Christians?") expresses a critique of the Jewish Christian classification of the Gospel of John.

12

The Persecutions of Christians and the Imperial Cult

From the beginning, emerging Christianity was subject to local repression (see above, 8.4). The persecution limited to the world capital city, Rome, under the caesar Nero marks a noteworthy turning point: Christians are now perceived to be a separate group and subject to the punishment of death, although they are explicitly depicted by Tacitus and Pliny as innocent. While the (local) persecution under Nero and the general persecution (in Asia Minor) under Trajan are undisputed, as the sources indicate, the question is controversial whether one can speak of a persecution under Domitian, that is, an action against Christians with a denial of their right to exist.[1] The starting point for the investigation should not be the later records of church history (esp. Eusebius)[2] with their schematization, but the pagan and NT traditions alone.

12.1 The Imperial Cult as a Political Religion

The Hellenistic ruler cult developed from the Greek hero cult, which finally made the transition into the Roman imperial cult.[3] One idea was determi-

---

1. Cf. Haug, *Politische Verfolgung*, 34–35, on the rejection of elementary rights to existence and of a person's freedom as the main criteria for persecution.

2. Eusebius wrote his *Historia ecclesiastica* in ca. 303–24 CE; in it he gives a genealogy of the persecutions against Christians: the first persecutor was Nero (cf. *Hist. eccl.* 2.25.4); the second was Domitian (cf. *Hist. eccl.* 3.17.2); on Trajan, cf. *Hist. eccl.* 3.33.

3. Cf. Funke, "Götterbild." The ideal ruler believes "not only in the gods, but also in good intermediate beings [δαίμονας] and heroes [ἥρωας]; these are the souls of virtuous men who have cast off their mortal nature" (Dio Chrysostom, *Or.* 3.54).

native: In the great cultural achievements and victories of history, the deity reveals himself in human form, or the gods choose individuals and elevate them to the level of the divine.[4] One may trace the beginnings of this imperial cult back to the fifth century BCE, where in the Greek cultural realm divine honors were granted to living rulers for the first time.[5] The reasons for the emerging veneration of rulers lie both in the political and in the economic-social area. Rulers were venerated especially for military victories and the related political, economic, and cultural period of flourishing. In terms of religions and culture, the ruler cult cannot be explained from a single cause; one prerequisite was Greek polytheism, and the hero cult probably played an important role. The deeds performed by a preeminent personality were rewarded with honors, and because aid and saving were basic functions of the divine, the thanksgiving and veneration took on a religious dimension. With Alexander the Great (356–323 BCE), the ruler cult took on a new quality. While the ruler cult in the Greek city-states always had only a limited reach, with Alexander a universal element became connected to the ruler cult. His extraordinary personality, his education, his political and military success, but also his early tragic end were the ideal material from which myths could arise. Already in his own lifetime, Alexander probably began with the propagation of the ruler cult, as his visit to the temple of Ammon in the oasis of Siwa in 331 BCE indicates; according to reports, he was addressed there by the deity as son of Zeus (cf. Plutarch, *Alexander* 27). In the Greek cities of Asia Minor, Alexander around 334/333 BCE was verifiably venerated already in his lifetime; it is unclear, however, whether he also demanded this from the Greek cities around the end of his life. Undoubtedly, the ruler cult took on a new quality with Alexander the Great; it is not a coincidence when, for example, Augustus used a seal with the image of Alexander (Suetonius, *Aug.* 50). The successors of Alexander continued the ruler cult. Indeed, the attributes of their names indicate the religious implications of their claim to power (σωτήρ, savior; εὐεργέτης, benefactor). The Ptolemies in particular advocated the ruler cult, taking into account the ancient Egyptian ideology of the pharaoh. Alexander became revered as a god by Ptolemy I within the framework of a new imperial cult. The Romans increasingly turned toward the eastern Mediterranean world and gradually conquered parts of Greece and Asia Minor. The inhabitants of these regions transferred their ruler cult now to the Romans. The Roman Republic, however, offered no possibility of venerating a ruler permanently as a god, but the cities of Greece and Asia

---

4. Cf. Burkert, *Griechische Religion*, 247–48.

5. According to ancient tradition, Lysander was the first Greek to whom an altar was dedicated in 404 BCE, and sacrifices were offered as to a god (cf. Plutarch, *Lysander* 18.3–4).

Minor could pay homage to Rome by venerating the Dea Roma (cf. Tacitus, *Ann.* 4.56.1), and individual Roman governors were praised in the provinces for their beneficence.

The Roman emperor cult was a new element in the Roman religion and developed in the transition from the republic to the principate. A central role belongs to Julius Caesar and Octavian (the later caesar, Augustus).[6] Julius Caesar was venerated already in the east of the empire in the last years of his rule, as inscriptions around 48 BCE indicate.[7] In Rome between 46 and 44 BCE, the veneration also accelerated. He allowed

> honours to be bestowed on him which were too great for mortal man: a golden throne in the House and on the judgment seat; a chariot and litter in the procession at the circus; temples, altars, and statues beside those of the gods; a special priest, an additional college of the Luperci, and the calling of one of the months by his name. (Suetonius, *Jul.* 76 LCL)

His murder in 44 BCE on March 15 indicates, of course, that this development was in no way undisputed. After his death Caesar received "all divine and human honors" (Suetonius, *Jul.* 84.2); he was ceremoniously exalted by apotheosis, recognized as a star[8] among the gods, and was now regarded as the god of the state.

Octavian/Augustus intentionally developed the caesar cult in order to install himself as a religious-political instrument for securing his rule.[9] The public space in large cities such as Ephesus or Corinth was characterized by temples, altars, or images of the imperial cult. Consequently, the early Christians were inevitably confronted with them (cf. 1 Cor. 8:5, "so-called gods"). In intentional connection to his stepfather,[10] Augustus demanded to be venerated both in Rome and in the east of the empire. "He had left small room for the worship of heaven, when he claimed to be himself adored in temples and in the image of

---

6. Inscriptions from the area of the emperor cult appear in Freis, *Inschriften zur römischen Kaiserzeit*, 17–30.

7. Cf. *SIG* 760 (trans. Leipoldt and Grundmann, *Umwelt des Urchristentums*, 2:105).

8. Cf. Bechtold, *Gott und Gestirn*. The deification took place through apotheosis and being recognized as a star; i.e., the caesar was venerated as an eternal star. As in the funeral games for caesar in July 44 BCE, a comet was sighted by ancient witnesses. Octavian interpreted this as a sign of the deification of his adoptive father and his relocation among the stars (cf. Suetonius, *Jul.* 88). Thus the *caterismi*, the placement among the stars, found an entry into the presentation of the rule of the Roman caesar and became a symbol of the apotheosis of the deceased predecessor.

9. On Augustus, cf. above, 3.3.1 under "Wisdom."

10. On the relationship of the names Augustus and Caesar, see Ovid, *Metamorphoses* 15.760, who around 8 CE declares: "So then, that his son might not be born of mortal seed, Caesar must needs be made a god."

godhead by flamens and by priests!"[11] Under Octavian/Augustus a restoration
of the Roman religion followed. Cults were again introduced, temples restored
and reopened. To express divine honor to the caesars, the names of months
and the beginning of the year were changed.[12] Divine attributes were applied
to the caesar: He is eternal, invincible; he cares for his empire; he is tirelessly
active and ever present.[13] Vergil connects a golden age with the appearance of
Augustus, and the critical intellectual Seneca can declare, "A god we believe
him to be, but not because we are commanded."[14] In 27 BCE Octavian received
the familiar divine attribute "Augustus" (exalted one); in 12 BCE Augustus was
chosen to be high priest (pontifex maximus). Augustus appears on numerous
inscriptions and coins as "god" or as "son of God"; he was equally venerated
by the Greeks as well as the Romans.[15] Vergil (Aeneid 6.791–97) was not alone
in connecting the appearance of Augustus with a golden age.

As inscriptions declared, the Roman caesar was the benefactor and savior
of the world; he not only guaranteed the political unity of the empire but
also preserved prosperity, salvation, and meaning.[16] The caesars demanded
to be celebrated as the peacemakers, benefactors, and saviors of the world.[17]
However, they had to demonstrate this quality; that is, the divinity of the
caesar was primarily a description of a function. The caesar cult, with its
veneration of the caesar as divine (in some instances during his lifetime, but
always divinization after death) found numerous followers in Rome, but especially in the provinces[18] it was the inner bond of the empire.[19] It was applied

11. Tacitus, Ann. 1.10.6. Cf. the contrary report in Philo, Legat. 154, according to which
Augustus "rejected . . . being addressed as God"; he was irritated "when anyone addressed
him in this way; and he conceded to the Jews, whose religious horror of such attempts he
recognized fully."

12. Cf. the calendar decree of the "Greeks in Asia"; OGIS 458 (NW I/2:246–47).

13. Cf. Clauss, Kaiser und Gott, 219–79.

14. Seneca, De clementia 1.10.3.

15. Cf. Hoff, Stroh, and M. Zimmermann, Divus Augustus, 186: "Some have interpreted the
circumstance that the Caesar cult was approved only at the level of the provinces in connection
with the Dea Roma as a gesture of ostentatious modesty. The contemporaries could hardly have
missed the true protagonist in the totality of all the signs that Augustus constantly sent out in
order to propagate his superhuman position. . . . The house of Caesar dominated not only the
cultic veneration of the living but also made exclusive claim for it."

16. Cf. the texts in NW I/2:239–57; additional texts and analyses in Jung, ΣΩΤΗΡ, 145–76.
From the numerous texts, an example—the inscription of a speech of Nero in the year 67 in
Corinth—is instructive (cf. NW I/2:249–50), where the altar of Zeus Soter (τῷ Διὶ τῷ Σωτῆρι
(cf. NW I/2:249f.) is dedicated to Nero, and the lord of the world appears as the only savior;
cf. Auffarth, "Herrscherkult und Christuskult."

17. Texts in NW I/2:239–56; also Horace, Carmina 1.12, 45–60 (NW I/1.2 [1]:123).

18. Cf. Cancik and Hitzl, Die Praxis der Herrscherverehrung.

19. Cf. Dahlheim, Die Welt zur Zeit Jesu, 232: "The cult of Caesar bound together all
people between Britain and Syria, and its liturgy was the same everywhere. That amounted to

in different ways by individual caesars. While Tiberius, Claudius, Vespasian, and Titus were rather reserved, Caligula (Suetonius, *Cal.* 22.2–3), Nero,[20] and Domitian intensified the caesar cult to accomplish personal and political aims. The caesar cult was in no way a purely external ritual matter but must be understood as a political-religious phenomenon that affected the inhabitants of the Roman Empire in almost every area in everyday life (temple, statues, and public places, cults, festivals, images, coins, formal dating in letters).

After a certain time, a confrontation between emerging Christianity and the Roman caesar cult was unavoidable, for a structural similarity existed between both: Both the Roman caesar and Jesus Christ were lord, savior, and son of God; they guaranteed salvation, peace, and meaning. These attributes could not permanently apply to two persons, even if the function with the caesar cult and not the nature of the caesar stood in the foreground.[21] Nevertheless, the Roman Empire in the imperial period was, at its core, religiously constituted, for "the Roman Caesar was deity. He was this from the beginning, from the time of Caesar and Augustus; he was this in his lifetime; he was so also in the west of the Roman Empire, in Italy, in Rome."[22] When the Christians, because of their exclusive monotheism, maintained their distance from the cult of caesar (and from the Roman cult as a whole) or even rejected him, they did not recognize the Roman imperial order and fell under political suspicion, for their Kyrios was crucified according to the law.

12.2 Persecution under Nero

The persecution of the Christians in Rome in 64 CE under Nero has a prior history, which began with the Edict of Claudius in 49 (see above, 6.5). With the expulsion of Jews and Jewish Christians from Rome, the situation of the Roman church changed significantly. Whereas the Jewish Christians formed the majority of the church until the Edict of Claudius, after 49 CE they were in the minority (cf. Rom. 1:5, 13–15; 10:1–3; 11:13, 17–31; 15:15, 16, 18). In 56 CE the Roman church must have become large inasmuch as Paul expected material and personal support from them. Finally, the persecution

---

a religious revolution. For the first time in the history of the Mediterranean world, men prayed to one God, who was shared by all."

20. As a classical witness, cf. Nero's declaration of freedom to the Greeks in 67 CE; *SIG* 814 = *NW* I/2:249–50. Cf. also Dio Cassius 63.5, where Nero allowed himself to be worshiped by the Armenian king Tiridates: "I have come to you, my god, in order to worship you as Mithras. I will be what you have determined for me; you are my good fortune and my fate."

21. Of course, in reference to Caligula, Philo, *Legat.* 162, points out: "But Gaius exalted himself, for he not only said, but also believed, that he was a god."

22. Clauss, *Kaiser und Gott*, 17.

in 64 CE presupposes an expanding church that was known in the whole city. Between 49 and 64 CE, a noteworthy process of differentiation may be assumed. (1) With the weakening of the Jewish Christian part of the Roman church, the gentile Christians gained in influence, forcing the separation from the Jewish communities in Rome and, possibly, making it more attractive for those who were Romans by birth to join the new movement from the East. (2) The dominance of gentile Christians probably led the Roman authorities to regard the Christians as an independent movement separate from Judaism. Furthermore, "the enormous multitude" of Christians arrested during the Neronian persecution mentioned by Tacitus (*Ann.* 15.55.4) presupposes that the Roman church had grown very quickly. If without further reasons and with the approval of the population Nero could make the Christians responsible for the fire of Rome, then this movement was already known in the entire city and regarded by the majority of the population as worthy of punishment. This is confirmed in the report of Tacitus (*Ann.* 15.44.2–5) about the fire of Rome and the Christians.[23] Tacitus, on the one hand, explicitly emphasizes that the Christians were innocent of the fire, but he declares with respect to the Christians:[24]

> But neither human help, nor imperial munificence, nor all the modes of placating Heaven, could stifle scandal or dispel the belief that the fire had taken place by order. Therefore, to scotch the rumour, Nero substituted as culprits, and punished with the utmost refinements of cruelty, a class of men, loathed for their vices, whom the crowd styled Christians.[25] Christus, the founder of the name, had undergone the death penalty in the reign of Tiberius, by sentence of the procurator Pontius Pilatus, and the pernicious superstition was checked for a moment, only to break out once more, not merely in Judaea, the home

23. Probably out of fear of Nero, Seneca nowhere mentions the fire of Rome in 64 CE explicitly, but an indirect reference may be present in *Ep.* 91.13: "Perhaps its destruction has been brought about only that it may be raised up again to a better destiny. . . . Timagenes [rhetor who was active in Rome from 55 BCE], who had a grudge against Rome and her prosperity, used to say that the only reason he was grieved when conflagrations occurred in Rome was his knowledge that better buildings would arise than those that had gone down in the flames" (LCL). Cf. also Statius, born in 40 CE, *Silvai* 2.7.60: "You will tell of the criminal firestorm of the guilty ruler that roared over the roofs of the Remus." Dio Cassius does not mention the Christians in his description of the fire of Rome but handed on this report: "One can devise no curse, which the population did not hurl against Nero, in which, of course, no one mentioned his name, as the men only generally cursed the one who started the fire in the city" (62.18.3).

24. On the sources and biases of Tacitus, cf. Cook, *Roman Attitudes toward the Christians*, 39–83.

25. Cf. Köstermann, *Cornelius Tacitus: Annalen*, 254: "The preterit *appellabat* . . . apparently indicates that the name 'Christian' had also been in circulation among the people at that time."

of the disease, but in the capital itself, where all things horrible or shameful in the world collect and find a vogue. First, then, the confessed members of the sect were arrested; next, on their disclosures, vast numbers were convicted, not so much on the count of arson as for hatred of the human race. And derision accompanied their end: they were covered with wild beasts' skins and torn to death by dogs; or they were fastened on crosses, and, when daylight failed were burned to serve as lamps by night. Nero had offered his Gardens for the spectacle, and gave an exhibition in his Circus, mixing with the crowd in the habit of a charioteer, or mounted on his car. Hence, in spite of a guilt which had earned the most exemplary punishment, there arose a sentiment of pity, due to the impression that they were being sacrificed not for the welfare of the state but to the ferocity of a single man. (LCL)

Behind the term flagitia (crimes) one understands the charges that had apparently been made against Christians for a considerable time: isolation, break with Roman tradition, absurd divine honors to a crucified one, foolishness, conspiracy, and what outsiders regarded as strange practices in the context of the Lord's Supper (thus the charges of incest, infanticide, and being a secret cult).[26] The accusations assumed in 1 Pet. 4:15 probably played a role from the beginning: "Let no one among you suffer as a murderer or thief or evildoer." The charge of "superstition" (superstitio) consistently appears in anti-Christian polemic, for, in the Roman view, it was strange and peculiar at the same time that the Christians worshiped a crucified political agitator.[27] Finally, this did not involve a strictly criminal matter, but a moral-political value judgment.[28] The charge, as expressed in the phrase odium humani generis (hatred of humanity) and the related view that Christianity was the cause of all misfortune, was politically explosive.[29] With their exclusive church organization, their social support of needy church members, and their refusal to participate in societal and political life, the Christians drew

26. According to Freudenberger, Das Verhalten der römischen Behörden, 78, flagitia is to be understood as acts/behavior and attitudes that violate good morals. Köstermann, Cornelius Tacitus: Annalen, 254, translates with "scandalous deeds" in his commentary and rejects any weakening of the term. Cook, Roman Attitudes toward the Christians, 49, summarizes his analysis of flagitia; yet it does indicate what pagans thought: that Christians were "bad" people, addicted to all kinds of sins.
27. Cf. also Plutarch, Mor. 140d, which perhaps is a reference to a secret sympathizer, a married woman: "Wherefore it is becoming for a wife to worship and to know only the gods that her husband believes in and to shut the front door tight upon all queer rituals and outlandish superstitions. For with no god do stealthy and secret rites performed by a woman find any favor" (LCL).
28. Cf. Lührmann, Superstitio, 206; also Cook, Roman Attitudes toward the Christians, 51–54. Cicero, Pro L. Valerio Flacco 67, had already called the Jewish faith a barbara superstitio.
29. Cf. Cook, Roman Attitudes toward the Christians, 62–68.

this accusation. Whether already the refusal of the caesar cult stands in the background remains an open question.[30] Tacitus makes similar accusations against the Jews (*Hist.* 5.3–5), who were, however, largely accepted by the Romans (especially by Augustus)[31] as an ancient religion and a national group.[32] The charges made by Tacitus probably reflect an anti-Christian polemic by the Roman elite at the beginning of the second century, but also the hostile attitude of many Romans against the Christians in 64 CE.

Suetonius (*Nero* 16.2) offers another accent in his description of the persecution of Christians under Nero:

During his reign many abuses were severely punished and put down, and new laws were made: a limit was set to expenditures; the public banquets were confined to a distribution of food; the sale of any kind of cooked viands in the taverns was forbidden, with the exception of pulse [legumes] and vegetables, whereas before, every sort of dainty was exposed for sale. Punishment was inflicted on the Christians, a class of men given to a new and mischievous superstition. He put an end to the diversions of the chariot drivers, who from immunity of long standing claimed the right of ranging at large and amusing themselves by cheating and robbing the people. The pantomimic actors and their partisans were banished from the city. (LCL)

Suetonius apparently sees in the persecution of Christians a new ban introduced by Nero and does not treat this persecution in connection with the fire of Rome, which he describes in chapter 38.[33] The description of the movement

30. Thus argued firmly by Hommel, *Tacitus und die Christen*, 182–89, who connects the charge *odium humani generis* with the *laesae maiestatis* ("violation of the majesty of the Roman people and its representative") and thus with the cult of caesar. "The required reverence for the genus humanum toward its protector and benefactor . . . found its legitimate expression in the cult of caesar" (Hommel, *Tacitus und die Christen*, 186). On the other hand, one may object that the texts in Tacitus and Suetonius do not actually indicate this.

31. Cf. Schuol, *Augustus und die Juden*. Schuol emphasizes the good relationship of Augustus to individual Jewish rulers and the imperial reforms that were energetically pursued by the caesar (particularly in procedures of law).

32. On the privileges of the Jews, cf. Philo, *Legat.* 152–58, 305, 311–16; Josephus, *Ant.* 16.162–65; cf. Delling, *Die Bewältigung der Diaspora-Situation*, 49–55; Schuol, *Augustus und die Juden*, 66–144. Among the exceptional rules involving the Jews, besides the freedom from military service and the right to observe the Sabbath, was that they were not forced to participate in the caesar cult; cf. Tacitus, *Hist.* 5.5.5, who wrote about the Jews and the installation/worship of images: "They do not pay such homage to kings, nor to the caesars." The Jews prayed for the caesar and venerated him but did not pray to him as a deity!

33. For the basis of this view, cf. Fiedrowicz, "Christen Verfolgung," 250: "This conclusion in Suetonius can be explained on the basis of compositional factors. He does not arrange his material chronologically, but treats the actions from a systematic standpoint and treats the state-sponsored actions and the transgressions of the caesar separately in order to enumerate

as "novel" and "dangerous to the public" probably is the result of the Christians' common perception as violators of tradition, that is, those who did not orient themselves to the *mos maiorum* (custom/tradition of the ancestors). It is disputed whether Nero gave a special mandate that, independent of the fire of Rome, classified the Christians as a politically dangerous group. This act was not unusual for Nero, for he acted against persons as well as movements that did not participate in the state cult and the veneration of his person.[34] Thus in the year 67 the Stoic Thrasea Paetus was driven to death by Nero because he, as a republican and philosopher, made a public display of his aversion to the caesar cult, which led to the charge against him: "He disdained the religious customs and disregarded the laws" (Tacitus, *Ann.* 16.22.3).

First Clement could confirm that the persecution of the Christians in Rome was not directly connected with the fire of Rome. He assumes the deaths of Peter and Paul in Rome (cf. 1 Clem. 5.2; 6.1) without claiming a connection with the fire. Of course, the precise circumstances of the deaths of Peter and Paul remain unclear (see above, 9.1). Finally, Dio Cassius reports about the fire of Rome[35] without, of course, mentioning the Christians anywhere in his work. The tensions between individual traditions cannot actually be resolved. One can observe the detailed report;[36] in favor of Suetonius, one may note the brief and generally remarkable sequence (sale of cooked food, death penalty for Christians, enjoyment of the charioteer) of the order of Nero.

Inasmuch as Tacitus explicitly calls them innocent and their high ethic was never in question, what led to the persecution of Christians? Probably four interwoven factors played a role.

1. The punishment and/or expulsion of religious groups was no exception but took place repeatedly in the history of the early imperial period. Besides the Edict of Claudius, there were also the expulsions of Jews and Isis devotees under Tiberius (19 BCE) and the prohibition of the practice of the Druid religion by Claudius[37] because this movement was regarded as barbarian! From the Roman perspective, the Christians could be considered only as a new, obscure movement from the Jewish environment. Under Nero's rule, actions were taken against numerous individuals. An event

first the sanctions against the Christians and then to account for the burning of Rome as the negative side of the Neronian government."

34. Nero was especially hostile to philosophers; cf. Philostratus, *Vita Apollonii* 4.35: "Nero was an opponent of every philosophy."

35. Cf. Dio Cassius 62.16–18.

36. According to Malitz, *Nero*, 73, "There is no sound reason to doubt the report of Tacitus."

37. Cf. Suetonius, *Claud.* 25.5, "He utterly abolished the cruel and inhuman religion of the Druids among the Gauls, which under Augustus had merely been prohibited to Roman citizens" (LCL).

from the year 57 CE is noteworthy; the distinguished Pomponia Graecina was prosecuted because of "foreign superstition" (*externa superstitio*; Tacitus, *Ann.* 13.32.) and was handed over to her husband for the verdict. He, of course, declared her innocent. Whether there was a connection to Christianity in Rome can neither be proved nor excluded. Around 61 CE a high jurist warns the senate about slaves: "But now that our households comprise nations—with customs the reverse of our own, with foreign cults or with none, you will never coerce such a medley of humanity except by terror" (Tacitus, *Ann.* 14.44). Here also one cannot exclude a reference to Christianity since the list of greetings in Rom. 16 contains the names of numerous slaves.

2. The Christians were apparently perceived as a group that turned away from the Roman tradition in blatant ways. The charge reported by Suetonius of the "novel" superstition is based on the basic Roman conviction that only the "old" and true Roman gods deserve veneration. Already it is indicated in the Bacchanalian trial in 186 BCE (see above, 6.5) about those who are aberrant: "These are the gods, which our forefathers had appointed to be worshiped, to be venerated, to receive our prayers, not those gods who would drive our enthralled minds with vile and alien rites, as by the scourges of the Furies, to every crime and every lust" (Livy 39.15.2–3 LCL). Especially Cicero repeatedly emphasizes that only the traditional gods should be venerated: "No one should have gods for himself, neither new nor foreign except for the officially recognized ones; at home one should venerate the gods, whose veneration was already inherited from the ancestors."[38] The religious laws/customs formed the basis of the empire (cf. Cicero, *Leg.* 2.19–23); they are the foundation and part of the cultural system, and not to observe them can be interpreted as the endangerment of the political and social order. Christians avoided most of the festivals and official celebrations because these events were always connected to pagan gods and the imperial cult, and thus they caused indignation.[39] From the Roman point of view, they were not a *religio*, but rather a *superstitio*, for early Christianity lacked all of the traditional attributes of an ancient "normal" religion (cf. Cicero, *Leg.* 2.19–41): (a) veneration of the gods according to the traditions of the ancestors; (b) sanctuaries; (c) sacred

38. Cicero, *Leg.* 2.19; cf. also 2.25–26: "When one worships his own, new, or foreign gods, this means a danger to the religious order and demands religious ceremonies that are unknown to our priests. The gods inherited from the fathers may be worshiped only if also the fathers obeyed this law." According to Cicero, the mystery religions, into which he and his conversation partners were initiated, are the only exception (cf. *Leg.* 2.35–36).
39. Cf. T. Schmitt, *Die Christenverfolgung unter Nero*, 530–31.

customs of the family and ancestors; (d) public sacrificial ceremonies; and (e) various priests for various gods. Thus the early Christians soon fell into a double conflict: from the Romans and from the Jews. The latter, people regarded by the Romans as an "ancient" and acceptable religion, had to distance themselves from the Christians in order not to lose their special privileges. It is scarcely coincidental that the Jews in Rome were not persecuted by Nero.

3. Nero intensified the ruler cult[40] and, like Caligula, depicted himself as divine. He demanded to be venerated as Mars and the sun god; temples and colossal statues were erected for the state god Nero, and the earthly home of a god was the "Golden House." In addition, the declaration of freedom for the Greeks and the homage to Nero by the great king Tiridates ("I come to you as my god") illustrate the absolute ruler cult.[41] The Christians probably maintained a distance from the caesar cult and thus were considered as a group that stood outside the society.

4. The practice of punishing religious minorities, the perception of Christians as enemies of Roman religious tradition, and the place of the caesar in Rome played an important role in the conflagration that broke out on July 18, 64 CE.[42] The fire raged for six days, and the caesar, who dwelled outside the city, came in only as his own palace was threatened by fire. This infuriated the people, and the rumor spread that the caesar himself, in his self-indulgence, had set the fire in order to build the world capital according to his plans.[43] In order to extinguish the erupting wrath of the people, a guilty party had to be found. The Jews would have been a possible group, but they had been protected as an ancient religion to a certain extent, and they had two powerful advocates: one was Nero's wife Poppaea, whom Josephus (*Ant.* 18.189–96) calls a "Godfearer" and who must have been in some form favorable to Judaism. Another advocate was the actor Aliturus, who was of Jewish descent and stood in high regard with Nero (cf. Josephus, *Life* 16). Two years before the outbreak of the Jewish War, moreover, it did not appear appropriate to fuel the conflict with the Jews/Judaism. Thus the obvious solution was to make the splinter group from Judaism, the Christians, responsible and to punish them. This may also have been the purpose of Tigellinus, the powerful prefect of the praetorium, and Balbillus, the palace astrologer, who was a known

40. A clear indication for this is the rapidly increased usage in the papyri of the title κύριος for the ruler at the time of Nero; cf. Arzt-Grabner, "Neues zu Paulus," 146–49.

41. Dio Cassius 63.5; extensive material is given by Clauss, *Kaiser und Gott*, 98–111.

42. Cf. Malitz, *Nero*, 69–81.

43. This claim appears independently in various traditions; cf. Seneca, *Ep.* 94.61; Tacitus, *Ann.* 15.67; Dio Cassius 62.18.3.

hater of the Jews.[44] What Nero or his advisers knew about Christianity must remain an open question. Probably a mixture from his proximity to Judaism and—from the Roman perspective—fully absurd teachings (a crucified man as son of God) sufficed to brand this group, known in the city and yet manageable, as the scapegoat for the fire. The savage punishments correspond to the punishments of those found guilty of arson (the arsonist was himself burned);[45] furthermore, one must consider a lynch-mob mentality that had been stirred up. Finally, however, it is crucial that the Christians were considered worthy of punishment because of their teachings, their faith, and their suspicious behavior. It is evident that already under Nero they were regarded as an un-Roman, dangerous movement. This aspect is strengthened when one takes the report of Suetonius as the starting point: The Christians were punished with death because they were Christians; that is, there was already the accusation with Nero of injury to the dignity of the Roman people and its representative (on *laesae maiestatis*, see below, 12.4), caused by a clear distance from the caesar cult.

Conclusion. In any case, one can speak of a Neronian persecution, for the action against the Christians was open, systematic, and intended for annihilation. It was limited to Rome, but all of the dramatic events in the world capital penetrated with some delay into the provinces. In addition, the new movement must have been known to the elite in 64 CE even if the knowledge about them varied. Thus the Neronian persecution cannot be minimized as an isolated case that was not significant for the early churches outside Rome.[46] From this point onward, the Christians were considered as an un-Roman movement worthy of punishment, whose existence was constantly in danger.[47]

44. The influence of the palace astrologers cannot be overestimated; their task was to interpret heavenly phenomena or catastrophes and recommend measures to the caesar, i.e., especially the punishments (cf. Suetonius, *Nero* 36).

45. Cf. Digesta 47.9; also Malitz, *Nero*, 75. Here one cannot establish the alternative, according to which Christians were punished as arsonists, but not as Christians (so Frenschkowski, "Nero," 867). Because they were Christians, they could be punished as (alleged) arsonists.

46. The historicity of the Neronian persecution has occasionally been disputed. See, for example, Shaw, "Myth of the Neronian Persecution," 73: "Although the passage is probably genuine Tacitus, it reflects ideas and connections prevalent at the time the historian was writing and not the realities of the 60s." Also Öhler (*Geschichte des frühen Christentums*, 286–88) speaks of an "ancient historical construction." The reference to the exchange of letters between Pliny and Trajan (around 110 CE), the differences with Tacitus and Suetonius, and the political-literary strategies (portrayal of Nero) of Tacitus around the year 115 CE are in no way sufficient to doubt the historicity of an event attested by two Roman historians (Tacitus and Suetonius) and by 1 Clement. On the historicity, cf. the good arguments of Fiedrowicz, "Christen Verfolgung," 250–52.

47. Cf. Vittinghoff, "'Christianus sum,'" 355: "From Nero's time, 'Christianus sum' was a latent political offense."

12.3 Persecution under Domitian?

The ancient pagan sources consistently portray a negative image of Domitian (born 51 CE; caesar 81–96 CE).[48] From 85 CE he had himself named "dominus et deus noster" ("our Lord and God," Suetonius, *Dom.* 13.2).[49] The satirist Martial (ca. 38–102 CE) repeatedly mocked Domitian as "Lord and God of the world"[50] and reports that, under Trajan (98–117 CE), this address was abolished (*Epigrams* 4.30; 8.2; 10.72: "I am not about to speak of 'lord and god'; there is no place for you anymore in this city"). Domitian is called "leader of human-kind and father of the gods"[51] by Statius (born first century CE), and on coins Domitian is the first Roman caesar to be depicted with the lightning flash of Jupiter.[52] Juvenal (born around 55 CE) ultimately calls the baldheaded Domitian a second Nero.[53] These are in no way only signs of a "bizarre vanity"[54] but also indications of an intensification of the caesar cult; likewise are the conferring of honorary titles on cities (especially in the province of Asia) and the associated (sacral) building activity.[55] This is confirmed by the contemporary witness and politician, Pliny the Younger (see below, 12.4), who describes the changes in the claim to power/caesar cult from Domitian to Trajan as a political action.[56]

48. A portrait of Domitian is given in L. Thompson, *Book of Revelation*, 96–115; Urner, *Kaiser Domitian*. Both scholars attempt to give a new evaluation of the (dark) image of Domitian.

49. Cf. also Dio Cassius 67.4.7: "For he even insisted upon being regarded as a god and took vast pride in being called 'master' and 'god.' These titles were used not merely in speech but also in written documents."

50. In Martial, the following designations have been given: *Epigramme* 5.5 and 7.2.5, "god"; 7.34, "Lord and God"; 8.2, "Lord of earth and God of all things"; 9.66, "imperial god."

51. Statius, *Silvae* 4.3.139; on the other hand, according to *Silvae* 1.6.83–84, in the framework of a drunken feast Domitian rejected the address "dominus." On the sacral elevation of Domitian by Statius, Calpurnius Siculus, and (in part) Martial, cf. Leberl, *Domitian und die Dichter*.

52. In Martial, *Epigramme* 7.70 and 8.24, Domitian is compared with Jupiter; on the enactment of Domitian as deity, cf. Clauss, *Kaiser und Gott*, 119–32.

53. Juvenal, *Sat.* 4.38: "As the last Flavian was flaying the half-dying world and Rome was enslaved to a baldheaded Nero . . ."

54. So Timpe, *Domitian als Christenfeind*, 217, who attributes the image of Domitian as the persecutor of Christians exclusively to later Christian history writing.

55. Cf. Dräger, *Die Städte der Provinz Asia*, 107–229; Tóth, *Der himmlische Kult*, 97–120. Among Ephesus, Smyrna, and Pergamum—the first three churches in the letters to the churches—an embittered dispute over rank developed at the time of Domitian, which was intentionally inflamed by the caesar.

56. Cf. Pliny the Younger, *Panegyricus* 2.3.4, where it is reported about Domitian, "Times are different, and our speeches must show this; . . . Nowhere should we flatter him as a divinity and a god"; in 52.3.4 Trajan is directly addressed and placed in a positive contrast to Domitian: "Of your statues, only one or two are to be seen in the vestibule of the temple of Jupiter Best and Highest, and these are made of bronze; whereas only recently every approach and step, every inch of the precinct, was gleaming with silver and gold, or rather, was casting pollution, since the figures of the gods were defiled by having statues of an incestuous emperor in their midst" (LCL).

Around the end of his time in power, Domitian intensified the pressure on the opposition (cf. Suetonius, *Dom.* 14.4; 10.5; 11.1–3). Besides the execution of opponents that had taken place throughout the year (cf. Dio Cassius 67.31.2), in 93 CE he had all of the philosophers driven from Rome and Italy (Suetonius, *Dom.* 10.3; Dio Cassius 67.13.1ff.),[57] and in 95 CE he arranged the execution of his cousin T. Flavius Clemens and the banning of his wife Flavia Domitilla, who were probably Christians:

> And the same year Domitian slew, along with many others, Flavius Clemens the consul, although he was a cousin and had to wife Flavia Domitilla, who was also a relative of the emperor's. The charge brought against them both was that of atheism [ἀθεότης], a charge on which many others who drifted into Jewish ways [τὰ τῶν Ἰουδαίων ἤθη] were condemned. Some of these were put to death, and the rest were at least deprived of their property. Domitilla was merely banished to Pandateria. (Dio Cassius 67.14.1–2 LCL)[58]

Domitian's attitude toward the Jews, which was critical and hostile to them, is reflected also in the intensification of the *fiscus Judaicus* around 96 CE (cf. Suetonius, *Dom.* 12.2). After the first Jewish War, the diaspora Jews in particular had to pay the Romans an annual tax of two denarii, analogous to the earlier temple tax (cf. Josephus, *J.W.* 7.218; Dio Cassius 64.7.2). Proselytes and Godfearers and individual Jewish Christians were probably affected by this measure (see above, 9.2).

The personal hostility between Dio of Prusa (ca. 40–120 CE) and Domitian is noteworthy. Dio Chrysostom was banned by Domitian (Dio, *Or.* 13.1) and expressed himself sharply about the caesar: "How I bore my exile, not succumbing to loss of friends or lack of means or physical infirmity; and, besides all this, bearing up under the hatred, not of this or that one among my equals, or peers as they are sometimes called, but rather of the most powerful, most stern man, who was called by all Greeks and barbarians both master and god [καὶ δεσπότην ὀνομαζόμενον καὶ θεόν], but who was in reality an evil demon" (Dio, *Or.* 45.1).[59]

---

57. Cf. also Epictetus, *Diatr.* 4.13.5, where Epictetus reports that Domitian's secret police are soldiers dressed as citizens and begins to complain about the caesar: "And then you too, just as though you had received from him some guarantee of good faith in the fact that he began the abuse, tell likewise everything you think, and the next thing is—you are led off to prison in chains" (LCL).

58. For the analysis of the text, cf. Lampe, *Die stadtrömischen Christen*, 166–72, who sees only a Christian in Domitilla. On the other hand, Flavius Clemens, as father and possibly a successor of Domitian, was executed (cf. Suetonius, *Dom.* 15.1).

59. Cf. also Perry, "Critiquing the Excess of Empire": Why the address "dominus ac deus" is to be considered "a false generalization of a common address by caesar's rabble" (thus Eck, "Domitianus," 749) is a mystery to me.

A reflection of the persecution of Christians under Domitian is probably present in Dio Cassius 61.1–2, in a report about the innovations of his successor, Caesar Nerva (96–98 CE):

Nerva also released all who were on trial for *maiestas* [ἐπ' ἀσεβείᾳ, insulting the sovereign] and restored the exiles; moreover, he put to death all the slaves and the freedmen who had conspired against their masters and allowed that class of persons to lodge no complaint whatever against their masters; and no persons were permitted to accuse anybody of *maiestas* or of adopting the Jewish mode of life [οὔτ' ἀσεβείας, οὔτ' Ἰουδαϊκοῦ βίου]. Many of those who had been informers were condemned to death, among others Seras, the philosopher. (LCL)

At the time of Domitian, apparently, an atmosphere of denunciation of political opponents and philosophers was rampant, but Christians also fell victim. Thus the combination of insulting the sovereign and "acceptance of a Jewish way of life" could scarcely have referred to open or hidden conversion to Judaism;[60] instead it refers to Christians.[61]

Whether Domitian initiated a major persecution is disputed.[62] His biographers were, as a rule, focused on the senate (Suetonius, Tacitus) and intentionally downplayed the image of the caesar.[63] Within the NT, 1 Peter and Revelation are the two writings in which allusions to the persecution under Domitian may be present.

1 Peter

First Peter presupposes a current conflict situation between the church and its environment. The terminology already signals this topic; of forty-two πάσχειν references in the NT, twelve appear in 1 Peter! Did the suffering of Christians in Asia Minor involve local repression, or must one assume that

---

60. Heemstra, *The Fiscus Judaicus and the Parting of the Ways*, 67ff., however, associates this statement with the *fiscus Judaicus*.

61. Cf. Kübler, "Maiestas," 551: "Ἀσέβεια is also lack of reverence, *reverentia*, and that is the *crimen maiestatis* (usually one translates ἀσέβεια with *impietas*). Thus sacrilege, Christianity, and later heresy are punished as *crimen laesae maiestatis*."

62. For skeptical to negative views, see, e.g., Freudenberger, "Christenverfolgungen," 25; K. Aland, *Das Verhältnis*, 224; A. Collins, *Crisis and Catharsis*, 69ff.; Ulrich, "Euseb, *HistEccl* III,14–20" (Eusebius portrays Domitian as a second Nero); Witulski, *Kaiserkult in Kleinasien*, 53–77; D.-A. Koch, *Geschichte des Urchristentums*, 468, "Neither for Rome nor for Asia Minor can one speak of a change in the danger for Christian communities between 75 and 100 CE." Stauffer, *Christ and the Caesars*, 172, represents the classical counterposition: "We read the apocalypse with entirely new eyes as an apostolic counterdeclaration against the declaration of war by the divine Caesar in Rome."

63. Cf. Hanslik, "Domitian," 125.

already comprehensive actions against the Christians are taking place? The textual evidence offers a differentiated picture. In 1 Pet. 2:21–25; 3:18; and 4:1 the suffering of Christ is connected to the suffering of Christians. The example of the suffering of Christ shapes the readiness to suffer among Christians. Suffering appears as a constitutive part of Christian existence, the natural result of the fact that believers are strangers in the world (cf. 1 Pet. 1:6–7; 5:9–10). The connection between "suffering" and "affliction" (1 Pet. 2:19), "bear patiently" (1 Pet. 2:20), "being slandered" (1 Pet. 2:23), and "do good" or "do evil" (1 Pet. 3:17; 4:15, 19) indicates a form of social discrimination. Christians publicly bear witness to their faith; they distinguish themselves from their environment by their ethos (cf. 1 Pet. 2:11–18; 3:1–4, 7, 16) and thus evoke unjust sanctions. A few passages in 1 Peter, however, cannot be sufficiently explained as a reaction to social tensions. According to 1 Pet. 4:15–16, Christians are condemned before a court like murderers, thieves, and evildoers because they are Christians (ὡς Χριστιανός); "Let no one among you suffer as a murderer or thief or evildoer, . . . but if anyone suffers as a Christian, do not be ashamed, but glorify God with this name." The explicit reference to the "name" could be a reference to the *nomen ipsum*, that is, Christians suffer like thieves and murderers only because they are Christians. They will be punished with death. A purifying fire is about to break out over the Christians (cf. 1 Pet. 4:12 NRSV, "Beloved, do not be surprised at the fiery ordeal that is taking place among you to test you, as though something strange were happening to you"). Christians should resist the devil, who goes around the entire world and inflicts the same suffering on all Christians (1 Pet. 5:8–9). Here suffering clearly has a different perspective and quality; it involves more than local repression.[64] If one takes this differentiation within 1 Peter seriously and does not minimize it as mere rhetorical figures, then the *nomen ipsum* and the metaphor of the "fiery ordeal" point to the late period of Domitian.[65] Moreover, an allusion to the caesar cult may be present in 1 Peter 2:13: The caesar appears as a human creation and is thus subordinated to the κύριος Ἰησοῦς Χριστός (Jesus Christ, the Lord).

Revelation

The Christians in Revelation saw themselves as subject to many afflictions. False teachers threatened the identity of the churches from the inside (cf. Rev. 2:2,

---

64. Cf. Reichert, *Eine urchristliche praeparatio ad martyrium*, 74–75; contra Brox, *Der erste Petrusbrief*, 30: "The letter can be explained adequately from the 'daily situation' of the early church."

65. For example, Feldmeier (*Der erste Brief des Petrus*, 27) dates 1 Peter in the time of Domitian (81–90); Gielen, "Der erste Petrusbrief." Contra D.-A. Koch, *Geschichte des Urchristentums*, 443, 477–79, who assumes the legal situation under Trajan and dates the letter ca. 115 CE.

6, 14, 20ff.). There was also concern about lukewarmness in faith (Rev. 2:4–5; 3:15–16); some churches were powerless (Rev. 3:8) and "dead" (Rev. 3:1). From the outside, there was not only the danger of war (Rev. 6:2–4),[66] inflation (Rev. 6:5–6), and pressure from the Jews (Rev. 2:9–10; 3:9) on the churches, but in Asia Minor the horrible beast, the Roman emperor, ruled (Rev. 12:18–13:10) and with him the second beast, the imperial priesthood (Rev. 13:11–17; 16:13–14; 19:20). It propagates the ruler cult as an obligatory declaration of loyalty for all citizens in the form of worship of the caesar's image (cf. Rev. 14:9: "Then another angel, a third, followed them, crying with a loud voice: 'Those who worship the beast and its image, and receive a mark on their forehead or on their hands . . .'").[67] Numerous institutions of the cult of caesar existed in the seven cities addressed in Revelation.[68] In Ephesus a statue of Domitian that was four times larger than life size stood in the temple of caesar;[69] in Pergamum a temple of Zeus towered over the city;[70] Smyrna was also a center of the emperor cult. The church sees itself subjected to the excessive claim to power by the Roman Empire and depicts that in a language detailed in its images and symbols. The seer describes the rage of the beast (Rev. 13; 17; 18); the letters to the churches provide the historical background.[71] Christians are oppressed (Rev. 2:9) and thrown into prison (Rev. 2:10), and one witness has already been killed (Antipas in Rev. 2:13; cf. Rev. 6:9–11). The hour of testing now comes over the world (Rev. 3:10).[72] Presumably in the churches were currents that advocated a moderate cooperation with the emperor cult. It undoubtedly had a great power of attraction, which is consistently portrayed as a seductive woman (Rev. 17:1, 5; 19:2; 21:8; 22:15). However, the seer demands a minimum of distance with respect to the pagan state and its various forms of religious activity in order to flee from idolatry.[73] He unmasks

66. Revelation 6:2 could refer to the Parthian invasions (cf. Rev. 9:13ff.; 16:12); Rev. 6:3–4 could refer to conflicts within the empire; U. Müller, *Die Offenbarung des Johannes*, 167; Roloff, *Die Offenbarung des Johannes*, 81.

67. While explicitly referring to Rev. 14:9–11, Bousset (*Die Offenbarung Johannis*, 386) observes a tendency in the Apocalypse: "It is a manifesto of war against the cult of Caesar."

68. Cf. the correct observation of Burkert, *Griechische Religion*, 248: "The entire political organization of Asia Minor orbited around the Emperor Cult."

69. Cf. Elliger, *Ephesos*, 96–99.

70. Deissmann, *Light from the Ancient East*, 13, E. Lohmeyer, *Die Offenbarung des Johannes*, 25, identifies this temple as the "throne of Satan" in Rev. 2:13; arguments for a sanctuary of the emperor cult are made by, e.g., U. Müller, *Die Offenbarung des Johannes*, 110; Klauck, "Das Sendschreiben nach Pergamon," 161; on the religious "infrastructure" of Pergamum, cf. Klauck, "Das Sendschreiben nach Pergamon," 157–59.

71. Within this mythological context, the references to persecutions or killings in Rev. 11:7–9; 13:15; 17:6; 18:24; and 20:4 cannot be connected with historical events with certainty.

72. Cf. Lona, "Treu bis zum Tod."

73. The distancing of Christians from the gods and the emperor cult was probably only one reason for the endangerment of the churches. Similarly problematic in the eyes of the seer was the

the allegedly all-powerful Roman state and propagates an alternative world in which God's power will prevail.[74]

Concrete references to Domitian and his claim to power are present in many passages. (a) The phrase ὁ κύριος καὶ ὁ θεὸς ἡμῶν (our Lord and God) in Revelation 4:11, as in John 20:28, is in direct antithesis to the address demanded by Domitian, reported in Suetonius (*Dom.* 13.2): *dominus et deus noster* (cf. also Rev. 15:4; 19:10; 20:4; 22:9). In addition, 1 John 5:21 ("Children, keep yourselves from idols") probably alludes to the emperor cult. (b) The eyes of Christ, the heavenly Son of Man, are described in Rev. 1:14 as "like a fiery flame," an image that corresponds both to the portrait of Augustus (Suetonius, *Aug.* 79.2) and to Domitian (Statius, *Silvae* 1.1.99–104. (c) The legend of Nero redivivus presupposed in Rev. 13 and 17 is most convincingly associated with the figure of Domitian.[75] (d) The description of God on his throne in Rev. 4:8b ("Holy, holy, holy is God the Lord, the Almighty, who was and is and who is to come") is contrasted to the imperial throne, which will fall in the eschatological battle. (e) The decree ordered by Domitian around 92 CE (Suetonius, *Dom.* 7.2; 14.2)—and then not carried out—to destroy the vineyards in the provinces is evidently referred to in Rev. 6:6. (f) The reception of Revelation in the ancient church likewise indicates a dating under Domitian. Eusebius (*Hist. eccl.* 3.39.6, 12) assumes that Papias (around 120 CE) knew Revelation. Justin mentions it in *1 Apol.* 28.1; and *Dial.* 81.4; Irenaeus, *Haer.* 5.30.3 dates it explicitly in the time of Domitian.[76]

Conclusion. A large-scale persecution of Christians under Domitian cannot be proved. However, the intensification of the emperor cult in Asia Minor led to local repression and persecution[77] that clearly went beyond isolated instances.[78]

---

silent assimilation to pagan religiosity in its various forms. It undermined the purity of individual churches; assimilation thus appeared as a subtle form of apostasy; cf. U. Müller, *Die Offenbarung des Johannes*, 113 and passim; Klauck, "Das Sendschreiben nach Pergamon," 181–82.

74. Cf. M. Labahn, "'Gefallen, gefallen ist Babylon.'"

75. Cf. Giesen, "Das Römische Reich," 2566–70.

76. Cf. Schnelle, *History and Theology of the New Testament*, 517–37; those who advocate a dating of Revelation under Domitian in contemporary exegesis include also Witetschek, "Ein weit geöffnetes Zeitfenster?"; Mucha, "Ein flavischer Nero"; M. Labahn, "'Gefallen, gefallen ist Babylon,'" 325. A different historical placement of Revelation is given by Thomas Witulski; for him it belongs to the time of Hadrian (117–38 CE) and was written between 132 and 135. "Against Christian circles, which considered the participation of Christians in the cultic-religious veneration of Hadrian and sought to justify it, the apocalyptist encourages his addressees toward uncompromising refusal and admonishes them to remain steadfast and faithful in the presence of a pagan environment." Witulski, *Die Johannesoffenbarung*, 350; cf. also D.-A. Koch, *Geschichte des Urchristentums*, 481–93.

77. Cf. U. Müller, *Die Offenbarung des Johannes*, 260.

78. Contra D.-A. Koch, *Geschichte des Urchristentums*, 483, who describes a persecution under Domitian as historical fiction.

This view is supported by the increased claim to power under Domitian,[79] statements in 1 Peter and Revelation, the repeated references to danger because of the emperor cult, and the simple *nomen ipsum* as a reason for persecution. In addition, the correspondence between Pliny and Trajan gives five references to persecution, which could have taken place already under Domitian.[80] (1) Pliny is unclear about the legal situation in trials against Christians (*Ep.* 10.96) but presupposes such trials. (2) If Christians are reported openly or anonymously (cf. *Ep.* 10.96.2, 5, 6), then the ones who report know that Christians can/must be reported and that action will be taken against them. (3) The well-considered action of Pliny to let Christians who were accused pray to the gods and caesar and offer sacrifices (*Ep.* 10.96.5) points to an established practice, for (4) it is reasonably assumed that genuine Christians would not let themselves be forced to do so. This presupposes that such a practice had been common in Asia Minor for a long time and that there had already been a considerable number of trials against Christians. (5) They are mentioned by Pliny himself: according to *Ep.* 10.96.6, those who were denounced had revoked their faith three years previously, and many a longer time in the past, and many even twenty years earlier, that is, during the reign of Domitian.[81] Indeed, a geographical connection also exists: 1 Peter is explicitly addressed to Christians in Pontus and Bithynia, where under Pliny there were persecutions against Christians.

12.4 Pliny and Trajan concerning Christianity

The correspondence between Pliny and Trajan is the earliest extant evidence for the legal bases of the persecution of Christians. Pliny the Younger (born 61 CE), dispatched by Trajan the emperor (98–117 CE) as a special envoy with extraordinary authority in the province of Bithynia-Pontus between 110 and 112[82] to restore public peace (*Ep.* 10.96), writes to the caesar:

[1]It is my custom to refer all my difficulties to you, Sir, for no one is better able to resolve my doubts and to inform my ignorance. I have never been present at an examination of Christians. Consequently, I do not know the nature or

79. Cf. also Eck, "Domitianus," 749: "The intensification of the veneration of the ruler is to be seen in the erection of the giant temple of Caesar in Ephesus and in the reaction that it received in Revelation."

80. For the basis of the following arguments and the discussion, see below, 12.4.

81. Cook, *Roman Attitudes toward the Christians*, 161, also thinks of isolated persecutions under Domitian.

82. According to Alföldy, "Die Inschriften des Jüngeren Plinius"; somewhat different is the view of Freudenberger, *Verhalten der römischen Behörden*, 17 (111–113 CE); Cook, *Roman Attitudes toward the Christians*, 143 (Pliny's arrival in 109 or 110 CE).

the extent of the punishments usually meted out to them, nor the grounds for starting an investigation and how far it should be pressed. [2]Nor am I at all sure whether any distinction should be made between them on the grounds of age, or if young people and adults should be treated alike; whether a pardon ought to be granted to anyone retracting his beliefs, or if he has once professed Christianity, he shall gain nothing by renouncing it; and whether it is the mere name of Christian which is punishable, even if innocent of crime, or rather the crimes associated with the name. For the moment this is the line I have taken with all persons brought before me on the charge of being Christians. [3]I have asked them in person if they are Christians, and if they admit it, I repeat the question a second and third time, with a warning of the punishment awaiting them. If they persist, I order them to be led away for execution; for, whatever the nature of their admission, I am convinced that their stubbornness and unshakeable obstinacy ought not to go unpunished. [4]There have been others similarly fanatical who are Roman citizens. I have entered them on the list of persons to be sent to Rome for trial. Now that I have begun to deal with this problem, as so often happens, the charges are becoming more widespread and increasing in variety. [5]An anonymous pamphlet has been circulated which contains the names of a number of accused persons. Among these I considered that I should dismiss any who denied that they were or ever had been Christians when they had repeated after me a formula of invocation to the gods and had made offerings of wine and incense to your statue (which I had ordered to be brought into court for this purpose along with the images of the gods), and furthermore had reviled the name of Christ: none of which things, I understand, any genuine Christian can be induced to do. [6]Others, whose names were given to me by an informer, first admitted the charge and then denied it; they said that they had ceased to be Christians two or more years previously, and some of them even twenty years ago. They all did reverence to your statue and the images of the gods in the same way as the others, and reviled the name of Christ. [7]They also declared that the sum total of their guilt or error amounted to no more than this: they had met regularly before dawn on a fixed day to chant verses alternately among themselves in honour of Christ as if to a god, and also to bind themselves by oath, not for any criminal purpose, but to abstain from theft, robbery and adultery, to commit no breach of trust and not to deny a deposit when called upon to restore it. After this ceremony it had been their custom to disperse and reassemble later to take food of an ordinary, harmless kind; but they had in fact given up this practice since my edict, issued on your instructions, which banned all political societies. [8]This made me decide it was all the more necessary to extract the truth by torture from two slave-women, whom they call deaconesses. I found nothing but a degenerate sort of cult carried to extravagant lengths. [9]I have therefore postponed any further examination and hastened to consult you. The question seems to me to be worthy of your consideration, especially in view of the number of persons endangered;

for a great many individuals of every age and class, both men and women, are being brought to trial, and this is likely to continue. It is not only the towns, but villages and rural districts too which are infected through contact with this wretched cult. [10]I think though that it is still possible for it to be checked and directed to better ends, for there is no doubt that people have begun to throng the temples which had been almost entirely deserted for a long time; the sacred rites which had been allowed to lapse are being performed again, and flesh of sacrificial victims is on sale everywhere, though up till recently scarcely anyone could be found to buy it. It is easy to infer from this that a great many people could be reformed if they were given an opportunity to repent. (LCL)

The text has a carefully planned structure. In §§1–2a Pliny appears to be submissive, but at the same time skillfully draws Trajan into the argument. Pliny has not yet participated in a trial against Christians (*cognitiones de Christianis*). He knows, however, that court cases against Christians have taken place for a period of time and were known to the Roman ruling class.[83] Pliny addresses three concrete questions to the caesar: whether age makes a difference; whether the remorse of (those who were previously) Christians, should be allowed; and whether they should be punished for the name "Christian" alone (*nomen ipsum*) or when the name is connected with a crime (*flagitia*). It is unclear, however, what exactly is meant by "crime."

The main part, §§2b–8, discusses four groups. (a) §§2b–3: Christians who do not lie and are led away to execution. (b) §4: Steadfast Christians who are Roman citizens are transferred to Rome. (c) §5: Those accused anonymously, who deny that they are Christians and confirm it by a proof of loyalty. (d) §§6–8: Anonymously accused former Christians, who have denied a long time ago that they were Christians[84] and also confirm this with a test of loyalty. In detail, the major section contains additional valuable historical references and information. (1) Although Pliny has not yet participated in a hearing against Christians, he is able to lay before the caesar a comprehensive and thoroughly considered process. This indicates an already-existing practice of reports against Christians to the governor. Thus the citizens know that being a Christian is punishable and have brought charges against the Christians.[85]

---

83. With Freudenberger, "Christenverfolgungen," 24: "Pliny [the Younger] complied with the legal mediation procedure" (*Ep.* 10.97.1). Thus it is certain that merely being a Christian was considered a matter of legal concern"; contra Reichert, "Durchdachte Konfusion," 244 (the text says nothing about previous hearings).

84. Reichert, "Durchdachte Konfusion," 245, understands the information about the years (three years, twenty years) merely as an indication of temporal distance.

85. Cf. Freudenberger, *Verhalten der römischen Behörden*, 94; Reichert, "Durchdachte Konfusion," 244, is not able to rebut this obvious argument when she emphasizes a minimal conclusion: "Strictly speaking, the reference indicates only that Pliny has learned from the personal

(2) With the particular steps taken, it probably involves those measures that had already been put into practice before and with Pliny: (a) Christians who affirmed that they were Christians a second and third time were led away to the death penalty. As a reason for this action, Pliny mentions the stubbornness and obstinacy of the people who believed in that absurd superstition. (b) On the other hand, Pliny set free Christians who denied their faith, of course, after they had called on the Roman gods, offered a sacrifice to the caesar's image,[86] and cursed Christ. In particular, the reason (real Christians do not do such a thing) points to an older practice that already existed.[87] Section 7 should indicate that the early practice of those who have now fallen away (resurrection worship service, ethical propriety, eucharistic celebration)[88] is regarded as harmless so that the caesar can forgive them.

The concluding section (§§8–10) indicates Pliny's essential motivation: Christianity had spread explosively in parts of Asia Minor. People of every social position and age have joined it; not only the cities but also the countryside was affected. Evidently whole families were arrested, likewise an indication of the great expansion of Christianity. At the end of the letter, furthermore, Pliny mentions the economic aspects as a cause for the resentment of the pagan population: the collapse of the pagan cultic sacrifice and the related losses for the pagan tradesmen.

The text indicates that the strong resistance against the growing Christianity took place at three levels: (1) At the local level were private individuals and perhaps also associations (cf. Acts 19:23–40) who directly reported or anonymously denounced the Christians for religious, political, or economic reasons. (2) The regional Roman authorities, all the way up to the governor,

---

report(s) of those accused of being Christians that this was the essential and only point of the accusation." Pliny would have first filtered out his conclusions to a certain extent from numerous charges against Christians; considering the dominant role of personal and anonymously written reports in the text and the prohibition of anonymous reports by Trajan (Pliny the Younger, *Ep.* 10.97.2), this argument is not convincing.

86. Cf. Freudenberger, *Verhalten der römischen Behörden*, 138–39, according to whom this tradition was introduced by Domitian and hardly originated under Trajan or Nerva. The tradition could not have originated under Trajan, for otherwise Pliny would not have asked in this way. Moreover, in his answer Trajan requires explicitly only the veneration of "our gods," not his own person. Nerva (96–98 CE), in his brief time in power, was very critical of the elevated emperor cult; his time was celebrated as a period of freedom (cf. Pliny the Younger, *Panegyricus*; Dio Cassius 67–68; Tacitus, *Agricola* 3.1).

87. Josephus offers a parallel, *J.W.* 7.46–53, which tells of a test of loyalty (sacrifice according to Greek custom) given to Jews in Antioch by the Greeks in the winter of 66/67 CE; those who refused were executed.

88. The prohibition of *hetaeriae* (clubs, assemblies/political-religious associations) in §7 indicates that the assemblies and common meals of Christians were regarded as potentially dangerous.

participated in the persecution of Christians. (3) Finally, the central Roman authorities, even including the caesar, saw themselves forced to act against the Christians as long as they did not demonstrate political-cultic loyalty to the Roman state.

The intention of Pliny is clearly evident; he wants to win over the caesar for a double strategy: harshness toward the unyielding and leniency to the liars. He hoped to be able to turn this development around and restore the former influence of the ancient faith. But why are the unfaltering Christians immediately condemned to death? Apparently the *nomen ipsum* sufficed for this,[89] for no specified "crime associated with the name" plays a role; to the contrary, Pliny explicitly praises the exemplary ethical conduct of Christians (§7). The accusation (*delatio*) concerned being a Christian and involved a special category of accusation *extra ordinem*. What was the reason for considering the *nomen ipsum* as a reason for accusation? What was hidden behind this accusation if no "further crimes" could be proved about the Christians? A reason could have been that the new movement of Christians through their ringleader, a political insurrectionist executed by the Romans, and through their strange teachings (a crucified person as Son of God) was regarded as deviant and potentially criminal.[90] However, does this reason alone account for the immediate verdict of the death penalty? Pliny himself gives an indication that the *confessio nominis* indeed sufficed as a basis for an accusation, but it was connected within a wider complex: If he demands the worship of the image of the caesar and the statue of the gods (§5), then the obviously known nonparticipation of the Christians in the emperor cult and the Roman cult as a whole would have been the basis for the accusation on the basis of the *nomen ipsum*. If the public exercise of the Roman emperor cult and cult of the gods served as a decisive proof for this sentiment, then the decisive point was evident in the position of Christians toward this cult. In legal terms, the refusal of the cult could be regarded as a crime against the state (*crimen laesae maiestatis*), that is, as a violation of the religious duty of citizens.[91] It must not be used with Christians as its own category of offense; at any rate, it should remain in

89. Cf. Reichert, "Durchdachte Konfusion," 238.

90. This aspect is emphasized by Vittinghoff, "'*Christianus sum*,'" 336; Freudenberger, "Christenverfolgungen," 24.

91. Cf. Kübler, "Maiestas," 549–51. This interpretation is supported by, not least, Cicero, *De republica* 4.12, where the central charge of *flagitia* (crimes) raised against the Christians is mentioned with a reference to the area of disrespect in the Law of Twelve Tables, which is punishable by death. Freudenberger, "Christenverfolgungen," 25–26, rejects this connection explicitly because neither Pliny the Younger nor Trajan says anything further about the crimes connected with Christianity, and Trajan did not explicitly require the veneration of his image.

the background.[92] The *nomen ipsum* cannot be treated in isolation or as an abstraction, for a massive negative view of Christians is necessarily connected with their distance from the Roman cult. The identity of the ruler with the state and the idea of the divine nature demanded, from the Roman perspective, a respectful veneration. Anyone who withdrew fell into suspicion of insufficient respect and thus of political disloyalty.

Caesar Trajan answers Pliny (*Ep.* 10.97.1–2):

> You have followed the right course of procedure, my dear Pliny, in your examina-
> tion of the cases of persons charged with being Christians, for it is impossible
> to lay down a general rule to a fixed formula. These people must not be hunted
> out; if they are brought before you and the charge against them is proved, they
> must be punished, but in the case of anyone who denies that he is a Christian,
> and makes it clear that he is not by offering prayers to our gods, he is to be
> pardoned as a result of his repentance however suspect his past conduct may
> be. But pamphlets circulated anonymously must play no part in any accusation.
> They create the worst sort of precedent and are quite out of keeping with the
> spirit of our age. (LCL)

The position of the Roman caesar Trajan is noteworthy,[93] for he first confirms the procedure of his representative, but then he formulates a very liberal
criterion for the conduct toward Christians. They do not need to be hunted
down, and only the one who is reported and found guilty should be punished.
But anyone who denies that he is a Christian can prove this by an act, that is,
by calling on the gods.[94] Trajan probably reduces Pliny's previous practice to
the calling on the Roman gods. Apostate Christians are thus spared of having to sacrifice before the caesar's image and of cursing Christ. The pressure
on the Christian churches would thus be reduced, for against this cultural
background it was still possible to invoke the Roman gods as a mere sign of
loyalty with the Roman state. It is, however, possible that Trajan tacitly assumes the worship of his image.[95]

---

92. At least T. Mommsen, "Der Religionsfrevel," supports this interpretation: "When anyone refuses homage to the gods of the Roman state, which every citizen is obligated to do, . . .
he injures the state and becomes an offender, provided that he does not, like the Jews, have an
exception, so, of course, for everyone who stands before the authorities and confesses that he
is a Christian and expresses this refusal, that witness leads legally to martyrdom."

93. On Trajan, cf. Schipp, *Die Adoptivkaiser*, 22–34, who emphasizes: "Trajan always
adopted a moderate position based on matters of fact" (29).

94. Philo (*Flacc.* 96) offers a parallel, where he reports about a persecution of Jews in Alexandria. Jewish women were given pork to eat: those who ate it were freed; those who resisted
were tortured.

95. Thus Speigl, *Der römische Staat*, 78 A 112.

The correspondence between Pliny and Trajan indicates that actions had been taken against Christians for a long time,[96] with the *nomen ipsum* as the basic charge. Indeed, Pliny and Trajan advocate the punishment of any Christians who were reported and are intransigent in their court hearing. Nevertheless, their attitude signals an easing of tension, for Pliny expresses caution in the procedure, and Trajan does not permit anonymous reports. However, it is clear that both already had practiced and established judgment about the new movement: confessing and thus recalcitrant Christians are worthy of death.

Under Hadrian (117–38 CE), local persecutions again occurred in Asia Minor, leading to an exchange of letters between the caesar and the governor Minicius Fundanus:[97]

> To Minucius Fundanus. I received a letter written to me from his Excellency Serennius Granianus, your predecessor. I think that the matter ought not to remain without inquiry, to prevent men from being harassed or helping the rascality of informers. If then the provincials can make out a clear case on these lines against the Christians so as to plead it in open court, let them be influenced by this alone and not by opinions or mere outcries. For it is far more correct if anyone wishes to make an accusation for you to examine this point. If then anyone accuses them and shows that they are acting illegally, decide the point according to the nature of the offence, but by Hercules, if anyone brings the matter forward for the purpose of blackmail, investigate strenuously and be careful to inflict penalties adequate to the crime.[98]

The crucial question is whether Hadrian changed the legal status of Christians, as suggested by the last statement just quoted. Doubts could be raised, of course, by the reports delivered by Justin about the persecution of Christians. Justin also passes on the imperial rescript, to which he adds an introduction: "And though from a letter of the great and illustrious Emperor Hadrian, your father, we could demand that you order judgment to be given as we have asked, yet we have made this address and explanation, not on the grounds of Hadrian's decision, but because we know that what we ask is just. And we have subjoined the copy of Hadrian's letter so that you may know that we are speaking the truth."[99] The introduction and the rescript that follows could indicate that under Hadrian the *nomen ipsum* was no longer the basis

---

96. Contra Reichert, *Durchdachte Konfusion*, 241–50, who emphatically describes the action of Pliny as a new procedure, which in no way is preceded by earlier practices.

97. For an analysis, see Engberg, *Impulsore Chresto*, 206–14.

98. Eusebius, *Hist. eccl.* 4.9.1–3 LCL.

99. Justin, *1 Apol.* 68, trans. Barnard, *St. Justin Martyr*.

for prosecution. However, Justin's *First Apology* (4) offers an opposing view, since Justin clearly assumes that Christians are still being persecuted because of their name: "In our case you take the name as proof against us [ἐὰν ἡμῶν δὲ τὸ ὄνομα ὡς ἔλεγχον λαμβάνετε], and although, as far as the name goes, you ought rather to punish our accusers" (4.4).

Conclusion. The Latin original of the rescript of Hadrian is not extant, and the versions in Eusebius and Origen are probably tendentious. In Justin (around 150 CE) Hadrian becomes, in recognizable apologetic discourse, practically a benefactor of Christianity, and Eusebius probably writes for his own time (beginning of the fourth century), portraying the great caesar Hadrian as a model. A fundamental change in the status of Christians under Hadrian did not take place.

> Contrary to attempts to minimize and relativize the persecutions, one may conclude: from 64 CE Christians were considered as potentially worthy of punishment on the basis of their existence or their name. The Romans allowed new cults as long as they were compatible with the official imperial cult.[100] It was crucial that these cults were not against the existing societal order and had no destabilizing effect. It was different with the two eastern religions that challenged the polytheistic foundation of the Roman state and societal order by their radical monotheism: Judaism and Christianity. While Judaism in principle was granted a special status as an "ancient religion," Christianity, with its rejection of the Roman cult, was perceived as hostile to the Roman Empire, law, and culture and was classified as an illicit association.

---

100. The Christians distinguished themselves fundamentally from the surrounding world by their basic refusal of a combination of cults; cf. T. Mommsen, *Der Religionsfrevel*, 403: "The Roman citizen who worshiped Isis and the divine Mithras by no means abandoned the temple of Jupiter."

13

Early Christianity
as an Independent Movement

Early Christianity had to find and articulate its place in the religious-symbolic world of its time and in the social reality of its environment. This process reached its first conclusion at the beginning of the second century CE, as the language, texts, and concepts proved to be historically significant. Particularly with the theology of Paul, the four Gospels, and Acts, early Christianity created an impressive new knowledge system that essentially determined its independence. Christianity now enters history as a recognizable movement (despite hostility) that was already consolidated externally and at the same time internally differentiated.

13.1 The New Narrative and the New Language of the Christians

Narratives define the self-understanding of individuals, groups, states, political systems, philosophies, and religions.[1] In the OT, the stories of Moses are the basis of a theological-political program whose significance extends into the present. Islam took up major parts of the Jewish narrative and transformed it, with Mohammed as the founder of a new discourse in the imperative. Ancient philosophy places the striving for virtue in the middle point of its narrative

1. Rüsen, "Kann gestern besser werden?," 30, speaks of "master narratives": "They follow contemporary events and reorganize the self-understanding of those who are affected so that the new experiences become integrated into the cultural orientation of its way of life."

453

and promises a successful life. Since the French and American revolutions, the striving of individuals for personal freedom, prosperity, and personal happiness has dominated the narrative of the modern era. The sciences place the conviction and the promise of serving progress at the center of their narrative. Without an existing narrative in the minds of people, there is, for ideological models, no permanent survival in history.

Early Christians also created a new narrative in order to transmit for themselves and others an image and a consciousness of what one believes and how one is obligated to live. The formation of their own new language was an essential contribution to this process of formation, for language is the absolute cultural identity marker. Language defines and transmits elements of knowledge.[2] Here early Christianity was creative, for it formed a rich and diverse language in the reception and transformation of Jewish and Greco-Roman terminology that can be described here with a few examples (especially in Paul, Mark, and John).[3] Paul and the evangelists were especially creators of new language and thought, and thus their linguistic power became a language event.

The Language of Christology

From the beginning, central theological insights and statements made with titles of majesty (see above, 4.2; 5.7) take on a central place in almost all NT writings. The title Χριστός (the Anointed One/the Christ) appears 531 times in the NT and was taken from Jewish messianic expectation but could be easily understood by Greeks and Romans in the context of common ancient rites of anointing. A linguistic new creation in the context of the title *Christ* is the phrase in Paul ἐν Χριστῷ (in Christ), which, besides the usage elsewhere, simply means "to be Christian" (see above, 8.7). The title of *son* about 41 times is the absolute υἱός, about 80 times υἱὸς τοῦ θεοῦ (Son of God), about 82 times υἱὸς τοῦ ἀνθρώπου (Son of Man), and 15 times υἱὸς Δαυίδ (son of David). Son has both a Jewish (e.g., Ps. 2:7) and a pagan background (sons of the gods, caesar as "Son of God"), and thus it was intelligible to people from different backgrounds. Similarly, the title κύριος (lord) is also intelligible to different cultures; with 719 appearances, it could refer to God or Jesus, or it could be used in the secular realm. In the Jewish (LXX) and pagan world it was widespread. What was crucial was the re-encoding of this title by the

---

2. Knoblauch, *Wissenssoziologie*, 171: "Language constitutes the most important element of culture. Languages contain specific worldviews."

3. On the Greek of New Testament authors, cf. Porter and Pitts, *Language of the New Testament*.

early Christians: As they worshiped a crucified man as the anointed Son of God and Lord, they abandoned the well-known cultural tradition (cf. 1 Cor. 1:23) and established something that was provocatively new.

This combination of a point of contact with a transformation of the content was apparently very successful; one can observe from it another central area of Christology: Jesus's representative death "for us."[4] Already in the words over the cup in the early tradition of the Lord's Supper (Mark 14:24, ὑπὲρ πολλῶν, for many/for all; 1 Cor. 11:24; Luke 22:19, 20: ὑπὲρ ὑμῶν, for you) this concept appears and was then developed in the pre-Pauline tradition (cf. 1 Cor. 15:3b) and especially by Paul himself. *Substitution* means to perform a deed for another and in the place of another and thus to obtain a saving effect. In Pauline usage, 1 Thess. 5:10 indicates the basic concept of the apostle: Jesus's death "for" makes possible the new creation and the salvation of humankind. Jesus Christ died "for us [ὑπὲρ ἡμῶν] so that, whether we are awake or asleep, we will live with him" (cf. also 2 Cor. 5:14b, 15; Gal. 2:20; Rom. 8:32). The death of Jesus, however, is no heroic performance (cf. Rom. 5:7, "Scarcely does one die for a righteous person; for a good person one might perhaps dare to die"),[5] but rather a dying "for the ungodly" (Rom. 5:6): "for us," for the sinner (Rom. 5:8). It was for the "condemnation/removal of sin" (περὶ ἁμαρτίας κατέκρινεν) that God sent his Son (Rom. 8:3), who entered into sin's sphere of power in order to overcome it. In terms of the history of tradition, the Christology of sending stands in the background (Gal. 4:4–5; 1 John 4:9; John 3:16–17) so that a general concept of atonement is present, not the OT sacrificial offering that is in the background.[6] The idea of cultic atonement does not shape the historical background of the Pauline ὑπέρ sayings;[7] rather, the Greek concept of the vicarious death of a just man whose death effects redemption/removal of guilt and thus averts calamity is probably the starting point of the tradition.[8] This conception already had a strong influence on the Jewish martyr theology, as, for example, is indicated in 2 Macc. 7:37–38; 4 Macc. 6:27–29; 17:21. In

---

4. Cf. G. Friedrich, *Die Verkündigung des Todes Jesu*; Breytenbach, "Versöhnung, Stellvertretung und Sühne"; Breytenbach, "Sühne"; Breytenbach, "Versöhnung"; Barth, *Der Tod Jesu Christi*; Janowski, *Stellvertretung*; Knöppler, *Sühne im Neuen Testament*; Eschner, *Gestorben und hingegeben*.

5. In Rom. 5:7 the basis of the image is clearly the Hellenistic idea of a dying to protect a person, the homeland, or a virtue; cf. the texts in *NW* I/2:592–97, 715–25; *NW* II/1:117–19.

6. Cf. Breytenbach, "Versöhnung, Stellvertretung und Sühne, " 71–72.

7. Cf. Eschner, *Gestorben und hingegeben*, 1:511, who argues "that Paul has created his formulations of 'dying for' and 'self-giving' in unmistakable echo of the death that averts calamity, which was widely attested in the Greek literature of Hellenism and in the imperial period."

8. Texts in *NW* I/2:592–97, 715–25; cf. also Hengel, *Atonement*, 8–18; Barth, *Der Tod Jesu Christi*, 59–64.

the background stands the concept of the universal vicarious death of the just person who breaks through the inseparable connection between sin and death and thus makes new, true life possible. In the dying (cf. 1 Thess. 5:10; 1 Cor. 1:13; 8:11; 15:3b; 2 Cor. 5:14–15; Gal. 2:21; Rom. 5:6, 8; 14:15) and self-giving formulas (cf. Gal. 1:4; 2:20; Rom. 4:25; 8:32)[9] this thought is compressed; Paul takes it up and emphasizes the universal dimensions of the event: as the one attested by God, the Crucified One suffered the violence of death in order to take away the destructive powers of sin and death from them; only he, as the resurrected Son of God, could bring about this liberation "for others."

The ὑπέρ phrase appears not only in Paul; it is prominent also in John and Hebrews. In John 10:11 ("I am the good shepherd. The good shepherd gives his life for the sheep"; cf. v. 15), Jesus donates life by the giving of his life. Thus he identifies himself as the eschatological good shepherd and indicates that he is the Messiah, the shepherd of the people of God. According to John 15:13, "Greater love has no one than he who gives his life for his friends." The love of Jesus is realized in his radical devotion for his own people. Thus as Jesus loved believers in his exemplary act to the point of death, so believers should also love each other. The death of Jesus for his friends is a vicarious death that gives life and opens up the new existence in love. In the context of the high-priest typology, the earthly high priest must continually offer the sacrifice "for the people" and "for himself" (Heb. 5:1ff.; 7:27a; 9:7), but the heavenly high priest, Jesus Christ, has overcome sin "for us" (Heb. 6:20; 9:24) once for all.

The Language of the Cross

Within the ancient world, the language of the cross in particular depicted something new and unique. Crucifixion, the preferred Roman death penalty for slaves and insurrectionists, was a particularly cruel and degrading punishment.[10] To develop from this a positive theology, a provocative and at the same time extremely creative act of early Christianity was required, as Paul affirms in 1 Cor. 1:23: "But we preach Christ crucified, to the Jews an offense, to the gentiles foolishness." As the central abbreviation of the narrative, the cross is already in Paul more than a kerygmatic statement; it always remains also a historical place and a gruesome manner of death, especially where Paul integrates it into mythological narratives (Phil. 2:6–11). Where the cross appears in Paul, it always includes the entire story of Jesus Christ, which is

9. For an analysis, cf. Wengst, *Christologische Formeln*, 55–86.

10. Basic studies here are Hengel, "Mors turpissima crucis"; H-W. Kuhn, "Die Kreuzesstrafe"; Cook, *Roman Crucifixion in the Mediterranean World*.

expressed in 1 Cor. 1:18 as "the word of the cross" (λόγος τοῦ σταυροῦ). The cross is a past event and an abiding saving reality at the same time, for in its true meaning, it can only be conceived as the act of God in Jesus Christ. In the letters of Paul, the cross appears (1) as a historical place, for Paul does not sever it from history: the cross is always the place of the death of Jesus of Nazareth. With the phrase σκάνδαλον τοῦ σταυροῦ (offense of the cross, 1 Cor. 1:23; Gal. 5:11), Paul refers to the concrete degrading manner of execution in a crucifixion, which identifies people as criminals, not as a son of God. To worship a crucified man as the Son of God was theologically offensive to Jews[11] and madness to the Greco-Roman world.[12] As the center of the new world of meaning, the cross evades common cultural interpretations and causes the divine wisdom to appear in a new and surprising light. The cross is (2) an argumentative theological topic that Paul introduces especially in the discussion with the Corinthian church. The wisdom of the cross is not compatible with the wisdom of the world (cf. 1 Cor. 1:18–25). The cross is the radical challenge to all human self-affirmation and individualistic striving for salvation because one finds salvation in powerlessness and not in power, in lament and not in jubilation, in shame and not in fame, in the forsakenness of death and not in glory. The foolishness of the cross can be neither philosophically nor ideologically received; it retreats from any instrumentalizing because it is based on God's love alone. Finally, the cross is (3) a theological symbol. It has the character of a reference, and at the same time through the power of the Spirit it brings the past into the present. As the place of the once-for-all transfer of Jesus Christ into the new being, the cross also shapes the present existence of those who believe in Christ. It designates the transfer of status from death to life and attains its actuality in a ritual context: in baptism is the incorporation into the continuing reality of the cross and resurrection, for the power of death and sin has been overcome, and the status of the new being is granted through the Spirit (cf. Gal. 2:19; Rom. 6:5, 6).

Mark also develops a language of the cross (see above, 10.2.1). For him the cross is the focal point of the entire gospel composition.[13] This fact is evident in three compositional levels.

1. The combination of Mark 1:11; 9:7 ("my beloved Son") or Mark 12:6 ("beloved son") already mentioned reaches its goal in Mark 15:39. It was only at the cross that a man, a Roman centurion, recognizes, unveils, and

11. On the translation of σκάνδαλον with "offense," cf. H.-W. Kuhn, "Jesus als Gekreuzigter," 36–37.
12. Cf. Pliny the Younger, *Ep.* 10.96.8, "misguided superstition."
13. Cf. Ebner, "Kreuzestheologie im Markusevangelium."

bears witness to the secret of the person of Jesus Christ: "This was truly the Son of God." The past tense ἦν signals that for Mark the earthly Jesus was the Son of God. At the end of this way, the acclamation of the Roman centurion under the cross provokes spontaneously a comparison with the imperial cult, for the highest power on earth is attributed not to the caesar, who is worshiped as son of God, but Jesus Christ, the Son of God.

2. In the middle of the Gospel, Jesus's role as the suffering Son of Man "on the way" to Jerusalem (Mark 8:27–10:52) comes to the foreground. Peter's confession of the Messiah (Mark 8:27–30) is followed by a three-fold parallel composition—(a) announcement of suffering in Mark 8:31; 9:31; 10:32–34; (b) understanding of discipleship in Mark 8:32b, 33; 9:32–34; 10:35–40; (c) instruction to the disciples in Mark 8:34–9:1; 9:35–37; 10:41–45—which indicates emphatically that the cross is the signature of the way of Jesus and Christian existence. The framing of the middle section by two healings of blind people (Mark 8:22–26; 10:46–52) strengthens this perspective: the eyes of the disciples and with them the Markan community should be opened about who Jesus of Nazareth is: the suffering Son of Man, who calls for a discipleship in suffering. After Mark 8:27 it is clear without reservation that Jesus is going to the cross and that Mark thinks about the cross; that is, the sayings about the suffering Son of Man are a form of Markan theology of the cross.

3. The Markan messianic secret as a whole is intended to orient the ministry and the work of Jesus the Son of God as a whole to the cross and to understand this work on the basis of the cross.

The language of the cross had to be understood within the surrounding world of early Christianity as strange and provocative, but at the same time it was attractive to many people because it turned common concepts of God upside down and integrated suffering into the idea of God.

The Language of Faith

New Testament statements about faith are directly connected to Christology,[14] especially in Paul and John. The linguistic evidence is significant: In Paul πίστις (faith) appears eighty-one times, and πιστεύειν (believe) appears forty-two times. In John πιστεύειν appears ninety-eight times.[15] On the one

---

14. For an overview, see Lührmann, *Glaube im frühen Christentum*; Schnelle, "Glaube"; Morgan, *Roman Faith and Christian Faith*.

15. Only Hebrews is comparable, of course, which has thirty-two of the instances, of which twenty-four are in Heb. 11.

hand, Paul takes over the term from Hellenistic Judaism and pagan Hellenism,[16] while on the other hand, he goes beyond this usage, for now πίστις/πιστεύειν become the central and exclusive terms for designating one's relationship to God and the mark of identity.[17] For Paul, faith is a new qualification of the "I," for in faith God's care for the world is opened for humankind. God's saving initiative in Jesus Christ is the foundation and enabling of faith. Faith does not rest on the decision of the person; it is a gift of God's grace.[18] This was the case already for Abraham: "Therefore, it depends on faith, in order that the promise may be based on grace and guaranteed to all of his descendants, not only to the adherents of the law, but also to those who share the faith of Abraham, who is our father" (Rom. 4:16). The basic structure of the Pauline concept of faith is indicated clearly in Phil. 1:29: "For it was granted to you, not only to believe in Christ, but also to suffer for him." Faith is a work of the Spirit, for "No one can say, 'Jesus is Lord!' except by the Holy Spirit" (1 Cor. 12:3b). Faith belongs to the fruit of the Spirit (cf. 1 Cor. 12:9; Gal. 5:22). A new relationship with God is opened up in faith, which one can accept with gratitude.

A second aspect is indicated in the orientation of faith to Jesus Christ. For Paul, faith is always faith in God, who raised Jesus Christ from the dead (cf. Rom. 4:17, 24; 8:11). Jesus Christ is the one who both initiates faith and is its content.[19] The focus of faith is thus not the believer but the object of faith. Because faith originates in the preaching of the gospel, it is ultimately and always an act of God, founded in the Christ event alone.

No other NT author thought so intensively about the nature of faith as the evangelist John.[20] In most instances πιστεύειν appears with εἰς ("believe in"), in which a fundamental aspect of the Johannine understanding of faith is revealed. The relationship of faith to the person of Jesus Christ means for

16. Cf. Lührmann, "Pistis im Judentum"; Barth, "Pistis in hellenistischer Religiosität," 173–76; Schunack, "Glaube in griechischer Religiosität," 299–317; Frey, Schliesser, and Ueberschaer, *Glaube*. A comprehensive portrayal of the Greek and Latin linguistic background is offered by T. Schumacher, *Zur Entstehung christlicher Sprache*, 199–299.

17. Cf. Barth, "πίστις."

18. Cf. the basic considerations by G. Friedrich, "Glaube und Verkündigung bei Paulus," 100ff. Contra Wolter, *Paul*, 71–94, for whom the subject of faith is the human interpretation or consent to the "assurance of reality"; cf. Wolter, *Paul*, 72, where he says of the Pauline preaching of the gospel: "The message is accepted by the person to whom it is extended. Paul calls this reaction from the side of the addressees and hearers of the proclamation of the gospel 'faith' (πίστις/πιστεύειν), or he expresses this response with the verb 'believe' (πιστεύειν)."

19. Cf. G. Friedrich, "Glaube und Verkündigung bei Paulus," 102–6.

20. Cf. here Schlier, "Glauben, Erkennen, Lieben"; F. Hahn, "Sehen und Glauben im Johannesevangelium"; F. Hahn, "Das Glaubensverständnis im Johannesevangelium"; Bergmeier, *Glaube als Gabe nach Johannes*; Hergenröder, *Wir schauten seine Herrlichkeit*; Schnelle, *Theology of the New Testament*, 717–22.

John at the same time "believe in his word" (John 4:41, 50; 5:24), "believe in Moses and the Scripture," which witness to Jesus (cf. John 5:46–47), and especially, believe in the one who sent him (cf. John 5:24; 6:29; 11:42; 12:44; 17:8). Jesus appears as the representative of God, and he can say: "Believe in God and believe in me" (John 14:1b; cf. 12:45; 14:9). Faith in God and faith in Jesus Christ are identical because Jesus Christ is the Son of God. The entire Gospel of John was written "so that you may believe that Jesus is the Christ, the Son of God, and that believing, you may have life in his name" (John 20:31).

The concept of faith is differentiated by three different motifs. (1) *Faith and miracles*. For the evangelist John, the miracle creates faith; the seeing of the σημεῖον (sign/miracle) is followed by the response πιστεύειν εἰς Ἰησοῦν Χριστόν (believe in Jesus Christ).[21] This fully undualistic connection between seeing and believing is explicitly stated in John 2:11, 23; 4:53; 6:14; 7:31; 9:35–38; 10:40–42; 11:15, 40, 45; 12:11; 20:8, 25, 27, 29a, and thus it plays a significant role in the understanding of faith in the Fourth Evangelist. Faith is the result of the miracle that has previously occurred, not the response that leads to the miracle. John does not see belief in response to miracles as only a "provisional faith": faith in response to the miracle is not only a substandard or imperfect faith,[22] but faith in the full sense of the word is to know and recognize that Jesus Christ is the Son of God. (2) *Believing and knowing*. For John, to believe in Jesus is the equivalent of "to know" (γινώσκειν) Jesus. Thus, according to John 14:7, "If you know me, you will know my Father. From now on, you do know him and you have seen him." Jesus says of himself, "I am the good shepherd. I know my own and my own know me" (John 10:14). Believers have known Jesus (1 John 4:16; John 6:69); they know him and know who he is: the One sent by God, the Son of Man, the truth (cf. John 7:17–18; 8:28; 14:6, 17, 20; 17:7–8, 25; 1 John 2:4; 3:19; 5:20). The promise is made to those who abide in the word of Jesus: "You will know the truth, and the truth will set you free" (John 8:32). The Johannine knowing is not oriented to external reality; it penetrates to the nature of what is known. (3) *Seeing*. An additional central dimension of faith in John involves "seeing" (ὁρᾶν, βλέπειν, θεωρεῖν).[23] In particular, "meeting" texts such as John 4:1–42; 5:1–15; 7:25–28; 9:35–38; and 20:1–10, 11–18 are shaped by the motif of "seeking" and "finding" and of the change from "not knowing/not seeing" to faith. The Johannine "seeing" is

---

21. Cf. here Schnelle, *Antidocetic Christology*, 182–94.

22. Contra Bultmann, *Theology*, 2:73, "Genuine faith must not be confused with a seeming faith that is aroused by Jesus's 'signs.'"

23. Detailed analyses of relevant texts are provided by Hergenröder, *Wir schauten seine Herrlichkeit*, 56ff.

developed in an exemplary way in John 9. While the man born blind receives his eyesight and through faith becomes one who truly sees, the Pharisees fall into judgment because they persist in unbelief and thus become the ones who are truly blind (John 9:39–41). John thus challenges his church to respond to Jesus's healing action. When this occurs, Jesus not only opens the eyes of the blind, but also the eyes of the church.

One may clearly observe how Paul and John in particular develop their own language of faith as they take established usage from the interpersonal area (faithfulness, reliability, trust) yet concentrate the terms christologically and give them a new content: faith becomes the exclusive appropriation of receiving the saving event.

The Language of Fraternal Community

The new self-understanding of the early Christians is indicated especially in their self-designation. First of all, the concept of the ἐκκλησία (assembly, community, church) is a self-designation.[24] Of the 114 references to ἐκκλησία in the NT, forty-four are in Paul, of which thirty-one are in the two Corinthian letters. A new language of brotherhood develops within the ἐκκλησία.[25] In Paul ἀδελφός/ἀδελφοί (brother/brothers) is used 113 times and ἀδελφή (sister) appears four times. Paul almost always means Christians,[26] addressing the church in its entirety (cf. 1 Thess. 1:4; 1 Cor. 1:10; 2 Cor. 1:8; Rom. 1:13; Phil. 1:12 and passim) or speaking of individuals (e.g., 1 Cor. 1:1, Sosthenes; 1 Cor. 16:12, Apollos; 2 Cor. 1:1, Timothy; Rom. 16:23, Quartus). While in pagan usage ἀδελφός is limited primarily to the realms of family and clans, Paul uses it universally for all believers and demands love and consideration among brothers and sisters (cf. Rom. 14:1–15:13). Additional self-designations in Paul are "the saints" (οἱ ἅγιοι)[27] and "the elect" (οἱ ἐκλεκτοί).[28] In the prescript of the letters the designation of the church appears frequently as ἅγιοι (1 Cor. 1:2; 2 Cor. 1:1; Rom. 1:7; Phil. 1:1), which, like ἐκκλησία θεοῦ, can be an alternative expression for individual churches (1 Cor. 16:1; 2 Cor. 8:4; Rom. 15:26) and the whole church (1 Cor. 14:33, ταῖς ἐκκλησίαις τῶν ἁγίων, the churches of the saints). Christians are "holy," according to Paul,

---

24. Cf. above, 8.3 under "*Ekklēsia*."

25. On the use of ἀδελφός in the New Testament, cf. esp. Trebilco, *Self-Designations and Group Identity*, 16–67.

26. Exceptions: 1 Cor. 9:5; Gal. 1:19; Rom. 9:3.

27. On the OT and Jewish background of this concept, cf. Deut. 33:3; Dan. 7:18, 21–22, 25, 27; T. Levi 18.11, 14; 1 Enoch 100.5 (Gk. fragment); Pss. Sol. 11.1; 1QM 10.10.

28. Cf. Isa. 65:9, 15, 22; Pss. 105:6, 43; 106:5; 1 Chron. 16:13; Sir. 46:1; 1QpHab 5.4; 9.12; 10.13; 1QH 14.15.

not on the basis of a special ethical quality but through incorporation into the saving act of God in Jesus Christ. In direct connection with ἐκκλησία and closely related to ἅγιος are the terms κλητός (called), κλῆσις (calling), ἐκλογή (election), ἐκλεκτός (elect). In 1 Thess. 1:4, Paul mentions his gratitude for the election of the Thessalonians, who were formerly pagans, but have now become examples for other churches. In 1 Cor. 1:26–28 Paul describes the calling (κλῆσις) of the weak, the foolish, and the despised as a confirmation of the paradoxical act of God at the cross. How closely calling and holiness belong together for Paul is indicated in 1 Cor. 1:2; Rom. 1:7, where he speaks of those who are "called to be saints."

Particular honorific or self-designations appear in the Johannine literature. In 3 John 15 the presbyter chooses φίλοι (friends) as a self-designation for his church and uses the title also for the addressees (cf. also John 11:11; 15:14–15). A common address within the Johannine school was τέκνα or τέκνα θεοῦ (children/children of God; cf. τεκνία in 1 John 2:1, 12, 28; 3:7, 18; 4:4; 5:21; John 13:33; on τέκνα θεοῦ, cf. 2 John 1, 4, 13; 3 John 4; 1 John 3:1, 2, 10; 5:2; John 1:12; 11:52). The disciples of Jesus appear as οἱ ἴδιοι (his own) in John 13:1, and an additional honorific designation in the Johannine school is ἀδελφός (brother; cf. 3 John 3, 5, 10; John 20:17; 21:23). In addition, John makes two incisive new formulations: (1) The Holy Spirit is called παράκλητος (the one called to stand by) in John 14:17, 26; 15:26; 16:13.[29] The use of the term παράκλητος in the sayings about the Paraclete (John 14:16–17, 26; 15:26; 16:7–11, 13–15) in John is probably derived from the genre of the farewell speech (John 13:31–16:33). Because the farewell situation was conceived as the preservation of the continuity and continuance of the admonition and teaching, John takes the term παράκλητος in this sense and extends it: the Paraclete receives especially a hermeneutical function. As teacher, witness, and interpreter for the church, the Paraclete develops the meaning of the person of Jesus Christ and leads the believers into the future. (2) Only in John is a particular disciple called "the beloved disciple" (13:23, "the disciple whom Jesus loved"). As a literary figure, the beloved disciple appears as a model disciple, a guarantor of the tradition and ideal witness of the Christ event. He functions as interpreter of Jesus and speaker for the group of disciples (John 13:23–26a); in the hour of temptation, he remains faithful to his Lord (18:15–18) and becomes the true witness under the cross and the exemplary follower of Jesus (19:25–27). The beloved disciple confirms the actual death of Jesus on the cross (19:34b–35) and is the first to recognize the eschatological dimension of the Easter event (20:2–10).

29. On the linguistic aspects, cf. Behm, "παράκλητος," *TDNT* 5:800–801.

The Language of Eschatology

Within the religious world of antiquity, early Christian eschatology (see above, 11.1) was somewhat new. It was no longer the capricious gods, the erratic power of fate, or destructive catastrophes that determined future expectation, but God's loving election in Jesus Christ (cf. 1 Thess. 1:4). The election to salvation took place in the creation of a new inner world of faith and the new external sign of baptism, both of which save from God's future wrath at the coming/second coming of the Resurrected One (cf. 1 Thess. 1:9–10; 5:9–10). Paul defines this fellowship with Christ with the new phrase "be with the Lord/be with Christ."[30] In 1 Thess. 4:13–18 the eschatological scenario culminates in the promise "and so we will all be with the Lord" (σὺν κυρίῳ ἐσόμεθα). Jesus's death "for us" has the goal that "we live with him" (1 Thess. 5:10). According to Rom. 8:17, the new status of the believers as "joint heirs of Christ" brings not only shared suffering but also the assurance that "we will be glorified with him" (συνδοξασθῶμεν). In Phil. 1:21–24 Paul contemplates being "with Christ" immediately after his death (v. 23, σὺν Χριστῷ εἶναι). In Phil. 3:20–21 Paul speaks of the transformation of our body of lowliness to be conformed (σύμμορφος) to the glorified body of Christ through God's power and thus signifies the post-mortal manner of existence of believers in continuity with 1 Cor. 15 and Rom. 8. With σὺν Χριστῷ Paul speaks comprehensively of the participation of believers in the entire destiny of Christ: from the crucifixion and burial (Rom. 6:3–4) to participation in his resurrection (cf. Rom. 8:11; Phil. 3:10).

In John the concept of life becomes the eschatological center.[31] It is newly encoded: because life is in the Logos (John 1:4), John defines the true life no longer in physical terms but in theological terms. Eternal life is present in faith; as a result, the step from death to life takes place not in the future; instead, for the believer it lies already in the past (John 5:24, "Truly, truly, I say to you, Whoever hears my word and believes in the one who sent me has eternal life; and he does not come into judgment, but has passed from death into life"). The entire saving act of God aims at the gift of true life for humankind: "For God so loved the world that he gave his only begotten Son so that everyone who believes does not perish but has eternal life" (John 3:16; cf. John 3:36; 6:47; 8:51; 11:25–26). In the Eucharist the Johannine community receives the bread of life that comes down from heaven: "I am the living bread that came down from heaven. Anyone who eats this bread will live eternally" (cf. John 6:51a–b; cf. 6:33, 50, 58). Because the decision about the future has been made,

---

30. Cf. Siber, *Mit Christus leben.*
31. Cf. here Mussner, *ZΩH: Die Anschauung.*

the believers have already passed through the judgment (John 3:18; 12:48). Faith now grants full participation in life; anyone who does not obey the Son will not see life, but the wrath of God remains over him (cf. John 5:14, 26). The decision over life and death takes place in the present encounter with Jesus Christ.

> New semantic forms and the reshaping of old forms belong to the necessary strategies of a new movement in order that it may form and solidify an identity. Early Christianity also shaped a new language as it took up Jewish and Greco-Roman terms and reshaped them, filled symbols with something new, or created a fully new discourse. The development of its own linguistic world was a crucial step toward the separate identity of the new movement of Christians and in this respect created the presupposition for its historical impact.

New Writings

The introduction of its own normative Scriptures was a further step toward an autonomous thought world and at the same time toward the separation from Judaism.[32] The letters of Paul already push this development forward, for along with the adoption of the conventions of ancient letters, Paul's letters differ considerably from ancient letters by their length and content (see above, 8.6). Furthermore, they contain clear accents in reference to the previous "Holy Scripture" of the movement, the OT.[33] The numerous citations from the OT demonstrate, on the one hand, the permanent anchoring of Paul in Judaism; on the other hand, it is not "the Scripture" that is cited, but single verses that, in the altered context, become witnesses to the gospel.[34] Paul arrives at the integration of citations in the new context, for the intertextual references that are created achieve two results: they place the OT reference in a new, normally christological horizon of meaning and at the same time legitimate the Pauline gospel. Paul thus transcends the horizon of understanding of scriptural exposition of the Hellenistic synagogue, for it is not the dead weight of the Scripture but God's eschatological saving act in Jesus

32. Cf. Theissen, *Die Religion der ersten Christen*, 233–80.

33. Cf. here Schröter, "Das Alte Testament im Urchristentum," 49–81, who emphasizes correctly "that one must distinguish between a Jewish and a Christian use of the Scriptures, and to speak of occasionally coming across the Old Testament as the common foundation of Judaism and Christianity appears to be too undifferentiated."

34. On the Pauline reception of the OT, cf. D.-A. Koch, *Die Schrift als Zeuge*; R. Hays, *Echoes of Scripture*; H. Hübner, *Vetus Testamentum in Novo*, vol. 2.

Christ that forms the actual center of his thought. Based on this reading, the central contents of Jewish theology (Torah, election) are reconsidered, and the scriptural text is incorporated into a productive intertextual process of interpretation. "Freedom in dealing with the wording of the Scripture, with which Paul departs from contemporary Jewish exegesis, is thus not to be separated from the content of his scriptural interpretation and signals a fundamental change in the understanding of the Scripture."[35] The letters of Paul also indicate how Paul creates an unsurpassed image of himself and establishes the authority of his letters: Both by God's foresight (cf. Gal. 1:15; Rom. 1:1–2) and by his own tireless engagement (cf. 1 Thess. 2:13; 1 Cor. 3:6–11; 9:1–2; 2 Cor. 2:14–3:3; 10:14–16; Rom. 15:18–21),[36] he became the prototype of the proclaimer of the gospel and an example for his churches.[37] Both the content of the letters and the person of Paul aim at a normative significance, which they attain at the latest in the deutero-Pauline letters and Acts (see above, 10.3.2).

The new movement of Christians reaches a new stage of self-discovery, self-presentation, and historical impact with the publication and dissemination of the Gospels and Acts (see above, 10.1–2). The evangelists formulate the new founding narrative of Christians and not only accelerate the separation from Judaism and its normative Scripture but their writings also take their place. The Gospels engage equally in the cultivation of text, tradition, and meaning as they attempt to preserve, form, and communicate their meaning out of the past into the present in a process of interpretation (see above, 9.4; 10.1). The Gospels have a crucial significance in forming and securing the identity of the early Christians in several respects:[38] (1) They communicate an image of Jesus of Nazareth, the originator of the founding narrative (see above, 4.3). They define the framework for understanding the story of Jesus Christ and thus determine its reception. (2) At the same time, the Gospels, with their preservation and transmission of the traditions, communicate the basic information about Jesus Christ. (3) An additional essential function of the writing of the Gospels consists in the formulation of an external and internal perspective. In the external perspective, the Gospels define the position

---

35. D.-A. Koch, *Die Schrift als Zeuge*, 198.

36. Cf. Backhaus, "'Mitteilhaber des Evangeliums,'" 46ff.

37. Epictetus, *Diatr.* 4.8.31–32, has the true Cynic say: "God has sent me to you as an example; I have neither house nor property, neither wife nor children, no, not so much as a bed or a shirt or a piece of furniture, and yet you see how healthy I am. . . . But see whose work it is. It is only the work of Zeus" (LCL); similarly, the philosophers make their pupils their imitators: cf. Xenophon, *Mem.* 1.6.3.

38. Cf. Theissen, *Die Religion der ersten Christen*, 233–53. On the sociological literature, cf. Escarpit, *Das Buch und der Leser*; Escarpit, *Elemente einer Literatursoziologie*.

of the new movement with respect to Judaism and the pagan environment. In the internal perspective, it was their task, in the first place, to define the image of God and Christ and to make it plausible; then there was the task of developing their own ethical code. (4) Furthermore, norms for a new authority and leadership structure had to be established, for with the gospel genre the strong wandering charismatic of the oral tradition lost its influence. The local churches became the bearers and interpreters of the Jesus tradition. (5) Beyond the functions of communicating and legitimating, the Gospels shape the new movement's understanding of its history as they describe their position in the history of the past, present, and future activity of God with humankind.

The Formation of the Canon

The formation of the canon was a further step toward the developing independent identity of early Christianity.[39] This process was essentially borne by the churches, defining the specific writings that possessed authority. It was not authoritative statements of individuals, movements, or synods that gave rise to the collection of Holy Scriptures[40] but rather a process with an inner consistency and necessity: the OT as the established canon, the authoritative claim of the Pauline letters and the Gospels, as well as the growing distance from the original events necessitated a reception of the relevant witnesses for the Christian faith. The formation of canon belongs within the process of the necessary and consistent self-definition of the church. The intention of the predominant arrangement is obvious: After the fourfold portrayal of the story of Jesus Christ, the book of Acts forms the transition and orientation for reading the Pauline letters,[41] which were then supplemented by the writings of the other

39. Cf. Zahn, *Geschichte des neutestamentlichen Kanons*; Harnack, *Das Neue Testament um das Jahr 200*; Leipoldt, *Geschichte des neutestamentlichen Kanons*; Campenhausen, *Formation of the Christian Bible*; Metzger, *Canon of the New Testament*; Schnelle, *Einleitung*, 426–42; Lips, *Der neutestamentliche Kanon*.

40. The word κανών (literally, a straight stick) in the sense of a "table of authoritative writings" appears first in Canon 59 of the provincial synod of Laodicea (around 360 CE); cf. Zahn, *Grundriss der Geschichte des neutestamentlichen Kanons*, 1–11; Metzger, *Canon of the New Testament*, 289–93.

41. The common claim that before Marcion (in Rome ca. 140; in his home in Sinope ca. 120 CE) no evidence exists for a Gospel (e.g., Vinzent, *Die Auferstehung Christi*, 119–20) is not convincing. The Didache (ca. 120 CE) presupposes the presence of the Gospel of Matthew and (indirectly) the Gospel of Mark (cf. Did. 15.3//Matt. 18:15; Did. 8.2//Matt. 6:7–13; Did. 9.5//Matt. 7:6a; Did. 7.1//Matt. 28:19; Did. 8.1–2//Matt. 6:2, 5; Did. 11.7//Matt. 12:31–32; Did. 16.1//Matt. 24:42; 25:1–13). For the detailed argument, cf. Wengst, *Didache*, 24–32. The Papias fragment (ca. 130 CE) in Eusebius (*Hist. eccl.* 3.34.15–16) attests Mark and Matthew as writers of Gospels. Justin, the contemporary of Marcion, cites from the written text of Matthew (Matt. 11:17) and presupposes readings from the Gospels each Sunday (*1 Apol.* 67.3). Moreover, the

apostles; the reading matter then finally flows into the eschatological perspective of the Revelation of John. Primarily with the letters of Paul and the Gospels, Jesus of Nazareth and Paul stand at the beginning of the tradition; they are to a certain extent accessible as a "book" and produce an unexpected effect.

In the process of collecting the books, the formation of the canon was at the same time a process of selection.[42] As the separation of individual units of meaning from the undifferentiated flow of life, they took on a high claim to validity; the process always functioned as the demarcation from other means of knowledge and value. In this process the ancient church resisted the temptation of reduction (Marcion) or harmonization (Tatian) and also the danger of inflation (gnosis) of relevant writings. With the canon of twenty-seven writings, the church affirmed plurality without accepting pluralism. The juxtaposition of the four Gospels along with the letters attributed to James, Peter, and John (cf. Acts 2:9) clearly indicates that the theological dialogue would be established at the level of the canon.

> Early Christian socialization took place significantly through literature! The early Christians were a creative literary movement; they read the OT (LXX) in a new context, created new genres (Gospels), and transformed existing genres (Pauline letters). In addition, they were to a considerable extent bilingual and able to read the highly demanding letters of Paul and to disseminate them. The significant position, function, and spread of literature in the early Christian churches became a defining factor for the independence and success of early Christianity.

13.2 New Perspectives about God

At the center of the new Christian narrative is the view of God. The development of a view of God is the core responsibility of every religion. Every

---

Lord's Supper tradition in *1 Apol.* 66.3 refers explicitly to the tradition of the Gospels (cf. Luke 22:19). The Gospel of John is attested in $\mathfrak{P}^{52}$ (middle of the second half of the second century CE) in Egypt and must have been written a considerable time before that. For the Gospel of Luke, Marcion is the first (indirect) witness. However this fact certainly does not preclude its being written considerably earlier. The classic dating of the Gospels (and Acts) between 70 and 100 CE is evident in the situation presupposed in them and the history of early Christianity. Without the Jesus traditions of the Gospels, the expansion of Christianity in this period is not conceivable.

42. This is a necessary and inevitable process; cf. Luckmann, "Religion—Gesellschaft—Transzendenz," 121: "The societal systematizing of the intersubjective reconstruction of the subjective experience of transcendence includes both selection and rejection, canonization and censorship."

worldview, every philosophy, and naturally every religion has an understanding of God.[43] God does not himself speak directly, but instead we have our own images of God that come from humankind and thus can naturally be compared and evaluated to establish greater or lesser plausibility. The image of God centered in Jesus Christ was of great significance for the expansion of Christianity.

Why did Jews and people who adhered to various Greco-Roman religions in a truly multireligious society turn to the Christian understanding of God? An essential reason lay in monotheism, which already created a fascination for Judaism in antiquity. Of course, monotheistic ideas were already present in Greek thought from the middle of the sixth century BCE (Xenophanes),[44] which could not, though, prevail either theoretically or practically. The variety of gods and portrayals of the gods in the Greco-Roman world[45] obviously led to a loss in plausibility, about which Cicero comments: "There are as many names for the gods as there are human languages."[46] Because the number of the gods could not be determined, the question arose regarding which deities and in what sense they must be worshiped.[47] Thus the philosopher asks: "Then, if the traditional gods whom we worship are really divine, what reason can you give that we should not include Isis and Osiris in the same category? And if we do so, why should we repudiate the gods of the barbarians? We shall therefore have to admit to the list of gods oxen and horses, ibises, hawks, asps, crocodiles, fishes, dogs, wolves, cats and many beasts besides" (LCL).[48] The absurdity of the argument is obvious: the conventional religions and cults neutralize each other and can no longer convincingly satisfy the religious needs of the economically and intellectually mobile classes. The Middle Platonist Plutarch attempts to avoid this danger with the suggestion that the deity has different names among the various peoples but is nevertheless the same.

So for that one rationality [Gk. *logos*] which keeps all these things in order and the one Providence which watches over them and the ancillary powers that are set over all, there have arisen among different peoples, in accordance with their customs, different honours and appellations. Thus men make use of consecrated

43. Cicero's statement in *De natura deorum* (around 44 BCE) already provided this insight, as the Skeptic Cicero questions all the views of God and the world in terms of their consistency.
44. Cf. Xenophanes, frag. 23: "One god greatest among gods and men, not at all like mortals in body or in thought"; on pagan monotheism, see Schrage, *Unterwegs zur Einheit und Einzigkeit Gottes*, 35–43; S. Mitchell and Nuffelen, *Pagan Monotheism*; Staudt, *Der eine und einzige Gott*, 22–70.
45. On the early period of Greek religion, cf. Jaeger, *Theology of the Early Greek Philosophers*.
46. Cicero, *Nat. d.* 1.84.
47. Cf. Cicero, *Nat. d.* 3.40–60.
48. Cicero, *Nat. d.* 3.47.

symbols, some employing symbols that are obscure, but others those that are clearer, in guiding the intelligence toward things divine. . . . Wherefore in the study of these matters it is especially necessary that we adopt, as our guide in these mysteries, the reasoning that comes from philosophy, and consider reverently each one of the things that are said and done.[49]

Because God is immovable and timeless, in which there is "neither earlier nor later, no future nor past, no older nor younger; but He, being One [ἀλλ' εἷς ὤν] has with only one 'now' completely filled 'forever'; . . . we ought, as we pay Him reverence, to greet Him and to address Him with the words 'You are'; or even, I vow, as did some of the men of old, 'You are one.' In fact, the deity is not many, . . . but being must have unity, even as unity must have being" (LCL).[50] The two sources of the knowledge of God[51] are (1) the idea of the divine implanted in humankind in light of the majesty of the cosmos, and (2) the concepts of God passed on in ancient myths and customs have lost plausibility. The more the anthropomorphisms of the Greek myths about the gods were subjected to skeptical critique, the more the faith in one god, henotheism as well as exclusive monotheism, necessarily grew in the power to convince.[52]

The fading of the binding power of Greco-Roman religions is indicated also in the widespread popular views about the gods, which Plutarch sharply attacks in his essay *Superstition*, written around 70 CE. In contrast to the atheists, the superstitious people reckon with the existence of the gods but mean that these bring first and foremost suffering and pain. They assume that the gods are "rash, faithless, fickle, vengeful, cruel, and easily offended" (*Mor.* 170d–e). All of the blows of fate such as "sickness in the body, loss of property, the death of children, or mishaps or failures in political activities" are understood as attacks by the deity (*Mor.* 168c). The rule of the gods

49. Plutarch, *Is. Os.* 67.68.
50. Plutarch, *Mor.* 393a–b.
51. Cf. Dio Chrysostom, *De dei cognitione* (*Or.* 12). The "Olympic Oration" of Dio of Prusa is an impressive example of the attempt to revive Greek religion and its cults. Zeus is praised as the universal, peaceful, and merciful God, who protects humankind as father and king and preserves for them everything that they need for a successful life. The terms used by Epictetus are also noteworthy, as he consistently speaks of θεός (God); cf., e.g., Epictetus, *Diatr.* 1.3.1–3; 9.1–6; 3.22.53; 4.1.98–102 and passim.
52. One may observe, of course, that already in the known beginning period of Greek theology, the canonization of anthropomorphic polytheism of Homer and Hesiod by Herodotus (*Hist.* 2.49–58) and the skepticism/atheism of a Protagoras (born around 490 BCE) stood alongside each other: "As to what concerns the gods, I am not able to know: neither that they exist nor that they do not exist, nor what they do with respect to their appearances" (80B4, Diels-Kranz numbering). In Diogenes Laertius 9.51 a good reason is given: "For many are the obstacles that impede knowledge: both the obscurity of the question and the brevity of human life" (LCL).

appears as "dark, relentless tyranny" (*Mor.* 166d) from which one cannot escape. When Plutarch offers the contrasting view of the goodness, world supremacy, benevolence, and caring of the gods (*Mor.* 167e–f), extols the encouraging and comforting philosophy as a physician (*Mor.* 168c), and recommends extremely elevated piety as the only appropriate attitude (*Mor.* 171e), he demonstrates a multilayered piety, which can be characterized by fear and insecurity with respect to the gods. At the turn of the millennium the traditional ancient teaching about the gods had obviously lost its convincing power, and their existence was now questioned.[53] No one trusted any more that the gods would give a positive direction to life; the blows of fate, the harshness of life, and the insecurity about the future oppressed humankind and abandoned the people to evil forces.

The Attractiveness of the Early Christian View of God

The attractiveness of the early Christian view of God is indicated in its (1) personal and (2) content-related new understanding.[54]

On point 1. Paul and John in particular stand firmly in the tradition of OT monotheism, but at the same time they challenge their hearers to accept a new view of the world and a new God. This god is one, but not alone; one knows his name and his story: Jesus Christ. Paul and John represent an exclusive monotheism in a binitarian form. The worship of the one God is extended to the Son. The view of God is vivid, for Jesus Christ is the image of God (2 Cor. 4:4). The God proclaimed by Paul is a personal God who acts in history, becomes a man, and cares for humankind. He is neither removed from the world nor immanent in the world, but in Jesus Christ has come into the world (cf. Gal. 4:4–5; Rom. 8:3). It was not the universal mythos, but the concrete action of God in Jesus Christ for humankind that defined the early Christian understanding of God. As the Resurrected One, he is the first of the new creation (1 Cor. 15:20–28); God made [Christ] to be [God's] righteousness for the forgiveness of human sins (Rom. 3:25), and through him God reconciled himself to the world (2 Cor. 5:18–21). In John the personal centering of the concept of God was similarly clear. Jesus is the exegete of God; he alone is able to bring real knowledge of the Father (John 1:18). With the incarnation (John 1:14), the unique and direct experience of God enters history in

53. Cf. Cicero, *Nat. d.* 1.94: "But none of these (i.e., the philosophers) discerned the truth about the divine nature; it is to be feared that the divine nature is entirely non-existent"; cf. also 1.63: "Did not Diagoras, called the Atheist, and later Theodorus, openly deny the divine existence?"

54. Essential aspects of the New Testament understanding of God are described in Feldmeier and Spiekermann, *God of the Living*.

Jesus and is perceptible as the revelation of the Son of God. Corresponding to John 1:18, John 20:28 emphasizes the deity of Jesus, which distinguished him from the beginning, remained visible in his earthly ministry, and shaped the appearances of the Resurrected One. Against the charge of ditheism (cf. John 5:18; 10:33, 36; 19:7), John emphasizes the unity of the Father and Son. It occurs in John 5:17–30 as a unity of the will, action, and revelation; John 10:30 stands in actual continuity with this passage: "I and the Father are one!" The statements claiming reciprocal immanence in John 10:38 ("so that you may know that the Father is in me and I in the Father") and John 14:10 (Jesus says to Philip: "Do you not believe that I am in the Father and the Father is in me?") express the Johannine conception fully. Because Jesus lives from the unity that comes from the Father, the Father himself is revealed in the words and works of Jesus.[55] Finally, the "I am" sayings (cf. John 6:35a; 8:12; 10:7, 11; 11:25; 14:6; 15:1) signal the special relationship of the Father and Son. Anyone who sees the Son also sees the Father (John 12:45; 14:9); anyone who hears the Son also hears the Father (John 14:24); anyone who believes in the Son also believes in the Father (John 14:1), and anyone who does not honor the Son does not honor the Father (John 5:23).

On point 2. Not only in a personal way, but also in terms of content, the early Christians create a new definition of the nature of God as they push two aspects to the center: God is life and God is love. The concept of life becomes a central interpretative dimension of the concept of God in early Christianity, for the act of God in the resurrection of Jesus Christ from the dead is understood as a victory of life.[56] Thus suffering is integrated into the concept of God, for the Resurrected One is and remains the Crucified One. In contrast to the Jewish and pagan world, early Christianity dared an unusual thought: God undergoes suffering, from which the true life comes into being. Paul speaks of the God "who gives life to the dead and calls into being the things that do not exist" (Rom. 4:17). Through Jesus Christ, life now has dominion (cf. Rom. 5:17, 21). The resurrection is not an isolated event but rather the beginning of a universal process, of which the end is the universal triumph of life when "God becomes all in all" (1 Cor. 15:28). In the present, believers already participate in this foundational event.[57] The powers of the resurrection of Jesus Christ are at work through baptism and the gift of the Holy Spirit and give rise to their own certainty: "But we know

55. Appropriately stated by Scholtissek, *In ihm sein und bleiben*, 371: "The theocentric nature of Jesus makes it possible for the Father to be present entirely in the Son. Jesus does not represent the Father, but presents him."

56. Cf. Feldmeier and Spiekermann, *God of the Living*, 519–50.

57. Cf. Schnelle, "Transformation und Partizipation."

that, if we have died with Christ, we shall also live with him" (Rom. 6:8; cf. 2 Cor. 1:9; 5:15). "The one who knew no sin God has made to be sin so that we might become the righteousness of God in him" (2 Cor. 5:21; cf. 2 Cor. 8:9). God identifies himself with the crucified Jesus so much that the power of his resurrection, which is being revealed, is still at work: "For this reason Christ died and has again come to life so that he might be the Lord of the dead and the living" (Rom. 14:9).

In John also the comprehensive term for the new existence of Christians is ζωή (life) or ζωὴ αἰώνιος (eternal life).[58] To be human becomes a reality only in faith: the life made possible through God. Life is for John, first of all, an attribute of the Father,[59] who gives life to the Son: "For as the Father has life in himself, so he has granted life to the Son to have life in himself" (John 5:26; cf. John 6:47). The Son in turn receives power over all humankind from the Father "so that he may give eternal life to all whom you have given to him" (John 17:2b). The preexistent Logos already had life in himself, which was the light of humankind (John 1:4; 1 John 1:2). Jesus comes from God as the embodiment of life; the divine life in the cosmos is present in a concrete historical person.[60] As the light of the world, Jesus is at the same time the light of life (John 8:12). As the basis for the salvation of humankind from destruction in death, the entire incarnation is intended to give eternal life to believers (cf. John 3:16, 36a). True life takes place only in the encounter with Jesus that gives rise to faith, for in him the divine power of life has broken into the world of death. Only he can say of himself that he is "the resurrection and the life" (John 11:25). Through the Son, the Father gives life that cannot be destroyed by biological death. As a relationship of the believer with God begins in the present, eternal life opens up a never-ending future. John does not promise immortality to believers, but an enduring, true life with God.

The second substantive new dimension of the view of God is indicated in Paul and the Johannine literature in the concept of love.[61] Paul can summarize the entire saving event in Rom. 5:8: "But God has shown his love toward us in that Christ died for us while we were yet sinners."[62] Thus for Paul crucial significance belongs to love as the fundamental basis and norm of Christian existence. Not coincidentally, 1 Cor. 13 stands between chapters 12 and 14, which is aimed at the danger of the misuse of the gifts. In 1 Cor. 13:1–3 Paul

58. Cf. Mussner, ZΩH: Die Anschauung; M. Thompson, "'Living Father.'"
59. Cf. Mussner, ZΩH: Die Anschauung, 70ff.
60. Cf. Mussner, ZΩH: Die Anschauung, 82ff.
61. Cf. Feldmeier and Spiekermann, God of the Living, 125–46. They indicate that the concept of the loving God is naturally also in the OT but, of course, limited to the elect people.
62. On the command to love in Paul, cf. Wischmeyer, Der höchste Weg; Wischmeyer, "Das Gebot der Nächstenliebe"; Söding, Das Liebesgebot bei Paulus.

illustrates the principle, indicating that extraordinary gifts are of no benefit if they are not permeated with love. Love is the most prominent fruit of the Spirit, and in love the believers fulfill the entire law (Rom. 13:8–10).

The concept of love takes on a system quality in the Johannine literature.[63] A full movement of love proceeds from the Father, which includes the Son (John 3:16, 35; 10:17; 15:9, 10; 17:23, 26) as well as the world (John 3:16) and the disciples (John 14:21, 23; 17:23, 26). It continues in the love of Jesus toward God (John 14:31) and the disciples (John 11:5; 13:1, 23, 34; 14:21, 23; 15:12, 13; 19:26) as well as in the love of the disciples for Jesus (John 14:15, 21, 23) and each other (John 13:34, 35; 15:13, 17). At the end, despite the unbelief of many, the world will recognize "that you sent me and loved them, as you have loved me" (John 17:23). The programmatic statement is made in 1 John 4:8b, 16b that "God is love." The central insight of this understanding is[64] that the love directed to the world is what God has sent. God demonstrates in his Son that God is love and the one who loves, for he gives his love, and it reaches its fulfillment and perfection in love among brothers and sisters. This concept is immediately insightful and exhibits a potential for religious philosophy: God can be thought of only as love; every other definition fails to grasp his nature. This view captivates not only by its incisive simplicity, great depth, and simple truth, but it is without explicit parallels in the history of religion;[65] that is, here nothing less than a totally new image of God is introduced in intellectual history! This view, however, is not merely an abstract idea: it is realized historically in the life, death, and resurrection of Jesus Christ, and it became a starting point for a remarkable historical development. In a remarkable way Jesus embodies the model of God as love, and his enduring significance consists of the fact that the intellectual idea of God as the embodiment of love and the good has been realized perfectly in a historical person. The idea and the event come together in Jesus Christ.

Early Christian monotheism in a binitarian form exercised a great power of attraction in the context of a declining polytheism. Particularly with the incarnation, early Christianity carried out a humanizing of the concept of God: In Jesus Christ, God

---

63. Cf. E. Popkes, *Die Theologie der Liebe Gottes*, 361, according to whom "the dramaturgic Christology of the love of God in the Gospel of John" embodies the climax in the development of early Christian theology. It reflects and expresses by way of analogy why love and the death of Jesus can be understood as an event of the love of God."

64. Cf. Schnelle, "Johanneische Ethik."

65. Similar to the Johannine statement is Plato, *Nomoi* (*Laws*) 900D: the gods "are perfect in every virtue and have the universal care for all things as their proper function"; they are "good and perfect" (901E).

has a face and a history that is totally shaped by love. The Christians were active
in the consciousness of serving the true God and life.

13.3 Serving as a Model of Success

Besides proving a framework of a coherent religious world, the deeds of the
early Christians made the movement attractive. At the latest around the beginning of the second century, they were perceived as a movement that was
distinguished by a high ethos and an extraordinarily powerful social engagement. Around 110 CE, Pliny (see above, 12.4) reports that the Christians
bind themselves by an oath "not to commit any crimes, but to the contrary
to commit no theft, robbery, or adultery, not to break their word and not to
refuse to return entrusted property that was demanded to be returned" (*Ep.*
10.96). Lucian (ca. 120–80 CE), in a satirical exaggeration in *The Passing of
Peregrinus* (11), gives a picture of Christianity that evokes the amazement
and astonishment of the world around 160 CE. The wandering philosopher
Peregrinus[66] temporarily joined the "Wisdom of the Christians" (σοφίαν τῶν
Χριστιανῶν) and was then arrested.

> Then at length Proteus was apprehended for this and thrown into prison, which
> itself gave him no little reputation as an asset for his future career and the
> charlatanism and notoriety-seeking that he was enamoured of. Well, when
> he had been imprisoned, the Christians, regarding the incident as a calamity,
> left nothing undone in the effort to rescue him. Then, as this was impossible,
> every other form of attention was shown him, not in any casual way but with
> assiduity; and from the very break of day aged widows and orphan children
> could be seen waiting near the prison, while their officials even slept inside
> with him after bribing the guards. Then elaborate meals were brought in, and
> sacred books of theirs were read aloud, and excellent Peregrinus—for he still
> went by that name—was called by them "the new Socrates." (*Peregr.* 12 LCL)

In addition, many other churches "with incredible speed" (*Peregr.* 13) set out
to support and to defend their brother in the faith. Behind the satirical exaggeration the Christians are visible as a group, in which each becomes involved
for his people and supports them. This distinguished the churches from the
beginning and eventually resulted in the success of Christianity (Matt. 25:36,

66. Cf. also Lucian, *Peregr.* 13, where it is reported that the Christians call each other "brothers," pray to "the crucified sophist," and have all possessions in common.

"I was naked, and you clothed me; I was sick and you visited me; I was in prison and you came to me"; Heb. 13:3, "Remember those who are in prison, as though you were in prison with them; those who are being tortured, as people who are in the body").[67]

The Beginnings and Paul

From the very beginning, *diakonia*, as a total concern for the neighbor, was a central feature of the life according to the gospel. An energetic support of brothers and sisters in the faith probably existed already in the Jerusalem church. The conflict over the care of the Hellenistic widows (Acts 6:1) presupposes an established social care in the Jerusalem church (see above, 5.5). The social-utopian texts about the community of goods in Acts 2:42–46; 4:32–35 can also be read as a reflection of the economic and social justice in the Jerusalem church. There were isolated instances of the renunciation of property for the sake of the church (cf. Acts 4:36f.), which is pictured by Luke as a powerful program (see above, 5.5). At the apostolic council (Gal. 2:10) the agreement on the collection for "the poor among the saints in Jerusalem" (Rom. 15:26) is also evidence of a very early consciousness of responsibility for the economic situation of individual churches (see above, 7.4). Characteristic of Paul is the theological anchor to social action, for not coincidentally the key terms διακονία (service) and διακονεῖν (serve) appear especially in the context of the collection (cf. 2 Cor. 8:4, 19–20; 9:1, 12, 13; Rom. 15:25, 31).[68] The collection appears as the "grace of God" (2 Cor. 8:1), which took shape in the Christ event and triggered a reciprocal giving and taking: "For you know the grace of our Lord Jesus Christ, that he became poor for your sake, that you might become rich" (2 Cor. 8:9). The idea of being dependent on one another and for each other is also the basic idea assumed in the concept of the body of Christ (1 Cor. 12:1–11, 28–31; Rom. 12:3–8), which avoids an instrumentalizing of the gifts, places them in the service of the edification of the entire community (cf. 1 Cor. 14:26), and concentrates on love (1 Cor. 13). The deep christological foundation of reciprocal caring is indicated also in Phil. 2:1–11, where the hymn in verses 6–11 serves as a model for the ethical conduct of the community: "Let each one of you look not to your own

---

67. The dictum of the emperor Julian (331–363 CE), who attempted to revive the ancient cults with reforms and affirmed the success of the Christians: "We should observe that it is their benevolence to strangers, their care for the graves of the dead, and the pretended holiness of their lives that have done most to increase *atheism* [the Christians]. To be silent about their strange way of life, whether it is merely external or not" (*Epistulae* 89 [or *Letters of Julian* 22, "To Arsacius, High Priest of Galatia"]; cited in Thraede, "Soziales Verhalten," 45).

68. Cf. T. Holtz, "Christus Diakonos."

interests, but to what serves the other" (Phil. 2:4). Hospitality is already for
Paul a central concern (Rom. 12:13, "Contribute to the needs of the saints;
practice hospitality"), a theme that also plays a central role in later writings
(cf. Heb. 13:2, "Do not forget hospitality. For by it some have entertained
angels without knowing it"; also 1 Pet. 4:8–9; 1 Tim. 3:2; 5:20–21; Titus 1:8;
1 Clem. 10.7; 11.1; 12.1, 13). The concrete form of Pauline communities also
indicates that from the beginning the early Christian preaching had an effect
on the daily social life of the believers. Galatians 3:26–28 annuls three fundamental social and cultural alternatives in antiquity: Jew-Greek, slave-free,
man-woman (see above, 8.3). The mission to the nations without demanding
circumcision, the Letter to Philemon with its new definition of the relationship between slave and free, and the elevated place of women in the Pauline
missionary work (see above, 8.3) indicate that in the house churches the new
existence was put into practice. In Roman society it was common to acquire
a position through one's origin or social position; the renunciation of such
within the early Christian churches led to an alternative, and at the same time
attractive, counterworld. Paul could not and did not intend to overcome the
divisions within society, but instead he wanted to overcome these divisions
within the churches (cf. 1 Cor. 11:17–22). As he anchored the social-diaconal
dimension of faith directly in theology/Christology, he made them the indispensable constituents of Christian thinking and conduct.[69]

The Gospels

The Synoptic Gospels adopted the strong diaconal impulse of Jesus[70] and
presented it as the continuing obligation of believers, making Jesus the model
of suffering and dying for others and the foundation and measure of diaconal
conduct. Jesus probably understood his fate as "serving for others" (Mark 10:45:
"For the Son of Man did not come to be served, but to serve and to give his life as
a ransom for many").[71] The disciples should follow the word of their Lord: "For
I am in your midst as one who serves" (Luke 22:27). Directly connected to this
concept is a new ideal of domination, which Jesus formulates to the disciples in

69. A social-psychological explanatory model is provided by Gerd Theissen ("Gemeindestrukturen und Hilfsmotivation," 427). In order to make both external and internal social stigmatiza-
tion tolerable, the early Christians took over the values of the upper class: "The grip of upper-
class values was important for the motivation for charity in early Christianity. Ancient ideas of
benevolence (*euergetism*), the idea of charity in the aristocratic classes, was such a value of the
upper class and then became accessible in Christianity for the lower classes."
70. Cf. Horn, "Diakonische Leitlinien Jesu."
71. Cf. Roloff, "Anfänge der soteriologischen Deutung," 141: "Furthermore, it can scarcely
be questioned that this interpretation, which was exercised in the context of the early Palestinian
churches, can be traced back to the self-designation of the earthly Jesus."

Mark 10:42b–44: "You know that among the rulers of the gentiles, those whom they recognize as their rulers dominate them. It will not be this way among you. Rather, anyone who wishes to be great among you should be your servant, and whoever wants to be first, should be the servant of all." The ancient practice of rulers is subjected to a radical critique, for what distinguishes the true ruler is not suppression and exploitation but service and caring.[72] In the Gospels, Jesus's care for the tax collectors and sinners (cf. Mark 2:15–16; Luke 19:1–10; Matt. 11:19) and the healings of the sick stand in the horizon of the kingdom of God (cf. Luke 10:9 par; Mark 1:40–42; Matt. 10:8; Luke 10:27; 11:20), and the explicit renunciation of power (cf. Mark 10:43f.) stands in the foreground. What is demanded is a conduct that overcomes religious or cultural barriers and orients itself exclusively to the concrete well-being of the other, as the parable of the good Samaritan emphatically indicates with its concluding demand: "Go and do likewise!" (Luke 10:37). In the parable of the world judgment (Matt. 25:31–46), the works of love (feeding the hungry, giving a drink to the thirsty, being hospitable to strangers, clothing the naked, visiting the sick and the imprisoned) explicitly describe the meaning of "serving" (v. 44). The judge of the world not only breaks through all consideration of works righteousness but also identifies himself without reservation with those who are in need (v. 40b: "What you have done to the least of these my brothers, you have done to me") and gives a dimension that has been unheard. With the command for love of enemies (cf. Matt. 5:44), Jesus makes love boundless; a boundary is no longer possible, nor a limitation on the definition of the neighbor. It knows no boundaries, and it is for the benefit of all people. God's radical, boundless love penetrates the everyday life of people who, with their love of enemies, participate in the love of God. The renunciation of revenge (Luke 6:29), the prohibition of judging (Luke 6:37), and the command, "Give and it will be given to you!" (Luke 6:38) are dimensions of love. The central place of *diakonia* in the churches comes into view in the story of Mary and Martha (Luke 10:38–42). When Martha sees her primary task in "serving" (v. 40) and is criticized for it (v. 41f.), then the concern is for the balanced relationship between *diakonia* and teaching and a limit of unrelenting acts of love.

Johannine Literature

In the Johannine school also, faith is demonstrated and proved in love.[73] In Johannine literature, love is integrated in a comprehensive communicative

---

72. This position corresponds substantively to the vision that Dio Chrysostom (*Or.* 1–3) gives of the ideal ruler.

73. On the Johannine ethic, cf. M. Pfeiffer, *Einweisung in das neue Sein*, 95–136; E. Popkes, *Die Theologie der Liebe Gottes*; Watt, *Ethics and Ethos*; Schnelle, *Die Johannesbriefe*, 162–67;

event. Anyone who knows God and is from God keeps God's commandments and lives not in the darkness but in the light, so that one lives in love and truth and is withdrawn from sin. The love of God facilitates and demands the love of community members for each other (cf. 2 John 6; 1 John 2:4ff.; 4:10, 19; 5:1–5; John 3:16; 13:31–35; 15:9–10). The crucial command is "that you love one another as I have loved you" (John 13:34). The action required of this entire event is explicitly summarized in 1 John: "We know love in this, that he laid down his life for us. We ought also to give our lives for one another. How does God's love abide in anyone who has the world's goods and sees a brother or sister in need and yet refuses to help? Little children, let us love, not in word or speech, but in deed and truth" (1 John 3:16–18). Love, life, light, and truth are here closely connected. The starting point is the love of Christ, which was expressed in the giving of his life for others. This exemplary conduct of Jesus is applied to the Johannine community. A concrete exemplary social conduct is required of the members of the Johannine school. It comes to realization in the support of needy members of the community, and these demands are far removed from an ethics of ideological conviction;[74] it involves a definite social behavior, a love that is realized in deeds.

The foot washing as a portal (John 13:1–20)[75] and the love command (John 13:34–35) as the direct beginning of the farewell speech confirm this insight. In the time of Jesus's absence, the foot washing, an anticipation and prefiguring of the fate of Jesus, should motivate the church members to conduct themselves in love. The use of ἀγαπᾶν in 13:1 indicates that the way of Jesus to the cross stands in continuity with his previous being and activity and in continuity with love. John intentionally chooses the foot washing in order to illustrate the level of action, the concrete content of the idea of love. For John, love also is an event that cannot remain within itself and comes to completion in deeds. The existence of the people is transferred by God into a new quality, which is realized in correspondence to the act of Jesus in the foot washing: "If I, the Lord and Teacher, have washed your feet, so you ought to wash each other's feet" (John 13:14). Jesus's act includes in itself the obligation for the disciples to act in the same way (John 13:15, "For I have given you an example so that you do as I have done to you"). The metaphor of bearing

---

Watt and R. Zimmermann, *Rethinking the Ethics of John*; Weyer-Menkhoff, *Die Ethik des Johannesevangeliums*.

74. See Käsemann, *Testament of Jesus*, 65: "The object of Christian love for John is only what belongs to the community under the Word, or what is elected to belong to it, that is, the brotherhood of Jesus."

75. On the foot washing, cf., in addition to the commentaries, Kohler, *Kreuz und Menschwerdung*, 192–229; Niemand, *Die Fußwaschungserzählung*; Zumstein, "Die johanneische Auffassung der Macht."

fruit in the speech about the vineyard is another center of the Johannine ethic of love that is expressed in deeds:[76] "I am the true vine, and my Father is the vinegrower. He cuts off every branch in me that bears no fruit; he cleanses every branch that bears fruit so that it might bear more fruit" (John 15:1–2). Bearing fruit is, on the one hand, concentrated in the abiding in his word; on the other hand, the level of action is maintained, "for without me you can do nothing" (John 15:5d). The choice of the disciples by Jesus (John 15:16) is the presupposition for bearing fruit and at the same time aims toward that goal. Without the continuing connection with the vine, it is impossible for the branches to bear fruit. "As the Father has loved me, so have I loved you. Abide in my love! If you keep my commandments, you will abide in my love, just as I have kept the commands of my Father and abide in his love" (John 15:9–10). The disciples may know that they are totally and continually sustained by the love between the Father and the Son.

Salvation and Healing

A particular area of the expression of care within the community was manifest in the healings of the sick, for eschatological salvation and bodily healing belonged together.[77] The exorcisms and healings of Jesus (Luke 13:32b: "See, I drive out demons and perform healings") prove the foundation. Their purpose is the deprivation of Satan's power and the restoration of life, conforming to the creation (cf., e.g., Mark 3:22; Luke 11:20; 13:16; Mark 1:29–31, 40–45; 5:25–34; 7:31–37; 8:22–26; etc.).[78] Mark 9:14–29, with its emphasis on the inability of the disciples and an instruction on successful healing (Mark 9:29: "This kind can come out only through prayer") is evidence of a more or less successful healing praxis in the churches with direct appeal to Jesus. In 1 Cor. 12:9, 28, 30, Paul assumes that gifts of healing are self-evident. According to 2 Cor. 12:12, he himself has performed healings (cf. also Acts 19:11: "And God did extraordinary miracles through the hands of Paul"). The miracles of Acts (Peter: Acts 3:1–10; 5:12–16; 9:32–43; Paul: Acts 13:4–11; 14:8–14; 19:11f.; 20:7–12; 28:1–10; summaries: Acts 2:43; 4:30, 33; 5:12; 14:3)[79] not only reflect the popular veneration of Peter and Paul but also demonstrate the healing power of faith and of prayer, in which the Crucified and Risen One is living. The prayer for the sick in James 5:15 explicitly confirms this

---

76. On the interpretation, cf. Ritt, "Der christologische Imperativ"; Watt, "'Metaphorik' in Joh 15,1–8"; M. Pfeiffer, *Einweisung in das neue Sein,* 265–303.

77. Cf. here Schrage, "Heil und Heilung im Neuen Testament."

78. Cf. Schnelle, *Theology of the New Testament,* 121–28.

79. On the miracles in Acts, cf. Schreiber, *Paulus als Wundertäter,* 13–158.

connection ("And the prayer of faith will save the sick, and the Lord will raise them up"). The instruction on petitionary prayer in James 5:7–18 takes up a regular practice within the church: "Is anyone among you sick? So call the elders of the church, and they will pray over him and anoint him with oil in the name of the Lord" (James 5:14). Bodily help and eschatological salvation both lie in the power of the Lord, who is at work in the prayer and service of the elders.

The Later Development

In the letters at the end of the first century, social problems within the churches come to the foreground and to some extent reflect the formation of an institutionalized diaconal Christianity. Colossians and Ephesians remain with the instruction to support the neighbor in word and deed (cf. Col. 3:17; Eph. 4:28), but in the household codes they introduce a further relevant diaconal element (Col. 3:18–4:1; Eph. 5:22–6:9).[80] Crucial here are the reciprocal obligations of the wives and husbands, children and parents, fathers, slaves and masters. In particular, the position of slaves within the Christian house was probably strengthened. The reciprocal duties now indicate to the masters that they all have a master and will receive their reward without respect of persons (Col. 3:24; 4:1; Eph. 5:21; 6:5, 9).

Throughout 1 Peter, the consistent strategy is to stabilize the church in its difficult situation through recognition and at the same time to make the recognition and convivial model of the letter attractive to outsiders.[81] The Christians must demonstrate their membership in the people of God through love for brothers and sisters, fear of God, and a conscious rejection of earlier relationships, which includes rather than excludes a loyal coexistence in the pagan society (1 Pet. 2:12: "Conduct yourselves honorably among the Gentiles"). Within this conception, visible good deeds take on a special significance: "For this is the will of God that you, through your good deeds, silence the ignorance of foolish people" (1 Pet. 2:15); "It is better to suffer for the good and not for evil deeds" (1 Pet. 3:17). Christians should be zealous for the good (1 Pet. 3:13) and be able to give an account to everyone (1 Pet. 3:15).

Second Thessalonians 3:6–13 speaks of the misuse of financial support within the church. Here the warning is explicitly made of church leaders' indulgence in idleness. When it is emphasized in verse 8 that "one has not taken bread from anyone free of charge" and the demand follows, "Whoever will not work, neither should he eat" (2 Thess. 3:10), then the church leaders who

---

80. See above, 10.3.2 under "The Deutero-Pauline Letters."
81. Cf. Popp, *Die Kunst der Konvivenz.*

receive gifts without doing anything to pay their financial costs are probably in view. The instruction concerning widows in 1 Tim. 5:3–16 is noteworthy. They apparently comprise a large group in the church,[82] and a church treasury existed for the care of widows (1 Tim. 5:16). Of course, this treasury should be used only for women who lead exemplary lives. The misuse of this institution (cf. 1 Tim. 5:4–15) is indicated not only by the capacity of the system of offering support but also in the conflict over who is to be regarded as a "widow" within the community. There was possibly a type of "widow's office": widows were provided for, and they, in turn, were given spiritual and social tasks within the community. This model was so attractive that it led to misuse and conflicts within the community.

The Old World and the New Conduct of Christians

The new and attractive aspect of Christian behavior is indicated especially in the comparison with the social conduct and benevolence in the Greco-Roman societies.[83] The worship of the gods of the imperial pantheon was focused on the correct exercise of the rituals in order to appease the gods. Thus the obligation to a definite ethical or social behavior was not connected with the exercise of the ritual.[84] Financial contributions were necessary for the performance of the cult. Cults or temples had at their disposal a sizeable fortune (e.g., the Artemis cult in Ephesus); in the context of local cults, the feeding of the poor and similar activities were practiced. All of this, however, did not involve a sustainable and continuing support of general welfare. While charity (*beneficia*) was highly regarded and welcome everywhere,[85] it was not an actual obligation made by the religion or philosophy. Within the framework of a reciprocal basic order, good works (εὐεργεσία) served as thankfulness/response for an elevated place in society. Poverty and wealth were not seen as phenomena determined by society but treated within the context of societal conventions or individual ethical matters. "Philosophical ethics considered

82. Cf. Dassmann, "Witwen und Diakonissen"; Wagener, *Die Ordnung des "Hauses Gottes,"* 115–233.

83. Cf. Thraede, "Soziales Verhalten und Wohlfahrtspflege."

84. Cf. Thraede, "Soziales Verhalten und Wohlfahrtspflege," 48–49.

85. A balanced portrayal is given by Longenecker, *Remember the Poor*, 60–107. A few positive examples: Strabo, *Geography* 14.2.5, reports about Rhodes: "The Rhodians are concerned for the people in general, although their rule is not democratic; still, they wish to take care of their multitude of poor people. Accordingly, the people are supplied with provisions and the needy are supported by the well-to-do, by a certain ancestral custom" (LCL); Musonius, *Diss.* 19, criticizes luxury buildings: "How much more commendable than living a life of luxury it is to help many people. . . . What would one gain from a large and beautiful house comparable to what he would gain by conferring the benefits of his wealth upon the city and his fellow citizens."

need as irrelevant for the self-realization of the wise or educated."[86] Concrete action for disadvantaged people or groups was rather secondary in the thought of the political, military, and intellectual elite.[87]

With the Christians, however, serving was an exemplary performance of being a Christian; it belonged as a natural consequence of faith in its very nature. If God is love (cf. 1 John 4:8, 16), then the consequence is the concrete concern of the believers for those in need and suffering. Social boundaries of status lost their significance. Even Christian slaves were incorporated into the ethos of conducting themselves as brothers, and a supraregional network of assistance was formed. Thus the early Christians introduced a new hierarchy of values, the head of which is active love.

13.4. Early Christianity as a Religion of the City and of Education

Early Christianity as an Urban Religion

Jesus ministered primarily in rural areas and villages in Galilee and apparently avoided larger cities, such as Sepphoris and Tiberias; he met his death in the big city of Jerusalem. For a long time after Easter, the new movement of Christ-believers developed both in rural Galilee and in Jerusalem and then rapidly became a predominantly urban phenomenon. The churches of Damascus and Antioch were the first large churches outside Israel, to which were added Rome (and perhaps also Alexandria) in the 40s CE. Finally, the Pauline mission is already an exclusively urban phenomenon (see above, 8.1).

The transition from an originally rural to a predominantly urban movement had several reasons:[88] (1) The relatively unified Greco-Roman Mediterranean culture in the first century CE was a basis for the rapid expansion of Christianity into different regions. This cultural form was found in Asia Minor as the crucial first region of expansion, especially in the cities. (2) A great portion of the rural population, living at the minimal requirement for their existence, was not open to radical changes.[89] Consequently, the predominantly conservative attitude of the rural population made the city the ideal area for mission. (3) Here people who were mobile, such as tradesmen or handworkers,

---

86. Thraede, *Soziales Verhalten und Wohlfahrtspflege*, 55.
87. Cf. Veyne, *Brot und Spiele*; Gehrke, "Euergetismus."
88. Cf. Meeks, *First Urban Christians*, 9–73.
89. Cf. Macmullen, *Roman Social Relations*. The contrasts between city and countryside, as maintained by Meeks, *First Urban Christians*, 9–10, should not be overemphasized; cf. Bendemann and Tiwald, "Das frühe Christentum und die Stadt," 25–26. In 1 Clem. 42.4 the villages and then the cities are mentioned as the places for the proclamation of the apostles and their successors.

were open to new ideas and ready to support new movements. Their frequent movements also encouraged the spread of early Christianity, for the good Roman network of roads to a certain extent created the possibility for the spread of the gospel. (4) While one could move effortlessly in the large cities with Greek as the world language, numerous dialects were spoken in the rural areas. (5) The large cities already had a great religious variety and infrastructure (especially in architecture), so that new religious movements at first were scarcely noticed. Furthermore, cities, with their anonymity (then as now), opened the possibility of practicing new ways of living in the form of house religion without being subject to the social control of the family or clan. (6) It was also possible for the early Christians to fit into the existing religious infrastructure since outsiders would perceive them as an association (see above, 8.3). (7) Successful early Christian missionaries such as Philip, Barnabas, Paul, Prisca and Aquila, and Apollos were already socialized in the city so that their concentration in cities can be explained by their urban background. (8) Cities offered early Christian missionaries not only possibilities for mission but also for finding work. They could remain financially independent, devote themselves to the new movement without outside pressure, and demonstrate their credibility.

The first urban church of the new movement of Christ-believers was formed in Jerusalem (see above, chap. 5). Jerusalem already had a long history as the "holy city" of Judaism and was transformed under Herod the Great into a Hellenistic metropolis by the expansion of the fortress Antonia and the building of a theater and hippodrome as well as a palace.[90] The expansion of the temple complex especially introduced a splendor that had not existed before. The living environment of this city is especially visible in the passion narrative of the Synoptic Gospels and the Lukan portrayal of the first church in Acts 1–6.[91] Jesus drives out those who were selling from the portico of the temple (Mark 11:15–16 par.), and on the temple grounds he engages in dispute with the Jewish authorities (Mark 11:27–33 par.). After the Last Supper in the large upper room of a house (Mark 14:15; Luke 22:12) and the arrest in the garden of Gethsemane, Jesus is brought to the house of the high priest Caiaphas. This event was followed by a trial before the high council, then before Pilate in the palace of the governor (cf. Luke 22:66–71; Mark 15:16; Matt. 27:27; John 18:28, 33; 19:9). From there Jesus was led away to Golgotha, a skull-shaped hill outside the ancient city (cf. Mark 15:22; John 19:17, 20). In his portrayal of the first Jerusalem church, Luke employs local traditions: After

90. On Jerusalem, cf. Küchler, *Jerusalem*; Keel, *Die Geschichte Jerusalems*, vol. 1.
91. Two archaeological sites identified with a precise location and connected with Bethesda/the Pool of Siloam are mentioned in the Gospel of John (5:1–7; 9:1–7).

the ascension the disciples assemble on the Mount of Olives (Acts 1:9–12); Peter and John go up to the temple at the "Beautiful Gate" (Acts 3:1–10) and preach in "Solomon's Portico" (Acts 3:11–26), after which they were led to a trial before the high council (Acts 4:1–22). They met regularly in the house of Mary, the mother of John Mark (Acts 12:12). The possibilities and the dangers of an urban religion are indicated clearly in Acts: on the one hand, the success of the first mission (cf. the symbolic number 3,000 in Acts 2:41; 5,000 in 4:4), but on the other hand, the increasing pressure from Jewish authorities against the new movement (cf. Acts 7:54–60).

The new movement experienced a remarkable expansion in Damascus and in Antioch (see above, 6.4), where churches were founded circa 31/32 or circa 34 CE. In both cities there was a large Jewish community and traditionally good economic and cultural connections with Jerusalem. It is no coincidence that even in a multicultural large city such as Antioch, the Christians were first recognized as a separate group (cf. Acts 11:19–30), for here (as also in Rome) economic independence, the formation of house churches, and the emancipation from cultural (Jewish) boundaries were most likely possible. Cities offered the early churches not only a good environment; they were also particularly the place in which the new identity of Christians was formed in an often painful and controversial, as well as a rapid, process. First Corinthians especially (see above, 8.1; 8.5) indicates the special challenges faced by urban churches.[92] The persistence of old cultural and religious values, the pressure from the pagan environment, and the practice of new norms frequently came into conflict. Especially in questions of sexual morality (cf. 1 Cor. 6:12–20: participation in cultic prostitution; 1 Cor. 7:1–16, 25–40: marriage, getting married, divorce, the place of widows), legal disputes among Christians (1 Cor. 6:1–11), and the (further) participation in pagan cultic meals (1 Cor. 8:1–13; 10:14–23: meat offered to idols), old mores and new insights came into conflict with each other. In addition, there were the independent theological concepts of the Corinthians (concepts of perfection and freedom: 1 Cor. 4:8; 6:12; 10:23; resurrection that has already occurred: 1 Cor. 15:12–19) as well as differing views of the meaning of baptism (cf. 1 Cor. 1:10–17), slavery (cf. 1 Cor. 7:17–24), conduct in the worship service (1 Cor. 11:1–6: the conduct of women; 1 Cor. 11:17–34: appropriate participation in the sacraments), and the meaning of the gifts (cf. 1 Cor. 12–14: their preference for glossolalia). Despite many problems, the cities were the ideal places to overcome the process of establishing an identity and securing the stability of the new movement.

---

92. On the situation in Corinth, cf. Baird, "'One against the Other'"; Horsley, "1 Corinthians: A Case Study"; Maschmeier, "Der Glaube auf dem Marktplatz."

Ephesus is an example of how cities, over generations and theological directions, became theological centers and hubs.[93] The church was probably founded by Apollos (see above, 6.2) and then became a center of the Pauline mission. Paul worked there methodically for several years (cf. Acts 19:9) and wrote 1 Corinthians from Ephesus (cf. 1 Cor. 16:8). Ephesus may have been the setting for the Pauline school, which began during Paul's lifetime and then continued in the deutero-Pauline letters (see above, 8.2), for at least the Letter to the Ephesians and the Pastoral Epistles were written there.[94] The married couple associated closely with Paul, Prisca and Aquila, also worked in Ephesus (cf. 1 Cor. 16:19; Acts 18:19, 26). The Johannine school may be located in Ephesus (see above, 10.4).[95] Various Johannine churches existed in the area of Ephesus (cf. 2–3 John), of which the primary community was in Ephesus. Three reasons support this conclusion: (1) According to ancient church tradition, the Gospel of John originated in Ephesus.[96] (2) The impact of the Fourth Gospel (*alogoi*, Montanists, Acts of John, reception by the Gnostics) points clearly toward Asia Minor and to the western part (Rom) of the Roman Empire.[97] First John is attested in Asia Minor soon after it was written (cf. Pol. *Phil.* 7.1). (3) The theological agreements between Pauline and Johannine theology (preexistence, theology of the cross, christological titles, pneumatology, anthropology, ethics) indicate that Ephesus was the common setting for Paul and the Johannine school. Here the history of traditions came together, for John relied on Paul for the formation of his theology.[98]

Beyond these, other theological streams may be connected with Ephesus. In Revelation, the first of the seven letters to the churches was written to the church in Ephesus (Rev. 2:7), a fact that suggests the continuing significance of the city. The church is praised by the seer, but at the same time he refers to the major conflict with the Nicolaitans (Rev. 2:6). How widely should one be open to the pagan environment and its religious and political claims (imperial cult)? The seer thus represents the position of clear separation: he rejects participation in any form of idolatry and prostitution (Rev. 2:14). In Ignatius also (see below, 14.1), the Letter to the Ephesians is the longest writing that, of course, presupposes a fully different church situation from the one in Revelation. Ignatius vehemently argues against radical docetists, who consider the divine nature only (cf. Ign. *Eph.* 7.2, 16; 18.2, 19; 20.2). He encourages the unity of the church (cf. Ign.

---

93. Cf. Tiwald, "Frühchristliche Pluralität in Ephesus."
94. Cf. Schnelle, *Einleitung*, 381–82, 410.
95. Cf. Tilborg, *Reading John in Ephesus.*
96. Cf. Irenaeus, *Haer.* 3.1.1 (= Eusebius, *Hist. eccl.* 5.8.4); 2.22.5 (= Eusebius, *Hist. eccl.* 3.23.3).
97. Cf. T. Nagel, *Die Rezeptionsgeschichte des Johannesevangeliums.*
98. Cf. below, 13.5.2 under "Paul and John."

Eph. 4), attempts to strengthen the office of bishop (cf. Ign. *Eph.* 1–6), and appeals explicitly to Paul (Ign. *Eph.* 12.2). Both Revelation and Ignatius indicate that several Christian churches must have existed in Ephesus at the same time. The singular ἐκκλησία (church, community) in Rev. 2:1 and the reference to the reputed apostles in Rev. 2:2 suggest this conclusion as does Ignatius's polemic against the autonomous assemblies of the docetists (cf. Ign. *Eph.* 5.2, 3; 7.1; 16.1). Besides, wandering prophets come (Ign. *Eph.* 9.1) who travel from church to church and create unrest with their teaching. Whether a connection existed between the separate churches of the "Pauline" type (Paul, deutero-Pauline letters, Ignatius) and of the "Johannine" type and whether all of them considered themselves "one church" of Christians remain open questions.

Finally, in a few NT writings, cities become (negative or positive) theological models. The Gospel of Mark is shaped by a tension between Galilee and Jerusalem.[99] Jerusalem appears from the beginning as a place of hostility to Jesus (cf. Mark 3:6; 7:1); the three passion predictions in Mark 8:31; 9:31; 10:33 interpret the path from Galilee to Jerusalem as a way of suffering and dying in lowliness and mocking. The conflict in Mark 11:15–18 reaches its climax, where Jesus attacks the religious authorities with the cleansing of the temple. While in Jerusalem the innocent Jesus of Nazareth is imprisoned and dies a shameful death (cf. Mark 14:1–3, 43–64; 15:1–41), Galilee becomes the place of the appearances of the Resurrected One (cf. Mark 14:28; 16:7). In Luke-Acts also Jerusalem has a special theological connotation, this time in interplay with Rome. God's historical action is an event aimed at a goal that is borne in all its epochs by his saving will. Jesus "must" go on the way to Jerusalem for the passion (Luke 9:31; 13:33; 24:26, 44). Likewise, the systematic expansion of the gospel in the world from Jerusalem to Rome is based on a divine plan, which the exalted Lord has given to the apostles (Acts 1:8): "You will be my witnesses in Jerusalem, in Judea and Samaria, and to the end of the earth." This program takes place as a great movement from Jerusalem to Rome, the center, interpreted and underlined with the "way" metaphor (cf. Acts 13:10; 19:23).[100] Luke first describes the initial period in Jerusalem (Acts 1–5) and then describes the spread of the gospel beyond Judea, Samaria, Caesarea, and Antioch in order to place Paul in the center. Luke emphasizes three times that Paul "must" go to Rome (Acts 19:21; 23:11; 27:24, "Do not be afraid, Paul! You must appear before Caesar").[101] Caesar also served the

---

99. The theological dimension of this contrast was first observed by E. Lohmeyer, *Galiläa und Jerusalem*.

100. Cf. J. Schäfer, "Vom Zentrum zum Zentrum."

101. Cf. Burfeind, "Paulus *muß* nach Rom," 83: "With the three journeys, Luke has given a structure to Acts according to a theological point of view: first he legitimates the gentile mission,

will of God, for it was in response to his decree that Mary and Joseph went to Bethlehem (Luke 2:1–21), and an appeal to Caesar brought Paul to Rome (Acts 25:11). For Luke, Jerusalem and Rome are both abiding centers and the crucial axis of the proclamation of the gospel to the whole world.

Revelation develops an impressive sacral architecture, which offers a view of history interpreting anew earthly events as a heavenly cult reality intelligible within the framework of an apocalyptic style.[102] Thus the central ecclesiological image is portrayed in the new Jerusalem coming down from heaven (cf. Rev. 21:1–22:5; cf. 3:12).[103] After the unholy city Rome/Babylon is destroyed (Rev. 18:1–24), the new Jerusalem appears as the eschatological antithesis and the new creation of God. The image of Jerusalem was taken by John from ancient Judaism[104] and the NT tradition (Gal. 4:21–31) and is inserted into continuity with Israel in salvation history, a theme that is important for him. At the end of time the idea of the city of God as the realization of the ideal kingdom of God and ideal community for believers appears in the place of the transitory imitation. God and Christ merge in their activity (Rev. 11:15; 22:3–4), and finally God and the Lamb will rule the new Jerusalem (21:22; 22:3b–4). Believers will enter into the eschatological reality of God, through the gates of the heavenly Jerusalem (Rev. 22:14), and the church is certain that "salvation [ἡ σωτηρία] comes from our God, who sits upon the throne, and the Lamb" (Rev. 7:10; cf. 12:10; 19:1). The seer makes a noteworthy accent in the form of the image: the description of the city (cf. Rev. 21:12ff.) echoes especially the vision of Ezekiel of the postexilic temple (Ezek. 40–48)[105] so that now the ideal city is the place of the abiding dwelling place of God.[106] There is no longer a temple there, for "the temple is the Lord, God the Almighty, and the Lamb" (Rev. 21:22). In the new Jerusalem as the ideal city, the communal life is opened for the brothers and sisters in the presence of God. This future

---

then the independence of the gentile mission from the synagogue; and finally, the political relevance of the universalization of Christianity becomes increasingly clear."

102. The various references to images, space, and time in Revelation are shaped by both Jewish and Hellenistic traditions; cf. Tóth, *Der himmlische Kult*, 48–156.

103. On the analysis, cf. Georgi, "Die Visionen vom himmlischen Jerusalem"; Roloff, "Neuschöpfung in der Offenbarung"; Söllner, *Jerusalem, du hochgebaute Stadt*; F. Hahn, "Das neue Jerusalem"; Wick, "Das Paradies in der Stadt."

104. Cf. Tob. 13:16–18; 14:5; 1 En. 90.28–29; 4 Ezra 7.26, 44; 8.52; 9.26 and passim.

105. For the seer, Ezekiel is the preferred OT reference; cf. Kowalski, *Die Rezeption des Propheten Ezechiel*; Sänger, *Das Ezechielbuch.*

106. Georgi, "Die Visionen vom himmlischen Jerusalem," assumes, probably correctly, that conceptions of the ideal Hellenistic polis lie in the background. A sketch of the new Jerusalem is given by Böcher, "Mythos und Rationalität," 169, who convincingly classifies the number symbolism, number riddles, knowledge of stones, astronomy/astrology, and angels/demons as rational elements of the interpretation of the world.

event is already a salutary reality in the church, which is a help for overcoming the open and hidden dangers in order to enter at the end of time.

Early Christianity and Education

If one places early Christianity within the reference points of Greco-Roman antiquity (with respect to politics, the military, religion, education), it is a phenomenon in which education plays an important role. The members of the new movement by no means came from the lowest classes at the beginning, but all levels were represented (see above, 8.3). Furthermore, with the passage of time, increasingly more rich and educated people joined the churches, as especially Luke-Acts, the deutero-Pauline letters, James, and Hebrews indicate (see above, 11.2). Besides, can one classify a movement as unliterary or uneducated[107] that, as early as the first fifty years of its existence, produced many writings and new genres like no other religion in its initial phase?

Education in antiquity was intended for the formation and maturation of people with respect to their intellectual and bodily capabilities. In addition, they learned basic technical skills (writing, reading, grammar, introduction to rhetoric, arithmetic),[108] especially for the communication and exercise of moral concepts,[109] which make possible a balanced life in sufficiency, sobriety, courage, and justice. Already in antiquity the concept of education involved far more than technical skill and had as its goal an ethical orientation. For Seneca alone, ethical perfection (*virtus perfecta*) was the goal of education, for which only the subjects of the seven *artes liberales* (grammar, rhetoric, arithmetic, geometry, astronomy, dialectic/logic, music) could prepare one.[110] Such a version of the concept of education is thoroughly adaptable to modern theories of education, especially for which formation of identity on the basis of a necessary communication of knowledge, acquisition of orientation for life and action, critical skills, and the development of a personal profile

---

107. Cf., e.g., Deissmann, *Light from the Ancient East*, 208: "Christianity did not begin as a literary movement. Its creative epoch was unliterary."

108. Cf. Quintilian, *Institutio oratoria* 1.4–10.

109. Cf. Plutarch, *Mor.* 2A, who indicates that the acquisition of virtue involved the concurrence of three aspects: "nature, reason, and habit [φύσιν καὶ λόγον καὶ ἔθος]. By reason, I mean the act of learning, and by habit, I mean constant practice."

110. Cf. Seneca, *Ep.* 88.20: "Why, then, do we educate our children in the liberal studies? It is not because they can bestow virtue, but because they prepare the soul for the reception of virtue"; *Ep.* 88.29: "I should like to pass in review the several virtues. Bravery [*fortitudo*] . . . Loyalty [*fides*] . . . Temperance [*temperantia*] . . . Kindliness [*humanitas*]." *Ep.* 88.33: "Wisdom is a large and spacious thing; it needs plenty of room; one must learn things about the divine and the human, the past and the future, the ephemeral and the eternal; and one must learn about Time" (LCL).

stand at the center.[111] Development of character and profile, ethical orientation, capacity for judgment and discernment (cf. Rom. 12:2; Phil. 4:8), and especially identity formation (cf. 2 Cor. 5:17) all undoubtedly stand at the center of the early Christian life of faith within the community, making early churches also a place of formation.

Who, though, in antiquity and especially in the churches could read and write? Here particular problems emerge, for the sources are random and diffuse. Thus it is not surprising that the optimistic older estimate, especially that of William Harris, must be reduced.[112] Harris maintained that about 10–15 percent of the entire population could read and write to some extent.[113] In the recent[114] and newest research the picture again changes, for here an altered perspective is dominant in the idea of "everyday writing":[115] away from the fixation on the book to a study of the various written and oral forms of communication in an ancient city. Here the dramatically increased number of archaeological discoveries over recent decades indicates that there were numerous statements (documents, brief texts of every kind, receipts, notes, graffiti of all kinds, programs for official events,[116] religious/public inscriptions, public announcements at the level of the city, province, or empire). These

111. One example from the myriad of definitions: "Education is the acquisition of a system of morally desired dispositions through the imparting and adopting of knowledge in such a way that people define their place, receive their personality profile, and attain their orientation for life and action through choice, assessment, and articulation within the reference system of their historical and social world. One can also say instead, education produces identity, having the relationship in mind that the subject 'education and identity' desires to establish." Kössler, "Bildung und Identität," 56.

112. Cf. Hatch, *Influence of Greek Ideas*, 25–49, for the first-century CE schools, as on 35: "It may be inferred from the extant evidence that there were grammar schools in almost every town. At these all youths receive the first part of their education"; Marrou (*History of Education*, 266) states, "But apart from these exceptions, most children went to school—the girls, apparently, on the same footing as the boys." He refers to a statement in Martial, *Epigrams* 9.68: "Cursed teacher, what have you done? You are an abomination to all of the boys, all of the girls! The roosters scarcely begin to crow, and you cry out, thrashing through the city."

113. Cf. Harris, *Ancient Literacy*, 328–29 (for the 5th cent. BCE he calculates 15 percent of the entire male population; for the period from 100 BCE he calculates 10 percent of the population, but in isolated Hellenistic cities 30–40 percent of the men who were born free). His conclusion: "The written culture of antiquity was in the main restricted to a privileged minority—though in some places it was quite a large minority—and it coexisted with elements of an oral culture" (337).

114. Cf. Millard, *Pergament und Papyrus*, 155–56, who emphasizes against a limitation of reading and writing to the elite: "In this chapter we will attempt to portray a positive view with consideration of Greco-Roman texts of every kind."

115. Cf. Bagnall, *Everyday Writing*; also W. Johnson and H. Parker, *Ancient Literacies*.

116. An example: Cicero, *Orationes philippicae* 2.97, mentions borrower's notes and then says: "For this there are dealers who publicly offer for sale such things as programs, entrance cards [*libellos*] for gladiator battles."

are made of various materials (papyrus, ostraca, parchment, stone, animal hides, wood) and are found in various places (e.g., public places, theaters, marketplaces, shops, sanctuaries, parks, entrances to houses).[117] Ancient society, particularly in the cities, was a society of communication, in which central places, lecture halls,[118] and theaters were places of public culture, that is, of lectures, meetings, promotion, and exchange. After Augustus, not only literature production increased, but also the number of public inscriptions was more prevalent.[119] Without a rudimentary knowledge of reading and writing, one could not actually move in an ancient city, as the inscriptions and graffiti at Pompeii confirm even today.[120] Inasmuch as the majority of the children probably attended elementary school,[121] one may assume various levels of reading and writing competence. In any case probably around 30 to 50 percent of the population in the towns and larger cities had an elementary knowledge of writing and reading.

For the early Christian churches also there was likewise no reason to be pessimistic. The following reasons support a relatively high rate of literacy in comparison with the total population in the early churches (more than 50 percent): (1) In the initial period the church was located in the city, where the literacy rate was clearly higher than in rural areas. (2) A considerable part of the church members came from Judaism's area of influence, which had a higher literacy rate than average in the Roman Empire.[122] The household slaves (cf. Philemon) who joined the early churches probably had a higher than average level of education. (3) In the early churches a lively literary and intellectual life was dominant: the Septuagint was studied, that is, read aloud

117. Cf. Dreyer, "Medien für Erziehung."

118. Philo, *Prelim. Studies* 64, reports about his time: "Hardly a day passes but the lecture-halls and theaters are filled with philosophers discoursing at length, stringing together their questions on virtue without stopping to take a breath."

119. Cf. Hoff, Stroh, and M. Zimmermann, *Divus Augustus*, 190: "About the same number of inscriptions have been preserved from the forty-four years of the rule of Augustus as from all 450 years of the Roman Republic, total inscriptions from the imperial period outnumbering those of the republic by roughly 10 to 1."

120. Cf. Hüttemann, *Pompejanische Inschriften*; Huninck, *Glücklich ist dieser Ort!*

121. Cf. Weeber, *Alltag im Alten Rom*, 312: "The literacy level of the city population was relatively high; most of the children attended an elementary school for somewhere around four years in the ages between roughly seven and eleven."

122. On the value placed on education, cf. Philo, *Spec. Laws* 2.61–62, where he combines the prohibition of work on the Sabbath with the challenge to be occupied with philosophy: "So each seventh day there stand wide open in every city thousands of schools of good sense, temperance, courage, justice, and the other virtues"; on the nature of contemporary Jewish instruction, cf. Safrai, "Education and the Study of the Torah"; Riesner, *Jesus als Lehrer*, 97–245. An alternative view is argued by Hezser, *Jewish Literacy in Roman Palestine*, who assumes that in Palestine even fewer people could read and write than in the rest of the Roman Empire.

13.1. The theater at Hierapolis

publicly, read privately, and discussed. Paul made use of a secretary (cf. Rom. 16:22), and the letters of Paul were not only read publicly (cf. 1 Thess. 5:27), but the apostle also assumes that people would read his letters with their own eyes (Gal. 6:11, "See with what large letters I write with my own hand"; also 1 Cor. 16:21; Philem. 19). (4) The texts indicate that in the churches—as was common in antiquity[123]—the letters were predominantly read aloud, giving the oral tradition a special importance so that church members with little capacity for writing and reading could participate intensively in church life. In addition, education was not identical (and is not in the present) with competence for reading and writing, for anyone who could not (or barely could) read and write was not automatically uneducated. (5) The existence of a Pauline and Johannine school also indicates (see above, 8.2; 10.4) that in many churches an intensive theological work took place, which is not conceivable without assuming an education. (6) Furthermore, education in the first century CE was not bound to social class.[124] (7) According to 1 Cor. 12:28; Gal. 6:6; Rom. 12:7b; and Acts 13:1, teachers were active in the churches from the beginning. Their tasks concentrated on the interpretation of the (oral or written)

123. Cf. Seneca, *Ep.* 95.2; Pliny the Younger, *Ep.* 1.13.
124. Thus, e.g., a large number of Epictetus's pupils were without means; he calls to them: "As soon as you have fed your fill to-day, you sit lamenting about the morrow, wherewithal you shall be fed" (*Diatr.* 1.19.9 LCL).

kerygma as well as the interpretation of written texts. The Gospels also indicate directly or indirectly the activity of early Christian teachers, portraying Jesus of Nazareth primarily as a teacher.[125] (8) The multilingual character (Greek/Latin, Hebrew/Aramaic/local languages) of many church members, the creation of new literary genres (Gospels; cf. above, 10.1), and the major themes treated in the letters (mostly Pauline) especially indicate that a great linguistic and intellectual creativity was dominant in the new movement (see above, 6.6; 10.1; 13.1–3). (9) Paul and John in particular worked intentionally with the educational traditions of their time and participated in religious-philosophical discussion (freedom, justice, logos, truth) in order to define the new faith in intellectual terms and to make the urban elite receptive to it.

Conclusion. Socialization within early Christianity took place largely through education and literature![126] No religious figure (earlier or later) gave rise to a literature as quickly and totally as Jesus Christ! From the beginning, the astonishing production of literature of early Christianity was a historic strategy[127] inasmuch as Christians both wrote history and made history. As a comprehensive program for life, meaning, and thinking, early Christianity presented a phenomenon in education, a creative movement that called for people to change their conduct and to think anew about God, the world, the neighbor, and oneself.

Early Christianity developed in the first century CE primarily as an urban religion. It could avail itself of all the advantages of urban life (equally public and intimate, relatively easy attraction of followers of all social levels, exercise in the practice of the Christian life). Anyone who joined the new movement entered into an already-formed world of teaching and language. Thus one may assume a definitely high intellectual level, because a comparison with local cults, the mystery religions, and the imperial cult indicates that early Christianity was a religion that possessed critical reflection and analysis. The letters of Paul contain proclamation but are primarily argumentative texts that make great demands on the hearer and reader (as is the case today). The Gospels are masterful narratives that present biographical and kerygmatic elements in a new genre and enable hearers to have

125. Cf., e.g., L. Schenke, "Jesus als Weisheitslehrer."

126. See Hurtado, *Destroyer of the gods*, 105–41, who describes early Christianity as a "bookish religion."

127. Augustus presents a certain political-religious parallel. His person, function, and work were depicted in a literary manner that was until then unknown; on Augustan literary politics, cf. Hoff, Stroh, and M. Zimmermann, *Divus Augustus*, 143–70.

a continuing memory of Jesus Christ. Anyone who has heard, read, or discussed such texts can scarcely be called "uneducated."

13.5 The Major Theological Currents and Networks near the End of the First Century

13.5.1 The Five Major Currents

Around 50 CE there were three major historical-theological currents: the Jerusalem church with the strong Jewish Christian standpoint of James the brother of the Lord, the Jesus movement with its concentration on the work of Jesus, and the universal conception of Antioch/Paul (see above, 6.9). The Jerusalem church perished (see above, 9.2), and with it the strict Jewish Christianity clearly lost influence. Although all three movements survived, they went through a process of total transformation. Around the end of the first century CE, two other bearers of tradition were added (cf. Gal. 2:9: "James and Cephas and John, considered to be pillars") so that five major streams defined theological thought.[128] They interacted with each other in various ways and then prevailed in the further historical development.

PAUL

The paramount place of Paul, the apostle to the gentiles in early Christianity, is undisputed and no accident. It was carried out by Paul himself (see above, 10.3.2) and rested on three pillars: (1) his theology, which to some extent was difficult to understand and at the same time stirring; (2) his successful mission to the gentiles, which formed the actual foundation for the expansion of Christianity around 100 CE; and (3) his martyrdom, which, in the view of later generations, confirmed the divine election of the apostle (cf. 1 Clem. 5.5; Ign. *Eph.* 12.2). Besides Paul himself was the Pauline school (see above, 8.2), and after his death deutero-Paulinism (see above, 10.3), which propagated and further developed the Pauline legacy, his historical achievement, and the significance of the person of the apostle in a changed era. At the center of the image of Paul around 100 CE was the memory of the great contender for the gospel and of the courageous martyr for Christ, who became an example of faith through his fearless and tireless engagement for the church. Acts and the deutero-Pauline letters (see above, 10.3) propagate this

---

128. Hebrews and the Revelation of John are independent witnesses (see above, 10.5.2) without either being considered one of the great theological streams.

image with differing accents; it is, however, dominant also in 1 Clement and in Ignatius of Antioch (see below, 14.1). Isolated accents of the theological argument in the Pauline letters are taken up in the deutero-Pauline letters and modified without reaching the level of the apostle. At the same time, however, the genuine theology was disseminated and propagated by the collection of the Pauline letters in a process that cannot be underestimated! Second Peter 3:15–16 ("so our beloved brother Paul has written to you")[129] documents that the letters, despite their difficult content, were read in the churches and discussed and thus had a lasting effect. Furthermore, the lasting significance of Paul is indicated in the fact that all relevant streams of early Christianity are influenced by him and respond either positively or negatively.[130]

THE SYNOPTIC GOSPELS

The traditions of the Jesus movement, the second stream at the beginning (see above, 6.9), flowed into the Synoptic Gospels (see above, 10.2), which became the crucial bearers of the Jesus tradition. The new literary genre, gospel, made it possible to formulate old traditions from and about Jesus as well as actual texts into its contemporary significance in a narrative of Jesus Christ. A theological plan based on narrative integrated various aspects of the ministry and death of Jesus and combined it with concrete internal and external problems in the church. All three Gospels agree in the basic narrative, but all had their own theological program and specific questions in their churches that needed to be answered.

Around 100 CE the Synoptic Gospels were primarily sources of information. As Justin, 1 *Apol.* 67.3, attests, they were read in the worship service: "On Sunday all who live in cities or in the country come together in one place, and the memoirs [τὰ ἀπομνημονεύματα][131] of the apostles or the writings of the prophets are read." A discourse, prayers, and the Eucharist followed the reading.[132] The function of the Gospels as Holy Scripture and their role as a source of information are not in contradiction; for a church that was expanding primarily in Asia Minor, Greece, and Italy, it was important to

---

129. Pervo, *Making of Paul*, 143, observes correctly that in the direct address in the deutero-Pauline letters, "Paul's words are directed to all believers."

130. Cf. below, 13.5.2: Networking, a type of "family tree" of the impact of Pauline literature, is offered by Pervo, *Making of Paul*, 242–44, who distinguishes between the "left" (e.g., Mark, Marcion), "moderate" (e.g., Colossians, Ephesians), "right" (e.g., Luke, Pastoral Epistles"), "Pauline," and "Anti-Pauline" (e.g., James, Matthew, Revelation) in the reception of Paul.

131. In Justin, *1 Apol.* 66.3, the "memoirs of the apostles" are explicitly identified with the Gospels.

132. Hengel, *Die vier Evangelien*, 197, correctly assumes that this practice is older than the *Apology*, written around 150 CE.

provide basic information about this Jesus of Nazareth from distant Palestine. That was the basic assumption for every form of church work and mission. An individual Gospel reading probably took place very early, as Luke 1:1–4 suggests. These created a demand for Gospels; every large church and prosperous patron wanted to have their own Gospels.[133] This process required the placing of titles on the Gospels as distinguishing characteristics: "The Gospel according to _____" (εὐαγγέλιον κατά + proper name in the accusative). Whether the names were added in the first decades of the second century or belonged to the original text is disputed.[134] The textual tradition does not actually answer this question, for the earliest relevant papyri are dated around 200 CE ($\mathfrak{P}^{66}$ $\mathfrak{P}^{75}$).[135] Three observations, however, support a later addition: (1) Mark 1:1; Matt. 1:1; Luke 1:1–4 (and John 1:1–18) do not need a supplement or interpretation with a title because they already have a title and develop a theological program from it. (2) Apparently the title is derived from Mark 1:1, "The beginning of the gospel of Jesus Christ, the Son of God." This introduction, or original "title," of the Gospel of Mark already points to the transition from the nonliterary to the literary concept of the gospel, lending itself to becoming a distinguishing title for the Gospel. (3) The remarkable uniformity of the titles and the unusual form of the title with κατά also suggest the secondary character of the titles of the Gospels.[136]

Roughly contemporaneous with the identification of the individual Gospels with titles, a process of legitimating the authors began. Papias of Hierapolis[137] is the first who assumes multiple Gospels and distinguishes them explicitly according to their authorship. He identifies himself as an intentional collector and transmitter of traditions that came to him first as oral traditions: "But if ever anyone came who had followed the presbyters, I inquired into the words of the presbyters, what Andrew or Peter or Philip or Thomas or James or John or Matthew, or any other of the Lord's disciples, had said, and what Aristion and the presbyter John, the Lord's disciples, were saying. For I did not suppose that information from books would help me so much as the word of a living

133. Hengel, *Die vier Evangelien*, 197–216, describes this development, emphasizing the practical effect of the parchment codex, which at first included only the Gospels.

134. Hengel, "Die Evangelienüberschriften"; Hengel, *Die vier Evangelien*, 88, represents this view regarding the Gospel titles: "In the second century they were already fully unified and, in my opinion, part of the text of the four Gospels, which from the beginning were not disseminated without titles."

135. Cf. Petersen, "Die Evangelienüberschriften," 253–60.

136. Cf. T. Heckel, *Vom Evangelium des Markus*, 208–9; Petersen, *Die Evangelienüberschriften*, 267–68.

137. On the person and work, cf. Vielhauer, *Geschichte der urchristlichen Literatur*, 757–65; Körtner, *Papias von Hierapolis*; Heckel, *Vom Evangelium des Markus*, 219–65.

and surviving voice" (Eusebius, *Hist. eccl.* 3.39.4 LCL). Papias received from it the highly treasured oral traditions from the pupils of the presbyter, from whom he inquired about the traditions of the apostles. The chain of traditions involved apostles → presbyters (apostolic pupils) → pupils of the presbyters → Papias.[138] Of course, the high evaluation of oral tradition is also a rhetorical topos,[139] but Papias does not stand alone, for the Didache (see above, under 10.5.2) also attests the juxtaposition of the oral traditions delivered especially by prophets and written traditions (Did. 15.3 refers to Matt. 18:15).[140]

Having gathered his traditions, Papias put them in writing and commented on them around 130 CE[141] in his five-volume work, "Interpretation of the Words of the Lord" (Λογίων κυριακῶν ἐξηγήσεως), extant only in fragments, in which he reports various traditions about the authorship of the Gospels. He wrote about Mark,

> Mark became Peter's interpreter and wrote accurately all that he remembered, not, indeed, in order of the things said or done by the Lord. For he had not heard the Lord, nor had he followed him, but later on, as I said, followed Peter, who used to give teaching as necessity demanded but not making, as it were, an arrangement of the Lord's oracles so that Mark did nothing wrong in thus writing down single points as he remembered them. For to one thing he gave attention, to leave out nothing of what he had heard and to make no false statements in them. (Eusebius, *Hist. eccl.* 3.39.15 LCL)

The Papias tradition, with its indirect attribution of the Gospel of Mark to Peter, indicates clearly that the name *Mark* as author of the Gospel was anchored firmly in the tradition. Only this fact can explain the striking state of affairs in which a Gospel was ascribed to a theologian who did not belong to the circle of disciples or apostles. Papias defends Mark in a twofold respect: (1) The lack of order in the Gospel of Mark presented no serious shortcoming. This charge probably originated from a comparison of the Gospel of Mark with other Gospels (especially Matthew, perhaps also John). (2) Mark was not an eyewitness of the life of Jesus, but his Gospel was based on the lectures of Peter, giving authenticity and credibility to his Gospel. Papias reports about the author of the Gospel of Matthew on the basis of the traditions of the presbyter: "Matthew collected the oracles in the Hebrew language, and each interpreted them as best he could" (Eusebius, *Hist. eccl.* 3.39.16 LCL). Papias

---

138. Cf. Heitmüller, "Zur Johannes-Tradition," 195.
139. Cf. Plato, *Phaedr.* 274c–75a.
140. Cf. J. Becker, *Mündliche und schriftliche Autorität.*
141. The dating fluctuates between 110 and 130 CE; with Vielhauer, *Geschichte der urchrist-lichen Literatur*, 758–59, the content of the fragments suggests a date of around 130.

offers no information about Luke. However, in the Armenian translation of the Apocalypse-Commentary of Andrew of Caesarea (around 600 CE), a fragment is included in which Papias cites Luke 10:18.[142] One may assume that the tradition that Paul's companion Luke was the author of the Third Gospel was widespread before 150 CE. As the oldest witness of the tradition in Asia Minor, Papias mentions the apostle John and John the presbyter but knows nothing about either one of them as author of the Fourth Gospel. Thus it is somewhat improbable that Papias knew the Gospel of John. Consequently, he is not the first witness to the four-Gospel collection.[143]

As a whole, the Papias traditions on the Synoptics reflect the tendency to give a historical classification of the authors of the Gospels, to legitimate them, and to make them direct (Matthew) or indirect (Mark, perhaps Luke) eyewitnesses. All of these processes demonstrate the expansion and significance of the Synoptic Gospels around 100 CE.

PETER

Around 100 CE, Peter is not only a central historical figure but also a literary-theological figure of early Christianity. The historical Peter played a predominant role (see above, 5.2) both in the pre-Easter circle of disciples and in the early history of emerging Christianity, but he left behind no written witness. However, he becomes the theological guarantor for several theological streams of early Christianity. The Papias tradition on the Gospel of Mark was cited above, according to which Mark was the interpreter of Peter and wrote down his preaching. Does the sequence Mark-Peter involve a reliable historical tradition[144] or an apologetic concern?[145] First, one must consider the anchor of a missionary with the name of John Mark in the circle of Pauline tradition, as Philem. 24; Col. 4:10; 2 Tim. 4:11; Acts 12:12, 25; 15:37, 39 indicate. No direct connection can be found between this tradition and the note in Papias. However, a possible connecting link could be present in 1 Pet. 5:13, where the author says, "The chosen [the church] in Babylon and Mark my son greet you." It is possible that the names of Mark and Silvanus/

---

142. Cf. Siegert, "Unbeachtete Papiaszitate," 606. See critique in Körtner, "Papiasfragmente," 15. All the material is treated in Gregory, *The Reception of Luke and Acts*.

143. Contra T. Heckel, *Vom Evangelium des Markus*, 263: "Papias probably knew the four Gospels: Matthew, Mark, Luke, and John." With certainty the historical and theological concept of the four-Gospel canon appears first in Irenaeus (cf. *Haer.* 3.11.8–9); in Justin the evidence is not certain (only Mark and Luke are definite; cf. e.g., *Dial.* 100.1).

144. As argued by Hengel, *Saint Peter*, 58–78.

145. The view of Niederwimmer, "Johannes Markus"; Vielhauer, *Geschichte der urchristlichen Literatur*, 260.

Silas (cf. 1 Thess. 1:1; 2 Cor. 1:19; 2 Thess. 1:1; 1 Pet. 5:12) from the Pauline tradition entered the Petrine tradition.[146] Then the combination Mark-Peter in the Papias tradition could have its starting point in 1 Pet. 5:13. The Papias tradition about Mark and Peter cannot be considered historically credible, for their legitimating character is evident, and the Gospel of Mark has no "Petrine" theology.

Peter takes a prominent position in the Gospel of Matthew (see above, 10.2.2).[147] He appears as the "first" apostle (Matt. 10:2) and as speaker for the disciples (Matt. 15:15; 18:21), and his conduct in Matt. 14:28–31 is portrayed as an instructive example for the proper relationship between faith and doubt. The word of Peter in Matt. 16:17–19 is foundational; the evangelist inserts it into the Markan sequence between the confession about Christ and the command for silence.[148] This is indicated by a multilayered structure. (1) The macarism in verse 17 ("Blessed are you, Simon Barjonah, for flesh and blood have not revealed this to you, but rather my Father in heaven") takes up the preceding confession directly. (2) Three comparably structured words are attached to the opening phrase in 18a and discuss the building of the church (v. 18b, "You are Peter, and on this rock I will build my church, and the gates of Hades will not prevail against it"), the conferring of the keys to the kingdom of heaven (v. 19a, "I will give you the keys to the kingdom of heaven"), and the total authority of binding and loosing (v. 19b: "And what you bind on earth will be bound in heaven, and what you loose on earth will be loosed in heaven"). A tradition that is probably very old is present in verse 18b, for it is based on a wordplay with Πέτρος (Peter) and πέτρα.[149] Closely connected are the conferring of the name and the meaning of the name; the name stands also for the function. This word was presumably formulated very early, but it can scarcely be traced back to Jesus, for the formulation μου τὴν ἐκκλησίαν (my church) reflects a post-Easter perspective.

The key word and the logion of binding and loosing (cf. John 20:23) present Peter as the guarantor of the Matthean tradition and the prototype for the confessing disciple and Christian teacher who, in contrast to the scribes and Pharisees (cf. Matt. 23:13), unlocks the kingdom of heaven through his interpretation and thus makes the Matthean *ekklēsia* a house with a firm

---

146. Cf. Körtner, "Markus der Mitarbeiter."

147. Cf. Luz, *Matthew*, 2:366–68; Roloff, *Die Kirche*, 162–65.

148. In addition to the literature cited above at 5.2 under "Peter," cf. Luz, *Matthew*, 2:366–68: "The nickname Cephas is old, but Matt. 16:18 is not"; Hengel, *Saint Peter*, 1–44 (Jesus himself had called the fisherman Simon and gave him the nickname Cephas); Böttrich, *Petrus*, 65–72 (the first appearance to Peter as the origin of the word of promise).

149. Besides Lampe, "Das Spiel mit dem Petrusnamen"; cf. Hengel, *Saint Peter*, 30–40.

foundation (cf. Matt. 7:24–27). The authority of binding and loosing, according to Matt. 18:18, applies to the whole church so that Peter becomes the exemplum for all disciples: what is attributed to him in knowledge, authority, strong faith, and even doubting faith, the church can apply to itself. The Gospel of Matthew documents the prominent place of Peter within strict Jewish Christian circles, who see in him the guarantor of the unbroken continuity with Jesus of Nazareth, and thus legitimates its tradition and claims (e.g., the keeping of the "whole" law in Matt. 5:17–20).

While in Matthew the authority of Peter is undisputed from the beginning, the evidence is very different in the Gospel of John. Here the "beloved disciple" (John 13:23, the disciple "whom Jesus loved") is the guarantor of the tradition and ideal witness of the Christ event.[150] The beloved disciple was called before Peter (John 1:37–40); he is the interpreter of Jesus and the speaker for the disciples (John 13:23–26a). In the hour of testing, he remains faithful to his Lord (John 18:15–18); he becomes the true witness under the cross and the exemplary disciple of Jesus (John 19:25–27). The scene at the cross is the founding legend of the Johannine community: Mary represents the believers of all times, who are directed to the beloved disciple as she was. From the cross Jesus addresses his church, which, like Mary, is now in the care of the beloved disciple. The beloved disciple confirms the actual death of Jesus at the cross (John 19:34b, 35) and first recognizes the eschatological dimension of the Easter event (John 20:2–10). Thus just as the Paraclete determines the community in the present and opens up its future (cf. John 14:15–17, 25–26; 15:26–27; 16:5–11, 12–14), the beloved disciple connects the church with the past of the earthly ministry of Jesus. John connects literary, theological, and historical strategies with the beloved disciple. In literary terms, the beloved disciple appears as a model disciple, in whose movements in the text the hearers/readers can identify themselves. Theologically, the beloved disciple is, because of his unique proximity to Jesus, the ideal interpreter of the Christ event; as the Son is close to the heart of the Father and makes him known (John 1:18), so the beloved disciple is near to the heart of Jesus (John 13:23). In historical terms, it is thoroughly plausible to see in the beloved disciple the presbyter of 2 and 3 John (see above, 10.4.1), who is identical with the presbyter John mentioned by Papias (cf. Eusebius, *Hist. eccl.* 3.39.4). As the founder of the Johannine school, the presbyter appears already in 2 and 3 John as a special bearer of the tradition, a function that the evangelist took up and expanded.

---

150. On the beloved disciple, cf. Kragerud, *Der Lieblingsjünger*; Lorenzen, *Der Lieblingsjünger*; Kügler, *Der Jünger*; Bauckham, "The Beloved Disciple"; Simon, *Petrus und der Lieblingsjünger*; Culpepper, *John, the Son of Zebedee*; Charlesworth, *Beloved Disciple*; Theobald, "Der Jünger, den Jesus liebte."

As he makes the founder of the Johannine school in the post-Easter period the true pre-Easter eyewitness and guarantor of the tradition, the beloved disciple represents the post-Easter disciples within the context of the pre-Easter disciples! As a historical person, the beloved disciple is not "entirely a fiction,"[151] for John 21:22–23 presupposes his unexpected death, giving the editor of the Gospel of John the occasion to correct the personal traditions about the beloved disciple and his relationship to Peter.

In the supplementary chapter 21, the precedence given to the beloved disciple in relation to Peter becomes corrected![152] Now Peter is the one who is loved above all others (John 21:15), and Peter receives from the Resurrected One the commission "Feed my sheep" three times (John 21:15–17). Jesus appoints Peter to the office of shepherd and thus, in an apparent correction to John 19:25–27, as his earthly representative. Peter now stands in the foreground, and the beloved disciple stands in the background; he no longer has direct access to his Lord, but instead Peter and Jesus talk about his fate (cf. John 21:20–23). With this addition, the editors of the Gospel of John document the continually growing influence of the figure of Peter within their circles. The Johannine traditions probably had to be placed under the authority of Peter in order to be considered a legitimate interpretation of the Christ event.

In 1 Peter, Peter appears for the first time as a (fictive) author.[153] The prescript indicates its supraregional character: "To the elect strangers in the diaspora of Pontus, Galatia, Cappadocia, and Bithynia" (1 Pet. 1:1). The writing is addressed to the churches of almost all of Asia Minor, that area in which most Christians lived around 100 CE. First Peter was obviously considered to be a letter of the apostle Peter in the ancient church from the beginning (cf. Pol. *Phil.* 8.1; Papias according to Eusebius, *Hist. eccl.* 3.39.17; Irenaeus, *Haer.* 4.9.2; 4.16.5; 5.7.2). However, this ascription of authorship is historically inaccurate. In 1 Pet. 1:1 the author calls himself an apostle, but in 1 Pet. 5:1 he is a "fellow elder." A member of the Twelve, an apostle, and first witness of the resurrection of Jesus Christ could scarcely have employed this title, which reflects early Christian ecclesiology at a later stage. It is noteworthy that the letter offers no personal profile. The passion narrative is described only in traditional early Christian language (cf. 1 Pet. 2:22–25), and the letter

151. Kragerud, *Der Lieblingsjünger*, 149.
152. For the evidence of the secondary character of John 21, cf. Schnelle, *Die Johannesbriefe*, 339–40, 396–98.
153. The authorization of Peter and related circles through writing continues unabated into the second and third centuries CE; noncanonical Petrine writings of Peter include, e.g., Kerygmata Petrou, Gospel of Peter, Apocalypse of Peter, Acts of Peter; cf. Karl M. Schmidt, *Mahnung und Erinnerung*, 410–18.

demonstrates no evidence of the primary knowledge of an eyewitness.[154] First Peter was probably written around 90 CE in Asia Minor, and the central message was the theological permeation of the individual and societal dimensions of the present suffering by believers.[155]

Although the Christians are challenged to practice proper conduct within societal institutions, they must suffer as strangers in the world because of their relation to God. The author attempts to encourage and strengthen (cf. 1 Pet. 5:12) Christians in Asia Minor who were being harassed, and he develops a threefold strategy in order to stabilize the new Christian identity and to secure the survival of the churches of Asia Minor in a hostile environment.[156] (1) Believers should recognize that their suffering is a sign of God's grace and not a result of sins committed (1 Pet. 2:19; 3:14). Thus they should submit to the will of God in humility (1 Pet. 3:8–9; 5:5).[157] (2) The theological and social-psychological strategy of stabilizing the community in its difficult situation and at the same time making the model of recognition and community life attractive to outsiders permeates all of 1 Peter. Thus specific early Christian authorities are claimed to secure legitimation, for 1 Peter places itself specifically in the stream of Petrine (and implicitly Pauline) tradition.[158] (3) The apostle Peter is already a model of the believers' endurance in suffering, and he made his way to the west of the Roman Empire (cf. 1 Cor. 1:12; 9:5), probably ministering also as a missionary. The pseudonym Peter was chosen because the apostle, according to Acts 10, was the founder of the gentile mission and was venerated as one of the first martyrs in early Christianity. His readiness to suffer predetermined him to be the author of this letter. The biographical-theological intention of 1 Peter is clear: the churches should orient themselves to Peter and adopt him as a model of humility, endurance, and readiness to suffer.

Second Peter claims to be the testament of the apostle Simon Peter (cf. 2 Pet. 1:1, 13–15). The reference to the transfiguration of Jesus (2 Pet. 1:18), the reference to 1 Peter (cf. 2 Pet. 3:1), and the image of Paul communicated in 2 Pet. 3:15–16 offer this impression. The almost total use of the Epistle of Jude indicates that the claim of authorship does not have a historical basis.

154. For the detailed argument, cf. Schnelle, *History and Theology of the New Testament*, 398–415.

155. Contra D.-A. Koch, *Geschichte des Urchristentums*, 477–79, who dates 1 Peter ca. 115 CE because he presupposes the legal situation that is reflected in the correspondence between Pliny and the caesar Trajan.

156. Cf. Popp, *Die Kunst der Konvivenz*; Guttenberger, *Passio Christiana*; T. Klein, *Bewährung in Anfechtung*.

157. Cf. Feldmeier, "'Basis des Kontaktes unter Christen.'"

158. Cf. below, 13.5.2 under "Paul and Peter."

The developed doctrine of inspiration and the reflection on the delay of the parousia (2 Pet. 3:8) point to a time around 110 CE.[159] Second Peter disputes intensively with false teachers; the selection of the pseudonym "Simon Peter" signals the standpoint and intention of the author: he understands himself as the speaker for the majority church and reclaims for himself the correct interpretation of Scripture, which is expressed in the reference to the synoptic tradition (particularly Matthew)[160] and 1 Peter (2 Pet. 3:1), and especially in the appeal to Paul (and his letters) in 2 Pet. 3:15. Second Peter makes the claim to have on his side this combination of witnesses for his refutation of the false teachers and his interpretation of the delay of the parousia. In 2 Peter, Peter and Paul appear as witnesses of unity and truth.[161]

> Around 100 CE, Peter is not only a significant historical figure from the beginning but also a theological factor who writes letters and legitimates and interprets other Scriptures. The martyrs Peter and Paul become regarded as a unity (cf. 1 Clem. 5.4–5; Ign. *Rom.* 4.3), and Peter guarantees the appropriate interpretation of the Pauline letters (2 Peter). A central figure of the circle of disciples and the Jerusalem church thereby becomes a historical and theological guarantor of the whole church.

John

The Johannine literature (letters and Gospel) portrays a new theological world within early Christianity (see above, 10.4). Jesus Christ comes on the scene in a new language and way of thinking and thus into the consciousness of the reader. With its memorable images, the Johannine theology makes a comprehensive visualization of Jesus and furthermore treats numerous acute problems in a surprising way around 100 CE, conducting a discourse for the outside as well as the inside. The relationship to the "Jews" and the "world" defines the discourse with the outsiders. The charge of ditheism[162] that was certainly raised from the Jewish side against all of early Christianity is a major theme in the Gospel of John (cf. John 5:18; 10:33, 36; 19:7) and refuted with a basic argument: the Father stands behind the Son, and thus all statements

159. Cf. Schnelle, *History and Theology of the New Testament,* 424–33.
160. Cf. the list in Dschulnigg, "Ort des Zweiten Petrusbriefes," 168–76. According to Dschulnigg, the author of 2 Peter was at home in the Jewish Christianity of the Gospel of Matthew, "whose theology he defends throughout his letter" (177).
161. Cf. T. Heckel, "Die Traditionsverknüpfungen des Zweiten Petrusbriefes," 193–95.
162. On the disputes between Judaism and Johannine Christianity, cf. above 10.4.3; 11.5.

about the Son are based on the will of the Father. It is not Christology but rather theology that is the essential level of the argument. The will of the Father enables and legitimates the work of the Son; Jesus does not act alone and from himself, but rather the Father is in him and works through him (cf. John 5:19ff.; 8:16, 29; 16:32).[163] John treats the rejection of the Johannine proclamation and the related discrimination with the concept of the cosmos (see above, 10.4.3). He interprets unbelief as well as hostility to the believers as a result of their existence from the cosmos (John 8:23, "And he spoke to them: You are from below, and I am from above. You are from [ἐκ] this world, I am not from [ἐκ] this world"). The fundamental difference between the revealer and the world is explained with the reference to the differing origin. In the background is the Johannine idea that the origin totally determines existence. Jesus's origin from the Father and the imprisonment of unbelief in the world are mutually exclusive, making it impossible for them to understand each other. Nevertheless, the Johannine conception is not intended for rejection but for the overcoming of the cosmos, the place of unbelief, within the world (John 17:5).[164] In the mission of the Johannine churches (John 20:21: "As the Father has sent me, so I send you"), the world should find faith and with it its original purpose, for the world was created by the Logos (cf. John 1:3). Johannine dualism between God and the world does not possess an ontological quality but results from the eschatological revelation of God in Jesus Christ, who establishes the dualism but at the same makes possible the triumph over it through faith.

The internal discourse involves primarily Christology and eschatology. The proto-Gnostic docetism, with its devaluation of the earthly nature of Jesus Christ (see above, 10.4.2), not only presents a challenge for Johannine theology but also signals a deep conflict that has lasted for centuries in the whole church. On the one hand, it was necessary not to undermine monotheism with a massive range of christological titles, but on the other hand, the divine nature of Jesus had to be defined beyond the categories of a prophet or one who had been sent. Thus the Gospel of John developed the significant model: It proclaimed an exclusive monotheism in a binitarian figure; the Son is incorporated into the worship of the Father. He is much more than an agent of the Father; he not only participates in God's nature, but he is of God's nature. Thus the emphasis on the incarnation of the preexistent Logos (John 1:14) and the orientation to the cross in the Gospel of John aim at an appropriate determination of the relationship between the divine and the human in Jesus

163. Cf. Schnelle, *Theology of the New Testament*, 684–85.
164. Cf. Balz, "κόσμος."

Christ, according to which the Preexistent and Incarnate One is nothing other than the Crucified and Exalted One (see above, 10.4.3).

In his eschatology, John makes two original new determinations:[165] (1) John reinterprets the delay of the announced parousia in the form in which it was expected with a readjustment of the end-time events, making a new perspective on faith. Traditional future events not only extend into the present (cf. John 5:25); instead, the eschatological events have an unlimited present reality. In the present encounter with the word of the revealer, the judgment takes place already; the decision about the future is made in the present (cf. John 8:51 and passim). Because in faith, eternal life is already present, the step from life to death is not only in the future, but for the believers it has taken place already in the past (cf. John 5:24). Thus faith does not annul time but gives it a new quality and orientation. John develops this theme primarily in the farewell speech, in which the primary addressees are the external readers of the text and the church as it listens. Thus John 14:2–3 looks toward the parousia of Christ, and John 14:18–21, 28; 16:13e, 16 discuss the expected return of Christ. What was determined in the present will endure into the future. (2) Both farewell speeches in John 13:31–14:31 and 15:1–16:33[166] treat central questions (not only) of the Johannine Christians around the year 100 CE: the fear stands before the church that it will be subjected to the present social and legal afflictions without a future. The farewell speeches confront this fear with the fundamental knowledge: the departure of Jesus is necessary, for only in this way will there be a future under the guidance of the Spirit. A new era has dawned that will be shaped by the Holy Spirit. The Paraclete is a Spirit of possibilities and potential. The distinguishing features of the Spirit are its origin from God, its divine nature, and thus its opposition to the world. Here the external perspective comes into view. In particular, the fourth and fifth Paraclete sayings in John 16:7–11, 13–15 signal an intensification of the conflict with the world, in the course of which increasingly greater juridical functions are attributed to the Paraclete (John 15:26; 16:7–11). The Paraclete intervenes actively for the believers in the present distress and stands with them in conflict with the world as it reveals the hostile attitude of the world, demands justice, and overcomes the powers that are hostile to God (John 16:8–14).

165. Cf. above 11.1 under "Realized Eschatology."

166. On the literary problems and theological dimensions of the farewell speeches, cf. U. Müller, "Die Parakletvorstellung"; Schnelle, "Die Abschiedsreden im Johannesevangelium"; M. Winter, *Das Vermächtnis Jesu*; Dettwiler, *Die Gegenwart des Erhöhten*; Hoegen-Rohls, *Der nachösterliche Johannes*, 82–229; Frey, *Die johanneische Eschatologie*, 3:102–239; Haldimann, *Rekonstruktion und Entfaltung*; Rahner, "Vergegenwärtigende Erinnerung"; Parsenios, *Departure and Consolation*.

James and Jewish Christianity

Strict Jewish Christianity became greatly weakened by the successful gentile mission of Paul and the fall of Jerusalem (see above, 9.2). Nevertheless, it remained a central stream of early Christianity (see above, 10.5). This stream is evident in the literary production in which the Letter of James played a central role.[167] Both the circles behind the Petrine letters and those behind the Letter of James were motivated by the enumeration of the relevant authorities at the apostolic council in Gal. 2:9 ("James and Cephas and John, who were considered as pillars") to ascribe their letters to their respective guarantors. They were evidently intended to lessen the predominance of the Pauline and deutero-Pauline letters and to secure the permanent influence of their own positions.[168] James the brother of the Lord (see above, 5.2), as the second leader of the Jerusalem church, represented a defined, strict Jewish Christian position, and he was a key person at the apostolic council (see above, chap. 7) and acted against the mission of Antioch/Paul (cf. Gal. 2:11–15), which did not require circumcision. Through his martyrdom in 62 CE (see above, 9.1), he attained a status similar to that of Paul and Peter as a founding figure. Consequently, he offered himself as a theological authority and letter writer for strict Jewish Christian circles. Of course, while after 70 CE Jewish Christianity was not a unified movement (see above, 10.5.2), four distinguishing characteristics appear in the Letter of James and in the Gospel of Matthew: (1) The observance of the "whole" Torah (James 2:10, Matt. 5:17–19) was the theological center. The phrase ὅλον τὸν νόμον already played a critical role (cf. Gal. 5:3) in the Galatian crisis (see above, 8.5), where it was connected with the opponents' demand for the circumcision of gentile Christians. (2) After 70 CE the requirement of circumcision is represented only in isolated cases (cf. Col. 3:11: Ebionites, Jewish Christians mentioned by Justin) but does not play a role in programmatic writings such as James and the Gospel of Matthew. One can speak of the tacit waiver of the requirement of circumcision inasmuch as strict Jewish Christian churches were open to the gentile mission (Matthew) and/or reliant on gentile sympathizers (James, Didache). (3) Nevertheless, in order to secure an aspect of strict Jewish identity, minimal ritual standards other than circumcision were required. This openness is indicated in Matt. 23:3 (about the scribes: "Whatever they teach you, follow it") and Did. 6.2–3 ("concerning foods: Bear what you are able"), where a clear boundary is drawn with respect to food offered to idols. There were probably churches

---

167. On the theological orientation of the Letter of James, cf. above, 10.5.2 under "The Letter of James" and 11.2 under "The Letter of James."

168. Cf. Lührmann, "Gal 2,9 und die katholischen Briefe"; Nienhuis, *Not by Paul Alone*.

that continued to keep the Sabbath (Matt. 24:20?; Ign. *Magn.* 9.1; Jewish Christians, according to Justin). (4) A more open (opponents in Colossians and the Pastoral Epistles; the Letter of James) or a more concealed (Gospel of Matthew) anti-Paulinism was a further characteristic of many strict Jewish Christian writings and/or groups. Paul was considered to be the falsifier of the normative Jewish origin of Christianity and the twofold apostate, who betrayed Judaism and Christianity by his opening to the gentile world.[169]

Strict Jewish Christianity could reclaim a historical and theological continuity to the initial event for itself, appealing to Jesus of Nazareth as a Jew and the Jewish origins of the new movement. Thus it was also a strong and continuing voice of Christianity around 100 CE.

13.5.2 Networks

From the beginning, early Christianity was characterized in its missionary work by significant mobility (see above, chap. 6). In addition to logistic and economic support (cf. Phil. 4:10, the collection), there was certainly an exchange of theological perspectives very early. Theology was an aspect of the communicative networking, as Paul's letters indicate! They were read publicly in the churches (cf. 1 Thess. 5:27) and evoked both agreement and rejection (by opponents), giving evidence of networking. The Synoptic Gospels (see above, 10.2) are a further prime example of networking in early Christianity. The Gospel of Mark and the logia source were present in the churches of Matthew and Luke and became the basis and a part of a new gospel. Thus the very different reception by Matthew and Luke indicates that networking was a multilayered phenomenon that took a variety of forms. It can involve full or partial adoption of thoughts or entire writings as well as the reception of citations, key terms, allusions, variations, and amplifications. It can also involve critique, rejection, or omissions. The presupposition for this process is, of course, first a chronological determination of the date of the writings;[170] for example, the seven authentic letters of Paul are certainly older than the deutero-Pauline letters or the Gospels. In addition, literary relationships, geographical proximity, personal contacts, terminological continuity, use of common traditions, or a recognizable influence of tradition history may be indications of intentional connecting links. Networking is an intentional process: relationships are established in a positive or negative way, always

169. On the anti-Paulinism of strict Jewish Christian circles, cf. Lüdemann, *Opposition to Paul*, 119–88; Lindemann, *Paulus im ältesten Christentum*, 101–9; Dassmann, *Der Stachel im Fleisch*, 108–25, 222–44; Pervo, *Making of Paul*, 187–98.
170. Cf. Wong, *Evangelium im Dialog mit Paulus*, 46–57.

connected with reception and redaction. All of this can take place in a recip-rocal process in various directions in which, as a rule, in early Christianity only the positions of the later writing can be ascertained. Whether and how, for example, genuine Pauline churches around 100 CE were influenced by the Gospels cannot be determined.

PAUL AND MARK

With the letter and the gospel genres, Paul and Mark represent the begin-ning of Christian literature and offer the critical impulse for Christology.[171] Furthermore, Paul and Mark are not chronologically far apart. Paul probably died in Rome around 64 CE; the Gospel of Mark could have been written after 70 CE in Rome (see above, 10.2.1). Although the narrative genre of gospel and the predominantly argumentative-oriented genre of the letter are very differ-ent, they have comparable features. Paul also narrates a story of Jesus Christ; his letters are permeated with narrative elements and references that treat the story of the earthly Jesus, his resurrection, and his parousia.[172] The tradition of the Lord's Supper in 1 Cor. 11:23b–25 and the confessional statement in 1 Cor. 15:3b–5, as narrative abbreviations in formed language,[173] include the basic data of the story of Jesus Christ, inasmuch as they treat the preexistence of the earthly Jesus directly and reflect on its theological significance:[174] his total dedication to his people in the time of his betrayal, his death, his burial, his resurrection on the third day, as well as his appearances. The earthly Jesus is not hidden away by Paul but is interpreted in view of the cross and Easter. In Mark also, the cross stands at the center, for Mark 9:9 indicates that the messianic secret must be considered as a form of the Markan theology of the cross (see above, 10.2.1). Jesus the Son of God remains the same in his suffering and in his authoritative works. Mark demonstrates how Jesus will

171. Werner, *Der Einfluß paulinischer Theologie*, 209, shaped the discussion long ago: (1) "Where Mark agrees with Paul, it always involves a general early Christian point of view. (2) Where particular, characteristically Pauline perspectives appear that go beyond this com-mon basis in the letters, the parallels are fully absent in Mark, or Mark represents a virtually opposite standpoint. (3) One cannot speak at all of an influence of Pauline theology in the Gospel of Mark."

172. Cf. Reinmuth, "Narratio und argumentatio," 21, according to which Paul does not nar-rate an abstract story of the historical Jesus, but he tells the story of Jesus Christ as he "knows and proclaims it—thus the story of Jesus Christ, which includes the story of the earthly Jesus as well as his preexistence and future parousia."

173. Cf. Straub, "Geschichten erzählen, Geschichte bilden," 123: "Narrative abbreviations include stories or refer to stories, without being narratives themselves. Narrative abbreviations can be interpreted hermeneutically only in reference to larger narratives to which they allude or refer."

174. Cf. Scholtissek, "'Geboren aus einer Frau,'" 211–12.

gather his people as the sign of the kingdom of God through his authoritative word, his healing activity, and his readiness to give his life for others. Thus the evangelist takes up the central thought of Pauline theology and makes it the center of his dramatic narrative: the crucified Jesus of Nazareth is the Son of God. Paul and Mark are close to each other in their basic christological perspective, for they proclaim Jesus Christ, the Crucified One (1 Cor. 1:23; Mark 16:6, ἐσταυρωμένον). The unity of the earthly, crucified, and resurrected Son of God, Jesus Christ, is the basis of their Christology. The narratival development of this basic insight is depicted in various genres[175] but still has no element that divides them. Paul and Mark are (besides John) the decisive representatives of a firm theology of the cross, as is indicated especially in a comparison with Matthew and Luke.[176]

In addition, there are other striking agreements. Paul and Mark are not only the bearers of the term εὐαγγέλιον (gospel), but Mark takes up the central term εὐαγγέλιον and shapes it literarily and theologically: within the narrative world of the gospel, Jesus Christ is now at the same time the proclaimer and content of the gospel. Furthermore, along with John, Paul and Mark are the bearers of the concept of faith as the central appropriation of the saving event in early Christianity. On the question of the law, Paul and Mark are, on the one hand, very different because of their respective historical situations; on the other hand, they are in substance close to each other on this question (cf. Rom. 14:14; Mark 7:15). The absence of the word νόμος in the Gospel of Mark is probably no coincidence. Mark presupposes the critical result of the Pauline debate about the law: the mission of the gentiles without the requirement of circumcision, which attaches to the law no soteriological significance but only an ethical significance (cf. Mark 2:1–3:6; 7:1–23; 12:28–34).

Even if a direct reference to the Pauline letters by Mark cannot be demonstrated, the conceptual and tradition-historical continuities and the agreements in the theological orientation suggest a knowledge and an independent processing of Pauline thought by the earliest evangelist.[177] This connection could have been established in Rome, where both were active in a period of time not far apart from each other. Here Mark probably acquired his knowledge of Pauline theology.

175. What Boring, *Mark*, 248, correctly says about Mark is also fundamentally true for Paul: "Jesus is the central and primary character, and he appears in almost every scene."

176. Cf. Berger, *Theologiegeschichte*, 317: "The agreement in this point is especially important inasmuch as there are no natural Jewish or other analogies."

177. In contemporary scholarship, the majority maintain a Pauline influence on Mark; cf. Wong, *Evangelium im Dialog mit Paulus*, 61–106; Bird, "Mark: Interpreter of Peter"; Ischmeyer, Sim, and Elmer, *Paul and Mark*; E.-M. Becker, Engberg-Pedersen, and M. Müller, *Mark and Paul*.

PAUL AND LUKE

Undoubtedly, Luke had at his disposal extensive Pauline traditions as he made the apostle to the nations the hero of the second part of Acts. Thus one can speak of a strong networking (see above, 10.3.1). Luke is an admirer of Paul and certainly also a pupil of Paul, but in what sense? Two strong signals make Luke a direct companion of Paul: (1) Luke, the name of the author, was probably indebted to this strategy. The first to mention Luke as the author of the Gospel was Irenaeus of Lyon: "But Luke, the companion of Paul, wrote down the gospel preached by him" (*Haer.* 3.1.1; cf. Eusebius, *Hist. eccl.* 5.8.3). The assumption is probably still correct that the name Luke as the name of the author of the two-volume work is based on a combination of statements in Acts and the Pauline and deutero-Pauline letters.[178] The name Luke appears in Philem. 24; Col. 4:14; and 2 Tim. 4:11, but it is not yet connected with the authorship of the Third Gospel. Thus the tradition probably presupposes these three letters. From the second part of Acts, it is evident that its author had extensive knowledge of the life of Paul until his imprisonment in Rome. Second Timothy (cf. 2 Tim. 1:17), originating, according to the claim of its author, in Rome, begins precisely where Acts ends (cf. Acts 28:30–31). According to 2 Tim. 4:11, Luke is the last coworker who has remained faithful to Paul, a fact that distinguishes him from all other coworkers and predetermined him to be the author of the two-volume work *ad Theophilum*. (2) The respective "we passages" that begin and end abruptly (Acts 16:10–17; 20:5–15; 21:1–18; 27:1–28:16) indicate a direct personal proximity of Luke to Paul. As a companion of Paul and author of Acts, according to his claim, he especially brings his own experiences and view of the events into the narrative.[179] However, one may raise important objections to the historicity of these two signals: (a) Luke is not correctly informed about important instances of the missionary activity of Paul; for example, Acts reports five trips to Jerusalem by Paul (Acts 9:26; 11:27–30; 15:2, 4; 18:22; 21:15), while the Pauline letters clearly presuppose only three trips to Jerusalem (Gal. 1:18; 2:1; Rom. 15:25). Furthermore, the differing depictions of the negotiating partners and the decision at the apostolic council indicate (see above, 7.3) that Luke was not a companion of Paul (cf. also Acts 16:1–3 with Gal. 2:3–4). Luke limits the title of apostle to the Twelve, while for Paul the recognition of his apostolate is the basis of his self-understanding and his

---

178. Cf. the argument in Wehnert, *Die Wir-Passagen*, 60–66; Schnelle, *History and Theology of the New Testament*, 240–43.

179. On the discussion of the possible explanatory theories, cf. Schnelle, *History and Theology of the New Testament*, 266–71.

missionary activity (see above, 5.2). According to the portrayal in Acts, the Petrine mission to gentiles precedes the Pauline mission (cf. Acts 10:1–11:18), which conflicts with Gal. 2:1–10, where Paul has to defend his mission to the gentiles to the "three pillars" and thus to Peter. (b) The rendering of Pauline theology by Luke and Paul's own statements are different at several points. If Luke had actually been a companion of Paul, he would have had more precise knowledge of Pauline theology. This fact is indicated especially in the understanding of the law and justification. In Acts, Paul appears to be faithful to the law without equal: he circumcises Timothy (Acts 16:3) and makes a Nazarite vow to rebut all accusations against him (cf. Acts 21:20ff.). Paul defends his faithfulness to the law to the Jewish people (Acts 24:14) and to the Roman authorities: "I have in no way committed an offense against the law of the Jews, nor against the temple nor against the Caesar" (Acts 25:8). However, echoes of Paul's doctrine of justification can be found in Luke. According to Acts 13:38–39, "Let it be known to you, therefore, brothers, that through this man the forgiveness of sins is being preached to you; by this man everyone who could not be justified by the law of Moses will be justified" (cf. also Luke 18:9–14; Acts 15:11, "But we believe that we will be saved by the grace of the Lord Jesus Christ, just as they will"; Acts 16:31). The lines do not exclude each other. Luke does not understand law and faith in antithetical terms, but one is added to the other.[180] Faith encompasses the law and integrates justification into the total event.[181]

Luke is definitely interested in the person and theology of Paul. In the first place, Luke is concerned about Paul's place in the history of the early Christian mission.[182] Here it is evident that networking, especially in the interpretation of central figures of the earliest history (particularly Paul), serves to legitimize his own position.[183] Thus Luke refers to the Pauline traditions and not to the letters of Paul, which he does not mention and probably did not know. Luke is (like some deutero-Pauline letters) an admirer of Paul and a representative of a "mild" Paulinism that has been shaped in the history of the tradition, which is not interested in the rather aggressive theology of the Paul that is conditioned by its circumstances (Galatians!), but in his historical achievement.

180. Cf. the comprehensive study of Wong, *Evangelium im Dialog mit Paulus*, 149–56.
181. Cf. F. Hahn, *Theologie*, 1:573, in response to H. Klein: "In this respect justification by faith complements and overlaps with justification by the law."
182. Cf. Burchard, "Paulus in der Apostelgeschichte," 136: "Luke describes Paul not primarily from historical or biographical reasons, but to answer the questions of the present."
183. Appropriately Löning, *Die Saulustradition in der Apostelgeschichte*, 204: "The major Lucan concern is the question of the legitimacy of gentile Christianity in the post-Pauline form."

Paul and Matthew

In contrast to Luke's depiction, references to Paul in Matthew are uncertain and only indirect. References to Christian opponents appear in Matt. 7:15; 24:11, where the evangelist warns about ψευδοπροφῆται (false prophets). The theological profile of these opponents remains unclear; for the most part (with references to Matt. 5:17–20; 7:12–27; 11:12f.; 24:10–13) they are regarded as Hellenistic antinomians/hyper-Paulinists.[184] Matthew accuses them of ἀνομία (lawlessness; cf. Matt. 7:23; 24:12); their fruits are evil (cf. Matt. 7:16–20), and they do not do the will of God. Evidently these opponents undermine the comprehensive ethical conception (oriented to the Torah) of Matthew (cf. Matt. 24:12) and thus endanger the unity of the community. An implicit polemic against Paul might be present in Matt. 5:19: "Whoever breaks one of the least of these commandments and teaches others to do the same, will be called the least in the kingdom of heaven. But whoever does and teaches them, will be called great." A reference to Paul (Latin: "small") can be seen in the superlative ἐλάχιστος (the least), which appears as Paul's self-designation in 1 Cor. 15:9.[185] Paul would come into heaven because of his undisputable achievement yet be only "the least" because of his "liberal" or even antinomian position. Such a side blow toward Paul is conceivable[186] and would form a sharp contrast to the Matthean position: he is the true trustee of the proclamation of Jesus of Nazareth, the teacher of the law (Matt. 5:17), and preserves it against falsification through his gospel, as it has emanated from Paul. Here, to a certain extent, is a "negative" networking as a demarcation and sharpening of the writer's own profile.

Paul and John

The relationship of Paul to John is very different from that between Paul and Matthew.[187] Of course, one can find no direct reference to a knowledge

---

184. Cf. Barth, "Das Gesetzesverständnis"; cf. also Schweizer, "Gesetz und Enthusiasmus." A list of various proposed solutions (Zealots, Pharisees, Essenes, strict Jewish Christians, Paulinists) appears in Luz, *Matthew*, 1:379–80, who asks whether the false prophets may be considered "Marcan."

185. Cf. Theissen, "Kritik an Paulus im Matthäusevangelium?," who offers the following additional arguments: the teacher of the law teaches "people" those things that fit with the universal perspective of Paul; the singular formulations in Matt. 5:19 point to a single person; similarly, Wong, *Evangelium im Dialog mit Paulus*, 123–28; cf. Sim, "Matthew's Anti-Paulinism."

186. Theissen, "Kritik an Paulus im Matthäusevangelium?," 476ff., sees a polemic against Paul also in Matt. 10:9; 13:25, 18:6; 23:15. This claim is not convincing because, except for Matt. 5:19, no actual linguistic or content-related signals of polemic are present.

187. An introduction to this topic is given by Hoegen-Rohls, "Johanneische Theologie im Kontext paulinischen Denkens?"

of the Pauline letters in John, but there are strong tradition-historical connections and agreements in the theological outlook.[188] Furthermore, Ephesus as the probable setting for the Pauline and Johannine schools suggests a geographical proximity.

The statements about the preexistence and sending of the Son of God (cf. Gal. 4:4–5; Rom. 8:3–4; 1 John 4:9, 10, 14; John 3:16) must be considered a central connecting element between the Pauline and Johannine Christology.[189] God sends his Son because of love (cf. Rom. 5:8; 8:39; 1 John 4:9–10; John 3:16), and this sending is meant for the whole cosmos (implicit in Gal. 4:4–5; Rom. 8:3; explicit in 1 John 4:9; John 3:17). The Son's mediation in creation (cf. 1 Cor. 8:6; John 1:3) is connected with his preexistence. The theology of the cross is a central christological feature in Paul and John. Along with Paul and Mark, the Gospel of John represents a theology of the cross (see above, 10.4.3). Paul and John develop a language of faith[190] and reflect basic agreements on their understanding of sin: sin rules the cosmos as a universal power, and thus both Paul and John use the singular ἁμαρτία (sin) to describe this power (cf. Rom. 5:12; also 1 Cor. 15:56; Rom. 3:9, 23; 8:2–4; etc.; John 1:29; 8:34; etc.). Humankind is ruled by sin; they are subject to the wrath of God (Rom. 1:18; John 3:36) and have fallen into death (Rom.1:32; 5:12; John 5:24; 8:21). Likewise, the entire cosmos has been given over to transience and judgment (cf. Rom. 3:6, 19; 1 Cor. 6:2; 11:32; John 9:39; 12:32; 16:8, 11). According to Paul and John, the transfer from the spheres of sin and death to the realm of life takes place in baptism. Here the πνεῦμα (cf. 1 Cor. 12:13; 2 Cor. 1:21–22; John 3:5–6) is granted as the life-giving gift of God or of the exalted Lord. The reception of the Spirit or the new birth in the water and the Spirit transfers the one who is baptized from the realm of *sarx* (flesh) and death (cf. Rom. 8:4ff.; 8:13; Gal. 5:16; 6:8; John 3:6; 6:63a). As a divine creative power, the Spirit constitutes a corporeality that is contrary to fleshly existence (cf. Rom. 8:6; John 6:63a). Only in Paul and John does the concept of mutual dynamic immanence of the believer in the deity and the deity in the believer exist in a developed form.[191] Paul consistently describes the new existence of the baptized person with the phrase ἐν Χριστῷ. In baptism, the believer enters into the realm of the pneumatic Christ and takes on a new existence (2 Cor. 5:17). In John also the consistently close connection between

188. Cf. D. Zeller, "Paulus und Johannes," 167–82; Schnelle, "Paulus und Johannes."

189. Cf. the comprehensive list in Schnackenburg, "Paulinische und johanneische Christologie."

190. See above, 13.1 under "The Language of Faith."

191. In 1 Pet. 3:16; 5:10, 14; and Rev. 14:13 the reference is only to being "in Christ" or "in the Lord," but not to a mutual dynamic immanence.

the believer and Jesus Christ or God is described as mutual dynamic immanence. Thus the union of Christians with God or Jesus Christ appears as an extension of the fellowship between the Father and the Son (cf. John 14:20; 17:21–23; 1 John 2:24; 5:20). As Christ is in God and God in him (John 14:10), the believer abides in Christ (John 6:56; 15:4–7; 1 John 2:6, 24; 3:6, 24) and Christ in the believer (John 15:4–7; 1 John 3:24). Similarly, God abides in the believer (1 John 4:16) and the believer in God (1 John 2:24; 4:16). Finally, basic agreements are present in the Pauline and Johannine understandings of the law. According to John 1:17, there is no continuity between Moses and Jesus in salvation history; Christians stand under grace and truth, but not under the law. Thus Moses is devalued (cf. also John 6:32; 7:22), and the law belongs to the Jews (cf. John 7:19; 8:17; 10:34). The Christians, on the other hand, have left behind this stage of a religion of law long ago (cf. John 4:20ff.). The law, the Scripture, bears witness to Jesus and confirms his messianic identity (cf. John 2:22; 5:39; 7:38, 42; 10:35; 17:12; 19:24, 28, 36–37; 20:9). Even Moses himself bears witness to the divine origin and sending of Jesus (cf. John 1:45; 5:45–47). For John, the law is revealed only by Jesus; he is the content, goal, and Lord of the law. The Johannine Christology deprives the law of its theological significance as the bearer of revelation and ethical norm. Thus the Fourth Evangelist takes up the consequence of the Pauline critique of the law like no other author in the NT.

The agreements between Paul and John are not sufficiently explained by suggestions of common traditions or comparable influences in the history of religions or early Christianity.[192] Instead, they point to a connection between Paul and John, which can be determined more precisely. It consists of a geographical and a theological link between Paul and John, the Pauline and Johannine schools. The geographical link is Ephesus,[193] and the theological link lies in the comparable views of the Christ event. For neither Paul nor John does the activity of the historical Jesus of Nazareth stand in the foreground, but rather the salvific meaning of the Christ event forms the center of their thought. They consider the Christ event consistently in all of its dimensions. The individual Christian participates in the entire Christ event in faith, in the sacraments. The individual believer is free from the power of sin and death and stands at a distance from the cosmos. The law no longer applies to him; he lives in an inner relationship to Jesus or God, and the saving gift of life is already present as a promise. These are the themes that concern Paul and John. Thus John does not stand in conflict with the

192. Cf., however, J. Becker, "Das Verhältnis des johanneischen Kreises zum Paulinismus."
193. Cf. here Schnackenburg, "Ephesus."

Synoptic Gospels, whose portrayal of the life of Jesus is similarly permeated by christological ideas. John, however, has another accent. For him, the life of Jesus is subordinated fully to the dominant christological ideas.[194] In the shaping of his theology, John relies on Paul, who had thought previously of the problems that confronted John and his community. That this linkage is not a mere repetition but is to be considered an independent treatment and continuation and transformation of Pauline thought is to be understood as the work of such a theologian as John himself.[195] John is thus not a pupil of Paul or one who completes his theology. He merely attests the fact that the networking in early Christianity was in no way a singular process: NT theologians and writers did not take over all existing or known traditions indiscriminately but submitted them to theological reflection and selected them according to their theological purpose and corresponding historical situation.

The Synoptic Gospels

A literary dependence exists between the Gospels of Matthew, Mark, and Luke, for they contain major agreements in language and sequence, but at the same time they differ in numerous points. This phenomenon is still best explained by the two-source theory,[196] which regards the Gospel of Mark as the earliest gospel, which Matthew and Luke used as a template and source. In addition, Matthew and Luke also used an additional source, which is no longer extant but can be reconstructed from the two Gospels. It consists primarily of sayings and speeches of Jesus and is called the logia source (abbreviated as Q, for *Quelle*, source); in addition, the two Gospels used their own sources, the special material. When such a network of relationships between texts exists, this is evidence for a close and intentional networking.

The Gospel of Matthew uses Mark as a basic narrative but is structured in such a way that the relationship between them is difficult to define. Of course, the extensive use of Markan material indicates a fundamental affirmation of the new gospel genre and of the Markan portrayal. Nevertheless, Matthew's own accent in the arrangement, editing, and correcting of the material is so great (see above, 10.2.2) that one has to ask about the intentions of Matthew. With the prehistory and the five major speeches, Matthew gives his own independent structure and only begins to follow the Markan

---

194. Cf. Strathmann, *Das Evangelium nach Johannes*, 23: "In his portrayal, John pays homage not to the historicism, but to the principle of the kerygmatic stylization."

195. One may note especially that a certain proximity to the deutero-Pauline letters is unmistakable in the cosmology (cf. Col. 1:15–20) and eschatology (cf. Col. 3:1–4; Eph. 2:4–9).

196. For the full argument, cf. Schnelle, *History and Theology of the New Testament*, 161–96.

outline for long sections in 12:1.[197] Different accents in content are further evident: The messianic secret that is central for Mark is passed over, being replaced at the center by another topic. While Mark does not use the word νόμος (law), nullifies the food laws (Mark 7:19c), limits the commandments to the social-ethical level (cf. Mark 10:17–22; 12:28–34), and ascribes a saving function to following Jesus (cf. Mark 10:21; 12:34), Matthew develops an opposite program.[198] For him the commands of the Torah are absolute (cf. Matt. 5:17–18; in addition, the omission of Mark 7:19c, declaring all foods clean, in Matt. 15:17), of course, within the framework of a hierarchy of smaller and greater commandments, in which a decisive role is attributed to mercy and faith (cf. Matt. 23:23; also Hosea 6:6 in Matt. 9:13; 12:7). Jesus's instructions are the binding interpretation of the will of God expressed in the Torah and the prophets (cf. Matt. 5:20–48). While Mark clearly relativizes the Torah, in Matthew the Torah claims continuing validity and is interpreted by Jesus Christ, the teacher, within the horizon of the imminent arrival of the kingdom of God (Matt. 23:10). Does Matthew consider the Markan portrayal of Jesus to be unacceptable?[199] Or does he want to give a hearing to his strict Jewish Christian position? Does the networking signify a correction or a supplement? These alternatives are probably inadequate, for Matthew does not rewrite the Gospel of Mark but primarily writes his own Gospel, in order to give a literary-theological voice to the strict Jewish Christianity and the central aspect of the work associated with the faith around the end of the first century.

Luke goes in an entirely different direction. He is the only NT author who confirms the networking and reflects: "Since many have undertaken to draw up an account of the events that have been fulfilled among us, as they have delivered them to us by those who from the beginning were eyewitnesses and servants of the word, I too decided to write an orderly account, having carefully investigated everything from the beginning" (Luke 1:1–3). The mention of predecessors or precursors in connection with eyewitnesses and of his own careful work suggests an indirect critique; whether he means the logia source and/or the Gospel of Mark must remain an open question. The categories of critique or improvement are in no way adequate for describing Luke's intention; he goes beyond Q, Mark, or Matthew in his own new way (see above,

197. Cf. Luz, *Matthew*, 1:10: "In other words, the newly narrated Gospel of Mark can be read only on the basis of chaps. 1–11."

198. Cf. Konradt, "Matthäus und Markus," who places the problem of the law, the Davidic messiahship of Jesus, and the portrayal of the disciples in the center.

199. So Konradt, "Matthäus und Markus," 232, who argues that Matthew intends to prevent the influence of the Markan story of Jesus.

10.2.3). He does not place the term εὐαγγέλιον or βίβλος at the beginning but instead speaks of a διήγησις (narrative/report); that is, he wants his work to be understood as a historical report. Thus he opens a new horizon, for the entire history of early Christianity, from the beginnings at the promised birth to the preaching of the gospel in Rome, is the subject of the portrayal. This expanded comprehensive perspective and the additional sources explain the particular outline of the Gospel of Luke. In contrast to Matthew, he omits many more Markan pericopes (Matthew takes 128 Markan pericopes, Luke only 96)[200] and employs extensive special material that he appropriates, primarily in the travel narrative (Luke 9:51–19:27). Furthermore, Luke does not, like Matthew, distribute his sources throughout his work;[201] instead, he places them next to each other, giving a totally different portrayal of the life of Jesus. Luke's theology is evident as he, like Matthew, ignores the Markan theory of the messianic secret. Unlike Matthew, however, he does not place the problem of the law in the center but, as a narrator, in his outline he orients himself to the topics of the logia source.[202] Luke's concern is the way of salvation (cf. Acts 16:17, "These men are servants of the most high God, who proclaim the way of salvation"), which he narrates from its beginnings in Jerusalem to its preliminary end in Rome.[203] The beginning of the exalted status of Jesus (Luke 1–2), faith, the call to discipleship and the associated lifestyle (Luke 6:20–49; 9:23–27), the care for outsiders (Luke 18:9–13), the warning against covetousness (Luke 12:13–21), and the actual security of life (Luke 13:22–30) stand in the center of the gospel. Although Matthew and Luke each write their own Gospel, with their process of editing Mark and Q they signal a literary and theological continuity. Despite the discernible individual orientation of each, they offer a new perspective: the life and ministry of Jesus of Nazareth as the basis of a narrative that is reported, interpreted, and proclaimed.

John and the Synoptic Gospels

While the independence of the Gospel of John from the Synoptics was almost unanimously assumed until about 1970,[204] the consensus has significantly changed. In contemporary scholarship, a clear majority maintains that John has a knowledge of one or more Synoptic Gospels (minimally Mark and/or

200. Cf. Morgenthaler, *Statistische Synopse*, 232.
201. On the source theories in Luke, cf. Fitzmyer, *Luke*, 1:63–106.
202. Cf. H. Klein, *Das Lukasevangelium*, 44: "Luke is theologically shaped by the logia source (Q). . . . He has preferred Q when it shared parallel traditions with Mark."
203. Cf. the list of topics in H. Klein, *Das Lukasevangelium*, 52–62.
204. In contemporary scholarship, Theobald, *Das Evangelium nach Johannes*, 76–81, represents this position.

Luke).[205] While the substantial agreements between John and individual Synoptic Gospels yield various interpretations in their details,[206] the reception of the gospel genre and the analogous composition suggest a knowledge of the Synoptics by John. If the Fourth Gospel were fully independent of Mark, the Johannine circle would have had to develop the gospel genre a second time. Of course, it must be considered historically improbable that about thirty years after the creation of the gospel genre and about ten to twenty years after its reception by Matthew and Luke, a second theologian would create the same genre without a knowledge of the Gospel of Mark. Furthermore, John adopts from Mark the two constitutive elements of the gospel genre: (1) Jesus Christ as the speaking and acting subject of the gospel (cf. Mark 1:1; 1:14; for John, the Paraclete sayings and the *ego-eimi* [I am] words); and (2) cross and resurrection as the focal points of the gospel composition (cf., e.g., Mark 1:11; 9:7; 15:39; John 1:29, 36; 2:1, 4, 14–22; 3:14–15; 19:30).[207]

Even more than the Synoptics, John writes his own gospel (see above, 10.4.3)! He introduces a world of language and image, has at his disposal numerous traditions of his own and other special traditions, and arranges the material in a new way so that a new perception of the life and ministry of Jesus becomes possible. Thus he develops two theological-political agenda items: (1) From the networking with Paul and Mark, he creates a new form of the gospel:[208] a consistent kerygmatically oriented story of Jesus Christ that does justice equally to the meaning of faith and of history. (2) With the introduction of the "beloved disciple," John consistently relativizes the claim of the Petrine circle of tradition that was becoming increasingly stronger around the end of the first century. The editors of the Gospel correct this in turn with John 21 but do not nullify the "beloved disciple," so that the two stand next to each other, and the readers/hearers of the gospel can form their own image.

Paul and Peter

The circles associated with Peter appropriated the figure of Paul either directly (2 Peter) or indirectly (1 Peter) in order to secure the legitimacy and

---

205. For the contemporary state of research, see M. Labahn and M. Lang, "Johannes und die Synoptiker"; cf. also Blinzler, *Johannes und die Synoptiker*; Schnider and Stenger, *Johannes und die Synoptiker.*

206. On the parallels, cf. Schnider and Stenger, *Johannes und die Synoptiker*, 26–170.

207. Representatives of moderate models of dependence are, among others, Schnelle, *Das Evangelium nach Johannes*, 20–21; Wilckens, *Das Evangelium nach Johannes*, 1–5; Dietzfelbinger, *Das Evangelium nach Johannes*, 1:11. Models that go further than this thesis of a moderate dependence see in the literary use of the Synoptics by John not only a question of sources but also a hermeneutical concept; cf. especially Thyen, *Das Johannesevangelium*, 4.

208. See above, 13.5.2.

acceptance of their writings.[209] Both apostles were already models of the steadfastness of faith in suffering and were active as missionaries in Asia Minor. The figure of Peter was employed because he was considered the founder of the gentile mission (cf. Acts 10) and was venerated as one of the first martyrs in early Christianity. Paul must, of course, be added as the indirect letter writer, for the churches that are addressed were in the area of his mission. The geographical information in 1 Pet. 1:1–2 and 5:13 (Babylon as a code name for Rome),[210] the dependence of the Pauline epistolary form, and the use of Silvanus/Silas (cf. 1 Thess. 1:1; 2 Cor. 1:19; 2 Thess. 1:1; Acts 15:22, 27, 32, 40; 16:19–25, 29; 17:4, 10, 14–15; 18:5) and (John) Mark (cf. Philem. 24; Col. 4:10; 2 Tim. 4:11; Acts 12:12, 25; 13:5, 13; 15:37, 39) lead the hearers/readers of the letter to think of Paul instinctively.[211] Central terms and concepts of Pauline theology define the theology of 1 Peter: χάρις (grace: 1 Pet. 1:2, 10, 13; 2:19–20; 4:10; 5:10, 12), δικαιοσύνη (righteousness: 1 Pet. 2:24; 3:14), ἀποκάλυψις (revelation: 1 Pet. 1:7, 13; 4:13), ἐλευθερία (freedom: 1 Pet. 2:16; cf. Gal. 5:13), καλεῖν for the call to salvation (call: 1 Pet. 1:15; 2:9, 21; 3:9; 5:10), and election (1 Pet. 1:1 with ἐκλεκτός; 2:9). The central Pauline conception ἐν Χριστῷ appears in 1 Peter only in 3:16; 5:10, 14! Finally, the numerous contacts between the paraenetic material of 1 Peter and Pauline paraeneses are evident in the major agreements between 1 Pet. 2:13–17 and Rom. 13:1–7.[212] Moreover, the Peter-Paul traditions are both located in Rome (cf. 1 Clem. 5.4; Ign. *Rom.* 4.3). The purpose of the networking of the Petrine circle with Paul is evident: along with the authorization of the writing, there is especially a theological intention: Paul is placed under the leadership of Peter. The churches look to Peter and Paul as models and humbly accept their own suffering as the will of God. In addition, an ecclesiastical-political signal is given: the unity of the distressed early Christian movement under the leadership of Peter and Paul. The reference to Paul in 1 Peter, which is only indirect, and the claim to interpret Pauline theology in 2 Peter clearly indicate that the claim is being made for Peter's primacy.

209. On 1 and 2 Peter, cf. above, 13.5.1 under "Peter."

210. Babylon appears as a cipher for Rome after 70 CE (cf. Rev. 14:8; 16:19; 17:5; 18:2, 10, 21); cf. also Sib. Or. 3.300–302; 4.119–20, 138; 5.143, 159; 2 Bar. 11.1; 67.7; 4 Ezra 3.1, 28, 31). For the discussion of this conclusion and other introductory questions, cf. finally Horn, "Die Petrus-Schule in Rom."

211. Herzer, *Petrus oder Paulus?*, is critical of the claim of Paulinism in 1 Peter; he maintains that the constellation of names in 1 Pet. 5:12–13 comes primarily from Acts 15 (particularly 15:22–23); cf. Herzer, *Petrus oder Paulus?*, 62–73.

212. These questions have been previously treated primarily as matters of tradition history; cf. the list and (critical) assessment of the parallels in Schröger, *Gemeinde im 1. Petrusbrief*, 212–16, 223–28; Goppelt, *A Commentary on 1 Peter*, 28–29; Brox, *Der erste Petrusbrief*, 47–51.

PAUL AND JAMES

The Letter of James deals critically with the understanding of the law and faith that he observes in Paul himself or at least in the impact of Paul.[213] Like the Gospel of Matthew, James evaluates the law in positive terms as the "law of liberty" (James 2:12) and vehemently demands the unity of faith and works (James 1:22, "Be doers of the word and not hearers only"). He thus concentrates on a possible weakness of the Pauline doctrine of grace, for the relationship between sin and grace, human deeds and God's role, could be misunderstood (cf. Rom. 6:1). The required correspondence to the will of God without a reference to the Torah stood in constant danger, since the social reality did not correspond to the theological theory. Behind the social misconduct, primarily by the rich, James sees a fundamentally anthropological problem: the divided person (James 1:8; 4:8) for whom the unity of faith and acts, along with speech and conduct, has been lost and who falls into a deceptive self-confidence (cf. James 4:13–17). James sees the deeper reason for these undesirable developments in a false theological position that he indirectly, but recognizably, connects with Paul; James counters the decentering of the Torah with the idea of ethical perfection in humility and lowliness by the fulfillment of the law, which is made possible by the divine gift of wisdom. James aims at overcoming the divided Christian existence. His concern is the totality and perfection of the Christian. Ethics and anthropology form the center of his construction of identity, which is shaped by the question of faith corresponding to wisdom and oriented to the law in the unity of being and doing. Here the law appears as the order of freedom in love. The battle over the significance of the Torah is led by James, with a defined theological conception that attempts to demonstrate or overcome the possible or actual deficits in the Pauline conception.

PAUL AND THE LETTER TO THE HEBREWS

Hebrews belongs to the great riddles of the NT. Its historical situation is fully unclear, for it has only vague references to the community's situation and no information about the author.[214] Pauline authorship and composition in Rome are suggested by the epistolary conclusion in Hebrews 13:23–24:[215] "Know that our brother Timothy has been set free. When he comes, I will see

---

213. On the Letter of James and his partial anti-Pauline argument, cf. above 10.5.2 under "The Letter of James."

214. On the introductory issues, cf. Schnelle, *History and Theology of the New Testament*, 365–82.

215. Cf. Karrer, *Der Brief an die Hebräer*, 35.

you. Greet all of the leaders and all of the saints. Those who are from Italy greet you." In view of the content of the preceding message, these reports are unexpected; thus the formal ending of the letter, oriented to the conclusion of Pauline letters (cf. 1 Cor. 16:19; Phil. 4:21–22; Rom. 16:21), was probably secondary, possibly added by the editor of a Pauline letter collection.[216] On the other hand, if the epistolary conclusion is considered original, this suggests only that the author of Hebrews wanted his writing to be understood within the realm of Pauline theology.[217] The impression is given by the epistolary conclusion that Hebrews was written by Paul or within the Pauline environment.[218] In addition to the epistolary conclusion, other agreements between Paul and Hebrews are present: Heb. 1:1–4 has agreements with Phil. 2:6–11; Rom. 1:3–4; 1 Cor. 8:6; Col. 1:15ff. Like Paul (cf. Gal. 3; Rom. 4), Hebrews takes up the promise to Abraham in 6:13–20; 11:8–19. Concepts of a sacrificial offering appear both in Rom. 3:25 and in Heb. 2:17–18; and like Paul (cf. 2 Cor. 3), Hebrews knows the antithesis between the first covenant and the new covenant. The terms ὁμολογία (confession: Heb. 3:1; 4:14; 10:23) and ὁμολογεῖν (confess: Heb. 11:13; 13:15), which appear also in Paul and his tradition (2 Cor. 9:13; Rom. 10:9; 1 Tim. 6:12–13; Titus 1:16), play a central role in Hebrews as the community's acceptance of God's address to the community.[219] At the same time, basic differences exist between Pauline theology and the theology of Hebrews (law, righteousness, the concept of faith).[220] Consequently, the author, despite Heb. 13:23–24, cannot be regarded as a pupil of Paul.

But what is the intention of the (secondary) ascription to Paul or the Pauline tradition by the epistolary conclusion? First of all is the legitimation of this anonymous writing that has no (identifiable) addressees.[221] The success of this strategy is indicated in the reception history of the book, for it was very early regarded (in the eastern part of the empire) as a letter of Paul. A second reason follows: Hebrews is intended to be read as a supplement to the

216. Cf. Grässer, *An die Hebräer*, 22. In favor of this argument is the fact that in the oldest witness to the text, 𝔓[46] (around 200 CE), Hebrews appears after Romans.
217. Grässer, *An die Hebräer*, 22, considers the partially pseudonymous character of Hebrews as no coincidence. "Here, for theological reasons, Hebrews appears from the outset in an anonymous form."
218. Contra Backhaus, *Der Hebräerbrief*, 488: "The similarities are the result of the social, spatial, and theological intersections, not the result of literary independence or intentional imitation."
219. Rothschild, *Hebrews as Pseudepigraphon*, 63–118, goes too far in finding additional Pauline "echoes" in Hebrews.
220. Cf. Backhaus, "Der Hebräerbrief und die Paulus-Schule."
221. The title Πρὸς Ἑβραίους is generally correctly regarded as secondary. Cf. Grässer, *An die Hebräer*, 1:41–45.

Pauline letters (with a theology of the cult). The intention is not to correct Paul (as in the Letter of James!) but to supplement his work. A moderate Jewish Christian voice[222]—one that does not polemicize against Paul, unites Jewish and Platonic thought,[223] and places the heavenly world at the center—would then expand the Pauline corpus.[224] Thus the postulated relationship of the author with Timothy and the greeting of the brothers from Italy serve this purpose.[225] Networking here means especially supplementation and balance, a strategy that was appropriate at the end of the first century.

THE REVELATION OF JOHN BETWEEN JOHN, PAUL, AND JAMES

The Revelation of John has a special place among the NT writings, not only because of its form.[226] This is indicated by the broad background in the history of religion but at the same time by the many inner Christian networkings. This is first evident naturally in the Johannine literature, in which it is noteworthy that the name Ἰωάννης (John) appears only in the text of Revelation (1:1, 4, 9; 22:8). Does this involve a secondary attribution,[227] or was the name of the seer really John but not the same as the author of the letters and the Gospel?[228] The claim of the book suggests the authenticity of the name John, who belonged to the circle of the Johannine school (see above, 10.4). Thematic connections between Revelation and the Fourth Gospel are indicated in the motif of living water (cf. Rev. 7:16–17; 21:6; 22:1, 17; John 4:10, 13–14; 7:37–39). In Rev. 19:13 Jesus, the one who returns, is called ὁ λόγος τοῦ θεοῦ (the word of God; cf. John 1:1), and the concept of Christ as the "Lamb" (of God) is of central significance for the Christology of Revelation (ἀρνίον 29 times) and of the Gospel of John

222. On the question of whether Hebrews can be considered a Jewish Christian witness, cf. above, 10.5.2 under "The Epistle to the Hebrews."

223. The dichotomy of earth and heaven, visible and invisible, transient and abiding, shakable and unshakable, changeable and unchangeable, strange land and homeland, time and eternity indicate the influence of Middle Platonism (cf., e.g., Heb. 8:5; 9:23; 11:3, 10, 13; 12:22–24, 25–29; 13:14).

224. Cf. Rothschild, *Hebrews as Pseudepigraphon*, 12: "The work was composed to be read alongside Paul's other letters," thus (incorrectly) regarding this as the original intention of the entire letter and not only of the closing.

225. Cf. Karrer, *Der Brief an die Hebraer*, 382: "Thus the author's acquaintance with Timothy gives great plausibility to the value of the theology of Hebrews in the Pauline churches."

226. Cf. Gradl, "Buch und Brief," who sees in the book and epistolary motifs a doubled medial version of Revelation.

227. The view of, e.g., Frey, "Erwägungen zum Verhältnis," 425–27, who attributes the giving of the name to a redactional framing and classifies Revelation as a pseudepigraphon.

228. The information about the author is considered original by, e.g., T. Holtz, *Die Offenbarung des Johannes*, 7–8, who does not postulate a connection to the other Johannine writings.

(ἀμνός in John 1:29, 36). The theme of victory stands in the foreground in Revelation (νικᾶν 17 times out of 28 occurrences in the NT) and in the Johannine corpus (νικᾶν 7 times; νίκη in the NT only in 1 John 5:4). The motif of witness (μαρτυρεῖν 76 times; μαρτυρία 37 times in the NT) is present in Revelation (μαρτυρεῖν 4 times; μαρτυρία 9 times) and the writings of the Johannine school (μαρτυρεῖν 43 times; μαρτυρία 21 times) with particular frequency.[229] These connecting links do not permit a more certain conclusion, for below the purely linguistic statistical evidence of common motifs, one may see either considerable isolated deviations in theological conceptions or agreements derived from a comparable background of tradition history. Moreover, major differences in language, Christology, ecclesiology, and eschatology are present.[230] The result is ambiguous: on the one hand, Revelation stands in a certain proximity to the Johannine corpus and could belong in the pre- or posthistory of the Gospel;[231] on the other hand, Revelation exhibits a high degree of independence in the horizon of its thought, its historical situation, its themes, and its theology.[232] This vagueness and associated independent standpoint are probably intended, for Revelation also exhibits a relationship to Paul.

The starting point here is the epistolary frame of Revelation: In Rev. 1:4–6 an independently accented prescript oriented to the Pauline epistolary convention[233] follows the opening that functions as a title.[234] It includes a superscript and an adscript (v. 4a), an expanded salutation (vv. 4b, 5a), and a doxology (vv. 5b–6), which appears in place of a thanksgiving. The concluding greeting in Rev. 22:21 is also formed under the influence of a Pauline epistolary formula (cf. 1 Thess. 5:28; 1 Cor. 16:23; Phil. 4:23). In accordance with the liturgical style of Revelation, the work concludes with a prayer for the coming of the Lord (22:21) and the response with the consolation of grace (cf. 1 Cor. 16:22–23). The epistolary form of Revelation must be understood as a direct expression of the entire book's address to the specific situation of the readers. The seer addresses churches in the Pauline tradition and opens the reception of his message with an intentional recourse to the Pauline epistolary convention.

229. The agreements are presented in detail and emphasized by J. Taeger, *Johannesapokalypse und johanneischer Kreis*.
230. Cf. the comprehensive study by Frey, *Erwägungen zum Verhältnis*, 336ff.
231. G. Strecker, *Literaturgeschichte des Neuen Testaments*, 275, argues for the prehistory position; maintaining the posthistory view (Revelation as a "trito-Johannine" writing) is J. Taeger, *Johannesapokalypse und johanneischer Kreis*, 206: "The question of the Apocalypse's belonging to the Johannine literary circle is not only presumably, but certainly, an open question."
232. Cf. Tóth, *Der himmlische Kult*, 493–510.
233. Cf. the analysis by Karrer, *Die Johannesoffenbarung*, 86–108.
234. Evidence provided by Karrer, *Die Johannesoffenbarung*, 66–83.

The letters to the churches also document the epistolary orientation of Revelation, for the seer writes in the style of epistolary communication:[235] addressee, information about the sender, the command to write, and knowledge of the church's situation (cf. 1 Thess. 1:3ff.) point in this direction. Like the apostolic letters, the prophetic letters appear as a substitute for the presence of the writer and enable the writer to maintain an influence on the situation of the church. The seer thus places himself intentionally within the Pauline tradition in order to receive a heightened acceptance by the churches that are addressed. This act could have been related to his conscious Jewish Christian orientation[236] and is indicated also by the seer's adoption of the apostolic decrees (cf. Acts 15:28f.) in Rev. 2:24, which were initiated by James the brother of the Lord. John is in favor of minimal ritual standards for gentile Christians, standards that prohibit food offered to idols and sexual immorality. The equally impressive as well as unconventional sacral architecture of Revelation, with its interpretation of earthly events and happenings in the heavenly cult, probably required a broad earthly networking.

The multiple dimensions of networking in early Christianity in its theological and historical significance can scarcely be overestimated. The almost constant reference to Paul is theologically significant. All NT authors positioned themselves in an open or hidden, polemical or conciliatory form with respect to Paul, whose prominent position as the one who shaped early Christianity as an independent movement (see above, 8.7) is thus indirectly confirmed. Networking opened an area for theological interpretation that was perceived as adoption, variation, supplementation, harmonization, conciliation, polemic, or opposition. The networkings were historically a crucial step in the consolidation of early Christianity. It made possible a conceptual stability that was unknown until then and prevented strands and threads of tradition from departing or breaking off. The connections were maintained even in the midst of contradiction, and the unique commitment to literature on the person of Jesus Christ in this early period was not conceivable without networking. The extensive production of literature was in turn the presupposition for the plurality of theological positions in early Christianity, which, in spite of continuing internal and external dangers, ensured its survival. Without its diverse literature, early Christianity would not have survived.

---

235. Cf. Karrer, *Die Johannesoffenbarung*, 160.
236. Cf. above, 10.5.2 under "The Revelation of John."

13.6 The Expansion of Early Christianity

The size of the early Christian churches and the expansion of early Christianity until about 130 CE are difficult to determine; one can offer only hypotheses because the sources give no actual information. The population of the Roman Empire in the first and second centuries CE as a whole and the populations of the individual provinces and larger cities permit an approximate estimation. A certain consensus exists of the total population of the empire (ca. 60 million),[237] and the approximate population of a few larger cities: Rome, 1 million; Alexandria, 300,000 to 500,000;[238] Antioch (Syria), 300,000; Damascus, 45,000;[239] Ephesus, 100,000;[240] Jerusalem, 60,000;[241] Thessalonica, 30,000;[242] Corinth, 12,000 to 16,000;[243] Athens, 10,000 to 20,000.[244]

Because there is no concrete information about the expansion of early Christianity, methodological considerations must be considered first.[245] The starting point can be (1) only the textual witnesses, combined with (2) general considerations and insights.

Concerning point 1. The statements of the undisputed Pauline letters and Acts are the basic textual witnesses, for they attest the existence of churches or describe the first history of the spread of early Christianity. Thus the situation around 60 CE offers information for an approximate assessment. In addition, one can observe isolated stories in the Gospels that can be claimed as local traditions or church aetiologies indicating the existence of a church

237. Cf. Christ, *Geschichte der römischen Kaiserzeit*, 373: "According to modern estimates (as by O. A. W. Dilke), the entire population of the *Imperium Romanum* in 14 CE was over 60 million inhabitants. Fourteen million were in Rome, Italy, and the three large islands, Sicily, Sardinia, and Corsica; around six million were in Spain, and five million in Gaul. In the provinces of the Danube there were more than two million, in Greece and the Greek islands three million, in Asia Minor thirteen million; in Syria, Palestine, and Cyprus six and one half million; in Egypt and Cyrenaica five and one half million; in the rest of Roman North Africa there were around six million." Cf. Wilken, *Christians as the Romans Saw Them*, 31; Stark, *Rise of Christianity*, 9–10.

238. Diodorus Siculus 17.52 reports that there were 300,000 who were born free; this suggests a total population of ca. 500,000; cf. Clauss, *Alexandria*, 17 (favoring a population there of 180,000 to 200,000).

239. Cf. Stark, *Rise of Christianity*, 137.

240. Cf. Corsten and Zangenberg, "Ephesos," 2:148.

241. See above, 5.3.

242. Cf. Brocke, "Thessaloniki," 2:173.

243. See Walters, "Civic Identity in Roman Corinth," 402.

244. Cf. Brocke, *Griechenland*, 157.

245. Stark, *Rise of Christianity*, 4–13 (cf. 12), selects for his calculation of the period from 40–350 CE an estimation of 1,000 Christians in 40 CE as a starting point and estimates a growth of 40 percent per decade (= 3.42 percent annually). As a control measure, he takes the growth rate of modern churches (e.g., Mormons). He estimates the Christian population in the empire for the year 40 at 1,000; for 50 at 1,400; for 100 up to 7,530; and for the year 150 at 40,496.

as it probably already existed around 60 CE (e.g., the centurion from Capernaum in Luke 7:1–10//Matt. 8:5–10, 13).

Concerning point 2. As a starting point for the size of churches, one should assume that about thirty to forty persons could assemble in a house.[246] When several house churches are evident in big cities, the number rises correspondingly. When several churches are addressed in the prescript (cf. Gal. 1:2), then one must assume two to three churches. Inasmuch as numerous churches had been in existence for a period of time around 60 CE and a certain growth is to be assumed, about fifty people appear to be estimated as the basic unit of a church. As a whole, these assumptions are restrictive; thus differences between urban and rural, larger and smaller, fast-growing and continuing or dying churches as a whole balance each other. Moreover, probably some churches are not mentioned in any strand of tradition.

Evidence exists or is probable, on the basis of the Pauline letters and Acts, that around 60 CE churches existed in the following locations:[247]

Table 7. Early Church Locations

Location	Reference
Jerusalem	Gal. 1:17; Acts 1:4ff.
Arabia?	Gal. 1:17
Damascus	Acts 9:10; Gal. 1:17
Ashdod	Acts 8:40
Gaza	Acts 8:26
Caesarea Maritima	Acts 8:40; 10:1–48; 21:8–9
Samaria[a]	Acts 8:4–25; Luke 10:25–37: several churches
Lydda	Acts 9:32–35
Joppa	Acts 9:36–43
Tarsus?	Acts 9:30; 11:25; Gal. 1:21
Antioch/Syria	Acts 11:19–30; Gal. 2:11–15; Acts 15:23: several churches
Cyprus	Acts 4:36; 13:4–12: Salamis, Paphos
Antioch of Pisidia	Acts 13:13–52
Iconium	Acts 14:1–7
Lystra	Acts 14:8–20a
Derbe	Acts 14:20b–21
Perga	Acts 14:25
Syria	Acts 15:23: several churches

Note: Also to be mentioned are Seleucia (Acts 13:4), Amphipolis, and Apollonia (Acts 17:1), although they may have been only places to stop on the journey.

a. Both the geographical location between Galilee and Judea and the independent traditions (Luke-Acts and Gospel of John; cf. above, 6.4 under "Samaria") make it probable that very early there were Christian churches in Samaria.

246. Cf. above, 8.3 under "House Churches."
247. Cf. the list in Harnack, *Expansion of Christianity*, 2:621–24; Schnabel, *Urchristliche Mission*, 1465–68.

Location	Reference
Cilicia	Acts 15:23: several churches
Philippi	Acts 16:11–40; Philippians
Thessalonica	Acts 17:1–9; 1 Thessalonians
Beroea/Berea	Acts 17:10–15; 20:4
Athens	1 Thess. 3:1; Acts 17:34
Corinth	Acts 18:1–17; 1 Corinthians; 2 Corinthians: several churches
Cenchreae near Corinth	Rom. 16:1
Achaia	2 Cor. 1:1: several churches
Ephesus	Acts 19; 1 Cor. 16:8: several churches
Galatia	Gal. 1:2: several churches
Illyricum	Rom. 15:19
Alexandria?	Acts 18:24
Troas	Acts 20:6–12; 2 Cor. 2:12
Miletus	Acts 20:17–38
Tyre	Acts 21:3–6
Sidon	Acts 27:3
Ptolemais	Acts 21:7
Puteoli	Acts 28:13–15
Rome	Acts; Romans: several churches

In the Gospel tradition there are indications of churches around 60 CE, particularly in local traditions and church etiologies that are clearly connected with missionary activities in these places: Capernaum (Luke 7:1–10//Matt. 8:5–10, 13; Mark 1:29–31); Bethsaida (Mark 8:22–26; Luke 9:10; John 1:44; 12:21); Caesarea Philippi (Mark 8:27–39); Cana (John 2:1–11; 4:46; 21:2); Nain (Luke 7:11–17); Decapolis (Mark 7:31–37; Mark 5:1–20//Matt. 8:28–34: Gerasa/Gadara);[248] Bethany (Mark 14:3–9//John 11:1–45//Luke 10:38–42); Jericho (Mark 10:46–52; Luke 19:1–10); Emmaus (Luke 24:13–35).

From the beginning, churches in Jerusalem and Rome had a special place because of their significance and their size. According to Luke, Paul persecuted the Jerusalem church around 32/33 CE before his call (cf. Acts 8:3); that is, they must have already had a certain size in this period and recognizable identity. If one assumes a size for the church of about one hundred people for this period until 40 CE, then they must have grown to five hundred people around 60 CE. One must assume a rapid growth also for the church in Rome, for around 56 CE there were at least four hundred people.[249] The persecution under Nero in 64 CE (see above, 12.2) presupposes, in the city of one million, a relatively large group of Christians that was already known in the city and identifiable (at least eight hundred people, perhaps as many as one thousand).

248. The Decapolis was a center of Hellenistic culture; cf. above, 3.2.1 under "Cynics."
249. Cf. above, 8.3 under "House Churches."

Based on these considerations, one may assume a total of about four thousand people as members in about fifty to sixty early Christian churches.[250] This number appears to be realistic for the entire empire on the basis of the textual witnesses and the missionary activities that are assumed as well as the networking among the churches.

Further development is also difficult to measure. In addition to the already-existing churches, the textual witness points to others: Colossae (Col. 1:2);[251] Laodicea (Col. 4:15; Rev. 3:14–22); Crete (Titus 1:5); Hierapolis (Col. 4:13; Papias); Magnesia (Ignatius, *To the Magnesians*); Pergamum (Rev. 2:12–17); Philadelphia (Rev. 3:7–13; Ignatius, *To the Philadelphians*); Sardis (Rev. 3:1–6); Smyrna (Rev. 2:8–11; Ignatius, *To the Smyrnaeans*); Thyatira (Rev. 2:18–29); Tralles (Ignatius, *To the Trallians*); Cappadocia (1 Pet. 1:1); Bithynia and Pontus (1 Pet. 1:1; Pliny, *Ep.* 10.96.1); Pella (Eusebius, *Hist. eccl.* 3.5.3); three churches/house churches in 2 and 3 John (the church of the presbyter, 2 John 1 and 3 John 1; the ἐκκλησία κυρία from 2 John 1; the church of Diotrephes, 3 John 9). The churches in Ephesus, which already existed, apparently had considerable growth (Ephesians; Rev. 2:1–7; Ignatius, *To the Ephesians*), which was also the case in Rome (Ignatius, *To the Romans*), Galatia (1 Pet. 1:1), the province of Asia (1 Cor. 16:19), and Corinth (1 Clement). The Letters of James and 1 Peter already took on a universal perspective. The prescript of 1 Peter identifies itself as a "diaspora letter" to churches in almost all of Asia Minor (Pontus, Galatia, Cappadocia, the province of Asia, Bithynia).[252] The Letter of James also understands itself as a teaching letter that is addressed with a conscious Jewish Christian standpoint to all of the Christian churches outside Palestine (James 1:1: "to the twelve tribes in the diaspora"). On the other side, the Jerusalem church does not exist any longer after 70 CE (see above, 9.2), and other churches in Palestine probably did not survive the catastrophe.

Besides the continuing growth of most churches/church associations and the loss of individual local churches, at the beginning of the second century CE a third phenomenon emerged: an explosive growth of local churches in some places. Three sources that are independent of each other give evidence of this growth: (1) In his correspondence with Caesar Trajan, Pliny describes the situation in Pontus and Bithynia (see above, 12.4):

250. More precisely: 4,100 people (36 churches each with 50 people = 1,800; eight times "several" churches [125 people] = 1,000; Jerusalem and Rome: 1,300 members). Similar to Wilken, *Christians as the Romans Saw Them*, 31; D.-A. Koch, *Geschichte des Urchristentums*, 420, calculates 50 churches in 150 CE.

251. After a possible earthquake in 60/61, Colossae remained a more significant place; cf. Bormann, *Der Brief des Paulus an die Kolosser*, 12–28.

252. Cf. T. Klein, *Bewährung in Anfechtung*.

It is not only the towns, but villages and rural districts too which are infected through contact with this wretched cult. I think though that it is still possible for it to be checked and directed to better ends, for there is no doubt that people have begun to throng the temples which had been almost entirely deserted for a long time; the sacred rites which had been allowed to lapse are being performed again, and flesh of sacrificial victims is on sale everywhere, though up till recently scarcely anyone could be found to buy it. It is easy to infer from this that a great many people could be reformed if they were given an opportunity to repent. (Pliny, *Ep.* 10.96.9–10f. LCL)

Even if one considers a certain rhetorical excess, the text clearly indicates three tendencies: (a) The number of Christians has until 100 CE continually grown, and (b) now it has reached the rural areas so that (c) even economic losses are recorded. (2) At the beginning of the second century, the Didache gives evidence of the existence of numerous Jewish Christian churches in Syria.[253] According to Did. 11.3–6, traveling charismatics, as a rule, should be received for a day; if, however, they remain three days or demand money, they demonstrate that they are false prophets. If an apostle travels farther, bread should be given to him to last until the next place to stay; that is, what is assumed is a larger association of churches in which the churches are fairly near to each other (one to two days' walk). (3) It is already noteworthy that Tacitus (*Ann.* 15.44.4), in the context of the Neronian persecution (see above, 12.2), speaks of a "huge number" (*multitudo ingens*) of Christians who were arrested. Undoubtedly, the Roman church was already large around 64 CE, even if they scarcely comprised a "huge number." Either this refers to the number of Jews in Rome,[254] or Tacitus assumes the situation of his own time (around 115 CE). The latter suggestion would fit the development of the Roman church well, as Ignatius, *To the Romans* (prescript), and 1 Clement assume.

Two further aspects may be added to these regional developments in the first third of the second century CE that indicate a rapid growth of Christianity:[255] the origin and the emerging expansion of early Gnosticism and the perspective of the early apologists. The early Gnostics (see below, 14.2) were active in Antioch (Menander, Satornilus), Asia Minor (Cerinthus), and Alexandria (Basilides), and soon in Rome (before 140 CE: Valentinus; 144 CE: the heretic

253. See above, 10.5.2 under "Didache."
254. As maintained by Köstermann, *Cornelius Tacitus: Annalen*, 256.
255. Cf. Harnack, *Expansion of Christianity*, 2:956: "The facts of the case do justify the impression of the church-fathers in the fourth century—of men like Arnobius, Eusebius, and Augustine—that their faith had spread from generation to generation with inconceivable rapidity."

Marcion breaks from the Roman church). The success of Gnostic theologians and the emerging production of their own writings also point to a counterreaction to the existence of numerous churches. The appearance of the first apologists (ca. 125/126 CE, Quadratus; ca. 127 CE, Aristides) with their confident appeal to Caesar Hadrian is also not at all conceivable without a perceptible number of Christians and an observable expansion of Christianity.

The center of early Christianity around 130 CE was undoubtedly Asia Minor, while other centers were in Syria, Greece, and Italy. The situation in Egypt (Alexandria) and Spain is unclear. One can assume an early church around 50 CE in Alexandria (cf. Acts 18:24: Apollos from Alexandria);[256] one can say with certainty that Christianity had set foot in Alexandria around 100 CE. This fact is suggested by the close connections between Palestine and Alexandria and by the appearance of Gnostic teachers around 130 CE, so a prehistory must be assumed.[257] The conditions in Spain are fully unclear, for on the one hand, the travel plans of Paul (Rom. 15:24, 28) must have had a certain background; on the other hand, evidence for Christian churches in Spain does not appear until the late second century. The land was in no way inviting, for there was no Jewish population there.[258] From the Roman perspective, Spain was considered wild and uncultivated,[259] and the situation with the language was complex.[260] Paul probably knew that in the Roman

256. On Alexandria, cf. above, 6.4 under "Alexandria"; on Apollos, cf. above, 6.2 under "Apollos."

257. On Christianity in Egypt, cf. Fürst, *Christentum als Intellektuellen-Religion* (accordingly, no Christianity in Egypt can be determined in the first century CE; it set foot in Alexandria as an intellectual religion in the second century); Markus Lang, "Das frühe ägyptische Christentum," also argues for the emergence of Christianity in Egypt in the early second century. The historical record suggests a late emergence; an early date is suggested especially by (besides Apollos) general considerations: considering the rapid development in Damascus, Antioch, and Rome around 40 CE, it would be amazing if Christianity did not come into Alexandria relatively early. If one rejects an early dating, then the last third of the first century remains especially a plausible period in which a church could have come into existence in Alexandria inasmuch as the developments at the beginning of the second century presuppose an earlier history.

258. Cf. Bowers, "Jewish Communities in Spain."

259. Cf. Strabo, *Geography* 3.4.13 (most Iberians are coarse rural residents); 3.4.19 (the hinterland is mostly unknown).

260. Cf. Bellido, "Die Latinisierung Hispaniens"; Untermann, "Hispania," 1–17. The Romanization (and thus also Hellenization) was undoubtedly more advanced in the east and south (cf. M. Koch, "Animus . . . Meus . . . Praesagit"); but at the same time, "when the direct witnesses of pre-Roman languages ebb away with the coming of the Augustan period, this is the case only for the official use and for the levels of the population who have at least acquired a minimal amount of civilization, who had at least acquired the art of writing. It is a priori entirely certain that in the lower and lowest levels, the Latinizing that took place with the beginning of the Middle Ages (except for the Basque area), would have to wait a long time" (Untermann, *Hispania*, 14).

church there were also those who had been born in Spain, who could support him in this regard. Whether and when there were missionary activities after Paul remains uncertain.

All developments give evidence of an unambiguous and continuing and partially volatile growth of early Christianity, although concrete numbers are difficult to determine. A combination of constant growth and sudden bursts of growth appears plausible in order to account for the rapid development in some regions of the empire. As a basic number, 4,000 Christians from the year 60 CE may be assumed; one may also assume an estimated growth of around 40 percent per decade.[261] Then the following development is the result:

Table 8. Estimated Growth
of Christianity per Decade

Date CE	Number of Persons
60	4,000
70	5,600
80	7,840
90	10,976
100	15,366
110	21,512
120	30,117
130	42,164

If one considers about 8,000 an additional number, then the result is a combined total of about 50,000 Christians in the empire around 130 CE.[262] The number of churches probably grew considerably, from about 50–60 to at least 100 churches.

261. This is the conclusion also of Stark, *Rise of Christianity*, 6; he suggests a comparison with the Mormons at 43 percent per decade in the last one hundred years as an external control.

262. For a comparison, cf. Stark, *Rise of Christianity*, 7, who calculates for 150 CE a total of 40,496.

14

The Transition to the Ancient Church

A round the end of the first century, two insights are unavoidable: (1) The parousia of Jesus Christ had not taken place in the manner in which the church had hoped; it was still awaited, but the expectation was no longer imminent. (2) One had to settle into the world and create viable structures. Consequently, the issues of office and appropriate teaching stood at the center. This process had already begun in the last quarter of the first century and accelerated in the second century.

14.1 Claims to Power and Established Structures

1 Clement

First Clement, written around 96 CE, is directed against a "rebellion" (1 Clem. 1.1, στάσις), an attempted coup within the Corinthian church. Younger people revolted against the elders (cf. 1 Clem. 3.3); younger church members probably deposed the presbyters because they considered them incapable of leading (1 Clem. 44.4: "It would be no small sin to depose them from office"). Whether all (cf. 1 Clem. 47.6) or only a few of the presbyters (cf. 1 Clem. 44.6) were deposed remains unclear. Similarly, the reasons for the revolt are not known; nevertheless, the repeated emphasis on the impeccable conduct of the officeholders (cf. 1 Clem. 44.3, 4, 6) suggests that precisely here is the cause of the conflict. A mixture of generational conflict, personal rivalries, and various concepts of the church probably led to the conflict.[1]

---

1. Three relevant interpretative models have been mentioned: (1) Adolf von Harnack (*Einführung in die alte Kirchengeschichte*, 73) speaks of "squabbling among cliques" and thus makes

Finally, the relationship of bishops/overseers (*episkopoi*) and deacons to
the presbyters cannot be clearly defined, for according to 1 Clem. 42.4, the
apostles have appointed "bishops and deacons," and the dispute involves the
"office of overseer" (ἐπισκοπή); thus the function of the presbyters as overseers is probably the issue.[2] This view is indicated by the sequence "deposing
from the bishop's office" and "expulsion of presbyters" in 1 Clem. 44.4, 50.
The revolt lasted until the time of the writing of the letter (cf. 1 Clem. 46.9),
causing the Roman church to intervene. The news of these events reached not
only Rome but also the pagan world, which now defamed the new movement
(47.6–7). The author argues against the events in Corinth at several levels.
His starting position is that presbyters appointed "with the consent of the
whole church" (1 Clem. 44.3) in an orderly way should not be deposed. Thus
he demands, "You, therefore, who laid the foundation for the revolt, must
submit to the presbyters" (1 Clem. 57.1). This clear demand is then supported
by numerous arguments. Thus 1 Clement considers the revolt the result of
"jealousy and envy," which began already in the OT (cf. 1 Clem. 4) and was
evident in examples from the lives of the apostles Peter and Paul (1 Clem.
5). Clement invokes the great tradition of Christians (1 Clem. 7.2) who were
looked after by the Roman church. The Corinthian church is challenged to
practice humility toward the word and will of God (cf. 1 Clem. 13.1–18.17).
Finally, the opponents in Corinth are accused of not acting in humility, like
the Lord Jesus Christ, but in boasting and arrogance (cf. 1 Clem. 16.2). The
strategy of 1 Clement consists evidently of distinguishing between the leaders
of the revolt and the whole church, whom Clement wanted to bring to his
side (cf. 1 Clem. 14.2). He recommends that those who resist should either
submit or leave the church and go away (1 Clem. 54.2).

---

personal matters responsible for the conflict. (2) Walter Bauer (*Orthodoxy and Heresy*, 95–110)
regards differences in doctrine and life as the starting point: "The office is not in danger; rather,
the officeholders desired by Rome are the ones, and thus Rome intervenes, arguing that the church
officers cannot be removed" (101). Rome especially becomes involved against reviving Gnostic
streams in Corinth. Against Bauer, one must affirm that doctrinal conflicts are not present in
1 Clement. (3) Hans von Campenhausen (*Ecclesiastical Authority and Spiritual Power*, 88–90)
emphasizes that for Rome the idea of order is crucial: "The innovators in Corinth have sinned
against this basic order of appropriate Christian living; they have dispossessed the elders and
elevated themselves over the flock of Christ" (88).

2. On the important terminology in this context: ἐπισκοπή in 1 Clem. 44.1, 4; ἐπίσκοπος in
1 Clem. 42.4, 5. Lindemann, *Die Clemensbriefe*, 130, translates ἐπίσκοπος/ἐπισκοπή in 1 Clem.
42.5; 44.1 as "overseer/inspector" and sees no reference to the office of bishop; according to his
thesis, "the presbyters . . . are apparently those who have taken over the legitimate succession
of the original *episkopoi* and deacons appointed by the apostles." Contrary to this view, the
text in 1 Tim. 3:1, written at approximately the same time, undoubtedly uses ἐπισκοπή for the
office of bishop, and 1 Tim. 3:2 uses ἐπίσκοπος for the bishop.

Based on God's almighty power (cf. 1 Clem. 27–28), the demand for humility and submission (cf. 1 Clem. 37.1–38.4) shapes the argument. First Clement is oriented in a theocentric way, as the numerous and extensive OT citations indicate. In contrast to this piety that has been shaped by the Septuagint, the Christology is clearly underdeveloped (cf. 1 Clem. 7.4; 13.1–4; 21.6; 22.18–8).[3] Thus the plausibility of the resurrection can be supported with the saga of the Phoenix:[4] "How then, can we consider it to be some great and marvelous thing, if the Creator of the universe shall bring about the resurrection of those who have served him in holiness, in the assurance borne of good faith, when he shows us—by a bird no less—the magnificence of his promise?" (1 Clem. 26.1). The reception of Pauline theology is also only rudimentary;[5] indeed, clear echoes of the doctrine of justification are present in 1 Clem. 31.1–32.4, which are then immediately superseded by a general morality, an ethic of good deeds: "Shall we idly abstain from doing good, and forsake love? Rather, let us hasten with earnestness and zeal to do every good deed" (33.1–2). Paul, like Peter, is the great witness of the beginning (cf. 1 Clem. 5). Both apostles justify the claim of the Roman church under the leadership of Clement[6] to establish the order of the church that will be pleasing to God. (cf. 1 Clem. 40.1–45.8). With 1 Clement, the Roman church appears before the public for the first time and claims to point the way for other churches. "We have written enough to you, brothers, about the things that pertain to our religion and are particularly helpful for a virtuous life, at least for those who wish to guide their steps in holiness and righteousness" (1 Clem. 62.1). Here and in 1 Clem. 45.7, the new movement of Christians is called a "religion" (θρησκεία); the Roman church undoubtedly played a leading role.

Ignatius of Antioch

Before 117 CE,[7] Ignatius wrote seven letters to the churches of Asia Minor on his journey to martyrdom in Rome, providing an insight into theological

---

3. Cf. Lindemann, *Die Clemensbriefe*, 112–13.

4. According to the core of the Phoenix saga, there is a holy bird Phoenix, which comes every five hundred years to Heliopolis in Egypt in order to die and to be reborn from its own decaying body; all relevant Phoenix traditions appear in Lindemann, *Die Clemensbriefe*, 263–77.

5. On the image and reception of Paul, cf. Dassmann, *Der Stachel im Fleisch*, 77–98.

6. In the list of bishops, Clement appears normally after Peter or Linus (and Anacletus) in the third place; cf. Irenaeus, *Haer.* 2.3.3 (the apostles build the church; the first bishop is Linus, followed by Anacletus and Clement); Eusebius, *Hist. eccl.* 3.4.8–9 (Peter-Linus-Clement); Eusebius, *Hist. eccl.* 21 (apostles: Linus, Anacletus, Clement).

7. On the argument for a date at the end of the period of Trajan's rule (98–117 CE), cf. most recently H. Löhr, *Die Briefe des Ignatius*, 108–9 (there also the treatment of other relevant introductory questions). The two main arguments: (1) Polycarp, in *Phil.* 13.2, presupposes a

argumentation and the political-ecclesiastical situation at the beginning of the second century. As bishop of Antioch, Ignatius was apparently taken prisoner in a local persecution of Christians, condemned to death, and transferred to Rome, where he was to be thrown to the wild animals (cf. Ign. *Eph.* 1.2; 11.2; Ign. *Magn.* 1.2; 12 and passim). Ignatius does not stand theologically within the tradition of the OT (cited only incidentally: Ign. *Magn.* 12; *Trall.* 8.2), but he considers himself to be a successor to Paul and John. He places his martyrdom consciously in the tradition of Paul (Ign. *Eph.* 12.2); and his demand to participate in the suffering and glory of Christ through martyrdom (cf. Ign. *Rom.* 2.1f.; 4.1; 5.3; 7.1–3; *Magn.* 1.2; 14.1; *Eph.* 1.2; 10.1; 12.2; *Trall.* 12.2f.; 13.1–3; *Phil.* 5.1; *Smyrn.* 9.2; 11.1) likewise points to a Pauline background (cf. Rom. 6:3–5; Phil. 3:10–11, 12–21). The contrast between "flesh and Spirit" (Ign. *Eph.* 8.2) has Pauline roots (Rom. 8:1–11). The Pauline tradition of the Pastoral Epistles continues to have an effect, especially in the issue of church office (cf. 1 Tim. 3:1–13; Titus 1:5–9). The vehement incarnation and redemption Christology (Ign. *Eph.* 7.2; 19 and passim; cf. John 1:14), the central motif of the unity of Christ and God (Ign. *Magn.* 7.1; cf. John 10:30), the sending of the Son by the Father (Ign. *Magn.* 7.2; 8.2; cf. John 3:16), the deity of Jesus Christ (Ign. *Eph.* 7.2; 15.3; cf. 1 John 5:20; John 20:28), and the unity of the church (John 10) are also based on John,

---

collection of the letters of Ignatius; (2) Eusebius, *Hist. eccl.* 3.36, locates the appearance of Ignatius and Polycarp in the late period of Trajan. A late dating of around 170 CE is represented by R. Hübner, "Thesen zur Echtheit und Datierung"; the counterargument is provided by Lindemann, "Antwort auf die 'Thesen zur Echtheit.'" Against a pseudepigraphic late dating are the following arguments: (1) Around 170 CE it makes no sense to appeal to Ignatius to battle against the Gnostics! Ignatius battled—around 170/180 in a diversity of forms—not against developed Gnostic systems but against a docetic Christology, which was partially taken over in later systems but was not identical with them (see below, 14.2). In addition, no protological dualism can be recognized for the opponents in Ignatius (as in the Johannine Letters), and there is no cosmogony evident, which must be considered a characteristic of Gnostic systems. The central polemic against opponents in Ignatius (exception: Ignatius, *To the Romans*) would miss the mark at a later date! (2) The attempt to introduce the monepiscopacy is not a late phenomenon of the second century, for the Pastoral Epistles already favor this model (see above, 11.4). (3) The transfer of Ignatius to Rome by ten soldiers is frequently regarded as unhistorical. However, the near contemporary, Pliny the Younger, *Ep.* 10.96.4, speaks explicitly of the transfer of Christians to Rome. As in the case of Ignatius, the fact that a group of Christians is mentioned explains the number of soldiers. Ignatius does not mention the fellow prisoners explicitly, but this fact corresponds to his self-description (again, oriented to Paul). According to Ign. *Phil.* 11.1, Rheus [Rhaius] Agathopus followed him from Syria, and Philo followed from Cilicia (in addition, delegates from the churches; cf. Ign. *Eph.* 2.1). The transfer of a prisoner to Rome is attested in numerous sources (e.g., Livy 39.41.6, where suspects within the context of a bacchanalian conflict were transferred to Rome). On all of this, cf. Krause, *Gefängnisse im Römischen Reich*, 4. The thought of the Ignatian letters reflects no particular ideas of the late second century but is rooted in an independent development of Pauline/deutero-Pauline and/or Johannine theology.

as is the claim of the Father's speaking through the Son (Ign. *Magn.* 7.2; 8.2; *Rom.* 8.2; cf. John 1:18).

The theology of Ignatius is defined by the idea of the unity of the church,[8] which should correspond to the unity of the Father and Son (cf. Ign. *Eph.* 5.1); that is, the Ephesian church is one with its bishop. "As the church is united with Jesus Christ and as Jesus Christ is united with the Father, so that all things may be harmonious in unity" (cf. also Ign. *Eph.* 4.1–2; Ign. *Magn.* 6.1–2; Ign. *Phil.* 2.1–2). The bishop is the guarantor of the unity, and Ignatius grants him a special place. Almost every letter begins (exception: Ignatius, *To the Romans*) with a detailed description of the nature of the office of bishop and the resulting consequences: because it is obvious that the church "must regard the bishop as the Lord himself" (Ign. *Eph.* 6.1), it should be subordinated not only to Jesus Christ, but also to the bishop and the presbyters, so "that they may be as attuned to the bishop as strings to a lyre" (Ign. *Eph.* 4.1; cf. Ign. *Magn.* 2; *Trall.* 2.1). The church is an image of the heavenly hierarchy: "Be eager to do everything with godly harmony, the bishop presiding in the place of God and the presbyters in the place of the apostles, and the deacons who are especially dear to me are entrusted with the service of Jesus Christ" (Ign. *Magn.* 6.1). The church in Magnesia is specifically to live in unity with the bishop, imitating heavenly incorruptibility (Ign. *Magn.* 6.2). The consequence is that the church can and should do nothing without the bishop (and the presbyters; Ign. *Phil.* 7.2, "Do nothing without the bishop"). Neither private assemblies nor special worship services are desired, but let all run to the one temple of God, to the one sacrificial altar (cf. Ign. *Magn.* 7.1–2; *Trall.* 7.2). Here the pragmatic dimension of the strengthening of the office of bishop by Ignatius is clear: it serves, in the first place, as a defense in the churches against widespread false teaching. These false teachings particularly involved Christology, but the opponents of Ignatius probably also represented a deviant ecclesiology (their own Lord's Supper/worship services),[9] which rejected the office of bishop or at least did not concede his primary role. Ignatius in turn declared emphatically that the office of bishop had a central place.[10] The numerous admonitions in this context indicate, however, that the monepiscopacy had by no means prevailed, for Ignatius battled for its introduction.

The false teachers are the traveling missionaries against whom Ignatius fought (cf. Ign. *Eph.* 7.1; 9.1; Ign. *Smyrn.* 4.1; 6.2), who operated successfully

---

8. Ἕνωσις in Ign. *Magn.* 1.2; 13.2; *Trall.* 11.2; *Phld.* 4.1; 7.2; 8.1; *Pol.* 1.2; 5.2; cf. H. Löhr, *Die Briefe des Ignatius*, 117–27.

9. In Ign. *Pol.* 3.1 the comment is explicit that the docetists represented a "deviant doctrine."

10. Contra R. Hübner, "Thesen," 65, who maintains that the form and function of the office of bishop in Ignatius is essentially an argument against the authenticity of the letters.

in house churches, so that Ignatius can describe them as "those who corrupted houses" (Ign. *Eph.* 16.1). They evidently represent a docetic Christology, whose view Ignatius vigorously disputes.[11] He accuses his opponents of denying the bodily nature of Jesus Christ. They do not confess "that the Lord had a body" (Ign. *Smyrn.* 5.2, μὴ ὁμολογῶν αὐτὸν σαρκοφόρον). Against this view, Ignatius emphasizes that Jesus Christ was really born to the virgin Mary, baptized by John, and "really" nailed in the flesh for us under Pontius Pilate (Ign. *Smyrn.* 1.1; cf. Ign. *Trall.* 9.1–2: Jesus Christ "who was really [ἀληθῶς] born, ate and drank, really [ἀληθῶς]] persecuted under Pontius Pilate, really [ἀληθῶς] crucified and died, . . . who was really [ἀληθῶς] raised from the dead"). Jesus Christ is at the same time flesh and spirit, born and unborn, "God appearing in the flesh" (ἐν σαρκὶ γενόμενος θεός), from Mary and from God, subject to suffering and beyond it (Ign. *Eph.* 7.2). Finally, Ignatius even maintains that Jesus Christ was in the flesh also after the resurrection (Ign. *Smyrn.* 3.1). Ignatius argued vehemently for the reality of the incarnation, suffering, and resurrection of Jesus Christ.

According to the opponents, Jesus only appeared to suffer. Ignatius says about them λέγουσιν, τὸ δοκεῖν πεπονθέναι αὐτόν (they say that he only appeared to suffer; Ign. *Trall.* 10; cf. *Smyrn.* 2; 4.2). Against them, he emphatically argued for the suffering and death of Christ (cf. Ign. *Eph.* 7.2; 20.1; *Trall.* 9.1; 11.2; *Rom.* 6.1; *Smyrn.* 1.1, 2; 6.2). If Jesus on earth is only τὸ δοκεῖν, an appearance, the opponents must also deny his resurrection. Only in this way is the vehemence with which Ignatius emphasizes the resurrection of Jesus Christ in response to the opponents (cf. Ign. *Smyrn.* 1.2; 3.1; 7.1; *Trall.* 9.2; *Eph.* 20.1; *Magn.* 11) to be explained. If the opponents deny the resurrection, then the Eucharist is deprived of its meaning, and the grace of Christ is diminished (Ign. *Smyrn.* 6.2). Then it is consistent with this view when the opponents are not present at the Eucharist (led by the bishop) and have their own worship service, including the Eucharist (cf. Ign. *Smyrn.* 6.2: "They abstain from Eucharist and prayer because they refuse to acknowledge that the Eucharist is the flesh of our savior Jesus Christ"; cf. also Ign. *Smyrn.* 8.1; *Eph.* 5.2–3; *Trall.* 6.1–2; *Phld.* 4).[12] The opponents possibly had another ecclesiological concept that was not concentrated in the bishop, as it was with Ignatius. As the opponents disputed the fleshly existence of Jesus Christ, his suffering, and the resurrection of the Crucified One, they drew the consequences for the Eucharist. Since they employed the keyword τὸ δοκεῖν,

---

11. Besides the analyses of the commentaries, a comprehensive study of the text is given by Uebele, *"Viele Verführer,"* 38–92.

12. They probably also held baptismal services; cf. Ign. *Smyrn.* 8.2.

this teaching can be called docetism.[13] Evidently, the entire earthly existence of Jesus can be summarized as δόκησις.[14] Jesus Christ was unborn, coming only in appearance. For Ignatius, the appropriate confession and the concrete acts of love belong together. With the false teachers, however, the two come apart; thus Ignatius accuses them of lacking brotherly love: "Note well those who hold heretical opinions about the grace of Jesus Christ that came to us; note how contrary they are to the mind of God. They have no concern for love, none for the widow, none for the orphan, none for the oppressed, none for the prisoner or the one released, none for the hungry or thirsty" (Ign. *Smyrn.* 6.2). Apparently the docetists believed that they were not responsible for concrete obligations of love because they involved only the body, which they disdained.

Ignatius argues against a strong false teaching that was influenced by Judaism (Ign. *Magn.* 8–11; *Phld.* 5–9). He criticizes "deviant doctrines and old fables" (Ign. *Magn.* 8.1) and affirms a clear principle: "If we until now live according to Judaism, we confess that we have not received grace." The old customs and the new hope do not get along with each other, and "it is out of place to say Jesus Christ and to live in a Jewish way" (Ign. *Magn.* 10:3). The false teachers make the case for the Sabbath (*Magn.* 9.1) and place their interpretation of the OT Scriptures even above the gospel (*Phil.* 8.2). Ignatius (*Phld.* 6.1) indicates that this teaching was successful not only among those who were Jews by birth but also among non-Jews within the church: "But if anyone espouses Judaism, do not listen to him! For it is better to hear Christianity from a circumcised man than Judaism from an uncircumcised person." It is often assumed that two heresies were present.[15] Although it is possible to regard docetism and Judaism as "two sides of the same heretical phenomenon,"[16] a differentiation is necessary: In the *Letter to the Magnesians*, the battle is against a radical Jewish Christian false teaching (cf. 8.1, 2; 9.1; 10.3), while in 9.1 and in 11 docetic motifs are also in view. In the *Letter to the Philadelphians* the polemic is predominantly against a Judaizing position (cf. 6.1; 8.2; 9.1). However, in *Phld.* 4 the allusion is to docetic positions. Therefore, one cannot speak of two fully different false teachings[17] but of particular developments in specific

13. On docetism, cf. above, 10.4.2; on the Ignatian churches, cf. W. Bauer and Paulsen, *Die Briefe des Ignatius*, 65; Schoedel, *Ignatius of Antioch*, 10–14; Uebele, *"Viele Verführer,"* 51, 57, and passim.
14. Cf. W. Bauer and Paulsen, *Die Briefe des Ignatius*, 239.
15. On the older history of research, cf. Rohde, "Häresie und Schisma," 229–30.
16. W. Bauer and Paulsen, *Die Briefe des Ignatius*, 240.
17. Thus W. Bauer and Paulsen, *Die Briefe des Ignatius*, 65; Schoedel, *Ignatius of Antioch*, 198–99.

churches. A docetic false teaching was dominant, which in Magnesia and Philadelphia had Judaizing motifs.[18]

Along with the central theme of unity, a clear hierarchical conception was dominant in the ecclesiology. At the pinnacle of the church stands the bishop, then the council of presbyters and the diaconate (cf. Ign. *Trall.* 7.2: "Anyone who does anything without the bishop, council of presbyters, and diaconate, does not have a clean conscience"; also *Trall.* 2.2; 3.1). "Without these one cannot speak of the church" (Ign. *Trall.* 3.1). The bishop is the likeness of God, the council of presbyters arranges the work of the church like the apostles, and the deacons are not only responsible for food and drink (cf. Ign. *Trall.* 2.3; 3.1). The submission to the bishop is absolutely necessary (cf. Ign. *Eph.* 20.2; *Trall.* 2.1; 13.2), for he is a mediator between God/Jesus Christ and the church. The sacraments given by the bishop "within the sanctuary" (Ign. *Trall.* 7.2) grant the φάρμακον ἀθανασίας (medicine of immortality, Ign. *Eph.* 20.2), eternal life, while the eucharistic celebration of the false teachers "outside the sanctuary" (Ign. *Trall.* 7.2) leads to death (Ign. *Trall.* 11.1).

Ignatius represents the first instance of a form of the church that later became the norm for the Catholic Church as it was being formed: suffering, but equipped with a great self-confidence and self-expectation (Ign. *Smyrn.* 8.2: "Where the bishop appears, there let the congregation be, just as wherever Christ Jesus is, there is the Catholic Church [ἡ καθολικὴ ἐκκλησία]"). The concentration in the office of bishop originated out of the necessity created by the disputes with the false teachers over Christology and ecclesiology. In addition, it sprang from the theology of Ignatius, who transferred heavenly realities ("one God," "one Lord") to the earth ("one bishop," "one church," "one Eucharist") and referred both to each other (cf. Ign. *Magn.* 6.1). Ignatius was shaped by a strong mysticism of suffering: "Let me be food for the wild beasts, through whom I can reach God" (Ign. *Rom.* 4.2). This mysticism of suffering defines his inner being and allows doubt to come into view (Ign. *Trall.* 4.2: "For while I earnestly desire to suffer, I do not know whether I am worthy"). He emphatically requests that his churches not stand in his way since he understands martyrdom as the test and demonstration of true discipleship (Ign. *Rom.* 6.1: "Permit me to be an imitator of the suffering of my God"). It is not coincidental that Ignatius develops in detail his theology of suffering and martyrdom in his letter to the Roman church, since Rome was not only the location of his anticipated martyrdom but was also especially distinguished by the martyrdoms of Peter and Paul (cf. Ign. *Rom.* 4.3).

---

18. Cf. Uebele, *"Viele Verführer,"* 76, who repeatedly speaks of a "Judaizing-docetic false teaching."

14.2. The Emergence of Another Message: Early Gnosticism

Gnosis is a religious-intellectual stream in late antiquity that arose from the second century CE onward in various literary-theological forms and historical movements.[19] The word γνῶσις means "knowledge," and for the Gnostic it means primarily self-knowledge of one's place in the world and in relation to God. This self-knowledge reveals the true (lost) situation of humankind, and its task was to answer fundamental questions. "It is not alone the bath that makes us free, but also knowledge: Who were we? What have we become? Where were we? Into what have we been thrown? Where are we going? From what have we been freed? What is birth? What is rebirth?"[20] For most Gnostics, faith in the redeemer Jesus Christ was the answer to these questions.

Sources and Definition

Recent Gnostic scholarship[21] has concentrated on two problem areas: the sources and the definition. The question of sources is thus particularly complicated because the tendencies and the age of the sources are determined in different ways. A writing of the NT (especially the Gospel of John)[22] is not to be considered, and there is no evidence of pre-Christian Gnosticism.[23] It is no longer possible to jump over the centuries (mentally) and postulate presuppositions about the NT on the basis of texts that are primarily from the third and fourth centuries CE—presuppositions for which evidence cannot be found in the NT![24] The only—variously detailed—reports about the earliest Gnosticism/Gnostics appear in Justin (died around 145 CE in

---

19. I am treating not the entire phenomenon of "gnosis" but only what is relevant with respect to the NT in the period up until 130 CE.

20. Clement of Alexandria, *Excerpts of Theodotus* 78.2.

21. A current survey is given by Brankaer, *Die Gnosis*, 11–21; B. Aland, *Die Gnosis*, 37–56.

22. In earlier scholarship, the Gospel of John (cf. Schottroff, *Der Glaube und die feindliche Welt*, 295: "With the Gospel of John the Gnostic teaching on salvation has entered the canon") and, in part, the Letters of Paul (cf. Schmithals, *Gnosticism in Corinth*) were thought to be influenced by Gnosticism. On John, cf. Tröger, "Ja oder Nein zur Welt"; on Paul, cf. M. Hengel, *Paulus und die Frage*, 487ff.; H.-F. Weiss, *Frühes Christentum und Gnosis*, 61–206, attempts, with reference to the Nag Hammadi texts not under Christian influence to keep the question open but never moves beyond mere speculation. He must also finally admit that "in fact there is not a single Gnostic source that one could call pre-Christian (in the sense mentioned)." H.-F. Weiss, *Frühes Christentum und Gnosis*, 185.

23. Cf. Markschies, "Gnosis/Gnostizismus," 869: "It is improbable that a pre-Christian Gnosticism ever existed; no sources for it have been preserved"; also Brankaer, *Die Gnosis*, 99: "In reference to the present existing information, the existence of a non-Christian Gnosticism has not been attested."

24. Thus in accordance with the history of religions school, Bultmann, "Johannesevangelium," 847, interprets the Fourth Gospel against the background of a fully developed Gnostic

Rome),[25] who mentions an antiheretical writing (*Syntagma*) that he had written,[26] but it is not extant. Information is found particularly in Irenaeus of Lyon (ca. 135–200 CE), who around 180 CE wrote a five-volume work, *Adversus Haereses* (*Against Heresies*). Additional sources are Tertullian (160–212 CE), Clement of Alexandria (died before 215 CE), Origen (ca. 185–254 CE), Hippolytus of Rome (died 235 CE), and Epiphanius of Salamis (315–402 CE). The church fathers were engaged in a massive conflict with Gnosticism, which had grown rapidly at the latest from the middle of the second century CE. Consequently, their reports are not only polemical, but generally speaking, they can also tend to be simplistic and distorted in their description. For the most part, it remains unknown where the early church fathers received their information; they are partially dependent on each other and sometimes transmit entirely different or contradictory traditions about the same person/school. Nevertheless, Irenaeus is especially significant as the one who passes on information about the earliest Gnosticism inasmuch as he offers the first comprehensive report about Gnostic systems, stands close in time to the beginnings of Gnosticism, and intentionally gathers traditions. In addition, through the polemic and the general description, the teachers of the first Gnostics become known. Gnostic original sources from the post-NT period that have been found since the nineteenth century include Corpus Hermeticum, Pistis Sophia, Odes of Solomon, and the Mandaean literature. The Nag Hammadi discoveries greatly expanded the information about Gnosticism.[27] Around 1945, thirteen codices with a total of fifty-one predominantly Gnostic writings, were found in upper Egypt at nome/district 13. Other discoveries included a receipt dated at 339/342

---

redeemer myth and points to the Mandaean writings as evidence, "whose final redaction comes from the seventh century, but contains older material."

25. On the chronology: The reference to the Alexandrian prefect Felix (Justin, *1 Apol.* 29), who was in office from 148 to 154, suggests a publication of *1 Apology* at the beginning of the 150s (second century). Justin's antiheretical work (*Syntagma*) was probably written a few years previously, thus around 145 CE.

26. Cf. Justin, *1 Apol.* 26.8: "I have a treatise against all heresies, which have arisen all composed, which I will give to you if you want to read it." In my estimation the arguments of Thornton, *Der Zeuge des Zeugen*, 38–40—that Justin's *Syntagma* is a source for Irenaeus, *Haer.* 1.23–27—have not been invalidated. On Justin's antiheretical polemic, cf. also Justin, *Dial.* 35.4–6: "There are therefore, and have been, dear friends, many who have taught others to say and to do things godless and blasphemous, coming to us in the name of Jesus, and are called by the surname of the man from whom each doctrine and opinion started. For some in some way and some in another teach men to blaspheme the maker of the universe and the Christ that was prophesied by Him as about to come, and the God of Abraham and Isaac and Jacob; . . . of these some are called Marcionites, others Valentinians, others Basilidians, others Saturnilians; . . . each has its name from the founder of its system. They conduct themselves like those who believe that they are philosophers."

27. All texts are accessible in Robinson, *Nag Hammadi Library*.

CE. The Nag Hammadi texts can be dated paleographically to the middle of the fourth century, although numerous of these writings contain older traditions, and editorial work makes it historically probable that some texts can be traced back to the second century CE.[28] A key text is the Gospel of Thomas, which is attested by Hippolytus at the beginning of the third century (*Ref.* 5.7.20); it is now dated to the middle of the second century.[29] It contains a collection of 114 Jesus logia that were originally written in Greek, connected with each other by catchwords, have no narrative framework, and end in an odd way.[30] In terms of the history of traditions, the Gospel of Thomas brings together various materials, including traditions that are possibly old[31] and sayings that have a Gnostic tinge.[32] The Gospel of Thomas probably originated gradually and took up logia from various sources and groups. The Gospel of Thomas, however, nowhere employs cosmological speculation and a separation between the highest god and the creator god ("demiurge" or "Jewish God").[33] Thus this gospel may not be considered as a witness to the earliest Gnosticism, although it includes a Gnostic element.

Manicheanism (Mani, 216–277 CE) and the Mandaean literature provide no information for the early history of Gnosticism.[34] The judgment of A. Böhlig may be considered as representative: "The New Testament is not to be interpreted with reference to Mani, but Mani depends on the New Testament."[35] The Mandaean literature was compiled in the seventh and eighth centuries in Babylon. Essential elements were present already in the third to fourth century CE, and the oldest parts of the Mandaean literature (hymnic literature) could extend into the second century.[36] The tracing of

28. Cf. Robinson, introduction in *Nag Hammadi Library*, 1–25.

29. On the Gospel of Thomas, see above, 6.9 under "Excursus."

30. Cf. logion 114: "Simon Peter said to them, 'Mary should leave us, for women are not worthy of life.' Jesus said, 'Behold, I myself will lead her in order to make her male, so that she too may become a living spirit resembling you males. For every woman who will make herself male will enter the kingdom of heaven.'"

31. Cf. logia 34, 54, 55, 73.

32. Cf. logion 27: "If you do not fast as regards the world, you will not find the kingdom"; logion 42: "Jesus says, 'Become passersby'"; logion 49: "Blessed are the solitary and the elect, for you will enter the kingdom. For you are from it, and to it you will return"; in logion 50, Jesus says: "If they say to you, 'Where do you come from?' then say to them, 'We have come from the light, the place where the light came into being of its own accord and established itself and became manifest through their image'"; in logion 87, Jesus says, "Wretched is the body that depends on a body. And wretched is the soul that depends on these two."

33. Cf. Plisch, *Das Thomas-Evangelium*, 35.

34. All important texts in A. Böhlig, *Der Manichäismus*.

35. A. Böhlig, "Neue Initiativen zur Erschließung," 255.

36. On the chronology of Mandaean texts, cf. Rudolph, *Die Mandäer*, 1:53–58.

traditions over several centuries is naturally burdened with uncertainty. All of the analyses of the tradition history depend on the Mandaean literature; these analyses begin with motifs in the middle of the second century CE and must be regarded as completely hypothetical.

An understanding of Gnosticism, its nature, and its proximity to the NT (particularly the Gospel of John) depends to a considerable extent on the definition of what Gnosticism is. The definition of Gnosticism as a specific ancient understanding of existence, which is based on the definition by Hans Jonas, has had great influence.[37] This broad definition of the term Gnosticism then leads to the subsuming of various movements of late antiquity under this term, making concrete religious historical scholarship more difficult. At the Messina Congress in 1966, the proposal was made of distinguishing between "Gnosticism" and "gnosis." "Gnosticism" is used for the one "group of systems in the second century CE." In contrast with this definition, "gnosis" is used for a "knowledge of divine mysteries, that is reserved for the elite."[38] This interpretation also cannot be maintained because, in fact, only terms were exchanged: what was earlier called "gnosis" should be called "Gnosticism." Only definitions that identify precisely what basic conception must be present in order to speak of gnosis are innovative.[39]

Similarly problematic in current scholarship is the observable tendency to construct the phenomenon "gnosis" with little use of the term[40] but instead to analyze specific streams of the late second century and the third century (Valentinian and Sethian Gnosticism),[41] which are dominant particularly in the Nag Hammadi texts.[42] With this limitation to church history (and the

37. Cf. Jonas, *Gnosis und spätantiker Geist*, 1:12ff.

38. Cf. Colpe, "Vorschläge des Messina-Kongresses von 1966."

39. On the discussion of the terms "gnosis/Gnosticism/Gnostic," cf. also H.-F. Weiss, *Frühes Christentum und Gnosis*, 34–59.

40. Michael Williams, *Rethinking "Gnosticism,"* 265, prefers to avoid this terminology and instead speaks of "biblical demiurgical": "It would include all sources that made a distinction between the creator(s) and controllers of the material world and the most transcendent divine being, and that in so doing made use of Jewish or Christian scriptural traditions." King, *What Is Gnosticsm?*, 218: "What will happen now to the category of Gnosticism? In the end, I think the term 'Gnosticism' will most likely be abandoned, at least in its present usage." I see no reason for this terminological restraint, for the English term "Gnosticism" is in fact unsuitable as a modern construct; but 1 Tim. 6:20 indicates that the Greek term γνῶσις is in no way a foreign designation, but was a given designation, and thus the German word "gnosis" is appropriate.

41. A description of Valentinian and Sethian Gnosticism is provided by Brankaer, *Die Gnosis*, 62–74, 75–84.

42. Cf. esp. Colpe, *Einleitung in die Schriften*. However, the phenomenon of "Gnosticism" cannot be reduced to the Nag Hammadi texts (so, e.g., the tendentious study by King, *What Is Gnosticism?*, 149–217); cf. B. Aland, *Die Gnosis*, 82: "As to what is the central concern of

exclusion of the NT), a historical explanation of the phenomenon is avoided,[43] and the church fathers (particularly Irenaeus) fall under the suspicion of applying an ideological perspective. Their distinction between orthodoxy and heresy[44] is considered unhistorical and provides the foundation for a mistrust of their portrayals.[45] Undoubtedly, Irenaeus engaged in oversimplification and inscribed his own standpoint in the texts, but the comprehensive, sharp polemic against Gnostic teachers had already begun with Justin. His lost work against the heresies was probably no less polemical than that of Irenaeus. Polemics belonged to the agonistic society as part of the common repertoire. Therefore, Irenaeus is definitely not obsolete as the central source of our knowledge of early Gnosticism. One must ask precisely where his portrayal is historically probable and where it is not; that is, one must distinguish strictly between plausible traditions and evaluations.[46]

Based on the preceding considerations, the following methodological consequences must be considered: (1) In the question of the origins of Gnosticism, one must proceed strictly chronologically; that is, the earliest references/sources/witnesses/representatives are to be consulted.[47] (2) The basic principles of early Gnostic thought must be determined from the common areas of thought among these texts. Thus sayings that are dualistic or critical of the world or the body are not sufficient, for dualism and a certain distance from the world belong to almost every religion and philosophy. (3) Furthermore, the potential "gnosticizing" of isolated terms and concepts (especially from the Gospel of John) in later Gnostic writings is not identical with "Gnosticism" in the NT or other early Christian writings! (4) On the other hand, it does not promote the knowledge of the phenomenon "Gnosticism" if one avoids the term, fully leaves out the NT, and leaves the early history of Gnosticism in the dark.

Gnosticism, I do not see a basic difference between Nag Hammadi and the writings of the church fathers."

43. See also D.-A. Koch, *Geschichte des Urchristentum*, 155, who makes Gnosticism and the apologists contemporaneous (around 130 CE) but at the same time assumes that the development did not begin until 150 CE and thus does not treat the phenomenon of "Gnosticism."

44. See above, 11.3 under "Orthodoxy and Heresy," where it is indicated that the distinction is in no way an invention of the church fathers but is already found in Paul.

45. Cf. King, *What Is Gnosticism?*, 218. According to her, it is important "to recognize and correct the ways in which reinscribing the discourses of orthodoxy and heresy distort our reading and reconstructing of ancient religion." The critical reading of the church fathers is undoubtedly appropriate, but this does not mean that they may not be used as sources and that the constructions of the exegetes of the twenty-first century are more reliable historically than the portrayals of the church fathers.

46. Cf. the prudent considerations in B. Aland, *Die Gnosis*, 57–65, according to whom the church fathers would not have reached their goal if pure polemic defined their portrayals.

47. That principle is emphatically maintained by Hengel, *Son of God*, 33–42.

The Beginnings of Gnosticism

The oldest literary reference appears in 1 Tim. 6:20: "O Timothy, guard the tradition and turn away from all ungodly chatter and contradictions of falsely called gnosis/knowledge [τῆς ψευδωνύμου γνώσεως], which many have professed and turned away from the faith." Around 100 CE, there was in the churches of the Pastoral Epistles apparently a movement that not only (1) claimed the catchword "gnosis" as a self-designation and a battle slogan (cf. also 1 Tim. 4:2; 2 Tim. 3:7; Titus 1:6; 1 Clem. 36.2), yet also (2) represented Gnostic teachings that, in the first place, used the catchword ἀντιθέσεις (antitheses).[48] This involves not only disputed points but also (3) a doctrinal system. That this includes their own designation and did not come from others is especially indicated in the fact that the author of the Pastoral Epistles speaks of a "falsely called gnosis" and thus attempts to claim this term for himself. The tenets of the opponents stand (4) in clear contrast to the tradition of the church of God; they lead (5) to separations and constitute a false path (ἀστοχέω, stray), about which (6) 1 Timothy gives a clear message that this is false teaching.[49] The seriousness with which the author of the Pastoral Epistles considered the danger to his churches[50] is indicated finally by (7) the rhetorically prominent place of this warning at the end of the letter.

These intrachurch false teachings were combined into several elements.[51] In addition to the catchword "gnosis," the ascetic demands of abstinence from marriage and certain foods (1 Tim. 4:3; cf. also Irenaeus, *Haer.* 1.24.2; 1.28.1) indicate an early form of Christian Gnosticism. Later Gnostic parallels are found in the claim of the opponents that the resurrection has already come (2 Tim. 2:18; cf. NHC I/4.49:15–16).[52] The false teaching also includes

48. In 1 Tim. 6:20, however, there is no allusion to the "antitheses" of Marcion; cf. Schlarb, "Miszelle zu 1 Tim 6,20."

49. Cf. also the warning in Titus 3:10: "After a first and a repeated warning, have nothing to do with a heretical person [αἱρετικὸν ἄνθρωπον]."

50. In recent scholarship on Gnosticism, 1 Tim. 6:20f. is greatly underestimated; in the work of Michael A. Williams, Karen L. King, and David Brakke, this text plays no role at all. Markschies, "Gnosis/Gnostizismus," esp. 1048, mentions 1 Tim. 6:20 briefly, in order to argue for those who advocated this "gnosis": "But it is improbable that they represented a developed system in the manner of the large schools." Here the later schools (e.g., Valentinus) of advanced Gnosticism become the criterion for describing the beginning, leaving the beginnings naturally to remain obscure.

51. A listing of all agreements between the sayings about the opponents that can be reconstructed in 1 Timothy and Gnostic texts appear in Herzer, "Was ist falsch?," esp. 84–90, who, however, dates 1 Timothy around 140 CE.

52. Cf. also Gospel of Thomas, logion 51: "The disciples said to him, 'When will the repose of the dead come about, and when will the new world come?' He said to them, 'What you look forward to has already come, and you did not recognize it.'"

myths and endless genealogies, according to 1 Tim. 1:4; 4:7; 2 Tim. 4:4; Titus 1:14; 3:9, both of which point to cosmological speculation. In later Gnostic texts, numerous mythological speculations are present. Jewish elements also shaped the false teaching. Thus the opponents make the claim to be teachers of the law and to be especially knowledgeable on Scripture (1 Tim. 1:7; cf. Titus 1:9–10). In terms of the history of religions, the opponents' teaching is to be classified as an early form of Christian Gnosticism.[53] The opponents, with their claim of a resurrection that has already happened, evidently represented an extensive understanding of salvation as already present,[54] a view that probably is derived from their interpretation of baptism and the related possession of the Spirit. The ascetic tendencies of the opponents' teaching indicate that the present world is understood as a place of imprisonment, from which the Gnostic attempted to be free through the knowledge of the redeeming God. Creation and the Creator God are judged negatively, for the overcoming of the hostile material world was the goal of the opponents' teaching. Against their view, 1 Tim. 4:4–5 emphasizes the good creative work of God, in which nothing is reprehensible. The mission of the false teachers took place predominantly in small house churches (2 Tim. 3:6–9), a practice that fit the esoteric character of Gnostic teaching.

Inasmuch as the development of Gnostic doctrine/doctrines in the Pastoral Epistles required a certain amount of time to develop, one may assume that early Gnostic teaching emerged slowly within the context of emerging Christianity around the end of the first century and then had an explosive growth in the second century CE.

The sharp polemic of Justin (*Syntagma* around 145 CE; *1 Apology* and *Dialogue with Trypho* between 150 and 160 CE) and especially of Irenaeus of Lyon, who in *Adversus Haereses* recorded the teachings/views of the earliest Gnostics in a polemical work, are evidence of the origin of early Gnosticism at the end of the first century CE[55] and its rapid expansion from the first half of the second century.[56]

---

53. On the history of research, cf. Schlarb, *Die gesunde Lehre*, 73–82; cf. also the cautious portrayal in Oberlinner, *Titusbrief*, 52–73.

54. Cf. Schlarb, *Die Gesunde Lehre*, 93; Oberlinner, *Titusbrief*, 54, who likewise regards 2 Tim. 2:18 as the center of the false teaching.

55. Cf. also Colpe, "Gnosis II," col. 560, who comments on the chronological demarcation: "For the time being, one can conclude that Gnosticism began in the first century, rather than later, but this does not mean that it began everywhere."

56. Irenaeus (*Haer.* 1.23.1–4), like Justin (*1 Apol.* 26.1–3), sees in Simon Magus the progenitor of all false teachers and Gnostics. The historical Simon Magus, however, was probably a magician (Acts 8:9–19), and the system reported by Irenaeus was probably transferred secondarily to Simon in the second century (the basic study is still that of Beyschlag, *Simon Magus*). In

Menander came from Samaria and taught at the turn of the first to the second century in Antioch.[57] According to Irenaeus,

> He affirms that the primary Power continues unknown to all, but that he himself is the person who has been sent forth from the presence of the invisible beings as a savior for the deliverance of humankind. The world was made by angels, who—like Simon, he maintains—have been produced by Ennoea. By means of that magic that he teaches, he confers the knowledge that one may have power over those very angels that made the world; for his disciples obtain the resurrection by being baptized into him, and can die no more, but remain in the possession of immortal youth. (*Haer.* 1.23.5, *ANF* 1:348)

Menander distinguished between the highest god and the lower angels as creator of the world,[58] connected to some extent with cosmological speculations. He maintained that he himself was the redeemer, who granted a "knowledge" through his magic powers that could even overcome angels. The third central element of his teaching was the resurrection of the one who has knowledge already (in baptism to him; cf. 1 Cor. 1:12–13; Justin, *1 Apol.* 26.4: "the followers of Menander believe that they will not die").

Satornilus (Saturninus) also came from Antioch and was active at the beginning of the second century:

> Saturninus, like Menander, set forth one father unknown to all, who made angels, archangels, powers, and potentates. The world, again, and all things therein, were made by a certain company of seven angels. Man, too, was the workmanship of angels. . . . He was accordingly formed, yet was unable to stand erect, through the inability of the angels to convey to him that power, but wriggled [on the ground] like a worm. Then the power above, taking pity upon him, since he was made after his likeness, sent forth a spark of life,

---

accordance with my basic approach, I limit myself to the early beginnings of Gnostic thought, i.e., the development until ca. 130 CE. This approach is justified, inasmuch as the first (according to later criteria) undisputed matured Gnostic system appears with Valentinus (in Rome from ca. 135). Marcion (in Rome from 140 CE) is likewise to be considered a representative of Gnosticism in a limited sense. Indeed, while he argued for two gods (the Creator God of the OT and the "alien" God who was the father of Jesus Christ), he does not have cosmological speculations, and Christ in no way becomes diminished. The letters of Paul (with Galatians at the top) and a "purified" Gospel of Luke formed the basis of his theological thought; cf. B. Aland, *Die Gnosis*, 199–201.

57. Justin, *1 Apol.* 26.4, makes Menander (probably incorrectly) a pupil of Simon Magus, in order to establish a family tree of heretics.

58. Cf. Colpe, "Gnosis II," col. 629: "A beginning of Gnostic fragmentation, if not between self and self, is present in the teaching of the Samaritan Menander." B. Aland, *Die Gnosis*, 162–64, classifies Menander (like Satornilus and Cerinthus) as a "pre-Gnostic" teacher because, in contrast to advanced Gnosticism, he offers no foundation for his system.

which gave man an erect posture, compacted his joints, and made him live. He declares, therefore, that this spark of life, after the death of a man, returns to those things which are of the same nature with itself, and the rest of the body is decomposed into its original elements. He has also laid it down as a truth, that the Saviour was without birth, without body, and without figure, but was, by supposition, a visible man; and he maintained that the God of the Jews was one of the angels; and, on this account, because all the powers wished to annihilate his father, Christ came to destroy the God of the Jews, but to save such as believe in him; that is, those who possess the spark of his life. This heretic was the first to affirm that two kinds of men were formed by the angels—the one wicked and the other good. And since the demons assist the most wicked, the Saviour came for the destruction of evil men and of the demons, but for the salvation of the good. They declare also, that marriage and generation are from Satan. Many of those, too, who belong to his school, abstain from animal food, and draw away multitudes by a feigned temperance of this kind. They hold, moreover, that some of the prophecies were uttered by those angels who made the world, and some by Satan; whom Saturninus represents as being himself an angel, the enemy of the creators of the world, but especially of the God of the Jews. (Irenaeus, *Haer.* 1.24.1–2, *ANF* 1:349; cf. Hippolytus, *Ref.* 7.28.1–5)

A defining element of this system is the separation between the highest god and the lower elements of the created order (here the angels, including the "Jewish God,"[59] combined with cosmological speculations and a strong anti-Jewish accent).[60] Satan also appears as a godless principle. There is, with the motif of the "life spark," the idea of an identity of substance between the highest nature and the "enlightened" person. In the Christology there is a combination of docetic elements (unborn, incorporeal, without form) with a double effect of salvation: against the "Jewish God" and the evil angels/people and redemption for the good people. Added to this are ascetic elements such as abstinence from procreation and marriage as well as abstinence from meat.

At the beginning of the second century, Cerinthus was active in Asia Minor and represented a Christology of separation:

Cerinthus, again, a man who was educated in the wisdom of the Egyptians, taught that the world was not made by the primary God, but by a certain Power far separated from him, and at a distance from that Principality who is supreme over the universe, and ignorant of him who is above all. He represented Jesus as

59. This is suggested by the citation of Gen. 1:26 in the report of Irenaeus (*Haer.* 24.1): "Thus the angels exhorted each other, saying, 'Let us make man after our image and likeness.'"
60. Cf. Colpe, "Gnosis II," col. 629: "Saturninus appears to have gone one step further, clearly describing the creation by angels as something against god and counting the Jewish god among the angels."

having not been born of a virgin, but as being the son of Joseph and Mary according to the ordinary course of human generation, while he nevertheless was more righteous, prudent, and wise than other men. Moreover, after his baptism, Christ descended upon him in the form of a dove from the Supreme Ruler, and that then he proclaimed the unknown Father, and performed miracles. But at last Christ departed from Jesus, and that then Jesus suffered and rose again, while Christ remained impassible, inasmuch as he was a spiritual being. (Irenaeus, *Haer.* 1.26.1, ANF 1:351–52)[61]

It remains disputed whether Cerinthus is to be classified as an early Gnostic or as a Jewish Christian with his own particular teaching.[62] Irenaeus and Hippolytus (*Ref.* 7.33; 10.21.2–3) attest for Cerinthus cosmological speculations and a protological dualism (separation of the first God—demiurge). In addition, a separation-Christology, which has a clear proximity to docetic conceptions, is also evident (cf. Epiphanius, *Pan.* 28.1.7, καὶ οὐ τὸν Ἰησοῦν εἶναι Χριστόν [and Jesus is not the Christ]). The connection of Cerinthus with the Johannine tradition is totally credible (cf. Irenaeus, *Haer.* 3.3.4; 11.1–2; Eusebius, *Hist. eccl.* 4.14.6; 3.28.6: the famous encounter of Cerinthus and John in the bath at Ephesus). Cerinthus could have interpreted the Gospel of John with Gnostic categories, and it is conceivable that John 1:32 might have been the point of departure. Jewish Christian motifs are already present in Irenaeus and Hippolytus (natural birth, righteousness, and wisdom); there may also have been chiliastic elements (Eusebius, *Hist. eccl.* 3.28.2, 4; 7.25.2–3). However, the portrayal of Cerinthus as a Judaizer and Ebionite (Epiphanius, *Anakephalaiosis* 2.28.30) is secondary,[63] probably triggered by the sequence "Cerinthus-Ebiones" in Irenaeus and Hippolytus. Cerinthus was a Gnostic-Jewish Christian teacher who primarily developed an independent separation Christology in a cosmological-speculative context.

Carpocrates appeared in the first decade of the second century in Asia Minor. The reports about his person, his teaching, and his followers are difficult to assess because the depictions of the system are strongly mixed with ethical value judgments.[64] According to Irenaeus,

61. All relevant texts on Cerinthus are discussed by Klijn and Reinink, *Patristic Evidence*, 3–19. The testimony of the Epistula Apostolorum 1.7ff. (middle of the second century) confirms an interpretation of Cerinthus within the context of early Gnosticism with the sequence: warning about Cerinthus; Jesus's true suffering under Pontius Pilate—true resurrection in the flesh.

62. With Hengel, *Johannine Question*, 59–62, I consider these elements original; for an alternative view, see Markschies, "Kerinth," 48–76, who does not classify Cerinthus as a Gnostic but emphatically as a Jewish Christian.

63. Texts in Klijn and Reinink, *Patristic Evidence*, 161.

64. All relevant texts are in Völker, *Quellen zur Geschichte*, 33–36 (Greek); Förster, *Die Gnosis*, 1:50–56 (German).

Carpocrates, again, and his followers maintain that the world and the things which are therein were created by angels greatly inferior to the unbegotten Father. They also hold that Jesus was the son of Joseph, and was just like other men, with the exception that he differed from them in this respect, that inasmuch as his soul was steadfast and pure, he perfectly remembered those things which he had witnessed within the sphere of the unbegotten God. On this account, a power descended upon him from the Father, that by means of it he might escape from the creators of the world. . . . They further declare, that the soul of Jesus, although educated in the practices of the Jews, regarded these with contempt. (*Haer.* 25.1, *ANF* 1:350).

Jesus becomes an example for purified souls, who at the end of the recurring wandering of the soul, escape and return to the highest God. Furthermore, the followers of Carpocrates are reported to have engaged in magical practices and represented an antinomian or libertine ethic.

Around 130 CE Basilides appeared in Alexandria. Perhaps he marks the transition to a developed Gnostic myth. However, the traditions about his teachings vary and can scarcely be reduced to a common denominator.[65] According to Irenaeus, Basilides distinguished strictly between the highest god and the god of the OT. The logos, prudence, wisdom, and power from which the powers and angels come are from the unborn Father. The angels formed heaven upon heaven until the number 365 was reached.

Those angels who occupy the lowest heaven, that, namely, which is visible to us, formed all the things which are in the world, and made allotments among themselves of the earth and of those nations which are upon it. The chief of them is he who is thought to be the God of the Jews; and inasmuch as he desired to render the other nations subject to his own people, that is, the Jews, all the other princes resisted and opposed him. Wherefore all other nations were at enmity with his nation. But the unborn and nameless father, perceiving that they would be destroyed, sent his own first-begotten Nous (he it is who is called Christ) to bestow deliverance on them that believe in him, from the power of those who made the world. He appeared, then, on earth as a man, to the nations of these powers, and wrought miracles. Wherefore he did not himself suffer death, but Simon, a certain man of Cyrene, being compelled, bore the cross in his stead; so that this latter being transfigured by him, that he might be thought to be Jesus, was crucified, through ignorance and error, while Jesus himself received the form of Simon, and, standing by, laughed at them. For since he was an incorporeal power, and the Nous (mind) of the unborn father, he transfigured himself as he pleased, and thus

65. All relevant texts are easily accessible in Förster, *Die Gnosis*, 1:80–110.

ascended to him who had sent him, deriding them, inasmuch as he could not
be laid hold of, and was invisible to all. Those, then, who know these things
have been freed from the principalities who formed the world; so that it is not
incumbent on us to confess him who was crucified, but him who came in the
form of a man, and was thought to be crucified, and was called Jesus, and
was sent by the father, that by this dispensation he might destroy the works
of the makers of the world. If anyone, therefore, he declares, confesses the
crucified, that man is still a slave, and under the power of those who formed
our bodies; but he who denies him has been freed from these beings, and is
acquainted with the dispensation of the unborn father. Salvation belongs to
the soul alone, for the body is by nature subject to corruption.[66] (Irenaeus,
Haer. 1.24.4–5, ANF 1:349–50)

Hippolytus (*Ref.* 7.20–27; 10.14) attributes to Basilides and his son Isidore
a comprehensive, complex, and enthralling myth.[67] Then the ineffable God,
who stands above being, decided to become active through the world seed,
in which neither an evil god nor evil matter plays a role. The world seed
includes a threefold sonship: "a part of this threefold sonship was light, the
other heavy, the third needing of purification" (*Ref.* 7.22). In addition, the
great archon was created by the world seed, which knew nothing of the god
that is above existence and also did not know that "the sonship left behind
in the seed" (*Ref.* 7.22) greatly surpassed it in wisdom. He learned from the
son that he was generated and was not the highest god of the cosmos. This
revelation that the true god is above the great archon and his upper world is
the gospel. This gospel comes only to the Jesus who was generated. His task
consists of separating what was mixed in the world.

The third sonship, which had been left behind in order to give good deeds and
to receive good deeds, was purified by Jesus and ascended through the universe
to blessed sonship. The entire purpose of these was the blending together of, as
it were, the conglomeration of seeds, and the distinction of the various orders
of created objects, and the restoration into their proper component parts of
things that had been blended together to their original place. Jesus, therefore,
became the original of the distinction of the various orders of created objects,
and his Passion took place for no other reason than to distinguish what had
been mingled together. (*Ref.* 7.27)

66. In Irenaeus, *Haer.* 1.24.5–7, statements about the angels and the arcane discipline follow
1.24.6: "One may not divulge their mysteries, for they must remain hidden in silence."
67. Here only the basic features can be described; a more detailed depiction of the myth is
in B. Aland, *Die Gnosis*, 173–82; the contradictions are noted by W. Löhr, *Basilides und seine
Schule*, 298–312, in which the original tradition is extensively expanded and the report of Hippolytus disappears as a source.

The true beneficiaries of this distinction are the pneumatics, for the Holy Spirit is the mediator between the upper and the lower worlds: "We, the pneumatics, are the sons of God, he said [υἱοὶ δέ, φησίν, ἐσμὲν ἡμεῖς οἱ πνευματικοί], left here in order to lead souls, to shape, to find the way and to bring to perfection, we whose nature is to abide in this distance" (*Ref.* 7.25). The removal of the mixture of the transient and eternal and the return made possible for the pneumatic into the highest level of being are the central content of the myth.

Other accents are in turn present in the fragments of Clement of Alexandria.[68] Here Basilides appears primarily as a philosophically educated theologian and pastor, whose teaching includes dual elements but is not strictly dualistic. In the center stands a doctrine of the soul that is influenced by Plato, in which the soul must engage in a spiritual battle (frag. 5: "Through the reasonable part of the soul, we must be superior and demonstrate that we rule over the lower creation in us").[69] Otherwise a wandering of the soul follows as punishment (frags. 16; 17: "There is no other punishment for sin than the reincarnation of the soul after death"; 18). The God of the OT as the archon of this world/this aeon (frags. 4; 14) is obviously to be regarded as a lower deity. Moses proclaims the one temple and cosmos, "and also—here Basilides no longer agrees—the one God." The highest deity, on the other hand, is good and just (frag. 7) and leads the Christians through temptations.

All three traditions have their own profile, so that the following explanatory models can be considered: (1) The reports of Irenaeus, Hippolytus, and Clement indicate a common profile and are harmonized (for the most part beyond the initial stages in Justin and/or the claim of subsequent expansions).[70] (2) The reports of Irenaeus and Hippolytus depict secondary interpretations, so that the fragments of Clement of Alexandria especially form the basis for the historical Basilides and his son Isidore.[71] (3) The report of Hippolytus is taken as a basis and made parallel to isolated fragments of Clement so that in Basilides (especially because of the agreements with Valentinus) the first detailed myth of advanced Gnosticism is found.[72] A clear explanation of this highly complex finding appears to be scarcely possible and is not attempted here. Methodologically one must consider that the report of Irenaeus cannot

---

68. A depiction in summary is in W. Löhr, *Basilides und seine Schule*, 324–37.

69. Enumeration and text according to W. Löhr, *Basilides und seine Schule*, 78–79.

70. So, e.g., Hilgenfeld, *Ketzergeschichte*, 195–230; Layton, *Gnostic Scriptures*, 418; Pearson, "Basilides the Gnostic," 3.

71. Cf. W. Löhr, *Basilides und seine Schule*, 324–35.

72. So B. Aland, *Die Gnosis*, 172–91; contra W. Löhr, *Basilides und seine Schule*, 284–323, who sees no connection of the Hippolytus report to the original teaching of Basilides.

simply be cast aside.[73] (1) He presents the chronologically oldest report and relies on traditions, possibly on the older *Syntagma* of Justin, which came thirty years earlier.[74] (2) The critics of the Irenaeus report must explain why the Christology in the fragments of Clement (and also in Hippolytus) is so insignificant, while they are dominant in the original in Irenaeus.[75] (3) The "cheerful exchange" with Simon of Cyrene and the apparent crucifixion[76] are original concepts that, in view of Basilides, cannot simply be considered unimportant. Every depiction of the teaching of Basilides will need to consider, along with the cosmology and ethics, the Christology and the anti-Jewish elements of his drama of salvation.

Basic Assumptions of Gnostic Thought

Using this complex system as well as the witness of the Pastoral Epistles, one can filter out in varying clarity and depth four basic ideas, which at the same time can be considered the crucial characteristics of early Gnostic thought/Gnostic systems as a whole:[77] (1) Both the highest god and the

73. So, e.g., brief and succinct is Mühlenberg, "Basilides"; B. Aland, *Die Gnosis*, 172; Brankaer, *Die Gnosis*, 60.

74. Cf. Pearson, "Basilides the Gnostic," 28, criticizing the methodological approach of Löhr, who considers the report of Irenaeus (the basis of which is Justin's *Syntagma*) and claims: "Basilides was a Gnostic. But, more importantly, he was a Christian."

75. This problem is at least mentioned by W. Löhr, *Basilides und seine Schule*, 334; all others pass over it in silence.

76. Variations of this motif are found in the Apocalypse of Peter (NHC VII,3.81: "The redeemer said to me, 'The one whom you see on the tree glad and laughing, that is the living Jesus. But the one whose hands and feet are pierced with nails, that is his fleshly part, the substitute'") and in the second logos of the great Seth (NHC VII,2.55): "They punished me, yet I did not actually die but only appeared to do so."

77. See other recent definitions of Gnosticism: Sellin, *Der Streit um die Auferstehung*, 200: "The world (and the earthly nature of humankind) is the creation of a being that has fallen from the light (demiurge) and thus a product of a godless power." Another definition is offered by Colpe, "Gnosis II," 559: "The distinctive feature of Gnosticism lies in the fact that everywhere in the ancient East, where syncretism and non-Gnostic Christianity would have formed a hypostasis, it actually created two hypostases. They are both to be characterized as 'self,' yet they have the same substance and even the same names. That it nevertheless involved two hypostases is indicated by the fact that a total process of redemption is considered necessary in order to bring together one hypostasis with the other; i.e., the salvator with the salvandum [the savior with those to be saved]." Markschies, "Gnosis/Gnostizismus," 870, lists characteristic motifs of Gnosticism: (1) the experience of a fully transcendent highest God; (2) the introduction of other divine figures; (3) the assessment of the world and matter as an evil creation; (4) the introduction of a lower creator God; (5) explanation of the negative present situation by a mythological drama; (6) the knowledge of this situation granted through a transcendent redeemer figure; (7) redemption through gnosis; (8) predetermination of the classes of humankind; (9) a developed dualism at all levels. B. Aland, *Was ist Gnosis?*, 2, gives this definition: "Gnosis presents the Christian experience of fall and rescue through a revelation that is hidden and then promised

redeemer figures are perfect transcendent beings. By definition, they do not come into contact with anything earthly, and they undergo no changes. (2) As a consequence, they hold to a protological dualism, according to which, even before the origin of the world, a division occurred at the level of the deity/ deities between the first/higher and a second/lower god (gods), who did not possess the purity of the first authority. The second/lower god (in most instances the "Jewish" God) appears as the creator of the earthly world. The good and true god cannot be held responsible for the deficient creation with all of its suffering and injustice. (3) From the negative understanding of the earthly world and its origin, cosmologies necessarily emerge that depict the nature of the highest deity, the becoming/nature of the world/worlds in the form of myths. (4) In the background of this worldview is the experience of world alienation and of the desire for overcoming the world/purification at the anthropological level, supported by the consciousness of belonging to "another," "better," and "higher" world, to which one returns with the help of the redeemer.[78]

All four basic principles indicate a background in Platonic thought that, with the Middle Platonism of the first century BCE to the second/third centuries CE, was very influential.[79] Philo, Plutarch, and Dio of Prusa indicate the great extent to which the Platonic philosophy was appropriated to engage religious-philosophical traditions and myths with respect to their deeper content and thus to actualize and make them intelligible.[80] The basic assumption of all models is that God/the gods alone belong to the ideal, transcendent, incorporeal and only real level: the world of ideas.[81] The highest deity is identical with the highest idea: the good ("Is God good in reality and to be spoken

---

through revelation. It is portrayed in graphic, mythical-narratival or philosophical-like form." Brankaer, *Die Gnosis*, 20, gives the following characteristics of Gnosticism: "1. It involves movements that developed beginning from the second century within—in the 'laboratory'— Christianity. 2. The Gnostics believe that they are redeemed and lifted above the world by a special knowledge, normally communicated by a redeemer figure from outside the world. 3. The positive anthropology—faith that one is bound to a higher reality—often results from a negative assessment of the world and matter. 4. Gnostics depict their understanding of the world in myths in which the origin of the world is explained by the fall from a higher nature; often they depict a lower creator God, who is unknowing or even evil."

78. Cf. Colpe, "Gnosis II," col. 571: "In Gnosis, however, the self must itself become redeemed, i.e., raised, brought to itself, be reminded of its essential character by its heavenly homeland."

79. On Platonic thought, cf. Erler, *Platon*; on the extraordinary impact of Plato in antiquity, cf. especially Dörrie, Baltes, and Pietsch, *Der Platonismus in der Antike*.

80. B. Aland, *Die Gnosis*, 21–36, correctly emphasizes the strong influence of philosophy on Gnosticism.

81. Cf. Erler, *Platon*, 390: "According to Plato, without the ideas, there is no knowledge, no explanation of reality, and no foundation for moral or political conduct."

of in this way?"; Plato, *Pol.* 379b).[82] God is perfect, undergoes no change, and does not approach humankind,[83] but remains in himself: "But that which is immovably the same forever cannot become older or younger by time, nor can it be said that it came into being in the past, or has come into being now, or will come into being in the future nor is it subject at all to any of those states which affect moving and sensible things and of which generation is the cause." (Plato, *Tim.* 38a). In contrast, the world and heaven have come into being, for they are visible and possess bodies. The Platonic body-soul dualism is based on this basic idea. The immortal soul represents one's true self and constitutes its true being.[84] "If no pure knowledge is possible when we are in the body, then it is totally impossible to acquire knowledge, or it is only possible after death" (*Phaed.* 66e). The soul has a divine origin and will return to its origin with the departure of the body.

This fundamental and insoluble contrast between body and soul dominates ancient thought beyond the boundaries of the school in numerous variations at the turn of the millennium. In all philosophical-theological systems, God is associated with the essential being, the good, the logos, the spirit, and separated categorically from the earthly world, from mutability, from becoming and decay. Epicurus already taught about God: "First, believe that god is a living being, immortal and blessed, in accordance with the general conception of god commonly held, and do not ascribe to god anything foreign to his indestructibility or repugnant to his blessedness. Believe of him everything which is able to preserve his blessedness and indestructibility" (*Letter to Menoeceus* 123). Diogenes Laertius (7.147) reports about the Stoics: "The deity, they say, is a living being, immortal, rational, perfect or intelligent in happiness, admitting nothing evil, taking providential care of the world and everything that is in it, but he is not in human form [μὴ εἶναι μέντοι ἀνθρωπόμορφον]." For Plutarch, god/the gods are the only reality that exists beyond time and becoming, and they are beyond movement, of becoming and decaying: "What, then, really is Being? It is that which is eternal, without beginning and without end, to which no length of time brings change. . . . But God is (if there be need to say so), and he exists for no fixed time, but for the everlasting ages, which are immovable, timeless, and undeviating, in which there is no earlier nor later, no future nor past, no older nor younger; but he, being one, has with only one 'now' completely filled 'forever'; and only what is being in this sense, is truly being, not having been nor about to be, nor has it had a

82. On the Platonic understanding of the gods/god, cf. Erler, *Platon*, 464–73.
83. Cf. Erler, *Platon*, 472: "An essential characteristic of Platonic theology is the rejection of a proximity of God to humankind. The divine is unapproachable and beyond human knowledge."
84. Cf. Erler, *Platon*, 375.

beginning nor is it destined to come to an end" (*Delphi* 19, 20 [*Mor.* 393]). Therefore, gods cannot be mortal: "It is against the (general) conception that humankind is immortal, as it is that God be mortal. Or rather: I do not see which distinctions between God and humankind exist if God is also rational and impermanent being."[85] According to Apuleius (ca. 125–170 CE), following Plato, the gods are incorporeal, living nature, without end and without beginning, but rather eternal with respect to before and after, separated from contact with the corporeal of their own nature, with perfect reason for their highest happiness (*De Deo Socratis* 123).[86]

Of great significance also is a development in Middle Platonism, which relies on various statements of Plato about the demiurge[87] that lead to a doctrine of two or, more precisely, three gods. Plutarch connects the origin of good and evil with two different gods and recognizes that he is in good company. "The great majority and the wisest of men hold this opinion: they believe either there are two gods, rivals as it were, the one the artificer of good and the other of evil. There are also those who call the better one a god and the other a daemon."[88] In particular, the Middle Platonist Numenius (middle of the second century CE)[89] teaches that there are two (or three) gods who stand in a relationship to each other like a father and son. While the first god is complete in himself, the second god is the essential demiurge who created the world and is in contact with matter:

The first god, existing in his own place, is simple, because, consorting with himself alone, he can never be divisible. However, the second and third god is one: but by being associated with matter which is duality, he gives unity to it, but is himself divided by it, because matter is prone to desire and flux. Therefore,

85. Plutarch, *De communibus notitiis adversus Stoicos* 31 (cited according to Dörrie, Baltes, and Pietsch, *Theologia Platonica*, 19). Cf. also Plutarch, *Mor.* 1022e–f, where Plutarch defines the divine as the indivisible and describes him positively as "simple and incapable of suffering" (τὸ γὰρ ἁπλοῦν καὶ ἀπαθές).

86. Cf. also Apuleius, *De dogma Platonis* 1.5f.: "Plato maintains about God that he is incorporeal [*quod sit incorporeus*]. He is one [*unus*], as he says, immeasurable, the creator and builder of all things, happy and making happy, the best, without any need, imparting everything. He is called the heavenly, ineffable, nameless, and as he himself says, invisible, invincible, whose nature it is difficult to find" (cited in Dörrie, Baltes, and Pietsch, *Theologia Platonica*, 65–67).

87. Plato, *Tim.* 28–29, especially stands in the background, making its distinction between being and becoming. In reference to the origin of the world, he says, "If the world is indeed fair and the maker good, it is manifest that he must have looked to that which is eternal . . . and must, of necessity, if this be admitted, be a copy of something" (*Tim.* 9a–b). If the existing world is a copy of a higher existence, then a higher deity is conceivable as the creator of the world.

88. Plutarch, *Is. Os.* 46 (written around 105 CE).

89. Cf. also Alcinous (middle of the second century CE); fragments in Dörrie, Baltes, and Pietsch, *Theologia Platonica*, 56–65, 88, 102f., 152f., 216.

by not being in contact with the intelligible (for so he would have been in contact with himself), because he looks toward matter and gives attention to it, he becomes unregarding of himself. And he lays hold of the sensible realm and ministers to it and he draws it up into his own moral nature, as a result of his yearning for matter.[90]

A division within the deity/deities is thoroughly consistent because the negative evaluation of the corporeal/material must lead also to a generally negative judgment of the deity that was active as creator and had to be engaged with matter in any form. Therefore, this concept probably did not originate in the second century CE, for Numenius and Alcinous probably stand in an older intellectual tradition of Middle Platonism.[91] In any case, this protological dualism is the second element (besides the devaluation of the corporeal/material) that the early Gnostics took from Platonism and combined with Jewish Christian concepts. The development/presentation of Gnostic theology in the form of myths is indebted to Platonic thought, for in the key dialogue *Timaeus*, the statement is made in the context of reflections on the nature of the gods and the origin of the universe, that "we are not able to give notions which are altogether and in every respect exact and consistent with one another, . . . so that we ought to accept the myth that is probable [εἰκότα μῦθος] and inquire no further" (Plato, *Tim.* 29c–d). The graphic (and speculative) account is thus the appropriate form for approaching these last questions.

The Origin of Gnostic Thought

Against this background, the origin of early Gnostic thought can be traced in its essential features: For members of the early Christian churches educated in Platonism or sympathetic to it (especially in the cities of Asia Minor),[92] some of the major teachings of Christianity were acceptable (God as the Good, God as love; Jesus Christ as the true redeemer; eternal life through faith; salvation from the existence dominated by sin; overcoming of the world through faith; the Holy Spirit as divine power), but for others it was not acceptable (God as creator of the earthly world; the actual incarnation of the Son of God, Jesus Christ, and his actual suffering; the presence of the

90. Numenius of Apameia, in Eusebius, *Praeparatio evangelica* 11.18.3–5 (cited according to Dörrie, Baltes, and Pietsch, *Theologia Platonica*, 139; cf. also the texts on 139–53).

91. A starting point of this development (according to Dörrie, Baltes, and Pietsch, *Theologia Platonica*, 471) might have been the Neopythagorean Euodorus of Alexandria (first century BCE).

92. On the educational and social-historical aspects of Gnosticism, cf. B. Aland, *Die Gnosis*, 203–15.

Crucified and Resurrected One in the sacraments; the identification of [the highest] god with this event). Because of this intellectual background, these church members sought a solution to their problem, attempting a synthesis of Platonic and Jewish Christian thought. They could not and did not want to deny the life and ministry of the earthly Jesus of Nazareth, but made of it an unessential, only apparent, event. In docetism (see above, 10.4.2), besides 1 Tim. 6:20, one may see a second close connection between the emerging Christianity and the earliest Gnostic systems. The docetists were also intellectuals shaped by Platonism, who regarded Jesus Christ as a purely transcendent redeemer and attributed to him only an unessential, apparent existence (cf. 1 John 4:1–3). In particular, the conflict of Ignatius of Antioch with docetists indicates how widely this thought had spread, particularly in churches of Asia Minor. Because docetism and later Gnostic systems drew their ideological foundation/understanding of reality likewise from Platonism, it is consistent when docetic views appear frequently among Gnostics. However, Gnosticism and docetism are not identical,[93] for while in docetism the concern is the relevance of the bodily, earthly historical appearance of Jesus for salvation, the crucial characteristic of Gnostic systems (protological dualism, cosmological speculations) are evident neither in the Gospel of John nor in the letters of Ignatius. Docetism is an independent form of Christology, that, however, may be regarded as an anticipation of Gnostic thought that was suitable for Gnostic reception.

Besides Platonism and the docetism associated with it, Judaism from the beginning shaped Gnosticism. The origin of Gnosticism in a primarily Jewish context is, however, improbable for two reasons.[94] (1) There are no sources supporting this claim and (2) central elements of the Jewish faith (strict monotheism, the Creator God, positive evaluation of the creation) can scarcely be combined with the basic negative view of creation in the Gnostic systems. However, the influence of isolated Jewish elements on early Gnostic systems is only natural, for some Gnostics were Jewish Christians, and all Gnostics had to debate with the Jewish foundation of Christianity from the beginning (especially with the belief in creation). For the early (and also later) Gnostics, the concern was, in accordance with their intellectual background, the capacity of early Christianity to connect with the culture. They were

93. Cf. Colpe, "Gnosis II," 611: "Rather, docetism is a presupposition of the Gnostic teaching of redemption." Cf. also the differentiation in Weigandt, "Der Doketismus im Urchristentum," 4–19; also Schoedel, *Ignatius of Antioch*, 155.

94. Cf. Tröger, "Gnosis und Judentum," 168: "As a result of our considerations, we can establish that the Gnostic movement reflects many contacts with Judaism (in the widest sense), but it is not derived from it"; cf. also the critique of a Jewish origin of Gnosis in Brakke, *Gnostics*, 84–86.

"modern" thinkers, trained exegetes, and thus representatives of an inquiring and scholarly Christianity.[95] At the same time, therefore, Gnosticism was from the beginning a speculative and syncretistic movement, as the variety of motifs and systems and the difficulty of establishing a singular derivation indicate. Furthermore, in the context of a philosophical theology determined by Platonism, the transitions are always fluid so that individual Gnostic writings served a purely philosophical logic and could be severed from Christianity. This is definitely the consequence of such an intellectual approach by which Gnosticism, the nous (mind/reason), or the logos could grant redemption fully independent of a Christian savior figure.[96] Theologically, despite all of the speculative systems among the Gnostics, a rational (Platonic) depiction of God is dominant.[97] This depiction does not actually bind God's activity within history. They portrayed the absoluteness, oneness, purity, foreignness, otherness, and eternity of God, who sends his redeemer (for the most part, Jesus Christ), in order to liberate the elect from the limitations of earthly existence. Therefore, they understand the work of Jesus Christ differently from the NT writings; that is, they do not understand it as the authentic interpretation of the one God of Israel and of all of humanity that was attested by God himself in the cross and resurrection. For them the new Christian-Platonic depiction of God was an absolute concept that is not realized historically in the life, death, and resurrection of Jesus Christ.

The earliest sources/witnesses suggest that Gnostic thought originated slowly around the end of the first century within early Christianity. At the turn of the century, it took on the quality of a system; and from the middle of the second century, it expanded explosively into advanced Gnosticism. No evidence exists for

95. Cf. Tertullian, *Prescription against Heretics* 7.5: "Where does evil [*unde malum*] come from? And why? Where does the human come from, and how did he come? But especially, Where does God come from?"

96. Non-Christian writings from Nag Hammadi (NHC III/3; V/5; VI/5, 6–8; VII/1, 2, 4; VIII/1; IX/2; X; XI/3; XII/1) or the *Corpus Hermeticum* (Colpe and Holzhausen, *Das Corpus Hermeticum Deutsch*; Eckart, *Das Corpus Hermeticum*) are in no way an indication of a pre-Christian Gnosticism. The absence of clear Christian conceptions indicates the possibility of its most important presupposition: Platonic philosophy.

97. Therefore, the starting point of Gnostic thought is to be seen in the premises of the Gnostic worldview. For the contemporaneous circumstances, see Hengel, "Paulus und die Frage," 502–10, who locates the origin of Gnosticism in the large cities such as Antioch and Alexandria, where, after the catastrophe of 70 CE, disappointed Jews, Samaritans, Godfearers, and Jewish Christians turned toward a new depiction of God in a mixture of apocalyptic and Platonism, and Gnosticism began to grow. A different accent is given by H.-F. Weiss, *Frühes Christentum und Gnosis*, 487–90, who sees the origin of Gnostic thought in the interpretation of Scripture.

a pre- or non-Christian origin of Gnosticism! From the beginning, Gnosticism was a movement of emancipation, which linked itself to various educational traditions, joined them with each other, could separate specific (e.g., Christian) elements again, and represented, from the perspective of the time, a "modern" view. The clarity of the analysis of the human situation and the simplicity of the solution corresponded to the purity of a fully transcendent understanding of God: the solution was salvation through knowledge. Inasmuch as the (later) writings accepted into the canon did not represent this conception or could not submit to them, the Gnostic groups produced their own Scriptures.

Table 9. Chronology of Early Christianity to 130 CE

after 70	accelerated separation of Jewish Christianity and Christians from the people; loss of meaning of Jewish Christianity
70–90	composition of the Synoptic Gospels; early deutero-Pauline letters
from 80	docetism; development of Gnostic thought
ca. 90–95	first larger persecution of Christians (1 Peter, Revelation)
90–100	Catholic Epistles; late deutero-Paulines; Hebrews; Acts; the Letters of John; 1 Clement
ca. 100	Gospel of John
ca. 100	Menander, Satornilus
beginning of the 2nd century	Cerinthus
before 117	martyrdom of Ignatius of Antioch
110–112	correspondence between Pliny and Trajan; transregional persecution of Christians
ca. 130	Basilides

15

Fifteen Reasons for the Success of Early Christianity

1. The Roman Empire, as a relatively unified cultural and political area without dividing boundaries, was a crucial presupposition for the success of early Christianity.
2. Greek as a world language and the good possibilities for travel in the first century advanced the expansion of Christianity.
3. A further reason was the initial close dependence on the existing infrastructure of Hellenistic Judaism (Paul). Here especially many sympathizers to the Jewish religion (Godfearers) were won to the faith.
4. The weakness of the existing religions also favored the spread of Christianity. Among Greeks and Romans there was no concept of a mission, but only regional or local cults (e.g., Delphi), which were not connected with each other. Similarly, no supraregional organized priesthood existed. The decline of the pagan cults (cf. Plutarch, Pliny) favored the success of Christianity.
5. Monotheism exercised a great appeal and already was the source of fascination about Jews in antiquity. The great number of gods and portrayals of the gods in the Greco-Roman world apparently led to a loss of plausibility. In addition, there was the continuing fascination with the figure of Jesus of Nazareth, who proclaimed and embodied a new understanding of God. The narratives of and about Jesus in the

Gospels produced a continuing proximity to the redeemer figure that was unknown until then.

6. Something new in the history of ancient religion appeared with early Christianity. Early Christian mission was not intended to offer people an additional religion but made an exclusive claim that involved the renunciation of all previous religious commitments. The goal of early Christian preaching was not the adhesion to another religion but the conversion to the one true God (cf. 1 Thess. 1:9–10). It involved a conscious decision with a level of commitment with no little success!

7. The success of the early Christian mission can be explained only with the assumption of a high capacity to connect with Jewish and Greco-Roman streams of tradition. The reception and transformation of Greco-Roman concepts began not with the ancient church but even earlier, with Paul! Like no one else, he was capable of combining Jewish and Greco-Roman thought and creating an open and argumentative system in which one could participate. This twofold capacity for connection could be attained, not by rejection, but only through a conscious participation in the debates that were taking place in the environment of the churches. The early Christian missionaries participated aggressively in the religious, ethical, and philosophical discussions of their time. A new cultural system like early Christianity could emerge only because it was in a position to connect with existing cultural movements and produce new organizations of concepts and traditions. Intentional communication and desired conviction are here at the beginning!

8. A high social, communicative, and informal network existed among the house churches; the five pillars of the network were letters, travel, coworkers, reciprocal material support, and a developed culture of hospitality (cf. Luke 14:12–14; Rom. 12:13; 1 Pet. 4:9; 1 Tim. 3:2; 5:10; Titus 1:8; Heb. 13:2; 1 Clem. 1–2; Did. 11–13). As a whole, the infrastructure of the Christians was new and effective. The development of communication and the formation of networks is what today is called by the old-fashioned word "mission."

9. Christians were participants in a local congregation and at the same time members of the worldwide church so that individuality and cosmopolitan breadth supplemented each other. In the entire Roman Empire, one could quickly as a tradesman, soldier, or slave find a church community in the centers and become at home.

10. Besides a novel teaching, a challenging love ethic (love of God, neighbor, self, and enemy) created new social forms. A key to the success of

Christian churches was the openness for people of all social classes, both men and women, and all occupations. This openness presented the greatest difference from pagan associations. The conversion of "entire houses" (cf. 1 Cor. 1:16; Acts 16:14; 18:8) indicates that members of all social classes could belong to the new community (cf. Gal. 3:26–28). There was no limitation on rank, standing, descent, or gender. Through the absence of formal conditions for admission, women and members of the lower levels of society (especially slaves) joined the new communities in great numbers.

11. Baptism, the weekly eucharistic celebration, and the small house churches created a strong bond and required the formation of an identity. Charismatic church services, new intensive experiences of the Spirit, miracles, and healings as well as charismatic personalities determined the life of the community. In the communities it was possible to live out the new identity and to expand as the "I" and "we" consciousness was brought into a balance. As individual persons, believers were equally beloved children of God and together members of the body of Christ. The churches created bonds within and were open to the outside.

12. Early Christianity appeared as a creative literary and intellectual movement; they read the OT in a new context, created new genres (gospels), and transformed existing genres (Pauline letters, miracles, parables). No figure in the ancient world so quickly caused the creation of a literary and intellectual tradition as Jesus Christ. Furthermore, within the early Christian churches a productive culture of debate was dominant. A productive tension between self-concept and reality was crucial: it was a small group, but held sway over the world. Utopia (the kingdom of God) and paradoxes became productive as starting points: in death is life; the poor are rich; the oppressed will rule. Here the principle of reversal was the driving force.

13. Like Pythagoras and Socrates, Jesus wrote nothing; at the beginning, there was no "holy book." This fact made possible the formation of various directions in interpretation. What was written limited the interpretation and did not allow the hermeneutic to affect the written texts.

14. The split into individual movements (Jerusalem church, Jesus movement in Galilee, Antioch and Paul, Johannine school) was a crucial presupposition for the survival of the new faith. This plurality made it possible to react to the different challenges so that the disappearance of one orientation (e.g., the community of the logia source) did not result in the downfall of the whole movement.

15. Christians had a direct access to God; there was no priestly class. De-mocratization was an essential element of the new faith; all are children of God. In addition, new instructions for conduct and emotions became adaptable for the culture, that is, love of enemies, forgiveness, sympathy, humility, and simplicity. Finally, the Christians conceived of the hereafter in a new way; the capricious power of fate and the fear of the hereafter were removed by a loving God, who raised Jesus Christ from the dead and promised to raise believers.

Early Christian missionaries moved within a realm of a political, economic, and language scene that, despite its regional manifestation, was perceived as a common world. These favorable external conditions were combined with a novel, expansive concept of mission as well as attractive teachings and lifestyle. The interplay of these factors considerably favored the spread of the new movement of Christians. In a society shaped by Greco-Roman ethnocentrism, the Christians practiced an exclusive model of fraternal openness and equality that included utopian elements and left behind basic values of antiquity. Early Christianity developed very quickly into a new cultural system. As a whole, one can describe early Christianity as an equally charismatic and intellectual movement. This double structure was the basis of its attractiveness and success.

Works Cited

Dictionary and Encyclopedia Articles

Aland, Kurt. "Das Verhältnis von Kirche und Staat in der Frühzeit." *ANRW* 2.23.1:60–246.

Auffahrt, Christoph. "Mysterien." *RAC* 25:422–71.

Balz, Horst. "κόσμος." *EDNT* 2:309–13.

Barth, Gerhard. "πίστις." *EDNT* 3:91–97.

Behm, Johannes. "παράκλητος." *TDNT* 5:799–801.

Betz, Hans Dieter. "Hellenismus." *TRE* 15:19–35.

———. "Paul." *ABD* 5:186–201.

Betz, Otto. "Beschneidung II," *TRE* 5:716–22.

Beyer, Hermann Wolfgang. "ἐπίσκοπος." *TDNT* 2:608–20.

Böcher, Otto. "Johannes der Täufer." *TRE* 17:172–81.

Breytenbach, Cilliers. "Sühne." *TBLNT* 1685–91.

———. "Versöhnung." *TBLNT* 1777–80.

Bultmann, Rudolf. "Johannesevangelium." *RGG*, 3rd ed., 3:840–50.

Burkert, Walter. "Geschichte und Religion." *TRE* 14:235–52.

Colpe, Carsten. "Gnosis II." *RAC* 11:537–659.

———. "υἱὸς τοῦ ἀνθρώπου." *TDNT* 8:400–477.

Cullmann, Oscar. "Πέτρος." *TDNT* 6:100–112.

Deines, Roland. "Pharisaer." *TBLNT* 1455–68.

Delling, Gerhard. "στοιχεῖον." *TDNT* 7:666–87.

Eck, Werner. "Domitianus." *DNP* 3:749.

Elliger, Winfried. "Korinth." *RAC* 21:579–605.

Figl, Johann, Udo Rütersworden, and Bernd Wander. "Universalismus/Partikularismus." *RGG* 8:774–78.

Fitzmyer, Joseph A. "κύριος." *EDNT* 2:328–31.

Frenschkowski, Marco. "Nero." *RAC* 25:839–78.

Freudenberger, Rudolf. "Christenverfolgungen." *TRE* 8:23–29.

Funke, Hermann. "Götterbild." *RAC* 11:659–828.

García y Bellido, Antonio. "Die Latinisierung Hispaniens." *ANRW* 1.1:462–91.

Giesen, Heinz. "Das Römische Reich im Spiegel der Johannes-Apokalypse." *ANRW* 26.3:2501–2614, esp. 2566–70.

Goulet-Cazé, Marie-Odile. "Kynismus." *RAC* 22:631–87.

Haacker, Klaus. "Die Stellung des Stephanus in der Geschichte des Urchristentums." *ANRW* 26.2:1515–53.

———. "Zum Werdegang des Paulus." *ANRW* 26.2:815–938.

Hahn, Ferdinand. "Gottesdienst III: Neues Testament." *TRE* 14:28–39.

———. "Χριστός." *EDNT* 3:478–86.

Hanslik, Robert. "Domitian." *KP-II*, 125.

Höcker, Christoph. "Straßen- und Brückenbau." *DNP* 11:1030–36.

Judge, Edwin A. "Kultgemeinde (Kultverein)." *RAC* 22:393–438.

Kasher, Aryeh. "Diaspora I/2." *TRE* 8:71–112.

Kötting, Bernhard. "Christentum I (Ausbreitung)." *RAC* 2:1138–59.

Kübler, Bernhard. "Maiestas." PW 14:542–59.

Kuhn, Heinz-Wolfgang. "Die Kreuzesstrafe während der frühen Kaiserzeit." *ANRW* 2.25.1:648–793.

Kuhn, Karl Georg, and Hartmut Stegemann. "Proselyten." PW 1248–83.

Lang, Bernhard. "Judentum (Frühjudentum)." *NBL* 2:404–9.

Leeuw, Gerardus Van Der. "Universalismus und Partikularismus I." *RGG*, 2nd ed., 5:1379. Tübingen, 1931.

Markschies, Christoph. "Gnosis/Gnostizismus." *NBL* 1:868–71.

———. "Gnosis/Gnostizismus." *RGG* 4:1045–53.

Meyer, Rudolf. "Σαδδουκαῖος." *TDNT* 7:35–54.

Meyer, Rudolf, and Hans-Friedrich Weiss. "Φαρισαῖος." *TDNT* 9:11–48.

Mühlenberg, Ekkehard. "Basilides." *TRE* 5:299.

Nestle, Dieter. "Freiheit." *RAC* 8:269–306.

Norris, Frederick W. "Antiochien I." *TRE* 3:99.

Radl, Walter. "παρουσία." *EDNT* 3:43–44.

Räisänen, Heikki. "Die 'Hellenisten' der Urgemeinde." *ANRW* 26.2:1468–1514.

Rengstorf, Karl Heinrich. "ἀπόστολος." *TDNT* 1:407–47.

Roloff, Jürgen. "Amt IV." *TRE* 2:509–33.

———. "Apostel I." *TRE* 3:430–45.

———. "ἐκκλησία." *EDNT* 1:410–15.

Schäfke, Werner. "Frühchristlicher Widerstand." *ANRW* 2.23.1.

Schnelle, Udo. "Taufe im NT." *TRE* 32:663–74.

Seifrid, Marc A. "In Christ." *DPL* 433–36.

Sellin, Gerhard. "Mythos." *RGG*, 4th ed., 5:1697–99.

Stemberger, Günter. "Juden." *RAC* 19:160–245.

Strecker, Georg. "Ebioniten." *RAC* 4:487–500.

———. "Elkesai." *RAC* 4:1171–86.

———. "Judenchristentum." *TRE* 17:310–25.

Thyen, Hartwig. "Johannesbriefe." *TRE* 17:186–200.

Timpe, Dieter. "Hellenismus." *RGG* 3:1609.

Wacht, Manfred. "Gütergemeinschaft." *RAC* 13:1–59.

Weeber, Karl-Wilhelm. "Reisen." *DNP* 10:858.

Wiseman, James. "Corinth and Rome I: 228 B.C.–A.D. 267." *ANRW* 2.7.1:438–548.

Zeller, Dieter. "Messias/Christus." *NBL* 3:782–86.

———. "Mysterien/Mysterienreligionen." *TRE* 23:504–26.

Zwickel, Wolfgang. "Hohepriester." *NBL* 2:181–83.

———. "Tempel." *NBL* 3:799–810.

Books and Articles

Ådna, Jostein. *Jesu Stellung zum Tempel: Die Tempelaktion und das Tempelwort als Ausdruck seiner messianischen Sendung.* WUNT 2/119. Tübingen: Mohr Siebeck, 2000.

Adna, Jostein, and Hans Kvalbein, ed. *The Mission of the Early Church to Jews and Gentiles.* WUNT 127. Tübingen: Mohr Siebeck, 2000.

Aland, Barbara. *Die Gnosis.* Stuttgart: Reclam, 2014.

———. *Was ist Gnosis? Studien zum frühen Christentum, zu Marcion und zur kaiserzeitlichen Philosophie.* WUNT 239. Tübingen: Mohr Siebeck, 2009.

Aland, Kurt. "Die Entstehung des Corpus Paulinum." Pages 302–50 in Aland, *Neutestamentliche Entwürfe.*

———, ed. *Neutestamentliche Entwürfe.* TB 63. Munich: Kaiser, 1979.

———. *Das Verhältnis von Kirche und Staat in der Frühzeit: Hermann Dörries zum 80. Geburtstag.* Berlin: de Gruyter, 1979.

Aland, Kurt, and Barbara Aland. *The Text of the New Testament: An Introduction to the Critical Editions and to the Theory and Practice of Modern Textual Criticism.* Translated by Erroll F. Rhodes. 2nd ed. rev. and enl. Grand Rapids: Eerdmans; Leiden: Brill, 1989.

Aland, Kurt, and Siegfried Meurer, eds. *Wissenschaft und Kirche: Festschrift für Eduard Lohse.* Bielefeld: Luther-Verlag, 1989.

Albani, Matthias. *Der eine Gott und die himmlischen Heerscharen: Zur Begründung des Monotheismus bei Deuterojesaja im Horizont der Astralisierung des Gottesverständnisses im Alten Orient.* ABG 1. Leipzig: Evangelische Verlagsanstalt, 2000.

Alexander, Loveday. "Acts and Ancient Intellectual Biography." Pages 31–63 in B. Winter and Clarke, *The Book of Acts in Its Ancient Literary Setting.*

———. "Paul and the Hellenistic Schools: The Evidence of Galen." Pages 60–83 in

Engberg-Pedersen, *Paul in His Hellenistic Context.*

———. *The Preface to Luke's Gospel: Literary Convention and Social Context in Luke 1.1–4 and Acts 1.1.* SNTSMS 78. Cambridge: Cambridge University Press, 1993.

Alföldy, Géza. "Die Inschriften des Jüngeren Plinius und seine Mission in der Provinz Pontus et Bithyniae." *Acta Antiqua Academiae Scientiarum Hungaricae* 39 (1999): 21–44.

———. *Römische Sozialgeschichte.* 4th ed. Stuttgart: Steiner, 2011.

———. *The Social History of Rome.* Translated by David Braund and Frank Pollock. Ancient Society and History. Baltimore: Johns Hopkins University Press, 1988.

Alkier, Stefan. *Urchristentum: Zur Geschichte und Theologie einer exegetischen Disziplin.* BHT 82. Tübingen: Mohr Siebeck, 1993.

———. *Wunder und Wirklichkeit in den Briefen des Apostels Paulus: Ein Beitrag zu einem Wunderverständnis jenseits von Entmythologisierung und Rehistorisierung.* WUNT 134. Tübingen: Mohr Siebeck, 2001.

Alkier, Stefan, and Hartmut Leppin, eds. *Juden—Heiden—Christen? Religiöse Inklusionen und Exklusionen im Römischen Kleinasien bis Decius.* WUNT 400. Tübingen: Mohr Siebeck, 2017.

Alkier, Stefan, and Michael Rydryck, eds. *Paulus—das Kapital eines Reisenden: Die Apostelgeschichte als sozialhistorische Quelle.* SBS 241. Stuttgart: Katholisches Bibelwerk, 2017.

Alkier, Stefan, and Annette Weissenrieder, eds. *Miracles Revisited: New Testament Miracle Stories and Their Concepts of Reality.* SBIR 2. Berlin: de Gruyter, 2013.

Alikin, Valeriy A. *The Earliest History of the Christian Gathering: Origin, Development and Content of the Christian*

Gathering in the First to Third Centuries. VCSup 102. Leiden: Brill, 2010.

Althaus, Paul. *Die Wahrheit des christlichen Osterglaubens: Einspruch gegen Emanuel Hirsch.* Gütersloh: Bertelsmann, 1940.

Ameling, Walter. "Die jüdischen Gemeinden im antiken Kleinasien." Pages 29–55 in Jütte and Kustermann, *Jüdische Gemeinden und Organisationsformen.*

Amir, Yehoshua. *Studien zum antiken Judentum.* Frankfurt: Lang, 1985.

André, Jean-Marie. *Griechische Feste, Römische Spiele: Die Freizeitkultur der Antike.* Leipzig: Reclam, 2002.

Andresen, Carl, and Günter Klein, eds. *Theologia Crucis, Signum Crucis: Festschrift für Erich Dinkler zum 70. Geburtstag.* Tübingen: Mohr Siebeck, 1979.

Arnal, William. "The Q Document." Pages 119–54 in Jackson-McCabe, *Jewish Christianity Reconsidered.*

Arzt-Grabner, Peter. "Gott als verlässlicher Käufer: Einige Papyrologische Anmerkungen und bibeltheologische Schlussfolgerungen zum Gottesbild der Paulusbriefe." *NTS* 57 (2011): 392–414.

———. "Neues zu Paulus aus den Papyri des römischen Alltags." *EC* 1 (2010): 131–57.

———. *2. Korinther.* PKNT 4. Göttingen: Vandenhoeck & Ruprecht, 2014.

Ascough, Richard S. *What Are They Saying about the Formation of Pauline Churches?* New York: Paulist Press, 1998.

Assmann, Jan, and Guy G. Stroumsa. *Transformation of the Inner Self in Ancient Religions.* SHR 83. Leiden: Brill, 1999.

Auffarth, Christoph. "Herrscherkult und Christuskult." Pages 283–317 in Cancik and Hitzl, *Die Praxis der Herrscherverehrung in Rom und seinen Provinzen.*

Auffarth, Christoph, and Jörg Rüpke, eds. Ἐπιτομὴ τῆς οἰκουμένης: *Studien zur römischen Religion in Antike und Neuzeit;*

Für Hubert Cancik und Hildegard Cancik-Lindemaier. Stuttgart: Steiner, 2002.

Aune, David E. *The New Testament in Its Literary Environment.* LEC 8. Philadelphia: Westminster, 1987.

———. *Prophecy in Early Christianity and the Ancient Mediterranean World.* Grand Rapids: Eerdmans, 1983.

Avemarie, Friedrich. "Die jüdischen Wurzeln des Aposteldekrets: Lösbare und ungelöste Probleme." Pages 5–32 in Öhler, *Aposteldekret und antikes Vereinswesen.*

———. *Die Tauferzählungen der Apostelgeschichte.* WUNT 139. Tübingen: Mohr Siebeck, 2002.

———. "Die Werke des Gesetzes im Spiegel des Jakobusbriefes." *ZTK* 98 (2001): 282–309.

Avemarie, Friedrich, and Hermann Lichtenberger, eds. *Auferstehung.* WUNT 135. Tübingen: Mohr Siebeck, 2001.

Ayuch, Daniel A. *Sozialgerechtes Handeln als Ausdruck einer eschatologischen Vision: Vom Zusammenhang von Offenbarungswissen und Sozialethik in den lukanischen Schlüsselreden.* MTA 54. Altenberge: Oros, 1998.

Baarlink, Heinrich. *Die Eschatologie der synoptischen Evangelien.* BWANT 120. Stuttgart: Kohlhammer, 1986.

Backhaus, Knut. "Entgrenzte Himmelsherrschaft: Zur Entdeckung der paganen Welt im Matthäusevangelium." Pages 75–103 in Kampling, *"Dies ist das Buch. . . ."*

———. *Der Hebräerbrief.* RNT. Regensburg: Pustet, 2009.

———. "Der Hebräerbrief und die Paulus-Schule." *BZ* 37 (1993): 183–208.

———. *Die "Jüngerkreise" des Täufers Johannes: Eine Studie zu den religionsgeschichtlichen Ursprüngen des Christentums.* PaThSt 19. Paderborn: Schöningh, 1991.

———. "Lukas der Maler: Die Apostelgeschichte als intentionale Geschichte der christlichen Erstepoche." Pages 30–66 in Backhaus and Häfner, *Historiographie und fiktionales Erzählen.*

———. "'Mitteilhaber des Evangeliums' (1 Kor 9,23): Zur christologischen Grundlegung einer 'Paulus-Schule' bei Paulus." Pages 44–71 in Scholtissek, *Christologie in der Paulus-Schule.*

———. *Der neue Bund und das Werden der Kirche.* NTA 31. Münster: 1996.

Backhaus, Knut, and Gerd Häfner, eds. *Historiographie und fiktionales Erzählen.* BTS 86. Neukirchen-Vluyn: Neukirchener Verlag. 2007.

Baeck, Leo. *The Essence of Judaism.* Translated by Victor Grubwieser. Revised and edited by Irving Howe. New York: Schocken Books, 1961. Original edition, 1948.

Bagnall, Roger S. *Everyday Writing in the Graeco-Roman East.* Berkeley: University of California Press, 2011.

Baird, William. "'One against the Other': Intra-Church Conflict in 1 Corinthians." Pages 116–36 in Fortna and Gaventa, *Conversation Continues.*

Balch, David L., and Annette Weissenrieder, eds. *Contested Spaces: Houses and Temples in Roman Antiquity and the New Testament.* WUNT 285. Tübingen: Mohr Siebeck, 2012.

Ballhorn, Geeske. "Die Miletrede—ein Literaturbericht." Pages 37–47 in Horn, *Das Ende des Paulus.*

Balode, Dace. *Gottesdienst in Korinth.* GTF 21. Frankfurt am Main: Lang, 2011.

Barclay, John M. G. "Die Diaspora in der Kyrenaika, in Antiochia, in Babylon, in Kleinasien und an der Schwarzmeerküste, in Rom." Pages 202–14 in Erlemann and Noethlichs, *Prolegomena, Quellen, Geschichte.*

———. *Jews in the Mediterranean Diaspora: From Alexander to Trajan (323 BCE—117 CE).* Berkeley: University of California Press; Edinburgh: T&T Clark, 1996.

———. "Mirror-Reading a Polemical Letter: Galatians as a Test Case." *JSNT* 31 (1987): 73–93.

———. *Obeying the Truth: A Study of Paul's Ethics in Galatians.* Edited by John Riches. STNW. Edinburgh: T&T Clark, 1988.

Bardy, Gustave. *Menschen werden Christen: Das Drama der Bekehrung in den ersten Jahrhunderten.* Edited by Josef Blank. Freiburg: Herder, 1988. Original French edition, 1949.

Barnard, Leslie William. *St. Justin Martyr: The First and Second Apologies.* ACW 56. New York: Paulist Press, 1997.

Barrett, Charles Kingsley. *Essays on John.* Philadelphia: Westminster, 1982.

———. *The Gospel according to St. John: An Introduction with Commentary and Notes on the Greek Text.* 2nd ed. Philadelphia: Westminster, 1978.

———. "Jews and Judaizers in the Epistles of Ignatius." Pages 133–58 in Barrett, *Essays on John.*

———. *The New Testament Background: Selected Documents.* Harper Torchbooks. New York: Harper & Row, 1961.

Barrett, Charles Kingsley, and Claus-Jürgen Thornton, eds. *Texte zur Umwelt des Neuen Testaments.* Tübingen: Mohr Siebeck, 1991.

Barth, Gerhard. "Das Gesetzesverständnis des Evangelisten Matthäus." Pages 149–54 in Bornkamm, Barth, and Held, *Überlieferung und Auslegung.*

———. *Neutestamentliche Versuche und Beobachtungen.* Wechsel-Wirkungen 4. Waltrop: Spenner, 1996.

———. "Pistis in hellenistischer Religiosität." Pages 169–94 in Barth,

Neutestamentliche Versuche und Beobachtungen.

———. *Die Taufe in frühchristlicher Zeit.* BTS 4. Neukirchen-Vluyn: Neukirchener Verlag, 1981.

———. *Der Tod Jesu Christi im Verständnis des Neuen Testaments.* Neukirchen-Vluyn: Neukirchener Verlag, 1992.

Barthes, Roland. *Mythen des Alltags.* 23rd ed. Frankfurt: Suhrkamp, 2003. Original edition, 1957.

Bauckham, Richard. "The Beloved Disciple as Ideal Author." *JSNT* 49 (March 1993): 21–44.

———. "For Whom Were Gospels Written?" Pages 9–48 in Bauckham, *Gospels for All Christians.*

———, ed. *The Gospels for All Christians: Rethinking the Gospel Audiences.* Grand Rapids: Eerdmans, 1998.

———. "Jesus and the Jerusalem Community." Pages 55–95 in Skarsaune and Hvalvik, *Jewish Believers in Jesus.*

———. *Jude, 2 Peter.* WBC 50. Waco: Word, 1983.

Bauer, Johannes B. "Der erste Petrusbrief und die Verfolgung der Christen unter Domitian." Pages 513–27 in Schnackenburg, *Die Kirche des Anfangs.*

Bauer, Thomas J. *Paulus und die kaiserzeitliche Epistolographie.* WUNT 276. Tübingen: Mohr Siebeck, 2011.

Bauer, Walter. *Orthodoxy and Heresy in Earliest Christianity.* Revised and augmented by Robert A. Kraft and Gerhard Krodel. Philadelphia: Fortress, 1971.

Bauer, Walter, and Henning Paulsen. *Die Briefe des Ignatius von Antiochia und der Brief des Polykarp von Smyrna.* Tübingen: Mohr, 1985.

Baum, Armin D. "'Babylon' als Ortsnamenmetapher in 1 Petr 5,13 auf dem Hintergrund der antiken Literatur und im Kontext des Briefes." Pages 180–220

in Heid and Haehling, *Petrus und Paulus in Rom.*

———. *Der mündliche Faktor und seine Bedeutung für die synoptische Frage.* TANZ 49. Tübingen: Francke, 2008.

———. *Pseudepigraphie und literarische Fälschung im frühen Christentum.* WUNT 2/138. Tübingen: Mohr Siebeck, 2001.

Baum, Armin D., Detlef Häusser, and Emmanuel L. Rehfeld. *Der jüdische Messias Jesus und sein jüdischer Apostel Paulus.* WUNT 2/425. Tübingen: Mohr Siebeck, 2016.

Baumgarten, Roland. *Heiliges Wort und Heilige Schrift bei den Griechen: Hieroi Logoi und verwandte Erscheinungen.* ScriptOralia. Tübingen: Narr, 1998.

Baur, Ferdinand Christian. *Paul the Apostle of Jesus Christ: His Life and Works, His Epistles and Teachings.* Peabody, MA: Hendrickson, 2003. Original German edition, 1845.

Bauspiess, Martin. "'Doketismus' als theologisches Problem: Zur Bultmann-Käsemann-Kontroverse um den Wirklichkeitsbezug der johanneischen Theologie." Pages 185–219 in Bauspiess, Landmesser, and Portenhauser, *Theologie und Wirklichkeit.*

Bauspiess, Martin, Christof Landmesser, and Friederike Portenhauser, eds. *Theologie und Wirklichkeit: Diskussionen der Bultmann-Schule.* TI 12. Neukirchen-Vluyn: Neukirchener Verlagsgesellschaft, 2011.

Bechtold, Christian. *Gott und Gestirn als Präsenzformen des toten Kaisers: Apotheose und Katasterismos in der politischen Kommunikation der römischen Kaiserzeit und ihre Anknüpfungspunkte im Hellenismus.* SPK 9. Göttingen: Vandenhoeck & Ruprecht, 2011.

Becker, Eve-Marie, ed. *Die antike Historiographie und die Anfänge der christlichen Geschichtsschreibung.* BZNW 129. Berlin: de Gruyter, 2005.

———. "Form und Gattung der paulinischen Briefe." Pages 141–49 in Horn, *Paulus Handbuch.*

———. "Der jüdisch-römische Krieg (66–70 n. Chr.) und das Markus-Evangelium." Pages 213–36 in E. Becker, *Die antike Historiographie.*

———. *Das Markus-Evangelium im Rahmen antiker Historiographie.* WUNT 194. Tübingen: Mohr Siebeck, 2006.

Becker, Eve-Marie, Troels Engberg-Pedersen, and Mogens Müller, eds. *Mark and Paul: Comparative Essays.* Vol. 2, *For and against Pauline Influence on Mark.* BZNW 199. Berlin: de Gruyter, 2017.

Becker, Eve-Marie, and Peter Pilhofer, eds. *Biographie und Persönlichkeit des Paulus.* WUNT 187. Tübingen: Mohr Siebeck, 2005.

Becker, Jürgen, ed. *Die Anfänge des Christentums: Alte Welt und neue Hoffnung.* Stuttgart: Kohlhammer, 1987.

———. *Die Auferstehung Jesu Christi nach dem Neuen Testament: Ostererfahrung und Osterverständnis im Urchristentum.* Tübingen: Mohr Siebeck, 2007.

———. *Das Evangelium nach Johannes: 1, Kapitel 1–10.* 3rd ed. ÖTK 4/1–2. Gütersloh: Mohn, 1991.

———. *Johanneisches Christentum: Seine Geschichte und Theologie im Überblick.* Tübingen: Mohr Siebeck, 2004.

———. *Maria: Mutter Jesu und erwählte Jungfrau.* BG 4. Leipzig: Evangelische Verlagsanstalt, 2001.

———. *Mündliche und schriftliche Autorität im frühen Christentum.* Tübingen: Mohr Siebeck, 2012.

———. *Paul: Apostle to the Gentiles.* Translated by O. C. Dean Jr. Louisville: Westminster/John Knox, 1993.

———. *Das Urchristentum als gegliederte Epoche.* Stuttgart: Verlag Katholisches Bibelwerk, 1993.

———. "Das Verhältnis des johanneischen Kreises zum Paulinismus." Pages 473–95 in *Paulus und Johannes.* Edited by Dieter Sänger and Ulrich Mell. WUNT 198. Tübingen: Mohr Siebeck, 2006.

Beckheuer, Burkhard. *Paulus und Jerusalem: Kollekte und Mission im paulinischen Denken des Heidenapostels.* EURHS 23/611. Frankfurt: Lang, 1997.

Belezos, Constantine J., ed. *Saint Paul and Corinth: 1950 Years since the Writing of the Epistles to the Corinthians; Exegesis, Theology, History of Interpretation, Philology, Philosophy, St. Paul's Time.* 2 vols. Athens: Psichogios, 2009.

Belle, Gilbert Van. *The Signs Source in the Fourth Gospel: Historical Survey and Critical Evaluation of the Semeia Hypothesis.* BETL 116. Louvain: Leuven University Press, 1994.

Bellen, Heinz. *Grundzüge der römischen Geschichte.* Vol. 2, *Die Kaiserzeit von Augustus bis Diocletian.* Darmstadt: Wissenschaftliche Buchgesellschaft, 1998.

Ben-David, Arye. *Talmudische Ökonomie: Die Wirtschaft des jüdischen Palästina zur Zeit der Mischna und des Talmud.* Hildesheim: Olms, 1974.

Bendemann, Reinhard von. "Die Auferstehung von den Toten als 'Basic Story.'" *GuL* 15 (2000): 148–62.

Bendemann, Reinhard von, and Markus Tiwald, eds. *Das frühe Christentum und die Stadt.* BWANT 198. Stuttgart: Kohlhammer, 2012.

———. "Das frühe Christentum und die Stadt: Einleitung und Grundlegung." Pages 9–42 in Bendemann and Tiwald, *Das frühe Christentum und die Stadt.*

Berger, Klaus. *Formgeschichte des Neuen Testaments.* Heidelberg: Quelle & Meyer, 1984.

———. *Die Gesetzesauslegung Jesu.* WMANT 40. Neukirchen-Vluyn: Neukirchener Verlag, 1972.

———. "Die impliziten Gegner: Zur Me-
thode des Erschließens von 'Gegnern'
in neutestamentlichen Texten." Pages
373–400 in Lührmann and G. Strecker,
Kirche.

———. "Streit um Gottes Vorsehung: Zur
Position der Gegner im 2. Petrusbrief."
Pages 121–35 in van Henten, *Tradition
and Re-interpretation in Jewish and
Early Christian Literature.*

———. *Theologiegeschichte des Urchristentums: Theologie des Neuen Testaments.*
Tübingen: Francke, 1994.

Berger, Klaus, and Carsten Colpe. *Religionsgeschichtliches Textbuch zum Neuen
Testament.* TzNT 1. Göttingen: Vandenhoeck & Ruprecht, 1987.

Berges, Ulrich, and Rudolf Hoppe. *Arm und
Reich.* Die Neue Echter-Bibel. Themen
10. Würzburg: Echter, 2009.

Bergmeier, Roland. *Glaube als Gabe nach
Johannes: Religions- und theologiege-
schichtliche Studien zum prädestinatiani-
schen Dualismus im vierten Evangelium.*
BWANT 112. Stuttgart: Kohlhammer,
1980.

Berner, Ulrich. "Religio und Superstitio."
Pages 45–64 in Sundermeier, *Den Fremden wahrnehmen.*

Bernett, Monika. *Der Kaiserkult in Judäa
unter den Herodiern und Römern.*
WUNT 203. Tübingen: Mohr Siebeck,
2007.

Betz, Hans Dieter. *Galatians: A Commentary on Paul's Letter to the Churches in
Galatia.* Philadelphia: Fortress, 1979.

———. *The "Mithras Liturgy": Text,
Translation, and Commentary.* STAC 18.
Tübingen: Mohr Siebeck, 2005.

———. *2 Corinthians 8 and 9: A Commentary on Two Administrative Letters of
the Apostle Paul.* Philadelphia: Fortress,
1985.

———. *The Sermon on the Mount: A Commentary on the Sermon on the Mount,*
*Including the Sermon on the Plain (Mat-
thew 5:3–7:27 and Luke 6:20–49).* Her-
meneia. Minneapolis: Fortress, 1995.

Betz, Hans Dieter, Don S. Browning, Bernd
Janowski, and Eberhard Jüngel, eds.
*Religion in Geschichte und Gegenwart:
Handwörterbuch für Theologie und
Religionswissenschaft.* 8 vols. Tübingen:
Mohr Siebeck, 2000.

Betz, Otto. "Rechtfertigung in Qumran."
Pages 17–36 in Friedrich, Stuhlmacher,
and Pöhlmann, *Rechtfertigung.*

Beyschlag, Karlman. *Simon Magus und die
christliche Gnosis.* WUNT 16. Tübingen:
Mohr Siebeck, 1974.

Bichler, Reinhold. "'Hellenismus': Geschichte und Problematik eines Epochen-
begriffs.* Darmstadt: Wissenschaftliche
Buchgesellschaft, 1983.

Bickermann, Elias. "Die römische Kaiserapotheose." *ARW* 27 (1929): 1–34.

———. *Die römische Kaiserapotheose.*
Leipzig: Teubner, 1929.

Bieringer, Reimund. "Die Gegner des Paulus
im 2 Korintherbrief." Pages 181–221 in
Bieringer and Lambrecht, *Studies on
2 Corinthians.*

Bieringer, Reimund, and Jan Lambrecht,
eds. *Studies on 2 Corinthians.* BETL 112.
Louvain: Leuven University Press, 1994.

Bieringer, Reimund, Didier Pollefeyt, and
Frederique Vandecasteele-Vanneuville,
eds. *Anti-Judaism and the Fourth Gospel.*
Louisville: Westminster John Knox; Assen,
the Netherlands: Royal Van Gorcum, 2001.

Bietenhard, Hans. "Die Dekapolis von Pompejus bis Trajan." *ZDPV* 79 (1963): 24–58.

Billerbeck, Margarethe, ed. *Epiktet: Vom
Kynismus.* Leiden: Brill, 1978.

———. *Der Kyniker Demetrius: Ein Beitrag
zur Geschichte der frühkaiserzeitlichen
Popularphilosophie.* PhAnt 36. Leiden:
Brill, 1979.

Bird, Michael F. "Mark: Interpreter of Peter
and Disciple of Paul." Pages 30–61 in

Paul and the Gospels: Christologies, Conflicts, and Convergences. Edited by Michael F. Bird and Joel Willitts. LNTS 411. New York: Bloomsbury, 2011.

Birt, Theodor. *Das antike Buchwesen in seinem Verhältnis zur Literatur: Mit Beitrag zur Textgeschichte des Theokrit, Catull, Properz und anderer Autoren.* Berlin: Hertz, 1882. Repr., Aalen: Scientia, 1974.

Blaschke, Andreas. *Beschneidung: Zeugnisse der Bibel und verwandte Texte.* TANZ 28. Tübingen: Francke, 1998.

Blass, Friedrich, Albert Debrunner, and Friedrich Rehkopf. *Grammatik des neutestamentlichen Griechisch.* 16th ed. Göttingen: Vandenhoeck & Ruprecht, 1984.

Blatz, Beate. "Das koptische Thomasevangelium." Vol. 1, pages 92–113 in Schneemelcher, *Neutestamentliche Apokryphen.*

Blatz, Heinz. *Die Semantik der Macht: Eine zeit- und religionsgeschichtliche Studie zu den markinischen Wundererzählungen.* NTA 59. Münster: Aschendorff, 2016.

Bleicken, Jochen. *Geschichte der römischen Republik.* Munich: Oldenbourg, 2004.

———. *Verfassungs- und Sozialgeschichte des römischen Kaiserreiches.* 2 vols. UTB 839. 3rd ed. Paderborn: Schöningh, 1989–94.

Blinzler, Josef. *Johannes und die Synoptiker.* SBS 5. Stuttgart: 1965.

Blomberg, Craig L. *Neither Poverty nor Riches: A Biblical Theology of Material Possessions.* Downers Grove, IL: InterVarsity; Leicester, UK: Apollos; Grand Rapids: Eerdmans, 1999.

Böcher, Otto. "Hellenistisches in der Apokalypse des Johannes." Pages 473–92 in Cancik, Lichtenberger, and P. Schäfer, *Geschichte, Tradition, Reflexion.*

———. "Mythos und Rationalität." Pages 163–71 in Hans Schmid, *Mythos und Rationalität.*

Bock, Darrell L. *Blasphemy and Exaltation in Judaism and the Final Examination of Jesus.* WUNT 2/106. Tübingen: Mohr Siebeck, 1998.

Böhlig, Alexander, ed. *Der Manichäismus.* Vol. 3 of *Die Gnosis.* Die Bibliothek der Alten Welt: Reihe Antike und Christentum. Zurich: Artemis, 1980.

———. "Neue Initiativen zur Erschließung der koptisch-manichäischen Bibliothek von Medinet Madi." *ZNW* 80 (1989): 240–60.

Böhlig, Hans. *Die Geisteskultur von Tarsos im augusteischen Zeitalter mit Berücksichtigung der paulinischen Schriften.* FRLANT 19. Göttingen: Vandenhoeck & Ruprecht, 1913.

Bond, Helen K. "Dating the Death of Jesus: Memory and the Religious Imagination." *NTS* 59 (2013): 461–75.

Boring, M. Eugene. *The Continuing Voice of Jesus.* Louisville: Westminster John Knox, 1991.

———. *I and II Thessalonians: A Commentary.* NTL. Louisville: Westminster John Knox, 2015.

———. *Mark: A Commentary.* NTL. Louisville: Westminster John Knox, 2006.

Borkowski, Josef-Friedrich, ed. *Socratis quae feruntur Epistolae: Edition, Übersetzung, Kommentar.* BAK 94. Stuttgart; Leipzig: Teubner, 1997.

Bormann, Lukas. *Der Brief des Paulus an die Kolosser.* THK 10.1. Leipzig: Evangelische Verlagsanstalt, 2012.

———. *Philippi: Stadt und Christengemeinde zur Zeit des Paulus.* NovTSup 78. Leiden: Brill, 1995.

Bornhäuser, Karl. *Das Johannesevangelium: Eine Missionsschrift für Israel.* BFCT 2/15. Gütersloh: Bertelsmann, 1928.

Bornkamm, Günther. "Der Auferstandene und der Irdische: Mt 28,16–20." Pages 171–91 in Dinkler, *Zeit und Geschichte* or pages 289–310 in Bornkamm, Barth, and Held, *Überlieferung und Auslegung*.

———. *Das Ende des Gesetzes: Paulusstudien*. 3rd ed. BEvT 16. Munich: Kaiser, 1961.

———. "Die Häresie des Kolosserbriefes." Pages 139–56 in Bornkamm, *Das Ende des Gesetzes*.

Bornkamm, Günther, Gerhard Barth, and Heinz Joachim Held, eds. *Tradition and Interpretation in Matthew*. Translated by Percy Scott. NTL. Philadelphia: Westminster; London: SCM, 1963.

———, eds. *Überlieferung und Auslegung im Matthäusevangelium*. Neukirchen-Vluyn: Neukirchener Verlag, 1960.

Bösen, Willibald. *Galiläa als Lebensraum und Wirkungsfeld Jesu*. Freiburg im Breisgau: Herder, 1985.

———. *Der letzte Tag des Jesus von Nazaret: Was wirklich geschah*. Freiburg im Breisgau: Herder, 1994.

Botermann, Helga. *Das Judenedikt des Kaisers Claudius*. Hermes 71. Stuttgart: Steiner, 1996.

Böttrich, Christfried. *Petrus: Fischer, Fels und Funktionär*. BG 2. Leipzig: Evangelische Verlagsanstalt, 2001.

Bousset, Wilhelm. *Kyrios Christos: A History of the Belief in Christ from the Beginnings of Christianity to Irenaeus*. Translated by John E. Steely. Nashville, Abingdon, 1970.

———. *Die Offenbarung Johannis*. KEK 16. Göttingen: Vandenhoeck & Ruprecht, 1966 (= 1906).

Bowers, W. P. "Jewish Communities in Spain." *JTS* 26 (1975): 395–402.

Boyarin, Daniel. *Abgrenzungen: Die Aufspaltung des Judäo-Christentums*. ANTZ 10. Berlin: Institut Kirche und Judentum, 2009.

———. "Als Christen noch Juden waren: Überlegungen zu den jüdischchristlichen Ursprüngen." *Kul* 16 (2001): 112–29.

Brakke, David. *The Gnostics: Myth, Ritual, and Diversity in Early Christianity*. Cambridge, MA: Harvard University Press, 2010.

Brandenburg, Hugo. "Die Aussagen der Schriftquellen und der archäologischen Zeugnisse zum Kult der Apostelfürsten in Rom." Pages 351–82 in Heid and Haehling, *Petrus und Paulus in Rom*.

Branham, R. Bracht, and Marie-Odile Goulet-Cazé, eds. *The Cynics: The Cynic Movement in Antiquity and Its Legacy*. Berkeley: University of California Press, 1996.

Brankaer, Johanna. *Die Gnosis: Texte und Kommentar*. Marixwissen. Wiesbaden: Marixverlag, 2010.

Braumann, Georg, ed. *Das Lukas-Evangelium: Die redaktions- und kompositionsgeschichtliche Forschung*. WdF 280. Darmstadt: Wissenschaftliche Buchgesellschaft, 1974.

Braun, Heike. *Geschichte des Gottesvolkes und christliche Identität*. WUNT 2/279. Tübingen: Mohr Siebeck, 2010.

Bremmer, Jan N. *Götter, Mythen und Heiligtümer im antiken Griechenland*. Darmstadt: Wissenschaftliche Buchgesellschaft, 1996.

———. *The Rise of Christianity through the Eyes of Gibbon, Harnack and Rodney Stark*. Groningen: University of Groningen, 2010.

Breytenbach, Cilliers. "Das Markusevangelium als episodische Erzählung." Pages 137–69 in F. Hahn, *Erzähler des Evangeliums*.

———. *Paulus und Barnabas in der Provinz Galatien: Studien zu Apostelgeschichte 13f.; 16,6; 18,23 und den Adressaten des Galaterbriefes*. AGJU 38. Leiden: Brill, 1996.

———. *Versöhnung: Eine Studie zur paulinischen Soteriologie.* WMANT 60. Neukirchen-Vluyn: Neukirchener Verlag, 1989.

———. "Versöhnung, Stellvertretung und Sühne." *NTS* 39 (1993): 59–79.

Breytenbach, Cilliers, and Henning Paulsen, eds. *Anfänge der Christologie: Festschrift für Ferdinand Hahn zum 65. Geburtstag.* Göttingen: Vandenhoeck & Ruprecht, 1991.

Breytenbach, Cilliers, and Jens Schröter, eds. *Die Apostelgeschichte und die hellenistische Geschichtsschreibung: Festschrift für Eckhard Plümacher zu seinem 65. Geburtstag.* AJEC 57. Leiden: Brill, 2004.

Bringmann, Klaus. *Augustus.* Gestalten der Antike. Darmstadt: Wissenschaftliche Buchgesellschaft, 2012.

Brocke, Christoph vom. *Griechenland.* Leipzig: Evangelische Verlagsanstalt, 2007.

———. "Thessaloniki." Vol. 2, pages 171–74 in Erlemann et al., *Neues Testament und antike Kultur.*

———. *Thessaloniki: Stadt des Kassander und Gemeinde des Paulus.* WUNT 2/125. Tübingen: Mohr Siebeck, 2001.

Brockhaus, Ulrich. *Charisma und Amt: Die paulinische Charismenlehre auf dem Hintergrund der frühchristlichen Gemeindefunktionen.* Wuppertal: Theologischer Verlag Brockhaus, 1972.

Brown, Colin, and Lothar Coenen, eds. *The New International Dictionary of New Testament Theology.* Grand Rapids: Zondervan, 1986.

Brox, Norbert. "'Doketismus—eine Problemanzeige.'" *ZKG* 95 (1984): 301–14.

———. *Der erste Petrusbrief.* EKKNT 21. Neukirchen-Vluyn: Neukirchener Verlag, 1979.

———. *Der erste Petrusbrief.* 2nd ed. EKKNT 21. Neukirchen-Vluyn: Neukirchener Verlag, 1986.

———. *Falsche Verfasserangaben: Zur Erklärung der frühchristlichen Pseudepigraphie.* SBS 79. Stuttgart: KBW, 1975.

Brox, Norbert, and Karl Kertelge, eds. *Mission im Neuen Testament.* QD 93. Freiburg: Herder, 1982.

Bruce, Frederick F. *Jesus and Christian Origins outside the New Testament.* Grand Rapids: Eerdmans, 1974.

Bultmann, Rudolf, *The Gospel of John: A Commentary.* Translated by G. R. Beasley-Murray. Philadelphia: Westminster, 1971.

———. *The History of the Synoptic Tradition.* Translated by John Marsh. New York: Harper & Row, 1963.

———. *Theology of the New Testament.* Translated by Kendrick Grobel. 2 vols. New York: Scribner, 1951–55.

Burchard, Christoph. "Das doppelte Liebesgebot in der frühchristlichen Überlieferung." Pages 3–26 in Burchard and Sänger, *Studien zur Theologie, Sprache und Umwelt.*

———. *Der dreizehnte Zeuge: Traditions- und kompositionsgeschichtliche Untersuchungen zu Lukas' Darstellung der Frühzeit des Paulus.* Göttingen: Vandenhoeck & Ruprecht, 1970.

———. *Der Jakobusbrief.* HNT 15.1. Tübingen: Mohr Siebeck, 2000.

———. "Paulus in der Apostelgeschichte." Pages 126–47 in Burchard and Sänger, *Studien zur Theologie, Sprache und Umwelt.*

Burchard, Christoph, and Dieter Sänger, eds. *Studien zur Theologie, Sprache und Umwelt des Neuen Testaments.* WUNT 107. Tübingen: Mohr Siebeck, 1998 (= 1970).

Burfeind, Carsten. "Paulus muß nach Rom: Zur politischen Dimension der Apostelgeschichte." *NTS* 46 (2000): 75–91.

Burkert, Walter. *Ancient Mystery Cults.* Carl Newell Jackson lectures. Cambridge, MA: Harvard University Press, 1987.

———. *Greek Religion*. Translated by John Raffan. Cambridge, MA: Harvard University Press, 1985.

———. *Griechische Religion der archaischen und klassischen Epoche*. RM 15. Stuttgart: Kohlhammer, 2011.

Burridge, Richard A. *What Are the Gospels? A Comparison with Graeco-Roman Biography*. 2nd ed. Grand Rapids: Eerdmans, 2004.

Bussmann, Claus. *Themen der paulinischen Missionspredigt auf dem Hintergrund der spätjüdisch-hellenistischen Missionsliteratur*. EURHS 23/3. Bern; Frankfurt: Lang, 1971.

Campbell, R. Alastair. *The Elders: Seniority within Earliest Christianity*. Edinburgh: T&T Clark, 1994.

Campenhausen, Hans von. *Der Ablauf der Osterereignisse und das leere Grab*. 4th ed. Sitzungsberichte der Heidelberger Akademie der Wissenschaften: Philosophisch-historische Klasse. Heidelberg: Winter, 1977.

———. *Ecclesiastical Authority and Spiritual Power in the Church of the First Three Centuries*. Translated by J. A. Baker. Peabody, MA: Hendrickson, 1997.

———. *The Events of Easter and the Empty Tomb*. Translated by A. V. Littledale. Philadelphia: Fortress, 1968.

———. *The Formation of the Christian Bible*. Translated by J. A. Baker. Philadelphia: Fortress, 1972.

Cancik, Hubert, and Konrad Hitzl, eds. *Die Praxis der Herrscherverehrung in Rom und seinen Provinzen*. Tübingen: Mohr Siebeck, 2003.

Cancik, Hubert, Hermann Lichtenberger, and Peter Schäfer, eds. *Geschichte, Tradition, Reflexion: Festschrift für Martin Hengel zum 70. Geburtstag*. 3 vols. Tübingen: Mohr Siebeck, 1996.

Carlson, Stephen C. *The Gospel Hoax: Morton Smith's Invention of Secret Mark*. Waco: Baylor University Press, 2005.

Cassirer, Ernst. *An Essay on Man: An Introduction to a Philosophy of Human Culture*. New Haven: Yale University Press, 1944.

———. *Versuch über den Menschen: Einführung in eine Philosophie der Kultur*. Hamburg: Meiner, 1996.

Charlesworth, James H. *The Beloved Disciple: Whose Witness Validates the Gospel of John?* Valley Forge, PA: Trinity Press International, 1995.

Christ, Karl. *Geschichte der römischen Kaiserzeit: Von Augustus bis zu Konstantin*. 4th ed. Beck's historische Bibliothek. Munich: Beck, 2002.

———. "Grundfragen der römischen Sozialstruktur." Vol. 3, pages 152–76 in Christ, *Römische Geschichte und Wissenschaftsgeschichte*.

———. *Römische Geschichte und Wissenschaftsgeschichte*. Vol. 1, *Römische Republik und Augusteischer Principat*. Vol. 2, *Geschichte und Geschichtsschreibung der römischen Kaiserzeit*. Vol. 3, *Wissenschaftsgeschichte*. Darmstadt: Wissenschaftliche Buchgesellschaft, 1982–83.

———. "Zur Herrschaftsauffassung und Politik Domitians." Vol. 2, pages 1–27 in Christ, *Römische Geschichte und Wissenschaftsgeschichte*.

Cineira, David Alvarez. *Die Religionspolitik des Kaisers Claudius und die paulinische Mission*. HBS 19. New York: Herder, 1999.

Clarke, Andrew D. "Another Corinthian Erastus Inscription." *TynBul* 42 (1991): 146–51.

Clauss, Manfred. *Alexandria*. 2nd ed. Stuttgart, 2004.

———. *Kaiser und Gott: Herrscherkult im römischen Reich*. Stuttgart: Teubner, 1999.

———. *The Roman Cult of Mithras: The God and His Mysteries*. Translated by Richard Gordon. Edinburgh: Edinburgh University Press, 2000.

Claussen, Carsten. *Versammlung, Gemeinde, Synagoge: Das hellenistisch-jüdische Umfeld der frühchristlichen Gemeinden*. Göttingen: Vandenhoeck & Ruprecht, 2002.

Coenen, Lothar, ed. *Theologisches Begriffslexikon zum Neuen Testament*. 2 vols. Wuppertal: Brockhaus, 1997–2000.

Coggins, Richard J. *Samaritans and Jews: The Origins of Samaritanism Reconsidered*. Atlanta: John Knox, 1975.

Colish, Marcia L. *The Stoic Tradition from Antiquity to the Early Middle Ages*. Vol. 1, *Stoicism in Classical Latin Literature*. Leiden: Brill, 1990.

Collins, Adela Yarbro. *Crisis and Catharsis: The Power of the Apocalypse*. Philadelphia: Westminster, 1984.

———. *Mark: A Commentary*. Herm. Minneapolis: Fortress, 2007.

Collins, Adela Yarbro, and John J. Collins. *King and Messiah as Son of God*. Grand Rapids: Eerdmans, 2008.

Collins, John J. *Jewish Wisdom in the Hellenistic Age*. Louisville: Westminster John Knox, 1997.

———. "The Son of Man in First-Century Judaism." *NTS* 38 (1992): 448–66.

Colpe, Carsten. "Die älteste urchristliche Gemeinde." Pages 59–79 in J. Becker, *Die Anfänge des Christentums*.

———. "Das deutsche Wort 'Judenchristen' und ihm entsprechende historische Sachverhalte." Pages 38–58 in Colpe, *Das Siegel der Propheten*.

———. *Einleitung in die Schriften aus Nag Hammadi*. JThF 16. Münster: Aschendorff, 2011.

———. "Die erste urchristliche Generation." Pages 59–79 in Becker, *Die Anfänge des Christentums*.

———. "Mithra-Verehrung, Mithras-Cult und die Existenz iranischer Mysterien." Vol. 2, pages 378–405 in *Mithraic Studies*. Edited by John R. Hinnels. Manchester: Manchester University Press, 1975.

———. *Das Siegel der Propheten: Historische Beziehungen zwischen antikem Judentum, Judenchristentum, Heidentum und frühem Islam*. Edited by Carsten Colpe. ANTZ 3. Berlin: Institut Kirche und Judentum, 1990.

———. "Vorschläge des Messina-Kongresses von 1966 zur Gnosis-Forschung." Pages 129–32 in *Christentum und Gnosis*. Edited by Walter Eltester. BZNW 37. Berlin: Töpelmann, 1969.

Colpe, Carsten, and Jens Holzhausen, trans. *Das Corpus Hermeticum Deutsch: Übersetzung, Darstellung und Kommentierung in drei Teilen*. CP 7. Stuttgart–Bad Cannstatt: Frommann-Holzboog, 1997.

Conrad, Christoph, and Martina Kessel, eds. *Geschichte schreiben in der Postmoderne: Beiträge zur aktuellen Diskussion*. Stuttgart: Philipp Reclam, 1994.

Conzelmann, Hans. *Acts of the Apostles: A Commentary on the Acts of the Apostles*. Edited by Eldon Jay Epp with Christopher R. Matthews. Translated by James Limburg, A. Thomas Kraabel, and Donald H. Juel. Herm. Philadelphia: Fortress, 1987.

———. *Gentiles, Jews, Christians: Polemics and Apologetics in the Greco-Roman Era*. Minneapolis: Fortress, 1992.

———. *Geschichte des Urchristentums*. Göttingen: Vandenhoeck & Ruprecht, 1978.

———. *Heiden—Juden—Christen*. Tübingen: Mohr, 1981.

———. *History of Primitive Christianity*. Translated by John E. Steely. Göttingen: Vandenhoeck & Ruprecht, 1973.

———. "Paulus und die Weisheit." Pages 177–90 in Conzelmann, *Theologie als Schriftauslegung*.

———. "Die Schule des Paulus." Pages 85–96 in Andresen and G. Klein, *Theologia Crucis*.

———. *Theologie als Schriftauslegung: Aufsätze zum Neuen Testament*. BEvT 65. Munich: Kaiser, 1974.

———. *The Theology of St. Luke*. Translated by Geoffrey Buswell. New York: Harper, 1961.

———. "Was glaubte die frühe Christenheit?" Pages 106–19 in Conzelmann, *Theologie als Schriftauslegung*.

———. "Was von Anfang war." Pages 207–14 in Conzelmann, *Theologie als Schriftauslegung*.

———. "Zur Analyse der Bekenntnisformel 1 Kor 15,3–5." Pages 131–41 in Conzelmann, *Theologie als Schriftauslegung*.

Cook, John G. *Roman Attitudes toward the Christians: From Claudius to Hadrian*. WUNT 261. Tübingen: Mohr Siebeck, 2010.

———. *Roman Crucifixion in the Mediterranean World*. WUNT 327. Tübingen: Mohr Siebeck, 2014.

Corsten, Thomas, and Jürgen Zangenberg. "Ephesos." Vol. 2, pages 147–53 in Erlemann et al., *Neues Testament und antike Kultur*.

Crossan, John Dominic. *The Birth of Christianity: Discovering What Happened in the Years Immediately after the Execution of Jesus*. New York: HarperCollins, 1998.

———. *Der historische Jesus*. Munich: Beck, 1994.

———. *In Parables: The Challenge of the Historical Jesus*. New York: Harper & Row, 1973.

Crossan, John Dominic, and Jonathan L. Reed. *Jesus ausgraben: Zwischen den Steinen—hinter den Texten*. Düsseldorf: Patmos, 2003.

Crüsemann, Frank. *Die Tora: Theologie und Sozialgeschichte des alttestamentlichen Gesetzes*. 4th ed. Gütersloh: Gütersloher Verlagshaus, 2005.

———. *The Torah: Theology and Social History of Old Testament Law*. Minneapolis: Fortress, 1996.

Cullmann, Oscar. *The Christology of the New Testament*. Translated by Shirley C. Guthrie and Charles A. M. Hall. 5th ed. London: SCM, 2009.

———. *Der johanneische Kreis: Sein Platz im Spätjudentum, in der Jüngerschaft Jesu und im Urchristentum: Zum Ursprung des Johannesevangeliums*. Tübingen: Mohr, 1975.

———. *The Johannine Circle*. Translated by John Bowden. Philadelphia: Westminster, 1976. = *The Johannine Circle: Its Place in Judaism, among the Disciples of Jesus and in Early Christianity; A Study in the Origin of the Gospel of John*. NTL. London: SCM, 1976.

Culpepper, R. Alan. *Anatomy of the Fourth Gospel: A Study in Literary Design*. Foundations and Facets. Philadelphia: Fortress, 1983.

———. *The Johannine School: An Evaluation of the Johannine-School Hypothesis Based on an Investigation of the Nature of Ancient Schools*. SBLDS 26. Missoula, MT: Scholars Press, 1975.

———. *John, the Son of Zebedee: The Life of a Legend*. Columbia: University of South Carolina Press, 1994.

Cumont, Franz. *The Oriental Religions in Roman Paganism*. Translated by Grant Showerman. New York: Dover, 1956.

Dahlheim, Werner. *Die Welt zur Zeit Jesu*. Munich: Beck, 2013.

Dalferth, Ingolf U. *Der auferweckte Gekreuzigte*. Tübingen: Mohr, 1994.

Dassmann, Ernst. *Ämter und Dienste in den frühchristlichen Gemeinden*. Here 8. Bonn: Borengässer, 1994.

———. "Hausgemeinde und Bischofsamt." Pages 74–95 in Dassmann, *Ämter* und Dienste in den frühchristlichen Gemeinden.

———. Der Stachel im Fleisch: Paulus in der frühchristlichen Literatur bis Irenäus. Münster: Aschendorff, 1979.

———. "Witwen und Diakonissen." Pages 142–56 in Dassmann, Ämter und Dienste in den frühchristlichen Gemeinden.

Dautzenberg, Gerhard. Urchristliche Prophetie: Ihre Erforschung, ihre Voraussetzungen im Judentum und ihre Struktur im ersten Korintherbrief. BWANT 104. Stuttgart: Kohlhammer, 1975.

Davies, William D., and Dale C. Allison. The Gospel according to Saint Matthew. Vols. 1–3. ICC. Edinburgh: T&T Clark, 1988–97.

Deines, Roland. Die Gerechtigkeit der Tora im Reich des Messias: Mt 5,13–20 als Schlüsseltext der matthäischen Theologie. WUNT 177. Tübingen: Mohr Siebeck, 2004.

———. Jakobus: Im Schatten des Größeren. BG 30. Leipzig: Evangelische Verlagsanstalt, 2017.

Deissmann, Adolf. Light from the Ancient East: The New Testament Illustrated by Recently Discovered Texts of the Graeco-Roman World. Translated by Lionel R. M. Strachan. London: Hodder & Stoughton, 1910.

———. Die neutestamentliche Formel "in Christo Jesu" untersucht. Marburg: Elwert, 1892.

Delling, Gerhard. Die Bewältigung der Diaspora-Situation durch das hellenistische Judentum. Berlin: Evangelische Verlagsanstalt; Göttingen: Vandenhoeck & Ruprecht, 1987.

———. Die Taufe im Neuen Testament. Berlin: Evangelische Verlagsanstalt, 1963.

———. Die Zueignung des Heils in der Taufe: Eine Untersuchung zum neutestamentlichen "Taufen auf den Namen." Berlin: Evangelische Verlagsanstalt, 1961.

Destro, Adriana, and Mauro Pesce. From Jesus to His First Followers: Continuity and Discontinuity; Anthropological and Historical Perspectives. BIS 152. Leiden: Brill, 2017.

Dettinger, Dorothee. Neues Leben in der alten Welt: Der Beitrag frühchristlicher Schriften des späten ersten Jahrhunderts zum Diskurs über familiäre Strukturen in der griechisch-römischen Welt. ABG 59. Leipzig: Evangelische Verlagsanstalt, 2017.

Dettwiler, Andreas. Die Gegenwart des Erhöhten. FRLANT 169. Göttingen: Vandenhoeck & Ruprecht, 1995.

Dettwiler, Andreas, and Jean Zumstein, eds. Kreuzestheologie im Neuen Testament. WUNT 151. Tübingen: Mohr Siebeck, 2002.

Dexinger, Ferdinand, and Reinhard Pummer, ed. Die Samaritaner. WdF 604. Darmstadt: Wissenschaftliche Buchgesellschaft, 1992.

Dibelius, Martin. Aufsätze zur Apostelgeschichte. FRLANT 60. Göttingen: Vandenhoeck & Ruprecht, 1951; 5th ed., 1968.

———. Der Brief des Jakobus. 6th ed. KEK 15. Göttingen: Vandenhoeck & Ruprecht, 1984 (= 1921).

———. Die Formgeschichte des Evangeliums. 6th ed. Tübingen: Mohr, 1971 (= 1919).

———. From Tradition to Gospel. Translated from the revised second edition of Die Formgeschichte des Evangeliums by Bertram Lee Woolf, in collaboration with the author. LTT. Cambridge: Clarke, 1971.

———. James: A Commentary on the Epistle of James. Translated by Heinrich Greeven. Herm. Philadelphia: Fortress, 1975.

———. "Paul on the Areopagus." Pages 26–77 in Greeven, Studies in the Acts of the Apostles.

———. "Paulus auf dem Areopag." Pages 29–70 in Dibelius, *Aufsätze zur Apostelgeschichte* (1951).

———. *Studies in the Acts of the Apostles.* Edited by Heinrich Greeven. Translated by Mary Ling. New York: Charles Scribner's Sons, 1956.

Diefenbach, Manfred. *Der Konflikt Jesu mit den "Juden": Ein Versuch zur Lösung der johanneischen Antijudaismus-Diskussion mit Hilfe des antiken Handlungsverständnisses.* NTA 41. Münster: Aschendorff, 2002.

Dienstbeck, Stefan. *Die Theologie der Stoa.* Theologische Bibliothek Töpelmann 173. Berlin: de Gruyter, 2015.

Dietrich, Walter, Martin George, and Ulrich Luz, eds. *Antijudaismus—christliche Erblast.* Stuttgart: Kohlhammer, 1999.

Dietzfelbinger, Christian. *Die Berufung des Paulus als Ursprung seiner Theologie.* WMANT 58. Neukirchen-Vluyn: Neukirchener Verlag, 1985.

———. *Das Evangelium nach Johannes.* Vol. 1. ZBK.NT 4.1. Zurich: Theologischer Verlag, 2001.

Dihle, Albrecht. *Die goldene Regel: Eine Einführung in die Geschichte der antiken und frühchristlichen Vulgärethik.* StA 7. Göttingen: Vandenhoek & Ruprecht, 1962.

Dihle, Albrecht, and Reinhard Feldmeier. *Hellas und der Orient: Phasen wechselseitiger Rezeption.* Julius-Wellhausen-Vorlesung. Berlin: de Gruyter, 2009.

Dillon, John. *The Middle Platonists: A Study of Platonism, 80 B.C. to A.D. 220.* London: Duckworth, 1996.

Dinkler, Erich. "Der Brief an die Galater." Pages 278–82 in Andresen and G. Klein, *Signum Crucis.*

———, ed. *Zeit und Geschichte: Dankesgabe an Rudolf Bultmann zum 80. Geburtstag.* Tübingen: Mohr, 1964.

Dittenberger, Wilhelm. *Sylloge inscriptionum graecarum.* Leipzig: Hirzelium, 1920.

Divjanović, Kristin. *Paulus als Philosoph: Das Ethos des Apostels vor dem Hintergrund antiker Popularphilosophie.* NTA 58. Münster: Aschendorff, 2015.

Dobbeler, Axel von. *Der Evangelist Philippus in der Geschichte des Urchristentums.* TANZ 30. Tübingen: Francke, 2000.

Dobbeler, Axel von, et al., eds. *Religionsgeschichte des Neuen Testaments: Festschrift für Klaus Berger zum 60. Geburtstag.* Tübingen: Francke, 2000.

Dochhorn, Jan. *Schriftgelehrte Prophetie: Der eschatologische Teufelsfall in Apc Joh 12 und seine Bedeutung für das Verständnis der Johannesoffenbarung.* WUNT 268. Tübingen: Mohr Siebeck, 2010.

Dodd, Charles Harold. *The Interpretation of the Fourth Gospel.* Cambridge: Cambridge University Press, 1978 (= 1951).

Doering, Lutz. *Ancient Jewish Letters and the Beginnings of Christian Epistolography,* WUNT 298. Tübingen: Mohr Siebeck, 2012.

———. *Schabbat: Sabbathalacha und -praxis im antiken Judentum und Urchristentum.* TSAJ 78. Tübingen: Mohr Siebeck, 1999.

Donfried, Karl P. "The Cults of Thessalonica and the Thessalonian Correspondence." *NTS* 31 (1985): 336–56.

———, ed. *The Romans Debate.* Peabody, MA: Hendrickson, 1977. Rev. and expanded ed., 1991.

Döring, Klaus. "Antisthenes, Diogenes und die Kyniker vor Christi Geburt." Pages 267–321 in *Sophistik, Sokrates, Sokratik, Mathematik, Medizin.* Vol. 2.1 of *Die Philosophie der Antike.* Grundriss der Geschichte der Philosophie. Basel: Schwabe, 1998.

———. *Exemplum Socratis: Studien zur Sokratesnachwirkung in der kynisch-stoischen Popularphilosophie der frühen Kaiserzeit und im frühen Christentum*. Hermes Einzelschriften 42. Wiesbaden: Steiner, 1979.

———. "Sokrates." Pages 141–78 in *Sophistik, Sokrates, Sokratik, Mathematik, Medizin*. Vol. 2.1 of *Die Philosophie der Antike*. Grundriss der Geschichte der Philosophie. Basel: Schwabe, 1998.

Dormeyer, Detlev. *Evangelium als literarische und theologische Gattung*. Erträge der Forschung 263. Darmstadt: Wissenschaftliche Buchgesellschaft, 1989.

———. *Das Markusevangelium*. Darmstadt: Wissenschaftliche Buchgesellschaft, 2005.

———. *Das Markusevangelium als Idealbiographie von Jesus Christus, dem Nazarener*. SBB 43. Stuttgart: Katholisches Bibelwerk, 1999.

———. *Das Neue Testament im Rahmen der antiken Literaturgeschichte*. Darmstadt: Wissenschafliche Buchgesellschaft, 1993.

———. *The New Testament among the Writings of Antiquity*. Biblical Seminar 55. Sheffield: Sheffield Academic, 1998.

Dörrie, Heinrich, Matthias Baltes, and Christian Pietsch, eds. *Theologia Platonica*. Vol. 7 of *Der Platonismus in der Antike*.

———, eds. *Der Platonismus in der Antike*. 7 vols. Stuttgart-Bad Cannstatt: Frommann-Holzboog, 1987–2008.

Doty, William G. *Letters in Primitive Christianity*. Guides to Biblical Scholarship. NTS. Philadelphia: Fortress, 1973.

Downing, Gerald. "A Cynic Preparation for Paul's Gospel for Jew and Greek, Slave and Free, Male and Female." *NTS* 42 (1996): 454–62.

Downs, David J. *The Offering of the Gentiles: Paul's Collection for Jerusalem in Its Chronological, Cultural and Cultic Contexts*. WUNT 2/248. Tübingen: Mohr Siebeck, 2008.

Dräger, Michael. *Die Städte der Provinz Asia in der Flavierzeit: Studien zur kleinasiatischen Stadt- und Regionalgeschichte*. EURHS 3/576. New York and Frankfurt: Lang, 1993.

Draper, Jonathan A. "Die Didache." Pages 17–38 in Pratscher, *Die Apostolischen Väter*.

———. "The Holy Vine of David Made Known to the Gentiles through God's Servant Jesus: 'Christian Judaism' in the Didache." Pages 257–83 in Jackson-McCabe, *Jewish Christianity Reconsidered*.

Drexhage, Hans-Joachim, Heinrich Konen, and Kai Ruffing. *Die Wirtschaft des Römischen Reiches (1.–3. Jahrhundert): Eine Einführung*. Studienbücher Geschichte und Kultur der Alten Welt. Berlin: Akademie Verlag, 2002.

Dreyer, Boris. "Medien für Erziehung, Bildung und Ausbildung in der Antike." Pages 223–50 in *Handbuch der Bildung und Erziehung in der Antike*. Edited by Johannes Christes, Richard Klein, and Christoph Lüth. Darmstadt: Wissenschaftliche Buchgesellschaft, 2006.

Droysen, Johann Gustav. *Geschichte des Hellenismus*. 3 vols. Orig. pub., 1836–43. Darmstadt: Primus, 1998.

———. *Historik: Vorlesungen über Enzyklopädie und Methodologie der Geschichte*. Darmstadt: Wissenschaftliche Buchgesellschaft, 1977.

———. *Outline of the Principles of History*. Translated by E. Benjamin Andrew. New York: H. Fertig, 1893. Repr., 1967.

Dschulnigg, Peter. "Der theologische Ort des Zweiten Petrusbriefes." *BZ* 33 (1989): 161–77.

———. "Warnung vor Reichtum und Ermahnung der Reichen: 1 Tim 6:6–10, 17–19 im Rahmen des Schlussteils 6:3–21." *BZ* 37 (1993), 60–77.

Dudley, Donald R. *A History of Cynicism: From Diogenes to the 6th century A.D.* Hildesheim: Olms, 1967 (= 1937).

Dulling, Dennis C. "Die Jesusbewegung und die Netzwerkanalyse." Pages 135–57 in Stegemann, Malina, and Theissen, *Jesus in neuen Kontexten.*

Dunderberg, Ingo, Christopher Tuckett, and Kari Syreeni, eds. *Fair Play: Diversity and Conflicts in Early Christianity; Essays in Honour of Heikki Räisänen.* NovTSup 103. Leiden: Brill, 2002.

Dunn, James D. G. *Beginning from Jerusalem: Christianity in the Making.* Vol. 2. Grand Rapids: Eerdmans, 2009.

———. *Christology in the Making: A New Testament Inquiry into the Origins of the Doctrine of the Incarnation.* 2nd ed. Grand Rapids: Eerdmans, 1996.

———. "The Incident at Antioch (Gal 2.11–18)." *JSNT* 18 (June 1983): 3–57.

———. *The Oral Gospel Tradition.* Grand Rapids: Eerdmans, 2013.

———. *The Parting of the Ways between Christianity and Judaism and Their Significance for the Character of Christianity.* London: SCM Press; Philadelphia: Trinity Press International, 1991.

———, ed. *Paul and the Mosaic Law.* WUNT 89. Tübingen: Mohr Siebeck, 1996.

———. *The Theology of Paul the Apostle.* Grand Rapids: Eerdmans, 1998.

Du Toit, David. *Der abwesende Herr: Strategien im Markusevangelium zur Bewältigung der Abwesenheit des Auferstandenen.* WMANT 111. Neukirchen-Vluyn: Neukirchener Verlag, 2006.

———. *Bedrängnis und Identität.* BZNW 200. Berlin: de Gruyter, 2013.

———. *Theios Anthropos: Zur Verwendung von theios anthropos und sinnverwandten Ausdrücken in der Literatur der Kaiserzeit.* WUNT 2/91. Tübingen: Mohr Siebeck, 1997.

Ebel, Eva. *Die Attraktivität früher christlicher Gemeinden.* WUNT 2/178. Tübingen: Mohr Siebeck, 2004.

———. *Lydia und Berenike: Zwei selbständige Frauen bei Lukas.* BG 20. Leipzig: Evangelische Verlagsanstalt, 2009.

———. "Regeln von der Gemeinschaft für die Gemeinschaft? Das Aposteldekret und antike Vereinssatzungen im Vergleich." Pages 317–39 in Öhler, *Aposteldekret.*

———. "Ein Verein von Christusverehrern? Die Gemeinde des 2. und 3. Johannesbriefes im Spiegel antiker Vereine." Pages 399–419 in *Studien zu Matthäus und Johannes: Festschrift für Jean Zumstein zu seinem 65. Geburtstag.* Edited by Andreas Dettwiler and Uta Poplutz. ATANT 97. Zurich: Theologischer Verlag, 2009.

Ebersohn, Michael. *Das Nächstenliebegebot in der synoptischen Tradition.* MTS 37. Marburg: Elwert, 1993.

Ebner, Martin. "Evangelium contra Evangelium: Das Markusevangelium und der Aufstieg der Flavier." *BN* 116 (2003): 28–42.

———. "Kreuzestheologie im Markusevangelium." Pages 151–68 in Dettwiler and Zumstein, *Kreuzestheologie im Neuen Testament.*

———. *Leidenslisten und Apostelbrief: Untersuchungen zu Form, Motivik und Funktion der Peristasenkataloge bei Paulus.* FB 66. Würzburg: Echter, 1991.

———. *Die Stadt als Lebensraum der ersten Christen: Konturen des Urchristentums.* USU. Göttingen: Vandenhoeck & Ruprecht, 2012.

Ebner, Martin, and Stefan Schreiber, eds. *Einleitung in das Neue Testament.* 2nd ed. K-ST 6. Stuttgart: Kohlhammer, 2013.

Eck, Werner. *Judäa—Syria Palästina: Die Auseinandersetzung einer Provinz mit römischer Politik und Kultur.* TSAJ 157. Tübingen: Mohr Siebeck, 2014.

———. "Der Kochba-Aufstand der Jahre 132–136 und seine Folgen für die Provinz Syria Palaestina." Pages 229–44 in Eck, *Judäa–Syria Palästina.*

———. "Die römischen Repräsentanten in Judäa: Provokateure oder Vertreter der römischen Macht." Pages 166–85 in Eck, *Judäa–Syria Palästina.*

———. *Rom und Judäa: Fünf Vorträge zur römischen Herrschaft in Palaestina.* Tria Corda: Jenaer Vorlesungen zu Judentum. Antike und Christentum 2. Tübingen: Mohr Siebeck, 2007.

Eck, Werner, and Johannes Heinrichs. *Sklaven und Freigelassene in der Gesellschaft der römischen Kaiserzeit.* Texte zur Forschung 61. Darmstadt: Wissenschaftliche Buchgesellschaft, 1993. Repr., 2005.

Eckart, Karl-Gottfried. *Das Corpus Hermeticum: Einschliesslich der Fragmente des Stobaeus.* MJS 3. Münster: Lit, 1999.

Eckhardt, Benedikt, and Clemens Leonhard. *Juden, Christen und Vereine im römischen Reich.* RVV 75. Berlin: de Gruyter, 2018.

Eckstein, Hans-Joachim. "Die Gegenwart im Licht der erinnerten Zukunft: Zur modalisierten Zeit im Johannesevangelium." Pages 187–206 in *Der aus Glauben Gerechte wird leben: Beiträge zur Theologie des Neuen Testaments.* By H.-J. Eckstein. BVB 5. Münster: Lit, 2003.

Eckstein, Peter. *Gemeinde, Brief und Heilsbotschaft: Ein phänomenologischer Vergleich zwischen Paulus und Epikur.* HBS 42. Freiburg im Breisgau; New York: Herder, 2004.

Egger, Rita. *Josephus Flavius und die Samaritaner: Eine terminologische Untersuchung zur Identitätsklärung der Samaritaner.* NTOA 4. Freiburg, Schweiz: Universitätsverlag; Göttingen: Vandenhoeck & Ruprecht, 1986.

Ego, Beate, Armin Lange, and Peter Pilhofer, eds. *Gemeinde ohne Tempel: Zur Substituierung und Transformation des Jerusalemer Tempels und seines Kults im Alten Testament; Antiken Judentum und frühen Christentum.* WUNT 118. Tübingen: Mohr Siebeck, 1999.

Eisele, Wilfried. *Ein unerschütterliches Reich: Die mittelplatonische Umformung des Parusiegedankens im Hebräerbrief.* BZNW 116. Berlin: de Gruyter, 2003.

Elliger, Winfried, *Ephesos: Geschichte einer antiken Weltstadt.* Urban-Taschenbücher 375. Stuttgart: Kohlhammer, 1985.

———. *Paulus in Griechenland: Philippi, Thessaloniki, Athen, Korinth.* 2nd ed. Stuttgart: Katholisches Bibelwerk, 1990.

Engberg, Jakob. *Impulsore Chresto: Opposition to Christianity in the Roman Empire c. 50–250 AD.* ECCA 2. Frankfurt: Lang, 2007.

Engberg-Pedersen, Troels, ed. *Paul in His Hellenistic Context.* Minneapolis: Fortress, 1995.

Epp, Eldon Jay. *Junia: The First Woman Apostle.* Minneapolis: Fortress, 2005.

Erlemann, Kurt. *Jesus der Christus: Provokation des Glaubens.* Neukirchen-Vluyn: Neukirchener Verlag, 2011.

———. *Naherwartung und Parusieverzögerung im Neuen Testament: Ein Beitrag zur Frage religiöser Zeiterfahrung.* TANZ 17. Tübingen and Basel: Franke, 1995.

Erlemann, Kurt, and Karl Leo Noethlichs, eds. *Prolegomena, Quellen, Geschichte.* NTAK 1. Neukirchen-Vluyn Neukirchener, 2004.

Erlemann, Kurt, Karl Leo Noethlichs, Klaus Scherberich, and Jürgen Zangenberg, eds. *Neues Testament und antike Kultur.* 5 vols. Neukirchen-Vluyn: Neukirchener Verlag, 2004–8.

Erler, Michael. "Epikur." Pages 29–490 in Flashar, *Die hellenistische Philosophie.*

———. *Platon*. Vol. 2.2 in *Die Philosophie der Antike*. Grundriss der Geschichte der Philosophie. Basel: Schwabe, 2007.

Ernst, Josef. *Herr der Geschichte: Perspektiven der lukanischen Eschatologie*. SBS 88. Stuttgart: Katholisches Bibelwerk, 1978.

———. *Johannes der Täufer: Interpretation, Geschichte, Wirkungsgeschichte*. BZNW 53. Berlin: de Gruyter, 1989.

Escarpit, Robert. *Das Buch und der Leser: Entwurf einer Literatursoziologie*. Kunst und Kommunikation 2. Cologne and Opladen: Westdeutscher Verlag, 1961.

———, ed. *Elemente einer Literatursoziologie*. KG 12. Stuttgart: Enke, 1977.

Eschner, Christina. *Gestorben und hingegeben "für" die Sünder: Die griechische Konzeption des Unheil abwendenden Sterbens und deren paulinische Aufnahme für die Deutung des Todes Jesu Christi*. 2 vols. WMANT 122. Neukirchen-Vluyn: Neukirchener Verlag, 2010.

Esler, Philip Francis. *Galatians*. New Testament Readings. London and New York: Routledge, 1998.

Evang, Martin, and Otto Merk. *Aufbruch und Verheißung: Gesammelte Aufsätze zum Hebräerbrief, zum 65. Geburtstag mit einer Bibliographie des Verfassers*. BZNW 65. Berlin: de Gruyter, 1992.

Evang, Martin, Helmut Merklein, and Michael Wolter, eds. *Eschatologie und Schöpfung: Festschrift für Erich Grässer zum siebzigsten Geburtstag*. BZNW 89. Berlin: de Gruyter, 1997.

Fander, Monika. "Frauen im Urchristentum am Beispiel Palästinas." *JBTh* 7 (1992): 165–85.

Fantham, Elaine. *Literarisches Leben im antiken Rom: Sozialgeschichte der römischen Literatur von Cicero bis Apuleius*. Translated by Theodor Heinze. Stuttgart and Weimar: Metzler, 1998.

Feldmeier, Reinhard. "'Basis des Kontaktes unter Christen': Demut als Schlüsselbegriff der Ethik des Ersten Petrusbriefes." Pages 249–62 in Du Toit, *Bedrängnis und Identität*.

———. *Der erste Brief des Petrus*. THK 15.1. Leipzig: Evangelische Verlagsanstalt, 2005.

———. *The First Letter of Peter: A Commentary on the Greek Text*. Translated by Peter H. Davids. Waco: Baylor University Press, 2008.

———. *"Salz der Erde": Zugänge zur Bergpredigt*. Biblisch-theologische Schwerpunkte 14. Göttingen: Vandenhoeck & Ruprecht, 1998.

———. "Verpflichtende Gnade: Die Bergpredigt im Kontext des ersten Evangeliums." Pages 15–107 in Feldmeier, *"Salz der Erde."*

Feldmeier, Reinhard, and Hermann Spiekermann. *God of the Living: A Biblical Theology*. Translated by Mark E. Biddle. Waco: Baylor University Press, 2011.

Fellmeth, Ulrich. *Pecunia non olet: Die Wirtschaft der antiken Welt*. Darmstadt: Wissenschaftliche Buchgesellschaft, 2008.

Fiedler, Peter, and Dieter Zeller, eds. *Gegenwart und kommendes Reich: Schülergabe Anton Vögtle zum 65. Geburtstag*. SBB 6. Stuttgart: Katholisches Bibelwerk, 1975.

Fiedrowicz, Michael. *Christen und Heiden: Quellentexte zu ihrer Auseinandersetzung in der Antike*. Darmstadt: Wissenschaftliche Buchgesellschaft, 2004.

———. "Christen Verfolgung nach dem Brand Roms im Jahr 64." Pages 250–56 in *Nero: Kaiser, Künstler und Tyrann*. Edited by Jürgen Merten et al. Darmstadt: Theiss, 2016.

Fieger, Michael. *Das Thomasevangelium: Einleitung, Kommentar und Systematik*. NTA 22. Münster: Aschendorff, 1991.

Fischer, Josef. *Sklaverei: Quellenreader Antike*. Darmstadt: Wissenschaftliche Buchgesellschaft, 2014.

Fischer, Karl Martin. *Das Ostergeschehen*. 2nd ed. Göttingen: Vandenhoeck & Ruprecht, 1980.

———. *Tendenz und Absicht des Epheserbriefes*. FRLANT 111. Göttingen: Vandenhoeck & Ruprecht, 1973.

———. *Das Urchristentum*. KE 1. Berlin: Evangelische Verlagsanstalt, 1985.

Fitzgerald, John T. *Cracks in an Earthen Vessel: An Examination of the Catalogues of Hardships in the Corinthian Correspondance*. SBLDS 99. Atlanta: Scholars Press, 1988.

Fitzmyer, Joseph A. *The Gospel according to Luke: Introduction, Translation, and Notes 1–2*. AB 28/28A. Garden City, NY: Doubleday, 1981–85.

———. "The 'Son of God' Document from Qumran." *Bib* 74 (1993): 153–74.

Flach, Dieter. *Römische Geschichtsschreibung*. 4th ed. Darmstadt: Wissenschaftliche Buchgesellschaft, 2013.

Flashar, Hellmut, et al. *Die hellenistische Philosophie*. Vol. 4 of *Die Philosophie der Antike*. Grundriss der Geschichte der Philosophie. Basel: Schwabe, 1994.

Fleddermann, Harry T. *Q: Reconstruction and Commentary*. BTS 1. Louvain: Peeters, 2005.

Flusser, David. *Judaism of the Second Temple Period*. Vol. 1, *Qumran and Apocalypticism*. Jerusalem: Hebrew University Magnes Press; Grand Rapids: Eerdmans. 2007.

———. "Das Schisma zwischen Judentum und Christentum." *EvT* 40 (1980): 214–39.

Förg, Florian. *Die Ursprünge der alttestamentlichen Apokalyptik*. ABG 45. Leipzig: Evangelische Verlagsanstalt, 2013.

Fornberg, Tornd, and David Hellholm. *Texts and Contexts: Biblical Texts in Their Textual and Situational Contexts; Essays in Honor of Lars Hartmann*. Oslo: Scandinavian University Press, 1995.

Forschner, Maximilian. *Die Philosophie der Stoa: Logik, Physik and Ethik*. Darmstadt: Wissenschaftliche Buchgesellschaft, 2018.

———. *Die stoische Ethik: Über den Zusammenhang von Natur-, Sprach- und Moralphilosophie im altstoischen System*. 2nd ed. Darmstadt: Wissenschaftliche Buchgesellschaft, 1995.

Förster, Werner. *Die Gnosis*. Vols. 1–3. 2nd ed. BAW: Reihe Antike und Christentum. Zurich: Artemis, 1979.

———. *Zeugnisse der Kirchenväter*. Vol. 1 of *Die Gnosis*. 2nd ed. BAW. Zurich: Artemis, 1979.

Fortna, Robert T. *The Gospel of Signs: A Reconstruction of the Narrative Source Underlying the Fourth Gospel*. SNTSMS 11. Cambridge: Cambridge University Press, 1970.

Fortna, Robert, and Beverly R. Gaventa, eds. *The Conversation Continues: Studies in Paul and John in Honor of J. Louis Martyn*. Nashville: Abingdon, 1990.

Frankemölle, Hubert. *Der Brief des Jakobus*. ÖTK 17.1. Gütersloh: Gütersloher Verlagshaus; Würzburg: Echter Verlag, 1994.

———. *Frühjudentum und Urchristentum*. Stuttgart: Kohlhammer, 2006.

———. *Jahwebund und Kirche Christi: Studien zur Form- und Traditionsgeschichte des "Evangeliums" nach Matthäus*. 2nd ed. NTA 2/10. Münster: Aschendorff, 1984.

Freedman, David Noel, ed. *Anchor Bible Dictionary*. 6 vols. New York: Doubleday, 1992.

Freis, Helmut, ed. *Historische Inschriften zur römischen Kaiserzeit: Von Augustus bis Konstantin*. 2nd ed. Darmstadt: Wissenschaftliche Buchgesellschaft, 1994.

Frenschkowski, Marco. "Galiläa oder Jerusalem? Die topographischen und politischen Hintergründe der Logienquelle." Pages 535–59 in Lindemann, *Sayings Source Q*.

———. *Mysterien des Urchristentums: Eine kritische Sichtung spekulativer Theorien zum frühen Christentum*. Wiesbaden: Marix, 2007.

———. *Offenbarung und Epiphanie*. WUNT 2/79–80. Mainz: Johannes Gutenberg-Universität, 1994. Tübingen: Mohr Siebeck, 1997.

———. "Pseudepigraphie und Paulusschule." Pages 239–72 in Horn, *Das Ende des Paulus*.

———. *Die verborgene Epiphanie in Spätantike und frühem Christentum*. Vol. 2 of *Offenbarung und Epiphanie*. WUNT 2/80. Tübingen: Mohr Siebeck, 1997.

Freudenberger, Rudolf. *Das Verhalten der römischen Behörden gegen die Christen im 2. Jahrhundert: Dargestellt am Brief des Plinius an Trajan und den Reskripten Trajans und Hadrians*. MBPF 52. Munich: Beck, 1967.

Frey, Jörg. "Apostelbegriff, Apostelamt und Apostolizität." Vol. 1, pages 91–188 in Schneider and Wenz, *Das kirchliche Amt*.

———. "Erwägungen zum Verhältnis der Johannesapokalypse zu den übrigen Schriften des Corpus Johanneum." Pages 326–429 in Hengel, *Die johanneische Frage*.

———. "Die Fragmente judenchristlicher Evangelien: Einleitung." Pages 560–92 in Markschies and Schröter, *Antike christliche Apokryphen*.

———. *Die Herrlichkeit des Gekreuzigten: Studien zu den Johanneischen Schriften*. WUNT 307. Tübingen: Mohr Siebeck, 2013.

———. "Der historische Jesus und der Christus der Evangelien." Pages 273–336 in Schröter and Brucker, *Der historische Jesus*.

———. *Die johanneische Eschatologie*. 3 vols. WUNT 96, 110, 117. Tübingen: Mohr Siebeck, 1997–2000.

———. "Die 'theologia crucifixi' des Johannesevangeliums." Pages 169–238 in Dettwiler and Zumstein, *Kreuzestheologie im Neuen Testament*.

———. "Von Paulus zu Johannes." Pages 235–78 in Rothschild and Schröter, *Rise and Expansion of Christianity*.

Frey, Jörg, Jens Herzer, Martina Janssen, and Clare K. Rothschild, eds. *Pseudepigraphie und Verfasserfiktion in frühchristlichen Briefen: Pseudepigraphy and Author Fiction in Early Christian Letters*. WUNT 246. Tübingen: Mohr Siebeck, 2009.

Frey, Jörg, James A. Kelhofer, and Franz Tóth, eds. *Die Johannesapokalypse*. WUNT 287. Tübingen: Mohr Siebeck, 2012.

Frey, Jörg, Ursula Schattner-Rieser, and Konrad Schmid, eds. *Die Samaritaner und die Bibel: Historische und literarische Wechselwirkungen zwischen biblischen und samaritanischen Traditionen = The Samaritans and the Bible: Historical and Literary Interactions between Biblical and Samaritan Traditions*. SJ 70. Berlin: de Gruyter, 2012.

Frey, Jörg, Benjamin Schliesser, and Nadine Ueberschaer, eds. *Glaube: Das Verständnis des Glaubens im frühen Christentum und in seiner jüdischen und hellenistisch-römischen Umwelt*. WUNT 373. Tübingen: Mohr Siebeck, 2017.

Frey, Jörg, and Udo Schnelle, eds. *Kontexte des Johannesevangeliums*. WUNT 175. Tübingen: Mohr Siebeck, 2004.

Frey, Jörg, and Jens Schröter, eds. *Deutungen des Todes Jesu im Neuen Testament*. WUNT 181. Tübingen: Mohr Siebeck, 2005.

Freyberger, Klaus S. "Damaskus." Vol. 2, pages 142–45 in Erlemann et al., *Neues Testament und antike Kultur*.

Freyne, Seán. *Jesus: A Jewish Galilean*. London: T&T Clark, 2004.

———. *The Jesus-Movement and Its Expansion*. Grand Rapids: Eerdmans, 2014.

Frickenschmidt, Dirk. *Evangelium als Biographie: Die vier Evangelien im Rahmen antiker Erzählkunst*. TANZ 22. Tübingen: Franke, 1997.

Friedländer, Ludwig. *Darstellungen aus der Sittengeschichte Roms: In der Zeit von August bis zum Ausgang der Antonine*. Revised and expanded by Georg Wissowa. 4 vols. 9th ed. Leipzig: Hirzel, 1919–21.

Friedrich, Gerhard. "Glaube und Verkündigung bei Paulus." Pages 93–113 in *Glaube im Neuen Testament: Studien zu Ehren von Hermann Binder anlässlich seines 70. Geburtstags*. Edited by Ferdinand Hahn and Hans Klein. BTS 7. Neukirchen-Vluyn: Neukirchener Verlag, 1982.

———. *Die Verkündigung des Todes Jesu im Neuen Testament*. BTS 6. Neukirchen-Vluyn: Neukirchener Verlag, 1982.

Friedrich, Johannes, Wolfgang Pöhlmann, and Peter Stuhlmacher, eds. *Rechtfertigung: Festschrift für Ernst Käsemann zum 70. Geburtstag*. Tübingen: Mohr, 1976.

Friedrich, Johannes, Peter Stuhlmacher, and Wolfgang Pöhlmann. "Zur historischen Situation und Intention von Röm 13,1–7." *ZTK* 73 (1976): 131–66.

Friesen, Steven J. "Poverty in Pauline Studies: Beyond the So-called New Consensus." *JSNT* 26 (March 2004): 323–61.

———. *Twice Neokoros: Ephesus, Asia and the Cult of the Flavian Imperial Family*. RGRW 116. Leiden: Brill, 1993.

———. "The Wrong Erastus: Ideology, Archaeology, and Exegesis." Pages 231–56 in Friesen, Schowalter, and Walters, *Corinth in Context*.

Friesen, Steven J., Daniel N. Schowalter, and James C. Walters. *Corinth in Context: Comparative Studies on Religion and Society*. NovTSup 134. Leiden: Brill, 2010.

Fuhrmann, Manfred. *Seneca und Kaiser Nero: Eine Biographie*. Frankfurt: Fischer-Taschenbuch-Verlag, 1999.

Fürst, Alfons. *Christentum als Intellektuellen-Religion: Die Anfänge des Christentums in Alexandria*. SBS 213. Stuttgart: Verlag Katholisches Bibelwerk, 2007.

Gäckle, Volker. *Die Starken und Schwachen in Korinth und Rom: Zu Herkunft und Funktion der Antithese in 1 Kor 8,1–11,1 und in Rom 14,1–15,13*. WUNT 200. Tübingen: Mohr Siebeck, 2005.

Gadamer, Hans-Georg. *Truth and Method*. 2nd ed. Revised and translated by Joel Weinsheimer and Donald G. Marshall. New York: Seabury, 1975.

Galling, Kurt, and Hans von Campenhausen, eds. *Die Religion in Geschichte und Gegenwart: Handwörterbuch für Theologie und Religionswissenschaft*. 3rd ed. Tübingen: Mohr, 1957–62.

Garleff, Gunnar. *Urchristliche Identität im Matthäusevangelium, Didache und Jakobusbrief*. BVB 9. Münster: Lit, 2004.

Garnsey, Peter, and Richard Saller. "Patronal Power Relations." Pages 96–103 in Horsley, *Paul and Empire*.

———. *The Roman Empire: Economy, Society, and Culture*. Berkeley: University of California Press, 1987.

Gathercole, Simon J. *The Composition of the Gospel of Thomas: Original Language and Influences*. SNTSMS 151. Cambridge: Cambridge University Press, 2012.

———. *Where Is Boasting? Early Jewish Soteriology and Paul's Response in Romans 1–5*. Grand Rapids: Eerdmans, 2002.

Gäumann, Niklaus. *Taufe und Ethik: Studien zu Römer 6*. BEvT 47. Munich: Kaiser, 1967.

Gebauer, Roland. *Paulus als Seelsorger: Ein exegetischer Beitrag zur praktischen Theologie*. CTM 18. Stuttgart: Calwer, 1997.

Geertz, Clifford. "Thick Description: Toward an Interpretive Theory of Culture." Chap. 1 of *The Interpretation of Cultures: Selected Essays*. New York: Basic Books, 1973.

Gehring, Roger W. *House Church and Mission: The Importance of Household Structures in Early Christianity*. Peabody, MA: Hendrickson, 2004.

Gehrke, Hans-Joachim. *Geschichte des Hellenismus*. Munich: Oldenbourg, 1995.

Gelardini, Gabriella. *"Verhärtet eure Herzen nicht": Der Hebräer, eine Synagogenhomilie zu Tischa be-Aw*. Leiden; Boston: Brill, 2007.

Gemeinhardt, Peter, and Sebastian Günther, eds. *Von Rom nach Bagdad: Bildung und Religion von der römischen Kaiserzeit bis zum klassischen Islam*. Tübingen: Mohr Siebeck, 2013.

Gemünden, Petra von, Matthias Konradt, and Gerd Theissen. *Der Jakobusbrief: Beiträge zur Rehabilitierung der "strohernen Epistel."* BVB 3. Münster: Lit, 2003.

Georgi, Dieter. *Der Armen zu gedenken: Die Geschichte der Kollekte des Paulus für Jerusalem*. 2nd ed. Neukirchen-Vluyn: Neukirchener Verlag, 1994.

———. *Remembering the Poor: The History of Paul's Collection for Jerusalem*. Nashville: Abingdon, 1992.

———. "Die Visionen vom himmlischen Jerusalem in Apk 21 und 22." Pages 351–72 in Lührmann and G. Strecker, *Kirche*.

Gese, Michael. *Das Vermächtnis des Paulus*. WUNT 99. Tübingen: Mohr Siebeck, 1997.

Giardina, Andrea, ed. *Der Mensch der römischen Antike*. Frankfurt: Campus Verlag, 1991.

Giebel, Marion. *Das Geheimnis der Mysterien: Antike Kulte in Griechenland, Rom und Ägypten*. 3rd ed. Düsseldorf: Patmos, 2003.

———. *Reisen in der Antike*. Darmstadt: Wissenschaftliches Buchgesellschaft, 1999.

Gielen, Marlis. "Der erste Petrusbrief." Pages 511–21 in Ebner and Schreiber, *Einleitung in das Neue Testament*.

———. *Die Passionserzählung in den vier Evangelien: Literarische Gestaltung—theologische Schwerpunkte*. Stuttgart: Kohlhammer, 2008.

———. *Tradition und Theologie neutestamentlicher Haustafelethik: Ein Beitrag zur Frage einer christlichen Auseinandersetzung mit gesellschaftlichen Normen*. BBB 75. Frankfurt: Hain, 1990.

———. "Die Wahrnehmung gemeindlicher Leitungsfunktionen durch Frauen im Spiegel der Paulusbriefe." Pages 129–65 in Schmelle, Ebner, and Hoppe, *Neutestamentliche Ämtermodelle*.

Gnilka, Christian, Stefan Heid, and Rainer Riesner. *Blutzeuge: Tod und Grab des Petrus in Rom*. Regensburg: Schnell & Steiner, 2010.

Gnilka, Joachim. *Das Evangelium nach Markus*. 2 vols. 5th ed. EKKNT 2/1–2. Zurich: Benziger; Neukirchen-Vluyn: Neukirchener Verlag. 1988–89.

———. *Die frühen Christen*. HTKNT, Supplement 7. Freiburg im Breisgau: Herder, 1999.

———. "Die Kollekte der paulinischen Gemeinden für Jerusalem als Ausdruck ekklesialer Gemeinschaft." Pages 301–15 in Kampling and Söding, *Ekklesiologie des Neuen Testaments*.

Goertz, Hans-Jürgen. *Umgang mit Geschichte*. Reinbek bei Hamburg: Rowohlt Taschenbuch Verlag, 1995.

———. *Unsichere Geschichte: Zur Theorie historischer Referentialität.* Stuttgart: Reclam, 2001.

Goldhahn-Müller, Ingrid. *Die Grenze der Gemeinde: Studien zum Problem der Zweiten Busse in Neuen Testament unter Berücksichtigung der Entwicklung im 2. Jh. bis Tertullian.* GTA 39. Göttingen: Vandenhoeck & Ruprecht, 1989.

Goodacre, Mark. *Thomas and the Gospels: The Case for Thomas's Familiarity with the Synoptics.* Grand Rapids: Eerdmans, 2012.

Goodenough, Erwin R. *The Church in the Roman Empire.* New York: Holt, 1931.

Goodrich, John K. "Erastus, Quaestor of Corinth." *NTS* 56 (2010): 90–115.

Goodspeed, Edgar J. *The Formation of the New Testament.* 2nd ed. Chicago: University of Chicago Press, 1927.

Goppelt, Leonhard. *A Commentary on 1 Peter.* Grand Rapids: Eerdmans, 1993.

———. *Der erste Petrusbrief.* KEK 7.1. Göttingen: Vandenhoeck & Ruprecht, 1977.

Görg, Manfred, ed. *Neues Bibel-Lexikon.* 3 vols. Zurich and Düsseldorf: Benziger, 1991–2001.

Görgemanns, Herwig, trans. and ed. *Plutarch: Drei religionsphilosophische Schriften, Griechisch-Deutsch.* Düsseldorf: Artemis & Winkler, 2003.

Görler, Woldemar. "Älterer Pyrrhonismus; Jüngere Akademie; Antiochos von Askalon." Pages 717–989 in Flashar, *Die hellenistische Philosophie.*

Goulet-Cazé, Marie-Odile. *Kynismus und Christentum in der Antike.* Edited by Marco Frenschkowski. Translated from French by Lena R. Seehausen. NTOA 113. Göttingen: Vandenhoeck & Ruprecht, 2016.

Gradl, Hans-Georg. "Buch und Brief: Zur motivischen, literarischen und kommunikativen Interdependenz zweier medialer Typen in der Johannes-Offenbarung." Pages 413–33 in Frey, Kelhofer, and Tóth, *Die Johannesapokalypse.*

Graf, Friedrich Wilhelm, and Klaus Wiegandt, eds. *Die Anfänge des Christentums.* Forum für Verantwortung. Frankfurt: Fischer Taschenbuch, 2009.

Graf, Fritz, and Sarah Iles Johnston. *Ritual Texts for the Afterlife: Orpheus and the Bacchic Gold Tablets.* New York: Routledge, 2007.

Grass, Hans. *Ostergeschehen und Osterberichte.* 2nd ed. Göttingen: Vandenhoeck & Ruprecht, 1962.

Grässer, Erich. *Der Alte Bund im Neuen.* WUNT 35. Tübingen: Mohr Siebeck, 1985.

———. "Der Alte Bund im Neuen." Pages 1–134 in Grässer, *Der Alte Bund im Neuen.*

———. *An die Hebräer.* EKKNT 17.1. Neukirchen-Vluyn: Neukirchener Verlag, 1990.

———. "Die antijüdische Polemik im Johannesevangelium." Pages 135–53 in Grässer, *Der Alte Bund im Neuen.*

———. "Kolosser 3,1–4 als Beispiel einer Interpretation secundum homines recipientes." Pages 123–51 in Grässer, *Text und Situation.*

———. *Das Problem der Parusieverzögerung in den synoptischen Evangelien und in der Apostelgeschichte.* 3rd ed. BZNW 22. Berlin: de Gruyter, 1977.

———. *Text und Situation: Gesammelte Aufsätze zum Neuen Testament.* Gütersloh: Gütersloher Verlagshaus, 1973.

———. "Das wandernde Gottesvolk: Zum Basismotiv des Hebräerbriefes." Pages 231–50 in Evang and Merk, *Aufbruch und Verheißung.*

———. "Das Wort als Heil." Pages 129–42 in Evang and Merk, *Aufbruch und Verheißung.*

Grässer, Erich, and Otto Merk, eds. *Glaube und Eschatologie: Festschrift für Werner Georg Kümmel zum 80. Geburtstag.* Mohr Siebeck, 1985.

Gregory, Andrew. *The Reception of Luke and Acts in the Period before Irenaeus.* WUNT 2/169. Tübingen: Mohr Siebeck, 2003.

Griffith, Terry. *Keep Yourselves from Idols: A New Look at 1 John.* JSNTSup 233. London: Sheffield Academic, 2002.

Gruben, Gottfried, Max Hirmer, and Albert Hirmer. *Griechische Tempel und Heiligtümer.* 5th ed. Darmstadt: Wissenschaftliche Buchgesellschaft, 2001.

Gruen, Erich S. *Heritage and Hellenism: The Reinvention of Jewish Tradition.* Berkeley: University of California Press, 1998.

Grund, Alexandra. *Die Entstehung des Sabbats: Seine Bedeutung für Israels Zeitkonzept und Erinnerungskultur.* FAT 75. Tübingen: Mohr Siebeck, 2011.

Gülzow, Henneke. *Christentum und Sklaverei in den ersten drei Jahrhunderten.* HthSt 16. Münster: Lit, 1999 (= 1969).

———. *Kirchengeschichte und Gegenwart.* Edited by Bärbel Dauber. Ausgewählte Werke 2. HThSt 17. Münster: Lit, 1999.

———. "Pontifikalreligion und Gesellschaft." Pages 13–34 in Gülzow, *Kirchengeschichte und Gegenwart.*

Günther, Matthias. *Die Frühgeschichte des Christentums in Ephesus.* ARGU 1. Frankfurt am Main: P. Lang, 1995.

Guttenberger, Gudrun. *Passio Christiana.* SBS 223. Stuttgart: Katholisches Bibelwerk, 2010.

Guyot, Peter, and Richard Klein, eds. *Das frühe Christentum bis zum Ende der Verfolgungen: Eine Dokumentation.* Vols. 1–2. Darmstadt: Wissenschaftliche Buchgesellschaft, 1997.

Haacker, Klaus. "Die Berufung des Verfolgers und die Rechtfertigung des Gottlosen." *TBei* 6 (1975): 1–19.

———. *Der Brief des Paulus an die Römer.* THK 6. 4th ed. Leipzig: Evangelische Verlagsanstalt, 2012.

———. *Stephanus: Verleumdet, verehrt, verkannt.* BG 28. Leipzig: Evangelische Verlagsanstalt, 2014.

Habicht, Christian. *Gottmenschentum und griechische Städte.* 2nd ed. Zet 14. Munich: Beck, 1970.

Hadot, Pierre. *Philosophie als Lebensform: Antike und moderne Exerzitien der Weisheit.* 2nd ed. Frankfurt: Fischer Taschenbuch, 2005.

Haenchen, Ernst. *The Acts of the Apostles: A Commentary.* Translated by Bernard Noble and Gerald Shinn, under the supervision of Hugh Anderson, and with the translation revised and brought up to date by R. McL. Wilson. Philadelphia: Westminster; Oxford: Blackwell, 1971.

———. *Die Apostelgeschichte.* 7th ed. KEK 3. Göttingen: Vandenhoek & Ruprecht 1977.

Haensch, Rudolf, and Jürgen Zangenberg. "Antiochia." Vol. 2, pages 133–39 in Erlemann et al., *Neues Testament und antike Kultur.*

Hafemann, Scott J. *Paul, Moses, and the History of Israel.* WUNT 81. Tübingen: Mohr Siebeck, 1995.

Häfner, Gerd. "Die Pastoralbriefe." Pages 463–65 in Ebner and Schreiber, *Einleitung in das Neue Testament* (2008).

Hahn, Ferdinand. "Das Apostolat im Urchristentum." *KuD* 20 (1974): 54–77.

———. *Christologische Hoheitstitel: Ihre Geschichte im frühen Christentum.* 5th ed. FRLANT 83. Göttingen: Vandenhoeck & Ruprecht, 1995.

———, ed. *Der Erzähler des Evangeliums: Methodische Neuansätze in der Markusforschung.* SBS 118–19. Stuttgart: Katholisches Bibelwerk, 1985.

———. *Exegetische Beiträge zum ökume-nischen Gespräch*. Göttingen: Vanden-hoeck & Ruprecht, 1986.

———. "Das Glaubensverständnis im Johannesevangelium." Pages 51–69 in Grässer and Merk, *Glaube und Eschatologie*.

———. *Mission in the New Testament*. London: SCM, 1965.

———. "Das neue Jerusalem." Pages 284–94 in Karrer, Kraus, and Merk, *Kirche und Volk Gottes*.

———. "Die Petrusverheißung Mt 16,18f." Pages 185–200 in F. Hahn, *Exegetische Beiträge zum ökumenischen Gespräch*.

———. "Sehen und Glauben im Johannes-evangelium." Pages 125–41 in *Neues Testament und Geschichte: Historisches Geschehen und Deutung im Neuen Testament; Oscar Cullmann zum 70. Geburtstag*. Edited by Heinrich Balten-sweiler and Bo Reicke. Zurich: Theologi-scher Verlag; Tübingen: Mohr Siebeck, 1972.

———. *Theologie des Neuen Testament*. 2 vols. Tübingen: Mohr Siebeck, 2011.

———. *The Titles of Jesus in Christology: Their History in Early Christianity*. Lut-terworth Library. Translated by Harold Knight and George Ogg. London: Lut-terworth, 1969.

Hahn, Ferdinand, and Hans Klein. *Die früh-christliche Prophetie: Ihre Voraussetzun-gen, ihre Anfänge und ihre Entwicklung bis zum Montanismus; Eine Einführung*. BTS 116. Neukirchen-Vluyn: Neukir-chener Verlagsgesellschaft, 2011.

Hahn, Horst. *Tradition und Neuinterpre-tation im ersten Johannesbrief*. Zurich: Theologischer Verlag, 2009.

Hahn, Johannes. *Der Philosoph und die Ge-sellschaft: Selbstverständnis, öffentliches Auftreten und populäre Erwartungen in der hohen Kaiserzeit*. Stuttgart: Steiner, 1989.

———. *Zerstörungen des Jerusalemer Tempels*. WUNT 147. Tübingen: Mohr Siebeck, 2002.

Hakola, Raimo. "The Johannine Commu-nity as Jewish Christians? Some Prob-lems in Current Scholarly Consensus. Pages 181–201 in Jackson-McCabe, *Jewish Christianity Reconsidered*.

Haldimann, Konrad. *Rekonstruktion und Entfaltung: Exegetische Untersuchungen zu Joh 15 und 16*. BZNW 104. Berlin: de Gruyter, 2000.

Hampel, Volker. *Menschensohn und histori-scher Jesus: Ein Rätselwort als Schlüssel zum messianischen Selbstverständnis Jesu*. Neukirchen-Vluyn: Neukirchener Verlag, 1990.

Hansen, Bruce. *"All of You Are One": The Social Vision of Gal 3,28; 1 Cor 12,13 and Col 3,11*. LNTS 409. New York: T&T Clark, 2010.

Hanslik, Robert. "Der Erzählungskomplex vom Brand Roms und der Christenverfol-gung bei Tacitus." *WS* 76 (1963): 92–109.

Hanson, Kenneth C., and Douglas E. Oak-man. *Palestine in the Time of Jesus: So-cial Structures and Social Conflicts*. 2nd ed. Minneapolis: Fortress, 2008.

Harding, Mark, and Alanna Nobbs, eds. *The Content and Setting of the Gospel Tradi-tion*. Grand Rapids: Eerdmans, 2010.

———. *Into All the World: Emergent Chris-tianity in Its Jewish and Greco-Roman Context*. Grand Rapids: Eerdmans, 2017.

Harnack, Adolf von. *Aus Wissenschaft und Leben*. Vol. 2. Giessen: Töpelmann, 1911.

———. *Die Briefsammlung des Apostels Paulus und die anderen vorkonstanti-nischen christlichen Briefsammlungen: Sechs vorlesungen aus der altkirchlichen literaturgeschichte*. Leipzig: Hinrich's Buchhandlung, 1926.

———. "Das doppelte Evangelium im Neuen Testament." Vol. 2, pages 211–24 in Harnack, *Aus Wissenschaft und Leben.*

———. *Einführung in die alte Kirchenge-schichte: Das Schreiben der römischen Kirche an die korinthische aus der Zeit Domitians (1. Clemensbrief).* Leipzig: Hinrich, 1929.

———. *The Expansion of Christianity in the First Three Centuries.* Translated and edited by James Moffatt. 2 vols. London: Williams & Norgate, 1904–5.

———. *The Mission and Expansion of Christianity in the First Three Centuries.* Translated and edited by James Moffatt. New York: Harper, 1962.

———. *Das Neue Testament um das Jahr 200: Theodor Zahn's Geschichte des neutestamentlichen Kanons (erster Band, erste Hälfte).* Freiburg im Breisgau: Mohr Siebeck, 1889.

———. *Über den 3. Johannesbrief.* TUGAL 14.3b. Leipzig: J. C. Hinrichs, 1897.

Harrill, James Albert. "Paul and Empire: Studying Roman Identity after the Cultural Turn." *EC* 2 (2011): 281–311.

———. *Slaves in the New Testament: Literary, Social, and Moral Dimensions.* Minneapolis: Fortress, 2006.

Harris, William V. *Ancient Literacy.* Cambridge, MA: Harvard University Press, 1989.

Hartmann, Lars. *Auf den Namen des Herrn Jesus: Die Taufe in den neutestamentlichen Schriften.* SBS 148. Stuttgart: Verlag Katholisches Bibelwerk, 1992.

Hatch, Edwin. *The Influence of Greek Ideas on Christianity.* London: Williams & Norgate, 1891.

Haug, Werner. *Politische Verfolgung: Ein Beitrag zur Soziologie der Herrschaft und der politischen Gewalt.* Grüsch: Rüegger, 1986.

Hawthorne, Gerald F., and Ralph P. Martin, eds. *Dictionary of Paul and His Letters.* Downers Grove, IL: InterVarsity, 1993.

Hays, Christopher M. *When the Son of Man Didn't Come: A Constructive Proposal on the Delay of the Parousia.* Minneapolis: Augsburg Fortress, 2017.

Hays, Richard B. *Echoes of Scripture in the Letters of Paul.* New Haven: Yale University Press, 1989.

———. "'New Covenantalism': Eine Wiederentdeckung." *ZNT* 29 (2012): 53–56.

Heckel, Theo K. "Die Traditionsverknüpfungen des Zweiten Petrusbriefes und die Anfänge einer neutestamentlichen biblischen Theologie." Pages 189–204 in *Die bleibende Gegenwart des Evangeliums (Festschrift für Otto Merk).* Edited by Roland Gebauer and Martin Meiser. MTS 76. Marburg: N. G. Elwert, 2003.

———. *Vom Evangelium des Markus zum viergestaltigen Evangelium.* WUNT 120. Tübingen: Mohr Siebeck, 1999.

Heckel, Ulrich. *Kraft in Schwachheit: Untersuchungen zu 2. Kor 10–13.* WUNT 2/56. Tübingen: Mohr Siebeck, 1993.

Heemstra, Marius. *The Fiscus Judaicus and the Parting of the Ways.* WUNT 2/277. Tübingen: Mohr Siebeck, 2010.

Hegermann, Harald. *Der Brief an die Hebräer.* THK 16. Berlin: 1988.

———. "Das Wort Gottes als aufdeckende Macht." Pages 83–98 in Seidel, *Das lebendige Wort.*

Heid, Stefan, and Raban von Haehling, eds. *Petrus und Paulus in Rom: Eine interdisziplinäre Debatte.* Freiburg im Breisgau: Herder, 2011.

Heil, Christoph. *Die Ablehnung der Speisegebote durch Paulus: Zur Frage nach der Stellung des Apostels zum Gesetz.* BBB 96. Weinheim: Beltz Athenäum, 1994.

———. *Lukas und Q: Studien zur lukanischen Redaktion des Spruchevangeliums Q.* BZNW 111. Berlin: de Gruyter, 2003.

———. "Die Q-Gruppe in Galiläa und Syrien." Pages 136–80 in *Spurensuche zur Einleitung in das Neue Testament: Eine*

Festschrift im Dialog mit Udo Schnelle. Edited by Michael Labahn. FRLANT 271. Göttingen: Vandenhoeck & Ruprecht, 2017.

Heil, Matthäus, and Klaus Wachtel, eds. *Prosopographia Imperii Romani: Saec. I. II. III. Pars VII. Fasciculus 2, [S].* Berlin: de Gruyter, 2006.

Heiligenthal, Roman. *Der verfälschte Jesus: Eine Kritik moderner Jesusbilder.* Darmstadt: Wissenschaftliche Buchgesellschaft, 1997.

———. *Zwischen Henoch und Paulus: Studien zum theologiegeschichtlichen Ort des Judasbriefes.* TANZ 6. Tübingen: Franke, 1992.

Heinen, Heinz. *Geschichte des Hellenismus: Von Alexander bis Kleopatra.* Munich: Beck, 2003.

Heininger, Bernhard. "Einmal Tarsus und zurück (Apg 9,30; 11,25–26): Paulus als Lehrer nach der Apostelgeschichte." *MTZ* 49 (1998): 125–43.

———. "Im Dunstkreis der Magie: Paulus als Wundertäter nach der Apostelgeschichte." Pages 271–91 in E.-M. Becker and Pilhofer, *Biographie und Persönlichkeit des Paulus.*

———. *Paulus als Visionär: Eine religionsgeschichtliche Studie.* HBS 9. Freiburg: Herder, 1996.

Heinrici, Georg. "Die Christengemeinden Korinths und die religiösen Genossenschaften der Griechen." *ZWT* 17 (1876): 465–526.

Heinz-Wolfgang Kuhn. *Ältere Sammlungen im Markusevangelium.* SUNT 8. Göttingen: Vandenhoeck & Ruprecht, 1971.

Heitmüller, Wilhelm. *"Im Namen Jesu": Eine sprach- und religionsgeschichtliche Untersuchung zum Neuen Testament, speziell zur altchristlichen Taufe.* FRLANT 2. Göttingen: Vandenhoeck & Ruprecht, 1903.

———. "Zur Johannes-Tradition." *ZNW* 15 (1914): 189–209.

Hellholm, David, ed. *Apocalypticism in the Mediterranean World and the Near East.* Proceedings of the International Colloquium on Apocalypticism, Uppsala, August 12–17, 1979. Tübingen: Mohr, 1983.

Hellholm, David, Tor Vegge, and Christer Hellholm, eds. *Ablution, Initiation and Baptism.* 3 vols. BZNW 176. Berlin: de Gruyter, 2011.

Hengel, Martin. "Abba, Maranatha, Hosanna und die Anfänge der Christologie." Pages 144–83 in *Denkwürdiges Geheimnis, Beiträge zur Gotteslehre: Festschrift für Eberhard Jüngel zum 70. Geburtstag.* Edited by Ingolf U. Dalferth, Johannes Fischer, and Hans-Peter Grosshans. Tübingen: Mohr Siebeck, 2006.

———. *The Atonement: The Origins of the Doctrine in the New Testament.* Translated by John Bowden. Philadelphia: Fortress; London: SCM, 1981.

———. "The Attitude of Paul to the Law in the Unknown Years between Damascus and Antioch." Pages 25–52 in Dunn, *Paul and the Mosaic Law.*

———. "Das Begräbnis Jesu bei Paulus und die leibliche Auferstehung aus dem Grabe." Pages 119–83 in Avemarie and Lichtenberger, *Auferstehung.*

———. *Between Jesus and Paul: Studies in the Earliest History of Christianity.* Translated by John Bowden. Philadelphia: Fortress, 1983.

———. "Die Evangelienüberschriften." Pages 526–67 in Hengel, *Jesus und die Evangelien.*

———. "Das früheste Christentum als eine jüdische messianische und universalistische Bewegung." *TBei* 28 (1997): 197–210.

———. "Der Jakobusbrief als antipaulinische Polemik." Pages 510–48 in Hengel, *Paulus und Jakobus.*

————. "Jakobus der Herrenbruder der erste 'Papst'?" Pages 71–104 in *Glaube und Eschatologie: Festschrift für Werner Georg Kümmel zum 80. Geburtstag.* Edited by Erich Grässer and Otto Merk. Tübingen: Mohr Siebeck, 1985.

————. "Jesus der Messias Israels." Pages 1–80 in *Der messianische Anspruch Jesu und die Anfänge der Christologie.* Edited by Martin Hengel and Anna Maria Schwemer. WUNT 138. Tübingen: Mohr Siebeck, 2001.

————. *Jesus und die Evangelien.* WUNT 211. Tübingen: Mohr Siebeck, 2007.

————. "Jesus und die Tora." *TBei* 9 (1978): 152–72.

————. *Die johanneische Frage.* WUNT 67. Tübingen: Mohr Siebeck, 1993.

————. *The Johannine Question.* London: SCM; Philadelphia: Trinity Press International, 1989.

————. *Judaism and Hellenism: Studies in Their Encounter in Palestine during the Early Hellenistic Period.* Translated by John Bowden. 2 vols. Philadelphia: Fortress, 1974, 1981.

————. "Literary, Theological, and Historical Problems in the Gospel of Mark." Pages 209–51 in *The Gospel and the Gospels.* Edited by Peter Stuhlmacher. Grand Rapids: Eerdmans, 1991.

————. "Mors turpissima crucis: Die Kreuzigung in der antiken Welt und die 'Torheit' 'des Wortes vom Kreuz.'" Pages 125–84 in J. Friedrich, Stuhlmacher, and Pöhlmann, *Rechtfertigung.*

————. "The Origins of Christian Mission." Pages 48–64 in Hengel, *Between Jesus and Paul.*

————. "Paulus und die Frage einer vorchristlichen Gnosis." Pages 473–510 in Hengel, *Paulus und Jakobus.*

————. *Paulus und Jakobus.* WUNT 141. Tübingen: Mohr Siebeck, 2002.

————. *The Pre-Christian Paul.* In collaboration with Roland Deines. Philadelphia: Trinity Press International; London: SCM, 1991.

————. *Property and Riches in the Early Church: Aspects of a Social History of Early Christianity.* Translated by John Bowden. Philadelphia: Fortress, 1974.

————. "Psalm 110 und die Erhöhung des Auferstandenen zur Rechten Gottes." Pages 43–73 in Breytenbach and Paulsen, *Anfänge der Christologie.*

————. *Saint Peter: The Underestimated Apostle.* Translated by Thomas H. Trapp. Grand Rapids: Eerdmans, 2010.

————. *The Son of God: The Origin of Christology and the History of Jewish-Hellenistic Religion.* Translated by John Bowden. Philadelphia: Fortress, 1976.

————. "Die Stellung des Apostels Paulus zum Gesetz in den unbekannten Jahren zwischen Damaskus und Antiochia." Pages 25–51 in Dunn, *Paul and the Mosaic Law.*

————. "Überlegungen zu einer Geschichte des frühesten." Pages 139–71 in Auffarth and Rüpke, Ἐπιτομὴ τῆς οἰκουμένης.

————. *Der unterschätzte Petrus: Zwei Studien.* Tübingen: Mohr Siebeck, 2006.

————. *Die vier Evangelien und das eine Evangelium von Jesus Christus.* WUNT 224. Tübingen: Mohr Siebeck, 2008.

————. *The Zealots: Investigations into the Jewish Freedom Movement in the Period from Herod until 70 A.D.* London: T&T Clark, 1989.

————. "Zwischen Jesus und Paulus." *ZTK* 72 (1975): 151–206.

Hengel, Martin, and Ulrich Heckel, eds. *Paulus und das antike Judentum: Tübingen-Durham-Symposium im Gedenken an den 50. Todestag Adolf Schlatters (19. Mai 1938).* WUNT 58. Tübingen: Mohr Siebeck, 1991.

———. "Der vorchristliche Paulus." Pages 177–293 in Hengel and U. Heckel, *Paulus und das antike Judentum*.

Hengel, Martin, and Anna Maria Schwemer. *Jesus und das Judentum*. GFC 1. Tübingen: Mohr Siebeck, 2007.

———. *Der messianische Anspruch Jesu und die Anfänge der Christologie: Vier Studien*. WUNT 138. Tübingen: Mohr Siebeck, 2001.

———. *Paul between Damascus and Antioch: The Unknown Years*. Louisville: Westminster John Knox, 1997.

———. *Paulus zwischen Damaskus und Antiochien: Die unbekannten Jahre des Apostels*. WUNT 108. Tübingen: Mohr Siebeck, 1998.

Henten, J. W. van, ed. *Tradition and Reinterpretation in Jewish and Early Christian Literature: Essays in Honour of Jürgen C. H. Lebram*. SPB 36. Leiden: Brill, 1986.

Hentschel, Anni. *Diakonia im Neuen Testament: Studien zur Semantik unter besonderer Berücksichtigung der Rolle von Frauen*. WUNT 2/226. Tübingen: Mohr Siebeck, 2007.

Hergenröder, Clemens. *Wir schauten seine Herrlichkeit: Das johanneische Sprechen vom Sehen im Horizont von Selbsterschliessung Jesu und Antwort des Menschen*. FzB 80. Würzburg: Echter, 1996.

Herrmann-Otto, Elisabeth. *Sklaverei und Freilassung in der griechisch-römischen Welt*. Studienbücher Antike 15. Hildesheim: Olms, 2009.

———. "Soziale Schichten und Gruppe." Vol. 2, pages 86–99 in Erlemann et al., *Neues Testament und antike Kultur*.

Herzer, Jens. "Juden—Christen—Gnostiker: Zur Gegnerproblematik der Pastoralbriefe." *BTZ* 25 (2008): 143–68.

———. *Petrus oder Paulus?* WUNT 103. Tübingen: Mohr Siebeck, 1998.

———. "Was ist falsch an der 'fälschlich so genannten Gnosis'? Zur Paulusrezeption des Ersten Timotheusbriefes im Kontext seiner Gegnerpolemik." *EC* 5 (2014): 68–96.

Hezser, Catherine. *Jewish Literacy in Roman Palestine*. TSAJ 81. Tübingen: Mohr Siebeck, 2001.

Hilgenfeld, Adolf. *Die Ketzergeschichte des Urchristentums, urkundlich dargestellt*. Darmstadt: Wissenschaftliche Buchgesellschaft, 1966 (= 1884).

Hill, Craig C. *Hellenists and Hebrews: Reappraising Division within the Earliest Church*. Minneapolis: Fortress, 1992.

Hirschberg, Peter. *Das eschatologische Israel*. WMANT 84. Neukirchen-Vluyn: Neukirchener Verlag, 1999.

Hirschfeld, Yizhar. *Qumran—die ganze Wahrheit: Die Funde der Archäologie—neu bewertet*. Gütersloh: Gütersloher Verlagshaus, 2006.

Hirsch-Luipold, Rainer. *Gott und die Götter bei Plutarch*. Berlin: De Gruyter, 2005.

Hock, Ronald F. *The Social Context of Paul's Ministry*. Minneapolis: Fortress, 1980.

Hoegen-Rohls, Christina. "Johanneische Theologie im Kontext paulinischen Denkens? Eine forschungsgeschichtliche Skizze." Pages 593–612 in Frey and Schnelle, *Kontexte des Johannesevangeliums*.

———. *Der nachösterliche Johannes: Die Abschiedsreden als hermeneutischer Schlüssel zum vierten Evangelium*. WUNT 2/84. Tübingen: Mohr, 1996.

———. *Zwischen Augenblickskorrespondenz und Ewigkeitstexten: Eine Einführung in die paulinische Epistolographie*. BTS 135. Neukirchen-Vluyn: Neukirchener Theologie, 2013.

Hoennicke, Gustav. *Das Judenchristentum im ersten und zweiten Jahrhundert*. Berlin: Trowitzsch & Sohn, 1908.

Hoff, Ralf von den, Wilfried Stroh, and
Martin Zimmermann. *Divus Augustus:
Der erste römische Kaiser und seine Welt.*
Munich: Beck, 2014.

Hoffmann, Paul. "Die historisch-kritische
Osterdiskussion von H. S. Reimarus bis zu
Beginn des 20. Jahrhunderts." Pages 15–67
in Hoffmann, *Zur neutestamentlichen
Überlieferung von der Auferstehung Jesu.*

———. "Markus 8,31: Zur Herkunft und
markinischen Rezeption einer alten Überlieferung." Pages 281–312 in Hoffmann,
Tradition und Situation.

———. "Der Petrus-Primat im Matthäusevangelium." Pages 94–114 in *Neues
Testament und Kirche: Für Rudolf
Schnackenburg [z. 60. Geburtstag am
5. Jan. 1974 von Freunden und Kollegen
gewidmet].* Edited by Rudolf Schnackenburg and Joachim Gnilka. Freiburg im
Breisgau: Herder, 1974.

———. *Tradition und Situation: Studien zur
Jesusüberlieferung in der Logienquelle
und den synoptischen Evangelien.* NTA
28. Münster: Aschendorff, 1995.

———, ed. *Zur neutestamentlichen Überlieferung von der Auferstehung Jesu.* WdF
522. Darmstadt: Wissenschaftliche Buchgesellschaft, 1988.

Hoffmann, Paul, and Christoph Heil. *Die
Spruchquelle Q: Griechisch und Deutsch
[griechischer Text nach der "Critical edition of Q" des International Q Project].*
4th ed. Darmstadt: Wissenschaftliche
Buchgesellschaft, 2013.

Hofius, Otfried. *Der Christushymnus Philipper 2,6–11.* WUNT 17. Tübingen: Mohr
Siebeck, 1976.

———. "Gesetz und Evangelium nach
2. Korinther 3." Pages 75–120 in Hofius,
Paulusstudien.

———. *Paulusstudien.* WUNT 51. Tübingen: Mohr Siebeck, 1989.

Hofius, Otfried, and Hans-Christian Kammler. *Johannesstudien: Untersuchungen*
zur Theologie des vierten Evangeliums.
WUNT 88. Tübingen: Mohr Siebeck,
1996.

Holmberg, Bengt, ed. *Exploring Early Christian Identity.* WUNT 226. Tübingen:
Mohr Siebeck, 2008.

———. "Understanding the First Hundred
Years of Christian Identity." Pages 1–32
in Holmberg, *Exploring Early Christian
Identity.*

Holmes, Michael W., ed. and trans. *The
Apostolic Fathers: Greek Texts and En-
glish Translations.* 3rd ed. Grand Rapids:
Baker Academic, 2007.

Holtz, Gudrun. *Damit Gott sei alles in allem.*
BZNW 149. Berlin: de Gruyter, 2007.

Holtz, Traugott. "Die Bedeutung des Apostelkonzils für Paulus." Pages 140–70 in T.
Holtz, *Geschichte und Theologie.*

———. "Christus Diakonos." Pages
127–43 in Schäfer and Strohm,
*Diakonie—biblische Grundlagen und
Orientierungen.*

———. *Geschichte und Theologie des
Urchristentums.* WUNT 57. Tübingen:
Mohr Siebeck, 1991.

———. *Die Offenbarung des Johannes.*
NTD 11. Göttingen: Vandenhoeck &
Ruprecht, 2008.

Hommel, Hildebrecht. *Sebasmata: Studien
zur antiken Religionsgeschichte und zum
frühen Christentum.* Vol. 2. WUNT 32.
Tübingen: Mohr Siebeck, 1984.

———. "Tacitus und die Christen." Vol. 2,
pages 174–99 in Hommel, *Sebasmata.*

Hoppe, Rudolf. "Arm und Reich im Jakobusbrief." Pages 106–15 in Berges and
Hoppe, *Arm und Reich.*

Horn, Friedrich Wilhelm. *Das Angeld des
Geistes: Studien zur paulinischen Pneu-
matologie.* FRLANT 154. Göttingen:
Vandenhoeck & Ruprecht, 1992.

———, ed. *Bilanz und Perspektiven gegenwärtiger Auslegung des Neuen Testaments: Symposion zum 65. Geburtstag*

von Georg Strecker. BZNW 75. Berlin: de Gruyter, 1995.

———. "Christentum und Judentum in der Logienquelle." *EvT* 51 (1991): 311 61.

———. "Diakonische Leitlinien Jesu." Pages 109–26 in Schäfer and Strohm, *Diakonie—biblische Grundlagen und Orientierungen.*

———, ed. *Das Ende des Paulus: Historische, theologische und literaturgeschichtliche Aspekte.* BZNW 106. Berlin: de Gruyter, 2001.

———. *Glaube und Handeln in der Theologie des Lukas.* 2nd ed. GTA 26. Göttingen: Vandenhoeck & Ruprecht, 1986.

———. "Die Gütergemeinschaft der Urgemeinde." *EvT* 58 (1998): 370–83.

———. "Die Kollektenthematik in der Apostelgeschichte." Pages 135–56 in Breytenbach and Schröter, *Die Apostelgeschichte und die hellenistische Geschichtsschreibung.*

———. "Die letzte Jerusalemreise des Paulus." Pages 15–35 in Horn, *Das Ende des Paulus.*

———. "Paulus, das Nasiräat und die Nasiräer." *NovT* 39 (1997): 117–37.

———, ed. *Paulus Handbuch.* Tübingen: Mohr Siebeck, 2013.

———. "Die Petrus-Schule in Rom." Pages 3–20 in Du Toit, *Bedrängnis und Identität.*

———. "Stephanas und sein Haus: Die erste christliche Hausgemeinde in der Achaia." Pages 83–98 in *Paulus und die antike Welt: Festgabe für Dietrich-Alex Koch zum 65. Geburtstag.* Edited by David C. Bienert et al. FRLANT 222. Göttingen: Vandenhoeck & Ruprecht, 2008.

———. "Der Verzicht auf die Beschneidung im Frühen Christentum." *NTS* 42 (1996): 479–505.

———. "Wollte Paulus 'kanonisch' wirken?" Pages 400–422 in *Kanon in Konstruktion und Dekonstruktion: Kanonisierungsprozesse religiöser Texte von der Antike bis zur Gegenwart—ein Handbuch.* Edited by Eve-Marie Becker and Stefan Scholz. Berlin: de Gruyter, 2011.

Horrell, David G. "Domestic Space and Christian Meetings at Corinth: Imagining New Contexts and the Buildings East of the Theatre." *NTS* 50 (2004): 349–69.

Horsley, Richard A. "1 Corinthians: A Case Study of Paul's Assembly as an Alternative Society." Pages 242–52 in Horsley, *Paul and Empire.*

———. "Die Jesusbewegung und die Erneuerung Israels." Pages 37–62 in *Die ersten Christen.* Edited by Richard A. Horsley. Gütersloh: Gütersloher Verlagshaus, 2007.

———, ed. *Paul and Empire: Religion and Power in Roman Imperial Society.* Harrisburg, PA: Trinity Press International, 1997.

———. *Paul and Politics: Ekklesia, Israel, Imperium, Interpretation.* Harrisburg, PA: Trinity Press International, 2000.

———. *Revolt of the Scribes: Resistance and Apocalyptic Origins.* Minneapolis: Fortress, 2010.

Horsley, Richard A., Jonathan A. Draper, John Miles Foley, and Werner H. Kelber, eds. *Performing the Gospel: Orality, Memory, and Mark; Essays Dedicated to Werner Kelber.* Minneapolis: Fortress, 2011.

Hossenfelder, Malte. *Antike Glückslehren: Kynismus und Kyrenaismus, Stoa, Epikureismus und Skepsis: Quellen in deutscher Übersetzung mit Einführungen.* Kröners Taschenausgabe 424. Stuttgart: Kröner, 1996.

———. *Epikur.* Beck'sche Reihe 520: Grosse Denker. Munich: Beck, 1991.

———. *Stoa, Epikureismus und Skepsis.* Vol. 3 of *Die Philosophie der Antike.* 2nd ed. Geschichte der Philisophie 3. Munich: Beck, 1995.

Hotze, Gerhard. *Paradoxien bei Paulus: Untersuchungen zu einer elementaren Denkform in seiner Theologie.* NTA 33. Münster: Aschendorff, 1997.

Hübenthal, Sandra. *Das Markusevangelium als kollektives Gedächtnis.* FRLANT 253. Göttingen: Vandenhoek & Ruprecht, 2014.

Hübner, Hans. *Vetus Testamentum in Novo.* Vol. 2, *Corpus Paulinum.* Göttingen: Vandenhoeck & Ruprecht, 1997.

Hübner, Kurt. *Die Wahrheit des Mythos.* Munich: Beck, 1985.

Hübner, Reinhard M. "Thesen zur Echtheit und Datierung der sieben Briefe des Ignatius von Antiochien." *ZAC* 1 (1997): 44–72.

Hulmi, Sini. *Paulus und Mose: Argumentation und Polemik in 2 Kor 3.* SFEG 77. Helsinki; Göttingen: Vandenhoek & Ruprecht, 1999.

Hüneburg, Martin. *Jesus als Wundertäter in der Logienquelle: Ein Beitrag zur Christologie von Q.* ABG 4. Leipzig: Evangelische Verlagsanstalt, 2001.

Huninck, Vincent, ed. *Glücklich ist dieser Ort! 1000 Graffiti aus Pompeji.* Stuttgart: Reclam, 2011.

Hunzinger, Claus Hunno. "Die Hoffnung angesichts des Todes im Wandel der paulinischen Aussagen." Pages 69–88 in *Leben angesichts des Todes: Beiträge zum theologischen Problem des Todes; Helmut Thielicke zum 60. Geburtstag.* Edited by Bernhard Lohse. Tübingen: Mohr Siebeck, 1968.

Hurtado, Larry W. *Destroyer of the Gods: Early Christian Distinctiveness in the Roman World.* Waco: Baylor University Press, 2016.

———. *Lord Jesus Christ: Devotion to Jesus in Earliest Christianity.* Grand Rapids: Eerdmans, 2003.

———. *One God, One Lord: Early Christian Devotion and Ancient Jewish Monotheism.* 2nd ed. Edinburgh: T&T Clark, 1998.

———. "Son of God." Pages 900–906 in Hawthorne and Martin, *Dictionary of Paul and His Letters.*

Hüttemann, Arno, ed. *Pompejanische Inschriften.* Stuttgart: Reclam, 2010.

Ischmeyer, Oda, David C. Sim, and Ian J. Elmer. *Paul and Mark.* BZNW 198. Berlin: de Gruyter, 2014.

Iser, Wolfgang. *The Act of Reading: A Theory of Aesthetic Response.* Baltimore: Johns Hopkins Press, 1978.

Jackson, Frederick J. F., and Kirsopp Lake, eds. *The Beginnings of Christianity.* 5 vols. London: Macmillan, 1920–33.

Jackson-McCabe, Matt, ed. *Jewish Christianity Reconsidered: Rethinking Ancient Groups and Texts.* Minneapolis: Fortress, 2007.

Jaeger, Werner. *The Theology of the Early Greek Philosophers.* Westport, CT: Greenwood, 1980.

Janowski, Bernd. *Stellvertretung: Alttestamentliche Studien zu einem theologischen Grundbegriff.* SBS 165. Stuttgart: Katholisches Bibelwerk, 1997.

Jeremias, Joachim. *Die Abendmahlsworte Jesu.* 4th ed. Göttingen: Vandenhoeck & Ruprecht, 1967.

———. *The Eucharistic Words of Jesus.* Translated by Norman Perrin from the 3rd ed. New York: Scribner, 1966.

———. *Jerusalem in the Time of Jesus: An Investigation into Economic and Social Conditions during the New Testament Period.* Philadelphia: Fortress, 1969.

Jervell, Jacob. *Die Apostelgeschichte.* KEK 3. Göttingen: Vandenhoeck & Ruprecht, 1998.

Jewett, Robert. *Romans.* Herm. Minneapolis: Fortress, 2007.

Johnson, Luke Timothy. *Among the Gentiles: Greco-Roman Religion and Christianity*. New Haven: Yale University Press, 2009.

———. *The Literary Function of Possessions in Luke-Acts*. SBLDS 39. Missoula, MT: Scholars Press, 1977.

Johnson, William A., and Holt N. Parker, eds. *Ancient Literacies: The Culture of Reading in Greece and Rome*. Oxford: Oxford University Press, 2009.

Johnson-Debaufre, Melanie. *Q, Eschatology, and the Construction of Christian Origins*. HTS 55. Cambridge, MA: Harvard University Press, 2005.

Jonas, Hans. *Gnosis und spätantiker Geist*. 2 vols. 4th ed. FRLANT 159. Göttingen: Vandenhoeck & Ruprecht, 1988–93.

Jones, F. Stanley, ed. *The Rediscovery of Jewish Christianity: From Toland to Baur*. Atlanta: Society of Biblical Literature, 2012.

Jones, Howard. *The Epicurean Tradition*. London: Routledge, 1989.

Jonge, Marinus de. *Christologie im Kontext: Die Jesusrezeption des Urchristentums*. Neukirchen-Vluyn: Neukirchener Verlag, 1995.

Jordan, Stefan. *Theorien und Methoden der Geschichtswissenschaft*. Paderborn: Schöningh, 2009.

Judge, Edwin A. *Social Pattern of the Christian Groups in the First Century: Some Prolegomena to the Study of New Testament Ideas of Social Obligation*. London: Tyndale, 1960.

Jung, Franz. ΣΩΤΗΡ: *Studien zur Rezeption eines hellenistischen Ehrentitels im Neuen Testament*. NTA 39. Münster: Aschendorff, 2002.

Jürgens, Burkhard. *Zweierlei Anfang: Konstruktionen heidenchristlicher Identität in Gal 2 und Apg 15*. BBB 120. Bodenheim and Berlin: Philo, 1999.

Jüthner, Julius. *Hellenen und Barbaren aus der Geschichte des Nationalbewusstseins*. EdA 2/8. Leipzig: Dieterich, 1923.

Jütte, Robert, and Abraham Peter Kustermann, eds. *Jüdische Gemeinden und Organisationsformen von der Antike bis zur Gegenwart, Aschkenas*. ZGKJ Beiheft 3. Vienna: Böhlau, 1996.

Kähler, Christoph, Martina Böhm, and Christfried Böttrich, eds. *Gedenkt an das Wort: Festschrift für Werner Vogler zum 65. Geburtstag*. Leipzig: Evangelische Verlagsanstalt, 1999.

Kaiser, Otto. "Die Botschaft des Buches Kohelet." Pages 126–48 in Kaiser, *Gottes und der Menschen Weisheit*.

———. *Gottes und der Menschen Weisheit: Gesammelte Aufsätze*. BZAW 261. Berlin: de Gruyter, 1998.

Kaiser, Otto, and Peter Oesterreich. *Die Rede von Gott und der Welt: Religionsphilosophie und Fundamentalrhetorik*. Ulm: Humboldt-Studienzentrum, Universität Ulm, 1996.

Kajanto, Iiro. "Minderheiten und ihre Sprachen in Rom." Pages 83–102 in G. Neumann and Untermann, *Die Sprachen im Römischen Reich der Kaiserzeit*.

Kammler, Hans-Christian. *Christologie und Eschatologie: Joh 5, 17–30 als Schlüsseltext johanneischer Theologie*. WUNT 126. Tübingen: Mohr Siebeck, 2000.

———. "Die Prädikation Jesu Christi als 'Gott' und die paulinische Christologie." ZNW 94 (2003): 164–80.

Kampling, Rainer. "*Dies ist das Buch . . .*": Das Matthäusevangelium; Interpretation—Rezeption—Rezeptionsgeschichte; Für Hubert Frankemölle. Paderborn: Schöningh, 2004.

Kampling, Rainer, and Thomas Söding, eds. *Ekklesiologie des Neuen Testaments: Für Karl Kertelge*. Freiburg: Herder, 1996.

Karrer, Martin. "Apoll und die apokalyptischen Reiter." Pages 223–51 in Labahn and Karrer, *Die Johannesoffenbarung*.

———. *Der Brief an die Hebräer*. ÖTK 20/1. Gütersloh: Gütersloher Verlagshaus, 2002.

———. "Christliche Gemeinde und Israel: Beobachtungen zur Logienquelle." Pages 145–63 in *Gottes Recht als Lebensraum: Festschrift für Hans Jochen Boecker*. Edited by Peter Mommer, Werner H. Schmidt, and Hans Strauss. Neukirchen-Vluyn: Neukirchener Verlag, 1993.

———. *Der Gesalbte: Die Grundlagen des Christustitels*. FRLANT 151. Göttingen: Vandenhoeck & Ruprecht, 1990.

———. *Jesus Christus im Neuen Testament*. GNT 11. Göttingen: Vandenhoeck & Ruprecht, 1998.

———. *Die Johannesoffenbarung als Brief*. FRLANT 140. Göttingen: Vandenhoeck & Ruprecht, 1986.

———. "Petrus im paulinischen Gemeindekreis." *ZNW* 80 (1989): 210–31.

———. "Das urchristliche Ältestenamt." *NovT* 32 (1990): 152–88.

Karrer, Martin, Wolfgang Kraus, and Otto Merk, eds. *Kirche und Volk Gottes: Festschrift für Jürgen Roloff zum 70. Geburtstag*. Neukirchen-Vluyn: Neukirchener Verlag, 2000.

Karwiese, Stefan. *Groß ist die Artemis von Ephesos: Die Geschichte einer der großen Städte der Antike*. Wien: Phoibos, 1995.

Käsemann, Ernst. *Commentary on Romans*. Translated and edited by Geoffrey W. Bromiley. Grand Rapids: Eerdmans, 1980.

———. *Exegetische Versuche und Besinnungen*. 6th ed. Göttingen: Vandenhoeck & Ruprecht, 1970.

———. *Jesu letzter Wille nach Johannes 17*. 3rd ed. Tübingen: Mohr, 1971.

———. "Ketzer und Zeuge." Vol. 1, pages 168–87 in Käsemann, *Exegetische Versuche und Besinnungen*.

———. *The Testament of Jesus: A Study of the Gospel of John in the Light of Chapter 17*. Translated by Gerhard Krodel. Philadelphia: Fortress, 1968.

Kasher, Aryeh. *Jews and Hellenistic Cities in Eretz Israel: Relations of the Jews in Eretz-Israel with the Hellenistic Cities during the Second Temple Period (332 BCE–70 CE)*. TSAJ 21. Tübingen: Mohr, 1990.

Keck, Leander E. *Romans*. ANTC. Nashville: Abingdon, 2005.

Keel, Othmar. *Die Geschichte Jerusalems und die Entstehung des Monotheismus*. Vol. 1. Göttingen: Vandenhoeck & Ruprecht, 2007.

Keller, Reiner. *Diskursforschung: Eine Einführung für SozialwissenschaftlerInnen*. 2nd ed. Wiesbaden: VS Verlag für Sozialwissenschaften, 2004.

Kertelge, Karl, ed. *Das Gesetz im Neuen Testament*. QD 108. Freiburg: Herder, 1986.

———, ed. *Das kirchliche Amt im Neuen Testament*. WdF 439. Darmstadt: Wissenschaftliche Buchgesellschaft, 1977.

———, ed. *Paulus in den neutestamentlichen Spätschriften: Zur Paulusrezeption im Neuen Testament*. QD 89. Freiburg: Herder, 1981.

———, ed. *Der Prozess gegen Jesus: Historische Rückfrage und theologische Deutung*. QD 112. Freiburg: Herder, 1988.

———. *Die Wunder Jesu im Markusevangelium: Eine redaktionsgeschichtliche Untersuchung*. SANT 23. Munich: Kosel, 1970.

Kienast, Dietmar. *Augustus: Prinzeps und Monarch*. 4th ed. Darmstadt: Wissenschaftliche Buchgesellschaft, 2009.

Kierspel, Lars. *The Jews and the World in the Fourth Gospel: Parallelism, Function, and Context*. WUNT 200. Tübingen: Mohr Siebeck, 2006.

Kiilunen, Jarmo. *Die Vollmacht im Widerstreit: Untersuchungen zum Werdegang von Mk 2,1–3,6*. AASF 40. Helsinki: Suomalainen Tiedeakatemia, 1985.

Kim, Byung-Mo. *Die paulinische Kollekte.* TANZ 38. Tübingen: Franke, 2002.

King, Karen L. *What Is Gnosticism?* Cambridge, MA: Belknap Press of Harvard University Press, 2005.

Kinlaw, Pamela E. *The Christ Is Jesus: Metamorphosis, Possession, and Johannine Christology.* AcBib 18. Atlanta: Society of Biblical Literature, 2005.

Kippenberg, Hans G. *Garizim und Synagoge: Traditionsgeschichtliche Untersuchungen zur samaritanischen Religion der aramäischen Periode.* RVV 30. Berlin: de Gruyter, 1971.

Kippenberg, Hans G., and Gerd A. Wewers, eds. *Textbuch zur neutestamentlichen Zeitgeschichte.* GNT 8. Göttingen: Vandenhoeck & Ruprecht, 1979.

———, eds. "Texte aus der samaritanischen Tradition." Pages 89–106 in Kippenberg and Wewers, *Textbuch zur neutestamentlichen Zeitgeschichte.*

Kittel, Gerhard, and Gerhard Friedrich, eds. *Theological Dictionary of the New Testament.* Translated by Geoffrey W. Bromiley. 10 vols. Grand Rapids: Eerdmans, 1964–76.

Klauck, Hans-Josef. *Ancient Letters and the New Testament: A Guide to Context and Exegesis.* With the collaboration of Daniel P. Bailey. Waco: Baylor University Press, 2006.

———. *Apocryphal Gospels: An Introduction.* New York: T&T Clark International, 2003.

———. *Apokryphe Evangelien.* Stuttgart: Katholisches Bibelwerk, 2008.

———. *Der erste Johannesbrief.* EKKNT 23.1. Neukirchen-Vluyn: Neukirchener Verlag, 1991.

———, ed. *Gemeinde, Amt, Sakrament: Neutestamentliche Perspektiven.* Würzburg: Echter, 1989.

———. "Gütergemeinschaft in der klassischen Antike, in Qumran und im Neuen Testament." Pages 69–100 in Klauck, *Gemeinde, Amt, Sakrament.*

———. *Hausgemeinde und Hauskirche im frühen Christentum.* SBS 103. Stuttgart: Katholisches Bibelwerk, 1981.

———. *Herrenmahl und hellenistischer Kult: Eine religionsgeschichtliche Untersuchung zum ersten Korintherbrief.* 2nd ed. NTA 15. Münster: Aschendorff, 1986.

———. *Die Johannesbriefe.* Erträge der Forschung 276. Darmstadt: Wissenschaftliche Buchgesellschaft, 1991.

———. "Junia Theodora und die Gemeinde in Korinth." Pages 42–57 in Karrer, Kraus, and Merk, *Kirche und Volk Gottes.*

———. *Magic and Paganism in Early Christianity: The World of the Acts of the Apostles.* Edinburgh: T&T Clark, 2000.

———. *Magie und Heidentum in der Apostelgeschichte des Lukas.* SBS 160. Stuttgart: Katholisches Bibelwerk, 1996.

———, ed. *Plutarch: Moralphilosophische Schriften.* Universal-Bibliothek. Stuttgart: Philipp Reclam, 1997.

———. *The Religious Context of Early Christianity: A Guide to Graeco-Roman Religions.* Translated by Brian McNeil. Minneapolis: Fortress, 2003.

———. "Das Sendschreiben nach Pergamon und der Kaiserkult in der Johannesoffenbarung." *Bib* 73 (1991): 153–82.

———. "'Ein Wort, das in die ganze Welt erschallt': Traditions- und Identitätsbildung durch Evangelien." Pages 57–89 in Graf and Wiegandt, *Die Anfänge des Christentums.*

———. *Der zweite und dritte Johannesbrief.* EKKNT 23.2. Zurich: Benziger; Neukkirchen-Vluyn: Neukirchener Verlag, 1992.

Klauser, Theodor, et al. *Reallexikon für Antike und Christentum.* Stuttgart: Hiersemann, 1950–.

Klein, Günter. "Galater 2,6–9 und die Geschichte der Jerusalemer Urgemeinde."
Pages 99–128 in G. Klein, *Rekonstruktion und Interpretation*.

———. "Lukas 1,1–4 als theologisches Programm." Pages 170–203 in Braumann,
Das Lukas-Evangelium.

———, ed. *Rekonstruktion und Interpretation: Gesammelte Aufsätze zum Neuen
Testament*. BEvT 50, Munich: Kaiser,
1969.

———. "Die Verleugnung des Petrus." Pages
49–98 in G. Klein, *Rekonstruktion und
Interpretation*.

———. *Die zwölf Apostel: Ursprung und
Gehalt einer Idee*. FRLANT 77. Göttingen: Vandenhoeck & Ruprecht, 1961.

Klein, Hans. *Das Lukasevangelium*. KEK
1/3. Göttingen: Vandenhoeck & Ruprecht, 2006.

Klein, Richard, ed. *Das frühe Christentum
im römischen Staat*. WdF 267. Darmstadt: Wissenschaftliche Buchgesellschaft, 1971.

Klein, Thorsten. *Bewährung in Anfechtung:
Der Jakobusbrief und der Erste Petrus-
brief als christliche Diaspora-Briefe*.
NET 18. Tübingen: Franke, 2011.

Klijn, Albertus F. J., and Gerrit Jan Reinink.
*Patristic Evidence for Jewish-Christian
Sects*. NovTSup 36. Leiden: Brill. 1973.

Klinghardt, Matthias. *Gemeinschaftsmahl
und Mahlgemeinschaft: Soziologie und
Liturgie frühchristlicher Mahlfeiern*.
TANZ 13. Tübingen: Franke, 1996.

———. *Gesetz und Volk Gottes: Das lukanische Verständnis des Gesetzes nach Herkunft, Funktion und seinem Ort in der
Geschichte des Urchristentums*. WUNT
2/32. Tübingen: Mohr Siebeck, 1988.

Kloft, Hans. *Mysterienkulte der Antike:
Götter, Menschen, Rituale*. Munich:
Beck, 1999.

Kloppenborg, John S. *Excavating Q: The
History and Setting of the Sayings Gospel*. Minneapolis: Fortress, 2000.

———. "Fiscal Aspects of Paul's Collection for Jerusalem." *Early Christianity* 8
(2017): 153–98.

———. *The Formation of Q*. SAC. Philadelphia: Fortress, 1987.

———. "Membership Practices in Pauline
Christ Groups." *Early Christianity* 4
(2013): 183–215.

Kloppenborg, John S., and Richard S. Ascough, eds. *Greco-Roman Associations*.
BZNW 181. Berlin: de Gruyter, 2011.

Klumbies, Paul-Gerhard, and David S. Du
Toit, eds. *Paulus: Werk und Wirkung;
Festschrift für Andreas Lindemann zum
70. Geburtstag*. Tübingen: Mohr Siebeck,
2013.

Knauf, Ernst Axel. "Zum Ethnarchen des
Aretas 2 Kor 11,21." *ZNW* 74 (1983):
145–47.

Knoblauch, Hubert. *Wissenssoziologie*. 3rd
ed. UTB 2719. Konstanz: UVK Verlagsgesellschaft, 2014.

Knoppers, Gary N. *Jews and Samaritans:
The Origins and History of Their Early
Relations*. New York: Oxford University
Press, 2013.

Knöppler, Thomas. *Sühne im Neuen Testament: Studien zum urchristlichen Verständnis der Heilsbedeutung des Todes
Jesu*. WMANT 88. Neukirchen-Vluyn:
Neukirchener Verlag, 2001.

———. *Die theologia crucis des Johannesevangeliums: Das Verständnis des Todes
Jesu im Rahmen der johanneischen In-
karnations- und Erhöhungschristologie*.
WMANT 69. Neukirchen-Vlyun: Neukirchener Verlag, 1994.

Koch, Dietrich-Alex. *Die Bedeutung der
Wundererzählungen für die Christologie
des Markusevangeliums*. BZNW 42. Berlin: de Gruyter, 1975.

———. *Bilder aus der Welt des Urchristentums: Das Römische Reich und die hellenistische Kultur als Lebensraum des frühen Christentums in den ersten zwei Jahrhunderten*. Göttingen: Vandenhoeck & Ruprecht, 2009.

———. "Die Christen als neue Randgruppe in Makedonien und Achaia im 1. Jahrhundert n. Chr." Pages 340–68 in D.-A. Koch, *Hellenistisches Christentum*.

———. "Die Einmaligkeit des Anfangs und die Fortdauer der Institution." Pages 197–210 in D.-A. Koch, *Hellenistisches Christentum*.

———. "Die Entwicklung der Ämter in frühchristlichen Gemeinden Kleinasiens." Pages 166–206 in Schmeller, Ebner, and Hoppe, *Neutestamentliche Ämtermodelle im Kontext*.

———. *Geschichte des Urchristentums: Ein Lehrbuch*. Göttingen Vandenhoeck & Ruprecht, 2013.

———. "The God-Fearers between Facts and Fiction." Pages 272–98 in D.-A. Koch, *Hellenistisches Christentum*.

———. *Hellenistisches Christentum: Schriftverständnis, Ekklesiologie, Geschichte*. NTOA. SUNT 65. Göttingen Vandenhoeck & Ruprecht, 2008.

———. *Die Schrift als Zeuge des Evangeliums: Untersuchungen zur Verwendung und zum Verständnis der Schrift bei Paulus*. BHT 69. Tübingen: Mohr Siebeck, 1986.

———. "Seid unanstößig für Juden und für Griechen und für die Gemeinde Gottes (1 Kor 10,32)." Pages 145–64 in D.-A. Koch, *Hellenistisches Christentum*.

Koch, Dietrich-Alex, and Hermann Lichtenberger, eds. *Begegnungen zwischen Christentum und Judentum in Antike und Mittelalter: Festschrift für Heinz Schreckenberg*. SIJD 1. Göttingen: Vandenhoeck & Ruprecht, 1993.

Koch, Michael. "Animus . . . Meus . . . Praesagit, Nostram Hispaniam Esse." Pages 1–40 in *Hispania Antiqua: Denkmäler der Römerzeit*. Edited by Walter Trillmich et al. Mainz: Von Zabern, 1993.

Koch, Stefan. *Rechtliche Regelung von Konflikten im frühen Christentum*. WUNT 2/174. Tübingen: Mohr Siebeck, 2004.

Kocka, Jürgen. "Angemessenheitskriterien historischer Argumente." Pages 469–75 in *Wissenschaft Objektivität und Parteilichkeit in der Geschichtswissenschaft*. Edited by Reinhart Koselleck, Wolfgang J. Mommsen, and Jörn Rüsen. BH 1. Munich: Deutscher Taschenbuch Verlag, 1977.

Kohler, Herbert. *Kreuz und Menschwerdung im Johannesevangelium: Ein exegetisch-hermeneutischer Versuch zur johanneischen Kreuzestheologie*. ATANT 72. Zurich: Theologischer Verlag, 1987.

Köhler, Wolf-Dietrich. *Rezeption des Matthäusevangeliums in der Zeit vor Irenäus*. WUNT 2/24. Tübingen: Mohr Siebeck, 1987.

Kolakowski, Leszek. *Die Gegenwärtigkeit des Mythos*. Munich: Piper, 1973.

Kolb, Frank. "Antiochia in der frühen Kaiserzeit." Vol. 2, pages 97–118 in Cancik, Lichtenberger, and P. Schäfer, *Geschichte, Tradition, Reflexion*.

———. *Rom: Die Geschichte der Stadt in der Antike*. 2nd ed. Beck's historische Bibliothek. Munich: Beck, 2002.

Kollmann, Bernd. *Jesus und die Christen als Wundertäter*. FRLANT 170. Göttingen: Vandenhoeck & Ruprecht, 1996.

———. "Paulus als Wundertäter." Pages 76–96 in Schnelle, Söding, and M. Labahn, *Paulinische Christologie*.

———. "Philippus der Evangelist und die Anfänge der Heidenmission." *Bib* 81 (2000): 551–65.

———. *Ursprung und Gestalten der frühchristlichen Mahlfeier*. GTA 43. Göttingen: Vandenhoeck & Ruprecht, 1990.

Kollmann, Bernd, Wolfgang Reinbold, and Annette Steudel, eds. *Antikes Judentum und frühes Christentum: Festschrift für Hartmut Stegemann zum 65. Geburtstag.* BZNW 97. New York: de Gruyter, 1999.

Konradt, Matthias. *Christliche Existenz nach dem Jakobusbrief: Eine Studie zu seiner soteriologischen und ethischen Konzeption.* SUNT 22. Göttingen: Vandenhoeck & Ruprecht, 1998.

———. *Das Evangelium nach Matthäus.* NTD 1. Göttingen: Vandenhoeck & Ruprecht, 2015.

———. "'Geboren durch das Wort der Wahrheit'—'gerichtet durch das Gesetz der Freiheit': Das Wort als Zentrum der theologischen Konzeption des Jakobusbriefes." Pages 1–15 in Gemünden, Konradt, and Theissen, *Der Jakobusbrief.*

———. *Israel, Church, and the Gentiles in the Gospel of Matthew.* Translated by Kathleen Ess. Baylor-Mohr Siebeck Studies in Early Christianity. Waco: Baylor University Press, 2014.

———. *Israel, Kirche und die Völker im Matthäusevangelium.* WUNT 215. Tübingen: Mohr Siebeck, 2007.

———. *Jesus—Gestalt und Gestaltungen: Rezeptionen des Galiläers in Wissenschaft, Kirche und Gesellschaft; Festschrift für Gerd Theissen zum 70. Geburtstag.* Edited by Petra von Gemünden et al. NTOA 100. Göttingen: Vandenhoeck & Ruprecht, 2013.

———. "Matthäus und Markus." Pages 211–35 in Konradt, *Jesus—Gestalt und Gestaltungen.*

———. "Stellt der Vollmachtsanspruch des historischen Jesus eine Gestalt 'vorösterlicher Christologie' dar?" *ZTK* 107 (2010): 139–66.

———. "Theologie in der 'strohernen Epistel.'" *VuF* 44 (1999): 54–78.

———. "Zur Datierung des sogenannten antiochenischen Zwischenfalls." *ZNW* 102 (2011): 19–39.

Kooten, George Van. "Ἐκκλησία τοῦ θεοῦ: The 'Church of God' and the Civic Assemblies (ἐκκλησίαι) of the Greek Cities in the Roman Empire: A Response to Paul Trebilco and Richard A. Horsley." *NTS* 58 (2012): 522–48.

Korn, Manfred. *Die Geschichte Jesu in veränderter Zeit: Studien zur bleibenden Bedeutung Jesu im lukanischen Doppelwerk.* WUNT 2/51. Tübingen: Mohr Siebeck, 1993.

Körtner, Ulrich H. J. "Markus der Mitarbeiter des Petrus." *ZNW* 71 (1980): 160–73.

———. "Papiasfragmente." Pages 3–103 in Körtner and Leutzsch, *Papiasfragmente: Hirt des Hermas.*

———. *Papias von Hierapolis.* FRLANT 133. Göttingen: Vandenhoeck & Ruprecht, 1983.

Körtner, Ulrich H. J., and Martin Leutzsch, eds. *Papiasfragmente: Hirt des Hermas.* Darmstadt: Wissenschaftliche Buchgesellschaft, 1998.

Kosch, Daniel. *Die eschatologische Tora des Menschensohnes: Untersuchungen zur Rezeption der Stellung Jesu zur Tora in Q.* NTOA 12. Freiburg, Schweiz: Universitätsverlag; Göttingen: Vandenhoeck & Ruprecht, 1989.

Koschorke, Albrecht. *Wahrheit und Erfindung: Grundzüge einer Allgemeinen Erzähltheorie.* Frankfurt am Main: S. Fischer, 2012.

Koskenniemi, Heikki. *Studien zur Idee und Phraseologie des griechischen Briefes bis 400 n. Chr.* Suomalaisen Tiedeakatemian Toimituksia 102.2. Helsinki: Academia Scientiarum Fennica; Wiesbaden: O. Harrassowitz, 1956.

Kössler, Henning. "Bildung und Identität." Pages 51–65 in Kössler, *Identität.*

———. *Identität: Fünf Vorträge.* Erlangen: Erlanger Forschungen, 1989.

Köster, Helmut. *Ancient Christian Gospels: Their History and Development.*

Harrisburg, PA: Trinity Press International, 2004.

———, ed. *Ephesos: Metropolis of Asia; An Interdisciplinary Approach to Its Archaeology, Religion, and Culture.* HTS 41. Valley Forge, PA: Trinity Press International, 1995.

———. "Imperial Ideology and Paul's Eschatology in 1 Thessalonians." Pages 158–66 in Horsley, *Paul and Empire.*

Köstermann, Erich. *Cornelius Tacitus: Annalen; 4 Buch 14–16.* WKGLS. Heidelberg: Winter, 1968.

Kowalski, Beate. *Die Rezeption des Propheten Ezechiel in der Offenbarung des Johannes.* SBS 52. Stuttgart: Katholisches Bibelwerk, 2004.

Kragerud, Alv. *Der Lieblingsjünger im Johannesevangelium.* Oslo: Osloer Universitatsverlag, 1959.

Krämer, Hans Joachim. *Platonismus und hellenistische Philosophie.* Berlin: de Gruyter, 1971.

Kramer, Werner. *Christ, Lord, Son of God.* SBT 50. Translated by Brian Hardy. London: SCM, 1966.

———. *Christos Kyrios Gottessohn: Untersuchungen zu Gebrauch und Bedeutung der christologischen Bezeichnungen bei Paulus und den vorpaulinischen Gemeinden von Werner Kramer.* Berlin: Evangelische Verlagsanstalt, 1969.

Kraus, Wolfgang, ed. *Beiträge zur urchristlichen Theologiegeschichte.* BZNW 163. Berlin: de Gruyter, 2009.

———. *Das Volk Gottes.* WUNT 85. Tübingen: Mohr Siebeck, 1996.

———. "Zur Ekklesiologie des Matthäusevangeliums." Pages 195–239 in Senior, *Gospel of Matthew at the Crossroads.*

———. *Zwischen Jerusalem und Antiochia: Die "Hellenisten"; Paulus und die Aufnahme der Heiden in das endzeitliche Gottesvolk.* Stuttgarter Bibelstudien 179.

Stuttgart: Verlag Katholisches Bibelwerk, 1999.

Krause, Jens-Uwe. *Gefängnisse im Römischen Reich.* HABES 23. Stuttgart: Franz Seiner Verlag, 1996.

Krauter, Stefan. *Studien zu Röm 13,1–7: Paulus und der politische Diskurs der neronischen Zeit.* WUNT 243. Tübingen: Mohr Siebeck, 2009.

Krautz, Hans-Wolfgang, ed. *Epikur: Briefe, Sprüche, Werkfragmente; Griechisch/Deutsch.* Universal Bibliothek 9984. Stuttgart: Reclam, 1993.

Kremer, Jacob, ed. *Les Actes des Apôtres: Traditions, rédaction, théologie.* BETL 48. Gembloux: J. Duculot; Louvain: Leuven University Press, 1979.

———. "Weltweites Zeugnis für Christus in der Kraft des Geistes." Pages 145–63 in Brox and Kertelge, *Mission im Neuen Testament.*

Kreplin, Matthias. *Das Selbstverständnis Jesu.* WUNT 2/141. Tübingen: Mohr Siebeck, 2001.

Kreuzer, Siegfried. *Geschichte, Sprache und Text.* BZAW 479. Berlin: de Gruyter, 2015.

Kristen, Peter. *Familie, Kreuz und Leben: Nachfolge Jesu nach Q und dem Markusevangelium.* MTS 42. Marburg: Elwert, 1995.

Krumbiegel, Friedemann. *Erziehung in den Pastoralbriefen.* ABG 44. Leipzig: Leipzig Evangelische Verlagsanstalt, 2013.

Küchler, Max. *Jerusalem: Ein Handbuch und Studienreiseführer zur Heiligen Stadt.* Orte und Landschaften der Bibel 4.2. Göttingen: Vandenhoeck & Ruprecht 2007.

Kügler, Joachim. *Der Jünger, den Jesus liebte.* SBB 16. Stuttgart: Katholisches Bibelwerk, 1988.

Kuhn, Heinz-Wolfgang. *Ältere Sammlungen im Markusevangelium.* SUNT 8. Göttingen: Vandenhoeck & Ruprecht, 1971.

———. *Enderwartung und gegenwärtiges Heil: Untersuchungen zu den Gemeindeliedern von Qumran mit einem Anhang über Eschatologie und Gegenwart in der Verkündigung Jesu.* SUNT 4. Göttingen: Vandenhoeck & Ruprecht, 1966.

———. "Der Gekreuzigte von Givcat hat-Mivtar." Pages 303–34 in Andresen and G. Klein, *Theologia Crucis.*

———. "Jesus als Gekreuzigter in der früh-christlichen Verkündigung bis zur Mitte des 2. Jahrhunderts." *ZTK* 72 (1975): 1–46.

———. "Jesus vor dem Hintergrund der Qumrangemeinde." Pages 50–60 in *Grenzgänge: Menschen und Schicksale zwischen jüdischer, christlicher und deutscher Identität; Festschrift für Diethard Aschoff.* Edited by Folker Siegert. Münsteraner judaistische Studien 11. Münster: Lit, 2002.

Kümmel, Werner Georg. "Äußere und innere Reinheit des Menschen bei Jesus." Pages 117–29 in *Heilsgeschehen und Geschichte.* Vol. 2. Edited by Werner Georg Kümmel. MTS 3/16. Marburg: Elwert, 1978.

———. *Promise and Fulfillment: The Eschatological Message of Jesus.* Translated by Dorothea M. Barton from the 3rd ed. SBT 23. Naperville, IL: A. R. Allenson; London: SCM, 1957.

Kytzler, Bernhard, ed. *Roma aeterna: Lateinische und griechische Romdichtung von der Antike bis in die Gegenwart.* Die Bibliothek der alten Welt 100. Zurich: Artemis, 1972.

Labahn, Antje, and Michael Labahn. "Jesus als Sohn Gottes bei Paulus." Pages 97–120 in Schnelle, Söding, and M. Labahn, *Paulinische Christologie.*

Labahn, Michael. "'Gefallen, gefallen ist Babylon, die Große': Die Johannesoffenbarung als subversive Erzählung." Pages 319–41 in *Worte der Weissagung: Studien zu Septuaginta und Johannesoffenbarung.* Edited by Julian Elschenbroich and Johannes de Vries. ABG 47. Leipzig: Evangelische Verlagsanstalt, 2014.

———. *Der Gekommene als Wiederkommender: Die Logienquelle als erzählte Geschichte.* ABG 32. Leipzig: Evangelische Verlagsanstalt, 2010.

———. "Paulus, ein homo honestus et iustus: Das lukanische Paulusportrait von Act 27–28 im Lichte ausgewählter antiker Parallelen." Pages 75–106 in Horn, *Das Ende des Paulus.*

Labahn, Michael, and Martin Karrer, eds. *Die Johannesoffenbarung: Ihr Text und ihre Auslegung.* ABG 38. Leipzig: Evangelische Verlagsanstalt, 2012.

Labahn, Michael, and Manfred Lang. "Johannes und die Synoptiker." Pages 443–515 in Frey and Schnelle, *Kontexte des Johannesevangeliums.*

Läger, Karoline. *Die Christologie der Pastoralbriefe.* HThSt 2. Münster: Lit, 1996.

Lampe, Peter. "Acta 19 im Spiegel der ephesischen Inschriften." *BZ* 16 (1992): 59–76.

———. "Das korinthische Herrenmahl im Schnittpunkt hellenistisch-römischer Mahlpraxis und paulinischer Theologia Crucis." *ZNW* 82 (1991): 183–213.

———. "Paulus—Zeltmacher." *BZ* 31 (1987): 256–61.

———. "Das Spiel mit dem Petrusnamen—Matt. XVI.18." *NTS* 25 (1979): 227–45.

———. *Die stadtrömischen Christen in den ersten beiden Jahrhunderten: Untersuchungen zur Sozialgeschichte.* WUNT 2/18. Tübingen: Mohr Siebeck, 1987.

———. "Urchristliche Missionswege nach Rom: Haushalte paganer Herrschaft als jüdisch-christliche Keimzellen." *ZNW* 92 (2001): 123–27.

Lampe, Peter, and Ulrich Luz. "Nachpaulinisches Christentum und pagane Gesellschaft." Pages 185–216 in J. Becker, *Die Anfänge des Christentums.*

Landmesser, Christof, ed. *Jesus Christus als die Mitte der Schrift: Studien zur Hermeneutik des Evangeliums; Festschrift für Otfried Hofius zum 60. Geburtstag.* BZNW 86. Berlin: de Gruyter, 1997.

Landwehr, Achim. *Historische Diskursanalyse.* Frankfurt: Campus, 2008.

Lang, Bernhard. *Jesus der Hund: Leben und Lehre eines jüdischen Kynikers.* Beck'sche Reihe, 1957. Munich: Beck, 2010.

Lang, Manfred. *Die Kunst des christlichen Lebens: Rezeptionsästhetische Studien zum lukanischen Paulusbild.* ABG 29. Leipzig: Evangelische Verlagsanstalt, 2008.

Lang, Markus. "Das frühe ägyptische Christentum: Quellenlage. Forschungslage und -perspektiven." Pages 9–44 in *Das ägyptische Christentum im 2. Jahrhundert.* Edited by Wilhelm Pratscher, Markus Öhler, and Markus Lang. Münster: Lit, 2008.

Lange, Joachim, ed. *Das Matthäus-Evangelium.* WdF 525. Darmstadt: Wissenschaftliche Buchgesellschaft, 1980.

Lanzillotta, Roig. *Plutarch in the Religious and Philosophical Discourse of Late Antiquity.* AMMTC 14. Leiden: Brill, 2013.

Larsson, Edvin. "Die Hellenisten und die Urgemeinde." *NTS* 33 (1987): 205–25.

Layton, Bentley. *The Gnostic Scriptures: A New Translation with Annotations and Introductions.* Garden City, NY: Doubleday, 1987.

Leberl, Jens. *Domitian und die Dichter: Poesie als Medium der Herrschaftsdarstellung.* Hyponemata 154. Göttingen: Vandenhoeck & Ruprecht, 2004.

Lehmeier, Karin. *Oikos und Oikonomia: Antike Konzepte der Haushaltsführung und der Bau der Gemeinde bei Paulus.* MTS 92. Marburg: Elwert, 2006.

Leipoldt, Johannes. *Geschichte des neutestamentlichen Kanons.* Vol. 1, *Die Entstehung.* Vol. 2, *Mittelalter und Neuzeit.* Leipzig: Hinrichs'sche, 1907–8.

Leipoldt, Johannes, and Walter Grundmann, eds. and trans. *Umwelt des Urchristentums.* Vol. 1, *Darstellung des neutestamentlichen Zeitalters.* 5th ed. Vol. 2, *Texte zum neutestamentlichen Zeitalter.* 5th ed. Vol. 3, *Bilder zum neutestamentlichen Zeitalter.* 4th ed. Berlin: Evangelische Verlagsanstalt, 1966–76.

Lemke, Hella. *Judenchristentum: Zwischen Ausgrenzung und Integration; Zur Geschichte eines exegetischen Begriffes.* Münster: Lit, 2001.

Leppin, Hartmut. "Imperial Miracles and Elitist Discourses." Pages 233–48 in Alkier and Weissenrieder, *Miracles Revisited.*

Leutzsch, Martin. *Die Bewährung der Wahrheit: Der dritte Johannesbrief als Dokument urchristlichen Alltags.* Stätten und Formen der Kommunikation im Altertum 2; Bochumer Altertumswissenschaftliches Colloquium 16. Trier: Wissenschaftlicher Verlag Trier, 1994.

Lichtenberger, Hermann. "Josephus und Paulus in Rom." Pages 245–62 in D.-A. Koch and Lichtenberger, *Begegnungen zwischen Christentum und Judentum.*

Lichtenberger, Hermann, and Gerbern S. Oegema, eds. *Jüdische Schriften in ihrem antik-jüdischen und urchristlichen Kontext.* Gütersloh: Gütersloher Verlagshaus, 2002.

Liefeld, Walter L. "The Wandering Preacher as a Social Figure in the Roman Empire." PhD diss., Columbia University, 1967 [Ann Arbor, MI: University Microfilms].

Lietzmann, Hans. *Mass and Lord's Supper: A Study in the History of the Liturgy.* Translated by Dorothy H. G. Reeve. Leiden: Brill, 1953.

———. *Messe und Herrenmahl: Eine Studie zur Geschichte der Liturgie.* 3rd ed. AKG 8. Berlin: de Gruyter, 1955.

Lieu, Judith M. *1, 2 and 3 John*. NTL. Louisville: Westminster John Knox, 2008.

———. *Neither Jew nor Greek? Constructing Early Christianity*. SNTW. New York: T&T Clark, 2002; London: T&T Clark, 2005.

Limbeck, Meinrad, ed. *Redaktion und Theologie des Passionsberichtes nach den Synoptikern*. WdF 481. Darmstadt: Wissenschaftliche Buchgesellschaft, 1981.

Lindemann, Andreas. "Antwort auf die 'Thesen zur Echtheit und Datierung der sieben Briefe des Ignatius von Antiochien.'" *ZAC* 1 (1997): 185–94.

———. *Die Clemensbriefe*. HNT 17. Tübingen: Mohr, 1992.

———. "Kinder in der Welt des frühen Christentums." *NTS* 56 (2010): 169–90.

———. *Der Kolosserbrief*. ZBK.NT 10. Zurich: Theologische Verlag, 1983.

———. *Paulus im ältesten Christentum: Das Bild des Apostels und die Rezeption der paulinischen Theologie in der frühchristlichen Literatur bis Marcion*. BHT 58. Tübingen: Mohr Siebeck, 1979.

———. "Paulus und die Rede in Milet (Apg 20,17–38)." Pages 175–205 in *Reception of Paulinism in Acts*. Edited by Daniel Marguerat. BETL 229. Louvain: Peeters, 2009.

———. "Samaria und Samaritaner im Neuen Testament." *WuD* 22 (1993): 51–76.

———, ed. *The Sayings Source Q and the Historical Jesus*. BETL 158. Louvain: Leuven University Press; Sterling, VA: Peeters, 2001.

Linke, Bernhard. *Antike Religion*. Enzyklopädie der griechisch-römischen Antike 13. Munich: Oldenbourg, 2014.

Lips, Hermann von. *Glaube, Gemeinde, Amt: Zum Verständnis der Ordination in den Pastoralbriefen*. FRLANT 122. Göttingen: Vandenhoeck & Ruprecht, 1979.

———. *Der neutestamentliche Kanon*. Zurich: Theologischer Verlag, 2004.

———. *Timotheus und Titus: Unterwegs für Paulus*. Leipzig: Evangelische Verlagsanstalt, 2008.

———. *Weisheitliche Traditionen im Neuen Testament*. WMANT 64. Neukirchen-Vluyn: Neukirchener Verlag, 1990.

Loader, William R. G. *Sohn und Hoherpriester*. WMANT 53. Neukirchen: 1981.

Lohfink, Gerhard. "Paulinische Theologie in den Pastoralbriefen." Pages 70–121 in Kertelge, *Paulus in den neutestamentlichen Spätschriften*.

———. *Die Sammlung Israels: Eine Untersuchung zur lukanischen Ekklesiologie*. SANT 39. Munich: Kösel, 1975.

Lohmeyer, Ernst. *Galiläa und Jerusalem*. FRLANT 34. Göttingen: Vandenhoeck & Ruprecht, 1934.

———. *Kyrios Jesus: Eine Untersuchung zu Phil. 2, 5–11*. SHAW 4. Heidelberg: Winter, 1928.

———. *Die Offenbarung des Johannes*. HNT 16. Tübingen: Mohr, 1926.

Lohmeyer, Monika. *Der Apostelbegriff im Neuen Testament: Eine Untersuchung auf dem Hintergrund der synoptischen Aussendungsreden*. SBB 29. Stuttgart: Verlag Katholisches Bibelwerk, 1995.

Löhr, Hermut. "Die Briefe des Ignatius von Antiochien." Pages 104–29 in Pratscher, *Die Apostolischen Väter*.

———. "Speisefrage und Tora im Judentum des Zweiten Tempels und im entstehenden Christentum." *ZNW* 94 (2003): 17–37.

Löhr, Winrich A. *Basilides und seine Schule: Eine Studie zur Theologie- und Kirchengeschichte des zweiten Jahrhunderts*. WUNT 83. Tübingen: Mohr Siebeck, 1996.

Lohse, Eduard. *Die Briefe an die Kolosser und Philemon*. 2nd ed. KEK 9.2.

Göttingen: Vandenhoeck & Ruprecht, 1977.

———. *Colossians and Philemon: A Commentary on the Epistles to the Colossians and to Philemon*. Translated by William R. Poehlmann and Robert J. Karris. Edited by Helmut Koester. Philadelphia: Fortress, 1971.

Lona, Horacio E. "'Petrus in Rom' und der Erste Clemensbrief." Pages 221–46 in Heid and Haehling, *Petrus und Paulus in Rom*.

———. "Treu bis zum Tod." Pages 442–61 in Merklein, *Neues Testament und Ethik*.

Long, Arthur A. *Epictetus: A Stoic and Socratic Guide to Life*. Oxford: Clarendon, 2002.

———. *Hellenistic Philosophy: Stoics, Epicureans, Skeptics*. London: Duckworth, 2001.

Long, Arthur A., and D. N. Sedley. *The Hellenistic Philosophers*. 2 vols. New York: Cambridge University Press, 1987.

Longenecker, Bruce W. *Remember the Poor: Paul, Poverty, and the Greco-Roman World*. Cambridge; Grand Rapids: Eerdmans: 2010.

Longenecker, Bruce W., and Kelly Liebengood, eds. *Engaging Economics: New Testament Scenarios and Early Christian Reception*. Grand Rapids: Eerdmans, 2009.

Löning, Karl. *Das Geschichtswerk des Lukas*. Vol. 1, *Israels Hoffnung und Gottes Geheimnisse*. Urban-Taschenbücher 455. Stuttgart: Kohlhammer, 1997.

———. *Das Geschichtswerk des Lukas*. Vol. 2, *Der Weg Jesu*. Urban-Taschenbücher 456. Stuttgart: Kohlhammer, 2006.

———. "Paulinismus in der Apostelgeschichte." Pages 202–34 in Kertelge, *Paulus in den neutestamentlichen Spätschriften*.

———. *Die Saulustradition in der Apostelgeschichte*. NTA 9. Münster: Aschendorff, 1973.

———. "Der Stephanuskreis und seine Mission." Pages 80–101 in J. Becker, *Die Anfänge des Christentums*.

Lorenz, Chris, Annegret Böttner, and Jörn Rüsen. *Konstruktion der Vergangenheit: Eine Einführung in die Geschichtstheorie*. BGK 13. Cologne: Böhlau, 1997.

Lorenzen, Thorwald. *Der Lieblingsjünger im Johannesevangelium*. SBS 55. Stuttgart: 1971.

Lowy, Simeon. *The Principles of Samaritan Bible Exegesis*. SPB 28. Leiden: Brill, 1977.

Luck, Georg. *Magie und andere Geheimlehren der Antike: Mit 112 neu übersetzten und einzeln kommentierten Quellentexten*. Kröners Taschenausgabe 489. Stuttgart: Kröner, 1990.

———. *Die Weisheit der Hunde: Texte der antiken Kyniker in deutscher Übersetzung mit Erläuterungen*. KTA 484. Stuttgart: Kröner, 1997.

Luckmann, Thomas. "Religion—Gesellschaft—Transzendenz." Pages 112–27 in *Krise der Immanenz: Religion an den Grenzen der Moderne*. Edited by Hans-Joachim Höhn. Frankfurt am Main: Fischer Taschenbuch, 1996.

Lüdemann, Gerd. *Die Auferstehung Jesu: Historie, Erfahrung, Theologie*. Göttingen: Vandenhoeck & Ruprecht, 1994.

———. *Die ersten drei Jahre Christentum*. 1st ed. Electronic resource. Springe: zu Klampen, 2014.

———. *Das frühe Christentum nach den Traditionen der Apostelgeschichte: Ein Kommentar*. Göttingen: Vandenhoeck & Ruprecht, 1987.

———. *Heretics: The Other Side of Christianity*. Louisville: Westminster John Knox, 1996.

———. *Opposition to Paul in Jewish Christianity*. Translated by M. Eugene Boring. Minneapolis: Fortress, 1989.

———. *Paul, Apostle to the Gentiles: Studies in Chronology.* Translated by F. Stanley Jones. Philadelphia: Fortress, 1984.

———. *Paulus, der Heidenapostel.* 2nd ed. 2 vols. FRLANT 130. Göttingen: Vandenhoeck & Ruprecht, 1990.

———. *Primitive Christianity: A Survey of Recent Studies and Some New Proposals.* Translated by John Bowden. London: T&T Clark, 2003.

———. *The Resurrection of Jesus: History, Experience, Theology.* London: SCM, 1994.

Ludwig, Helga. "Der Verfasser des Kolosserbriefes: Ein Schüler des Paulus." PhD diss., University of Göttingen, 1974.

Lührmann, Dieter. *Fragmente apokryph gewordener Evangelien.* MTS 59. Marburg: Elwert, 2000.

———. "Gal 2,9 und die katholischen Briefe." *ZNW* 72 (1981): 65–87.

———. *Glaube im frühen Christentum.* Gütersloh: Mohn, 1976.

———. *Das Markusevangelium.* HNT 3. Tübingen: Mohr, 1987.

———. "Pistis im Judentum." *ZNW* 64 (1973): 19–38.

———. "Superstitio: Die Beurteilung des frühen Christentums durch die Römer." *TZ* 42 (1986): 191–213.

———. "Tage, Monate, Jahreszeiten, Jahre (Gal 4,10)." Pages 428–45 in *Werden und Wirken des Alten Testaments: Festschrift für Claus Westermann.* Edited by Rainer Albertz et al. Göttingen: Vandenhoeck & Ruprecht, 1980.

Lührmann, Dieter, and Georg Strecker, eds. *Kirche: Festschrift für Günther Bornkamm zum 75. Geburtstag.* Tübingen: Mohr Siebeck, 1980.

Luz, Ulrich, "Das 'Auseinandergehen der Wege': Über die Trennung des Christentums vom Judentum." Pages 56–73 in Dietrich, George, and Luz, *Antijudaismus—christliche Erblast.*

———. *Matthew: A Commentary.* 3 vols. Translated by Wilhelm C. Linss. Herm. Minneapolis: Augsburg, 1989–2005.

———. "Rechtfertigung bei den Paulusschülern." Pages 365–83 in Friedrich, Pöhlmann, and Stuhlmacher, *Rechtfertigung.*

———. *The Theology of the Gospel of Matthew.* Translated by J. Bradford Robinson. New Testament Theology. Cambridge: Cambridge University Press, 1995.

Maas, Wilhelm. *Die Unveränderlichkeit Gottes: Zum Verhältnis von griechisch-philosophischer und christlicher Gotteslehre.* Paderborner theologische Studien 1. Paderborn: Schöningh, 1974.

Macmullen, Ramsay. *Christianizing the Roman Empire.* New Haven: Yale University Press, 1984.

———. *Roman Social Relations.* New Haven: Yale University Press, 1974.

Maier, Johann. *Jüdische Auseinandersetzung mit dem Christentum in der Antike.* EdF 177. Darmstadt: Wissenschaftliche Buchgesellschaft, 1982.

———. *Zwischen den Testamenten: Geschichte und Religion in der Zeit des zweiten Tempels.* NEB.AT 3. Würzburg: Echter, 1990.

Maier, Johann, and Josef Schreiner, ed. *Literatur und Religion des Frühjudentums.* Würzburg/Gütersloh: Echter, 1973.

Maisch, Ingrid. *Der Brief an die Gemeinde in Kolossä.* THK 12. Stuttgart: Kohlhammer, 2003.

Malamat, Avraham. *Von den Anfängen bis zum 7. Jahrhundert.* Vol. 1 of *Geschichte des jüdischen Volkes.* Edited by Haim Hillel Ben-Sasson. 2nd ed. Munich: Beck, 1981.

Malbon, Elisabeth Struthers. *Mark's Jesus: Characterization as Narrative Christology.* Waco: Baylor University Press, 2009.

Malherbe, Abraham J. *Ancient Epistolary Theorists.* SBibSt 19. Atlanta: Scholars Press, 1988.

———, ed. *The Cynic Epistles: A Study Edition.* SBibSt 12. Atlanta: Scholars Press, 1977.

———. *The Letters to the Thessalonians.* AB 32B. New York: Doubleday, 2000.

———. *Paul and the Popular Philosophers.* Minneapolis: Fortress, 1989.

Malitz, Jürgen. *Nero.* Translated by Allison Brown. BAL. Malden, MA: Blackwell, 2005.

———, ed. *Nikolaos von Damaskus: Leben des Kaisers Augustus.* TzF 80. Darmstadt: Wissenschaftliche Buchgesellschaft, 2003.

———. "Philosophie und Politik im frühen Prinzipat." Pages 151–79 in *Antikes Denken—Moderne Schule.* Edited by Hans-Werner Schmidt and Peter Wülfing. Heidelberg: University Heidelberg Forschungsprojekt, 1988.

Marguerat, Daniel. *Paul in Acts and Paul in His Letters.* WUNT 310. Tübingen: Mohr Siebeck, 2013.

Marjanen, Antti, and Petri Luomanen, eds. *A Companion to Second-Century Christian "Heretics."* VCSup 76. Leiden: Brill, 2005.

Markschies, Christoph. *Christian Theology and Its Institutions in the Early Roman Empire: Prolegomena to a History of Early Christian Theology.* Translated by Wayne Coppins. Baylor-Mohr Siebeck Studies in Early Christianity. Waco: Baylor University Press, 2015.

———. *Kaiserzeitliche christliche Theologie und ihre Institutionen: Prolegomena zu einer Geschichte der antiken christlichen Theologie.* Tübingen: Mohr Siebeck, 2007.

———. "Kerinth." *JAC* 41 (1998): 48–76.

Markschies, Christoph, and Jens Schröter, eds. *Antike christliche Apokryphen in deutscher Übersetzung.* Tübingen: Mohr Siebeck, 2012.

Marrou, Henri I. *A History of Education in Antiquity.* Translated by George Lamb. New York: Sheed & Ward, 1956.

Martyn, James Louis. *History and Theology in the Fourth Gospel.* 2nd ed. Nashville: Abingdon, 1979.

Marxsen, Willi. *Der Evangelist Markus.* 2nd. ed. FRLANT 67. Göttingen: Vandenhoek & Ruprecht 1959.

———. *The Resurrection of Jesus of Nazareth.* Translated by Margaret Kohl. London: SCM, 1970.

Maschmeier, Jens-Christian. "Der Glaube auf dem Marktplatz: Freiheitskämpfe in Korinth." Pages 146–63 in Bendemann and Tiwald, *Das frühe Christentum und die Stadt.*

Mason, Steve. "Das antike Judentum als Hintergrund des frühen Christentums." *ZNT* 37 (2016): 11–22.

———. *A History of the Jewish War, A.D. 66–74.* Cambridge: Cambridge University Press, 2016.

Matera, Frank J. *New Testament Christology.* Louisville: Westminster John Knox, 1999.

Maurer, Michael, ed. *Aufriss der Historischen Wissenschaften.* Vols. 1–6. Stuttgart: Reclam, 2001–5.

Mayer, Günter. *Die jüdische Frau in der hellenistisch-römischen Antike.* Stuttgart: Kohlhammer, 1987.

Meade, David G. *Pseudonymity and Canon: An Investigation into the Relationship of Authorship and Authority in Jewish and Earliest Christian Tradition.* Grand Rapids: Eerdmans, 1986.

Meeks, Wayne A. *The First Urban Christians.* 2nd ed. New Haven: Yale University Press, 2003.

Meggitt, Justin J. *Paul, Poverty and Survival.* SNTW. Edinburgh: T&T Clark, 1998.

Mehl, Andreas. "Sprachen im Kontakt, Sprachen im Wandel: Griechisch, Latein, und antike Geschichte." Pages 191–230 in *Zur Evolution von Kommunikation und Sprache—Ausdruck, Mitteilung, Darstellung*. Edited by Max Liedtke. Schriftenreihe der Forschungsgemeinschaft Wilhelminenberg. Graz: Austria-Medien-Service, 1998.

Meier, John P. *Companions and Competitors*. Vol. 3 of *A Marginal Jew: Rethinking the Historical Jesus*. ABRL. New York: Doubleday, 2001.

———. *Mentor, Message and Miracles*. Vol. 2 of *A Marginal Jew: Rethinking the Historical Jesus*. ABRL. New York: Doubleday, 1994.

———. *The Roots of the Problem and the Person*. Vol. 1 of *A Marginal Jew: Rethinking the Historical Jesus*. ABRL. New York: Doubleday, 1991.

Meissner, Burkhard. *Hellenismus*. Darmstadt: Wissenschaftliche Buchgesellschaft, 2007.

Mell, Ulrich, and Ulrich B. Müller, eds. *Das Urchristentum in seiner literarischen Geschichte: Festschrift für Jürgen Becker zum 65. Geburtstag*. BZNW 100. Berlin: de Gruyter, 1999.

Mensching, Gustav. *Soziologie der Religion*. Bonn: Röhrscheid, 1966.

Merk, Otto. "Das Reich Gottes in den lukanischen Schriften." Pages 272–91 in *Wissenschaftsgeschichte und Exegese: Gesammelte Aufsätze zum 65. Geburtstag*. Edited by Roland Gebauer. BZNW 95. Berlin: de Gruyter, 1998.

Merkel, Helmut. *Die Pastoralbriefe: Übersetzt und erklärt*. NTD 9.1. Göttingen: Vandenhoeck & Ruprecht, 1991.

Merkelbach, Reinhold. *Die Hirten des Dionysos: Die Dionysos-Mysterien der römischen Kaiserzeit und der bukolische Roman des Longus*. Stuttgart: Teubner, 1988.

———. *Isis regina—Zeus Sarapis: Die griechisch-ägyptische Religion nach den Quellen dargestellt*. Stuttgart: Teubner, 1995.

———. *Mithras*. Königstein: Anton Hain Meisenheim, 1984.

Merklein, Helmut. *Der erste Brief an die Korinther*. Written with Marlis Gielen. 3 vols. ÖTK 7. Gütersloh: Mohn, 1992–2005.

———. "Erwägungen zur Überlieferungsgeschichte der neutestamentlichen Abendmahlstraditionen." Pages 157–80 in Merklein, *Studien zu Jesus und Paulus*.

———, ed. *Neues Testament und Ethik: Für Rudolf Schnackenburg*. Freiburg: Herder, 1989.

———. "Paulinische Theologie in der Rezeption des Kolosser- und Epheserbriefes." Pages 409–47 in Merklein, *Studien zu Jesus und Paulus*.

———. *Studien zu Jesus und Paulus*. WUNT 43. Tübingen: Mohr Siebeck, 1987.

———. "Der Theologe als Prophet." *NTS* 38 (1992): 402–29.

Merten, Jürgen, ed. *Nero: Kaiser, Künstler und Tyrann*. SRLT 40. Darmstadt: Theiss, 2016.

Merz, Annette, and Teun L. Tielemann, eds. *The Letter of Mara bar Sarapion in Context: Proceedings of the Symposium Held at Utrecht University, 10–12 December 2009*. CHANE 58. Leiden: Brill, 2012.

Metzger, Bruce M. *The Canon of the New Testament: Its Origin, Development, and Significance*. Oxford: Clarendon; New York: Oxford University Press, 1987.

Metzler, Dieter, and Frank Kolb. *Die Stadt im Altertum*. MBAH. Munich: Beck, 1984.

Metzner, Rainer. *Das Verständnis der Sünde im Johannesevangelium*. WUNT 122. Tübingen: Mohr Siebeck, 2000.

Meyer, Rudolf. *Der Prophet aus Galiläa: Studie zum Jesusbild der drei ersten Evangelien*. Leipzig: Lunkenbein, 1940.

Meyers, Eric M. "Jesus und seine galiläische Lebenswelt." *ZNT* 1 (1998): 27–39.

Michel, Hans-Joachim. *Die Abschiedsrede des Paulus an die Kirche Apg 20,17–38: Motivgeschichte und theologische Bedeutung*. SANT 35. Munich: Kösel, 1973.

Michel, Otto. "Der Abschluß des Matthäusevangeliums: Ein Beitrag zur Geschichte der Osterbotschaft." *EvT* 10 (1950/51): 16–26.

Millard, Alan R. *Pergament und Papyrus, Tafeln und Ton: Lesen und Schreiben zur Zeit Jesu*. Giessen: Brunnen, 2000.

Miller, Colin. "The Imperial Cult in the Pauline Cities of Asia Minor and Greece." *CBQ* 72 (2010): 314–32.

Minear, Paul S. *Images of the Church in the New Testament*. Repr., Cambridge: Clarke, 2007.

Mineshige, Kiyoshi. *Besitzverzicht und Almosen bei Lukas: Wesen und Forderung des lukanischen Vermögensethos*. WUNT 2/163. Tübingen: Mohr Siebeck, 2003.

Mitchell, Margaret. "The Letter of James as a Document of Paulinism? A Study in Reception-History." Pages 75–98 in *Reading James with New Eyes: Methodological Reassessments of the Letter of James*. Edited by Robert T. Webb and John S. Kloppenborg. London: T&T Clark International, 2007.

Mitchell, Stephen. *Anatolia: Land, Men, and Gods in Asia Minor*. 2 vols. Oxford: Clarendon; New York: Oxford University Press, 1993–95.

———. *The Rise of the Church: Land, Men, and Gods in Asia Minor*. Vol. 2 of *Anatolia*. Oxford: Clarendon, 1993.

Mitchell, Stephen, and Peter van Nuffelen, eds. *One God: Pagan Monotheism in the Roman Empire*. Cambridge: Cambridge University Press, 2010.

Mitton, C. Leslie. *The Formation of the Pauline Corpus of Letters*. London: Epworth, 1955.

Molthagen, Joachim. "Die ersten Konflikte der Christen in der griechisch-römischen Welt." *Historia* 40 (1991): 42–76.

Mommsen, Theodor. "Der Religionsfrevel nach römischem Recht." Pages 389–422 in T. Mommsen, *Gesammelte Schriften*, vol. 3, *Juristische Schriften*. Berlin: Weidmann, 1907.

———. *Römische Kaisergeschichte: Nach den Vorlesungs-Mitschriften von Sebastian und Paul Hensel 1882/86*. Edited by Barbara Demandt and Alexander Demandt. Munich: Beck, 1992.

Mommsen, Theodor, Barbara Demandt, Alexander Demandt, Thomas E. J. Wiedemann. *A History of Rome under the Emperors*. New York: Routledge, 1996.

Moore, George F. *Judaism in the First Centuries of the Christian Era: The Age of the Tannaim*. 3 vols. Cambridge, MA: Harvard University Press, 1927–30.

Moreland, Milton C. "The Jesus Movement in the Villages of Roman Galilee." Pages 159–80 in *Oral Performance, Popular Tradition, and Hidden Transcript in Q*. Edited by Richard A. Horsley. Semeia 60. Atlanta: Society of Biblical Literature, 2006.

Morgan, Teresa. *Roman Faith and Christian Faith: Pistis and Fides in the Early Roman Empire and Early Churches*. New York: Oxford University Press, 2015.

Morgenthaler, Robert. *Statistische Synopse*. Stuttgart: Gotthelf-Verlag, 1971.

Moyise, Steve. *The Old Testament in the New*. Continuum Biblical Studies Series. New York: Continuum, 2001.

Moyise, Steve, and Martten J. J. Menken, eds. *The Psalms in the New Testament*.

NTSI. New York: T&T Clark International, 2004.

Mucha, Robert. "Ein flavischer Nero: Zur Domitian-Darstellung und Datierung der Johannesapokalypse." *NTS* 60 (2014): 83–105.

Müller, Gerhard, et al. *Theologische Realenzyklopädie*. 36 vols. Berlin: de Gruyter, 1976–2004.

Müller, Klaus E., and Jörn Rüsen, eds. *Historische Sinnbildung: Problemstellungen, Zeitkonzepte, Wahrnehmungshorizonte, Darstellungsstrategien*. Reinbek bei Hamburg: Rowohlt, 1997.

Müller, Mogens. *Der Ausdruck Menschensohn in den Evangelien: Voraussetzungen und Bedeutung*. ATDan 17. Leiden: Brill, 1984.

Müller, Peter. *Anfänge der Paulusschule: Dargestellt am zweiten Thessalonicherbrief und am Kolosserbrief*. ATANT 74. Zurich: Theologischer Verlag, 1988.

———. *Der Brief an Philemon*. KEK 9/3. Göttingen: Vandenhoek & Ruprecht, 2012.

———. "Das frühe Christentum und die Bildung." Pages 17–28 in *Zukunftsfähige Bildung und Protestantismus*. Edited by Hartmut Rupp, Christoph Th. Scheilke, and Heinz Schmidt. Stuttgart: Calwer, 2002.

———. "Gegner im Kolosserbrief." Pages 365–94 in Kraus, *Beiträge zur urchristlichen Theologiegeschichte*.

Müller, Ulrich B. *Johannes der Täufer: Jüdischer Prophet und Wegbereiter Jesu*. Leipzig: Evangelische Verlagsanstalt, 2002.

———. *Die Menschwerdung des Gottessohnes: Frühchristliche Inkarnationsvorstellungen und die Anfänge des Doketismus*. SBS 140. Stuttgart: Verlag Katholisches Bibelwerk, 1990.

———. *Die Offenbarung des Johannes*. 2nd ed. ÖTK 19. Gütersloher Taschenbücher

510. Gütersloh: Mohn; Würzburg: Echter-Verlag, 1995.

———. "Die Parakletvorstellung im Johannesevangelium." *ZTK* 71 (1974): 31–77.

———. *Zur frühchristlichen Theologiegeschichte: Judenchristentum und Paulinismus in Kleinasien an der Wende vom ersten zum zweiten Jahrhundert n. Chr.* Gütersloh: Mohn, 1976.

Murphy-O'Connor, Jerome. *St. Paul's Corinth: Texts and Archaeology*. Collegeville, MN: Liturgical Press, 2002.

———. *St. Paul's Ephesus: Texts and Archaeology*. Collegeville, MN: Liturgical Press, 2008.

Müseler, Eike, ed. *Die Kynikerbriefe*. 2 vols. Paderborn: F. Schöningh, 1994.

Mussner, Franz. *The Historical Jesus in the Gospel of St. John*. Translated by W. O'Hara. QD 19. New York: Herder & Herder, 1967.

———. *ZΩH: Die Anschauung vom "Leben" im vierten Evangelium, unter Berücksichtigung der Johannesbriefe: Ein Beitrag zur biblischen Theologie*. Munich: Zink, 1952.

Nagel, Peter. *Codex apocryphus gnosticus Novi Testamenti*. WUNT 326. Tübingen: Mohr Siebeck, 2014.

———. "Das Evangelium des Judas." *ZNW* 98 (2007): 213–76.

Nagel, Titus. *Die Rezeption des Johannesevangeliums im 2. Jahrhundert: Studien zur vorirenäischen Aneignung und Auslegung des vierten Evangeliums in christlicher und christlich-gnostischer Literatur*. ABG 2. Leipzig: Evangelische Verlagsanstalt, 2000.

Neirynck, Frans. *Evangelica: Collected Essays*. Vol. 2, *1982–1991*. BETL 99. Louvain: Leuven University Press, 1991.

———. "The Miracle Stories in the Acts of the Apostles." Pages 169–213 in Kremer, *Les Actes des Apôtres*.

Nestle, Dieter. *Die Griechen.* Vol. 1 of *Eleutheria: Studien zum Wesen der Freiheit bei den Griechen und im Neuen Testament.* HUT 6.1. Tübingen: Mohr Siebeck, 1967.

Neuendorfer, Heinz-Werner. *Der Stephanuskreis in der Forschungsgeschichte seit F. Chr. Baur.* Giessen: Brunnen, 1983.

Neugebauer, Fritz. *In Christus = En Christo: Eine Untersuchung zum Paulinischen Glaubensverständnis.* Göttingen: Vandenhoeck & Ruprecht, 1961.

Neumann, Günter. "Kleinasien." Pages 167–85 in G. Neumann and Untermann, *Die Sprachen im Römischen Reich der Kaiserzeit.*

Neumann, Günter, and Jürgen Untermann, ed. *Die Sprachen im Römischen Reich der Kaiserzeit: Kolloquium vom 8. bis 10. April 1974.* BBJ 40. Cologne: Rheinland-Verlag; Bonn: Habelt, 1980.

Neumann, Nils. *Armut und Reichtum im Lukasevangelium und in der kynischen Philosophie.* SBS 220. Stuttgart: Katholisches Bibelwerk, 2010.

Neusner, Jacob. *Judaism in the Beginning of Christianity.* Philadelphia: Fortress, 1984.

———. *Judentum in frühchristlicher Zeit.* Stuttgart: Calwer Verlag, 1988.

———. "Die pharisäischen rechtlichen Überlieferungen." Pages 43–51 in Neusner, *Das pharisäische und talmudische Judentum.*

———. *Das pharisäische und talmudische Judentum: Neue Wege zu seinem Verständnis.* TSAJ 4. Tübingen: Mohr Siebeck, 1984.

Neusner, Jacob, and Bruce D. Chilton, eds. *In Quest of the Historical Pharisees.* Waco: Baylor University Press, 2007.

Nickel, Rainer. *Epikur: Wege zum Glück, griechisch-lateinisch-deutsch.* Düsseldorf: Artemis & Winkler, 2003.

———, ed. *Stoa und Stoiker.* 2 vols. Düsseldorf: Artemis & Winkler, 2008.

Nickelsburg, George W. E. *Jewish Literature between the Bible and the Mishna: A Historical and Literary Introduction.* 2nd ed. Minneapolis: Fortress. 2005.

Niebuhr, Karl-Wilhelm. *Heidenapostel aus Israel: Die jüdische Identität des Paulus nach ihrer Darstellung in seinen Briefen.* WUNT 62. Tübingen: Mohr, 1992.

———. "'A New Perspective on James'? Neuere Forschungen zum Jakobusbrief." *TLZ* 129 (2004): 1019–44.

Niederwimmer, Kurt. *Die Didache.* Göttingen: Vandenhoeck & Ruprecht, 1993.

———. *The Didache: A Commentary.* Translated by Linda M. Maloney. Edited by Harold W. Attridge. Minneapolis: Fortress, 1998.

———. "Johannes Markus und die Frage nach dem Verfasser des zweiten Evangeliums." *ZNW* 58 (1967): 172–88.

Niehues-Pröbsting, Heinrich. *Die antike Philosophie: Schrift, Schule, Lebensform.* Europäische Geschichte. Frankfurt: Fischer-Taschenbuch-Verlag, 2004.

Niemand, Christoph. *Die Fußwaschungserzählung des Johannesevangeliums.* StAns 114. Rome: Pontificio Ateneo S. Anselmo, 1993.

———. *Jesus und sein Weg zum Kreuz: Ein historisch-rekonstruktives und theologisches Modellbild.* Stuttgart: Kohlhammer, 2007.

Nienhuis, David R. *Not by Paul Alone: The Formation of the Catholic Epistle Collection and the Christian Canon.* Waco: Baylor University Press, 2007.

Nissen, Andreas. *Gott und der Nächste im antiken Judentum: Untersuchungen zum Doppelgebot der Liebe.* WUNT 15. Tübingen: Mohr, 1974.

Noethlichs, Karl Leo. *Das Judentum und der römische Staat: Minderheitenpolitik im antiken Rom.* Darmstadt: Wissenschaftliche Buchgesellschaft, 1996.

Oakes, Peter. *Philippians: From People to Letter*. SNTSMS 110. Cambridge: Cambridge University Press, 2001.

Oberlinner, Lorenz. *Die Pastoralbriefe*. 3 vols. HTKNT. Freiburg im Breisgau: Herder, 1994–96.

———. *Titusbrief*. Vol. 3 of Oberlinner, *Die Pastoralbriefe*.

Öhler, Markus, ed. *Aposteldekret und antikes Vereinswesen*. WUNT 280. Tübingen: Mohr Siebeck, 2011.

———. *Barnabas: Der Mann in der Mitte*. BG 12. Leipzig: Evangelische Verlagsanstalt, 2005.

———. *Barnabas: Die historische Person und ihre Rezeption in der Apostelgeschichte*. WUNT 156. Tübingen: Mohr Siebeck, 2003.

———. "Das ganze Haus: Antike Alltagsreligiosität und die Apostelgeschichte." *ZNW* 102 (2011): 201–34.

———. *Geschichte des frühen Christentums*. UTB 4737. Göttingen: Vandenhoeck & Ruprecht, 2018.

———. "Römisches Vereinsrecht und christliche Gemeinden." Pages 51–71 in *Zwischen den Reichen: Neues Testament und Römische Herrschaft*. Edited by Michael Labahn and Jürgen Zangenberg. TANZ 36. Tübingen: Franke, 2002.

Okure, Teresa. *The Johannine Approach to Mission*. WUNT 2/31. Tübingen: Mohr Siebeck, 1989.

Ollrog, Wolf-Henning. *Paulus und seine Mitarbeiter: Untersuchungen zu Theorie und Praxis der paulinischen Mission*. WMANT 50. Neukirchen: Neukirchener Verlag, 1979.

Olsson, Birger, and Magnus Zetterholm, ed. *The Ancient Synagogue from Its Origin until 200 C.E.: Papers Presented at an International Conference at Lund University, October 14–17, 2001*. CBNT 39. Stockholm: Almqvist & Wiksell International, 2003.

Omerzu, Heike. *Der Prozess des Paulus*. BZNW 115. Berlin: de Gruyter, 2002.

———. "Das Schweigen des Lukas." Pages 151–56 in Horn, *Das Ende des Paulus*.

Oorschot, Jurgen van. *Gott als Grenze: Eine literar- und redaktionsgeschichtliche Studie zu den Gottesreden des Hiobbuches*. BZAW 170. Berlin: de Gruyter, 1987.

Opper, Thorsten. *Hadrian: Empire and Conflict*. Cambridge, MA: Harvard University Press, 2008.

———. *Hadrian: Machtmensch und Mäzen*. Darmstadt: Wissenschaftliche Buchgesellschaft, 2009.

Oster, Richard. "The Ephesian Artemis as an Opponent of Early Christianity." *JAC* 19 (1976): 24–44.

Ostmeyer, Karl-Heinrich. "Armenhaus und Räuberhöhle? Galiläa zur Zeit Jesu." *ZNW* 96 (2005): 147–70.

Otto, Walter Friedrich. *The Homeric Gods: The Spiritual Significance of Greek Religion*. Translated by Moses Hadas. New York: Pantheon, 1954.

Paesler, Kurt. *Das Tempelwort Jesu: Die Traditionen von Tempelzerstörung und Tempelerneuerung im Neuen Testament*. FRLANT 184. Göttingen: Vandenhoeck & Ruprecht, 1999.

Pagels, Elaine. *Beyond Belief: The Secret Gospel of Thomas*. New York: Random House, 2003.

———. *Das Geheimnis des fünften Evangeliums: Warum die Bibel nur die halbe Wahrheit sagt; Mit dem Text des Thomasevangeliums*. 3rd ed. Munich: Deutsch Taschenbuch-Verlag, 2007.

Paget, James Carleton. "The Definition of the Terms Jewish Christian and Jewish Christianity in the History of Research." Pages 22–52 in Skarsaune and Hvalvik, *Jewish Believers in Jesus*.

———. "Jewish Christianity." Pages 731–75 in *The Early Roman Period*. Vol. 3 of *The Cambridge History of Judaism*. Edited by William Horbury, W. D. Davies, and John Sturdy. Cambridge: Cambridge University Press, 1999.

Painter, John. *The Quest for the Messiah: The History, Literature, and Theology of the Johannine Community*. 2nd ed. Nashville: Abingdon; Edinburgh: T&T Clark, 1993.

Panzram, Sabine. "Der Jerusalemer Tempel und das Rom der Flavier." Pages 166–82 in J. Hahn, *Zerstörungen des Jerusalemer Tempels*.

Pardee, Nancy. *The Genre and Development of the Didache: A Text-Linguistic Analysis*. WUNT 2/339. Tübingen: Mohr Siebeck, 2012.

Parker, David C. *New Testament Manuscripts and Their Texts*. Cambridge: Cambridge University Press, 2008.

Parsenios, George L. *Departure and Consolation: The Johannine Farewell Discourses in Light of Greco-Roman Literature*. NovTSup 117. Leiden: 2005.

Parsons, Talcott. *Societies: Evolutionary and Comparative Perspectives*. FMS. Englewood Cliffs, NJ: Prentice-Hall, 1966.

———. *The System of Modern Societies*. FMS. Englewood Cliffs, NJ: Prentice-Hall, 1971.

Passow, Franz. *Handwörterbuch der Griechischen Sprache*. Vol. 2.2. 5th ed. Leipzig: Vogel, 1857.

Patsch, Hermann. *Abendmahl und historischer Jesus*. CTM A1. Stuttgart: Calwer, 1972.

Paulsen, Henning. "Zur Wissenschaft vom Urchristentum und der Alten Kirche— ein methodischer Versuch." *ZNW* 68 (1977): 200–230.

———. *Der zweite Petrusbrief und der Judasbrief*. KEK 12.2. Göttingen: Vandenhoeck & Ruprecht, 1992.

Payne, Philip B. *Man and Woman, One in Christ: An Exegetical and Theological Study of Paul's Letters*. Grand Rapids: Zondervan, 2009.

Pearson, Birger A. "Basilides the Gnostic." Pages 1–31 in Marjanen and Luomanen, *A Companion to Second-Century Christian "Heretics."*

Peerbolte, L. J. Lietaert. *Paul the Missionary*. Contributions to Biblical Exegesis and Theology 34. Leuven: Peeters, 2003.

Peres, Imre. *Griechische Grabinschriften*. WUNT 157. Tübingen: Mohr Siebeck, 2003.

Perkins, Pheme. *Introduction to the Synoptic Gospels*. Grand Rapids: Eerdmans, 2007.

Perry, Peter S. "Critiquing the Excess of Empire: A Synkrisis of John of Patmos and Dio of Prusa." *JSNT* 29 (2007): 473–96.

Pervo, Richard I. *Acts*. Herm. Minneapolis: Fortress, 2009.

———. *The Making of Paul: Constructions of the Apostle in Early Christianity*. Minneapolis: Fortress, 2010.

Pesch, Rudolf, ed. *Das Markus-Evangelium*. Darmstadt: Wissenschaftliche Buchgesellschaft, 1979.

———. *Das Markusevangelium*. 3rd ed. HTKNT 2. Freiburg: Herder, 1984.

Petersen, Silke. "Die Evangelienüberschriften und die Entstehung des neutestamentlichen Kanons." *ZNW* 97 (2006): 250–74.

———. *Maria aus Magdala: Die Jüngerin, die Jesus liebte*. BG 23. Leipzig: Evangelische Verlagsanstalt, 2011.

Petracca, Vincenzo. *Gott oder das Geld: Die Besitzethik des Lukas*. TANZ 39. Tübingen: Franke, 2003.

Pfeiffer, Matthias. *Einweisung in das neue Sein*. BEvT 119. Gütersloh: 2001.

Pfeiffer, Stefan. *Die Zeit der Flavier: Vespasian, Titus, Domitian*. Darmstadt: Wissenschaftliche Buchgesellschaft, 2009.

Pichler, Josef, and Christine Rajič, eds. *Ephesus als Ort frühchristlichen Lebens: Perspektiven auf einen Hotspot der Antike*. Regensburg: Pustet, 2017.

Pilhofer, Peter. "Livius, Lukas und Lukian: Drei Himmelfahrten." Pages 166–82 in *Die frühen Christen und ihre Welt: Greifswalder Aufsätze 1996–2001*. Edited by Peter Pilhofer, Jens Börstinghaus, and Eva Ebel. WUNT 145. Tübingen: Mohr Siebeck, 2002.

———. *Philippi*. Vol. 1, *Die erste christliche Gemeinde Europas*. WUNT 87. Tübingen: Mohr Siebeck, 1995.

———. "Städtische Wurzeln des frühen Christentums." *TPQ* 161 (2013): 158–65.

Plisch, Uwe-Karsten. *The Gospel of Thomas: Original Text with Commentary*. Translated by Gesine Schenke Robinson. Stuttgart: Deutsche Bibelgesellschaft, 2008.

———. *Das Thomas-Evangelium: Originaltext mit Kommentar*. Stuttgart: Deutsche Bibelgesellschaft, 2007.

Plümacher, Eckhard. *Lukas als hellenistischer Schriftsteller: Studien zur Apostelgeschichte*. SUNT 9. Göttingen: Vandenhoeck & Ruprecht, 1972.

———. "Neues Testament und hellenistische Form: Zur literarischen Gattung der lukanischen Schriften." *TheolViat* 14 (1977/78): 109–23.

Plutarch. "Über die eingegangenen Orakel." Pages 106–69 in *Über Gott und Vorsehung, Dämonen und Weissagung*. Edited by Konrat Ziegler. Zurich: Artemis, 1952.

Pohlenz, Max. *Griechische Freiheit: Wesen und Werden eines Lebensideals*. Heidelberg: Quelle & Meyer, 1955.

———. *Die Stoa. Geschichte einer geistigen Bewegung*. 2 vols. 7th ed. Göttingen: Vandenhoeck & Ruprecht, 1992.

Pokorný, Petr. *Theologie der lukanischen Schriften*. FRLANT 174. Göttingen: Vandenhoeck & Ruprecht, 1998.

Popkes, Enno Edzard. *Das Menschenbild des Thomasevangeliums*. WUNT 206. Tübingen: Mohr Siebeck, 2007.

———. *Die Theologie der Liebe Gottes in den johanneischen Schriften: Zur Semantik der Liebe und zum Motivkreis des Dualismus*. WUNT 2/197. Tübingen: Mohr Siebeck, 2005.

Popkes, Wiard. *Der Brief des Jakobus*. THK 14. Leipzig: Evangelische Verlagsanstalt, 2001.

———. *Paränese und Neues Testament*. SBS 168. Stuttgart: Katholisches Bibelwerk, 1996.

———. "Traditionen und Traditionsbrüche im Jakobusbrief." Pages 143–70 in *The Catholic Epistles and the Tradition*. Edited by Jacques Schlosser. BETL 176. Louvain: Leuven University Press; Dudley, MA: Peeters, 2004.

Popp, Thomas. *Die Kunst der Konvivenz: Theologie der Anerkennung im 1. Petrusbrief*. ABG 33. Leipzig: Evangelische Verlagsanstalt, 2010.

Porter, Stanley E., ed. *Paul and His Opponents*. Leiden: Brill, 2005.

———, ed. *Paul and the Ancient Letter Form*. PaSt 6. Leiden; Boston: Brill, 2010.

Porter, Stanley E., and Andrew W. Pitts, ed. *Language of the New Testament: Context, History and Development*. LBS. Leiden: Brill, 2013.

Prast, Franz. *Presbyter und Evangelium in nachapostolischer Zeit: Die Abschiedsrede des Paulus in Milet (Apg 20, 17–38) im Rahmen der lukanischen Konzeption der Evangeliumsverkündigung*. FB 29. Stuttgart: Katholisches Bibelwerk, 1979.

Pratscher, Wilhelm, ed. *Die Apostolischen Väter: Eine Einleitung*. UTB 3272. Göttingen: Vandenhoeck & Ruprecht, 2009.

———. "Der Beitrag des Herrenbruders Jakobus zur Entstehung des Aposteldekrets." Pages 33–48 in Öhler, *Aposteldekret und antikes Vereinswesen*.

———. *Der Herrenbruder Jakobus und die Jakobustradition*. FRLANT 139, Göttingen: Vandenhoeck & Ruprecht, 1987.

Price, Simon R. F. *Rituals and Power: The Roman Imperial Cult in Asia Minor.* Cambridge: Cambridge University Press, 1984.

Pummer, Reinhard. *The Samaritans: A Profile.* Grand Rapids: Eerdmans, 2016.

Radl, Walter. *Paulus und Jesus im lukanischen Doppelwerk.* EURHS 23/49. Bern: Lang, 1975.

Rahner, Johanna. "Vergegenwärtigende Erinnerung." *ZNW* 91 (2000): 72–90.

Räisänen, Heikki. "The 'Hellenists': A Bridge between Jesus and Paul?" Pages 242–301 in Räisänen, *The Torah and Christ.*

———. *The "Messianic Secret" in Mark's Gospel.* Edinburgh: T&T Clark, 1990.

———. *Das "Messiasgeheimnis" im Markusevangelium: Eine Redaktionskritischer Versuch.* Schriften der Finnischen Exegetischen Gesellschaft 28. Helsinki: Finnischen Exegetischen Gesellschaft, 1976.

———. *The Torah and Christ.* SESJ 45. Helsinki: Finnish Exegetical Society, 1986.

Ranke, Leopold von. *Geschichten der romanischen und germanischen Völker von 1494–1514.* Leipzig: Duncker & Humblot, 1874. In L. von Ranke's *Sämtliche Werke: Zweite Gesamtausgabe* 33/34. Leipzig: Duncker & Humblot, 1877.

Rapp, Christof, ed. *Epikur: Ausgewählte Schriften.* Stuttgart: Kröner, 2010.

Rapske, Brian. *The Book of Acts and Paul in Roman Custody.* BAFCS 3. Grand Rapids: Eerdmans, 1994.

Rau, Eckhard. *Das geheime Markusevangelium: Ein Schriftfund voller Rätsel.* Neukirchen-Vluyn: Neukirchener-Verlag, 2003.

———. *Von Jesus zu Paulus: Entwicklung und Rezeption der antiochenischen Theologie im Urchristentum.* Stuttgart: Kohlhammer, 1994.

Reck, Reinhold. *Kommunikation und Gemeindeaufbau: Eine Studie zu Entstehung, Leben und Wachstum paulinischer Gemeinden in den Kommunikationsstrukturen der Antike.* SBB 22. Stuttgart: Katholisches Bibelwerk, 1991.

Reed, Jonathan L. *Archaeology and the Galilean Jesus: A Re-examination of the Evidence.* Harrisburg, PA: Trinity Press International, 2002.

Reichert, Angelika. "Durchdachte Konfusion: Plinius, Trajan und das Christentum." *ZNW* 93 (2002): 227–50.

———. *Der Römerbrief als Gratwanderung: Eine Untersuchung zur Abfassungsproblematik.* FRLANT 194. Göttingen: Vandenhoek & Ruprecht, 2001.

———. *Eine urchristliche praeparatio ad martyrium: Studien zur Komposition, Traditionsgeschichte und Theologie des 1. Petrusbriefes.* BBET 22. New York: Lang, 1989.

Reinbold, Wolfgang. *Propaganda und Mission im ältesten Christentum.* FRLANT 188. Göttingen: Vandenhoeck & Ruprecht, 2000.

Reinmuth, Eckart. "Narratio und argumentatio: Zur Auslegung der Jesus-Christus-Geschichte im Ersten Korintherbrief." *ZTK* 92 (1995): 13–27.

Reiprich, Torsten. *Das Mariageheimnis: Maria von Nazareth und die Bedeutung familiärer Beziehungen im Markusevangelium.* FRLANT 223. Göttingen: Vandenhoeck & Ruprecht, 2008.

Reiser, Marius. "Hat Paulus Heiden bekehrt?" *BZ* 39 (1995): 78–91.

Rengstorf, Karl Heinrich, ed. *Das Paulusbild in der neueren deutschen Forschung.* 2nd ed. Darmstadt: Wissenschaftliche Buchgesellschaft, 1969.

Reuters, Franz Heinrich, ed. *Die Briefe des Anacharsis: Griechisch und deutsch.* SQAW 14. Berlin: Akademie, 1963.

Ricken, Friedo. *Antike Skeptiker.* Munich: Beck, 1994.

Riedo-Emmenegger, Christoph. *Prophetisch-messianische Provokateure der Pax Romana: Jesus von Nazaret und andere Störenfriede im Konflikt mit dem Römischen Reich*. NTOA 56. Göttingen: Vandenhoeck & Ruprecht, 2005.

Riesner, Rainer. "Apostelgeschichte, Pastoralbriefe, 1 Clemens-Brief und die Martyrien der Apostel in Rom." Pages 153–79 in Heid and Haehling, *Petrus und Paulus in Rom*.

———. *Essener und Urgemeinde in Jerusalem: Neue Funde und Quellen*. Giessen: Brunnen, 1998.

———. *Jesus als Lehrer*. 3rd ed. WUNT 2/7. Tübingen: Mohr Siebeck, 1988.

———. *Paul's Early Period: Chronology, Mission Strategy, Theology*. Translated by Doug Stott. Grand Rapids: Eerdmans, 1998.

———. "A Pre-Christian Jewish Mission?" Pages 211–50 in Ådna and Kvalbein, *The Mission of the Early Church to Jews and Gentiles*.

———. "Die Rückkehr der Augenzeugen." *TBei* 38 (2007): 337–52.

———. "Zwischen Tempel und Obergemach—Jerusalem als erste messianische Stadtgemeinde." Pages 69–91 in Bendemann and Tiwald, *Das frühe Evangelium und die Stadt*.

Rigaux, Béda. "Die 'Zwölf' in Geschichte und Kerygma." Pages 468–86 in Ristow and Matthiae, *Der historische Jesus und der kerygmatische Christus*.

Rist, John M. *Epicurus: An Introduction*. Cambridge: Cambridge University Press, 1972.

———. *The Stoics*. Berkeley: University of California Press, 1978.

Ristow, Helmut, and Karl Matthiae, eds. *Der historische Jesus und der kerygmatische Christus: Beiträge zum Christusverständnis in Forschung und Verkündigung*. Berlin: Evangelische Verlagsanstalt, 1960.

Ritt, Hubert. "Der christologische Imperativ: Zur Weinstock-Metapher in der testamentarischen Mahnrede (Joh 15,1–17)." Pages 136–50 in Merklein, *Neues Testament und Ethik*.

Robinson, James M. *The Gospel of Jesus: In Search of the Original "Good News."* San Francisco: HarperSanFrancisco, 2005.

———. "ΛΟΓΟΙ ΣΟΦΩΝ: On the Gattung of Q." Pages 71–113 in *Trajectories through Early Christianity*. Edited by Helmut Köster and James M. Robinson. Philadelphia: Fortress, 1971.

———, ed. *The Nag Hammadi Library in English*. 3rd ed. San Francisco: Harper & Row, 1988.

Robinson, James M., Paul Hoffmann, and John S. Kloppenborg, ed. *The Critical Edition of Q*. Minneapolis: Fortress, 2000.

Rohde, Joachim. "Häresie und Schisma im Ersten Clemensbrief und in den Ignatius-Briefen." *NovT* 10 (1968): 217–33.

Roller, Otto. *Das Formular der paulinischen Briefe: Ein Beitrag zur Lehre vom antike Briefe*. BWANT 4.6. Stuttgart: Kohlhammer, 1933.

Roloff, Jürgen. "Anfänge der soteriologischen Deutung des Todes Jesu (Mk. X. 45 und Lk. XXII. 27)." Pages 117–43 in Roloff, *Exegetische Verantwortung in der Kirche*.

———. *Die Apostelgeschichte*. NTD 5. Göttingen: Vandenhoeck & Ruprecht, 1988.

———. *Apostolat, Verkündigung, Kirche: Ursprung, Inhalt und Funktion des kirchlichen Apostelamtes nach Paulus, Lukas und den Pastoralbriefen*. Gütersloh: Mohn, 1965.

———. *Der erste Brief an Timotheus*. EKKNT 15. Neukirchen-Vluyn: Neukirchener Verlag, 1988.

———. *Exegetische Verantwortung in der Kirche*. Göttingen: Vandenhoeck & Ruprecht, 1990.

———. *Die Kirche im Neuen Testament.* GNT 10. Göttingen: Vandenhoeck & Ruprecht, 1993.

———. "Neuschöpfung in der Offenbarung des Johannes." *JBTh* 5 (1990): 119–38.

———. "Die Paulusdarstellung des Lukas." *EvT* 39 (1979): 510–31.

———. "Das Reich des Menschensohnes: Ein Beitrag zur Eschatologie des Matthäus." Pages 275–92 in Evang, Merklein, and Wolter, *Eschatologie und Schöpfung.*

———. *The Revelation of John.* Translated by John E. Alsup. CC. Minneapolis: Fortress, 1993.

Rordorf, Willy. *Sunday: The History of the Day of Rest and Worship in the Earliest Centuries of the Christian Church; Der Sonntag.* Translated by A. A. K. Graham. Philadelphia: Westminster, 1968.

Rosén, Haiim B. "Die Sprachsituation im Römischen Palästina." Pages 215–39 in G. Neumann and Untermann, *Die Sprachen im Römischen Reich der Kaiserzeit.*

Rothschild, Clare K. *Hebrews as Pseudepigraphon.* WUNT 235. Tübingen: Mohr Siebeck, 2009.

Rothschild, Clare K., and Jens Schröter, eds. *The Rise and Expansion of Christianity in the First Three Centuries of the Common Era.* WUNT 301. Tübingen: Mohr Siebeck, 2013.

Rottloff, Andrea. *Lebensbilder römischer Frauen.* KGAW 104. Mainz: P. von Zabern, 2006.

Rudolph, Kurt. *Die Mandäer.* Vol. 1. FRLANT 74. Göttingen: Vandenhoeck & Ruprecht, 1960.

Ruffing, Kai. *Wirtschaft in der griechisch-römischen Antike.* GK. Darmstadt: Wissenschaftliche Buchgesellschaft, 2012.

Rüpke, Jörg. *Die Religion der Römer: Eine Einführung.* Munich: Beck, 2001.

Rupp, Hartmut, ed. *Zukunftsfähige Bildung und Protestantismus*: [Eckhart Marggraf zum 60. Geburtstag]. Stuttgart: Calwer, 2002.

Rusam, Dietrich. *Die Gemeinschaft der Kinder Gottes: Das Motiv der Gotteskindschaft und die Gemeinden der johanneischen Briefe.* BWANT 133. Stuttgart: Kohlhammer, 1993.

———. "Neue Belege zu den στοιχεῖα τοῦ κόσμου (Gal 4,3.9; Kol 2,8.20)." *ZNW* 83 (1992): 119–25.

Rüsen, Jörn. "Faktizität und Fiktionalität der Geschichte—Was ist Wirklichkeit im historischen Denken?" Pages 19–32 in *Konstruktion von Wirklichkeit.* Edited by Jens Schröter and Antje Eddelbüttel. Berlin: de Gruyter, 2004.

———. *Historische Vernunft: Die Grundlagen der Geschichtswissenschaft.* Grundzüge einer Historik 1. Göttingen: Vandenhoeck & Ruprecht, 1983.

———. *History: Narration, Interpretation, Orientation.* MSH 2. New York: Berghahn Books, 2004.

———. *Kann gestern besser werden? Essays zum Bedenken der Geschichte.* Kulturwissenschaftliche Interventionen 2. Berlin: Kadmos, 2003.

———. "Kann gestern besser werden? Über die Verwandlung der Vergangenheit in Geschichte." Pages 17–44 in Rüsen, *Kann gestern besser werden?*

———. *Lebendige Geschichte: Formen und Funktionen des historischen Wissens.* Grundzüge einer Historik 3. Göttingen: Vandenhoeck & Ruprecht, 1989.

———. *Rekonstruktion der Vergangenheit: Die Prinzipien der historischen Forschung.* Grundzüge einer Historik 2. Göttingen: Vandenhoeck & Ruprecht, 1986.

———. "Was heißt: Sinn der Geschichte?" Pages 17–47 in Müller and Rüsen, *Historische Sinnbildung.*

Rutgers, Leonard V. *The Jews in Late Ancient Rome: Evidence of Cultural*

Interaction in the Roman Diaspora. Leiden: Brill, 1995.

Rydryck, Michael. "Das Kapital des Paulus: Ein Beitrag zur sozialhistorischen Plausibilität der Apostelgeschichte." Pages 59–84 in Alkier and Rydryck, *Paulus—das Kapital eines Reisenden.*

Safrai, Samuel. "Education and the Study of the Torah." Pages 945–70 in *The Jewish People in the First Century: Historical Geography, Political History, Social, Cultural and Religious Life and Institutions.* Edited by Samuel Safrai and Menachem Stern. 2 vols. CRINT. Assen: Van Gorcum; Philadelphia: Fortress, 1976.

Sandt, Huub Van De, and Jürgen Zangenberg, eds. *Matthew, James, and Didache: Three Related Documents in Their Jewish and Christian Settings.* SBL Symposium 45. Atlanta: Society of Biblical Literature, 2008.

Sänger, Dieter, ed. *Das Ezechielbuch in der Johannesoffenbarung.* BTS 76. Neukirchen: Neukirchener Verlag, 2006.

———. "Ἰουδαϊσμός, ἰουδαΐζειν, ἰουδαϊκῶς: Sprachliche und semantische Überlegungen im Blick auf Gal 1,13f. und 2,14." *ZNW* 108 (2017): 150–85.

———, ed. *Der zweite Korintherbrief: Literarische Gestalt, historische Situation, theologische Argumentation: Festschrift zum 70. Geburtstag von Dietrich-Alex Koch.* FRLANT 250. Göttingen: Vandenhoeck & Ruprecht, 2012.

Sato, Migaku. *Q und Prophetie.* WUNT 2/29. Tübingen: Mohr Siebeck, 1988.

Schäfer, Gerhard Karl, and Theodor Strohm, eds. *Diakonie—biblische Grundlagen und Orientierungen: Ein Arbeitsbuch zur theologischen Verständigung über den diakonischen Auftrag.* Heidelberg: Heidelberger Verlagsanstalt, 1990.

Schäfer, Jan. "Vom Zentrum zum Zentrum: Die Achse der Apostelgeschichte von Jerusalem nach Rom." Pages 189–207 in Bendemann and Tiwald, *Das frühe Christentum und die Stadt.*

Schäfer, Peter. *Geschichte der Juden in der Antike: Die Juden Palästinas von Alexander dem Großen bis zur arabischen Eroberung.* 2nd ed. UTB 3366: Geschichte, Theologie, Judaistik. Tübingen: Mohr Siebeck, 2010.

———. "Die sogenannte Synode von Jabne." *Jud* 31 (1975): 54–64, 116–24.

———. "Der synagogale Gottesdienst." Pages 391–413 in Maier and Schreiner, *Literatur und Religion des Frühjudentums.*

———. "Der vorrabbinische Pharisäismus." Pages 125–72 in Hengel and U. Heckel, *Paulus und das antike Judentum.*

Schaller, Berndt. "4000 Essener—6000 Pharisäer: Zum Hintergrund und Wert antiker Zahlenangaben." Pages 172–82 in Kollmann, Reinbold, and Steudel, *Antikes Judentum und Frühes Christentum.*

Schenke, Hans-Martin, Hans-Gebhard Bethge, and Ursula Ulrike Kaiser, eds. *Nag Hammadi Deutsch.* 2 vols. Berlin: de Gruyter, 2001–3.

Schenke, Ludger. "Jesus als Weisheitslehrer im Markusevangelium." Pages 125–38 in *Die Weisheit: Ursprünge und Rezeption; Festschrift für Karl Löning zum 65. Geburtstag.* Edited by Martin Fassnacht et al. NTA 44. Münster: Aschendorff, 2003.

———. "Jesus als Wundertäter." Pages 148–63 in *Jesus von Nazaret—Spuren und Konturen.* Edited by Ludger Schenke. Stuttgart: Kohlhammer, 2004.

———. *Die Urgemeinde: Geschichtliche und theologische Entwicklung.* Stuttgart: Kohlhammer, 1990.

———. *Die Wundererzählungen des Markusevangeliums.* Stuttgart: Katholisches Bibelwerk, 1974.

Schenke, Ludger, Rainer Feige, and Johannes Neugebauer. *Das Johannesevangelium: Einführung, Text, dramatische Gestalt.*

Urban-Taschenbücher 446. Stuttgart: Kohlhammer, 1992.

Schiefer-Ferrari, Markus. *Die Sprache des Leids in den paulinischen Peristasenkatalogen.* SBB 23. Stuttgart: Katholisches Bibelwerk, 1991.

Schille, Gottfried. *Das älteste Paulus-bild: Beobachtungen zur lukanischen und zur deuteropaulinischen Paulus-Darstellung.* Berlin: Evangelische Verlagsanstalt, 1979.

———. *Das vorsynoptische Judenchristentum.* Berlin: Calwer Verlag, 1970.

Schimanowski, Gottfried. "Alexandria." Vol. 1, pages 127–32 in Erlemann et al., *Neues Testament und antike Kultur.*

———. *Juden und Nichtjuden in Alexandrien: Koexistenz und Konflikte bis zum Pogrom unter Trajan (117 n. Chr.).* MJS 18. Münster: Lit, 2006.

Schinkel, Dirk. *Die himmlische Bürgerschaft.* FRLANT 220. Göttingen: Vandenhoeck & Ruprecht, 2007.

Schipp, Oliver. *Die Adoptivkaiser: Nerva, Trajan, Hadrian, Antonius Pius, Marc Aurel und Lucius Verus.* GK. Darmstadt: Wissenschaftliche Buchgesellschaft, 2011.

Schlange-Schöningen, Heinrich. *Augustus.* Darmstadt: Wissenschaftliche Buchgesellschaft, 2005.

Schlarb, Egbert. *Die gesunde Lehre: Häresie und Wahrheit im Spiegel der Pastoralbriefe.* MTS 28. Marburg: Elwert, 1990.

———. "Miszelle zu 1 Tim 6,20." *ZNW* 77 (1986): 276–81.

Schlier, Heinrich. "Glauben, Erkennen, Lieben nach dem Johannesevangelium." Pages 290–302 in Schlier and Trilling, *Aufsätze zur Biblischen Theologie.*

Schlier, Heinrich, and Wolfgang Trilling. *Aufsätze zur Biblischen Theologie.* Leipzig: St.-Benno-Verlag, 1968.

Schmeller, Thomas. *Brechungen: Urchristliche Wandercharismatiker im Prisma soziologisch orientierter Exegese.* SBS 136. Stuttgart: Katholisches Bibelwerk, 1989.

——— *Hierarchie und Egalität: Eine sozialgeschichtliche Untersuchung paulinischer Gemeinden und griechisch-römischer Vereine.* SBS 162. Stuttgart: Katholisches Bibelwerk, 1995.

———. "Mission im Urchristentum: Definition—Motivation—Konkretion." *ZNT* 15 (2005): 2–11.

———. *Schulen im Neuen Testament? Zur Stellung des Urchristentums in der Bildungswelt seiner Zeit.* HBS 30. Freiburg: Herder, 2001.

———. *Der zweite Brief an die Korinther.* EKKNT 8.1. Neukirchen-Vluyn: Neukirchener Theologie, 2010.

Schmeller, Thomas, Martin Ebner, and Rudolf Hoppe, eds. *Neutestamentliche Ämtermodelle im Kontext.* QD 239. Freiburg im Breisgau: Herder, 2010.

Schmid, Hans Heinrich, ed. *Mythos und Rationalität.* Gütersloh: Mohn, 1988.

Schmid, Hansjörg. *Die Gegner im 1. Johannesbrief? Zu Konstruktion und Selbstreferenz im johanneischen Sinnsystem.* BWANT 159. Stuttgart: Kohlhammer, 2002.

Schmid, Konrad. *Literaturgeschichte des Alten Testaments: Eine Einführung.* Darmstadt: Wissenschaftliche Buchgesellschaft, 2014.

———. *The Old Testament: A Literary History.* Translated by Linda M. Maloney. Minneapolis: Fortress, 2012.

Schmid, Ulrich. "Die Buchwerdung des Neuen Testaments." *WuD* 27 (2003): 217–32.

Schmidt, Johann Michael. *Die jüdische Apokalyptik: Die Geschichte ihrer Erforschung von den Anfängen bis zu den Textfunden von Qumran.* 2nd ed. Neukirchen-Vluyn: Neukirchener Verlag, 1976.

Schmidt, Karl Ludwig. "Die Stellung der Evangelien in der allgemeinen Literaturgeschichte." Pages 37–130 in Schmidt and Sauter, *Neues Testament, Judentum, Kirche*.

Schmidt, Karl Ludwig, and Gerhard Sauter, eds. *Neues Testament, Judentum, Kirche: Kleine Schriften*. TB 69. Munich: Kaiser, 1981 (= 1923).

Schmidt, Karl Matthias. *Mahnung und Erinnerung im Maskenspiel: Epistolographie, Rhetorik und Narrativik der pseudepigraphischen Petrusbriefe*. HBS 38. Freiburg: 2003.

Schmithals, Walter. *Gnosticism in Corinth*. 3rd ed. FRLANT 66. Göttingen: Vandenhoeck & Ruprecht, 1969.

Schmitt, Hatto H., and Ernst Vogt, ed. *Lexikon des Hellenismus*. Wiesbaden: Harrassowitz, 2005.

Schmitt, Rüdiger. "Die Ostgrenze von Armenien über Mesopotamien, Syrien bis Arabien." Pages 187–214 in G. Neumann and Untermann, *Die Sprachen im Römischen Reich der Kaiserzeit*.

Schmitt, Tassilo. "Die Christenverfolgung unter Nero." Pages 517–37 in Heid and Haehling, *Petrus und Paulus in Rom*.

Schnabel, Eckhard J. *Early Christian Mission*. 2 vols. Downers Grove, IL. InterVarsity, 2004.

———. *Urchristliche Mission*. Wuppertal: Brockhaus, 2002.

Schnackenburg, Rudolf. "Ephesus: Entwicklung einer Gemeinde von Paulus zu Johannes." *BZ* 35 (1991): 41–64.

———. *The Gospel according to St. John*. 3 vols. Translated by Cecily Hastings et al. New York: Seabury, 1980–82.

———. *Die Johannesbriefe*. 6th ed. HTKNT 13.3. Freiburg: Herder, 1979–84.

———. *Das Johannesevangelium*. 4 vols. HTKNT 4.1–4. Freiburg: Herder, 1981–84.

———. *The Johannine Epistles: Introduction and Commentary*. 7th ed. Translated by Reginald and Ilse Fuller. New York: Crossroad, 1992.

———, ed. *Die Kirche des Anfangs: Für Heinz Schürmann*. ETS 38. Freiburg: Herder, 1978.

———. *The Moral Teaching of the New Testament*. Translated by J. Holland-Smith and W. J. O'Hara. New York: Herder & Herder, 1965.

———. "Paulinische und johanneische Christologie." Vol. 4, pages 102–18 in Schnackenburg, *Das Johannesevangelium*.

———. *Die urchristlichen Verkündiger*. Vol. 2 of *Die sittliche Botschaft des Neuen Testaments*. HTKSup 2. Freiburg: Herder, 1988.

Schneemelcher, Wilhelm, ed. *Neutestamentliche Apokryphen*. 2 vols. Tübingen: Mohr, 1959–64. Repr., 1987.

———, ed. *New Testament Apocrypha*. 2 vols. London: Lutterworth, 1961–63. London: SCM, 1973–74.

———. *Das Urchristentum*. Stuttgart: Kohlhammer, 1981.

Schneider, Carl. *Die Welt des Hellenismus*. Munich: Beck, 1975.

Schneider, Gerhard. "Anbruch des Heils und Hoffnung auf Vollendung bei Jesus, Paulus und Lukas." Pages 25–60 in G. Schneider, *Lukas, Theologe der Heilsgeschichte*.

———. *Die Apostelgeschichte*. 2 vols. HTKNT 5.1–2. Freiburg: Herder, 1980–82.

———. *Das Evangelium nach Lukas*. Vol. 1. ÖTK 3.1. Gütersloh: Mohn 1977.

———. *Lukas, Theologe der Heilsgeschichte: Aufsätze zum lukanischen Doppelwerk*. BBB 59. Bonn: Hanstein, 1985.

———. *Parusiegleichnisse im Lukas-Evangelium*. SBS 74. Stuttgart: Katholisches Bibelwerk, 1975.

Schneider, Theodor, and Gunther Wenz, ed. *Das kirchliche Amt in apostolischer Nachfolge*. Vol. 1, *Grundlagen und Grundfragen*. DK 12.1. Freiburg: Herder, 2004.

Schnelle, Udo. "Die Abschiedsreden im Johannesevangelium." *ZNW* 80 (1989): 64–79.

———. *Antidocetic Christology in the Gospel of John: An Investigation of the Place of the Fourth Gospel in the Johannine School*. Translated by Linda M. Maloney. Minneapolis: Fortress, 1992.

———. *Antidoketische Christologie im Johannesevangelium: Eine Untersuchung zur Stellung des vierten Evangeliums in der johanneischen Schule*. FRLANT 114. Göttingen: Vandenhoeck & Ruprecht, 1987.

———. *Apostle Paul: His Life and Theology*. Translated by M. Eugene Boring. Grand Rapids: Baker Academic, 2005.

———. "Denkender Glaube: Schulen im Neuen Testament." Pages 81–110 in Gemeinhardt and Günther, *Von Rom nach Bagdad*.

———. *Einführung in die neutestamentliche Exegese*. 8th ed. Göttingen: Vandenhoeck & Ruprecht, 2014.

———. *Einleitung in das Neue Testament*. 9th ed. Göttingen: Vandenhoeck & Ruprecht, 2017.

———. "Ethik und Kosmologie bei Paulus." Pages 207–29 in *Biblical Ethics and Application: Purview, Validity, and Relevance of Biblical Texts in Ethical Discourse*. Edited by Ruben Zimmermann and Stephan Joubert. WUNT 384. Tübingen: Mohr Siebeck, 2017.

———. *Das Evangelium nach Johannes*. 5th ed. THK 4. Leipzig: Evangelische Verlagsanstalt, 2009.

———. *Gerechtigkeit und Christusgegenwart: Vorpaulinische und paulinische Tauftheologie*. 2nd ed. GTA 24.

Göttingen: Vandenhoeck & Ruprecht, 1986.

———. *Die getrennten Wege von Römern, Juden und Christen: Religionspolitik im 1. Jarhundert n. Chr.* Tübingen: Mohr Siebeck, 2019.

———. "Gibt es eine Entwicklung in der Rechtfertigungslehre vom Galater- zum Römerbrief?" Pages 289–309 in Klumbies and Du Toit, *Paulus: Werk und Wirkung*.

———. "Glaube." Pages 275–93 in *Neues Testament: Zentrale Themen*. Edited by Lukas Bormann. Neukirchen-Vluyn: Neukirchener Theologie, 2014.

———. "Heilsgegenwart: Christologische Hoheitstitel bei Paulus." Pages 178–93 in Schnelle, Söding, and M. Labahn, *Paulinische Christologie*.

———. "Historische Anschlussfähigkeit: Zum hermeneutischen Horizont von Geschichte und Traditionsbildung." Pages 47–78 in Frey and Schnelle, *Kontexte des Johannesevangeliums*.

———. *The History and Theology of the New Testament Writings*. Translated by M. Eugene Boring. Minneapolis: Fortress, 1998.

———. *Introduction to the New Testament*. London: SCM, 1998.

———. "Johanneische Ethik." Pages 309–27 in *Eschatologie und Ethik im frühen Christentum: Festschrift für Günter Haufe zum 75. Geburtstag*. Edited by Christfried Böttrich. GTF 11. Frankfurt am Main: Lang, 2006.

———. "Die johanneische Schule." Pages 198–217 in Horn, *Bilanz und Perspektiven gegenwärtiger Auslegung des Neuen Testaments*.

———. *Die Johannesbriefe*. THK 17. Leipzig: Evangelische Verlagsanstalt, 2010.

———. "Johannes und die Synoptiker." Pages 1799–1814 in Segbroeck et al., *The Four Gospels*, 1992.

———. "Die Juden im Johannesevangelium." Pages 217–30 in Kähler, Böhm, and Böttrich, *Gedenkt an das Wort*.

———, ed. *The Letter to the Romans*. BETL 226. Louvain: Peeters, 2009.

———. *Neutestamentliche Anthropologie: Jesus, Paulus, Johannes*. BTS 18. Neukirchen-Vluyn: Neukirchener Verlag: 1991.

———. "Paulus und die Anfänge einer christlichen Überlieferungskultur." Pages 191–219 in *Paulus und Paulusbilder: Konstruktion, Reflexion, Transformation*. Edited by Manfred Lang. ABG 31. Leipzig: Evangelische Verlagsanstalt, 2013.

———. "Paulus und Epiktet—zwei ethische Modelle." Pages 137–58 in *Jenseits von Indikativ und Imperativ*. Edited by Friedrich Wilhelm Horn and Ruben Zimmermann. WUNT 238. Tübingen: Mohr Siebeck, 2009.

———. "Paulus und Johannes." *EvT* 47 (1987): 212–28.

———. "Die Reihenfolge der johanneischen Schriften." *NTS* 57 (2011): 91–113.

———. "Der Römerbrief und die Aporien des paulinischen Denkens." Pages 3–23 in Schnelle, *The Letter to the Romans*.

———. "Der 2. Korintherbrief und die Mission gegen Paulus." Pages 300–322 in Sänger, *Der zweite Korintherbrief*.

———. "Die Tempelreinigung und die Christologie des Johannesevangeliums." *NTS* 42 (1996): 359–73.

———. "Theologie als kreative Sinnbildung: Johannes als Weiterbildung von Paulus und Markus." Pages 119–45 in Söding, *Johannesevangelium—Mitte oder Rand des Kanons?*

———. *Theologie des Neuen Testaments*. 3rd ed. Göttingen: Vandenhoeck & Ruprecht, 2016.

———. *Theology of the New Testament*. Grand Rapids: Baker Academic, 2009.

———. "Transformation und Partizipation als Grundgedanken paulinischer Theologie." *NTS* 47 (2001): 58–75.

———. *Wandlungen im paulinischen Denken*. SBS 137. Stuttgart: Katholisches Bibelwerk, 1989.

Schnelle, Udo, Thomas Söding, and Michael Labahn, eds. *Paulinische Christologie: Exegetische Beiträge; Hans Hübner zum 70. Geburtstag*. Göttingen: Vandenhoeck & Ruprecht, 2000.

Schnider, Franz. *Der Jakobusbrief*. RNT 20. Regensburg: Pustet, 1987.

Schnider, Franz, and Werner Stenger. *Johannes und die Synoptiker*. Munich: Kösel, 1971.

———. *Studien zum neutestamentlichen Briefformular*. NTTS 11. Leiden: Brill, 1987.

Schoedel, William R. *Die Briefe des Ignatius von Antiochien: Ein Kommentar*. Munich: Kaiser, 1990.

———. *Ignatius of Antioch: A Commentary on the Letters of Ignatius to Antioch*. Herm. Philadelphia: Fortress, 1985.

Schoeps, Hans-Joachim. *Theologie und Geschichte des Judenchristentums*. Tübingen: Mohr, 1949.

Schöllgen, Georg. "Die Didache als Kirchenordnung." *JAC* 29 (1986): 5–26.

Scholtissek, Klaus, ed. *Christologie in der Paulus-Schule: Zur Rezeptionsgeschichte des paulinischen Evangeliums*. SBS 181. Stuttgart: Verlag Katholisches Bibelwerk, 2000.

———. "'Geboren aus einer Frau, geboren unter das Gesetz' (Gal 4,4): Die christologisch-soteriologische Bedeutung des irdischen Jesus bei Paulus." Pages 194–219 in Schnelle, Söding, and M. Labahn, *Paulinische Christologie*.

———. *In ihm sein und bleiben: Die Sprache der Immanenz in den Johanneischen Schriften*. HBS 21. Freiburg: Herder, 2000.

Schorch, Stefan. "The Construction of Samari(t)an Identity from the Inside and from the Outside." Pages 135–49 in *Between Cooperation and Hostility: Multiple Identities in Ancient Judaism and the Interaction with Foreign Powers*. Edited by Rainer Albertz and Jakob Wöhrle. JAJSup. Göttingen: Vandenhoeck & Ruprecht, 2013.

———. "Der Pentateuch der Samaritaner: Seine Erforschung und seine Bedeutung für das Verständnis des alttestamentlichen Bibeltextes." Pages 5–30 in Frey, Schattner-Rieser, and K. Schmid, *Die Samaritaner und die Bibel*.

Schottroff, Luise. *Der Glaube und die feindliche Welt*. WMANT 37. Neukirchen-Vluyn: 1970.

Schottroff, Luise, and Wolfgang Stegemann. *Jesus and the Hope of the Poor*. Translated by Matthew J. O'Connell. Maryknoll, NY: Orbis Books, 1986.

———. *Jesus von Nazareth—Hoffnung der Armen*. 3rd ed. Stuttgart: Kohlhammer, 1990.

Schowalter, Daniel N., and Steven J. Friesen, ed. *Urban Religion in Roman Corinth: Interdisciplinary Approaches*. HTS 53. Cambridge, MA: Harvard University Press, 2005.

Schrage, Wolfgang. *Der erste Brief an die Korinther*. 4 vols. EKKNT 7.1–4. Neukirchen-Vluyn: Neukirchener Verlag; Zurich: Benziger, 1991–2001.

———. *The Ethics of the New Testament*. Translated by David E. Green. Philadelphia: Fortress, 1988.

———. *Ethik des Neuen Testaments*. 2nd ed. Göttingen: Vandenhoeck & Ruprecht, 1989.

———. "Heil und Heilung im Neuen Testament." Pages 327–44 in Schäfer and Strohm, *Diakonie—biblische Grundlagen und Orientierungen*.

———. *Unterwegs zur Einheit und Einzigkeit Gottes: Zum "Monotheismus" des Paulus und seiner alttestamentlich-frühjüdischen Tradition*. BTS 48. Neukirchen-Vluyn: Neukirchener Verlag, 2002.

Schramm, Gottfried. *Fünf Wegscheiden: Der Weltgeschichte; Ein Vergleich*. Göttingen: Vandenhoeck & Ruprecht, 2004.

Schreiber, Stefan. *Die Anfänge der Christologie: Deutungen Jesu im Neuen Testament*. Neukirchen-Vluyn: Neukirchener Theologie, 2015.

———. "Arbeit mit der Gemeinde (Röm 16,6.12)." *NTS* 46 (2000), 204–26.

———. "Häresie im Kanon? Zum historischen Bild der dritten christlichen Generation." *BZ* 58 (2014): 186–210.

———. *Paulus als Wundertäter: Redaktionsgeschichtliche Untersuchungen zur Apostelgeschichte und den authentischen Paulusbriefen*. BZNW 79. Berlin: de Gruyter, 1996.

Schröder, Bernd. *Die "väterlichen Gesetze": Flavius Josephus als Vermittler von Halachah an Griechen und Römer*. TSAJ 53. Tübingen: Mohr, 1996.

Schröger, Friedrich. *Gemeinde im 1. Petrusbrief*. Passau: Passavia Universitätsverlag, 1981.

———. *Der Verfasser des Hebräerbriefes als Schriftausleger*. BU 4. Regensburg: Pustet, 1968.

Schröter, Jens. *Das Abendmahl: Frühchristliche Deutungen und Impulse für die Gegenwart*. SBS 210. Stuttgart: Katholisches Bibelwerk, 2006.

———. "Das Alte Testament im Urchristentum." Pages 40–81 in *Das Alte Testament in der Theologie*. Edited by Elisabeth Gräb-Schmidt and Reiner Preul. Marburger Jahrbuch Theologie 25. Leipzig: Evangelische Verlagsansalt, 2013.

———. *Erinnerung an Jesu Worte*. WMANT 76. Neukirchen-Vluyn: Neukirchener Verlag, 1997.

———. "Jesus im frühen Christentum: Zur neueren Diskussion über kanonisch und apokryph gewordene Jesusüberlieferungen." *VuF* 51 (2006): 25–41.

———. *Der versöhnte Versöhner: Paulus als unentbehrlicher Mittler im Heilsvorgang zwischen Gott und Gemeinde nach 2 Kor 2,14–7,4.* TANZ 10. Tübingen: Franke, 1993.

Schröter, Jens, and Hans-Gebhard Bethge. "Das Evangelium nach Thomas (NHC II,2)." Vol. 1, pages 153–57 in H. Schenke, Bethge, and Kaiser, *Nag Hammadi Deutsch.*

Schröter, Jens, and Ralph Brucker, eds. *Der historische Jesus: Tendenzen und Perspektiven der gegenwärtigen Forschungen.* BZNW 114. Berlin: de Gruyter, 2002.

Schulz, Siegfried. "Gottes Vorsehung bei Lukas." *ZNW* 54 (1963): 104–16.

Schumacher, Leonhard. *Sklaverei in der Antike: Alltag und Schicksal der Unfreien.* Beck's archäologische Bibliothek. Munich: Beck, 2001.

Schumacher, Thomas. *Zur Entstehung christlicher Sprache: Eine Untersuchung der paulinischen Idiomatik und der Verwendung des Begriffes πίστις.* BBB 168. Göttingen: Vandenhoeck & Ruprecht; Bonn: Bonn University Press, 2012.

Schunack, Gerd. "Glaube in griechischer Religiosität." Pages 296–326 in Kollmann, Reinbold, and Steudel, *Antikes Judentum und frühes Christentum.*

Schuol, Monika. *Augustus und die Juden: Rechtsstellung und Interessenpolitik der kleinasiatischen Diaspora.* SAG 6. Frankfurt am Main: Verlag Antike, 2007.

Schur, Nathan. *History of the Samaritans.* BEATAJ 18. Frankfurt am Main: P. Lang, 1989.

Schürer, Emil. *The History of the Jewish People in the Age of Jesus Christ.* Revised and edited by Fergus Millar, Géza Vermès, Matthew Black, Martin Goodman, and Pamela Vermes. Vols. 1, 2, 3.1,

3.2. New York: Bloomsbury T&T Clark, 2014.

Schürmann, Heinz. *Gottes Reich, Jesu Geschick: Jesu ureigener Tod im Licht seiner Basileia-Verkündigung.* Freiburg: Herder, 1983.

———. "Jesu Tod im Licht seines Basileia-Verständnisses." Pages 185–245 in Schürmann, *Gottes Reich, Jesu Geschick.*

Schwankl, Otto. *Die Sadduzäerfrage (Mk 12,18–27 parr): Eine Exegetisch-theologische Studie zur Auferstehungserwartung.* BBB 66. Bonn: Athenäum, 1987.

Schwartz, David R. *Agrippa I: The Last King of Judaea.* TSAJ 23. Tübingen: Mohr Siebeck, 1990.

Schweitzer, Friedrich. *Religion, Politik und Gewalt: Kongressband des XII; Europäischen Kongresses für Theologie, 18.–22. September 2005 in Berlin.* Edited by Friedrich Schweitzer. Gütersloh: Gütersloher Verlagshaus, 2006.

Schweizer, Eduard. "Altes und Neues zu den 'Elementen der Welt' in Kol 2,20; Gal 4,3.9." Pages 111–18 in Aland and Meurer, *Wissenschaft und Kirche.*

———. "Gesetz und Enthusiasmus bei Matthäus." Pages 350–76 in J. Lange, *Das Matthäus-Evangelium.*

———. "Röm 1,3f. und der Gegensatz von Fleisch und Geist bei Paulus." Pages 180–89 in *Neotestamentica: German and English Essays, 1951–1963.* Edited by Eduard Schweizer. Zurich: Zwingli, 1963.

Schwemer, Anna Maria. "Verfolger und Verfolgte bei Paulus: Die Auswirkungen der Verfolgung durch Agrippa I. auf die paulinische Mission." Pages 169–91 in E.-M. Becker and Pilhofer, *Biographie und Persönlichkeit des Paulus.*

Schwier, H. *Tempel und Tempelzerstörung: Untersuchungen zu den theologischen und ideologischen Faktoren im ersten jüdisch-römischen Krieg (66–74 n. Chr.).*

Novum testamentum et orbis antiquus 11. Göttingen: Vandenhoeck & Ruprecht, 1989.

Scott, James M. *Paul and the Nations* WUNT 84. Tübingen: Mohr Siebeck, 1995.

Segbroeck, Frans van, et al., eds. *The Four Gospels, 1992: Festschrift Frans Neirynck*. BETL 100. Louvain: Leuven University Press, 1992.

Seidel, Hans, ed. *Das lebendige Wort: Beiträge zur kirchlichen Verkündigung; Festgabe für Gottfried Voigt zum 65. Geburtstag*. Berlin: Evangelische Verlagsanstalt, 1982.

Sellin, Gerhard. "Hagar und Sara." Pages 116–37 in Sellin, *Studien zu Paulus und zum Epheserbrief*.

———. "Die Häretiker des Judasbriefes." ZNW 77 (1986): 206–25.

———. *Der Streit um die Auferstehung der Toten: Eine religionsgeschichtliche und exegetische Untersuchung von 1 Korinther 15*. FRLANT 138. Göttingen: Vandenhoeck & Ruprecht, 1986.

———. *Studien zu Paulus und zum Epheserbrief*. FRLANT 229. Göttingen: Vandenhoeck & Ruprecht, 2009.

Senior, Donald P., ed. *The Gospel of Matthew at the Crossroads of Early Christianity*. BETL 243. Louvain: Peeters, 2011.

Sevenich-Bax, Elisabeth. *Israels Konfrontation mit den letzten Boten der Weisheit: Form, Funktion und Interdependenz der Weisheitselemente in der Logienquelle*. Münsteraner theologische Abhandlungen 21. Altenberge: Orlos, 1993.

Shaw, Brent D. "The Myth of the Neronian Persecution." *Journal of Roman Studies* 105 (2015): 73–100.

Siber, Peter. *Mit Christus leben: Eine Studie zur paulinischen Auferstehungshoffnung*. ATANT 61. Zurich: Theologischer Verlag, 1971.

Siegert, Folker. "Gottesfürchtige und Sympathisanten." *JSJ* 4 (1973): 109–64.

———. "Unbeachtete Papiaszitate bei armenischen Schriftstellern." *NTS* 27 (1981): 605–14.

Sim, David C. *Apocalyptic Eschatology in the Gospel of Matthew*. SNTSMS 88. Cambridge: Cambridge University Press, 1996.

———. "Matthew's Anti-Paulinism: A Neglected Feature of Matthean Studies." *HTS* 58 (2002): 767–83.

Simon, Lutz. *Petrus und der Lieblingsjünger im Johannesevangelium*. Theologie 498. Frankfurt: P. Lang, 1994.

Skarsaune, Oskar, and Reidar Hvalvik, eds. *Jewish Believers in Jesus: The Early Centuries*. Peabody, MA: Hendrickson, 2007. Reprint, Grand Rapids: Baker Academic, 2017.

Smith, Dennis E. "What Do We Really Know about the Jerusalem Church?" Pages 237–52 in *Redescribing Christian Origins*. Edited by Ron Cameron and Merrill P. Miller. Atlanta: Society of Biblical Literature, 2004.

Söding, Thomas. *Das Christentum als Bildungsreligion: Der Impuls des Neuen Testaments*. Freiburg: Herder, 2016.

———, ed. *Der Evangelist als Theologe: Studien zum Markusevangelium*. SBS 163. Stuttgart: Katholisches Bibelwerk, 1995.

———, ed. *Johannesevangelium: Mitte oder Rand des Kanons? Neue Standortbestimmungen*. QD 203. Freiburg: Herder, 2003.

———. *Der lebendige Gott: Studien zur Theologie des Neuen Testaments; Festschrift für Wilhelm Thüsing zum 75. Geburtstag*. Edited by Thomas Söding. NTA 31. Münster: Aschendorff, 1996.

———. *Das Liebesgebot bei Paulus: Die Mahnung zur Agape im Rahmen der paulinischen Ethik*. NTA 26. Münster: Aschendorff, 1994.

———. "Starke und Schwache." *ZNW* 85 (1994): 69–92.

———. "Die Tempelaktion Jesu." *TTZ* 101 (1992): 36–64.

———. *Das Wort vom Kreuz: Studien zur paulinischen Theologie.* WUNT 93. Tübingen: Mohr Siebeck, 1997.

Söllner, Peter. "Jerusalem." Pages 2:153–59 in Erlemann et al., *Neues Testament und antike Kultur.*

———. *Jerusalem, du hochgebaute Stadt: Eschatologisches und himmlisches Jerusalem im Frühjudentum und im frühen Christentum.* TANZ 25. Tübingen: Francke, 1998.

Späth, Thomas, and Beate Wagner-Hasel, eds. *Frauenwelten in der Antike: Geschlechterordnung und weibliche Lebenspraxis; Mit Quellentexten und Bildquellen.* Stuttgart: Metzler, 2006.

Speigl, Jakob. *Der römische Staat und die Christen: Staat und Kirche von Domitian bis Commodus.* Amsterdam: Hakkert, 1970.

Speyer, Wolfgang. "Hellenistisch-römische Voraussetzungen der Verbreitung des Christentums." Pages 25–35 in *Der neue Mensch in Christus.* Edited by Johannes Beutler. QD 190. Freiburg: Herder, 2001.

———. *Die literarische Fälschung im heidnischen und christlichen Altertum.* HAW 1.2. Munich: Beck, 1971.

Städele, Alfons, ed. *Die Briefe des Pythagoras und der Pythagoreer.* BKP 115. Meisenheim am Glan: Hain, 1980.

Standhartinger, Angela. *Studien zur Entstehungsgeschichte und Intention des Kolosserbriefes.* NovTSup 94. Leiden: Brill, 1999.

Stark, Rodney. *The Rise of Christianity: A Sociologist Reconsiders History.* Princeton: Princeton University Press, 1996.

Starnitzke, Dierk. *Diakonie in biblischer Orientierung: Biblische Grundlagen, ethische Konkretionen, diakonisches Leitungshandeln.* Stuttgart: Kohlhammer, 2011.

Staudt, Darina. *Der eine und einzige Gott: Monotheistische Formeln im Urchristentum und ihre Vorgeschichte bei Griechen und Juden.* NTOA 80. Göttingen: Vandenhoeck & Ruprecht, 2012.

Stauffer, Ethelbert. *Christ and the Caesars: Historical Sketches.* Translated by K. and R. Gregor Smith. Philadelphia: Westminster, 1955.

Stegemann, Ekkehard, and Wolfgang Stegemann. *The Jesus Movement: A Social History of Its First Century.* Translated by O. C. Dean Jr. Minneapolis: Fortress, 1999.

———. *Urchristliche Sozialgeschichte: Die Anfänge im Judentum und die Christusgemeinden in der Mediterranen Welt.* Stuttgart: Kohlhammer, 1995.

Stegemann, Hartmut. "Die des Uria." Pages 246–76 in *Tradition und Glaube: Das frühe Christentum in seiner Umwelt; Festgabe für Karl Georg Kuhn zum 65. Geburtstag.* Edited by Gerd Jeremias and Hartmut Stegemann. Göttingen: Vandenhoeck & Ruprecht, 1971.

———. *Die Essener, Qumran, Johannes der Täufer und Jesus.* Herder Spektrum 4128. Freiburg: Herder, 1993.

———. *The Library of Qumran: On the Essenes, Qumran, John the Baptist, and Jesus.* Grand Rapids: Eerdmans, 1998.

Stegemann, Wolfgang. "War der Apostel Paulus ein römischer Bürger?" *ZNW* 78 (1987): 200–229.

Stegemann, Wolfgang, Bruce J. Malina, and Gerd Theissen, ed. *Jesus in neuen Kontexten.* Stuttgart: Kohlhammer, 2002.

Steinmetz, Peter. "Die Stoa." Pages 490–716 in Flashar, *Die hellenistische Philosophie.*

Stemberger, Günter. "Birkat ha-minim and the Separation of Christians and Jews." Pages 75–88 in *Judaea-Palaestina, Babylon and Rome: Jews in Antiquity.* Edited by

Benjamin Isaac and Yuval Shahar. TSAJ 147. Tübingen: Mohr Siebeck, 2012.

———. *Geschichte der jüdischen Literatur: Eine Einführung.* Beck'sche Elementarbucher. Munich: Beck, 1977.

———. *Jewish Contemporaries of Jesus: Pharisees, Sadducees, Essenes.* Translated by Allan W. Mahnke. Minneapolis: Fortress, 1995.

———. "Die Juden im Römischen Reich: Unterdruckung und Privilegiene einer Minderheit." Pages 6–22 in *Christlicher Antijudaismus und jüdischer Antipaganismus: Ihre Motive und Hintergründe in den ersten drei Jahrhunderten.* Edited by Herbert Frohnhofen. Hamburger theologische Studien 3. Hamburg: Steinmann & Steinmann, 1990.

———. *Juden und Christen im spätantiken Palästina.* Hans-Lietzmann-Vorlesungen 9. Berlin: de Gruyter, 2007.

———. *Das klassische Judentum: Kultur und Geschichte der rabbinischen Zeit (70 n. Chr. bis 1040 n. Chr.).* Beck'sche Elementarbücher. Munich: Beck, 1979.

———. *Pharisäer, Sadduzäer, Essener.* Stuttgarter Bibelstudien 144. Stuttgart: Katholisches Bibelwerk, 1991.

———. "Die sogenannte 'Synode von Jabne' und das frühe Christentum." *Kairós* 19 (1977): 14–21.

Stendahl, Krister. *The School of St. Matthew and Its Use of the Old Testament.* 2nd ed. Philadelphia: Fortress, 1968.

Stern, Menaham, ed. *Greek and Latin Authors on Jews and Judaism.* Vol. 1, *From Herodotus to Plutarch.* Jerusalem: Israel Academy of Sciences and Humanities, 1974.

Steudel, Annette, and Hans-Ulrich Boesche. *Die Texte aus Qumran.* Vol. 2. Darmstadt: Wissenschaftliche Buchgesellschaft, 2001.

Stibbe, Mark W. G. *John as Storyteller: Narrative Criticism and the Fourth Gospel.* SNTSMS 73. Cambridge: Cambridge University Press, 1992.

Still, Todd D., and David G. Horrell, eds. *After the First Urban Christians: The Social-Scientific Study of Pauline Christianity Twenty-Five Years Later.* London: Continuum, 2009.

Stökl Ben Ezra, Daniel. *Qumran: Die Texte vom Toten Meer und das antike Judentum.* UTB 4681. Tübingen: Mohr Siebeck, 2016.

Stowers, Stanley K. *Letter Writing in Greco-Roman Antiquity.* LEC 5. Philadelphia: Westminster, 1986.

Strathmann, Hermann. *Das Evangelium nach Johannes.* 4th ed. NTD 4. Göttingen: Vandenhoeck & Ruprecht, 1959.

Straub, Jürgen. "Geschichten erzählen, Geschichte bilden." Pages 81–169 in *Erzählung, Identität und historisches Bewusstsein: Die psychologische Konstruktion von Zeit und Geschichte.* Edited by Jürgen Straub. Frankfurt am Main: Suhrkamp, 1998.

———. "Über das Bilden von Vergangenheit." Pages 45–113 in *Geschichtsbewusstsein.* Edited by Jörn Rüsen. Cologne: Böhlau, 2001.

Strecker, Christian. *Die liminale Theologie des Paulus.* FRLANT 185. Göttingen: Vandenhoeck & Ruprecht, 1999.

Strecker, Georg. "Die Anfänge der johanneischen Schule." *NTS* 32 (1986): 31–47.

———. *Die Bergpredigt.* Göttingen: Vandenhoeck & Ruprecht, 1984.

———, ed. *Eschaton und Historie.* Göttingen: Vandenhoeck & Ruprecht, 1979.

———. *The Johannine Letters: A Commentary on 1, 2, and 3 John.* Translated by Linda M. Maloney. Edited by Harold Attridge. Herm. Minneapolis: Fortress, 1996.

———. *Die Johannesbriefe.* KEK 14. Göttingen: Vandenhoeck & Ruprecht, 1989.

———. *Das Judenchristentum in den Pseudoklementinen.* Texte und

Untersuchungen zur Geschichte der
altchristlichen Literatur 70. Berlin:
Akademie-Verlag, 1958.

———. *Literaturgeschichte des Neuen Testaments*. Göttingen: Vandenhoeck &
Ruprecht, 1992.

———. "Redaktionsgeschichte als Aufgabe
der Synoptikerexegese." Pages 9–32 in G.
Strecker, *Eschaton und Historie*.

———. *The Sermon on the Mount: An Exegetical Commentary*. Translated by O.
C. Dean Jr. Nashville: Abingdon, 1988.

———. *Theologie des Neuen Testaments*.
Berlin: de Gruyter, 1995.

———. *Theology of the New Testament*.
Edited by Friedrich Wilhelm Horn.
Translated by M. Eugene Boring. New
York: de Gruyter, 2000.

———. "Der vorchristliche Paulus." Pages
713–41 in Fornberg and Hellholm, *Texts
and Contexts*.

———. *Der Weg der Gerechtigkeit*. 3rd ed.
FRLANT 82. Göttingen: Vandenhoeck
& Ruprecht, 1971.

Strecker, Georg, Udo Schnelle, et al., eds.
*Neuer Wettstein: Texte zum Neuen
Testament aus Griechentum und Hellenismus*. Berlin: de Gruyter, 1996–. Cited
as NW.

Strobel, August. "Der Termin des Todes
Jesu." ZNW 51 (1960): 69–101.

———. "Zum Verständnis von Röm 13."
ZNW 47 (1956): 67–93.

Strobel, Karl. *Kaiser Traian: Eine Epoche
der Weltgeschichte*. 2nd ed. Regensburg:
Pustet, 2019.

Stuhlmacher, Peter, ed. *The Gospel and the
Gospels*. Grand Rapids: Eerdmans, 1991.

Suhl, Alfred. *Paulus und seine Briefe: Ein
Beitrag zur paulinischen Chronologie*.
SNT 11. Gütersloh: Mohn, 1975.

Sumney, Jerry L. *Identifying Paul's Opponents: The Question of Method in
2 Corinthians*. JSNTSup 40. Sheffield:
JSOT, 1990.

Sundermeier, Theo, ed. *Den Fremden wahrnehmen*. Gütersloh: Gütersloher Verlagshaus, 1992.

Taeger, Fritz. *Charisma: Studien zur Geschichte des antiken Herrscherkultes*.
Vol. 1–2. Stuttgart: Kohlhammer,
1957–60.

Taeger, Jens W. *Johannesapokalypse und
johanneischer Kreis*. BZNW 51. Berlin:
de Gruyter, 1988.

———. "Der konservative Rebell." ZNW 78
(1987): 267–87.

———. *Der Mensch und sein Heil: Studien
zum Bild des Menschen und zur Sicht
der Bekehrung bei Lukas*. SNT 14. Gütersloh: Mohn, 1982.

Tannehill, Robert C. *The Narrative Unity of
Luke-Acts: A Literary Interpretation*. 2
vols. Foundations and Facets. Minneapolis: Fortress, 1986–90.

Tàrrech, Armand Puigi, John M. G. Barclay,
and Jörg Frey, eds., *The Last Years of
Paul*. WUNT 352. Tübingen: Mohr Siebeck, 2015.

Teichmann, Frank. *Der Mensch und sein
Tempel*. 3rd ed. Darmstadt: Wissenshaft-
liche Buchgesellschaft, 2003.

Tellbe, Michael. *Christ-Believers in Ephesus:
A Textual Analysis of Early Christian
Identity Formation in a Local Perspective*. WUNT 242. Tübingen: Mohr Siebeck, 2009.

Teppler, Yaakov Y. *Jews and Christians in
Conflict in the Ancient World*. TSAJ 120.
Tübingen: Mohr Siebeck, 2007.

Theissen, Gerd. "Das Doppelgebot der
Liebe: Jüdische Ethik bei Jesus." Pages
57–72 in Theissen, *Jesus als historische
Gestalt*.

———. "Evangelienschreibung und Gemeindeleitung." Pages 389–414 in Kollmann, Reinbold, and Steudelin, *Antikes
Judentum und frühes Christentum*.

———. "Die Gegenmission zu Paulus in
Galatien, Philippi und Korinth." Pages

277–306 in Kraus, *Beiträge zur urchristlichen Theologiegeschichte*.

———. "Gemeindestrukturen und Hilfsmotivation: Wie haben urchristliche Gemeinden zum Helfen motiviert?" Pages 413–40 in *Anthropologie und Ethik im Frühjudentum und im Neuen Testament Wechselseitige Wahrnehmungen: Internationales Symposium in Verbindung mit dem Projekt Corpus Judaeo-Hellenisticum Novi Testamenti (CJHNT), 17.–20. Mai 2012, Heidelberg*. Edited by Matthias Konradt and Esther Schläpfer. WUNT 322. Tübingen: Mohr Siebeck, 2014.

———. *The Gospels in Context: Social and Political History in the Synoptic Tradition*. Translated by Linda M. Maloney. Minneapolis: Fortress, 1991.

———. "Hellenisten und Hebräer (Apg 6,1–6): Gab es eine Spaltung in der Urgemeinde?" Pages 3:323–43 in Cancik, Lichtenberger, and P. Schäfer, *Geschichte, Tradition, Reflexion*.

———, ed. *Jesus als historische Gestalt*. FRLANT 202. Göttingen: Vandenhoeck & Ruprecht, 2003.

———. *Die Jesusbewegung: Sozialgeschichte einer Revolution der Werte*. Gütersloh: Gütersloher Verlagshaus, 2004.

———. "Judentum und Christentum bei Paulus." Pages 331–56 in Hengel and U. Heckel, *Paulus und das antike Judentum*.

———. "Kirche oder Sekte? Über Einheit und Konflikte im frühen Urchristentum." Pages 81–102 in *Einheit der Kirche im Neuen Testament: Dritte europäische orthodox-westliche Exegetenkonferenz in Sankt Petersburg, 24.–31. August 2005*. Edited by Anatoly A. Alexeev et al. WUNT 218. Tübingen: Mohr Siebeck, 2008.

———. "Kritik an Paulus im Matthäusevangelium? Von der Kunst verdeckter Polemik im Urchristentum." Pages

465–90 in Wischmeyer and Scornaienchi, *Polemik in der frühchristlichen Literatur*.

———. "Legitimation and Subsistence: An Essay on the Sociology of Early Christian Missionaries. Pages 27–67 in Theissen, *The Social Setting of Pauline Christianity*.

———. *The Miracle Stories of the Early Christian Tradition*. Translated by Francis McDonagh. Edited by John Riches. SNTW. Philadelphia: Fortress, 1983.

———. "Nächstenliebe und Egalität." Pages 120–42 in Gemünden, Konradt, and Theissen, *Der Jakobusbrief*.

———. *The New Testament: A Literary History*. Translated by Linda M. Maloney. Minneapolis: Fortress, 2011.

———. *Die Religion der ersten Christen: Eine Theorie des Urchristentums*. Gütersloh: Kaiser/Gütersloher Verlagshaus, 2000.

———. "Röm 9–11—Eine Auseinandersetzung des Paulus mit Israel und sich selbst: Versuch einer psychologischen Auslegung." Pages 311–41 in Dunderberg, Tuckett, and Syreeni, *Fair Play*.

———. "Simon Magus—die Entwicklung seines Bildes vom Charismatiker zum gnostischen Erlöser." Pages 407–32 in Dobbeler et al., *Religionsgeschichte des Neuen Testaments*.

———. *The Social Setting of Pauline Christianity: Essays on Corinth*. Edited and translated and with an introduction by John H. Schütz. Philadelphia: Fortress, 1982.

———. "Social Stratification in the Corinthian Community: A Contribution to the Sociology of Early Hellenistic Christianity." Pages 69–119 in Theissen, *The Social Setting of Pauline Christianity*.

———. "The Strong and the Weak in Corinth: A Sociological Analysis of a Theological Quarrel." Pages 121–43 in

Theissen, *The Social Setting of Pauline Christianity*.

———. "Urchristlicher Liebeskommunismus." Pages 689–712 in Fornberg and Hellholm, *Texts and Contexts*.

———. "Die urchristliche Taufe und die soziale Konstruktion des neuen Menschen." Pages 87–114 in Assmann and Stroumsa, *Transformation of the Inner Self in Ancient Religions*.

———. "Die Verfolgung unter Agrippa dem I. und die Autoritätsstruktur der Urgemeinde." Pages 263–85 in Mell and U. Müller, *Das Urchristentum in seiner literarischen Geschichte*.

Theissen, Gerd, and Annette Merz. *The Historical Jesus: A Comprehensive Guide*. Translated by John Bowden. Minneapolis: Fortress, 1998.

———. *Der historische Jesus: Ein Lehrbuch*. Göttingen: Vandenhoeck & Ruprecht, 1996.

Theobald, Michael. *Das Evangelium nach Johannes: Kapitel 1–12*. RNT. Regensburg: Friedrich Pustet, 2009.

———. "Der Jünger, den Jesus liebte." Vol. 3, pages 219–55 in Cancik, Lichtenberger, and P. Schäfer, *Geschichte, Tradition, Reflexion*.

———. "Vom Text zum 'lebendigen Wort' (Hebr 4,12)." Pages 751–90 in Landmesser, *Jesus Christus als die Mitte der Schrift*.

Thiessen, Werner. *Christen in Ephesus: Die historische und theologische Situation in vorpaulinischer und paulinischer Zeit und zur Zeit der Apostelgeschichte und der Pastoralbriefe*. TANZ 12. Tübingen: Franke, 1995.

Thompson, James W. *The Beginnings of Christian Philosophy: The Epistle to the Hebrews*. Washington, DC: Catholic Biblical Association of America, 1982.

———. *Moral Formation according to Paul*. Grand Rapids: Baker Academic, 2011.

Thompson, Leonard L. *The Book of Revelation: Apocalypse and Empire*. Oxford: Oxford University Press, 1997.

Thompson, Marianne M. *The Humanity of Jesus in the Fourth Gospel*. Philadelphia: Fortress, 1988.

———. "The Living Father." Pages 19–31 in *God the Father in the Fourth Gospel*. Edited by Adele Reinhartz. Semeia 85. Atlanta: Society of Biblical Literature, 1999.

Thornton, Claus-Jürgen. *Der Zeuge des Zeugen: Lukas als Historiker der Paulusreisen*. WUNT 56. Tübingen: Mohr Siebeck, 1991.

Thorsteinsson, Runar M. *Roman Christianity and Roman Stoicism: A Comparative Study of Ancient Morality*. Oxford: Oxford University Press, 2010.

Thraede, Klaus. "Soziales Verhalten und Wohlfahrtspflege in der griechischrömischen Antike." Pages 44–63 in Schäfer and Strohm, *Diakonie—biblische Grundlagen und Orientierungen*.

Thümmel, Hans Georg. *Die Memorien für Petrus und Paulus in Rom: Die archäologischen Denkmäler und die literarische Tradition*. AKG 76. Berlin: de Gruyter, 1999.

Thyen, Hartwig. *Das Johannesevangelium*. HNT 6. Tübingen: Mohr Siebeck, 2005.

Tilborg, Sjef van. *Reading John in Ephesus*. NovTSup 83. Leiden: Brill, 1996.

Tilly, Michael. *Einführung in die Septuaginta*. Darmstadt: Wissenschaftliche Buchgesellschaft, 2005.

Timpe, Dieter. "Domitian als Christenfeind und die Tradition der Verfolgerkaiser." Pages 213–42 in *Heil und Geschichte*. Edited by Jörg Frey, Stefan Krauter, and Hermann Lichtenberger. WUNT 248. Tübingen: Mohr Siebeck, 2009.

Tiwald, Markus. "Frühchristliche Pluralität in Ephesus." Pages 128–45 in Bendemann and Tiwald, *Das frühe Christentum und die Stadt*.

———. *Das Frühjudentum und die Anfänge des Christentums: Ein Studienbuch.* BWANT 208. Stuttgart: Kohlhammer, 2016.

———. "Die vielfältigen Entwicklungslinien kirchlichen Amtes im Corpus Paulinum und ihre Relevanz für heutige Theologie." Pages 101–28 in Schmeller, Ebner, and Hoppe, *Neutestamentliche Ämtermodelle.*

———. "Der Wanderradikalismus als Brücke zum historischen Jesus." Pages 523–34 in Lindemann, *The Sayings Source Q.*

———. *Wanderradikalismus: Jesu erste Jünger—ein Anfang und was davon bleibt.* ÖBS 20. Frankfurt: Lang, 2002.

Tödt, Heinz Eduard. *Der Menschensohn in der synoptischen Überlieferung.* Gütersloh Mohn, 1958.

———. *The Son of Man in the Synoptic Tradition.* Translated by Dorothea M. Barton. NTL. London: SCM, 1965.

Tóth, Franz. *Der himmlische Kult: Wirklichkeitskonstruktion und Sinnbildung in der Johannesoffenbarung.* ABG 22. Leipzig: Evangelische Verlagsanstalt, 2006.

Trebilco, Paul. *The Early Christians in Ephesus from Paul to Ignatius.* WUNT 166. Tübingen: Mohr Siebeck, 2004.

———. *Self-Designations and Group Identity in the New Testament.* Cambridge: Cambridge University Press, 2012.

Trobisch, David. *Die Endredaktion des Neuen Testaments: Eine Untersuchung zur Entstehung der christlichen Bibel.* NTOA 31. Freiburg: Universitätsverlag; Göttingen: Vandenhoeck & Ruprecht, 1996.

———. *Die Entstehung der Paulusbriefsammlung: Studien zu den Anfängen christlicher Publizistik.* NTOA 10. Freiburg, Switzerland: Universitätsverlag; Göttingen: Vandenhoeck & Ruprecht, 1989.

———. *The First Edition of the New Testament.* Oxford: Oxford University Press, 2012.

———. *Paul's Letter Collection: Tracing the Origins.* Minneapolis: Fortress, 1994.

Tröger, Karl-Wolfgang. *Altes Testament, Frühjudentum, Gnosis: Neue Studien zu "Gnosis und Bibel."* Berlin: Evangelische Verlagsanstalt, 1980.

———. "Gnosis und Judentum." Pages 155–68 in Tröger, *Altes Testament, Frühjudentum, Gnosis.*

———. "Ja oder Nein zur Welt: War der Evangelist Johannes Christ oder Gnostiker?" *Theologische Versuche* 7 (1976): 61–80.

Trummer, Peter. "Corpus Paulinum—Corpus Pastorale." Pages 122–45 in Kertelge, *Paulus in den neutestamentlichen Spätschriften.*

Tsuji, Manabu. *Glaube zwischen Vollkommenheit und Verweltlichung: Eine Untersuchung zur literarischen Gestalt und zur inhaltlichen Kohärenz des Jakobusbriefes.* WUNT 2/93. Tübingen: Mohr Siebeck, 1997.

Tuckett, Christopher. "Thomas and the Synoptics." *NovT* 30 (1988): 132–57.

Turner, Victor. *The Ritual Process: Structure and Anti-Structure.* Lewis Henry Morgan Lectures. Somerset: Taylor & Francis, 1969.

———. *Das Ritual: Struktur und Anti-Struktur.* Frankfurt: Campus-Verlag, 2000 (= 1969).

Uebele, Wolfram. *"Viele Verführer sind in die Welt ausgegangen": Die Gegner in den Briefen des Ignatius von Antiochien und in den Johannesbriefen.* BWANT 151. Stuttgart: Kohlhammer, 2001.

Ulrich, Jörg. "Eusebi, *HistEccl* III, 14–20 und die Frage nach den Christenverfolgungen unter Domitian." *ZNW* 87 (1996): 269–89.

Untermann, Jürgen. "Hispania." Pages 1–17 in G. Neumann and Untermann,

Die Sprachen im römischen Reich der Kaiserzeit.

Urner, Christiana. *Kaiser Domitian im Urteil antiker literarischer Quellen und moderner Forschung.* Diss., University of Augsburg. Book, Augsburg: [C. Urner], 1993.

Vegge, Tor. *Paulus und das Antike Schulwesen.* BZNW 134. Berlin: de Gruyter, 2006.

Verheyden, Jozef, R. Bieringer, Jens Schröter, Ines Jäger, eds. *Docetism in the Early Church: The Quest for an Elusive Phenomenon.* Tübingen: Mohr Siebeck, 2018.

Verhoef, Eduard. *Philippi: How Christianity Began in Europe; The Epistle to the Philippians and the Excavations at Philippi.* London: Bloomsbury, 2013.

Vermaseren, Maarten J. *Cybele and Attis: The Myth and the Cult.* London: Thames & Hudson, 1977.

Vermès, Géza. *The Complete Dead Sea Scrolls in English.* New York: Allen Lane/ Penguin Press, 1997.

———. *Jesus the Jew: A Historian's Reading of the Gospels.* Philadelphia: Fortress, 1981.

Verweyen, Hans Jürgen. *Philosophie und Theologie: Vom Mythos zum Logos zum Mythos.* Darmstadt: Wissenschaftliche Buchgesellschaft, 2005.

Veyne, Paul. *Brot und Spiele.* Darmstadt: Wissenschaftliche Buchgesellschaft, 1990.

———. *Die griechisch-römische Religion: Kult, Frömmigkeit und Moral.* Stuttgart: Reclam, 2008.

Vielhauer, Philipp, ed. *Aufsätze zum Neuen Testament.* TB 31. Munich: Kaiser, 1965.

———. "Erwägungen zur Christologie des Markusevangeliums." Pages 199–214 in Vielhauer, *Aufsätze zum Neuen Testament.*

———. *Geschichte der urchristlichen Literatur: Einleitung in das Neue Testament,* *die Apokryphen und die Apostolischen Väter.* Berlin: de Gruyter, 1975.

———. "Oikodome." Vol. 2, pages 1–168 in Vielhauer, *Oikodome.*

———. *Oikodome: Aufsätze zum Neuen Testament.* Edited by Günter Klein. TB 65. Munich: Kaiser, 1979 (= 1939).

———. "Zum 'Paulinismus' der Apostelgeschichte." Pages 9–27 in Vielhauer, *Aufsätze zum Neuen Testament.*

Viering, Fritz, ed., *Die Bedeutung der Auferstehungsbotschaft für den Glauben an Jesus Christus.* Berlin: Evangelische Verlagsanstalt, 1967.

Vinzent, Markus. *Die Auferstehung Christi im frühen Christentum.* Freiburg: Herder, 2014.

Vittinghoff, Friedrich. "'*Christianus sum*': Das 'Verbrechen' von Außenseitern der römischen Gesellschaft." *Historia* 33 (1984): 331–57.

———. "Gesellschaft." Vol. 1, pages 163–277 in *Handbuch der Europäischen Wirtschafts- und Sozialgeschichte.* Edited by Hermann Vittinghoff et al. Stuttgart: Klett-Cotta, 1990.

Vogel, Manuel. *Commentatio mortis: 2 Kor 5,1–10 auf dem Hintergrund antiker ars moriendi.* FRLANT 214. Göttingen: Vandenhoeck & Ruprecht, 2006.

———. "Der Hebräerbrief als ständiger Gast im Haus der Kirche." *ZNT* 29 (2012): 46–52.

———. *Das Heil des Bundes: Bundestheologie im Frühjudentum und im frühen Christentum.* TANZ 18. Tübingen: Francke, 1996.

Vögtle, Anton. *Die "Gretchenfrage" des Menschensohnproblems Bilanz und Perspektive.* QD 152. Freiburg: Herder, 1994.

Voigt, Emilio. *Die Jesusbewegung.* BWANT 169. Stuttgart: Kohlhammer, 2008.

Völker, Walther. *Quellen zur Geschichte der christlichen Gnosis.* Sammlung ausgewählter kirchen- und dogmengeschichtlicher quellenschriften 2/5. Tübingen: Mohr Siebeck, 1932.

Vollenweider, Samuel. *Freiheit als neue Schöpfung*. FRLANT 147. Göttingen: Vandenhoeck & Ruprecht, 1989.

———. "Der 'Raub' der Gottgleichheit: Ein religionsgeschichtlicher Vorschlag zu Phil 2,6(–11)." *NTS* 45 (1999): 413–33.

Vollenweider, Samuel, Manuel Baumbach, Eva Ebel, Maximilian Forschner, and Thomas Schmeller. *Epiktet: Was ist wahre Freiheit? Diatribe IV 1*. Tübingen: Mohr Siebeck, 2013.

von Rad, Gerhard. *Weisheit in Israel*. 2nd ed. Neukirchen-Vluyn: Neukirchener Verlag, 1982.

———. *Wisdom in Israel*. Nashville: Abingdon, 1972.

Voss, Florian. *Das Wort vom Kreuz und die menschliche Vernunft: Eine Untersuchung zur Soteriologie des 1. Korintherbriefes*. FRLANT 199. Göttingen: Vandenhoeck & Ruprecht, 2002.

Wagener, Ulrike. *Die Ordnung des "Hauses Gottes": Der Ort von Frauen in der Ekklesiologie und Ethik der Pastoralbriefe*. WUNT 2/65. Tübingen: 1994.

Wagner, Jochen. *Die Anfänge des Amtes in der Kirche: Presbyter und Episkopen in der frühchristlichen Literatur*. TANZ 53. Tübingen: Franke, 2011.

Wahlde, Urban C. von. *Gnosticism, Docetism, and the Judaisms of the First Century: The Search for the Wider Context of the Johannine Literature and Why It Matters*. LNTS 517. London: Bloomsbury, 2015.

Waldherr, Gerhard H. *Nero: Eine Biographie*. Regensburg: Pustet, 2005.

Walker, Rolf. *Die Heilsgeschichte im ersten Evangelium*. FRLANT 91, Göttingen: Vandenhoeck & Ruprecht, 1967.

Walter, Nikolaus. "Apostelgeschichte 6,1 und die Anfänge der Urgemeinde in Jerusalem." Pages 187–211 in Walter, *Praeparatio Evangelica*.

———. "Leibliche Auferstehung? Zur Frage der Hellenisierung der Auferweckungshoffnung bei Paulus" Pages 109–27 in *Paulus, Apostel Jesu Christi: Festschrift für Günter Klein zum 70. Geburtstag*. Edited by Michael Trowitzsch. Tübingen: Mohr Siebeck, 1998.

———. *Praeparatio Evangelica*. Edited by Nikolaus Walter. WUNT 98. Tübingen: Mohr Siebeck, 1997.

Walters, James. "Civic Identity in Roman Corinth and Its Impact on Early Christians." Pages 397–417 in Schowalter and Friesen, *Urban Religion in Roman Corinth*.

Wander, Bernd. *Gottesfürchtige und Sympathisanten*. WUNT 104. Tübingen: Mohr Siebeck, 1998.

———. *Trennungsprozesse zwischen frühem Christentum und Judentum im 1. Jh. n. Chr.: Datierbare Abfolgen zwischen der Hinrichtung Jesu und der Zerstörung des Jerusalemer Tempels*. 2nd ed. TANZ 16. Tübingen: Franke, 1997.

Wasserberg, Günter. *Aus Israels Mitte Heil—für die Welt: Eine narrativ-exegetische Studie zur Theologie des Lukas*. BZNW 82. Berlin: de Gruyter, 1998.

Watt, Jan G. van der. "Ethics and Ethos in the Gospel according to John." *ZNW* 97 (2006): 147–76.

———. "'Metaphorik' in Joh 15,1–8. *BZ* 38 (1994): 67–80.

Watt, Jan G. van der, and Ruben Zimmermann, eds. *Rethinking the Ethics of John*. WUNT 291. Tübingen: Mohr Siebeck, 2012.

Weber, Reinhard. "Christologie und 'Messiasgeheimnis': Ihr Zusammenhang und Stellenwert in den Darstellungsintentionen des Markus." *EvT* 43 (1983): 108–25.

———. *Das "Gesetz" bei Philon von Alexandrien und Flavius Josephus: Studien zum Verständnis und zur Funktion der Thora bei den beiden Hauptzeugen des hellenistischen Judentums.* ARGU 11. Frankfurt: Lang, 2001.

———. *Das "Gesetz" im hellenistischen Judentum: Studien zum Verständnis und zur Funktion der Thora von Demetrios bis Pseudo-Phokylides.* ARGU 10. Frankfurt: Lang, 2000.

Wechsler, Andreas. *Geschichtsbild und Apostelstreit: Eine forschungsgeschichtliche und exegetische Studie über den antiochenischen Zwischenfall (Gal 2,11–14).* BZNW 62. Berlin: de Gruyter, 1991.

Weder, Hans. *Einblicke in das Evangelium, exegetische Beiträge zur neutestamentlichen Hermeneutik: Gesammelte Aufsätze aus den Jahren 1980–1991.* Göttingen: Vandenhoeck & Ruprecht, 1992.

———. *Das Kreuz Jesu bei Paulus: Ein Versuch, über den Geschichtsbezug des christlichen Glaubens nachzudenken.* FRLANT 125. Göttingen: Vandenhoeck & Ruprecht, 1981.

———. "Die Menschwerdung Gottes." Pages 363–400 in Weder, *Einblicke in das Evangelium.*

———. *Die "Rede der Reden": Eine Auslegung der Bergpredigt heute.* 2nd ed. Zurich: Theologischer Verlag, 1987.

Weeber, Karl-Wilhelm. *Alltag im Alten Rom: Das Stadtleben.* 7th ed. Düsseldorf: Artemis & Winkler, 2003.

———. *Luxus im alten Rom.* Darmstadt: Primus, 2003.

Wehnert, Jürgen. "Die Auswanderung der Jerusalemer Christen nach Pella—historisches Faktum oder theologische Konstruktion?" *ZKG* 102 (1991): 231–55.

———. *Die Reinheit des "christlichen Gottesvolkes" aus Juden und Heiden: Studien zum historischen und theologischen Hintergrund des sogenannten*

Aposteldekrets. FRLANT 173. Göttingen: Vandenhoeck & Ruprecht, 1997.

———. *Die Wir-Passagen der Apostelgeschichte.* GTA 40. Göttingen: Vandenhoeck & Ruprecht, 1989.

Weigandt, Peter. "Der Doketismus im Urchristentum und in der theologischen Entwicklung des zweiten Jahrhunderts." Diss. theol., Ruprecht-Karls-Universität Heidelberg, 1961.

Weikert, Christopher. *Von Jerusalem zu Aelia Capitolina: Die römische Politik gegenüber den Juden von Vespasian bis Hadrian.* Hypomnemata 200. Göttingen: Vandenhoeck & Ruprecht, 2016.

Weinkauf, Wolfgang, ed. *Die Philosophie der Stoa: Ausgewählte Texte.* Stuttgart: Philipp Reclam, 2001.

Weischedel, Wilhelm. *Wesen, Aufstieg und Verfall der philosophischen Theologie.* Vol. 1 of *Der Gott der Philosophen: Grundlegung einer philosophischen Theologie im Zeitalter des Nihilismus.* 2nd ed. Munich: Deutsches Taschenbuch, 1985.

Weiser, Alfons. *Die Apostelgeschichte.* 2 vols. ÖTK 5.1–2. Gütersloh: Mohn, 1981–85.

———. "Zur Gesetzes- und Tempelkritik der 'Hellenisten.'" Pages 146–68 in Kertelge, *Das Gesetz im Neuen Testament.*

Weiss, Alexander. "Der Aufruhr der Silberschmiede (Apg 19,23–40) und das Edikt des Paullus Fabius Persicus (I. Ephesos 17–19)." *BZ* 53 (2009): 69–81.

———. "Keine Quästoren in Korinth." *NTS* 56 (2010): 576–81.

———. "Paulus und die *coloniae*: Warum der Apostel nicht der einzige römische Bürger unter den frühen Christen war." Pages 341–56 in Baum, *Der jüdische Messias Jesus und sein jüdischer Apostel Paulus.*

———. "Sergius Paullus, Statthalter von Zypern." *ZPE* 169 (2009): 188–192.

———. *Soziale Elite und Christentum: Studien zu ordo-Angehörigen unter den frühen Christen*. Millennium Studies 52. Berlin: de Gruyter, 2015.

Weiss, Hans-Friedrich. *Der Brief an die Hebräer*. KEK 13. Göttingen: Vandenhoeck & Ruprecht, 1991.

———. *Frühes Christentum und Gnosis: Eine rezeptionsgeschichtliche Studie*. WUNT 225. Tübingen: Mohr Siebeck, 2007.

Weiss, Wolfgang. *Eine neue Lehre in Vollmacht*. BZNW 52. Berlin: de Gruyter, 1989.

Wellhausen, Julius. *Kritische Analyse der Apostelgeschichte*. Abhandlungen der Königlichen Gesellschaft der Wissenschaften zu Göttingen 15. Berlin: Weidmannsche Buchhandlung, 1914.

Wengst, Klaus. *Anspruch und Wirklichkeit: Erfahrungen und Wahrnehmungen des Friedens bei Jesus und im Urchristentum*. Munich: Kaiser, 1986.

———. *Bedrängte Gemeinde und verherrlichter Christus: Ein Versuch über das Johannesevangelium*. 4th ed. Kaiser Taschenbücher 114. Munich: Kaiser, 1992.

———. *Christologische Formeln und Lieder des Urchristentums*. 2nd ed. SNT 7. Gütersloh: Mohn, 1973.

———. *Didache (Apostellehre), Barnabasbrief, Zweiter Klemensbrief, Schrift an Diognet*. SdU 2. Darmstadt: Wissenschaftliche Buchgesellschaft, 1984.

———. *Der erste, zweite und dritte Brief des Johannes*. ÖTK 16. Gütersloh: Mohn; Würzburg: Echter Verlag, 1978.

———. *Häresie und Orthodoxie im Spiegel des ersten Johannesbriefes*. Gütersloh: Mohn, 1976.

———. *Das Johannesevangelium*. TKNT 4.1–2. Stuttgart: Kohlhammer, 2000–2001.

———. *Pax Romana and the Peace of Jesus Christ*. London: SCM, 1987.

Wenning, Robert. "Dekapolis." Vol. 2, pages 145–47 in Erlemann et al., *Neues Testament und antike Kultur*.

Werner, Martin. *Der Einfluß paulinischer Theologie im Markusevangelium: Eine Studie zur neutestamentlichen Theologie*. BZNW 1. Giessen: A. Töpelmann, 1923.

Weyer-Menkhoff, Karl. *Die Ethik des Johannesevangeliums im sprachlichen Feld des Handelns*. WUNT 2/359. Tübingen: Mohr Siebeck, 2014.

Wick, Peter. "Das Paradies in der Stadt." Pages 238–50 in Bendemann and Tiwald, *Das frühe Christentum und die Stadt*.

Wider, David. *Theozentrik und Bekenntnis: Untersuchungen zur Theologie des Redens Gottes im Hebräerbrief*. BZNW 87. Berlin: de Gruyter, 1997.

Wiefel, Wolfgang. *Das Evangelium nach Matthäus*. THK 1. Leipzig: Evangelische Verlagsanstalt, 1998.

———. "Die Hauptrichtung des Wandels im eschatologischen Denken des Paulus." *TZ* 30 (1974): 65–81.

———. "The Jewish Community in Ancient Rome and the Origins of Roman Christianity." Pages 85–101 in Donfried, *The Romans Debate* (1991).

Wilckens, Ulrich. *Auferstehung: Das biblische auferstehungszeugnis historisch untersucht und erklärt*. TdT 4. Stuttgart: Kreuz-Verlag, 1970.

———. *Der Brief an die Römer*. Vol. 2. EKKNT 6.2. Neukirchen-Vluyn: Neukirchener Verlag, 1980.

———. *Die Briefe des Urchristentums: Paulus und seine Schüler, Theologen aus dem Bereich judenchristlicher Heidenmission*. Vol. 3 of *Theologie des Neuen Testaments*. Neukirchen-Vluyn: Neukirchener Verlag, 2005.

———. *Das Evangelium nach Johannes*. NTD 4. Göttingen: Vandenhoeck & Ruprecht, 1998.

———. "Die Gegner im 1. und 2. Johannesbrief, 'die Juden' im Johannesevangelium
und die Gegner in den Ignatiusbriefen
und den Sendschreiben der Apokalypse."
Pages 89–125 in Wilckens, *Der Sohn
Gottes und seine Gemeinde.*

———. *Resurrection: Biblical Testimony
to the Resurrection; An Historical Examination and Explanation.* Translated
by A. M. Stewart. Atlanta: John Knox,
1978.

———. *Der Sohn Gottes und seine Gemeinde.* FRLANT 200. Göttingen: Vandenhoeck & Ruprecht, 2003.

———. *Theologie des Neuen Testaments:
Studienausgabe in 6 Teilbänden.* Neu-
kirchener Theologie. Neukirchen-Vluyn:
Neukirchener, 2003–9.

———. *Weisheit und Torheit: Eine
exegetisch-religions-geschichtliche Untersuchung zu 1. Kor. 1 und 2.* BHT 26.
Tübingen: Mohr, 1959.

Wilhelm, Friedrich. "Diakonische Leitlinien Jesu." Pages 109–26 in Schäfer and
Strohm, *Diakonie—biblische Grundlagen und Orientierungen.*

Wilk, Florian. *Die Bedeutung des Jesajabuches für Paulus.* FRLANT 179. Göttingen: Vandenhoek & Ruprecht, 1998.

Wilken, Robert L. *The Christians as the
Romans Saw Them.* New Haven: Yale
University Press, 1984.

Will, Wolfgang. *Caesar.* Gestalten der
Antike. Darmstadt: Wissenschaftliches
Buchgesellschaft, 2009.

Williams, Margaret H. "The Shaping of
the Identity of the Jewish Community
in Rome in Antiquity." Pages 33–46 in
Zangenberg and Labahn, *Christians as a
Religious Minority.*

Williams, Michael A. *Rethinking "Gnosti-
cism": An Argument for Dismantling a
Dubious Category.* Princeton: Princeton
University Press, 1996.

Williamson, Ronald. *Philo and the Epistle
to the Hebrews.* ALGHJ 4. Leiden: Brill,
1970.

Windisch, Hans. *Johannes und die Synoptiker: Wollte der vierte Evangelist die älte-
ren Evangelien ergänzen oder ersetzen?*
UNT 12. Leipzig: Hinrichs, 1926.

———. *Der zweite Korintherbrief.* 9th ed.
KEK 6. Göttingen: Vandenhoeck & Ruprecht, 1924.

Winn, Adam. *The Purpose of Mark's Gospel: An Early Christian Response to
Roman Imperial Propaganda.* WUNT
2/245. Tübingen: Mohr Siebeck, 2008.

Winter, Bruce M. *After Paul Left Corinth:
The Influence of Secular Ethics and Social Change.* Grand Rapids: Eerdmans,
2001.

———. *Divine Honours for the Caesars:
The First Christians' Responses.* Grand
Rapids: Eerdmans, 2015.

Winter, Bruce M., and Andrew D. Clarke,
eds. *The Book of Acts in Its Ancient
Literary Setting.* Vol. 1 of *The Book of
Acts in Its First Century Setting.* Grand
Rapids: Eerdmans, 1993.

Winter, Martin. *Das Vermächtnis Jesu und
die Abschiedsworte der Väter.* FRLANT
161. Göttingen: Vandenhoeck & Ruprecht, 1994.

Winterling, Aloys. *Caligula: A Biography.*
Translated by Deborah Lucas Schneider,
Glenn W. Most, and Paul Psoinos. Berke-
ley: University of California Press, 2011.

Wischmeyer, Oda. "Das Gebot der Nächstenliebe bei Paulus." *BZ* 30 (1986):
153–87.

———. *Der höchste Weg.* SNT 13. Gütersloh: Mohn, 1981.

———. "Die paulinische Mission als religi-
öse und literarische Kommunikation."
Pages 90–121 in Graf and Wiegandt, *Die
Anfänge des Christentums.*

———. "Polemik im Jakobusbrief: Formen,
Gegenstände und Fronten." Pages 357–79

in Wischmeyer and Scornaienchi, *Polemik in der frühchristlichen Literatur*.

Wischmeyer, Oda, and Lorenzo Scornaienchi, eds. *Polemik in der frühchristlichen Literatur: Texte und Kontexte*. BZNW 170. Berlin: de Gruyter, 2011.

Wissowa, G., K. Mittelhaus, and K. Ziegler, eds. *Paulys Realencyclopädie der classischen Altertumswissenschaft*. Supplement vol. 9. Stuttgart: Stuttgart Drukkenmüller, 1962. Cited as PW.

Witetschek, Stephan. "Ein weit geöffnetes Zeitfenster? Überlegungen zur Datierung der Johannesapokalypse." Pages 117–48 in Frey, Kelhoffer, and Tóth, *Die Johannesapokalypse*.

———. *Ephesische Enthüllungen*. Vol. 1. BTS 6. Louvain: Peeters, 2008.

Witulski, Thomas. *Die Johannesoffenbarung und Kaiser Hadrian: Studien zur Datierung der neutestamentlichen Apokalypse*. FRLANT 221. Göttingen: Vandenhoeck & Ruprecht, 2007.

———. *Kaiserkult in Kleinasien: Die Entwicklung der kultisch-religiösen Kaiserverehrung in der römischen Provinz Asia von Augustus bis Antoninus Pius*. NTOA 63. Göttingen: Vandenhoeck & Ruprecht; Fribourg: Academic Press, 2007.

Wlosok, Antonie. "Die Rechtsgrundlagen der Christenverfolgungen der ersten zwei Jahrhunderte." Pages 275–301 in R. Klein, *Das frühe Christentum im römischen Staat*.

———, ed. *Römischer Kaiserkult*. WdF 372. Darmstadt: Wissenschaftliche Buchgesellschaft, 1978.

Wolff, Christian. *Der erste Brief des Paulus an die Korinther*. 2nd ed. THK 7. Leipzig: Evangelische Verlagsanstalt, 2000.

Wolter, Michael. "Apokalyptik als Redeform im Neuen Testament." *NTS* 51 (2005): 171–91.

———. "Apollos und die ephesinischen Johannesjünger (Act 18,24–19,7)." *ZNW* 78 (1987): 49–73.

———. *Der Brief an die Kolosser; Der Brief an Philemon*. ÖTK 12. Gütersloh: Mohn; Würzburg: Echter Verlag, 1993.

———. *Der Brief an Philemon*. ÖTK 12. Gütersloh: Mohn, 1993.

———. "Israels Zukunft und die Parusieverzögerung bei Lukas." Pages 405–26 in Evang, Merklein, and Wolter, *Eschatologie und Schöpfung*.

———. *Das Lukasevangelium*. HNT 5. Tübingen: Mohr Siebeck, 2008.

———. *Die Pastoralbriefe als Paulustradition*. FRLANT 146. Göttingen: Vandenhoeck & Ruprecht, 1988.

———. *Paul: An Outline of His Theology*. Translated by Robert Brawley. Waco: Baylor University Press, 2015.

———. "'Reich Gottes' bei Lukas." *NTS* 41 (1995): 541–63.

Wong, Eric K. C. *Evangelium im Dialog mit Paulus: Eine intertextuelle Studie zu den Synoptikern*. NTOA 89. Göttingen: Vandenhoeck & Ruprecht, 2012.

———. *Interkulturelle Theologie und multikulturelle Gemeinde im Matthäusevangelium: Zum Verhältnis von Juden- und Heidenchristen im ersten Evangelium*. NTOA 22. Freiburg, Switzerland: Universitätsverlag; Göttingen: Vandenhoeck & Ruprecht, 1992.

Woolf, Greg. *Rom: Die Biographie eines Weltreichs*. 2nd ed. Stuttgart: Klett-Cotta, 2015.

Wördemann, Dirk. *Das Charakterbild im bíos nach Plutarch und das Christusbild im Evangelium nach Markus*. SGKA 1. Paderborn: Schöningh, 2002.

Woyke, Johannes. *Die neutestamentlichen Haustafeln: Ein kritischer und konstruktiver Forschungsüberblick*. SBS 184. Stuttgart: Katholisches Bibelwerk, 2000.

Wrede, William. *The Messianic Secret*. Cambridge: Clarke; Greenwood, SC: Attic, 1971.

———. *Paul*. London: P. Green, 1907.

———. "Paulus." Pages 1–97 in Rengstorf, *Das Paulusbild in der neueren deutschen Forschung.*

Wright, N. T. *Paul and the Faithfulness of God.* COQG 4. Minneapolis: Fortress, 2013.

———. *The Resurrection of the Son of God.* COQG 3. Minneapolis: Fortress, 2003.

Wurm, Alois. *Die Irrlehrer im ersten Johannesbrief.* Biblische Studien 8.1. Freiburg im Breisgau: Herder, 1903.

Xeravits, Géza G., and Peter Porzig. *Einführung in die Qumranliteratur.* Berlin: de Gruyter, 2015.

Yavetz, Zvi. *Tiberius: Der traurige Kaiser: Biographie.* Munich: Beck, 1999.

Zager, Werner. *Begriff und Wertung der Apokalyptik in der neutestamentlichen Forschung.* Theologie 358. Frankfurt: Lang, 1989.

Zahn, Theodor. *Geschichte des neutestamentlichen Kanons.* Vols. 1–2. Leipzig: Deichert, 1988–92.

———. *Grundriss der Geschichte des neutestamentlichen Kanons.* Wuppertal: Brockhaus, 1904. Repr., 1985.

Zangenberg, Jürgen. "Δύναμις τοῦ θεοῦ: Das religionsgeschichtliche Profil des Simon Magus aus Sebaste." Pages 519–40 in Dobbeler, *Religionsgeschichte des Neuen Testaments.*

———. "From the Galilean Jesus to the Galilean Silence." Pages 75–108 in Rothschild and Schröter, *The Rise and Expansion of Christianity.*

———. *Frühes Christentum in Samarien: Topographische und traditionsgeschichtliche Studien zu den Samarientexten im Johannesevangelium.* TANZ 27. Tübingen: Francke, 1998.

———. "Gebeine des Apostelfürsten? Zu den angeblich frühchristlichen Gräbern unter der Peterskirche in Rom." Pages 108–38 in Zangenberg and Labahn, *Christians as a Religious Minority in a Multicultural City.*

———. "Mission in der Antike und im antiken Christentum." *ZNT* 15 (2005): 12–21.

———. ΣΑΜΑΡΕΙΑ: *Antike Quellen zur Geschichte und Kultur der Samaritaner in deutscher Übersetzung.* TANZ 15. Tübingen: Francke, 1994.

Zangenberg, Jürgen, and Michael Labahn, eds. *Christians as a Religious Minority in a Multicultural City: Modes of Interaction and Identity Formation in Early Imperial Rome; Studies on the Basis of a Seminar at the Second Conference of the European Association for Biblical Studies (EABS) from July 8–12, 2001, in Rome.* JSNTSup 243. London: T&T Clark International, 2004.

Zeller, Dieter. "Der eine Gott und der eine Herr Jesus Christus." Pages 34–49 in Söding, *Der lebendige Gott.*

———. *Der erste Brief an die Korinther.* KEK 5. Göttingen: Vandenhoeck & Ruprecht, 2010.

———. "Jesus, Q und die Zukunft Israels." Pages 351–69 in Lindemann, *The Sayings Source Q.*

———. "New Testament Christology in Its Hellenistic Reception." *NTS* 46 (2001): 312–33.

———. "Paulus und Johannes." *BZ* 27 (1983): 167–82.

———. "Der Zusammenhang der Eschatologie in der Logienquelle." Pages 67–77 in Fiedler and Zeller, *Gegenwart und kommendes Reich.*

Zeller, Eduard. *Die Philosophie der Griechen in ihrer geschichtlichen Entwicklung.* Part 3.1, *Die nacharistotelische Philosophie.* 1st half. Darmstadt: Wissenschaftliche Buchgesellschaft, 2006 (= 1923).

Zetterholm, Magnus. "The Didache, Matthew, James—and Paul: Reconstructing Historical Developments in

Antioch." Pages 73–90 in Sandt and Zangenbert, *Matthew, James, and Didache.*

Zgusta, Ladislav. "Die Rolle des Griechischen im römischen Kaiserreich." Pages 121–45 in G. Neumann and Untermann, *Die Sprachen im Römischen Reich der Kaiserzeit.*

Ziegler, Konrat, Walther Sontheimer, Hans Gärtner, and August Friedrich von Pauly. *Der Kleine Pauly: Lexikon der Antike.* 5 vols. Munich: Deutscher Taschenbuch Verlag, 1979.

Zimmermann, Alfred E. *Die urchristlichen Lehrer.* WUNT 2/12. Tübingen: Mohr Siebeck, 1984.

Zimmermann, Heinrich. *Die Hohepriester-Christologie des Hebräerbriefes.* Paderborn: Schöningh, 1964.

Zimmermann, Johannes. *Messianische Texte aus Qumran.* WUNT 104. Tübingen: Mohr Siebeck, 1998.

Zimmermann, Ruben, ed. *Kompendium der frühchristlichen Wundererzählungen.* Vol. 1, *Die Wunder Jesu.* Gütersloh: Gütersloher Verlagshaus, 2013.

———. "Unecht—und doch wahr? Pseudepigraphie im Neuen Testament als theologisches Problem." *ZNT* 12 (2003): 27–38.

Zintzen, Clemens, ed. *Der Mittelplatonismus.* Darmstadt: Wissenschaftliche Buchgesellschaft, 1981.

Zmijewski, Josef. *Die Eschatologiereden des Lukasevangeliums: Eine traditions- und redaktionsgeschichtliche Untersuchung zu Lk 21,5–36 und Lk 17,20–37.* BBB 40. Bonn: Hanstein, 1972.

Zugmann, Michael. *"Hellenisten" in der Apostelgeschichte.* WUNT 2/264. Tübingen: Mohr Siebeck, 2009.

Zumstein, Jean. "Ausgrenzung aus dem Judentum und Identitätsbildung im Johannesevangelium." Pages 383–93 in Schweitzer, *Religion, Politik und Gewalt.*

———. "Die johanneische Auffassung der Macht, gezeigt am Beispiel der Fußwaschung (Joh 13,1–17)." Pages 161–76 in Zumstein, *Kreative Erinnerung.*

———. "Das Johannesevangelium: Eine Strategie des Glaubens." Pages 31–45 in Zumstein, *Kreative Erinnerung.*

———. *Kreative Erinnerung: Relecture und Auslegung im Johannesevangelium.* 2nd ed. ATANT 84. Zurich: Theologischer Verlag Zurich, 2004.

Zwierlein, Otto. "Kritisches zur Römischen Petrustradition und zur Datierung des Ersten Clemensbriefes." *GFAW* 13 (2010): 87–157.

———. *Petrus in Rom: Die literarischen Zeugnisse, mit einer kritischen Edition der Martyrien des Petrus und Paulus auf neuer handschriftlicher Grundlage.* 2nd ed. UaLG 96. Berlin: de Gruyter, 2010.

Index of Authors

Index of Selected Subjects

Index of Selected References

658